MAY 9 5

D0021123

DATE DUE

JUN 1 7 1995	
JUL 1 1 1995	FEB 2 8 2003
AUG 1 2 1995	JUN 1 3 2003
SEP 0 8 1995	MAY 2 0 2004
DEC 0 5 1995	JUN 0 9 2005
JAN 1 6 1996	
FEB 0 6 1996	MAR 1 7 2006
	MAY 0 7 2008
FEB 2 7 1996	FEB 19 2010
JUN 2 7 1996	
AUG 0 9 1996	
NOV 0 7 1996	
JUL 1 8 1998	
OCT 0 8 1998	
JAN 1 1 2000	
JAN 2 9 2000	
NOV 3 0 2002	

GAYLORD   PRINTED IN U.S.A.

San Rafael Public Library
1100 E Street
San Rafael, CA 94901

LYTTON STRACHEY

Books by the same author

Hugh Kingsmill
Unreceived Opinions
Augustus John
Bernard Shaw 'The Search for Love'
Bernard Shaw 'The Pursuit of Power'
Bernard Shaw 'The Lure of Fantasy'
The Shaw Companion

Edited by the same author

The Best of Hugh Kingsmill
Lytton Strachey by Himself
The Art of Augustus John
(with Malcolm Easton)
The Genius of Shaw
The Shorter Strachey (with Paul Levy)
William Gerhardie's *God's Fifth Column*
(with Robert Skidelsky)

LYTTON STRACHEY

The New Biography

MICHAEL HOLROYD

San Rafael Public Library
1100 E Street
San Rafael, CA 94901

Farrar, Straus and Giroux

New York

Copyright © 1994 by Michael Holroyd
All rights reserved
Printed in the United States of America
Published simultaneously in Canada by HarperCollins*CanadaLtd*
First published in the United Kingdom by Chatto & Windus
First American edition, 1995

Library of Congress Cataloging-in-Publication Data
Holroyd, Michael.
Lytton Strachey : the new biography / Michael Holroyd.—1st ed.
p.   cm.
Includes bibliographical references (p.   ) and index.
1. Strachey, Lytton, 1880–1932—Biography. 2. Authors,
English—20th century—Biography. 3. Biographers—Great Britain—
Biography. 4. Critics—Great Britain—Biography.   I. Title.
PR6037.T73Z595   1995
828'.91209—dc20   [B]   94-24632   CIP

Lytton Strachey: A Critical Biography by Michael Holroyd was
originally published in two volumes, *The Unknown Years 1880–1910*
and *The Years of Achievement 1910–1932*, by William Heinemann Ltd
in 1967 and 1968. The two volumes were published in the United States
by Holt, Rinehart & Winston Inc., in 1968.
The contents of these volumes, revised and rearranged,
were published in paperback in two different volumes,
Lytton Strachey: A Biography and *Lytton Strachey and the
Bloomsbury Group*, by Penguin Books Ltd. in 1971
(the former reprinted 1979, 1980, 1987)
copyright © Michael Holroyd 1967, 1968, 1971.
Lytton Strachey: A Biography was first published
in hardcover as a single volume
by William Heinemann Ltd in 1973.
This present edition combines the contents of all
previous editions, revised, rearranged and cut,
with substantial new material added by the author.

CONTENTS

LIST OF ILLUSTRATIONS

Colour plates, between pages 380 and 381

Lytton Strachey, painted by Simon Bussy, 1904.
Carrington's portrait of Strachey, 1914.
The Mill at Tidmarsh, by Carrington, 1918.
Henry Lamb's portrait of Strachey, 1914.

Black and white plates, between pages 220 and 221

1 Lytton, aged three.
2 The Strachey family, c.1886.
3 Lytton as Queen of the Amazons, Christmas 1893.
4 Marie Souvestre.
5 dr cecil reddie.
6 Professor Walter Raleigh.
7 G.E. Moore.
8 Vanessa Stephen.
9 Virginia Stephen.
10 Clive Bell.
11 Leonard Woolf.
12 Duncan Grant and Maynard Keynes, 1912.
13 George Mallory, c.1912-13.
14 Lady Ottoline Morrell.
15 Lytton Strachey.
16 Henry Lamb.
17 Lytton Strachey in his Augustus John period.
18 Mark Gertler.
19 Gerald Brenan.
20 David Garnett.
21 Bernard Penrose.

The winter of 1963–4 was for me a crucial one. After two years' work, and a further two years of waiting, I had had my first book published: a biography of Hugh Kingsmill, the novelist, biographer and critic. But two weeks after publication I was being theatened with an action for libel. The situation seemed perilous. My chief witness, Hesketh Pearson, who had encouraged me to write, suddenly died. I could muster other supporters, but they would hardly figure as star witnesses. There was Malcolm Muggeridge, who had contributed a marvellous introduction to my book, but who had elsewhere attacked the Queen and whose appearance in court was guaranteed to stir up violent antipathy in a jury. There was John Davenport, the critic, who at that time had chosen to wear a prejudicial black beard. And there was William Gerhardie, the distinguished novelist who had not actually published a novel for the last quarter of a century and who, besides denying that he spoke with a slight Russian intonation, would certainly turn up at the wrong courtroom or on the wrong day whatever precautions I took.

Altogether it was not a pleasant prospect. Yet my publisher, Martin Secker, who was nearing eighty, appeared to find the predicament wonderfully invigorating. It brought back to him, evidently, the good old fighting days of D.H. Lawrence, Norman Douglas and early Compton Mackenzie, all of whom he had published. While the old man seemed splendidly rejuvenated, I, still in my twenties, tottered towards a nervous senility. For nights on end I would start awake from dreadful courtroom scenes – rhetorical but unavailing speeches from the dock – to the dreary horror of early morning and the next batch of solicitors' letters.

But out of this nightmare something had been born. The first of the sixteen publishers to whom I had submitted my Kingsmill manuscript was Heinemann. Fortunately it had fallen into the hands of James Michie, the poet and translator. He had liked it, had sent for me, and gently explained that were his firm to make a practice of bringing out books about almost unknown writers by totally unknown authors, it would very soon be bankrupt. However, I might become better known myself were I to choose a less obscure subject. Had I any ideas?

This was the opportunity for which I was looking. Kingsmill was said to be one of those biographers who had imitated Lytton Strachey and so helped to bring his literary reputation into disrepute. In order to demonstrate the injustice of this charge I had examined Strachey's books in some detail. To my surprise I found there was no literary biography of him. Was there not, I wondered, a need for such a book? James Michie agreed there was, and a contract was drawn up in which I undertook to make a re-evaluation of Strachey's place as a biographical historian. It would be about 70,000 words long and take me, I estimated, at least a year.

A year later I had read everything published by and about Strachey, and I had produced an almost complete manuscript. But I had come to the conclusion that Strachey was one of those non-fiction writers whose work was so personal that it could be illuminated by some biographical commentary. It was impossible, from published sources, to reconstruct any worthwhile biography. As for unpublished sources, Clive Bell had sounded an ominous warning. 'Lytton could love, and perhaps he could hate,' he had written.

'To anyone who knew him well it is obvious that love and lust and that mysterious mixture of the two which is the heart's desire played in his life parts of which a biographer who fails to take account will make himself ridiculous. But I am not a biographer, nor can, nor should, a biography of Lytton Strachey be attempted for many years to come. It cannot be attempted till his letters have been published or any rate made accessible, and his letters should not be published till those he cared for and those who thought he cared for them are dead. Most of his papers luckily are in safe and scholarly hands.'[1]

This passage conjured up an almost impregnable stronghold into which I had to make a breach. But I had no doubt that within these fortifications lay solutions to many of the problems that my literary researches had raised. I knew none of the surviving members of the Bloomsbury Group, but I had been given the address of a certain Frances Partridge, a friend of Strachey's who had collaborated with him on the eight-volume edition of *The Greville Memoirs*. To write to her out of the blue and ask for assistance seemed as good a start as any.

I wrote. In her reply she explained that the person I should first get in touch with was James Strachey, Lytton's younger brother and literary executor. He was the key figure to any critical and biographical study such as I wanted to write. For if he were prepared to cooperate then she too would be ready to help me, and so also, she implied, would most of Lytton's other friends.

I met James Strachey a fortnight later. In the meantime various unnerving rumours concerning him had reached me. He was a psychoanalyst, who had been analysed by Freud, had subsequently worked for him in Vienna, and who, during the last twenty years, had been engaged on a monumental translation of the Master's works. This twenty-four volume edition, with its maze of additional footnotes and introductions, was said to be so fine as a work both of art and of scholarship that a distinguished German publishing house was endeavouring to have it retranslated back into German as their own Standard Edition. He was married to another psychoanalyst, Alix Sargant-Florence, author of *The Unconscious Motives of War*, a once brilliant cricket player and dancer at night clubs. Together, I was inaccurately informed by Osbert Sitwell, they had rented off the attics of their house to some unidentified people on whom they had practised their psychoanalytical experiments so that these wretched tenants no longer knew anything except the amount of their rent and the date it was due.

It was with some qualms that I approached their red-brick Edwardian house, set in the beech woods of Marlow Common. I arrived at mid-day, prepared for practically anything – but not for what I found. Though it was frosty outside, the temperature within the house seemed set at a steady eighty degrees Fahrenheit. No windows were open and, to prevent the suspicion of a draught, cellophane curtains were drawn against them. There was an odour of disinfectant about the rooms. I felt I had entered a specially treated capsule where some rare variety of *homo sapiens* was being exquisitely preserved.

James Strachey was almost an exact replica of Freud himself, though with some traces of Lytton's physiognomy – the slightly bulbous nose in particular. He wore a short white beard because, he told me, of the difficulty of shaving. He had had it now for some fifty years. He also wore spectacles, one lens of which was transparent, the other translucent. It was only later that I learnt he had overcome with extraordinary patience a series of eye operations that had threatened to put an end to his *magnum opus*. In a more subdued and somewhat less astringent form, he shared many of Lytton's qualities – his humour, his depth and ambiguity of silence, his rational turn of mind, his shy emotionalism and something of his predisposition to vertigo. As he opened the front door to me, swaying slightly, murmuring something I failed to overhear, I wondered for a moment whether he might be ill. I extended a hand, a gesture which might be interpreted either as a formality or an offer of assistance. But he retreated, and I followed him in.

Of all his Stracheyesque characteristics, it was his silence that I found most dismaying during the hour's 'interview', as he called it, before lunch.

I could not tell whether he produced these silences spontaneously, or whether they were in some manner premeditated. Had he heard what I said? Or did he disapprove? Or again, was he pondering, indefinitely, upon some singular reply? It was impossible to tell. To fill the vacuum, I began jabbering nonsense.

His wife came in, austere and intellectual, very thin, with a deeply-lined parchment face and large expressive eyes. We all drank a little pale sherry and then moved in procession past Stephen Tomlin's bust of Lytton to the dining-room.

Lunch was a spartan affair. Though generous in spirit, my hosts were by temperament ascetic and lived frugally. We ate spam, a cold potato each, and lettuce leaves. In our glasses there showed a faint blush of red wine from the Wine Society, but I was the only one who sipped any. After the spam, some cheese was quarried out from the cold storage, and some biscuits extracted from a long row of numbered tins ranged like files along a shelf in the kitchen. Everything, spam, potato, lettuce, cheese and biscuits, was, like the windows, swathed in protective cellophane.

During lunch we talked of psychoanalysis – not the subject but the word, its derivation and correct spelling. Should it have a hyphen? Did it need both the central 'o' and 'a'? It was a topic to which I could contribute little of brilliance.

After lunch, Alix Strachey excused herself. She was going upstairs to watch a television programme for children. Recently she had decided to learn physics, she explained, and found these kindergarten classes instructive. James said nothing. In silence we filed back the biscuits on the shelf, dashed the rest of the wine down the sink, re-inserted the cheese into its wrappings and its frozen chamber. Then James announced that we were to visit the 'studio wilderness', a large building with a stone floor, standing some ten yards to the rear of the house. He put on boots, a scarf, gloves, a heavy belted overcoat down to his ankles, and we started out on our journey.

The studio wilderness housed much of Lytton's library and collection of papers. The bookcase along one of its walls was filled with French and English volumes going back to the year 1841. In the middle of the building were two great wooden tables piled high with boxes and files, and on the floor were littered innumerable trunks and suitcases – all full of letters, diaries and miscellaneous papers. Cobwebs and a pall of dust blanketed everything. Spiders – of which I have a particular horror – scuttled about the walls and floor, or swam suspended from the ceiling. James stared at this carefully accumulated debris with fascinated wonder. He had made Herculean efforts to organize it all, but it had got the better of him.

Sometimes he felt like putting everything in the fire, or sending it all to the archives of some far-off university. Meanwhile he stored every item, however minimal, and had persistently done so for the last thirty years. He was waiting for a time when civilized opinion had advanced far enough to make the revelations which these papers contained acceptable to the public. One of the ways he would determine whether such a time had arrived was to be the reaction of any potential biographer. I was not the first to approach him. Several years before, Guy Boas had done so. But it had not worked out since Boas considered the material too scandalous for publication. James Strachey suggested he might get the book printed in Holland, but Boas, not liking to risk it, had backed down. Then Michael Goodwin, editor of *Twentieth Century*, had applied, and even been permitted to start his research, but had soon vanished driven, in James's expert opinion, insane by the project. Much pioneer work had been done by Professor Charles Richard Sanders in the United States. Then Professor Gabriel Merle had come over from Paris and taken back a large number of confidential microfilms of Lytton's letters in order to compose a thesis for the Sorbonne. So what I saw in front of me was only some of the source material. There was still more besides, James added, in his study. We must go there now.

We travelled back and went upstairs. The study was a long rectangular room surrounded on three sides by books and gramophone records, with a narrow window running above them. At the farther end of the room stood a desk on which lay the intimidating engines of James Strachey's *oeuvre*. Two massive metal radiators, to which I politely extended my hands, turned out to be stereophonic loudspeakers – James was an authority on Haydn, Mozart and Wagner, and contributed notes and commentaries for Glyndebourne programmes. Above the fireplace hung a portrait of Lytton relaxing in a deck-chair, painted by Carrington. Next to the fireplace was an armchair, draped in cellophane. James showed me more papers, including his own correspondence with Rupert Brooke, and several reels of microfilm. 'Do you *still* want to write about Lytton?' he at length inquired. I replied that I did. 'I see,' was all he said.

I left the house late that afternoon in profound depression. The mass of unpublished material made my previous year's work seem futile. But I could not think I had made a good impression. It appeared likely that I had been wasting my time.

Forty-eight hours later I received a letter from James. He and his wife had decided to assist me so far as possible. But there were practical difficulties. Since 'this Freud translation business is in a rather specially hectic state', they were both bound to avoid being diverted. Therefore, I would have to bring my own food and drink each day. There was also the problem of travel. I should have to journey up and down by a relay of trains and buses. However, if I could face such horrors as these, I was free to start whenever I liked – preferably before the snow set in. I would be allowed access to the studio wilderness and permitted to inspect anything in the house itself.

So began what, for the next five years, was to prove not simply the composition of a large book but a way of life and an education.

I started work at Marlow in October 1962. The hexagonal room where we had first had lunch was given over to me, and as soon as I entered it I would strip off as many clothes as I thought practicable, begin reading through the correspondence, copying out sections, taking notes. From time to time there was a knocking at the hatch which communicated with the kitchen. I would open it to find a steaming cup of coffee and a numbered biscuit, presumably left by Alix. From time to time James would quietly manifest himself in the doorway on the other side of the room, stand there awhile regarding me, deposit some notebook or sheaf of papers he had come across, then disappear. Apart from this there was little to disturb me – occasionally some music from the radiator-like loudspeakers upstairs, and very occasionally the sound of scuffling feet as the top-floor tenants descended the stairs. Nothing else.

Very soon I realized that this must be one of the major caches of literary papers in modern times. Lytton was never a voluble conversationalist and had disliked the telephone. But he had loved to write and to receive letters. Here, in holograph, typescript and microfilm, were very many of his letters, preserved since the age of six, and the correspondence of his Bloomsbury friends.

All this was tremendously exciting. But it posed for me equally tremendous problems – problems of how to treat this colossal quantity of unpublished documents and of how to organize my life around it. Near the outset I had to make the difficult decision that the subject was worth several years' labour, and I had to persuade my publisher that I had made the right decision. James Michie had left Heinemann, but I was fortunate in that David Machin, his successor, was equally sympathetic. I outlined my plan. I wanted to accomplish four things – to provide a selection of the best of Strachey's letters; conduct a reappraisal of his work; present a panoramic view of Bloomsbury life; and write a modern biography. I would endeavour to shape all this into a conversation piece around the figure of Lytton Strachey. 'Discretion', he had said, 'is not the better part of biography.' I should not be discreet.

I had received from Heinemann an advance on royalties of fifty pounds, and although this was double what I had been paid for my life of Kingsmill, I could see that there would be something of a financial shortfall if my plans were to go ahead. There were no Arts Council bursaries in those days, no Authors' Foundation grants, for British authors to buy the extra time they needed to write their books. It was difficult, too, for my publisher to pay me very much more since Bloomsbury was so unfashionable. E.M. Forster's reputation had not then been revived by the film industry; Virginia Woolf was not yet the inspiration she was to become, with the rise of the feminist movement; the art criticism of Clive Bell and Roger Fry was considered somewhat insignificant; the paintings of Vanessa Bell and Duncan Grant lay in the cellars of many galleries; even the professional reputation of Maynard Keynes was in retreat before Milton Friedman and the Chicago economists.

The best day's work I did for my own economy was at the United States Embassy in Grosvenor Square, looking through lists of fellowships that offered money to non-American citizens for work done outside the United States. By the end of the day I had found two: the Eugene Saxton Fellowship[2] and the Bollingen Fellowship. I applied for each in succeeding years and, by virtue, I imagine, of there being no competition whatsoever, was given both of them. The trustees seemed disturbed by my approach and shortly afterwards closed down both institutions. But their grants enabled me to live and work, with the odd job thrown in, for some three years.

Part of a biographer's research can have about it an inevitable sameness. When one has examined ten thousand letters, one may be forgiven for eyeing the next ten thousand with a certain lacklustre. While I was examining Lytton's early and most plaintive correspondence, with its microscopic details of faulty digestion, neurasthenia, apathy, self-loathing and other unhappy qualities that made up what he termed 'the black period' of his life, I did feel seriously infected with many of these same ailments. If symptoms like these were posthumously contagious, then my next subject must, I resolved, be someone of astonishing virility and euphoria. However, I soon became absorbed in this life, and over the years I was writing my book I do not think I was ever more than half aware of the outside world. The world in which I lived was that of the Bloomsbury Group during the early part of this century. My work held something of the excitement of an archaeological discovery. The vast *terra incognita* represented by the Strachey papers seemed like a lost way of life that was gradually emerging into the light.

Fortunately the routine of my research was widely variegated. One of my most interesting finds took place in the basement of 51 Gordon

Square, the Strachey family's home from 1919 to 1963. The house was being vacated, having been bought by University College, London. But I had been given authority to explore everything. On my first visit I noticed a tablet in the entrance hall listing the various members of the family with the captions 'In' and 'Out'. The word 'Out' had been slotted against those who (some of them half a century ago) had died. By the time I finished reconnoitring the basement, the dustmen had turned up to carry off the rubbish for burning, and I won a fierce tug-of-war with them for Lytton's bulky long-lost Fellowship dissertation on Warren Hastings. Among other things I came across was a letter in the near-illegible Gothic hand of Sigmund Freud, written on Christmas Day 1928, and giving his thoughts on *Elizabeth and Essex*.

The research was enlivened, too, by a great deal of travel. One of the first things I did on leaving Marlow was to fly to Paris. There I met Gabriel Merle, a charming taciturn French scholar, who handed me the microfilms he had been lent by James. These microfilms contained Lytton's correspondence with his family, with Virginia Woolf (unabridged) and with Duncan Grant and Maynard Keynes. Having negotiated the Customs and returned home, I hired from Kodak a huge black machine, like an astronomer's telescope, and fed the reels of microfilm into it. For two months my life orbited round this monstrous object, which stood in the centre of my one-room flat, dwarfing the furniture. I ate, slept, washed and dressed under its shadow. And for twelve or fifteen hours a day I would sit projecting the films on to a screen, and copying down anything I needed.

Later on I travelled through France to La Souco, the house overlooking Monte Carlo which had belonged to Lytton's brother-in-law, the painter Simon Bussy, and where Lytton had often stayed and worked. It was deserted when I called, with a notice that it was up for sale. So I boldly made my way in and looked round until captured by a voluble French neighbour who accused me of being a burglar. My French not being up to providing a truthful explanation, I gave her to understand that I was a prospective purchaser, and in the guise of a man of wealth was lavishly entertained.

A number of people had disliked Lytton Strachey – Harold Nicolson for instance. I went to see him in his rooms at the Albany one evening. He was sitting in a chair when I entered, open-eyed and apparently examining me critically. He said nothing. I stood before him shuffling my feet, shifting my weight from one side to another, murmuring something about the uncontroversial weather. He continued to glare. Suddenly a sort of convulsion ran through him, and he blinked. 'I'm afraid I've been asleep,' he said. 'Would you like a drink?' I said that I would. But the question was apparently to satisfy his curiosity rather than my thirst. We began to talk. Lytton, he told me, had resembled a bearded and bitchy old woman, rude rather than witty in society, injecting with his unnaturally treble voice jets of stinging poison into otherwise convivial gatherings. After about a quarter of an hour he looked across at his own large empty glass, which stood on the table between us, and asked: 'Another drink?' Hesitantly I agreed. But once again he made no move, and since I could see no sign of drink in the room, we went on talking. Ten minutes later his gaze again fell on the glass, this time with incredulity. 'Do you want *another* drink?' His tone was so sharp I thought it prudent to refuse.

Next day I told this story to Duncan Grant. Without a word, he leapt up and poured me a strong gin and tonic. It was half-past ten in the morning.

Another near-contemporary of Lytton's who was reputed to disapprove of him was Bertrand Russell. He invited me to Plas Penrhyn, his remote house in North Wales, high up on a hill overlooking the Irish sea. There, in the drawing-room, he regaled me with mildly indecent stories of Frank Harris and Oscar Wilde, showed me the typescript of his then unpublished autobiography and several Strachey letters. Had he disliked Lytton? I asked. No, he answered, never. And so smiling, diminutive and gently nostalgic did he appear that it was difficult to believe that he had upbraided Lytton for having degraded G.E. Moore's ethics into 'advocacy of a stuffy girls'-school sentimentalizing' – a piece of invective that earned him a rebuke from E.M. Forster.

Frances Partridge had intimated that James Strachey's approval would guarantee me the help of many other friends, and so it turned out. Over the years I met or corresponded with over a hundred people, and the great majority of these generously helped me. This was all the more remarkable in view of the controversial material involved. For here was I, a stranger from a different generation, proposing to investigate their past with probing intimacy. I was setting out to give Lytton's love-life the same prominence in my book as it had had in his career, to trace its effect on his work, and to treat the whole subject of homosexuality openly – in the same way as I would have treated heterosexuality. But my plan depended on the cooperation of a band of mercurial octogenarians. It was for all of us a daunting prospect. 'Shall I be arrested?' one of them asked after reading through my typescript. And another, with pathos, exclaimed: 'When this comes out, they will never again allow me into Lord's.' In particular, it says much for the courage and integrity of Duncan Grant and Roger Senhouse that they did not censor what I had written. Each of them had been central to an understanding of part of Lytton's life. But neither, perhaps, had known the full extent of the role he had played in Lytton's emotions until he read my account based largely on what Lytton wrote to other friends. It was hardly surprising that this should be the cause of some agitation. But neither of them put any obstacle in my way, and Duncan Grant set his seal of approval on the first volume by drawing for its jacket a portrait of Lytton based on an early photograph, and giving it to me.

By the crucial winter of 1963–4, I had reached in my first volume what is for me one of the most difficult stages in a book. I was two-thirds of the way through it. A great deal remained to be done, but the temptation to relax slightly, together with the accumulating strain of the Kingsmill affair, made the last third very arduous. I had often been haunted by fears that I would not be able to do the book, that it was beyond me. Now these fears multiplied. I inched my way forward, writing in the mornings, typing or doing extra research work every afternoon. This last section of the book took me almost a year to finish, and by the time I had done so, my two index fingers, the only ones I used for typing, were numb.

I returned to Marlow in the autumn of 1964, taking with me the typescript of volume one. While James unhurriedly read through it in his study, I worked below preparing for the second volume. Occasionally, in late afternoon, the electricity supply would fail, and the regime became candles in champagne bottles. James did not say much while he was reading the typescript, but when he had completed it his reaction was devastating. I had, he felt, been far too hostile to his brother. He suspected that I harboured an unconscious dislike of him, probably on moral grounds. This suggestion seemed to me fantastic, but there is no appeal against the accusation of an *unconscious* attitude. One's natural rejoinder – that one is *unconscious* of it – seems only to corroborate the allegation. For my own part, I had come to feel that James resented any criticism of Lytton, to whom he had been intimately attached. 'I'm in a bit of a conflict,' he told me. On the one hand, he explained, he had grown rather friendly towards me, but on the other he rather violently objected to many passages in the book. He didn't enjoy being unpleasant to someone he quite liked. What, therefore, were we to do?

What we agreed to do was to go through the book sentence by sentence trying to hammer out a mutually acceptable text. In return for what he called 'a bribe' of five hundred pounds, I agreed not to publish this first volume until I had finished the whole work. Both volumes could then be brought out together or with only a short interval between them. Despite James's generosity, this was undeniably a setback. I felt like a marathon runner who, on completing the course, is asked whether he wouldn't mind immediately running round it all over again.

I returned to London, to my portable typewriter, and the start of another quarter of a million words. Over the next two and a half years, James went through both volumes, in microscopic detail, twice. I stayed with him and Alix a number of times in Marlow; he occasionally came to London; we exchanged a hundred letters; he sent me many pages of closely written notes. When he was especially cross, I noticed, he would switch from blue to red ink, and on one fearful occasion the envelope itself was addressed in red. Nothing escaped his attention. One character had 'short' not 'small' shin bones; 'extrovert' was a word that derived from Jung and was meaningless; another person's ability was not 'considerable' but '*very* considerable'; 'pratter' was a mistyping of 'prattle'; and so on. These notes, queries and comments took up an infinite amount of James's time. But they were of incalculable value to me. By nature he was uncommunicative, yet now he was being provoked into divulging all sorts of information known to almost no one else that would greatly enrich the biography. Sometimes, of course, we did not agree. In these cases I stuck to my guns and put James's dashing comments in the footnotes.

In April 1967, shortly after having completed his final notes, James died suddenly of a heart attack. I felt stunned. I had thought he would live to be at least a hundred. Although he would on occasions criticize me sharply over something I had or hadn't written, our differences had been argued out in the best of spirits. His mind and scholarship could appear daunting, but they were mixed with a humour and gentleness that were unforgettable, and that made working with him a lesson in civilized behaviour.

Readers of the biography might well deduce from some of the footnotes that James greatly disliked the book from beginning to end. He was never one to cover up opinions so that I knew it was true when he told me at the end he appreciated the seriousness of purpose and approved of the structure and length of the book. The figures and situations, though not always as he saw them, had seemed to force their way through, he added, by a continuous pressure of permeation, and some of the narrative, especially towards the close, he liked. Since I had never blindly accepted his opinions, and since I knew his approval was extremely hard to win, nothing could have pleased me more.

*

The above preface was written for the first paperback edition of this biography in 1971. To preserve the reputation of the binders, I had divided the biographical narrative from the literary criticism (which appeared as a separate publication) and reduced the original two-volume baggy monster to a slim 1,044 pages. It was this version, with a few revisions made in subsequent reprints, that went marching through the next twenty years until, unable to endure any longer slinking past bookshops which stocked it, I hurried to my publishers one day and begged them to put it out of print. It was an unusual scene and needs some explanation.

Reviewing *Lytton Strachey* on its first publication in 1967, Raymond Mortimer had called it 'the first post-Wolfenden biography'. Some readers today may need to be reminded that, ten years after the Wolfenden Report on prostitution and homosexuality was published in 1957, the Sexual Offences Act became law. This replaced the Labouchère Criminal Law Amendment Act of 1885 under which Oscar Wilde had been sentenced to two years' hard labour, and legitimized homosexual acts in private between consenting adults over twenty-one years of age – providing they were not in the armed services. The ten-year delay between the Report (which was not unanimous) and its legal implementation gives an indication of how sensitive the subject was still felt to be at the time my biography first appeared.

The amiable habit publishers have of copying out the most favourable passages from reviews and reproducing them on the jackets of books can produce a rather sentimental impression of how those books were actually received. Even a reader such as Frances Partridge, who could not 'see any sense in biographies that suppress or distort the truth', has recorded in her diary 'a sort of horror' as part of her reaction to reading my typescript. 'Perhaps he has probed too unmercifully,' she wrote (28 March 1966), 'even the bedrooms and beds are explored for data.'

Everyone agreed that I had written *Lytton Strachey* in prose and not in verse; but after that opinions divided sharply. 'Rather wonderful & terrible how *all* that can now be said,' Nancy Mitford wrote (2 March 1968).[3] I was charged with 'cruelty' and praised for 'candour'. W.H. Auden and Sir Roy Harrod, biographer of Maynard Keynes, believed the book should not have been written. Dame Helen Gardner declared it to be a 'directory for consenting adults'. My mail became filled with apoplectic accusations and curious invitations (one poet even composed his envelope in verse as if he were Lytton Strachey addressing Roger Senhouse). 'I have been reading your book on Lytton Strachey,' volunteered another enthusiast from that pre-Aids world, 'and I do think you have done a service to humanity in general by showing how far degradation can go . . . One can only be truly thankful that one never met him . . . he set the worst possible example. Homosexuality is not being "civilised" or "rational". It is the filthiest trick ever devised by man: it is anti-social, it often leads to cancer.'

What particularly incensed some people was the revelation that

Maynard Keynes, whose economic theories had revived Western capitalism in its fight against the 'red menace' of communism, had been an active homosexual. I was said to have given comfort to the enemy, to have subverted the Free World. When President Nixon announced in a public speech: 'We are all Keynesians now,' there was a ripple of laughter round the world. Not very long afterwards he left office.

'I don't suppose Lytton will ever, or should ever, get explained to the general public,' E.M. Forster had written to Ottoline Morrell (27 January 1932). Within Bloomsbury, reactions to my typescript were so hostile that it seemed doubtful for a time whether it would be published. As Virginia Woolf indicated in her diary and letters, James Strachey believed that, had his brother lived longer, he would have turned what was implicit in his biographies into an explicit autobiographical campaign to achieve the same treatment under the law for homosexuality as for heterosexuality. I can see now, though I did not see it then, that he would have liked my biography to perform something of the work Lytton might have done between the 1930s and 1950s. He did not tell me that his first idea in the 1930s had been for himself 'to set about a very long life of Lytton with all the letters', and, as Virginia Woolf explained in her diary (5 April 1935), for her to 'write a character of Lytton as introduction'. But Virginia knew a different Lytton and doubted James's prediction of the things, such things, his brother would have done. He was evidently disappointed that Virginia never wrote this 'character' of Lytton, and in a letter to me he dismissed her judgement of character with much the same finality as he swept aside many of my own judgements. James was disappointed with my book partly because, though I made no moral distinction between homosexuality and heterosexuality, I did not offer as a subtext the unfulfilled life he had foreseen.

Yet, as many letters I was to receive show, the book was read by homosexuals. Kenneth Williams in his diary (13 January 1969) wrote of being deeply moved by 'this strange, gentle, unhappy and wonderfully civilized man who was so unable to find complete & shared love, and who was, at the end, surrounded by love. I think there are things in this book which have affected me deeply ... I think this book will go on affecting me, and will reverberate for the rest of my life.'[4] I believe this would have silently pleased James.

When James was confronted by something particularly idiotic from me, he would go pink in the face and fall silent. David Garnett, on the other hand, seeing something outrageous, grew full of 'red-faced truculence, and talk about libel actions', so Alix Strachey said. His objections were precisely the opposite of James's. His own autobiography had been enlivened by many amorous exploits, but he had confined himself on the page to heterosexual exploits. My revelations, he believed, would be incalculably harmful to anyone associated with them. So, in the summer of 1966, he 'violently entered the lists', Frances Partridge records, 'in favour of wholesale suppression'.

Fourteen years later, having heard a radio broadcast I made on Strachey, David Garnett wrote to me to explain that there had been two reasons why he so disliked my biography. He thought that I was 'quite wrong' about Lytton's attitude to his family, and that I had given an 'inaccurate impression of the Apostles' at Cambridge. He may have been right, but since these subjects were covered in less than one twentieth of my book, they hardly constituted grounds for 'wholesale suppression' – indeed they were not really the main cause of his antagonism. But his letter was, I believe, signalling something else. Written a year before his death, it saluted a change in the climate of opinion, a change that had started in the late 1960s.

This change profoundly affected what was seen as admissible material in non-fiction. In 1968 an article appeared in the *Spectator* warning biographers of the dangers of further advances in Stracheyesque indiscretion. People likely to be the subjects of such biographies would, it was argued,

'destroy their most intimate letters and be very careful what they write in their journals. Diarists will be identified and suspect. The very keeping of a diary will be regarded as an unsocial act. So the private records of our times, perhaps the most articulate in history, will be paradoxically sparse unless we impose on ourselves some sort of limitation on what is to be published and when.'

The author of the *Spectator* article, called 'A Problem of Discretion', had recently edited his own father's diaries for publication. 'My only cause for hesitation', he wrote, 'was whether to reveal my father's racial prejudices and my mother's extreme conservatism.' But a number of readers reacted in horror when, in 1973, this same author revealed his father's complaisance and his mother's sexual radicalism by publishing and adding to his mother's autobiography, in a now famous book called *Portrait of a Marriage*. It was ten years since his mother's death; five since his father's; and one year since the death of Violet Trefusis about whose love-affair with his mother, Vita Sackville-West, the book tells. In his Foreword, Nigel Nicolson wrote: 'Let not the reader condemn in ten minutes a decision which I have pondered for ten years.' This ten-year span includes the year in which Nigel Nicolson wrote 'A Problem of Discretion' for the *Spectator*, and what is more significant than praise or blame is the barometric change this decision registers in modern non-fiction.

Besides the changes taking place in biography itself, there were other changes, in newspapers and the arts, that were to affect my book. Frances Partridge had noted, with some qualms, the confidence of my literary judgements. I remember this as being little more than a confidence trick to help me over the obstacle course before publication. 'I think on the whole Holroyd has got it right,' Frances Partridge concluded (20 November 1968). But none of us had foreseen, in an age of growing journalistic power, the aggressive use some reviewers were to make of the biography, all the more difficult when praising me in order to season their disparagement of Bloomsbury. 'I have just seen [Malcolm] Muggeridge's sniggering review of your book on Lytton Strachey,' Geoffrey Keynes wrote to me (1 October 1967). '. . . I do not know your motives but I cannot regard them, whatever they may be, as creditable.' I pointed out that writers of books are not responsible for the reviews of their books, but Geoffrey Keynes regarded this as a trivial point. I had given these reviewers an opportunity for exercising a venom and malevolence they would not otherwise have had. 'The harm is done', he wrote (4 October 1967), '& there's no more to be said.'

The second development we had not foreseen was that, as the performing arts began to enjoy a renaissance, there would be proposals from Christopher Hampton, Peter Luke, John Osborne, Ken Russell, Gore Vidal and others to make films and plays, and even a musical, from the Strachey and Carrington story. 'The book was made possible by the collaboration of the many who lent Holroyd letters,' Noel Carrington protested to the BBC (2 December 1968) on reading that Oliver Reed was flexing his muscles to take on the part of Strachey. '. . . I am sure that most of us would have declined to let him have such access had we known that a film dramatisation of the characters was to follow . . . I feel there is a valid distinction between a biography and the televised dramatisation of a life, especially one that ended in tragedy still exceedingly painful to those concerned.' Neither Noel Carrington nor Alix Strachey nor Frances Partridge objected to a documentary. But a fictional dramatization was for the time being unacceptable because, as Frances Partridge explained, 'no actor's performance, however good, can be other than grotesque to those who knew the originals intimately'.

Had my biography been published ten years later, it would have had a much less bumpy ride. Angelica Garnett, for example, whom I saw while doing my research and who came to the American publisher's launch of the book in 1968, had, unknown to me, been adamant that 'one couldn't publish such things about living people'. Duncan, she told Frances Partridge, 'has a lot of conventional friends who'll be horribly shocked'. This was the same reason that had been given by her mother Vanessa Bell for maintaining the pretence, while Angelica was growing up at Charleston in the 1920s and 1930s, that Clive Bell was her father. My biography did not then reveal Duncan Grant as her real father, but it was perhaps a useful prologue to the remarkable and necessary autobiography, *Deceived with Kindness* (1984), that she began writing in the 1970s. This book set her free from a deception practised for the benefit of an 'innocent and conventional' generation of people, such as Clive Bell's and Duncan Grant's parents, and posthumously restored Duncan as her father.[5] The question that confronted her and others in the 1960s was whether such pretences spring up inevitably and indestructibly from generation to generation, or whether Bloomsbury had helped to reduce the need for them.

Having been handed such unsettling material by James Strachey and having worked on it in private for almost five years, I assumed far too innocently that everyone would naturally agree it should be published. I knew little of what was going on after I circulated my completed typescript round Bloomsbury in 1966 – and indeed I did not fully realize the alarm it was causing until the publication in 1993 of Frances Partridge's diaries, *Other People 1963–1966*. It was fortunate for me that she felt strongly in favour of unbowdlerized biographies. Feeling 'uneasy at the thought of the chopper ready to fall' on my head, she was prepared to defend my book in principle at a time when others 'had not a good word for it', arguing that Bloomsbury should have the courage to uphold its own standards publicly. 'I'm more than faintly surprised', she wrote, 'at their [the homosexuals'] secretiveness just when their position seems to be about to be legally ratified.' Nevertheless, she acknowledged the subject to be 'complicated and difficult' because of the personal feelings of those directly involved. Eventually, when everyone had had their say, it was agreed that the main people in question, Duncan Grant in the first volume and Roger Senhouse in the second volume, must have the last word.

An atmosphere of fatalism prevailed. There was a pause, and as the pause lengthened so the publishers themselves became agitated. On the advice of their lawyers, I was asked to get written permission from both Duncan Grant and Roger Senhouse. When I approached Roger Senhouse, he immediately asked me down to stay the weekend with him at his house in Rye. There would be no difficulty, he assured me, over permission, and he repeated this assurance while placing the vital piece of paper to one side during the first evening I was there. Over the next forty-eight hours, at breakfast, or out walking, and again in his library (where I saw the books Strachey had left him), I would produce this paper like a policeman producing a warrant, and Roger would greet it with genial familiarity before passing on to more entertaining subjects. He was determined to see me off at the railway station on the Sunday evening. As we got into the taxi I apologetically flourished the permission statement once more, and he eagerly seized it. Then, as we got out of the taxi I retrieved it from the seat and, on the platform, as my train was coming in, presented it yet again – and he finally signed it, saying with a smile that it was 'a fair cop'. What he had to put up with from me I only came to see some half-dozen years later when, endeavouring to do some small favour for the novelist William Gerhardie, I received from Gerhardie a portrait of myself conveying what it was like to be on the receiving-end of my attentions. In short I appeared as 'a *smilingly* impenitent, pig-headed, bloody-minded, bigoted, intolerant, unyielding, inelastic, *hard*, inflexible, opinionate, fanatical, obsessed, pedantic, rook-ribbed, *unmoved*, persistent, incurable, irrepressible, intractable, impersuadable, cross-grained ruffian – no offence implied'.[6]

Roger Senhouse also, miraculously, took no offence. Only now do I appreciate quite how painful was his and Duncan Grant's position,[7] or understand the indignation towards me of those who rallied round them. 'I think you will agree, it puts Duncan Grant in a rather awkward position,' Quentin Bell explained to me (11 July 1966).

'He is certainly not an enemy of historical truth or, I think, at all ashamed of his erotic adventures; but I don't think that anyone could fail to be rather taken aback by contemplating the publication of such very intimate details of his early loves, and, what is more, of his very youthful expressions of feeling . . . he is very much torn between a desire not to be unfair and obstructive and a natural reluctance to see very private emotions made so very public.'

A Bloomsbury compromise was proposed based on Strachey's own treatment of Florence Nightingale's early love which 'tells one practically nothing and yet says everything'. I was not very happy with this, and Duncan finally decided to ask for no excisions. So, as the art historian Richard Shone later wrote, he made 'his own contribution to the emancipated climate of the Sixties just as he had participated in a similar movement half a century before'.[8] Not all of us have our principles tested in this awkward fashion late in life, and none of us can feel confident of passing such a test. At the time I did not quite realize how difficult their decision must have been, and not knowing what was happening while I anxiously waited, did not adequately acknowledge the courage needed to make that decision. This act of acknowledgement I now belatedly perform.

Immediately after publication, my book received its most torrid greeting from a number of heterosexuals and their families. Lady Ottoline Morrell's daughter, Julian Vinogradoff, had guardedly shown me Lytton's correspondence with her mother and praised my first volume, the severity of which she picked out for special commendation. She also lent one or two Bloomsbury pictures in her private collection for a party given by Miss Dillon, the owner of Dillons bookshop, to mark the completion of my second volume. I sent Mrs Vinogradoff what is called a 'complimentary' copy of this second volume but, finding nothing complimentary in it about her mother, she arrived early at the party and, to the delight of various waiting journalists, removed her pictures from the wall.

Her objections, which were strong and sincerely felt, burst into the *Times Literary Supplement* and found loyal support from such eminent littérateurs as Lord David Cecil. This resentment was still simmering six years later when the second volume of Ottoline's memoirs, *Ottoline at Garsington* (1974), was published with a nine-page introduction by its editor, Robert Gathorne-Hardy, attacking the 'derisive and derogatory' portrait I had drawn of Ottoline comprehensively based on 'every misleading source'. What Ottoline had suffered in her lifetime at the hands of so many writers from D.H. Lawrence to Aldous Huxley, and so many artists from Henry Lamb to Augustus John, was now being gratuitously visited on her family: that was the feeling of Julian Vinogradoff's friends. In preparing this revised edition of my biography I have looked carefully at these objections, re-examined the correspondence, read two new biographies of Ottoline and made whatever corrections, reinterpretations or amplifications I have come to feel are genuinely needed. But I cannot guarantee their acceptability to those who knew and loved Ottoline.

Among the several solicitors' letters I received, the most threatening came from a firm representing Bernard Penrose, known to everyone as 'Beacus'. What I had usually done was to send pages of my typescript to anyone who appeared in them and who might find them hurtful. However I had not been able to send anything to Bernard Penrose because he had been seriously ill in hospital. On the advice of a solicitor, I therefore invented a new name for him and added a few fanciful touches, as if I were an unbridled novelist, to conceal his identity. He then came out of hospital fighting fit and demanding to know through his lawyers whether I could deny that he was the 'Piers Noxall', nicknamed 'Snipe', who I claimed had made Carrington pregnant in the late 1920s. I could not deny it, and though Carrington's diary made it clear that he was the father of her unborn child, I could not prove the truth of this to any lawyer's satisfaction forty years later. Here was an example of the maxim 'the greater the truth the greater the libel'. To my relief, Bernard Penrose did not want damages. What he wanted was for me to publish an extended apology drafted by his solicitors in the reprint of my biography, and to rewrite the passages referring to himself, using his name but eliminating him as Carrington's lover and leaving her pregnancy suspended mysteriously in the narrative. This I was obliged to do. 'Honour is satisfied!' he wrote cheerfully after I had paid for the insertions and amendments together with his solicitor's costs (equivalent to £2000 in 1994).

Later I found out that this legal action had been primed by Bernard Penrose's wife who, though not married to him at the time, had never been told of his early relationship with Carrington and resented having to learn of it from a book. Bernard Penrose's refusal to ask for damages perhaps reflected his unease at the situation, and the help he was to give me over my biography of Augustus John during the next couple of years was his way of making things up to me.

There is no doubt that Beacus made Carrington pregnant. In his unpublished autobiography, which he wrote in 1987 and I read in 1993, he virtually claims as much. 'When I fell in love with another woman,' he wrote, 'Carrington was nearly 40. I found out only later that she had become pregnant and had an abortion. I wished I had married her, but she said she did not believe in having children.'

For this edition I have removed the lawyer's apology and rewritten the pages in which Beacus appears, using a good deal of material that I had not seen all those years ago.

Some of my other pseudonyms were so successful that they took on lives of their own. I have met people who claim to have known these creations and told me vivid stories of their exploits. They also found their way into a number of later publications. In a scholarly work published in the United States, for example, one of them enjoyed an enterprising relationship with his non-fiction original. This game has gone on long enough and since the need for such devices has now passed, I have done away with all pseudonyms.

Not everyone with whom James Strachey had been in contact agreed to help me. For instance, Leonard Woolf. James had lent Leonard Woolf the letters Leonard had sent Lytton from Ceylon between 1904 and 1911 to help him prepare the second volume of his autobiography, *Growing*, which was published in 1961. James asked Leonard to show me Lytton's correspondence over this period. Leonard agreed to see me, but showed me nothing. 'I am very doubtful about lending the letters,' he wrote to me (2 December 1962); and again (3 April 1963): 'I have looked through such letters as I have and I cannot at the moment find anything which would be of any use to you.' When my first volume came out in the autumn of 1967, he reviewed it in the *New Statesman* (6 October 1967), congratulating me on my 'conscientious industry', but regretting that I had wasted a 'wonderful opportunity for writing a first-rate biography'. Later he told Professor Bernard Blackstone that he had thought better of me than I evidently did of him, quoting what Voltaire had said in a similar circumstance: 'Perhaps we are both wrong.'[9]

It is possible, though I was unaware of this, that Leonard Woolf's initial unhelpfulness had prejudiced me against him. In any event, I was surprised to receive a generous letter from him at the beginning of 1968 telling me that he was reviewing my second volume. I was delighted to hear that he thought it in every way much better than the first. 'A few weeks ago in turning out some papers,' he wrote the following month (1 February 1968), 'I found some letters from Lytton to me and also some of his poems in his own handwriting. I have had them typed and I thought it may interest you to see the typescripts.' These were the letters that James Strachey had asked him to show me over five years earlier. I slipped something from them into the 1971 edition of my biography, and have been able to see and use more of that correspondence now.

Leonard Woolf's second review in the *New Statesman* (23 February 1968) was one of those happily chosen by the publisher to advertise my book. I can say of his criticism what he said of both volumes of my biography: that it was honest criticism throughout. He was honest, too, when asked why his autobiography had silently passed over the fact that so many of his friends were homosexuals. The editor of *Encounter* sent round a questionnaire to a number of authors, from Roy Harrod to Maurice Bowra, who had written biographies and memoirs of those times asking them this question. Was it oversight or *suppressio veri*?[10] Leonard Woolf replied that his friends' homosexuality was irrelevant to the subject treated by him in his autobiography and, since he himself was not homosexual, irrelevant to his relation to them. Furthermore, 'when I wrote, it was still unusual to reveal facts which might be painful to living people unless it was absolutely vital to mention them.' No one else who was sent this questionnaire from *Encounter* replied.

There is one criticism of my biography made by Leonard Woolf that I still don't accept. 'I do not think that he [Lytton] had any very strong passions or emotions,' he wrote, '. . . he was hardly ever completely serious when he had a pen in his hand, writing the tragedy or comedy of his perpetual love affairs to Maynard Keynes, James [Strachey], or me . . . Mr Holroyd should remember what Rosalind said some 350 years ago: "Men have died from time to time, and worms have eaten them, but not for love."'

It is true that in the air of pure romantic comedy which fills the Forest of Arden, there are no deaths for love. But we cannot go far into Shakespeare's tragedies without coming across both men and women dying for love. In Lytton Strachey's life, comedy and tragedy were not separated, nor does his sense of humour imply a lack of seriousness – indeed quite the contrary. Homosexuality was 'irrelevant' to Leonard Woolf and, to my mind, he underrated its significance in releasing Strachey from lonely confinement in his own body. He also underrated the intensity and precariousness of Strachey's passions during the long shadowy period of history that followed Wilde's imprisonment. In the 'mausoleum talks' after Strachey's and Carrington's deaths, with what later appeared a tragic irony, Leonard Woolf described Carrington's suicide as 'histrionic'. But however much one may not like it, her ending (which is the end of my biography) conclusively refutes Leonard's use of Rosalind's happy assertion.

It is a risky affair, meddling with a book that is remembered with affection by some of its early readers in order to hand it on to a new generation. The present version is still long, but not so immensely long: in short, it is almost 250,000 words less long than my original double-decker publication. Part of this reduction was made in 1971 by simply removing the literary criticism and sewing up what remained. The present operation has been far more complicated. Although the book comes out at 100,000 words shorter than the 1971 edition, it also contains 100,000 new words. The miracle which I am attempting to bring off is the creation of a comparatively shorter book with much more in it.

'There is a chagrin of authors, not realised by readers and ignored by librarians,' wrote William Gerhardie in the Prefatory Note to a new edition of his novel *Of Mortal Love* (1949), 'a pious wish, for ever thwarted, to withdraw from circulation earlier, unpurified, inferior texts and versions of his books, to be replaced by a revised edition, and frustrate the nonsense of first editions.' Such acts of piety and purification are looked on with considerable suspicion by critics. Writers, they feel, should live with their mistakes (which may well be more enlivening than embalmed texts), and their endeavours to eliminate these errors from their past arise from either the vanity of altering our appearance or the ambition to control history.

The precedents of those who have famously rewritten their work are certainly not encouraging. George Moore, it is said, in a mad act of justification, remodelled his paragraphs so that their last printed lines, beating back the invasion of blank spaces, exactly reached the margin of the page.

Henry James, that terrified revisionist, imposed his late manner on his earlier novels as a process of what he called 'beautification'. But this fingering of the past from the near side of the grave, intended as an enhancement of textual detail and surface expression, is generally seen now as a self-deluded attempt at regaining access to early emotions and exerting authority over them – elderly improvements which actually smothered the life from his prose.

W.H. Auden, too, in his determination to weed out the 'false emotions, inflated rhetoric, empty sonorities' that had entered his work through the influence of Yeats ('a symbol of my own devil of inauthenticity') repeatedly revised some poems and omitted others 'false to my personal and poetic nature' from the canon of his work. But his claim to know his poetic intention better than his readers aroused the ire of those readers' 'minders', the critics, who levelled accusations at him ranging from insensitive and wilful misunderstanding of his past work to political reworking of the facts.

I refer to these distinguished examples because, as I hurried past the bookshops to my publisher, I was well aware of the lesson they presented against ever turning back. Such warnings seemed relevant because I too felt what Henry James had felt when he said about *Roderick Hudson*: 'the thing is positively in many places *vilely* written!' I also recalled what Auden wrote when he set about revising his *Collected Shorter Poems*, 'gnashing my teeth at my clumsiness in the old days. To-day, at least, I think I know my craft.'

But there was also the matter of scholarship, and in this respect the precedents of revised biographies – Richard Ellmann's *James Joyce*, Leon Edel's *Henry James*, George Painter's *Marcel Proust* – are more auspicious. Part of my embarrassment came from the fact that in some places my biography had grown categorically misleading. Over more than twenty-five years there has been a great deal of new and informative Bloomsbury non-fiction published in the letters of Max Beerbohm, Vanessa Bell, Carrington, E.M. Forster, Roger Fry, D.H. Lawrence, Katherine Mansfield, Bertrand Russell and Leonard Woolf; in the correspondence between Rupert Brooke and Noel Olivier, Lydia Lopokova and Maynard Keynes, Ralph Partridge and Gerald Brenan, James and Alix Strachey; as well as in Ottoline Morrell's diaries and the diaries and letters of Virginia

Woolf. In addition to this primary source material there have been numerous valuable and authoritative memoirs and biographies. This accumulation of material, together with a good deal of unpublished documentation now in public collections, has enabled me to correct simple errors of fact, alter some sequences of facts, and reconsider my interpretation of facts. Some letters that I saw in private in the 1960s seem to have disappeared; other letters, such as those from Lytton to Sebastian Sprott, I have seen for the first time. I have been able to build up the subsidiary characters and sometimes hand over the narrative to them. Describing the triangular relationships in which Bloomsbury specialized I often used correspondence from only two sides. Now I am able to complete the triangle and give a multi-faceted account of what was happening.

I have taken advantage of these opportunities to give new accounts of Carrington's early life, in particular her involvement with the painter Mark Gertler, and of Lytton's long-lasting friendship with Virginia Woolf. I have also attempted to chart Bloomsbury's changing relationship with some of its neighbours: its attitude to Henry James's world and the world of D.H. Lawrence; its dalliance with the bohemianism of Augustus John and its mingling with Rupert Brooke's Neo-Pagans, as well as its scepticism and growing interest in the advance of psychoanalysis. Above all I have been able to re-examine what Carrington called the 'Triangular Trinity of Happiness' at Tidmarsh and Ham Spray House and show, as I could not do before, the parts that many men and women played in this comedy of manners and the changes made to their lives as it developed into tragedy. Finally, I have tried to demonstrate that Bloomsbury's belief in 'a great deal of a great many kinds of love' was an essential part of Lytton Strachey's point of view as a historian.

The question may be asked as to whether Lytton Strachey is worth all this extra labour, and whether a new generation will be interested in his life and work. I believe that the extraordinary story of his life holds a continuing interest and that this interest is reinforced by the lasting change he brought to the craft of biography, technically and also culturally, by smuggling in deviant behaviour as part of our heritage.

Dr Johnson suggested that fame was a shuttlecock that needed determined play from the opposite side of the net to keep it in contention. If this is true, then Strachey has been doing well enough. 'With his pacifism, his homosexuality and his bohemianism', his anticipation of the modern plea 'Make love, not war', he might, the historian Piers Brendon suggests, have been clearly seen as a patron saint of the 1960s 'flower power'. But this was obscured by the influence of F.R. Leavis who during the previous decade, Dr Brendon remembers, would tell his Cambridge pupils that Strachey had been 'responsible, through his malign influence on Maynard Keynes, for the outbreak of the Second World War'.[11]

It is the reward of a successful ironist to be paradoxically acclaimed in such grand style. In his book, *A History of the Modern World* (1983), Paul Johnson pictures Strachey, 'the unofficial leader of Bloomsbury . . . [and] a propagandist of genius', as an English equivalent to Lenin, who used G.E. Moore's *Principia Ethica* as Lenin used J.A. Hobson's *Imperialism*, to 'create and fashion a new God'. In Paul Johnson's view, Strachey aimed at an intellectual takeover of the modern world. We see him grasping the principle of power and running the Bloomsbury coterie with 'an iron, though seemingly languid, hand' until it grew into a mafia which was 'far more destructive to the old British values than any legion of enemies'. The influence of this ruling mandarin reaches, in Paul Johnson's pages, 'upwards and downwards by the 1930s to embrace the entire political nation'. In some respects this is a similar interpretation of his influence to James Strachey's, though from the very opposite standpoint. For Paul Johnson accuses Lytton Strachey of destroying the virtues of patriotism and leaving behind a national emptiness which became the homosexual recruiting-ground at Cambridge for Soviet espionage.[12] It is perhaps appropriate for a work identifying Strachey's parental attack on the generation brought up on Carlyle's *Heroes and Hero Worship* as one of the most powerfully decadent forces of the twentieth century, to be dedicated to the influence and achievements of the author's father.

For a biographer to write about another biographer presents peculiar layers of complexity that become more mysterious when the Life is unpicked and restitched many years later. The situation lends itself to one of those Max Beerbohm caricatures in which the Young and the Old Self confront each other. In our case we met as strangers. This has been part of the fascination, not to say the exasperation, of the exercise. My obstinate and opinionated Young Self has insisted on retaining passages which I would never write today but which, despite their deformities, still have (he maintains) some irregular beat of life in them. The Old Self, arguing for a new aesthetic, has patiently explained that the original plan to contrast Strachey's 'black period' with the 'Spiritual Revolution' that led to his illuminating success is too simple and has the initial disadvantage of beginning with 300 pages of blackness.

Emerging from that blackness, the Young Self learnt to write biography rather as people learn to skate, by making mistakes, falling down, picking himself up, trying again and stuttering on until, somewhere near the end, he could move with fair fluency. The Young Self allows that quicker and less haphazard progress can now be made, especially since more is known about Bloomsbury by the general reader. But he is suspicious of the Old Self's professional tricks. Changing the metaphor, he impatiently asks what is the point of ring craft and shadow play, the use of ropes and clinches, if no knock-out blow is ever delivered. Eventually we were able to work out an accommodation because we had a similar end in view.

What I hope to have done is to approach nearer to writing the book I would like to have written all those years ago. Reading the early chapters in 1964, Alix Strachey complained that there was something 'froglike and unfeeling' about them. This is my final attempt to change that frog into a prince.

PART I

'We begin life in a very odd manner – like shipwrecked sailors. The world is our desert island.'

Lytton Strachey to Leonard Woolf (July 1904)

ONE

Lancaster Gate

'To reconstruct, however dimly, that grim machine, would be to realize with some real distinctness the essential substance of my biography.'

Lytton Strachey, 'Lancaster Gate' (1922)

I

PAPA AND MAMA

'The Stracheys are most strongly the children of their fathers, not of their mothers,' Amy St Loe Strachey wrote in 1930. '"It does not matter whom they marry," said one of St Loe's aunts to me when I was quite young, "the type continues and has been the same for three hundred years."' This was not obviously true of St Loe's cousin, Lytton Strachey. 'You'd never think he was a general's son,' the head porter at the Great Gate of Trinity sighed to Clive Bell, as Lytton's drooping silhouette moved across the quadrangle.

Richard Strachey had been born at Sutton Court near Chew Magna, Somerset, on 24 July 1817 and passed much of his active career in India. It was largely to him that the country owed its extensive railways and canals. He established the first adequate forest service in the country; he reorganized the public works department of which, in 1862, he became the head; he was the first to advise amendment of the currency; and in his spare time he developed a talent for watercolours. But his real leaning was towards the sciences, and he liked to think that his lasting achievements lay in meteorology. He was also a fine geographical scholar, for two years President of the Royal Geographical Society, and was awarded the highest scientific honour in Britain, the Royal Society's Gold Medal. In an empire of polymaths Richard Strachey more than held his own. Yet his imagination remained largely matter-of-fact.

His marriage to Jane Maria Grant took place on 4 January 1859. She was the daughter of Sir John Peter Grant and Henrietta Chichele, a prominent member of a rather more aristocratic Anglo-Indian family. Jane Maria had been born on 13 March 1840, on board the East India

3

Company's strong ship, *The Earl of Hardwicke*, in the middle of a violent storm off the Cape of Good Hope. Eighteen years later, in a sedate Indian withdrawing-room, she met Richard Strachey, a black-haired widower[1] of forty-two, seated on a yellow sofa, displaying the exact 'colours of a wasp'.

They were not an obviously well-matched pair. He, like most Stracheys, was rather short,[2] highly methodical at work but of an abrupt social temperament; she was stately in appearance, and had more artistic interests. His influence with the children seems to have declined with time, while Jane Maria became increasingly the dominating figure within the family. 'It was my mother who counted,' Lytton's sister Dorothy wrote.

Giles Lytton Strachey was born at Stowey House, Clapham Common, on 1 March 1880, the eleventh of thirteen children, three of whom died in infancy. He was christened Giles Lytton after a sixteenth-century ancestor, Giles Strachey, and his godfather, the first Earl of Lytton, Viceroy of India, who as 'Owen Meredith' achieved some distinction as a poet. As a young child he was high-spirited and loquacious. 'Giles is the most ridiculous boy I ever saw,' Jane Maria wrote to her daughter Dorothy shortly after his third birthday: 'he said to me, "Yesterday in the streets I saw a cow eating the birds!" He then enacted a drama of which the punishment of the unnatural cow was the motive; as a policeman he flung himself on one knee and upraised his arms at the cow with a most fine dramatic gesture of Command; a terrific combat then ensued in which he wielded the peacock broom with might, and finally cried sternly, "Go to be dead." He never ceases talking for a single minute.'

Giles liked to march up and down Stowey House chanting what was apparently an epic poem full of high-sounding phrases, which always began the same way but varied unpredictably in its later stages. 'It is interspersed with morsels in rhyme called "Dickey Songs",' his mother noted in her diary on 25 March 1884, 'and sung by the "Bugyler" – the chief hero "Brynorma", the drummer boy is "Shiptenor", there is "Tellysin" and a "Calorum" and a "Sunsence"; as far as we can ascertain these names are entirely of his own construction. It looks rather as if he were one of the "many children" who could have written Ossian!'[3]

Lytton's father was by this time nearing seventy, though his wife was only forty-three. Terminating his short, impersonal letters in which the formality is relieved by drawings of odd botanical specimens to be seen at Kew, and which accompany mathematical booklets and packets of strange foreign stamps, Richard Strachey would sign himself 'Your affnt father, Rd. Strachey'; while Jane Maria, spreading herself over far longer and more frequent letters, remained, even after Lytton was grown up, 'ever darling, your loving Mama'. But his father's remoteness seemed to heighten Lytton's admiration.

Lytton's earliest memories of his father recalled little but voluminous sheaves of papers covered with calculations which encumbered his desk. During the day he would sit working at railway or atmospheric matters before this enormous desk in his study; and Lytton was often sent up from the dining-room to persuade him to descend for lunch. As the child grew, so his father seemed to shrink into 'a little man with a very beautiful head', as Leonard Woolf later described him, 'sitting all day long, summer and winter, in a great armchair in front of a blazing fire, reading a novel'.[4] Over the last few years of his life he was seldom seen without a novel in his hand. Six a week were brought to him on a silver tray, and these would apparently absorb him until, shortly after ten o'clock at night, Ellen, the maid, appeared with a shawl to take him up to bed. Meanwhile Mrs Strachey, as she sat playing patience on the opposite side of the elaborately tiled fireplace, kept an agonized eye on her husband to see if he was going to be good. Occasionally, very occasionally, he *was* good, soon closed his book, rose with a smile and shuffled off to bed on Ellen's arm. More often than not, however, he was naughty and resolved to finish the chapter before becoming aware that Ellen was in the room. After waiting patiently for several minutes, Ellen would bend forward and whisper to him that it was late. No notice whatever would be taken of this announcement. Silent looks of sympathy were then exchanged between Ellen and Mrs Strachey, who shook her head in helpless disapproval. But never did she interfere or address any remark to her husband, and if the proceedings became unusually protracted, one of her daughters would put her book down, firmly advance and say, 'Papa, it's bedtime!' Realizing the game was up, the General would raise his spectacles over his forehead and with an engaging smile pretend that this was the first he had heard of it.

During the day, the old man seemed unaware of the terrific din from the swarms of creatures in spectacles, his sons and daughters. He sat through it unmoved, occasionally smiling affectionately, Leonard Woolf recalled in his autobiography, 'when it obtruded itself unavoidably upon his notice, for instance, if in some deafening argument one side or the other appealed to him for a decision. He was usually a silent man [but] . . . extraordinarily friendly and charming to an awkward youth such as I was, and he was fascinating when now and again he was induced to enter the discussion or recall something from his past.'[5]

Part of this benevolent remoteness came from deafness which afflicted his later years and which forced him to relinquish several of the official appointments he still held. Up to the age of ninety, he continued to go to the City and to the Meteorological Office. But he was a dangerous pedestrian, and occasionally collided with hansom cabs – impacts which,

5

though sometimes bringing on attacks of gout and spreading family anxiety, always left him in high spirits. He passed the last active period of his life perfecting his instruments for measuring the movements of clouds, and in giving expression to one or two laws of meteorology. But that the rules of ethics, the laws and customs of social morality, the psychological complexities of his own children could be subjected to a similar scrutiny apparently did not occur to him.

Beside her husband, Jane Maria Strachey appears an unconventional figure. Only a remarkable woman would have struck up a friendship with Robert Browning or been asked by George Eliot to enter upon a correspondence. She had little taste in the plastic arts, and was no intellectual. Yet she was a figure in her own right – and not unaware of the fact. When on 22 June 1897, the date of Queen Victoria's Diamond Jubilee, she opened *The Times* and saw that her husband had been made Grand Commander of the Star of India, she complained that this had been done without his first being asked. Previously he had declined honours. Now she would be known as plain Lady Strachey – one of several – instead of *the* Mrs Richard Strachey.

From her earliest years she loved literature, particularly French literature and Elizabethan drama. Her own publications consisted mostly of verses for children,[6] though she also edited her aunt Elizabeth Grant's celebrated *Memoirs of a Highland Lady*,[7] and in old age composed 'Some Recollections of a Long Life'.[8] She enjoyed classical music, sitting Lytton on her knee while she played songs on the piano; and inspired him too with her passion for parlour games, amateur theatricals, puzzles, and with something of her zest for billiards. Long before women were generally permitted such habits she smoked, not just ordinary cigarettes, but ultra-modern American cigarettes. She grew more 'advanced' in her old age than she had been in her youth – for which Lytton was partly responsible. She had been brought up a Christian but, after reading John Stuart Mill's work *On Liberty* at the age of nineteen, became his fervent disciple. In her sixties she tried to match Lytton's rather aggressive paganism. 'I should not be surprised', she wrote hopefully to him, 'if the decay of Christianity led to some really interesting appreciations of the New Testament that might stimulate perceptions which, like mine, have been blunted by ceaseless iteration and vitiated by the theological standpoint.' Lytton listened to what she said, but they were divided by gender and a generation. 'Oh how dreadful to be a mother,' he exclaimed to Maynard Keynes. 'How terrible to love so much and know so little! Will it always be like this to the end of the world?'

In public Lady Strachey worked for the Women's Progressive

Movement, regularly marching at the head of processions; at home she instinctively put her husband before herself. Like him, she preferred the scientists of their acquaintance – Francis Galton, T.H. Huxley – to the artists and men of letters. Although she met many eminent writers, including Carlyle, Ruskin and Tennyson, her recorded observations on them were unexceptional. She never noticed anything to suggest that the Carlyles were not on the very best of terms.

She dressed in bunchy unfashionable black satin clothes. Though statuesque in appearance, her movements were ungainly. She was energetic, but absent-minded and short-sighted, sometimes entering a room and after gazing round it in distraction, being obliged to walk out vacantly. She suffered also, this majestic-looking woman, from attacks of vertigo and after one attack near Marble Arch was arrested by the police on suspicion of drunkenness.

'Our conventionality,' wrote Lytton, 'slightly mitigated by culture and intelligence, was impinged upon much more seriously by my mother's constitutional vagueness and immateriality, and by a vein in her of oddity and caprice. Her feeling for what was right and proper was unsupported by the slightest touch of snobbery; and, while it was very strong and quite unhesitating, it was surprisingly peculiar to herself. That her daughters should go into mourning for the German Emperor, for instance, appeared to her essential; but her own dresses were most extraordinary, designed by herself, quite regardless of fashion. She had all her children christened, but she never went to Church – except in the country, when she went with the utmost regularity. She was religious in the payment of calls; but the arrangements of the household, from the point of view of social life, were far below the standard.'[9] Amid the tribal hubbub of talkative Stracheys, she would station herself at a writing-desk and pursue a slow, immensely elaborate, system of household accounts.

The private education which Lady Strachey oddly fastened on her sons and daughters seemed haphazard. Though they remained uninstructed and, in the case of the daughters, unenlightened regarding the facts of life, she read them the bawdiest Elizabethan dramatists, together with such novels as *Tom Jones*. Many years later, however, when Lytton brought up the question of Shakespeare's sonnets, she sent two of his sisters – then in their twenties – out of the room, while she argued in favour of Shakespeare's sexual purity. Degradation and horror had no place in her life, and she somehow avoided coming in contact with the lust and savagery of the Elizabethans of whom she was so fond. She learnt long passages of Milton off by heart, and, enjoying the music of the poetry, paid not the least attention to the doctrines. Similarly, despite being a

7

freethinker, she liked to read Robert South's sermons aloud to her children to give them an ear for rhythm in English prose. Literature was an excellent recreation, but it had little connection with her family's lives. According to her eldest daughter Elinor, she had a 'reverence' for the family 'as an entity'. But for all the pleasure she took in managing this family, she remained curiously ignorant of what any of them were thinking or feeling.

2

ELEPHANTIASIS AND UNCLES

When Lytton was four years old the Stracheys moved from Stowey House to 69 Lancaster Gate. This cliff-like Victorian terrace, with its pillared porticoes, just north of Kensington Gardens, was described by Nikolaus Pevsner as a 'monumentally planned composition of tall well-to-do houses' in his *Buildings of England*. Here Lytton was to spend the next twenty-five years. 'My remembrances of Stowey House are dim and sporadic,' he wrote long afterwards, '– Jim Rendel[10] with a penny in a passage – a miraculous bean at the bottom of the garden – Beatrice Chamberlain[11] playing at having tea with me, with leaves and acorns, under a tree. But my consecutive existence began in the nursery at Lancaster Gate ... [and] was to continue till I was twenty-eight – a man full grown – all the changes from childhood to adolescence, from youth to manhood, all the developments, the curiosities, the pains, the passions, the despairs, the delights, of a quarter of a century having taken place within those walls.'

A portentous establishment, dark, rambling, badly planned, ugly both within and without, Lancaster Gate[12] filled Lytton with foreboding. He felt submerged by its solemn and prodigious bulk. But it was not mere size alone which chilled him, Lytton believed; 'it was size gone wrong, size pathological; it was a house afflicted with elephantiasis that one found one had entered, when, having mounted the steps under the porch, having passed through the front door and down the narrow dark passage with its ochre walls and its tessellated floor of magenta and indigo tiles, one looked upwards and saw the staircase twisting steeply up its elongated well – spiralling away into a thin infinitude, until, far above, one's surprised vision came upon a dome of pink and white glass, which yet one judged, with an unerring instinct, was not the top – no, not nearly, nearly, the top.'[13]

8

There were, considering the space occupied, astonishingly few rooms. Lytton's father was the only member of the family to have a sitting-room of his own; while his daughters led an oddly communal existence in a tiny apartment behind the dining-room, far higher than it was long or broad, and styled the 'young ladies' room'. For the boys there was not even this doleful sanctuary. The house contained seven layers of human habitation: a basement, a ground floor, and a drawing-room that filled out almost all the first floor, above which were placed four further floors of bedrooms. These were all small, of enormous height and, except for one on each floor that looked out on to the street, very gloomy, since there was no garden or even courtyard. So lugubrious was the outlook from the two back rooms that the windows had been made of a desperately cheerful, pink and impenetrable frosted glass. Borrowing an idea from her husband's office in the City, Lady Strachey had 'reflectors' put up – vast plates of shiny material, slightly corrugated, which hung opposite the windows from chains. The windows themselves were so huge and cumbersome that no one could force them open, and little circular ventilators, working by means of cords and pulleys, had to be cut in the panes. All this made a weird impression on Lytton as he sat in his bedroom, dwarfed by its sombre altitude, or in the schoolroom at the end of the passage on the ground floor – the mammoth windows of pale ground glass with their complex machinery of string and ventilator, and a dim vision of discoloured yellow bricks, looming through the London fog outside.

There were other alarming inconveniences, such as the 'one and only bathroom, for instance,' Lytton remembered, 'perched, with its lavatory, in an impossible position midway between the drawing-room and the lowest bedroom floor – a kind of crow's nest – to reach which, one had to run the gauntlet of stairs innumerable, and whose noises of rushing water were all too audible from the drawing-room just below.'

By the late 1880s, it was obvious that the Strachey family was in decline. As the Victorian age crept into antiquity and the grumblings of serious reaction to it made themselves heard, they looked around and found themselves stranded. Within Lancaster Gate everything remained as before. To go there for the first time was like stepping into a previous age. The first chill was cast upon one by the butler who drew open the massive mahogany doors. Uncouth and unpresentable – the promoted gardener's son of Stowey House – Frederick was a gentle creature whose fearsome appearance, accentuated by his great mouth ill-concealed beneath a straggling moustache, belied his inner excellence. Later he was replaced by Bastiani, a figure even more characteristic of the subtle *dégringolade* – 'a fat, black-haired, Italianate creature,' as Lytton described him, 'who eventually took to drink, could hardly puff up the stairs from the basement, and as he handed the vegetables, exuded an odour of sweat and whisky into one's face. He disappeared – after a scene of melodramatic horror – to be replaced by Mr Brooks who, we could only suppose, must have been a groom in earlier life, since all his operations were accompanied by a curious sound of *sotto voce* hissing.'

The child brought up within this strange mausoleum took it for granted that here was the only world in existence. Lytton was aware that something was wrong with this world – that it was an unpleasant shape. As the bad drains and dampness of the house gradually affected the growing boy, his cheerfulness ebbed away, his health mysteriously deteriorated. The disintegration of the house seemed to be casting a physical and emotional spell on him.

The focal point of Lancaster Gate was its monumental drawing-room. This great assembly hall, with its lofty eminence, its towering door, its glowing *portière* of pale green silk, filled him with religious awe. 'The same vitality, the same optimism, the same absence of nerves,' he wrote, 'which went to the deliberate creation of ten children, built the crammed, high, hideous edifice that sheltered them.

'And so it was inevitable that the most characteristic feature of the house – its centre, its summary, the seat of its soul, so to speak – should have been the room which was the common meeting-place of all the members of the family – the drawing-room. When one entered that vast chamber, when, peering through its foggy distances, ill-lit by gas-jets, or casting one's eyes wildly towards the infinitely distant ceiling overhead, one struggled to traverse its dreadful length, to reach a tiny chair or a far-distant fireplace, conscious as one did so that some kind of queer life was clustered thick about one ... then, in truth, one had come – whether one realized it or no – into an extraordinary holy of holies.'

Here Lytton grew mesmerized by the riddle of the Victorian age. If the drawing-room was a temple erected to the spirit of Victorianism, its altar was undoubtedly the elevated and elaborate mantelpiece. This was an expanse of painted wood, designed by Halsey Ricardo, with pilasters and cornices and various marble and multicoloured tiles. Having reached this citadel through the waves of persons ebbing and flowing around it, you could see, from the vantage-point of a mottled hearth, that this was in no sense a romantic room. Yet there was something here which continued to fascinate Lytton. Like the age whose history will never be written, it was familiar to him yet at the same time a little surprising, as though perpetually withholding some secret. 'Up to my last hour in it,' he later confessed, 'I always felt that the drawing-room was strange.'

By character and usage it was primarily a family room, built to contain not only Sir Richard and Lady Strachey and their ten children, but also all the other branches of the clan, in particular a large quantity of paternal uncles. The most senior of these, Sir Edward Strachey – the third baronet and father of St Loe Strachey, future editor of the *Spectator* – seldom left the fortified manor of Sutton Court in Somerset, behind whose walls he laboured gallantly at his *Materials to Serve for a History of the Strachey Family*. The second of Lytton's uncles, Colonel Henry Strachey, whose tenacity was to carry him through to his ninety-sixth year, would, though blind, frequently find his way up from Sutton Court to talk over old times. He was a very polite old gentleman, Lytton later recalled, and 'very dim, poor man, but his shoes exquisitely polished'. Yet another uncle, Sir John Strachey, who as finance minister to three successive Indian viceroys had fostered a measure for the introduction of metrical weights throughout India – a Trollopian edict never put into effect[14] – visited Lancaster Gate regularly in the summer months from his house in Cornwall Gardens. He had by this time become a philosophic radical after the style of Mill, while, as an ardent supporter of Garibaldi, he wintered in Florence.

But perhaps the general state of decomposition was best embodied by Lytton's two junior uncles, George and William. George, having been a diplomat, contributed in his later years prolix articles to the *Spectator*. In the drawing-room of Lancaster Gate he presented a peculiar spectacle, 'bent double with age and eccentricity, hideously snuffling and pouring out his opinions on architecture to anyone who ventured within his reach'.

The most outlandish uncle of all was William Strachey. Notwithstanding his having lived in India only five years, and his association with the British Empire having been slight and undistinguished, he persevered in upholding Eastern customs with far greater rigidity and a finer disregard for common sense than any other Strachey. Having once visited Calcutta, he became convinced that the clocks there were the only reliable chronometers in the world, and kept his own watch resolutely set by Calcutta time, organizing the remaining fifty-six years of his life accordingly. The results were disconcerting for his friends and family in England. He breakfasted at afternoon tea and lived most of his waking hours by candlelight. On visits to Sutton Court, his strange nocturnal habits earned him a reputation in astrology among the embedded Somerset folk. He had once bought a mechanical bed at the Paris Exhibition which upset the occupant at an appointed hour. Using it for the first time, he was thrown into his bath next to the bed, and in a rage smashed the bed and clock, and resumed his old Calcutta habits. He had been well known at Holland House in the middle of the century, and having once exchanged the time of day with Palmerston, was in his later years immoderately fond of attributing his own opinions to the late prime minister. At the age of seventy he impressed his nine-year-old nephew Lytton as being an utterly fantastic figure, dressed always in spats and a coat and waistcoat of quaint cut and innumerable buttons – the very same that he might have worn in the eighteen-forties – and, whatever the weather, attired in a pair of goloshes. When he died in his mid-eighties, he left Lytton a legacy of unworn and prettily coloured underclothes including 'some exquisite drawers or "pants"'.

Lytton also saw something of the Scottish side of his family. The Grants of Rothiemurchus traced their ancestry back to John Grant, Chief of Grant, who in 1539 had married Lady Marjorie Stuart, making Lytton a potential claimant to the Scottish throne. The laird, Lady Strachey's eldest brother John Peter Grant, was rather remote, but numerous other uncles and aunts often visited Lancaster Gate. Lytton's favourite was Uncle Trevor, a very friendly and uncomprehending fellow, married to a native of India, Aunt Clementina, who was said to make chapattis on the drawing-room carpet. Together they brought up a large, unfortunate family, the most unfortunate of all ending his life being hugged by a bear. There was also Uncle Bartle, a military gentleman who, on periods of leave from his regiment, edited a famous cookery book and compiled a scholarly volume on the orchids of Burma; Aunt Hennie, a most prominent figure who had been dropped on her head when an infant; and Uncles Charles and George who both had sons named Pat. 'White' Pat was thought by the family to be a good character, 'Black' Pat a bad one, until 'White' Pat ran off with 'Black' Pat's wife. Most spectacular of all these maternal relations was 'Aunt Lell', the wife of Sir James Colvile. Whenever Lady Strachey was away, Lytton would be left in the care of Aunt Lell, 'a demi-lunatic, harmless and wonderfully funny', who had learnt the piano under Madame Schumann and whose well-conducted social life, moving round her smart Park Lane house – so different from the knockabout regime of Lancaster Gate – immensely impressed him.

As for the people who came to Lancaster Gate, observed Lytton's sister Dorothy, 'many of them highly distinguished, we admired them without listening to them'. On Sunday afternoons the family atmosphere was at its most bizarre. 'Then the drawing-room', wrote Lytton, 'gradually grew thick with aunts and uncles, cousins and connections, with Stracheys,

Rendels, Plowdens, Battens, Ridpaths, Rowes.' Since most of the Stracheys had peculiarly penetrating voices, and Lady Strachey's children inherited all her Scottish love of argument, the general volume of noise, of turmoil and excited chatter at these weekly gatherings was terrific. On one afternoon Bertrand Russell, whom Lady Strachey had met as a fellow member of a committee designed to secure votes for women, was invited to call. 'All the children', he records, 'were to my unpractised eyes exactly alike except in the somewhat superficial point that some were male and some were female. The family were not all assembled when I arrived, but dropped in one by one at intervals of twenty minutes (one of them, I afterwards discovered, was Lytton). I had to look round the room carefully to make sure that it was a new one that had appeared and not merely one of the previous ones that had changed his or her place. Towards the end of the evening I began to doubt my sanity, but kind friends afterwards assured me that things had really been as they seemed.'[15]

'My ideal life', Lady Strachey once confided to Virginia Woolf, 'would be to live *entirely* in boarding houses.' All her homes resembled boarding houses. When one of her sons or daughters invited a friend back to lunch, no one would pay the guest any attention. Innumerable Stracheys would sit in solemn silence round the dinner table, Sir Richard wrapped in a shawl at the centre of them reading a novel, and everything proceeded with a ceremonious absence of communication. Then, once the meal was completed, uproar broke out again.

Unless someone of importance stayed on, none of the family troubled to dress for the long serious family dinner. The butler of the moment, assisted by a liveried boot-boy, waited upon them during these formidable sessions. 'At the end,' Lytton wrote, 'the three mystic bottles of port, sherry, and claret were put at the head of the table and solemnly circulated – the port, sherry and claret having come from the grocer's round the corner.'

These visitors to Lancaster Gate were quietly observed by the thin pale boy. One of the most habitual was an amateur musician, Sir William Ward. Besides having been Governor of the Straits Settlements he was, Lytton records, 'an executor, of astonishing brilliancy, on the pianoforte. Pressed to play, he would seat himself at the piano and dash into a Chopin waltz with the verve of a high-stepping charger, when suddenly a very odd and discordant sound, rising and falling with the music, would make itself heard. It was something between a snore and a whistle, and nobody could think what it could be. But the mystery was at last explained – the ex-Governor suffered, in moments of excitement, from a curious affection of the nose. While the family listened, a little hysterically, to this peculiar combination of sounds, all at once yet *another* sound – utterly different – burst upon their ears – the sound, this time, of rushing water. There was a momentary shock; and then we all silently realized that someone, in the half-way landing upstairs, was using the w.c.'

This mixture of heavy punctilio and extenuating farce, which made up the routine of life at Lancaster Gate, was curiously unsettling. Though his sisters remembered Lytton as 'giggling fairly continuously from the age of three to nineteen', darker emotions were also gathering within him. 'It was not a question of unhappiness,' he explained, 'so much as of restriction and oppression – the subtle unperceived weight of the circumambient air.' But then these mists of pessimism would dissolve, the sun shine through and flood his world with light. At such moments 'some magic spring within me was suddenly released, and I threw off that weight, my spirit leaping up into freedom and beatitude.'

3

MARIE SOUVESTRE

The most pleasurable periods of Lytton's childhood were those he spent in the Scottish Highlands. For many years his mother would take her children up to the Doune,[16] the Grants' family home in Rothiemurchus, during part of the holidays. These were always happy excursions for Lytton. To the end of his life he remained susceptible to 'its massive and imposing landscape, its gorgeous colouring, its hidden places of solitude and silence, its luxuriant vegetation, its wilderness of remote and awful splendour'. Though surrounded as usual by hordes of Grants and Stracheys, he could go off for day-dreaming walks among the pine-woods and the mountains.[17]

An early diary shows Lytton on one of these summer holidays playing on the grass with a cousin, eating strawberries fresh from the garden, riding ponies, dancing, playing cricket and robbers, vaulting streams and climbing the slopes of the Cairngorms. In more recognizable moods he would listen to his mother reciting extracts from the *Iliad*, and to his sister Dorothy reading from Walter Scott's *The Abbot*. And at other times he is sketching the landscape or working out puzzles.

More frequently as time went on the family would rent a large country house for the summer in one of the Home Counties, and here, amid the shrill young Stracheys, Lytton played croquet and starred in amateur theatricals. But these southern holidays never pleased him so much as the hills and corries of the Highlands.

In the summer of 1886 he was sent, with his younger sister Marjorie, to the Hyde Park Kindergarten and School at 24 Chilworth Street. Here he remained for some eighteen months and in the words of the headmistresss, Miss E. Fisher Brown, 'worked exceedingly well and was very intelligent'.

In one of his earliest surviving letters, dated 7 May 1887, Lytton wrote to his mother: 'I have just begun French, it is very exciting. I know the French for Lion – it is Lion but pronounced differently. Marjorie smudged this letter.'

'I am very glad you like French,' she answered; 'the further you go the more exciting you will find it. There are beautiful stories and books of all sorts in it.'

Lytton's enthusiasm for French, and the literature of France, expanded under the encouragement of his mother, who helped him to write French verses and often presented him on his birthdays with one of the French classics. She also saw to it that the first school which was to help in shaping the course of his career, was a French girls' school near Wimbledon.

Many years earlier, while in Italy, Lady Strachey had met Marie Souvestre (daughter of the French writer Emile Souvestre) who conducted a celebrated school for girls at Fontainebleau, called Les Ruches. 'She fell in love with me at once,' she innocently wrote. So impressed had Lady Strachey been by this woman's charm and intelligence that she sent her two eldest daughters, Elinor and Dorothy, to Les Ruches when they were each aged about sixteen. When Marie Souvestre left France to become the headmistress-proprietor of Allenswood, at South Fields not far from Wimbledon Common, both the younger Strachey daughters, Joan Pernel and Marjorie, were entered there, while Dorothy was employed on the teaching staff, giving lessons on Shakespeare.

A handsome, keen-witted, irreligious woman, Marie Souvestre had been an habituée of intellectual society in Paris and Berlin, as well as being on friendly terms with many of the radical free-thinking set in London – John Morley, Joseph Chamberlain, Leslie Stephen. 'A remarkable woman,' Beatrice Webb described her in a diary entry for March 1889:

'Purely literary in her training, with the talent of brilliant expression, and the charm of past beauty and present attractiveness. She is a student of individual human natures, but she is deficient in the personal experience of religious feeling and public spirit; she watches these qualities in others with a strange combination of suspicion, surprise, and unappreciative admiration. You feel that every idea is brought under a sort of hammering logic, and broken into pieces unless it can be sound metal, and if it belongs to the religious order and is proof against ridicule, it is looked at critically and laid carefully on one side for some future hostile analysis.'[18]

The relationship between the Stracheys and Marie Souvestre in the 1880s and '90s was very close. Comings and goings between Lancaster Gate and Allenswood were frequent, and sometimes the whole Strachey family spent part of their holidays at the school. Lytton, of course, was never enrolled as a pupil of Marie Souvestre, but her influence on him was long-lasting. During later adolescence, when he was critical of almost everyone, he never mentions 'cette grande femme' pejoratively.

Marie Souvestre was approaching sixty when Lytton first got to know her. She was watched over with loving care by Mlle Samaia, a very tiny, dynamic woman who had been with her at Les Ruches, and whose adoration now took the form of seeing that she breakfasted in her bedroom and was never vexed by having to look after the business side of the school. Marie Souvestre was already by this time white-haired and rather stout. She had clear-cut features, a strong almost masculine face, good forehead and dark piercing eyes. She never married, but appeared to find emotional and intellectual fulfilment in looking after her girls. The school was the nucleus of her life, but she was by no means a typical headmistress, not by English standards. She had no veneration for outdoor sports. She was a declared atheist, a humanist and, in politics, fervently pro-Boer. Though she never attempted to indoctrinate Lytton, it was not in her nature to conceal her feelings.

Eleanor Roosevelt, who was a student at Allenswood during the 1890s, recalled that 'she had a very soft spot for Americans and liked them as pupils. This was not surprising as a number of her pupils turned out to be rather outstanding women.' In particular she was drawn to girls who were intelligent or good-looking or who loved literature. Sometimes she would make the children read poems and plays to her in French. For her favourites, sitting on little chairs on either side of her library fireplace, the walls behind them lined with books and the room filled with flowers, these were times of great happiness, as they listened to her voice and strove to imitate it.

Lytton found himself occupying a favoured place in Marie Souvestre's esteem, and he benefited from the best she had to offer. His views on public school education, his anti-religious convictions and his special feeling for French writers, in particular Racine, can be partly traced to her early influence. Dorothy, Lytton's elder sister, has left a vivid picture of this ageing woman in an anonymously published novel, *Olivia*.[19] Marie Souvestre appears under the name of Mlle Julie, the joint principal of a girls' boarding school in France, Les Avons. On the first occasion that Mlle Julie makes her appearance, she is described giving a remarkable reading from Racine's *Andromaque*. 'I have heard many readers read Racine, and famous men among them, but I have not heard any who read him as well as Mlle Julie,' wrote Dorothy. 'She read simply and rapidly, without any of the actor's arts and affectations, with no swelling voice, with no gestures beyond the occasional lifting of her hand, in which she held a long ivory paper-cutter. But the gravity of her bearing and her voice transported me at once into the courts of princes and the presence of great emotions.' Dorothy concludes: 'What is certain is that it gave me my first conception of tragedy, of the terror and complication and pity of human lives. Strange that for an English child that revelation should have come through Racine instead of through Shakespeare. But it did.'

In another autobiographical passage Dorothy contrasts Marie Souvestre with Lady Strachey. Despite her shrewdness and good sense, Lytton's mother had an extraordinarily ramshackle mind. The social code under which she had been brought up remained a permanent obstacle to her capacity for absorbing fresh ideas or unconventional emotions. Marie Souvestre was pleasantly free from such inhibitions. When she entered the drawing-room at Lancaster Gate and began to talk, everything changed and the children became aware of what they had always instinctively felt – that there existed beyond the boundaries of their home a quite different and more congenial world.

'I have no doubt been accustomed, or ought to have been accustomed, to good talk at home,' wrote Dorothy. 'But at home one was inattentive . . . When one did listen to it, it was mostly political, or else took the form of argument. My mother and my aunt, who was often in the house, had interminable and heated discussions, in which my mother was invariably in the right and my aunt beyond belief inconsequent and passionate. We found them tedious and sometimes nerve-racking. My father, a man, in our eyes, of infinite wisdom and humour, did not talk much . . . As for the people who came to the house, many of whom were highly distinguished . . . their world seemed hardly to impinge upon ours.

'How different it was here! Mlle Julie was witty. Her brilliant speech darted here and there with the agility and grace of a humming-bird. Sharp and pointed, it would sometimes transfix a victim cruelly. No one was safe, and if one laughed with her, one was liable the next minute to be pierced with a shaft of irony. But she tossed her epigrams about with such evident enjoyment, that if one had the smallest sense of fun, one enjoyed them too, and it was from her that I, for one, learnt to realize the exquisite adaptation of the French tongue to the French wit. To sit at table at her right hand was an education in itself.'

4

SPELLBOUND

Most of Lady Strachey's children inherited something of her love of letters; but in Lytton she soon recognized a boy of special promise. He would bring out programmes for the plays produced by his elder brothers and sisters, and illustrate their notebooks and magazines. His first recorded verses were written at the age of five; and two years later he composed some ingenious 'Songs of Animals, Fishes and Birds'. He also copied out poems from Shakespeare, Marlowe and Blake which his mother taught him.

Lady Strachey collected her children's verses in a family book. They are almost all playful, decorative pieces. But from among these pages of light-hearted rhyming, one of Lytton's pieces, written in April 1890, strikes an odd note. It is addressed to the sister who died in infancy.

> To me Life is a burden
> But to thee
> The joyous pleasures of the world
> Are all a gaiety.
> But if thou did'st perceive my thoughts
> Then thou would'st sigh and mourn,
> Olivia, like me.

From early on the children had been encouraged to work in couples, and Lytton was usually paired off with his younger sister Marjorie. They collaborated in editing a literary magazine, *The Gazelle Gazette*; a book of songs, *Carmina Exotica*; and the beginning of a French comedy. They also corresponded with each other as husband and wife in *The Itchingham Letters*, and produced a play with a sea captain and a detective. A photograph of Lytton taken at about the age of three shows a small figure gorgeously attired, chubby and with long dark locks reaching below his shoulders. For many years his mother dressed him in petticoats, thinking them prettier and less absurd than knickerbockers.

Lytton was always in the company of his mother and sisters. His elder brothers were seldom at Lancaster Gate. Richard John Strachey,[20] the eldest of all, was a commissioned officer in the Rifle Brigade, while Ralph Strachey,[21] having failed to get into the army owing to defective eyesight, ultimately became chief engineer in the East Indian Railway. The third son, Oliver Strachey,[22] was away for much of the year at Eton. In his daydreams, Lytton longed for a time when he too could play some part in this masculine life. For several years he kept a map on which he charted the movements of his brothers around the world.

At home he still worshipped his father from afar, and was jubilant when, during the holidays, the old man occasionally took him to the circus, or to the Royal Naval Exhibition of 1891, or the Crystal Palace to see 'The Wonderful Performance of Wild Beasts', or even to inspect the *Stracheya tibetica* and other lesser botanical specimens at Kew Gardens. Sometimes on these expeditions, and greatly to his son's delight, his father would interrupt his godlike silence and make jokes. But the two of them were never close.

A sequence of illnesses beginning in his eighth year, after the birth of his younger brother James, may have been a means of regaining attention. If Lytton was the most brilliant of the children, James, born when his father was seventy and his mother forty-seven, was the adored *enfant miracle*. His mother's letters to him were full of special endearments: 'my loveling', 'my darling bird'. At the same time no one seemed to know what was the cause of Lytton's maladies. He was subjected to a variety of cures: obliged to consume at every meal a plate of porridge; then dosed with glasses of port; and for several months fed on raw meat. But no remedy was successful.

When he was nine years old Lytton was told by his mother that he was to be sent out of London to continue his education at a small private school on the south coast. The prospect filled him with a conflict of emotions. He pined for the affection and comradeship of boys his own age: yet he was full of apprehension. He already felt towards his home the contradictory impulses of dependence and dislike. In his paper read to the Memoir Club in 1922, he spoke of persistently dreaming that he was back at Lancaster Gate surrounded by his family. Everything is unchanged.

'We are in the drawing-room, among the old furniture, arranged in the old way, and it is understood that we are to go on there indefinitely, as if we had never left it. The strange thing is that, when I realize that this has come about, that our successive wanderings have been a mere interlude, that we are once more permanently established at number 69, a feeling of intimate satisfaction comes over me. I am positively delighted. And this is strange because, in my waking life, I have never for a moment, so far as I am aware, regretted our departure from that house, and if, in actuality, we *were* to return to it, I can imagine nothing which would disgust me more. So, when I wake up . . . I have the odd sensation of a tremendous relief at finding that my happiness of one second before was a delusion.'[23]

These contrasting layers of waking and dreaming match his ambivalent attitude towards the Victorian age. Lancaster Gate, which became his personal symbol of Victorianism, exuded security. Its grim recesses inspired in him an involuntary fascination he never outgrew. A strong awareness of this rationally objectionable heritage was early ingrained in him. The huge mansion gave off a faintly musty air of superannuated traditionalism; and many of the family embodied something antagonistic to youthful enjoyment.

'What had happened', he told members of the Memoir Club, 'was that a great tradition – the aristocratic tradition of the eighteenth century – had reached a very advanced state of decomposition. My father and my mother belonged by birth to the old English world of country-house gentlefolk . . . But their own world was different: it was the middle-class professional world of the Victorians, in which the old forms still lingered, but debased and enfeebled . . . And then, introducing yet another element into the mixture, there was the peculiar disintegrating force of the Strachey character. The solid bourgeois qualities were interpenetrated by intellectualism and eccentricity . . .'

'Disintegration and *dégringolade*, no doubt, and yet the total effect, materialized and enormously extended, was of a tremendous solidity. Lancaster Gate towered up above us, and around us, an imperturbable mass – the framework, almost the very essence – so it seemed – of our being. Was it itself, perhaps, one vast filth-packet, and we the mere *disjecta membra* of vanished generations, which Providence was too busy or too idle to clear away? So, in hours of depression, we might have unconsciously theorized; but nevertheless, in reality, it was not so. Lancaster Gate vanished into nothingness, and we survived.'

While it lasted, the notion that this regime would, in the course of things, come to an end was dreadful; though by the time the family's diminished income eventually brought about this catastrophe, it no longer mattered. The house had already put its spell upon him, so that, wherever he might travel, the same dream, only slightly varying in its details and always transporting him back within the sombre walls of No. 69, would recur. At the age of nine the chance of moving beyond its embrace was already disturbing. What lay beyond? What would, what *could* happen, when he went away?

TWO

'Funny Little Creature'

'At school, friendship is a passion. It entrances the being; tears the soul. All loves of after life can never bring its rapture, or its wretchedness; no bliss so absorbing, no pangs of jealousy or despair so crushing and so keen! What tenderness and what devotion; what illimitable confidence; infinite revelations of inmost thoughts; what ecstatic present and romantic future; what bitter estrangements and what melting reconciliations; what scenes of wild recrimination, agitating explanations, passionate correspondence; what insane sensitiveness, and what frantic sensibility; what earthquakes of the heart, and whirlwinds of the soul, are confined in that simple phrase – a schoolboy's friendship!'

Benjamin Disraeli, Coningsby

I

SEA AIR

Lady Strachey was determined that all her sons and daughters should distinguish themselves. She knew that Lytton might need special attention, but what that attention might be she could never really decide. She seems to have been swayed by the educational history of Lord Lytton, his godfather, whom she had first met in India a few years before Lytton's birth.[1] 'He was extremely unconventional,' she wrote, 'and not having been brought up at a public school, or in ordinary English society, was quite unable to understand the importance attached to conventionalities by the ordinary English public.' She wanted Lytton to enjoy similar advantages and even to pursue a comparable career to that of the great Indian viceroy and poet.

Lytton was first sent, probably in the summer term of 1889, to Henry Forde, who took in a few boys for private teaching at his house at Parkstone, on Poole Harbour in Dorset. His mother believed in the beneficial effects of Victorian 'sea air', and during the holidays, when the family did not go up to Rothiemurchus, she would make sure that Lytton visited some seaside resort, Torquay or Dover or Broadstairs. He was to remain at Parkstone, with one interval spent travelling abroad, until the summer of 1893.

Henry Forde was a Dickensian character, extravagantly obsequious and literary-minded. He was harried continuously by an invalid wife, Grace, who resented the rival claims of her husband's few pupils. 'What a trial the boys are, Henaree!' she would chide him. 'Why don't you *whip* them?' The school reports sent to Lady Strachey sometimes contain more information about their own son who, in contrast to the sickly Lytton, was 'roughing it' at a boarding school at Tonbridge. 'I do not consider Giles behind the average of the ordinary boy at his age,' Henry Forde wrote (December 1890), 'indeed I think he is rather in advance of it; but he is much behind what a boy of his powers should have reached, *if* he had had health.'

Though he did not excel in the Classics as Henry Forde expected, and though he developed a faculty for rapidly forgetting the technicalities of grammar, Lytton began to develop his style. 'It would not at all surprise me, if he were to become literary,' Henry Forde told Lytton's mother shortly after his twelfth birthday.

'I do not mean merely fond of letters – that he is sure to be – but a contributor to them, a writer. He has an ear for, and a knack of hitting off queer and picturesque phrases and turns of expression, and I could quite easily fancy his developing a marked style of his own in the future, and one that would "stand out". He is a distinctly unusual and original kind of boy; and I should think had best be let develop his own way; his education should be chiefly directed to giving him help to evolve himself, not to forcing him into ordinary moulds. Owing to his bid-able-ness and – one must at present say – his timidity, he might be easily moulded after the average standard, with the result I believe of docking and thwarting what is special in him.'

Tall for his age and terribly thin, he looked odd but was not unpopular with the other boys. 'He's always so absurd,' decided his five-year-old brother James. 'He's a funny little creature!'

In his letters home, there are accounts of 'delightful bathes ... I can swim a little' (9 July 1893); of sailing in a big boat called *The Lulu*, striking a rock in the sea, and being stuck there till rescued at nine o'clock at night; of watching 'Mr Gladstone in a tug-boat going to pool. They actually rang the church bells!' (16 June 1889); of playing a 'lovely game of going round the room without touching the floor; it makes one get into a fever'

(15 December 1889); of listening politely to Mr Forde as he read *Gulliver's Travels* – 'it is rather sickening but it can't be helped' (2 February 1890); and of starting 'a Small Naval and Military Exhibition which I hope will be a success' (7 June 1891).

He seems to have been active in the school's plays, which included a boisterous production of *Blue-Beard*, and several Shakespearian tableaux – Lytton playing Romeo in one, while in another 'I was Othello with my face blackened and a pillow and Cecil in bed being smothered'. His impersonation of female parts was specially convincing and sometimes overflowed into real life.

'On Sunday Dora was going to the Thompsons so she dressed me up in her short skirt and Mrs Forde's fashionable cape, bonet and she also put her boa round my neck wich hid my short hair behind we then went to the Thompsons and I was introduced by the name of Miss Miller – a friend of Dora's. After a little Mrs Thompson recognized me but as Mr Thompson had not come in yet so I was arranged with my back to the light. Soon Mr Thompson came in with a friend of his called Mr Pike, he is very frightened of ladies, so when the two entered I was introduced to them they were both unaware of what was going on. Soon the *whole* room was in suppressed laughter and the *unfortunate* Mr Pike didn't know what to do he grew redder and redder in the face and from red to purple and from purple to – I don't know what at last Miss Webb, perceiving his embarrassment said, "I think you'd [better] examine Miss Miller more carefully" – so he did – and then of course he recognized me.'

Though Henry Forde reported that Lytton 'eats with capital appetite' and did some 'spirited painting', his mother was worried by his continuing infirmities. During the summer holidays of 1892, she told Lytton that she was arranging for him to go on a five-month visit to Uncle Charlie in Gibraltar to inhale saltier air and escape the worst of the English winter. He returned to Parkstone in September full of suppressed excitement.

This voyage did not start until two days before Christmas when he and his sister Dorothy set sail on board the *Coromandel*. A diary which he now started tells how he began to feel seasick a few miles out of port, but cured himself by drinking champagne – a tip given him by his father before embarking. Soon they reached Gibraltar, and he noted that 'with the aid of spectacles, I could see what the place looked like. All the houses were like toy houses scattered about the rock and to complete the smallness, the water became filled with little toy boats.'

Having 'affected a landing successfully', they went to live for the next month with their uncle, Charles Grant, a captain in the Black Watch; his wife, 'Aunt Aggie'; and their son, 'Black Pat' – a 'horrible snouted and absurdly mendacious' little boy of about the same age, with whom he got on very well. 'It is perfectly lovely here,' Lytton wrote to his mother. 'All kinds of flowers are in bloom, there are roses and oranges!' It was a happy time. The two boys drove everywhere in a cab 'like a four post bed' and spent their days going to parties, playing bezique, climbing trees, inspecting the guns in the public park, watching football matches and soldiers parading about the barracks, and being taught the Highland Fling by a Scottish piper named Smith. With Pat's mother and father, they also crossed over into Spain where they visited an empty but 'most interesting' bull ring, after which they would play each morning at bull fights – 'We squat on the ground,' Lytton explained to his mother, 'and charge against each other.'

At the end of January the Black Watch was moved to Egypt, and Lytton travelled with the regiment on board the troop-ship HMS *Himalaya*, attired in a diminutive variant of the Highland costume. At Alexandria they disembarked, travelling on by train to Cairo. The three weeks they spent here were among the best of the whole journey. The carnival atmosphere appealed enormously to Lytton. The streets and buildings seemed like illustrations from some fabulous story book. 'It is a delight here,' he told his mother (6 February 1893). 'We don't know what is going to happen to us.' He explored the bazaars, the museums, the tomb of the Mamalukes, the Citadel Mosque, and Joseph's well, down which he and Pat dropped stones. The two boys went everywhere on donkeys which were even more novel than four-post-bed cabs. 'The donkeys flew and I greatly enjoyed myself,' Lytton noted after his first ride. 'These donkeys would be priceless in England they hold their heads up and never think of stopping till they are told to and even then sometimes they won't.'

He had particularly wanted to see the Pyramids. 'Vast and grand and towering above all things near them, they rose against the blue sky solemn and majestic,' he wrote in his diary. But he was even more impressed by the modern hotel, 'the most beautiful in the world' he called it. His good opinion of the Pyramids revived after a hectic expedition to inspect them close at hand. 'We were surrounded by Arabs,' he narrated, 'and one seized each arm and hauled us up the pyramid. The steps are from three to four feet high. My two Arabs helped me along very well and I rested two or three times during the ascent. . . . Coming down was easier than going up I thought but other people didn't. I simply jumped from step to step, the Arabs holding my hands.'

Then they were off again, this time to examine the Sphinx. 'Aunt Aggie', Lytton recounted, 'said she thought it would be a good idea to go to the sphinx on camels, directly she mentioned this word fifteen camels were on us, all making the most awful noise when sitting down.'

'We were all seized by at least four men who pulled us in four different directions I got to a Camel and an Arab said it was a lady's one, which it was not so I was hussled off and two men came and lifted me into the air and put [me] on a camel, at this moment the sheik interfered and I got on to the one that was supposed to have had a lady's saddle. It was a rather ghastly sensation when the camel got up and you thought you were going to tumble off. We walked on our camels to the sphinx where we dismounted and walked to a place just opposite its face. Although its nose had entirely gone it looked as if all its features were there. What an exquisite face it is – how solemn – how majestic you look, your eyes looking out into the desert with that beautiful expression always on your face so collosal and so perfect. You, who have been there for thousands and thousands of years, you, who have gazed and gazed at that endless sea of sand ever since you existed, tell me oh tell me how to look with that sublime expression on your face at all that comes and all that goes, careless of everything for ever.'[2]

As he looks up into the staring eyes, the first whisper of a poem comes to him, as he feels the sensation of transferring his identity through species and gender. Not composed in its final form until ten years later, 'The Cat' was the only one of his verses to be anthologized.[3]

> An ampler air, a warmer June
>   Enfold me, and my wondering eye
> Salutes a more imperial moon
>   Throned in a more resplendent sky
> Than ever knew this pagan shore.
>   Oh, strange! For you are with me too,
> And I who am a cat once more
>   Follow the woman that was you.

Towards the end of February, Lytton left Cairo and returned by train to Alexandria. 'How interesting it all has been,' he wrote in his diary. 'How glad I am I came to Egypt and saw all these wondrous sights.' On 27 February, he embarked once more on the *Himalaya*, arriving in the afternoon of the following day at Port Said. By 1 March, his thirteenth birthday, he was sailing along the Suez Canal, suffering under the intense heat but relishing the sensation of such an unusual birthday. 'My birthday today,' he wrote, '– how odd – a birthday in the Suez Canal! . . . Every now and then we pass a little red-brick house with a brown roof and green trees growing round it, they look so pretty. At 4 p.m. we arrived at Suez a wee town on the edge of the desert. We couldn't have the birthday cake today as it was not iced.'

The *Himalaya* stopped long enough at Suez for Lytton to watch a cricket match, collect some shells and ride a few more donkeys. Then they were all off again, this time to Aden which they reached in the second week of March. Here he occupied himself wandering through the exotic camel market 'crowded with camels in different attitudes', throwing stones at an octopus and coins into the water for the little black boys who 'dived down and brought up the sixpences in their mouths, they swam exquisitely and were quite at home in the water as in their boats'.

The party continued its journey to Mauritius, putting up at the town of Curepipe for two days. Lytton was not impressed. 'The hills', he recorded, 'were most extraordinary they looked as if they were going to fall down every minute, they were not at all grand, but looked drunk and misshapen.'

Cape Town, on the other hand, where the *Himalaya* arrived on 23 April, was properly symmetrical. 'It is a most magnificent place,' Lytton decided, 'with palacial buildings and shops worthy of Bond Street but it is very small, everything is next door to everything else.' The six weeks he spent there were tremendously exciting. He climbed the slopes of Table Mountain which was 'exquisite and looked just as I'd expected it to be', went off on fishing trips, played croquet and billiards – at which he considered he had done exceedingly well whenever he failed to rip the cloth – and, helped by his cousin Pat, brought out an illustrated magazine, *The Comet*, which was 'a great success, with poems and stories'.

Lytton's gift for treating grown-ups as his equals caused him to be made the hero of a farewell party given by the officers of the Black Watch, with whom he had spent much of the voyage.[4] On 12 May, shortly before he was due to go back to England, both he and Pat received an invitation to dine in the Mess. Lytton was attired in 'my best Etons and a white waistcoat and black tie' and Pat was equally smart. Neither of them was allowed alcoholic drinks, except to toast Queen Victoria's health, and contented themselves with lemon squash. After the Queen's health had been drunk, and much to the two boys' astonishment, the officers rose again to their feet. 'We did not know in the least what was happening,' Lytton confessed, '[and] were going to follow their example, when they told us to sit down.

'Capt. Gordon then said, "I beg to propose the health of the Rt. Hon. Prime Minister Lytton Strachey and Field Marshal Sir Patrick Grant! Hear, hear was heard from several voices – soon afterwards we went into the anteroom . . . Then it was discovered that it was very late and that if we did not hurry we should miss our train; so we hastily put on our coats and dashed out . . . As we left we were cheered by the officers! We ran with all speed to the station, my tie streaming in the breeze!'[5]

A few days later Lytton sailed for England. He had relished military life.[6] These five months abroad, with their aura of heat and their perpetual stimulus of fresh excitement and companionship, were a wonderfully liberating interval from the routine of childhood and helped to quicken his lifelong passion for travel. 'I enjoyed the voyage very much indeed,' he wrote, 'it was so entertaining and interesting – oh! it is like some beautiful dream.'

2

'GLAD DAY, LOVE AND DUTY'

He re-entered the darkness of Lancaster Gate, and in the second week of June went back to Parkstone, where rumours of his world-wide adventures had already made him a hero with the other boys. But the novelty was over. Henry Forde soon noticed a change. 'He certainly does look grown in every way: his cheeks are quite plump,' he wrote to Lady Strachey. 'I am rather surprised to see that he is not at all tanned by the suns and seas of the journey. He bears his return to the humdrum work and life like the philosophical boy he is; set to at his Virgil this morning as if he had only left off the day before, and is taking the ovation the boys are giving him – and which seems likely to continue for days, like a Roman Triumph – with dignity and as if it too were quite in its place and to be expected, and altogether is possessing his soul in blandness and calm. He is a most admirable boy.'

Lytton's mother had also observed a general toughening in her son's mental attitude and physique. It was now time, she judged, for him to be removed from the educational backwaters of Parkstone. By August she had made the arrangements. 'We are very, very sorry to part with Giles,' Henry Forde wrote to her, 'we have all grown really fond of him. *I* also think it will be best for him, as he has grown so much stronger, to try his wings in a wider sphere, and more robust air . . .'

Lytton himself was not sorry to leave. Parkstone was not much of a place. 'There is a dead mouse under the schoolroom I think, because of the dreadful smell – so bad we can't write our letters there!' After almost five years he was bored with it, and looked forward to joining a real school.

*

The New School, Abbotsholme, in Derbyshire, to which Lytton was sent in September, described itself as an advanced 'Educational Laboratory' which aimed at producing wholesome citizens by what was known as 'the natural method'. No day-boys or girls were admitted since they tended to befoul the moral climate of a school. Founded only four years previously by Dr Cecil Reddie, it originated what for a time was known as 'The New School Movement', and became the progenitor of the better-known Bedales, and the Landerziehungsheime Schule of Germany, respectively under Dr Badley and Dr Hermann Lietz, both of whom were for a time assistant masters at Abbotsholme. Among its offspring were L'Ecole des Roches, Salem and Gordonstoun.

Abbotsholme was a strange choice.[7] The prospectus issued that year should in itself have given a warning. 'The aim', one passage ran, 'is to provide an ideal home and life for the sons of parents who can afford to have the best for their boys' physical, mental, and moral welfare, and who realize that Education spells Empire.' The fees amounted to about fifty pounds a term, but added charges were imposed on those parents whose children were found to have deficiencies. These extra sums were in the nature of reminders that 'the School is intended for boys who are in all respects normal'.

It seems likely that Lady Strachey was influenced by the personality of Dr Reddie himself. She met him through Charles Kegan Paul,[8] a mutual friend who, after serving as an assistant master at Eton, had been appointed one of the trustees of the New School. As founder and headmaster of Abbotsholme, Reddie was in all ways its moving spirit. A dynamic figure of sturdy proportions, with stern eyes and a thundering flow of talk, he was worshipped by many of his pupils and held in extreme terror by others, including the teaching staff, none of whom – except the biology master – was permitted to marry. He was six foot tall, but rather stocky, owing apparently to his legs, which were shorter than they should have been. His autocratic manner and fierce idealism concealed from many the crankiness of his schemes for remoulding national life from the gymnasium at Abbotsholme. He was a man, or so he believed, whose mission was to rescue late Victorian England from degeneracy by filling the country's key positions with Old Abbotsholmians. Lytton must have seemed poor material for this social reconstruction. But still in the experimental stages of building up his 'school for English boys of eleven to eighteen belonging to the directing classes', Dr Reddie was anxious to attract references from influential parents. Even the most unlikely specimen from two distinguished Anglo-Indian families was welcome.

Initially he had based his ideas of a reconstituted society on the writings of Disraeli, Carlyle and Ruskin. But it was in Germany, he wrote, that 'notwithstanding our English prejudices, we at once observed strong evidence of superior intellectual life and social order'. There he had made a thorough study of 'Boy Nature', and made plans for diverting the downward plunge of England's national life and forming the pattern of a new English master race.

Dr Reddie was a Utopian, and his ideal boys were to be cultural athletes, glorified all-rounders, who cast no shadows and were divested of everything which vexes the spirit in its partnership with the flesh. Yet there was a morning light on this miniature colony which gave it a pastoral charm. He had sought out an idyllic setting: 'We must place first and foremost', ran his opening manifesto, 'the magnificent position of the school amid unparalleled scenery – mountains and sea, woods and fields, and gorgeous skies, with its spectacle spread out before us of one of the loveliest cities in the world. Next we must place the spacious grounds and stately buildings, an atmosphere of dignity and culture, and a free and open life.'

The chapel was seen as the source from which all other school activities gained their illumination. Here the corbels were carved with the heads not of saints but of redoubtable men of action and vision – Nelson and Shakespeare – while from the wall shone a five-pointed star, Solomon's seal, the sign of wisdom. Behind a simple altar cross stood the statue of a naked youth transfixed in a Blakean pose (later concealed by curtains). 'It was Dr Reddie's attempt to express something of his faith in his boys,' wrote a later headmaster, 'of their power to rise to great heights by truth and self-dedication.' In secular matters he encouraged these qualities by 'natural methods' that regulated the most essential functions of the boys. He dispensed with the decadent water-closet and reintroduced the earthier squatting employed by the beasts of the field. Some concessions, however, were made to the higher status of the human being. As they sat in a long military row, the boys looked over a flowerless but well-weeded garden.

When Lytton went to Abbotsholme, the school numbered a little over forty boys. School House itself was a large country mansion in the Victorian-Elizabethan style surrounded by orchards and gardens. The Abbotsholme estate covered one hundred and thirty acres and was set on the western slope of Dove Ridge in Derbyshire, overlooking the River Dove. The nearest village – about a mile away – was Rocester, once a Roman camp, and later the seat of the Abbey from which Abbotsholme took its name.

Lytton's weekdays, during the winter term of 1893, were divided into three sections. His morning was given mainly to class-work; his afternoon to manual work out of doors; his evening to music, poetry, art and social recreation. Reveille sounded at five minutes to seven (in summer it was ten past six), and after a gasping cold bath Lytton would fall in on the parade ground for drill and work with dumb-bells. From here he hurried off for a ten-minute thanksgiving service in the chapel where he was able to recover a little before breakfast at twenty to eight. Twenty minutes later he was upstairs again standing by his bed while the dormitory was inspected by the masters. Following dormitory parade came the first class of the day which was called Second School – First School in the summer being at six forty-five. The lessons differed from those of the ordinary public school in two respects: few of them exceeded forty minutes; and in the teaching of languages priority was given to German and French over Latin and Greek. The classes which Dr Reddie took were sometimes eccentric. Many a period supposedly given over to physics or chemistry was sure to be occupied by the subject of hygiene – and he was strong on the importance of mental as well as bodily cleanliness. 'On one occasion,' wrote Stanley Unwin, 'in a state of fury at our incompetence, he broke the pointer across the table and said that if we did not learn to think and to take more pains we should end by blacking the boots of the Germans.'

The physical training at Abbotsholme made a feature of manual labour which, Dr Reddie believed, instilled a broader social feeling than the traditional team spirit. He strove to banish the notorious psychological troubles afflicting those who lacked continuous occupation. Only a good deal of agrarian effort supported by a programme of tonic exercises could 'stimulate the healthy growth of the body in supple grace and compact symmetry, and promote that frank, hearty, and instinctive appreciation of its beauty, which is essential to the true education. Moreover, to render the body strong, clean, and lovely is a religious duty.'

From twelve to one o'clock, when studies were interrupted by a brief lunch and a lengthy piano recital, and again from two o'clock to half-past four, Lytton took part in various other tasks: drawing, carpentry, basket-making, bee-culture. In order to rouse a manly interest in clothing and its proper relation to the human body, he was coached in the processes of boot-making and tailoring, and occasionally instructed in the preparation of butter. A quota of tree-felling was obligatory too. Bringing in the potato harvest, cleaning out the cowshed, damming the streams in the Dingle, erecting pigeon houses, he was gleaning the ways of nature at first hand and availing himself – should it prove necessary – of a sound preparation for colonial life.

Afternoon school lasted from half-past four till six o'clock, when the boys were allowed their tea. There followed thirty minutes of freedom before the final part of the school day reserved for artistic training. Since Dr Reddie possessed 'neither talent, time, nor taste for literary composition', which exerted 'an exaggerated influence in our lives, producing new perils to body, mind, and character', Lytton's literary gifts received no encouragement. Music, as the most social of the arts, had the highest priority, and from seven to seven-thirty he pitched into compulsory glee-singing, his voice, by this stage of the day, being described as 'rather weak'. Each evening, too, the boys assembled in Big School to meet any visitors who had arrived, and would conduct themselves in adult fashion. The day ended with another short thanksgiving service in the chapel; and then, at ten minutes to nine, Lytton was free to go up to bed.

On Sundays, the service would follow a pattern laid out by Dr Reddie in a publication of startling prolixity: 'The Abbotsholme Liturgy, with Special Services for Christmas, Good Friday, Easter, the Ascensions, Whit-tide, Trinity; also for Waterloo Day and Trafalgar Day; also David's Lament for Saul and Jonathan, the Seven Beatitudes, the Ten Laws, and a number of Canticles and a large number of the Psalms, all retranslated, pointed and noted; also part of the anthology in the school chapel.' No boy, were he Protestant, Catholic, Hindu or Muslim, was permitted to escape these celebrations.

An organ recital followed lunch, while the remainder of the afternoon was left officially free. In practice it was not free for Lytton. The school was segregated into Fags, Mids and Prefects, and as a new boy he naturally came into the first category. This fagging, with which he busied himself through the long afternoon, had been set up by Dr Reddie in a special effort to educate the boys' affections. All boys 'are *trained* to understand their relation to one another', he explained in his prospectus. 'At Abbotsholme this natural relation of boys to one another is recognized and carefully organized.' The prefects were empowered to beat the fags. The masters also, Dr Reddie continued, 'catch the same spirit and learn to use the same methods. The result is greater co-operation in the teaching and greater harmony in the boys' deportment. Both are humanized.' In this way Abbotsholme became a family unit, with Dr Reddie himself as God the Father hammering home the school motto: 'Glad Day, Love and

Duty'. During his time at Abbotsholme Lytton must also have witnessed one of the awful floggings administered by Dr Reddie before the assembled school.

Something of the strain imposed by this curriculum comes out in Lytton's letters home. 'I enjoy myself greatly on the whole. Of course there are some things which I don't much like, such as cold baths and paperchases! – but still I'm sure I shall get used to them' (5 October 1893); 'Yesterday [18 November] we had a run because we could not play football as it was snowing. So we sallied forth – oh! it was dreadfully cold, and the wind and the snow hit you – and altogether it was most unpleasant! . . . I had my first round of boxing on Wednesday in which I was knocked flat on the ground!'; 'The baths *were* cold, I assure you! Everyday we change entirely into jersies and flannel knickers. One is allowed to put on as many jersies as you like – but no shirt or vest or draw!' (1 October 1893). 'I think you will get used to the cold bath in time,' his mother wrote hopefully. But by the time her letter arrived Lytton was in bed with a high fever. After ten days he recovered, only to faint away with a spell of dizziness, being carried unconscious from the chapel back to the sick-room. His pulse quickened alarmingly and he lost weight. He seems to have outgrown his strength, being already five feet two inches tall, but weighing only a few pounds over five stone. By December he had made a second recovery and, wearing a 'lovely' dress and 'a beautiful yellow wig', gave a memorable performance as Hippolyta, Queen of Amazons, in *A Midsummer Night's Dream*.[9] 'I remember you very well,' Dr Reddie wrote to him twenty-eight years later; 'I still have that photograph of you as "a fascinating female" in the little play we gave, as we sat in the conservatory.'

From the report which Lady Strachey was sent at Christmas two facts emerge. First, Lytton was extremely eager to succeed in this new environment and had made a special effort to do well at athletics, drill and farming. Secondly, in his anxiety that Lytton should not be removed from Abbotsholme, Dr Reddie glossed over his weak constitution while trying to shelter him from the New School's Spartan syllabus. Lytton's work was dismissed rather cursorily as 'good', and his health described as 'fair'. 'I have not pressed this boy,' he wrote. 'He neither needs it nor can he safely stand it. He has been twice ill this term, once when most were suffering from similar feverish colds in October, and again lately during the *hot weather* feeling faint for two days. He has otherwise been in good health and in excellent spirits – I believe the climate suits him – As regards work and general development, nothing more can be desired.'

Lytton returned to Abbotsholme in January 1894, when life proved even harder. 'He is not in the picture captioned potato digging,' one of Lytton's contemporaries, Gerald Brooke, observed. 'It was a bitterly cold day with a wind from the snow-clad hills driving over the valley. It nearly put me out! Strachey was probably talking to matron in the sick-room.'[10]

'He was', another pupil, G. Lissant Cox, recalled, 'a strange bird from my point of view.' This appears to have been the general opinion. 'My recollection of him is that he seemed to be older than I was, with a very grown-up air for a boy. He must have lived with grown-ups,' another Old Abbotsholmian remembered. 'I think he must have been much above the school average in taught knowledge. He could talk to anyone who would listen to him but not to me. I was only interested in bird's-nesting ... I remember seeing him talking about the play while he washed, then turning round stark naked to continue the discourse. He was circumcised but quite unconscious of the fact that he did not look like all the other boys in the dormitory.'

During this second term his health collapsed and he was sent back home. When older, he would sometimes speak with intense dislike of his Abbotsholme days. But it is perhaps significant that he never broke off his connections with the school. When at Cambridge, he attended more than one of the annual Old Abbotsholmian dinners given at Christ's College, and received several visits from Dr Reddie himself, much dazed by the great height of his ex-pupil.

'Teachers and prophets', Strachey wrote in *Eminent Victorians*, 'have strange after-histories.' The fortunes of Abbotsholme were soon bedevilled by sinister plots and counter-plots. Suspicious of everyone, Dr Reddie dismissed five masters in a single term, convinced that they were conspiring to take control of his miniature kingdom under the leadership of a mysterious bankrupt Dutchman who, escaping from the bailiffs out of the window of an adjacent building which he had hoped to make a rival establishment to Abbotsholme, fled to Holland and was heard of no more. The greatest blow of all, however, fell with the declaration of war in 1914. Many parents who had previously supported the Germanic mode of school life now hurriedly withdrew their sons until Dr Reddie was left in sole charge of two pupils. Various schemes, which Lytton supported, were implemented by the old boys to reinstate the school. Though he did not give his old headmaster a copy of *Eminent Victorians*, Lytton did send him *Queen Victoria* and was warmly complimented for his courage in praising at such a time the Prince Consort, a German.

By the late 1920s a group of old boys finally persuaded Dr Reddie to sell the school, and under Colin Sharp it became more successful and more orthodox. At this time Lytton contributed generously to an annuity for the ex-headmaster on condition that he did not go near Abbotsholme again. It was a bitter pill for the ageing man to swallow. During his years of retirement he became a figure of increasing pathos and peculiarity. While his self-esteem shrank, so also did his very name. As dr cecil reddie, a leading 'member of the league for abolition of capital-letters to save everybody's eyesight and to simplify education', he retired to welwyn-garden-city in hertfordshire, from where he wrote 'dear giles' a number of letters complaining of the invalid female relatives who now pressed in on him. He was to die within a few days of Lytton himself.

3

'SCRAGGS'

'At school I used to weep – oh! for very definite things – bitter unkindness and vile brutality.' So wrote Lytton in a letter to Leonard Woolf. The eccentricity of Abbotsholme was succeeded in the summer of 1894 by the more traditional philistinism of Leamington College, then ranked as one of the minor public schools. Lytton's awkwardness and odd appearance were seized on by his new companions. Just as his younger brother had thought him 'absurd' and described him as a 'funny little creature' so the boys at school gave him the nickname 'Scraggs' and made him a victim of bullying. 'I am not getting on very well at present,' he admitted, 'as on[e] of the boys (Phipps) as well as talking nasty things is rather a bully, which is rather painful.'

Something of his distress comes out from a letter written to his mother at the beginning of June. Naïvely and ambiguously phrased, hinting at rather than complaining of bullying, it gave a glimpse of life at Leamington which raised some alarm back at Lancaster Gate where Lady Strachey, feeling that the situation was moving beyond her competence, placed it before her husband. 'I am glad to hear that you are now off the Sick List and beginning again to get on to your work,' Richard Strachey wrote back. 'If you steadily stick at this you will find it in the end the best protection from annoyances such as you seem to have to submit to, from what you have written to your mother.

'I shall try as soon as possible to come up and see you, when you can explain if necessary more exactly what you have to complain of. Of course it is a very disagreeable position for a boy to be placed in to have to ask for protection against other boys, but there are some things which should not be put up with. If anything occurs that you feel any difficulty in writing

35

about to your mother let me know or merely say that you think it better that I should see you and talk about it and I will come. As to mere petty bullying you may be able to grin and bear it – but certainly on no account put up with any absolute acts or attempts at indecency such as is well known are not unheard of at schools. You may feel quite confident that we will protect you completely against any unpleasant consequences to yourself if you resist all evil influences to the best of your ability, and do not hesitate to let it be known that you will not submit to what you feel you should resist.'

This letter gave Lytton some sense of security against his afflictions.

'My dear Papa,
I think mine is a case of "petty bullying" so I will to the best of my ability grin and bear it, which, I think, is the only thing to be done.
As to the other matter all I know is that conversations frequently take place without any regard to decency, but whether it is carried on further than this I do not know as I have only been here such a short time. But I hope that matters will clear up, and that I will have a happy issue out of my difficulties . . .
Your letter cheered me greatly for you see I am not *very* happy and its so nice to feel there's a place from where I can be sure of help in time of need.'

After this first term the bullying diminished. Soon he is entering chess competitions, joining 'a glee society and on Saturday evenings we sing glees, which is rather amusing' (21 October 1894), and being dragooned into the choir – 'every Sunday – arrayed in a white robe I stalk into the chapel – feeling most grand!' He reassures his mother: 'Yes, things are getting smoother now which is a great comfort.' The amateur theatricals enabled him to exploit his idiosyncrasies. He played in Sheridan's farce *The Critic* ('I come in at the end as Tilburina, stark mad in white muslin, accompanied by my confidant stark mad in white calico'); and in a production of *The Frogs* by Aristophanes ('The Scene is Dionysus and his slave being rowed across the Styx by Charon, who I am').
Although Lytton's spirits improved during the three years he spent at Leamington, his illnesses continued and he had to be taken away for the whole of the 1896 Easter term. He was allowed to return by the family doctor once special arrangements had been made for his welfare. These included extra food – 'My luxurious tea', he reported happily, 'is eyed by my fellows with looks of covetousness.' About this time, too, he learnt to

ride a bicycle 'with some fluency though I have not yet mastered the art of mounting', and in the latter part of the day would go off for solitary excursions around the country. On one of these adventures he caught sight of a figure who was to play a minor part in his *Queen Victoria*, recording the encounter in mock-Pepysian fashion: 'I also went to see the Prince of Wales, who had been on a visit to the Warwicks,' he wrote to his mother (21 May 1895). 'His Royal Highness was so gracious as to take off his august hat to me, and I returned the compliment. My lady Warwick looked very pretty but it struck me that her hat was not of quite the latest fashion.'

Considering the number of classes he missed over the years, his scholastic record is impressive. His reports show him to have done well in mathematics, French and English; to have been fairly good at Classics, and useless at science. In the late summer of 1895, when he was fifteen and a half, he took the Oxford and Cambridge Lower Certificate Examination, passing in seven subjects. Lady Strachey, who had been in a state of anxiety as to how he would emerge from this first major test of his abilities, was delighted. 'The Exam is for boys of sixteen years of age and a First or Second Class is given in *each* subject,' the headmaster explained.

'I am very pleased to say that Lytton obtained a First Class in Arithmetic and English, and a Second Class in Latin, Greek, French, Additional Mathematics and Scripture Knowledge – thus passing in seven subjects while five are only necessary for the Certificate. I think the result is highly satisfactory, and is due to the steady way in which he has worked. If he had been a stronger boy and able to bear more pressure, he might have got a First Class in other subjects. I think he might work for this next year and take the Higher Certificate the year after.'

Within twelve months Lytton appears to have settled down quite comfortably. The occasional letters which Richard Strachey received contain nothing more alarming than bulletins of the latest botanical developments in his son's window-box; while Lytton's correspondence to his mother tells of cricket matches, plays, natural history expeditions that were 'distinctly unnatural and could never become history', and editing the school magazine. He also learnt to skate and 'Now,' he informed his sister Pippa, 'I am certainly able to fly at a descent rate, but occasionally falling, when performing the most brilliant feats.' At most other forms of sport his failure was less spectacular if as complete, and he spent much of his free time composing an Ibsenesque tragedy 'which is not only bloodthirsty, but dull, so dull that I cannot read it myself'. Such pastimes, together with his fondness for using out-of-the-way words, made him an object of contempt, amusement, surprise and sometimes admiration to the other boys. In general, he was more at home with the masters, some of whom he would occasionally invite to supper in his room.

By the autumn of 1895 Lytton had been made head of his house. He was entitled to wear a tin mitre on his cap, to sport a walking-stick, take roll-calls and read the lesson in chapel – his maiden performance, from the First Epistle of Paul the Apostle to Timothy, being an exhortation to widows. 'The agility of my voice', he wrote to Philippa, 'is not particularly convenient in this respect; as at one moment it is plunged in the depths below, and at the next is soaring with the lark at Heaven's gate – much to the alarm of the congregation.'

It was characteristic of Lady Strachey, an agnostic, to see that her son went to schools that emphasized Christian teaching. The school visitor was the Lord Bishop of Worcester; three of its vice-presidents were elevated clergymen; the headmaster, described by Lytton as 'somewhat of a crock', was the Very Reverend R. Arnold Edgell; and two of the half-dozen assistant masters had taken holy orders. For this body of men Lytton had not a good word: with one exception, the Reverend (later Bishop) E.J. Bidwell – 'an excellent man as well as being a clergyman'.[11] His letters home are sprinkled with contemptuous references to the men of God who instructed him.

7 October 1895

'We've had rather a painful missionary down here, converting us to the true faith! He religiously presented me with tracts, which I religiously presented to the waste paper basket! ... The general opinion here is that the man has done more harm than good by making the boys think of things they would never have before, and which they'd do very well without.'

31 May 1896

'Two of the masters are engaged to be married – one of them Mr Jones, the mathematical wallah – is engaged to a sister of one of the boys. The other Mr Suthery (classics) to an unknown. I am sorry to say the latter is going to be a clergyman – not so the former.'

10 November 1896

'Mr Suthery, the master who has distinguished himself by becoming a clergyman, preached on Sunday, not remarkably.'

23 November 1896

'Yesterday a special clergyman, very much like a goat, came to preach on Foreign Missions. He meandered through many a path of idiocy, and then quite suddenly – and luckily – stopped. I think he was seized with a sudden desire to go to Thibet and begin converting Grand Lhamas, or we would be listening with rapt attention to his bland remarks e'en now.'

It was now that Lytton began to read Gibbon. During his last term at Leamington he composed a nicely overweighted parody of Gibbonian rhetoric, called 'The Decline and Fall of Little Red Riding Hood'. Having been warned by her mother against the terrible beasts of the forest, Red Riding Hood sets out for her grandmother's house. She has not gone far when she is terrified to behold 'the crafty eye, the sinister jowl, and the gaunt form of a wolf, aged alike in years and in deceit'. This cunning and malign creature soon banishes her fears, however, by chivalrously offering her flowers, and then, learning of her destination, conjures up a scheme of devastating evil – 'as harmless in appearance as it was diabolical in reality'. He races off to the grandmother's cottage:

'At last, having traversed twice as quickly as Red Riding Hood a road twice as short as that which she had taken, he arrived in triumph at the house of the redoubtable though comatose octogenarian. History does not reveal the details of the interview. It can only be gathered that it was a short and stormy one. It is known for certain, however, that the wolf obtained at the same moment a victory and a meal, and that when Little Red Riding Hood entered her grandmother's abode, the arch deceiver, occupying the bed, and arrayed in the nightgown of his unfortunate victim, was prepared to receive the child with a smile of outward welcome and of inward derision.'

Once Red Riding Hood arrives, the famous dialogue ('What big teeth you have!') is neatly recast and leads to the climax of the story in a paragraph of imitation-Gibbon:

'"The better," answered the wolf, seeing the culmination of his plan coincide with the humour of the situation, "the better to eat you with, my dear!" Suiting the action to the word, he leapt out of bed and with incredible savageness threw himself upon his victim. Then he divested himself of his borrowed raiment and slipped quietly out of the cottage.'

Once he had turned away from Christianity, Plato's *Symposium* became Lytton's Bible. In this dialogue he found a philosophy of love, sympathetic yet strict, which seemed to satisfy his confused state of mind. A short diary which he kept during part of November 1896 shows him reading the *Symposium* 'with a rush of mingled pleasure and pain . . . of surprise, relief, and fear to know that what I feel now was felt 2,000 years ago in glorious Greece. Would I had lived then, would I had sat at the feet of Socrates, seen Alcibiades, wondrous Alcibiades, Alcibiades, the abused, but the great, felt with them all!'

Lytton's infatuations at Leamington were platonic and inconclusive. Yet they stirred up feelings so vivid and complex that the memory of them lingered into adult life and formed a pattern for his later love relationships. He idolized young men who were good-looking and self-assured. This was how he would like to have been. But since he could not transform himself into this version of an ideal self, he attempted the next best thing: to mislay himself in the all-absorbing contemplation of someone who inspired this spell of wish-fulfilment. While still in his first year at Leamington, he became devoted to one of the older boys. This seems to have induced a state of temporary self-oblivion, releasing him from the prison of his own sickly body. It was his first real passion and it involved what he always considered to be his purest emotions – 'that good kind exquisite abolition of oneself in such a heaven-born hero', as he described the sensation to Leonard Woolf. '. . . Part of it, don't you think, came from what we certainly can never get again – that extraordinary sense of corporal hugeness of our God? To be able to melt into a body literally twice as big as one's own.'

At the age of sixteen he experienced another delicious passion – 'the second of my desperate businesses at school', he later called it. In many respects this infatuation was similar to the first – unrequited, and focused upon someone quite different from himself. His hero was a dashing young batsman, head of the averages, a rather plump popular boy named George Underwood, very freckled and with red hair that dazzled Lytton during the bright summer months. Getting himself appointed as scorer to the cricket eleven, Lytton travelled round with the team to the opposing schools, lying in the long tickling grass under the sun amusing himself recording the runs amassed by his glamorous batsman. Altogether it was a rapturous affair, entirely one-sided, leaving him with a powerful nostalgia. As late as September 1931, four months before his death, he summoned up this friendship in his diary.

'I was older, and enormously devoted and obsessed; he was very sweet and very affectionate, but what he really liked was going off somewhere with Ruffus Clarke and the chic older boys, while I was left in the lurch, ruminating and desperate. How I loathed Ruffus Clarke! – a biggish, calm, very fair-haired boy – wicked and irresistible. I based my objections on purely moral grounds. I was a romantic prig, and the only wonder is how poor Underwood put up with me for a moment . . .

Ruffus Clarke and Fell! I can see them with absolute distinctness. Both with that curious softness which some boys of about seventeen seem to be able to mingle with their brutality. Fell was handsome, dark and slightly sinister, though not nearly so sinister as his younger brother, who, sandy and hatchet-faced, had devilry written all over him . . . As for me, I never knew what really happened – nobody told me – I couldn't even guess.'[12]

The type of boy to whom he was attracted tended to despise him, as indeed he despised himself, for being weak. When the infatuation faded, this contempt remained, cold and real inside Lytton, reinforcing the agony of his own self-contempt, forming a fuel for his ambition. He remained outwardly timid as, inwardly, his spirit grew more anarchical and strong. By the end of 1896, being no longer in love with his cricketer, he was eager to quit this 'semi-demi public school'. Over Christmas there was much excitement and activity at Lancaster Gate, where preparations were in full swing for a family performance of Ibsen's *John Gabriel Borkman* in William Archer's new translation. Lytton himself played the part of Vilhelm Foldal, the ageing government clerk, with great success. This minor triumph added to his confidence. Without great difficulty he prevailed upon his mother to tell the headmaster that her son would not be returning to Leamington after the Easter holidays.

Arnold Edgell was dismayed by Lady Strachey's decision, and did what he could to change her mind. But she was adamant, and Lytton himself felt delighted. The years were moving on and he was resolved not to be left behind. On 1 March 1897, his seventeenth birthday, he wrote to his mother: 'I am quite appalled by my great age. The man who instituted birthdays was a criminal.'

The following month he left Leamington determined to force those who had despised him in the past to acknowledge his qualities. Yet public ambition would never be enough. He would always want something more, pushing past obstacles for some whispered words alone.

THREE

Liverpool

'The truth is I want *companionship*.'

Lytton Strachey, *Diary* (April 1898)

I

PREPARATIONS

For six months after leaving Leamington College Lytton prepared himself
for university life. Every week he would go off for isometric exercises with
a Scottish doctor who had constructed a system of weights and pulleys to
develop the muscles. He also studied with his sister Dorothy, the part-
time schoolmistress at Allenswood, who coached him in English, history
and French.

There were times during these months when he regretted his decision
to leave school. He missed the comradeship. Buried alive in Lancaster
Gate, he felt a vague feeling of uneasiness. Even the splendours of
Rothiemurchus no longer banished his dissatisfaction. Nature had only
sublimities and vastitudes and water and leaves. His desires were for
something more intimate: for affection, an answering smile, the eye that
understood and the secret touch of someone special.

Mistrustful of strangers, Lytton sensed their presence like a separating
wall; and retreated into silence. He made himself feel superior to what he
considered their smug mediocrity. What right had they to feel so self-
satisfied? Already, at seventeen, he longed to make them squirm and twist
in their seats with his derision.

Something of the impression he gave was recorded by the artist and
writer Graham Robertson.

'He was a mere boy of eighteen or nineteen when we came across each
other, with all his laurels yet ungathered and his character (presumably)
unformed, but in its unformed condition it was, to me, singularly
objectionable, and we violently disliked each other – if violence in any
form could be attributed to so limp and flaccid a being as was the Lytton of

those days. As to the "strong, deep voice" mentioned by Max [Beerbohm] as reserved for his intimates . . . I suppose his parents, brothers and sisters must be reckoned among his intimates, but I never heard him address them otherwise than in a breathless squeak of an asthmatic rabbit. Voices were not the family strong point. I think they all talked so continuously as to have exhausted the small allotment of voice originally accorded to them.'[1]

In September 1897 Lytton passed the Preliminary Examination of the Victoria University of Manchester. To Dorothy Strachey, who had written to offer her congratulations, he replied: 'Let me add my congratulations for your admirable coaching, and also let me bring before you the fact that it is AGAINST MY PRINCIPLES to fail in an examination.'

Since he was still rather young to go to Oxford or Cambridge, his mother decided that he should first attend a smaller university. The family had a special connection with Liverpool University College (as it then was) through Lytton's cousin, Sir Charles Strachey, who had married Ada Raleigh, sister of Professor Walter Raleigh. It was because of Raleigh's position there as King Alfred Professor of English Literature that in October 1897 Lytton was sent for two years to Liverpool. He studied Greek, Latin, mathematics, history and English literature. 'Five burly men spend their days in lecturing me,' he told his mother, 'so I really ought to be well instructed.' The best lecturer of all these, he added, was Walter Raleigh himself, who taught him English literature: 'He is thoroughly good.'

Lytton soon grew friendly with Raleigh. His wife too delighted him with her outspokenness. 'What do you think of Mrs Raleigh?' he asked a friend. 'Don't you like her brimstone and vitriol? Have you talked to her about [Bertrand] Russell? They hate each other like poison; he's a moralist, and she's an anarchist. And secretly I'm on her side.' Raleigh was a distinct relief from the more pedantic type of don. Now nearing his forties, he had already written books on *The English Novel* and *Robert Louis Stevenson* which Lytton admired, and was then working on a study of Milton. He nourished a secret faith, he admitted, 'not in refinement and scholarly elegance, those are only a game, but in blood feuds, and the chase of wild beasts, and marriage by capture. In carrying this last savage habit into effect there would be an irresistible dramatic temptation to select the bluest lady of them all.' His image of himself living on the decks of the world rather than confined in a stuffy cabin was to find an echo in Lytton's own romanticism. 'Can anything be more bitter than to be doomed to a life of literature and hot-water bottles,' Lytton later (1913) asked the mountaineer George Mallory, 'when one's a Pirate at heart?'

Raleigh had convinced himself that, by virtue of his piratical spirit, he was for ever being threatened with dismissal from one university post after another. It seemed to be a psychological device by which he reconciled himself to his steady academic career. When alone, immersed in the drudge of authorship, Raleigh's freedom of expression faltered; but in conversation all his exuberance and wit were released. He loved an audience and excelled before a good one, however large or small, for only then could he translate literature back into the actual movement of life going on around him. Few people who heard him lecture forgot the sparkle and subtlety of these performances. First you saw the spread of his smile announcing that he was coming out with something he knew to be good; then it would burst forth, pointed, epigrammatic, conclusive; and he would stop suddenly, as if in delighted astonishment at his own fluency, glancing round as though to compliment everyone for their cleverness in drawing out of him such pith: '*There! You've got it! That's the point!*' Lytton was delighted by these theatrical accomplishments.

The Raleighs took a special interest in him while he was at Liverpool, and would invite him to dinner or take him to concerts and theatres. But Lytton often left their company reflecting on his own contrasting lack of charm and energy. His squeaky voice and long, ungainly body preyed more than ever on his mind. He felt that he looked like some zoological specimen. Though wanting desperately to shine, he was more moved by a fear of public humiliation.

In his letters and in occasional diary entries Lytton gave thumb-nail sketches of the other dons whose lectures he attended. The most striking of these was John Macdonald Mackay, Rathbone Professor of Ancient History. 'Professor Mackay is very weird and somewhat casual,' he wrote shortly after arriving at Liverpool. 'The first difficulty is to hear what he's saying as he speaks in a most extraordinary sing-song. When that has been mastered the connection must be traced between the lecture and Roman History. Lastly, but most important, to prevent and curb shrieks of laughter.' The professor himself never curbed these outbursts, and as he grew friendly with Lytton – having been at Balliol with his cousin St Loe Strachey – his mannerisms became embarrassing. 'M is rather too much inclined to think himself funny and laugh at his own jokes. He *will* look at me when he means to be witty, which is most inconvenient as I feel that I must smile and yet do not like pandering.'

Lytton enjoyed the lectures on Greek by Professor P. Hebblethwaite. 'H is quite a character,' he observed, 'very stout and lame of a leg; with handsome features and grey beard and hair. His eye-glasses are a constant source of amusement to me; and his continual "yes?" which is quite unintended to be answered.'

The other dons were more ordinary. At mathematics he had always been proficient, and he described Professor Frank Carey, the mathematical don, as 'thoroughly good'. His least favourite subject was Latin. These lectures were consistently dull and Professor Herbert Strong, who gave them, was, Lytton told his mother, the least likeable of all his five burly instructors.

2

THE MELANCHOLY OF ANATOMY

The two years Lytton passed at Liverpool were among the bleakest of his life. He was unable either to excel as he had dreamed of doing, or to find those few intimate friends who would have transformed his existence. 'My life is a turmoil of dulness,' he wrote in his diary. 'My days are spent in a wild excitement over the most arrant details. The putting on of boots is thrilling; the taking off of coat, hat and gloves more so; the walk to the College and back a very procession of agitation. And all carried on with a feverish haste, and a desire to be done with it. As for letters – the expectation of one, no matter from whom is the subject of frenzy.'

With his allowance of one pound a month from his mother, Lytton hired a bicycle which he called 'the Graphic'. After lunch he would set off for prodigious rides into the country, or to explore distant second-hand bookshops. In less than a year he pedalled a thousand miles on the Graphic – an impressive measurement of his urge to escape from the place. On Tuesdays, Thursdays and Saturdays he sweated through a course of strengthening exercises directed by a Dr Blüm who 'is a Swede, and decent enough. The system is entirely different from the Macphearson, and much more scientific. No pulleys, no weights, merely movements of the arms, legs and body, he presses in the opposite direction. Thus the resistance is regulated by the man himself.' Most evenings he spent alone in his room, writing up the day's lectures and trying to write poetry until at about eleven he retired to bed.

He was lodging at No. 80 Rodney Street – across the road from where Gladstone had been born. It was a sombre, dignified street of Georgian houses, full of dignified professional men with their sombre families. Typical of the district were Lytton's landlords, Dr and Mrs Alexander

45

Stookes. They had been apprehensive of having a rowdy student in the house, but 'the boy has proved a delightful companion and no trouble to either of us,' Dr Stookes wrote to Lady Strachey after Lytton's first term. 'We could hardly have imagined that it would have been possible to have a stranger guest with so little friction.'

With Dr Stookes himself – whom he nicknamed 'Spookes' – Lytton eventually grew quite friendly. They would discuss literature, religion, sociology and all manner of subjects. It was Dr Stookes who introduced him to some of the local social problems, taking him round Liverpool's slums. Though Liverpool was growing prosperous as it emerged as one of the largest ports in the world, its new grandness and prosperity did not touch the starving children and drunken beggars in the streets. 'Nearly every street is a slum in this town, except those with the fine shops,' Lytton noted in his diary. 'Here is nothing intermediate. Hardly anyone lives in the town if they can possibly help it. Pitt Street was painful to me in the extreme; it stank; dirty "furriners" wandered in groups over it; and a dingy barrel organ rattled its jargon in a yard.' Sometimes he would wander through these gloomy slums alone. The dirt and drabness filled him with loathing, seeming to mirror his internal wretchedness. 'In the afternoon walked down to the docks and thence to the landing-stage,' one diary entry runs. 'The crowds of people were appalling. The landing-stage blocked; and *all* hideous. It gave me the shivers in two minutes and I fled. My self-conscious vanity is really most painful. As I walk through the streets I am agonized by the thoughts of my appearance. Of course it is hideous, but what *does* it matter? I only make it worse by peering into people's faces to see what they are thinking. And the worst of it is I hate myself for doing it.'[2]

Hoping to find companionship Lytton joined several of the undergraduate societies. Tempted by the promise of light refreshments, he told his mother, 'I attended the University College Christian Union meeting, thus becoming acquainted with some of the students. A very good thing I thought, but why Christian? A prayer terminated the proceedings. The undergraduates are not, I think particularly enlightened, but as yet I have only spoken to the less advanced ones.' A little later he was elected to the debating society, where he had higher hopes of making friends. For several months he continued going to these debates without uttering a word. Then, in March 1898, to his dismay, he was scheduled to make a speech in defence of slang. 'The day of the debate on Slang,' he noted in his diary. 'I was alarmed, as I had only been able to scribble a few remarks by 2.30. The debate was at 4.30 with a tea at 4. I managed to put down some absurd notes and then, palpitating with horror, started off for the College. I arrived late of course. The tea was in the Ladies' Debating Room which was a most charming apartment. I stood dumbly and swallowed a cup of tea. Then, after a long pause while everyone else was talking, we adjourned to the literature room, which was soon pretty well filled. I was horrified to see the swells of the place such as Grundy, Burnett, etc., accumulated there.' Lytton's opponents opened the proceedings with the proposition that slang was undesirable, so that as seconder he spoke last. When it was time for him to rise and address the meeting, all went well. 'Fortunately for me,' he explained afterwards, 'I have come to be considered a funny man, so that the audience began to laugh even before I spoke. Perhaps my appearance accounted for this however. I stumbled through my very short oration somehow, and was relieved that it should have gone down so well.'[3]

After this initial address, he gave several speeches to the society. His strangeness enhanced these performances on the debating platform, and he generally became adept at anticipating and reversing derision. 'The other day as I was sitting in the drawing-room with my back to the light,' he told his mother, 'a lady visitor who had been to inspect the twins, suddenly entered. Rushing up to me she said, "Oh my dear Dr Stookes, I really must congratulate you on your *charming* children! So pretty; so sweet!" Without a word I slowly rose to my full majestic height and the lady, giving one gasp of horror, fled wildly from the room!'

One new friend was Lumsden Barkway, later Bishop of St Andrews. 'He is the son of a presbyterian clergyman, and is going in for that profession himself,' Lytton wrote. 'But he tries his best not to be bound down, and takes an interest in pictures and such. He is rather melancholy, and has hardly ever been out of the suburb of Liverpool where he lives.' Another friend was a Miss Combe, the 'austerely flighty' headmistress of a large school for girls, whose sister had married Oliver Strachey's friend, Roger Fry. Miss Combe was a fiery cyclist and had a fund of pastoral sagas involving 'spring foliage' and 'autumn tints'. Their friendship was conducted precariously from two bicycles. Despite a number of these 'not altogether unsuccessful' trips, Lytton did not really warm to Miss Combe. 'Women are such strange creatures,' he remarked. 'Miss Combe is not so pleasant. She appeared to me to possess the qualities of a groveller.'

But he met no one who answered his needs. 'Miss C is not good enough,' he concluded; 'besides I want someone who can go out for walks with me at any time. Barkway? Dear me, is that all University College can give me? If I could only make friends with Grundy or Bird![4] But my "habitual reserve" is too much for them. Well, well, well, perhaps I shall find someone some day. And then I am sure he – or she – will not belong to University College. Talking of shes, I think it is too much that one cannot speak to a member of "the sex" without being looked upon askance by somebody or other. If only people were more sensible on this point, half the so called immorality would come to an end at once. I wonder if I shall ever "fall in love". I can't help smiling at the question – if they only knew – if they only knew! But it is tragedy also.'

3

DIARIES AND DECISIONS

On 3 March, two days after his eighteenth birthday, Lytton began a new diary. 'Many times before have I got a book and written in it my thoughts and my actions,' he put down. 'But my previous attempts have always been crowned with failure: – inasmuch as after 2, 3, or possibly 4 entries the diary came to an end. Another effort! God knows there is small enough reason for it. My other autobiographical writings were the outcome of excitements really quite out of the commonplace; but this is *begun*, at any rate, in the veriest dog days imaginable.'[5]

This diary covers a period of about six weeks. Though it contains some amusing sketches, many of its pages make depressing reading. 'My character', he wrote, 'is not crystalized. So there will be little recorded here that is not transitory; and there will be much here that is quite untrue. The inquisitive reader, should he peep between the covers, will find anything but myself, who perhaps after all do not exist but in my own phantasy.' Unwilling to contemplate his image directly, he uses Shakespeare as a convenient looking-glass. 'Had Shakespeare any character? of his own, that is to say?' The answer, he goes on, is that he had not, and that Shakespeare was 'a cynic in his inmost of hearts'. He pretends to rejoice in his enforced isolation. 'Better so, perhaps; in fact necessarily so. And there are quite sufficient of the other sort.'

The purpose of keeping this diary was to redress the balance between the glamour of his secret dreams and the greyness of actual life. Within its pages he had no fear of making an exhibition of himself, of boring others instead of impressing them. It was, he points out, 'a safety valve to my morbidity'. Although no longer bullied as he had been at school, his sense of loneliness was more overwhelming. He could not avoid focusing on his appearance, and expressed his misery in terms of physical self-disgust: 'When I consider that I am now 18 years of age a shudder passes through my mind and I hardly dare look at the creature* those years have made me.'

This feeling of wretchedness was aggravated by his failure to get any of his poetry accepted by the university magazine, *The Sphinx*. The poems which he submitted – sonnets and epigrams – are not personal like his diary entries, but some of them are competent metrical exercises, such as 'On being asked for a description of a Roundel'. This was intended perhaps as a parody of Swinburne's description of a Roundel published in 1883 (and so harmless compared to Swinburne's earlier 'Rondel' which reeked of rotten poppies and white death). But it was not printed until Lytton had gone up to Cambridge, and though eventually coming out in *The Granta* and not *The Sphinx*, it belongs to this Liverpool period.

> A Roundel is a thing that's not
> So *very* irksome to compose.
> It's something that one throws off hot -
> A Roundel is.
> The first thing needful, I suppose,
> Is some slight sentiment or plot,
> Then start off with a fitting close
> Add rhymes (with luck you'll find a lot)
> And, my inquiring friend, – who knows? -
> Perhaps you may have here just what
> A Roundel is.

At the end of March 1898, Lytton took the Intermediate BA examination and two months later learnt that he had passed in all subjects – mathematics, ancient history, Greek, Latin and English literature. That summer, Lady Strachey arranged for him to spend some weeks with a French family, the Renons, who lived at Loches, about a hundred and thirty miles south-west of Paris, near the gently flowing Indre.

Early in June, with his baggage and bicycle, Lytton set out, travelling by train to Paris and then the next day to Loches itself. Twenty-four hours after arriving there he sent a long letter to his mother describing his adventures.

---

* It seems possible that Lytton had Marfan syndrome, a disorder caused by a mutated gene which was discovered in 1896 by the French paediatrician Antoine Marfan. Symptoms include above average height, spidery hands, a long face, narrow feet, thin limbs, short sight, sometimes a curved spine and a high-arched palate creating a squeaky voice. It is particularly common among children of elderly fathers.

49

'Yesterday morning I sallied forth from the hotel, and, marching down the Avenue de l'Opéra found myself opposite the Hôtel du Louvre ... After making a tour of the building seven or eight times I found an entrance, and, giving up my umbrella to a gendarme, was soon lost among the majestic remnants of the Ancient World. I found it all too difficult to tear myself away ... But at length, seizing my umbrella, I dashed into a chabriolet ... What need be said of the wild journey through the metropolis of the great Republic, the fearful jolts of the vehicle threatening at every moment to snatch me from my bicycle which I still held clasped to my breast? Twice we were nearly killed; twice we escaped death by a hairsbreadth. We reached the Gare d'Orléans a quarter of an hour before time and ... proceeded to Tours (changing at St-Pierre) where I had lunch, and took a walk in the town which appeared charming. Thence to Loches. I was met by a jeune homme aged 19, a son of M. Renon. We then drove in an omnibus here – 6 miles – where I was received by the family circle with open arms. M. Renon, Madame, Mademoiselle (15?) et bébé (fils 10) ... The house is charming, quite small, with all the rooms opening out of doors. My room is on the ground floor, and can only be approached by a door leading into the garden. Everyone is as polite as peculiar – much more gentle (in its true sense) than in England in corresponding circumstances. I am lured on to talk, and can understand fairly well, though the speed distresses me ...'

Much of his time he spent composing a hilarious blank verse tragedy, catching frogs in the garden pond and, during the evening, playing cards. Every day, too, he repeatedly mislaid, until finally smashing, his spectacles. He inspected the dungeons at Loches where Louis XI confined his unfortunate friends, 'most gloomy and ghastly, with the walls covered with the inscriptions of the prisoners'.

Lytton was struck by the un-English way in which the Renons organized their lives. 'Life here is more like that on board ship than anything else,' he explained to his mother. 'I rise from my couch at 8.30. At 9 I have a petit déjeuner of coffee au lait and toast and butter. At 11.30 Déjeuner, consisting of lots of vegetables, soup, a small quantity of meat and strawberries. At half-past six is dinner, pretty well the same as déjeuner ... I don't much approve of the French system of meals which elongates the afternoon abnormally and abolishes the morning and evening. Before déjeuner I do "traductions" which are quite harmless and amusing. After déjeuner I sleep for one hour – the rarity of meals rendering a vast absorption necessary when there is one.'

On Sundays Lytton went with the rest of the family to church, welcoming the opportunities which the *pain bénit* afforded him of augmenting his meals. He would later write up accounts of these services in letters to his mother, some of them reading like theatre reviews of amateur musicals. 'I sat behind the altar, at the very back of the building. From this position the show appeared tawdry. The robes of the Curé were truly splendid, but the tinsel, and the sham marble wallpaper were incongruous. A young man played vilely on the harmonium and the singing rivalled that of an English village church. On the whole I was not impressed, though I ate the holy bread like a martyr.' As for the Roman Church in general, he was sadly disappointed. 'I think I shall remain protestant,' he reassured Lumsden Barkway.

Far more to his liking were the pagan festivities. Often during these Sunday afternoons a fair was set up in the market-place at Loches where the whole town, reinforced by the floating population of several villages near by, would assemble to enjoy themselves late in the long summer evenings. The sight of all this merrymaking exhilarated Lytton. Yet he is always a spectator at the revelries. 'An awning has been erected beneath which the people were dancing to the sound of clockwork music. It was a most amusing spectacle. The paysannes with their white lace caps, and handkerchiefs tied round their waists to keep their dresses clean, hanging on to their partners with both arms round their necks. When the music stopped they kissed and parted! It was a great relief to see all this happening on a Sunday.'

It had been Lytton's intention to spend four weeks at Loches, but life there was so congenial that he stayed two months. 'France is not so bad as it might be,' he admitted to Lumsden Barkway. 'I was not so absolutely dumb as I expected to be; the country is charming and the people most kind and polite. The only drawback I have discovered as yet is in what I call the "sanitary arrangement". It is dark and dank, and full of blue-bottles! I hardly dare to venture in – most inconvenient.'

He returned to English civilization in early August, joining his family at Ardeley Bury, 'a really delightful country house' near Stevenage in Hertfordshire. Here he spent several weeks reading Tacitus, Thucydides, Thackeray and *Paradise Lost* which, he told Lumsden Barkway, was 'the best thing in the English language!'

In early October, he went back to Liverpool. He was now confronted with the decision of whether to read history at Oxford or Cambridge. The family had assumed that he would go to Cambridge, but recently his mother had begun to wonder whether he should prepare himself for entry into the Civil Service, in which case he ought to follow his brother, Oliver, up to Balliol College. 'If your object is the Civil Service,' she wrote to him (4 December 1898), 'you are likely to be better prepared for the examination at Oxford than at Cambridge. So we have settled it that way. Your father met Mr A.L. Smith – the Balliol tutor – at the Royal Society dinner, and he says you are to go to him and he will put you through your paces, and advise accordingly – which is his function; and this you will do during the Christmas holidays. We propose that you should enter at the next October term, and go up for the entrance exam before the Easter term.'

Lytton much preferred the prospect of going to Cambridge, but acquiesced meekly enough to his mother's plans which involved taking his responsions in March and then, in June, trying for a Christ Church scholarship which would automatically make him eligible for entry to Balliol in the autumn of 1899. His spirits were further lowered by the ordeal of a family Christmas at Lancaster Gate which appears to have been celebrated by the Stracheys one day earlier than normal, and was something he struggled to avoid in later life. 'My time has been spent as follows,' he informed Lumsden Barkway,

'– Dec. 16th–Dec. 24th. Preparations for Christmas festivities, and visits to the National Gallery. Dec. 24th. Official Christmas (very terrible). Dec. 25th. My cousin Charles and his wife Ada (sister of Raleigh) came to dinner (at which I ate and drank *far* too much). They afterwards sang a charming song called the "Kensit Battle Hymn" written by Charlie and Raleigh. *Delightful*! Dec. 25th–28th. Severe illness resulting from Xmas festivities.'

Next day some of the family left London and moved to the Bank House in the High Street at Guildford, which belonged to one of Lytton's uncles who was transferred to fill the vacuum at Lancaster Gate. 'The house is over a shop,' Lytton explained to Lumsden Barkway, '– rather peculiar, isn't it? – but charming for all that, though the beds are rather short and hard.'

When he returned to Liverpool in the New Year, he began preparing himself for the Christ Church scholarship in which his special subject was to be the Early Roman Empire, with eighteenth-century England thrown in as an extra. He continued studying Gibbon. 'I have been reading the Great Gibbon lately,' he wrote to his mother in February, 'and have just finished the two chapters on Christianity. They are the height of amusement – his attitude throughout so unimpeachably decorous; but I can't help thinking it all rather unfortunate. If he had not been so taken up with his scorn of superstition, he might have paid some attention to the extraordinary change which was coming over the world, the change from the pagan idea to the christian idea, which, however unsound the doctrines that contributed to its success, was still dominating Europe (I suppose) at the time Gibbon wrote. He might at least have cast a glance at the old paganism that had gone for ever. But he never touches more than the externals. I suppose his mind was unable to appreciate the real spirit of Christianity.' This response was similar to some critical reviews he would read of 'Cardinal Manning', the first essay in his *Eminent Victorians*.

On 21 March, Lytton travelled to Oxford, spending four days in a bleak lodging house, No. 4 St John Street. Before the Balliol tutor for responsions, J.L. Strachan-Davidson, he cut an awkward figure. This ordeal over, he went for ten days to Lancaster Gate, bringing with him his Presbyterian friend, Lumsden Barkway, who had just won a scholarship to a theological college. 'I wish I were you!' Lytton told him. 'I have Oxford still before me. Alas.'

A little later he visited Cambridge for a few days in company with Walter Raleigh, who 'gave a most witty lecture on Chesterfield'. He wished that his mother had decided to send him here. Already he seemed to belong to the place, and his letters home are full of social calls on friends and relations. 'On Sunday I lunched in Clough Hall where the Sidgwicks[6] were present, also the Freshfields[7] who were staying with them. On Monday I had dinner with Miss Stephen[8] in Sidgwick Hall. The Raleighs also came and paid Pernel [Strachey] a visit in her chamber.'

In the third week of June Lytton finally left University College, Liverpool. Although his time there had not been happy, he felt little excitement at leaving, for he no longer faced the future with quite the same brave spirit as when he had left Leamington. 'The thought of final departure is indeed painful,' he wrote to his mother (12 June 1899). 'Packing will be a sad business.' But Lady Strachey was well pleased with his progress. He had passed all the examinations, and this in spite of his illnesses. It had been a creditable performance. 'I think the Liverpool plan has been a success on the whole,' she told him.

At the end of June, Lytton returned to Oxford where he took the Christ Church scholarship examination. From here he travelled alone to Rothiemurchus, where he stayed in lodgings. 'In the evening, when the sun is setting, one cannot help being a little sad,' he wrote in a stilted rhapsody to Lumsden Barkway, 'it is the sadness of regret. The days of childhood, with their passionate pains and pleasures, are with us; days nearer to us, too, with their precious moments of bitterness and love; and the present day that is fading beneath the hills for ever.' His examinations no longer seemed important. He idled pleasantly through the summer days. 'Here, among the mountains,' he wrote, 'the Vision of Balliol itself seems to dwindle and appear insignificant.'

The actuality of Balliol was also dwindling. While he was in Rothiemurchus the result of his entrance examination came through. In the course of a long letter to Lady Strachey, J.L. Strachan-Davidson wrote:

'We have read the papers, and have come to the conclusion that the Essay is decidedly promising, but that the Classical work is insufficient. The Latin translation was fair but the Greek was not up to the mark, and the Latin Prose was bad.

I am not sure that this disappointment will not prove all for the best. I was struck by the extreme shyness and nervousness displayed by Mr Strachey, and much doubt whether he would be happy in a large College like Balliol. I am afraid that the pace would be too quick for him, and that he would find himself outside of the life and society of the place.'

As an alternative to Balliol Strachan-Davidson suggested Lincoln College which, with his special recommendation, would almost certainly accept him. This college, he explained, consisted of about sixty-five undergraduates, most of whom had not passed through the great public schools, and its more modest climate would be better suited to a boy like Lytton, silent, maladroit and literary.

Lady Strachey was angered by this exclusion of her son from Balliol based, she felt convinced, on a superficial estimate of his character. She rejected absolutely the notion that Lytton would be better placed at Lincoln College, and in her reply to Strachan-Davidson she made a shrewd analysis of Lytton's personality.

'I am sure you are mistaken in your diagnosis of his disposition, though I am not surprised at the impression produced. He has a very unfortunate manner which was no doubt at its worst in circumstances where a certain amount of nervousness is not inexcusable; but as a matter of fact it is more manner than anything else; he is both self-reliant and equable in a rather unusual degree. He has hitherto got on exceedingly well with other boys and young men wherever he has been placed, so that I should not feel very anxious about his eventually settling down comfortably in such a society as that of Balliol. At any rate, in sending him to College we look for the advantage to be gained by a larger, fuller life than would be obtained in one of the smaller colleges.'

Up in Scotland Lytton received the news with mixed feelings. He hated failure of any kind and, as he had joked to his sister Dorothy, it was AGAINST HIS PRINCIPLES to miss the mark in an examination. But once he let his mind contemplate the life which might await him at Cambridge, he felt happier. His mother had made up her mind to send him to Trinity which, with over six hundred undergraduates, was the largest college in Cambridge. She could no longer see her son in the role of Lord Lytton, but might he not be another Lord Tennyson? 'I think you are to be congratulated on the change,' she told him, 'especially as it is a sign from above that you are to be a poet – the coming man in that line could never have been allowed to be anywhere but at Cambridge.'

Lytton returned to Lancaster Gate early in August and then moved down with the family to Selham House, near Petworth. Surrounded by books and sisters, he spent his mornings preparing for the Previous Examination (then commonly known as the 'little-go'), and reading Swinburne who was 'VERY GOOD' and Boswell's *Johnson* which was 'most delightful'. But dominating all other thoughts was the prospect of Cambridge. 'As to Cambridge,' he told Lumsden Barkway, 'I am looking forward to it with more dread than you. Though I am sure it will be charming in the long run – but the beginning I fear will be painful – as most beginnings are to me.'

Towards the end of September, he left Petworth and, having passed both parts of the little-go, was admitted to Trinity. At about the same time, a letter from Walter Raleigh arrived at the college announcing that among its freshmen that Michaelmas would be a certain ex-pupil of his, an undergraduate of unusual promise.

FOUR

Fratribus

'Have you noticed that one's always waggling between two extremes – one's own opinion of oneself, and everyone else's? Sometimes I get so fascinated by the latter that I'm quite carried away and begin to act up to it, as if I really thought it true ... We are all cupboards – with obvious outsides which may be either beautiful or ugly, simple or elaborate, interesting or unamusing – but with insides mysteriously the same – the abodes of darkness, terror and skeletons.'

Lytton Strachey to John Sheppard (1902)

I

ONCE UPON A MIDNIGHT

Late Victorian Cambridge was a pretty market town in the Fen country populated by East Anglian shopkeepers who supplied the university. Bicycles, trams and horses shared the streets, gently coming and going as though in some holiday resort, while through the courts and quadrangles floated the strange crustacea of academic life. Students in their summer straw boaters, flannels and high collars, and professors in their brilliant plumage, paraded over the Palladian bridges and along the college lawns in a predominantly male procession.

For the fifth time in six years, Lytton faced the ordeal of being a new member of an unknown community. But on this occasion, owing partly to Walter Raleigh's thoughtfulness, his solitude did not last long. At Cambridge he seemed to know from the first that he had entered a milieu which suited him. The civilized sunny atmosphere was wonderful after the damp breezes of Liverpool. His letters home are almost jovial: 'Ho! Ho! Ho! How proud I was as I swept through the streets of Cambridge yesterday, arrayed for the first time in cap and gown!' he wrote to his mother on 3 October. 'To my great surprise and delight the gown is blue! Lovely!' A fortnight later, he wrote again: 'I am enjoying myself deeply ... and am just beginning to enter into things. Everyone is the pique of politeness and kindness.'

After a few days, Lytton came across his Liverpool friend Lumsden Barkway, who was studying near by at the Westminster Theological College. In these weeks, before he made any new friends, the two of them would have tea in Lytton's rooms. These rooms, like everything else at Cambridge, immediately delighted him. 'They are very nice – on the 2nd floor – the sitting-room facing the Court [New Court], the bedroom the backs – with a beautiful view of weeping willows.' The following term he was transferred to rather darker rooms on the ground floor of New Court. These he did not care for so much and since, in the opinion of his mother, they were detrimental to his health, arrangements were made early in 1901 for him to lodge at a set of first-floor attics on Staircase K (where Byron had rooms, in the topmost one of which he was said to have kept a bear) within the south-east corner turret of the Great Court of Trinity – 'rather quaint with sloping roofs, etc.' Here, in what for unknown reasons used to be known as 'mutton-hole corner', he remained for over four years.

Lytton's tutor at Trinity was J.D. Duff,[1] nicknamed 'Plum Duff'. He 'cooes like a dove', Lytton told his mother, and was fond of long soothing conversations 'chiefly about persons – ranging from Heine to Sidney Lee'. The professor from whom he learnt history, (Sir) Stanley Leathes – 'Mr Stand-at-ease'[2] – was 'rather severe, and hideously ugly, but very much on the spot'. Every week Lytton took him an essay which he had to read aloud – a painful experience which he later turned to use as a means of testing his publications.

With his ungainly body, short sight and rather prim manner, Lytton was an intimidating undergraduate. 'His impact upon Cambridge when he came up was of a man from a different planet,' wrote H.O. Meredith, 'human, but not of our humanity, who belonged in his speech, gestures, poses and opinions to no recognized category of adolescence or maturity. The Strachey "voice" (which became so deservedly famous: faint echoes of it are still discoverable in contemporary society) was only one of his "differentials". His ways of standing, or sitting in a chair, or helping himself to bread and butter – briefly everything about him differentiated him from the crowd. The impression was *not* however (*at least not primarily*) one of originality; there was about him not much suggestion of a genius and still less of a crank. He gave rather the feeling of one who brought with him the ways and manners of an unsurmised and different civilization.'

Inevitably such a man charmed some and irritated others. The most usual reaction was to be more or less intrigued: here was a new animal in their midst, alien yet inoffensive, whom it was not easy to accept and impossible to ignore.

Despite the ripples of disturbance he produced, the Cambridge community, with its many vocational bachelors,[3] accommodated Lytton far better than anything he had yet experienced. Within a few weeks he had struck up several new friendships; and during the six years he was there, the number of his friends increased as his influence within the university widened. These companionships were often lifelong and, as Desmond MacCarthy observed, very like loves.

*

Early in Lytton's second term, he and four other undergraduates marshalled themselves into a small society which met in Clive Bell's rooms. 'The Reading Club consists of 5 members,' Lytton wrote to his mother soon after its formation (February 1900). 'Myself, Robertson,[4] Sydney-Turner (very distinguished and with immense knowledge of English Literature), Bell (a curious mixture of sport and reading) and Woolf (nothing particular). Last night we read J[ohn] G[abriel] B[orkman] – my Foldal being considered very life-like. I died of internal laughter every 5 minutes . . . They are all very amusing and pleasant.'

With Robertson, whom he originally described as 'a most entertaining personage . . . very tall, with a round cherubic face', Lytton's friendship did not develop far after he made the discovery that his father was a clergyman. But he quickly introduced into the group a sixth member, Thoby Stephen, who, he told his mother (18 October 1899), 'looked a charmer, and the image of the others[5] . . . He is rather strange but I think sensible and the best I have yet met.'

They called themselves the Midnight Society since it was their custom to meet each Saturday night at twelve o'clock. Having first strengthened themselves 'with whisky or punch and one of those gloomy beef-steak pies which it was the fashion to order for Sunday lunch', Clive Bell recounts, they would proceed 'to read aloud some such trifle as *Prometheus Unbound*, *The Cenci*, *The Return of the Druses*, *Bartholomew Fair* or *Comus*. As often as not it was dawn by the time we had done; and sometimes we would issue forth to perambulate the courts and cloisters, halting on Hall steps to spout passages of familiar verse, each following his fancy as memory served.'

Perhaps the most unlikely member of the group was Clive Bell himself. 'A gay and amiable dog', as Maynard Keynes described him, he seemed a 'mixture between Shelley and a sporting country squire' according to Thoby Stephen. Before baldness had begun prematurely to advance, his hair was luxuriant golden-brown above a spacious, pink and polished face and most of his friends belonged to the hunting and shooting set.

When Bell was his natural breezy self, flamboyantly holding forth in his 'so-happy-that-I-don't-care-whether-I-impress-you-or-not' sort of mood, Lytton thought him splendid, writing after one evening together: 'He was *divine* – in a soft shirt, & hair & complexion that lifted me & my penis to the heights of heaven. Oh! Oh! Oh!' In due course Bell planned to deliver himself of a *magnum opus* on modernism, the importance of which seemed to justify its eternal postponement. The grandeur of these aspirations displeased Lytton, whose own romantic ideals they parodied: 'He's really rather a mystery,' he told Leonard Woolf (July 1905), '– what can be his *raison d'être*? He takes himself in deadly earnest, I've discovered, as Art Critic and litterateur. Very queer – and he likes, or says he likes, such odd things – Gluck, Racine, Pope and Gibbon. If it's mere imitation of us, the question remains – why the dickens should he imitate us?'

Booming and rubicund, Bell was unrestrained in general conversation. After knowing him for some five or six years, Lytton concluded (1 July 1905) that:

'his character has several layers, but it is difficult to say which is the *fond*. There is the country gentleman layer, which makes him retire into the depths of Wiltshire to shoot partridges. There is the Paris decadent layer, which takes him to the quartier latin where he discusses painting and vice with American artists and French models. There is the eighteenth-century layer, which adores Thoby Stephen. There is the layer of innocence which adores Thoby's sister. There is the layer of prostitution, which shows itself in an amazing head of crimped straw-coloured hair. And there is the layer of stupidity, which runs transversely through all the other layers.'

Clive Bell got to know the original members of the group through Saxon Sydney-Turner, whose rooms were near his own, and he soon became friendly with Thoby Stephen. The presence within this intellectual fraternity of someone like Thoby Stephen, with his athletic prowess and love of the open air, must have facilitated Clive Bell's bold faltering footsteps into the world of the literati. The two of them would smoke cigars and discuss points of hunting, watched by the others with a mingling of envy and disapproval. 'Lytton, however, liked us for that,' Clive Bell shrewdly observed; while Leonard Woolf noticed that 'in those early days, and indeed for many years afterwards, intellectually Clive sat at the feet of Lytton and Thoby'.

Thoby Stephen was the elder son of Sir Leslie Stephen. Over six feet tall and of a somewhat ponderous build, he had a physical magnificence that put some of his friends in mind of Samuel Johnson, without the Doctor's infirmities yet with the same monumental good sense. He was a frequent target of hero-worship. It was really his masculinity that enchanted Lytton. In a letter (1 July 1905) written to an Oxford undergraduate, B.W. Swithinbank, he describes the admiration Thoby inspired in him: 'He has a wonderful and massive frame, and a face hewn out of the living rock. His character is as splendid as his appearance, and as wonderfully complete. In fact, he's monolithic. But, if it were not for his extraordinary sense of humour, he would hardly be of this world. We call him the Goth; and when you see him I'm sure you'll agree that he's a survival of barbaric grandeur. He'll be a judge of great eminence, and, in his old age, a sombre family potentate. One day we composed each other's epitaphs. He said that mine should be "The Universal Exception"; and mine for him was "The Forlorn Hope".'

Lytton idealized Thoby. Different in almost every respect from himself, he represented what was unattainable in life. He seemed the perfect human specimen, an aesthetic ideal. 'Don't you think that if God had to justify the existence of the world,' he asked Leonard Woolf, 'it would be done if he were to produce the Goth?'

In Leonard Woolf the Midnight Society had a freshman who was, so he later explained, in a curious psychological state. Having inherited a highly-strung intellect from his father, and rejected his mother's squeamish sentimentality, he was growing up a rather dry, nervously repressed young man, in appearance lean, with a long nose, sombre eyes and pale ascetic lips. The pendulum of his emotions appeared to swing through a fairly small arc, but in moments of stress they found an outlet in the involuntary trembling of his hands. To Lytton's relief, he never believed in God, and considered the whole paraphernalia of prayer as 'one of the oddest freaks in human psychology'.

It was Woolf whom Lytton singled out to act as his confessor, the reliable friend to whom, during his first three years at Cambridge, he confided his secret passions. This outlet to his feelings provided a relief which his early diaries had failed to give him. For diaries, as he now knew, tended to redouble one's self-preoccupation. Through communion with a sympathetic friend, he hoped to lose part of his isolation. The reasoning was sound; and the choice of Leonard Woolf was partially successful. He had much to recommend him – a good brain, a lack of prejudice, a detachment of manner, an impressive honesty. But his puritanism stood as an obstacle to complete and spontaneous confidence. Often Lytton would tease him about it, suggesting that he should join a League for the Advancement of Social Purity, or refusing to send him 'an Etude quasi sadiste' which he had written, 'as I'm afraid you might think it improper'. Leonard Woolf reacted indignantly to such jibes. But whenever Lytton tested him with some specially obscene piece of gossip, he would sense Leonard's fractional recoil. 'It is hopeless,' he told his brother James, his next confessor but one, '– what can one expect in even a remote future, when *Woolf* thinks that people ought to be "punished" for incest?'

The remaining member of the Midnight Society, Saxon Sydney-Turner, was still-born into the Midnight. 'When I first knew him he was a wild and unrestrained freshman,' Lytton remembered, 'who wrote poems, never went to bed, and declaimed Swinburne and Sir Thomas Browne till four o'clock in the morning in the Great Court at Trinity. He is now . . . quite pale and inanimate, hardly more than an incompletely galvanized dead body.' To those who had not known him early on he seemed an automaton of a man, endlessly crossword puzzling and opera-accumulating as he moved indecisively through the shadows until the last years of his life when, in retirement from the Treasury, he took disastrously to gambling. With the members of the Midnight Society he would talk on subjects of the greatest tedium, such as the use by Tacitus of the dative case. Everything around him was static. The furniture in his room never moved. He ate little, without relish, infrequently. He was short, thin, with an anaemic pallor and fading hair.

At times Lytton felt that he might go under in the same way as his friend. 'It would never do to become Turnerian,' he wrote to his brother James (October 1912), 'and I feel it's a danger that hangs over all of us.' To Saxon himself a few years earlier he had written: 'Time and Space for you do not exist, and perhaps not for me either, who feel myself fleeting towards your philosophy. What this is you have never told me, but it occurred to me the other day, and though it made me feel very ill, perhaps I agree.'

Occasionally Lytton and the others would catch a glimpse of the Saxon they first knew. 'He looks sometimes', wrote Leonard Woolf, 'like a little schoolboy whom life has bullied into unconsciousness;' while to Lytton he appeared 'like some puzzled night-animal blinking in the unaccustomed daylight'. So they stayed loyal to him, though in their fashion denouncing him violently to his other friends.

One other companion Lytton met during his first months at Trinity. This was the historian, George Trevelyan, who was some four years older than himself and from a similar West Country landed dynasty. He would be invited over to Trevelyan's rooms for breakfast and a lengthy walk; and when he inquired whether he might enjoy the food without the exercise, was told: 'No walk, no breakfast.' Lytton thought him rather earnest, 'and somewhat patristic towards me', as he told his sister Pernel.

Sometimes the two of them went off bicycling together, Trevelyan talking about Cromwell, Milton, Cardinal Newman, Oxford and the Early Christians. 'He is most friendly and kind,' Lytton wrote to his mother (March 1900), 'and very like what I imagined his father to be.'[6] But in time, this kindness, with its overtones of avuncular authority – so welcome when he still felt lonely and unknown in Cambridge – began to pall. He seemed set on a career as the nation's chronicler that would crown him Historian Laureate. He was gravely methodical, and rather tedious too when taking it on himself to explain that the pleasure which people derived from dancing came from the legitimate physical contact it afforded partners of the opposite sex. Lytton did not dance. Besides it was impossible as yet to explain that his preference lay in contact with his own sex.

2

PALPITATIONS, FRENCH AND ENGLISH

During the Easter term of 1900, there was always something happening. Lytton went to hear Stephen Phillips read his *Paolo and Francesca*[7] in a sonorous monotone which hushed the jangling ornaments of his female audience, but sent Lytton off to sleep. Less soporific, though rather more disagreeable, was a Newnham lecture given by Edmund Gosse on Leigh Hunt. 'Law! He *did* think himself clever!' Lytton wrote to Pernel. 'After 3 sentences he suddenly said, "I was never in such a draught in the whole course of my life!" Katherine [Stephen] and Sharpley ran forward and screwed ventilators (apparently). After a long time he said, "Oh, it really doesn't matter." Grossly rude, I thought.' Every Wednesday and Thursday, he attended lectures on Early Florentine Art given by Roger Fry. 'These are very interesting and good though somewhat abstruse,' he told his mother (15 May 1900).

When the summer vacation came he joined his family at a country house they had rented at Kingston Lisle Park, 'in the Berkshire downs near the White Horse,' he wrote to Lumsden Barkway, '– a beautiful park and beautiful country.' While here, during the hot weather of July, he was assailed by violent palpitations of the heart. A doctor was called to examine him, but could find no specific cause for these attacks, which he put down to 'nerves'.* Sir Richard Strachey was also laid up at the time, and two

---

* It is possible that he was suffering from what is called paroxysmal tachycardia. The cause of this condition is not accurately known, though it is probably of nervous origin and can be aggravated by physical wear and tear. The symptoms are sometimes alarming, but it is not considered dangerous.

nurses moved into the house, which was converted into a makeshift sanatorium. Doses of digitalis and bromide were prescribed for Lytton. 'The disease is mysterious', he explained to Lumsden Barkway from his sick-bed, '– of no very definite nature – fainting and general weakness. Nothing is radically wrong say the doctors, but it has been settled that I shall not go back to Cambridge next term so as to make a complete recovery. This is I suppose the wisest thing – but I am very, very sad at the thought of it.'

Instead of returning to Cambridge that autumn he was mewed in by female relatives who forbade him all exertion, even reading. 'Everyone and thing missed you last term,' wrote Leonard Woolf, to whom, in his letterless condition within Lancaster Gate, Lytton had cried out for the lifeblood of Trinity gossip, 'and I am sure the temporary death of the Midnight Society might have been avoided if we had had you to back up those members who are not afraid of late hours.'

By the middle of October he felt better. He had been moved to a nursing home in Queen's Gate Terrace[8] where Dr Roland Brinton, the family physician, gave him a thorough examination before reporting to Lady Strachey (18 October 1900) that he could 'have a little light literature – after the business of the day is over – and before it is time for him to settle down for the night. He still has occasional attacks of palpitations – and his heart certainly has a tumultuous action – but I can find no reason to think that there is any structural disease there. So I feel fairly confident that all his uncomfortable sensations will disappear. He likes a little claret – but a pint bottle lasts him two days – so there is no excess.'

After six weeks Lytton's weight increased from nine to eleven stone, his old clothes now failing conspicuously to meet across his manly chest. 'I feel much stronger,' he assured Lumsden Barkway (23 November 1900), '– but not yet quite natural or ordinary – something of a portent or monster still . . . last Summer still remains a nightmare.'

At the beginning of December he went down to St-Jean-de-Luz, near Biarritz, in the Basses Pyrénées. His mother went with him, and having deposited him at the Hôtel d'Angleterre and introduced him to some cousins living near by, she returned to England.

There was little to do but write letters. 'The only man of amusement (barring a decayed millionaire and a gouty Baron)', he wrote to Leonard Woolf, 'is an Oxford person who teaches little boys and in intervals writes poems for the *Spectator* . . . He gives me his poems to read (bad enough), and good advice (rather worse) and his views on Shakespeare (quite ridiculous). We talked the other day of people we should like to meet – I mentioned Cleopatra. He said, "I should rather see Our Lord to anyone else." I had to reply, "Oh, I put him on one side as inhuman."

'The people at the hotel are more than fearful. I often wish I was a snake and could wriggle on the ground.'

The few residents of the hotel would seat themselves for meals at a long table and stare hopelessly into a looking-glass past tall pots with strangled chrysanthemums peeping out and a few bleak cruet-stands. At breakfast, lunch and dinner Lytton listened to monotonous golf and social gossip. 'I have no one on my right,' he wrote to Lumsden Barkway, 'on my left an old Irish squire of sorts – dull as ditchwater but good-natured enough – as I suppose all dullards are. He repeats indefinitely, and I dare say winds himself up before he hops into bed at night. Next him an old maid – very thin, and rather pitiful, then her two nieces – vulgar, *very* good, and *very*, *very* stupid. Poor people! At the head of the table a Captain (Caulfield by name) in the Navy – but *I* believe the Marines – or even Horse Marines. Terrible! Impossible to mention anyone who is not his bosom friend. As conceited as a cock-a-doodle-do, and as brainless. These are the English inhabitants of this house. Oh! I've forgotten one – Miss Roper, who looks like a governess, but who isn't, and wears curious tails to her jackets, and talks sensibly enough. I fear I am rude to some of them sometimes. I often want to make faces, and sometimes do – when nobody's looking.'

The town itself, with its old narrow streets, its quay, its square, and the ancient galleried church where Louis XIV was married, delighted him. But nothing happened there. Sometimes he would go for long walks to surrounding villages and 'once I got on a merry-go-round at a fair and revolved to my heart's content'. His happiest hours were spent bicycling among the hills. One day he went by train to Biarritz which, as a fashionable seaside resort, had a splendid sea-front with magnificent waves coming up in a continual procession. 'Their thunder was enormous, and their foam beautiful,' he wrote to Lumsden Barkway.

'. . . Talking of great volumes of sound, isn't it extraordinary that some poetry really makes as much noise as anything else? I mean Milton for instance – the *quantity* of sound appears to me often as vast as that of a full symphony of Beethoven or the enormous roaring of the sea . . .

Coming back in the train the sunset was miraculous – hardly credible – dark purply grey – rose – pale saffron – altogether with the mountains an effect of great peace. I wondered why all the heads I passed were not turned towards it – but nature grows familiar and so I suppose contemptible to country-dwellers – and this is one of the advantages of travelling – one is woken up to the marvel of things.'

Lytton's days were made congenial by the hospitality of his cousins, Mrs King[9] – Lady Strachey's first cousin – Irish and gay and bright, and her daughter Janie – married to a young Irishman named McGusty – an amusing girl with gold hair and a pink-and-white complexion. They introduced him to some of the inhabitants at St-Jean-de-Luz including several bachelors 'or people who ought to be bachelors – generals, bankers, loungers of all sorts. The man of business is Bellairs – half French and half English – talks French with an English accent, and English with a French, as Janie says, lays down the law on everything, says "damn it my dear fellow" a good deal, and is altogether a windy but not unimaginative fool ... Have I mentioned Mr Penny? a commercial gentleman staying here with a wife and child. He has, as he says, "knocked about all over the world", and now I suppose is settling down. His wife leads a sad life I fear, for even to us he is liable to give long lectures on the Roman Catholic religion and how to drive an omnibus. He is a Master of Platitude.'

Chaperoned by his cousins, Lytton went off once a week to play roulette which he described as 'very soothing'. On one occasion a tremor of excitement went around at the arrival of ex-Queen Nathalie of Serbia, at that time living in retirement near by. Lytton marked the waves of thrilled obsequiousness produced by her regal entry:

'As the game was proceeding, suddenly "la Reine" was whispered, and everyone rising to their feet, Her Majesty, accompanied by her suite, entered the apartment. She looked pleasant and stupid – rather bulky and well-dressed – stayed for so long that I was late for dinner and consequently fined a franc and relegated to a side-table. People kissed her gloved hand when saying How-do-you-do, and curtseyed and shook hands at the same time on her leaving. I must say if I were a retired sovereign I should give up such airs and graces, and try to slip into a room like an ordinary mortal.'

On 9 January 1901 Lytton travelled back to London and a little later returned to Trinity where the Midnight Society resumed its nocturnal readings, Lytton taking the part of Cleopatra in *Antony and Cleopatra*. He was now studying Walter Pater. 'As for Pater,' he wrote to Lumsden Barkway, 'though I have not read much of him he appears to me so deathly – no motion, no vigour – a waxen style ... And after all does he say so very much that is worth hearing? In short I do not like the man.' In the vacation his mother read to him from *The Ring and the Book*, which pleased him more. 'What a work!' he commented. 'No one but R[obert]

B[rowning] could ever have dreamt of writing it.' With Henry James, whose early novels Lady Strachey was also fond of reading aloud, he was even more fascinated, opening one of his letters to Leonard Woolf in imitation of the master:

'In settling the great question, at any rate, is there more than one answer of the many which, as a serious solution, can add more than nothing to an after all admitted ignorance? Do not, in their hubbub, the thousand vociferations only succeed in missing the failure by which they are self-condemned by satisfactorily proving even to the least experienced auditor the correctness of the one? Will you not agree that boredom is, essentially, life? Sleep, I think, and death are the only states of which a limited consciousness can speak without it.'

That year Lytton passed the summer holidays with his family at Cuffnells, a country house with vast gardens, near Lyndhurst, ten miles from Southampton. Much of this time was occupied in writing an essay on Warren Hastings for the Greaves Prize at Trinity (which he failed to win), and in attempting to learn German. In his solitary moments he was 'reading Keats in raptures' and going off for long walks in the Hampshire countryside. His happiness over these weeks was increased by the presence of the Stephen family, including the radiant Thoby, whom he saw several times, once at a fair where the Goth was sporting himself very splendidly among village boys and coconuts. 'Here it is delicious,' he told Leonard Woolf, 'the New Forest – beautiful trees and weather. The Goth within five miles with his family. It is a school they live in, and the Goth at night retreats to the dormitory where he magnificently sleeps among the small surrounding beds.'

Once or twice he was invited across by Thoby to the Stephen schoolhouse where, for the first time, he met Thoby's two aloof and lovely sisters, Vanessa – later to marry Clive Bell – and Virginia – who subsequently married Leonard Woolf – together with Adrian, their brother, and the awe-inspiring Leslie Stephen – 'quite deaf and rather dangerous' – who insisted on Lytton repeating all his falsetto remarks down a formidable ear-trumpet.[10] 'It is a nice though wild family,' Lytton reported to Leonard Woolf, '– 2 sisters very pretty – a younger brother Adrian, and Leslie with his ear-trumpet and tam-o'-shanter. What is rather strange is the old man – older than he really is – among so young a family. He is well kept in check by them, and they are well bustled by him. They know each other very well I think.'

For the Christmas vacation of 1901, Lytton was packed off to the Villa

Himalaya, above Menton in the South of France with two of his sisters, Dorothy and Marjorie. The blue sea, the sky and the hills were so enchanting that he dreaded returning to England. 'This is heavenly! Yes, heavenly! The best of what one imagines the Riviera!' he enthused to Lumsden Barkway (on 29 December 1901). '. . . Mountains! Yes! And some with snow! They tower! The sea glows and shimmers and swells! The sky is a marvel! . . . we continue our rounds of pleasure – among which I don't think I mentioned to you the fascination of food. Omelettes! Wines – sparkling and sweet like ginger-beer! Rolls! All quite absolute! Especially after one has been toiling on legs or donkeys up precipitous paths under tropical suns. One falls on food voracious as lions.' In such conditions the first necessity was idleness. It was a time for dreaming rather than work. 'I turned the Cape the other day, and there was Monte Carlo,' he wrote to Leonard Woolf. 'One wouldn't go there.' All the same, he went there several times, gambled and lost a little, listened to the orchestra, took his ease in the Royal Palace, and saw the delicious orangeries – trees crowded together on bright grass and the wall dropping to the sea a thousand feet below.

Out of the idleness and dreaming emerged a riotous three-act tragedy to be performed by the Midnight Society in the Lent term. But writing did not come easily. 'The air is strangely lowering,' he told Leonard Woolf who had inquired after the progress of the play. 'I write the tragedy and walk – either strollingly or up steep hills to absurd villages.' A favourite destination was Eze-en-haut, which hangs dramatically from a cliff top between Cap Ferrat and Monte Carlo. 'There are the ruins of a Moorish Castle there,' he wrote to his mother, 'also the foundations of a temple to Isis, now converted to a Church to the Holy Virgin.' One other village also caught his imagination. This was Castellar, 'in the depths – or heights? – of the hills. Very small and pleasant. With 4,000 children all shrieking and yelling – also a damp, tinsel R.C. Church – also one room of a mediaeval palace belonging to a family whose last descendant was hung from its own window in the time of the Revolution.'

With his sisters he crossed the frontier into Italy reaching the old Roman post, Ventimiglia. 'Italy pleases me,' he wrote to Leonard Woolf.

'But everything is strange, almost lurid with contrasts, and the sense of abounding life. Coming down a winding hill-road through a valley, we heard the other day the noises of a butchery. The surroundings were so bathed in country peace, the sky was so blue, the vegetation so green and florid, that the sound struck as a horror. I imagined, in some recess, whence – believe it! – rose shouts of fiendish human exultations, an

67

obscene and reeking sacrifice to a still remembered pagan god. Above us perhaps loomed (beneath the walls of Madonna's edifice) the hoary temple of Isis; who knows whether through the remoteness of these secluded years some worship had not lingered; some mystic propitiation and reconciliation of the hideous mysteries of life and death.'

3

CHARACTERS

The death of the Midnight Society[11] was hastened by the regular week-end visits from London of three former undergraduates, Desmond MacCarthy, Bertrand Russell and E.M. Forster, all of whom got to know Lytton well during his early years at Cambridge. After the conversation of MacCarthy, especially, it was difficult to carry on with the formality of prepared literary readings. He would bring along his friend, the philosopher G.E. Moore, not primarily to debate questions of philosophy but to play with gusto upon the piano and to sing. After this musical entertainment, MacCarthy himself would come forward with a string of stories, often admittedly unfinished, but always ending in laughter. When he and Moore had done with their cabaret performance, the volumes of *Bartholomew Fair* and *The Cenci* remained unopened.

MacCarthy's reputation as a brilliant raconteur was partly rooted in his skill as a practised listener. He achieved the feat of talking just enough to suggest a beguiling flow of story telling, and was at his best with people to whom he owed no special obligation. On these Saturday visits to Trinity, the apparent play of his soft Irish humour, the seeming grace and quickness of his speech, cast round him a haze of geniality.

In later years, as literary editor of *The Speaker*, the *New Quarterly* and the *New Statesman* he was punctilious in giving his friends commissions. But other reviewers were sometimes reduced to despair by his invariably courteous procrastination; and one of them, A.G. Macdonell, was eventually moved to retaliate with a satirical portrait of him as Charles Ossory in his celebrated comic novel, *England, Their England*.

MacCarthy soon took to Lytton and began to draw him out. But it was a long business. At first Lytton remained suspicious. He had an automatic disdain for those who could command instant popularity, and did not feel really at home in MacCarthy's vague and expansive presence. MacCarthy's stories, while they lasted, soothed him. But when they trailed off, and MacCarthy left, he felt the burden of his solitude reinforced. 'The curious thing,' Lytton observed, 'is that when one's with him it all seems very amusing, and that afterwards one can only look back on a dreary waste.' In a letter to Maynard Keynes (18 November 1905), he described the same paradox. 'He's a curious figure – very dull and amusing. Also rather desolate.' This feeling of desolation arose from the sense that talking with MacCarthy meant little more than carrying on an animated dialogue with oneself – in Lytton's case the one person from whom he wished to escape.

But gradually he thawed. 'I liked him much better than before,' he was able to tell Leonard Woolf by the end of 1904. 'He seemed to understand a good deal, and want to be liked.' 'The thing is to keep him off literature,' Lytton later explained to Virginia Woolf, 'and insist on his doing music-hall turns: if only he'd make that his profession he'd make thousands. Can't you see him coming on in a macintosh?'

Bertrand Russell, who used to travel down with MacCarthy at weekends, was, in the opinion of D.H. Lawrence, 'all Disembodied Mind'. Actually the dazzling clarity of his mind was to be exceeded by the violence of his moral and sexual passions. He had, in James Strachey's phrase, a 'most marvellous mental apparatus', his intelligence appearing to shine through his large dark eyes. But as a young man he suffered greatly from loneliness, abandoning himself to the beauty of mathematics 'because it is *not* human'.

Later on, reading *Eminent Victorians* in Brixton gaol, Russell was to record that, 'It caused me to laugh so loud that the officer came to my cell, saying I must remember that prison is a place of punishment.'[12] But his amusement did not blind him to other facets of Lytton's writing – the rhetorical flourishes borrowed from Macaulay, the girls' school sentimentality. It may have been, as James Strachey believed, that he resented the greater influence of G.E. Moore over Lytton. Moore would sometimes rebuke Desmond MacCarthy for inviting Russell to his reading parties during the Cambridge vacations, feeling that his own patient method of analysis was disrupted by Russell's quick-fire arguments. Russell must have been aware of this coolness. He once asked him: 'You don't like me, do you, Moore?' Moore deliberated for several minutes, and then replied with a pregnant monosyllable: 'No.' After which the two philosophers went on chatting amiably enough. Russell never actively disliked Moore, but he seems to have considered that Lytton perverted Moore's ethics so as to exalt his own homosexuality.

He disliked, too, the arrogant tone which Lytton sometimes assumed in these undergraduate days and the deliberate affectation with which he fashioned his idiosyncrasies into a subtly pervasive style.

This style also disconcerted E.M. Forster. His alarming silences, spread like an eiderdown over frivolous chatter, and the piercing little shrieks with which he would greet any vaguely mystical observation unnerved Forster who was already, as Maynard Keynes described him, 'the elusive colt of a dark horse'. He reacted towards Lytton with the wariness of unspoken intimacy. In some of his letters to mutual friends, Lytton criticized Forster fiercely – his quaint timidity, his old-maidish liberalism. But what he really objected to was having a mirror held up to the more negative features of his own image. 'Excessive paleness is what I think worries me most,' he wrote to Leonard Woolf. 'The Taupe [Forster] in his wonderful way I imagine saw this about me, and feeling that he himself verged upon the washed-out, shuddered.'

Forster was by no means the only person to be criticized in Lytton's correspondence. No one escapes. It is the writing of someone hypersensitive and insecure. Surrounded by many new friends, Lytton could never be certain that they liked him or be sure that he admired them for liking him. There is often something forced about his relationships. He is impatient for intimacy, on guard against rejection. His life, after coming up to Trinity, was for the most part dominated by two types of people. There was the young man who, approximating to his ideal, excited his lust and adoration; there was the person to whom he confessed these feelings, and on whose sympathy, commiseration and encouragement he relied. Sometimes variations appear in the pattern and the borderline between these two is not distinct.

Among others who shared the risky distinction of appearing in Lytton's correspondence were C.P. Sanger,[13] a gnomelike figure with bright sceptical eyes, rather older than Lytton, who had shown exceptional promise at Trinity and was now a barrister; Walter Lamb who was 'like a fellow with one leg who's not only quite convinced that he's got two but boasts of his walking exploits'; R.C. Trevelyan (usually referred to as Bob Trevy), the whimsical, bookish poet and elder brother of George Trevelyan, whose poetry no one liked and whose personality was 'amusing but vague to a degree'; and J.E. McTaggart, the redoubtable Hegelian philosopher, whose rooms Lytton, in company with Leonard Woolf, Saxon Sydney-Turner and a few other chosen undergraduates, would visit every Thursday evening. McTaggart[14] was a shy immobile figure with an artillery of rapid talk as well as a limitless capacity for provocative silence. An atheist who believed in God, he intrigued Lytton until, coming under the greater influence of G.E. Moore, he was to see him off in four lines:

McTaggart's seen through god
And put him on the shelf;
Isn't it rather odd
He doesn't see through himself.

4

BLANK, BLANK, BLANK

After matriculating in the autumn of 1899, Lytton was made an
Exhibitioner the following year. In between the meetings of the Midnight
and other societies, he was reading history in a rather desultory manner,
and in June 1901 he took the first part of his History Tripos. 'My tripos
begins tomorrow,' he wrote to his mother (21 May 1901), 'and lasts till
Thursday. I am calm and with the aid of chocolate will I hope weather it.'
To the general disappointment, he obtained only a Second Class. 'It was
exactly what I expected', he wrote to Lumsden Barkway, '– and I think on
the whole inevitable.'

Early in the Lent term he embarked on his most ambitious exercise in
verse. Entitled 'Ely: An Ode', the piece was written for the Chancellor's
Medal which is awarded each year for the best ode or poem in heroic verse
and of less than two hundred lines submitted by a resident undergraduate.
'Ely' is set in the strophes, antistrophes and epode of the Pindaric metre.
The subject of Lytton's entry was the cathedral of Ely, and throughout the
composition one feels that he is on his very best behaviour. It is the only
Cambridge poem in which he addresses God with a capital 'G'.
Characteristically he left himself very little time to complete this ode. 'Ely,
if it is, will have to be written by next Saturday,' he told his mother (26
January 1902). But all went well and the next month he learnt that he had
won the award, narrowly beating Sheppard of King's into second place.[15]
'I could dance with joy,' Lady Strachey wrote to him from Lancaster Gate,
'and we are all in the greatest delight.'[16] On 2 June the family came up to
Cambridge and heard him read his winning ode in the Senate House.

Despite his Second Class, he was elected to a Scholarship at Trinity,
receiving a homily from G.M. Trevelyan that stressed his obligation to 'do
credit to us'. He must 'get a First now', Trevelyan insisted (22 March
1902). 'To do that, you will have to work reasonably hard ... Your
answers are all essays – clever essays to cover a good deal of ignorance.
Please regard yourself as married to the College and to History – bigamy
has its duties as well as privileges.' His fellow scholar was Thoby Stephen.

'The ceremony was not particularly impressive,' he informed his mother (28 April 1902), 'in fact particularly absurd. We all had to be dressed in black and white ties and bands – mystical articles which much increased the ludicrosity of the performance. We all assembled at the Lodge first, where the Master received us in his usual charming method. We then proceeded to Chapel. Various grinning dons occupied the pews. Each scholar advanced and read aloud his names in a book, and then knelt down on both knees before the Master, placing his hands between his, while he (the M) said in Latin, "I admit thee a scholar of the College." But the whole thing was hurried over as quickly as possible – no pomp or even pomposity.'

It was generally expected that Lytton would obtain a First Class in Part II of the History Tripos and then go on to become a Fellow of the College. Already, by the autumn of 1902, he had a particular Fellowship dissertation in mind and asked his mother to find out from Sir John Strachey – the author of *Hastings and the Rohilla War* (1892) – whether he considered Warren Hastings and the Begums of Oude a good subject. Neither his uncle's book, nor the work of the other great champion of Hastings, James Fitzjames Stephen, dealt with the charge made against Hastings in the House of Lords that he had engineered the despoliation of the Begums of Oude, the mother and grandmother of the reigning Vizier. 'Lytton's idea seems to me an excellent one,' his uncle replied. 'With the exception of Stephen's *Nundkomar*[17] and my own Rohillas there has been, in my belief, little or no original research into the history of these times. I never looked into the great mass of Hastings's papers at the British Museum or the India Office Records for any time after that with which I was concerned, but there can be no doubt that they are a mine out of which a vast amount of knowledge can be dug.'

Lytton took the second part of the History Tripos in the early summer of 1903, and once again, to everyone's dismay, he obtained only Second Class Honours. In a letter to Lady Strachey (30 June 1903), J.D. Duff described the result as coming as a complete surprise. 'That he is a First Class man is a point on which I feel no doubt at all,' he wrote. 'Of course I have never seen his work, except an Essay on Warren Hastings some years ago; but I judge from our personal intercourse, and say that in quality of intellect he is superior to any pupil I have had in my four years; and I have had dozens of Firsts and Double Firsts.

'Nor do I think it was a matter of health. He was not pressed for time: most men have only one year for the second part of the Tripos: and he kept well during the two years and I don't think he suffered during the examination.

'From what he has said to me, I believe the real reason to be that his
Tripos involved a good deal of task work, books to be got up and definite
facts to remember, and that he did not do this work. I had no notion of this
beforehand, though perhaps I should have found it out.'

Though Lytton affected not to care much about the Tripos result, a
Double Second could well influence Fellowship Electors against him.
They were a body of about sixteen dons representing all subjects, and all
keen for their own candidates. Two, probably, would represent history;
but all heard the evidence for each candidate before voting. 'I think Lytton
might do so good a Dissertation as to overcome this prejudice,' Duff told
Lady Strachey, 'but it will undoubtedly be felt and expressed.'

Lady Strachey was also anxious lest this indifferent degree should
impede his entry into the Civil Service, her original choice of career for
him when he was applying to Balliol and one which she now revived.
Cambridge at this time trained a large proportion of its undergraduates for
careers in public service, and several of Lytton's friends were conscripted
into some branch of the Civil Service – A.R. Ainsworth, Ralph Hawtrey
and Robin Mayor going to the Education Office; Theodore Llewelyn
Davies and Saxon Sydney-Turner to the Treasury; Maynard Keynes for a
couple of years to the India Office; and Leonard Woolf, for seven years, to
the Ceylon Civil Service. Competition was keen and most successful
applicants had been awarded Firsts or Double Firsts. 'Personally,' wrote
G.M. Trevelyan to Keynes, 'I think it most distressing the way the civil
service swallows nearly all the best Cambridge men.'

Lytton felt no desire to join the Civil Service. His mother, however,
wanted him to join the Board of Education, as it was then called, and
Lytton appeared to fall in with her wishes. For the next few months she
waged an energetic campaign on his behalf, knowing that these things
were still largely arranged by private influence. While his parents were
sending letters to their friends and relations, Lytton busied himself getting
testimonials from the dons under whom he had studied. These letters of
recommendation are naturally flattering. But, after allowances are made
for the spirit of helpfulness normally motivating such testimonials, they do
seem to show that he was held in high esteem. J.D. Duff, more well-
meaning than well-informed, wrote again along the lines of his earlier
letter to Lady Strachey. Stanley Leathes, who had been an examiner for
both parts of the History Tripos, wrote of him as an undergraduate whose
abilities deserved a higher place than that recorded in his examination
results:

'He is a man of unusually wide culture, of considerable originality, and unusual literary gifts ... he is in every sense a well-educated man, and worthy to rank with first-class men, as is shown by his being elected to a Scholarship to Trinity. I think that his intelligence, wide reading, versatility, and cultivation would render him a good public servant in the Education Department. His intellectual capacity is far above his University degree.'

From the University of Glasgow, where he was now Professor of English Language and Literature, Walter Raleigh added a more personal note in support of Lytton's application:

'I have known Mr Strachey for years and I cannot think of anyone among my numerous past pupils, whom I should prefer to him for work requiring ability, tact and judgement. He has a mind of rare power and distinction, a character of great decision, and a temper so reasonable and gentle that it is a delight to work with him. I hope that he may be successful in obtaining the appointment that he seeks, where I am sure he would quickly gain the confidence and esteem of all who should have to do with him.'

The briefest and least helpful testimonial was provided by William Cunningham, a Trollopian clergyman, later Archdeacon of Ely, known as 'Parson Bill', who had succeeded Stanley Leathes as Lytton's director of studies.

While Lytton was canvassing these opinions, Lady Strachey got in touch with Sidney Webb, who was chairman of the London County Council's technical education board; and he in turn introduced her at a dinner given on 18 November to Sir Robert Laurie Morant, Permanent Secretary of the Board of Education, who agreed to interview Lytton once he returned to London for the vacation. Lady Strachey was jubilant. 'I believe I have done the trick,' she wrote to Lytton the day after meeting Morant.

What transpired at Lytton's meeting with Sir Robert Morant is not now known. He was never invited to join the Board of Education and Lady Strachey finally abandoned her hopes of a career for him in the Civil Service. The similarity between this unsuccessful petition and his equally fruitless application to Balliol is striking. In each case it is his mother who, as the driving force behind the scheme, brings it near completion. Both plans ultimately depend upon the personal impression created by Lytton. It was the maladroit figure he presented in these interviews that seems to have damned his chances of gaining the advancement he did not want. Was it shyness or an obstinate line of subterfuge? Either would account for these failures and both were characteristic.

With a career in public service gone, Lytton now prepared himself to pursue another of his mother's schemes – a Fellowship. Once again he was not entirely pleased by the prospect. He had no great desire to be a don. But Cambridge itself he loved as no other place. With rooms at Trinity he could escape the gloom of Lancaster Gate. Besides, what future could there be for him beyond the university?

'After Cambridge,' he wrote to Leonard Woolf, 'blank, blank, blank.'

FIVE

Beetles and Water-spiders

'I feel I should go mad when I think of your set, Duncan Grant and Keynes and Birrell. It makes me dream of beetles. In Cambridge I had a similar dream. I had felt it slightly before in the Stracheys. But it came full upon me in Keynes and in Duncan Grant. And yesterday I knew it again in Birrell – you must leave these friends, these beetles.'

D.H. Lawrence in a letter to David Garnett (19 April 1915)

'I can see us as water-spiders, gracefully skimming, as light and reasonable as air, the surface of the stream without any contact at all with the eddies and currents underneath.'

John Maynard Keynes, 'My Early Beliefs' (1938)

I

CONVERSAZIONE

The most notorious of all university societies, to which Lytton had been elected in his third year up at Trinity, was the 'Cambridge Conversazione Society', better known as the 'Apostles' or simply 'the Society'. Unlike the Midnight, the Apostles were not confined to Trinity and did not cease attending meetings once they had graduated or gone down. Most weekends Lytton would meet them for tea or dinner on the Saturday – and Sunday breakfasts were always an event.

Since its original foundation almost a century earlier, the Apostles had been a 'secret' body, attracting on that account a great volume of publicity. At the same time, there was a reason for concealment. Although it was known to readers of memoirs, few of the undergraduates realized that the society still existed. Consequently, the Apostles were protected from those who, aspiring to be elected, would behave in special ways to ingratiate themselves.

Lytton jubilantly proclaimed his election, which officially took place on 1 February 1902, in a heavily marked 'Private and Confidential' letter to his mother who already knew of the eminence and mystique of the Society.[1]

'My dearest Mama – This is to say – before I am committed to oaths of secrecy – that I am now a brother of the Society of Apostles – How I dare write the words I don't know! – I was apparently elected yesterday, and today the news was gently broken. The members – past and present – are sufficiently distinguished. Tennyson was one of the early ones. But I shall know more when I visit the Ark – or closet in which the documents of the society are kept. It is a veritable Brotherhood – the chief point being personal friendship between the members. The sensation is a strange one. Angels are Apostles who have taken wings – viz. settled down to definite opinions – which they may do whenever they choose. I feel I shall never take wings ... Another person whom I don't know called Sheppard (King's) was elected at the same time as me. We meet each other tonight! ...'

The Society had been founded as a small, comparatively humble debating club in St John's College. But during the 1820s, it fell under the control of two formidable undergraduates, F.D. Maurice and John Stirling, who transferred its rendezvous to the larger and more fashionable Trinity. Its members met behind locked doors on Saturdays when, after tea and anchovy toast, they would read papers, and hold discussions, on moral questions.

The inner world of the Apostles was sacrosanct. Accounts of its workings given by two nineteenth-century brethren, Dean Merivale and Henry Sidgwick, 'show that its nature and atmosphere have remained fundamentally unaltered throughout its existence', wrote Leonard Woolf, who was elected in the same year as Lytton. Dean Merivale describes its activities as follows:

'Our common bond has been a common intellectual taste, common studies, common literary aspirations, and we have all felt, I suppose, the support of mutual regard and perhaps some mutual flattery. We soon grew, as such youthful coteries generally do, into immense self-conceit. We began to think that we had a mission to enlighten the world upon things intellectual and spiritual. We lived, as I said, in constant intercourse with one another, day by day, meeting over our wine or our tobacco; but every Saturday evening we held a more solemn sitting, when each member of the society, about twelve in number, delivered an essay on any subject, chosen by himself, to be discussed and submitted to the vote of the whole number. Alas! Alas! what reckless joyous evenings those were. What solemn things were said, pipe in hand; how much serious emotion was mingled with alternate bursts of laughter, how everyone hit his neighbour, intellectually, right and left, and was hit again, and no mark left on either side; how much sentiment was mingled with how much humour!'

Henry Sidgwick, a friend of Maynard Keynes's parents, who was elected in 1856–7, gives a picture of Apostolic ethics three decades later.

'Absolute candour was the only duty that the tradition of the society enforced. No consistency was demanded with opinions previously held – truth as we saw it then and there was what we had to embrace and maintain, and there were no propositions so well established that an Apostle had not the right to deny or question . . . it was rather a point of the apostolic mind to understand how much suggestion and instruction may be derived from what is in form a jest.'

'It's all or nothing with us,' Lytton wrote to Maynard Keynes (4 November 1905), 'Oxford's the glorification of the half-and-half.' This denunciation of Oxford had a serious meaning. Under Gerald Balfour,[2] brother of the Prime Minister and himself a senior politician, Alfred Lyttelton,[3] a Conservative cabinet minister, and Henry Cust, a distinguished art-historian, the Apostles had for a time evolved into a more urbane group, and it was only in about 1890 that it reacted against this 'top hat epoch' and reintroduced more austere doctrines. By the time Lytton and Sheppard joined, the principles and aims were well understood. They sought to establish a rival influence to the worldly climate of Benjamin Jowett's Balliol.[4] They placed self-fulfilment before self-advancement, preferred philosophy to politics, valued thought above action.

Lytton was sympathetic to this Apostolic ideology. He believed that a lust for fame contaminated the search for truth, and a love of power distorted human affections. Yet he was not altogether unambitious. He therefore welcomed a set of values that discountenanced the worldly success he was unsure of attaining. Self-effacement had an authentic appeal to him; but obscurity was a constant irritant. He was never truly Apostolic as men like Ralph Hawtrey,[5] G.E. Moore and C.P. Sanger were, but, in Apostolic jargon, slightly 'tinged with the phenomenal'. He revered the Society, and considered the values it upheld to be the real ones. But fame was later to make him a happier man.

78

A few days after their election Lytton and Sheppard attended their first formal meeting and inscribed their names in the official ledger. 'I am number 239,' Lytton informed his mother (10 February 1902).

'We have previously inspected the ark in which the papers and books of the Society are kept. It is a charming cedar-wood chest – presented by Oscar Browning.[6] A paper of Arthur's[7] is preserved in it – also a speech by Uncle Raleigh. The minute books are very amusing. The procedure is as follows. A subject is chosen on which the next paper is to be read; but as a matter of fact the paper need have nothing to do with the subject chosen ... Everyone speaks (though in a purely conversational way) in turn after the paper is read. There were a good many distinguished persons present – among them Goldie Dickinson – and I, being the last elected, had to speak last. They seemed fairly amused.[8] We then voted on this (which, though you wouldn't expect it, seemed to be the main point at issue) – Shall we be anti-vivisectionists? Most I think (including me) said no. Sometimes people add notes to their negatives or affirmatives – and this is what makes the minute books amusing ... everything's so mysterious, one doesn't always know exactly the thing that's wanted. What at present alarms me is the thought that I, as junior member, will have, at the annual dinner in June, to fulfil the function of Vice-President, and return thanks for the health of the Society proposed by the President, who will probably be either Sir Richard Jebb or the Earl of Carlisle!'

A bolder spirit of revolt soon began to surface in the papers Lytton read to the Apostles. Perhaps the most outspoken of them was 'Christ or Caliban?' (25 October 1902), a Swinburnian essay in which Caliban symbolized freedom from restraint, and Christ the repression of the nineteenth century. In essence it is a tract against a Victorian society which had turned its back on his own deepest problems and classed him an outcast.

Yet even before his fellow Apostles, Lytton could not really speak his mind. His meaning can be interpreted between the lines of his speeches and his idealization of the 'savage races' in 'Christ or Caliban' is offset by a vein of self-conscious humour. At the same time the crusading spirit which flows through the speech is as real as Rousseau's call to mankind to throw off its chains and revert to primitive life. As real and as romanticized. Lytton did not have a truly speculative mind; he was not deeply interested in religious, philosophical or even historical theory. Yet there is a force of feeling which thrusts its way through these lines – a belief in the freedom of the individual, his dignity, her rights.

'I, at any rate, would be willing with all the alacrity in the world to put myself back into one or other of those more violent ages where railways and figleaves were equally unknown.

– "But if you were a slave?" I would be willing to risk that, for I should perhaps creep in to see the first performance of the Birds, or I might be doorkeeper at the Globe, or with some luck I might get to a Gladiatorial show. – How terrible! But supposing you were a gladiator yourself. You wouldn't enjoy that! – Perhaps not; but at any rate I should die a violent death . . . at least I should have no braces . . .

'We still have our field sports, we still hunt; and if I had ever been allowed to choose my life anywhere in my own age I should have been a stout athletic boxer . . .

'But if external help is lacking, is there no chance of some swift internal disintegration? Is there no possibility of a break-up so general and so complete that the entire reorganization of society would be a necessary sequence? Personally, I welcome every endeavour, conscious or unconscious, to bring about such an end. I welcome thieves, I welcome murderers, above all I welcome anarchists. I prefer anarchy to the Chinese Empire. For out of anarchy good may come, out of the Chinese Empire nothing.'

This iconoclasm appears in much of his Apostolic oratory. 'Shall we be Missionaries?' (undated) is an attack on imperialism: 'I believe, indeed, that some Englishmen do sincerely hold that if England conquered the whole world the greatest possible amount of good would be produced.' Another paper, 'Is Death Desirable?' (January 1903) reaffirms his agnosticism: 'It is no longer, for me at any rate, either interesting or profitable to pretend to believe in the immortality of the soul.' In 'Ought the Father to grow a Beard?' (10 May 1902) he looks at the effect of changes in fashion on the history of art. A year after Queen Victoria's death, he invites his Apostolic audience to:

'Suppose tomorrow morning nursery-maids in Kensington Gardens, clerks on buses, ladies and gentlemen driving in their carriages and cabs to the shops and to the City, were to notice that an extraordinary change had, during the night, come over the central figure of the Albert Memorial. Suppose their astonished eyes were to perceive that the imposing golden form was no longer in the sitting posture, had risen to its feet. But that is not all. Imagine they saw too that it had discarded that princely robe, those knee-breeches, those stockings which we have all admired so, that it stood there in the garb of nature, in the garb in which Augustus and Hadrian and Marcus Aurelius thought fit to appear before the millions of their subjects, thought fit to be remembered when they had long since ceased to walk the earth, had long since passed to the abode of the immortal gods. Imagine this, and imagine the accumulated force of horror and disgust and fury in the breasts of the passers-by. Imagine the indignant rush up those sacred steps, the blind fingers tearing, overturning, destroying . . . but to contemplate our late beloved Prince in such a situation is too painful; I draw a shuddering veil.'

In an early paper for the Apostles, Lytton imagines a 'new heaven, new earth' where there is no more censorship even on subjects such as defecation (about which he was to write a poem).

'For me at least that mysterious and intimate operation has always exercised an extraordinary charm. I seem to see in it one of the few last relics of our animalic ancestry – a strange reminiscence of the earth from which we have sprung. The thought of every member of the human race – the human race which has produced Shakespeare, and weighed the stars – retiring every day to give silent and incontestable proof of his matinal mould is to me fraught with an unutterable significance. There, in truth, is the one touch of Nature which makes the whole world kin! There is enough to give the Idealist perpetual pause! There – in that mystic unburdening of our bodies – that unanswerable reminder of mortality!'

By using defecation – or 'forthing' as it was called – Lytton broke one of the last Apostolic taboos, marking out their territory as his own as he imagines a time when Apostolic morals rule the world. 'Do not imagine that I am less aware than you of what quicksands I am setting foot upon . . . I am quite aware of it; but I am bold, and I proceed.'

Not all his Apostolic papers proceeded so boldly. In 'Does Absence Make the Heart Grow Fonder?' (19 November 1904), he wrote: 'I cannot help confessing that if I had the chance of marrying in quite the ordinary way the person whom I wanted to, I wouldn't hesitate for a moment.' But the chances of this actually happening were remote. For as he admitted a year later – 'Shall we take the Pledge?' (December 1905) – 'My acquaintance among women is small: I know very few with anything approaching intimacy; and I must confess that I have never been in love with one.'

The greatest delight of belonging to the Society was that after years of silent constraint, one might say something of what one felt and thought. This was a marvellous release from the suppressions of polite society, a sudden expanding joy. 'It was a principle in discussion that there were to be no *taboos*, no limitations, no barriers to absolute speculation,' recalled Bertrand Russell in his autobiography. 'We discussed all manner of things, no doubt with a certain immaturity, but with a detachment and interest scarcely possible in later life.' 'We were at an age', remembered Maynard Keynes in 'My Early Beliefs', a paper delivered in 1938 to the Memoir Club, 'when our beliefs influenced our behaviour, a characteristic of the young which it is easy for the middle-aged to forget.'

Over the years Lytton delivered almost twenty papers to the Apostles on sex and aesthetics, individualism and emancipation. Drawing on an Apostolic tradition then influenced by the philosopher G.E. Moore, he learnt to spread a layer of wit over his deepest convictions and develop an informal way of combining irony with allusiveness. These were the sophisticated and oblique tactics he was later to recommend in his preface to *Eminent Victorians*. 'It is not by the direct method of a scrupulous narration that the explorer of the past can hope to depict that singular epoch. If he is wise, he will adopt a subtler strategy. He will attack his subject in unexpected places; he will fall upon the flank, or the rear; he will shoot a sudden, revealing searchlight into obscure recesses, hitherto undivined.'

The Apostolic system resembled a religious system; clearly was, in fact, a parody of religion. Here were the distinctive characteristics of all religions: the codes, dogma, ritual procedures which made up the fundamental sanctity of the Society. Beyond this philosophical free-masonry lay the 'phenomenal' world of unreality. Not to be Apostolic was not to exist. The formalities of meetings and of elections, beginning with a solemn curse, were designed to caricature the mystique of a religious service. There was no pulpit, but the hearthrug fulfilled a similar function and was spoken of in the same respectful fashion. There were, too, secret words and secret meanings of words – 'whales', for instance, which referred to the sardines now consumed in lieu of the original anchovies, and which were held to have been the object of a fantastic law of transubstantiation. And there was a mystical hierarchy from 'embryos' – those who were in the running for election – up the scale to those who 'took wings' and became 'angels'.

A religious secrecy also, full of paradox, fed the legend. Theoretically, they wanted everyone to be Apostolic; yet very few there were who were chosen, behind those locked doors, to join the Cambridge Conversazione Society.

2

FATHER FIGURES

Like radicals seeking a replacement for communism in the late twentieth century, the nineteenth-century Apostles had sought some guide to conduct after the collapse of Christianity. By the turn of the century the debates had become a battle-ground for the younger Cambridge philosophers, J.E. McTaggart, A.N. Whitehead,[9] Bertrand Russell and G.E. Moore. There was still a small political element within the group, but it was very far from being in the ascendant. Christian socialism had been left behind. Moral philosophy so overshadowed other preoccupations that fierce radicals like George Trevelyan and Nathaniel Wedd[10] would sometimes doze off to sleep during the involved proceedings; while Leonard Woolf's anxiety to make arrangements for G.E. Moore to be appointed president of the Board of Education found little support among his brethren and none at all from Moore himself. For Lytton, politics seemed little more at this stage of his life than, in Keynes's words, 'a fairly adequate substitute for bridge'.

'It was owing to the existence of the Society', wrote Bertrand Russell, 'that I got to know the people best worth knowing.' Lytton too spent as much of his time as possible in the company of these 'new and important friends' as he described them in a letter to Lumsden Barkway. In the Easter vacation of 1902 he was invited to a reading-party at Ventnor on the Isle of Wight, with a select band of brothers, including Charles Sanger, Desmond MacCarthy – who turned up late – G.E. Moore and his future brother-in-law, A.R. Ainsworth.[11]

Lytton looked forward to the Isle of Wight, so pleasantly small, with amiable quantities of sea all round and nice white chalk downs. The party stayed at the Blackgang Chine Hotel, where rooms were to be had at two guineas a week, and followed a daily programme of work and entertainment. The mornings were consecrated to serious writing and reading – Moore slowly penned philosophy; Ainsworth read Plato and *Anna Karénine* in French, and Lytton sat with *Père Goriot, Madame Bovary*, Montaigne's essays, Swinburne's poems and Webster's plays. The afternoons were given over to walking expeditions to Carisbrooke and Freshwater, and the evenings to games of jacoby and picquet. This is always the most peaceful part of the day – Moore at the piano singing Brahms in his Germanic tenor; the tall bespectacled Bob Trevelyan standing by him swaying vaguely with the melody; MacCarthy in front of the fire deep in a rocking chair, his feet on the mantelpiece; Ainsworth still poring over his *Anna Karénine*; Lytton perfectly motionless.

'Can you imagine the scene?' he writes to Leonard Woolf. 'We have a sitting-room to ourselves – a table in the middle, very comfortable red plush chairs, pictures of whores on the walls, a piano (at/on which Moore plays and sings) a marble mantelpiece, and 43 red and yellow glass ornaments ... We are all very nice and happy I presume – though sometimes your humble servant sinks into demi-depression.'

Frequent attacks of indigestion are soon interrupting his mornings and eventually reduce him to a diet of bread and milk. In the afternoons he is regularly chilled to the bone as, together with the rest of the party, he makes his way joylessly round blustery twisting hillocks into sunken Victorian villages. He nearly quarrels with the harmless Ainsworth, then loses his temper on being told by him that George Trevelyan shares Bernard Shaw's low opinion of Webster. 'My view of the world', he tells Leonard Woolf, 'becomes black when I think of it.'

The world grows brighter when Goldie Dickinson and Roger Fry turn up. 'The latter – as of course you know – is a sort of art-critic,' he reminds Lumsden Barkway. 'He began as a scientist but threw up that for painting. His quaker relations were a good deal agitated and fussed, and his father offered to increase his allowance by £100 if he'd promise not to study from the nude. But the charming offer was refused.'

Among non-Apostles Lytton still felt ill-at-ease. In July 1902 he went with some of his family to Oxfordshire to stay with Ianthe, Ina and Angelica Homere, 'my Greek Lady friends' as he called them. The Homeres had once lived next door to the Stracheys in No. 70 Lancaster Gate, but now subsisted on the wrecks of a fortune lost by their father on the stock market. After the old man's death, his three daughters – the severely practical and embittered Ianthe, the nondescript Ina, and Angelica, a nymphomaniac of great beauty apparently infatuated with Lytton – had moved to a modest house between Kingham and Chipping Norton into which they took paying guests. The peaceful life at Kingham rapidly provoked in Lytton an intense boredom as he sat among 'the evening gnats under a tree on a lawn ... The sound of a brass band is only wafted to me occasionally'. 'For me I dribble on among ladies whom I *cannot* fall in love with,' he complained to Leonard Woolf (July 1902). 'One of them is beautiful, young, charming – oughtn't I to be in love with her? We go for walks together, read each other sonnets, sit out together at nights, among moons, stars, and the whole romantic paraphernalia – oughtn't I to be in love? We talk about it. Oughtn't I? It's *my* disease, I'm afraid, not to be.'

At the end of the month, he went to stay with Walter and Lucie Raleigh at Stanford-in-the-Vale in Berkshire. The general air of clergymen and bicycles reminded him unpleasantly of Liverpool. Uncle Raleigh, of course, was very brilliant; his talk bubbled away like champagne. Yet something was wrong. Raleigh was an Apostle, but with an important difference; he was a *Victorian* Apostle, and curiously out of date. That generation were altruists and enthusiasts. Their high-minded integrity seemed somehow theoretical, their idealism insensitive. They were always eager to offer up real suffering individuals for the sake of some noble abstraction. Yet Raleigh was one of the best of them. '*He* is very eminent, but frantically taken up with a book on Wordsworth,' he told Leonard Woolf (August 1902), 'and at other times paralysing conversationally.' To Lytton's dismay the farmhouse also contained four children. Like most shy persons he liked to avoid '*le petit peuple*', though he noticed that one of them was 'most inviting'.

A week later, he was a critical spectator along the route of Edward VII's much-postponed coronation. Parades of this sort appealed to his romantic imagination as a kind of civic ballet in the streets. All the same, he was not in the festive vein. 'Their Majesties of England had the honour to be cheered by me on Saturday,' he informed Leonard Woolf (11 August 1902). 'A purely mechanical stimulus. Kitchener looked almost absurdly proud. Roberts of course absolute. To have been in the Abbey would have repaid. My mother reports sumptuosities of dresses and trains unspeakable – also other things.'[12]

At Cambridge Lytton was elected secretary to the Apostles that autumn. 'The position is eminent and interesting,' he wrote off to his mother (15 November 1902), 'as the S. has to keep a good many of the Society's papers, and generally arrange matters. I have got a book begun by Harry Wilson of biographies of brothers, which I hope to go on with. Much is mysterious and difficult to find out about the beginning part (1820, etc.). There is also a photograph book which we want to make as complete as possible.'

One advantage of belonging to the Society was that as an undergraduate Lytton got to know better some of the senior members such as Goldsworthy Lowes Dickinson and G.E. Moore.

Like Lytton at Abbotsholme and early Leamington, Lowes Dickinson had hated his schooldays at Charterhouse. At Cambridge, where he could choose his companions with more freedom, he was in a position to observe the barbarities of life from a decent distance. He should have been in his natural element, for, as one of his critics put it, 'his hatred of school had not sprung from any aversion to the young of his own sex'. In the papers he read to the Apostles, leading on to his blueprint for the League of Nations, Lowes Dickinson aired his dreams of a better-behaved society. But Lytton, who was reinterpreting the history of the Apostles and bringing out their latent homosexuality for use as a weapon against Victorian morality, sometimes felt impatient with Lowes Dickinson's sentimentality. He preferred G.E. Moore. 'What a brain the fellow has!' Dickinson wrote of Moore in a letter to R.C. Trevelyan. 'It desiccates mine! Dries up my lakes and seas and leaves me an arid tract of sand. Not that *he* is arid – anything but; he's merely the sun. One ought to put up a parasol – I do try to, one of humour, but it has so many rents in it.'

Moore was seven years older than Lytton. Though they saw a lot of each other, Lytton never seems to have developed a close friendship with him. In a letter to Leonard Woolf (April 1905), he describes Moore as 'quite inaccessible on his cold, restrictive searchlight heights'. For some time he cherished the hope that Moore might marry his sister Pippa and this excited him since Moore fulfilled his ideal of genius. Many years later he told a friend that of all the eminent people he had met in his life, only Moore impressed him as being, without question, really great.

'About the greatest men', one of Lytton's aphorisms reads, 'there is always something incredible.' The unworldliness of Moore's thought appeared to illuminate his face with an incredible beauty. He was still young enough to share many of Lytton's own enthusiasms, yet went his way unconscious of the risk of ridicule. He appeared to be a philosopher by divine vocation. In conversation he was neither witty nor quick. Every sentence was considered. An incorrectly employed word, Leonard Woolf recalls, would draw from him a gasp as at some obscenity; he would gaze at the speaker as if one or other of them must surely be mad. And later he would confess: 'I *simply* don't understand *what* he means!' But 'when Strachey made one of his subtle, perhaps cynical, perhaps shocking utterances, the flavour of which even his clever undergraduate friends did not at first appreciate at its full value, Moore was to be seen shaking with laughter', Keynes's biographer Roy Harrod records. The young had 'no inhibitions in his presence [and] ... the veneration which his young admirers accorded him almost matched that due to a saint'.

Whether it was the discussion of ethics, or the singing of a Beethoven song, or an energetic game of fives, or simply a tide of uncontrollable laughter, Moore would be caught up in it with total concentration, the sweat pouring from his face, enthralled as a boy, oblivious of everything. When he was with Lytton, Desmond MacCarthy and Bertrand Russell, his pipe, alternately gripped in his hand and clenched between his teeth, would remain unlit all evening, though he might have exhausted a full box of matches burning his fingers. Lytton and the other Apostles were entranced by his sudden passions and aura of 'divine absurdity'.

In 1902, while his apostles watched and waited, Moore was hard at work on the book which, the following year, was to match their expectations. Meanwhile: 'I hope for the New Age – that is all – which will cure all our woes,' wrote Lytton, 'and give us new ones, and make us happy enough for death.'

3

A ROSE-WATER REVOLUTION

Early in the year 1903, Lytton's attention was diverted from the affairs of the Society by a family drama which shook the régime of Lancaster Gate to its foundations.

When his sister Pernel was studying at the Sorbonne in 1898, she had met a destitute painter called Simon Bussy who, she told Lytton (4 November 1899), 'is very small, rather like a frog to the outward view but . . . he is evidently rather a genius'. In the autumn of 1901, 'Little Bussy', as Lady Strachey called him, came over to London and, despite speaking almost no English, made friends with William Rothenstein and settled into a studio in the West Cromwell Road. Soon he became a regular visitor at the Stracheys' home and did pastel portraits of Sir Richard and one or two of his daughters. Then came the bombshell as he suddenly announced his engagement to Dorothy Strachey who, aged thirty-seven, was five years older than Bussy.

No one denied that he could paint very nicely – he had studied at Gustave Moreau's atelier with Marquet, Rouault and Matisse (of whom he was a close friend all his life). Nevertheless he was the son of a shoemaker from the Jura town of Dôle, and Lady Strachey's liberalism faltered at the sight of him *actually cleaning up his plate with pieces of bread*. But all the silent disapprobation of older Stracheys was to no avail. With what Lytton later called 'extraordinary courage' Dorothy remained determined to marry her penurious artist. Disapproving, resigned, yet not without some humour, Lady Strachey broke the catastrophic news to Lytton in a letter dated 8 February 1903:

'You will doubtless be more astonished than pleased to hear that Dorothy is engaged to marry S. Bussy. She is very much bent on it, and of course must do as she chooses, and we must all do our best to help her with it.

The terrible feature of the case is the smallness of means, but this will doubtless improve as years go on. If you ever have occasion to mention him do say he is an artist of genius, one of the rising young painters of the modern school in France – which is strictly true . . .

P.S. Oh la! la!

P.P.S. I now understand the expression in her portrait.'

By the very same post Lytton received a letter from Dorothy herself announcing the same news in rather different fashion:

'Dearest Lyt,

Please give me your fraternal blessing. I am going to marry Simon Bussy. Most people I am afraid will think it exceedingly wild, but in reality it is an action of the highest wisdom. (vide Maeterlinck.)

We shall have 2d. a year but we shall be very gay and sensible – and live if possible in a minute house near Roquebrune.'

At first Lytton found it hard to get on with his future brother-in-law. There was of course the language barrier: Bussy still refused to speak much English and Lytton was too shy to utter a syllable of French. What, he wondered, did his astonishing sister see in this Frenchman? He was very *spirituel*, had a great deal of *esprit*, and – *bouffe*! – nothing more that anyone else could detect. Still, on principle, he supported Dorothy rather than his mother. Her act was a significant break-through of supreme importance in the Strachey anthropology. Under a feeble plea of difference of nationality, a full-scale wedding ceremony was dispensed with later that year, and the family gathered instead at a stiff and uneasy party in the mammoth drawing-room.[13]

Despite this cut across those fetters of convention, life was to carry on for a while much as before. 'The boredom of respectable, or un-respectable, persons (especially ladies) is so intense that my soul sinks far below my stomach, below my bottom, below my boots,' Lytton complained to Sheppard (22 March 1903). 'The people who enter this house are mainly respectable, and nearly all females, which if you come to think of it is *écrasant*.' Instead of returning home for the Easter vacation, he veers off with another of Moore's reading-parties to Penmenner House, at the Lizard in Cornwall. Among the other Apostles there are Leonard Woolf, C.P. Sanger and Desmond MacCarthy – who turns up late. 'Others ex-pected later,' Lytton informs his mother (3 April 1903), 'including Bob Trevelyan, whose play[14] has just come out. I have read it – it is, I'm afraid, sad stuff. Moore has also brought the last volume of Charles

Booth's new book – on religion in London.[15] It looks very interesting and full of details – which are charming things.'

'Nose to nose with the sea', among geraniums and tiger-lilies, Lytton languishes in contentment. The sun shines, the blue sea stretches away in almost every possible direction, Moore sings and laughs, some 'Oxford gents' leave the house and all is very pleasant – no illnesses, no arguments and no necessity to shave. On bright days they stroll along the coast, eating sandwiches among the rocks, while a few of the more intrepid readers paddle and the others have bad fits of the giggles. One afternoon they walk to Mullion, a village about seven miles away, to watch Desmond MacCarthy and Bob Trevelyan play in a football match for the Lizard.

His summer vacation that year was phenomenally un-Apostolic. Every day he walked to the British Museum and worked at the Hastings papers. 'I'd always rather be doing something else,' he told Leonard Woolf. But as he wrote to Saxon Sydney-Turner, 'My life depends on what I find there.'

4

THE GOOD LIFE

By far the most significant event of the year 1903 for all Apostles was the publication of G.E. Moore's *Principia Ethica*. 'I expected when I read it,' Lytton told John Sheppard (11 October 1903), 'to see posters in the street announcing the Death of Herbert Spencer and the Fall of Kant. But there was only something about the Duke of Devonshire.' Moore's views on moral questions had, of course, been known for some time, but the Socratic passion of his book was a revelation. Discussion of its ethical concepts dominated, for a time, everything else. The effect on Lytton was instantaneous. He saw Moore as another Plato, and *Principia Ethica* as a new and better *Symposium*. On 11 October he wrote Moore a rhapsodic letter.

'Dear Moore,

I have read your book, and want to say how much I am excited and impressed. I'm afraid I must be mainly classed among 'writers of Dictionaries, and other persons interested in literature', so I feel a sort of essential vanity hovering about my 'judgements of fact'. But on this occasion I am carried away. I think your book has not only wrecked and shattered all writers on Ethics from Aristotle and Christ to Herbert Spencer and Mr Bradley, it has not only laid the true foundation of Ethics, it has not only left all modern philosophy bafouée – these seem to me small achievements compared to the establishment of that Method which shines like a sword between the lines. It is the scientific method deliberately applied, for the first time, to Reasoning. Is that true? You perhaps shake your head, but henceforward who will be able to tell lies one thousand times as easily as before? The truth, there can be no doubt, is really now upon the march. I date from Oct. 1903 the beginning of the Age of Reason.

The last two chapters interested me most, as they were newer to me than the rest. Your grand conclusion made me gasp – it was so violently definite. Lord! I can't yet altogether agree. I think with some horror of a Universe deprived for ever of real slaughters and tortures and lusts. Isn't it possible that the real Ideal may be an organic unity so large and of such nature that it is, precisely, the Universe itself? In which case Dr Pangloss was right after all.

. . . It was very pleasant to be able to feel that one came into the Dedication.[16] But expression is so difficult, so very difficult, and there are so many cold material obstructions, that the best of Life seems to be an act of faith.

This is a confession of faith, from

your brother
Lytton Strachey'

It is obvious that this letter is very far from being flattery. All Lytton's correspondence strikes the same eulogistic note. 'The last two chapters – glory alleluiah!' he exclaimed to Leonard Woolf (October 1903). 'And the wreckage! That indiscriminate heap of shattered rubbish among which one spies the utterly mangled remains of Aristotle, Jesus, Mr Bradley, Kant, Herbert Spencer, Sidgwick and McTaggart! Plato seems the only person who comes out even tolerably well. Poor Mill has, simply, gone.'

Moore's *Principia Ethica* is known to philosophers for its initial chapters; but to Lytton and the younger Apostles it was for the uplift of the conclusion that it came to be specially revered. Compared with the unworldliness of its last pages, Keynes observed, the New Testament was a handbook for party politicians. The final two chapters – which Lytton singled out in his letters to Leonard Woolf and to Moore himself – 'Ethics in Relation to Conduct' and 'The Ideal' – are different in tone from the rest of the book. The rigmarole of meticulous argument, of cross-examination, assertion and counter-assertion, becomes less concentrated, while, particularly in the last chapter of all, the judgements grow more frankly personal. In a key passage Moore writes: 'By far the most valuable things, which we know or can imagine, are certain states of consciousness which may be roughly described as the pleasures of human intercourse and the enjoyment of beautiful objects. No one probably, who has asked himself the question, has ever doubted that personal affection and the appreciation of what is beautiful in Art or Nature, are good in themselves.'

Moore's first impact on the young Apostles, his biographer Paul Levy tells us, was not doctrinal but personal. To Bertrand Russell he appeared 'beautiful and slim, with a look almost of inspiration [and] ... a kind of exquisite beauty.' Leonard Woolf remembered his face as being 'amazingly beautiful, almost ethereal' and felt him to be 'the only great man whom I have ever met or known in the world'. Keynes experienced a similar exhilaration. 'It is *impossible* to exaggerate the wonder and *originality* of Moore,' he wrote to Lytton (21 February 1906). For them all he was a lovable, slightly intimidating, always illuminating presence.

'Moore's influence on the Society gave, I think, increased depth and meaning to our relationship,' wrote Leonard Woolf. By the time Woolf left for Ceylon and Keynes had read *Principia Ethica* a second time (having described it as a 'stupendous' work, '*the greatest* on the subject'), Moore's influence had developed into a cult. For Keynes it was 'the beginning of a new renaissance, the opening of a new heaven on earth'. Like Russell, MacCarthy and the others he felt liberated as from a mental prison. The old heaven and the old hell suddenly passed away in what Lytton called 'the wreckage', and the Apostles were left with the rudiments of a true theory of ethics to use as a compass through the century of relativism that lay ahead. Moore gave them a method for trusting to intuitions rather than rules, and a language for evaluating human relationships.

The leaders of this cult of personal relationships were Lytton and his friend Maynard Keynes. For the time being Lytton was the senior partner. He treated *Principia Ethica* as an extension of Moore's beguiling personality. His 'Method', shining like a sword between the lines, was an apparatus of question-and-answer that united the rational and romantic elements in Lytton's nature and was to find its way into his rhetorical prose style. He saw *Principia Ethica* as providing a scientific framework[17] for his emotional impulses and giving a moral basis for the love that, since Oscar Wilde's imprisonment, dared not speak its name. On several occasions he was on the point of asking Moore whether he had experienced any homosexual feelings, but could never pluck up the courage. 'Dear Moore,' he had written, 'I hope and pray that you realise how much you mean to us.'

Moore became a moral centre of the Society within a hostile society, a focus for an alternative sexual code. 'We repudiated entirely customary morals, conventions and traditional wisdom,' Keynes later wrote. 'We were, that is to say, in the strict sense of the term, immoralists.' By 1911 Beatrice Webb was describing the Apostles as 'a pernicious set . . . which makes a sort of ideal of anarchic ways in sexual questions', and *Principia Ethica* as 'a metaphysical justification for doing what you like'.

It was this sexual revolt that made a repressed homosexual like D.H. Lawrence antagonistic, and that later drew from F.R. Leavis the charge of perpetual immaturity. In the opinion of Bertrand Russell, Keynes (unlike Lytton) eventually escaped from this coterie into the great world. But as his biographer, Robert Skidelsky shows, 'Keynes always remained a Moorite.' After the First World War, he was much tinged with phenomenal matters and somewhat defensive. But in these early years, when expectations were high, he and Lytton were on the offensive – and offended many of the older brethren. Moore was their prophet and they were his crusaders. 'Our great stumbling-block in the business of introducing the world to Moorism is our horror of half-measures,' Lytton wrote to Keynes (8 April 1906).

'We can't be content with telling the truth – we must tell the whole truth; and the whole truth is the Devil. Voltaire abolished Christianity by believing in god. It's madness of us to dream of making dowagers understand that feelings are good, when we say in the same breath that the best ones are sodomitical. If we were crafty and careful, I dare say we'd pull it off. But why should we take the trouble? On the whole I believe that our time will come about a hundred years hence, when preparations will have been made, and compromises come to, so that, at the publication of our letters, everyone will be, finally, converted.'

5

HASTINGS'S CREATURE

During his first years at Cambridge most of Lytton's close friends belonged to his own college, Trinity. In his last three years he made so many excursions into King's College that when one of the university papers later published a reproduction of Henry Lamb's early portrait above the caption 'Lytton Strachey (*King's*)' hardly anyone noticed the error. All the members of the original Midnight Society had gone down long before Lytton himself left – Thoby Stephen to set up house in Gordon Square with his brother and two sisters after the death of their father; Clive Bell to shoot at animals in British Columbia, and then to work at a dissertation in Paris on British policy during the Congress of Verona; Saxon Sydney-Turner to a shadowy, civil servant's attic in Somerset House; and, last of all, Leonard Woolf to Ceylon, becoming as Lytton phrased it to Moore 'absolute Lord there of a million blacks'. His own college now depressed him. 'Trinity is like a dead body in a high state of putrefaction,' he wrote in his last year there. 'The only interest of it is in the worms that come out of it.' So he turned for companionship to King's.

One of the most intimate of his new friends was John Sheppard, whom he liked to call Frank – 'my first, last, and only Frank!' Sheppard's theatricality delighted Lytton. He could never be relied on to present himself as only twenty-four hours older than on the previous day. 'He is generally, I think, about his fifteenth birthday,' wrote an interviewer from *The Granta*, 'but sometimes he has just passed his hundred and fifteenth.' By leaning on a stick and affecting a slight limp he could, with his white hair and diminutive frame, momentarily appear senile: but his cherubic face and high-pitched preposterous laughter always ruined the performance.

They first got to know each other at the Decemviri, an undergraduate society that used to meet in one another's rooms for coffee and debate. One evening the subject for debate was 'that this house would rather be Drake than Shakespeare'. The motion was proposed by Donald Robertson, a great Alpine climber of splendid physique and a scholar of Trinity, who gave a spirited account of the life of action and adventure. After he had sat down, a pair of heavy curtains, concealing a window-seat, were drawn open, and Lytton's falsetto voice cried out: 'Utterly ridiculous!' The tall frail figure spoke of the supreme value of Shakespeare. It was a performance Sheppard never forgot.

For almost two years Sheppard remained the chief figure in Lytton's emotional life. They used to go off to the rooms of a middle-aged widow, near Emmanuel College, to be instructed in the mysteries of dancing, each of them solemnly circling the room in the arms of this unsmiling lady whose equally stern sister sat in the corner strumming slow melodies on the piano. These classes were not a success. On attending their first ball at Lancaster Gate,[18] both pupils were hopelessly outclassed by their partners and obliged to retire from the floor.

Sheppard was a fine classical scholar, but appeared to prefer the athletic activities for which he had no aptitude. Like Lytton he worshipped Thoby Stephen, and loved to chide him with being a 'muscular Christian', for which taunt he would be exquisitely chased round the Great Court at Trinity, or the fountain at King's. But Lytton did not approve, and rigorously set out to make Sheppard a person fit for his love. 'If I hadn't liked Lytton,' Sheppard explained, 'I couldn't have endured it.' Lytton attacked Sheppard for keeping company with his intellectual inferiors, jealously objecting to his friend going off on walks with non-Apostolic companions. But Sheppard was an incorrigible sentimentalist. He couldn't seem to help it; he actually *liked* everyone.

Lytton's tactics tended to produce more panic than affection. 'What frightens *me*', he wrote to Sheppard (22 March 1903), 'is the idea that you're sometimes frightened of *me*. I'm almost sure you are. That desolates me – you believe it? – and makes me want to kick down the walls of the Universe. My dear soaring Pig, put me at as high a figure as you like, you know quite well that for *you* I'm not in the market at all – I'm simply a gift.'

Lytton experimented with all sorts of fantastical approaches. 'Shall we all of us go to sleep for centuries, and wake up like young giants? Or never at all?' he inquired. Sometimes he was anatomically confiding. 'Most of the time I suffer a dull pain in the bowels. When I die and my stomach is opened, my intestines will be found knotted into more horrible contortions than have ever been known ... my knotted entrails are entwined in spiritual convolutions. My dear child, do my entrails begin to bore you?' At other moments he essayed purest romance. 'What quality is it that contains at once this simplicity and this majesty, this softness and this strength? ... It is what all of Us – the terribly intelligent, the unhappy, the artistic, the divided, the overwhelmed – most intimately worship, and most passionately, most vainly love.'

Sheppard loved his humour but had qualms about his humanity. 'I am human,' Lytton reassured him (3 April 1903), 'too human, and I can hardly control my thoughts.' He tried to explain the paradox between his yielding heart and critical mind. 'Dear Frank ... it's so much easier to say filthy things than charming ones, which one may feel just as much if not more. It'd take fourteen years to say *everything* one thought about *anyone*. So one just says the things which are amusingest and of course the nastiest as well. All this, when one doesn't have any really very definite feelings either of like or dislike about the person. Because when the feelings are fairly engaged – la!' But Sheppard was not wholly convinced.

In the winter vacation of 1903–4 the two of them went down to the Mermaid Inn at Rye, where they spent a week together, reading, talking, walking to Romney and Winchelsea and keeping an unavailing eye open for the legendary Henry James who lived a few yards away at Lamb House. Surrounded by retired field officers, billiard-playing clergymen, and the occasional antiquarian golfer, there was little chance for Sheppard to stray.

But after Christmas Lytton's infatuation began to fade and the two of them drifted apart. 'I'm fairly bored by him,' Lytton admitted to Leonard Woolf the following summer, 'and as frigid as if he were a lovely young lady.'

Since the University Library did not stock some of the books he needed for his Fellowship dissertation, Lytton spent part of the Lent and almost all the Easter term of 1904 in London working at the British Museum. 'The B. Museum and India Office are imperative,' he told Saxon Sydney-Turner. 'Whether I shall ever get to Cambridge next [Easter] term God knows ... I shall be a mere ghost till the damned dissertation is written.' He did, however, accept an invitation that March to the wedding of George Trevelyan and Janet Ward. The celebrations were staged in Oxford and did not disappoint Lytton's gloomiest expectations. 'Have you heard of the arrangements for the Trevelyan-Ward wedding?' he inquired in a note to his sister Pippa (9 February 1904). 'Bride and bridegroom wanted *office*, Bride's mother (Mrs Humphry Ward) wanted *Church*; compromise arrived at – An Oxford Unitarian Chapel with a service drawn up by Bride, Bgroom, and B's mother – at present chiefly Emerson. The happy pair are to lead the Simple Life, and will go to Oxford in a special train.' Lytton himself travelled over from Lancaster Gate with several members of his family, and the following day wrote up an account of the proceedings in the course of a long letter to Leonard Woolf (20 March 1904):

'My mother said we were a "cultured crowd" and we were. Mostly matrons, in grey silk and hair – Henry James, Sheppard, Hawtrey, Theodore L.D.,[19] etc., filled in the gaps. The lunch was free, and at separate tables, but the whole train was inter-connected so that there was a good deal of moving about. A High char-à-banc, with a horn, drove us from the station; flags were waved of course, and there was some cheering ... Mr Edward Carpenter officiated. He began with an address composed of quotations and platitudes, during which, as Miss Souvestre said, the bride and bridgroom looked at the windows as much as they could ... The bride and bridegroom were almost completely hideous. But I suppose one must let copulation thrive. The service was practically all balls in both senses.'

Ten days later, in another letter to Leonard Woolf, he added a postscript: 'I didn't tell you Henry James's *mot* on the occasion – "The ordinary service binds, and makes an impression – it's like a seal; there was nothing more than a wafer."'

At the start of the Easter vacation, he went down to a reading-party at

Hunter's Inn, not far from Lynton on the north coast of Devon, with Moore, Sanger, Ainsworth and Desmond MacCarthy (who arrived late). 'This place is more like a hotel than an Inn,' he wrote to Pippa (4 April 1904). 'There is a large party of Oxford men with an elderly tutor . . . The country is highly beautiful, the weather tolerable. We go for long walks, and usually quarrel about the way.'

On 8 April he left Hunter's Inn some time during the afternoon on his way to the South of France and, following a brilliant short cut, lost himself on a vast and misty common. At last he came across a group of three men sitting in a field skinning a dead pig and shouted across to them in a reedy treble to ask for the station. 'The tavern?' they queried. By the time he turned up at Woody Bay station his train had long since gone and he sat dozing and dreaming before the fire. 'For the next four hundred years', he wrote from the waiting-room to Moore, 'I shall be voyaging.'

Four days later he turned up at La Souco, the little house in Roquebrune where the Bussys had recently installed themselves. He was enchanted with the place: so small, so pretty, so charmingly proportioned, so pink and yellow coloured that it might have been an illustration in a children's book. 'The house is perfectly divine,' he wrote to his mother (13 April 1904), who had not yet visited Dorothy since her marriage. 'The pink of beauty reigns – marble staircases, Chippendale chairs, Louis XIV cabinets, impressionist pictures, and the best view in Europe . . . My bedroom looks out on to the neighbouring banker's and baron's garden, whose chief object is a gigantic red umbrella under which the bankers and barons sit.'

On the same day he also wrote to Leonard Woolf. 'It is a most extraordinary place. The house is 3 inches square[20] – and a dream of beauty. The floors are tiled with smooth red hexagonal tiles, and partially covered with matting; the walls are white, the furniture replete with every beauty . . . If the whole place was taken up and plunged 400 miles away from everywhere and everything but the flowers and the frogs, I could live in it for ever; as it is there are too many Germans whirling past it through the air – too many terrific English driving tandems from Mentone just below and just above us.'

Conversation with his brother-in-law was still out of the question. Besides, what was there to talk about? From his sister, the rebel of the family, he expected some great things once he had given her a copy of *Principia Ethica*. To his dismay, however, she informed him that the last chapter omitted all the difficulties and was untrue. This, it seemed to Lytton, was most discouraging. Perhaps intelligent women were too bound up these days with the suffrage movement to see anything else. Naturally he too believed, if more tepidly, that women should be given the vote – the poor things wouldn't have much else before long. Yet he felt irritated by the Bussys' heterosexual contentment. Their show of love made him feel an outsider again. 'I must say that I am sometimes a little annoyed at their affectionateness,' he complained to Leonard Woolf (13 April 1904). 'Wouldn't you be? Two people loving each other so much – there's something devilishly selfish about it. Couples in the road with their silly arms round their stupid waists irritate me in the same way. I want to shake them.'

The place seemed crowded with foreign peasants and enormous goats. 'This is a wonderful, fascinating country,' he told Leonard Woolf, 'but as for living in it – ! I don't think I could live anywhere out of England – I should always be moving on.' He soon resigned himself to working on his dissertation. But here too he was confronted by monotony. The task of perpetually renewing his original enthusiasm, of elucidating for the benefit of examiners information already stalely familiar was tiresome. 'I am lost', he confessed, 'over Warren.' But he forced himself to go on with it, and was painted by Simon Bussy, a blue study in pastels, at his labours.

Early in May he returned to England, dividing the next six weeks between Lancaster Gate and the British Museum. By the second week of June he had completed the bulk of his research work, and went off for a few days to Ivy Lodge, near Tilford, three miles from Farnham in Surrey, with Bertrand Russell, his wife Alys and her brother Logan Pearsall Smith, who was then working on his *Life and Letters of Sir Henry Wotton*. 'Everyone talks without stopping on every subject,' he reported to his mother (16 June 1904). 'Ping Pong S reads poetry aloud in a wailing voice, which is rather depressing. I believe he thinks all poetry should be mildly melancholy, and has no more idea of drama than a cow. Russell is writing a chapter on the Improper Infinitive.'

On his return he resumed his work, inching his way forward with the Warren Hastings thesis. 'My dissertation is assuming most unwieldy proportions,' he told Maynard Keynes (14 July 1904). 'You don't know how superb one feels – writing a real book, with real chapters.'

On 15 July, he moved out of London to Morhanger Park, a country house at Sandy in Bedfordshire, within half an hour of Cambridge. He now immersed himself in the final stages of his work. 'I want to see everyone very much,' he appealed to Keynes. All the same he could spare no time to visit Cambridge, not even to hear C.P. Sanger read a paper to the Society on copulation: 'I feel', he told Keynes (21 August 1904), 'that if I left off writing for a single second all would be lost.' Instead, he invited a few of his friends, including Sheppard and Moore, to visit him at his retreat. 'Be prepared for doing nothing but sit in the garden and read novels,' he warned Moore (8 August 1904). 'Won't you like that? I am ploughing on with my dissertation; it's now very boring! But it looks beautiful all typewritten out.' As each sheet was finished it was passed to his sister, Pippa, who typed it out on foolscap. At one point the table at which he was working, bent low by the accumulation of reference books, collapsed with a bang, flighting papers everywhere and giving rise to pandemonium. But the chaos was beaten back and tidied up by a flutter of female relatives, and the slow progress resumed. 'I am in a fairly hellish state which makes me seem rather magnificent to myself,' he wrote to Leonard Woolf (July 1904). 'Horrible illnesses attack me, and I sometimes think all's lost. But really perhaps the only supremacy is the supremacy of effort. I feel occasionally like an unchained tiger . . . But by God! one does have hours of hideous collapse! Also, I find, of a sort of wonderful, sublimated sentimentality . . . I have it often at breakfast when my stomach is all wobbly with being up so early. I don't know – I seem to have a physical feeling in my abdomen of spiritual affection. But perhaps it is merely lust.'

He had left his final effort rather late and now had serious doubts as to whether the thesis would be completed in time. He broke off all correspondence with his friends, making only one exception, on a pale wan scrap of a letter, to ask Maynard Keynes for a copy of Rosebery's biography of Pitt quotations from which, he admitted (21 August 1904), 'should have been part of Chapter V, with quotations from Sir Eyre Coote, and information upon William Markham – hush! – I think he *must* have been Hastings' creature – and the police of Benares.'

With a couple of days to spare, the dissertation was finished, and Lytton went off until the end of the month to join C.P. Sanger in Caernarvonshire, and catch up with his theories on copulation. Sanger's company suited him well, never more so than now in his exhausted and anxious state. Refreshed by this short holiday he returned to Trinity on 1 September to assemble with the other Fellowship candidates. 'I handed in my Dissertation all right, having corrected everything – with one exception remembered afterwards – and added a note on the spelling of proper names,' he told his mother (2 September 1904). 'I find that there are about seven other people going in for fellowships, which is fewer than usual, and that there will be perhaps four fellowships – which is more than usual. There are very few people up, and those who are seem to be declining into perpetual melancholy.'

When he got back a few days later to Morhanger Park Lytton was in a state of well-concealed optimism. Although the opposition likely to be encountered from the scientists was stiff, his chances of obtaining a Fellowship would never be better. But for the moment he felt utterly sick of Anglo-Indian politics. Compulsory reading that autumn for all Apostles were the posthumously selected essays of Henry Sidgwick who, half a century before, had refertilized the spirit of the Society in a fashion similar to Moore's by moving its debate from Christianity to ethics. From these miscellaneous papers Lytton returned to Sidgwick's *Methods of Ethics*. 'He [Sidgwick] seems to make hardly any false propositions, and the whole thing seems to be extraordinarily weighty and interesting,' he told Leonard Woolf (September 1904). 'But Lord! What a hopeless confused jumble of inarticulate matter. It is a vast vegetable mass of inert ponderosity, out of which the Yen[21] had beaten and welded, and fused his peerless flying-machine. Don't you think Sidgwick contains the embryonic Moore?'

In the third week of September Lytton returned to Trinity to compose an essay for the Fellowship Examination in the form of a dialogue between Johnson, Gibbon and Adam Smith on the uses and abuses of universities, and to dine at the Master's Lodge with the other candidates. It was now that the awful news was broken to him that the electors, headed by a don with the sinister name of Moriarty, had referred his dissertation to a clergyman – none other than that high-minded Tory divine and pioneer of economic history, the Rev. William Cunningham, who the previous year had given him a muted testimonial for the Board of Education.

He was sure that all was lost. Ten days later he arrived back at Trinity to be told by Cunningham that he had failed to win the Fellowship. 'Things are less satisfactory than I think might have been hoped,' he wrote to his mother (12 October 1904), whom he had earlier forewarned of his likely failure. 'Cunningham's main objection to my dissertation was that its subject did not allow sufficient scope for original treatment. That is to say, the main point of view from which it is proper to regard H's administration has now been satisfactorily established by James Fitzjames and Uncle John, and hence all that a subsequent worker has to do is to follow along the line which they have indicated. This, Cunningham thought, I had done exceedingly well; but he saw no evidence to show that a man who was not first class might not have done the work which I had done ... The reverend Doctor was very kind, and persisted strongly that my work was well and thoroughly done – but he thought that it had not brought out the qualities which were to be looked for in a fellowship candidate.'

Lytton had worked harder on his dissertation than he liked to tell his friends. He wanted to be elected a Fellow of Trinity almost, as it were, against his will, and certainly without apparent effort. Besides, it was still AGAINST HIS PRINCIPLES to fail in an examination. His immediate disappointment was so bitter that he could hardly bear to stay in Cambridge. 'My misery is complete,' he confided to Leonard Woolf who had done relatively poorly in the Civil Service examination. 'I have never felt more utterly desolate and now can hardly imagine that I shall be able to stick out the term. However, I presume it will at any rate never be worse than this, as there is absolutely not a soul or a cat in the place . . . Shall we ever recover? Is this the end of all? Well, Lord have mercy upon us!'

After reading the typescript of his dissertation, Leonard Woolf wrote back endeavouring to raise his friend's spirits (October 1904): 'W.H., I thought, was enthralling, but I believe I see what those asses mean. It's too enthralling, and not enough like a dissertation. It's a little too graceful for them, and if you made it all seem more laborious and magnified all the points, they would have elected you.'

Lytton at once responded to this encouragement, soaring into reviving fantasy. 'Yes; our supremacy is very great, and you've raised my spirits vastly by saying so,' he replied.

'I sometimes feel as if it were not only we ourselves who are concerned, but that the destinies of the whole world are somehow involved in ours. We are – oh! in more ways than one – like the Athenians of the Periclean Age. We are the mysterious priests of a new and amazing civilization. We are greater than our fathers; we are greater than Shelley; we are greater than the eighteenth century; we are greater than the Renaissance; we are greater than the Romans and the Greeks. What is hidden from us? We have mastered all. We have abolished religion, we have founded ethics, we have established philosophy, we have sown our strange illumination in every province of thought, we have conquered art, we have liberated love. It would be pleasant to spend our days in a perpetual proclamation of our magnificence.'

So Lytton wrote at a time when his misery and disappointment were complete; for the more wretched he felt, the more marvellous had to be his dreams.

A few days later, after Cunningham's verdict, he left for the consoling wilds of Rothiemurchus. There, amid the lochs and mountains, he could forget his troubles. 'I have banished almost everything from my mind,' he wrote to Leonard Woolf (October 1904) after a few hours. Then he thought that something might still be saved from the ruins. Cunningham had told him that there would probably be very few Fellowships next year and that it would be an outside chance if he got one. He had nevertheless urged him to go on with this work. If he could remould his account of the

Begums so as to combine it with the story of Cheyt Sing, Rajah of Benares, whom Hastings had been accused of driving into revolt, he might exonerate Hastings from all four charges brought against him in the House of Lords – including the incidental accusations that he had been guilty of accepting bribes and rewarding favourites with wasteful contracts. It was the logical extension of his original idea. Even if it didn't win him a Fellowship, the thesis ought to be published. Methuen was already interested. Besides, what else could he do? He must try again. 'On the whole,' he wrote to his mother (12 October 1904), 'I believe this is the best thing I can do.' Perhaps, one day, G.L. Strachey's 'Warren Hastings' would be acknowledged a *magnum opus* – a fine revenge on the Trinity electors.

Also, there was always that outside chance.

6

A NEW FRIEND AND RIVAL

When he first went up to Trinity, Lytton had been frail and lonely, self-consciously aware of his many peculiarities. But in his final two years he had grown to be so much of an intellectual force that his influence is said to have left its mark on three generations of undergraduates. As Noël Annan has pointed out, although he showed little sign of publishing anything beyond *belles lettres*, he was recognized as an arbiter. He was unauthorized yet taken as an authority, and his influence was spreading beyond Cambridge. 'My own view is that Lytton's Cambridge years had an important effect on the subsequent mental life in England; especially on the attitude of ordinary people to religion and sex,' James Strachey told the author. 'The young men in my years (though also interested in socialism) were far more open-minded on both those topics than their predecessors – and I believe they handed on what they derived from Lytton, and this (taken in conjunction with Freud, who was totally unknown till much later) is, I think, what has resulted in the reform of the general attitude to sex.'

Evidence of his influence upon other undergraduates comes from their letters in which they aimed at a style of semi-pornographic humour. His reputation for decadence was gaining notoriety. 'You must be careful next term for "the College" is really enraged with us,' Leonard Woolf had written to him in the summer vacation of 1903. 'They think you are a witch and given up to the most abandoned and horrible practices and quite ready to burn us alive at the slightest provocation ... a scholar of the college

[Arthur S. Gaye], it is now a well-known fact, once went to tea with you and came out white to the lips and trembling. "The Conversation", he said, "was too horrible! And the pictures and atmosphere."'

Lytton was delighted. Nor was Leonard Woolf exaggerating the sinister prestige which roused this hostility. An imaginary interviewer from *The Granta* pictured him reclining on a sofa, robed in a négligé costume of silk pyjamas, with his eyes half-closed over the *oeuvre* of a French poet. Several bottles of absinthe and similar concoctions stand near by, and from these, with trembling hands, he replenishes his glass. The room is wreathed in smoke from heavy black tobacco cigarettes. 'As I came in,' the interviewer wrote, 'he directed towards me the listless gaze of his cold, glassy eyes, but made no attempt to simulate the least interest in my presence.' The fictitious colloquy proceeds quietly, with Lytton still lying on the sofa, his hands bright yellow and his cheeks hollow and chalky, until suddenly everything accelerates to a climax. Rising to his feet, Lytton dances about the room 'after the manner of a lunatic who imagines himself to be an inebriated Bacchante in a frenzy of Greek orgy, but cannot find any liquor of sufficient strength to give the necessary realism to his performance.' He then falls back, mumbling that he has found what he has been searching for all his life, an original sin – 'a corkscrew to open the bottle of an hitherto untasted draught of life'.

This caricature brings to mind Oscar Wilde's rooms some thirty years earlier at Oxford. To an extent Lytton was carrying on Oscar's business of challenging conventional morals. Like Wilde's dandyism and bold check suits, Lytton's sartorial devices, which later came to a head under the influence of Augustus John, were both a means of drawing attention to himself and of emphasizing in the most theatrical manner his departure from the orthodoxies of the past. Yet his eccentricities[22] were less easy-going than Wilde's. Wilde had made an art of unorthodoxy; Lytton set out to make of it an asset. Both wanted to provoke the dull-witted conformist and make social life less formal.

It was the custom for people to call each other by surnames, never Christian names, though nicknames were quite proper. Lytton was responsible for inventing many of these nicknames. Maynard Keynes, to his evident dislike, was dubbed 'Pozzo', possibly on account of his figure, or it has been suggested after the devious Corsican diplomat, Pozzo di Borgo, or possibly after the Italian word for 'well' or 'fount', or perhaps indicating a sewer; Forster was known as 'the Taupe' because of his resemblance to a mole; the inscrutable wisdom of G.E. Moore was suggested by 'the Yen'; the officiousness of Walter Lamb conveyed by 'the Corporal'. Despite looks which lent themselves easily to caricature, Lytton's friends never gave him a lasting nickname.[23]

Lytton gave as his reason for staying up a further year at Cambridge the need of the Society to be put back on its feet. The Michaelmas term of 1904 marked the end of Moore's six-year tenure of his Prize Fellowship. To the dismay of his admirers, the most elevated angel of them all showed no inclination to remain at Trinity, but in September floated off with A.R. Ainsworth to Edinburgh. 'He has gone,' Lytton wrote to Keynes during the Christmas vacation (11 January 1905). 'The wretched creature said he had no intention of coming to Cambridge next term, but that he would have to in the May term, as he's examining the Tripos. This is rather disappointing, isn't it?'

Just as Moore had succeeded McTaggart as the dominating influence among the young Apostles, so now Lytton and then Keynes supplanted Moore. 'The tone of the generation some ten years junior to my own was set mainly by Lytton Strachey and Keynes,' Bertrand Russell wrote. 'It is surprising how great a change in mental climate those ten years had brought. We were still Victorian; they were Edwardian. We believed in ordered progress by means of politics and free discussion. The more self-confident among us may have hoped to be leaders of the multitude, but none of us wished to be divorced from it. The generation of Keynes and Lytton did not seek to preserve any kinship with the Philistine . . .'

At their reading parties they could be seen, in Keynes's words, 'sunk deep in silence and in basket chairs on opposite sides of the fireplace in a room which was at all times pitch dark'.[24] There, in the smoky obscurity they sat upon their waists, with their buttocks protruding far beyond the front edge of their chairs, their ankles on the fender, discussing their livers and hearts and the hearts of their friends – all broken. During this time 'the Society changed in one respect', Bertrand Russell wrote in his autobiography. 'There was a long drawn out battle between George Trevelyan and Lytton Strachey . . . in which Lytton Strachey was on the whole victorious. Since his time, homosexual relations among the members were for a time common, but in my day they were unknown.'

From going through the Society's papers in his role as secretary, Lytton had become convinced that many past Apostles were undercover homosexuals. Some of them had not even been aware of their predilections; others had suppressed these feelings and lived out lives of miserable celibacy. Reconstituting the Society was a first step towards easing forward the gradual advance of sexual tolerance. But Lytton was not alone. In Maynard Keynes, who had been elected an Apostle during February 1903, there existed a worthy if rather more cautious lieutenant. Of all Lytton's new friends at King's, Keynes was the most significant. At Eton he had been both scholastically and socially successful. A long spoonbill nose, slightly *retroussé*, which had earned him the nickname of 'Snout' at school, was surmounted by a pair of brilliant eyes. Dark-haired, still fairly slim, with a receding chin and sensual lips partly camouflaged by a trim moustache, he looked infinitely sly and was impatient with fools. His own health, like Lytton's, was never good, and he suffered too from a sense of being physically unattractive. After their first meeting Lytton described him as 'stiff and stern'; but under this reserved manner ran a powerful stream of emotion. During his first year at Cambridge, he felt the need of friends, and in Lytton he soon found someone in whom he might trustingly confide; for to the intellectual affinity which existed between 'Scraggs' and 'Snout' was added a deeper sexual communion.

Already, by the time he was elected to the Apostles, Keynes's cleverness was prodigious, and his mind, in the opinion of Bertrand Russell, 'was the sharpest and clearest I have ever known'. In spoken argument only Russell himself could match the young undergraduate. Keynes, however, seemed more clinical. Whereas Russell attributed motives of black villainy to those who disagreed with him, Keynes dismissed opponents as idiots. There seemed little obvious connection between his feelings and the workings of his mind. Years later, in a letter to Ralph Partridge, Lytton was to describe him as an 'immensely interesting figure – partly because, with his curious typewriter intellect, he's also so oddly and unexpectedly emotional'.

But Keynes's emotionalism was well-concealed. Desmond MacCarthy said of him that his object in life was to impress men of forty (men whom Bernard Shaw defined as scoundrels), and Lytton felt inclined to agree. 'I don't believe he has any very good feelings', he wrote to Leonard Woolf (December 1904), '– but perhaps one's inclined to think that more than one ought because he's so ugly. Perhaps experience of the world at large may improve him. He has been ill, and I have been twice to see him in Harvey Road.[25] Really the entourage is shocking. Old ladies call, and gossip with Mrs Keynes. He joins in, and it flashed upon me that the real horror of his conversation is precisely that it's moulded on maiden aunts.'

Yet Lytton grew increasingly friendly with him. 'Keynes is the best person to talk to,' he admitted to Woolf later that same month, 'for he at any rate has brains, and I now believe is as kind as his curious construction allows him to be.' When Woolf had sailed for Ceylon six weeks earlier, he left vacant the role of confessor in Lytton's life. Keynes was an obvious contender, and by the beginning of the Lent term of 1905 the substitution had been completed. 'You are the only person I can speak to,' Lytton now told Keynes. And to Leonard Woolf he wrote (February 1905), making amends for previous slighting observations: 'There can be no doubt that we are friends. His conversation is extraordinarily alert and very amusing.

He sees at least as many things as I do – possibly more. He's interested in people to a remarkable degree. N.B. He doesn't seem to be in anything aesthetic, though his taste is good. His presence of character is really complete. He analyses with amazing persistence and brilliance. I never met so active a brain (I believe it's more *active* than either Moore's or Russell's). His feelings are charming, and, as is only natural, in perfect taste ... he perpetually frightens me. One can't be sentimental about a person whose good opinion one's constantly afraid to lose. His youth chiefly makes itself obvious by an overwhelming frankness, and of course often by a somewhat absurd naïveté.'[26]

The frankness which Lytton and Keynes exchanged in their correspondence, with its frequent references to buggery and rape, its oscillation between higher and lower sodomy, was part of the new Apostolic code. What they were looking for almost as urgently as sexual licence and homosexual love was freedom of speech as a sympathetic source of disclosure. Often they were nervous of their letters going astray, for according to the law they were both criminals – hideous criminals in the public's opinion. This danger, and the atmosphere of hostility, accounts for the obliqueness and protective arrogance in their letters. Lytton set the tone, but in the politics of sex he was perhaps more naïve than his new friend.

By the summer of 1904 the two of them were already established in joint ascendancy over the Apostles. A visiting Oxford student that Michaelmas term, J.D. Beazley,[27] recorded nearly fifty years later that 'when I went over to Cambridge at that time I thought Keynes and Strachey were the two cleverest men I had ever met; and looking back over the years, I still think they are the two cleverest men I ever met.' Sir Roy Harrod, to whom he was speaking, then asked him whether he received the impression that one was leading or dominating the other. 'No,' he replied, 'they seemed to me to be equals, peers, different and complementary.'

Despite corresponding with Keynes at this time, Lytton led something of a solitary existence. A receiver of confidences, he had none of his own to impart. Now that all those with whom he had originally formed friendships were gone, life seemed empty. 'I have had practically every experience,' he sighed. 'Nothing can come to me new again.' Illness still haunted him, 'but I dare say that by being always on the edge of the grave, one manages to avoid falling into it,' he wrote to Woolf at the beginning of the New Year. 'Our bodies are like Comets' tails, trailing behind us as we whirl towards the stars; when we lose them we turn into dead coals and drop into the earth.'

That winter a new star appeared on the Cambridge horizon, suddenly filling his world with its light. This was Arthur Lawrence Hobhouse, known then as 'Hobby' or 'Hobber', a freshman at Clare College which nestles between King's and Trinity, though more closely to the former. Here, it seemed to Lytton, was the perfect embryo to fill that emotional vacancy left by Sheppard. 'Hobhouse is fair, with frizzy hair, a good complexion, an arched nose, and a very charming expression of countenance,' he wrote to Leonard Woolf (30 November 1904). 'His conversation is singularly coming on, he talks a good deal, in a somewhat ingenuous way, but his youth is balanced by great cleverness and decided subtlety in conversation. He's interested in metaphysics and people, he's not a Christian, and sees quite a lot of jokes. I'm rather in love with him, and Keynes, who lunched with him today at [Walter] Lamb's, is convinced he's all right ... He was at Eton, but at 17 he insisted on going to St Andrews to learn medicine, which he does up here. This in itself shows a curious determination. But he doesn't look determined; he looks pink and delightful as embryos should.'

The task of securing Hobhouse's election to the Society occupied much of Lytton's time. There was among the Apostles an understanding that no freshman might be admitted. Undeterred, Lytton went to see Henry Jackson, Regius Professor of Greek at Cambridge, a sexually cautious but influential senior Apostle, and persuaded him that this custom needed the odd exception to establish its general efficacy, and that, in any case, 'two years at a Scotch University' (Jackson had also been at St Andrews) corresponded to a full year at Cambridge. Once this was accepted, Lytton set about introducing the new embryo to other Apostles. 'Our embryo Hobhouse is still as satisfactory as ever,' he reported to Moore (13 December 1904). 'I had arranged that MacCarthy should meet him at lunch last Friday, but at the last moment that evil person telegraphed to say that he couldn't come ... I feel rather like a buzzing Chimaera, but Hobhouse is a *vast* encouragement.'

In the middle of this canvassing, his attention was caught by the emergence of a figure from his past. 'Marie Souvestre – the eminent woman – is ill with no one knows what,' he wrote to Leonard Woolf (21 December 1904). 'She refuses to let any doctor examine her – no one knows why – but they guess it may be because she's afraid she's got cancer – but writhes in agony. They think she hasn't got cancer – but can't tell. It would be a sad loss if so eminent a person were to die.' In fact her instinct was surer than that of her doctors, and within three months she was dead. Her friends, the Stracheys included, visited her in the last months, and though the approach of death showed on her face, she seemed as passionately alive as ever. 'Veracity, an undeviating directness of intelligence, faithfulness and warmth of affection, were her most delightful qualities; dignity of manner and brilliancy of speech her chief ornaments,' wrote Beatrice Webb in her diary for 31 March 1905.

'An amazing narrowness of vision for so intelligent a person; a total inability to understand religion; a dogmatism that was proof against the spirit of scientific investigation; a lack of charity to feelings with which she did not sympathize – in short, an absence of humility – was, perhaps, the most disabling of her characteristics. It narrowed her influence to those whom she happened to like and who happened to like her.'[28]

Early in this new year, Lytton went to stay with his brother Oliver, at Howe Hill, near Harrogate. Oliver, rather peremptorily removed from Balliol, had been sent on a tour round the world under the tutelage of Robert Bridges. On his return, he had persuaded his mother to let him study the piano under Leschetizky in Vienna, where he had been one of only two Englishmen at Brahms's funeral. From Vienna he returned again in disgrace to England, his piano playing not being up to concert standards, and was dispatched to India, to join the East India Railway. Recently he had returned home yet again, this time with a Swiss wife,[29] and set up home with Ralph Wedgwood, 'a sort of railway person'[30] who had procured him a job. This was Lytton's first visit to their house, where G.E. Moore was a frequent guest. In the middle of some heated arguments Lytton remained mostly sleepy. Compared with the illuminating reality of Hobhouse, such dialectical fireworks appeared dim. 'The household consists of Oliver and Ruby and Julia[31] (his wife and child), and Wedgwood,' he wrote to Woolf (January 1905).

'. . . Wedgwood is a quasi Goth, large, strong, ugly, and inordinately good natured. He is rather stupid, but argumentative and jocose; and much better than it's possible to convey in description. His face is often positively wreathed in kindness of a strange fatherly sort. He likes music and has no perceptions. Moore has been much the same as usual, and of course rather wearing – especially with his damned Turnerisms [silences]. He has sung a good deal and played very violent duets with Oliver. I find it rather difficult to talk to him, and he has said nothing of much interest to me. Tonight he came out in a grand discussion with W and O with all the usual forms and ceremonies – the groans, the heaves, the tearing of hair, the startings up, the clenching of fists, the frowns, the apoplectic gaspings and splutterings.'

The Lent term of 1905, to which Lytton had impatiently looked forward as witnessing the unprecedented election of a freshman and the consummation of his new relationship, began with a shock when the secretary of the Shakespeare Society mentioned that 'a man called Hobhouse smashed himself up last night on a bicycle'. After cross-examining his bed-maker as to the dangers, generally speaking, of this type of accident, Lytton hovered about the Great Court, then plunged into Hobhouse's room. He was in bed, being read to by a friend, and declared that the doctor had pronounced him to be only bruised. 'Oh dear!' Lytton wrote to Keynes (2 February 1905). 'The appearance. He was flushed, embarrassed, exquisite. I fled after three seconds, cursing everything and everybody . . . and wondering how soon the news would spread abroad, and how many people his bedroom would be able to hold. These thoughts still agitate and blast me. I am consumed by terrors. We live upon a cataract; and at any moment, while we are yawning at the Decemviri, or maundering at McT's, the Hope of the World may be crushed to smithers by a cart in Trinity Street.'

That night he composed his agitations into verse:

> O the darkness! O the stillness!
> All our world is closed in sleep.
> I in sadness, you in illness
> Solitary vigil keep.
>
> You, with happy head and tired,
> Lie around your silent room,
> Feel your heart still vaguely fired
> Paint with splendour all the gloom . . .
>
> Ah! You bring to gentle sleeping
> Smiles that once were my smiles too;
> Now I smile no more, but weeping,
> Lonely, write these songs for you.

This incident was the prelude to a greater shock. By accident Lytton discovered that his friend and confidant, Maynard Keynes, was also enamoured of Hobhouse. At once a bitter rivalry broke out between them. Who should act as sponsor for Hobhouse's Apostolic 'birth'? The struggle was, in Lytton's words to Leonard Woolf, 'very much like a Homeric battle over a wounded hero'. By the third week of February it was all over. Keynes, in victory, embraced the new Apostle, and Lytton was left to brood abjectly over 'my own unutterable silence – my dead, shattered, desiccated hope of some companionship, some love'.

Never, it seemed, had his sexual loneliness been so bleak as over the next few weeks. 'Hobhouse . . . was duly elected last Saturday,' he wrote to Moore (21 February 1905). '. . . Oh Moore! I feel like a primeval rock, indifferent and venerable. I am too old ever to take wings. The only passion I have left me is the Black Rage. My stomach struggles through endless sloughs of dyspepsia. Alas!'

Some relief he did obtain by channelling his despair into a series of unhappy love poems after the style of Donne – 'The Conversation', 'The Speculation', 'The Situation', 'The Resolution', 'To Him', 'The Category', 'The Reappearance', 'The Exhumation'. In 'The Two Triumphs' he contrasts the fading joys of lust with the limitlessness of unrequited love. Writing in the first person, Lytton imagines his rival tasting the fruit of carnal passion to its bitter core. By contrast his own love flourishes in platonic adversity:

> Yet listen – you are mine in his despite.
> Who shall dare say his triumph mine prevents?
> My love is the established infinite,
> And all his kisses are but accidents.
> His earth, his heaven, shall wither and decay
> To naught: my love shall never pass away.

The theme running through many of these poems is the decay of physical love and its implied inadequacy according to Moore's ethical principles. In 'The Exhumation', as in 'Knowledge' and other verses written later, the word 'lust' conveniently rhymes with 'dust'.

For some two months following the election of Hobhouse, Lytton was consumed with hatred for Keynes. On 25 February, only a week after the election, he launched an extraordinary onslaught upon his friend before the assembled Apostles: 'For it is one of his queer characteristics that one often wants, one cannot tell why, to make a malicious attack on him, and that, when the time comes, one refrains, one cannot tell why. His sense of values, and indeed all his feelings, offer the spectacle of a complete paradox. He is a hedonist and a follower of Moore; he is lascivious without lust; he is an Apostle without tears.' He could endure neither to see nor speak to Keynes and their correspondence was broken off. 'He repels me so much', Lytton wrote to Leonard Woolf that month, 'that I can hardly prevent myself ejaculating insults to his face.'

Hobhouse was the first love of Keynes's adult life. At the end of March the two of them went for a three-week working holiday to Truro. 'You know my feelings – I shall know yours in time,' Keynes had written to him. But their sexual passions proved unsatisfactory, and whenever Keynes's 'demonstrations of feeling became very intense', Hobby told James Strachey, 'I couldn't help suffering a revulsion in time'. 'That episode is over,' Keynes reported prematurely a month later, '. . . I swear I had no idea I was in for anything that would so utterly uproot me. It is absurd to suppose that you would believe the violence of the various feelings I have been through.'

Keynes's pain and disappointment had a curious effect on Lytton. 'For a week or two,' he later revealed, 'I hated you like hell.' But as Keynes confided his ups and downs with Hobby, so Lytton began to feel closer again. By growing infatuated with the same man were they not showing what they had in common? During the summer Keynes was still Hobby's 'constant true love' – to an extent. 'I have a clear head,' he wrote to Hobby, 'a weak character, an affectionate disposition and a repulsive appearance.' The clear head he reserved for Lytton to whom he confided that Hobby 'simply does not know what the thing means'.

By his confidences Keynes was to win back Lytton's trust. 'Poor Keynes,' he wrote. 'It's only when he's shattered by a crisis that I seem to be able to care for him.' This was the beginning of a new lease of friendship. Their correspondence started up again and sometimes their affection grew so warm that they wondered – could it be possible? – whether they might actually be in love with each other.

7

SALE VIE AND A GLIMPSE OF HEAVEN

During the terms and vacations, Lytton worked steadily at the second part of his dissertation. 'My history has been – perpetual labour, interspersed with an occasional Symphony,' he wrote at the beginning of April. Moore's reading-party that Easter was to be held at the Crown Hotel, Pateley Bridge, in Yorkshire, 'eight miles away from a station, and a hundred from anywhere else'. High up above sea and civilization, the natives 'live on strange meats', Lytton reveals to Sheppard (14 April 1905). 'Yesterday we had the inside of a she-goat for breakfast, and to-day at lunch Moore found himself opposite – he didn't quite know what – it was smothered in thick white sauce – he explored – yes! it was a sow's udder, trimmed with tripe and parsley . . . Goodbye! They're serving the horse-tail soup.' Perhaps it is only in heaven that one is never bored when other people are talking. 'Isn't it ridiculous', he writes to Woolf, 'that after a week one should find one's dearest friends quite insupportable.' But boredom stimulates the appetite, and each day he devours 'vast slabs of salt bacon, chunks of mutton, plates of "tea-cake" (at breakfast), pints of foul "ale" and hot jam pudding, deluged with cream. It's sickening in the abstract; but I manage to look forward to every meal . . . We don't laugh much, and we play two games of jacoby every evening. This is a tolerable life for a fortnight.'

It was late spring by the time Lytton got back to Trinity. The laburnum and lilac were out along the Cam; roses bloomed again outside King's Chapel; the early peaches dropped from the walls of the Senate House; the scorpions reared their heads in the sunlight of the Great Court and all Cambridge came alive with the scents and colours of an early English summer. It was to be his last term. The familiar beauty of each street and building, the glamour and high spirits of so many young men, stirred feelings of premature nostalgia. 'I am restless, intolerably restless, and Cambridge is the only place I never want to leave,' he sighed, 'though I suffer there more than anywhere else.'

The first news was not encouraging. His essay on 'English Letter Writers'[32] had failed to win the fifty pounds which went with the Le Bas Prize. 'That Devil the Vice Chancellor[33] had awarded the Le Bas prize to – no one,' he wrote to Leonard Woolf (May 1905). 'So here am I penniless after my titanic efforts.' Still gloomier rumours were to follow. 'I also gather that my chance for a fellowship is now merely nil – for 2 reasons. i, There are only two to be given, and ii, Laurence[34] is to be my examiner. Amen!' Vere Laurence, a lanky bearded history don at Trinity, was as unhappy a choice, Lytton felt, as Cunningham had been the previous year. They had never been friendly. But hopeless though the prospects seemed, he had no alternative but to press on. 'I try to write my dissertation, and fail,' he told Keynes (7 July 1905). 'I die daily, as the Scriptures have it. But then I die in so many different ways.'

By June, after an Apostolic debate on 'Is Life Worth Living?', Lytton retreated to Lancaster Gate. Three months' hard labour awaited him – to be crowned with almost certain failure. Life, as he now knew it, was certainly *not* worth living. 'Oh lord, lord, lord!' he lamented to Woolf (June 1905). 'I do feel that I'm extraordinarily misty – a sort of coloured floating film over the vicissitude of things. The mere business of carrying on one's life seems something so overwhelming and exhausting that it's all one can do to get along from hour to hour. One sleeps, washes, dresses, eats, forths, reads, eats, walks, talks, eats, reads, eats, despairs, yawns, and sleeps again, and all one's energies have been used up, and one is exactly as one was before. If one were a disembodied spirit there'd be some sort of hope . . .'

In mid-June, he visited Balliol College, Oxford, as the guest of an undergraduate, Bernard Swithinbank, who, 'tall and handsome', we learn from Roy Harrod, '. . . an elegant, even exquisite schoolboy', had been Keynes's closest friend at Eton. Keynes, in fact, had introduced him to Lytton, who began to cultivate his friendship soon after Hobhouse's election to the Apostles. He was particularly anxious to get on well with Swithinbank, who was also in correspondence with Keynes. 'I want to tell you that I enjoyed my visit to Oxford more than I've enjoyed anything for ages and ages,' he wrote the day after returning to London (20 June 1905). 'I hope you'll believe this in spite of what I'm afraid may have seemed appearances to the contrary. It's almost impossible ever to express one's feelings properly, so that when I say that I shall always remember your rooms with pleasure, will you make allowances for my inadequate statement? It was really exciting to meet the people whom I met there.'

By the same post he sent off a letter to Leonard Woolf in Ceylon, describing his new Oxford friend who, it seems, was probably as shy as Lytton himself.

'In appearance he's tall (taller than me, I believe) and rather large footed and essentially solid; but by no means looks a strong and bulky person, his face is pale, ill and intellectual. The expression is often cat-like – the eyelids droop, and the mouth broadens; the features are all well-shaped, the nose arched. His hair is fair and thick, his voice rather shrill and boyish. The general impression he gives is undoubtedly one of vagueness. One sees at once that he's kind, nervous and impractical; and one's a little inclined to think that that's all. But it by no means *is* all. To begin with, there's his humour, which is always faultless and always wonderfully his own. Then his character is a real character. It's poetical – untrammelled. I mean by actualities; and quite unafflicted by contortions and affectations; it shines with a pale sincerity.'

'I live in the bosom of a large and vivacious family,' he told Swithinbank. At the end of June the Stracheys joined the Stephens in Sussex, as guests of the mountain explorer Douglas Freshfield. It was a sumptuous interval. 'Their house is incredibly vast and new,' Lytton wrote to Swithinbank

(1 July 1905), 'and packed with priceless cabinets, rugs, china vases and pictures. I was horribly depressed by the magnificence, and by the conversation, which was always on the highest levels. We discussed Henry James and Cymbeline and the essence of Architecture from morning till night.' From the other guests he singled out one with exceptional qualities – the twenty-three-year-old Virginia Stephen. Their reaction to the house seemed to coincide, and she put into words what was for him the true cause of his depression there when, in mock-horror, she exclaimed: 'There's not an ugly thing in it!' Lytton could only add: 'Except the owners.'

These weeks were impregnated with thoughts of Bernard Swithinbank. It gave Lytton peculiar pleasure to be 'nose to nose' with Keynes's poetic Eton friend, now his own friend. He wrote to Swithinbank, received an immediate reply, and straightway wrote off again suggesting an expedition to Richmond Park. 'So today I went, and we punted (or rather he) up to Twickenham, had tea there, and came back,' he notified Keynes (7 July 1905), to whom Swithinbank was also reporting events:

'It was perfectly charming. I said very little and he a good deal. When I left him, I was in a condition. Lord, lord. I didn't know one could have such affection without lust. But there it is. He's unique – exquisite. Only I'm jealous of anyone else thinking so, almost. I only know one other work of the Creator equally beautiful as an aesthetic whole – the Goth. And heavens, what a difference!'

Lytton had always found it difficult to work in Lancaster Gate and was thankful when, in the third week of July, he was able to move out to a large country house, six miles from Kettering, which the Stracheys had rented that summer. Great Oakley Hall was a Tudor mansion, with gardens, bowling-greens and box-hedges, all encompassed by magnificent elm trees. The rooms were complete with family portraits, carved doors and sliding panels; and there was also a large insignificant library which was found to contain several yards of collected sermons and an edition of Pope's Homer. The spacious air of comfort suited Lytton well, soothing and amusing him. 'The Church is on the croquet lawn,' he explained to Swithinbank (15 July 1905), 'so I'm afraid our games may be interrupted by psalms and sermons. I expect there's a family pew in the church, which my mother will occupy in state, as she insists upon going to Church in the country, in order to keep up (I believe) the Established Religion. This seems a queer form of atheism, but harmless. As for me, I think I am a

Christian, who never goes to Church, in order to encourage Freedom of Thought.'

For six weeks he was closeted here with Warren Hastings. 'I work like hell, and live a regular life,' he told Woolf, but 'I have no hopes' (July 1905). To Clive Bell also he wrote complaining of his hopelessness (28 July 1905): 'My dissertation oppresses me horribly,' he admitted, 'but I cast it off as much as I can. I read Sir Charles Grandison in the intervals between wishing I were alive and wishing I were dead.' For recreation he promenaded among the flowering rose bushes, languished among the back numbers of *Punch* and gossiped about Clive Bell's unsuccessful proposal of marriage to Vanessa Stephen, which he was keen one day to make the basis of a comic novel. 'I'm here, in the ordinary condition of exhaustion, and doomed to death though fated not to die,' he wrote to Keynes announcing an exciting literary discovery (18 July 1905). '. . . Have you read [Benjamin Constant's] Adolphe? It's superb. The point of view is original – i.e. that of the lovee. Don't you think rather a good idea? He's so dreadfully bored, and yet likes and doesn't want to give pain. It's wonderfully done – all in epigrams.'

The weeks went by; his mood remained suspended. 'I feel like a condemned criminal awaiting the chaplain's visit,' he told Saxon Sydney-Turner. And to Clive Bell he wrote (28 July 1905): 'The country has closed in upon me, and I'm gasping in the vacuum. Quelle sale vie! Nothing but village school treats on the lawn, and rectors to lunch, and not a word about any part of the body that happens to come between the waist and thighs.' Keynes invited him to come and stay at Cambridge where he was living with his parents. Lytton's reply, written on 27 July, almost exults in his wretchedness:

'Dear Keynes
  Total cash – 1/3½
    „ hope – ditto. i.e. hope of finishing dissertation, of ever seeing you again, of learning how to spell correctly, and of being in anything but a damned trance. I spend hours, days, and weeks in simply staring at blank sheets of paper – hopeless, helpless, utterly incompetent, completely vague, absolutely comatose, physically morally and spiritually, DEAD. Oh my brethren! Take warning by this sad spectacle of a ruined soul. Such are the results of moral looseness. Cambridge, with its sad atmosphere of paradox and paederasty, is doubtless much to blame; but it would be idle to pretend that the fault does not mainly lie with a perverse intellect which has wantonly squandered the talents supplied by an all-wise Creator.

Lord! This garden is wreathing and writhing with a school treat. It keeps on blowing motor horns, or things like motor horns, whose blasts pierce my entrails like so many swords. This is the quiet of the country ...

I have no news, except that the rector is married, that yesterday there was a flower show at Rockingham Castle, that today we had haddock for breakfast, and that tomorrow I shall stab myself...

Friday. Suicide postponed. I shall risk all, and come tomorrow ...'

He could not tell whether his low spirits came from invalidism, sexual loneliness, or the prospect of an empty future. 'I so often feel that all is absolutely lost,' he told Swithinbank (15 July 1905). 'The Lord knows I take no pride in this; I'm not Byronic. I'm not even decadent; it's only the truth.'

At the beginning of August his romantic young cousin, Duncan Grant, arrived. 'He's wonderfully nice, and nice looking,' Lytton informed Woolf. Thoughts of Swithinbank faded. Perhaps, after all, this lanky, shy Oxonian friend of Keynes had only been a substitute for Hobber. In any case he was too similar to Lytton himself, a companion in loneliness rather than a means of escape from it. To fall in love with Swithinbank would have been like preparing for a journey to the ends of the earth – and then moving next door. But with the beautiful, talented Duncan, an affair might lead to another universe. Of all his associates Lytton chose Maynard Keynes to whom to confide the wonder and agony of this secret: 'As for me – I don't quite know what I'm doing – writing a dissertation presumably,' he told Keynes (3 August 1905). 'But I've managed, since I saw you last, to catch a glimpse of Heaven. Incredible, quite – yet so it's happened. I want to go into the wilderness of the world, and preach an infinitude of sermons on one text – "Embrace one another." It seems to me the grand solution. Oh dear, dear, dear, how wild, how violent, and how supreme are the things of this earth! – I am cloudy, I fear almost sentimental. But I'll write again. Oh yes, it's Duncan. He's no longer here, though; he went yesterday to France. Fortunate, perhaps, for my dissertation.'

Duncan Grant's failure to reply to his letters kept Lytton glued to his dissertation. When at last he did receive an answer it brought on a supreme attack of indigestion. Only the fleeting appearance of Hobhouse distracted Lytton's attention. He had happened to be passing near by and was invited to lunch with the Stracheys. By now Lytton was able to observe him with detachment. He was as vain as a peacock and obviously had feelings of quite the wrong sort. On the whole Hobhouse's short visit was amusing for the effect it produced on Lytton's sisters – one of dazzled fascination. 'Everyone bowed before him, and talked to me after he'd gone about his hair,' he informed Keynes (7 September 1905). After lunch they sat out on the lawn together and Lytton noticed that he looked rather pale as they discussed, in the abstract, the dark question of physical love. 'Poor thing,' Lytton lamented to Keynes after he had gone (7 September 1905), 'he doesn't seem to understand much! He says he's repulsed by it – what can one reply? All the same he understands more than most.'

On 30 August, Lytton completed his encyclopaedic dissertation and dispatched it to Cambridge by the last possible post. 'The weight is now off my spirit,' he wrote to Woolf (31 August 1905). 'The last week has been one of the most unpleasant of my life. Perpetual constipation, nervous irritation, headaches even, utter boredom, desperate hurry, incapacity to think – all the most sordid nuisances the flesh is heir to. I am now more or less happy, and at any rate lazy, though a good deal wrecked.'

The completion of this two-part thesis, which had occupied him for some two and a half years, was a tremendous relief. He felt a new energy creeping through him. Whatever the electors might decide, there was nothing more he could do about it. 'The Begums have at last been vanquished,' he wrote triumphantly to Duncan Grant (30 August 1905), 'and today they were dispatched to Cambridge, where they may rot at ease till the judgement day. Your letter came just in time to see the tail ends of them, whisking out of Great Oakley like so many witches on broomsticks. The result is that I am now considerably re-animated.' He was especially keen to see Duncan again and conjured him to leap on a train and come for the last few days of the summer – if not to see him then at least to meet his great friend Keynes, whom he was sure to like. 'I think I am very disgracefully behaved not to have written before to you in answer to your invitation to stay,' Duncan replied (24 September 1905). 'I am afraid I cannot manage it . . . I should like to have seen Canes (?) very much.'

Two days later Lytton set off for Trinity, and the following evening attended his second ceremonial dinner with the examiners, sitting next to his own examiner, R. Vere Laurence. 'Laurence was wicked as usual,' he wrote to Woolf. 'I thought at times obviously hostile – well, well. What's so curious, I find, when I talk to these people is that I simply roar with laughter at my own jokes. I suppose it's to encourage myself.'

The Fellowship decisions were not to be announced for another week. Lytton rejoined his family back at Lancaster Gate, passing the days listlessly waiting. Then in the last week of October he returned to Trinity. 'I could see everything,' he wrote to Woolf (25 October 1905), 'and Rosy's[35] enraged disappointed red face told me at once all was over.' His failure did not come as a shock, yet he was dismayed.

It was not an unfair verdict. 'Warren Hastings, Cheyt Sing and the Begums of Oude' is structurally weak and methodologically flawed. In his

Preface, Lytton argued the merits of using long verbatim quotations from primary sources. He made little attempt to sift this evidence, and the general effect, obscuring his argument, is of a glorified anthology rather than a work of revisionist historiography. Throughout, Lytton appears happier with his villains than his heroes. He successfully undermines the reputation of the historian-philosopher James Mill, but never pulls off a convincing portrait of Warren Hastings himself.

The retrospective interest of these 833 holograph pages lies in their exposition of the methods he later renounced as a historical biographer. Though there was a suggestion that the 'wicked Mephistophelean myth' that had arisen round him affected his chances of a Fellowship, he had been working against the grain of his natural talent. As James Strachey was to express it, 'the Cambridge authorities had enough foresight and self-restraint to spare my brother the corrupting influences of an academic career.' But the immediate blow was severe. Once again, he had failed in an examination and encountered a setback to his precarious self-confidence. 'But when Cambridge is over,' he had written to Leonard Woolf (April 1905), 'when one has been cast into the limbo of unintimacy, of business, of ugly antiquity – is there any hope?' As it became populated by his special friends, Cambridge had acquired a magic quality. 'Body and spirit, reason and emotion, work and play, architecture and scenery, laughter and seriousness, life and art – these pairs which are elsewhere contrasted were there fused into one,' wrote E.M. Forster. 'People and books reinforced one another, intelligence joined hands with affection, speculation became a passion, and discussion was made profound by love.'[36] All this Lytton was now leaving.

His writings over the next twenty-five years are sprinkled with bitter-sweet references to Cambridge, 'whose cloisters', he wrote in *Eminent Victorians*, 'have ever been consecrated to poetry and common sense'. Elsewhere he wrote: 'The real enchantment of Cambridge is of the intimate kind; an enchantment lingering in the nooks and corners, coming upon one gradually down the narrow streets, and ripening year by year. The little river and its lawns and willows, the old trees in the old gardens, the obscure bowling-greens, the crooked lanes with their glimpses of cornices and turrets, the low dark opening out on to sunny grass – in these, and in things like these, dwells the fascination of Cambridge.'

Before the Michaelmas term started, Lytton packed up everything and left his rooms on staircase K in the Great Court of Trinity. 'The wicked dons of Trinity have refused to make me a fellow,' he told Duncan Grant (9 October 1905). 'I'm sorry, but resigned. I had imagined so many splendid things for us, if it had come off. Poverty, drudgery must now be faced.'

The companionship for which he had longed at Liverpool and cherished at Cambridge seemed in danger of being forfeited. For six years he had frequented doctor and saint, and heard great argument, but finally, like FitzGerald's Khayyám, had gone out by the same door as in he went. His departure from Trinity marked, so he felt, the end of his youth. At twenty-five, nearly twenty-six, he was back almost where he had been at the age of eighteen, and in much the same style as his diary entry for the spring of 1898, his thoughts turned bitterly inwards. With his spidery legs and arms, large nose, his dismal moustache and calamitous teeth, he felt himself to be handicapped by a hideous appearance. So it was natural for him to express his sense of failure in terms of physical denigration: 'You don't know what it is to be twenty-five,' he told Duncan Grant (11 October 1905), 'dejected, uncouth, unsuccessful – you don't know how humble and wretched and lonely I sometimes feel . . . Oh God, these are wretched things to be writing.'

PART II

'The middle-aged fill me with frigid despair – they have so little to recommend them – really only their vague sense of the past. I feel that I am dimly dwindling into that terrible condition – a sort of dying process. One struggles – but one sinks.'

Lytton Strachey to Maynard Keynes (21 January 1906)

SIX

Post-Graduate

'I feel desperately homesick – but for what home?'
Lytton Strachey to Leonard Woolf (1905)

I

BUBBLES, OYSTERS AND POTATOES

During the autumn of 1905, and for several succeeding years, a solitary young man, the son of an English general, was to be seen journeying between London and Cambridge. His striking figure, long and limp, with its half-languorous, half-drifting motion, gave him the look of an overgrown adolescent. But the pallid complexion was that of a seasoned scholar. He was apparently engaged in elucidating two problems – the kind of things that ought to exist for their own sake, and the kind of actions we ought to perform. He believed, indeed, that he possessed the solution to these problems, as a reference to some passages in the book he was carrying would show.

This singular person was Lytton Strachey, and the book was reputed to be his bible, *Principia Ethica*.

On his arrival back at Lancaster Gate that autumn, Lady Strachey had given over to him a bed-sitting room where he was to do much of his writing over the next two years. 'I am established in a room here,' he told Leonard Woolf (25 October 1905), 'with a folding bed, and all my books ranged in 2 bookshelves. It's pretty dreary, and when I'm to do any work heaven alone knows.' In this upper chamber he sat, bent over a hissing gas fire, while beyond the steamed-up pink and frosted window-panes, the life of London ebbed past. Already the enchantments of Cambridge seemed remote, half real, half fairyland, like Prospero's island. 'I find Cambridge already hardly more than a vision,' he told Keynes (13 October 1905).

He was nominally a journalist, but 'really, as far as I can see, a complete drifter, without any definite hopes, and the New Age as far off as ever,' he wrote to Leonard Woolf. '. . . I pray to God, though, that I may miraculously take a turn towards the practical – for a year or two – which I believe would be enough.'

As always when discussing his own work, Lytton understated his conscientiousness. There was something ridiculous about hard work. But easy writing's vile hard reading, and the readability of Lytton's essays shows the attention he gave his narrative construction. His output at this time, however, was not large. In his last two years at Cambridge he had contributed about half a dozen reviews to the *Spectator* and some more elaborate articles to the *Independent Review*, an intellectual monthly largely financed by the Trevelyans, with a strong Apostolic input and a violent commitment to Free Trade. During the following two years, until he was taken on to the regular staff of the *Spectator*, he produced about one article every six weeks at three guineas apiece (equivalent to £140 in 1994). 'I spend my days here trying to be a journalist,' he gloomily informed Swithinbank (15 October 1905), 'but I seem to lack the conviction and energy which I feel are necessary. Other things are much more interesting than reviews! But daily bread must be obtained somehow . . .'

Part of the horror of giving up Cambridge had simply been the actual process – which vanished once it was over. He still had his friends. Above all others came Duncan Grant. He was also seeing quite a lot of the Stephen family, gazing in rapture at the magnificent Goth, and with curiosity at the enigmatic Virginia. Then there was Clive Bell – still hopelessly, it seemed, in love with Vanessa Stephen. He had recently returned from Paris, and having failed to obtain a Fellowship himself, confidently assured Lytton that he was well out of Trinity. 'It's shocking about Cambridge,' Lytton wrote to Keynes (8 November 1905). 'I've been having tea with Bell – very dim and decadent in a blue dressing-gown in his wonderful Temple chambers – and he tells the same story . . . What's of course chiefly lacking is intellect, and that's lacking in Oxford too – only they make up for it by culture and indecency.'

He longed for some honest indecency himself, and after extracting the Cambridge gossip from Keynes, he would pass it on to Leonard Woolf in Ceylon. 'The freshmen sound most exciting,' he answered Keynes after a few days at Lancaster Gate (16 October 1905), 'and I can hardly contain myself – I burst with impatience and curiosity.' Keynes was now (27 November 1905) 'my only Evangelist, and I watch the posts for news from the Only Place'.

The most exciting new discovery was a freshman by the name of Goodhart.[1] The grandson of Lord Rendel, and cousin of Lytton's eldest brother-in-law, Goodhart was reckoned to be 'possibly a genius, certainly remarkable and almost certainly nice', in Lytton's words to Leonard

Woolf. 'Even James was excited when I saw him, about a "wonderful" conversation they'd had, after which Goodhart had fallen back with spasms and palpitations and had had to send for a doctor. He's violently musical and wildly architectural, he talks in torrents, and believes in medieval Christianity.' But it soon turned out to be a South Sea Bubble. Goodhart was taken up by the Society like an oyster, then damned and dropped like a hot potato after it was discovered that his belief in Christianity was not confined to medieval times. But there were always new embryos to take the place of the duds – the young Charles Darwin,[2] for example, whose election Lytton supported; and Dillwyn Knox,[3] one of the famous brothers, with whom Keynes had had a sexual fling at Eton, but of whom Lytton did not approve: 'Did I tell you that I took a pretty violent zid against Knox?' he asked Keynes. 'He seemed to me too gravely inconsiderate, in the regular damned Etonian way. It's impossible not to dislike someone a little, who so obviously dislikes one so much.'

Another freshman was Harry Norton, a brilliant mathematician destined to become a generous friend of Lytton's. 'I'm sure he has a very good logical kind of mind,' Keynes gravely reported to Lytton (15 October 1905); 'his own view, however, is that he is cultured – and he is incredibly. His whole person is girt about by a writhing mess of aesthetic and literary appreciations, which I have – so far – discovered no means of quelling. He's very proud of all this, but it's really rather nonsense: what saves him is his strong comprehension – I hardly ever caught him really stupid. There is nothing to say about his appearance – ordinary public school.'

A public school appearance was 'rather ugly'. But Norton was 'undoubtedly nice', talked incessantly with intermittent yells of laughter, and had an innocent habit of indecency which endeared him to Lytton. Unknown to his friends, Norton was suffering from what is technically known as hypomania, which later turned into severe depression. 'He had an extremely high-grade mental apparatus,' James Strachey wrote. 'He was one of the only three or four people I have ever known in the same intellectual category as Russell – with whom he was perfectly able to argue on equal terms.'

Lytton hoped that Norton might be able to draw out his younger brother James, an enigmatic and impassive character, much given, it was felt, to laziness. But to his dismay, James began to associate more with the much-vilified Walter Lamb, while Norton was seen on more than one occasion talking to that 'blind confused charming affectionate creature' Sheppard. As for Lytton, he was powerless to do anything unless he were to commit the Sin of Parentage.

Of all the new friends Lytton met that autumn and who were eventually elected to the Society, perhaps the most spectacular was Rupert Brooke. He had attended Hillbrow, the same private school as James Strachey, and had later gone on to Rugby with Maynard Keynes's younger brother Geoffrey.[4] His father, William Parker Brooke, was the housemaster of School Field, the house at which Rupert was entered and where every hour, he later said, was 'golden and radiant'. But living in his father's house at school had been 'a peculiar and anxious situation', wrote the biographer Paul Delaney. 'He was one of the boys, and one of the family; he had to conceal from his parents what his friends felt about them. Leading two lives under the same roof, his personality developed along two separate lines.' Accomplished at work and sport, and with good looks of a type which are at their height in the late teens and early twenties, he attracted extreme adulation. Lytton had heard much of Brooke before meeting him in September at Kettering.[5] 'He has rather nice – but you know – yellow-ochre-ish hair, and a healthy young complexion,' he explained to Duncan Grant (5 September 1905), who had also known Brooke at Hillbrow. 'I took him out for a walk round the Park this morning, and he talked about Poetry and Public Schools as decently as could be expected.' Brooke, for his part, rather took to Lytton: 'Lytton Strachey I found most amusing,' he wrote to Geoffrey Keynes, 'especially his voice.'

'The genius at school is usually a disappointing figure,' Lytton was to write in his essay on the macabre nineteenth-century poet Thomas Lovell Beddoes, 'for as a rule, one must be commonplace to be a successful boy. In that preposterous world, to be remarkable is to be overlooked.' It is not clear to what extent Lytton may have been envious of the younger man's triumphal progress. Because of the reverence felt for him by their younger brothers, Lytton and Maynard spent some time assessing Brooke's character. On the basis of an hour or two's acquaintance and an examination of some of Brooke's letters to James, Lytton censured his 'vile diction', feeble epigrams and jokes and general aesthetic tinge, but allowed that he had an interest (though not perhaps a deep one) in interesting things. 'Something might be done,' he thought.

After Keynes, there were no further elections to the Apostles for two years, when Keynes had introduced Hobhouse. Early in 1906 James Strachey and Harry Norton joined the Society, and two years later, as a result of James's campaigning, so did Rupert Brooke. By then he was shedding his *fin de siècle* dandyism and taking up socialism. A wave of Fabian politics was sweeping over undergraduate life. This new tide caught up many of Lytton's friends – including James, Maynard, and Rupert Brooke himself.[6] Rupert was a born play actor, Lytton a spectator.

The theatre, with its centre at the Royal Court in Sloane Square showing the plays of Shaw, Ibsen and Granville Barker, was part of this Fabian movement. At Cambridge, Rupert (with his namesake Justin Brooke) founded the Marlowe Dramatic Society whose performance of Milton's *Comus* was treated to a modest review by Lytton.[7]

'Rupert Brooke,' he wrote to Virginia Stephen in April 1908, 'isn't it a romantic name? – with pink cheeks and bright yellow hair – it sounds horrible, but it wasn't. The conversation is less political than you think, but I dare say you would have found the jokes a little heavy – as for me, I laughed enormously, and whenever I began to feel dull I could look at the yellow hair and pink cheeks of Rupert.' Virginia Stephen, who had also met Brooke, remembered he 'was very keen on living the "free life"'. But she was less struck by Rupert's trick when bathing of emerging from the water with an instant erection than was James Strachey, who thought him 'absolutely beautiful' and who feared getting an erection himself 'as I was naked too'.

The Stephens, Stracheys and their friends were to be called 'Bloomsberries'.[8] But Virginia singled out Rupert and his friends as a separate group of post-Pre-Raphaelite 'Neo-Pagans'.

2

THE LIMBO OF UNINTIMACY

When Lytton left Cambridge, his rooms at Trinity were violently redecorated and taken over by his younger brother. 'Grotesquely changed – an *art nouveau* symphony in green and white,' Lytton described them to Leonard Woolf, 'with James, very prim and small,[9] sitting in the extreme corner of the sofa, which is covered with green sack-cloth.'

Lytton had chosen the apple colour himself – a fact which he omits in his description of it to Leonard Woolf. What actually maddened him was the sight of his brother, a preposterous caricature of his past self, sitting there silent, contemptuous, ineffectual – a mere reflection of a reflection.

James's withdrawn nature and youthful appearance earned him the name of 'the Little Strachey', while Lytton now figured as 'the Great Strachey'. At Lancaster Gate, James had been known as 'Jembeau', and even 'Uncle Baby' by some of his nieces and nephews considerably older than himself. But these nicknames were exclusively family matters. Lytton had always preferred nicknames to 'the pomposity of real Christian names'. Nevertheless, owing to the difficulty of differentiating in conversation between himself and his younger brother, who was now entering his world, he suggested to his friends that they should in future address each other by Christian names.

The presence of an enigmatic younger brother in his old rooms swelled Lytton's post-graduate reputation. 'I see you're rapidly becoming a kind of distant, eminent brilliant wicked Mephistophelian myth,' Maynard wrote to him (5 November 1905). Lytton replied with a touch of foresight: 'It's rather alarming to find oneself a myth. I feel as if I ought to wear very peculiar clothes – *à la* Tennyson . . . a fur cap, and eyeglasses at the end of a stick. But of course the first necessity is a beard!'

During this winter Lytton was seeing more of Duncan Grant and Desmond MacCarthy. He would sometimes have lunch with the former at his new studio in Upper Baker Street, which appealed to his bohemian notions of how a painter should live – an almost completely bare room, ornamented solely with his sketches and drawings. 'They're superb,' he told Maynard after his first visit there (24 November 1905), 'and I've no doubt of his supremacy qua artist. He made an omelette in a frying-pan over the fire, and we ate it on the bare wooden table with bread and cheese and beer. After that we drew our kitchen chairs up to the fire, and smoked cigarettes and talked . . .'

Desmond MacCarthy had recently become drama critic and assistant literary editor of the Liberal weekly, *The Speaker* (edited by the Fabian historian J.L. Hammond), and he arranged for Lytton to contribute unsigned book reviews to the paper. Whenever they met, Desmond liked to read to Lytton who sat languidly beside him. 'I've rarely been read aloud to so much,' Lytton complained in a letter to Leonard Woolf, '– and have rarely heard anyone read aloud so badly.'

The regime of Lancaster Gate seemed to sap his energy. It was not that he disliked his family, but that regular family life corroded family affection. There were simply too many women. 'I have a sister-in-law – she's now in the house – Lord!' he wrote to Maynard in despair (9 December 1905). 'She talks incessantly balderdash of the lowest description. She tries to flirt with me. She ogles, and wonders what I can possibly mean. If you come on Thursday she'll be here to flirt with you.'

Lytton envied his brother Oliver who, despite resenting the absence in India of anyone who 'has ever read a book, or looked at a picture, or ever thought, or even spoken to anybody, who has ever thought about anything but horses', was nevertheless returning there to join the Indian Traffic Department. 'How he hates it! How he longs to stay! Ah! how much I'd like to go instead of him.' As the weeks dissolved into months Lytton took every opportunity of getting away, visiting James twice and being introduced to all the new embryos. But the great days of the Apostles had surely passed – even Maynard admitted this. 'If things go on at this present rate, I shudder to think what our sons may or may not be doing twenty years hence,' Lytton wrote to Swithinbank. 'But perhaps by that time the fashion will have changed, and they'll all be womanizers. Well, it will be a great triumph to be thought indecent by one's son.'

Was Oxford any better? Early in November he went to find out and see Walter Raleigh who was now a professor of literature there. 'Here I am, a little shattered,' he told Maynard (2 November 1905). 'Last night I spent with the Raleighs, partly at a rather dull concert, and partly listening to his consummate brilliance. It's so great that it practically amounts to a disease. But in any case he belongs to the age before the flood – the pre-Dickinsonian era – which is really fatal. He's not interested in the things which absorb us – result, dead silence on my part, and blank boredom on his – though of course there are compensating moments.'

From the Raleighs, he sauntered across to Balliol, spending a few days with Bernard Swithinbank with whom he felt happier. 'The amusement has been and continues great,' he told Duncan (3 November 1905). 'Life here swims through a beautiful sea of gentleness and *politesse*. I was not surprised, when the door opened and someone who looked like a freshman glided in, to hear him addressed as Gabriel. The angel Gabriel, I thought, of course.' He peered at many of Swithinbank's friends – including Daniel Macmillan[10] and J.D. Beazley – went to the Union, and attended a meeting of the Pleiads – a society of seven ('perhaps too many') founded by Swithinbank – where he heard a paper read on 'Les amours de Chopin et de George Sand'. But in comparison with the proceedings of *the* Society it seemed pretty feeble stuff, gleaned from text books. As to Oxford in general, its cultivation and impropriety made for a peculiar charm which Lytton found lacking in the more decadent spirit of Cambridge.

He would have liked to establish a close relationship with Swithinbank who, he instinctively felt, would cause him less pain than Duncan Grant. But the more he saw of him, the more he came to realize the unlikelihood of any intimate friendship. Swithinbank was too shy – too *intellectually* shy. 'There are awkward silences,' he reported apologetically to Maynard (2 November 1905); 'you see we really do at present have very few topics in common – I mean easy topics; though very often it's charming, and we can giggle without restraint. But what I think is the chief horror is his incapacity to analyse. He seems almost frightened and sheers off . . . [into] a sort of tormented resignation.'

It was an aimless and unsatisfactory life he was now leading. 'I feel', he wrote, 'like the Israelites who wandered in sight of the Promised Land for forty years.' His tenuous connection with the Only Place was still being preserved primarily through Maynard Keynes, who was 'certainly now', he informed Leonard Woolf (November 1905), '– though I hardly expect you to believe it – the most important person there. He maintains a curious aloofness.' In many of his references to Maynard, there is a tone of aversion. 'Keynes sits like a decayed and amorous spider in King's,' he wrote to Clive Bell (17 January 1906), using the imagery which he was later to apply to King Philip of Spain, the spider of the Escurial, in *Elizabeth and Essex*, 'weaving purely imaginary webs, noticing everything that happens and doesn't happen, and writing to me by every other post.'

The truth was that their respective circumstances had changed since Maynard was elected to the Society. Then Lytton had been indisputably the major figure, listening to the younger man's confidences and providing the benefit of his magnanimous understanding. But the quick and eager Apostle soon began to develop a confidence of his own. Whereas Lytton's influence at Cambridge did not extend far beyond the Apostles and some intimate friends at Trinity and King's, Keynes became not only a leading Apostle, but also president of the Union and of the University Liberal Club – a person of wide authority. Lytton had only obtained Second Class Honours; Maynard, with a minimum of hard work, had won a First. Lytton half-heartedly failed to be accepted by the Education Board; Maynard went on to pass the Civil Service examination with some ease. Lytton was not elected as a Fellow of Trinity; Maynard was awarded a lectureship and then a Fellowship at King's. And when, in time, the fashionable conversation switched from metaphysics and literature to economics and political philosophy, Maynard could still more than hold his own, while Lytton, despite laughing enormously at jokes he found a little heavy, remained something of an outsider. This reversal in the pattern of their fortunes strained their old comradeship. Although Lytton was to admire the author of *The Economic Consequences of the Peace*, he did not like what he took to be the mechanical salt-butter rogue who treated his love-affairs statistically and took the doings of the Liberal Party with great seriousness. Lytton's spasms of sexual jealousy were something separate, which nevertheless stimulated his periodical aversions. What aggravated matters during these early years was his own lack of money. The room he had been given at Lancaster Gate (it had previously been Dorothy's bedroom) was depressingly squalid. The comparison with Maynard's more prosperous circumstances unsettled him, and it was only when Maynard suffered momentary setbacks that their former intimacy returned.

The pattern of their friendship shows through their correspondence. Hating London, Lytton is ever thirsty for information about Cambridge youth, anxious to absorb himself in their activities. But Maynard replies casually and with a disconcerting echo of Lytton's own sentiments a year earlier: 'I really believe I would leave Cambridge and come up to London at once – but for one reason. I suppose the Society must be put on its legs again – or at any rate one has to try.' Lytton's letters expatiate on the twists and turns of his own shadowy passions and preoccupations. Maynard writes at length of his new successes in economics, the flattering remarks on his papers, and his intention to study ethics for the Civil Service examination. Lytton answers with mixed feelings: 'I suppose it doesn't matter very much whether you get into the C.S. or not, does it? If you didn't, wouldn't you get a fellowship, and take rooms in the Temple? That you might do in any case – very charming. Oh dear me!' Deliberating on his course of action, Maynard wonders whether he should stay on at King's as an economist. 'I could get employment here,' he writes, 'if I wanted to.' But Lytton, who hopes to leave Lancaster Gate and set up home with his friend somewhere in London, is appalled at the notion. 'Oh no, it would be surely mad to be a Cambridge economist,' he replies. 'Come to London, go to the Treasury, and set up house with me. The parties we'd give!' Soon, however, Lytton realizes that Maynard has no intention of getting a flat with him in town, and reflects that in these circumstances his rooms in King's might be very useful. But already it is too late. Maynard is determined to quit the stagnant atmosphere of Cambridge and embark on the adventure of life in London as soon as possible. He will conquer the metropolis as he has the university. He even confesses himself a little taken with Ray Costelloe,[11] who was later to become Oliver Strachey's second wife; he takes up mountaineering in the company of Geoffrey Winthrop Young[12] (recently sacked from his post as a master at Eton), and is immediately triumphant. Lytton's consternation rises and he sadly admits to Duncan that he has no faith in Maynard's power of penetrating below the surface of life.

In due course the result of the Civil Service examination comes through. Maynard is second. 'A wonderful achievement,' his father noted in his diary. But Maynard, who has worked only intermittently, is furious – and writes to Lytton at length to tell him so[13] – whereupon Lytton sorrowfully confesses to Duncan: 'I used to tell Keynes everything, but his commonsense was enough to freeze a volcano, so now I've stopped.' At this point, however, Maynard encounters a period of adversity, becomes careworn and is re-admitted as the repository of Lytton's emotional problems. For the next two years, 1907 and 1908, Maynard works in the

India Office, but even before his first twelve months are up he is already consumed with ennui and thinking about moving on again. 'I'm thoroughly sick of this place,' he writes to Lytton in September 1907, 'and would like to resign. Now the novelty has worn off, I am bored nine-tenths of the time and rather unreasonably irritated the other tenth whenever I can't have my own way. It's maddening to have thirty people who can reduce you to impotence when you're quite certain you are right.' Lytton, at once responding to this familiar blend of boredom and arrogant frustration, is enthusiastically sympathetic. It is more like old times again. 'I feel it's a great mercy,' he wrote later, 'having you as Brother Confessor.'

How pleasant it was divulging what he felt. For his feelings were now centred strongly on Duncan Grant, to whom he had succeeded in introducing Maynard in the very first month of his return to Lancaster Gate. And he had much to divulge about Duncan and his world.

3

DUNCAN GRANT AND HIS WORLD

Duncan Grant was some five years younger than Lytton. His father, Major Bartle Grant, Lady Strachey's younger brother, had married Ethel McNeil, a beautiful but penniless Scottish girl, and Duncan, who was born in Rothiemurchus, was their only child. His early years had been spent in India where Major Grant was serving with his regiment. But once the boy was old enough to attend preparatory school he was shipped back to England, spending his holidays with the Stracheys at Lancaster Gate. In this strange house, among children of his own age, he was happy. 'The paved floors, the glass-coloured dome on the staircase, the little hidden servants' room, endless bedrooms, nurseries and hidden kitchens and all sorts of basements, made it a most fascinating haunt for a child.' Destined for a military career, he had in due course been entered with James Strachey as a day boy at St Paul's School, where he was placed in the army class and taught mathematics, of which he understood nothing. But Lady Strachey persuaded his parents to let him study at the Westminster School of Art. 'The great excitement is about Duncan,' she wrote to Lytton in December 1901, 'who appears likely to turn out a genius as an artist, at least so the experts say. But what to do with him is the difficulty.' In the style of genius, Duncan seemed to benefit little from orthodox teaching and eventually failed to gain admission to the Royal Academy School.

From his father, Duncan Grant had inherited a love of music and an aesthetic sensibility; from his mother, his beauty. 'His face is outspoken,' Lytton declared to Leonard Woolf (October 1905), 'bold, and just not rough. It's the full aquiline type, with frank gray-blue eyes, and incomparably lascivious lips.' As a youth he often wore a dirty collar, usually upset his afternoon tea, and never knew what time it was. When he spoke he blinked his eyes, and generally convinced his uncle, Trevor Grant, that he was a simpleton. But Duncan was so easy-going he did not seem to mind. With his charm and talent and appealing looks, he was fated to be the love-object of many men and women.

Lytton's feelings for Duncan were not simply physical. 'I know there's a sort of passion,' he wrote, '– an animal feeling, a passion without affection, which is merely bodily pleasure, and doesn't count.' It was certainly not this that he desired, but rather an ideal union of sex and affection, fantasy and companionship, that embodied Moore's ethics of beauty.

In these early years of exile from Cambridge, Lytton wished above all else to be a literary artist. The man of action was beginning to seem too immature a vision of perfection, and as it slowly faded so it was replaced by a different kind of hero, the painter, the musician, the creative literary genius. But fears of his own inadequacy pressed in on him as he laboured over his *belles lettres*. 'Perhaps,' he wrote, 'the truth is that I'm not an artist. But what the devil *am I*?' In his perplexity he looked for someone on whom to centre his complicated longings. And it was on Duncan that he fastened.

In all his infatuations, even those at school, Lytton was endeavouring to relinquish his own personality and assume the identity of the person loved. It was therefore only to be expected that he should now fall in love with an artist. 'Let's both be great artists and great friends,' he exhorted Duncan. 'Je t'embrasse de tout mon coeur.' Once he had established himself as a writer, the direction, though not the nature, of his desires would change, aiming once more for the impossible. After *Eminent Victorians* he would again worship blue-eyed rowing Blues and handsome young Old Etonians. But those days were still far off.

Now, while his self-confidence was at a low ebb and he followed an aimless existence, haunted daily by the thought of failure, the figure of Duncan Grant seemed like a star shining in the black vault of the heavens. 'He sees everything, you know,' Lytton told Maynard excitedly (18 November 1905), 'and he's probably better than us. I have a sort of adoration. When I hear people talking about him I'm filled with a secret pride.'

The other side of this adoration was an exultant self-abasement. All his life Lytton tended to move naturally towards the role of victim. At school he had attracted bullying; and he sometimes magnified his illnesses. In his love-affairs he often manoeuvred himself into states of distress. Sometimes his complaints were well-founded, sometimes they were delusions; but often he was their own architect. Duncan Grant was genuinely fond of him, but Lytton's intensity produced an atmosphere of claustrophobic possessiveness. For it was not simply that Lytton longed to assimilate his body, but to take, as it were, vacant possession of his soul. Duncan, on the other hand – and he was unlikely to have attracted Lytton's attentions had it been otherwise – felt little wish to surrender his own identity. He set about defending himself by reversing the current of eulogy and self-abasement. Lytton, he wrote, was 'too good, too true, too great'. He despised himself 'for not being of the fine clay that could fly with you into limitless space for ever', though, of course, he still felt for him 'a very great friendship and the utmost regard'. Over and above this modest degree of fondness, he suggested, Lytton's sentiments were wasted. As for himself, he was little better than a brute; his affection was on a lower level – nothing more than a perverted calf-love; he could never match the nobility of Lytton's passion.

But to all these evasions and dissimulations Lytton had an answer. Duncan, he explained, overestimated his emotions simply because he, Lytton, was better able to express them. It was merely a matter of being older. And all the while he seemed partially to thrive on this ill-treatment. Towards anyone who was absurd enough to think highly of him or hold him in great affection Lytton automatically felt less. He returned admiration with a diminution of feeling. After all, he despised himself so utterly that he could not think well of a person who was taken in. What, in a sense, he demanded from those on whom he fixed his love was a contempt so powerful as to blast and obliterate his own personality. He laments repeatedly that Duncan Grant is stand-offish, unkind, indifferent: and he worships him all the more. 'Duncan tortures me. But a crisis must happen soon. I find him perfect,' he writes. He was in a torment lest the unbearable torture should cease; lest he should fall out of love, and back into nothingness.

In the intervals between these painful spasms, he reflected lingeringly on his own heightened reactions. Any excess of emotion threatened to overwhelm his fragile body. He had fits of dizziness. Describing the sensations Lytton frequently couples the words 'dim' and 'intense', to indicate how violent feelings brought about a fading of his consciousness. From boyhood onwards, it was this self-consciousness that he sought to eradicate. To transfer consciousness from his own body to that of his partner was the unrealizable fulfilment of his passions.

Lytton's love for Duncan was probably never more intense than during the winter of 1905–6. 'I have fallen in love hopelessly and ultimately,' he confided to Clive Bell (17 January 1906). 'I have experienced too much ecstasy, I want to thank God, and to weep, and to go to sleep.' While Duncan persisted in acting 'almost as though he were afraid of me, of my affection – as if he didn't dare to face something he couldn't reciprocate', Lytton grew more deeply obsessed. The affair prompted his most romantic vein, in which radiant happiness is fused with delirious misery. 'He [Duncan] is the full moon of heaven. I rave, and you may judge of my condition when I tell you that it's 4 p.m. – the most utterly prosaic hour of the day,' he confided to Maynard (8 December 1905). '. . . At the present moment I feel capable of achieving every wonder, of rising to incomparable heights! Good heavens, last night my despair was too absolute.' As the strength of his affections mounted so he would feel liberated from the husk of GLS, floating in a shadowy paradise. 'I live in a mist,' he told Maynard on 21 December, '– perhaps a golden one – where most ordinary things are fluctuating and dim. My nerves have quite gone. I seem to be in direct and mystic contact with the Essence of the World. The air is full of divinity, and the music of the spheres enchants me as I walk.'

Lytton and Duncan had been invited by Lady Colvile to spend the first week of January at her home, Park Cottage, at Ledbury in Herefordshire. Lytton should have been delighted. But he was not. Everything was going rather too well. Love was like faith – one didn't like to lose it until one had, when one couldn't understand why one ever wanted it. 'I begin to wonder whether his [Duncan's] intellect is satisfying enough,' he queried in a letter to Maynard (31 December 1905). 'I can imagine myself bored . . . and I almost dread five days tête-à-tête.' He was beginning to suffer the pangs of requited love.

Lytton's fears proved unjustified. It was impossible not to offend someone who almost cherished persecution. 'Nothing definite has happened,' he reported to Maynard. 'I was blissfully happy till suddenly he said something which brought it over me in a sudden shock that he didn't care for me, and wanted to escape.' On the instant Lytton gave himself up to thoughts of death. Duncan, in response, complained of his moodiness and immediately Lytton was infatuated again. No question of boredom now. 'He's a *genius* – a colossal portent of fire and glory,' he wrote to Maynard.

'His feelings transcend all – I have looked into his eyes, and the whole universe has swayed and swum and been abolished, and we have melted into one indescribable embrace. His features were moulded by nothing intermediary, but by the hand of God itself; they are plastic like living marble, they clothe a divinity, a quintessential soul. I rave; but I weep too. Looking at his face, I imagined last night the marks of Time upon it. I saw the lines and the ruins and the desolations of Age, I saw Death too, and the face composed in Death; and I prayed that the whole world might stand still for ever.'

In the second week of January 1906, Lytton returned alone to London and took up the bare threads of his existence. He tried to be cheerful, welcoming minor illnesses which enabled him to trace his defects to a definite cause. People who experience a kind of tension over nothing, or at least nothing they can pin down, were, he believed, the ones who suffered most. 'I'm pretty ill,' he explained to Duncan on succumbing to a cold in the head, 'and in the very highest spirits.' But the cold passed and the symptoms of debility persisted.

Each week he saw Duncan once or twice, enough to revive and exhaust his passion. In the blank periods between their meetings, he was sucked back into self-absorption. Everything revolted him. 'The whole world stinks in my nostrils,' he cried out to Maynard (1 February 1906). 'I stench in my own nostrils.'

4

MEN IN LOVE

'At moments,' Lytton explained to Maynard Keynes (14 February 1906), 'I give up hope and long for an all but infinite separation.' To his dismay he had suddenly been granted this wish when Duncan, having been given a hundred pounds for his twenty-first birthday by his aunt, Lady Colvile, decided to use it on his artistic education in Paris. Staying on at Lancaster Gate while Duncan was enjoying himself on the other side of the Channel was a bleak prospect, and Lytton secretly hoped that Lady Colvile would make the separation easier by inviting him down to her villa in Menton.

Early in February Lady Colvile did write to Lady Strachey suggesting that Lytton should visit her. 'I'm going to the South of France in a few days,' he wrote happily to Swithinbank (4 February 1906). 'This I feel to be wicked, as I've positively no excuse, and I can't see why I should bask in sun and roses, and other people not. However I suppose the world is arranged on these principles.' As the date of his departure drew near he was filled with agitation. 'I'm sad because I'm so futile and incompetent,' he told Duncan (5 February 1906), 'and because the thought of parting from you is a dull agony. I feel like a schoolboy at the end of his holidays, who knows that tomorrow he must go away from home. How dreadful to be an exile!'

Since they were both going to France, Lady Strachey arranged for the two of them to travel together. They set off on 18 February by train to Paris, and stayed one night at the strangely named Hôtel de l'Univers et du Portugal. The next day, Lytton left Duncan 'up 42 flights of stairs in the hotel', a little alarmed, but glad to be in France, and continued his journey south, alternately sleeping and writing regretful letters back to Paris. 'It's very nice now – gliding along by the shore in a demi-trance. I often turn round to say something to you; why aren't you here?'

On his arrival at Menton, Lytton was met by Lady Colvile and Trevor Grant, 'a dowager aunt and a vagabond uncle', as he described them to Swithinbank, '(they're brother and sister not husband and wife)', who took him up to their home, Villa Henriette. 'This is a very small house,' he wrote to his mother (20 February 1906), 'but charmingly placed, the front rooms looking over olive-trees to the sea.' As so often, the sea-climate was a solace after the emotional wear and tear. The rocks and mountains seemed to absorb his regrets which evaporated in the quivering air. 'I pass along in a dream,' he told Maynard (21 February 1906), 'looking at peacock-blue seas, and talking to imbecile dowagers, and eating artichoke omelettes . . .'

He bought himself a rather dashing pair of green-yellow gloves and a splendid Monte Carlo hat, and sat long motionless hours on the terrace looking at the blur of the sea and sky through palms, olives and cypresses. 'Imagine, if you possibly can, my infinite silence,' he invited Maynard. '. . . I respond if I'm spoken to, I give out reciprocal sounds; voilà tout!

'I've lost count of everything, the day of the week, the number of reviews I ought to be writing, the length of time I've been without seeing Duncan, the name of the founder of the Society – all, all has gone. I can only think of whether the Protestant Church ought to have a new organ loft, and of how much Mrs Trollope loses per week at bridge. The word reminds me – I believe I was once – I have some memory – I don't know though – *was* I once at Cambridge? Are you there now? I wonder. No, no, I think it must be the colour of the sea that I'm thinking of – if it really is sea and not scene-painting. – But after all, what can one expect of one's state of mind when one's reduced to reading the works of W.W. Jacobs? – "The captain turned in his chair and regarded his daughter steadily. She met his gaze with calm affection.

"'I wish you were a boy,' he growled.

"'You're the only man in Sanwick who wishes that,' said Miss Nugent complacently."'

He thought about Duncan constantly and looked forward to their days together in Paris on his return journey. He was disappointed by the appearance of the boys round Menton. Their olive complexions and bare necks looked enticing, but on closer inspection they nearly all turned out to be dirty and dense. 'I have seen no one of even respectable looks for almost a week,' he complained to Maynard (24 February 1906), 'and I am becoming a little impatient.' He sank back into lethargy. 'A quiet married life is all I look forward to, for myself, and for everyone else.'

Some entertainment was provided by Lytton's aunt and uncle, both of whom were extravagant characters. About his mother's elder sister Lady Colvile, a figure of Elizabethan grandeur, he would recite all sorts of stories in his letters to Duncan. 'La tante Elinor has so far been fairly well under control,' he reported back during the first week of his visit. 'There is a wretched imbecile of a French maid called Nina whom she worries at meals rather, but that's all. I relapse into the pathetic silence of a delicate youth, whenever I see anything like a crisis approaching. This has an excellent effect, and Nina (who deserves it) is immediately blown up for serving the curry before the rice, or for not putting the Oriental Pickles on the table.' A little later 'Aunt Lell' began suffering from *twinges*. Even then she struck Lytton as 'exquisite – perhaps tragic. Her hands are enough in themselves to prostrate one; and even her face I find absorbing. I saw her the other day in bed, without her wig. You can't conceive the difference. She looked terribly old.'

As a result of his aunt's sickness, Lytton was thrown together with his uncle, Trevor Grant, Lady Strachey's favourite brother. To keep out the heat he surrounded himself with an enormous overcoat (even in winter), spent many hours noisily draining down cups of coffee and reading the day before yesterday's copy of *The Times*. Lytton was half fascinated, half repelled. 'We get on pretty well,' he assured Duncan, '– he talks, and I do my best to listen appreciatively – it's not very difficult, as it's all about old Indian days, and fairly amusing.

'. . . He's rather trying in some ways. He makes the most disgusting swilling and squelching noises when he's eating, and I sometimes feel that I shall shriek if it goes on for a second longer. It does, and I never do –

such is my virtue, or cowardice. The truth is that he is a vagabond, not an ordinary civilized human being accustomed to live in houses, behave at table and so on. He ignores all that, and floats dimly on in his dim self-centred way. Sometimes I see him at dusk prowling along the sea-shore in his long flapping overcoat – a mystic solitary figure. What can he be thinking of? His sons? His photography? Old India days? Clementina's Death? Nothing at all? . . .'

Shortly after Lytton's arrival, Trevor Grant retreated to England, and his place at the Villa Henriette was taken by another of Lady Colvile's brothers, George – the complete antithesis of Trevor, very spruce and haughty and English. Removed from his natural habitat, he seemed pathetically out of place, and no one could find anything to say to him.

Presently another member of the family joined the household. This was a cousin of Lytton's, Alfred Plowden, a magistrate of Marylebone Police Court.[14] Most of his holiday was spent at Monte Carlo, where he went for the sake of the tables and his smart friends, all of which Lytton deplored. 'Everything there [at Monte Carlo] is made out of painted cardboard,' he told Swithinbank (9 March 1906); 'the palm-trees are cut out of tin, there is always a band playing, and one feels as if one ought to be in tights and spangles.' As for Alfred Plowden himself, he struck Lytton as being one of the silliest creatures he had ever come across – 'a sort of hopelessly non-existent character who simply walks about on the stage and vanishes into space when no one else is there', he described him to Duncan (7 April 1906). 'A Personnage de Comédie, I think, pure and simple.'

As Alfred Plowden was leaving, an incident took place on the railway platform which suggests the glimmerings of some sympathy between them. 'I saw him to the station the other evening,' Lytton recounts (8 April 1906), 'and as we waited for the train the fearful noise of the croaking frogs made him say, "I wonder what they can be doing?" I couldn't help bursting out with, "I think they *must* be copulating." The Police Magistrate did smile.'

*

'I write a few reviews,' Lytton told G.E. Moore, 'and spend the rest of the day having tea with ladies of sixty.' In fact he wrote just two pieces for publication in these weeks – his essay on Blake which appeared in the *Independent Review*,[15] and a review of Augustine Birrell's *Andrew Marvell* for the *Spectator*. Much of his morning was given over to the writing of letters – to G.E. Moore on Society matters, filial and fraternal letters to the family assuring them that Dorothy Bussy, then about to bear her first child, was being properly looked after, patriarchal letters reassuring his aunt, Ethel Grant, about the supposed degenerative influence of Paris on her son Duncan, love letters to Duncan, and letters about love letters to Maynard. But his oddest correspondence was with Edmund Gosse. An essay he had written on Sir Thomas Browne, published in the February issue of the *Independent Review*, had been based on a volume of Gosse's, recently issued in the 'English Men of Letters' series. On 3 February, MacCarthy's *Speaker* printed Lytton's unsigned review of this book which was somewhat disparaging to Gosse. In Lytton's view Browne's works (unlike those of Byron) were not of the kind that needed a biography of the author to serve as commentary. 'The Glasgow merchant who read through *Don Juan*', he wrote, 'and asked at the end whether the author was a married man was surely in need of some enlightenment.' For writers like Browne, on the other hand, it was sufficient to know that they had lived, and Gosse's book would have gained if it had told its readers 'a little more about Sir Thomas's style and a little less about his sons'. Chronologically, Browne belonged to the seventeenth century but his idiom had much in common with the Elizabethans. What could be more futile, then, than to seek for simple constructions and homely words in the pages of Browne's prose? In attempting to do exactly this Gosse had attacked the central principle of Browne's style, 'its employment of elaborate and gorgeous latinisms'. Gosse was like a man who admired the beauty of a butterfly but did not care for the wings: 'To the true Browne enthusiast, indeed, there is something almost shocking about the state of mind which could exchange "pensile" for "hanging" and "asperous" for "rough", and would do away with "digladiation" and "quodlibetically" altogether. The truth is, that there is a great gulf fixed between those who naturally dislike the ornate, and those who naturally love it.'

As a correspondent Lytton found Gosse no less uncongenial than as a critic. In defending the use of biography as an aid to literary criticism, Gosse seemed to be upholding an enlightened principle, which is nevertheless contradicted by the example of his own tactful life of Browne and partly by his cloyingly polite style; while Lytton, dealing deftly with all points of the controversy, writes in a more amusing manner in order to defend a somewhat pedagogic stance. Perhaps Gosse had the best of the exchange, if only because each of his letters was written on House of Lords cream-laid, extra thick, imperial octavo notepaper, and brought with it an excess charge of fifty centimes.

Besides writing reviews and letters, Lytton read prolifically. 'I'm now reading Lockhart's *Life of Scott*, Blake's poems, and the Correspondence of Voltaire,' he wrote to G.E. Moore (28 March 1906). 'It's a frightful mixture – but if one's a JOURNALIST what can one do? I read the first because I want to have read it, the second because they do me good, and the third because I like it – or because I think I might. How charming it would be to "tear the heart out" of books, like Dr Johnson! That's to say, if one liked hearts. I think I prefer the spinal marrow.'

Of all the books he was reading, his favourite was Voltaire's Correspondence. Letters, he later told Lady Ottoline Morrell (31 October 1916), were 'the only really satisfactory form of literature', because they give us the facts so directly and draw us right into the world where they were written. 'I'm reading Voltaire's Correspondence,' he wrote to Maynard (27 February 1906), 'which is the greatest fun to me imaginable.

'There's a poor Abbé Desfontaines whom he hated like hell because he criticized his wretched tragedies, and he works himself up into a splendid fury. At first he merely says the Abbé had been in prison; then that it was for Sodomy; then that it was for Sodomy with a chimney-sweeper's boy for Cupid – and so it goes on in letter after letter. At last comes a little poem describing the rape, and how the Abbé was seized by the police in flagrante delicto, stripped and birched – 20 strokes for sodomy and 30 for his bad verses. It's really all very scandalous; and I think it's pretty clear that Voltaire himself had had affairs.'

Another book he read during these months was *Henry Sidgwick: A Memoir* by A. and E.M. Sidgwick. All the Apostles were reading it. Their impatience with its lack of intimacy, of boldness in thought, lucidity and crispness in style, was part of the twentieth-century revolt against the approved standards of the nineteenth. The free-thinking Sidgwick was a most eminent Victorian, and the Apostles' revaluation of him as man and philosopher has been seen by some as a key to the general change in attitude among thinking people at about this time. Yet, perhaps because the break with the Victorian age was not complete, the *Memoir* provoked an involuntary fascination. 'I have never found so dull a book so absorbing,' Keynes told Swithinbank. The same note of paradoxical interest is more elaborately sounded by Lytton in a letter to Moore: 'I found it extraordinarily fascinating – though I can't think why, as *every* detail was inexpressibly tedious. I never realized before what a shocking wobbler the poor man was; but my private opinion is that his wobble was not completely honest – I believe he did it because he wanted to, and not because he thought it reasonable. Really his ethical reason for postulating an Almighty is a little too flimsy, and I don't see how an intelligent and truly unbiased person could have swallowed it. His letters irritated me a good deal – but perhaps you wouldn't find them so. The conscientiousness and the lack of artistic feeling combined occasionally drove me wild. Also the tinge of donnishness – however, I suppose one must forgive a good deal quia multum amavit.'

Sidgwick was to be one of Strachey's original twelve candidates for the book that became *Eminent Victorians*. His *Methods of Ethics* had anticipated Moore's *Principia Ethica* by postulating good as indefinable and stepping away from primitive fundamentalism. But then he had edged backwards. As Keynes put it in his letter to Swithinbank (27 March 1906): 'He never did anything but wonder whether Christianity was true and prove it wasn't and hope that it was . . . I wonder what he would have thought of us; and I wonder what we think of him.'

To the first of these questions F.R. Leavis was to give a trenchant answer in *Scrutiny* (June 1951) when, attempting to rescue the representative great Cambridge men of the past from the coterie power of their Bloomsbury descendants, he scathingly inquired: 'Can we imagine Sidgwick or Leslie Stephen or Maitland being influenced by, or interested in, the equivalent of Lytton Strachey? By what steps, and by the operation of what causes, did so great a change come over Cambridge in so comparatively short a time?'

Lytton believed that the change was based on the benefit of individual need. In a paper to the Apostles (20 May 1911) delivered after reading a biography of Maitland, he lamented the 'gay horror' of that previous generation. 'The brave concealment of tragedy! The profound affection just showing, now and then, with such delicacy, between the lines . . . What a world, what a life, passing in these dimnesses! I see once more the bleak and barren plain, and the dreadful solitary castles, with their blinds drawn down.'[16]

Maynard and Lytton discussed frankly what they thought of Sidgwick and Maitland in their correspondence. 'What an appalling time to have lived!' Lytton exclaimed. 'It was the Glass Case Age:

'Themselves as well as their ornaments, were left under glass cases. Their refusal to face any fundamental question fairly – either about people or God – looks at first sight like cowardice; but I believe it was simply the result of an innate incapacity for penetration – for getting either out of themselves or into anything or anybody else. They were enclosed in glass. How intolerable! Have you noticed, too, that they were nearly all physically impotent? – Sidgwick himself, Matthew Arnold, Jowett, Leighton, Ruskin, Watts. It's damned difficult to copulate through a glass case.'

*

Almost daily Lytton went to see the Bussys at La Souco, where he had stayed two years earlier. The house, with its french windows opening on to terraces of olive trees, seemed even more delightful. 'You can't imagine how exquisite their tiny garden is – all intricacies, covered with every variety of growing things,' he wrote to Duncan (5 March 1906). 'There are brilliant orange and lemon trees quite close to the house, and a large cluster of large white daisies, and clumps of wallflowers. Too divine, and all seen at a glance in the brilliant sun.'

The austere and gentle Dorothy, with her encyclopaedic knowledge of French, remained a quintessential Strachey; and Simon was a quintessential French peasant. They lived a life of profound, affectionate detachment, and were radiantly happy. But Dorothy's pregnant state affronted Lytton, and he was vastly relieved once he had been delivered of a niece, Jane Simone, in the first week of March. He had always liked Dorothy, though he had not, until now, thought very highly of her husband. The change in his attitude was another instance of his new veneration of the artist, accompanied by an abasement of himself as an unfulfilled literary artist. This is clearly conveyed in a passage from one of his letters to Duncan, which also hints at that admiration of the unlettered man of action which had been paramount at school and would rise again later. 'I admire Simon very much,' he wrote (25 February 1906), 'and I wish I could speak to him. I think he thinks me lazy – and I am – and he can't bear the idea of people being lazy.

'He urged me to begin a great work. It was a curious moment or two, in the twilight, at the window, looking out over the splendid Monte Carlo bay. I didn't know what to do, I couldn't speak French, and, even in English, what could I have said? – "Allons, Lyttone, allons!" – He was superb, and I was perfectly out of my depth. How could I explain – oh! what I can hardly explain to you – my utter inability to take "art" and "literature" and the whole bag of tricks seriously?* . . . I nearly burst out to him – "Je suis obsédé! Obsédé par les personnages!" Only I didn't, because it couldn't have done any good, and the French seemed more than doubtful. So it ended up in an awkward silence and I went away half in tears.'

With Simon Bussy, too, he discussed the problem of whom Duncan

---

* In a later part of this letter, which was written the following day, Lytton added a significant amendment. 'I find that I didn't quite say what I meant last night, about my not taking "art" seriously. I suppose I do, in some way or other, though not in the way that "artists" do. But I can't quite make out what I mean.'

should elect to study under in Paris, and how he should plan his year there. It was as a result of their deliberations that Duncan became a pupil of Jacques-Emile Blanche.

The English residents of Menton gave him many fits of the giggles. It was as if they had stepped out of the pages of Flaubert. As if unable to credit his senses, he went again and again to their tea-parties. Perhaps it might prove good material for some dramatic comedy he would compose making him and his friends millionaires.

'Oh heavens!' he wrote to Duncan after staggering away from the first of these gatherings (25 February 1906). 'All the females were so much alike that I hardly knew whether I was talking to complete strangers or to the Countess [Pallavicino] or Harriet [Codrington] herself. Mrs Hodgson is a relief, as her nostrils are apparently amputated, so that I can recognize her pretty well. But Miss Scott, and Miss Egerton, and Miss Duparc! – They have all long red noses, they are all 45, and they are all hopelessly respectable and insufferably cheerful.' Brightest of all these bright-nosed quadragenarians was Lady Dyer, something between a vicar's wife and an ex-governess, dressed in a long velvet cloak with fur edges and a round yellow straw hat trimmed with mauve chrysanthemums who was 'a complete vulture. Her red pointed nose and her moulting fur added to the effect.'

The men of Menton were mostly plain old paralysed majors. In the forefront of this troupe were Mr Bax Ironside, a distant cousin of Lytton's, nicknamed 'Mr Iron Backside'; a doddering inhabitant by the name of Stainforth who collected spiders; and Major Horrocks who, though blind, always spotted the lurking figure of Lytton from the opposite end of every crowded drawing-room, and compelled him to listen to descriptions of his many diseases, eczema especially.

'I strolled into Italy the other day – I honestly believe there's something different in the atmosphere over the border,' Lytton reported to Duncan (5 March 1906). 'At any rate it's a great change to go from the dreary respectable villas of this side to the cabarets, guitars, singings, and dancings of the other. The comble was reached when I met a highly respectable personnage in overcoat and felt hat, who suddenly drew up in the middle of the road opposite me, and began to jump. The dear man! I really believe I should have joined him, if I had happened to have the wherewithal.'

Back at the Villa Henriette, gazing over the Mediterranean – 'any colour from peacock to an incredible *pâleté*' – he watched a huge steam yacht belonging to the Rothschilds, and dreamt of owning it himself, of christening it *La Belle Espérance* and floating over purple seas, reading

Voltaire and drinking champagne with his chosen companions and occasionally carrying off Moore for a trip through the Hebrides. 'We'ld laugh all day, and at night, when the stars were out and it was time to be romantic, we'ld make Lysias sing to us, till at last there'ld be nothing for us to think of but Beauty and Love.'

'Venez, venez vite!' Lytton summoned Maynard (14 March). Both of them had been invited by the Berensons to 'whirl through Italy in a motor-car' and to put up at their villa, I Tatti, at Settignano. Lytton 'judiciously declined', but Maynard accepted with alacrity, and the two of them arranged to meet for a few preliminary days in Genoa before Maynard went on to join his hosts. And so, in the third week of March, Lytton boarded a steamer at Monte Carlo. It was 'packed with Germans who talked at the tops of their voices to each other without intermission', he wrote to his mother (20 March 1906); 'but there was an old American who came up and talked to me, telling me his life history, etc. How he had made his pile, and was now travelling with his wife and daughters. He told me that he thought Europe was a very interesting place, and that he reckoned the Mediterranean was one of the oldest seas on this planet. I agreed; but when he went on to say that in his opinion the gambling rooms at Monte Carlo exemplified Our Lord's saying as to the danger of building houses on the sand, I felt obliged to demur. His final conclusion was that I was "a lord in disguise", and I didn't deny it.'

At Genoa the wind blustered and the rain poured. He was glad to have Maynard to talk to in the dark interior of the Hotel Helvetia, and would have been happy to stay all day in those Helvetian recesses, eating omelettes and discussing sodomy. Some sightseeing, however, was compulsory. 'The palaces were simply écrasant,' he wrote to Duncan (26 March 1906). 'We felt like miserable marionettes, beneath their vast and endless bulks.

'The staircases were particularly incredible. I tried to imagine Marchionesses, etc., sweeping up them, but could hardly believe that they'd ever reach the top. The pictures were mostly of the Bolognese school, and they certainly didn't come up to the Roger Fry level. But among the 40,000 that we saw in the 40 palaces that we went into there were about 6 which it would have been delightful to have.'

These few days in Genoa with Maynard unsettled Lytton. On his return he felt more keenly the limitations of his life at Menton. Accompanied by his aunt, he let himself be solemnly driven round the 'Battle of Flowers', was pelted by every hand, and pelted back as hard as he could. But it was a chaste affair. All the while he scanned the crowd for a decent-looking boy, and saw not one.

'I began to talk to myself as I believe prisoners do in solitary confinement,' he confessed to Maynard (8 April 1906). Above all he longed for some warm words from Duncan, and felt increasingly depressed at being able to do nothing but express his love by post. There was one compensation: the absence of emotional stress was so excruciating it *had* to be good for his health.

That was how matters stood when, early in April, Duncan did write. It was a short letter, but it had something to communicate, which 'I suppose I must blurt out as fast as possible. Hobhouse as you know has been staying here and I have fallen in love with him and he with me.' This, he hurriedly went on, made no difference to his affection for Lytton, and he hoped that Lytton himself would not feel differently. He signed himself 'your ever loving Duncan'.

Lytton knew that Duncan wanted to be reassured, but suspected their friendship had been dreadfully damaged. In what he later described as 'a hysterical letter', he wrote back to Duncan: 'I think you may think me cruel, or sentimental – or both; especially, I think, if the "you" is in the plural number. – No, no! Don't be angry! Think of me, please, as a poor damned daffed human being, but a human being still, who would give his ears to be talking to you.'

He wrote at once, of course, to Maynard. 'I'm still gasping,' he admitted. 'I don't know what to feel – I only have the sensation of the utter unreality of everything, and even this blessed landscape, when I look at it, seems to waver in a wild mirage. God forgive us all! What a hideous muddle! – I have wept and laughed alternately and at the same time, wildly, hysterically, ever since I read it . . . I think what I mainly feel at present is a sort of stupor. I have subsided; I'm waiting to see what will happen next.'

Maynard, curiously exultant, genuinely sympathetic, wrote back at once. 'Great God, it's more wild and more mad than anything that ever happened in the world before. Oh and we have created it. It has sprung and sprouted from the tips of our penes – from yours and mine. And it will spread and grow over the whole world . . . As for you and D[uncan] . . . You know – as always, how much I am in love with you and Duncan as a unity – that I can't help feeling that this is only an episode.'

Lytton believed in a great deal of many kinds of love. But it really was a drawback to the New Style of loving that the chance of complications appeared to be doubled, and the resulting vertigo of confusion grew so giddy. On the other hand perhaps the extra amusement made it all worthwhile. How would anyone be able to remember who was meant to be in love with whom? Or whom they were in love with themselves? The combinations of throbbing molecular structures seemed limitless.

Duncan's revelation extinguished the soothing dullness of Menton. In a half-hearted way Lytton was longing to see Duncan in Paris again, especially since Hobhouse had returned to England. But he did not know whether his arrival would be an embarrassment, and in any case doubted whether he had the courage to tell his aunt that he wanted to leave. Two days later his health had deteriorated so markedly that it provided a legitimate excuse for his return. 'I cannot stay here in relaxation and solitude,' he wrote to Maynard (15 April 1906) '. . . Anyhow it is now *certain* that D is not and was not in love with me. I dare say in our old age we'll come together again. His charmingness in his letters is incredible, and I love him à l'outrance.'

Later that week Lytton left Menton. On reaching Paris he dragged himself round to the Hôtel de l'Univers et du Portugal, where he summoned a doctor who prescribed quinine in large doses to bring down his soaring temperature. 'I am here,' he scribbled to Maynard (23 April 1906), 'I think recovering, but I have been ill. How I got here I hardly know; my weakness was complete, and my depression almost absolute.' He looked so wretchedly ill that Duncan sent for his sister Pippa. 'It would be the greatest comfort if you could [come],' Lytton added, 'though I'm afraid the trouble involved is enormous . . . I don't feel as if I could face the journey back by myself.' She came, nursed him back to health, but no sooner were they ready to leave than a railway strike crippled the whole of Paris, and they were obliged to stay a further week.

It was a time of torment. In his fevered state, Lytton thought a lot about Hobber. There was an aphrodisiac quality about the role he had played in all their lives – a grain of love-powder that worked hell. Then an unexpected letter arrived from Hobber in England. It said nothing much; but how the handwriting shocked him, rekindling his excitement when he first saw it on a letter. What a muddle!

Each day Duncan would come up to his room, sit at the foot of his bed, and talk. He was kind, amusing, gentle, considerate. But it was not the Duncan he used to know – the boy in the orchard at Great Oakley, or during those wonderful few days at Ledbury, or the young painter in his romantic studio in Hampstead, or even, less than two months back, up those forty-two flights of stairs in this same hotel. Never could Lytton have believed that he might actually come to fear his presence, and long to escape from it. Then abruptly his mood would change, 'for why should I be distracted and humiliated and lost? Why should I madly beg for strange unwilling kisses, and be happy for a moment amid that warmth and that delusive sweetness? Why should I cast you from me with horror and mortal anguish, and with unsatiable adoration, and with intolerable desire? Oh yes, I know you are Duncan still.'

By the first week of May, Lytton and Pippa were at last free to return home. At the Gare du Nord Duncan came to see them off, and they all embraced. They travelled by easy stages, spent one night at Dover, and the next day were re-engulfed into the noise and gloom of London.

5

INFLUENCE FUNESTE

The family were mystified by Lytton's sudden illness, and there was nothing he could tell them that might account for it. 'I am trying to calm myself down,' he confided to Maynard, but he feared 'all sorts of doctoring and wretchednesses'. After examining him thoroughly, the family physician came up with a new diagnosis and course of treatment. 'He says that my disease is that there is not sufficient room in the lower part of my torso for my lungs, liver and lights, so that they are liable to press in an inconvenient way upon the heart, which is in itself superb,' he reported on 16 May. 'The cure is to be a course of terrific "exercises" of the most ghastly and depressing type, which it is hoped will expand the frame to a more reasonable size.' The effect of these exercises was indeed spectacular, and a week later he was writing in panic to Maynard:

'I have reason to believe that there's something wrong with my balls. I have curious feelings in them, & my wet dreams have become intolerably frequent . . . But what can I do? To tell my wretched doctor seems to me complete purgatory – I can't face it. He's an alien mind, and it would be too fearful to have him groping me . . . I'd give anything to see you, Maynard . . . if you came – if only for a minute or two – I should feel very much eased . . . I feel as if people will think I'm a criminal . . . I suppose I've exceeded – but I can't bear what they may silently think . . . do, do, consider my sad case!'

Maynard arrived at Lancaster Gate and stayed two nights. He urged Lytton to consult his doctor and was generally so adult and responsible about everything that Lytton feared his friend was growing middle-aged. 'I'm afraid', he had written to Duncan (16 May 1906), 'that in three years I

146

may find it impossible to speak to him [Maynard].' As yet, however, there was no one remotely suitable to take his place. 'You are the only person I can speak to,' he assured Maynard again in October. 'Pippa is unconscious. And my mother!'

Maynard also prescribed a visit to the Apostles, and at the end of May Lytton rose from his bed and hobbled off to Cambridge. He felt sure that he could count on some scandal to revive his spirits. At Trinity he spent five fine days with his old friends. Everything enchanted him. Cambridge was more beautiful now than ever it had been when he was an undergraduate. But then it was always fatal to live in a place: better to keep continually on the move. At one point he caught sight of Hobber, looking, he thought, rather unhappy. Altogether, it was an entirely satisfactory week. 'It was delightful to feel conscientiously lazy,' he wrote to Duncan (31 May 1906), 'and to glide about in the canoes among the lilac and laburnum and horse-chestnuts, and to watch the cricket, and to eat strawberries, and to talk about whatever one liked.'

That summer the Stracheys had rented Betchworth House, near Dorking. It was a large country mansion with a magnificent long gallery, and stood in park lands which enclosed a trout stream, golf course and tennis courts. Here Lytton lingered for seven weeks, 'embosomed in my family', visited by Maynard Keynes and Harry Norton, reading Madame du Deffand's letters and writing an essay on 'Mademoiselle de Lespinasse' for the *Independent Review*. 'The hours pass in a melancholy, almost charming mist,' he wrote. 'It's so fine & hot & idle – one lies dreaming of kisses, among long perspectives, half trees and half imagination, half sunset and half love . . . at the present moment, I am purged and quieted.'

To avoid Lancaster Gate, he decided to visit Clive Bell and his family who were shooting in the north of Scotland, stopping off on the way in Edinburgh, with G.E. Moore and A.R. Ainsworth at 11 Buccleuch Place. 'Moore', he reported, 'was quite cheerful, and played most of the Eroica with the greatest verve.' The next day he journeyed to Lairg and was met at the station by a wonderfully golden-bearded Clive Bell, sitting, like Toad of Toad Hall, at the wheel of a dangerous-looking motor-car;[17] and together they whirled away for twenty tremendous miles over breakneck roads round mountains, lochs and the reflections of sunsets. 'One bumps and leaps and shrieks as I imagine one might on a buck-jumper,' Lytton wrote to Pippa (11 September 1906). 'But the fascination of the movement is intense, and I am glad to say that every journey has to be made on it.'

The Bells appeared to be camped in a tiny 'shooting-box', set loftily on the edge of Loch Merkland 'with nothing but moors and mountains for 20 miles in any direction', Lytton wrote to Pippa the day after his arrival.

'Lairg is 22 miles away, and there is only one house between here and it. The country is exquisite, with vast long lakes streaming one after the other, and beautiful pale hills. It is quite unlike Rothiemurchus – far less distinguished of course, but also far more completely remote and inhuman. The house is quite small, mostly made of tin, and entirely lined with pitch-pine walls, floors and ceilings ... I intend secretly to have a shot at a stag, or at any rate to try to, before I come away. Everyone is very "hearty", and one's appetite is too.'

After ten invigorating days, Lytton travelled south to Feshiebridge, to join Maynard, Harry Norton and James Strachey for what Keynes's biographer Roy Harrod called 'a last wild excess ... of talk upon the old subjects'. 'What they discussed is unknown,' writes Keynes's biographer D.E. Moggridge, 'but one doubts that they discussed Maynard's two instances of actual as opposed to theoretical sodomy with James Strachey' that summer. Maynard had recently been staying with Hobhouse in Somerset and, while making a start on his Theory of Probability, been receiving letters from Harry Norton 'in which sodomy and mathematics are inextricably mixed'. But Norton, unlike Lytton, James and Hobhouse, is not on Maynard's list of loves for 1906. He was, in fact, in love with James. The four of them found rooms in a cottage six miles south of Inverdruie, from which they would set out on testing excursions into the mountains – one of them, to Ben Muich Dhui, being a twenty-five-mile walk as well as a stiff climb. Lytton suggested making a comprehensive tour of the Western Highlands, but none of his companions was keen. 'I could find no one adventurous enough to share the perils,' he complained to Moore, 'and what are perils unshared?'

Presently he was back at Lancaster Gate. 'I don't know whether I've become sentimental in my old age, but when, in the evening, I thought of you all, I found myself literally in tears,' he had written to Maynard. '. . . I can't think why I continue to live here, in this desolation.' Sanger, Swithinbank and Saxon Sydney-Turner, Norton, MacCarthy and Thoby Stephen all came to see him in his 'vale of desolation'; and letters poured in from Woolf in Ceylon, Moore in Edinburgh and Maynard at Cambridge. 'I have been turning over old letters – a shocking occupation,' he told Maynard. 'All one's old crises rise up like ghosts before one.' Both of them were rather nervous that summer after reading about a pact made by two young men to commit suicide at Clapham Junction. The one who survived knew James, who had written him an indiscreet letter. 'I feel sick and angry,' Lytton confided to Maynard (19 June 1906). '. . . I want to destroy my papers ... my rage is violent against most of this world.' But Maynard thought there was little risk 'so long as no one has anything to do with the lower classes or people off the streets, and there is some discretion in letters'.

Then, in late November, a 'dreadful thing' happened. 'You must be prepared for something terrible,' Lytton wrote to Leonard Woolf. 'You will never see the Goth again. He died yesterday.' He had read the announcement of Thoby Stephen's death in *The Times* on 21 November. 'I am stunned,' he wrote immediately to Maynard. 'The loss is too great, and seems to have taken what is best from life.' The following week he was invited by Vanessa and Virginia Stephen to their home at 46 Gordon Square and told all the details: how Thoby on holiday in Greece had been suffering from what was supposed to be pneumonia, but how his illness had turned out to be typhoid. 'I am overwhelmed, crushed,' Woolf replied to Lytton (12 December 1906). '. . . he was an anchor. He was above everyone in his nobility.' Such an end did not, despite their certain knowledge, ring true. 'I seem to see & hear the Goth all day,' Leonard wrote a month after his death. But Maynard, who had known Thoby mainly through Lytton's legendary accounts, wrote: 'He seems to me now, I don't know why, the kind of person who is doomed to die.'

Lytton was now seeing a lot of Maynard, who had just come down from King's. The two Cambridge exiles planned to spend part of December together in Paris, where Maynard could get to know Duncan better. But since Lytton would not receive payment for his last batch of reviews until January and Maynard had not enough money to pay for them both, they decided to go instead for a week to Rye, putting up at the Mermaid Inn where Lytton had previously taken Sheppard. 'We go out for duty-walks in order to get up appetites for too-constant meals,' Lytton wrote to Saxon Sydney-Turner. 'I am halfway through the Brides' Tragedy; as you said, it's not a patch on the Jest Book[18] – but it has some superb things. – "I've huddled her into the wormy earth!"'

After finishing Beddoes, Lytton turned to Charles Darwin and was enthralled. During the next weeks he read little but the works of Darwin, whom he came to consider one of the greatest stylists in English literature. 'I'm reading the Descent of Man,' he told Duncan on 30 December, '– it's most entertaining, with any number of good stories about Parrots, Butterflies, Capercailzies and Barbary Apes.

'The account of how the Peacock grew his tail is a masterpiece. But the chief charm is Darwin's character, which runs through everything he wrote in a wonderful way. I should like to show you some passages in his Autobiography – really magnificent! He was absolutely good – that is to say, he was without a drop of evil; though his complete simplicity makes him curiously different from any of us, and, I suppose, prevents his reaching the greatest heights of all.'

This discovery of Darwin was the single bright spot to a year which closed for Lytton in much confusion and anguish. During the six months since his return from Menton he had been composing reviews with 'Venus', his fountain pen* – reviews of literary criticism for the *Spectator* and of biographies for *The Speaker*. 'Reviews dribble from Venus somewhat in the manner of Hobber's semen,' he revealed to Maynard who remarked on his growing professionalism as a literary journalist. He was also writing longer pieces for the *Independent Review* which published his 'Mademoiselle de Lespinasse', 'The Poetry of Blake', and an article on Birkbeck Hill's edition of Johnson's *Lives of the Poets*. 'I ought to be making a fortune – at any rate enough to pay off every bill,' he wrote. 'But what an occupation!'

He filled his mind with journeyman work to drive out ill thoughts of Duncan and Hobber. But he was not always successful. His review for *The Speaker* (28 July 1906) of J.E. Farmer's *Versailles and the Court under Louis XIV* 'concludes with a description that could have been inspired by a personal visit', wrote the Indian scholar K.R. Srinivasa Iyengar many years later. In fact Lytton had gone there only in imagination, his heart following Duncan who was staying in Versailles for part of that summer and who had invited Hobhouse to visit him there. Writing letters to him was like dancing on egg shells, and Lytton used Farmer's book to help with this delicate feat. 'It is full of plans and pictures, and I think it ought to be amusing to write about,' he wrote. 'I hope, with the aid of your descriptions, to be able to make it appear that I have constantly been there. The poor deluded public!'

When his genitals ceased troubling him and there were no arrests for buggery reported in the papers, when he was cooped up in Lancaster Gate without distractions and 'Venus' ran dry, then Duncan would occupy his mind. He read his letters again and 'I feel a physical pain inside me', he confessed to Maynard (21 May 1906). 'I imagine everything, and can hardly breathe . . . how long is it to last? When he comes back, what Hell! And when he goes away, what damnation!'

Duncan came and went and came again. 'I have never known such anguish,' Lytton cried out to Maynard (21 October 1906). '. . . I am a fool, and lose myself in treacherous dreams.' His emotional turmoil prompted a multitude of familiar ailments. 'I think it's a disease that I've got . . . Rabies

---

* So called because, to make it write, he had to twist its bottom, causing the nib to rise from the waves.

amantis.' Sometimes he thought it would be better to break away and have done with it. But the one thing he dreaded more than his present wretchedness was falling out of love. 'Oh my dear,' Maynard replied, 'I don't see any hope of your ever falling out of love with him.' Lytton knew that he should not always be complaining to Maynard, but could not help himself. 'That that little devil should despise me, and with justice, is my lowest infamy,' he wrote on 28 November. 'That he should register my tears, and dishonour my abandonments, my failures, the miserable embraces I can't withhold! – That he should say that he pities me perhaps! – I want to shake the universe to dust and ashes! Hell! Hell! Hell!'

In contrast to these letters to Maynard, is the moderation of his correspondence with Duncan himself. 'How I manage to write to him, & keep up a cheerful face as I do, I can't conceive.' These two concurrent and complementary sets of letters show Lytton's peculiar duality, the layer of shyness which conceals his palpitating feelings helping to convey the misconception of him as dry and aloof.

After a family dinner at Lancaster Gate Lytton writes to apologize in case he may inadvertently have said something – anything – during the course of the long dismal meal to offend Duncan. If he has been hurt, Duncan must forgive Lytton's stupidity; if not, then he must forgive these troublesome apologies. Whatever the case, Lytton demands forgiveness. Duncan, however, doesn't remember being pained, and is sure that Lytton would never hurt or offend him. Perhaps, he suggests, he had failed to comprehend something. Incomprehension can, physiognomically speaking, resemble pain – doesn't Lytton agree? In any event he himself intended to write to apologize about his beastly behaviour the previous week at a picture gallery they had visited together. He had felt out of sorts – and the pictures hadn't helped. But probably Lytton, with that incomparably generous nature of his, had already forgiven him. Anyway, Lytton must not, he begs, bother to answer this note.

Lytton's reply comes by return of post, expressing his gratitude both for the letter itself, and for the knowledge that his mania for inferences had led him astray. But he is horrified at Duncan referring to his earlier behaviour as beastly. On the contrary it was he, Lytton, who was at fault. He ought to have overcome his wretched sensitiveness – no, *selfishness* – and saved Duncan from feeling that he had behaved badly.

The tussle for forgiveness and blame now warms up. Duncan at once counters Lytton's claim of selfishness with the plea that he himself is without a sense of humour. Not only that, but he had got into the absurd way of crediting Lytton with special powers of telepathy. This had, in fact, once led him to be put out by a joke Lytton made about Hobber, with whom he was still hopelessly in love, but whom he was trying to forget. It was foolish of him to have done anything but laugh. In his answer Lytton again quickly shoulders all the available guilt. He had got into the habit, he explains, of making jokes at serious things; it relieved (to his mind) the heaviness of existence, like the drops of lemon on a pancake. He was truly sorry. 'I don't want you ever to think of my feelings, but I did hope that you simply *knew* how much I cared.'

The last unforgiving word belongs to Duncan. 'My brutality was rather a bitter return for your perfect goodness. When I look back and see what I have ever given you in return for it, I nearly collapse at my perfect unworthiness. O! Lytton I really mean it, when was there anyone so unselfish and noble as you. If it weren't for you I am sure I should not be able to bear life now.'

The labyrinthine pattern of Lytton's emotional life seemed to be set irrevocably in the original passions and inspirations of the past. True, Thoby had gone – but his need for a distant pedestal-hero was now less urgent than before; and besides, Thoby would later be replaced by George Mallory, the handsome mountaineer also fated to die young. The brief reappearance in London of Duncan had proved to him, if proof were needed, that the other figures remained as dominant as ever. At any rate he could see no one as yet to take their place. 'What will happen to me?' he had asked Maynard; and so far as he himself could tell, the answer was: Nothing. He would go on living at 69 Lancaster Gate; he would go on visiting Cambridge; he would continue his career as journalist and also his revolutions round the far-off Duncan, sending out incoherent messages to Maynard.

Duncan disappeared back to Paris on 19 January without saying goodbye. The next day Lytton wrote to him: 'Last night, when I came down to dinner and saw that you had taken away grandpapa's portrait, I knew that you had gone, and was utterly crushed. It was all I could do not to burst into tears at dinner, and afterwards Mama asked me if I was ill, and I nearly gave way altogether.' A few days later his bewilderment and sense of loss arranged themselves into a sonnet, 'The Enigma', which he composed while walking between Piccadilly and the Charing Cross Road. It is a characteristic example of the rhetorical innuendo he used to record the crises of his love life:

> Oh, tell me! – I have seen the strangest things:
> I know not what: beginnings, threads and shears.
> And I have heard a moaning at my ears,
> And curious laughter, and mysterious wings.

Have friends or angels tricked me? Oh, what brings
This river of intolerable tears
Over my soul? And all these hopes and fears?
These joys, and these profound imaginings?

Will no one tell me? Ah! Save me, it seems,
The puzzle's plain to all. I am as one
Who wanders in an unknown market-place,
Through bustling crowds with business to be done.
Vain are my words, and my conjectures dreams,
I cannot greet the unremembered face.

SEVEN

Intentions

'The dangers of freedom are appalling!'
Lytton Strachey to Duncan Grant (12 April 1907)

I

THE TRAVAILS OF A JOURNEYMAN

The year 1907 was to see the first links in a tightening chain of events that would split apart Lytton's old routine. No sign of these changes, however, was evident in the predictable beginnings to this year. Soon after Duncan Grant had returned to Paris – 'that DAMNED TOWN' as Lytton called it – he limped off to the Homeres at Chipping Norton. Here he was given a little upstairs sitting-room and, alone with 'Venus', he remained quietly working at a memorial essay on his godfather, the first Earl of Lytton. Crouching over the hot gas-fire, his spirit seemed to vaporize and curiously re-form so that he could do and say all the things a woman could do and say. If only he had been a woman! In these androgynous trances he seemed contented 'and I really think that if I had three wishes, I should wish for three fires – one behind me and one on each side of me – as hot as the one in front'.

The Homere sisters, noticing his wistful expression, concluded that he must be unhappily in love with the beautiful Vanessa Stephen. It was Ianthe – 'who always talks about interesting things' – who came out with their suspicions. Lytton shrilled with amazed laughter, at the same time secretly wondering whether it ought not to be as they imagined.

His meditations were brought up short by the advances of Angelica Homere, the amorous youngest sister and a prime beauty, who, inflamed by sudden jealousy, flirted with him so boldly that Lytton grew terrified lest she should launch a physical assault on him. He was thus obliged to play an ironically familiar role – that of Duncan Grant to her Lytton Strachey. Even so, the dialogues he failed to avoid!

Angelica: 'Will you be in London when I'm there in March?'
Lytton: 'I'm afraid I shall be in the country on a visit.'

Angelica: 'Oh dear! I had looked forward to seeing you so much …
D'you know that you're perfectly beautiful?'

Lytton (casual and unmoved): 'Of course. I've always known that.'

Angelica (in tears): 'Do you hate me very much?'

While he was still in 'Homereland', a letter arrived from Desmond MacCarthy. That summer he was going to marry Molly Warre-Cornish, a talented daughter of the Vice Provost and Librarian at Eton (Lytton sent some candlesticks as a present) after which he would earn his living by editing, in Micawber fashion, a periodical to be called the *New Quarterly*. This paper was the whim of a wealthy, boorish friend and patron of MacCarthy's, a man of grand literary pretensions called George Arthur Paley. MacCarthy promised Lytton about one hundred pounds a year (equivalent to £4300 in 1994) if he would become a regular contributor – also promising that he need not write about anything that did not interest him. This represented a real opportunity for Lytton. He wanted to sever his connections with the *Spectator* and, in the intervals between his *New Quarterly* contributions, devote himself to some major literary work: perhaps reconstruct his *Warren Hastings*, and, more exciting, compose a play – a tragedy on Queen Elizabeth. And then, of course, he would have to live apart from the family, on whom, at the same time, he must still remain to some extent dependent financially. The trouble was that the Secretary of State for India, 'honest John Morley', had refused to give Sir Richard Strachey a pension, and no one knew what was to happen. MacCarthy's letter, in spite of all the quandaries it uncovered, cheered Lytton. 'I am trying to shake myself free of most of my entanglements,' he wrote to Dorothy Bussy, 'and when I've succeeded in doing so – ho! for the chef-d'oeuvre!'

Soon after his return to London, he went to see MacCarthy and they discussed the new paper, enthusing over its prospects. 'It's probably to be called the London Quarterly,' Lytton told Duncan (11 February 1907), 'and may possibly come out in July … [MacCarthy's] a very wild editor, but he's cheerful and seems to believe in me. The publisher is Dent, who will do it free of charge in order, MacCarthy thinks, to get the reputation of dealing with first-class literary gents.'

Although nothing was yet settled, Lytton felt that he ought to inform St Loe Strachey, his cousin and editor of the *Spectator*. Though it was by far the most widely read of all the political weeklies (selling twenty thousand copies each week mainly, it was rumoured, to all the country vicarages), the *Spectator* was something of a joke among the intelligentsia. On coming down from Cambridge Lytton had been taken on as a reviewer largely owing to St Loe's fondness for Lady Strachey. But he was never comfortable in its somewhat pompous pages, especially since St Loe loved altering everyone's prose and applying his resounding editorial first person plural.

'I interviewed him in his office,' Lytton wrote afterwards to Duncan (21 February 1907), 'and told him that for the present I should not review any more books for him – the first step towards Liberty! He was most gracious, and said that if ever I wanted to begin again he'd be charmed to let me.' He also invited Lytton to call on him at Herbert House, a large, archetypal Victorian mansion in Belgrave Square, with faded carpets, red plush curtains and coloured glass chandeliers, where he lived with his wife 'Oriental Amy'. The place was full of bourgeois hangers-on 'all in laced boots', including Sidney Lee whose *Shakespeare and the Modern Stage* Lytton had recently criticized in the *Spectator* for treating the sonnets as literary exercises rather than the flowering of sexual passion. 'Poor dear old St Loe strikes me now as a trifle *épuisé*,' Lytton commented to James shortly afterwards, 'with moustaches more than ever fading, and even spectacles (when no one's there). Amy is *une matrone* in blue silk with amber necklaces . . .'

Finally, it was agreed that Lytton should, after all, continue his reviewing for the *Spectator* until his appointment as a regular contributor to the *New Quarterly* began. He could hardly wait.

*

As if to celebrate his new hopes, Lytton at once embarked on a succession of London gaieties – lunch at the Savoy, dinner at the Carlton and the Ladies' Athenaeum, a French play, performances of *The Gondoliers* and *The Marriage of Figaro*. His hostess on all these occasions was that noble woman, Lady Colvile. 'In the intervals of these orgies,' he confided to Duncan, 'I hope to finish my review of Lord Lytton for the Independent, but it's damned difficult. I lay on the butter as thick as I can – there's such precious little bread.'

The one topic of conversation among the Stracheys at this time was the first large-scale demonstration which the Society for Women's Suffrage was to stage in their nation-wide campaign for emancipation – three thousand ladies proceeding from Hyde Park Corner, flanked by mounted police, to Exeter Hall, in what became known as the 'Mud March'. Lytton's sister Pippa, who was later a dynamic secretary of the Fawcett Society,[1] had commandeered family and friends to assist with the organization of this parade. James Strachey and Harry Norton were summoned from Cambridge to waft the ladies to their places in the hall; Maynard Keynes was conscripted to help marshal them in the park; and even Swithinbank was fetched up from Oxford as a supernumerary volunteer. Pippa, who interviewed the police at Scotland Yard daily, persuaded the apprehensive Lytton to join the men's league for the promotion of female suffrage. 'I believe the ladies will try to forbid prostitution,' he wrote to James; 'and will they stop there?'

The grand procession was held on the second Saturday in February. As the date approached, Lytton realized that he could not face it and fled away to Cambridge. But here, too, he was solicited by inviting women, being pressed into tea at Newnham with Mrs Sidgwick,[2] 'a faded monolith of ugly beauty, with a nervous laugh, and an infinitely remote mind, which, mysteriously, realizes all'. He also saw the remnants of his friends – those who had managed to escape Pippa's enlistment – Sheppard, Walter Lamb, and the shy and fantastic Dilly Knox, about whom he had now changed his mind. 'His beauty was transcendent, and his feelings seemed to me superb.'

A few months earlier the 'divine ambiguous Knox' had produced a little farce called *The Limit*, bicycling on to the stage as 'Screachey', an aesthete with a long black beard. Cambridge was still 'suffused with the golden glow of homosexuality', Knox's biographer Penelope Fitzgerald writes. '... The amiable abstracted figure of Dilly, among many shifting intrigues, impressed Lytton Strachey, with his highly developed comic structure.' Then, after seeing him 'wonderfully décolleté' in Sheppard's rooms, Lytton felt himself becoming infatuated with Dilly. Otherwise this quick bird's-eye view of Cambridge was rather lowering – days of frost and slush, fires faint and few, and the appalling sight of James's half-demolished breakfast with its broken eggshells and spilt tea over the table to greet him on arrival and again each morning when he rose at twelve from his icy bed. Left unaided to put coals on the fire, he was unable to find a shovel, the tongs broke, and he was obliged to bend down and prise out each monstrous black lump with trembling fingers. Even the miraculous divinity of Knox did not quite atone.

Under Pippa's management the Suffrage procession went off without a hitch and once it was safely over, Lytton rushed back to London. The round of dissipations started up again and he was 'as cheerful as a Kangaroo'. Life seemed full of exciting possibilities. Those waiters, for instance, at the Carlton. He almost fainted when they bent smartly over to serve him with brussels sprouts and peas and roast potatoes.

One worry was the reluctant decision of the family to leave Lancaster Gate. The news left Lytton feeling curiously empty. He had never known a time when the great brooding mansion was not looming over him. Now he was simply told that the upkeep was too expensive for the family with its depleted fortunes – a common-sense explanation which hardly matched the significance of the change. Lady Strachey decided that they should move later that year to a dilapidated house in Belsize Park Gardens, Hampstead. 'There is a basement billiard-room,' Lytton wrote to Duncan after inspecting the new house, '– the darkest chamber I've ever seen in my life, and without a billiard table. Your mother, mine and I found ourselves locked into it, and thought we'd be discovered three crumbling skeletons – forty years hence. Fortunately I was able to leap a wall and attract a caretaker.'

Towards the end of February, Lytton was offered a room at Trinity and hurried back to Cambridge and to 'my beloved Adolphe' as he now called Dilly Knox. He was determined to make 'a declaration' and put the 'Knox question' to the test. Dilly had 'a wonderful veil of ugliness' that he was able to lower at any minute over his face. His method was 'to lure you on with his beauty, until at last, just as you step forward to seize a kiss, or whatever else you may want to seize, he lets down a veil, and you simply fall back disgusted. Isn't it a horrid trick? And then, of course, when you ... begin to wonder what you could have found in him, he removes the veil, and says he must go back to King's.'

What struck him about Knox was his resemblance to Swithinbank; and he was confronted with the same difficulties in their relationship – the embarrassments, the tantalizing ambiguities. To take an example: one evening they held a discussion on the relative merits and demerits of sapphism and sodomy – a fruitful subject, Lytton would have thought, under almost any circumstances. And yet, though it was taken up as the most natural thing in the world, it simply petered out, the veil came down and Dilly disappeared in a puff of pipe smoke. Then there was the dreadful discovery that he had taken to wearing black spectacles. Sitting with Swithinbank a little later in the sunshine of St James's Park, Lytton had discussed the crisis and Swithinbank revealed that he had a passion for Dilly too – 'sometimes'. 'You'll never have one again!' Lytton told him. 'You'll never get over the eye-glasses.' But Swithinbank claimed he would solve the problem by snatching them off. For Lytton, however, they symbolized dusty middle-age and arid academicism. He had noticed the same thing happening to Harry Norton, whose end would surely be 'the Solicitor's Office, a wife, and £60,000 a year.' As for Dilly, he was as charming as ever, liking everyone equally, but would never be more than an 'Endless Possibility'. Lytton could see his future all too clearly; he'd be elected a Fellow of King's, and waste away his life in a dim miasma of mathematical mazes and the ancient metres of Herodas.

Lytton's failure to strike up any new friendships, or to extend the boundaries of his old associations during these Cambridge weeks, came as a setback. The world was one vast negative, he reflected, and he was its full stop. There was no startling new embryo, no Rupert Brooke to gaze at and wonder over. 'I linger on vaguely from day to day,' he confessed to Maynard (27 February 1907), 'partly in the dim hope of excitement, and partly from being too lazy to pack. I see now, though, very very clearly that nothing will ever happen, and that life is all a cheat.'

In the third week of March, he tore himself away and went to stay with Desmond and Molly MacCarthy at the Green Farm, Timworth, near Bury St Edmunds. This was a large farmhouse (its back windows overlooking the cowsheds with their great clattering of milk churns) with a somewhat decayed garden, and fine flat sweeping fields of turnips and cabbages all around. The newly married MacCarthys had only recently moved in, and Molly was still hanging chintz curtains and arranging furniture. It was not wholly comfortable. The meals, for one thing, were never punctual; and the fires, for another, were continually going out. Desmond talked much about the *New Quarterly* and whether the *Nation* was better than the *Speaker*, and in the evenings they strolled together round the splendid park near by, with its great lake and wood. This was the part of each day that Lytton enjoyed most, the domestic inconveniences forgotten in the dream-like landscape – the wide stretch of water with the light on it, and the surrounding forms of trees vanishing in haze. It was enchanting and he wondered whether he too should live in the country.

Molly MacCarthy's mother, Mrs Cornish,[3] was also staying with them, and could be offered up as a figure of amusement in Lytton's letters to Duncan Grant. She was, he wrote (23 March 1907), 'incredibly affected, queer, stupid and intelligent. She flowed with reflections on life, and reminiscences of George Eliot, and criticisms of obscure French poetesses who flourished in 1850:

'She was damned difficult to answer though. What is one to say when a person says – "Ah, isn't it delightful to think of all those dear animals asleep around us?" Do you know her remark to an Eton youth when he was introduced to her? "Oh, Mr Jones, has it ever occurred to you how very different a cow is from a thrush?" I dare say she's mad, and I'm pretty sure she's a minx, and a minx of sixty. "Can't one tempt you to Eton, Mr Strachey? You'd find all Walpole's letters in the library, and a great many delightful boys." What was one to say to that?'

Lytton was already deep in negotiations with G.E. Moore about another Easter reading-party. The problems were endless. Where should they go?

Yorkshire would almost certainly be too cold; Lytton could still vividly recall the snowstorms of two Easters ago, and those vast slabs of salt beef at the Crown Hotel. What about the Lizard once more? 'I long to see the charming place again,' he wrote to Moore. But Penmenner House had unfortunately been snapped up by a party of Christian young gentlemen. Eventually they engaged rooms at Court Barton, in the village of North Molton, near Exmoor in Devon. The ethical intricacies of choosing 'the elect of the elect' were even more difficult than usual. Too many people would distress Moore; too few would distress the landlady. Besides, they must be the *right* people. Moore would naturally bring Ainsworth, as always; and, as always, Lytton would bring James. But after that the composition of the party was uncertain. How could they make sure that Hobby, for example, was given the impression – without any actual lies being told – that there was to be no reading-party that year? How to ensure that Bob Trevy did not stay the full three weeks? Would MacCarthy come at the last minute? Then what of Saxon Sydney-Turner? And how, on top of all these dilemmas, to fit in Norton and Keynes?

Harry and Maynard had decided to spend the week beforehand in Paris, together with James. Lytton thought this an excellent scheme. They ought, he said, to do the thing *en grand seigneur*, and put up at the St James Hotel in the rue St-Honoré. Harry and James were silent, but Maynard gently demurred. Perhaps, he suggested, it might be cheaper, and rather more friendly to stay with Duncan at 22 rue Delambre near the Boulevard Raspail. Lytton was at once enthusiastic. Why hadn't *he* thought of it? – especially since that very week he had written to Vanessa Stephen urging her 'to look up my little cousin, when you're in Paris'.

He waved the three of them off at Charing Cross station, and returned home to dream. It gave him a stab of vicarious pleasure, this day-dreaming, heightened by just a shade of melancholy. He was anxious that Maynard, with his dry aloofness, should not bore Duncan. He saw visions of them all crowding through the Louvre, or lingering among the fountains and the oranges which he had lovingly described but never actually seen at Versailles, or again, if it was warm and the sun shining, wandering in the Tuileries Gardens where Mademoiselle de Lespinasse walked not so very long ago hearing the same *che farò* that they might hear that very night. Were they in danger of falling into the clutches of the police? If they did, then of course they must at once telegraph him so that he might busy himself collecting certificates of good character from Hobhouse, Knox, Sheppard and the rest. Maynard, with his multifarious connections, would be quite safe, as he could get the son of a bishop to swear to his exemplary behaviour while at Eton. Duncan would be let off as an artist; and no one could look at James and find him guilty of anything. So that poor Harry Norton was really the only one of them at risk, and he, very probably, would be excused as an *anglais fou*.

Now that Maynard had quit King's and was languishing on his stool at the India Office, Lytton felt more kindly towards him. Poor old Maynard! It really was more like the old times now that things were going wrong again. He felt closer to him than for many months. Yet the check to Maynard's progress was only momentary, and soon enough good fortune was to blaze down on him again. More successful mountain-climbing would follow, and, if that were not enough, more golf. By June 1908, when he resigned from the India Office to take up a lectureship at Cambridge, his role as Lytton's brother confessor was already being partly taken over by James. And before the following March, when Maynard was finally elected a Fellow of King's, the substitution would pretty well be complete. Once Maynard's triumph was assured, their old intimacy never fully revived.

The reading-party at North Molton was to begin in the final week of March and last for three weeks. Within its limitations – of comfort, warmth, good company but no love – it would be one of their most agreeable gatherings. 'This country is in the region of Exmoor (except that there is no moor to be seen),' Lytton writes to Duncan, 'and I like it, with its rolling hills vanishing away to the horizon, and its valleys with streams and trees in them, and its general air of health. We are in a farmhouse, touching a church, and there are some rather nice turkeys to be seen strutting about and gobbling outside my bedroom window, and there is plenty of Devonshire cream at meals, and there are a good many amusing (and instructive) books, and there is a piano which Moore plays in the evening.'

There is a 'surplusage of beef and Devonshire cream' to be disposed of by country walks; there is a village shop with bull's-eyes in it; there are two sitting-rooms and a garden; and upstairs there are feather beds and books. They read novels and go to sleep in the sun dreaming of masterpieces they will one day create. 'In a few minutes we shall all be tramping through the sun. And then more cream, and then more beef, and then somnolence, and then bed – solitary bed.'

Lytton had taken with him his Warren Hastings dissertation, intending to prepare the typescript for future publication. He spends one hour a day emending and rewriting parts of it and adding an Introduction.[4] He also writes a good deal of verse, including a long satire in the manner of Pope. Long ago, it recounts, a great dearth of things to say afflicted the human race. The situation baffled human intelligence until one day a young quick-minded shepherd put forward a startling innovation.

O mortals! Would you know the one sure way
Of saying much when there is naught to say?
Imitate me! Construct the flowing line,
With numbers' art your syllables entwine,
Swell out the pompous verse with stress and pause,
And govern all by metre's mystic laws!
Then shall your wandering words move sweetly on
When the last shred of meaning has quite gone,
Then empty feet transport you where you will,
And simple rhythm waft you forward still,
Then rhyme, self-spun, shall wrap you round and round
And all your folly vanish in a sound.

This speech was considered blasphemy, and the shepherd was hanged
from the nearest tree by a crowd of indignant citizens. Generations later,
however, an altar is erected where this tree stood to the poor shepherd's
martyrdom. The articulate religion which subsequently flourishes there
encourages the ennui to which Lytton felt so susceptible, and exalts the
cliché of which he makes intimate use in his writing.

Here maudlin lovers seeking how to spin
Poetic cobwebs from their faint and thin
Imaginations, found inspirèd aid,
Murmuring nonsense in the holy shade.
Here many a pompous simpleton pursued
Through its dull coils the eternal platitude,
Found out that what was fated came to pass,
That mortal beings perished like the grass,
That all the world was subject to decay,
That he who gave might likewise take away,
That much was known to men, yet more was not,
And naught was certain in the human lot.
Here too would hired laureates fill their lays
With ever-fresh incontinence of praise,
Proclaiming in the same insipid breath
A royal birth, or victory, or death,
Then hymn aloud in strains as void as air
The copulation of a princely pair.

After their few days with Duncan, the Parisian Apostles arrived at North
Molton. This was the first time Maynard had been invited to one of

Moore's reading-parties. 'At this moment Keynes is lying on the rug beside me,' Lytton tells Swithinbank (31 March 1907), 'turning over the leaves of a handbook on obstetrics which seems to keep him absorbed. Norton is next to him on a camp-stool, and it is he who is writing mathematics. Next to him is Bob Trevy, under an umbrella, very vague and contented . . . I should have mentioned that I am on a basket chair (with plenty of cushions in case of accidents), and that I am perfectly happy, as I am writing to you instead of doing what I ought to be doing, viz., composing a preface to Warren Hastings . . .'

Then everything breaks up. Keynes and Norton leave for London, the weather deteriorates into ceaseless rain, Sanger retires upstairs to his feather bed with a severe cold, and James collapses with toothache. Lytton huddles in the smaller sitting-room with Ainsworth and Moore, who, in the throes of a philosophical crisis, finds relief in declaiming the novels of Captain Marryat. 'Has the rumour reached you of the astounding news?' Lytton asks Maynard.

'Moore has shivered his philosophy into atoms, and can't for the life of him construct a new one. He "doesn't know what to think" – about *anything* – propositions, eternal being, Truth itself! In fact he's pretty well chucked up the sponge. Isn't it shocking? Christ denying Christianity! Hegel gapes for him, and shuddering worlds hide their horror-stricken heads. He's a great man, and if he's not got water on the brain he'll come through, and soar to even more incredible heights. But has he got water on the brain? Shall we ever know?'

Moore's volte-face is in fact the outcome of a succession of growing doubts and qualifications with which he has been wrestling since Christmas. But by the end of the reading-party he is emerging from his perplexity. 'The Yen has discovered that when you say "So and so is so and so's father", the word "father" in the sentence has no meaning whatever. It's a rather important discovery; but I suppose it'll be blasted soon enough.*

The reading-party disperses on 18 April. 'London is a shocking-place as far as people go,' Lytton complained to James the following month. But a few distractions, mostly pictorial, lightened the gloom. There was an exhibition of Simon Bussy's paintings at Leighton House which Lytton

---

* In an explanatory postscript to this letter, Lytton added: 'When you say "So and so is so and so's father", you mean "So and so occupies a relation towards so and so to which the word 'father' may be properly applied" – and that's all; you needn't (and probably don't) know what "father" means.'

advised everyone to see – 'They are all pastels, and most of them dreams of beauty' – also a private view at the National Gallery more remarkable for the onlookers than the pictures – 'That astounding creature Pinero[5] was there ... Large red face, immense black eyebrows, rolling eyes, vast nose, theatrical manner, bandanna handkerchief, trousers *à la rigueur*, and patent leather boots with brown fronts' – and finally, at the Carfax Gallery, 'a charming collection of Max Beerbohm's caricatures – many of them really beautiful, and some like Blake – all (to my mind) the height of amusement'.

That spring and early summer Lytton read the reminiscences and letters of Carlyle – 'a psalm-singing Scotchman with a power of observation which knocks you flat' – and the novels of Joseph Conrad whom he described as 'very superb – in fact the *only* superb novelist now, except old Henry James, etc. – and Lord Jim is full of splendid things. The Nigger of the Narcissus is another very wonderful one, and perhaps the best of all is a shortish story called Heart of Darkness in a book called Youth.' Among recently published books there was his friend E.M. Forster's *The Longest Journey*. 'I don't think you know Forster,' he wrote to Duncan (30 April 1907), '– a queer King's brother, and a great friend of Hom's.

'He's just written his second novel, and there's a rather amusing account of Cambridge in it, and Cambridge people. One of the very minor characters is asked to breakfast by one of his friends and replies by putting his hand on his stomach, to show that he's breakfasted already. MacCarthy thinks that this is me. Do you? But the rest of the book is a dreary fandango. After the hero (who's Forster himself), the principal figure is Hom.'

As for his own writing, he was planning two major essays, one biographical, the other critical. The first of these, his final contribution to the *Independent Review* which was now re-forming under the name of the *Albany Review*, was on Lady Mary Wortley Montagu, 'a magnificent 18th-century lady, who wrote letters, and introduced inoculation into Europe', he explained to Duncan (13 May 1907). 'She was sublime, and no one knows it nowadays ... She had only two tastes – intellect and lust. Imagine her pessimism! But her honesty and courage were equal to every emergency, and she never gave into anything or anybody, and died fighting. Great Lady Mary!'

The second of these essays reflects a complementary taste. He had been introduced to the writings of Beddoes by Saxon Sydney-Turner. Like

Lady Mary Wortley Montagu, Beddoes, he felt, was an unjustly disregarded figure. His long reappraisal of Beddoes's work was commissioned for the opening number of MacCarthy's *New Quarterly*, now due out in the autumn.

He had many other plans, too, though 'I regret to say that I go to sleep after lunch more often than not', he admitted to Duncan (18 June 1907). 'The other day I actually did it after breakfast! But that undoubtedly was a sign of disease – I wonder, though of *what* disease? – "The disease, sir, of sloth!" a vicar would probably say. But one need pay no attention to vicars.

'I am in my room. James is opposite, reading Chinese poetry. I'm sure I must have shown you the book – one of the most charming in the world.[7] I want to write about Madame du Deffand,[8] and Baudelaire, and Beddoes, and Marivaux and God knows who. Why on earth don't I? "Sloth, sir, sloth!"'

2

THE SPECTATORIAL EXPERIENCE

On 22 May, Lancaster Gate was put up for public auction. Lady Strachey wanted the place to go for not less than a magnificent three thousand pounds (equivalent to £130,000 in 1994). Lytton, who liked to imagine that they could let it furnished for the season to some wealthy American 'and live on the proceeds in lodgings for the next ten years', thought this too high a price, and his view seemed to be proved right when the auction came to nothing. However, it soon turned out that there was a prospective purchaser hanging in the wind, with whom Lady Strachey eventually succeeding in coming to terms, and so the family postponed their move until September.

In the meantime, day-to-day life at Lancaster Gate took on a more desperate air. 'I have now read through all meals steadily,' Lytton told Maynard two days after the abortive auction, '. . . I think I may have spoken three sentences today.' And to Duncan he grumbled: 'I really haven't the vaguest idea what I've done since I came back to London. The only certain thing is that I've done no work. Oh, devils! devils! – I've been to no plays, and heard no music, and hardly talked to anyone but Keynes (and him I believe only twice). On Thursday I had dinner with Clive and Vanessa . . . They seemed somewhat less insistent on the fact that they were in love with each other, which made it easier to talk to them, and I enjoyed myself pretty well.' Such a passage, with its grudging admission of enjoyment, is characteristic of Lytton at this time. He did not want anyone to underrate his discontent.

Among the more interesting of his social engagements was a dinner-party with the artist William Rothenstein, his wife Alice, and Isabel Fry, a younger sister of Roger, who had been refused permission to study at Cambridge on the grounds that her father's conversation at dinner was education enough, but who later went on to become a brilliant educationist. 'The dinner was remarkable', Lytton wrote to Duncan (13 May 1907), 'chiefly because Rothenstein and his wife were there.

'It was *the* Rothenstein – very Jewish and small and monkey-like; I believe the one who was at the Friday Club,[9] and who annoyed me, must have been his younger brother [Albert], because wasn't he rather podgy and hubristic? At any rate, I was annoyed almost as much this time – and by very much the same style of vagueness. I rather peevishly dissented, and I fear he was offended! He was nice, and extraordinarily meek, but oh! the rot he talked! Madam[10] was a blonde, somewhat devoid of [undecipherable], worshipping him, and enraged with me for daring to disagree with him! My philistinism was increased by the frightful fact that I alone of the party was in evening dress! A haughty and exclusive aristocrat was what I appeared to be, no doubt, trampling poor artists underfoot as if they were so many beetles! And I unfortunately let out that I lived in Lancaster Gate! "Horribly rich," I'm sure she murmured to him, or rather "Orribly rich". Shall I call on them, when we've settled in a bijou residence in Hampstead, dressed in my third best brogalines and without a collar? But even then I should never be able to agree that Nature was only one aspect of Art, that Beauty was the expression of True Emotions, and that Music, Poetry, and Painting were the plastic embodiments of Life.'

William Rothenstein also left a description of this meeting in his *Men and Memories*,[11] though his account is somewhat qualified by judicious afterthoughts. 'Lytton Strachey's look in those early days was very unlike his later appearance,' Rothenstein recalled:

'Long, slender, with a receding chin, that gave a look of weakness to his face, with a thin, cracked voice, I thought him typical of the Cambridge intellectual. Dining one night with Isabel Fry, I recollect saying that poetry, usually regarded as a vague and high-falutin' art by many, was in fact the clearest expression of man's thoughts. Strachey replied acidly.

Who, indeed, was I to talk of matters with which I was not concerned? And I thought that here was the cultured University man, who lies in wait, hoping one may say something foolish, or inaccurate, and then springs out to crush one, in high falsetto tones. But I was mistaken. Of course Lytton Strachey was much more than a cultured Cambridge man; he was to become a master of English prose; and with reputation came a beard, and long hair, and a cloak and sombrero, which gave weight and solemnity to an appearance previously not very noticeable. I think Lytton Strachey was of so nervous a temper, that he needed some defensive armour to cover his extreme sensitiveness, and a weapon with a sharp edge, with which to protect himself. He suffered fools less genially than Max [Beerbohm], to their faces at least.'

While preparations for the move to Hampstead were being made, Lytton felt obliged to remain in London[12] with only one weekend in Cambridge, and another in Oxford. At Cambridge the lilacs were in full bloom, the horse chestnuts flowering, 'the backs and river pullulating with undergraduates in flannels, and prostitutes in tights and spangles – the whole thing really delightful'. The Apostles crowded into Sheppard's rooms to redemolish Christianity, but the sight of Dilly Knox in heavy black spectacles was a shock. Though they were to remain friendly – Knox was keen for Lytton to write a biography of that 'deluded individual' Jesus Christ – the veil of academicism had finally descended.

Another shock awaited him at Oxford. He dined off cold duck and champagne with the governor of the Seychelles; he breakfasted with Granville Proby,[13] a fat, aristocratic Old Etonian friend of Maynard's, with Geoffrey Scott,[14] 'a bad character, all egoism and love of amusement and importance for their own sakes ... clever, and amusing and extremely scandalous', with Dillwyn Knox's younger brother Ronnie,[15] 'a christian and a prig, and a self-sufficient little insignificant wretch!' and with James Elroy Flecker,[16] whom he looked forward to meeting and who made no particular impression on him; he lunched with Swithinbank on strawberries and cream, and saw Jack Beazley, resplendently beautiful with high complexion, and curling red-golden hair; he had tea with the Raleighs, and met a professor of Greek and a doctor who had recently examined a notorious murderer. Everything was as agreeable as he could have wished. In the evening he strolled with Swithinbank round the Magdalen College cloisters. It was not difficult to imagine among those medieval stones the monks and novices of the Middle Ages with their paternosters, atonements, penances, secret preoccupations. Had he been alone in that oppressive gloom he might have felt quite nervous. But he was with 'Swithin', at the sight of whom, if the Universe were conducted as it should be, the sinister antiquities of Magdalen would scatter like remnants from a dream when one wakes up. He was lucky to have such a friend.

As the two of them walked in the evening sun, Swithinbank let drop the news that he had applied for the post of sanitary inspector in the Fiji Islands. It was a job for which, he believed, there was little competition. Once he had been convinced that this was not some new style of joke, Lytton did what he could to dissuade his friend from such a scatterbrained exploit. But Swithinbank, having failed to get a Fellowship at Balliol, was curiously adamant. 'He has taken it into his head', Lytton wrote to James with what, it seemed to him, was only slight exaggeration, 'that there is only one thing for him to do – viz. to become Inspector General of Brothels in the Fiji Islands. Did you ever hear of such a thing? Nothing will induce him to change his mind; and he hopes to sail in July!'

Lytton's consternation was all the greater since the heavily bespectacled Knox – the only possible successor to Swithinbank, waiting in the wings of his amatory life while Duncan still hovered elusively on-and-off-stage – had been eliminated as a romantic understudy that very month. The absurdity of it was that Swithinbank could quite easily become a master at Winchester which he would thoroughly enjoy, whereas the drainage system of Fiji really *couldn't* please him. Something must be done.

Hurrying back to London, Lytton conferred with Maynard, and both agreed that here was a matter for decisive intervention and counterplot. Lytton went off to see his cousin, Sir Charles Strachey, in the Colonial Office, who condemned the idea as absurd. Lytton handed this official verdict to Maynard who wrote off to Swithinbank's father, a clergyman, imploring him in the name of God to prevail upon his son not to go, and painting all the vices and horrors of Fiji in their most lurid lights. A silence followed. Then came a telegram from poor Swithinbank – 'Fijis are off!' So the situation was saved.

In London another crisis was approaching. Towards the end of June, St Loe Strachey wrote inviting Lytton to join the *Spectator* staff. He proposed that, with effect from October, Lytton should review a book each week for a salary of one hundred and fifty pounds per year (equivalent to £6,500 in 1994). It was a difficult and depressing decision for Lytton to have to make. The emolument was not great, but with MacCarthy's *New Quarterly* starting up at the same time and taking the place of the now defunct *Independent Review*, it would amount to a livelihood of two hundred and fifty pounds a year (equivalent to £10,750 in 1994). For a few days he deliberated. He asked Maynard, who advised him to accept: 'It is hardly possible to overestimate the importance of money.' He asked James, who was later to become a member of the *Spectator* staff himself, and who advised him to refuse because sooner or later pressure was pretty certain to be put on him to become a full-time journalist – *et voilà tout*. All his dreams of plays, novels, even biographies, would have to be abandoned.

In the end Lytton accepted. 'It seemed on the whole the wisest thing to do,' he told Duncan (25 June 1907), 'though I'm still not sure whether it wasn't simply the most cowardly. I had hoped to begin doing something worth doing, but the money, and the obvious fact that Mama wanted me to accept it, and the conceivable possibility that I might at least *think* of things, and the certainty that I could always chuck it when I liked – these considerations turned the melancholy balance, and shattered my dreams of ease and comedy. However, the splendid thing is that I shall be wonderfully rich next year (if I survive the stress and strain of composition!) and, as there's no particular reason why I should be pinned to London, I shall be able to travel.'

*

As soon as the *Spectator* appointment had been confirmed, and his 'Lady Mary Wortley Montagu' completed, Lytton began to make plans for spending a week with Duncan at Versailles. This was something he had often dreamed of doing. Now, before it was too late, he would make his dream a reality.

He set off in the second week of July, and for seven idyllic days he lived with Duncan in La Bruyère's house. They passed most of their time in the wonderful gardens – those of the Grand Trianon for choice. Though he had been prepared for much, the beauty was still astonishing. 'What I want to know is why anyone lives anywhere else,' he wrote to Clive Bell. 'I suppose one wouldn't be up to it for more than a week or so at a time. The ghosts would begin to grow more real than oneself.'

Encircled by these splendid gardens, and enchanted by the company of Duncan, Lytton was wonderfully happy. 'We spend most of our time beside a basin in the Trianon,' he informed James, 'but one day was given to Paris, on which I looked at every picture in the Louvre, and every statue, and then went off and had a blow out, and we viewed a farce in the Boulevard Montmartre, and then we steamed back to Versailles.'

He returned to London on 17 July and sank into a benevolent trance. 'I seem to be remarkably contented,' he told Maynard who visited him for a few days, and who was, so he informed Duncan, 'rather uglier than usual'.

Whenever he felt that family life was growing too much for him, he would prescribe for himself a letter from *Les Liaisons Dangereuses* before going to bed, and a 'Fleur du Mal' the first thing in the morning. It seldom failed. 'I've just got a book', he told Clive Bell (9 August 1907), 'in which some notes by Baudelaire on the Liaisons Dangereuses are printed – do you know them? They're really splendid – all his wonderful sanity, precision, and grasp of the situation are finely displayed. He says, comparing modern life to the eighteenth century – "En réalité, le satanisme a gagné. Satan s'est fait ingénu. Le mal se connaissant était moins affreux et plus près de la guérison que le mal s'ignorant. G. Sand inférieure à de Sade."'

But reading books could not prolong the happiness of his idyll at Versailles. 'I have been grunting and sweating over a filthy article on Beddoes the whole time,' he wrote to Swithinbank. Yet his curiosity was provoked by the mysterious undertones in Beddoes's life. Here was a strangely distant character – a throwback to the Elizabethan age – yet Lytton felt oddly close to him. 'I am trying to write on Beddoes,' he told Maynard (30 July 1907), 'and become daily more persuaded that he was a member of our sect. What do you think? It occurred to me yesterday that Degen[17] is probably still alive, and that we've only got to go over to Franckfort and inquire for a respectable old retired baker, aged seventy-seven, to hear the whole history! Won't you come?'

At the end of August, 'The Last Elizabethan', as he entitled his Beddoes essay, was finished. The family's furniture was now being transferred from Lancaster Gate across to 67 Belsize Park Gardens, and Lytton went to stay at Hurst Court, near Twyford in Berkshire, which Harry Norton's family had rented that summer. All the Nortons repeated aimless jokes and greeted them with trilling laughter which was sustained throughout a series of senseless meals like something in the *Inferno*. No wonder Harry was 'so utterly done for – beyond reach of human aid', Lytton lamented to Maynard (10 September 1907).

'. . . Oh! The horror of Sunday! And to see him appearing at breakfast, rather ashamed of being four minutes late, dressed in the complete vulgarity of "best clothes" with a dreadful fancy waistcoat and a revolting tie! Oh, oh! And then "church" – ugh! Fortunately no attempt was made to induce me to go – I think if there had been I should have said something gross. As it was, I hardly opened my mouth once. He is a weak-willed creature, very good-natured and very clever, but content to be his mother's puppet, and the rest of the family's buffoon.'

After his week at Hurst, Lytton fled to the Homere sisters at Kingham where 'swallowed by the waters of female oblivion' he revived himself 'among my Greek ladies', he wrote helplessly to Swithinbank (13 September 1907).

'I am on a deck-chair (very uncomfortable) in a misty garden, looking at nothing but a tree or two, and listening to a Greek lady (very fine and fat) practising scales on a grand piano ten yards off. I feel as if I were hardly more than a scale myself, or at least an arpeggio. Here comes a glass of milk for me, and a couple of rusks. I believe I am perfectly happy.'

On 20 September, he hurried on to join Clive and Vanessa at Curfew Cottage in Watchbell Street, Rye, close to the Mermaid Inn where he had stayed on separate occasions with Sheppard and Keynes. He had always loved Rye, with the mysterious presence of Henry James brooding over it, and it was especially enjoyable to be there among real friends with whom one could do as one pleased, come down late for breakfast, go to sleep on the drawing-room sofa, use bawdy and indecent language. Virginia and Adrian Stephen who were staying near by at Playden regularly came over. 'They *are* nice,' he told Duncan, 'and Bell, too, really, if one isn't put off rather by a thick layer of absurdity.'

The death of his friend Thoby had drawn Lytton closer to the Stephen family. 'He came and was such an inexpressible help,' Vanessa later recalled (25 January 1932), 'and made one think of the things most worth thinking of ... he seemed to see further into things than anyone else could.' It was impossible to use formal language once their hearts had been opened by common grief, and the growing informality of these friends was to be seen as a contribution to the changing social history. Lytton 'released Vanessa from guilt and the need to conform', wrote her biographer Frances Spalding. Her sister Virginia recorded a famous incident the following year when, entering the drawing-room at Gordon Square, Lytton pointed his finger at a stain on Vanessa's dress and inquired 'Semen?' Could one really say it, they wondered, '& we burst out laughing'. Only those getting to know Lytton well in those days when freedom of mind and expression were almost unknown, Vanessa wrote, 'can understand what an exciting world of explorations of thought and feeling he seemed to reveal. His great honesty of mind and remorseless poking fun at any sham forced others to be honest too and showed a world in which one need no longer be afraid of saying what one thought, surely the first step to anything that would be of interest and value.'[18]

One development was the formation of Bloomsbury's Play Reading Society which met for the first time that December to put on Vanbrugh's *The Relapse, or Virtue in Danger* in which Lytton excelled as Lord

Foppington. It was as if the prim interlude of Victorianism had never existed.

*

Number 67 Belsize Park Gardens was a smaller house than Lancaster Gate, but still spacious enough to cater for the rather depleted numbers of the family. As before, Lytton was assigned a bed-sitting-room where he was to compose his reviews and articles. 'Rousseau and his bag of tricks have absorbed me,' he wrote to Clive and Vanessa at the end of the month. 'I spend my days in the British Museum, and my nights in my Hampstead chamber, poring over Grimm, Madame D'Epinay; Mr John Morley, and Mrs Frederika Macdonald,[19] and trying to determine which is the silliest. It's a dreadful occupation, and I shall probably end by being the silliest of all.'

On 1 October, he began working for both St Loe Strachey's *Spectator* and Desmond MacCarthy's *New Quarterly*. The *Spectator* occupied most of his time and over the next nineteen months he contributed seventy-five articles and reviews, usually eighteen hundred words long, to its literary section. At first he found this employment invigorating. Once a week he called at the *Spectator* offices to collect a new book, wondering desperately whether he could complete his piece on it in time. It was a straightforward challenge to his capabilities. Overcoming the hurry and the drudgery of weekly journalism acted as a tonic to his system. He could do it! Not only that, he could do it better than most others. 'I walk on the Heath pretty nearly every afternoon and feel amazingly young and cheerful,' he wrote to Maynard towards the end of October. 'I do really feel seventeen – with all the tastes of that age, and all the vices. Very queer indeed.'

The *Spectator* gave Lytton a focus for his continuing education. He read volumes on French and Elizabethan literature which were to be useful preparation for his *Landmarks in French Literature* and *Elizabeth and Essex*; he wrote on Alexander Pope, the subject of his Leslie Stephen Lecture in 1925, and on Carlyle and Macaulay, who would be among the 'Six English Historians' in *Portraits in Miniature*. He reviewed many new works of history and biography too and began forming his own non-fiction ideology.

At the *Spectator* Lytton was also able to read contemporary poetry and keep up with contemporary literary theory. The one living poet whose genius he considered to be indisputable was Kipling. He was somewhat dismissive of Austin Dobson and Edmund Gosse, enjoyed A.E. Housman but felt he had narrowed his territory and 'was content to reign over a tiny kingdom',[20] and though charmed by Yeats's earlier poems defined them as 'romance in process of decomposition'. His criticism of Yeats recalls the aesthetic judgement of Dr Johnson on Gray's *Odes*,

172

Milton's *Lycidas* and the poetry of Donne. 'The poem is not only divorced from the common facts of life,' he writes, 'but its structure is essentially unreasonable, because it depends on no causal law, and thus the effect which it produces is singularly fragmentary and vague. It is full of beauties, but they are all unrelated, and slip out of one's grasp like unstrung pearls.'[21]

Once or twice when the *Spectator* art critic, St Loe's younger brother Henry Strachey, could not struggle up from Somerset, Lytton would go off to the London exhibitions with his undetected collaborator Duncan Grant. His rather cautious art notices, like his book reviews, were unsigned. But on 30 November 1907, the *Spectator* printed the first of his theatre criticisms, above the pen-name 'Ignotus'. In its previous forty years the *Spectator* had occasionally published reviews of current stage performances, but Lytton was the paper's first drama critic. Very special measures had to be provided, James Strachey remembered, 'for blanketing the shock to vicarage nerves'. At the end of Lytton's first piece of dramatic criticism, St Loe weighed in with an announcement that 'we desire to take this opportunity of pointing out that the critic in question expresses his personal views, and that we are not to be held editorially responsible for his judgments.'[22]

Lytton's judgements on the Edwardian theatre were often severe. He disliked the stereotyping of British actors in contrast to the freedom of some of their European counterparts. He championed the theatre of ideas and school of naturalistic acting ushered in at the Court and Savoy theatres by Harley Granville Barker as 'something like a revolution in the art of dramatic production in England';[23] and he derided the staginess of the powerful actor-managers such as Beerbohm Tree at His Majesty's.

'A leaf dropped, and he clutched the air with frantic fingers; he could never speak without first looking over his shoulder, and he could never look over his shoulder without first rolling his eyes ... It is hardly an exaggeration to say that Mr Tree is fundamentally a great dumb-show actor, a master of pantomime, and nothing more ... He is so acutely conscious of his audience that he is blind to everything else.'[24]

Despite his admiration for Granville Barker, he opposed Barker's and William Archer's proposals for a National Theatre, on the grounds that such an institution would be collared by State control and dictate a style of orthodox acting throughout the country. Among contemporary playwrights he described J.M. Barrie as 'a master in the art of theatrical bluffing',[25] criticized John Galsworthy for giving his audiences sociological problems instead of human beings, and, though he praised the 'brilliant dialogue and paradoxical wit' of Bernard Shaw as being 'for the most part the expression of high originality and vivacity of thought', concluded (perhaps with the help of St Loe Strachey) that 'the question of marriage is too complex to be treated in a light manner'[26] after seeing *Getting Married.*

Working under pressure at the *Spectator*, Lytton quickened and condensed his style. He also learnt another ingenious skill. The younger members of the Strachey family liked to apply the word 'spectatorial' to any particularly pompous pronouncements in the paper. These were often attributable to the autocratic editorship of St Loe Strachey. James Strachey, who was to work as his private secretary for six years, remembered how he would settle down on Thursday afternoons and read through the galley proofs of the forthcoming issue. 'He altered a word here and there, he scribbled a fresh sentence in the margin, he struck out a whole paragraph and replaced it by one of his own.'[27] Lytton became adept at forestalling this intervention by using a method of pre-censorship. But it is difficult to know whether some of the rather conservative romanticism is supplied by St Loe, introduced by Lytton so as to appease him, or part of Lytton's own semi-spectatorial personality in his twenties.

Lytton's trustworthiness received the highest accolade when, at the beginning of 1908, he was offered the editorship of the *Spectator*. This was the sort of temptation his brother had predicted would happen, but Lytton had little difficulty in refusing on the grounds that his business was literature, not politics. St Loe replied that, though he regretted the decision, he realized it to be the right one, leaving Lytton wondering whether St Loe 'wishes that he too had chucked it'. Lytton was already beginning to weary of writing for money against time. 'I shouldn't mind being a journalist if it really paid; but does it?' he had earlier asked Sheppard (11 October 1903). 'I'd rather be a cabin boy on a sailing ship, whether it paid or no. Romance is the only thing worth living for ... Our poor imaginations are tired out with the construction of worlds so different from our own, we are exhausted, we give up, we take to journalism, we are contented, we are rich, we exist no more.'

With the money he was now beginning to earn, he was able to repay various loans he had received from Keynes and Norton, and to take them to lunch at Simpson's in the Strand, for many years his favourite London restaurant, and conveniently placed round the corner from the *Spectator* office in Wellington Street, almost on Waterloo Bridge. But pleasant as this was, he did not feel contented. He was to sum up his predicament a year later in a letter to his sister Dorothy (25 February 1909): 'My condition is not encouraging. With this damned *Spectator* every week I see no hope of ever doing anything. It's pretty sickening. On Monday I shall be in my 30th year, and if I happened to die there'd be precious little to show for them all . . . occasionally I'm absolutely in despair. If I had decent health I should go into a garret and starve until I'd done something, but that's impossible. The only consolation is that as it is I lead a very tolerable life.'

The *Spectator* seemed infested with Stracheys: the back numbers were crowded with forebears; current contributors ranged from Lytton's eighty-year-old uncle George to his twenty-year-old brother James; and there were plenty of nephews and cousins lining up to join its columns. Living with his family, working with his family, however tolerable his life, Lytton felt stifled. During his twenties he continued to take a sentimental interest in the role of his family in the history of British India. In his thirties, when he grew more politically minded, his ideas changed. His break with the past, culminating in *Eminent Victorians*, was to take one of St Loe Strachey's great friends, Sir Evelyn Baring (Lord Cromer), as representing that part of his inheritance he had shed. In his autobiography, *The Adventure of Living*, St Loe placed Baring first in the chapter called 'Five Great Men'. Baring was a reviewer for the *Spectator* at the same time as Lytton, and St Loe bracketed them together as the two most brilliant critics in his employment. But Baring, it seems, did not have to use the same pre-censorship as Lytton, since he and St Loe 'wanted the same good causes to win, and we wanted to frustrate the same evil projects'. As his social and political opinions changed, Lytton came to see Baring (in the last chapter of *Eminent Victorians*, 'The End of General Gordon') as a man whose 'ambition can be stated in a single phrase; it was to become an institution; and he achieved it. No doubt, too, he deserved it.'

There were no arguments, no show of irritation, between the two cousins while Lytton was working for the *Spectator*. But later St Loe would inform Lady Strachey that it was the moral duty of the *Spectator* to attack *Eminent Victorians*. 'This is certainly quite as it should be,' Lytton assured his mother. 'I only hope that St Loe was not personally annoyed by my remarks on Lord Cromer.' A contributory factor in this process was the sacking of James from the *Spectator* at the end of 1914 on account of his pacifism. 'I was very sorry to part with him for I like him very much,' St Loe told Lady Strachey (December 1914), 'and I feel most awfully sorry for him in the position into which he has got himself, owing I fear, alas, to his sophisticated, socialistic point of view:

'. . . I suppose I am a monster, but to me the notion that it is so dreadful to take human life, or indeed life, seems so amazingly foolish that I get quite rabid and unjust about it . . . I feel sure James will grow out of his follies . . . the rock-bed of his trouble is a sort of indecision and a sort of intellectual fastidiousness which makes him unable to take any course . . .'

Lytton shared James's intellectual fastidiousness, embraced the same 'sophisticated socialistic point of view', and was also a pacifist during the war. He did not keep quiet, but threw off indecisiveness in the 'Spiritual Revolution' that led to *Eminent Victorians* for which the Spectatorial St Loe acted as a hidden catalyst. It was an appealing irony that this book would help to introduce a new historical perspective, revealing much of Britain's amazing foolishness to have lain with St Loe's generation.

3

A POCKET HANDKERCHIEF ON MONT BLANC

Lytton had likened his reviewing to the taking up of weekly essays to his history tutor at Trinity. But the *Spectator* which held him in the family net so fast (before casting him so far), also moved him a little farther off from Cambridge. Meeting Saxon Sydney-Turner in London, he reflected that there was probably no one less entertaining in the world. What had they ever found to talk about in those studious cloisters of Trinity, he and Woolf and Bell and the others? 'We reviewed old days, of course,' he wrote to Duncan, 'as you may imagine, and said what we always have said for the last hundred years. Friendship is a queer business.'

'At the present moment, as usual, I take more interest in Duncan than in anyone else,' he told his sister Dorothy. Their *affaire* had started up again early in 1907 after Duncan confided to James that his involvement with Hobby was 'all over'. Poor Hobby had been terrified that his mother would find out. He returned from a visit studying 'business methods' in the United States to be confronted by his mother waving an opened letter 'rank with sodomy' and demanding an explanation. 'She stormed and raved,' Lytton recounted to Leonard, 'and . . . wound up by accusing the Society, if you please, of being a hotbed of unnatural vice.' After this Hobby appeared to Duncan, as well as to Maynard and Lytton, beset by unnecessary duties, anxious to live by rules and do what was expected of him. So he faded from their world, destined to become a respectable farmer and Liberal politician, with a wife and eventually a knighthood.

Duncan was now living with his family in Fellows Road, round the corner from Belsize Park Gardens. His alternating presence and absence greatly agitated Lytton. At times, reading *Mansfield Park*, going for walks on Hampstead Heath, catching mild influenza together, they were happy. Then Lytton would fall into an unholy state of nerves. 'Such nightmares as I had last night! Duncan, it's not you that's the cause,' he confided on 23 November. 'I have a devil inside me – perhaps seven. I occasionally feel that I'm done for, and that I shall really smash up, and "go under", as they say, like a decadent poet. It's my imagination, my awful imagination. I should like to go to sleep for ages and ages. Oh God, what a miserable thing is a human being! There's no hope for a human being outside love. That I shall never get now, and it's all I want.'

Cast back in the solitary confinement of his own body, he fell easily into the roles of victim and invalid. It was while convalescing from one of these bouts early in 1908 at his aunt's house in Russell Square that the news came of his father having fallen seriously ill. He returned home at once. A few days later, on the morning of 12 February, Sir Richard Strachey died in his sleep. Although Lytton had never succeeded in getting close to the old man, he had always been fond of him. For a time he contemplated writing his biography. But it would have meant, he told James, writing the whole history of India in the nineteenth century. His father had always been a shadowy personage with whom it was inconceivable to deal except on formal terms. Though he had long ceased to reach out to him as any kind of companion, Sir Richard's silent presence in the house had acted as a lodestone, drawing him back from his frequent trips out of London. Now that magnetic power was gone, and a rock of masculinity standing out from the eternal sea of females finally submerged. Soon, Lytton resolved, he too must leave and set up home elsewhere.

To recover from her husband's death, Lady Strachey left with her brother Trevor for the South of France at the end of February. Lytton and Pippa accompanied them as far as Calais and saw them into their train. Then they went on to Boulogne. The trip did them both good, especially Pippa, who had been nursing her father. Soon after their return to England, and while their mother was still abroad, they both went down for a short visit to St Loe Strachey's country house at Newlands Corner, near Guildford. 'A most gorgeous newly-painted scarlet motor-car took us to and from the station,' Lytton wrote to his mother (11 March 1908), 'and St Loe insisted on my wearing one of his numerous fur-coats, so I felt very grand.

'In the evening we all went to the Parish room in the village, where Amy's "Masque of Empire" was performed – mainly by village boys and girls. Amabel[28] was Britannia, which was the leading part. She looked nice but her acting was too much in the regular affected "recitation" style, which Pippa thinks she must have learnt from Amy. I can't imagine anyone acting so by the light of nature ... Amy was most affable and not at all prononcée. When I went she insisted on my taking away the Masque to suggest any improvements that might occur to me. It is in the main quite harmless – the chief blot to my mind is that at the end Britannia and all the Colonies and Dependencies fall on their knees, repeating R.K.'s poem "Lest we forget" and praying for mercy, etc. .... One thing annoyed me. She talked of Queen Victoria as Britain's "grandest queen". I begged her to put "long-lived" instead – or any other disyllabic adjective – pointing out that that could only apply to Queen Elizabeth. But she wouldn't hear of it.'

In numbers the family at Belsize Park Gardens was greatly reduced. There was Lady Strachey and her three daughters, the admirable Pippa, Marjorie, high-spirited and often shocking people with her outrageous opinions, and occasionally Pernel, quiet, observant and witty. Ever since the earliest Lancaster Gate days, Lady Strachey had liked to read at lunch and dinner copies of *Home Chat* and *Tit-Bits*, from the pages of which, with cries of laughter, she would shout out jokes. Everyone deprecated this practice, and the arguments with her daughters, in particular Marjorie, were high-pitched and continuous. Lytton became in time a little deaf to all this din, but the noise was nerve-racking.

Earlier in the year, before his father's death, he declined an invitation from Moore to join his Easter reading-party, to be held this time in the Green Dragon at Lavington on Salisbury Plain. Now he quickly changes his mind and, in the third week of April, speeds into Wiltshire. Despite the magical charm of Moore himself – still 'a colossal being' as he describes him to Virginia Stephen – who plays the piano and sings in the old inimitable way with the sweat pouring down his face, this congregation of 'intellect upon Salisbury Plain' only adds to his sense of isolation. Hawtrey, Sanger, Bob Trevy – it is the same crowd as always; but, individually, they are changing. And perhaps he, too, is changing. The nostalgia he feels for Cambridge now mingles with a new bitterness. Only that month, in the columns of the *Spectator*, he has launched a slashing attack on the fifth volume of *The Cambridge Modern History*, likening its learned authors – one of whom is his old tutor, Stanley Leathes – to 'the barbarians of the Dark Ages'.

In any event, whether it is he or his Cambridge companions who have changed, Lytton seems left out of things. There is a feeling of alienation born out of some obscure sense of rivalry with Maynard, and a lessening contact with the younger undergraduates with their brave camp fires and *plein air* socialism, led by Rupert Brooke. Even his own brother, James, appears 'very mysterious and reserved, and either incredibly young or inconceivably old'. He spends much of his time re-reading Racine who, unlike the Apostles these days, occupied himself with the only worthwhile subject in the world. 'Oh, adventures! Does one ever have them nowadays?' he exclaims in a letter to Virginia Stephen.

He had recently been asked by the Oxford University Press to write an introduction to a book of his choice. For several weeks he racked his brains for something that was both suitable and worth republishing and, after discussing it with Walter Raleigh, at last decided on *A Simple Story* by Mrs Inchbald. But finding no time to fit this in he was obliged to write off to the publishers begging for an extension. Whatever happened, the 'dreadful introduction' could no longer be delayed after he returned to London.

Overworked and overwrought, he slumped into an acute fit of family fever. 'It's impossible to think and impossible to breathe,' he complained to James. 'Oh! Oh! I have serious thoughts of flight. But how? Where? – Could I ever face poverty, journalism, and solitude?' He would have liked to join Maynard, but Maynard had now left his flat at 125B St James's Court, before settling into King's College where Alfred Marshall had offered him a lectureship in economics with a salary of a hundred pounds a year. Since Duncan was so unreliable, with whom else could Lytton share a flat? To live alone was uneconomic – indeed unthinkable.

Temporary respite came in June, almost all of which he spent in pleasant rooms at King's. Between reviews, and when the weather was fine, he entertained himself gliding up and down the river very slowly in a punt which James worked with a paddle, or simply eating too much, or wandering along Trinity Street with a fixed lack of purpose. 'The only disadvantage of this place are the beauties', he confided to Swithinbank (5 June 1908), 'who are everywhere and ravish one's heart in the most unpleasant manner . . .[I] spend all I get in reckless luxury. It's the only way of consoling oneself for the ruins of life.'

He tried to take a special interest in Rupert Brooke with whom his relationship was complicated by the unhappy devotion of his brother who had declared his passion after a performance of *Eumenides*. 'As for Rupert,' Lytton told Duncan (12 June 1908), '– I'm not in love with him, though it's occasionally occurred to me that I ought to be – but there really are too many drawbacks to him, though of course there are charms and pleasantries too. His self-conceit is écrasant, and his general pose merely absurd. He's also, I *think* – but I'm not sure – rather brutal to me, who'm

an innocent friendly person, and no fool . . . It's disappointing – a little –
but certainly my heart's not broken – only rather pricked.'

Lytton was also getting to know some of the other younger men now up
at Cambridge – in particular Gerald Shove,[29] Hugh Dalton and again
James Elroy Flecker ('whom we now don't much like'), but with none of
them was he able to communicate freely. It was easy to be free when one
was twenty, and life was an affair of plain sailing. But approaching thirty,
when Spectatorial responsibilities and a ruined digestive system combined
to harness and perplex one, what could be expected? For hours he would
sit writing in a small inner sanctum, solitary but not altogether
undisturbed. Often he seemed to hear the door of the outer room open,
and someone enter, and – did footsteps approach the inner door? Was it
the bedmaker? Or the wind outside? Or simply imagination – spectres
from the old days? He could not tell; only the inner door never opened and
he sat there listening, and then bent himself again over his poems for the
idealized Duncan.

> One day you found me – was I there?
>   Perhaps it was my ghost you found –
> I know not; but you found me fair
> And love was in my lips and hair
>   And in my eyes profound.
>
> You kissed me, and you kissed me oft.
>   – Was it my ghost or was it me? –
> Your kisses were so sweet, so soft,
> The happy cherubim aloft
>   Wept that such things should be.
>
> You vanished then – I know not why;
>   But that you vanished 'tis most true.
> Yet did you vanish? – Till I die
> Methinks I'll doubt (my ghost or I)
>   If 'twas your ghost or you.

*

On his return to Hampstead at the begining of July, Lytton discovered that
for some time past Duncan had been in love with Maynard, and that they
were having an affair.

Of all the amorous crises sprinkled through his life, this was perhaps the
most wretched. It came as a complete shock. The two points between
which his unstable emotional existence had been delicately poised were

rooted up. Adding to his agony was the realization that he had been made to look so foolish. As he retraced the pattern of events in his mind, it was this thought which tormented him most. He could now see their swelling affection for each other through their letters to him. 'Anyone could fall in love with Duncan if he wanted to,' Maynard had written as early as 1906. Then, a year later, while packing up some of the clothes Maynard had left after his visit to Versailles, Duncan confided (7 April 1907): 'I did seem to like Keynes much more than before.' But Lytton had noticed nothing until, after returning from Cambridge, he took them both to lunch at Simpson's on 14 July, and observed them together. A whispered aside told him everything. 'Ils s'aiment,' he burst out to James. Next day he went over to question Maynard. It appeared that they had become lovers early the previous month when Lytton had left for King's – indeed they had even made a secret journey to Cambridge while he was there! 'I feel quite shattered by the interview,' Maynard told Duncan after Lytton had left, '. . . ill and rather distraught. I wish there was no one else in the world but you.' Lytton's cross-questioning had struck him as quite cynical, as if he were 'much interested as a student of human life'. But after getting home, Lytton's control gave way. 'They've kept it horribly secret,' he reported to James. 'He [Maynard] has come to me reeking with that semen he has never thought that I should know.'

Now that Lytton knew the truth, everything slipped into place. It had been he who, almost against their will, had driven them together. And to think that all the time he had been confiding to Maynard about Duncan's elusiveness, and joking with Duncan on the subject of Maynard's lack of passion, they could have been comparing notes. Then, too, while he was cautiously meditating on the relative merits of living with either Maynard or Duncan, they had gone off – so he now discovered – and found accommodation together in Belgrave Road.[30]

James was his one support in this crisis, assuring him that Duncan and Maynard could not possibly be in love. 'There's hardly any affection,' he explained (16 July 1908). 'And so irritation's bound to set in – and be fatal too.' This was a pleasant thought, but though it soothed a little, he could not banish the sense of treachery, the pain. Lytton hoped that 'they are all playing, and taking themselves in'. Yet the fact was that Maynard's feelings for Duncan were very similar to his own. 'Dear Duncan I love you too much and I can't now bear to live without you,' Maynard wrote to him this summer. Duncan was the most intense sexual and emotional male love of both their lives.

With Maynard, whom he now described as 'a safety-bicycle with genitals', Lytton sensed it was vital to keep up polite relations. 'I only know that we've been friends far too long to stop being friends now,' he wrote (21 July 1908). 'There are some things that I shall try not to think of, and you must do your best to help me in that; and you must believe that I do sympathize and don't hate you and that if you were here now I should probably kiss you, except that Duncan would be jealous, which would never do!'

Maynard's response was all that Lytton could have wished. 'Your letter made me cry,' he wrote back, 'but I was very glad to get it.' He wanted to write something more, but he did not know what to say. Might he come to Hampstead? This was the very last thing Lytton wanted. All sorts of disasters might ensue. Maynard would eloquently put his case and make himself appear innocent and upstanding; the mere sight of him might stir Lytton into losing his temper and humiliating himself. Far better to keep Maynard at a disadvantage. He therefore replied saying that on the whole – if Maynard did not mind – he thought it best that he should *not* come and see him at present. He was not very well, still most horribly *accablé* with the Inchbald introduction, and would not really have anything to say. Soon perhaps he would be going away – he did not know where or with whom.

But Maynard still pressed resolutely for a meeting and postponed his journey to Cambridge in order to force one. Would Lytton, he inquired, like to go with him to see *Isadora* Duncan dance, and forget the real Duncan, whom no one in the world could help but adore?

Ignoring both pun and invitation Lytton replied saying he had sent Maynard a present of some books to adorn *his rooms at King's*. Probably they were waiting for him now. He asked his friend to examine the binding which, he believed, was of a kind that he particularly admired. He hoped that Maynard would be pleased with this little gift; the book on walking-sticks was especially entertaining.

There was nothing that Maynard could do but concede a tactical defeat, quit London and pick up his books at Cambridge. 'Dear Lytton, why have you given them me? They show something you couldn't write, and they made me feel a great deal which you must understand without my saying it. Oh Lytton, it is too good of you to behave like this.'

There remained one final card for Lytton to play – he thanked Maynard lavishly for the letter thanking him for the books. 'I'm glad you liked them, and it's very nice of you to feel what you say. Duncan is very kind, too. I'm sure of one thing, and that is that affection makes everything right. So I'm really extraordinarily happy now.'

In his simultaneous dealings with Duncan, Lytton began by striking the loftiest note of altruism yet. Duncan, he knew, was considering taking art lessons in London. What gesture could be finer than to offer to pay for these lessons? It drew from his cousin an almost identical response to Maynard's. 'Lytton you're *too* kind,' he told him, 'you made me burst into tears; I cannot bear your being so completely good and generous. I think it cruel of you to plunge me into such contradictory emotions.'

And there, perhaps, Lytton should have left it. But he could not. Duncan had praised him for his kindness, and he could not forbear to send off a rueful answer: 'Oh, Duncan, I have thought of unkind letters, unkind words – and heaven knows you may have them from me yet; but now it is not with that in my heart that I want to speak. It is not for you that I am feeling, but for myself; and I should like you to know my thoughts . . .

'Concealment would have been easier now too, as you may guess, since if I am to speak all it must be to one more than I want to speak to. He [Maynard] will tell you, no doubt, that I am wrong, that I am foolish because I am jealous, and that I am to be pitied because I am in love. I am ready to face even pity, even the pity of both of you, on the condition that Duncan knows my mind.

There are things in me, I knew very well, which are beastly; and there are things in you Duncan, which irritate me, which pain me, which I even dislike. If you understand that, will you understand this besides – that I am your friend? It would be irrelevant to say more.'

Once this much had been said it was impossible not to say more. The dams of self-restraint had been opened a crack, and self-pity, anger, recrimination cascaded through. On the evening of the day – 17 July – that Duncan received this letter, he called round unannounced at Belsize Park Gardens. Lytton could not refuse to admit him, but said very little and did not attempt to stop him when, after a brief uneasy session, Duncan rose to leave. Later that night he sent off a short note, saying that he had thought it best that Duncan should leave when he did. Otherwise 'I might have been stupid'.

What really pained Lytton, however, was Duncan's ensuing silence. Unlike the persistent Maynard, he did not write for days to expatiate on Lytton's self-effacing goodness. After the first, rather short letter, there was nothing. It was typical of this maddeningly elusive young man. What was he thinking? Lytton's imagination kept revolving until, after a fortnight of waiting, he could no longer contain himself.

'Dearest Duncan,

I want to say something, though I'm afraid it may annoy you, and I daresay I've said it already – but I feel an uneasy suspicion that I may not have made myself quite clear. It is this – though I like Maynard, I cannot think of him as you do, or else, I suppose, I should be in love with him too! The result is that I don't take your affair as seriously as you do either, and therefore imagine that you will some day or other return from Cythera.[31] But that, I feel, is neither here nor there, and so long as you *are* in Cythera, I don't see why that fact should prevent my liking both of you as much as I always have. Please realize what I mean, if it's not too vilely expressed, and forgive me if it's all obvious and I'm merely harping on what you know . . .

. . . Oh lord, lord, why do we live in such a distorted coagulated world? I feel all topsy-turvy and out of place, as if I were a pocket handkerchief that somebody had dropped on the top of Mont Blanc. It's all too preposterous, and what's worse, I'm well aware that I do very little but add to the preposterousness. But I believe that a just God – a *really* just God – would completely bear me out. Oh! You're laughing.

This is an absurd kind of letter, you must admit; I'll write again perhaps more sensibly, from somewhere or other. And you must write to me. It'll be forwarded. Adieu!

> Your
> Lytton'

Early in August, Lytton travelled up to Scotland on a voyage of recovery. Accompanied by James, who himself hoped to wear off the ill-effects of his 'dumb deaf and blind adoration' of Rupert Brooke, he went first to the Isle of Skye, putting up for a week at the Sligachan Inn, a strange and desolate place, some nine miles from Portree. On all sides lay deserts of bumpy green morass, sea-lochs, and, farther off, blunt black mountains bulging into the sky and wrapped in a pale wet mist – a dehumanized spectacle that suited Lytton well. Occasional blazing sunbursts would light up within him unsuspected wells of hope; and even the days of perpetual rain seemed soothing and merciful.

Soon he felt ready to make his first step back south. He was beginning to grow more critical and complaining – a sign of improvement. The Sligachan Inn was filled to bursting point with fishers and climbers throwing glances at the two thin-legged bespectacled gentlemen who sat paralysed by the fire. After a week of torture in the smoking-room, the continual scrutiny from this crowd of weather-beaten Alpinists and fishers of fish impelled them southwards to Rothiemurchus.

They arrived in the second week of August. 'The "accommodation" is, as people say, rather primitive,' Lytton explained to Swithinbank (13 August 1908), '. . . a smallish sitting-room, where I have to sleep, and a sort of cave adjoining it, where brother James sleeps ... and there is an exceedingly amiable Scottish matron who does everything; and that's all.' The cottage – almost touching the road to Loch an Eilein[32] – was in a strategic position for observing travellers. All day and every day the world swept past his window in carriages, brakes and motors; and as the road divided just in front of the house, many of them stopped to ask the landlady the way to the loch, so that Lytton could press his nose against the glass and stare his fill. It was, for the time being, as close as he wished to be.

He was out of doors so much that his nose grew red and raw as Bardolph's. On one boiling day, he told Swithinbank, 'I returned to savagery and plunged wildly into a mountain pool, lost my eyeglasses, and very nearly perished miserably of exposure. Imagine the fearful scene. I tore over hill and dale, and then lay out in the sun having erections. It was very odd.' 'We are tapis here (brother James and I)', he wrote to Clive Bell (13 August 1908), 'in a hut near a lake, like so many lop-eared rabbits. The beauties of nature satisfy me (for the moment); I go out before breakfast in pumps and brood over the lake; I walk in the heat of the day on to the summits of mountains.'

He was also writing again – things other than his essays and reviews, which he had somehow managed to keep up throughout the crisis. Over these weeks, in a long series of letters to Maynard, he fabricated an ingenious love-adventure. Maynard – now passing two months in the Orkneys with Duncan and working at *A Treatise on Probability* while having his portrait painted[33] – was by turns curious, amazed, *almost* incredulous. Then came the dénouement. Not a single word was true. Everything had been recounted in the lightest manner; but there can be no doubt as to the motive behind this elaborate piece of invention, with all its enticing scandal and melodrama. Maynard had been used as a Brother Confessor for something that never took place; his old role had been falsified, and Lytton had got a little of his own back in fiction for the way he had been deceived in fact. From now on, James, who had helped him each evening over their peat fire to concoct this plot, would be his confidant.

While in Scotland he became re-immersed in H.A. Giles's charming anthology of Chinese poetry about which he wrote a long essay for MacCarthy's *New Quarterly*. He had had a surfeit of drama. Now he wanted to lose himself in pure art, where every loose end, that weighs on the heart like a broken assignation, is satisfactorily tied up, where tragedy is rounded into song, and love and lust become an interplay of syllables. In this anthology, the fragility of human relations is transmuted into something delicate and lasting. It was comforting to be reminded that morbid affairs of the heart had been going on for centuries now that he, in his turn, was weathering the storm and sailing into smoother waters. Lytton concludes his essay, not with a translation, but with his own verses.

'In these lyrics of China the stress and fury of desire are things unknown, and, in their topsy-turvy Oriental fashion, they are concerned far more with memories of love than expectations of it. They look back upon love through a long vista of years which have smoothed away the agitations of romance and have brought with them the calm familiarity of happiness, or the quiet desolation of regret. Thus, while one cannot be certain that this love is not another name for sublimated friendship, one can be sure enough that these lovers are always friends. Affection, no doubt, is the word that best describes such feelings; and it is through its mastery of the tones and depths of affection that ... its pages, for all their strange antiquity, are fresh to us; their humanity keeps them immortal. The poets who wrote them seem to have come to the end of experience, to have passed long ago through the wonders and tumults of existence, to have arrived at last at some mysterious haven where they could find repose among memories that were for ever living, and among discoveries that were for ever old. Their poetry is the voice of civilization which has returned upon itself, which has ... learnt to say some things so finely that we forget, as we listen to it, that these are not the only things that can be said.

> We parted at the gorge and cried 'Good cheer!'
> The sun was setting as I closed my door;
> Methought, the spring will come again next year,
> But he may come no more.

The words carry with them so much significance, they produce so profound a sense of finality, that they seem to contain within themselves a summary of all that is most important in life ... it is far from frigid; but it is dry – dry as the heaped rose-leaves in a porcelain vase, rich with the perfume of how many summers! The scent transports us to old gardens, to old palaces; we wander incuriously among forsaken groves; we half expect some wonder, and we know too well that nothing now will ever come again. Reading this book, we might well be in the alleys of Versailles; and our sensations are those of a writer whose works, perhaps, are too modern to be included in Professor [Herbert] Giles's anthology:

> Here in the ancient park, I wait alone.

The dried-up fountains sleep in beds of stone;
The paths are still; and up the sweeping sward
No lovely lady passes, no gay lord.

Why do I linger? Ah! perchance I'll find
Some solace for the desolated mind
In yon green grotto, down the towering glade,
Where the bronze Cupid glimmers in the shade.'[34]

These poems seemed to purge Lytton's bitterness for a time. But by mid-September the commotion revived. James was not only his confessor but also over the next six months his fellow conspirator. That summer Duncan was writing to Maynard: 'You are the only person I feel I can speak to . . . It's not only that one's a sodomite that one had to hide but one's whole philosophy of life . . . I wish you were here to stand between me and the world.' This was how they all felt. Under the law, male homosexuals in consenting relationships were judged to be criminals and subject to two years' imprisonment with hard labour. It was difficult not to see yourself as an outcast from your family, or an enemy of your country. You were open to blackmail, denied the alleviations of unhappy love affairs used by heterosexuals, and a prey to feelings that could easily fester. Certainly Lytton could not get over his obsession. 'It was all ashes and dry bones,' he complained to James (27 October 1908) after staying with Maynard in King's that autumn. In a conspiracy of 'Pozzophobia' the two brothers plotted their revenge. James was the leader. 'Popular opinion seems to be smashing him [Maynard],' he reported (15 February 1909). '. . . His face becomes so thin on these occasions he's quite pathetic . . . He said it was awful that you hated him.'

It was true that Lytton did hate Maynard. He could not seem to help himself. 'Looking back I see him, hideous and meaningless,' he wrote to Leonard Woolf (5 February 1909), 'a malignant goblin gibbering over destinies that are not his own . . .' None of this venom was very helpful in itself and there were times when 'I can't help feeling rather guilty', he confessed to James (14 February 1909). But only when Maynard wilted under the force of his friends' disapproval and went through the same course of thwarted expectations over Duncan, could Lytton feel any warmth for him. By March he had come to see him as 'an almost tragic figure', telling James (11 March 1909) that 'I'm afraid he must be quite dreadfully in love . . . I believe he's simply living on the accumulations of intensely private passion . . . The more I consider this, the more certain it seems to me that I'm the only person who can support him . . . and that when the time comes I should be there.' A week later, on hearing that Maynard had been given a Fellowship at King's, he wrote to congratulate him (17 March 1909), adding:

'I've been wanting to write to you for some time, though really I think it's hardly necessary – only to say that you must always think of me as your friend. I shall think of you in the same way. But I've been rather afraid that lately you may have felt that things have become different. I don't think it's the case. The only thing is that I'm sometimes uneasy and awkward perhaps, partly I suppose because of my nervous organization which isn't particularly good – but I don't see how it can be helped. I can only beg that you'll attend to it as little as possible, and believe me to be a sensible decent person who remembers and knows.'

Though Maynard was '*very* glad' to read this, he sent only 'a sterile letter' back. From time to time, incited by his brother, Lytton would find that, despite his wish to be sensible and decent, his nervous organization would get the better of him and 'my rage against Pozzo only seems to have increased'. When Duncan somewhat prematurely confided to James (22 April 1909) that he was 'no longer in love' with Maynard, and James passed on this confidence, Lytton swung the searchlight of his criticism on his past lover. 'I wonder if you will allow *me* to be fond of Maynard,' Duncan ironically inquired. 'It seemed as if you would put it down to my now seeing him as he is . . . that you would go on always finding fault with me until I became a second you.' To make people become a version of himself was Lytton's form of revenge. His lingering antagonism was to delay Maynard's acceptance as a friend by the 'Visigoths', as Lytton called the Goth's two sisters Vanessa and Virginia. It was Duncan who was to introduce Maynard to their houses and make him part of what became known as the Bloomsbury Group.

For by now the course of all their lives was flowing into Bloomsbury.

4

A BAD END

From 'the rigours of a Scotch summer and the sanitary arrangements of a Scotch cottage', Lytton had eventually reached Edinburgh where, two years earlier, he had stopped off with Ainsworth and heard Moore cheerfully playing the Eroica. 'I spent two nights in Edinburgh', he wrote to Moore who was now living in Richmond, 'and took a walk to look at Buccleuch Place – it seemed very deserted and grey.'

He had begun reading Condorcet whose *éloges* he was to cite in his preface to *Eminent Victorians* as evidence of the inferiority of British biography to French. In Britain we relegated this humane branch of literature to the journeyman. 'I think France is on the whole a more civilized place than England,' he now wrote (2 September 1908) to his mother, 'and it seems to me that may be the result of their having had their superstitions and prejudices rooted up once and for all by the philosophers. What a disgrace that the education of the country should depend upon the squabbles of non-conformists and anglicans! But what else can happen so long as everyone goes on taking these people at their own valuations?'

Back in London he attended second-rate plays, devoured solitary lunches at Simpson's, collected consignments of books from the *Spectator* (going on to the London Library for more books to help him with his reviews) and divided his remaining hours between Hampstead and Bloomsbury. 'There are moments – on the Heath, of course – where I seem to myself to see life steadily and see it whole,' he wrote to Virginia Stephen, who was in Paris with Clive and Vanessa, 'but they're only moments; as a rule I can make nothing out.

'You don't find much difficulty, I think. Is it because you *are* a virgin? Or because, from some elevation or another, it's possible to manage it, and you happen to be there? Ah! there are so many difficulties! So many difficulties! I want to write a novel about a Lord Chancellor and his naughty son, but I can't for the life of me think of anything like the shadow of a plot, and then – the British public! Oh dear, let's all go off to the Faroe Islands, and forget the existence of Robin Mayor and Mrs Humphry Ward,[35] and drink rum punch of an evening, and live happily ever after!'

He seldom went to King's or Trinity now. There were too many people it was painful to see. When Virginia Stephen returned from Paris, he arranged to go off with her and her brother Adrian not on a reckless expedition to the Faroe Islands, but quietly down to Penmenner House, at the Lizard in Cornwall. He wished to postpone his return to London for as long as possible, staying on after Virginia and Adrian left 'in extraordinary solitude, willing to sell my soul for a little conversation . . . but Saint-Simon supports me, wonderful as ever.'

It had been a bad year, but it was not over yet. The time had come for

Swithinbank, the understudy, to step into a principal role in his life. Meeting him that month for the first time, Duncan found him 'the most beautiful person I've ever seen', and Lytton felt cautiously inclined to agree. He could at least congratulate himself on having successfully scotched that mad venture to the Fiji Islands. Remembering all this, he wrote him an affectionate letter, and received in reply the news that his friend was making arrangements to take service in India. It was another painful shock. Again he tried to change Swithinbank's mind. The letter he sent was written in an unusually earnest tone, particularly interesting in someone who, not so long ago, had envied his brothers for their Anglo-Indian careers. 'I believe as strongly as I believe anything that you oughtn't to go,' he wrote.

'Have you thought enough of the horror of the solitude and the wretchedness of every single creature out there and the degrading influences of those years away from civilization? I've had experience – I've seen my brothers, and what's happened to them, and it's sickening to think of. Oh! You've got your chance – your chance of being well off and comfortable among the decent things of life, and among your friends.'

But this time there was no dissuading him and Lytton was forced to capitulate. 'But go away', he exclaimed in irritation, 'and be a great man, and rule the blacks, and enjoy yourself among apes and peacocks.' Swithinbank's departure – like that, apparently, of Leonard Woolf four years before – was the end of their friendship. Their correspondence lingered into the following year and then trailed off.

It had really been a terrible year, and at the end of it, here he was, left alone with projects for a vague infinity of things, but no likelihood of bringing any of them to fulfilment. Deserted and grey; the words which had come to him as he stood before Buccleuch Place, dismal and uninhabited in the autumn wind and rain, epitomized the condition he had reached after almost twenty-nine years.

EIGHT

The Wrong Turning

'My heart . . . it seems strange that things should still be so singularly active – and at such an age too (106 last birthday). Well! Perhaps this time . . . Only, so different, so different . . . like all other times, in fact.'

Lytton Strachey to Leonard Woolf (1911)

I

A PROPOSAL OF MARRIAGE

Lytton restored himself after the blank, blank, blank of leaving Cambridge with many visions of an apostolic afterlife. 'When will my heaven be realised? my Castle in Spain,' he had asked Maynard (11 March 1906). 'Rooms, you know, for you, Duncan, and Swithin, as fixtures – Woolf, of course, too, if we could lure him from Ceylon; and several suites for guests. Can you conceive anything more supreme? I should write tragedies, you would revolutionise political economy, Swithin would compose French poetry, Duncan would paint all our portraits in every conceivable combination & permutation, and Woolf would criticise us & our works without remorse.'

After three years of emotional turmoil only Leonard Woolf still held a secure place in this dreamscape. 'We are the true Aristotelian friends,' Leonard had written to him (30 December 1905) – and he went on believing this to be true. 'I must feel my cable,' Lytton assured him; 'and my anchor is in Ceylon.' This anchor was buried in the past and the cable held him timelessly. Nothing changed. In Leonard's imagination Lytton was still the undergraduate who 'corrupted Cambridge just as Socrates corrupted Athens', who used Victorian standards to subvert Victorian ethics by accepting the valuation of men above women and then innocently arguing that a relationship between two men must be doubly superior. He was not, in Leonard's memory, a weekly reviewer but an inspirational spirit which could perform miracles. 'You may write a masterpiece when you are forty but I insist upon your writing one also before you are thirty,' Leonard exhorted him (15 September 1907). So far as Lytton knew,

Leonard also had not changed: 'If you came back tomorrow you would be simply what [you]'ve always been – a person of sense,' he reassured him (2 October 1908).

There were other reasons for the durability of their friendship. 'We are females, nous autres, but your mind is singularly male,' Lytton had written (9 September 1904). In the awful monotony of civil service life, Leonard reached out to 'the wonder of your letters', confiding to Lytton that 'I have never felt so lonely in my life . . . if you only knew how I want to see you! . . . Do you feel my isolation, the continual creeping of depression . . . God, how I wish I could talk to you! . . . you are the only one to whom I really wish to talk.' Lytton quickly realized that to whatever depths he might descend, a lower deep stood threatening to devour his friend. 'I am stunned by the madness and bitterness of life,' Leonard burst out in March 1906. '. . . I sometimes wonder whether I should commit suicide.' He did in fact make a will, take out his gun and prepare to shoot himself. 'God knows why I didn't.' Lytton exerted himself to bring comfort. 'I can only hope that we will get through this someday,' he wrote (13 April 1906), 'that we will live to inhabit our castles in Spain.' He made his letters as entertaining as he could, telling Leonard of the regular Thursday evening soirées Thoby Stephen had started up in his 'Gothic Mansion' at 46 Gordon Square and then, after the Goth's death, how his sisters Vanessa and Virginia, 'the Visigoths', were continuing them for Thoby's Cambridge friends. Virginia 'is rather wonderful', he had written (January 1905), '– quite witty, full of things to say, & absolutely out of rapport with reality.' Clive Bell, he reported, was still wildly in love with Vanessa, and had fallen into 'a sort of distraction – it seems at times to be almost a mania. When he's alone I'm convinced that he's haunted, desperately haunted, by visions of Vanessa; his frightened pathetic face shows it; and his small lascivious body oozes with disappointed lust.'

This was troubling news for Leonard. He vividly remembered seeing the Goth's two sisters one spring day at Cambridge with their large hats, white dresses, parasols: 'their beauty literally took one's breath away . . . It was almost impossible for a man not to fall in love with them, and I think that I did at once.' Lytton, however, was taken aback to learn of Leonard's secret adoration. 'As for your having been in love with Vanessa, it's really scandalous, I think – I mean to allow such things to come out only about 2 years after their occurrence . . . I feel that I shall never get used to the contortions of life.'

These contortions seemed to tighten after Vanessa at last accepted Clive Bell's proposal of marriage. 'It seems to me that in every way it would be best if you were to go away,' she had written to him on 8

November 1906, '– I thought for a year.' A fortnight later, forty-eight hours after Thoby's death, she changed her mind, and they were married on 7 February 1907. 'Do you feel now that we have grown irreparably old?' Leonard wrote to Lytton. '. . . Bell? & Vanessa? I am too weary to mind the mockery of it all.' Shortly afterwards Virginia and her younger brother, the long lawyerish Adrian, moved to 29 Fitzroy Square (where the Fabian firecracker Bernard Shaw had lived with his mother twenty years earlier). 'If ever such an entity as Bloomsbury existed,' wrote Clive Bell, 'these two sisters with their houses in Gordon and Fitzroy Squares, were the heart of it.'

The atmosphere of these two Bloomsbury salons was very different. The Bells 'are a wild sprightly couple', Lytton told Duncan (2 June 1907). 'The drawing-room has no carpet or wall-paper, curtains some blue and some white, a Louis XV bed (in which they lie side by side), two basket chairs, a pianola, and an Early Victorian mahogany table!' Vanessa filled the house with light, painting its walls with pale colours and draping bright Indian shawls over the sparse furniture; Clive filled it with simple joviality that contrasted oddly with the pictures by Picasso and Vlaminck. 'When the door was opened,' remembered David Garnett, who joined this circle of friends shortly before the war, 'a warm stream of Clive's hospitality and love of the good things of life poured out, as ravishing as the smell of roasting coffee on a cold morning.'

At Fitzroy Square there was only a Dutch picture of a lady and Watts's portrait of Sir Leslie Stephen. They were like a giraffe and ostrich, Adrian and Virginia. On the ground floor, Adrian's drawing-room was well ordered, neatly lined with legal volumes; upstairs Virginia's study was littered with books all over the floor and from this rubble rose her tall desk where she stood writing each day, positioned near the window like her sister's easel. Vanessa 'overflows in all ways': but Virginia, struggling for self-control, kept on guard. Upon an unforeseen introduction, 'there was an expression of blazing defiance, a few carefully chosen banalities and a feeling of awkwardness', recalled Duncan Grant. He had got to know Virginia after joining her sister's Friday Club for artists, the more literary Thursday evenings being transferred from Gordon to Fitzroy Square. 'About ten o'clock in the evening people used to appear and continue to come at intervals till twelve o'clock at night,' he wrote, 'and it was seldom that the last guest left before two or three in the morning. Whisky, buns and cocoa were the diet, and people talked to each other. If someone had lit a pipe he would sometimes hold out the lighted match to Hans the dog, who would snap at it and put it out. Conversation; that was all. Yet many people made a habit of coming, and few who did so will forget those evenings.'

'In that world of many men, coming and going,' wrote Virginia in 'A Sketch of the Past', 'we formed our private nucleus.' It was a nucleus of privileged rejects and outsiders from the Victorian grand era, an informal coming together of young people who were cutting family ties and beginning to run their lives with unconventional freedom. Individually their needs were for 'five hundred a year each of us and rooms of our own', as Virginia later wrote. 'Good God!' Lytton exclaimed in a letter to Duncan (23 August 1909), 'to have a room of one's own with a real fire and books and tea and company, and no dinner-bells and distractions, and a little time for doing something! – It's a wonderful vision, and surely worth some risks!' It seemed as if the whole country was on the verge of some convulsive social change and that as artists and intellectuals they would soon be forming a new society. 'It was to be a society of people of moderate means,' wrote Virginia in her biography of Roger Fry, 'a society based on the old Cambridge ideal of truth & free speaking, but alive, as Cambridge had never been, to the importance of the arts . . .'

These Thursday evenings in Gordon and Fitzroy Squares, and the Friday Club meetings which involved many lay members, were the nearest Vanessa and Virginia came to experiencing undergraduate life. They soon lost their awe of male education. For they were a melancholy lot, these preoccupied young men, who folded themselves up in the corners of sofas, silently pulling at their pipes and chuckling at some Latin joke. 'I detest pale scholars and their questionings about life,' Virginia wrote impatiently, 'and the message of the classics, and the bearing of Greek thought upon modern problems.' Yet they were better than the men she had known in her own family with their bullying self-indulgence, agonizing suppressions, sinister prurience.

Lytton found a good substitute for the courts of Trinity and King's in these Bloomsbury squares. The rooms were different, but the same tobacco smoke stole up the windows against the night sky, and there was the same talk of Greeks and Romans – mostly Greeks. 'Talking, talking, talking,' sighed Virginia in recollection of these nights, '– as if everything could be talked . . .' Yet there was a difference in their talk. The silent domestic jungle, concealing so much illicit sexual trespass which both sisters had known, was cut away by open bawdiness and a new humour. 'Lytton seems to carry on a good deal with his females,' Maynard observed to Duncan (2 August 1908). 'He has let Vanessa see his most indecent poems – she is filled with delight, has them by heart, and has made many typewritten copies for Virginia and others.'

Vanessa relished Lytton's sexual explicitness. Since her marriage, she had flowered into 'the most complete human being of us all'. Virginia, reading these proudly unprintable verses ('a pretty occupation for a virgin on the Sabbath!'), criticized everything that was empty and pretentious in them. So the Cambridge milieu of the Apostles became enlarged and enriched by these Visigoths who were, Lytton told Leonard Woolf, 'the two most beautiful and wittiest women in England!'

Leonard seemed to be in two minds over what Lytton was telling him. It was like reading by instalments a *roman à clef* about characters from his own past – an unsettling experience. Eventually he returned Lytton's correspondence: for if he died in Ceylon their scatological contents should not be revealed to the world; and if he returned to England one day he could take them back as a symbol of recovering his old life.

Meanwhile it was more pleasant to read other people's novels and correspondence, and share this reading with Lytton. They read La Bruyère's *Les Caractères* and Voltaire's correspondence ('the only completely satisfactory thing in the world'), Roger Fry's edition of *The Discourses of Sir Joshua Reynolds* and the fiction of E.M. Forster. But above all, they read the late elusive novels of Henry James. 'The strange, Jamesian, convoluted beauty and subtlety of them act upon those who yield to them like drink or drugs,' recalled Leonard Woolf in his autobiography; 'for a time we became addicted . . .' Saxon Sydney-Turner appeared to them the perfect Jamesian figure, and *The Wings of the Dove* seemed to be about their respective homes at Lancaster Gate and Lexham Gardens. 'Did he invent us or we him?' Leonard asked Lytton after reading *The Golden Bowl* (23 July 1905). 'He uses *all* our words in their most technical sense & we can't have got them all from him.' 'I entirely agree,' answered Lytton, '– it's too extraordinary about his use of words. I suppose there must be some common cause . . . I also wonder whether it's because he's so horribly like us that I, at any rate, can't read him.'

James, too, could hardly bear these awful Bloomsberries. He was like them in the psychological insights that arose from mysterious dark places in himself, and unlike them in belonging so obviously to their parents' world. He saw Vanessa and Virginia as vestal virgins attending their old father, strange figures haunted by the ghost of Thoby. But when they stepped into their future, they disturbed him. How could the wondrous Vanessa, in the crushed strawberry glow of her beauty, marry that 'dreadful-looking little stoop-shouldered, long-haired, third-rate Clive Bell'; how could the ethereal Virginia, with all the promise of her printed wit, take up with such grubby poodles of young men because they had been friends of 'the big mild mastiff' Thoby? It was regrettable. Yet he loved watching them with his staring blank eyes as they sat on his lawn at Rye.

Lytton was down at Rye at the beginning of 1909 staying at the Mermaid Inn again 'in a semi-stupor among mists and golfers'. Through two dense filters, those of rain and dimness outside, pomp and fatuity within, emerged the remarkable silhouette of Henry James. 'He came in here to show the antique fireplace to a young French poet and you never saw such a scene – the poor man absolutely *bouche béante*, and all the golfers and bishops sitting round quite stolidly munching buttered buns. He has a colossal physiognomy, and it's almost impossible to believe that such an appearance could have produced the Sacred Fount. I long to know him.'

Even more impressive was a second sighting of Henry James – at a window of Lamb House. He made his appearance there, as Lytton passed by, to examine more minutely some momentous manuscript – a masterly performance, silent, serious, extraordinarily slow. 'So conscientious and worried and important,' Lytton described him to Virginia, '– he was like an admirable tradesman trying his best to give satisfaction, infinitely solemn and polite. Is there any truth in this? It has since occurred to me that his novels are really remarkable for their lack of humour . . . Perhaps if one talked to him one would understand.'

On his return to London, Virginia invited Lytton to dine at Fitzroy Square. He was to meet her cousin, H.A.L. Fisher, the historian and Oxford don whose father had married into the Stephen family. 'Summoned from the writing of history', as one of his pupils at New College described his elevation to president of the Board of Education, 'to a share in muddling it', his obsequiousness towards those who converted him into a subject for future historical research, combined with the book-learning he was anxious to put at their disposal, gratified some politicians who might otherwise have regarded a history don indifferently. 'You are going to meet the Fishers on Thursday,' Virginia had written to Lytton (4 June 1909). 'You and Herbert must talk about Voltaire, and I shall say how I have been seeing his waxwork at Madame Tussaud's. I can't help thinking he is rather a fraud (H.F. I mean). He is impossibly enlightened and humane. She is a bright woman.'

'I shall be able to speak of nothing but cleeks and greens,' Lytton replied from the Mermaid, 'though no doubt Herbert would be very well able to cope with that. Besides the golfers there are some of the higher clergy – bishops and wardens – and two lawyers at the chancery bar. Of course these are all golfers as well, so it all comes to very much the same thing.'

H.A.L. Fisher turned out to be less interested in golf than in riding, and after some false starts, the conversation switched to the subject of French literature, about which everyone professed to know something. Lytton struck Fisher as being 'a sensitive ungainly youth; awkward in his bearing, and presenting an appearance of great physical debility, as if he had recently arisen from the bed of an invalid. His voice was faint and squeaky. His pale face was at that time closely shaven . . . He was very silent, but uncannily quick and comprehending.'

Although no one realized it at the time, this meeting marked a pivotal change in Lytton's career.

Lytton's correspondence over these weeks is full of lively complaints about the 'ghastly solitude' of Belsize Park Gardens. Some of his days were spent up in his bed, dosed with Sanatogen and quinine; others, huddled in front of the fire, reading the notebooks of Samuel Butler and an eighteenth-century life of Madame de Maintenon. He looked forward to a journey he was planning to Italy. In the meantime, he must save every penny. He even had to refuse Moore's invitation to the Lizard for that year's Easter reading-party: 'I've got to choose one thing or the other.'

Whenever he emerged into the outside world and suffered himself to be taken to concerts or picture galleries, he would forget his ailments and become absorbed in the sights. 'I looked in for an hour at the New Gallery,' he wrote to Duncan (21 February 1909), '. . . and was carried away with excitement.

'. . . There are Whistlers and Reynoldses, and a divine Gainsborough, and Wattses that even I found charming, and amazing Monticellis, and a superb Manet, and a John à faire mourir de peur. The Simon [Bussy] I found rather a difficult affair to take in at the first go off, but I seemed to be making progress as time went on. The excitement was increased for me by the immense distinction of the audience. – Among others, Mrs Carl Meyer was present, in ermine, the Duchess of Portland and Lady Ottoline Morrell, the Marquis de Soveral, accompanied by Señor Villaviciosa, Lord Musk and Master Musk. Mrs George Batten was talking to Lady Strachey, while Mr Lytton Strachey, who was wearing some handsome Siberian furs, was the centre of an animated group. Mr E. Marsh came in later with the President of the Board of Trade[1] – to say nothing of Mr Edmund Gosse and Mr Sidney Colvin. – The Rothenstein woman, even more painted than usual, flowed in your praises to her Ladyship.'

Intellectually he repudiated this upper-class world. Nevertheless it seemed to defy all reason, and persist in its romantic hold over him. Part of the allure lay in his preoccupation with success; and part again in his curiosity over the more exaggerated antics of human beings.

This exaggerated world fills the pages of *Lord Pettigrew*, a novel which Lytton had begun to work on that winter. Written after the style of Anatole France's *M. Bergeret à Paris*, it is ostensibly a satire directed against the snobbery and the intrigue of fashionable society and reactionary politics.[2] He completed four chapters, that is between eight and nine thousand words, before giving it up. For a time he felt excited by the book's possibilities. He would lie in bed in the morning imagining its various dramatic incidents, and each day they would grow more extraordinary. 'You have never heard such conversations or imagined such scenes!' he wrote to Virginia, who had urged him to persist with it. 'But they're most of them a little too scabreux, and they're none of them written. What's so remarkable is the way in which I penetrate into every sphere of life. My footmen are amazing, and so are my prostitutes. There's a Prime Minister who should be fine, and there's a don's wife à faire mourir de rire. But it's impossible to get any of it together.'

Lord Pettigrew, so far as it went, was a fantasy which his mind fertilized with ideas far removed from experience, and it may be regarded as another symptom of his desire to escape the drudgery of life in London. His need for independence was now more urgent than ever, filling the letters he wrote from Belsize Park Gardens with adolescent day-dreams. 'If I could have my way,' he wrote after returning from Rye, 'I should go out to dinner every night, and then to a party or an opera, and then I should have a champagne supper, and then I should go to bed in some wonderful person's arms.'

Another aspect of Lytton's longing for a new life is revealed in his friendship with Virginia Stephen. She was already working at her first novel, *The Voyage Out*, which contains a portrait of Lytton under the name St John Hirst. Naturally cautious, irretrievably intellectual, an admirer of Gibbon and a confirmed misogynist, Hirst cherishes his memories of Cambridge and finds his own family oppressive. 'They want me to be a peer and a privy councillor.' When he leans against a window-frame he looks like 'some singular gargoyle'; when he subsides into a chair, he seems 'to consist entirely of legs'. He tells another character that 'there will never be more than five people in the world worth talking to'. He is filled with thwarted ambition: 'I hate everyone. I can't endure people who do things better than I do – perfectly absurd things too.' When he stings Rachel Vinrace, the heroine based on Virginia herself, with some criticism to which she can find no quick repartee, she reflects that he is 'ugly in body, repulsive in mind'.

For the most part, St John Hirst presents an unflattering likeness to Lytton, and Virginia was probably reflecting on the improbability of any intimate relationship between them when she describes a party at which they attempted to dance together.

'"We must follow suit",' said Hirst to Rachel, and he took her resolutely by the elbow. Rachel, without being expert, danced well, because of a good ear for rhythm. But Hirst had no taste for music, and a few dancing lessons at Cambridge had only put him in possession of the anatomy of a waltz, without imparting any of its spirit. A single turn proved to them that their methods were incompatible; instead of fitting into each other their bones seemed to jut out at angles making smooth turning an impossibility, and cutting, moreover, into the circular progress of the dancers.

"Shall we stop?" said Hirst. Rachel gathered from his expression that he was annoyed.'

Yet Virginia felt a kinship with Lytton's unhappiness. Both were unstable, thin-skinned, hostile as well as diffident. While out of step with the outside world, they were forming their own detached and syncopated rhythms. She admired his 'mind like a torpedo', was touched by his jokes, grew more interested in him.

Ever since Vanessa's marriage people had been speculating on Virginia's prospects. 'The world is full of kindness and stupidity, I wish everyone didn't tell me to marry,' she exclaimed to her friend Violet Dickinson. 'Is it crude human nature breaking out? I call it disgusting.' A marriage between a 'sapphist' and a 'sodomist' would be a most subversive way of responding to the pressure of conventions. Sometimes Virginia envied her voluptuous married sister. But marriage held little appeal for her. Walter Lamb, who courted her for a season, received no encouragement; and when Hilton Young proposed to her in a punt on the Cam, he was told that she could only marry Lytton – though she did not love him. 'He is in some ways perfect as a friend,' she later explained to Molly MacCarthy (March 1912), 'only he's a female friend.'

From this friendship arose many rumours and an atmosphere of expectancy. 'Did Lytton propose to you this afternoon?' Vanessa inquired on 30 July 1908. '. . . I would rather you married him than anyone else.' But perhaps, she vaguely conjectured, the most likely means of reaching such a relationship 'would be if he [Lytton] were to fall in love with Adrian'. Virginia and Adrian's quarrelsome ménage at Fitzroy Square was becoming rather unsatisfactory, but there were other reasons why Vanessa wanted her sister to marry Lytton. Her husband Clive had described herself and Virginia as 'the two people I love best in the world'. But after the birth of their son Julian in February 1908, Clive seemed to be giving

more of his love to his sister-in-law than to his wife. 'I see nothing of
Nessa,' he complained to Virginia at the end of that year. 'I do not sleep
with her; the baby takes up all her time.'

'Nessa has all I should like to have,' Virginia had written after her
sister's marriage to Clive. She saw Clive as a somewhat ludicrous figure –
she called him Parakeet (Lytton referred to him as a canary) – but he was
also quite lovable sometimes and genuinely helpful over her writing. It was
not difficult to lead him on – up to a point – and there was a perverse
satisfaction in doing so. With her cock-teasing treatment of a brother-in-
law perhaps she was avenging the sexual invasion by her half-brother
George Duckworth, which had made her shiver with shame in her
adolescence – as well as inflicting a love-injury on her sister. Later she told
Gwen Raverat that 'my affair with Clive and Nessa turned more of a knife
in me than anything else had ever done'.

At the beginning of 1909, Lytton and Virginia, Clive and Vanessa, and
several other close members of Bloomsbury, began a letter-writing game,
using pseudonyms, that they hoped might develop into an epistolary novel
along the lines of Aphra Behn or Samuel Richardson. Under cover of their
fictional names, after an evening together with the Bells, Lytton wrote to
Virginia (31 January 1909) springing elliptically 'to the most extraordinary
conclusions' about Clive's attitude to her. 'So you've noticed it then?' she
replied, admitting that it had become 'rather uncomfortable' for Vanessa
and herself. She knew that Vanessa wanted her to marry Lytton, but had
assured Clive at the end of 1908 that 'you will be glad to hear that I am not
in love with him [Lytton], nor is there any sign that he is in love with me.'

Lytton appears to have felt the same. 'The people I see and like most
are two women,' he wrote to his sister Dorothy Bussy that February, '– viz.
Vanessa and Virginia, with neither of whom I'm in love (and vice versa).'
Towards Vanessa, to his surprise, he had experienced a mild flutter of
sexual attraction, but between Virginia and himself the attraction was
intellectual. They seemed to understand each other. 'Virginia is I believe a
more simple character than appears on the surface,' Lytton was to tell
Ralph Partridge (1 September 1920). 'Her cleverness is so great that one
doesn't at first see a kind of ingenuousness of feeling underneath.' When
they were apart they hoarded up things to say to each other. He was
'infinitely charming', Virginia wrote years later to Vita Sackville-West,
'and we fitted like gloves'. But would they ever make a pair? Both of them
were anxious to escape their present ways of living. Life in Bloomsbury
with Virginia would surely be a better alternative for Lytton than living
with his mother in Hampstead. What else was there – loves apart? Now
that the two emotional supports of his life, Duncan and Maynard, had

collapsed and Swithinbank had gone, his relationship with Virginia took on a special importance. 'As I advance through life,' he had written to her (31 January 1909), 'I grow more and more convinced that extraordinary conclusions are the only things I care for.' And she replied (1 February 1909): 'You always tempt me to run on ... with your hints and subtleties and suggestive catlike ways.' The truth was that they found each other extraordinarily sympathetic.

On 17 February, despite a heavy cold, Lytton made his way from Belsize Park Gardens to Fitzroy Square and proposed marriage to Virginia. To his dismay she immediately accepted him. It was an awkward moment, for the very second it was happening, he sensed it was out of the question. 'As I did it, I saw it would be death if she accepted me, and I managed, of course, to get out of it before the end of the conversation,' he wrote to Leonard (19 February 1909). 'The worst of it was that as the conversation went on, it became more and more obvious to me that the whole thing was impossible. The lack of understanding was so terrific! And how can a virgin be expected to understand? You see she *is* her name. If I were either greater or less I could have done it and could either have dominated and soared and at last made her completely mine, or I could have been contented to go without everything that makes life important ... Her sense was absolute, and at times her supremacy was so great that I quavered ... I was in terror lest she should kiss me.'

In a letter to his brother James, he describes the proposal as a decided reverse 'in my efforts to escape'. The escape he was looking for was not only from his family at Belsize Park Gardens, but also from his two most regular visitors there, Duncan and Maynard. It was almost eight months since the crisis between them had come to a head, yet still nothing was resolved. Fluctuating between many moods and emotions – anger and resignation and magnanimity and jealousy – Lytton presented a formidable face to Maynard who, that February, had broken down and cried in front of James. A mounting tension darkened this 'black period' of Lytton's life which he seemed to be communicating to everyone. His proposal to Virginia, arising from an uprush of despair, was partly an effort to break this circle of unhappiness, and amounted to a renunciation, hurriedly withdrawn, of his homosexual ties and of homosexuality itself. All this he confided at the time to Vanessa Bell 'who's quite unparalleled', he told Leonard, 'but she doesn't see the real jar of the whole thing – doesn't take in the agony of Duncan, and the confusion of my states. I copulated with Duncan again this afternoon, and at the present he's in Cambridge copulating with Keynes. I don't know whether I'm happy or unhappy.'

The next day, 20 February, the affair with Virginia was concluded. 'I've had an éclaircissement with Virginia,' Lytton explained to Leonard. 'She declared she was not in love with me, and I observed finally that I would not marry her. So things have simply reverted.'

What Lytton quickly realized was that Virginia had as much need to escape as himself. So had Leonard in Ceylon. Two months earlier, on Christmas Day 1908, Lytton had launched one of his thunderbolts with a melodramatic letter suggesting that Leonard should propose to Virginia and rescue them both. Leonard's reply arrived forty-eight hours after his own proposal. 'Most wonderful of all would have been to marry Virginia,' Leonard wrote. 'She is I imagine supreme ... Do you think Virginia would have me? Wire to me if she accepts. I'll take the next boat home; & then when I arrived I should probably come straight to talk with you.'

Lytton was delighted. 'You are perfectly wonderful, and I want to throw my arms round your neck,' he replied (19 February 1909).

'. . . Isn't it odd that I've never been really in love with you? And I suppose never shall . . . If you came and proposed she'd accept. She really would. As it is, she's almost certainly in love with me, though she thinks she's not. I've made a dreadful hash, as you see, but it was the only way to make sure of anything. I was brought to it by the horror of my present wobble and the imagination of the paradise of married peace. It just needed the *fact* of the prospect to show me that there simply isn't any alternative to the horror, that I must face it, and somehow get through or die.'

Lytton advised Leonard that 'there's no doubt whatever that you ought to marry her. You *would* be great enough, and you'd have too the immense advantage of physical desire.' He then passed on the news of this proposal to Vanessa. But Vanessa was doubtful. She still believed that her sister would probably marry Lytton within a couple of years 'or at any rate be practically engaged to him', she insisted to Clive. For she knew what Lytton knew: that in her fashion Virginia loved Lytton. 'Oh I was right to be in love with him 12 or 15 years ago,' Virginia was to confide in her diary in 1925. 'It is an exquisite symphony his nature when all the violins get playing . . . so deep, so fantastic.'

Not until the autumn of 1910 did Vanessa and Virginia finally agree that 'an alliance with him [Lytton] was impossible & that marriage with somebody was quite possible.' But with whom? Leonard had written to say that 'I have no connection with yesterday: I do not recognize it nor myself in it.' But Lytton pressed on with his matchmaking. 'If you come [home],' he wrote in May 1909, '. . . you could marry Virginia, which would settle nearly every difficulty in the best possible way. Do try it. She's an astounding woman, and I'm the only man in the universe who would have refused her; even I sometimes have my doubts.' He urged Leonard to propose by telegram and after getting no answer to this suggestion, wrote again on 21 August to insist that his friend's destiny was clearly marked out for him.

'You must marry Virginia. She's sitting waiting for you, is there any objection? She's the only woman in the world with sufficient brains; it's a miracle that she should exist; but if you're not careful you'll lose the opportunity. At any moment she might go off with heaven knows who – Duncan? Quite possible. She's young, wild, inquisitive, discontented, and longing to be in love.'

'Of course,' Leonard replied the following month, 'I know that the one thing to do would be to marry Virginia.' But he shrank from the 'ghastly complications' of marriage, with all its horrible preliminaries of courtship. Besides he had left that world behind. 'I find I become hopelessly enmeshed in my surroundings, but what can I do?' he had written to Lytton. '. . . I work, God, how I work. I have reduced it to a method & exalted it to a mania.' Lytton warned him that he must come back and see Virginia before the end of 1910. But their letters lapsed and Leonard was not to return for a year's leave until the following summer.

'I'm still rather agitated and exhausted,' Lytton had written to Virginia immediately after his proposal. '. . . I do hope you're cheerful! As for me, I'm still of a heap, and the future seems blank to me. But whatever happens, as you said, the important thing is that we should like each other: and we can neither of us have any doubt that we do.'

2

ON GRAY AND PURPLE SEAS

Longing to be 'hundreds of leagues away from everything, and everybody, floating alone on purple seas', Lytton purchased a large bottle of medicine and took himself off for a weekend to the grey seafront of Brighton. To repair his nerves he was writing poetry and on the last day of his visit (Sunday, 21 February 1909) reported to Duncan that 'the combination of Brighton and Sanatogen has done the trick.'

His reversal with Virginia – a full realization of the practical limits to *that* kind of association – produced two effects: first, that of re-emphasizing the value of his old friendships; and second, that of reviving temporarily his passion for Duncan. Who else was there? Perhaps, even now, he might salvage something from the shipwreck. But it would be impossible to rekindle their intimacy without regenerating his feelings for Maynard. He was in no frame of mind to ignore the faintest chance of happiness. His ambassadorial letter to Maynard had been a difficult one to write, but it made him feel better – indeed he felt oddly, almost ominously, cheerful. It must be due to the astonishing quantities of Sanatogen he was consuming. 'By every rule,' he explained to Duncan (4 March 1909), 'I ought to be shivering on the edge of moral and physical annihilation, and I find I'm a healthy, energetic, efficient and resourceful member of society. How dreadful it sounds! I expect before the week's out I shall have joined the territorial army, and become a tariff reformer.'

He had three concurrent plans in mind. The first was a scheme to set up house with his brother James somewhere in London – possibly Bloomsbury. Pending this house-hunting, Lytton was putting into effect an interim plan and spending as much time as conveniently possible away from 67 Belsize Park Gardens. With this in mind, he decided to join the Savile Club, then in Piccadilly.[3] But his first appearance there was a fiasco, as he recounted to James (6 April 1909):

'My adventures on Friday, when I arrived here for the first time, were extremely painful. After having been certified as a member by a purple-bottle-nosed servitor in a guichet in the hall, I didn't in the least know what to do. There was a door, a staircase, and a notice-board; I was in my hat and coat, carrying an umbrella; the servitor merely stared from his guichet. In a moment of weakness I began to read the notices on the notice-board, and while I was doing so the servitor became involved in an endless conversation with an imbecile Major. I was therefore lost. I couldn't ask him where I was to put my hat, coat and umbrella. I had read every notice six times, and there seemed no hope. At last I made a wild plunge at the door – opened it, entered, and found myself in the dining-room, nose to nose with a somewhat surprised and indignant waiter. I then fled upstairs, and so managed to get here* safely. But there are further mysteries still to be explained – the second floor? – dare I penetrate there? . . .

A more serious proposition was his third plan – to liberate himself finally from the clutches of the *Spectator*. 'Perhaps Duncan has told you of

* 'The Smoking Room, overlooking Green Park.' [Strachey's footnote]

my probable abandonment of the *Spectator*,' he wrote to Maynard (29 March 1909). 'At present it had better not be mentioned. I think it's the only thing to do, though it terrifies me out of my wits.' Maynard, as usual, agreed. 'I think you're much to be congratulated on getting rid of the *Spectator*,' he replied (4 April 1909), '– if you're prepared to risk poverty and pawn your coat.' It was, he implied, easy to overestimate the importance of money. Nevertheless, Lytton's apprehensions were understandable. From the *Spectator* he received almost all his independent means of livelihood. Yet while he continued pumping so much precious energy into it, there could be little chance of writing anything else.

The last of his regular pieces for the *Spectator* – a rather indifferent article on the love letters of Thomas Carlyle and Jane Welsh – appeared on 10 April 1909; though in the course of the next five years he did contribute five long essay-reviews to the paper specially commissioned by James in his capacity as St Loe Strachey's private secretary. Lytton's decision to break free was hastened by 'some unpleasant diseases, among which is vertigo!' he told James (12 April 1909). 'The man Roland has been called in, and has ordered a complete cessation of work, and absolute mental rest ... I'm not even allowed out, for fear of falling down in the middle of Piccadilly, and I sit all day trying to read, and not succeeding very well.'

Once more, his plan for establishing himself on some permanent basis apart from his family was postponed. As soon as he was allowed out of doors, he went to stay for two weeks at King's and was whirled into the throbbing vortex of undergraduate romance. The colleges seemed thick with amorous crises and swirling rumours. Lytton rolled from one to another in fits of laughter and tears. Eclipsing all else was his meeting with the legendary George Mallory, a figure cut authentically in the heroic mould. 'His body – vast, pink, unbelievable – is a thing to melt into and die,' Lytton wrote to Leonard. As with Thoby Stephen, everything about him appeared larger than life – the manly shoulders, the magnificent torso, the wide smile, white teeth, blue eyes – so large indeed that Lytton felt he could curl up within Mallory's shadow and sleep like a child. He had first heard of him from James, who was said to treat him rather severely, and from Duncan, who placed him 'easily first' of all the handsome young men there. But their stories had conspicuously failed to do him justice.[4] Mallory was not so much a person with whom you slipped into an intimate friendship as someone whom you worshipped. 'Mon dieu! – George Mallory!' Lytton exclaimed to Clive and Vanessa Bell (21 May 1909):

'When that's been written, what more need be said? My hand trembles, my heart palpitates, my whole being swoons away at the words – oh heavens! heavens! I found of course that he'd been absurdly maligned – he's six foot high, with the body of an athlete by Praxiteles, and a face – oh incredible – the mystery of Botticelli, the refinement and delicacy of a Chinese print, the youth and piquancy of an imaginable English boy. I rave, but when you see him, as you must, you will admit all – all! The amazing thing, though, was that besides his beauty, other things were visible, more enchanting still. His passion for James was known, but it so happened that during my visit he declared it – and was rejected . . . Poor George! I met him for the first time immediately after this occurrence, and saw in my first glance to the very bottom of his astounding soul. I was écrasé. What followed was remarkable – though infinitely pure. Yes! Virginia alone will sympathize with me now – I'm a convert to the divinity of virginity, and spend hours every day lost in a trance of adoration, innocence, and bliss. It was a complete revelation, as you may conceive. By God! The sheer beauty of it all is what transports me . . . To have sat with him in the firelight through the evening, to have wandered with him in the Kings Garden among violets and cherry blossom, to have – no, no! for desire was lost in wonder, and there was profanation even in a kiss . . . For the rest, he's going to be a schoolmaster, and his intelligence is not remarkable. What's the need?'

Early in May, Lytton left Cambridge. 'I've grown used to annihilation,' he admitted to James, 'and have at last learnt the art of not expecting very much.' Calm was not life's crown, but calm was best. 'I'm beginning to understand the sentimentality of poets on the spring,' he told Duncan (7 May 1909). 'Their preposterous descriptions are here, actually existing, under my very nose. Beds of violets, choirs of birds, blossoms and butterflies and balmy breezes and scents and everything else.'

He was trying to declare a truce on his passions and to think carefully about his future. He possessed, he felt sure, the essential qualities that in the long run should give him success – a decent competency and the desire for doing genuinely interesting work. Love might be the very devil, but it *was* Time's fool; and once it had flown out of the window, he was astonished to find how well he got along without it.

His hopes of escaping to the sunshine of Italy had now been given up. But his mother, feeling that he needed some sort of restorative programme, decided that he should spend a few weeks in Sweden, a clean enlightened country, notorious for its up-to-date clinics. This was something of an anti-climax after his Roman dreams, but at least he would be out of Hampstead. And if the Swedish doctors could work a cure, he might then build up the strength to make a successful bid for liberty, for happiness and a new career.

3

SWEDISH EXPERIMENT, FRENCH SOLUTION

Lytton started out on his quest for health in mid-July. With him went two female attendants – an eccentric aunt of Duncan Grant's called Daisy McNeil who ran a private nursing home in Eastbourne for the infirm members of well-to-do families; and one of her elderly affluent patients, a woman by the name of Elwes, 'a poor dried-up good-natured old stick with an odd tinge of excitability, alias madness'. Both ladies were extraordinarily obliging, offering to mend Lytton's socks, presenting him at all times of the day with cups of weak tea, and insisting that he read the out-of-date newspapers before themselves. He repaid them by cracking polite jokes and elaborately admiring, for their benefit, the scenery. 'Even La Elwes's conversation has its charms,' he reported back to Duncan (1 August 1909). 'At first I was terrified by her hatchet nose and slate-pencil voice – and I still am occasionally – but on the whole I now view her with composure. Never have I met a more absolutely sterile mind – and yet how wonderfully cultivated! It's like a piece of flannel with watercress growing on it.'

On their arrival in Stockholm, Daisy McNeil, who spoke Swedish, arranged for Lytton to have some medical tests – fearful intimate encounters carried on in broken French. 'Pas de laxatifs, monsieur!' were the doctor's first and last words; and he sent Lytton down with his retinue of ladies to Badanstalten, a health sanatorium for 'physical therapeutics' at Saltsjöbaden, by the sea, not far from Stockholm. This sanatorium specialized in the treatment of heart conditions, nervous illnesses, stomach, intestinal and digestive complaints and was presided over by a charming cello-playing Dr Zander who attended personally to Lytton.

The water was undoubtedly the best feature of Saltsjöbaden, and if he had only owned a small sailing boat, life might have been tolerable. He saw a great many boats, but they were all private and it seemed out of the question to hire one. 'I believe I'm the only person of our acquaintance who could do what I'm doing,' he boasted to James.

'The dullness is so infinite that the brain reels to think of it, and yet I might almost be called happy . . . I had quite a shock when I entered the dining-room for the first time and saw the crowd of middle-aged and middle-class invalids munching their Swedish cookery. For complete second-rateness this country surpasses the wildest dreams of man. I sometimes fear that it may be the result of democracy, but imagine really that it's inborn, and brought to its height by lack of cash. All the decent Scandinavians, no doubt, left the place a thousand years ago, and only the dregs remain. Yet they're amazingly good-looking; and the sailors in Stockholm, with their décolleté necks, fairly send one into a flutter. The bath-attendants, however, so far, have not agitated me, and this in spite of the singular intimacies of their operations. Even the lift boys leave me cold. My health seems to be progressing rather well, but my experiences have been more ghastly than can be conceived, medical experiences, I mean – oh heavens!'

It was the improvement in his health that made the tedium supportable. He had started off the first week with nothing more strenuous than some insignificant baths ('Finsenbad'), but almost immediately he began to gain in weight, his digestion improved – also his temper – and other departments. 'Conceive me if you can a healthy and pure young man,' he wrote to Maynard (13 August 1909). 'My only terror is that none of it'll last.' After the first successful week he graduated from the bathroom to the gym. 'I hope when I get on to the mechanical gymnastics, etc., that I shall swell out of my clothes,' he told Duncan. By the third week his female attendants were letting out his waistcoats.

The regime now grew more formidable. At eight o'clock each morning Lytton was called by sister Fanny who brought him a glass of 'Carlsbad water' – a mild tonic. Half an hour later he breakfasted off a locally concocted simulacrum of porridge and sour cream. At nine-thirty he paraded at the gym for a thirty-minute period of mechanical exercises – gadgets and appliances of a gruesome medieval appearance. 'The hall where one does them [the exercises] looks exactly like a torture chamber,' he explained to his mother (3 August 1909), '– terrific instruments of every kind line the walls, and elderly gentlemen attached upon them go through their evolutions with the utmost gravity.'

When the sun shone, the air would glow miraculously light and clear, and he was able to sit out on his special deck-chair among the pines and the perspiring Swedish patients, dreaming and doing nothing. At the back of every dream stood the heroic figure of George Mallory. To his friends he poured out a stream of letters describing the rigours and incongruities of this 'Swedish experiment'. And when he had wearied of writing, he would read Tolstoy, Saint-Simon, Voltaire, Swinburne. 'I only regret that

I forgot to bring a copy of the Holy Bible,' he wrote to his mother. He eagerly devoured imported copies of the *Gloucester and Wilts Advertiser* and began to get quite heated over far-off local affairs. Swedish politics also tried to claim his attention when, early in August, a general strike was called. However there was scarcely a ripple of disruption in the medicinal halls.

It was during these morning periods of reading and writing letters, that Lytton conceived a plan for compiling an anthology of English heroic verse. 'One might get a great many good extracts which people don't know of,' he wrote to his mother (21 August 1909). 'The interest would be to trace the development up to Pope, etc., and then the throw back with Keats and Shelley.

'I think Pope made more advance on Dryden – in the mere technique of the line – than is usually recognized. Dryden's line, though of course it's magnificent, lacks the weight of Pope's. I once analysed some passages in the Dunciad, and found that the number of stressed syllables in each line was remarkable – sometimes as many as seven or eight. It's difficult to believe that this is the same metre as Epipsychidion which rushes along with three stresses to a line at most. I've written to Sidgwick[5] proposing to do this. I hope he'll accept.'

Nothing came of this plan, though fifteen years later Lytton incorporated some of his reflections on the heroic couplet into his Leslie Stephen Lecture on Pope.

Lunch took place at one o'clock, and once the patient was judged to have properly digested his food, he was plunged into a medicinal bath. These were rather strict affairs, meticulously supervised by stewards and officials, and always too cold for pleasure. After tea at four, Lytton was allowed two hours' rest until dinner which, to his disgust, was served at the unbelievably *bourgeois* time of six o'clock. Communal walks were permitted after dinner, under the pallid sky and among the mangy conifers of the so-called 'English Park'. It was a shocking experience to be hedged in on these slow expeditions by the elderly inhabitants. There were so many of them – all Swedes or Finns – and, despite their middle-class habits, suspected by Lytton of being counts and countesses incognito, as in a comic opera. Wherever he looked he saw them: dotted across the nondescript countryside, wandering in the scrubby woods or bobbing about in boats, streaming endlessly through the corridors to their various meals and cures, or chattering over their symptoms in the 'Salong'. There was no escaping them.

In the later evening, after promenading around in the park, Lytton usually played a few games of billiards with Daisy. He soon gained an immense reputation as a billiards expert among the inmates. 'Directly we begin to play,' he informed his mother (21 August 1909), 'crowds enter the room, and take seats to watch the Englishman playing "cannon-ball" as they call it. As the table is very small and the pockets are very large I occasionally manage to make a break of 15 or 20 which strikes astonishment in the beholders. Apparently the Swedish game consists entirely of potting the red ball with great violence, so that cannons and losing hazards brought off with delicacy appear to these poor furriners wonderful and beautiful in the extreme.'

At half-past nine play was interrupted for an evening bowl of pseudo-porridge; and an hour later Lytton retired upstairs to his bedroom, drew down his special blinds and went off into dreamless sleep. He had experienced nothing like this since Abbotsholme. After six weeks he became so attuned to the monotony that he could hardly believe in any mode of living which did not comprise dinner-at-six, mechanical gymnastics, porridge and cold baths, and perambulations with dubious Scandinavian countesses. It was not the unremitting hell it sounded, but rather a purgatory where he had absolved himself through suffering.

Early in September Daisy McNeil and 'La Elwes' gave up the struggle and fled to England; but James bravely came out to stay with his brother for the remaining days of his treatment. 'It was very fortunate,' Lytton explained to Maynard (17 September 1909), 'as otherwise I should have been alone and moribund in this ghastly region.'

The brothers left Saltsjöbaden on 23 September, arriving back in London two days later. After a week at Belsize Park Gardens, suffering from piles and carrying an air cushion, Lytton travelled down with his mother and Harry Norton to Brighton, where he set about trying 'to recover from the effects of Sweden'.

*

With Lytton's return to London came a new scheme to gain his independence. This entailed going to live at Grantchester as a neighbour of Rupert Brooke's, in 'my moated grange' as he called it, happily anticipating his tenancy. From Saltsjöbaden he had already written to Rupert inquiring after the Old Vicarage, next to The Orchard where Rupert was then living. This house, which Rupert himself later occupied and made famous with his Grantchester poem, was owned by a Mr and Mrs Neeve, who were at that time anxious to find lodgers. 'So far they have been singularly unsatisfied,' Rupert reported in his acquired Stracheyesque style.

'Mr Neeve is a refined creature, with an accent above his class, who sits out near the beehives with a handkerchief over his head and reads advanced newspapers. He knows a lot about botany. They keep babies and chickens; and I rather think I have seen both classes entering the house. But you could be firm. The garden is the great glory. There is a soft lawn with a sundial and tangled, antique flowers abundantly; and a sham ruin, quite in a corner; built fifty years ago by Mr Shuckbrugh,[6] historian and rector of Grantchester; and *most* attractive . . . There are trees rather too closely all round; and a mist. It's right on the river.'

James was in his fashion sceptical about this plan. 'I gather Lytton's corresponding with you about a house in Grantchester,' he wrote. 'Would you hate anyone being near you? though I suppose you both dislike one another too much to meet often.' But Rupert was as yet unaware of disliking Lytton; and Lytton himself felt enthusiastic about the venture. It would be exciting to see more of Rupert's pink picnicking friends. 'If I can, I shall stay there for ever,' he told Virginia (13 October 1909).

All this, however, was before he had gone down to reconnoitre the place. He spent one night as Rupert's guest at The Orchard where he was observed 'to have a habit of sitting with his back against the book-shelves, reaching a hand over his shoulder, and bringing forward without looking the first book he touched, reading a snatch of it, putting it back, and grabbing another, all without turning round'. Everything seemed fixed for a new phase in his life until Rupert casually let on that the house was frequently flooded in all seasons, and famously frigid in the winter. The Old Vicarage was obviously no place for Lytton; and so yet another scheme had to be let go.

He had almost resigned himself to another arid stretch of family life, when to his rescue came George Mallory, with the news that his old rooms in Cambridge were empty. Lytton hurried round there, and secured the place relatively cheaply 'at 35/- a week for board and lodging', he wrote to his mother (18 October 1909). 'I think they will do very well, but I can only have them for this term . . . I forgot to mention the charming name of my new abode – Pythagoras House.'

Pythagoras House became Lytton's headquarters for the next ten weeks. 'I occasionally wish that I could glide on here for ever,' he told Duncan (1 November 1909). 'Won't you come up for a week-end?' he invited Clive Bell (21 October 1909). Clive and Vanessa did come and visit him the following month, and so did Virginia. 'We were very intimate and easy and I have no doubts of his charm,' she wrote the following month.

Lytton was also seeing more of Rupert Brooke (still the impossible object of James's love), Harry Norton (impossibly infatuated with James), and the silent Saxon Sydney-Turner. Most notable among his new Cambridge friends was Francis Birrell:[7] 'I have made the acquaintance of Mr Birrell's small son, who is at King's,' he informed his mother. 'He is very gay, and has apparently never heard of Ireland.'[8]

At Pythagoras House Lytton composed a blank verse tragedy for a Stratford-upon-Avon Prize Play Competition. From the sixteenth century onwards nearly every would-be poet would attempt to write at least one blank verse drama. *Essex: A Tragedy* is competently, even ingeniously constructed, but rather lifeless. Perhaps the most interesting lines are those given to Queen Elizabeth as she reflects on the difference between her own age and that of the youthful Essex, since they convey something of Lytton's own worship of masculine youth, and the sense of premature middle-age which hung around him in his blacker moods.

> For I was old
> Ere he was young, and years before he breathed
> These locks had worn the coronet of a queen.
> Rather it was that in my age I knew him,
> And to my setting skies he came to lend
> The freshness of a star. Am I a dotard
> Dreaming on fantasies? Or is it true
> That frozen years can snatch from fiery youth
> Some palpable warmth and the reflected radiance
> Of life's meridian splendour? No, 'tis no dream;
> For often in the midst of my dull days,
> My councils, and my creeping policies,
> I have known a look from Essex light the clouds,
> And make earth glory.

Such soliloquies were to play a large part in *Elizabeth and Essex*, which Lytton subtitled 'A Tragic History'; and the chief interest *Essex: A Tragedy* now holds lies in its relationship to the biography. Lytton believed that the enigma of the Queen's relationship with her famous courtier was ideally suited to theatrical treatment. *Elizabeth and Essex* was to be conceived in dramatic form, unlike all his other books – even *Queen Victoria* – which are constructed as interrelated essays. *Essex: A Tragedy* shows that his attitude towards Essex and Elizabeth herself, notwithstanding the added

Freudian interpretations incorporated into the biography, remained pretty well consistent.

During the autumn evenings at Pythagoras House, Lytton would read out scenes from his competitive tragedy to his friends. Shortly before Christmas the play was completed and sent off to Stratford in the vain hope that it would be performed there during the Festival Week. 'When it's acted,' he optimistically wrote to Moore, 'I'll send you a box.'

Life at Pythagoras House was wonderfully harmonious. 'I suppose the result of the end of term,' he told James. 'People seem to draw closer.' A constant pleasure was the proximity of George Mallory. 'It's a surprising thing, after the experience of – I won't tell you how many years – to find oneself with someone who really likes things.' Yet were not Mallory's good looks beginning to go off? Was his complexionless face not becoming slightly washy and bulbous, its contours lunar like a cheese? Mallory could still look exquisite if you blurred over certain corpulent developments, but Lytton felt saddened by such melancholy deterioration. Also Mallory was planning to go off on one of his dangerous Alpine expeditions. 'It's not only the love affairs that are bound to fail!' Lytton wrote to James. 'And now I shall never see him again, or if I do, it'll be an unrecognizable middle-aged mediocrity, fluttering between wind and water, probably wearing glasses and a timber toe.'

He returned to Hampstead at the beginning of February, but almost at once escaped again, for 'a dream of a week' to Clive and Vanessa in Gordon Square. 'Dignity, repose, and medical consolations,' he wrote to them after leaving (15 February 1910), '– I feel that I shall never find the divine conjunction again.' James had by now started full-time work as St Loe Strachey's private secretary, and most of Lytton's friends – Clive and Vanessa, Ralph Hawtrey, Bertrand Russell, C.P. Sanger, Gerald Shove, R.C. Trevelyan, and Virginia – had gone down to Cornwall, so that instead of spending his evenings in Bloomsbury, he would wander dispiritedly off to the Savile Club to sit among the old gentlemen there and gaze forlornly at the footmen. 'The future seems very black,' he wrote to Duncan from Hampstead (4 April 1910). '. . . I've been almost perpetually ill here since I came back in December – and there seems now no possible reason, except the place and entourage, for this happening. If I was well, I should like London far better than Cambridge; but it's too much never to be able to work for more than a fortnight at a time. I've been too feeble to do a stroke . . .'

Meanwhile he wrote off diffidently to Rupert Brooke to ask if he might consider going to the country with him (31 March 1910) for a week. 'James thinks there may be, and says that you know of a cottage on

Dartmoor ... I want to go off somewhere; but I fear it's hardly possible that you're still free. If you were I could go as soon as you liked, with songs of Thanksgiving.'

Rupert at once agreed to go, but as the Dartmoor cottage, Becky House, was not vacant, he made arrangements for them to spend the second week in April at the Cove Hotel, at West Lulworth in Dorset. Rupert was a charming and decorative companion, and the hotel was warm and cosy, with a pulley for developing the biceps which both poet and dramatist laboured at vigorously. 'Rupert read me some of his latest poems on a shelf by the sea,' Lytton wrote to James, 'but I found them very difficult to make out, owing to his manner of reading. I could only return the compliment by giving him the first act of Essex to read – he didn't seem quite so bitter about it as you; but that may have been his politeness. I found him, of course, an extraordinarily cheerful companion. I only hope though, that he won't think me (as he does George Trevy) "an old dear". I thought I saw some signs of it.'

But he had found no solution to his long-term difficulties. By the summer he was back in London. 'Such is my low ebb', he admitted to Saxon Sydney-Turner, 'that I'm reduced to reading the life of Cardinal Manning!'

Lady Strachey had run out of new ideas to contend with her son's illnesses, and the only remedy that anyone could think of was a second sojourn at the Saltsjöbaden sanatorium. Accordingly Lytton set off in the second week of July for another ten weeks' spell in Sweden accompanied by his sister Pernel and Jane Harrison, the fifty-nine-year-old classical anthropologist and scholarly spirit behind the Cambridge Marlowe Society and Rupert Brooke's Garden-City Neo-Pagans, who was using this pharmaceutical holiday 'to get new heart' for the writing of *Themis*, her celebrated study on the social origins of Greek religion. When he entered the clinic, there, to welcome him, was the veteran brigade of patients going through the same hectic programme of porridge and baths. 'I already feel as if I'd been here for twenty years,' he began a letter to James written on his first day (18 July 1910).

While Jane Harrison took advantage of her stay to learn Swedish, principally from the writings of Selma Lagerlöf, Lytton concentrated on mastering Italian – for his dreams had revived of travelling south. He was going through the same pantomime of billiards, gymnastics and massage, but this time the medical treatment was more stringent. He was placed under the care of Dr Olof Sandberg, a specialist in digestive complaints, who insisted that Lytton should eat a great deal – 'as much as possible and sometimes a little more' – and who favoured a liberal use of the stomach pump. By the middle of August he reported to Pippa: 'My cure has been going very well.'

For Jane Harrison, suffering under a similar course of treatment, there were no redeeming features. She could not attune herself to the colourless oddity of the place; and Pernel fared little better. 'They both find the place very singular,' Lytton explained to his mother (5 August 1910), 'and I should think the place returns the compliment so far as Jane is concerned – she makes a strange figure among the formal Scandinavians, floating through the corridors in green shawls and purple tea-gowns, and reciting the Swedish grammar at meals.' Before long the two women surrendered and hastened back to England. 'This is the last anyone will hear of my health,' remarked Jane Harrison ruefully.

Lytton's invalidism was made of sterner stuff, and for him the rigorous cure continued unchecked. He was joined by his sister Pippa, but even she could only endure a fortnight of the sanatorium. Yet still Lytton stayed on. Then he suffered a relapse, the cause of which none of the specialists could diagnose. 'I've stayed on here week after week,' he complained to Maynard (26 September 1910), 'lured by the hope of attaining eternal health: on Friday I shall drag myself away ... I feel that this has been a wasted summer for me.'

To while away the hours he had been working spasmodically at a rather heavy *facétie* on the Suffrage Movement. 'I fear, even if it's finished, that it will never see the light of day,' he confessed to Pippa. 'The scene is the infernal regions, and the principal character so far Queen Victoria.' But now, in these last days at Saltsjöbaden, he received a letter from H.A.L. Fisher asking him to write a fifty thousand word panoramic study of French literature for a series that he and Gilbert Murray were editing. 'Herbert Fisher and Gilbert Murray have asked me to write a history of French lit for upperclass citizens,' was how he announced the news to James on a postcard (21 September 1910), 'and I shall accept. It will amuse me, and perhaps pay better than reviews. "If", Herb says, "75,000 are sold you will get £290." Isn't it a bright prospect? But at any rate I gather I'll get £50' (equivalent to £2100 in 1994).

Lytton returned to England at the beginning of October and succeeded in arranging his autumn and winter programme to such effect that hardly more than a week was to be passed in Hampstead. His peregrinations had about them an air of desperation. Waiting for him on his arrival back from Sweden was an invitation from Maynard to spend a couple of days at the Little House at Burford in Oxfordshire where, while working at his *Treatise on Probability*, he vainly hoped to lure Duncan away from his new love Adrian Stephen – meanwhile making do with the 'frivolous young butterfly' Frankie Birrell. Desmond MacCarthy too had invited Lytton for a week's visit, but on arriving from Burford, he found that his host had absent-mindedly left for Paris. However, he passed an agreeable time with Molly MacCarthy in the Cloisters at Eton waiting for Desmond's possible return. From there he went to Charterhouse, where George Mallory had taken up a temporary post as schoolmaster. Then he progressed for a further week to the Homere sisters at Kingham 'in a state bordering on collapse – mental and physical', he told Duncan (19 October 1910), though 'in spite of the hounds, the piano, and the intellectual annihilation, I'm now beginning to pull round.'

During these itinerant weeks he squeezed in an afternoon's discussion of his projected history of French literature with Herbert Fisher, 'who struck me as an academic fraud', he informed Maynard (9 October 1910), echoing Virginia's opinion of him. Fortunately, Fisher's view of Lytton was unrepentantly high. When, earlier that summer, the editors of the Home University Library, casting round to find the right person to compose a short one-volume survey of the literature of France, asked Fisher for his nomination, he had recalled his conversation in Fitzroy Square eighteen months previously. The favourite candidate for the authorship of this book was Edmund Gosse. But Fisher submitted Lytton's name, recommending him as the writer of 'Two Frenchmen', his first contribution to the *Independent Review*, and pointing to the superior versions of the original French which Lytton had offered in order to bring out shades of meaning in the work of La Bruyère and Vauvenargues. Fisher also drew the attention of the editors to the aesthetic cohesion of his essay, since the policy of the Home University Library was to select authors for their literary skill as well as academic distinction.

Fisher explained the details of this commission to Lytton, showing him J.W. Mackail's *Latin Literature*, 'with which he was not then acquainted, as a model which he might be content to follow. He assented to my proposal with rare economy of speech, and with none of the usual expressions of diffidence, which an editor is accustomed to hear from an untried author to whom he has offered a task of exceptional difficulty.'

His plans now took on an immediacy and purposefulness. During the autumn he would read a large number of French classics; while for the winter he decided to go off and live with Simon and Dorothy Bussy at Roquebrune, where from past experience he knew he could work in peace. His years of lethargy and aimlessness were almost at an end.

PART III

'I suppose I ought to feel ... a general sense of lamentation – but somehow I don't. My spirit refuses to be put down.'

Lytton Strachey to David Garnett (23 June 1915)

NINE

The Changing Past

'The greatest crime against youth is the crime of accelerating puberty.'

Cecil Reddie

'We'll be children seventy years, instead of seven.'

Rupert Brooke to Jacques Raverat (3 November 1909)

'The past seems to me the only thing we have which is not tinged with cruelty and bitterness ... the only pang I feel is the pang of approaching age.'

Lytton Strachey to John Sheppard (17 March 1906)

I

'CHÈRE MARQUISE' AND 'CHER SERPENT'

During the autumn of 1910, two people, who between them were to dominate the next few years of Lytton's life, emerge into prominence. Lady Ottoline Morrell he had encountered casually some years earlier at Haslemere, where his mother had taken him to see the Berensons. 'His tall, bending figure and a rather long, cadaverous face, with long nose and a drooping moustache, made him then a not very attractive figure,' recalled Ottoline, 'but I found him most sympathetic and everything he said was of interest.'

In Lytton's correspondence there are occasional references to Ottoline after this meeting which suggest a latent curiosity about her. But it was not until they met one evening as fellow guests of Charles Sanger and his wife Dora, that their friendship began. The Sangers were living near the Strand, high up above the noise of the traffic. Amid the group of young intellectuals Ottoline felt rather out of place. But her uncertainties were quickly dispelled by Lytton. 'I see him now,' she wrote of that first evening, 'sitting in a long basket-chair by the Sangers's gas-fire leaning forward as he would still do, holding out his long, thin hands to warm. I think he had just come from one of Bernard Shaw's plays ... [I] came home quite excited.'

Some seven years older than Lytton, Ottoline was the daughter of General Sir Arthur Cavendish-Bentinck and his wife, Lady Bolsover. Her childhood had been lonely, lavish and discontented, and she grew up determined to shake off her plush philistine background. First she plunged into evangelical religion; next she persuaded her family to allow her to travel to Italy, absorbing the beauties of art and nature; and then she had fallen miserably in love with Axel Munthe. 'How much was my fault, how much his fickleness, I never knew,' she wrote. Returning to England, she decided briefly on an academic career studying logic at the University of St Andrews, but soon abandoned logic and secured her freedom through marrying Philip Morrell, a shadowy picturesque lawyer who became the Liberal member of Parliament for South Oxfordshire.

It was only now, as a married woman, that she was able to find a satisfying outlet for her energies – in the political activities of her husband and, more completely, by entering Bloomsbury. Her introduction to the Bloomsberries came largely through Virginia Stephen, at whose evenings in Fitzroy Square she began to appear. Here she would regularly see Lytton, and though she did not get to know him well, the impressions of him she carried away that were sensitive and acute. 'Of Lytton Strachey I used to feel most shy,' she wrote, 'for he said so little and he seemed to live far away in an atmosphere of rarefied thought.

'His voice so small and faint, but with definite accentuations and stresses of tone, giving a sense of certainty and distinction, appeared to come from very far away, for his delicate body was raised on legs so immensely long that they seemed endless, and his fingers equally long, like antennae. It was not till I knew him better that I found how agile those long legs could be, and what passion and feeling lay in that delicate body...'[1]

It was not long before Ottoline made herself hostess to a circle of writers, artists and politicians. Once a week she would invite them to her home at 44 Bedford Square. In a great double room on the first floor, decked with modern pictures on pale grey walls, yellow taffeta curtains, soft lights and banks of flowers, they would intrigue over their coffee and cigarettes, listen to chamber music or dance in their pullovers and corduroy trousers. 'You have the most delightful salon in London,' William Rothenstein assured her. During the four or five years before the war, Lytton was among the most frequent of her guests at these occasions, and also at her more formal dinner-parties.

aged three, 1883.

The Strachey family. Back row Pippa (Philippa), Dorothy, Richard, Oliver; middle Ralph, Lytto
Lady Strachey (with Elinor's daughter Frances), Sir Richard (with Marjorie), Elinor (holding her
daughter Elizabeth); front (Joan) Pernel (holding racket), William (Elinor's son), c. 1886.

Lytton 'in a beautiful yellow wig' as Hyppolyta, Queen of the Amazons, Christmas 1893.

Souvestre, 'cette grande femme', an early
nce on Lytton.

dr cecil reddie, Utopian headmaster of
Abbotsholme.

or Walter Raleigh, 'he might be one's

G.E. Moore, 'I became…his captive slave'.

TOP *The 'Visigoths', Vanessa and Virginia Stephen.*

ABOVE *Clive Bell.*

RIGHT *Leonard Woolf.*

ßOVE *Duncan Grant (left) and*
ynard Keynes in 1912.

ßHT *'Mon Dieu! – George*
llory!' at 38 Brunswick
uare. c.1912-13 (Photo by
ncan Grant).

LEFT *Lady Ottoline Morrell, drawing by Henry Lamb* (Courtesy of Lady Pansy Lamb).

RIGHT *Lytton Strachey, drawing by Henry Lamb* (Courtesy of Lady Pansy Lamb).

Lytton Strachey in his *Augustus John period.*

Henry Lamb.

Mark Gertler.

Gerald Brenan.

David ('Bunny') Garnett.

Bernard ('Beacus') Penrose.

Ottoline Morrell has been described as an impresario rather than a creator. She 'has the head of a Medusa', wrote Virginia on first meeting her in 1909; 'but she is very simple & innocent in spite of it, & worships the arts.' Ottoline had seized upon the names and addresses of Virginia's 'wonderful friends' and swept them into her exotic whirlpool. Observing their gyrations from an upper landing in Bedford Square, Henry James put a restraining hand on her arm and cautioned: 'Look at them. Look at them, dear lady, over the banisters. But don't go down amongst them.' He was shocked to hear that she wanted to meet Conrad. 'But dear lady . . . he has lived his life at sea . . . he has never met "civilised women".' But Ottoline wanted to live dangerously, gorgeously, on the grand scale. 'Conventionality is deadness,' she wrote in her diary. Besides: 'I was already too far down the stairs to turn back.' Indeed she had several times fallen into, and risen out of, an anguished yet revitalizing love affair with Augustus John who was to paint a flamboyant portrait of her, like the prow of a ship in full sail over tempestuous seas – which she hung over her mantelpiece. 'Whatever she may have lacked,' John testified, 'it wasn't courage.'[2]

What she lacked was moderation. She was a big woman, six feet tall, brilliantly painted ('You beat us all for colour,' the painter Henry Lamb acknowledged), and she nursed a passion for exotic clothes. 'Ottoline was never afraid of looking extraordinary,' her biographer Miranda Seymour wrote. She used this sensational presentation of herself to attract friends and lovers, and to conceal illness, nerves, lack of self-esteem. In her enormous hats, high-heeled scarlet shoes, voluminous pink Turkish trousers, she became a creation of fantasy. 'She gave me a complete mental reorientation,' wrote Aldous Huxley. Virginia was so overcome that 'I really felt as if I'd suddenly got into the sea, and heard the mermaids floating on their rocks.' To Gertrude Stein she seemed like a 'marvellous female version of Disraeli'; to Henry James she appeared 'like some gorgeous heraldic creature, – a Gryphon perhaps or a Dragon Volant!' Her head, covered with masses of dark Venetian curls and uplifted as if scenting the air for scandal, appeared with its powdered cheeks, baronial nose and long jutting chin, to have been artificially attached to her tall and stately body. It was her 'distinctive desire', she declared, to live her life 'on the same plane as poetry and music'. She was determined to infiltrate the lives of these artists and intellectuals who turned up at her parties, share their 'experiences of the soul', perform as their ministering angel, *femme inspiratrice*, lover, champion.

Needing to help them, she gate-crashed into their world with imperious directness. Overcoming her fastidiousness, loudly sucking and crunching between her prominent equine teeth a succession of bull's-eye peppermints, she would subject some of the shyer poets and more inarticulate painters to a series of questions concerning their work and the specific details of their love-affairs. 'M-m-m. Does your friend have *no* love-life?' she once complained in her deep drawling voice to a poet who had brought some particularly reticent friend to tea. Sometimes, intolerant of delay, and despite little enthusiasm for sex, she would supply the missing love affair herself. 'Loving you is like loving a red-hot poker,' Bertrand Russell was to cry out in 1912, 'which is a worse bedfellow than even Lytton's umbrella: every caress brings on agony.' Many of her friendships exploded into extravagant quarrels, in the aftermath of which she would see herself caricatured in her late friend's next novel – as Priscilla Wimbush in Aldous Huxley's *Crome Yellow*, Lady Septugesima Goodley in Osbert Sitwell's *Triple Fugue*, or Hermione Roddice in D.H. Lawrence's *Women in Love* – or even perhaps as Lady Chatterley herself.

In Lytton, Ottoline recognized someone who could help her unpick the lock to the writers' secret chamber. She was also, in some respects, well-suited to act as Lytton's confidante and to give him encouragement. 'Ottoline has moved men's imaginations,' stated D.H. Lawrence, 'and that's perhaps the most a woman can do.' Certainly she moved Lytton's imagination. He found her alternately exhilarating and embarrassing. She exercised to perfection Bloomsbury's methods of interleaving affection with malice, and was transformed in Lytton's letters, Virginia's diaries, Augustus's portraits, into an exotic illusion reflecting their own heightened moods and needs.

It was at her parties in Bedford Square that Lytton now renewed his acquaintance and began to develop a friendship with another of Ottoline's protégés, Henry Lamb. Lamb had been educated at Manchester where his father was Professor of Mathematics at the university. He himself wished to be an artist, but his father would not hear of this, and a compromise had been reached whereby Henry agreed to study at medical school. Encouraged by his friend Francis Dodd,[3] he had nevertheless persisted in drawing in his spare time, and several of his pictures shown at the Manchester City Art Gallery had been praised by critics. But it was not until he met a dazzling young student at the University Ball in the summer of 1905 that he decided to throw up his studies and abscond with her to London. Euphemia, as he called her (Nina Forrest was her actual name), seemed the bohemian ideal of an artist's mistress-model, with a natural sense of comedy and adventure. She lived through men, many of whom found her charming figure and husky voice, her oval face and honey-coloured hair, pneumatically memorable.

Henry and Euphemia were a spectacular pair when they came to London that summer. Lytton's interest in Henry had been roused by his elder brother Walter who spoke tantalizingly of his beauty. Soon Henry joined Vanessa's Friday Club (so did Euphemia 'to the indignation of the more strait-laced members') and was invited to Gordon Square where Lytton first set eyes on him. 'He's run away from Manchester, become an artist, and grown side-whiskers,' he reported to Leonard Woolf (October 1905). 'I didn't speak to him, but wanted to, because he really looked amazing, though of course very very bad.'

Lytton had no opportunity of getting to know him then, since Henry suddenly married Euphemia and together they eloped to Paris where he embarked upon his artistic training and 'amatory wanderings' in company with Augustus John. These were crucial years in his life, and Lytton used occasionally to hear something of them from Duncan. 'That Lamb family sickens me and that man John,' he wrote (7 April 1907), 'I'm convinced now he's a bad lot.' 'What a "warning"! as the Clergy say,' Lytton replied (12 April 1907). 'When I think of him, I often feel that the only thing to do is to chuck up everything and make a dash for some such safe secluded office-stool as is pressed by dear Maynard's happy bottom.' Henry was largely overshadowed by the figure of John. 'I should have been Augustus John,' he was reported to have said. But the comparison often vexed his spirit. While Augustus commandeered Euphemia (whom he rechristened 'Lobelia'), Henry fell long-lastingly in love with Augustus's Dorelia. It was the end of his marriage, though his divorce from Euphemia did not come through for another twenty years.[4]

According to John's biographer, Henry took his apprenticeship to Augustus very seriously. 'He let his hair grow long; he failed to shave; he fastened on gold ear-rings ... With his hypnotic deep-blue eyes he fascinated men and women alike, and his entrance into any gathering was almost as striking as that of his master.' 'He is no ordinary personage and has the divine mark on his brow,' Augustus had assured Ottoline (20 September 1908). What better person was there than this brilliant understudy to fill Augustus's role in the theatre of Ottoline's romantic life? After his return to London in 1909, Dorelia had introduced Henry to Ottoline at Augustus's old studio in Fitzroy Street, and by the spring of 1910 she had fallen for him. 'It was perhaps a half maternal instinct that pushed me towards this twisted and interesting figure,' Ottoline wrote. Yet he was wonderfully attractive, sometimes like 'a vision of Blake', sometimes a version of Stendhal's Julien Sorel. 'I *was* in love with him,' she testified at the end of her life. But 'all his heart is given to Dorelia' (May 1910).

At first Lytton seems to have hardly differentiated between their various attractions. 'Ottoline has vanished to her cottage, but tomorrow she begins her parties again, and I shall drag myself there if I can,' he wrote to Duncan (4 April 1910). 'My last view of her was at a dim evening party full of virgins given by the Russells in a furnished flat. I was feeling dreadfully bored when I suddenly looked up and saw her entering with Henry. I was never so astonished, and didn't know which I was in love with most. As to *her*, though, there seems very little doubt. She carried him off to the country with her under my very nose, and I was left wishing that Dutch William and his friends had never come to England.'[5]

Eight months later Lytton himself was invited to stay at Peppard, Ottoline's cottage near Henley-on-Thames. One Sunday in October, they had met at a tea-party given at Newnham by Jane Harrison. Ottoline, half-laughingly, suggested that Lytton should come and visit her, adding that Henry would be the other guest. Lytton appeared to ponder this suggestion, drifted away, then came back to ask: 'Do you really mean me to come to Peppard?' 'Of course I do,' replied Ottoline, all at once dreading the responsibility of entertaining him at her home. So it was settled.

Away from the fogs of London and the noisy General Election fever that autumn, enjoyment came spontaneously to Lytton. He could find no fault with anything. He ate enormous meals, went for enormous walks through the beech-woods (where Henry had sketched Ottoline naked among the leaves), and had his portrait painted indoors by Henry, who had set up his studio in the stables. 'This is altogether exquisite,' he wrote rhapsodically to his brother James (18 November 1910), who was suspicious of this new attachment.

'Such comforts and cushions as you never saw! Henry, too, more divine than ever, plump now (but not bald) and mellowed in the radiance of Ottoline. The ménage is strange. Fortunately Philip is absent, electioneering in Burnley.[6] Henry sleeps at a pub on the other side of the green, and paints in a coach-house rigged up by Ottoline with silks and stoves, a little further along the road. She seems quite gone – quite! And on the whole I don't wonder . . .

. . . I'm afraid I have now been permanently spoilt for country cottage life. How does the woman do it? Every other ménage must now seem sordid . . .

Ah! She is a strange tragic figure. (And such mysteries!)'

It was during these weeks at Peppard that the pattern of their triangular relationship was fixed and defined. Both Ottoline and Lytton had fallen uncompetitively in love with Henry who returned their attentions with a mixture of gratitude and exasperation. Lytton's feelings are easily enough accounted for: Henry had now come to occupy in his scheme of things the position recently vacated by Duncan. 'That he's a genius,' he wrote to James (30 November 1911), 'there can be no doubt, but whether a good or an evil one?' Such romantic speculation excited Lytton, who, half-cherishing the role of unrequited lover, was still drawn to people whom he instinctively felt might use him badly. Henry was heterosexual and a prey to aggressive moods of depression. 'I cannot answer to his temper,' Ottoline had written to Lytton when renewing her invitation to Peppard (16 November 1910). Henry often felt himself to be the victim of dark powers, but 'I feel sure you could tame me & that with your help I could overcome myself', he told Ottoline, who nevertheless observed his temper to be growing more unreasonable. 'The more I suffered from it the more he delighted in tormenting me.'

All this fascinated Lytton who was not so sure he wanted Henry tamed. E.M. Forster was to describe them 'bounding like kittens in the corridor' of Covent Garden one night and attracting much attention. Sometimes Lytton would think of Henry as a cat which he loved to stroke and which would come with a soft pad 'onto my thigh – oh so soft and caressing! – and then – the sudden stiffening and the claws starting out and drawing blood right through my trousers.' It made him an unpredictable lover. 'He is the most delightful companion in the world,' Lytton confided to James (11 November 1911), '– and the most unpleasant.'

Henry treated Ottoline as a creative flame and Lytton as a prize-winning model. 'When are you coming to sit?' he constantly asked them. But he was a slow impatient worker. 'Must I wait for the age & fame of a Henry James?' he demanded in one of his intemperate letters to Ottoline. After working hard and long, interrupted by sickness and with mounting frustration, he blamed the dwindling creative flame, the feeble sitter, for his disappointments. 'None of my friends have any really imaginative affection for me, they all love me lazily & after their own halting fancy.'

But Ottoline was optimistic that she could make Henry a better person. 'I believe there is something in our friendship, something that unites our souls,' she wrote (29–30 January 1911). Nevertheless, for the time being, he 'certainly cares more for L[ytton].' Lytton's fancy was much tickled by Henry's bawdiness. Both of them had what Ottoline called 'a love of indecency' mixed with their literary and artistic interests, and possibly connected to their unruly digestions and what Maynard referred to as the regular visits from 'Inspector Piles'. Their correspondence and conversation were full of balls and buggeries, farting and phalluses. 'Fart for me under the nose of Maynard,' Henry implored Lytton. But it was less amusing when he metaphorically farted under Lytton's nose. While Ottoline believed, in the words of her biographer Sandra Jobson Darroch, that Lytton 'might yet be saved for the female sex', Lytton himself was convinced that Henry, with his angelic smile, his feminine skin and moments of incredible charm, could be converted to bisexuality. What did all this bawdiness mean if it didn't issue into action? It was provoking to find out that Henry was writing to Ottoline, 'I burn to embrace you and cover all your body with mine,' while he was waiting in vain for such letters himself and only allowed an occasional tepid embrace. Henry, it was true, liked to give him descriptions of French boys looking like ripe plums, silent and flirtatious, and photos of the Bluecoat Boys with their yellow stockings at Christ's Hospital, or send him postcards of 'that lovely serpent' Nijinsky and the young Prince George inscribed, 'With love from me & George'. All this, of course, was no more than teasing and when Lytton's advances grew bolder he was abruptly told to 'cork up your arse'. Yet he did not give up hope.

Henry was suspicious of the Bloomsbury Group, though he seemed to have a soft spot for Saxon Sydney-Turner (who at least never interrupted him). 'I get suffocated by those people,' he complained, 'why must they go on talking about their bloody little group.' In particular he was hostile to what he called 'the false aesthetics of the Clive–Fry coalition,' feeling ostracized as Matthew Smith occasionally (and Wyndham Lewis permanently) were to feel. 'I hear Duncan Grant's very famous in London,' he wrote from France in 1911, '& Clive Bell declares him the greatest artist since Cézanne.' More important, from Lytton's point of view, Henry did not value human relationships. 'His state of mind baffles me,' Lytton admitted to James (August 1911). 'He seems to be completely indifferent to everything that concerns me, and yet expects me to be interested in every trifle of his life.'

Nevertheless Henry's appeal was potent. He offered both Ottoline and Lytton admission into a superbly bohemian set – the world of all-night Chelsea parties with exorbitant artists such as Augustus John and the Russian mosaicist Boris Anrep,[7] both of whom assumed in Lytton's mind the proportions of myths. Henry was, too, a man of salamander-like good looks, pale, slim, with long flowing hair, and a mesmerizing Pan-like beauty. Ottoline, so close to the pair of them, saw clearly how Lytton was being tossed about on a sea of emotion.

'Lamb enjoyed leading him forth into new fields of experience. They would sit in pubs and mix with "the lower orders", as Lytton called them, picking up strange friends. And so great is the imitative instinct in the human breast that he even altered his appearance to please Lamb, wearing his hair very long, like Augustus John . . . He discarded collars and wore only a rich purple silk scarf round his neck, fastened with an intaglio pin. They were a surprising pair as they walked the streets of London, as Lamb wore clothes of the 1860 period with a square brown hat, Lytton a large black Carlyle felt hat and a black Italian cape.'[8]

Lytton's relationship with Ottoline was as picturesque but psychologically less straightforward. A rumour spread through Bloomsbury that he was romantically inclined towards her – a piece of gossip which Virginia, who pictured the great hostess when absent from Lytton as 'languishing like a sick and yellow alligator', helped to popularize. There were stories that appeared to give body to these rumours. Henry, it was said, had come upon them fixed in a fierce embrace, witnessing when they sprang apart, blood flowing down Lytton's lip. But then this might have become confused with the occasion when Lytton found Henry and Ottoline embracing, and Ottoline turned to explain: 'I was just giving Henry an aspirin.' In any event, it was all good pseudo-robust Elizabethan stuff, more stagey than real and with curious transvestite casting. 'I often wish I was a man,' Ottoline confessed to Lytton, 'for then we should get on so wonderfully.' But since Ottoline was the more masculine of the two, they did get on curiously well. She belonged to that breed of overruling imperious women – a breed which included Florence Nightingale, Lady Hester Stanhope, Queen Victoria and Queen Elizabeth – that lit up Lytton's androgynous imagination.

'What a pity one can't now and then change sexes!' Lytton had once written to Clive (21 October 1909). 'I should love to be a dowager Countess.' In the company of Ottoline, this desire could partly be gratified. Ottoline's aristocratic air appealed to his eighteenth-century respect for noble birth. She was his 'plus chère des Marquises'; he was her 'dear Monsieur Le Comte'. Together they soared high above middle-class rules and regularities. Sometimes they would step outside the drawing-room to play at tennis in Bedford Square gardens, and their huge slow lobs over the net were accompanied by such convulsive shrieks of laughter that crowds of passers-by would assemble and stare.

By themselves they were naturally giggling and easy-going, one hungering after secret confidences, the other so eager to impart them. But introduce a third person and their friendship was made subject to uneasy strain. To Lytton's eyes, Ottoline would then change from a beautiful, stately woman of genuine artistic sensibility into a bespangled monstrosity, with a hat (as Desmond MacCarthy noted) 'like a crimson tea cosy trimmed with hedgehogs'. Once, coming from a particularly sportive tête-à-tête with Ottoline, he began to extol her virtues to Duncan and Vanessa. 'She was majestic!' he cried. 'She was splendid! Magnificent! Sublime!' But when Duncan and Vanessa demurred at so excessive praise, he quickly added a string of qualifications to dim the opening eulogy. He mistrusted Ottoline's often-denied talent for gossip, and never used her as his sole confidante, apportioning the part between her and his brother James, who was less stimulating but more reliable and who deplored Ottoline's frivolous influence on Lytton.

Lytton had gone to Peppard expecting to stay a few days; but the atmosphere of so many pugs, cushions and erections held him there, the days dissolved into weeks, November slipped by and December came – and still he lingered on. Some of this time he spent reading up for *Landmarks in French Literature*, and also, in French, the novels of Dostoyevsky, to which he had been introduced by Lamb.[9] He also diligently transcribed his poems in a manuscript book, beautifully bound in orange-vermilion vellum, with which Ottoline had presented him. Towards the end of November she went off to help her husband's electioneering in Lancashire, and Lytton was left with Henry, dressed in Cossack boots and an amazing maroon suit, as his sole companion. Almost daily they wrote affectionate letters, telling Ottoline of all they were doing and how Henry's portrait of Lytton was progressing. 'He sits admirably & doesn't mind. But we are inclined to talk too much,' Henry wrote. '. . . I have not had such stirring conversation since the early days when I had just left school.'

As for Lytton, these weeks at Peppard, he told Ottoline, had been like 'an interlude from the Arabian nights'. He felt that he was on the brink of something curiously enticing. 'My existence here', he told James (30 November 1910), 'is something new. I tremble to think what an "idyll" it might be, if only – and even as it is – in fact I really have no notion *what* it is. It seems to me more like Country House Life in the thirties than anything else. I feel like George Sand – shall I write an Indiana?'

2

MUMPS AND A BEARD

Shortly before Christmas, Lytton left England and set off for the South of France to stay with the Bussys. At Roquebrune he hoped to avoid the hardships of an English winter and press ahead with his writing of *Landmarks in French Literature*.

Now that he was in France, England seemed infinitely desirable. 'You can imagine how I long to be at Peppard,' he wrote to Henry (21 February 1911), 'and rejoice in the honest warmth of an English winter – it all sounds so heavenly that I hardly dare to think of it.' He consoled himself with the French translations of Dostoyevsky, reading *L'Idiot*, *Le Crime et le châtiment* and *Les Possédés* which he liked best of all. 'I'm as converted as you could wish about Dostoievsky,' he wrote in another letter to Henry (5 January 1911). 'The last half of Vol 2 of the Possédés quite knocked me over. Colossal! Colossal! It's mere ramping and soaring genius, and all possible objections are reduced to absurdity. I shudder to think that I might never have read it, and I never should if it hadn't been for you ...'

At the beginning of March the Bussys left for Sicily, and Lytton's sister Marjorie came down to look after him and his child niece, Jane Simone. Life went on much as before, 'a mere blank of utter nothingness punctuated by a few horrors and rages here and there'. He was getting on with his book, and had completed the chapters on 'Louis XIV' and 'The Eighteenth Century'. 'I am in an almost complete stupor,' he admitted to James. But out of this struggle to advance was born a greater resilience. 'I feel quite reckless,' he added, '– more I think than I ever have before. It came to me quite suddenly the other day – how little anything matters ... and then that really, after all, one has a confidence.'

Early that April, Lytton returned to England. After a week with Henry at the Dog Inn, near Henley, he went on with James to Corfe Castle in Dorset, putting up at the Greyhound Inn. The evening of their arrival, a Friday, he complained of being ill. James took his temperature with the thermometer he always carried and saw that it was 104. Next day, to the general relief, an attack of mumps declared itself. James looked after him to start with, but had to go back to the *Spectator* on Tuesday morning. So Oliver Strachey, having just returned from India on short leave, was ordered to take his place at Corfe. He was furious. To save money they were obliged to transmigrate from the relatively comfortable Greyhound to the poky little Castle Inn, cramming themselves into a small closed carriage piled high and wide with luggage, and balancing every sort of treasured object in their arms – oil cans, ink bottles, safety-razors and Russian novels. Because of the risk of infection, Lytton was entombed in his bedroom at the Castle Inn for almost three weeks, attended by Oliver who, very kind and incompetent, endeavoured to look after him without succumbing to the disease himself. While he sat downstairs writing love-letters to his fiancée Ray Costelloe, upstairs in his bed Lytton lay composing love-letters to his '*très-cher* serpent' Henry, who had gone off to stay with Boris Anrep in Paris, and letters about love-letters to his 'Chère Marquise' Ottoline. The only book he had to read was a French edition of Dostoyevsky's letters which tended to deepen the gloom of his quarantine. 'For one thing his [Dostoyevsky's] portrait – most infinitely abattu – with eyes – oh! – but almost, I thought, as if he had been too much crushed – which was also the effect of the letters,' he reported to Henry (4 May 1911).

'His life was perfect hell till six years before he died; and his letters are almost entirely occupied with begging for money – always "pour l'amour du Christ". At last whenever you see Christ on a page you skip it because you know that an appeal for 125 roubles will follow. It's deplorable and it's impossible not to have rather a lower opinion of the man. He was not at all souterrain – very simple and at all times silly. On Christianity he writes the most hopeless stuff.'

There were occasional visits from friends. Clive Bell came for a day and waved up cautiously at the invalid's window; and Ottoline blew an elaborate kiss to him from the roadway and he responded 'out of the window, Romeo fashion' as she travelled up to London. 'It was very touching,' he commented, 'but insubstantial.' He was experiencing difficulty in catching up on all the winter's gossip. While he had been away in France, Ottoline had started two new *affaires*: a passionate and demanding one with Bertrand Russell who, finding 'to my amazement that I loved her deeply', was pressing her to leave Philip and had already told his wife Alys, who threatened to cite Ottoline in divorce proceedings; and a brief but awkward entanglement with Roger Fry who, emerging 'amazed and wondering' out of the hopelessness following his wife's confinement in a mental hospital, was now reacting in some panic as he formed a deeper emotional commitment to Vanessa Bell. Philip Morrell and Clive Bell (who had equipped himself with a pre-marital lover, the luxurious Mrs Raven-Hill, as his post-marital mistress) were the complaisant husbands in these *affaires*. But Alys's brother Logan Pearsall Smith, and Vanessa's sister Virginia, were to flavour the well of gossip with many fantastical stories.

It was during these weeks of illness at Corfe that Lytton grew his beard.[10] At first he was baffled as to its merits. Did it, for example, make him appear *too* ridiculous? 'The beard question is becoming rather dubious – but you shall judge,' he wrote to Ottoline. She, and all his friends, begged him to keep it; and soon enough he agreed to do so. 'The chief news is that I have grown a beard,' he informed his mother (9 May 1911). 'Its colour is much admired, and it is generally considered extremely effective, though some ill-bred persons have been observed to laugh. It is a red-brown of the most approved tint, and makes me look like a French decadent poet – or something equally distinguished.'

The growing of this celebrated beard was one sign of Lytton's more challenging attitude to life. Though he still remained outwardly diffident, and tended to exaggerate his setbacks, his self-assurance was growing. Under the influence of his brother James he had become more interested in politics, and was in the gradual process of rejecting his romantic Conservatism in favour of a more combative left-wing position. 'Have you noticed there are three classes of human beings?' he asked Sheppard, '– the rich, the poor and the intelligent. When the poor are serious they're religious, when the intelligent are serious they're artistic, but the rich are never serious at all.'

Something of this changing attitude was also implicit in a paper he delivered to the Apostles (20 May 1911) at Cambridge, where he and Oliver went after leaving Corfe Castle. Near the opening, he confesses his sentimentalism and the rather reactionary form it took: 'I even have a secret admiration for the typical Englishman – the strong silent man with the deep emotion – too deep – oh! far too deep ever to come to the surface; I can't help being impressed.' Victorian conventions seemed to have been slipping in the seven years since he had come down from Trinity. But with expanding freedom came a somewhat prosaic world. Now that the bishops had started going to the music halls the community seemed to be faced not with a growing sense of humour among the clergy, but an increasing solemnity on the variety stage. The managers of those places had taken to writing to newspapers to assure everyone that no *risqué* jokes were to be heard in their establishments – one could only hope they were not telling the truth. Again, eminent literary critics were pulling long faces over the more outspoken classics, wondering how Boccaccio or even *Tristram Shandy* could be so immoral. In Lytton's view it was high time that some light-hearted jester shook his cap and bells a little in the faces of such intruding Malvolios.

Lytton's manner, as well as his appearance and his political opinions, was also undergoing some change. The long body, which had for years proved such an embarrassment to him, was more coordinated, his ungainliness manipulated into part of a stylized personality. His scarecrow figure too was in the process of being shaped by the same alchemy into strange symmetrical proportions, radiating a spidery fascination. Of course, some people – Angelica Homere was one – had always found his

231

looks compelling; others – Wyndham Lewis for example – would always be revolted by him. From the beginning, Lytton had sadly accepted this latter view. Now he did so less readily. To some extent, his external appearance *had* changed; but there were also internal changes to account for his more optimistic attitude and to influence the way in which others regarded him. He was also better able to reflect embarrassment back on others. Shortly after his beard had grown to its full magnificence, a lady came up and asked him: 'Oh, Mr Strachey, tell me, when you go to bed, do you keep that beard of yours inside or outside the blankets?' Using his most insinuating voice – which always reminded Desmond MacCarthy of the gnat in *Alice in Wonderland* – he piped: 'Won't you come and see?' At another party, the conversation turned to the question of which great historical character the people there would most have liked to go to bed with. The men voted for Cleopatra, Kitty Fisher and so on, but when it came to Lytton's turn he declared shrilly: 'Julius Caesar!'

Ottoline, whom he visited at Peppard for a few days that June, noticed a change in him.

'He was franker with me than he used to be and I was less timid and nervous with him than I had been . . .

It is hard to realize that this tall, solemn, lanky, cadaverous man, with his rather unpleasant appearance, looking indeed far older than he is, is a combination of frivolity, love of indecency, mixed up with rigid intellectual integrity . . .

The steeds that draw the chariot of his life seem to be curiously ill-matched: one so dignified and serious, and so high-stepping, and of the old English breed, so well versed in the manners and traditions of the last four centuries; the other so feminine, nervous, hysterical, shying at imaginary obstacles, delighting in being patted and flattered and fed with sugar.

In general he takes little part, rather lying in wait than giving himself away – only occasionally interrupting, throwing in a rational and often surprisingly witty remark. But tête-à-tête he is a charming companion – his feminine quality making him sympathetic and interested in the small things of life, and with those who know him well he is very affectionate.'[11]

Leaving Peppard, Lytton returned once more to Cambridge, where he installed himself, with Oliver, in lodgings at 12 King's Parade, and the history of French Literature advanced another chapter. At Cambridge he was 'a different & happier person', Henry had noticed, 'calculating', as his brother Walter Lamb put it, 'the capacities of the well-dressed genitals around him'. From the vantage point of a punt near King's, 'propped up by the innumerable cushions, and surrounded by innumerable books which we never read', he inspected the parade of undergraduates flocking down to the bank, smoking their cigarettes and eating *langues-de-chat* as they sat down, row upon row, on the grass in the sunshine. The willows, the parasols, the blue skies, the white flannels all conspired to make a perfect décor for this pastoral court. Then, at weekends he would tear himself away to visit Lady Lytton at Knebworth, or, avoiding 'the terrors of the Coronation', George Mallory at Charterhouse, or, once again, his 'Chère Marquise' at Peppard, 'where it was all very idyllic, dining out in the moonlight with purple candle-sticks'.

But Cambridge, though delightful, was not conducive to hard work. At the beginning of July, Oliver having left to marry Ray Costelloe, Lytton decided to travel down to Becky House, near Manaton in Devon, which Rupert Brooke had recommended for its inexpensive peace and comfort. A largish country cottage, set in a rocky Dartmoor valley next to a famous Victorian waterfall and small rushing stream, it was occupied by a labourer and his family who let lodgings – a large sitting-room and a few bedrooms. Here he settled down to complete the final chapters of *Landmarks in French Literature*, working for five or six hours every day, and describing himself as 'extraordinarily healthy and industrious'. It confirmed what he instinctively believed: that the country was the place for him in which to live and work.

While at Becky House, he was joined for a week by two old friends, G.E. Moore and Leonard Woolf who had at last returned from Ceylon, his ascetic features burnt up by the tropical sun. 'He has a long, drawn, weather-beaten face,' Lytton rather morosely observed in a letter to James (15 June 1911), 'and speaks (when he does) very slowly, like one re-risen from the tomb – or rather on the other side of it.'

So much had happened in the six or seven years since they had been really close. Ottoline, like some theatrical impresario, had opened up the gorgeous world of smart dinner-parties and country house weekends; Henry had introduced him to the rough-and-tumble life of Augustus John with his bohemian crew of jokers and drinkers, gypsies and magicians; and through Rupert he was glimpsing a sportive group of nymphs and sylphs and dryads, bright innocent creatures, all children of the sun, who camped in the fields at night and bathed naked in the rivers. In comparison with all this, his old Apostolic friends seemed dull. Apprehensively he wrote off to Henry (5 July 1911): 'My heart quails at the thought of their conversation. Oh dear! How things must have changed since the days when I thought it was the absolute height of pleasure and glory! But now there is something cold and dry – I don't know what – the curiosity of existence seems to vanish with them; it's not that I don't like them – only that they are under the sea.'

But Moore and Woolf turned out to be less submarine than he feared. While his life and personality had been changing, theirs had not been static. 'I find them – oh! quite extraordinarily nice – but . . . if they are no longer under the sea, perhaps it's I who am somewhere else now – in the clouds, perhaps,' he told Henry (14 July 1911); 'at any rate I find myself dreaming of more congenial company. However we are very happy, and go out for walks, and discuss this and that, and do a great deal of work.' It was, in fact, Leonard Woolf to whom this Apostolic atmosphere seemed most foreign. 'I am beyond flux – I really am on a fixed course probably to damnation or beyond it,' he had written to Lytton shortly before sailing back. 'I expect you when we meet to pass me by because of it.' Everything in England was new to him in 1911 – the Post-Impressionist pictures, the Russian ballet, the theatre of Shaw and Granville Barker. After his deliberate shutting-down of intellectual curiosity in Ceylon, he feared the astringent company of Moore and Lytton in this bleak Dartmoor cottage. 'In the morning Lytton used to sit in one part of the garden, with a panama on his head, groaning from time to time over his literary constipation as he wrote *Landmarks in French Literature* for the Home University Library,' he recalled; 'in another part of the garden sat Moore, a panama hat on his head, his forehead wet with perspiration, sighing from time to time over his literary constipation as he wrote *Ethics* for the Home University Library. Lytton used to complain that he was mentally constipated because nothing at all came into his mind, which remained as blank as the paper on his knees. Moore on the contrary said that his mental constipation came from the fact that as soon as he had written down a sentence, he saw that it was just false or that it required a sentence to qualify the qualification.'

In the afternoons the three of them went for long walks across Dartmoor, and Moore, who had a passion for bathing, would strip off his clothes whenever they came to one of the cold black rock pools, and plunge in. 'Nothing would induce Lytton to get into water in the open air,' Leonard records, 'and so I felt I must follow Moore's example. It nearly killed me.' In the evenings, 'Moore sang Adelaide, Schubert songs, or the Dichterliebe, or he played Beethoven sonatas. It was good to see again the sweat pour down his face and hear the passion in the music as he played the Waldstein or the Hammerklavier sonata.'[12]

By the middle of August *Landmarks in French Literature* was nearly completed. 'I've only seven more centuries to do,' Lytton boasted to James (22 August 1911). He had moved to Woodstock Road, Gilbert Murray's house in Oxford, which Lady Strachey had taken for the month and where Pippa typed out the earlier chapters for him. He hoped to complete the book by the end of the month, but failing in this, fled back to the solitude of Becky House for another fortnight to finish off Chapter VII – 'The Age of Criticism' – and his short 'Conclusion'. By 10 September he was able to report to Maynard: 'I am feeling very lazy, as I've just this minute finished my poor book, after a solid two months of perpetual labour; and the thought of more such inventions is not attractive.'

*

Far more attractive was the thought of Rupert's radiant young friends, especially the remarkable-looking progressively educated Olivier sisters, all fearless tree-climbers, mad moonlight divers, elusive creatures of the woods. Rupert loved them all – Bryn, Noel, Marjorie and Daphne, the four daughters of Sir Sydney Olivier, an aristocratic Fabian now Governor of Jamaica. But particularly he loved Noel. He loved her idealistically, sexlessly, stereotypically, as one might love a wild rose or the setting sun. With many evasions Rupert kept this outdoor life, with its virginal assemblies of ageless boys and girls, separate from his brotherly congregations with the pipe-smoking Apostles, as he had earlier separated the school playing fields from his parents' home in School House at Rugby. He led a double life: that of a schoolboy hero with the Neo-Pagans; and a college pin-up with the Apostles. Both had their appeal, for both wanted to prolong youth. In his Neo-Pagan world the educationist ideals of Edward Carpenter and J.H. Badley seemed to have reached perfection. All the girls were honorary boys and, like Polixenes and Leontes,

> . . . thought that there was no more behind
> But such a day to-morrow as to-day,
> And to be a boy eternal.

It was a life of everlasting skies and eternal afternoons, camping and canoeing, sun-filled, free-floating, a fairy tale of innocence, immune from adult complexities. The Apostles too dreaded middle-age and the loss of potent youth. But they stopped the clock at later than ten-to-three, recognizing much of what was suppressed under 'innocence', 'purity' and the 'respectability' of parents, and in the darker hours of the evening celebrating its release in a new marriage of male intellect and sex.

It was James Strachey who was largely responsible for bringing these two milieux together. He had procured Rupert for the Apostles, but never succeeded in going to bed with him. He followed him everywhere, even into the fields and woods and round the evening fires and lake-side camps of his other friends. He appeared to them a pitiable object, indeed hardly a man at all with his unathletic ailments and awkwardnesses. 'He had the face of a baby and the expression of an old man,' wrote one of the group, Ka Cox; 'he seemed to take no pleasure or interest in material life or the physical world, and to exist only in the realms of pure intellect.' Nevertheless they grew curious about the catlike James, while he stirred the curiosity of Lytton and Virginia and Maynard when he came back with tales from Rupert's Neo-Pagan tents, like a miniature arcadian version of the German youth movement.

The first mingling of these two communities took place in August and September 1911 in a meadow on the bank of the Teign, not far from Becky House where Lytton was staying. Virginia strode down to sample camp life, 'sleeping on the ground, walking at dawn, and swimming in a river'; the economist Gerald Shove spent the night there in his suit and trilby hat, and James lay wretchedly awake under a gorse bush wrapped in a blanket. Maynard also turned up, seeking a casual substitute for Duncan that would be safer than his rough trade ('Auburn haired of Marble Arch', 'Lift boy of Vauxhall') in London. He found no one, though 'camp life suits me very well', he reported to his father. 'The hard ground, a morning bathe, the absence of flesh food, and no chairs, don't make me nearly so ill as one would suppose.' But Lytton would not risk it. Patrolling nearby in his knickerbockers and tam-o'-shanter like 'Christ on a walking tour', he concluded that the ground was too awkwardly shaped for relaxation.

After eighteen days of camping, a strange tension shimmered in the air round Rupert. He drove it off with long scrambling walks over the rocks and wet green boulders round Becky Falls, slitheringly pursued by James together with Lytton whose leg muscles hardened into granite, causing him exquisite pain.

There was more tension at Studland, in Dorset, where Lytton next went to stay with Clive and Vanessa, who had recently suffered a miscarriage. Roger Fry was also there, like some medieval saint in attendance upon Vanessa who seemed unconscious of everyone. 'Are you changing with all the rest of the world?' she had written to ask Lytton, the previous month. Their undiagnosed changes, during this glorious hot summer, were painful. Ottoline had retired to Marienbad that August seeking a cure for her persistent headaches – she was suffering from what was called 'neuritis' and had been ordered to sleep. On Roger's advice, Vanessa had been put under the care of a controversial psychiatrist or 'nerve specialist', Dr Maurice Craig of Harley Street, who prescribed six months of relaxation and good food. Helen Fry was now permanently confined to an asylum for an illness which after her death was found to have been caused by ossification of a cartilage. Virginia, too, had spent part of the previous year in a 'polite madhouse for female lunatics', fearful that she might become insane like her poor mad half-sister Laura, 'Her Ladyship of the Lake', who had lived apart in the family home, the symbol of Victorian *terra incognita*. Even now Virginia was ravaged with headaches, and seemed to Lytton so shrivelled up that she had hardly any real being. The lease of Fitzroy Square was coming to an end, and she planned to take a larger house (it would be 38 Brunswick Square) where she and Adrian could occupy separate floors, where Duncan could have a studio, Maynard a *pied-à-terre* and, at thirty-five shillings a week, Leonard might rent the attic. It was unconventional, but seemed to promise a happier way of life. Clive had hardly forgiven her for her momentary engagement to Lytton whom he wanted to forbid entry to Gordon Square. The two men's antagonism fretted her nerves. 'Clive presents a fearful study in decomposing psychology,' Lytton wrote to James while at Studland (24 September 1911). 'The fellow is much worse – burgeoning out into inconceivable theories on art and life – a corpse puffed up with worms and gases. It all seems to be the result of Roger, who is also here, in love with Vanessa. She is stark blind and deaf. And Virginia (in dreadful lodgings) rattles her accustomed nut. Julian [Bell] is half-witted.'

On the spur of the moment Lytton decided to make a dash to see Henry in Brittany. Borrowing five pounds from the loyal Pippa, he started out on his adventure, travelling by boat from Plymouth to Brest, and the following day from Brest by train to Quimperlé, and on to Doëlan by pony and trap.

'Did you hear he [Henry] raped Dorelia's sister,' Ottoline had politely inquired (21 July 1911). Henry had carried off Dorelia John's younger sister to paint and paint again that summer in Brittany. But the work was slow and difficult, and as the summer days went by she began to change from the Virgin Goddess of the John caravan, 'picturesque, kind-hearted Ede', into an 'effigy of sloth and obstinacy'. She was a perfect model, an impossible companion. Boris Anrep joined them, and Henry, welcoming this diversion, had resented the distraction. Now Lytton turned up to take Anrep's place. This was the first time Henry had seen his beard, though he did not immediately recognize its painterly virtues. 'He arrived well and with armsful of gossip,' Henry reported. But some of the gossip they had to exchange was oddly irritating. In Paris, four months earlier, Ottoline had confided to Henry that she was comforting Bertrand Russell because he was a tortured soul in need of her help (she had said almost exactly the same thing to Russell about Henry). The business was complicated by Ottoline's mother-in-law who suspected Lytton of being her lover. 'Shall I write to him,' Russell inquired, 'telling him to appear dying of love – doing his best to conceal his grief, but alas unable to do so?'

This news of Ottoline and Bertie had electrified Henry who became dementedly charming and high-spirited. 'O do not stint me!' he cried to Ottoline. 'I am insatiable for more life with you and in you.' Now he was sunk in aggressive depression, already suspecting that he must initiate a parting from the woman he had believed would be his salvation. He seemed to be on the verge of a breakdown. Suffering from sickness and headaches, he accused Lytton of getting into 'a silly panic' about his own health. 'I felt', Lytton wrote to Ottoline (15 October 1911), 'like a white man among savages in Central Africa.' Henry was certainly savage. 'Lytton's visit was a failure,' he wrote, 'he simply moped and whined and funcked in his room except for the days of his arrival and departure. I was . . . glad to shunt him on to Paris.'

But Lytton had greater resilience. At the end of a night-journey through Nantes, he arrived at the Hôtel des Saints-Pères. Walking through the Luxembourg Gardens next day, in the brilliant morning light, he saw all he loved best in France. It was crowded, happy, well-ordered; the leaves on the trees were beginning to change colour and everything looked vivid and alive. After the emotional failure of his week in Brittany, 'an extraordinary sense of vitality and excitement came upon me; a spring of self-confidence gushed up . . . it was delightful and astonishing.' He had finished his book on French Literature, he was thirty-one, 'and life was still before me . . .'

3

THE STRANGE CASE OF RUPERT BROOKE

While waiting for the publication of his book, Lytton found London fluctuating and misshapen that winter after the invigorating glory of Paris. He wandered between cocoa parties in Fitzroy Square and the more effulgent hospitality of Bedford Square. Meanwhile Henry returned from France that November and began renting a strange new studio in the sky, on the top floor of the Vale Hotel, in the Vale of Health, on Hampstead Heath, where Lytton began again to sit for him. 'I think I have a good design for his portrait,' he wrote, 'it will be very big.'

Then there were Leonard Woolf's uncertainties, which mirrored Lytton's own. 'I have been having an exhausting day with Woolf looking for lodgings in Bloomsbury. Like everyone else he doesn't know where to live; but the rooms we saw to-day were enough to make one despair of all human habitations. Filthy darkness and hideousness combined – I quite sink back with a sigh of relief among the new cretonnes of the poor old shooting-gallery.' It seemed that Leonard really would have to lodge in Virginia's new attics.

Otherwise Lytton bent over the proof-sheets of *Landmarks in French Literature* 'which I find a very soothing occupation. But the printers seem to sniff vice everywhere. As there's so much talk about "literature", I sometimes use the phrase "letters" as a variation – "men of letters" – and so on. And once or twice I refer to "French letters" – So and so "inaugurated a new era in French letters" – and the words are underlined and queried. My innocent mind failed at first to grasp the meaning of it . . . there are singular pitfalls for unwary authors.'

After Lytton's proofs had been corrected and following the publication of Rupert Brooke's *Poems*, Bloomsbury and the Neo-Pagans planned a second coming-together at Lulworth in Dorset. The prospect alarmed Rupert, threatening to break through the compartments of his life – even his *Poems* were divided into homosexual and spiritual sections. Maynard was invited. He had shocked these children of nature by openly propositioning Justin Brooke – and was now becoming an unlikely object of Bryn Olivier's admiration. Harry Norton would be there, sunk with his three chins between paralysed adoration of Vanessa Bell and James Strachey who, in disconcerting imitation of Rupert, was falling in love with Noel Olivier. Lytton was to bring Henry over and be joined by his younger sister Marjorie Strachey, a big fat romantic novelist-to-be, already famous for her lewd readings of nursery rhymes, who, like Maynard, had taken a shine to Justin Brooke, and like so many others was rumoured to have been seduced by Henry. Finally there was to be a brilliant young bisexual poet and Apostle, a Hungarian aristocrat called Ferenc Békássy. Rupert resented Békássy, though he could not object since he had been recommended by Noel Olivier. But then Békássy too was in love with 'cette éternelle Noel'.

Rupert had loved Noel since she was fifteen. She was now twenty and they were secretly engaged. But this engagement involved no sexual relations, nor even, it appeared, the promise of sexuality in the foreseeable future, since his love depended upon not 'dirtying' the purity of their relations with sex. His letters to her were full of poetic bluster and bravado. 'I know how superb my body is, & how great my bodily strength,' he wrote to her (28 August 1912). 'I know that with my mind I could do anything. I know that I can be the greatest poet and writer in England.'[13] Yet the strain within Rupert by his twenty-fifth year was unendurable. 'I know for certain I can't go on like this.' The fact was that he still found it easier to have erections with men than with women. Not long ago he had gone to bed with a schoolfriend, or so he alleged, and later sent a vivid description of what may have taken place to James Strachey, who was further tormented by rumours that Rupert was also engaged in an *affaire* with, of all people in the world, Hobhouse! Yet Rupert treated homosexuals as a Victorian paterfamilias might treat prostitutes, and his puritanism sealed off these experiments from the mainstream of his life. 'We must give it up,' Noel wrote to him (28 December 1911) after almost four years of short platonic meetings and long absences, ' . . . until you love less, or I love more.' But unless she committed herself to him sexually he could not break his love for her. As his frustration mounted, however, he edged towards another experiment that might be more easily absorbed into his general experience and set him free. He had found out all he could about contraception and was on the brink of taking the plunge with another of the Neo-Pagans, Ka Cox.

It was Ka Cox who had arranged the camp and reading-party at West Lulworth – a fact that may have persuaded the Olivier sisters at the last minute not to come. Ka was the daughter of a Fabian stockbroker, 'a broad bottomed, sensible, maternal woman', Virginia described her, with strong shoulders, a pince-nez and long brown hair gathered at the back. Her rather squashy appearance was far removed from the lyrical beauty of the Olivier sisters, but no one thought of her as ugly – she had the same powers of attraction as Miss Joan Hunter Dunn for John Betjeman's subaltern. Her parents had died before she was out of her 'teens and, after completing her education at Newnham, she was in the unusual position of being free and financially independent. She was also more mature than the other Neo-Pagans. 'Ka treated us all like children,' wrote Gwen Darwin, 'with easy affection.' She had been courted by Jacques Raverat who, complaining of 'the whip of Eros', urged her 'to love and yet to be *perfectly* free'. But she thought him too babyish for marriage and he had become engaged instead to Gwen Darwin whose cousin Frances Darwin married the anthropologist Francis Cornford). Rupert hated these engagements and marriages which broke their vows of friendship and rites of perpetual youth and made him feel 'so awfully lonely'. As he later confessed to James Strachey (10 July 1912): 'Solitude is my one unbearable fear.'

The way out of Rupert's predicament seemed to lie with Ka who was 'fine & wise', he informed Noel, and who 'arranges & satisfies everyone'. Nevertheless the tension that had been mounting in him during the previous summer camp revived. The weather was so wonderfully mild that some of the party bathed in the sea – but not Rupert, who on the last day of the year, after receiving Noel's letter of recantation, retired to his room with a cold.

Henry, who had been spending Christmas a few miles off with Augustus and Dorelia John at their new home, Alderney Manor, in the New Forest, was intending to join the Lulworth camp for the New Year. Lytton met him with a carriage at Wool station and they were driven to the Lulworth Cove Inn. It was 'divinely beautiful – almost too poetical and sweet', Henry wrote to Ottoline; 'dreamy white, graceful cliffs, with fantastic caves & arches, orange-red beach & green sea. The sky is like Giotto's blue . . . the hedges fawn & blood red against it.'

Ka had met Henry in London that autumn and been 'fascinated' by him. Here was a truly bohemian artist not afraid of women but actively involving them in his life and work. Hearing of her 'madness' over Henry, Rupert had been put out; but this did not prevent her inviting him to Lulworth and planning to flirt with him there. On New Year's Eve, while Rupert lay on his sick-bed, Henry and Ka went off together into the country. When she came back, Ka told Rupert that she wanted to marry Henry. Inflamed with jealousy, Rupert immediately proposed to Ka, and when she refused, he descended into 'the most horrible kind of Hell; without sleeping or eating – doing nothing but suffering the most violent mental tortures [which] . . . reacted on my body to such an extent that after the week I could barely walk'.

Henry soon left Lulworth for London, leaving a wake of disaster behind him. Ka wanted to follow him, but she was persuaded by Lytton to stay and help look after Rupert. For this was a serious mental collapse, a sexual hysteria arising from the collision of his two long-separated lives. 'Despite his own dabblings in the homosexual milieu, Rupert could not bear the idea of its escaping its bounds and mingling itself with heterosexual love – the school dormitory invading the family bedroom,' wrote the biographer Paul Delaney. '. . . His peculiar upbringing had made him abnormally sly and secretive; these qualities clashed with Lytton's open-minded and rational approach to sex . . . the merger of Bloomsbury and Neo-Paganism made them into rival masters of ceremonies.'[14]

'I hate Lytton,' Rupert told Ka a few weeks later (27–29 February 1912), '. . . for having worked to get the man [Henry] down there, and having seen the whole thing being engineered from the beginning, – and obligingly acquiesced in it as one of the creature's whims.' He described Henry as 'Someone more capable of getting hold of women than me, slightly experienced in bringing them to heel, who didn't fool about with ideas of trust or "fair treatment" . . . The swine, one gathers, was looking round. He was tiring of his other women, or they of him. Perhaps he thought there'd be a cheaper and pleasanter way of combining fucking with an income than Ottoline ... He cast dimly round. Virgins are easy game ... He marked you down.' But the author of this crude seduction was, in Rupert's imagination, Lytton, arch-manipulator of vice, hovering over the lovers, eyeing them at their sport. 'It was the filthiest part of the most unbearably sickening disgusting blinding nightmare,' he burst out, '– and then one shrieks with the unceasing pain that it was *true*.'

But how much of it was true? Lytton was still greatly attracted to Henry and 'would grope [him] under the table at meal-times in view of all the ladies', as Maynard reported to Duncan (5 January 1912). Yet he must have realized that sexual relations between them could not proceed much further than this. He was not jealous of Henry's womanizing and might even have welcomed a liaison with someone sensible and easy-going like Ka who would not cut him out. At any rate he could not have been surprised by her becoming infatuated with him 'like a fish fascinated by the glitter of some strange bait'. But as soon as he realized the emotional wreckage this was likely to cause, he behaved very differently from the monster of Rupert's fantasy. It was, in fact, to Lytton that Ka first confessed her infatuation; and it was Lytton who immediately wrote off to Lamb (4 January 1912):

'Ka came and talked to me yesterday, between tea and dinner. It was rather a difficult conversation, but she was very nice and very sensible. It seemed to me clear that she was what is called "in love" with you – not with extreme violence so far, but quite distinctly. She is longing to marry you. She thinks you may agree, but fears, with great conscientiousness, that it might not be good for you. I felt at moments, while she was with me – so good and pink and agreeable, – that there was more hope in that scheme than I'd thought before. But the more I consider, the more doubtful it grows. I can't believe that you're a well-assorted couple – can you? If she was really your wife, with a home and children, it would mean a great change in your way of living, a lessening of independence – among other things a much dimmer relationship with Ottoline. This might be worth while – probably would be – if she was an eminent creature, who'd give you a great deal; but I don't think she is that. There seems no touch of inspiration in her; it's as if she was made somehow or other on rather a small scale (didn't you say that?). I feel it's unkind to write this about Ka, and it's too definite, but I must try and say what I think ... Henry, I almost believe the best thing she could do now would be to marry Rupert straight off. He is much nicer than I had thought him. Last night he was there and was really charming – especially with her. Affliction seems to have chastened him, and he did feel – it was evident . . . they seemed to fit together so naturally – even the Garden-City-ishness.'

This letter has the ring of truth and exonerates Lytton from any Machiavellian plotting against Rupert. Though he felt rather two-faced about receiving Ka's confidences and then making use of them to dissuade Henry from marriage, and though it is just possible – if unlikely – that this advice was partly coloured by his own feeling for Henry, there can be no doubt that he was endeavouring to act honourably. One fact which appears to have been forgotten by everyone is that Lamb was still married to Euphemia. Far from recommending marriage, Lytton strongly advised both of them against even having an affair, on the grounds that it might break up Ka's much more suitable relationship with Rupert. 'If you're not going to marry her,' he wrote to Henry (6 January 1912), 'I think you ought to reflect a good deal before letting her become your mistress.

'I've now seen her fairly often and on an intimate footing, and I can hardly believe that she's suited to the post. I don't see what either of you could really get out of it except the pleasures of the obelisk. With you even these would very likely not last long, while with her they'ld probably become more and more of a necessity, and also be mixed up with all sorts of romantic desires which I don't think you'ld ever satisfy. If this is true it would be worth while making an effort to put things on a merely affectionate basis, wouldn't it? I think there's quite a chance that . . . everything might blow over, and that she might even sink into Rupert's arms. Can you manage this?'

Characteristically Lytton felt closer to Rupert in his misery and frustration. 'The situation, though, seems to be getting slightly grim,' he told Henry in another letter (5 January 1912). '. . . Rupert is besieging her – I gather with tears and desperation – and sinking down in the intervals pale and shattered. I wish I could recommend her to console him . . .

'As for Rupert – it's like something in a play. But you know his niceness is now certain – poor thing! I never saw anyone so different from you – in caractère. "Did He who made the Lamb make thee?" I sometimes want to murmur to him, but I fear the jest would not be well received.'

By February, Henry was being treated by Dr J.M. Bramwall, a specialist in hypnosis and a pioneer psychotherapist. He had earlier 'cured' Jacques Raverat (who was later discovered to have been suffering from multiple sclerosis) by ministering to his 'subliminal self'. Over Henry he performed 'a mumbo-jumbo game of quackery' and recommended outdoor exercise.

But Henry, who obediently went riding with Leonard Woolf in Richmond Park, kept falling off his horse. Lytton and Ka, applying fomentations, were the 'kindest nurses', but he was trying ill-humouredly to follow Lytton's advice and had decided that Ka was 'too good & a tiny bit slow & plodding'.

So Ka turned back to Rupert. He had been taken by Jacques Raverat to see the psychiatrist, Dr Maurice Craig, who had attended to Vanessa Bell's headaches and whom Leonard Woolf later consulted over Virginia. He was a man of 'the highest principle', Leonard judged, who 'knew as much of the human mind and its illnesses' as any mental specialist in England – which was 'practically nothing'. For Rupert, Dr Craig prescribed early bed, no work, but plenty of milk, stout and what was innocently called 'stuffing', that is eating 'all sorts of patent foods'. Ka was again an excellent nurse, feeding and cosseting Rupert who turned out to be even more difficult and demanding than Henry. He looked to her to restore his sanity and achieve his manhood – after which he would be ready to go off, marry Noel Olivier, and be a great poet and dramatist. But Rupert's self-dislike, which seemed to go back to his very conception, followed the course of his semen and once it had entered Ka (while they were safely in Germany), and she was emotionally allied to him, he projected his dislike on to the contaminated Beatrice who had led him from his 'mountain height' into the 'mist and mire'.

He was even more irrationally aggressive towards Lytton who, in Rupert's paranoid outbursts against women, homosexuals and Jews, featured as a pseudo-jew and carrier of typhoid. 'I'm glad Lytton has been having a bad time,' he wrote to Ka (27 February 1912). 'Next time you have one of your benignant lunches with him you can make it clear to him I loathe him – if there's any chance of that giving him any pain.' In his moral confusion, he could still write to Lytton (27 March 1912) proposing to 'abduct Bryn [Olivier] for Sunday to the Metropole at Brighton – and go Shares', and still count on James's sustaining loyalty. 'You know how the Stracheys feel?' he asked Ka (3 March 1912). 'James *is* better than the rest. But one can't tell.' By the summer Rupert's hatred of Lytton had overflowed and poisoned his friendship with James. 'To be a Strachey is to be blind – without a sense – towards good and bad, and clean and dirty,' he upbraided James (6 August 1912); 'irrelevantly clever about a few things, dangerously infantile about many; to have undescended spiritual testicles; to be a mere bugger ... It becomes possible to see what was meant by the person who said that seeing you and any member of the Olivier family together made them cold and sick.'

'The explosion', James reported to Lytton (12 August 1912), 'has had every motive assigned to it except the obvious one . . . the dreadful thing is that he's clearly slightly cracked and has now cut himself off from everyone.'

Rupert longed to regain the simple Neo-Pagan life that Bloomsbury had corrupted. The Stracheys '*are* parasites, you know, all of them', Gwen Raverat confidently declared (27 March 1912). '. . . I for one am a clean Christian & they disgust me.' Rupert too was disgusted by the suppressed part of himself represented by Lytton, and the incomplete part of himself mirrored by James's love of Noel Olivier. But he knew that such disgust was not 'clean' and 'Christian'. 'God damn you,' he had written to James (14 March 1912). 'God bum roast castrate bugger and tear the bowels out of everyone . . . You'd better give it up, wash your bloody hands. I'm not sane.'

This sickness persisted for much of 1912 and was superficially cleared up by what appeared to be a complete change of character. In mid-October he gave the Apostles a statement of his new creed. A 'passion for goodness and loathing of evil is the most valuable and important thing in us. And therefore it must not be in any way stifled, nor compelled to wait upon exact judgement. If, after ordering your life and thoughts as wisely as possible, you find yourself hating, as evil, some person or thing, one should count five, perhaps, but then certainly hit out . . . I see the world as two armies in mortal combat, and inextricably confused.'

Though Rupert acknowledged that 'one cannot completely distinguish friend from foe', he treated Lytton as a foe for the rest of his life. On 18 June 1914, at the Drury Lane première of Stravinsky's *Le Rossignol*, he began talking in a perfectly friendly way to James who, noticing that Lytton was approaching them, said jocosely: 'I believe you know my brother Lytton,' to which Rupert replied, 'No!' and walked away. 'The number of beastly people at Drury Lane is the only good reason for going there,' Rupert wrote afterwards. 'One can be offensive to them.' Noel Olivier had been there and Ottoline Morrell; and James felt 'decidedly awkward because it happened in an extremely visible place, with everyone one knew standing round . . . this showed very plainly Rupert's paranoia, though I was so ignorant then that I had no notion of it.'

A few weeks later, at the beginning of the war, Rupert's paranoia (or wish to be offensive) resolved itself into a patriotic loathing of the 'pro-German' Stracheys and pacifist Bloomsbury. His series of five war sonnets published at the end of 1914 amounted to what D.H. Lawrence called a 'great inhalation of desire' for death. 'Let them know the poor truths,' Rupert honourably pleaded at the end (17 March 1915). But by 1915, 'with his felicities all most promptly divinable' as Henry James wrote, his disordered mind was being mythologized and made a symbol of clean-living militant young England. 'Joyous, fearless, versatile, deeply instructed,' Winston Churchill was to write, 'with classic symmetry of mind and body, he was all that one would wish England's noblest sons to be . . .' [15]

4

A SPIRITUAL REVOLUTION

Landmarks in French Literature, dedicated 'to JMS' (Strachey's mother), was reviewed not widely but well. Publication date in Britain was 12 January 1912 (it came out in the United States three months later) and by April 1914 twelve thousand copies had been sold worldwide. After the war, demand for this 'Shilling Shocker', as Ottoline called it, was to increase with Strachey's growing fame. It went through eight new impressions during his lifetime, was translated into Hungarian and Japanese, and was still selling fifty years after his death. 'Oh so good,' exclaimed E.M. Forster (6 February 1912). H.A.L. Fisher too wrote of it as Lytton's finest book, a critical *tour de force*, and John Lehmann praised it as a 'luminous little masterpiece of interpretative criticism'. In *The Whispering Gallery* (1955), Lehmann recounts a conversation which he had during a train journey from France to England with an unknown travelling companion who identified herself on reaching Calais as Dorothy Bussy. 'It taught me, as no other book could have,' he told her, 'how to find excellence in the French tradition even if one were a devoted believer in the English tradition, and why Racine was a great poet and dramatist even though his greatness was so totally different from Shakespeare's.'

Landmarks in French Literature is impressionistic criticism, brilliant in its powers of summary and attractive in the imagery Strachey uses to convey his admiration. Baudelaire is 'the Swift of poetry', Marivaux is 'Racine by moonlight'; Chénier's poetic world is 'that of some lovely bird flitting on a sudden out of the darkness and the terror of the tempest, to be overcome a moment later, and whirled to destruction'; Saint-Simon's historical *Mémoires* are like 'a tropical forest – luxuriant, bewildering, enormous – with the gayest humming-birds among the branches, and the vilest monsters in the entangled grass'. There are some surprising omissions (Mérimée, Nerval, Mallarmé, Zola) and the occasional burst of dislike – Victor Hugo's *Hernani* is 'a piece of bombastic melodrama, full of the stagiest clap-trap and the most turgid declamation'. But the shortcoming of the book, partly occasioned by the series, lies in the fact that it is really the criticism of simile rather than metaphor. Eventually these similes become interchangeable (literally so when Lytton uses the same elaborate culinary likeness to describe La Fontaine's *Fables* as he had used for Molière's comedies five years earlier in the *Spectator*) and this makes some pages resemble what Desmond MacCarthy called 'a little textbook of enthusiastical critical clichés'. It is the congestion of similes, too, that gave Ludwig Wittgenstein the impression of short difficult breathing in the prose style; like the gasps of someone suffering from asthma. Opposition to the book was led by D.H. Lawrence. 'I still don't like Strachey,' he told Ottoline,'– French literature neither – words – literature – bore.'

To Dorothy Bussy, who thought highly of *Landmarks*, Lytton wrote (6 February 1912): 'James of course says that it's rubbish, Ottoline that it is a work of supreme genius, Virginia that it's merely brilliant, Woolf that it is bluff carried a little too far for decency, and Clive that it is almost as bad as "Sainte-Beuve" (I haven't heard him say so, but I'm sure he must have).'

Landmarks in French Literature marks a point of transition in Lytton's career. Later in the same letter to his sister he observes: 'For the last year I have been going through a Spiritual Revolution – which has been exciting and on the whole pleasant. I had feared that after 30 one didn't have these things, Ah! – But now I shall be glad of a little recueillement.' He was determined, he added, to do some 'creative work' and still dreamed of it being poetic drama. The phrase, Spiritual Revolution, was intended by Lytton as a joke – but a joke with some meaning. Over the last twelve to fifteen months, he had found himself pitched into a bohemian environment that represented a break with Cambridge and was more anarchic than Bloomsbury. The change was precipitated by a number of other events. His brother Oliver, who had always led a knock-about sort of life, was badgering him for spending 'all your life between Cambridge and the Reading Room of the British Museum'. There was also the effect of Dostoyevsky, whose powerful character analysis presented Lytton with a new attitude to human beings and opened his mind to subconscious forces in himself. He was beginning to see life more in terms of motives than morality, with good and bad impulses irrationally mixed. Dostoyevsky's novels suggested how literature might be liberated from traditional forms, and how the unexplored elements in human behaviour could be conveyed by the power of humour which was not simply reductive, as the English believed, but re-creative.

Lytton had entered upon a period of his literary development which, beginning with a rhapsodic acclamation of men and women of letters, would lead to his flank and rear attack on the reputation of men and women of action. It was a time of advancing confidence in the application of his own powers. Scattered throughout the pages of *Landmarks in French Literature* are signs and assurances of this counter-attack. In a passage describing the formation and influence of the French Academy, he goes out of his way to expound his opposition to the indifference shown by the English establishment towards the arts.

'The mere existence of a body of writers officially recognized by the authorities of the State has undoubtedly given a peculiar prestige to the profession of letters in France. It has emphasized that tendency to take the art of writing seriously – to regard it as a fit object for the most conscientious craftsmanship and deliberate care – which is so characteristic of French writers. The amateur is very rare in French literature – as rare as he is common in our own. How many of the greatest English writers have denied that they were men of letters! – Scott, Byron, Gray, Sir Thomas Browne, perhaps even Shakespeare himself. When Congreve begged Voltaire not to talk of literature, but to regard him merely as an English gentleman, the French writer, who, in all his multifarious activities, never forgot for a moment that he was first and foremost a follower of the profession of letters, was overcome with astonishment and disgust. The difference is typical of the attitude of the two nations towards literature . . .'

Lytton seldom misses an opportunity of asserting that literature expresses more richly than any form of transitory action the history and genius of a nation. 'Montesquieu's great reputation', he writes, 'led to his view of the constitution of England being widely accepted as the true one; as such it was adopted by the American leaders after the War of Independence; and its influence is plainly visible in the present Constitution of the United States. Such is the strange power of good writing over the affairs of men!'

Elsewhere, he joins in the acclamation which greeted Voltaire's last appearance in Paris, the like of which is reserved in England for military and political figures. The scene is presented as a dramatic curtain-call to Voltaire's life and work.

'One day, quite suddenly, he appeared in Paris, which he had not visited for nearly thirty years. His arrival was the signal for one of the most extraordinary manifestations of enthusiasm that the world has ever seen. For some weeks he reigned in the capital, visible and glorious, the undisputed lord of the civilized universe. The climax came when he appeared in a box at the Théâtre Français, to witness a performance of the latest of his tragedies, and the whole house rose as one man to greet him. His triumph seemed to be something more than the mere personal triumph of a frail old mortal; it seemed to be the triumph of all that was noblest in the aspirations of the human race. But the fatigue and excitement of those weeks proved too much even for Voltaire in the full flush of his eighty-fourth year. An overdose of opium completed what Nature had begun; and the amazing being rested at last.'

Like Voltaire, Lytton wished to devote himself to a humane and polemical art. His destiny did not lie in penning tiny verses in Ottoline's vellum manuscript book; it was to be more iconoclastic and contentious. He felt, too, the need to clarify what underlay his languid manner, and disabuse his friends of misconception. 'You understand a great deal, and very wonderfully,' he wrote to Ottoline (24 February 1912). 'But perhaps there's one thing that you don't quite realize about me – I mean what I feel about my work. Perhaps you don't see that the idea of my really not working is simply an impossibility. Sometimes you have admonished me on the subject, and I think I have been rather curt in my answers; it was because I felt so absolutely sure of myself – that you might as well talk of my not breathing as not writing. It's so happened that just the last month or two, when we've been getting to know each other, I've been having a time of transition and hesitation ... And then my health has been a vile nuisance – You see I'm making quite a case for myself! But I want you to understand this. From my earliest days I've always considered myself as a writer, and for the last ten years writing has been almost perpetually in my thoughts.'

In an address he delivered to the Apostles that spring (11 May 1912), entitled 'Godfrey, Cornbury or Candide',[16] Lytton explained his newly-developed beliefs. Essentially, they were a method of eradicating self-abasement and transforming himself into the sort of person he could admire. It was a move away from the good states of mind inculcated by *Principia Ethica* towards justification by work. In the course of his paper he points to three main motives which shape our ends – the thirst for pleasure, the desire to do good, and the need for self-development. Though sensitive to the force of these first two impulses, Lytton places himself in the third category of human being, whose satisfaction may come through literary achievement. It was a Voltairian creed. 'It seems to me that I live neither for happiness nor for duty,' he told the Apostles.

'I like being happy. I scheme to be happy; I want to do my duty, and I sometimes even do it. But such considerations seem to affect me only sporadically and vaguely; there is something else which underlies my actions more fundamentally, which guides, controls and animates the whole. It is ambition. I want to excel, to triumph, to be powerful, and to glory in myself. I do not want a vulgar triumph, a vulgar power; fame and riches attract me only as subsidiary ornaments of my desire. What I want is the attainment of a true excellence, the development of noble qualities, and the full expression of them – the splendour of a spiritual success. It is true that this is an egotistical conception of life; but I see no harm in such an egotism. After all, each of us is the only person who can cultivate himself; we may help on our neighbour here and there – throw him a bulb or two over the garden wall, or lend a hand with the roller; but we shall never understand the ins and outs – the complication of the soils and subsoils – in any garden but our own.'

*

In May 1912, Max Beerbohm, who had recently returned to England after a two-year stay in Italy, was lunching at the Savile Club when he first caught sight of Lytton, seated at a table with Duncan. He saw:

'an emaciated face of ivory whiteness above a long square-cut auburn beard, and below a head of very long sleek dark brown hair. The nose was nothing if not aquiline, and Nature had chiselled it with great delicacy. The eyes, behind a pair of gold-rimmed spectacles, eyes of an inquirer and cogitator, were large and brown and luminous. The man to whom they belonged must, I judged, though he sat stooping down over his table, be extremely tall. He wore a jacket of brown velveteen,[17] a soft shirt, and a dark red tie. I greatly wondered who he was. He looked rather like one of the Twelve Apostles, and I decided that he resembled especially the doubting one, Thomas, who was also called Didymus. I learned from a friend who came in and joined me at my table that he was one of the Stracheys; Lytton Strachey; a Cambridge man; rather an authority on French literature; had written a book on French Literature in some series or other; book said to be very good. "But why", my friend asked, "should he dress like that?" Well, we members of the Savile, Civil Servants, men of letters, clergymen, scientists, doctors and so on, were clad respectably, passably, decently, but no more than that. And "Hang it all," I said, "why *shouldn't* he dress like that? He's the best-dressed man in the room!"[18]

During these early winter and spring months of 1912, Henry was embarking on his series of portraits.[19] 'Do come as early as you can,' he summoned Lytton to his Vale of Health studio in the first week of January. 'I want to make an elaborate drawing to scale, so that I need only have to paint hands & face from you.' Though he planned to do much of the painting away from his model so that Lytton need visit him at 'decently rare intervals', he would lose his temper whenever Lytton deserted him for too long ('you're a bloodier ass and a feebler one than I imagined'). This was to be Henry's largest, most ambitious picture. Its progress was agonizingly slow 'and I get unduly spleenful and impatient', he admitted. His impatience was exacerbated by Lytton's 'perpetual raising of the question of our relationship', though it was the strangeness of their relationship that ultimately gave these portraits their peculiar tension.

Early in 1913, after some fifteen months, Henry ordered a new stretcher for the giant canvas and completed a 'colour rehearsal sketch'. He was 'dying to leap ahead' and believed that three or four days 'should be enough'. By the spring it was 'very nearly finished'. It 'fills me with incredulous pride – that I could ever get it so far complete . . . You would scarcely believe how amazingly unified the later operations have made it look . . .' He felt confident that his surreally formal style was exactly right for Lytton's italicized looks. Suddenly in April he discovered that the picture 'became finished at an unexpected juncture'. Despite all manner of obstacles, 'I watched, prayed, starved & took Sanatogen and did somehow manage to wind the thing up to a sort of conclusion . . . I have hardly dared to look at it since.'

When he did look closely again a year later, he saw that though there was indeed 'a sort of completeness . . . the whole thing must be repainted in quite another vein'. In fact, he concluded, 'it will be a new picture', needing 'a multitude of studies', which meant of course extra sittings. Lytton would sometimes bring along his brother Oliver, sometimes Saxon Sydney-Turner. 'I believe that the proper attenuated & subtle expression of the piece will prevail the stronger for it,' Henry encouraged him. The sittings went on during the spring and summer of 1914 while Henry replaced a pot and brushes with a chair and hat, made fresh studies of the trees and bushes in the background, recoloured the floor, re-marked the tartan rug, and instructed Lytton to bring his brown slippers and new reading glasses in place of the original *pince-nez*. 'The picture goes forward very slowly and I have never had a fair opportunity to do another head on it,' he complained that summer. But on 28 August 1914, a few days before he enlisted for wartime medical duties, he saw that it was 'alarmingly complete' . . .[20]

. . . But not *absolutely* complete. After the war, from 1919 to 1921, he continued making minor adjustments until in 1922, its colour somewhat sunk, it was exhibited in his first one-man show at the Alpine Club, and then loaned to the Tate Gallery. Here it immediately divided the generations, provoking a similar set of reactions to *Eminent Victorians*. The young Stephen Spender went to see it with his father, the author Humphrey Spender, who stared in silence at the sinuously reclining figure in front of the toy-like landscape. 'Then hatred for the painter suddenly clicked in his mind with hatred of the most irreverent and iconoclastic of modern essayists, as he said in a loud voice: "Well, Lytton Strachey deserves it! He deserves it!" And he strode away, meditating on the poetic justice which had ordained Henry Lamb to place Lytton Strachey in the inferno of those rooms which my father labelled "the lunatic asylum" in the Tate.'[21]

Sir George Sitwell was another member of the older generation provoked by Lytton's formidable looks. 'In an age when people tended to look the same,' explained his son Osbert, 'his [Lytton's] emergence into any scene, whether street or drawing-room, lifted it to a new plane, investing it with a kind of caricatural Victorian interest.'[22]

Henry himself had hovered between thinking the portrait 'far below our collective deserts' and believing its existence was 'to the immortal glory of us both', until at length he came to resent the way it outshone his other work in the public imagination. In the later version, though there are the same boneless interminable legs, the same spade-like beard, the same astonished eyebrows, the face has grown less thin, the figure appears a little less enfeebled, the eyes, though not so sad, stare yet more alarmingly. Lytton still reclines, apparently without energy, on the edge of a basket-chair, a green and black plaid rug over his arms, against a view of ordered parkland. But he is no longer quite alone. In the background, two figures have emerged from behind a tree and are wandering along a path away from the house – perhaps Mrs Humphry Ward and St Loe Strachey, having called to inquire after his well-sounding new book. In both portraits Henry displays a mingling of affection and irony from which Lytton emerges, in the words of David Garnett, as 'an etiolated plant soon to die for lack of fresh air, light and the watering-can'. The lofty room and vast window give the impression of a case in which Lytton is preserved as a rare specimen of the Bloomsbury culture, what Virginia called 'the essence of culture . . . exotic, extreme in every way'.

This vision of a 'major Bloomsbury idol' has, in Osbert Sitwell's words, the 'air of someone pleasantly awakening from a trance . . . a pagod as plainly belonging as did the effigies to a creation of its own.

'Humour and wit were very strongly marked in the quizzical expression of his face, and also, I think a kind of genuine diffidence as well as a certain despair and, always, a new surprise at man's follies . . . It is important to look the part one plays, and he gave consummately the impression of a man of letters, perhaps rather of one in the immediate past: a Victorian figure of eminence, possibly. Yet ... he would have been at ease in the England of an earlier age, when his beard might have been tinted a carnation hue. It was an Elizabethan as well as a Victorian head that peered aloft.'

Before his Spiritual Revolution, Lytton's dependence upon those he loved had been absolute. Now he was less wholly vulnerable. After the terrors and quarrels between him and Henry, there came, not the cringing apologies he had offered Duncan, but explanations that placed their differences in a more reasonable context.

'I know I'm exaggerated and maladif in these affairs,' he wrote to Henry after one reconciliation (19 February 1912). 'I wish I could say how I hate my wretched faiblesses. But I think perhaps you don't realise how horribly I've suffered during the last 6 or 7 years from loneliness, and what a difference your friendship has made for me. It has been a gushing of new life through my veins – enfin. I sometimes get into a panic and a fever, and a black cloud comes down, and it seems as if, after all, it was too good to be true ...'

Similarly, he would write off to his confidante, Ottoline (25 January 1912): 'He [Henry] has been charming, and I am much happier. I'm afraid I may have exaggerated his asperities; his affection I often feel to be miraculous. It was my sense of the value of our relationship, and my fear that it might come to an end, that made me cry out so loudly the very minute I was hurt.'

These letters to Ottoline are not so full of perdition and recrimination as those to Maynard. While they celebrate the value to him of Lamb's affection, which Lytton was never sure of retaining for long, yet one is made aware of a feeling – as one seldom was in the Duncan Grant affair – that, when the final separation comes, life will go on and that all kinds of new experiences lie in wait for him.

TEN

Town versus the Country

'Why is London the only place to live in . . .?'
Lytton Strachey to Virginia Woolf (8 November 1912)

'My theory is that if only I could get a cottage on these Downs, and furnish it comfortably, I could live and work in comparative happiness.'
Lytton Strachey to James Strachey (September 1912)

I

THE ANGEL, THE DEVIL AND *A SON OF HEAVEN*

It was during the spring and summer months of 1912 that Lytton wrote his only play to be performed on the London stage. *A Son of Heaven* was a four-act melodrama, the action of which passes on the 14th and 15th August 1900 at the Imperial Palace, Peking, during the Boxer Rebellion. 'The difficulties are too horribly great; and about half the time I feel simply incompetent,' he told Ottoline Morrell (18 March 1912). 'Well! Racine wrote two bad plays before Andromaque – so I suppose there's some hope.'

Was his life as a newly-published literary critic not sufficiently dazzling? Ottoline wondered. She pictured him prancing the streets flaunting a purple coat with green velvet collar. These games with Ottoline still lifted his morale. 'You won't vanish altogether with an Apollo from Transylvania who'll whisk you off to his castle in a chariot and six?' he demanded (7 June 1912) when she left for Paris. 'Shall I see you before the end of the month?'

By May he had completed the first act and almost completed the second. When not writing, he used his solitude for reading – Flaubert's letters, Maupassant's *Bel-Ami* ('a profoundly depressing book') and *The Brothers Karamazov* which, he informed his severely atheistic brother James, nearly converted him to Christianity. After his first rush of enthusiasm for Dostoyevsky in French, he had begun to take Russian lessons; but it was the recently issued Constance Garnett translation into

English which now absorbed him. 'It's been very exciting,' he told Henry Lamb (30 April 1912), 'but on the whole I was – disappointed!

'I don't think it's better than the other great ones – I hardly think it as good ... I think it's the *ablest* – the mass and the supremacy of the detail, and the concatenation of the whole thing – the mastery of the material is complete. But the material itself – those tremendous overwhelming floods of unloosed genius that pour out of Les Possédés and L'Idiot – that was what I missed. Of course there are great heights, but only once, at the very end, did I feel the knife really in between my ribs, and turning. For one thing, I think there's too much of the detective-story apparatus. The Christianity also is slightly trying at times.'

Later that year he reviewed *The Brothers Karamazov* for the *Spectator*,[1] remarking how Dostoyevsky's psychological insight replaced the quiet, sane, common sense of the English novel with a dark underworld of unconscious desires: yet 'Dostoievsky, with all his fondness for the abnormal and the extraordinary, is a profoundly sane and human writer.'

Lytton planned regular expeditions into the country with Henry this year. At Easter they stayed at the New Inn in the main street of Cerne Abbas, above which, on a steep hill dominating the small Dorset town, was drawn 'a vast obscene Giant ... with his club & his OBELISK' which, Henry believed, 'accounts for the absence of lady visitors'. Though Lytton's 'treatment & intolerance of the poor fumbling Inn people revolts me occasionally', he was generally behaving so well that Henry rewarded him with a visit to Augustus and Dorelia near by at Alderney Manor. 'I think John liked him,' Henry reported to Ottoline. At any rate they were both 'in vigorous health & were able to booze valiantly with John without subsequent disaster'. Henry believed it would be to Augustus's advantage to rub shoulders with a genuine literary intellectual like Lytton. But the earrings which Lytton began wearing shortly afterwards (and which are revealed in Henry's drawings of him) testify to John's paramount influence. For Augustus this flashing jewellery was a symbol of the gypsies, by whom he had longed to be kidnapped when a child. It was an ornament that would have outraged his father, a respectable Pembrokeshire solicitor ('We are the sort of people', Augustus told another Welsh artist Nina Hamnett, 'our fathers warned us against!'). For Lytton earrings became for a while the insignia of his homosexuality, which he was fashioning into a weapon against Victorian morality, as well as a sign of his wish to move further from the intellectual plains of Cambridge, and enter the knockabout world of British bohemia of which

Augustus, who held court in Chelsea rather than Bloomsbury, was the acknowledged Emperor.

In the last week of May, Lytton and Henry set off on a ten-day walking holiday in Cumberland. At the end of a tremendous trek of thirty miles across mountains and moors from Carlisle to the country town of Alston, they settled down for a few days' relaxation at Handy House, a lodging-house 'with a Scotch mist out of the window, plush brackets on the walls, furniture draped à la Roger [Fry] and Henry in the middle of it all, fuming over a picture'.

Despite good food and delightful country ('hills are ranged round on every side; and various streams rush by') their relationship was still precarious. Lytton longed to get closer to Henry, but feared to arouse his aggressive melancholia. 'At times,' he confessed to Ottoline (7 June 1912), 'I feel terrified when I think of him – he seems like some desperate proud fallen angel, plunging into darkness and fate. Oh why? Why? He nourishes himself in bitterness, and wraps himself up in his torments as if he loved them.'

He liked to think that the horrors which tormented Henry would dissolve, and his temperament grow easier, if the two of them could set up house together. For a while he contemplated moving to Milton Cottage in Rothiemurchus, with both Henry and James; and at various other times that summer he inspected houses in Gordon Square, Mecklenburgh Square and Woburn Square. But always there was some overriding objection – too close a proximity of relations, too great a remoteness from friends, or else simply the noise, expense and uncertainty.

Back at Belsize Park Gardens he advanced well into the third act of *A Son of Heaven*. It was pleasant to imagine himself a successful playwright. Wearing a deerstalker hat, tortoiseshell spectacles, a carnation in his button-hole, he would stroll down Piccadilly with an elastic tread, swinging his cloak. He drank tea at Rumpelmayer's, picked his way nimbly through picture galleries, whirled along in taxis . . .

Or perhaps he should be a biographer? A lady by the name of Marzials had got in touch asking whether he would write a life of St Evremond, with the aid of material collected by her late husband. 'I don't think I shall,' he told Ottoline (12 June 1912), '– unless the materials turn out to be very exciting; and that is unlikely. St Evremond was a pleasant gentleman; but that was all, I fancy. If I must write somebody's life, it had better be Voltaire.'

More exciting was the news that his friend Leonard Woolf was finally engaged to Virginia Stephen. 'To be in love with her – isn't that a danger?' Leonard had asked Lytton after getting back from Ceylon. Then on 2 June he wrote: 'Virginia is going to marry me . . . it is difficult to put one's happiness into words & it was so damned easy to put the miseries of life into them from Ceylon. At any rate after 13 years & the silences in them, youre the person I turn to first in the world to try to tell you of either.'[2] 'It is magnificent,' Lytton replied (6 June 1912). 'I am very happy; and je t'aime beaucoup.' He celebrated the event with a burst of gossip. 'I am *very* glad,' he told Ottoline (12 June 1912). 'I've not seen either of them yet; but I know that he's in ecstasies of happiness.

'He had to besiege her a good deal before she accepted him. I feel rather a fool because I kept on urging him to propose, while he was doing it all the time; but why didn't he tell me? I suppose he thought I wouldn't be discreet enough. There's a story that a week or two before the engagement he proposed in a train, and she accepted him, but owing to the rattling of the carriage he didn't hear, and took up a newspaper, saying "What?" On which she had a violent revulsion and replied "Oh, nothing!" – She was very much disappointed at everyone taking the news so calmly. She hoped that everyone would be thunderstruck. Duncan alone came up to her expectations – he fell right over on the floor when she told him: and of course really he had been told all about it by Adrian before.'

At the beginning of July he returned to Neo-Pagan pastures for a month's exile at Becky Falls. Every day he would rise at seven and work all morning at *A Son of Heaven*; would doze, dream and read in the afternoon, then walk in the evening through the woodlands and down the steep cleft with its cascading water. Each night he went on absorbing himself in Peking politics. 'My brain seethes like a witch's cauldron,' he wrote to Henry (13 July 1912), '– I keep ladling out the contents into my Chinese, but it continues to boil and bubble and sometimes I hardly know whether I'm on my head or my heels . . . I've now finished my 3rd Act, and so only have one more to do. It ought to be the most exciting and therefore the easiest, and I hope to reel it off in a week, and then proceed to the grand revision.'

For relaxation he read Anatole France, Gray, Dostoyevsky's *La Maison des morts* (not yet translated by Constance Garnett into English), Van Gogh's letters, and Lanfrey's life of Napoleon, which drew from him a tirade in one of his letters to Ottoline (6 July 1912).

'I think he [Napoleon] was the embodiment of all that is vilest in the character of man – selfishness, vulgarity, meanness, and falseness of every kind pushed to the furthest possible point. The *lowness* of him! If he had

had one touch of the eminence of vice that Milton's Satan had, he would not have been utterly damnable; but the wretch was base all through. That so many people should have admired him so much seems to me one of the bitterest satires on humanity. It is the ape adoring its own image in the looking-glass.'

After two weeks, G.E. Moore came to join him. On fine afternoons they would go for walks together along deep, narrow, aromatic Devonshire lanes, thick with summer flowers, and then up high on to the moor, away to far horizons, with the heather under their feet and great piled-up rocks on the tops of the hills. In the evenings they read aloud to each other from Froude's *Short Studies on Great Subjects* and Mahan's *Influence of Sea Power upon the French Revolution and Empire*; and sometimes Moore would sing.

Over these weeks Lytton drafted a petition on behalf of the sculptor, Jacob Epstein, which enabled him to work closely with Henry. Early the previous year Epstein had been commissioned to carve the tomb of Oscar Wilde. For over nine months he had laboured in his London studio at an immense monolith weighing some twenty tons. Eventually this work was transported to Paris, and had recently been erected over Wilde's remains in the Père Lachaise cemetery. The Préfecture of the Seine, however, had considered the tombstone indecent, and ordered it to be covered with a tarpaulin. In an effort to reach some compromise, Robert Ross, the trustee for the monument and Wilde's literary executor, had (without consulting Epstein) arranged for a large plaque to be modelled and cast in bronze; and this was then applied to the offending regions of the sculpture in the manner of a fig-leaf. But one night the plaque was removed by a marauding band of artists and poets; whereupon the tarpaulin had been replaced over the tomb by the authorities, and a gendarme stationed on duty near by.

At once a protest went up in the French newspapers. Lytton had been drawn into the affair by Francis Dodd and Ada Leverson.[3] Epstein's art, with its basic sexual instincts, had shocked genteel British culture, and Lytton himself was shocked by the French establishment's prudery. He was in favour of angels having genitals. The petition he composed took the form of a modest proposal to the French Government, asking them to refund the money which Epstein had been obliged to spend on the Customs duties in order to take the monument to France. One copy was sent to Dorothy Bussy who translated it into French and forwarded it to Auguste Bréal with an informal letter explaining the circumstances of Epstein's poverty, and asking him to get up a small committee to see the thing through. The second copy was presented from the English side.

Lytton hoped to obtain some official representation from the Foreign Office, but this failed. Many prominent names were considered as signatories to the petition, names which might impress the French Government – among others Henry James, W.B. Yeats, Charles Ricketts and C.H. Shannon: 'As to the English signatures,' he very properly concluded, 'Holroyd would of course be the very thing.'[4] But in the end none of these people was to be associated with the venture. The final version, which Lytton completed early in August, reads as follows:[5]

'Mr Epstein, the sculptor, has now completed the tomb of Oscar Wilde, which will shortly be placed in the Père Lachaise cemetery. It is estimated that the duty, levied by the French customs on the importation from England of the large blocks of stone composing the tomb, will amount to at least £120. The monument is a serious and interesting work of art, it is to be erected in a public place in Paris and it is dedicated to the memory of an English poet and littérateur of high distinction. In consideration of these facts, it has been suggested to us that the French Government might be approached with a view to the remission of the customs duty. The aesthetic merit of Mr Epstein's sculpture and the public interest attaching to it lead us to hope that he may be relieved from a considerable financial burden, which falls upon him owing simply to the commercial value of the mere stone of which his work is composed. The granting of the proposed remission of duty would, we feel, be in accordance with those traditions of enlightened munificence in all matters connected with the arts, for which the French Nation is so justly famed. George Bernard Shaw, H.G. Wells, John Lavery, Robert Ross, Léon Bakst.'

The French Government, however, was unmoved by this rhetorical flattery and the petition failed. But two years later, at the outbreak of war, the tarpaulin was removed from the tomb without remark and never replaced.

By the end of July, Lytton had finished and completely revised his Chinese play. All that remained to be added were the stage directions, and then it would be ready for typing. In style it owes something to Racine, and although Lytton did not take it altogether seriously, he rather fancied a spectacular production in the manner of Beerbohm Tree. Meanwhile, he put the manuscript to one side, left Becky House and with 'a map, a hat, a pair of pants' set off with Henry for Scotland. Their destination was the small cottage, owned by the Glass family, near Loch an Eilein where Lytton and James had stayed in August 1908. Early each morning, they had to light the kitchen fire and make their own breakfast; but this they were happy to do, since they had already been woken at four o'clock by solos on the fiddle. 'Willie Glass would play the violin outside our bedroom from 4 to 5 a.m. in the morning,' Lytton complained in a letter to his mother (24 August 1912), 'and Annie never by any chance had a meal ready within 2 hours of the appointed time . . . Willie told endless stories dated usually 1450, and was otherwise very cultured and agreeable – but the horrors were too great in the long run.'[6]

After a few days they departed for the Alexandra Hotel in Inverness. 'So far the journey has not been a great success,' Lytton admitted to Ottoline (7 August 1912). But already he was cheered by another brainwave. Henry loved remote places, so they would go to a fishing village called Helmsdale on the east coast of Sutherland where the bracing North Sea winds would soon blow Henry's doldrums away. 'We shall probably be there', Lytton informed Ottoline, 'for a few days at least.' They set off, arrived at Helmsdale in the evening – and, by the first train next morning, they fled. Lytton had pictured a romantic village between the mountains and the sea, filled with young fishermen in earrings. What he found was a squalid street in desolate country, and not an earring in sight. His distress mounted as Henry burst out that this was precisely what he had expected.

Amid terrible agitations they hurried on via Glasgow, Belfast and Londonderry to Middletown, on the north-west coast of Ireland. For four days they were perpetually on the move, their money pouring out, their tempers frayed. Finally they came to rest at a small detached house, McBride's Hotel. They could go no further. 'At present I am almost killed with various fatigues,' Lytton lamented to James (12 August 1912). He doubted whether he would be up to travelling again for two or three weeks. After all, they were comfortably housed, and the countryside, facing the Atlantic, was of a kind which Henry relished – vast stretches of treeless, peaty land covered with multitudes of small cottages, remote mountains in the background, and, on the other side, the sea, with island after island, sand-dunes and bays and creeks innumerable. The unified impression was huge, full of complexity and coloured in those vivid browns and greens that Henry was so fond of using in his pictures. Surely now he must be happy.

Henry indeed had started to regain his spirits. But not for long. The rain, it rained every day, the wind, it blew, and Henry sank into the blackest sulks, while Lytton took to his bed and read through the complete works of Tennyson. 'Henry I suspect is daft,' he wrote to Ottoline (14 August 1912), '– that's the only explanation I can see for his goings on . . . And then, of course, when he's not a devil, he's an angel – oh dear, what a muddle of a world we drag ourselves along in, to be sure! I sit here brooding over the various people – Woolf and Virginia, Duncan and Adrian, Vanessa and Clive and Roger, and James and Rupert and Ka – and the wildest Dostoyevsky novel seems to grow dim and ordinary in comparison.'

In the disordered novel of their lives everything did indeed seem 'agitated, feverish, intense', like the world of Dostoyevsky whose characters, Lytton wrote that summer, 'appear to be always trembling on the verge of insanity'. Henry had given up seeing his expensive hypnotist Dr Bramwall, but Ottoline who had been prescribed 'thought control' was now consulting a ferocious neurologist, Dr Combe, who, to banish her multiplying headaches, cut bits of bone out of her nose and stuck red hot wires into her nostrils, when she visited him in Lausanne. This barbaric treatment went by the grand name of 'rhinosurgery'. Lytton wrote (12 June 1912) offering to come out and 'be your maid – I'm sure I'd make a very good one ... I should arrange your petticoats most exquisitely, and only look through the crack now and then.' But Ottoline already had a companion in Lausanne, Bertrand Russell, who was sharing her bedroom. He too had been reading Dostoyevsky, recognizing a likeness between Myshkin in *The Idiot* and G.E. Moore who 'always speaks the truth because it does not occur to him to do otherwise, and he does it so simply that nobody ever minds'.

Meeting Bertie the previous summer with Ottoline, Henry had made a great effort to be polite, appearing 'really angelic'. Bertie unhappily admitted to Ottoline, '– I don't feel as if he disliked me, though one would suppose he must.' And it was true he did. He complained of Bertie's pedagogic talk as being 'like a file working on a thin iron-sheet', and of 'the necessity Bertie evidently feels to snub me every now & then'. But what he most resented was Bertie's inability to take him seriously as a rival.

Keeping her lovers in diplomatic accord gave Ottoline ever more excruciating headaches. Henry was sexually attractive, but Bertie (who had halitosis and pyorrhoea) needed her more. On learning that she had probably seen Henry in Paris earlier in 1912, Bertie wrote threatening to fling himself under a motor car (30 and 31 May 1912): 'I have longed for death, even when things seemed happy.'[7]

To pacify Henry while she spent more time with Bertie, Ottoline offered to give him dancing lessons. 'I will learn anything that involves you hugging my neck!' Henry had replied (April 1912). But his letters grew more provocative as their relationship was further clouded by a tactless muddle over a naked self-portrait he gave her.

Lytton did what he could to urge Henry's charm and genius, but this became difficult once Henry confided that he had 'resigned my post as eclave non favori' and would rarely be going to 'Throne Hall' as he called Bedford Square after the 'Throne Hall of Heavenly Purity' where Lytton had set *A Son of Heaven*. 'You need not ask me for explanations,' he told Lytton before starting on their Scottish journey together: 'the amputation was done without anaesthetics and I have lost enough blood.' So too, he made sure, had Ottoline, as he performed the final cut with a savage letter (12 July 1912), 'so bitter and odious the wording is engraved on my memory', advising her to 'keep for your own benefit a little of all this overflowing soul'. Meanwhile, he concluded, 'I shall go on my way cheerfully – and slightly weathered, yet enormously wiser as to the validity of feminine assistance in Life.'

Certainly Henry looked weathered enough during their holiday. But Lytton could not see any cheerfulness or renewed faith in the validity of male assistance. Henry had lost Ka and Ottoline, and was tied to an adoring homosexual who was to be the inspiration for a picture on which his artistic reputation would largely depend. It was a predicament worthy, in its own way, of a Russian novel.

'Don't be surprised if I suddenly arrive at Broughton pale and trembling – I should send a telegram first,' Lytton wrote to Ottoline from his sick-bed in Ireland. Yet even now he had not given up hope of a miraculous ascension transforming Henry from devil to angel again. He thought he saw signs of it – in which case there was no reason why they should not stay in Ireland together until the end of August, until September . . . Four days later he telegraphed to Ottoline:

Shall arrive tomorrow wire train later in need of your corraggio as well as my own.

What then happened was described by Ottoline herself:

'He arrived soon after the telegram and fell into my arms, an emotional, nervous and physical wreck, ill and bruised in spirit, haunted and shocked. I comforted him and diverted him as much as I could . . . we gave him a sitting-room to write in, and he stayed some time. I had many an enchanting talk with him and we grew very intimate. He read aloud to me, poetry – Shakespeare, Racine and Crashaw (who carried me away by his intense passion) . . .

At night Lytton would become gay and we would laugh and giggle and be foolish; sometimes he would put on a pair of my smart high-heeled shoes, which made him look like an Aubrey Beardsley drawing, very wicked. I love to see him in my memory tottering and pirouetting round the room with feet looking so absurdly small, peeping in and out of his trousers, both of us so excited and happy, getting more and more fantastic and gay.'[8]

His recuperation was gradual, however, for he was full of vain regrets. 'I seem to have been moving ceaselessly and quite pointlessly for the last 3 weeks,' he confessed to James (21 August 1912). 'Among other things I am almost ruined financially.' He did little work, feeling altogether too sick and exhausted. 'I think that I am not in a really healthy and competent state for more than half my days,' he wrote to his mother (3 September 1912).

Henry had posted a letter after Lytton, accusing him of staging a quarrel as an excuse for his retreat. 'I didn't want you to go away and I was aghast at the rapid failure of our holiday,' he wrote. With this letter he enclosed a drawing which shows a mischievously angelic version of himself cushioned in a cloud and holding a rope in each hand from which the lugubrious figures of Lytton and Ottoline are suspended. They are sighing in unison: 'When will he realize what he makes us SUFFER?'

Ruminating together, it was sometimes difficult for Ottoline and Lytton to know who was responsible for all this suffering. 'I think he is partly insane from egotism and vanity,' Ottoline had written to Bertie. But to Lytton she confided that she would continue loving him whatever happened. Lytton felt the same. Over the following weeks he tried to absorb as much of the blame as possible. He accused himself of being a tiresome companion; he offered Henry separate bedrooms in future; he promised to show more self-restraint. He was submissive, apologetic, coy and cajoling:

'Won't you take me back under your charge again, and cure me with the severest of your régimes? . . . I feel like a naughty child. Am I one? – At any rate a whipped one. Perhaps one who has been flogged hard for some mysterious naughtiness he hasn't understood, and then been shut up in a dark room to repent – Well, there is no trace of rancour in my heart now. Won't my papa come and open the door, and take me into his arms again?'

Henry's replies are more terse. In another cartoon, he depicts the two of them as ape-like creatures in the jungle, Lytton studying his vast penis and Henry farting a message into his dismayed face: 'Best friends are not always Best Companions.' Was it true? Lytton did not really believe that Henry was blameless. It was not actually a matter of blame, but of compatible games and fantasies that human nature needs. The most moving sentences in his letters are those which state his bewildered sense of failure in human relationships, and the darkness all round. 'The longer I live the more plainly I perceive that I was not made for this world. I think I must belong to some other solar system altogether.' His loneliness was compounded by a deep strangeness. He could find ease only in his imagination. So he came to live in other worlds, to stretch out and re-create other lives.

Back in London he shrugged off such thoughts as his days filled up with literary schemes and propositions. Following the success of *Landmarks in French Literature*, he was being solicited by publishers. With nothing to lose, he felt able to play the part of the Great Author employing, so he told Ottoline, 'all the signs of genius – a rolling eye, a melancholy abstractedness, no notion of business'. This charade went down so well that one publisher offered earnestly to print *anything* by him. He felt tempted, he told his mother, to unload on him 'the old Hastings lucubration which I should be glad to get off my hands'. More productive was an invitation from Harold Cox to write for the *Edinburgh Review*. Lytton accepted the offer and contributed four of his most ambitious biographical essays to this journal.

'I *am* happy, excited, delighted, prancing, optimistic, impudent, and youthful, now I'm in London again,' he assured Ottoline forty-eight hours after leaving her. The next day he left town with James to spend a fortnight at Van Bridge, a cottage near Haslemere in Sussex, which Alys Russell had lent them. 'It all seems a sort of Paradise – incredibly provided at the critical moment, like a conjuring trick,' he told Ottoline. There was a housekeeper to look after them, and they had every luxury down to the last hot-water bottle at night. There was 'only one flaw', Lytton informed his mother (9 September 1912), '– the extreme lowness of the rooms. Most of the ceilings come down to the level of our shoulders, and we have to creep about on all fours.'

He was now putting the final touches to his Chinese play. At first he had rather scoffed at the custom of writing out long stage directions, a fashion which had been introduced by Shaw to make his plays read like novels and then developed by Harley Granville Barker to the point where playwrights gave not only descriptions of the scenery and actions but also accounts of the characters and their feelings. On this system, it seemed to Lytton, Shakespeare should have written: 'Lear (*angrily*): Blow, winds, and crack your cheeks!' However, James persuaded him that agents and actor-managers would never be able to make out what was going on unless he stuck in explanations.

In the next two years there were to be many attempts to get *A Son of*

Heaven produced. The agent to whom Lytton sent it thought highly of its chances. It was an excellent play, he said, exciting and picturesque, full of dramatic appeal, certain to make money. James Barrie and John Masefield, who also read it, echoed this favourable verdict. The long list of actor-managers to whom it was submitted – Oscar Asche, Harley Granville Barker, Frederick Harrison, Norman Wilkinson and others – cordially agreed. He had written, they all maintained, a very good and interesting play. However, it was not precisely what was *needed* just then. The previous year might have been better. Or the next. Fashion was always changing. They would continue rigorously to bear it in mind; perhaps the year after next . . . In January 1914, Lytton gave the typescript to his brother James, then on his way to Moscow, and he handed it on to Dudley Ward who was the *Manchester Guardian* correspondent in Berlin and had connections with Max Reinhardt. Max Reinhardt liked *A Son of Heaven*. He declared it to be an excellent play, most exciting and picturesque. It was, he added, full of dramatic appeal, certain to make money. Unfortunately he was already committed for that year, and it would be unfair to the author to hold on to his work. He therefore returned it. After a while, Lytton grew resigned. It seemed, if one were to believe all that these distinguished men had written about his melodrama, that *A Son of Heaven* was fated to be the finest play never performed: and with that he would have to be content. He put it in a drawer and forgot about it.

Meanwhile, acting on what he called 'inspiration', Lytton shouldered a knapsack and marched off to Salisbury. The next few weeks he spent wandering over the Wiltshire and Berkshire Downs, to Amesbury, Marlborough and Wantage. 'It really was a heavenly experience,' he afterwards chided Henry (9 November 1912). 'I found that there were joys in solitude that I'd hitherto hardly dreamt of.'

On his travels, he sported a conspicuous yellow coat worn over a new suit of 'mouse-coloured corduroys' and a bright orange waistcoat. His brilliant heavily-haversacked figure caused some stir among the populace as he stepped out gaily along the roads and fields, especially since he was also wearing a brace of golden earrings. These, he told James, were a great solace to him, though they evidently worried the good citizens of Wiltshire. 'They eyed me with the greatest severity,' he wrote from Amesbury (21 September 1912), 'but I bearded them.' He felt eighteen rather than his full thirty-two years, 'a very young youth on a gay holiday' was how he described himself to Ottoline (25 September 1912), '– reckless & debonair & not caring a brass farthing for the rest of humanity.'

One of the highlights of this journey was his raid on Stonehenge. From the hotel at Amesbury he stole out at dusk, and with the moon bright and rising behind him, approached the dark cluster of awkward shapes which looked as if they had somehow been forgotten and left behind in the empty plain. At a distance it all appeared disappointingly small and squat; but, drawing nearer, he realized that in this peculiar compactness lay its power and beauty. The great old stones, faintly blue in the twilight, seemed to have come huddling together in a melancholy little group, like the last fragment of an army. They had the ominous look of contraction which extreme age can give. The barbed wire fence was easy to negotiate, and on entering the ring, under the darkening sky, he found the effect inexplicably compelling. Each stone was in reality a gigantic bulk while, in the blackness stretching away beyond the pillared circle, the twentieth century invisibly receded.

After inspecting the Wiltshire Downs, Lytton turned north towards Churn where Ottoline, having temporarily taken up water-colour painting, was residing at a little farmhouse lent to her by her brother Henry. He had already warned her at the start of his tour that he might be straying in this direction. 'So if one fine morning', he had written (18 September 1912), 'you perceive a dishevelled tramp, with melancholy marked upon every limb, wearing a small black hat, a ragged beard, a pair of odd-looking spectacles . . . if you see a figure coming creeping upon a stick over your airy down – it may be . . . a certain eminent young literary gentleman.' Ten days later he made a flying descent upon Churn. Ottoline noted his hurried arrival and departure in her diary.

28 September
Lytton arrived from Wantage with a huge pack on his back . . . as excited as a boy, for he had had his ears pierced and was wearing gold earrings, which he kept hid under his long hair, and he was wearing his new suit of corduroys, which were very short in the legs. What squeals of laughter and giggles and fun we had about it all . . . I was sad when he left, he was so well and full of fun and life and youth, adorable; and he and I and Philip had such delightful talks together. I watched his tall, thin back striding off with its rather quick nervous walk, vanishing into the distance. What a solitary figure he seemed then, seeking rather timidly and nervously for human adventure. I stood and waved to him and quite felt hurt that he didn't turn back.[9]

During this pilgrimage Lytton had made a companion of the solitude which had so frightened him after his falling-out with Henry – it was no longer a threat but an intermittent strength. Happiness was inexplicable,

the way it came and went, like the wind. All August he had actively
pursued it over England, Scotland and Ireland, emerging bruised and
broken; now, in September, when he had almost grown resigned to failure,
and his plans and movements were haphazard, happiness had come
bubbling up. So much of his life had been spent in a void, escaping from
or chasing after something. Ottoline had suggested marriage,
recommending Ethel Sands as an eligible partner. She was rich, sociable,
lesbian, and owned a beautiful manor house at Newington and a town
house in Chelsea.[10] But could one really marry a house? On the whole
Lytton thought not. 'I suppose a wife would settle such affairs for one,' he
wrote to James from his temperance hotel, '– oh dear! the length of time
this wobble has been going on – five years at least, I believe. I suppose I'm
extraordinarily incompetent . . . Oh for a little rest! – A little home life, and
comfort, and some soothing woman! Supposing one married Ka? –'

Such moments of dishonesty were now comparatively rare. He felt
certain that if he could write something worthwhile, then all these
weaknesses and futilities would melt away. 'Do you know how passionately
I desire to do this?' he asked Ottoline (6 September 1912). 'To achieve
something – not unworthy of my hopes, my imaginations, and the spirit
that I feel to be mine? Only the difficulties and terrors are so great –
overwhelming sometimes. Oh, to bound forward and triumph!'

2

THE CHESTNUTS

By the autumn of 1912, Lytton's wanderings had led him to one practical
conclusion. He would avail himself of a standing offer from Harry Norton
of a hundred pounds, and settle down in some small farmhouse in
Berkshire or Wiltshire – like the one where Ottoline was living at Churn.
'My theory is that if only I could get a cottage on these Downs,' he
explained to James, 'and furnish it comfortably, I could live and work in
comparative happiness. I believe it would cost very little, and I should be
able to afford another rat-hole in Hampstead, to fly to when the solitude
became oppressive . . . It seems to me my health *must* get all right in this
air, which is amazing; and if I was really settled down properly with my
books, etc. etc. I believe I should be able to work – and then people would
come down for week-ends, and I could go up from time to time and
gallivant – oh! it strikes me as a paradise.'

Lytton's choice fell on The Chestnuts, a small farmhouse in the village of East Ilsley, set high up on the edge of the Berkshire Downs, and owned by a racehorse trainer and his Norwegian wife, Mr and Mrs Lowe. He moved in on 10 October, and remained there for the next three months.

Though his published output was not large – a Spectatorial review of H.J.C. Grierson's *The Poems of John Donne*, and his long essay on Madame du Deffand for the *Edinburgh Review* – these months mark a change in his career. 'Madame du Deffand' opens a new phase in his development as a writer – the transition from literary criticism to biography – and one symbolized by his use of a new combination of names. No longer was he to write anonymously or appear as 'G.L. Strachey'. From this time onwards he was 'Lytton Strachey', a name – 'rather theatrical, I think' – that signalled a different attitude to his work, partly brought about by his reading of Dostoyevsky. He wanted to explore ways of writing with more dramatic force, obliquely yet with precision, and with less reliance on impressionistic effects. Already he felt an exhilaration at tackling the problems and complexities thrown up by his subject-matter, sorting out the disordered rubble and giving it an internal unity. When Henry asked him whether he was pleased with the Deffand essay, he replied (9 November 1912) that he was neither pleased nor displeased – 'but I notice with relief that I rather like writing it, which is something quite new'.

He read everything about Madame du Deffand that he could lay his hands on – far more than the three volumes of letters on which his essay was ostensibly based. The more he read, the more 'difficult and alarming' his task appeared. But once he started to write the terrors fell away and he became absorbed. 'It is a dreadful story,' he wrote to Ottoline (31 October 1912), 'and on the whole very gloomy, though wit, cold wit, plays over it almost unceasingly.

'There are the most déchirant moments, and as for Horace Walpole a more callous fiend never stepped the earth. It is impossible to forgive him – quite impossible. His brutality reminds one of – Henry! But he had none of the redeeming qualities; he was a thoroughly selfish and also a rather stupid man. She, au fond, was not much better: but anyway she loved much. It is a disillusioning spectacle – a woman with nearly everything that life can give – wealth, consideration, intellectual brilliance, experience of the world – reduced to such a pitch of cynicism, pessimism and despair. But it is also terribly pathetic. The last letter of all is ghastly.'

He finished the eight thousand words by the end of November, corrected proofs the following month, and it appeared in the *Edinburgh Review* in January 1913. 'I meant to suggest', Lytton wrote to his mother

(20 December 1912), 'the kind of nasty turn that the easy-going optimism of everyday life gets, when it comes face to face with her sort of disillusionment.'

It was while living at The Chestnuts this autumn, that the idea of *Eminent Victorians* came to him. The first title which suggested itself was *Victorian Silhouettes*, a book which, as he envisaged it, was to contain highly condensed biographies of about a dozen Victorians – some (mostly scientists) to be admired, others exposed. Preserved among his papers is a list of the twelve most likely candidates for this volume: Cardinal Manning, Florence Nightingale (whose official biography he had been asked to write), General Gordon, Henry Sidgwick, the patriotic portrait painter George Watts, the eighth Duke of Devonshire (who as Lord Hartington was to become a splendidly comic figure in 'The End of General Gordon'), Charles Darwin, J.S. Mill, the Oxford theologian and Master of Balliol Benjamin Jowett, Carlyle, Lord Dalhousie (who laid the foundations of modern India) and Thomas Arnold. The First World War would change the writing of *Eminent Victorians*, making it an ironic meditation on those nineteenth-century values that led civilization into such slaughter. Already something of this feeling was rising in him. 'Is it prejudice, do you think, or is it the truth of the case?' he asked Virginia (8 November 1912) after reading Meredith's letters. 'They seem to me a set of mouthing bungling hypocrites; but perhaps really there is a baroque charm about them which will be discovered by our great-great-grandchildren, as we have discovered the charm of Donne, who seemed intolerable to the 18th century. Only I don't believe it.'

Although his gallery of Victorians was to include a select number painted in attractive colours – apostles of inquiring intelligence and unobtrusive achievement (men somewhat like Lytton's father) – the first happened to be drawn in satirical vein. 'I am ... beginning a new experiment in the way of a short condensed biography of Cardinal Manning – written from a slightly cynical standpoint,' he explained to Ottoline in his first week at The Chestnuts (17 October 1912). 'My notion is to do a series of short lives of eminent persons of that kind. It might be entertaining, if it was properly pulled off. But it will take a very long time.' The writing of 'Cardinal Manning' persuaded him that he would have to reduce the number of biographies, if the work were not to occupy a lifetime. Round him at The Chestnuts he gathered the engines of his project – a suffocating assortment of treatises upon the English and Roman Church, fat studies on Manning, Newman, Keble, Pusey and other divines. 'I can't make out what Mrs Lowe thinks of me,' he wrote (17 October 1912); 'but I expect she judges that I am going into the Church –

from the number of books on cardinals, the Oxford Movement, etc., etc., that I have brought with me.'

Whatever her secret thoughts, Mrs Lowe – who claimed to be an intimate of Björnson and Grieg – looked after Lytton very well; while her husband, during the afternoons, endeavoured to teach him riding. 'To-day I had my first riding-lesson with Mr Lowe,' he wrote excitedly to Ottoline (31 October 1912). 'He is infinitely gentle and sympathetic – just what I wanted. I circled round the paddock in the mildest way, and got hardly at all tired. I shall gradually increase the dose until – hunting, steeple-chasing, polo. No Spanish Cavalier will be in it.' This was a fine and spirited beginning, but his progress was less rapid than he hoped. Three times a week Mr Lowe would take him out, quivering with apprehension, on a small well-behaved black cob. Together they would proceed unsteadily across the fields, walking, and triumphantly trotting. Then, one afternoon, he suddenly seemed to get the hang of it. 'I shall come galloping into Bedford Square in a peaked cap & striped silk breeches,' he promised Ottoline. His letters to James, Henry and Ottoline are full of his equestrian exploits: 'I can sometimes trot for several minutes together with absolute equanimity,' he claimed (25 November 1912). 'The joys of cantering make me turn pale with ecstasy merely to think of . . . Mr Lowe does not say much either in approval or disapproval except that my legs are perfect! I should never have suspected it. Full many a leg is born to blush unseen.'

Despite his belief that 'my breeches and "leggings" are much admired', he was regarded with suspicion in the village of East Ilsley. Whether spotted whirling like some mythical four-hoofed beast across the long line of the Downs, or encountered as a pedestrian when he descended into the village itself, a bearded man, like the tall Agrippa, 'so tall he almost touched the sky', Lytton was an intimidating spectacle, and one from which the villagers shied away. He too paled with fear, as he walked the streets among these staring strangers. If only he possessed some capacity for making friends with people. 'I am quite tongue-tied,' he admitted to Ottoline (17 October 1912). 'I think it is caused by something in the blood – some sluggish element; but oh! I do desire to expand – I really do.'

This loneliness was the chief disadvantage of living in the country. On some days he spoke to no one at all. His only connection with the world at large, he told Maynard, was via *The Times*, which arrived just after lunch and soothed him into a *post meridiem* slumber. ' You are not to suppose from this that I am unhappy here,' he assured Virginia (8 November 1912). 'No, my hours pass in such a floating stream of purely self-regarding comfort that that's impossible, only one does have regrets.'

These regrets grew most oppressive in the evenings when, the day's work done, he dearly felt the want of a companion.

Occasionally he would invite a friend down to stay – his sister Marjorie who had invented a party game which involved making up satirical obituaries of the guests, or even Henry over whose indiscretions an act of oblivion had now been passed.[11] Sometimes at weekends he would leave The Chestnuts and go to London, where the Second Post-Impressionist Exhibition was being held at the Grafton Galleries. On the first of several visits there he arrived late, and on asking the porter whether Leonard Woolf – the exhibition's secretary – was still inside, was urged to 'pass through, Mr Augustus John, pass through and see!'

Once inside, there was no chance of further mis-identification, since one of the exhibits was Lamb's first large portrait of him. Collected round it, more often than not, was a ring of old gentlemen berating his moral character based, so far as he could overhear, upon the fact that he did not wear a linen collar. 'I suppose he does it to save his laundress's bills,' was the guess of one lady. 'No, madam, no!' she was speedily corrected by her white-haired escort. 'I am told that he is quite well off. It is affectation – mere affectation!' One Dublin newspaper, after describing the portrait, added that more extraordinary than any of the pictures were the people who went to look at them: 'There may be seen the autumn poet, his long overcoat, his large Quaker hat, and his strange black tie, gazing in rapt admiration at his own portrait!'

Lytton too seemed more interested in the effect produced by Post-Impressionism than in the pictures themselves. The Matisses he did find interesting, and their colour was thrilling. Otherwise Picasso's analytical cubism was merely Futuristic and incomprehensible; Duncan, imitating Matisse, a fish out of water; Vanessa rather pathetic; Wyndham Lewis execrable. He deplored the negation of all literary appeal, the aesthetic torturing of the human figure to achieve ideological significance. But he was fascinated by the ripples of irritation among the spectators. His mind was becoming preoccupied by the ingredients of publicity, by the ways and means of animating public feeling, and the methods of amalgamating literature with journalism, art with polemics, imagination and will. 'Why do people get so excited about art? It made me feel very cold and cynical. I must say I should be pleased with myself, if I were Matisse or Picasso – to be able, a humble Frenchman, to perform by means of a canvas and a little paint, the extraordinary feat of making some dozen country gentlemen in England, every day for two months, grow purple in the face!'

The main feeling left by these weekends in London was that he had been wise to settle in the country. He no longer felt quite the same towards

Bloomsbury. He was dismayed that Roger Fry – 'a most shifty and wormy character' – had quarrelled with Ottoline, offended his brother-in-law Simon Bussy and insulted Henry. And, so often, where Fry led, Clive Bell and the others hotly pursued. He also disliked their collective hostility to Boris Anrep, on whom he now had a rather schoolgirlish crush.[12] 'The Bloomsbury Gang have been most vile about him – including I'm sorry to say Duncan,' he told Henry (20 November 1912). 'Their lack of prescience seems to be infectious.' Individually he still got on well with them, especially Leonard and Virginia, who had established themselves in small cosy rooms in Clifford's Inn, off the north side of Fleet Street. They seemed singularly unchanged – and it was specially interesting talking with Virginia, who had just completed *The Voyage Out*. Leonard too had written a novel, *The Village in the Jungle*, that had been welcomed rhapsodically by a publisher, though not by Lytton himself, who read it in typescript. 'Can you imagine what it's like?' he asked Henry (20 November 1912).[13] 'It's painful to see how completely he seems at home on the niveau of that Bloomsbury gang.' The full horror of Bloomsbury was to be experienced among the turbulent crowds of friends and enemies at the Grafton itself. 'When last I went it was most painful,' Lytton wrote to Ottoline (18 October 1912).

'Clive was strutting round in dreadful style, without a hat, as if he owned the place. It was impossible not to talk to him, and of course he would shout his comments, so that crowds collected – all so ridiculous and unnecessary. At last, when he began to explain the merits and demerits of the [Eric] Gill statue, and positively patted it with his fat little hand, I had to disown him, and become absorbed in a Matisse drawing. Poor Woolf sits at his table and sustains the bombardments of the enraged public – how he keeps his temper I can't think. Irate country gentlemen and their wives rush up to him purple in the face, as if *he* had painted all the pictures with the deliberate intention of annoying them.'

Some weekends, Lytton would travel up to Cambridge instead of London and stay with Maynard, or Moore, or Harry Norton. The chief excitement during these months centred round the election to the Apostles of the Austrian philosopher, Ludwig Wittgenstein, and another undergraduate named Francis Bliss, a Rupert Brooke *doppelgänger* from Rugby.[14] Having studied engineering for a period at Manchester, Wittgenstein had come to Cambridge where he became interested in Bertrand Russell's lectures on Mathematical Logic. An intense friendship sprang up between the two men.

News of this remarkable student soon spread through Cambridge. But though he was Russell's protégé it was through Moore that Lytton had got to hear of him. On 2 May 1912, Russell told Ottoline that Lytton had come to tea with Wittgenstein who, having only dullness and brilliance in his repertoire, had taken the trouble to be brilliant. One of the purposes of Lytton's visit was to look him over for the Apostles. But Russell argued that Wittgenstein would not like the Society. 'I'm quite sure he wouldn't really,' he confided to Ottoline. 'It would seem to him to be stuffy, as indeed it has become, owing to their practice of being in love with each other, which didn't exist in my day – I think it is mainly due to Lytton.' Despite Wittgenstein's having disrupted Russell's seminar by his refusal to exclude the possibility of a rhinoceros being present, 'I like Wittgenstein more and more,' Russell told Ottoline (16 March 1912, 5 June 1913). 'He has pure intellectual passion in the highest degree; it makes me love him ... His faults are mine.' Russell knew Wittgenstein was homosexual, yet he felt protective as if Wittgenstein were his son. 'If only you had Lytton's composition,' Ottoline replied (11 June 1912), 'how satisfactory.'

For his part Lytton also believed that the Apostles were growing stuffy – mainly due to Russell. Philosophy was becoming a subject for specialists to such a hermetic extent that non-philosophical unmathematical intellectuals apparently had no correct position on really interesting questions but to admit they were too complicated to discuss. Lytton wanted Wittgenstein to be elected largely because (as Desmond MacCarthy reported to Moore) he was 'a passionate arguer'. The Apostles had been 'most indignant with Russell', MacCarthy wrote (4 December 1912) for having spoken to Wittgenstein 'in a way likely to dissuade him from accepting election'. Eventually it was Maynard who, meeting Wittgenstein at the end of October, had pushed through his election the following month (though Wittgenstein, on the edge of a nervous breakdown, had been 'too ill to argue properly', Russell recorded).

The effect on Russell was terrible to see – at least through Lytton's eyes. 'The poor man is in a sad state,' he wrote to Saxon Sydney-Turner (20 November 1912). 'He looks about 96 – with long snow-white hair and an infinitely haggard countenance. The election of Wittgenstein has been a great blow to him.* He clearly hoped to keep him all to himself, and

* Bertrand Russell, in a letter to the author (14 September 1966), made it clear that, to the best of his recollection, he was never worried about Wittgenstein and the Apostles. Lytton's account of this episode, he wrote, 'completely surprised me, and I know nothing whatever about the matter concerning which you write. I knew nothing at the time about Wittgenstein's relations with the

indeed succeeded wonderfully, until Keynes at last insisted on meeting him, and saw at once that he was a genius and that it was essential to elect him.

'The other people (after a slight wobble from [Ferenc] Békássy) also became violently in favour. Their decision was suddenly announced to Bertie, who nearly swooned. Of course he could produce no reason against the election – except the remarkable one that the Society was so degraded that his Austrian would certainly refuse to belong to it. He worked himself up into such a frenzy over this that no doubt he got himself into a state of believing it: – but it wasn't any good. Wittgenstein shows no sign of objecting to the Society, though he detests Bliss, who in return loathes him. I think on the whole the prospects are of the brightest. Békássy is such a pleasant fellow that, while he is in love with Bliss, he yet manages to love Wittgenstein. The three of them ought to manage very well, I think. Bertie is really a tragic figure, and I am very sorry for him; but he is most deluded too. Moore is an amazing contrast – fat, rubicund, youthful, and optimistic ... Hardy[15] was there – p.p. and quite dumb. Sheppard was of course complaining that nobody liked him ...'

The lassitude of recent Society meetings was due, in Lytton's opinion, to the fact that present Apostles were more mature than his generation had been. It was an intellectual and emotional mistake, he believed, to abandon immaturity while still very young. He hoped that the election of a mysterious genius like Wittgenstein, who was also homosexual, would have a revivifying effect on the Society. The period of politeness was over: it was time for controversy. 'The hopeful aspect of affairs for the future was particularly exhilarating,' Lytton wrote to Maynard (20 November 1912). 'Our brothers Bliss and Wittgenstein are so nasty and our brother Békássy is so nice that the Society ought to rush forward now into the most progressive waters. I looked in on Bliss on Sunday night and he seemed quite as nasty as Rupert ever was. It was indeed charming!'

Yet Russell had been right. 'All the difficulties I anticipated have arisen with Wittgenstein,' he wrote to Maynard (11 November 1912). At his first

---

Society, nor had I any strong views as to whether he should be elected or not. I was interested in his intellectual potentialities, but I should have been glad of any outside influences that distracted him from the long monologues, lasting sometimes through the night, well into morning, during which he examined his own mind and motives. I do not think that I ever "worked myself into a frenzy" or "got quite ill" with any private worry, and, though I had anxieties at that time which were severe, they had nothing to do with the Society. I cannot imagine how the people whom you cite got these impressions of me, unless they thought the affairs of the Society were more important than I did at that time. I never felt any "mortification" at Wittgenstein being elected, nor can I think why I should have felt any such emotion.'

meeting, hearing Moore speak 'On Conversion', Wittgenstein pronounced it to be merely a way of getting rid of worry. He liked Maynard, Moore, Russell; he couldn't stand the undergraduates they had procured like Bliss, Békássy, and Sheppard's young man Cecil Taylor, whose claim to fame was that he had three balls. Besides, Wittgenstein did not see ethics as a branch of logic but as an activity that was a condition of the world. Really interesting questions were not matters of gossip – they called for self-communion: 'Whereof one cannot speak, thereof one must be silent.' By the end of November he was 'trembling on the verge of resignation,' James told Lytton. No one had ever resigned from the Society. In this emergency, the Apostles turned to Lytton. Maynard had already written in mid-November saying that he believed it 'might be a very good thing if you were to come to the Society this week, or if not then the week after'. Moore too urged him (4 December 1912) to come down and 'make him [Wittgenstein] see the point of the Society', adding characteristically: 'I wish you could explain to me, at the same time, what the real point is.'

By the time Lytton arrived in the second week of December it seemed too late. 'He has resigned some time this week,' Moore reported (8 December 1912). 'But I hope it is not too late for you to have a chance of making him change his mind.' Though he failed to change Wittgenstein's mind, Lytton helped to negotiate a compromise whereby Wittgenstein was suspended in Apostolic limbo, somewhere between an embryo and an angel, with no resignation recorded. What did it matter that, no longer troubling to be brilliant, Wittgenstein was now 'a fearful bore'? Most of the Apostles, according to James, thought 'the Witter-Gitter man' would be 'too awful for words'. But awfulness was better than bland agreeableness, when allied to integrity and talent.

So Wittgenstein was saved for the Apostles. He returned to Cambridge after the war ('God has arrived. I met him on the 5.15 train', Maynard announced in 1929). Formally 'absolved from his excommunication at the appropriate time', he took wings and eventually rose to succeed Moore himself as Professor of Philosophy at Cambridge.

3

OSCILLATIONS

The Chestnuts was never anything more than a temporary solution to Lytton's problems, but it gave him a permanent taste for country-cottage life. Without disrupting the flow of his work he was able to see his friends, especially Henry, who rode with him on the Downs, and who, as a special mark of favour, allowed Lytton to trim his hair; and also Ottoline, who, now encamped some ten miles off at Breach House, Cholsey, plied him with a stream of bewildering upper-class gifts: a massive bottle of hair water and a special tooth-brush ('I haven't yet dared to use it, as I've no notion how to ... how does one apply a tooth-brush to the head?'), a tortoiseshell snuff-box to match his spectacles ('I shall have to take to snuff, in order to be able to produce it with a rap and astound the world'); a voluminous embroidered red handkerchief ('I haven't yet dared to use it – it seems a profanation'); or simply a batch of sweet-smelling leaves to act as book-markers, which he put to use with more courage.

All this was very pleasant, and Lytton soon decided to find a furnished cottage somewhere in the neighbourhood, where he could settle down. 'I perceive that the path of the cottage-finder is not strewn with roses,' he wrote to Hilton Young (24 October 1912). Hilton, an Old Etonian barrister, then editing the City pages of the *Morning Post*, had volunteered to clear away some of the thorns and invited him down to his own cottage, The Lacket, which lay in a large estate at Lockeridge, near Marlborough. This estate belonged to a horse-trainer who took little interest in the property value of his land and was ready to let his houses without protracted negotiations.

Lytton hated the drudgery of house-hunting. But Hilton Young was so obliging that he could not find it in his heart to refuse. There were too, as he soon saw, many pretty cottages near by that made his mouth water. As for The Lacket itself, this was disappointing. 'Dear me! the poor fellow has not been brilliantly successful,' he wrote to Ottoline (22 October 1912). 'It is all so correct – so scrupulously in the dullest and flattest taste – and, mon dieu! the drab dullness – the lack of inspiration – of colour even. I find myself feasting my eyes on my orange waistcoat. And in the country what gay clean and bright colours one might have.

'He himself was here for the week-end – exactly like his cottage. Is it Cambridge, or is it England that makes some of one's friends so spiritually anaemic? The bounce has quite gone – if they ever had any. I felt like a Spanish bull-fighter, prancing round him, and sticking darts into his hide. And the good-natured old bull came up mooing, and positively liked having them put in. His kindness was extraordinary – showing me round everywhere, and making endless enquiries. He begged me to stay on here as long as I liked. I am longing to be off, but it is difficult to move ... I don't see why I shouldn't stay here for the rest of my life; I'm sure Hilton wouldn't venture to raise any objections. I might begin re-decorating. It would be a nice surprise for him when he next came down, to find the place done up in orange and magenta!'

One surprising item on this visit was the discovery of an article by Wyndham Lewis among some back numbers of the *English Review*. This article contained a description of the innkeeper with whom he and Henry had stayed during those few disastrous days in Brittany. It was the first piece of writing by that arch-enemy of Bloomsbury that Lytton read. 'It was cleverly done – I could no more have written it than flown – fiendish observation, and very original ideas,' he told Ottoline (22 October 1912). 'Yet the whole thing was most disagreeable; the subtlety was curiously crude, and the tone all through more mesquin than can be described ... It seemed to me that Henry had picked up some of his beastly mean notions from that source. Ugh! the total effect was affreux. Living in the company of such a person would certainly have a deleterious influence on one's moral being. All the same I should like to see more of his work – though not his paintings ...'

In the second week of January, his landlady at The Chestnuts, Mrs Lowe, collapsed and was taken to a nursing-home, suffering from consumption. For some weeks Lytton had been nervously eyeing the poor woman. Was consumption (which he already suspected) contagious? After three leisurely months there, he fled hurriedly away, and having found no other cottage, was forced to return to Belsize Park Gardens.

'My vision of the future is dim,' he admitted to Henry. *Victorian Silhouettes* would take him years to complete – even now he had hardly begun the Manning biography. Could he stay the course? Harry Norton, generous as ever, had promised to make over to him a quarterly allowance, and 'you may be glad to hear that I'm almost ready to believe there may be something in me after all,' Lytton told Ottoline (18 January 1913).

Uncertainties still kept assailing him, as Ottoline saw when he visited her a few days later at Cholsey. 'I had a long talk with Lytton last night as I was on my way to bed,' she noted in her diary (24 January 1913). 'I sat on my bed and he stood beside me, looking so dejected and despondent, for he seems to feel baulked in his life, doubtful about his writing: he says that he is no good at conversation so that he could never be a social success, that his small voice would prevent his going into politics, which he would rather like to do, but how could he ever make speeches with his thin tiny voice? I did my best to encourage him with his writing, as I am sure that is his real *métier*. Poor Lytton, how dejected he becomes, and yet he is really very ambitious.'

His spirits and moods continued to oscillate. Since he and Henry were both living in Hampstead, they met regularly. Lytton felt himself to be under no illusions as to Henry much wanting to see him, but that, he told Ottoline, 'makes me feel more grateful for his friendliness. I do really feel it intensely.' The bond between them was now Henry's painting. 'The last two days have been spent almost solid in sitting for Henry for the big portrait,' Lytton recorded (13 March 1913), 'the result is rather shattering.'

In the eighteen months leading up to the Great War, a frantic merriment was fretting the party-giving population of London. Lytton's letters during the early months of 1913 show him caught up in a frisson of sociality. There were 'hilarious' lunches at Simpson's with James, Harry Norton, Gerald Shove and others; teas in solitary pomp at the Savile or in overcrowded Bloomsbury, or again with Ethel Sands in her magnificent Chelsea house where (13 February 1913) 'I found George Moore ... Miss [Gertrude] Stein and ... a Spanish-Jew-American lady[16] – a friend of Miss Stein ... I gleaned a certain amount of information about Picasso, which interested me ... G.M. I rather liked. He reminded me of one of those very overgrown tabbies that haunt some London kitchens.' Finally, in the evening, there were dinners with Henry and his patrons, J.L. and Mary Behrend, who 'move in a queer stratum – I think rather like the sort of world that Wells describes in some of his novels – Fabian, and cultured, and oddly aimless and unsatisfactory. But the personal shades are many, and I think Mrs Behrend is really nice.'

Among the highlights of these weeks was an announcement that the Russian Ballet was arriving in England, and that they would be dancing *Petrushka*. Was there any chance of seeing the gorgeous Nijinsky? Lytton asked Ottoline (13 March 1913), who had met him in Paris and promised to introduce them. Perhaps they could throw Henry to Diaghilev, Ottoline speculated, so as to leave Nijinsky free for Lytton. In preparation he ordered a new suit ('no frills') of darkest purple. Between visits to his tailor, there were other distractions. With Leonard and Virginia – she 'looking very pink and very attractive', he, in a yellow beard, somewhat less so – he went to Shaw's *John Bull's Other Island* at the Kingsway Theatre 'and was positively rather amused. But I console myself with the reflection that, after all, the play was second rate.' With James he went to the English première of Richard Strauss's *Der Rosenkavalier* and then, to James's indignation, walked out after the first act, complaining there were no tunes in it.

More memorable was a visit to the Aristotelian Society, where Karin Costelloe (who married Adrian Stephen two years later) was reading a paper. It seemed an odd affair – Bertie Russell very brilliant; Moore supreme; Ethel Sands, having come for the sake of Karin's *beaux yeux*, silent and watchful. 'There was the strangest collection of people,' he wrote to Henry (4 February 1913), '– sitting round a long table with Bertie in the middle, presiding like some inquisitor, and Moore opposite him, bursting with fat and heat, and me next to Moore, and [Sidney] Waterlow next to me, and Woolf and Virginia crouching, and a strange crew of old cranky Metaphysicians ranged along like half-melted wax dolls in a shop window and – suddenly observed in the extreme distance, dressed in white satin and pearls and thickly powdered and completely haggard . . . Miss Sands! – the incorrigible old Sapphist – and Karin herself, next to Bertie, exaggeratedly the woman, with a mouth forty feet long and lascivious in proportion.

'All the interstices were filled with antique faded spinsters, taking notes . . . Bertie, no longer the Grand Inquisitor, but the Joconde, with eyelids a little weary, delivered some pungent criticisms, but the excitement came with Moore. I wish you'd been there. I think you would have been converted. As for me I became (for the first time for ages) his captive slave. The excitement was extraordinary, and the intellectual display terrific. But display isn't the right word. Of course it was the very opposite of brilliant – appallingly sensible, and so easy to understand that you wondered why on earth no one else had thought of it. The simplicity of genius! But the way it came out – like some half-stifled geyser, throbbing and convulsed, and then bursting into a towering gush – the poor fellow purple in the face, and beating his podgy hands on the table in desperation. The old spinsters in the background tittered and gasped at the imprévu spectacle. He is really really a grand maître.'

At weekends Lytton was still pressing on with his quest for some cheap and attractive cottage. During the week he read the works of Strindberg, and also G.M. Trevelyan's three-volume life of Garibaldi about which his feelings were mixed. Trevelyan's radicalism was too pious and pontificating for his taste. The story itself was wonderfully thrilling. Yet he did not really enjoy the biography. It was old-fashioned: a simple hagiography, without intimacy, celebrating the epic story of Italy's rise to nationhood as a liberal monarchy. 'There is much interest in it,' he informed Henry (15 February 1913), 'but tiresomely told.'

He shrank from making a full assault upon *Victorian Silhouettes* and, during February and March, composed instead a *conte drôlatique* entitled 'Ermyntrude and Esmeralda'. It is reminiscent of 'The Itchingham

Letters' which he and his sister Marjorie had written when children, pretending to be husband and wife. 'Will you believe me when I tell you that I have begun and got well under way with a new facétie?' he asked Henry, to whom he dedicated the work (18 February 1913). 'Don't I deserve at least a lead medal for this? I'm actually enjoying it; but I see all too clearly that it's a mere putting-off of the worst moment – but enough!'

'Ermyntrude and Esmeralda' was written as a correspondence between two inquisitive seventeen-year-old upper-class girls, one – Esmeralda – living in the country, the other in town. At school they pledged themselves to discover as much as possible about the mysteries of sex, and in their holiday letters they report to each other the dramatic results of their investigations.

At first these investigations are academic, involving dictionaries and some naïve speculation. But then things warm up. Ermyntrude, the daughter of an MP, is a cynical solitary girl, having some affinities with Lytton. Her parents are away and she is often bored. But one day there arrives a handsome new footman, with clean fingernails and the angelic name of Henry. Soon she is writing to Esmeralda describing her vibrant sensations as he makes love to her on a flight of stairs. That night he goes to bed with her and not long afterwards so does the butler. This leads on to a confusion of sexual relationships that outside Bloomsbury might have seemed excessive – especially when Ermyntrude's governess, Mrs Simpson, also makes a valiant attempt to climb into her bed and is only refused because the footman is under it at the time. Esmeralda, who lives in the country among a flurry of clergymen, generals, stump-cricket and charades, is a romantic scatterbrain. Coming across her younger brother and his tutor making passionate love, she wonders whether they will have babies and is mystified by the disgrace into which they fall when their affair is found out. Her fate is a parody of social convention.

There are many private jokes and autobiographical references in 'Ermyntrude and Esmeralda', a good number of which (including the fetish for ears that will reappear in *Elizabeth and Essex*) would have been familiar to Henry Lamb and can be read in Lytton's correspondence to him. The reality which lay behind this piece of fantasy gives the story its authenticity. It is not simply that schoolgirls are curious about babies, sex and love, but that their curiosity takes this physical form. By using nursery terms for genitals Lytton makes society's automatic fear of sex, and horror of sexual deviation, ludicrous. It was true, as he said, that he was 'putting off the worst moment' by postponing 'Cardinal Manning', but in its whimsical fashion this lightly written satire makes fun of the same repressions that were to be his target in *Eminent Victorians*. It is Lytton's most entertaining fiction, a genuine work of soft pornography.[17]

4

GRAND TOUR

'Ermyntrude and Esmeralda' was completed in March, by which time
Lytton had hit on a further means of 'putting off the worst moment'. For
several years he had dreamed of travelling through Europe, especially
Italy, visiting places of which he had read. Now he determined to make
this dream a reality. He would spend two months on his grand tour and
then return in the late spring or early summer, full of stamina, straining to
be at his work. It might be expensive, but he had made up his mind to live
on crusts and water for the rest of the year. He wrote to E.M. Forster to
find out about *pension* life in Italy, and received a discreet reply; he also
sent off for information about Sicily to Maynard who, a little less
discreetly, recommended him to go to Tunis where 'bed and boy' were
inexpensive.

On the morning of 15 March, he set off via Boulogne for Paris. To
amuse himself on this solitary journey he decided to write up an account of
his adventures. His attention was taken early on by two young gentlemen
from Eton, aged about seventeen or eighteen, both wearing monocles.

'Their faces', he wrote, 'were like joints of mutton – so full-blooded and
fleshy ... A casual observer might have thought they were dressed
shabbily ... but really everything they had on – their cloth caps, their short
waterproofs, their old flannel trousers, and their old brown shoes – was
impregnated with expensiveness. There was a look in their faces which
showed both that they were born to command and that none of their
commands would ever be of any good to anybody.'

Apart from these Etonians there was 'a plutocrat' on board – possibly
Sir James Mackay[18] – followed everywhere by four or five women in furs,
for whom he took cabin after cabin, into which they eventually retired one
after another, while he himself, spied on by the ever-attentive Lytton,
stood stonily on the deck in a yachting cap, 'looking like an old cock with
his hens in the background'.

There were also two aristocrats on board remarkable for their overcoats.
'The first was perhaps a baronet,' he noted, 'about 35, with ginger hair and
high colouring, and a blonde wife with ineffectual diamond earrings, who
no doubt was considered pretty.

'He fussed a great deal as we were getting near Boulogne, about his
luggage, walking to and fro, and instructing stewards – with that queer,
pointed, almost German-goose-step walk which must be the right thing
when one's travelling, because James and I saw Lord Portsmouth doing it

in exactly the same way, on the platform at Inverness in his tailcoat of grey flannel.

But what was particularly striking about the Baronet was his very big and very thick and very brilliant ultramarine overcoat, which one had to look at as much as one could whenever he passed, so that it was only after he'd passed several times that one noticed that he was wearing spats and that his brown boots were almost incredibly polished. At the buffet at Boulogne afterwards, sitting with his wife next to him and the maid opposite, he seemed to be quite frightened by the foreign language.

The second man was no doubt a Lord – tall, dark and angular – rather like Victor Lytton;[19] and *he* had on an immense *white* overcoat. The odd thing about both overcoats was that they had evidently been got for effect, and yet there was only one thing about them over which any care had been taken – and that was the quality of the material. The blue one was a bad blue, and the white one was a poor white; and neither had any shape; and each was provided with the vulgar strap and button at the back that happens to be common now . . . Perhaps it is this inability to be interested in anything but the mere quality of materials that has made the English what they are. One sees it everywhere – in their substantial food with its abominable cooking, in their magnificent literature with its neglect of form, in their successful government with its disregard of principle.'

There were many other classes and other nations represented among the passengers – a number of seasick Polish young ladies, some pedantic French youths and, on the upper deck, an academician (or possibly Russian prince) retching systematically into a basin – but none of these roused Lytton's curiosity for long. It was a rough and windy crossing. By the time the boat had reached mid-channel Lytton too felt a little sea-sick. As the storm grew, so all these lesser breeds without the titles, spats and overcoats seemed to suffer a strange diminution. But the British Upper Classes remained life-size to the end.

He stayed only one full day in Paris, during which he saw *King Lear* at the Odéon – a bad translation, feebly acted, which filled the audience with amazement. 'C'est d'un romantisme!' they repeated incredulously to each other. He also found time to see an exhibition of Renoir's paintings. 'Some of the early things were exquisite,' he wrote to Ottoline (17 March 1913), 'but the late ones are too horrid for words. I gather the poor old man's hand has grown very shaky. It seems a shame to show them.'

From Paris he went by train to Dijon. He had planned to move quickly south, but the thick snow and the cold intimidated him, and he decided to make his journey in shorter stages. There was, he thought, a dismaying dishonesty about *foreign* bad weather. 'It's slightly grim to be wandering all alone,' he confessed to Ottoline (17 March 1913). 'But there are compensations.' He remained in Dijon for two days, at the Grand Hôtel de la Cloche in the Place Darcy, which he described (19 March 1913) as 'splendid – with masses of food and wine, and such delightful rotund Burgundian fellow-guests – all with hooked noses and light eyes'. Roaming the streets with a Kodak camera which Henry had lent him, he went around snapping old buildings and young boys. 'I felt', he wrote to Henry (19 March 1913), 'as if one could well live and die in one of those heavenly "hôtels", in some street off the tramline, wrapped in infinite repose. Probably one could get one for the cost of a country cottage! – They are not large, but the proportions are perfect and the feeling of space supreme. But I suppose one would really have to be a 17th Century Magistrate to carry it off properly – and on the whole I don't think I am.'

The next stage of his journey took him through Avignon to a bright and bustling Marseilles, whose population seemed to be continually passing and re-passing him in a frantic hurry as he sat, with Kodak uncertainly poised, inspecting them from a café table outside the Grand Hôtel de Noailles et Métropole in the rue Noailles-Canebière. In the evenings he would retire up to his bedroom and read Samuel Butler's *The Way of All Flesh*: 'To my surprise I find it cheering.'

As his expenses had already mounted above the estimates he had made back in Hampstead, he decided to miss out Tunis and sail to Naples. He set sail from Marseilles on Thursday, 20 March, and arrived in Naples after a painful sea passage on Easter Saturday. Within twenty-four hours of landing there, he thought that he would never be able to leave. It was pure romance. He rattled around in taxi cabs, 'with my eyes bursting out of my head and my brain in a whirl of ecstasy', he told Ottoline (24 March 1913). 'I try to take snapshots, but my hands shake so with excitement that no doubt they're all failures.' In the evenings he would return, fatigued but happy, to Parker's Hotel which was crowded with *bourgeois* English majors and their ladies, all in evening dress, listening stonily to Italian love-songs sung by smiling Italian minstrels with mandolins. 'Everything is extraordinarily large,' he explained to James, 'especially the town, which is infinite, and packed with wonders – people, not things.

'In spite of my deathly exhaustion I took two excursions through it to-day in cabs – the rattling and the surrounding hubbub and general remuement are indeed intoxicating. Then you look up at Vesuvius – (not erupting! I had fully expected a tuft of smoke) . . . One of the oddities is this hotel, quite filled with English of the most English – what on earth are they doing here? I look at them, and look at them, but it remains an impenetrable mystery.'

He scarcely stepped into a church, never went to Capri, and only hurriedly visited the museum. The mere effort of existing in those astonishing long streets with that ever-flowing river of people was enough. The one excursion he did make was to Pompeii. 'It was an enchanting experience,' he told Ottoline (26 March 1913).

'The heat of an English July – can you imagine it – and the hills all round – and that incredible fossilization of the past to wander in. What a life it must have been! Why didn't we live in those days? Oh! I longed to stay there for ever – in one of those little inner gardens, among the pillars and busts, with the fountain dropping in the court, and all the exquisite repose! Why not? Some wonderful slave boy would come out from under the shady rooms, and pick you some irises, and then to drift off to the baths as the sun was setting – and the night! What nights those must have been!'

In spite of much bad taste, Lytton imagined there to have been great beauty in Pompeii – walls of deep reds, yellows and blacks seen between white pillars in the brilliant sunshine, green-blue figures round square fountains, flowers of all colours in the courtyards, and a vision of Vesuvius at the end of a street. Most disappointing to him were the erotic pictures, so feeble and anaemic, on some of the walls. These were concealed from the public and only unlocked by winking custodians for the benefit of respectable bachelors such as himself. Some, however, they would not unlock, even in the face of Lytton's eager imprecations; after which his interest palled.

His plans had by now evaporated and since he had heard alarming reports of overcrowding in Sicily, he proposed instead to go off for some days to Ravello, which Hilton Young had recommended.

On the morning of Sunday, 30 March, after a journey of three and a half hours along the shores of the Mediterranean, he arrived in the precipitous high hills above Amalfi. His *pensione* stood over a thousand feet above the sea which lay perfectly blue and smooth below. Hilton Young had not misled him. Beyond the sea, looking south over the Gulf of Salerno, lay distant misty mountains with Paestum at their foot; and inland, steep cliffs covered with chestnut woods and fruit trees in full bloom; and in the foreground, Norman and Saracen church towers, terraced gardens with hyacinths and freesias, wallflowers and red roses. What a place for adventures!

In another letter to Ottoline (4 April 1913) he writes in a vein reminiscent of his earlier letter (11 March 1906) to Maynard depicting 'My Castle in Spain' – the dream, revised in the light of seven years' further experience. 'Why not come here?' he invites her. 'We could collect a société choisie in this pleasant place – and dream away 2 years delightfully. Henry would be given a studio at the extreme end of the village. Desmond and Molly would have an apartment in the very centre. Duncan would lie out among the fruit trees. Virginia would prance in after dinner. And even [Augustus] John might occasionally appear. I should insist on having James [Strachey] but not Henry James – except for a week-end once a year. Don't you think it would do very well?'

The *pensione* Palumbo, where Lytton stayed, was a plain unpretentious lodging-house which had originally been built as a bishop's palace. His room in the annexe opened on to a spacious platform with views in all directions, and was reached by a marble staircase. Since he had this annexe practically to himself, and had brought with him several books on Cardinal Manning, there seemed to be an opportunity for settling down to work. He had arrived in intense heat, 'a blazing sun', he told Henry (31 March 1913), 'and such a mass of light reflecting and refracting – one can sit for indefinite hours with one's head in the shade and the rest of one grilling.' His well-being depended on the climate. When the skies were blue, the sun hot, he was sprightly and smiling; but the passing of a cloud could bring on indigestion or worse. So when the rain began to fall in Ravello and the temperature suddenly dropped, he decided that he must hurry on to Rome.

He arrived in Rome on Monday 7 April under a clear sky, feeling revitalized. For three days he stayed at a small hotel but 'one's fellow-travellers are death indeed,' he complained to James, 'the human race at its lowest ebb – mon dieu! Fit only for Forster's novels, but he hasn't got them. Oh!' On Thursday he moved to the *pensione* Hayden, in the Piazza Poli, which was 'pretty thick with Americans'. He was nursing a grudge against Forster. 'My experience of Pension life is most painful,' he grumbled in a letter to Saxon Sydney-Turner (14 April 1913), 'and I find that Forster has quite misrepresented it – whitewashed it absurdly. For sheer, stark ignorance, imbecility, and folly the conversations here can't be beaten. I'm rapidly becoming a second Flaubert under these influences. I can think of nothing but la Bêtise Humaine.'

Rome reminded him of Cambridge. There were the same sort of surprises in the street, a similar air of fancy-dress – even the Forum and the Palatine seemed like capricious college gardens. He went to the Pantheon; to the Castel Sant'Angelo (a Piranesi engraving of which had hung on the wall of his nursery at Lancaster Gate); to St Peter's, the huge exterior of which delighted him; to Hadrian's Villa; to the Colosseum; to the Medici Gardens, and the lake of Nemi and the Baths of Caracalla 'like some strange impossible dream materialised'. He also saw the Sistine Chapel which, he told Henry, 'quite désorientéd me at first. In the end I think I liked it – but it's very queer. As an effort of constructive skill the ceiling is terrific, but it seems rather thrown away. I believe if each morceau could be taken away separately and framed, it would be better. The difficulty of seeing any of it is very great. There are some lovely other frescoes round the walls, by Perugino, Botticelli, etc.' But of all these wonders, the most marvellous was the Forum, covered with green trees and shrubs, with lilac and wistaria, and whole choruses of singing birds – altogether different from anything he had expected.

All day Lytton busied himself inspecting the curiosities of the town. Between tea and dinner he usually wandered over to the Pincio and after listening to the band playing Rossini, strolled in the Borghese Gardens and meditated on Cardinal Manning's mysterious meeting with Pius IX in 1848. After dinner, and with the utmost regularity, he dashed off to the silent cinema. One afternoon, by way of a change, he went to hear Beethoven's 'Pastoral' Symphony, conducted by Richard Strauss who (13 April 1913) 'looked like a prematurely-aged diplomat, and I thought did his best to add somnolence to an already somnolent affair. After that came his own things – Hero etc., but I didn't stop.'

There was a peculiar luxury in being able to savour his sensations as he floated behind squadrons of Roman youths, past so many small piazzas and palace gardens, towards some obelisk or church. Yet unremitting solitude carried its disadvantages too. 'I feel that I shall have left a multitude of things unseen,' he wrote to Ottoline (17 April 1913). 'I should like to linger on for weeks and weeks – but the expense is really getting too great, and also the silence! I haven't spoken one word to an intelligent human being for a month, and I'm beginning to feel it.'

He had hoped to go on to Florence, but a financial seal was set on this scheme when he purchased a large Piranesi print – 'I think it's rather magnificent,' he concluded his last letter from Rome to Ottoline. 'Well, someday we *must* come here together, that's certain, isn't it? What fun it'll be! . . . The Pope is dying. Shall I apply for the post? Then you could come and stay with me at the Vatican.'

5

PEREGRINATIONS AND ANGOISSES

Like other European capitals, London was bursting with extravagant entertainments that summer. There were afternoon dances, risqué American revues, wild all-night parties. To the indignation of the older generation, young people everywhere were flinging themselves into these entertainments as if they already sensed that peace was almost at an end. Against the murmurings of war, they danced themselves to a standstill in the Ragtime, the Tango, the immodest Bunny Hug and fabulous Turkey Trot. One special feature of this brilliant season was the proliferation of fancy-dress balls, inspired by the exotic costumes of Léon Bakst, which seemed to give them all new ways of escape.

Lytton too was caught up in this hectic swan song. James took him to *Tristan and Isolde* and *Ariadne on Naxos*; he heard Paderewski play the 'Emperor' Concerto, and Nikisch conduct the 'Eroica'. And he was overwhelmed by *The Magic Flute*, though it was only performed by 'the poor Carl Rosa Company at the Coronet'. Most of his entertainment after arriving home from Italy was provided by 'Our Lady of Bedford Square'. The turns within Ottoline's flower-decked drawing-room appeared more exotic than ever. Of all the new stars there, the one to catch his attention was the novelist Gilbert Cannan. 'The poor fellow must have a dim time of it with his wife, who's 20 years older than him, and very distressing,' he remarked after their first meeting. Mary Cannan had formerly been married to J.M. Barrie, who still gave her an annual allowance of money on which the couple largely subsisted and which was handed over each year at a private dinner held, at Barrie's suggestion, on the divorced pair's wedding anniversary. At first Lytton confessed himself to be 'furiously prejudiced against G.C.', mainly, it appears, on account of Ottoline's recent patronage of him. When, early in May, Ottoline left England with her family for Lausanne (where Dr Combe had given her a course of ghastly cocktails – radium in milk – for a troublesome liver), a month passed without the exchange of any letters between them. At the end of this unprecedented silence, Lytton declared himself to be quite converted to Cannan, owing chiefly to his statuesque appearance. Tall and handsome, Cannan had known Henry Lamb at school in Manchester, gone to Cambridge after Lytton had come down (he was four years younger) and become drama critic of the *Star*. He had written plays and novels, and was spoken of as a prodigy, a Hamlet, a Galahad. The following year, in a leading essay for the *Times Literary Supplement* (19 June

1914), Henry James would choose his work, along with that of Compton Mackenzie, Hugh Walpole and 'in the dusty rear' D.H. Lawrence, as representing the best creative writing of a new generation soon to take the place of Conrad, Galsworthy, Wells and Bennett. This famous pronouncement, which James told Cannan (20 March 1914) conveyed 'the reflections of an aged novelist upon a craft he for a good many years practised', gave rise to much envy among excluded authors. James praised Cannan's 'admirably genuine young pessimism ... his straight communication of his general truth', singling out his novel *Round the Corner* which Ottoline had admired and Lytton had also been persuaded to read. 'Perhaps it would have been wiser not to,' he confided to Henry (5 May 1913), ' ... I stuck to it, and read every word of the blasted thing, but while I was doing so I felt a cloud over my life. The poor fellow is so modern and broad-minded too! But oh! the taste! – and the pointlessness.' Nevertheless 'in a moment of épanchement' Lytton invited Cannan over to tea at Belsize Park Gardens. The visit went off fairly well, though it was evidently not the preliminary to a close friendship. He was, Lytton disdainfully told Henry (17 May 1913), 'an empty bucket, which has been filled up to the brim with modern ideas – simply because it happened to be standing near that tap. The good thing about him is a substratum of honest serviceableness – but that is not enough in my line to excite me. *He* no doubt found me far too rarefied for him. I daresay if I took the trouble I could induce in him a culte for me which would replace the one he at present has for Rupert [Brooke]. But of course I shan't.'

While Ottoline was in Switzerland, most of Lytton's entertainment came in the form of Bloomsbury evening parties. These were extravagant affairs with all the guests in fancy-dress – among them Saxon Sydney-Turner got up as a eunuch. 'Karin [Costelloe] was the leading figure,' Lytton reported to Henry (16 June 1913), '– in white flannel cricketing trousers and shirt. Duncan was appalling as a whore great with child, and Marjorie incredible as a post-impressionist sphinx. Oliver was a Harlequin, Roger a Brahmin, and I Sarastro. The gambols were extraordinary and in the middle of them Gerald [Shove] appeared, drunk, in evening dress and a top-hat. He and Karin sang a Vesta Tilley song together and carried on a good deal. I was considerably in love with both.'

Sometimes, in his more fragile moods, this rowdiness jarred on Lytton. 'The dissipations of our circle are approaching a vertige,' he wrote to Henry (23 June 1913) who was then in Ireland.

'The last party was at Adrian's. Owing to an accident I couldn't bring myself to go – further than the door in the square – whence I heard such a

Comus uproar that I slipped away again. I had been having dinner with the Sangers, and felt that my condition was too hopelessly inadequate. The accounts of the proceedings made me glad I didn't venture. The nudity reached a pitch – Duncan in bathing-drawers, and Marjorie with nothing on but a miniature of the Prince Consort. Next time – next time is on Thursday, at Karin's, 10 o'clock. If you started at once, couldn't you be there?'

Lytton himself was very much there at Karin's party, during which a one-act farcette he had composed called *The Unfortunate Lover or Truth Will Out* – written in the manner of a Chekhovian burlesque – was given its première. Set at a country inn during the year 1840, the fun of the piece resides in the fast-changing multiple relationships assumed by the Bloomsbury actor-guests, the entire cast comprising two pairs of elopers – Duncan Grant playing a young boy disguised as a woman (a part originally intended for Molly MacCarthy), Clive Bell apparently his homosexual lover and dressed initially as a male, Marjorie Strachey as a girl wearing the clothes of a man, and Vanessa Bell attired simply, but misleadingly, as a woman. In the final scene, most of the characters were revealed to have been in double-disguise, men originally got up as men later assuming women's clothes and vice versa, and so complicated was the sequence of split-second accidents uncovering one layer of masquerade after another, that everyone lost hold of their identities and embraced in general laughter.

To win a little recuperation from frenzies such as these, Lytton now made his first weekend visit to Asheham, a strange isolated farmhouse in the Ouse Valley, near Rodmell in Sussex, which Leonard and Virginia had lately rented, set among great elm trees and meadows in a corner of the South Downs. Virginia was correcting proofs of *The Voyage Out* and the other guest, Desmond MacCarthy, 'produced the first chapter of a novel on school life', but could not 'make up his mind, he says, "how far to go"!'[20]

On his arrival back from the Continent the entire scheme of *Victorian Silhouettes* had presented itself clearly to his mind. 'An idée has suddenly crystallized,' he told Henry (5 May 1913), 'and I mean to attack it immediately.' But only twelve days later 'the crystal that formed itself so suddenly and beautifully has melted into a sticky little puddle at the bottom of my brain.' He now wrote off to Harold Cox proposing an article in the *Edinburgh Review* on Samuel Butler. But Harold Cox was dubious and succeeded, without ever rejecting the idea, in postponing a decision indefinitely. Between January and November of 1913, Lytton published nothing, falling back instead on a satire about Roger Fry's new Omega Workshops[21] and the phenomenon of Post-Impressionism – a sketch thrown off quickly and light-heartedly in the Molière vein. 'A crank always wanting to be up to date – in the hands of a pseudo-impostor who would put him through all sorts of paces, and try to have his daughter,' was how he described it in a letter (28 July 1913) to Henry.

'The 2 Academicians, always coming in together and talking in unison – and all sorts of other cranks – Miss Stein, Rupert perhaps, and others – A General whom it was important not to offend, because of legacies, coming in at the critical moment while all the queer creatures were parading about, reciting poems, painting pictures, etc. – in the midst of a room newly furnished in the P-I manner – they in desperation having to dash into the said furniture, to conceal themselves from his wrath – Rupert into a commode, and Miss Stein into the Grand Piano. Then perhaps after all the General himself getting impressed and converted by the arch-impostor – and so on.'

Leonard and Virginia's success in finding Asheham had stimulated once again his own desire for a country cottage. Hilton Young had spied out a likely plot of land for building it, and Lytton got hold of a friend of Henry's, George Kennedy, who had recently given up painting for architecture and was to design the new Chenil Galleries where Augustus John exhibited, as well as (through his friendship with Maynard) an extension to King's College, and the celebrated Arts Theatre in Cambridge. Everything seemed set fair. Kennedy inspected the site and agreed to design the building himself; and to celebrate the venture they all three drank warm champagne at eleven o'clock one May morning on the platform of Marlborough railway station. Then a surprising discovery was made: the land in question, so carefully selected, happened to belong to the National Trust and was therefore not for sale.

Lytton had spent part of the summer down at The Lacket, reading almost every book there and discovering the works of Chekhov, which seemed to catch so well the comical futility of his own life. 'The more I think of them [Chekhov's plays],' he wrote to Henry (23 June 1913), 'the more eminent they seem.' Gradually the atmosphere of The Lacket grew more appealing. 'I find myself quite beginning to like the matting on the walls,' he admitted (1 June 1913), 'and in a day or two I foresee that I shall be seeing some merit in Arnold-Forster's[22] water-colours.' Towards the end of July, Hilton Young wrote to tell him that he was not going to use his cottage for a year, so that, from the end of September, Lytton was free to move into it and remain there till the following autumn at a rent of thirty pounds (equivalent to £1200 in 1994). For an extra sum, the housekeeper, the excellent Mrs Templeman, would stay on and look after him. Lytton joyfully accepted the offer. 'I was in the greatest doubt as to how I could conveniently dispose of myself in the coming year,' he replied (28 July 1913), 'and I never dreamed that such a piece of good luck would come my way. It ought really to save my life, I think – temporarily if not permanently; and the most distinguished life-saving apparatuses can do no more. Of course Mrs Templeman must be included. Is she frightfully expensive? But it doesn't matter – I would sell out all my East India Stocks to keep her.'

There could be no reason now to postpone *Victorian Silhouettes*. 'I'm rather terrified by the prospect,' he confided to Ottoline (16 August 1913), 'but I think on the whole it's a good thing ... I dread the bleakness of the wintry downs, and shall have to rush up from time to time and fling myself into the arms of the yellow drawing-room.'

In mid-July he again visited Asheham, this time for a full week, feeling 'infinitely more cheerful – in fact altogether perky and insouciant'. But Virginia's health had deteriorated when she finished the proofs of *The Voyage Out* and shortly after he left, she had to be taken to a nursing-home, with violent headaches, sleeplessness, depression.

Back in London at another of Ottoline's parties, Lytton finally met the legendary Nijinsky who was 'certainly not a eunuch' and who, he told Henry (24 July 1913), 'was very nice, though you won't believe it, and much more attractive than I'd expected – in fact very much so, I thought ... as the poor fellow cannot speak more than 2 words of any human language it's difficult to get very far with him ... there was another Russian who acted as interpreter and the conversation was mainly conducted by Granville Barker.' Duncan had at once become what Ottoline called the 'pet' of both Nijinsky and Diaghilev: 'I saw Nijinsky looking him all over!' she reported (20 July 1913). The previous week, Lytton had gone to see *Le Sacre du Printemps*,[23] 'one of the most painful experiences of my life', he called it. 'I couldn't have imagined that boredom and sheer anguish could have been combined together at such a pitch. Stravinsky was responsible for this.' Yet Nijinsky, coming before the curtain at the end, dazzled and delighted him: 'I sent him a great basket of magnissime flowers, which was brought on to the stage and presented to him by a flunkey.'

He retreated to the Plough Inn, Holford at the foot of the Quantock hills, where Leonard and Virginia sometimes stayed. He had not intended to remain for more than a few days, but the weather was so radiantly hot, the food so sumptuous ('Sir Walter Scott alone could describe it properly, and even my greed finds itself nonplussed'[24]), the country so green and undulating, that he seemed to fall into a kind of trance. He went for long walks, often to Alfoxton House, which Wordsworth had rented for seven pounds a year less than The Lacket, and would let his thoughts follow Wordsworth and Coleridge as they were tracked by Home Office agents on suspicion of being secret agents of the French Revolution.

He sped up to join Henry in the Lake District. For a week they stayed at an inn at Brampton, in Westmorland, and every day went for fifteen-mile walks, sweating and toiling in the August haze, in their pockets sandwiches which they would eat under a hedge talking and sketching, until by the afternoon they had arrived at some place for tea; then home again over the mountains, Henry well ahead and sometimes barefoot. 'I have practically no money left,' Lytton confessed complacently to James (18 August 1913), 'and I shall be ruined by these absurd journeys backwards and forwards across England, but it can't be helped.

On Monday, 19 August, Henry went to Ireland, and Lytton veered off to Norfolk where the Bells and Olivier sisters were camping. Many of the Bloomsbury Group were down there in their tents, including Adrian Stephen – who turned up from Dieppe where he had been staying with Wyndham Lewis and Frederick Etchells – Duncan Grant, who arrived with an easel and a bottle of champagne, Molly MacCarthy, Saxon Sydney-Turner – rather eerie with his rheumatic flittings to and fro – Roger Fry with his children and Maynard who, with Vanessa, had arranged this reminder of the earlier Neo-Pagan camp.

Suddenly the fun was extinguished by the news that Virginia had attempted to commit suicide at Brunswick Square, being rescued fortuitously by Leonard and by Geoffrey Keynes using a stomach pump. 'There has been a horrible occurrence,' Lytton wrote to Henry (13 September 1913). 'Virginia tried to kill herself last Tuesday, and was only saved by a series of accidents.'

'She took 100 grains of veronal and also an immense quantity of an even more dangerous drug – medinal. The doctors at one time thought there was very little hope. But she recovered, and is apparently not seriously the worse for it. Woolf has been having a most dreadful time for the last month or so, culminating in this ... The doctors all agree that the only thing required is feeding and rest, so really now the prospect seems to be pretty hopeful. George Duckworth has lent them his country home in Sussex, and they intend to go there in about a week.'

Remembering, perhaps, his own proposal of marriage to Virginia, and his part in bringing Leonard and her together, Lytton felt acute sympathy for them both. He went to see Leonard at Asheham where, in blinding fauviste sunlight, Duncan, Roger and Vanessa had simultaneously painted Lytton's portrait. Then he went north: first to Redcar in Yorkshire to stay with his old Liverpool friend Lumsden Barkway, now a Presbyterian clergyman; then on to Milton Cottage, Rothiemurchus, where James had invited two of the Olivier sisters, Noel and Bryn, together with the latter's new husband, Hugh Popham.[25] Rain pelted down outside; discomfort stalked within. 'The arrival was worst of all,' Lytton told Henry (24 September 1913). 'A DOG! – One of those dreadful vast ones, standing higher than a table – ugh – belonging to the young woman – imagine my anguish, cooped up in the pouring rain in the tiny sitting-room with four other persons, and IT coiled about my ankles – day after day – Splitting headaches, nerves racked, yellow eyes revolving wildly in despair – and then at night having to make my way through the mist to a dark wooden outhouse where a bed had been rigged up for me, and where my agonised soles were pierced with icy oilcloths.'

With the aid of paraffin and calomel, regular doses of Dr Gregory's malodorous rhubarb tablets, some drops of ammoniated quinine, Seidlitz powders and cascara eased down with spoonfuls of Fellows Syrup, there was little difficulty for Lytton in regaining his health. 'I liked the Popham couple,' he told Henry. 'Noel is of course more interesting, but difficult to make out; very youthful, incredibly firm of flesh, agreeably bouncing and cheerful – and with some sort of prestige.'

Rupert was safely out of the country, 'Somewhere in the Sierra Nevada', but Noel was able to revive his enmity with a 'beastly' letter describing these 'perfect' three weeks in Scotland. 'The Strachey – the long dreaded [Lytton] Strachey – turned out to be a good-natured, slightly dotty buffoon; & in so far as the ridiculous makes the world brighter – an excellent fellow,' she wrote (25 September 1913). 'I haven't yet detected the poison in young [James] Strachey, though his attachment to me and my deadly slight affection for him is the most distressing thing . . .'[26]

When the party broke up at the end of the month, Lytton returned to London. 'Of course I've done not a stroke of work in these peregrinations and angoisses,' he admitted to Henry (24 September 1913). 'It's very annoying. I shall make for Lockeridge as soon as possible and sit down steadily there.' The worst moment could no longer be put off. He had treated himself to a long holiday but also prepared himself for the solitary conditions of writing. He had a better idea too of how to shoot a revealing searchlight through the complacency and into the repressed fear of nineteenth-century society. And he had also developed his conversational literary style, so unexpectedly potent, by daily letter-writing during his travels. His skills and ambitions were finally being submitted to a practical test.

ELEVEN

The Lacket

This is an age whose like has never been
Since Jahveh made the world, and lo! 'twas green.
Through all the mouldy chronicle of Time
Scribbled in prose, or furbished up in rhyme,
Or in the pomp of monuments expressed
(Like some plain woman who is over-dressed),
Where shall we find, ye grim and dreary Powers
Of Human Folly, folly such as ours?
The bronze age and the iron age, we're told,
Were once; and was there once an age of gold?
Perhaps: but now no learning of the schools
Need we to know this age the Age of Fools.

Lytton Strachey (1915)

I

ALONE WITH A WINDOW

The Lacket was a compact, rather isolated and romantic-looking thatched cottage, sheltering behind a huge box hedge with a boulder-strewn hillside rising behind it. A few hundred yards away lived the philosopher and mathematician, A.N. Whitehead, and his imposing wife Evelyn, with both of whom Lytton became friendly. He was to remain at The Lacket until the end of 1915, and it was here that he wrote two of the four essays in *Eminent Victorians*.

He was immediately taken charge of by Mrs Templeman – a 'discreet old lady', as Virginia Woolf described her, 'who is as noiseless as an elephantine kind of mouse'. This formidable old woman seemed to comprehend all his wishes – she was reassuring even on the matter of economy. He still had a little of the hundred pounds that Harry Norton had given him, and to this sum his mother added a further hundred. With what he could earn from contributions to periodicals, he hoped to pay for enough time to complete his *Eminent Victorians*. The solitude was comfortless at times; and Mrs Templeman, for all her massive qualities, could be appallingly severe. 'She places the vegetables upon the table with a grimness . . . an exactitude . . .,' Lytton complained to James (April 1914). 'When she calls me in the morning she announces the horrors of the day in a tone of triumph: – "Rain, as usual, sir." – "Oh, Mrs Templeman, Mrs Templeman!" – "Yes sir; old fashioned weather; that's what I call it."' Otherwise the two of them got on very well, though Mrs Templeman believed the 'darkness' to be bad for Lytton. 'When I observed that the darkness in London was worse,' he wrote to Hilton Young (9 January 1914), 'she said "Yes, sir, but then in London you have the noise" – to which no reply seemed possible.'

Despite the severities of his housekeeper and the bleakness of winter in the country, Lytton was content. 'I wish the place were mine,' he told Henry (27 October 1913), 'that I might mould it nearer to my eyes' desire.' He had implored Hilton Young to have an 'owl stuffed with wings outspread, so that I may hang it up over my bed and confuse it with the Holy Ghost in my last moments'. To Duncan he wrote (28 October 1913) explaining how he was leading 'a singularly egotistical life here, surrounded by every luxury, waited on by an aged female, and absorbed completely in Eternal-Peace. In the intervals of my satisfaction I struggle to justify my existence by means of literary composition, but so far the justification has not been so convincing as might be wished.'

His main work during these first winter months was not 'Cardinal Manning', but some minor pieces on contemporary politics and culture for the recently founded *New Statesman* (to which Desmond MacCarthy had been appointed drama critic); and, for the *Edinburgh Review*, a long essay on Stendhal which had been commissioned by Harold Cox in reply to Lytton's request to write on Samuel Butler. The subject necessitated a return to the impressionistic style of *Landmarks in French Literature*, as opposed to his more incisive biographical narrative, but he had no hesitation about taking it on, and, having assembled his library at The Lacket, began reading through the whole of Stendhal's work. 'I am beginning to gird up my loins for the wrestling bout with Stendhal,' he announced (27 October 1913) after ten days of intensive reading; and by 10 November he was able to report that 'I have plunged into the writing of the Stendhal affair and find it far less unpleasant than I'd expected – in fact I'm so far enjoying doing it very much.'

Concurrently with this he had also sent to J.C. Squire at the *New Statesman* a short piece on the subject of toleration entitled 'Avons-nous changé tout cela?' To his mingled pleasure and alarm, the article was immediately accepted for the sum of three guineas (equivalent to £125 in 1994). 'As for the New Statesman,' he told Henry (17 November 1913), 'I am getting to loathe it; and the worst of it is I now seem to be in imminent danger of becoming a regular contributor to its pages. The fellow Jack Squire, who is its editor or sub-editor, is most unpleasant, and I am trying hard to pick a quarrel with him, so as to escape having anything further to do either with him or it.' The quarrel between Lytton and Squire held fire for almost five years, while Lytton wrote ten articles and reviews on subjects ranging from Thomas Hardy and Matthew Arnold to Shelley and Frederick and Great for this Fabian weekly competitor to the *Spectator*. In a number of these he is evidently spoiling for a fight, forcing in references to the Bible which he felt sure *must* prove too strong for the editor who, by demanding their excision, would provide him with a legitimate excuse to leave. What actually happened was less satisfactory. His contributions appeared with all their more audacious criticisms intact, but marred by many smaller changes, omissions of quite trivial words or insertions of Squire's own, almost always fractionally inferior to the original text, and, though intensely irritating, never drastic enough to supply Lytton with a high-principled reason for cutting off this small source of income.

Every morning, he wrote at his desk; every afternoon, he would set off in a thick overcoat, gloves, scarf and earrings, to trudge through the woods where the gamekeeper, 'a grimy old fellow with a nice bare breast', would hold him in talk about football; every evening he would read and go through a programme of digestive exercises.

He sometimes travelled up to London at weekends, staying at Belsize Park Gardens or with the Bells in Gordon Square, and timing his visits to coincide with some concert, art exhibition, lecture or play. One weekend he spent with the St Loe Stracheys at a spectacular house-party in Surrey, full of reactionary ambassadors and their ladies, and an exquisite footman. There was plenty of 'copy' for his letters, yet no discoverable romance. The ambassadors, he told Pippa, were 'the acme of unimportance'; and much of the conversation was taken in charge by Leo Maxse, 'a mere spider in mind and body', who was still raving obsessionally on about the Marconi scandal and discharging his venom against the Cabinet.[1] Among the guests was a couple whom he would get to know better once he himself was better known – the Colefaxes.[2] 'He is a dreadful pompous lawyer and politician with a very dull large face pétri with insincerity,' he explained to Henry (4 November 1913). '. . . She too is a thoroughly stupid woman.'

The hostility of these observations indicates how awkward a figure Lytton still was in the smart world of the upper classes. People who, half-a-dozen years later, would entreat him to lunch or dine with them, now viewed him with unconcealed distaste or overlooked him altogether. Such mediocre performances in society tended to disrupt his peace of mind, yet he could not suppress a growing desire to enter and be courted by this extraordinary world. 'The result of it all is that I'm now feeling singularly solitary,' he confided to Ottoline (6 November 1913) on his return to The Lacket. 'But as I'm trying to work, it's so much the better.'

Less disturbing in their after-effects were the weekends when he invited James, Pippa and Pernel, Duncan, Maynard and Henry over to The Lacket. Leonard also came down a couple of times with reports that, though Virginia's condition was still serious enough to warrant a team of four nurses, the doctors were confident she would recover. 'Poor Woolf!' Lytton wrote to Ottoline (4 October 1913). 'Nearly all the horror of it has been and still is on his shoulders. Ka gave great assistance at the worst crisis, but she is now in London. Apparently what started this attack was anxiety about her novel coming on top of the physical weakness. The Doctors say that all depends upon rest and feeding-up.' Leonard himself had by this time finished a second novel, *The Wise Virgins*, the typescript of which he sent to Lytton early in the New Year. But Lytton decided that he' could not recommend his friend to publish it. By nature Leonard was not a novelist. He was wonderfully nice, which made matters all the more difficult when he arrived down at The Lacket asking for a candid opinion on his typescript. 'He was very sympathique, as ever, but there were some thorny moments during the discussion of his novel,' Lytton admitted to Henry (19 January 1914). 'I don't think the poor fellow is in his right assiette – though what the right one is I can't imagine. Perhaps he should be a camel merchant, slowly driving his beasts to market over the vast plains of Baluchistan. Something like that would I'm sure be more appropriate than his present occupations of Fabianising and novel-writing, and even than his past one of ruling blacks.'

So many guests came to The Lacket that Mrs Templeman soon began disintegrating. Before each new arrival she would sweep the chimneys, scrub all the floors and spread an air of ruin. It looked as if she might sink under her load of unnecessary duties. But Lytton's resourcefulness eventually carried the day, and after several confidential chats, the handsome tip of a golden sovereign at Christmas, and a promise that whenever he was away her sister might come over from Newbury to stay, all was well.

'I am enjoying myself very much here,' he wrote to his mother after a couple of months (7 December 1913), 'and feel as if I should like never to move away . . . I try to write a certain amount every day, and the rest of the time is spent in eating, sleeping, walking and reading. In the evenings I struggle with Italian. My occasional wish is for a wife – but it is not easy to be suited in that matter.'

'Whoever thought', he asked Ottoline, 'that I should end my days alone with a widow?'

2

SCENES FROM POST-EDWARDIAN ENGLAND

One unlooked-for effect of rustic chastity was the change of attitude it brought about towards London. Only recently it had been somewhere from which to escape; now it was transformed into an arena where no encounter was impossible and every adventure for the asking.

Such adventures as did come Lytton's way were inconclusive. 'After I left you I went to the Tube,' he told Henry (20 February 1914), 'and saw there a very nice red-cheeked black-haired youth of the lower classes – nothing remarkable in that – *but* he was wearing a heavenly shirt, which transported me. It was dark blue with a yellow edge at the top, and it was done up with laces (straw coloured) which tied at the neck. I thought it so exactly your goût that I longed to get one for you. At last on the platform I made it an épreuve to go up to him and ask him where he got it. Pretty courageous, wasn't it? You see he was not alone, but accompanied by two rather higher-class youths in billycock hats, whom I had to brush aside in order to reach him. I adopted the well-known John style – with great success. It turned out (as I might have guessed) that it was simply a football jersey – he belonged to the Express dairy team. I was so surprised by that I couldn't think what enquiries I could make, and then he vanished.'

It was only on paper that he could carry things through triumphantly. When it came to a black-haired youth and a football jersey, he could not cross the class frontier. But there were always plenty of more restricted activities. In January he stayed with his family, who were then making preliminary arrangements to move from No. 67 to No. 6 Belsize Park Gardens. 'I flew from Square to Square, from Chelsea to Hampstead Heath with infinite alacrity,' he told Duncan (6 February 1914). 'I even went to the Alpine Club.[3] I could not look much at the pictures there, as I found myself alone with [Nina] Hamnett,[4] and became a prey to the desire to pass my hand lightly over her mane of black hair. I knew that if I did she'd strike me in the face – but that, on reflection, only sharpened my desire, and eventually I was just on the point of taking the plunge when Fanny Stanley[5] came in and put an end to the tête-à-tête.'

Early in February he rushed up to town again, 'my excuse being that Swithin had just returned from Burma', he explained to Duncan (6

February 1914), 'but the truth is that I can't resist Piccadilly – though how it's spelt I've never been able to discover.' Swithinbank treated him to a magnificent lunch at Simpson's, with such quantities of Burgundy that he was ill for a week. He had not seen Swithin for nearly five years, and the change was devastating. Was this the young man with whom Lytton had once seriously contemplated falling in love? It seemed scarcely credible now as he sat regarding the 'very benevolent, medical man' lunching opposite him, so quiet, so respectable, so dazed. 'All youth gone,' he lamented in a letter to James (14 February 1914), '– and so sad – so infinitely sad and gentle: I suspect some tragedy – or would suspect one if there was anything in his character to allow of such a thing. Perhaps he's simply become a Buddhist. As for talking to him, it was quite impossible, and he was pained by my get-up.'

Another old friend he met by chance that week was E.M. Forster. He was scarcely more satisfactory than Swithinbank. 'We went all over London together,' he told James (3 February 1914), 'wrapped in incredible intimacy – but it was all hollow, hollow. He's a mediocre man – and knows it, or suspects it, which is worse; he will come to no good, and in the meantime he's treated rudely by waiters and is not really admired even by middle-class dowagers.'

Desmond MacCarthy had arranged for him to lunch with Kenneth Bell, 'half-wit and publisher',[6] at the Devonshire Club in St James's Street. 'It was a singular function,' Lytton observed to James (3 February 1914), 'chiefly in my honour, as Mr Bell, the young and advanced partner of the old-fashioned firm of Bell, wished especially to get in touch with me. I accordingly thought it would please if I appeared in a fairly outré style – cord coat, etc. – and the result was an extreme nervousness on the part of Kenneth.

'However, he suggested that I should write one of a new series of biographies of modern persons, to be written in a non-official manner; I suggested Cardinal Manning as a good subject; he appeared to be enthusiastic at the notion; but now I don't know (a) whether he really wanted it done by me, or (b) whether I really want to do it. I hope to find out when I interview him in a few days' time – if possible at his office; these club lunches with claret and kummel flowing through them in all directions don't make for lucidity.'

Their second discussion took place ten days later at the Savile Club. Though subjected to some pressure, Lytton could only be induced to propose schemes that amounted to slight variations of what he was already writing or planning to write. He had been ruminating too long over his Victorian portraits to abandon them, and wanted to persuade Bell to forget his own projects and fix up a contract for *Eminent Victorians*. For this second meeting he decided to adopt a peevish manner but was disarmed by the reverential style in which he was received, and which brought to the surface his more natural modesty. 'It's very queer how they're all after me so frantically,' he commented to James (14 February 1914).

'I interviewed Mr Basil Williams at the Savile (he's the editor of the new Biographical Series) and he fairly crouched.[7] It was plain that the series – "Creators of the 19th Century" – would not suit me, so I was firm and resisted all his pleadings. He begged me to write on Victor Hugo, Pius IX, Ibsen, and I really forget how many others, but I only smiled mysteriously, and a great deal, and so left him. However, at tea, Mr Bell appeared and pretty well bowled me over with his bonhomie (B. Williams is a sad, cheerful, compact and strangely uninspired little man, I forgot to mention.) The result is that I was led to suggest a series of 19th century essays on great men, in one volume, which he (K.B.) eagerly seized upon – though so far the financial arrangements are in the vague.'

For several weeks negotiations dwindled along, then finally broke down altogether, leaving Lytton to work at his volume of Victorian essays without a contract or publisher, wondering whether they would ever be more than silhouettes.

Business entertainment of a more unusual kind was provided by a meeting of *New Statesman* subscribers towards the end of April at the Kingsway Hall. Lytton turned up out of simple curiosity to see the Fabian junta. 'The so-called editor was "in the chair",' he told James, 'a most nauseous creature,[8] I thought – with Mr and Mrs Webb and B. Shaw on each side of him.

'I've no notion of what the point of the meeting was – no information of any kind was given, and I could only gather from some wails and complaints of the Webbs that it wasn't paying. B. Shaw made a quite amusing speech about nothing on earth. I'd no idea that the Webb fellow was so utterly without pretensions of being a gentleman. *She* was lachrymose and white-haired. Altogether they made a sordid little group. At the end there were "questions" from the audience – supposed to be addressed to the Editor qua Chairman, but the poor man was never allowed to get in a word. The three Gorgons surrounding him kept leaping to their feet with most crushing replies.'

These spring and early summer months of 1914 seemed to glow with miraculous lightness, as if the atmosphere were electrically charged. Foreigners flocked to London, which was enjoying an extraordinarily extended social season. The new Russian ballets, the operas at Covent Garden, the sporting calendar appeared more spectacular than ever before. Everything moved with an odd ease and brilliance.

The bohemians of this Edwardian pageant were taking their last curtain call. That May, Augustus John had moved into the large square studio-house in Chelsea which he had had specially constructed for him by a man he met in a pub; and it was here that he gave an all-night house-warming party in fancy dress. 'The company was very charming and sympathetic, I thought,' Lytton wrote to James '– so easy-going and taking everything for granted; and really I think it's the proper milieu for me – if only the wretches had a trifle more brain . . . John was a superb figure. There was dancing – two-steps and such things – so much nicer than waltzes – and at last I danced with him – it seemed an opportunity not to be missed. (I forgot to say that I was dressed as a pirate.) Nina Lamb was there, and made effréné love to me. We came out in broad daylight.'

Ottoline's *salon* in Bedford Square had by this time reached the height of its fame as a rallying point for artists and writers. Among the most frequent *habitués* besides Lytton himself were Gilbert Cannan; Stanley Spencer; the handsome, volatile, Jewish painter Mark Gertler; Arnold Bennett and Augustus John (both dressed extravagantly in Ottoline's clothes); Desmond MacCarthy reclining on a peripheral sofa; Vanessa Bell stepping out naked from the waist up; Bertrand Russell, taut and upright, dancing the hornpipe; a troupe of Slade School girls; and Nijinsky, who was soon to be married, and with whom Lytton had become disenchanted, but who still enthralled Ottoline 'gaping and gurgling like a hooked fish'. Indeed Ottoline's advances, and his unresponsiveness, were by this time causing ripples of merriment among her friends. She plied him with her most sentimental attentions. On one occasion the two of them were sitting in a tiny inner room when Lytton entered the house. As he advanced down the drawing-room he overheard Ottoline's husky voice, with its infinitely modulated nasal intonations, utter the words: 'Quand vous dansez, vous n'êtes pas un homme – vous êtes une idée. C'est ça, n'est-ce pas, qui est l'Art? . . . Vous avez lu Platon, sans doute?' The reply was a grunt.

The principal guest at the most glittering of these receptions was Asquith, the prime minister, who had been offering a number of brave but unrewarded gallantries to Ottoline. The party early in May represented her last bid to secure an under-secretaryship for her husband, and might ultimately have proved successful had they not both embraced pacifist convictions at the outbreak of the war three months later. The gathering itself was brilliant and Lytton's head spun alarmingly at finding himself close to so many celebrated people. Ottoline had warned him in advance that the prime minister was to be there, 'but I was rather surprised', he told James, 'to be rushed, the very minute I arrived into the dear man's arms. It was most marked; someone else whom he was talking to was scattered to the winds, and we were then planted together on a central sofa.

'He was considerably less pompous than I'd expected, and exceedingly gracious – talked about Parnell and such reminiscent matters at considerable length. I could see no sign of the faintest spark of anything out of the common in cet estimable Perrier Jouet. He seemed a pebble worn smooth by rubbings – even his face had a somewhat sand-papered effect. He enquired about my next book, and I gave him a sketch of it. At the end he said with slight pomp "Well, you have a difficult and interesting task before you." I said "*You* have a difficult and interesting task before *you*!" He grinned and said, "Ah, we do what we can, we do what we can" ... The company was most distinguished and the whole affair decidedly brilliant. Henry James of course loomed in the most disgusting way. The Raleighs were also there, and – very extraordinary – Sir M. Nathan ... [9] Ottoline was in a vast gold brocade dress, and seemed remarkably at her ease, and in fact at moments almost tête-montée. In the middle of it all she fell upon me, and charged me with infidelity, breaking her heart, etc.'

The Ulster crisis was then at its height, and Asquith had dramatically taken over the War Office. His graciousness struck Lytton as being partly that of genuine good humour, and partly the professional manner of a man whose business in life it was at all times to create a favourable impression. They talked about various public figures – Lord Randolph Churchill among others – and Asquith then turned the conversation back to Parnell who, he declared, was the most remarkable man he had known. Lytton wished later he had suggested that Gladstone was surely even more remarkable; then, after Asquith recounted how he had met Parnell in the Temple one morning when the divorce proceedings had just become public and how Parnell had shown that he had no notion of the hubbub this would produce, the talk pausing a moment with a slight embarrassment, he got up, cordially shook Lytton's hand, and sauntered into another room. The entire meeting had lasted about ten minutes. 'If I hadn't known who he was,' Lytton afterwards wrote (May 1918), 'I should have guessed him to be one of those Oxford dons who have a smattering of the world – one of those clever, cautious mediocre intelligences, who made one thank heaven one was at Cambridge.

'Two particulars only suggested a difference. His manner was a little nervous – it was really almost as if he was the whole time conscious with a slight uneasiness, that he was the Prime Minister. And then, though his appearance on the whole was decidedly donnish – small and sleek and not too well made in the details – his hands were different. Small and plump they were too; but there was a masterfulness in them and a mobility which made them remarkable.'

Though Lytton's manner had grown relaxed, he sometimes bristled awkwardly. 'He doesn't say anything, except *tête-à-tête*,' Walter Raleigh wrote to Logan Pearsall Smith after seeing him that June at Newington. 'I wish he would write a book called *Life Among the Man-haters*, or *Out against God*.'[10] During these weeks and months, Lytton was busy distilling this animosity against God and man into his 'Cardinal Manning'. 'I'm at present devoting 3 hours a day to Cardinal Manning,' he wrote to Clive Bell on 22 February. His letters record the progress he was now making after his long preparation.

Lytton Strachey to Henry Lamb, 22 February 1914
'I sit here buried in books on Cardinals and Theologians, and am rapidly becoming an expert on ecclesiastical questions. For instance, I now know what Papal Infallibility means – or rather what it doesn't – the distinction is highly important. I think that dogmatic theology would make a much better subject for a Tripos than most. Fine examination papers I could set – Discuss the difference between "definitionists" and "inopportunists". – Explain with examples the various meanings of "minimism". – Give a brief account of *either* Newman's attitude towards the Syllabus *or* Dollinger's relations with the Vatican Council. State clearly the interpretations put by (a) W.G. Ward, (b) Veuillot, (c) Dupanloup, upon the words "Ex cathedrâ". Doesn't it sound entrancing?'

Lytton Strachey to Henry Lamb, 14 March 1914
'I'm enjoying my Manning a good deal so far; the chief drawback seems to be that it's such a slow business. And of course I'm quite prepared to find when it's done that it's all a fantasia; but the only way of knowing that is to go through with it to the bitter end, and hope for the best.'

Lytton Strachey to Ottoline Morrell, 27 March 1914
'I'm trying to work, and even succeeding to some extent. My task is rather a strange one. I think it may have some vestiges of amusement in it – but it's difficult to say as yet. I won't, I fear, be quite as bright as the Chartreuse de Parme, though, in any case!'

Lytton Strachey to James Strachey, April 1914
'If one had the thews of a bull and the pen of a ready writer, one might get something done. As it is everything takes such a devil of a time. One has to sleep, eat, digest, take exercise – and after all that, one has to squeeze out one's carefully moulded sentences.'

At the beginning of the year he had applied to Harold Cox asking whether he might write two articles for the *Edinburgh Review*, one on Dryden and the other on Byron. The reply was flattering but unspecific. His 'Henri Beyle' had been much liked, he was told; but no mention was made of Dryden and none of Byron. Instead, over the next eighteen months, he was to publish two long biographical essays on a favourite subject, Voltaire, while continuing with his irregular articles for the *New Statesman* and, in April 1914, sending in his very last contribution to the *Spectator* – a leading review of Constance Garnett's translation of *The Possessed*.

Voltaire and Dostoyevsky were important influences on *Eminent Victorians*. In 'Voltaire and England', written at the same time as 'Cardinal Manning' and 'Florence Nightingale', he describes Voltaire's 'epoch-making book', *Lettres Philosophiques*, as 'a work of propaganda and a declaration of faith' that carried over England 'a whispered message of tolerance, of free inquiry, of enlightened curiosity'. This was Lytton's ambition, too, in *Eminent Victorians*. He steeped himself in Voltaire's spirit of Humanism, and studied his proselytizing raids on Christian theology. Whatever quips and mockeries played upon the surface, he was, like Voltaire, 'in deadly earnest at heart.'

The reading of Dostoyevsky encouraged him to experiment with drama, irony and psychological suggestion. 'While Tolstoy, Ibsen and Nietzsche sent waves of fresh thought across the Continent,' Virginia was to write, 'the English slept undisturbed . . .' But, to the distress of Henry James, the impact of Dostoyevsky's novels in Constance Garnett's translations was experienced as a liberating force among younger writers in these years before the war. 'It is directly obvious that he is the greatest writer ever born,' Virginia wrote to Lytton (1 September 1912). Dostoyevsky's material which, as James Strachey was to say, 'reveals a lot of the same material as Freud,' uncovered a richly comic irrational world which suggested to Lytton that ridicule was a valid historical attitude and literary aesthetic for his own work. In 'A Russian Humorist', he writes: 'Dostoievsky's mastery of this strange power of ridicule, which, instead of debasing, actually ennobles and endears the object upon which it falls, is probably the most remarkable of all his characteristics.' Lytton was to use ridicule most endearingly in *Portraits in Miniature*. In *Eminent Victorians* it plays gently on some of the minor characters, but is otherwise sharpened by Voltairian wit to produce a deft attacking style.

Since coming to The Lacket he felt more confident of carrying this long project to its end – unlike a previous tenant of Hilton Young's – Desmond MacCarthy. 'Desmond is a great study,' Lytton explained to James (9 February 1914):

'I've never seen anyone so extraordinarily incapable of pulling himself together. He'll never write anything, I'm afraid, in that hopeless miasma. He rode eighteen miles yesterday with Hilton, came back almost dead, and stretched his now vast bulk on a chair in a stertorous coma. At last we somehow got him to bed. He rose at 11.30 this morning, refused to have anything for breakfast, and then ate the whole of a pot of marmalade with extreme deliberation. He's wonderfully good-natured, affable, and amusing, but there are moments when dullness seems to exude from him in concentrated streams.'

Another visitor to The Lacket was Leonard Woolf, who stayed a week. 'He has been having a nervous breakdown in a mild way,' Lytton confided to Henry (12 March 1914), 'and seemed to want repose. He says he's now much better, and goes away on Saturday. Virginia is apparently all right now, and there are no nurses any more.'

So Lytton's life went amiably on – supported by his friends on Saturdays and Sundays, and by Cardinal Manning, Dostoyevsky, Voltaire and others during the rest of the week. There seemed no reason why this rhythm of living should not continue until he completed *Eminent Victorians*. After all those wandering years since Cambridge, the ordered days and weeks stretched purposefully ahead.

But on 4 August 1914 the social afterglow of Edwardian England was finally extinguished.

3

TWO TYPES OF PATRIOTISM

The Great War cast over Lytton's life a shadow that coloured much of his writing. With his invalidism, there was no question of his being called up for service, even of a more subsidiary kind. Logically, therefore, the wisest course he could take might have been to cut himself off entirely from political and military affairs. Yet this he could not do. Painfully and unwillingly he found himself involved. War filled the horizon, darkening the days and disturbing his troubled nights.

> Last night I dreamt that I had gone to Hell.
> I seemed to know the *milieu* pretty well.
> The place was crammed as tight as it would hold
> With men and hatred, folly, lust and gold.
> And lies? Ah, I'd forgotten: without fail
> Red hot for breakfast came *The Daily Mail*.
> Well, thought, they say, is free. I wish it were!
> Can you think freely in a dentist's chair?
> Then so can I, when, willing or unwilling,
> All Europe on my nerves comes drilling, drilling.
> I do my best; I shut my eyes and ears,
> Try to forget my furies and my fears,
> Banish the newspapers, go out of town,
> And in a country cottage settle down,
> Far from the world, its sorrow and its shame;
> But, though skies alter, still the mind's the same.[11]
> What comfort, when in every lovely hour
> Lurks horror, like a spider in a flower?

Most people, while paying lip-service to peace, welcomed this outbreak of war. Lytton's hatred of it was never assumed; he was not excited by the fighting. Though he loved the English countryside, feeling that he could not be happy living anywhere else, he never transmutes this love into a national superiority. 'On the whole I don't care much about England's being victorious (apart from personal questions),' he wrote to James (27 September 1914), '– but I should object to France being crushed. Mightn't it be a good plan to become a Frenchman?'

France, to his mind, was the most civilized country in Europe and therefore the one least likely to provoke a war. All war was a return to barbarism and, in a modern world, all wars should be avoidable. They reinstated medievalism, substituting injustice, cruelty, hypocrisy for the virtues of tolerance and enlightened inquiry. They disrupted much that made life worth living; art degenerated into puerile propaganda; friendships were callously wrenched apart.

Field Marshal Sir John French, head of the British Expeditionary Force which landed in France on 17 August, predicted that the Allied Powers would be victorious by Christmas. Throughout the country an unashamed howl went up for conscription. But the Liberal Government remained firm. In an official statement in *The Times* of 15 August, Kitchener, newly appointed Secretary of State for War, announced that voluntary territorials were to be divided into two categories – those serving abroad and those at home. He was looking for 100,000 volunteers for his new army. But his announcement stressed the importance of home defence and made it clear that the Government 'does not desire that those who cannot, on account of their affairs, volunteer for foreign service, should by any means be induced to do so'.

Lytton himself seems to have believed that all physically fit intellectuals should be prepared to defend the shores of England, but that no intellectuals were physically fit. He appeared eager to save the military services from the incompetence of writers and artists – let others do the dirty work. It was an attitude which Ottoline, a resolute pacifist, found 'quite inhuman and cruel'. 'I think one must resist,' Lytton explained to James early that September, 'if it comes to a push. But I admit it's a difficult question.

'One solution is to go and live in the United States of America. As for our personal position, it seems to me quite sound and coherent. We're all far too weak physically to be of any use at all. If we weren't we'd still be too intelligent to be thrown away in some really not essential expedition, and our proper place would be – the National Reserve, I suppose. God has put us on an island, and Winston [Churchill] has given us a navy, and it would be absurd to neglect those advantages – which I consider exactly apply to able-bodied intellectuals. It's no good pretending one isn't a special case.'

At the beginning of the war Bloomsbury and its friends were not wholly pacifist. That September, Clive Bell, whose *Peace at Once* (1915) was to be publicly burnt by order of the Lord Mayor, asked James Strachey for information on how to join the Army Service Corps or some other non-fighting unit. Duncan Grant immediately entered the National Reserve. Adrian Stephen spoke of enlisting. E.M. Forster volunteered as a Red

Cross Observer in Egypt. Wittgenstein joined the Austrian army. Rupert Brooke prepared to go to Belgium. 'I cannot see the use of intellectual persons doing this,' Lytton commented on hearing the news, 'as long as there are enough men in any case, and the country is not in danger. Home defence is another matter, and I think I should certainly train if I had the strength.' But of all his friends the one caught up by the call to arms was, to his great sadness, Henry Lamb who, in the first week of September (after withdrawing his name from the recruiting office at Putney), enrolled as an assistant at Guy's Hospital. His return to medical practice was an odd result, Lytton reflected, of Austria declaring war on Serbia. 'The horror and repulsiveness of it all seem far greater than they used to be,' Henry wrote. '. . . I am getting used to blood. It is much harder to bear when the people are not anaesthetised.' Lytton was relieved that Henry's common sense had overcome his initial militarism; but 'he's so fearfully undependable,' he complained to James (27 August 1914). 'Also his words have no connection with his feelings, nor his acts with anything; and he's constitutionally incapable of constancy . . . It seems to me that really – from any point of view – it's grotesque for a person of his health to go into the army: and I don't think this has been sufficiently emphasised. I hope to goodness he'll get fixed into something fairly harmless before long, as otherwise there'll always be this terror.'

Despite the columns of patriotic journalism, Lytton did not believe that ordinary men and women were really warlike. He blamed the newspapers – particularly those of Lord Northcliffe – for deluding credulous people like Henry who did not know their own minds, and whipping up a blind animosity against the Germans. Disregarding the newspapers, the condition of things seemed reasonably calm during these first weeks. In the remoteness of the country there was hardly a detectable change, but within London it was obvious from the grave faces of the people in the streets that something grim was happening. Their expressions denoted no lust for conflict, only sorrow and despondency. 'So far as I can make out there isn't the slightest enthusiasm for the war,' Lytton reported to Dorothy Bussy (21 August 1914). 'I think the public are partly feeling simple horror and partly that it's a dreadful necessity. But I think there will be a change when the casualties begin – both in the direction of greater hostility to the Germans and also more active disgust at the whole thing. Though of course a great deal will depend on the actual turn of events.'

Lytton tended to disassociate himself from the more belligerent pacifists, not because he disagreed with what they said but because he believed their fulminations, directed for the most part against the foreign secretary Sir Edward Grey, to be an error of tactics. 'Those anti-Grey people are really too senseless,' he complained to James (18 August 1914). 'Can't they see that they do nothing at this moment if they appear as pro-Germans? The only hope is to appear anti-German and also pro-peace. The more they worry Grey the more rigid he'll become.'

Everyone was declaring war on everyone else – Germany on Russia and France; France and Britain on Austria-Hungary; Austria-Hungary on Russia; Serbia on Germany . . . it was an epidemic. On 14 August Russia, having invaded East Prussia, promised Poland autonomy in return for aid. The following day Japan issued an ultimatum to Germany (which became a declaration of war eight days later). 'I agree that the Japanese and Polish affairs are very bad – especially the latter, it seems to me,' Lytton wrote to James. 'I didn't expect those Muscovites would show their hand so soon. That manifesto was a wonderful piece of blatant hypocrisy. Is it possible that the Poles will be such fools as to put their faith in the Tsar? Also won't it be plain pretty soon even to E. Grey that the war's being run for the aggrandisement of Russia? I don't believe the English public would stand that.'

The English public, Lytton considered, should be stirred up about peace. Instead of wasting energy blaming the Government, as Bertrand Russell was busy doing in the *Nation*, intelligent people ought to institute a Stop the War party in the Cabinet, backed by public opinion. Far from canvassing this support, Russell's passionate denunciations were, Lytton suspected, alienating the populace. Nevertheless, despite the crowds in Downing Street cheering Asquith and singing the National Anthem, there remained a fundamental good sense about people's attitude which he found heartening. 'I haven't seen anyone', he told James (16 August 1914), 'who hasn't agreed on the main lines – viz: that we should take nothing for ourselves, and insist on ending it at the earliest possible moment.'

There seems little doubt that Lytton was being optimistic. Before the carnage begins, the idea of military action is not horrific, but simple and inspiriting. Grey and Asquith were personally responsible for bringing Britain into the war. The House of Commons would have had no debate at all on the question had not Philip Morrell courageously got to his feet and made a protest. His speech, by all accounts the finest he ever made, did no good and put an end to his political career – though nothing had so become that career as his leaving of it. 'I can never forget seeing him standing alone,' Ottoline noted in her diary (3 August 1914), 'with nearly all the House against him, shouting at him to "Sit down!"'

Momentarily, Lytton himself would feel the faint vibration of war fever, instantly to be checked and corrected. Yet feeling it, he understood something of its appeal, and the force with which it was soon surging through the country, unerringly picking upon non-combatants. 'I walked into Marlborough to-day,' he wrote to James (18 August 1914), 'and found there the news of the continued French advance in the Vosges, and the "confusion" of the German army. Is this possibly the beginning of a great movement? It is appalling to have to *wish* for such horrors – but now it's the only way.

'. . . Yesterday I felt for the first time a desire to go out and fight myself. I can understand some people being overcome by it. At any rate one would not have to think any more.'

For the most part, however, the war affected him as a personal tragedy. He felt helpless. One of his sisters was in Germany and he was worried about getting her out. But when Evelyn Whitehead advised him to appeal to the British ambassador in Germany, he was nonplussed. 'But how can I?' he asked in his most penetrating voice. 'I have never met him.'

On a more public level he was equally incredulous. He followed the news carefully, growing more amazed and disgusted at each new communiqué and report. His political attitude in these early days of the war is nicely caught in a letter he wrote (21 August 1914) to Dorothy Bussy, after reading through a White Paper that reproduced the official dispatches between Sir Edward Grey and the ambassadors.

'It's like a puppet-show, with the poor little official dolls dancing and squeaking their official phrases, while the strings are being pulled by some devilish Unseen Power. One naturally wants to blame somebody – the Kaiser for choice – but the tragic irony, it seems to me, really is that everyone was helpless. Even the Austrians were no doubt genuinely in terror of the whole regime being undermined by Slavism, and the Russians couldn't allow the Austrians to get hold of the Balkans; the crisis finally came when the Germans found out that the Russians were secretly mobilizing – that frightened them so much that the war party became supreme, and all was over. The real horror is that Europe is not yet half-civilized, and the peaceful countries aren't strong enough to keep the others quiet.'

*

For the time being Lytton continued 'living the life of a complete St Anthony', as he described it to Ottoline (24 October 1914), 'with Mrs Templeman in the role of the Queen of Sheba – and I can't say she plays the part with conviction'. On most evenings he would spend a solitary hour or two, crouched over the fire 'knitting mufflers for our soldier and sailor lads,' so he informed Clive, 'but I expect that by the time I've finished them the war will be over, and they'll be given to Henry and Duncan'. Acknowledging the possibility of the country being overrun by the enemy, and feeling that it was essential to be ready with words of propitiation, he gave up Italian and began to take lessons in German.

Over the next four years there was to be no more travelling abroad, though he went between Wiltshire and the metropolis much as before. There were still the Thursday evening parties at Bedford Square, where wartime anxieties could be relieved for a few hours. To assist in the pretence that things were otherwise than they actually were, everyone would robe up in fancy-dress and, while Philip Morrell thumped out Hungarian dances or Russian ballet music at his pianola, fling themselves into fantastic dances. 'Now and then,' recalled Ottoline, 'Lytton Strachey exquisitely stepped out with his brother James and his sister Marjorie, in a delicate and courtly minuet of his own invention, his thin long legs and arms gracefully keeping perfect time to Mozart – the vision of this exquisite dance always haunts me with its half-serious, half-mocking, yet beautiful quality.'

There were also Bloomsbury parties to which Lytton had started going again. Clive and Vanessa gave one of the most spectacular of these affairs. It began with Mozart chamber music played by Adila and Jelly D'Arányi (who, as Hungarians, were looked upon with hostile suspicion by some English people, but to whom Bloomsbury was particularly hospitable). Afterwards the guests went upstairs to see the last scene from Racine's *Bérénice*, acted by three titanic puppets eight feet tall, painted futuristically and cut out of cardboard by Duncan. The words of the play were spoken by members of the Strachey family, whose fearful Gallic mouthings before 'several eminent frogs' were as bold in their way as the puppets themselves.[12]

But something had begun to go wrong with these parties. Cigarettes were ground out under the heels of the dancers at Bedford Square; bottles clinked and crashed as they were smuggled in under overcoats. Everything was moving from romantic comedy into ghastly farce. Gilbert Cannan's friend, the painter Mark Gertler, stamped on Marjorie Strachey's foot on the dance floor, then bruised Aldous Huxley's future wife so badly that her arm turned purple, and smashed another guest's spectacles. 'One young lady,' Miranda Seymour writes, 'attempting a spirited pirouette, struck David Garnett in the face and gave him a black eye. Another guest, embarking on a high-stepping dance with his hostess, tripped on her skirt and brought her crashing to the ground in his arms.'[13]

Practical jokes were the vogue. One of the more ingenious was played by Duncan on Lytton. At breakfast one morning, while he was staying with his family in Hampstead, he received through the post a poem in French purporting to come from a rather taciturn French actor named Delacre, a man whom he had met at several of Ottoline's parties and whose conversation was made up of long sombre stories beginning: 'Figurez-vous, mon cher . . .' This poem, composed in rhymed couplets and written with ominous capital letters on a single sheet of paper, implied that the writer had recently seen Lytton in a compromising situation.

SI UN VIEUX
VEUT BAISER DANS LA RUE
UN JEUNE HOMME
VAUT MIEUX
PRENDRE UN FIACRE
AVANT QU'APRES
TON AMI DELACRE
DEMEURE TOUT PRES
DE KNIGHTSBRIDGE CHER MAÎTRE?
CA BIEN PEUT ETRE

Although he was at a loss as to what indiscretion Delacre was claiming to have observed, Lytton's imagination began to canter away. He felt terrified that the story – whatever it was – might get out. Already he could see the newspaper headline – '*Astonishing Accusation!*' In panic he rushed round to Delacre's hotel, and implored him not to show it to anyone.

Lytton confided to his new friend David Garnett at tea that same afternoon what happened next. 'Delacre had then behaved in a most extraordinary and alarming manner. He had listened to Lytton's little speech without making any comment whatever. He then excused himself and left the room. After waiting three-quarters of an hour Lytton had asked a waiter to find Delacre and had been told that he had left the hotel. Lytton was completely baffled by this behaviour and felt that he had not improved matters by his *démarche*.'[14]

After listening to Lytton's story, David Garnett examined the lines again and pointed out that it was highly improbable that such a vain and solemn actor would select the word *fiacre* as a rhyme for his own name. 'You don't think that Duncan wrote it by any chance?' he hazarded.

Lytton stared in dismay. The notion had briefly occurred to him, but he had dismissed it. The French seemed so idiomatic and it rhymed so ingeniously. Yet this was the obvious explanation.

'What, that monster!' he exclaimed. '. . . I believe if the truth were known all the preposterous predicaments in the Universe might be traced back to him.'

To all appearances Bloomsbury was the same as ever; but appearances were misleading. Beneath the striving high spirits lay a darker mood deepened by news of the first fatalities. 'For myself I am absolutely and completely desolated,' Maynard wrote to Lytton from King's (27 November 1914). 'It is utterly unbearable to see day by day the youths going away first to boredom and discomfort and then to slaughter. Five of this College, who are undergraduates or who have just gone down, are already killed, including to my great grief Freddie Hardman, as you may have seen from the papers.' Lytton had seen Hardman only a few weeks earlier at one of Ottoline's parties. 'I think what the Greeks meant by that remark of theirs about those who die young was that they escape the deterioration of growing old; and perhaps if Freddie had gone on living he could hardly have gone on being so nice,' he wrote in his reply to Maynard (1 December 1914). 'But I'm afraid this reflection isn't much of a consolation to you.'

The war also ended Lytton's intimacy with Henry who, after being commissioned as a Lieutenant in the Royal Army Medical Corps in the summer of 1916 – serving in Palestine and France, winning a Military Cross and being badly gassed – was appointed an official war artist only as he lay in hospital after the signing of the armistice. Their flow of correspondence trickled on until the end of 1915. 'There is not a spoonful of brains to be found in the whole collection, beau-monde, doctor, matron, or nurses,' Henry complained that summer from L'Hôpital Anglais du Casino at Fécamp. '. . . I can see no hope of wars ceasing while such people abound.' There was no one, during these war years, to take Henry's special place. Lytton was always having infatuations – 'a violent, short, quite fruitless passion' for the twenty-one-year-old painter Geoffrey Nelson, for example, and a romantic affection for Ted Roussell, a young plough-boy from Sussex, who enlisted in 1917 and was killed in the last week of the war* – but these attachments, though sometimes highly charged, were of little lasting significance.

Two men of whom he soon grew particularly fond were Maynard's

---

* 'Dear Ted,' Lytton wrote to him on 13 November 1918, 'I wonder how you are. I haven't heard from you for a long time – and I hope you are well and flourishing. Now that the war's over, I expect you'll be coming back quite soon – which I daresay you won't be sorry for. Let me hear from you when you have time to write. Always your friend, L. Strachey.' This letter was returned to Lytton, its envelope marked 'Deceased.' 'His mother wrote me a most pathetic letter,' Lytton told Mary Hutchinson (11 December 1918). 'How hideous, how senseless . . . The field behind Eleanor [House] that late September, the plough & the horses, the seagulls, the boy at the plough – but it's better to talk of something else.'

charming Apostolic lover Francis Birrell and David ('Bunny') Garnett, themselves close friends. With both of them he enjoyed what was partly a friendship, partly a flirtation. 'I think he's a nice fellow at bottom,' he wrote to James about Francis Birrell (21 January 1915), 'but the overlaying paraphernalia are distinctly trying. He seems a sort of secondary Clive – and in the Dostoievsky style, half knows it.' To David Garnett, Birrell seemed a secondary Mr Pickwick, with all 'the innocence of Mr Pickwick which revealed itself as an incapacity for selfish calculation'. While Birrell chattered on, Garnett would remain exasperatingly silent until eventually achieving utterance with extreme rustic slowness, his sentences pock-marked with 'ghastly pauses', as Lytton later complained to Roger Senhouse (2 February 1929), '– each long enough to contain Big Ben striking midnight – between every two . . . words'. Even so, Lytton grew very close to Bunny Garnett. 'No, the world is not agreeable,' he wrote to James six months after meeting him (11 June 1915). 'And then again I think of dear Bunny – and the fact that such a person should exist in it fills me with delight. Charming!'

It was Francis Birrell who in December 1914 had introduced Lytton to Bunny Garnett. That Christmas, Lytton held a party at The Lacket. Daphne and Noel Olivier, James and Duncan all came down to stay with him in the cottage, while Birrell and Garnett took rooms at a local inn. 'Daphne liked it awfully,' Noel Olivier had written (7 January 1915) in her last letter to Rupert before his death. ' . . . I don't know why I shd inflict the information on you though.' But if so many were going to die nothing much mattered, and it was good to refresh oneself in the company of friends. David Garnett wrote of Lytton in his autobiography:

'I was struck first of all by his gentleness and his hospitality. Then I could see he was very much alive and very responsive. That evening the response may sometimes have concealed boredom, for Lytton was easily bored and the prospect of Christmas with two young women in the house – one of whom often spoke in tones of indignant emotional idealism – may have seemed rather appalling. James had let him in for them, and his curiosity and affection for Frankie [Birrell] had let him in for the shy, but good-looking hobbledehoy he had brought with him.'[15]

Bunny Garnett had a foot in all camps. His mother was Constance Garnett, the translator of Dostoyevsky, Tolstoy and Chekhov; his father Edward Garnett, a famous publisher's reader and editor of D.H. Lawrence. Bunny had been educated as a botanist, though he was to make his reputation after the war as a novelist. He was good-looking, with a tall muscular body, fair hair and intense blue eyes. Outgrowing his shyness, he enjoyed a range of sexual experiences. He had pitched his tent with the Neo-Pagans and seduced the youngest of the Olivier girls, Daphne. But though a famous womanizer, he was also part of the 'sodomitical' world. When asked towards the end of his life about his 'homosexual leanings', he replied: 'I was more leant against than leaning.' He was leant against a little by Frankie Birrell with whom he was to go to France later in 1915 to work with the Friends' War Victims Relief Mission. But he was leant against more seriously by Duncan whom he met for the first time at The Lacket this Christmas.

One evening Lytton assembled his guests round the fire and read them 'Ermyntrude and Esmeralda'. The story, which reminded Bunny Garnett of Laclos's *Les Liaisons Dangereuses*, persuaded him to be a libertine, he writes – 'that is a man whose sexual life is free of the restraints imposed by religion and conventional morality'.

The results of this conversion became apparent in the first week of the New Year. On 6 January 1915, at a Café Royal dinner preceding a party given by the Bells in Gordon Square, Maynard placed Bunny between Vanessa and Duncan. 'Vanessa is a darling,' Bunny wrote in his diary. She was now in her mid-thirties and still beautiful. 'Her face had a grave beauty in repose: the perfect oval of a sculptured Madonna,' he remembered. 'Her straight dark brown hair, parted in the middle, was swept in wings over her ears to be fastened in a loose knob on the back of the angled pedestal of her neck. Her mouth was lovely, not small or too large, rather turned down at the corners, often impudent and full of humour. The eyes, under deeply hooded lids, were ... blue-grey and deceptively innocent.'[16] Bunny Garnett, then twenty-two, felt much attracted to her. He must have heard that, over the last couple of years, Vanessa had been painfully disengaging herself from Roger Fry, whose forceful intellect and wild enthusiasms, mixed with sudden spells of irrational pessimism, had begun to jar on her nerves. She liked men – but not dominating men. She needed someone younger than herself, someone to love, her biographer Frances Spalding writes, 'as a younger brother or even son'. In some of his writings David Garnett hints at an affair between them. And it was true that Vanessa was transferring her love to someone at the Café Royal that evening – not Bunny but Duncan.

Duncan was, unusually for him, at a loss. Like Lytton, he had been dazzled by the Botticelli-like beauty of George Mallory and got as far as painting him naked – but George had recently married. He had also been enjoying an affair with Adrian Stephen – though Adrian was now becoming engaged to be married. He accepted gratefully enough the bonus of

Vanessa's growing love for him, but was not yet certain if he could reciprocate it. At The Lacket he had felt himself becoming passionately attracted to Bunny. Then, following the Café Royal dinner, late at night, he declared his passion, and Bunny, with the themes and ideas of 'Ermyntrude and Esmeralda' reverberating in his mind, consented to go to bed with him. So began one of the most extraordinary of Bloomsbury's *ménages à trois*, a truly dangerous liaison played out during the war against a changing set of beautiful farmhouses, and reaching out to haunt the next generation.

After the initial shock of war, writes Maynard's biographer Robert Skidelsky, 'Bloomsbury was recovering its nerve.'[17]

4

UNDERTONES OF WAR

Though the war sharpened his critical faculties, the magnitude of world events threatened to burst through Lytton's careful plans. How could he concentrate on nineteenth-century culture and politics in the middle of such grief and disaster? By the last week of August the German army had overrun Namur which, with its garrison of forts, was the hinge of the French outflanking movement. Twenty-five thousand soldiers lay dead. 'Namur is terrible,' Lytton wrote to James (August 1914). 'I suppose it's certain now it will be a long business. As for my private hopes, they're almost gone.'

When he did manage to settle down to some literary work he found it, as he told Henry (5 September 1915), 'a considerable sedative'. But the Manning biography, which should have been finished by the end of August, was giving him difficulty. Twenty-seven foolscap pages of it had to be rewritten, and it was not completed until shortly before Christmas. His letters contain repeated avowals of his determination to 're-attack the Cardinal', but it was only in the New Year that he could show his friends the finished essay. 'I have seldom enjoyed myself more than I did last night, reading Manning,' wrote Virginia who seemed that January to have recovered her health. 'In fact, I couldn't stop, and preserved some pages only by force of will to read after dinner. It is quite superb – It is far the best thing you have ever written, I believe – To begin with, what a miracle it is that such a group should have existed – and then how divinely amusing and exciting and alive you make it. I command you to complete a whole series . . .'

Encouraged by this and other enthusiastic letters, Lytton started on the second of what Duncan called his 'eminently disagreeable Victorians'.[18] The previous year Lytton had read Sir Edward Cook's official biography of Florence Nightingale, telling his mother (15 January 1914) that although the lady with the lamp was a fascinating woman, he did not really like her. Having turned down the offer of writing this book himself, he was particularly interested to see what kind of woman Edward Cook had depicted. 'I have just been reading the book I might have written – the Life of F. Nightingale,' he told James (16 January 1914). 'I'm glad I didn't, as I couldn't have satisfied anybody. She was a terrible woman – though powerful. And certainly a wonderful book might have been made out of her, from the cynical point of view. Of course the Victorian age is fairly reeking all over it. What a crew they were!'

From this point of view, he wanted to make a short unofficial biography of Florence Nightingale, giving his selection of information from the official Life a dramatic unity. 'I'm beginning to attack Florence Nightingale,' he told Henry (3 January 1915) who had stayed up nearly all night reading 'Cardinal Manning'. 'I want it to be very much shorter than the Cardinal, which will involve rather a different method, I think. I'm not quite sure whether the damned thing will be possible, but I hope for the best.'

The progress of 'Florence Nightingale', which occupied Lytton for almost six months, is charted in his correspondence. 'I wish I didn't dislike hard work quite so much,' he admitted to Henry (12 January 1915). ' . . . I think it's chiefly the starting that's so unpleasant.' A month later he is describing Florence Nightingale as 'a hard nut to crack', but assuring Ottoline (11 February 1915) that he was 'struggling with extraordinary persistence'.

Lytton Strachey to Virginia Woolf, 28 February 1915
'I am in rather a state just now with Miss Nightingale, who is proving distinctly indigestible. It's a fearful business – putting pen to paper – almost inconceivable. What happens? And how on earth does one ever manage to pull through in the end?'

In the early summer Lytton moved his books and papers into the garden where he sat all day locked in struggle.

Lytton Strachey to James Strachey, 11 June 1915
'I've been getting into a frantic state with F. Nightingale – working

incessantly until my brain spun round and round, and then in its usual dim unexplained way my health went groggy, and yesterday Lady S. arrived.

. . . the F.N. affair has been much more terrific than I could have expected. I imagined originally that I'd be able to do the whole thing in a fortnight. It's still not nearly done; and I'm in terror lest after all it should turn out quite illegible – I imagine Eddie Marsh trying to read it and saying afterwards, "It bored me stiff." I feel there would be no appeal from that.'

Lytton Strachey to Henry Lamb, 13 June 1915
'I am submerged by Nightingale, which has turned out a fearful task. I'm now within sight of the end, though, I hope.'

Lytton Strachey to Ottoline Morrell, 23 June 1915
'F. Nightingale has at last been polished off, I'm glad to say. So I'm feeling very gay and chirpy –'

The events of the war gave him the sense of living on a perpetual volcano. He was appalled by the suggestions he read in *The Times* about the possibility of a coalition Government. Could the rumours be true? His head buzzed with unanswered questions. Why should the Cabinet contemplate such a move? Had everyone come to the conclusion that the war was hopeless without conscription? If *that* were true, then the country would find itself in a jungle of militarism. Already there was a sinister augury in the riots directed against civilians of Germanic extraction still living in England. The most alarming feature of these incidents had been the conduct of the authorities who made use of them as an excuse for further maltreatment of those miserable people. 'Doesn't it all make one want to go and bury oneself somewhere far, far away – somewhere so far away that even the Times will never get to one?' he asked Ottoline. '"Où me cacherai? Fuyons dans la nuit infernale!"'

But worse than all this political uncertainty at home was the awful finality of news from the front. In June, Ferenc Békássy was killed in Bukovina after only two days' fighting. Two months earlier Rupert Brooke had died. This tragedy affected him probably more than any other: so much of his past was raked up by it. He had felt sure that, in normal circumstances, Brooke's aggressive malaise would have faded. 'I feel his state is deplorable,' he had written three years earlier to Ottoline (22 October 1912), 'and something ought to be done to bring him back to ordinary cheerful ways of living . . . I feel it particularly because once when I was very low – in health and spirits – Rupert helped me a great deal, and was very charming. And then besides, how wretched all those quarrels and fatigues are! Such opportunities for delightful intercourse ruined by sheer absurdities! It is too stupid.'

That Rupert should have ended his life with all the old quarrels and intrigues unresolved held a peculiar pathos, and brought home with added force the futility of this war. 'I suppose by the time you get this you will have seen about Rupert's death,' he wrote to Duncan (25 April 1915). 'James is a good deal shattered, and altogether it's a grim affair. It was impossible not to like him, impossible not to hope that he might like one again; and now ... The meaninglessness of Fate is intolerable; it's all muddle and futility. After all the pother of those years of living, to effect – simply nothing. It is like a confused tale, just beginning and then broken off for no reason, and for ever. One hardly knows whether to be sorry even. One is just left with a few odd memories – until they too vanish.'

Lytton tried not to discuss the war with anyone. He opened *The Times* every morning with dread; and in the evenings struggled to immerse himself in books which had little or no association with war – *Memoirs of Lady Hester Stanhope*, H.G. Wells's *Boon*, and *The Voyage Out*. Had the war contributed to Virginia's breakdown? He did not know. He saw everything in terms of the individual and felt that he was growing increasingly sensitive, instead of gradually turning, as he once half-humorously predicted, into a solid rock of a man. Yet he could not show his feelings. He used his writing both to obliterate the surrounding horrors and also, indirectly, to make sense of them. But the writing itself was agonizingly slow. 'The slowness of my work is alarming,' he had written to Henry while writing 'Florence Nightingale' (2 February 1915). 'I fully intend to do another play when this affair is finished, and after that I daresay a novel – by which time, at the present rate of progress, I shall be 75.'

The novel he never attempted, but a Chekhovian *jeu d'esprit*, *Old Lyttoff*, the scene of which was set at Eleanor House, a cottage which Clive and Vanessa had taken, surrounded by farm buildings and a boathouse-studio, near the Sussex village of West Wittering, he composed later that year. It was, he told Bunny Garnett (18 May 1915), 'a horrible melancholy story, ending with a pistol-shot, of course'.

He was re-reading *War and Peace* in Constance Garnett's translation with ever-increasing admiration. 'It is an amazing work,' he told Ottoline (21 August 1915), 'and I really think the best chance of putting a stop to the War would be to make it obligatory for everyone to read it at least once a year. In the meantime I think it ought to be circulated broadcast, though to be sure it would make rather a bulky pamphlet! But, oh dear me! in between whiles, what an ass the poor man makes of himself! "Matter and impertinency mixed", but luckily there's a good deal more matter than impertinency.'

Here was a subject that could be turned to anti-war propaganda. Before he was half-way through the novel, he had sounded out the editor of the *Edinburgh Review*. 'In a moment of rashness I wrote to Harold Cox, suggesting that I write an article on him [Tolstoy],' he told Bunny Garnett (7 August 1915). 'I don't know whether he'll accept, but if he does it'll be a fearful job – rather like writing on God. Have you read "Family Happiness" – in the Ivan Ilytch book? After that, one's left wondering how anyone can dare to write anything else ever again. And then – one remembers – Dostoievsky!'

As usual, Harold Cox countered Lytton's proposal with one of his own. Tolstoy, he replied, was out of date. And Lytton, who in the meantime had been reading Aylmer Maude's biography, experienced some relief at this preposterous decision. 'I have no patience with a man who decides to commit suicide because he can't see the object of existence,' he confided to Bunny Garnett (23 August 1915), 'and then decides not to because everything becomes clear to him after reading the Gospel according to St Mark. But I suppose one may forgive a good deal to the author of War and Peace.'

The outcome of his negotiations was that Harold Cox commissioned 'Voltaire and Frederick the Great', which appeared in the *Edinburgh Review* that October. It was natural, Lytton argued, for everyone's attention to be fixed on soldiers and statesmen in time of war, yet there was solace, and perhaps other advantages, to be gained by turning one's mind to dramas of the past. He offered his nine thousand word essay as an instructive entertainment. In his interpretation, Frederick the Great becomes a one-eyed man who, though observing things close at hand with great clarity, was limited in the perspective that Voltaire, with both eyes open, could command. By showing the most powerful man of action of his day outwitted by the most celebrated writer and philosopher, he hoped to refocus his readers' minds more optimistically. The present-day realists were not Asquith or Lloyd George, but men like Bertrand Russell and, he hoped, Maynard Keynes. 'My Voltaire-Frederick article occupies me to the exclusion of all else,' he reported to Ottoline (21 August 1915), '. . . I feel like a negro slave; whenever I look up from my writing table, I seem to see Mr Harold Cox over my shoulder whirling a cat-o'-nine-tails.'

The atmosphere in the country that summer was oppressive. Rumours of a German invasion were everywhere and women distributed white feathers to men, including farm labourers, who were not in uniform. Against this hostile background Bloomsbury appeared determinedly capricious and irresponsible. Lytton, going down to stay with Clive and Vanessa at Eleanor House, was treated as an old gentleman (author of *Old Lytoff*) and butted into the sea by Duncan with a fearful cacophony of roars and growls.

Eleanor House had been rented the previous year by Clive's friend St John ('Jack') Hutchinson. He was a strawberry-red ebullient barrister famous for his 'deadly' broadmindedness which Clive employed while making his friend's wife his new mistress. Mary Hutchinson was a cousin of Lytton's.[19] Her silences – so unlike Bloomsbury's continual story-telling – were considered examples of the highest sophistication. But though Vanessa felt that Mary was better made for fashionable salons than their own ramshackle world, she welcomed her affair with Clive since it gave a reassuring balance to her own affair with Duncan. 'When Vanessa realized that Duncan loved her and would give her what he could in return,' wrote David Garnett, 'she was wildly happy and so was he.' What she wanted from Duncan was a child to add to her two sons, Julian and Quentin, by Clive. What she feared was that Bunny Garnett's relentless pursuit of artists' models and Slade students, especially James Strachey's future wife Alix Sargant-Florence, would provoke Duncan's jealousy and imperil their triangular relationship.

At Eleanor House, Lytton could see how sensitively Vanessa had weaved together this relationship. The two parties spent a good deal of the time in the boatshed-studio on Chichester harbour, painting Bunny. 'I feel as if I had spent years in that shed with you and Duncan,' Vanessa wrote to him (25 August 1915) after he had left for France with Frankie Birrell. '. . . The life there was quite unlike anything else.' Duncan's portrait gave Bunny 'the beauty of a god', writes Frances Spalding, 'Vanessa portrayed a rather inert, red-nosed young man, colouring his lumbering body a luminescent pink.'[20] But though this unappetising picture may have conveyed her resentment of Bunny's physical appeal for Duncan, she was careful to amuse and flatter Bunny, and defer to him when the three of them were together. 'After all, if you have your nights together it seems to me your days can be spent *à trois*,' she cheerfully told Clive (28 April 1915). Only to Roger Fry did she reveal some of her qualms and uncertainties. 'I can't pretend I was always happy for it's impossible not to mind some things some times' (2 May 1915). Ever since Vanessa turned to Duncan, Roger had felt 'with a fresh bitterness how utterly I am out of it' (21 September 1914). It seemed impossible to devise an emotional arrangement that included everyone all the time, though 'a great deal of a great many kinds of love'[21] was a Bloomsbury ideal.

Every now and then Lytton would return to his family in Hampstead.

The 'Temptations of London' were still very hard for him to resist, and in spite of the sternest resolutions he seldom got to bed before one o'clock each morning. 'Life here seems to continue in an agreeable manner,' he wrote to Bunny Garnett from 6 Belsize Park Gardens (14 July 1915), 'one can't help feeling rather guilty about it, with these surrounding horrors; but there it is . . . a beneficent Deity appears to have provided suitably for every moment of the day and night. You need not suppose that I am idling far from it. I am working hard . . .'

Sometimes, back at The Lacket, he became vulnerable to war pessimism. The spring of 1914 had been idyllic – 'peonies and poppies in the garden, feathered songsters on every bough, and flannelled Marlborough boys in the middle distance'. But this year it was full of unforeseen terrors. 'The Spring has set in with all its hatefulness,' he announced to Henry (6 March 1915). '. . . the birds wake one up at three o'clock in the morning with their incomplete repertories; and Mrs Templeman's fancy turns to thoughts of – I don't know what, but certainly something pretty astringent.' With the summer a continuous firing of guns started up on Salisbury Plain – heavy, massive, booming guns that acted as a perpetual reminder of what, in any case, he could never forget. He likened himself to a solitary desert cactus. 'I am alone – desolate and destitute – in a country of overhanging thunder clouds and heavy emptiness,' he wrote to Francis Birrell (August 1915). 'I've got so low that I can hardly bear the thought of anything else, like the prisoners who beg not to be let out of their sentence.'

In the last weeks of his tenancy, he summoned his family and friends. Pippa and Pernel came down to The Lacket, and so did James with his new girlfriend Alix Sargant-Florence, 'an absolute boy' from Newnham, as well as Clive Bell, Roger Fry who was reading the poems of Mallarmé (a poet missing from *Landmarks in French Literature*) and E.M. Forster[22] who cut Lytton's hair crooked, but recovered himself walking through the 'scabious, harebells and white rabbits' of the Wiltshire Downs. Almost the last visitor was G.E. Moore. 'I feel that in my present state he'll reduce me to tears with his incredible reasonableness,' Lytton admitted to Francis Birrell (August 1915). 'When I last saw him I asked him whether the war had made any difference to him. He paused for thought, and then said – "None. Why should it?" I asked whether he wasn't horrified by it – at any rate at the beginning. But no; he had never felt anything about it at all.'

Lytton had planned to stay on at The Lacket until the beginning of October, but when an opportunity arose for sub-letting the cottage for the last three weeks he seized upon it (being hard up for money), and moved back to London in the second week of September. 'By a stroke of genius I got Forster to do my packing up at The Lacket,' he gleefully told James (17 September 1915), 'and actually to transport the 10 million packages to B.P.G. for me!'

'I'm feeling some twinges of regret, too, at leaving these remote regions,' he confessed to Ottoline (21 August 1915), 'but on the whole I'm not sorry – and anyhow it must be done. Adieu, adieu, adieu, remember me

Your

Lytton.'

TWELVE

War and Peace

'Garsington must be the retreat where we come and knit ourselves together.'

> D.H. Lawrence to Lady Ottoline Morrell (20 June 1915)

'Here one feels the real England – this old house, this countryside – so poignantly.'

> D.H. Lawrence to Edward Marsh (10 November 1915)

'I should beware of Garsington.'

> D.H. Lawrence to Mark Gertler (21 February 1918)

I

GARSINGTON

'I seem to have plunged into others' lives – Roger Fry, Lamb, Lytton, Bertie,' Ottoline Morrell wrote, surveying the year 1915, 'but from some cause they all seem to have come to an end.' Was her health responsible? she wondered. Or those formidable remedies – the devastating programme of red hot needles and the awful diet of starch and radium milkshakes that Dr Combe had prescribed over these pre-war years. It was the radium that alarmed Lytton. 'One day there'll be an explosion on your balcony, if you're not careful,' he had warned her (18 October 1912). 'The boots will rush up – too late! too late! Miladi will have been dissipated into a thousand fragments and the reputation of Dr Combe at last ruined for ever.'

Dr Combe had advised Ottoline to remove herself from London and live in the country – and so had a Swiss psychiatrist she consulted on how to eliminate 'unnecessary thoughts'. Were Roger, Henry, Lytton, Bertie unnecessary? It was sometimes difficult for Ottoline's friends to respond to her condition with sympathetic seriousness. But when Lytton heard that she and Philip had begun looking for a country house, he took the news hard. 'I suppose it won't make much difference to you,' he had remarked to Henry (9 November 1912); 'to me it will be desolating. It was the one

325

centre where I had some chance of seeing amusing and fresh people – my only non-Cambridge point of rapport in London. I was looking forward to rushing up from time to time and mingling with the beau monde! – All dashed. But I'm sure it's the only thing for her health, and I don't think she'll much mind.'

Lytton was equally frank with Ottoline herself. 'I am altogether écrasé by your new regime,' he declared, '– chiefly from a selfish point of view – for I am sure it is the one thing to do you real good, and I think you'll probably on the whole enjoy the country. I had counted so enormously on Bedford Square for the future that I feel quite shattered. London will be almost a perfect blank now.'

Bedford Square had offered romantic adventure in a grey metropolis. He felt like a child cheated of some promised treat. 'I suppose you hardly felt it,' he wrote to Virginia (1 December 1912). 'I think you've never taken to the caviare.'

Ottoline's move to the country, however, was continually being postponed, and the illuminations of Bedford Square shone ever more garishly as the streets filled up with marching soldiers. Yet the war had thrown deeper shadows over Ottoline's life. Some of her friends, considering pacifism to be unpatriotic, refused to see her any more. Though she had ended her quarrel with Roger Fry by planting a passionate kiss on Vanessa's lips ('nice though muddle-headed,' Vanessa felt), she seldom spoke to Roger now. She seldom spoke to Henry Lamb either, and her relationship with Bertie Russell was often being interrupted by his other romances and the pull of his political work. Though Lytton was always curious to know what she was up to ('An escapade with John? Or an amorous adventure with an ice-cream boy?') she saw less of him since he had been living at The Lacket. And now that he had come back to town she was finally preparing to move into the country.

For a long time she had had her eye on a certain house which she used to pass when driving out to Philip's political meetings from Oxford. 'The vision of this house as we passed it one night touched some spot of desire,' she narrates, 'and I exclaimed, "That is the only country house I could live in." It had a wonderful beauty and mystery.' Accordingly, when this house came up for sale in March 1913, Philip Morrell bought it – though they could not take possession for two years. 'So this day our die was cast – for better or worse,' wrote Ottoline in her *Memoirs*. 'That which had been a misty castle was now a solid possession.'

Lytton hardly knew if it were good news or bad: '2 years hence!' he exclaimed (4 April 1913), '– where shall we all be by then? – and what? –

infinitely grey-haired, respectable, crutch-supported antiquities – or bankrupts – or exiles with ruined reputations . . . Or do you think we shall be altogether rejuvenated & sprightly?' Two years later, as the Morrells left Bedford Square, Lytton was back with his family at Belsize Park Gardens reflecting that a misty castle in Oxfordshire might be a very agreeable place to hide out.

Garsington Manor was a Tudor house built in Cotswold stone and set in two hundred acres of garden and farmland. Here Ottoline was to live for fourteen years. Here she became a legend. It was Bedford Square all over again, but on a far more spectacular scale. The early months of 1915 she spent supervising the redecoration of the house and the landscaping of the garden. She removed floorboards, ripped out windows, replaced doors. She brought in a wonderful confusion of Chelsea porcelain, Chippendale chairs, eighteenth-century Italian furniture, Persian carpets, Samarkand rugs, a Welsh oak dresser, a huge Chinese jar of pot-pourri, and her collection of contemporary British paintings by Charles Conder, Duncan Grant, Augustus John, Henry Lamb, Gilbert and Stanley Spencer. She dug up the garden, creating dark corridors and bright flower-beds, planting yew and box hedges, an avenue of lime trees, cypresses, and brilliant congregations of phlox, marigolds, sunflowers, snapdragons. She transformed the old fishpond into a miniature Italianate lake overlooked by ranks of Classical statues. By June everything was more or less ready and the old manor lifted its mullioned windows, its fair stone, among the trees and foliage. 'I imagine wonder,' Lytton wrote (8 June 1915), '– ponds, statues, yew hedges, gold paint . . . I'm sure you needn't be afraid of my Critical Eye – for the simple reason that it won't be able to find anything to criticize!'

Nevertheless Ottoline was apprehensive of her friends' reactions, particularly the reaction of Lytton, whose malice at other people's expense she had so often enjoyed. On 16 June, her forty-second birthday, she launched Garsington with a small party, inviting Bertie Russell, Gilbert Cannan and Mark Gertler, D.H. Lawrence and his wife Frieda – but not Lytton and his Bloomsbury friends. Cannan had lent her *Sons and Lovers* and *The White Peacock* the previous autumn, and she had been enthralled by the re-creation of Nottinghamshire and its mining villages – though worlds apart socially, she and Lawrence had grown up within twenty miles of each other. Then Bertie and Ottoline had read *The Prussian Officer* that winter. 'I am amazed how good it is,' she told Bertie, '– quite wonderful some of the Stories – He has great passion – and is . . . a far better writer than Cannan.' Early in 1915 she invited Lawrence to Bedford Square. Like Lytton, he had recently grown a beard. It was the colour of strong tea and worn as a protest against the false standards of manhood raised by the war. 'He was a slight man, lithe and delicately built, his pale face rather overshadowed by his beard and red hair falling over his forehead,' Ottoline saw. '. . . I was extraordinarily happy and at ease . . . it was impossible not to feel expanded and stimulated by the companionship of anyone so alive . . . I felt when I was with him as if I had really at last found a friend.'[1]

Lawrence too was charmed by Lady Ottoline. Though 'I don't belong to any class now', as he told E.M. Forster (28 January 1915), he was still 'perceptively over-eager in aristocratic company', Katherine Mansfield had sharply observed. 'It is rather splendid that you are a great lady,' he was soon writing to Ottoline (c. 11 February 1915). '. . . I really do honour your birth . . . I would give a great deal to have been born an aristocrat.' Previously he had been taken up, along with Rupert Brooke, as one of Eddie Marsh's band of struggling writers and artists. But Brooke's death, which lit up Marsh's patriotism, filled Lawrence with a sense of futility. 'I cannot get any sense of an enemy – only of a disaster,' he had written to Eddie Marsh (13 September 1914). '. . . it is not *fine* but an awful necessity that these young men lose their chance of life . . . I used to think war glorious . . . You *are* not to hate the Germans, you can understand how it is – We are frightfully nice people, but it is *so* difficult for the English to understand anything that is *not* English.' His position was made still more awkward by his recent marriage to a German Baroness following a controversial divorce from her first English husband and separation from her children. In his misery Lawrence yearned to escape from England. With his friends Katherine Mansfield, Middleton Murry and others, he invented a Coleridgean dream of setting up an ideal community in Florida or on some faraway island, which prospered in their minds until his wife Frieda arrived with some maps of islands.

Lawrence was armed with a powerful fundamentalist vocabulary, but the ingredients of his fundamentalism were often changing. Meeting Ottoline, getting to know Bertrand Russell, he cancelled his utopian island-plans and conceived a new fantasy of sowing the seeds of a regenerated England at Garsington – so much nearer than Florida if no less far-fetched. 'I want you to form the nucleus of a new community which shall start a new life amongst us – a life in which the only riches is integrity of character,' he instructed Ottoline (1 February 1915). '. . . It is communism based, not on poverty, but on riches, not on humility, but on pride, not on sacrifice but upon complete fulfilment in the flesh of all strong desire, not on forfeiture but upon inheritance, not on heaven but on earth.' Having elected Ottoline as his new patron, he felt nervous of her other recruits, such as Lytton who, Ottoline told him, was demolishing Christianity in the person of Cardinal Manning and setting up a religion in the flesh of his own desire. 'Curse the Strachey who asks for a new religion – the greedy dog,' Lawrence added in the same letter to Ottoline. 'He wants another juicy bone for his soul, does he? Let him start to fulfil what religion we have.'

Probably there were 'enough people to make a start with', Lawrence calculated. 'We cuckoos, we shall plume ourselves, in such a nest of a fine bird,' he assured Ottoline. But when these decent people, these plumed cuckoos, Cannan and Gertler, Bertie and Ottoline, Frieda and Lawrence himself, began nesting at Garsington that June, a terrible flurry and commotion broke out. Resenting Ottoline's new role as Lawrence's muse, Frieda quarrelled violently with her 'Lorenzo' and quit the house, leaving Lawrence, an 'unhappy, distraught, pathetic figure', to trail after her back to London.

Three weeks later, Lytton made his first entry into Garsington accompanied by Duncan and Vanessa. They were welcomed by Ottoline swathed in a Turkish cloak and hung with ropes of pearls. Vanessa was to take the line that Ottoline 'has a terrifically energetic and vigorous character with a definite rather bad taste,' as she later (c. May 1916) explained to Roger Fry. This 'was different from having any creative power – but Lytton thinks Garsington a creation'. And in truth Lytton was amazed by what he saw. Ottoline's personality, reinforced by the influences of Bakst and Beardsley, overwhelmed the old mixture of seventeenth-century and Victorian baronial styles. Instead of varnishing the Elizabethan oak panelling, or leaving it sombre and bare, she had defied tradition and covered it with vivid coats of paint, dove-grey in the hall, sea-green (matching her eyes) in one of the drawing-rooms, and in the other a Chinese scarlet that occasionally matched her hair. Silk curtains, patterned hangings and an abundance of cushions gave an atmosphere of oriental magnificence to the rooms which were filled with the aroma of pot-pourri and cloves and orris root from bowls of incense on the side-tables and window-sills. Garsington was, as Ottoline herself wrote, 'a theatre, where week after week a travelling company would arrive and play their parts'. But was it a stage for tragedy, comedy, history, pastoral, pastoral-comical, historical-pastoral, tragical-historical, tragical-comical-historical-pastoral? Probably the last. But whatever the genre Ottoline was always the star, whether pursued as she stalked from scene to scene by her trotting pack of pug dogs or, when in the geometry of the garden, pursuing a dishevelled peacock, its quills drily rattling among the gallery of antique statuary and stone pineapples or uttering its screams from the branches of an ilex above her nasal laughter.

Ottoline was less wealthy than her visitors supposed and whenever a choice arose between a new statue or a second bathroom, the statue not the bathroom was added, and exoticism prevailed over comfort. So Garsington expanded into a Renaissance court or Arcadian colony rather than a home, and into a fantasy in her writers' imaginations – another Castle of Otranto or Nightmare Abbey. Leonard Woolf was to recognize its counterpart in Peacock's *Crotchet Castle*; D.H. Lawrence thought it 'like the Boccaccio place where they told all the *Decamerone*'; to Aldous Huxley it appeared as an Oriental palace from a story by Scheherazade; to Desmond MacCarthy it looked like 'a wonderful lacquered box, scarlet and gold, containing life-size dolls in amazing dresses'; and Lytton called it 'Shandygaff Hall'.

Though Garsington was flamboyantly Ottoline's creation, she had also created a magic reflection of her visitors' dreams and illusions. Whenever these dreams and illusions vanished, her guests would take their revenge on her. Where Lawrence saw a sacred precinct for England's mystical rebirth, Lytton looked for the reincarnation of Madame du Deffand and a miraculous transplantation of eighteenth-century French civilization. Behind the silvery-grey stone front, the lofty elms and tall iron gates, he pictured another Sceaux 'with its endless succession of entertainments and conversations – supper-parties and water-parties, concerts and masked balls, plays in the little theatre and picnics under the great trees of the park'.

Lytton wanted Ottoline to reach maturity as one of the leaders of contemporary society. It was here at Garsington – where the prime minister, entering with Maynard Keynes, was announced as 'Mr Keynes and another gentleman' – that literature and the arts could secure their true worth. It was here that Bloomsbury could mingle with the floating company of diplomats and aristocrats and practise 'those difficult arts which make the wheels of human intercourse run smoothly – the arts of tact and temper, of frankness and sympathy, of delicate compliment and exquisite self-abnegation'. Through their literature, their art, their manners, they would be an example to the world. This was Lytton's dream.

But the radiant atmosphere of Sceaux was only parodied, and the gifts of tact and temper proved beyond Ottoline's placatory powers. Instead of recapturing the grace of Madame du Deffand's *salon* – like 'dancers balanced on skates, gliding, twirling, interlacing, over the thinnest ice' – they floundered and pushed and fell into envious gossip and bickering. It was not delicate compliment and exquisite self-abnegation that were practised, but perpetual rumour and intrigue.

Lytton's Critical Eye soon found much to fix upon. 'It was not particularly enchanting,' he complained to David Garnett (14 July 1915). 'Such fussifications going on all the time – material, mental, spiritual . . . *Dona nobis pacem, dona nobis pacem*, was all I could murmur. The house is a regular galanty-show, whatever that may be; very like Ottoline herself, in fact – very remarkable, very impressive, patched, gilded and preposterous. The Bedford Square interior does not suit an Elizabethan Manor house in the wilds of Oxfordshire. It has all been reproduced, and indeed redoubled. The pianola too, with Philip, infinitely Philipine, performing, and acrobatic dances on the lawn. In despair I went to bed, and was woken up by a procession circumnavigating my bed, candles in hand . . . the rear brought up by the Witch of Endor. Oh! *Dona nobis pacem!*'

To Ottoline herself Lytton sent a letter by the same post telling her how deliriously enjoyable Garsington had been – and to prove that this was not simply politeness, he invited himself back there a fortnight later.

The other guests on this second visit were Mary Hutchinson and her lover Clive Bell to whom Garsington appeared a 'fluttering parrot-house of greens, reds and yellows'. They came with a young art student, Barbara Hiles, and an ex-Newnham undergraduate, Faith Bagenal, who were encouraged to scamper off together leaving their elders to discourse on life and literature. A sudden loneliness descended upon Lytton: 'a sort of eighteenth-century grim gaiety comes upon me, and I can hardly distinguish people from pugs,' he confided to Bunny Garnett (25 July 1915). 'I wish they'd all turn into embroidered parrots, neatly framed and hanging on the wall – but they won't; they will keep prancing round, snorting, and (one after another) trying to jump up into one's lap. It's most tiresome – one pushes them down in vain – the wriggling wretches! . . .'

Ottoline was a dog person, Lytton a cat person: in such simple ways the world divides. It is divided too by other people's expectations of us. Lytton had encouraged Ottoline in their games together to treat him as a French count. He played the part nicely but felt restricted by such repetitive casting. Besides, they could not play games all the time. 'Now I must go down on to the lawn,' he continued to Bunny Garnett, 'and have tea with them all, and practise my grim gaiety again with them, as if I were a M. le Marquis circa 1770. What fun it would be to be one really! – Or at least infinitely convenient. But I'm not. I'm circa 1915 or nothing . . .'

To Ottoline he then (31 July 1915) wrote to express his gratitude and delight. 'I find even my vigorous health taking on new forces, so that I am seen bounding along the glades of Hampstead like a gazelle or a Special Constable.' He was looking forward, so he assured her, to many more Garsington weekends. 'I shall come again,' the letter concluded.

He did go there again, very often, almost always leaving behind him the same backwash of alternating flattery and complaint. These pages of glorification and disparagement, when read through eighty years later, show Lytton diverting ridicule from himself as an inexplicably persistent guest by ridiculing Ottoline as an overwhelmingly possessive hostess. Virginia, who was the recipient of so many of Lytton's skits on Ottoline, and who also disparaged her while insisting that 'she deserves some credit for keeping her ship in full sail', wondered at Lytton's double-attitude. It matched what she called 'the blend of one's own mind of suavity & sweetness with contempt & bitterness'. She questioned the suavity rather than the bitterness. 'I suppose the danger lies in becoming too kind,' she wrote to Lytton (14 September 1919). 'I think you're a little too inclined that way already – take the case of Ottoline. It seems to me a dark one.'

Some justification of Lytton's strategy was to follow his death when Ottoline proudly showed Virginia the letters he had written to her. 'Now Lytton is dead how comforting it is to be with you who loved him. We must always hoard the memory of him up together,' Virginia answered (8 February 1932), ' . . . with you, who loved him, some reality comes back.' Ottoline always loved hearing from Lytton. 'Oh, if you only knew the happiness your letters bring!' she had written to him (22 March 1912). Virginia could see from this correspondence how Ottoline had depended on Lytton's love, demanding more and more of it. 'I live in dread', Ottoline told him after Roger Fry's estrangement (25 October 1912), 'of you also shaking me and casting me off. Oh please don't. I should mind it too much.' So he had reassured her that he would always be there. 'Our great-grand-children will see us gallivanting down Bond Street as nonagenarians, and gnash their teeth with envy.' It was fantasy, of course, and in the narrative of their actual lives they would be drawn in different directions. But Ottoline had felt she needed Lytton's adoration to gush forth like a cascading hot tap; and Lytton needed to moderate this steamy flow of sentiment with jets of criticism.

Garsington was a blessing for Lytton. A mixed blessing. It provided 'the mixture he wants of town and country', Vanessa thought. But the mixture soon curdled. Virginia 'was astonished that he wrote so affectionately to me', Ottoline later noted in her diary (23 November 1932). '. . . I was very much afraid that she would be slightly jealous, so that I said all I could about Lytton's devotion to her.' So Virginia entered the conspiracy to protect Ottoline. She had been 'looking through his old letters, but cant find the ones we want,' she lied (14 February 1932), '. . . you need never doubt his affection for you.'

Would it have been better to cast her off as Henry and Roger had done, or caricature her openly like Augustus, Duncan and Simon Bussy? This was how Ottoline moved artists' imaginations. She felt bitter at the published treacheries of Aldous Huxley and Osbert Sitwell, Gilbert Cannan and D.H. Lawrence. In his partial portrait of her as the macabre Hermione Roddice ('tall and rather terrible, ghastly') in *Women in Love*, Lawrence attributed her difficulties to an absence of natural sufficiency concealed beneath her dominating will. 'There was a terrible void, a lack, a deficiency of being within her. And she wanted someone to close up this deficiency. To close it up forever.'

Women in Love was to end their friendship which already seemed to be in retreat by the summer of 1915. One reason was Lawrence's experience of meeting Ottoline's and Bertie's friends, particularly their Bloomsbury friends. Forster turned out to be 'bound hand and foot bodily', and so reticent, so moribund, as to be useless for their revolutionary purposes. 'The man is dying of inanition.' Duncan Grant, though likeable, was foolishly wasting away his life. 'He looks as if he dissipates and certainly doesn't enjoy it,' Lawrence explained to Ottoline. 'Tell him to stop.' But there was no stopping these people. Even David Garnett, who was 'adorable', had fallen in with that 'horrible and unclean' Francis Birrell. 'You can come away, and grow whole, and love a woman, and marry her, and make life good and be happy,' he advised Garnett (19 April 1915), '. . . in the name of everything that is called love, leave this set and stop this blasphemy against love.' Russell had taken him to Cambridge in March 1915 and introduced him to Keynes one evening. Seeing him next morning at eleven o'clock in pyjamas nauseated Lawrence. 'I am sick with the knowledge of the prevalence of evil, as if it were some insidious disease,' he wrote to Ottoline (24 March, 19 April 1915). '. . . I *will not* have people like this – I had rather be alone. They made me dream in the night of a beetle that bites like a scorpion . . . It is enough to drive one frantic . . . Sometimes I think I can't stand England any more.' This meeting 'had been one of the crises in my life', he told David Garnett. It was the climax of a nightmare that had begun to steal over him 'slightly before, in the Stracheys'.

Although Lawrence had met his brother James and two of his sisters at Cambridge, he had never seen Lytton himself until they unexpectedly encountered each other one Friday night early in November that year at a party in the Earl's Court studio of Dorothy Brett, the painter.[2] Arriving there late, Lytton was thrust into the centre of a large crowd – Brett herself looking, with her *retroussé* nose and childish hands, about seventeen (less than half her age), and spoken of as the 'virgin aunt' of her two companions, Mark Gertler, who rushed about the room acting as assistant-host, and another artist Dora Carrington 'like a wild moorland pony', as Ottoline described her, 'with a shock of fair hair, uncertain and elusive eyes, rather awkward in her movements', standing speechless next to a large silent dog. While poor Brett, terribly deaf, laboured energetically at the pianola, her drunken guests lay around the studio – 'dreadful women on divans trying to persuade dreadful men to kiss them, in foreign accents (apparently put on for the occasion),' Lytton afterwards told his brother James (8 November 1915).

Among this jumble of humanity, Lawrence and Frieda caught his attention. 'There were a great many people I didn't know at all,' Lytton wrote to Bunny Garnett (10 November 1915), 'and others whom I only knew by repute, among the latter, the Lawrences, whom I examined carefully and closely for several hours, though I didn't venture to have myself introduced. I was surprised to find that I liked her looks very much – she actually seemed (there's no other word for it) a lady; as for him I've rarely seen anyone so pathetic, miserable, ill, and obviously devoured by internal distresses. He behaved to everyone with the greatest cordiality, but I noticed for a second a look of intense disgust and hatred flash into his face . . . caused by – ah! – whom? Katherine Mansfield was also there, and took my fancy a good deal.'[3]

What caused Lawrence this intense disgust on seeing Lytton, and brought on his crisis after meeting 'that satyr Keynes', as Ottoline called him, was the Bloomsbury cult of 'higher sodomy'. Lawrence was preaching a contrary creed: 'The great living experience of every man is his adventure into the woman,' he had exhorted Russell (24 February 1915). '. . . The man embraces in the woman all that is not himself, and from that one resultant, from that embrace, comes every new action.' The actions and reactions in Lawrence's life – his urge to seek new places, to form new societies, to find the pentecostal inspiration of a new life – were impelled by the need for self-escape. Women, he liked to believe, were wholly alien to men, and the great adventure into them amounted to a total loss of self in the dark unconscious of the womb. He was ill and disgusted by himself as well as by homosexuality which duplicated the ill self instead of transcending or obliterating it. Yet he was sexually aroused by the act of buggery which did not violate the womb, and 'something dreadful was going on inside him', David Garnett saw, as he contemplated these Bloomsbury friends of Ottoline and Russell. 'He was in the throes of some dark religious crisis and seemed to shrink in size with the effort of summoning up all his powers, all his spiritual strength.' From this struggle emerged the covert smuggling of the act of buggery into some of his novels, and the ideal allegiance in his life of male blood brotherhood which he attempted to impose on Middleton Murry and Bertrand Russell.

'Lawrence has the same feeling against sodomy as I have,' Russell explained to Ottoline; 'you had nearly made me believe there is no great harm in it, but I have reverted.' In these early war years Lawrence was to take the place of Wittgenstein in Russell's emotional life. 'Lawrence is wonderfully lovable,' he told Ottoline. '. . . I love him more and more.' The two of them planned to give a series of lectures in London during the summer of 1915. Russell was to speak on ethics; Lawrence would tackle immortality. But already Lawrence had begun to feel that both Ottoline and Russell were tainted – 'they filch my life,' was how he phrased it to Lady Cynthia Asquith, whom he saw as a possible replacement for Ottoline as his patron. Tearing up Russell's lectures, he wrote to Lady Cynthia (16 August 1915): 'I've got a real bitterness in my soul, just now, as if Russell and Lady Ottoline were traitors – they are traitors. They betray the real truth . . . I had hoped to get a little nucleus of living people together. But I think it is no good.'

What brought Lawrence back to Russell and Ottoline, and drafted Bloomsbury to his cause, was the mounting war fever. It was the autumn of Edith Cavell's execution, the Gallipoli failure and Winston Churchill's resignation from the government. At the front, British casualties exceeded half-a-million, and in London the big Zeppelin raids were beginning. The Bishop of London spoke of 'a kind of glorying in London at being allowed to take our little share of danger in the Zeppelin raids'. There was a rising demand for compulsory conscription. In private conversation at Garsington, the belletrist Augustine Birrell expressed surprise at so much fuss made over the soldiery. 'After all, the men out there will be returning some day.' In a public speech, however, delivered in his capacity as Chief Secretary for Ireland, he declared that the government should 'forbid the use, during the war, of poetry'.

The most dramatic act of literary censorship was the prosecution and suppression of Lawrence's novel *The Rainbow*, ostensibly on grounds of obscenity, but chiefly because of its denunciation of war. Clement Shorter asked readers of *The Sphere* whether Lesbianism was 'a fit subject for family fiction'; James Douglas in *The Star* decided that 'this kind of book has no right to exist' and called for preventative action from 'the sanitary inspector of literature'; and J.C. Squire, writing under the pseudonym of 'Solomon Eagle' in the *New Statesman*, suggested that Lawrence might be 'under the spell of German psychologists'. It was Ottoline who rallied Bloomsbury to Lawrence's defence, and Bloomsbury, recognizing a common enemy in police censorship, responded. While Philip Morrell raised questions in Parliament about the book's suppression, David Garnett wrote angrily to Augustine Birrell, E.M. Forster signed a letter of protest to *The Times* which was not published, and Lytton wrote ironically in favour of suppression to the *New Statesman* which suppressed his letter. 'It seems strange that they [the police] should have the leisure and energy for this sort of activity at the present moment,' he commented in a letter to Bunny Garnett (10 November 1915).

'But no doubt the authorities want to show us that England stands for Liberty. Clive is trying to get up an agitation about it in the newspapers but I doubt if he'll have much success. We interviewed that little worm Jack Squire, who quite failed to see the point: he thought that as in his opinion the book wasn't a good one it was difficult for him to complain about its suppression. Damn his eyes! In vain we pointed out that it was a question of principle, and that whether that particular book was good or mediocre was irrelevant – he couldn't see it. At last, however, he agreed to say a few words about it in his blasted paper – on one condition – that the book had not been suppressed because it mentioned sapphism – he had heard that that was the reason – and in that case, well, of course, it was quite impossible for the *New Statesman* to defend perversity.'

Lawrence made his last two visits to Garsington that November while the campaign was going on. 'It will always be a sort of last vision of England to me,' he wrote to Ottoline (11 November 1915), 'the beauty of England, the wonder of this terrible autumn.' It was his premature farewell to England before misanthropy rose up and he called down fire and brimstone on his native land. Driving from Garsington 'with the autumn falling and rustling to pieces, I am so sad', he told Lady Cynthia Asquith (9 November 1915), ' . . . this house of the Ottolines – It is England – my God, it breaks my soul . . . these elm trees, the grey wind with yellow leaves – it is so awful, the being gone from it altogether, one must be blind henceforth.'

Over Christmas, Garsington filled up with Bloomsberries – Maynard and Lytton, Clive and Vanessa with their two sons – and there were games and a dance and a charade, 'The Life and Death of Lytton' in which all the children acted. Then on Christmas Day there was a grand festivity in one of the barns, which was rigged up with decorations on a Christmas tree, 'and all the children in the village came and had tea there', Lytton wrote to his mother (28 December 1915). 'It was really a wonderful affair. There were a hundred children, and each one had a present from the tree; they were of course delighted – especially as they had never known anything of the kind before, since hitherto there haven't been any "gentry" in the village. Every detail was arranged by Ottoline, whose energy and good-nature are astonishing. Then in the evening there was a little dance here, with the servants and some of the farmers' daughters, etc. which was great fun, her Ladyship throwing herself into it with tremendous brio. It takes a daughter of a thousand Earls to carry things off in that manner.'

Within a year, Ottoline had changed from a defender of *The Rainbow* to the prosecutor of *Women in Love*. Russell 'wrote to me that "our ways are separate". Soit – I never wrote to him again,' Lawrence explained to Forster (30 May 1916). '. . . Lytton Strachey is the chief friend of Ottoline's just now . . . Lytton, Duncan Grant, and all that set . . . What they will do now, God knows.'

2

CONSCRIPTION

'My life here has been rather dissipated of late,' Lytton wrote to David Garnett from Belsize Park Gardens (8 November 1915). One of his dissipations was a new series of German lessons under the supervision of an astringent English spinster in Mecklenburgh Square, whom he called on once a week. In the intervals he would struggle with Heine; but it proved uphill work. Apart from this, 'I am also engaged on a short life of Dr Arnold (of Rugby), which is a distinctly lugubrious business, though my hope is to produce something out of it which may be entertaining,' he wrote to his mother (12 December 1915), who was spending the winter in Menton. 'He was a self-righteous blockhead, but unlike most of his kind, with enough energy and determination in him to do a good deal of damage – as our blessed Public Schools bear witness!'

Still it was an active if idle winter. 'I attend lectures by Maynard and Mr Shaw,' he told Francis Birrell (November 1915).

'The latter function was an odd one, Bertie in the chair, and a large audience eager for a pacifist oration and all that's most advanced – and poor dear Mr Shaw talking about "England" with trembling lips and gleaming eyes, and declaring that his one wish was that we should first beat the Germans, and then fight them again, and then beat them again, and again, and again! He was more like a nice old-fashioned Admiral on a quarter-deck than anything else. And the newspapers are so stupid that, simply because he's Mr Shaw, they won't report him – instead of running him as our leading patriot.'

The dusky streets of London, so invitingly blacked out, had grown extraordinarily attractive to him. 'How I adore the romance and agitation of them!' he exclaimed in a letter to Ottoline (21 January 1916). 'Almost too much I fear!' Periodically he would feel a need for the more peaceful attractions of the country, spending several weekends with Clive and Vanessa Bell at Eleanor House, with Leonard and Virginia Woolf down at Asheham, and with Ottoline and her court at Garsington. 'The country is certainly the place for peaceful happiness – if that's what one wants,' he explained to Ottoline (24 February 1916). 'I think one wants it about half the time; and the other half *un*peaceful happiness. But happiness *all* the time.'

Much of the talk during these winter weeks centred around conscription. To solve the task of bringing enough men to the Colours, within a country the bulk of whose population was still believed to be hostile to the idea of military service, the Government had, in October 1915, started the notorious Derby Scheme. This was a voluntary plan, on the continental pattern, the purpose of which was to persuade men of serviceable age to 'attest' – that is, to undertake to join up whenever called upon to do so – by means of a moral rather than a legal obligation. Almost all Bloomsbury was opposed to the blandishment and blackmail on which the Derby Scheme operated, and felt alarmed by the compulsory conscription that was threatened if this scheme failed. 'The conscription crisis has been agitating these quarters considerably,' Lytton had written to James from Garsington as early as 23 September. '. . . Some say that Lloyd George is verging towards the madhouse cell. Others affirm that E. Grey is "immovable" against conscription. Personally I feel despondent – about that and most other things.'

By December, the Derby Scheme was seen to have failed, and, in the first week of January 1916 the Government introduced a Military Service Bill, under which all single men were automatically deemed to have enlisted and been transferred to the Reserve, from which they could be called up when needed. The Labour members of the Coalition Government threatened resignation – then withdrew their threat. Nothing then stood in the way of the Bill, though Lytton still hoped for some last-minute uprising against it. 'Philip [Morrell] now seems to think that it may take a fortnight or even 3 weeks getting through the committee stage,' he informed James; 'and in that case isn't it still possible that something should be done? Surely there ought to be a continual stream of leaflets and pamphlets. Also if possible meetings all over the country, and signatures collected against the bill.'

To help disseminate anti-conscription propaganda, Lytton joined the

No Conscription Fellowship or NCF as it was called, and the National Council against Conscription, or NCC – the two societies that had been formed to resist the Act, to campaign for pacifism, and, subsequently, to urge that out-and-out conscientious objectors be given unconditional exemption from participating in the war, instead of being forced either into prison or into government occupations. Several other members of Bloomsbury including James Strachey – recently sacked from the *Spectator* by the militaristic St Loe – assisted at the NCC offices in Bride Lane, addressing envelopes, sticking on stamps, and writing leaflets. One of these (Leaflet No. 3), which stated that the Government's motive for bringing in compulsory service was to prevent strikes and crush labour, was drafted by Lytton.

CONSCRIPTION

WHY they want it, and why they say they want it.
THEY SAY THEY WANT IT to punish the slackers
THEY WANT IT to punish the strikers.
THEY SAY THEY WANT IT to crush Germany
THEY WANT IT to crush Labour.
THEY SAY THEY WANT IT to free Europe
THEY WANT IT to enslave England.
DON'T LET THEM GET WHAT THEY WANT BECAUSE THEY KEEP SAYING THEY WANT SOMETHING DIFFERENT.
The Cat kept saying to the Mouse that she was a highminded person, and if the Mouse would only come a little nearer they could both get the cheese.
The Mouse said 'Thank you Pussy, it's not the cheese you want; it's my skin!'

Shortly after this leaflet had been printed, H.W. Massingham[4] saw it, decided it was seditious, and rushed round to the Bride Lane office to get it withdrawn from circulation. Sir John Simon, who had resigned from Asquith's Cabinet to lead the opposition to the Military Service Bill, and who, according to Maynard, was rather regretting his hasty decision, also disapproved. And so it was agreed to send out no further copies, though half-a-million had by then been distributed. The *Morning Post* had already got hold of a copy and blazoned it across a page of anti-pacifist propaganda. After quoting some sentences from Lytton's leaflet, the paper demanded: 'Would it be possible to imagine a more wanton and malicious indulgence in false witness?' 'Queer fellows they are,' he remarked to Ottoline on reading the article. There seemed no intelligible point of contact between the two sides.

It was a comfort for Lytton to find himself in a solid phalanx of agreement with his friends. Bloomsbury, as a whole, believed that the war had been entered into to refute militarism, and that to introduce compulsory military service would contradict Britain's original intentions. Distrusting the political management of the war, they favoured, from 1916 onwards, the policy of a negotiated peace settlement. In his prepared statement as a conscientious objector, Lytton explained how he had arrived at his pacifist conclusion. Before 1916, he declared:

'I was principally concerned with literary and speculative matters; but, with the war, the supreme importance of international questions has been forced upon my attention. My opinions have been for many years strongly critical of the whole structure of society; and after a study of the diplomatic situation, and of the literature, both controversial and philosophic, arising out of the war, they developed naturally into those I now hold. My convictions as to my duty with regard to the war have not been formed either rashly or lightly; and I shall not act against these convictions whatever the consequences may be.'

Among the men in command of political operations, few were moved by philosophical ideals towards decent ends. Woodrow Wilson meant well, but was a simpleton; Clemenceau appeared to be a worldly and ambitious cynic; and as for Lloyd George, Lytton's one ardent desire, he told Francis Birrell, was, once the war had ended, to see him publicly castrated at the foot of Nurse Cavell's statue. Nor did Churchill inspire him with confidence.

> Though Time from History's pages much may blot,
> Some things there are can never be forgot;
> And in Gallipoli's delicious name,
> Wxxxxxx, your own shall find eternal fame.

Asquith, too, though in some ways more appealing than Churchill, was equally unprincipled and, Lytton had come to feel, of even vaster incompetence. 'Nothing is more damning than his [Asquith's] having told Maynard (who told me of it at the time) that "the Conscriptionists were fools", and that he was giving them enough rope to hang themselves by", three weeks before he was himself forced by them to bring in a bill for

Conscription,' Lytton later commented in an essay on Asquith (May 1918). 'If it was true (as Maynard assured me it was, on what I gathered was the best authority) that in December 1916, after he had been turned out with ignominy and treachery by Lloyd George and Bonar Law, he was willing and in fact anxious to act under them as Lord Chancellor, his wits must have sunk even lower than his sense of decency. I think eventually he must have grown too positively fuddled – with too much food and drink, too much power, too much orotund speechifying, too many of those jovial adventures of the "lugubre individu".'

Lytton believed that the world was still governed not by extremists, but by moderate men. The sight of these men, with their pin-stripe plausibility, controlling events, posed for him a profoundly menacing spectacle. It was a revelation of what the multitudes of ordinary respectable men and women were capable of thinking. Amid the bigotry and hysteria of war, people on both sides too easily relinquished their individuality and with it their humanity. Even before conscription, the British Government had undertaken to improve recruitment by means just as discreditable as those of the Germans. 'Is your "best boy" wearing Khaki? . . . If your young man neglects his duty to his King and Country, the time may come when he will NEGLECT YOU!' This was advocacy 'limited neither by the meagre bounds of the actual nor by the tiresome dictates of common sense'. A form of patriotism which justified mendacity to ensure national unity sprang not from too much love of one's country, Lytton argued, but from too little. A propagandist now himself, he used similar methods to popularize his convictions. In 'The Claims of Patriotism', an article published in the pacifist periodical *War and Peace*, he wrote:

'The lover who loved his mistress with such passionate ecstasy that he would feed her on nothing but moonshine, with disastrous consequences – did he, perhaps, in reality, not love her quite enough? That, certainly, is a possible reading of the story. And it might be as well for patriots . . . to reflect occasionally on that sad little apologue, and to remember that nothing sweetens love – even love of one's country – so much as a little common sense – and, one might add, even a little cynicism.'

To Lytton's commonsensical and cynical mind, the passing that spring of the new Conscription Bill for establishing National Service made Britain as ardent a supporter of the principle of militarism as Germany herself. 'What difference', he asked, 'would it make if the Germans *were* here?' His quarrel was with the whole militarist point of view, whether emanating from allied or enemy officialdom.

During the eighteenth century Voltaire had waged a constant fight against religion – then the dominating factor in human affairs. Stendhal had continued this struggle into the nineteenth century. By the early twentieth century, the 'powers of darkness' were no longer led by theologians, but by their modern counterparts, political warmongers. It was with this breed of men that the Voltaire of the twentieth century had to do battle. Despite the wartime rash of intolerance, Lytton believed that the odds were not set quite so heavily against him as against previous crusaders. War did not obsess or unnerve the human mind so ceaselessly as religious superstition. To moderate men with their limitations of average passions and average thoughts, it might still appear that 'militarism and the implications of militarism – the struggles and ambitions of opposing States, the desire for national power, the terror of national ruin, the armed organization of humanity – that all this seems inevitable with the inevitability of a part of the world's very structure; and yet it may well be, too, that they are wrong, that it is not so, that it is the "fabric of a vision" which will melt suddenly and be seen no more'.

If, as Lytton believed, war was seen as justifiable only as the last means of defence and never as an assertion of nationalism, then the days of aggressive patriotism were already numbered. Lloyd George stalked the political arena like some prehistoric monster, doomed to extinction. At the end of the war Lytton was to write to Maynard: 'To my mind the ideal thing would be to abolish reparations altogether – but of course that is not practical politics – at any rate just yet; perhaps in the end it will become so.'

These were opinions on which nearly all his friends, from Maynard Keynes to Bertrand Russell, seemed in agreement. 'Bertie was most sympathetic,' Lytton wrote to Ottoline (31 December 1915) on the eve of the introduction of the first Military Service Bill. 'I went to see him this morning and we had lunch with Maynard in an extraordinary underground tunnel, with city gents sitting on high stools like parrots on perches, somewhere near Trafalgar Square. Maynard is certainly a wonder. He has not attested, and says he has no intention of doing so. He couldn't tell us much – except that McKenna is still wobbling; but he seemed to think it not unlikely that he and Runciman would resign – in which case he would resign too and help them to fight it.'

But after compulsory military service had been introduced Reginald McKenna, Chancellor of the Exchequer, made no move to resign; nor did the President of the Board of Trade, Walter Runciman; and nor did

Maynard. Certainly both Lytton and Russell felt that he had 'ratted', and they both pressed him to leave the Treasury, reasoning that it must be impossible to reconcile his sympathy for conscientious objectors with the job of demonstrating how to kill Germans as cheaply as possible: 'the maximum slaughter at the minimum expense'. Maynard now found himself situated awkwardly between his Bloomsbury friends and his colleagues at the Treasury.

On 20 February, Lytton placed on Maynard's plate at Gordon Square 'the conscientious objector's equivalent of a white feather'. This was a newspaper report of a violent militaristic speech by the Financial Secretary to the Treasury Edwin Montagu – with a short covering note: 'Dear Maynard, Why are you still at the Treasury? Yours, Lytton.' In a letter to his brother James (22 February 1916), Lytton described Maynard's reaction: 'He really *was* rather put out when he read the extract . . . He said that 2 days before he had a long conversation with Montague [*sic*] in which that personage had talked violently in exactly the opposite way . . . I said . . . what was the use of his going on imagining that he was doing any good with such people? I went on for a long time with considerable virulence, Nessa, Duncan and Bunny sitting round in approving silence . . . The poor fellow seemed very decent about it, and admitted that *part* of his reason for staying on was the pleasure he got from being able to do the work so well [and] . . . saving some millions per week.'

Maynard agreed with Lytton that the war was futile and should be ended as 'peace without victory' rather than pursued as a fight to the finish. If Lloyd George was determined to do this, then there would come 'a point at which he would think it necessary to leave – but what that point was he couldn't say', Lytton explained to James. Next day Maynard sent fifty pounds to the National Council against Conscription. Though he was granted exemption from military service by the Treasury, he also applied at the end of February for exemption on grounds of conscientious objection, but was 'too busy' to attend the Tribunal hearing a month later. This suggests that after his virulent lecture from Lytton he had considered resigning from the Treasury, but decided against this at the last moment. He was also under pressure from his parents to stay in his job. Besides, he believed the war could not go on much longer and, while it did, he was well placed to save Duncan and his other Bloomsbury friends from imprisonment under the new Act. When Lytton and Russell seized on the inconsistencies of his position to attack his weak moral perspective, he parried them pragmatically. Only by the end of the following year did he bleakly admit to Duncan: 'I work for a government I despise for ends I think criminal.'

Although at one in their repudiation of Maynard, Lytton and Russell went separate ways as the war progressed. The passing of the Military Service Bill, which took the wind out of Lytton's sails as a political crusader, redoubled the force of Russell's activity. 'The anti-conscription movement has been rather fading out as far as I'm concerned,' Lytton wrote to Ottoline (21 January 1916). Russell, by contrast, was embarking on a series of crowded pacifist lectures. Lytton attended all of them and was unstinting in his praise. 'Bertie's lectures help one,' he wrote (16 February 1916). 'They are a wonderful solace and refreshment. One hangs upon his words, and looks forward to them from week to week, and I can't bear the idea of missing one – I dragged myself to that ghastly Caxton Hall yesterday, though I was rather nearer the grave than usual, and it was well worth it. It is splendid the way he sticks at nothing – Governments, religions, laws, property, even Good Form itself – down they go like ninepins – it is a charming sight! And then his constructive ideas are very grand; one feels one had always thought something like that – but vaguely and inconclusively; and he puts it all together, and builds it up, and plants it down solid and shining before one's mind. I don't believe there's anyone quite so formidable to be found just now upon this earth.'

Two months later, Russell's campaigning reached a crisis. On 10 April, Ernest F. Everett, a conscientious objector and member of the NCF, was sentenced to two years' hard labour for disobedience to military orders. Nine days afterwards the NCF issued a leaflet protesting against this sentence, whereupon six men were arrested and imprisoned for distributing it. On learning this Russell immediately sent off a letter to *The Times* declaring that he was the author of the leaflet and that, if anyone should be prosecuted, it ought to be himself. This letter made prosecution unavoidable and Russell duly appeared before the Lord Mayor, Sir Charles Wakefield, at the Mansion House on 5 June 1916, charged with making, in a printed publication, 'statements likely to prejudice the recruiting discipline of His Majesty's forces'. A.H. Bodkin[5] appeared for the prosecution; Russell defended himself; and the proceedings were brightened by the startling arrival of Lytton and Ottoline Morrell dressed in an astonishing hat and cashmere coat of many colours. 'B.R. spoke for about an hour,' Lytton recorded, '– quite well – but simply a propaganda speech. The Lord Mayor looked like a stuck pig. Counsel for the prosecution was an incredible Daumier caricature of a creature – and positively turned out to be Mr Bodkin. I felt nervous in that Brigand's cave.' Russell was found guilty and fined £100 (with £10 costs and the alternative of sixty-one days' imprisonment), a sentence that was confirmed on appeal.[6]

Russell despised Lytton's inability to persevere with the cause of pacifism, to stick at nothing. But Lytton suspected that Bertie had almost come to want bad conditions, so that he might have the joy of altering them. Conscription filled Lytton with no joy. 'It's all about as bad as it could be,' he wrote to Vanessa from Garsington (17 April 1916).

'Bertie has been here for the week-end. He is working day and night with the N.C.F., and is at last perfectly happy – gloating over all the horrors and the moral lessons of the situation. The tales he tells make one's blood run cold; but certainly the N.C.F. people do sound a remarkable lot – Britannia's One Hope, I firmly believe – all so bright and cheery, he says, with pink cheeks and blithe young voices – oh mon dieu! mon dieu! The worst of it is that I don't see how they can really make themselves effective unless a large number of them do go through actual martyrdom: and even then what is there to make the governing classes climb down? It is all most dark in every direction.'

Towards the end of 1917 Russell himself decided to withdraw from pacifist agitation, believing – as did Lytton – that it was by then more important to work for a constructive post-war peace. Yet he could point to some courageous achievements as a propagandist. In the Everett case, for example, his own leaflet and the ensuing trial had caused the Government to commute Everett's original sentence to a hundred and twelve days' detention.

Lytton had no such triumphs to his credit. He preferred to campaign by writing *Eminent Victorians*. The worsening conditions appear at times to have released his mind from its absorption in his own ill-health and he felt his spirits rising, he told Virginia (25 February 1916). 'I don't know why – perhaps because the horrors of the outer world are beginning to assert themselves – local tribunals, and such things – and one really can't lie still under *that*.' To Ottoline he wrote (16 February 1916): 'At moments I'm quite surprised how, with these horrors around one, one goes on living as one does – and even manages to execute an occasional pirouette on the edge of the precipice!'

After the two Military Service Acts had been passed (the second enlisting married men in addition to bachelors and childless widowers between eighteen and forty-one), he at once appealed for absolute exemption on the grounds of health and conscience, expecting that, after a medical examination and an interview with the tribunal, he would be placed in Class IVb, and made liable for clerical work. Once this had happened he intended to appeal and, in the event of this appeal failing,

345

he was prepared to be sent to prison. 'The conscience question is very difficult and complicated,' he wrote to James who was in a similar predicament (28 February 1916), 'and no doubt I have many feelings against joining the army which are not conscientious; but *one* of my feelings is that if I were to find myself doing clerical work in Class IVb – i.e. devoting all my working energy to helping on the war – I should be convinced that I was doing wrong the whole time; and if that isn't a conscientious objection I don't know what is . . . I'm willing to go to prison rather than do that work.'

He was subject to much nervous strain while waiting for the Hampstead Tribunal. 'I am still in a most half and half state – with a brain like porridge, and a constant abject feeling of exhaustion,' he reported to Bunny Garnett. 'However, I am now on a diet, and drink petroleum o'nights, and even try now and then to do a Swedish exercise or two . . . I wish I could go away from this bloody town and its bloodier tribunals – I should like to go to sleep for a month; but it's no good thinking of moving till the first stage of the affair, at any rate, is over.'

His apprehension rose after making a number of visits to watch the proceedings of the Hampstead Tribunal. 'It was horrible, and efficient in a deadly way,' he told Ottoline (March 1916). 'Very polite too. But clearly they had decided beforehand to grant no exemptions, and all the proceedings were really a farce. It made one's flesh creep to see victim after victim led off to ruin or slaughter.' And to Dorothy Bussy he wrote (25 March 1916): 'I believe the name of the tribunals will go down to History with the Star Chamber.'

These tribunals had become a means of venting public horror at the mounting slaughter on the Western Front upon the 'shirkers'. Very few of the papers dared refer to them, while the debates in the House of Commons were scarcely reported at all. It was really only by reading Hansard that anyone could find out what was going on. Perhaps it was not surprising that such scratch bodies, without judicial training or defined procedure, armed with immense powers and subject to the most violent animus, should find it difficult to interpret the conscience clauses of a complicated Act of Parliament. Yet it was not just with conscientious objectors that they abused their powers; they were almost as unrelenting with cases of hardship. 'I don't think that even if you had mentioned God in your application it would have had much effect,' Lytton wrote to Francis Birrell (March 1916), '– he is quite out of fashion; and as for Jesus he's publicly laughed at. Odd that one should have lived to find oneself positively on that fellow's side.'

On 7 March Lytton appeared as a claimant for exemption before the local Advisory Committee. These Advisory Committees had no legal basis, though in effect they controlled the administration of the law, at the same time shrugging off admitted responsibility. When an applicant appeared before one of these bodies, he was not allowed to argue his case, since the Committee maintained that it existed for advice, not decision. Yet the Tribunal invariably carried out the recommendation of the Committee, so that, when each applicant subsequently came up before it, he would find its mind already made up on the motion of a body that had refused to consider his case judicially. Lytton stated that he had an ineradicable conscientious objection to assisting in the war.

'I have a conscientious objection to assisting, by any deliberate action of mine, in carrying on the war. This objection is not based upon religious belief, but upon moral considerations, at which I have arrived after long and painful thought. I do not wish to assert the extremely general proposition that I should never, in any circumstances, be justified in taking part in any conceivable war; to dogmatize so absolutely upon a point so abstract would appear to me to be unreasonable. At the same time, my feeling is directed not simply against the present war: I am convinced that the whole system by which it is sought to settle international disputes by force is profoundly evil; and that, so far as I am concerned, I should be doing wrong to take part in it.

These conclusions have crystallised in my mind ... and I shall not act against those convictions whatever the consequences may be.'

To all this the Committee listened politely. At the end, they made no comment whatever, but simply informed him that they would recommend the Tribunal to grant him 'no relief'. The only logical assumption to be made was that they had spontaneously decided that his objection was fraudulent. He bowed coldly and left the room.

Between these court appearances, his social life helped to quell his anxieties. 'Ottoline has been up this week, receiving a series of visitors in her bedroom at Bedford Square, in a constant stream of exactly-timed tête-à-têtes – like a dentist,' he wrote to Bunny Garnett (10 March 1916).

'Yesterday there was a curious little party at Maynard's, consisting of her ladyship, Duncan with a cold, Sheppard with a beard, James and me. There she sat, thickly encrusted with pearls and diamonds, crocheting a pseudo-omega quilt, and murmuring on buggery.

I have also met Mr Ramsay MacDonald lately – not I thought a very brilliant figure, though no doubt a very worthy one. He struck me as one of

Nature's darlings, whom at the last moment she'd suddenly turned against, dashing a little fatuity into all her gifts.'

Nourished by special foods, fortified by Swedish exercises, Lytton prepared for his examination before the Hampstead Tribunal like an athlete. The conduct of the Advisory Committee had given him an opening for saying something scathing, and he spent his days drawing up imaginary cross-examinations of Military Representatives. But although, as he told Ottoline (11 March 1916), 'I am beginning to tighten my belt, roll up my sleeves and grind my teeth', he did not relish the prospect of putting his case without the aid of counsel, without hope of justice being done or even the elementary rules of fairness kept. 'I don't feel as if I had sufficient powers of repartee, and sufficient control of my voice, or my temper,' he wrote to Francis Birrell (March 1916); 'and public appearances of any kind are odious to me.'

The spectacle he presented was considerably odder than his appearances at previous oral examinations, for entry to Balliol and to the Civil Service. The proceedings, in view of his unfitness for soldiering or even manual work in a factory or farm, grew farcical, as each side endeavoured to make his opponent feel acutely silly.

'There was a vast crowd of my supporters surging through the corridors of the Town Hall, and pouring into the council chamber,' Lytton recounted in a letter to Pippa (17 March 1916). 'My case was the very last on the list. They began at about 5, and I appeared about 7.30, infinitely prepared with documents, legal points, conscientious declarations etc.' His friends and family now put in a strong appearance. First there entered Lytton's character witness, Philip Morrell, bearing a light blue air cushion. Following him, innumerable Strachey brothers and sisters, including James, Elinor, Marjorie, Pernel and Oliver, trailed in and lined themselves up opposite the eight members of the Tribunal, seated at a long table. Meanwhile, in other parts of the small courtroom, some fifteen attendant spirits, painters and pacifists, took their seats amid a miscellaneous sprinkling of the general public. Finally, the applicant himself, 'a wonderful sight . . . looking terribly dignified' though suffering from piles and carrying a tartan travelling rug, made his entrance. Philip Morrell gravely handed him the air cushion which he applied to the aperture in his beard and theatrically inflated. Then he deposited his cushion upon the wooden bench, lowered himself silently upon it facing the mayor, arranged the rug carefully around his knees, 'reared his head like some great sea lion and looked slowly round at all the old gentlemen'.[7]

The examination could now commence. In the course of it the military representative fired a volley of awkward questions from the bench.

'I understand, Mr Strachey, that you have a conscientious objection to all wars?'

'Oh no,' came the piercing reply, 'not to all. Only this one.'

'Then tell me, Mr Strachey, what would you do if you saw a German soldier attempting to rape your sister?'

Lytton turned and forlornly regarded his sisters. Then he confronted the Board once more and answered ambiguously: 'I should try and come between them.'

The Tribunal, however, was not amused, and his application for absolute exemption on the grounds of conscience was adjourned pending an examination by the military doctors. This examination took place a few days later at the White City. From eleven in the morning until half-past three in the afternoon he sat, among crowds of rowdy young men, bent over S.R. Gardiner's *History of England*. For once his disabilities did not let him down. He was rejected as medically unfit for any kind of service and formally pronounced a free man. 'It's a great relief,' he confessed to Ottoline that evening. '. . . Everyone was very polite and even sympathetic – except one fellow – a subordinate doctor, who began by being grossly rude, but grew more polite under my treatment. It was queer finding oneself with four members of the lower classes – two of them simply roughs out of the streets – filthy dirty – crammed behind a screen in the corner of a room, and told to undress. For a few moments I realized what it was like to *be* one of the lower classes – the appalling indignity of it! To come out after it was all over, and find myself being called "sir" by policemen and ticket collectors was a distinct satisfaction.'

He straightway set off for Garsington. 'I am still infinitely délabré,' he wrote to Virginia (15 April 1916), 'in spite of the infinite solicitudes of her Ladyship. It is a great bore. I lie about in a limp state, reading the Republic, which I find a surprisingly interesting work. I should like to have a chat with the Author.'

When he left Garsington it was to spend Easter at Asheham with the Woolfs. 'Virginia is most sympathetic, and even larger than usual, I think,' he wrote back to Ottoline (23 April 1916); 'she rolls along over the Downs like some strange amphibious monster. Sanger[8] trots beside her, in a very short pair of white flannel trousers with blue lines, rattling out his unending stream of brightness. Woolf and I bring up the rear – with a couple of curious dogs, whose attentions really almost oblige me to regret the charms of Socrates.'*

He returned to Belsize Park Gardens at the end of the month to see his mother who had returned from wintering in Menton. Lady Strachey was

* Ottoline's chief pug dog.

now in her seventy-fifth year and had recently lost the sight of one eye. 'The news of Mama is very appalling,' Lytton had written to Pippa (10 February 1916). 'The only hope is that in spite of everything it will be possible to read with the other eye.' For the time being this other eye remained all right, and her vigorous spirit continued to shine out unimpaired. 'Really I consider, apart from illness, and apart from the present disgusting state of the world, that I'm an extraordinarily happy person,' Lytton had written to her on his thirty-sixth birthday. 'One other reflection is this – that if I ever *do* do anything worth doing I'm sure it will be owing to you much more than to anyone else.'

Shortly after his return to London, Lytton took his mother down to Durbins, Roger Fry's somewhat austere house at Guildford, which Oliver and Ray Strachey had rented, and where Lady Strachey was to pass most of the next eighteen months. Before long, the distinctive Strachey regime was in full swing. 'Several members of the Strachey family were staying there,' wrote Nina Hamnett, another guest that summer. 'In the evening Lady Strachey would read us restoration plays and we would play games. Everyone would choose a book from the library and hide the cover. They read a passage from their books and the others had to guess who had written it.'[9] Outside, among the hollyhocks and lavender, Lytton pressed on with his work on Thomas Arnold; inside, Fry painted him still reading, in purples, blues and greys.

Much of this summer Lytton spent at Garsington, which had recently been converted into a reserve for conscientious objectors, who lived at the Bailiff's House or in one of the farm cottages. Philip Morrell was an enthusiastic pig-farmer and was able to offer these non-combatants the sort of labour described in the Military Service Acts as being work of national importance. Gerald Shove, recently married to Virginia Woolf's cousin Fredegond Maitland, was transformed into a wonderfully inept keeper of poultry; Clive Bell became an erratic hoer of ditches and cutter of hedges. As an encampment for 'agricultural dilettantes', Garsington grew still more fantastical. Part-guests, part-workers, these semi-residents would invite their families, friends, lovers, and at weekends a convoy of cars, motorcycles, bicycles and taxis would draw up and erupt in non-combative fighting over bathing-costumes, tennis rackets, towels and food. By day Ottoline appeared as a 'kind manageress of a hotel', by night she seemed what Goldie Lowes Dickinson called 'a rare and gentle pagan saint' spreading goodwill through a series of love-affairs. 'There was love-making everywhere from the pugs and peacocks to Ott and the Prime-minister,' reported Vanessa Bell to her ex-lover Roger Fry, having heard this from her husband's mistress Mary Hutchinson. And Fry himself (once the platonic love-object of Goldie Dickinson) lamented to Vanessa after one weekend that there had been 'no chance for me to do any lovemaking, so I had to listen all night long to doors opening and shutting in the long passage, though in common decency I suppose I ought to have gone out to the WC once or twice to keep up appearances'.

Amid this 'assemblage of Bloomsbury and Crankdom', Lytton soon got to know a younger generation of writers, artists and students, including Katherine Mansfield, 'very amusing and sufficiently mysterious'; Aldous Huxley, 'young and peculiarly Oxford'; and the beautiful refugee, Maria Nys, daughter of a Belgian industrialist, later to become Aldous Huxley's wife, whom Lytton was now coaching in Latin for her entrance examination to Newnham.[10] Both Katherine Mansfield and Maria Nys, with her vulnerable look of a child in a mature body, stirred in him a strongly indecisive attraction. 'Why on earth *had* I been so chaste during those Latin lessons?' Lytton asked himself in an autobiographical essay later that year (26 June 1916). 'I saw how easily I could have been otherwise – how I might have put my hand on her bare neck, and even up her legs, with considerable enjoyment; and probably she would have been on the whole rather pleased. I became certain that the solution was that I was restrained by my knowledge that she would certainly inform "Auntie" of every detail of what had happened at the earliest opportunity.'

All over the country there were rumours of conscientious objectors being shut up in underground cells, fed on bread and water, transported as cannon fodder to the front line. But in the early summer stillness, from behind those high yew hedges and the placid grey stone façade, such rumours faded as echoes in the air, faint and improbable. 'It's been unusually peaceful,' Lytton wrote to Maynard (10 May 1916), 'and I'm lying out under my quilt of many colours in the sun. I hope soon to have accumulated enough health to face London again for a little. It is horrid to sit helpless while those poor creatures are going through such things. But really one would have to be God Almighty to be of any effective use.'

3

THE VIRGIN AND THE GIPSY

In the autumn of 1915 Lytton had gone down for a few days to Asheham which Vanessa was briefly borrowing from the Woolfs. Duncan was there of course, and also Mary Hutchinson. And two art students, Barbara Hiles and Dora Carrington, had been invited. Barbara, 'a nice springing and gay girl', as Ottoline described her, was pretty and good-natured, and much admired by Saxon Sydney-Turner who (Virginia later noticed) gave off the sound of a simmering kettle whenever he went near her. Her friend Carrington was not really pretty, having a broken nose, moonlike face, uneven teeth – and being, in Virginia's imagination, 'green & yellow in the body, & immensely firm & large all over'. Her voice was flat, somewhat mincing and precise, and from time to time she would give an affected little gasp. She seemed a mass of odd moods: impulsive, self-conscious, restless, eager to please – losing herself in ceaseless activity. 'You are like a tin of mixed biscuits,' Iris Tree told her. 'Your parents were Huntley and Palmer.'

Though Carrington had little glamour, she reached towards people out of her mystery; and they, responding to a strange allure, circled round, moved closer. Her manner was naturally flattering: she had a dazzling smile; and she made up to – almost flirted with – anyone she liked. She appeared extraordinarily alive at every point, consumed by the most vivid and confusing feelings about people, places, even objects.

There was something childlike about her – the round apple cheeks, the large intense blue eyes so full of light, the pink and cream complexion smooth as china, her bouncy straw-coloured hair tinged with gold, worn short and straight, like a Florentine page-boy's. She was shy of photographs, veering erratically off like a butterfly from a net. But her paintings show a passionate involvement with nature and her letters, 'like the rustling of leaves, the voices of birds, the arrangement of natural forms' (as Gerald Brenan described them), reveal how she had carried her instincts miraculously intact from childhood into adult life. She was twenty-two – thirteen years younger than Lytton. Though she had accepted Ottoline's invitations, refused Bunny Garnett's advances, and worked a little for Roger Fry's Omega Workshops, this was her first plunge into Bloomsbury. 'I was much happier than I expected,' she wrote to Mark Gertler (December 1915). Early each morning she was up walking over the hills and 'huge wild downs', returning to find the others all still asleep in their beds. During the day she helped Vanessa in the kitchen where they lived and ate – 'everyone devoid of table manners. The vaguest cooking . . .' In the evenings they drank rum punch and gossiped. 'What traitors all these people are!' she exclaimed in a letter to Gertler. 'They ridicule Ottoline! . . . I think it is beastly of them to enjoy Ottoline's kindness & then laugh at her.' Duncan was 'much the nicest of them', she told another friend (6 December 1915), 'and Strachey with his yellow face and beard. Ugh!'

One day they went for 'a fine walk over tremendous high downs. I walked with Lytton . . .' Attracted to her, as he had been to Katherine Mansfield and Maria Nys, he suddenly stopped and embraced her. She broke away; and later that day complained to Barbara Hiles that 'that horrid old man with a beard kissed me!' Her friend tried to reassure her that his advances would go no further, but she refused to understand and the giggling Barbara spelt out the word H-O-M-O-S-E-X-U-A-L. 'What's that?' Carrington asked. But no amount of explanation could wash away her resentment. Planning to pay him out she tiptoed very early the next morning into Lytton's bedroom, taking a pair of scissors with which she intended to snip away his beard while he slept. It was to be one of those devastating practical jokes of which she was so fond – a perfect revenge for his audacity. But the plan misfired. As she leant over him, Lytton opened his eyes and looked at her. It was a moment of curious intimacy, and she, who hypnotized so many others, was suddenly hypnotized herself.

*

'I had an awful childhood', Dora Carrington later (18 November 1928) told Alix Strachey. She was the daughter of Samuel Carrington, a civil engineer with the East India Railway Company, who had travelled the world, returned to England in his fifties, 'an Odysseus . . . home at last', and married a governess, Charlotte Houghton. Dora idealized her father, but detested her mother whom she saw, her biographer Gretchen Gerzina writes, as an example of 'conventional, domestic and repressive English womanhood'.[11] In 1908, when Dora was fifteen, her father had a stroke which left him paralysed and very deaf. This affliction gave special poignancy to his qualities in Dora's eyes, and reinforced her hatred for her governess-mother. 'I can't forgive [her] for taming him as she did, & for regarding all his independence, & wildness as "peculiarities",' she confided (January 1919) to Mark Gertler.

She was determined never to be tamed herself. Yet involuntarily she had absorbed a fear of sex from her mother to whom (her younger brother Noel remembered) 'any mention of sex or the common bodily functions was unthinkable'.[12] To escape this suffocating gentility, she began to devise a system of alibis, white lies, half-truths, evasions which developed into 'a complicated calendar of deceptions' on which her emotional life became suspended. 'It is often a burden to me my deceit,' she later confessed to Gerald Brenan. Being financially dependent on her mother she made an art of devious self-protection until 'I couldn't speak the truth if I wanted to'. Sometimes she felt like H.G. Wells's eponymous heroine Ann Veronica, a new woman striving to be free. 'It's just like being in a bird cage here,' she wrote from home (May 1915), 'one can see everything

353

which one would love to enjoy and yet one cannot. My father is in another cage also, which my mother put him in, and he is too old to chirp or sing.' Dora could sing enchantingly and many enraptured young men came to her cage offering to liberate her. But could she trust them? She yearned for liberation – 'and yet one cannot'. It was as if she feared, like one of the early doves from the ark, being lost for ever. Perhaps it was better to wait, to use her battery of alibis, white lies, half-truths, evasions to hide at the crucial moment in her secrecy and reserve. So, unlike Ann Veronica, she did not fly off; rather she seemed paralysed, like her father.

For her elder sister, Lottie Louise, a nurse who quickly exchanged the humdrum home for a humdrum marriage to an orthopaedic surgeon, she had little liking. On the whole she was closer to her brothers. Sam, the eldest, was a rather hopeless red-faced young man who enlisted as a regular soldier. During the war he was badly shell-shocked, and afterwards took a job looking after dogs at the Knightsbridge Kennels. Sam was always a joke to her. But 'Teddy', her charming 'sailor-brother' soon to be killed in the battle of the Somme, she came to love for his beauty and strength, 'so brown with his black shining eyes and hair . . . so immense and solid'. She was closest of all to her younger brother Noel, who later became a publisher and farmer.[13] Forced into independence by these brothers, she came to feel that she ought to have been a boy too. Her letters are full of disgusted complaints at being female. It was all so pointless. She did not want children. She did not want sexual intercourse with any man. 'I have never felt any desire for that in my life', she wrote (16 April 1915).

Visual experiences made up for much that was otherwise unhappy. At school she had been in perpetual need of discipline. Her reports stated that she was no good at anything except drawing, and, since she also caused trouble at home, her mother packed her off to the Slade School of Fine Art, where she won a scholarship.[14] Rejoicing in her new freedom, she cut her hair short and dropped the use of her feminine baptismal name Dora – 'a sentimental lower class English name' as she described it to Noel (27 December 1916), which only her mother continued to use. For the rest of her life, even after her marriage, she was known simply as Carrington.[15]

From the moment she left home, 'there was a constant struggle to avoid returning for holidays and to evade by some ruse maternal discipline and inquisition', her brother Noel remembered. Their mother never ceased to regret this loss of control over her daughter or lose her dread of Dora's artistic friends.

Among the students at the Slade, she soon became 'the dominating personality', the artist Paul Nash wrote, '. . . a conspicuous and popular figure'. She was popular with the other girls and more than popular among the young men. Paul Nash who, while riding on the top of a bus, lent her his braces for a fancy dress party, was not the only one attracted by her. For many months, Albert Rutherston longed to speak his love – and then suddenly declared it in an apologetic letter from France. 'I've loved you, & all of you, yes, your talent, your delightful insight and wit . . . have brought me golden hours.' C.R.W. Nevinson, too, had grown infatuated with her. 'I do not recall ever having been in such an exotic condition,' he admitted. '. . . I do like you abominably . . . & am absolutely yours.' Mark Gertler also was consumed with sexual passion. 'To touch her hand is bliss!' he rhapsodized, 'to kiss it Heaven itself! I have stroked her hair and I nearly fainted with joy.' Unfortunately Gertler addressed this rhapsody to Nevinson. The two talented young artists were close friends until this entanglement with Carrington changed them into rivals. It was a wretchedly painful time. 'We were both very young,' Gertler remembered after his marriage many years later, and it had been 'nobody's fault'.[16] But at the time he blamed Carrington. 'I hated you for playing with the feelings of two men,' he told her (January 1913).

But Carrington did not really understand all this misery and commotion. She liked them all – Nash and Rutherston and Nevinson and Gertler – indeed she admired them and needed them as fellow-artists from whom she could learn. What was the need for all this sexual frenzy? She felt 'heartily sick' of it. The only advantage of having so many wooers was that it made a commitment to any one of them almost impossible. Nevertheless, by the time she left the Slade, Gertler had scattered his rivals and gained the thankless position as Carrington's special suitor.

'You are the *Lady* and I am the East End boy,' he wrote to her (December 1912). He was the son of devout Jewish parents, had passed an impoverished childhood in Whitechapel, and been sent to the Slade on the advice of William Rothenstein by the Jewish Education Aid Society. Like Carrington, he struggled with an inability to adapt himself to Slade standards, and he elected her, another outsider, as his *femme inspiratrice*. 'Your friendship INSPIRES MY WORK,' he proclaimed. '. . . I think of you in *every* stroke I do.' As Nevinson observed, Gertler was 'popular with the girls and adored by them'. But Carrington was unlike any of the actresses and East End Jewish girls he had known. 'I don't know anybody to equal you,' he wrote. She was his ideal of beauty. 'I think you are the purest and *holiest* girl I have *ever* met and as long as you remain with me you will remain so,' he assured her. 'I am going to devote my whole life to try and make you happy.' She became not only the focus of his painting, but also

'my most intimate friend'; not only his inspiration but an obsession. She
was unique, he thought, in her sudden enthusiasms, her air of simplicity,
her trustfulness. Yet a veil of mystery still enclosed her, and when she
spoke in that strange breathless voice, stealing looks out of her forget-me-
not blue eyes, he felt as if she were confiding some special secret to him.
After she left, he could not erase the image of her face 'like some beautiful
flower encased in a form of gold'. He was enchanted, but also disturbed.
'You are the *one* thing outside painting worth living for,' he told her. But
increasingly his preoccupation with her was exhausting him and spoiling
his painting. He decided to solve the problem masterfully and propose
marriage to her. But incredibly she turned him down. Was it true that their
'roads lie in different directions' and their differences in class, which had
so excited him, would inevitably come between them? He was struggling to
reconcile himself to this bitter rejection when she added that she loved
him.

He did not know where he was, and in his bafflement began discussing
his troubles with D.H. Lawrence, Gilbert Cannan, Aldous Huxley,
Ottoline Morrell and others. So he and Carrington were to find their way
into the literature of the times. In Aldous Huxley's *Crome Yellow* (1921)
Gertler becomes the painter Gombauld, 'a black-haired young corsair of
thirty, with flashing teeth and luminous large dark eyes'; while Carrington
may be seen in the 'pink and childish' Mary Bracegirdle, with her clipped
hair 'hung in a bell of elastic gold about her cheeks', her 'large china blue
eyes' and an expression of 'puzzled earnestness'. In D.H. Lawrence's
Women in Love (1921), some of Gertler's traits are used to create Loerke,
the corrupt sculptor to whom Gudrun is attracted (as Katherine Mansfield
was to Gertler), while Carrington is caricatured as the frivolous model
Minette Darrington – and Lytton too may be glimpsed as the effete Julius
Halliday. Lawrence became fascinated by what he heard of Carrington.
Resenting the desire she had provoked and refused to satisfy in his friend
Gertler, he took vicarious revenge by portraying her as Ethel Cane, the
gang-raped aesthete incapable of real love, in his story 'None of That'.
'She was always hating men, hating all active maleness in a man. She
wanted passive maleness.' What she really desired, Lawrence concluded,
was not love but power. 'She could send out of her body a repelling
energy,' he wrote, 'to compel people to submit to her will.' He pictured her
searching for some epoch-making man to act as a fitting instrument for
her will. By herself she could achieve nothing. But when she had a group
or a few real individuals, or just one man, she could 'start something', and
make them dance, like marionettes, in a tragi-comedy round her. 'It was
only in intimacy that she was unscrupulous and dauntless as a devil

incarnate,' Lawrence wrote, giving her the paranoiac qualities possessed by so many of his characters. 'In public, and in strange places, she was very uneasy, like one who has a bad conscience towards society, and is afraid of it. And for that reason she could never go without a man to stand between her and all the others.'

But was that man to be Mark Gertler? There was something striking and intense about him – the shock of hair, amazing vitality, his beautiful hands, those extraordinary gifts of draughtsmanship, his sense of humour and mimicry, 'the vivid eyes of genius and consumption'. His eager response to everything he saw found an immediate echo in Carrington's own heart. She was almost sure she loved him. And if she did, then he could wait for her. She saw nothing wrong in waiting. She loved him as a friend, as an artist, as a sister loves a brother. 'I do not love you physically, that you know,' she reminded him (November 1915), 'but I care for you far more than I do for anyone else.' But would this caring ever ripen into love? Sometimes he wondered if she understood sexual passion at all.

A vein of unconscious comedy ran through the intimate struggle of their wills. Gertler impatiently declared his total love, and urged her without delay to become his mistress or his wife. Carrington, finding herself unable to speak of such matters in any but the most oblique terms, reassured him that he was the mainland from which she made expeditions across the seas to remote islands, but to which she would always return. And when, growing tired of this metaphorical eloquence, he tried to cross-question her more precisely as to the date on which he might expect to be accepted as her lover, she would murmur 'next summer' or 'next winter', depending upon whether it was autumn or spring. Yet whenever the season appointed arrived, Carrington would ascend once more into flattering evasions about islands and continents. Finally, when Gertler demanded to know why 'you allow that barrier – Sex – to stand between us', she informed him that he was not ready yet for her 'corporeal body'.

He would almost despair of ever winning her love, when, out of the blue, she would send him a parcel of spotted ties or a jar of honey or some freshly picked flowers or an arousing photo of herself accompanied by a letter stating her determination to be less selfish, and make him happier. So he would be encouraged to take up the struggle again. But her repeated exhortations to him to be happy depressed Gertler. He could never make her out. When she smiled, he imagined she was mocking him and was amazed at his terrible dependence on her.

For a long time Gertler had only two themes to offer Carrington: first, he explained his passion as being 'not lustful, but *beautiful*!' and that she was wrong to 'think that I was vulgar and dirty'; then, he would assure her that although he was 'not worthy of her company', being '*far* too vulgar and rough for you', he was nevertheless hoping 'through my work to reach your level'. During 1915 he changed these tactics and invited her to spend weekends with him in the country – at Gilbert Cannan's millhouse, Ethel Walker's cottage, Ottoline Morrell's manor – and she was delighted. Whenever she could not leave her mother's house, he would send her enticing descriptions of his adventures in London. 'We are having exciting times here in London just now,' he wrote. At one party, he had been paired off with 'that little German girl you drew nude' and found that she 'dances *excellently*. She has a lovely little figure to clasp.' At another party, he played a love scene with the poet Iris Tree, 'very beautiful in a pale-lemon coloured evening dress . . . I like Iris more than is good for me.' At a third party 'Katherine [Mansfield] and myself – both very drunk – made passionate love to each other in front of everybody!' When not party-going he was painting. 'My pictures, apparently, have created a tremendous uproar!' he reported. Clive Bell and Roger Fry had praised him, Eddie Marsh was taking him up and Lady Cunard 'assures me that I am "the talk of London".'

These letters 'excited me terribly,' Carrington replied. '. . . You are famous, and also infamous.' She felt 'jealous that all these other people' should be seeing his pictures before she did, and sad to be missing all the fun. 'You must not forget me,' she pleaded. ' . . . I am afraid I miss you terribly . . . I am longing to come up.' They had shared so much, nearly everything, for so long that perhaps, after all, she could make a life with this artist who loved her. He had been so patient and his friendship was now a necessity. 'Do you miss my soups?' she asked. She promised to 'make some puddings and good dishes to cook for you when I come back', and when she did come back she also promised to go to bed with him. They did go to bed, once, in Gertler's new studio in Hampstead that summer, and Carrington emerged from their lovemaking a virgin, vexing and perplexing not only Gertler but also whole ranks of Bloomsbury scholars down the century. The experience, like an earlier assault he had made on her, 'made me inside feel ashamed, unclean. Can I help it?' she had asked him. 'I wish to God I could. Do not think I rejoice in being sexless, and am happy over this. It gives me pain also.'

Gertler's predicament was worse now than ever. 'You are a sort of person with whom one never gets beyond a certain point of intimacy, or if one for a moment oversteps the boundary line, one finds that you have immediately rushed back, leaving one alone gaping. You are in some ways amazingly inhuman.' He was determined to leave her – only he could not leave her. What was he to do? 'If only you could give yourself up in love,'

D.H. Lawrence advised him (20 January 1916), 'she would be much happier. You always want to dominate her, which is no good. One must learn to relinquish oneself . . .' But Lawrence, too, wanted to dominate people. So, turning instead to a scholar of the human heart, Gertler consulted Lytton Strachey.

*

Gertler had met Lytton at one of Ottoline's parties after which Lytton seems to have cherished some hopes that the young painter might succeed Henry Lamb as the artist in his life. He put himself out to be generous and gallant to Gertler, pressing on him copies of Virgil's *Pastorals*, *Tristram Shandy*, *Hamlet*, the poems of Thomas Hardy, Keats's letters and the novels of Dostoyevsky. Gertler was flattered and read hard. He did more: responding with invitations to tea, going off for walks with Lytton in Kensington Gardens, speaking French, visiting The Lacket and Belsize Park Gardens. Often they were uphill work, these classics and tea-parties and French lessons. Yet he was grateful for Lytton's attentions. 'I have become great friends with Lytton Strachey,' he boasted to Carrington (March–April 1915). '. . . We carry on a correspondence. He is a very intellectual man – I mean in the right sense. He is splendid to talk to . . . [he] talks a great deal to me when we are alone.' Slightly in awe of Lytton's sophistication, he was on his best behaviour. On one occasion Lytton sent him several of his own poems and a typescript of 'Ermyntrude and Esmeralda'. Some of these pieces were bewildering, but Gertler was determined to be impressed. '"Ermyntrude and Esmeralda" I thought extremely amusing. But the poems I thought were fine. I wonder if you have any more work you could let me read? I should like to.'

What author could resist such an appeal? More poems quickly followed, interspersed with volumes of Shelley, and these helped to establish Lytton as a man of enlightened sexual views in Gertler's mind and serious artistic intent. He was proud to have such a friend. 'I am unhappy. Come and see me soon,' he invited Lytton. But this had been a mistake, since Lytton took it as a sexual invitation. 'Since then I feel uncomfortable when I am with him,' Gertler explained to Carrington, and when Lytton, refusing to be put off, hurried round to his studio again, Gertler peeped through the hole in the door but didn't let him in. 'You can't think how uncomfortable it is for a *man* to feel he is attracting another man in that way . . . to any decent man to attract another physically is simply revolting!' Despite this difficulty, 'I like Lytton,' he told Carrington. Perhaps unwisely, she confided to him what had taken place between herself and Lytton at Asheham – and immediately regretted it. 'I am sorry I told you about Lytton, I did not mean to,' she apologized. 'Only I would rather you knew about it from me . . . a man so contemptible as that ought not ever to make one miserable or happy.' But Gertler could not take the incident seriously. Over the months that followed Carrington seemed more happy than miserable, and Gertler began to benefit. From all his swotting under Lytton's tutorship he was growing, like Monsieur Jourdain, marvellously improved – especially in Carrington's eyes. Having little education herself, she valued book-learning highly.

Early in 1916 a plot of astonishing craftiness occurred to Gertler for breaking down Carrington's resistance. He had tried, on his own behalf, every trick in the book: he had left her for three months at a time; he had bombarded her with his extremest attentions; he had spoken openly of his love for her; he had lied to her; he had lost his temper; he had reasoned; he had pleaded – all in vain. But might not Lytton's scholarship succeed where his own crude ardour had failed? If this apostle of sexual licence could use his learning and authority to unravel the knot of Carrington's virginity, then she might at long last give herself to Gertler. The more he thought about it the more this scheme recommended itself. Lytton, he felt sure, regarded him highly as a painter and would obviously have no interest in replacing him in Carrington's affections. The plan seemed foolproof.

Gertler therefore offered no objections to Carrington seeing Lytton alone. He did not know the 'incredible internal excitement' (20 April 1916) that sprang up in her whenever she went to see him – indeed he would not have believed it; and she never revealed that she sometimes deserted him in order to be with Lytton. Her happiness was unlike anything else she had experienced. It was inexplicable. It was extraordinary. She set out to make herself indispensable to him without at the same time relinquishing Gertler's friendship. The obstacles in her way must have appeared almost insurmountable. The anticipated hostility of the terrifying Bloomsberries, the disapproval of her formidable mother and the jealous anger of Gertler himself – all of whom must consequently be kept in ignorance of her devotion to Lytton – would have deterred some women. But not Carrington. Even more discouraging was Lytton's giraffe-like aloofness. So in awe of him did she feel that she would seldom risk even a telephone call, since he sounded 'so very frigid and severe on that instrument'. Often, too, he terrified her with his silences.

Lytton's feelings towards Carrington changed as their relationship progressed. He felt pleased by her adoration; but at other times she alarmed him. Observing this strange liaison with the man she might have married, Virginia noticed how, in his late thirties, Lytton was becoming 'curiously gentle, sweet tempered, considerate'. 'Intimacy seems to me possible with him as with scarcely anyone,' she wrote. So what was the nature of his intimacy with Carrington? Would he marry her, as Ottoline was telling everyone? 'God!' he exclaimed, 'the mere notion is enough – One thing I know – I'll never marry anyone – '

'But if she's in love with you?' Virginia pressed him.

'Well, then she must take her chance.'

'I believe I'm sometimes jealous – '

'Of her? thats inconceivable.'

'You like me better, don't you?'[17]

Then they had both laughed and he said that of course he liked Virginia better. In her diary she recorded that he had spoken 'with a candour not flattering, though not at all malicious'. Yet his candour had been somewhat tempered by his 'most sympathetic & understanding' knowledge of Virginia's wishes. For he was 'one of the most supple' of her friends, 'whose mind seems softest to impressions'. Perhaps then he knew how secretly pleased she would be when he spoke of his fear that Carrington might not 'let me write, I daresay'; and also on another occasion, when the two of them were calling on her, he whispered that 'he would like to stay with us without her'. Virginia was delighted, too, some years later when he dedicated his *Queen Victoria* to her. 'You ought to have dedicated Vic[toria] to C[arrington]', she reproved him.

'Oh dear no – we're not on those terms at all.'

'Ottoline will be enraged.'[18]

On the whole, he thought Ottoline might be enraged. But not Carrington.

What mystified Virginia, when she contemplated the unappealing aspects of the Strachey character – its prosaic scholarship 'lacking magnanimity, shorn of atmosphere', its meagre physical warmth, its failure of vitality, its orderliness, dustiness, its tacit assumption of the right to superior comfort and opulence to protect a nature 'infinitely cautious, elusive & unadventurous' – what mystified Virginia, in view of all this, was the source of Carrington's overpowering admiration for Lytton. 'I wonder sometimes what she's at,' Virginia was to write in her diary (6 June 1918). '. . . I suppose the tug of Lytton's influence deranges her spiritual balance a good deal.'

Gradually Virginia's suspicions of Carrington lifted. She was the easiest of visitors and she looked at pictures like a genuine artist. With Lytton she was 'ardent, robust, scatterbrained, appreciative, a very humble disciple, but with enough character to prevent insipidity'. By 1918 Virginia came to the conclusion that Lytton had improved Carrington, and she complimented him on the improvement. 'Ah, but the future is very dark –

I *must* be free,' he answered. 'I shall want to go off.' Yet what if Carrington herself might want to go off? she volunteered, and saw that he was not pleased by this hypothesis. The fact was, she thought, that Carrington had also improved Lytton. 'If he is less witty, he is more humane,' she noticed (22 January 1919). '. . . I like Carrington though. She has increased his benignity.' Nevertheless the future of this unlikely attachment did indeed seem dark, and from time to time Virginia would ask herself, 'But whats to happen to C[arrington] . . . What is to happen now to Carrington?'

Lytton was surprised by how much he enjoyed teaching Carrington the pleasures of English literature. Though he could make her feel her ignorance acutely, she would eagerly absorb these lessons and sometimes pass them on to the vainly waiting, still attentive Gertler, who was soon receiving a double quota of prose and poetry. As the months passed and summer came, Carrington's attachment to Lytton grew still stronger until it seemed to infect every particle of her being. She almost lost her identity, caring for him as others care for themselves. When he was with her, she was alive; when he was away for a week, a day, she ceased to exist except in her letters to him – sprawling, unpunctuated, misspelt letters, scribbled urgently on page after page of foolscap paper or the torn-out leaves of children's exercise books, and lit up by Edward Lear-like drawings that illustrated her stories, her predicament. She partly attributed this mysterious happiness with Lytton to the very different nature of their intimacy from her stormy affair with Gertler. Lytton made few demands on her and never interfered with her freedom. If she was no longer free, it was because she made such extraordinary demands upon herself. Unlike the tortured Gertler, Lytton was gentle and courteous. She felt safe with him. She felt at peace. He became her 'Chère Grandpère'; she was 'Votre grosse bébé'. Seeing them together, Virginia later observed (23 July 1918): 'Lytton very amusing, charming, benignant, & like a father to C[arrington]. She kisses him & waits on him & gets good advice & some sort of protection.'

News of how Lytton had become a father substitute was to reach Wyndham Lewis. A prolific and elusive father himself, he saw Lytton's honorary status as a characteristically Stracheyesque method of asserting his revolutionary pseudo-manhood, and Carrington's mission to establish, rather belatedly and inadequately, the paternal dominance that had been absent from her childhood. In his novel, *The Apes of God* (1930), this arch-enemy of the Bloomsbury 'Pansy-clan' caricatured the caricaturist under the name Matthew Plunkett. The crane-like Plunkett walks with an affected anarchical gait, adopts mannerisms reminiscent of his father, puts on in front of strangers an owlish ceremony of regulation shyness, and articulates with two distinct voices, one a high-piping vixenish shriek, the other of a more fastidious percussion – 'a nasal stammer modelled upon the effects of severe catarrh'. Being a modern man much taken up with psychology, this hero conceives the intensely original idea of submitting himself to psychoanalytical treatment in the Zürich consulting-den of the Jewish Dr Frumpfsusan – a bizarre notion suggested by the career of James Strachey, Freud's patient, pupil and English-language translator. Plunkett's aim, expressed in Jungian terms, is to get himself extroverted so that he can overcome a 'virulent scale complex of psychical-inferiority'. Dr Frumpfsusan explains that he must falsify nature to his personal advantage. 'Inferiority-feeling', he flatteringly suggests, 'may result from an actual superiority! The handicap of genius, isn't it?' For successful extroversion Plunkett should contrive to be a Gulliver in Lilliput. 'For that truly uppish self-feeling,' he concludes, '. . . you must *choose your friends small* . . . believe me, *you cannot choose your lady friend too small* . . .'

It is therefore on doctor's orders that Plunkett takes up with Betty Blythe, his Carrington-like girlfriend, a petite doll-woman. Of the magical puppet prescription, her tiny figure is dwarfed by the fairy giant of this Bloomsbury legend. Towering far above her, he strives to assume a buccaneering manner. When she calls on him one afternoon, he manages to caress one of her flaxen curls with the extreme fingertips of a tapering hand, and feeling at last 'a distinct vibration, in the recalcitrant depths of his person', swoops down and picks her up 'as though she had been a half-ton feather'. His knees bent and trembling, he staggers against the wall and then into his bedroom, only to drop Betty on the floor at the sudden shock of seeing, stretched out fast asleep on his bed, his last year's boyfriend.

In this farcical drama Lewis ingeniously implies that the acquisition of an awed and submissive girlfriend, like the growing of a beard, was meant to promote Lytton as a man of virility. But this extravaganza does not follow the biographical events. It was true that Lytton's boyfriends would still lie upon the bed. But he did not drop Carrington before reaching this bed which in due course would become loaded with a Vorticist conglomeration of intertwined figures.

For some months Carrington had continued to write to Lytton 'with the censor inside' (June 1916). Yet her letters still made him laugh out loud, even at breakfast. Though she did not wholly trust him yet, she could not help growing more openly loving, telling him '(since this disgusting cult of truth has begun)' how much she longed 'to be with you again'.

Her letters to Gertler over a similar period are less consistent. In one she suggests parting from him at least temporarily, 'as it nearly sends me mad with grief, at seeing you so miserable'. In another she urges him to read Keats. She struggles to explain their differences: 'You are too possessive, and I too free. That is why we could never live together.' But in April she writes: 'I am longing to see you again. Like a hungry person who has been waiting for [a] meal a long time . . . We will see a great deal of each other now.' Then in a pencilled note the following month, she is even more encouraging. 'You will not love me in vain,' she promises him (16 May 1916), '– I shall not disappoint you in the end.'

*

The last ten days of May Lytton and Carrington spent together at Garsington during one of Ottoline's most ambitious house-parties. Among the guests were Philip Snowden[19] and his wife, Bertie Russell, Maynard Keynes and various young ladies either deaf or French. 'The Snowden couple were as provincial as one expected,' Lytton wrote to James (31 May 1916), '– she, poor woman, dreadfully plain and stiff, in stiff plain clothes, and he with a strong northern accent, but also a certain tinge of eminence. Quite too political and remote from any habit of civilized discussion to make it possible to talk to him – one just had to listen to anecdotes and observations (good or bad); but a nice good-natured cripple . . .' Into this anti-Cabinet conclave, during the Sunday afternoon torpor while the peacocks were setting up their continuous howling like damned souls about the garden, the prime minister and his party arrived, just in time for one of them to effect the rescue of a servant who for a joke pretended to be drowning. The atmosphere was more like a campaign in Flanders than an English garden-party, but when the excitement had died down and tea was served, Lytton was able to study Asquith's entourage. 'They *were* a scratch lot,' he reported to James. It was the prime minister himself who chiefly interested him. Asquith seemed to have grown redder and bulkier since their last encounter in the summer of 1914. Then they had met at the height of the Ulster crisis; now they met again a few days after the Irish Rebellion. 'I studied the Old Man with extreme vigour,' Lytton wrote to James, 'and really he is a corker.

'He seemed much larger than he did when I last saw him (just two years ago) – a fleshy, sanguine, wine-bibbing, medieval Abbot of a personage – a glutinous lecherous cynical old fellow – oogh! – You should have seen him making towards Carrington – cutting her off at an angle as she crossed the lawn. I've rarely seen anyone so obviously enjoying life; so obviously, I thought, *out* to enjoy it; almost, really, as if he'd deliberately decided that he *would*, and let all the rest go hang. Cynical, yes, it's hardly possible to doubt it; or perhaps one should say just "case-hardened". Tiens! One looks at him, and thinks of the War . . . And all the time, *perpetually*, a little pointed, fat tongue comes poking out, and licking those great chops, and then darting back again. That gives one a sense of the Artful Dodger – the happy Artful Dodger – more even than the rest. His private boudoir doings with Ottoline are curious – if one's to believe what one hears; also his attitude towards Pozzo [Keynes] struck me – he positively shied away from him ("Not much juice in *him*", he said in private to her ladyship . . . so superficial we all thought it!). Then why, oh why, does he go about with a creature like Lady Meux? On the whole, one wants to stick a dagger in his ribs.'

Enjoyment was the keynote of Asquith's personality. He had clearly enjoyed a good lunch with several glasses of good wine. 'There was a look of a Roman Emperor about him (one could imagine a wreath on his head),' Lytton afterwards remembered (2–6 May 1918), 'or a Renaissance Pope ("Well, let me enjoy the world, now that I am Vicar of Christ") . . . It was disgusting; and yet, such was the extraordinary satisfaction of the man that, in spite of everything, one could not help feeling a kind of sympathetic geniality of one's own.'[20]

In calmer moments at Garsington, Lytton went 'for some enormous walks', he told James, '– "expeditions" – with, precisely, Carrington. One was to the town of Abingdon, a magical spot, with a town-hall by Wren perhaps – a land of lotus-eaters, where I longed to sink down for the rest of my life, in an incredible oblivion . . .

'As for Carrington, she's a queer young thing. These modern women! What are they up to? They seem most highly dubious. Why is it? Is it because there's so much "in" them? Or so little? They perplex me. When I consider Bunny . . . or even Gertler, I find nothing particularly obscure there, but when it comes to a creature with a cunt one seems to be immediately désorienté. Perhaps it's because cunts don't particularly appeal to one. I suppose that may be partly the explanation. But – oh, they coil, and coil; and, on the whole, they make me uneasy.'

From Garsington, where Asquith had made his accelerating advance on her, Carrington wrote scolding Gertler for casting 'a cloud of doubt on our trust in each other', and promising 'not to kiss anyone since it causes you pain'. She cared little for anything except making him happy, she assured him, and she cared for no one else. She ended with a simile that may have heartened him. 'It has felt like a lock on the river, with our two boats up against the lock. Now, it is open, and we can rush so swiftly down the river.'

When Carrington spoke about Gertler, Lytton hardly knew for whom he felt most. He was disquieted by Gertler who had written a despairing account of himself. It appeared that he was nearly bankrupt. 'I've just heard from Gertler, who says he's on the brink of ruin,' Lytton wrote from Garsington to Clive Bell (12 May 1916), '– has taken his last £2 out of the bank, and will have nothing at all in another week. Do you think anything can be done? I'm sure £10 would make a great difference to him, and I thought perhaps you might be able to invest some such sum in a minor picture or some drawings. Or perhaps you could whip up somebody else. If you do anything, of course don't mention me, as his remarks about his finances were quite incidental, with no idea of begging.'

On the same day Lytton wrote a somewhat stilted but generous letter to Gertler himself. 'I have long wanted to possess a work by you – so will you put aside for me either a drawing or some other small piece, which is in your judgement the equivalent of the enclosed [£10] – And I'll carry it off when I'm next in London. I only wish I could get one of your large pictures – what idiots the rich are! And how I loathe the thought of them swilling about in their motors and their tens of thousands, when people like you are in difficulties. What makes it so particularly monstrous is that the wants of artists are so very moderate – just for the mere decencies of life. All the same, though I'm very sorry that you're not even half as well off as an ordinary Civil Servant, you may be sure that I don't pity you – because you *are* an artist, and being that is worth more than all the balances at all the banks in London.'

Carrington was delighted that her new Bloomsbury friends, especially Lytton, were helping Gertler, and wrote enthusiastically to say how happy she was to hear that he was at last selling some of his pictures. But this was not the sort of letter he wanted from her. 'Don't write and congratulate me on having money,' he chided her (20 May 1916). 'I hate money and the people I get it from . . . If you could give me one night do, as you would make your unhappy friend happier!' She did give him one night in London, but afterwards wrote apologizing 'because in trying to help you out of your wretchedness last night, I feel that I only succeeded in being nasty to you'. She felt easier writing to him about 'the wonderful blue flowers, and so many birds singing all day'. She has been painting tulips, she writes, and is returning to Garsington in order to paint more – 'such tulips I feel weak with excitement'. She has also swum in the swimming-pool twice before breakfast. 'The children wear no clothes and run over the grass, and stand in the tulips, thigh deep in yellow tulips. It has made me depressed for they are so beautiful and I wished for the impossible to be more like them, and I hated this bulk of a body which surrounds my spirit . . . Are you happy now because I love you?'

But Gertler was not happy. All he got were descriptions of flowers and birds, and copies of Keats's poems. 'I have no use for Keats in my present mood,' he had told her. He was confused by those grand metaphors that led nowhere. 'You are always writing to me of the many ships on the sea,' he protested. Sometimes he felt he might die if he opened another envelope full of metaphors. Moreover, he had begun to suspect that she was concealing something from him, and accused her of being too friendly with Gilbert Cannan, who was then finishing *Mendel*, his novel built round the Gertler–Carrington love-affair. Carrington repudiated this accusation. It was true that Cannan had given her a brotherly kiss on the cheek – like a handshake – but the incident was not worthy of discussion, being nothing more than a novelist's legitimate research.

Nevertheless Gertler's suspicions had acted as a warning to Carrington and she veered hastily into harmless topics. She wished she could share with him her love of Rimbaud, but it was all too new and enthralling for her to speak about yet. Also she had shared a taxi with Augustus John who, she volunteered, had made no assault at all on her famous virginity.

Gertler was little comforted. If even Augustus quailed before her virginity, what hope was there for him? 'It gets more and more complicated with C[arrington],' he wrote to his friend Koteliansky (20 June 1916). '. . . If only the torment would end. It is like a terrible disease and incurable. We both put our heads together to try to end it, but we can't . . . because it has neither beginning nor end.'

4

UNREGARDED HOURS

After the hurricane of guests moved on, the rag-time and whirlpool abated, Garsington became once more a House of Rest for Lytton. Since his tribunal he had been 'like a sick dog', as he described it to Gertler (10 May 1916), 'dragging about from cushion to cushion, or creeping out into the sunshine to lie there dreaming'. Ottoline herself had departed, and Lytton was free to sit out alone in the kitchen garden, idling, reading, and writing letters. 'I feel as if I were gradually turning into a pear-tree on a South Wall,' he wrote to Vanessa Bell (2 June 1916), 'and unless you come and pull me up by the – root, before long, I shall very likely be doomed for the rest of my life to furnish fruit for her ladyship's table.'

In the third week of June he eventually left for Wissett Lodge, a Suffolk farmhouse with a large half-timbered façade which Duncan had rented so as to set himself up as an official fruit farmer with David Garnett and discharge their obligations under the National Service Act. After the pugs and cushions of Garsington, the atmosphere of bees and blackberries suited Lytton's mood, and he hesitated here until the end of the month, with Harry Norton as the other guest. 'Is it the secret of life or of ... something else ... I don't quite know what? ... Oblivion? Stupor? Incurable looseness? – that they've discovered at Wissett?' he asked Virginia (28 July 1916). 'I loved it, and never wanted to go away.'

Vanessa certainly believed that they could be 'perfectly happy' in such a place. 'I feel our ways are changing,' she had told Lytton (27 April 1916). Lost in its six acres of orchards and fields, Wissett was 'amazingly remote from the war and all horrors' (though Bunny swore he heard a Zeppelin, sounding like a threshing machine, pass by). It felt even more isolated than Asheham. Duncan and Bunny worked in the fields all day, while Lytton lay writing under the rambler-roses and laurel bushes, Norton went about thinking loudly about prime numbers, and Vanessa laboured to make Wissett a rival outpost to Garsington. It was inconceivable to her that they would ever wish to go back to London. Their only adventure occurred one Sunday morning when the four of them set out for a long walk towards the sea – an unwise direction, they discovered, when an agitated corporal rushed up and threatened to frogmarch them all into a military gaol because of their collective Germanic appearance and the incorrect Suffolk accent in which they answered his questions.[21] Otherwise 'everything and everybody seems to be more or less overgrown with vegetation', Lytton informed Ottoline (20 June 1916), 'thistles four feet high fill the flower garden, Duncan is covered with Virginia (or should it be Vanessa?) creeper, and Norton and I go about pulling up the weeds and peeping under the foliage. Norton is in very good spirits, having evolved a new theory of cubic roots.'

One afternoon, as they walked together in the shrubbery, Lytton, in strictest confidence, told Bunny something about Carrington. His curiosity roused, Bunny urged him to invite her down. But she could not abandon Gertler again so soon, and a temporary lull settled over their triangular relationship.

Lytton filled in this pause with an experiment in autobiography[22] describing the minutiae of a single not extraordinary day, Monday, 26 June. The essay uncovers a few disturbances in his emotional life – a slight breach with Ottoline, which, though quickly healed, heralded a more serious division between them; an uneasiness with Vanessa over their mutual attraction to Duncan, and some hint of awkwardness with Duncan over their mutual liking for Vanessa; a tremulous flirtation in the garden with Bunny; and, arising from this episode, an awareness that, although he was fortunate in knowing so many friends, Lytton could never be sure if any of them really liked him.

Vanessa believed that Lytton 'had very little sense of anything but the human interest in painting'.[23] On leaving Wissett, he called on Gertler at his studio in Rudall Crescent to choose the drawing for which he had sent ten pounds. Gertler's famous 'Merry-Go-Round' (a title as ironic as *Eminent Victorians*), which reflects both the dehumanization of war and the repetitive pattern of his affair with Carrington, was there. 'Oh lord, oh lord have mercy upon us! It is a devastating affair isn't it?' Lytton wrote to Ottoline (3 July 1916). 'I felt that if I were to look at it for any length of time, I should be carried away suffering from shellshock. I admired it, of course, but as for *liking* it, one might as well think of liking a machine gun. But fortunately he does all that for himself – one needn't bother with one's appreciations. He said it reminded him of Bach – Well, well!'

While Lytton was at Belsize Park Gardens, Carrington came over one afternoon. She had been invited to Garsington later that July, this time with Gertler. Lytton himself was expecting to return there about the same time, and wrote to Ottoline confirming this arrangement. 'I want to get my Arnold life done,' he had told her earlier from Wissett (20 June 1916), 'and I think under your peaceful shades it might be accomplished.' After his few days in London, he was eager for the country once more. 'I am accumulating writing material,' he wrote (3 July 1916), '– and mean to be very industrious for the next month or so.'

A week later he arrived at Garsington, where he was able, for more than a fortnight, to do no work whatever. Presided over by Ottoline, her face covered by peeling flakes of white chalk, her body swathed in a stiff gown of peacock silk, her throat encased in baroque pearls, innumerable guests spiralled round the house and overflowed into a cottage and the village inn. Most of them, Lytton complained to Mary Hutchinson (10 July 1916), were 'so damned political and revolutionary that I got quite sick of the conscientious objector and the thought of Ireland's wrongs'. Among the non-political guests were Evan Morgan,[24] 'a tall bright-coloured youth with a paroqueet nose, and an assured manner, and the general appearance of a refined old woman of high birth'; and, once again, the alluringly impassive Katherine Mansfield – 'an odd satirical woman behind a regular mask of a face . . . very difficult to get at; one felt it would take years of patient burrowing, but that it might be worth while.'

The weekend passed, the party went on. 'I came here with the notion of working,' he protested to Barbara Hiles (17 July 1916). 'Mon Dieu! There are now no intervals between the week-ends – the flux and reflux is endless – and I sit quivering among a surging mesh of pugs, peacocks, pianolas, and humans – if humans they can be called – the inhabitants of Circe's cave. I am now faced not only with Carrington and Brett (more or less permanences now) but Gertler, who ... is at the present moment carolling a rag-time in union with her Ladyship. I feel like an open boat in a choppy sea – but thank goodness the harbour is in sight.'

The Gertler–Carrington situation struck him as gloomy and complicated, he confided to Mary Hutchinson (23 July 1916). 'The poor thing [Carrington] seems almost aux abois with Gertler for ever at her, day in, day out – she talks of flying London, of burying herself in Cornwall, or becoming a Cinema actress. I of course suggested that she should live with me, which she luckily immediately refused – for one thing, I couldn't have afforded it. And there she is for the present at Garsington, with Mark gnashing his teeth in the background, and Brett quite ineffectual, and her Ladyship worming and worming for ever and ever, Amen.' At the same time, Lytton noticed that Carrington still admired Gertler. Lytton also sympathized with him over the perpetual virginity question – 'unless she's the most horrible liar'.

At the end of the month he sailed to another anchorage with Oliver and Ray Strachey at Durbins. Since Oliver only returned in the evenings from the Foreign Office to play Bach at the piano, Lytton was left with his mother, his sister-in-law Ray and his sister Pippa, who competed in looking after him as he worked away at 'Dr Arnold'. The only interruption was provided by the brief appearance of Ray Strachey's uncle, Logan Pearsall Smith, who, Lytton told a grateful Ottoline (21 August 1916), 'is really now *more* than middle-aged – senile, one's inclined to say, poor old fellow – doddering on with his anecdotes and literature, which, in spite of the efforts of a lifetime, remain alas! American. I was rather amused by his view of Vernon [Lee]. "I think on the whole she's the best talker I know" – I gave paralysed assent, and then ventured to add, "But perhaps at times she tends to be slightly boring" . . . He wouldn't have it though. Well, well, de gustibus non est disputandum, which may be translated:

'Tastes differ: some like coffee, some like tea;
And some are never bored by Vernon Lee.'[25]

Another visitor to Roger Fry's house was his old friend Walter Raleigh. 'He was far less outré and bloodthirsty about the war than I'd expected –

chiefly just childish; rather timid too, it seemed, on controversial questions; and I really liked him more than I ever had before.'

While Lytton was at Durbins, Carrington and Gertler had arranged to stay at Eleanor House as guests of Mary Hutchinson. Here they swam in the sea, Carrington told Lytton, and 'even Mark came in. Looking very absurd, in a bathing dress.' These were unusually happy days. 'Wittering was a very wonderful time for me, and all through you,' she afterwards reminded Gertler, ' . . . how much I loved being with you in those fields, and for showing me so much.' Perhaps it was because they were both painters that 'the intimacy we got at lately makes other relationships with people strangely vacant'. At such moments, doubting her secret liaison with Lytton, Carrington became silent. 'Are you in the Jew's arms at the present moment,' Lytton wondered. 'So near, and yet so far. Oh! Ah!' In the past he would have envied her being in Mark's arms, but now he felt a curious jealousy. The absurd fact was that he missed her, even missed her letters (which he 'perused in the privacy of my four-poster'). 'Write, write, write for Jesus' sake,' he demanded.

When Virginia invited him over to Asheham after leaving Durbins in mid-August, he refused because 'I have engaged myself to go [to] Wales then, with a small juvenile party' (28 July 1916). He would, he added, be at large again in September, when he hoped to see Leonard and Virginia in Cornwall.

This journey to North Wales was occasioned by Nicholas Bagenal, a young man who had just then come out of hospital after recovering from a wound in the hip. He was in love with his future wife, Barbara Hiles, who persuaded Lytton to act as chaperon during a fortnight's holiday they were to spend together at her father's cottage near Llandudno, before Nicholas returned to the front. Agreeing to this, Lytton had inquired whether he might in turn bring Barbara's friend, Carrington. 'You *must* come to Wales,' he insisted (28 July 1916) to Carrington. And so the juvenile party was formed – 'though really', Lytton confessed to Mary Hutchinson, 'I sometimes begin to wonder what the diable I am doing in this galère of grandchildren'.

Difficulties and anxieties abounded. 'Oh Lytton I'm so excited and so afraid you will be unhappy or bored,' Barbara wrote to him (5 August 1916). He endeavoured to set her mind at ease, though his own doubts gleam clearly through. 'I pray for this weather to last,' he answered (8 August 1916). 'But if it doesn't, we can always shut the doors and windows, and cook and eat and cook and eat indefinitely. In the intervals we can hum tunes and recite ballads. But if it's fine we must scale the mountains with gazelle-like tread . . . I'll bring some books.'

The chief difficulties, however, were provided by Carrington, whose fears outmatched the sum of Lytton's and Barbara's and possibly those of the wounded Nicholas Bagenal. The invitation had arrived at the end of July, while she was at 'Shandygaff Hall'. She wanted 'so much to go to this land of mountains,' in silks or rags, on foot or by rail. But she was penniless; she would have to invent a story for her mother; and then, would Mark mind? After her recent lecture on trust, surely he would not dare to object. Eventually she resolved to *walk* to North Wales, or possibly to bicycle there. But was it all going to be worth this tremendous effort? 'It would be awful to walk so far', she admitted to Lytton (30 July 1916), 'and then be met with the chilly eye of criticism!' She was training herself as best she could, assiduously reading Donne and, like Gertler, taking lessons in French. But her real fear was that after the strain of two or three weeks together, their peculiar relationship might snap.

The Morrells, meanwhile, were doing all they could to assist Gertler.

'Ottoline insists on trying her best to get my state of virginity reduced, and made me practically share a bedroom with Norton! ... I was dismal enough about Mark and then suddenly without any warning Philip after dinner asked me to walk round the pond with him and started without any preface, to say, how disappointed he had been to hear I was a virgin! How wrong I was in my attitude to Mark ... Ottoline then seized me on my return to the house and talked for one hour and a half in the asparagrass bed on the subject ... and told me truthfully about herself and Bertie. But this attack on the virgins is like the worst Verdun on-slaught ... Mark suddenly announced he is leaving ... and complicated feelings immediately came up inside me.'

'What Devils they all are, with their proddings & preachings, & virginity-gibberings,' Lytton replied (1 August 1916). '. . . Have you looked at Donne's Satires? *They're* rather in that style ... (aspara*grass*?).'

While Carrington tried to rise above this 'mass of intrigue', climbing out of her unbearably hot attic room and spending her nights chastely on the roof with Aldous Huxley ('Strange adventures with birds, and peacocks, and hordes of bees,' she reported to Lytton. 'Shooting stars, other things'), Ottoline below was writing to Gertler querying whether Carrington 'will ever find a mate that fulfils all she desires ... I love Carrington too and you. I hope you will always tell me anything you feel like and when you feel like it.' Lytton had once told her everything, but now he was growing most ungratefully secretive.

Before Wales, Carrington had to return to her parents' home at Hurstbourne Tarrant in Hampshire. She was in a fiercely rebellious mood, vanishing out of the house for long walks over the hills with a dog named Jasper, and at night sleeping out on the roof as she had at Garsington. Her mother, she complained to Gertler, 'was more awfull than ever', and her father more pitifully ill and old: 'I hate him for living as he does or rather I hate life for making him live. It is so undignified an end like this.'

Meanwhile negotiations over the holiday were growing more tightly knotted. Lytton had offered to pay for Carrington's travelling expenses, but, unable to write to her at her parents' home he communicated the news to Barbara. 'I am rather rich just now, I find,' he lied (8 August 1916), 'so it would be absurd for her [Carrington] to go by foot, or worse, for lack of money.' This was passed on to Carrington, but still she hesitated, until her mother, learning of her expedition now for the first time, absolutely forbade it. Her mind was then made up. She would burn her boats and go.

It was settled that at four o'clock on the afternoon of Saturday, 12 August, the four of them would converge on the platform of Llandudno Junction – Barbara and Nicholas travelling from Westbury-on-Severn in Gloucestershire, Lytton via Guildford in Surrey, and Carrington from Andover in Hampshire.

Leaving Durbins for Belsize Park Gardens on the first stage of his journey, and pausing for a few moments in the Haymarket, Lytton was swept up in an atmosphere of sudden cheerfulness. The streets were empty, but 'I became aware of a curious sensation of "bien-aise" in the air,' he recounted. 'Looking round I saw a motor coming up the hill; it was open, and in it was Asquith, alone, with a look of radiant happiness upon his face – happiness which was indeed literally radiant, for I had actually felt it when my back was turned. He passed on without seeing me – he really looked too happy to see anything. I think there was a portmanteau in the car, and I suppose he was off somewhere for the weekend.'[26]

As the prime minister, glowing with joy, glided away into the distance, like – the simile is Lytton's – a seraph in a heavenly ecstasy, the euphoria flooding the Haymarket drained away, and Lytton was left with a sense of amused and astonished envy. How the devil did he manage it? He wished that he could feel so buoyant over his own holiday. It was impossible to withhold a grudging feeling of amiability – despite Lytton's disapproval of Asquith's conduct over the recent treason trial of Roger Casement. 'I should be very glad if they didn't hang him [Casement], but I can't believe there's much chance of that – especially with Asquith prime minister,' he had written to Ottoline (3 July 1916). 'That old buffer has certainly been distinguishing himself lately. Is he a coward, or a fiend, or simply a dunderhead I wonder?'

Still pondering on this, he arrived at Llandudno. The cottage itself, very small and sequestered, with bees-waxed parquet floors and spring mattresses, was painted white outside and had a tiny garden filled with flowers. It was perched half-way up one of the chain of mountains which on all sides shut them in. Along the flat valley directly below ran a broad and shallow river. Lytton was reminded of Rothiemurchus. 'You can't think how kind they all were to me – and how wonderfully nice. Barbara managed the cottage, and the cooking with the greatest skill,' he wrote to Bunny Garnett (2 September 1916). '. . . Nick was really charming – his gaiety of spirits never ceased. It will be too horrible if he is forced back into that murderous whirlpool. As for Carrington – we seemed to see a great deal of each other. But this let me remark at once – my attitude throughout in relation to *all*, has been of immaculate chastity, whatever the conduct of others may have been.'

Increasingly as he got older, Lytton loved being in the company of people younger than himself. They helped him to shrug off his own 'antique spirit', as he called it. One half of him, he told Ottoline, felt as if it had gone back ten years or twenty, while the other half, he was pretty sure, had moved forward by about the same amount; with the result that – 'me voici, a mixture of 18 and 52'.

Great bundles of cloud would come toppling down the mountains and envelop the cottage; and not a day passed without some rain. Indoors Lytton lay reading Donne and Shakespeare while Carrington painted his portrait. In the sunnier intervals, the party, released from its hideout, sprang up into the mountains or made expeditions to Conway and Llandudno.

One highlight of the holiday was a bottle of champagne. Nick withdrew the cork with a pop – and Lytton, flinging his arms wildly in the air, shrieked: 'God! What the war must be like!'

'I am most happy here,' Carrington reassured Gertler, who had gone off to stay with Gilbert Cannan. '. . . Lytton sends his love. You must like him, because I do, so very much.'

'Remember me to Barbara,' Gertler replied, 'and my *love* to Lytton.'

But Carrington did not like such sarcasm, and wrote to reprove him, 'because that other objection [homosexuality] comes so much always before you. I have altered my views about that . . . one always has to put up with something, pain or discomfort, to get anything from any human being.'

Gertler, who felt he did not need a sermon on pain and discomfort, took exception to this, and a competition developed between them as to who genuinely liked Lytton better. No one had recently read more Donne and Dostoyevsky than Gertler and even 'my French is getting on better. I do half-an-hour a day.'

'Of course you liked Lytton and praised him before I did, because I did not know him in those days when you did'. Carrington countered.

The holiday drew to an end. 'What do you fancy?' Lytton had asked Carrington. 'Perhaps we might walk back to England through Wales? It would then be September . . .' In the final days of August the two of them set off together for Bath – 'a most charming town', Lytton told Bunny Garnett (2 September 1916). 'How one bounds along those elegant streets, and whisks from Square to Circus and Circus to Crescent! One almost begins to feel that one's on high heels, and embroidery sprouts over one's waistcoat. And then – the infectious enthusiasm of my youthful companion . . . you smile; but you are mistaken.

Carrington, too, was passing on news of their progress – to Gertler. 'Yesterday we investigated the whole town,' she wrote to him (29 August 1916). 'Every house nearly! and sat for about two hours in a 2nd hand book shop.

'I discovered accidently an early Voltaire which gave Lytton great joy, as he had been looking for it a long time. After tea we walked through the city upon to a high hill because we had seen in one of the books on architecture, (that I studied all Sunday), a wonderful house. Called "Widcomb House". and indeed it was beautiful! – Fielding lived in this village also – We boldly asked the maid if we might go over the garden. She fetched after a long time an incrediably old lady. Who said we might. But seemed utterly bewildered why anyone should want to see her house! The garden with a deep valley very big with high trees, distant hills gave me strange emotions. It was a sad morbid place, and deadly quiet – Lytton read the Voltaire to me an account of Frederick the Great, and Voltaire's relationship with his son.'

From Bath they moved to Wells – 'What a pity it is that it should now be the fashion for clergymen to believe in Christianity,' Lytton later wrote to his mother (3 September 1916). 'I should so have enjoyed being Bishop of Bath and Wells!' – and from Wells they went to Glastonbury. 'We are staying here,' Carrington wrote to Maynard from the George Hotel on 29 August. '. . . I doubt if Lytton will ever return.' On the opposite page Lytton added a few lines of verse for Maynard.

When I'm winding up the toy
Of a pretty little boy,
– Thank you, I can manage pretty well;
But how to set about
To make a pussy pout
– *That* is more than I can tell.[27]

Below these lines Carrington drew a picture of a pussy cat curled up and
fast asleep. They had shared a hotel bed the previous night, and from that
night, scholars have dated the end of Carrington's virginity. She felt
burdened with gratitude to Lytton. She had been with him for three
consecutive weeks, had lived with his moodiness, his invalidism, and loved
him more than ever. 'I did enjoy myself so much with you,' she wrote after
getting back to Hurstbourne Tarrant at the beginning of September,
'– you do not know how happy I have been, everywhere, each day so
crowded with wonders . . . Dear Lytton. I have been so happy, incrediably
happy!'

Still at Wells, 'sunk down into lodgings under the eaves of this
somewhat démodé Cathedral', Lytton wrote of his loneliness apart from
her. 'Lunch is over, tea is over, dinner is over, and here I am lying in my
solitary state on the sofa among the white cushions – silent, nieceless, sad!'
They had agreed to try and find a country cottage where they could spend
part of their lives together. It was to be a commitment that would never
exclude other emotional commitments, but give them both an
androgynous enlargement of experience. 'What excitements in store for us
all,' Carrington exclaimed (8 September 1916). Lytton, too, writing a
short poem in these 'unregarded hours', was cautiously excited.

Who would love only roses among flowers?
 Or listen to no music save Mozart's?
Then why not waste life's unregarded hours
 With fragile loves and secondary hearts?

Ah! Exquisite the tulips and the lilies!
 The Schuberts and the Schumanns, how divine!
Then kiss me, kiss me quickly, Amaryllis!
 And Laurie, mix your wantonness with mine!

5

FRAGILE LOVES AND SECONDARY HEARTS

It was not long before strange and disturbing rumours of Lytton's affair with Carrington were breezing through Bloomsbury. Had Bunny Garnett passed on his suspicions to Duncan and Vanessa at Wissett? On the whole Lytton thought not. Was it possible that Carrington herself had broken down and confessed before Ottoline and Clive's fusillade of questions at Garsington? She swore she had spoken only of the landscape. Even so, enveloped in mystery as Carrington was, Ottoline clearly spied the truth. 'Ottoline dislikes me!' Carrington revealed to Lytton (6 September 1916). 'Rather plainly.' Whenever something unpleasant happened, Ottoline usually blamed the woman rather than the man. She was to blame Frieda Lawrence for *Women in Love* and Maria Huxley for *Crome Yellow*. Now she blamed Carrington for alienating Lytton's affections. 'Her ladyship loves and fondels me no more! and Brett[28] was rather severe,' Carrington told Gertler (September 1916).

Though she had committed herself to Lytton, Carrington still could not bear to give up Gertler. 'I find you such an inspiring person to know,' she assured him (1 September 1916) on returning from Glastonbury. 'Without you all my life would collapse – like a punctured balloon.' Even when she feared seeing him, she loved to dream about him and write letters to him. She wrote as many letters to him that autumn as she did to Lytton, telling him of her happiness, though not the reason for it. 'I am excited over everything lately,' she exclaimed (3 September 1916). 'The fullness of life ... the things to come ... the wonder of it all!' She dispatched fresh tokens of her love: presents of flowers and plums, and more allegorical endearments. She asked Gertler for a new photograph; admitted that 'my moods vary like a sky of clouds!' and exulted in the wonder of wearing trousers like a boy. 'How I hate being a girl ... tied – with female encumbrances, and hanging flesh.'

These letters had a terrible effect on Gertler. With their denial of the body he longed to possess, they struck from him a long despairing cry – a tirade of pleas and recriminations which he let loose in the first week of September, but never sent Carrington.

'God, I am lonely – so lonely. I can't bear my loneliness ... Do you love me? Can you love? Is there nothing between us except my own fiery love? ... God save me from this Hell that I have been living in for so long. Save me soon, I can't bear it much longer! Your body seems most beautiful to me. Most painfully I long for it . . . How can you bear to let your beauty pass by, when you know there is a man dying for it! . . . There is only one period of Youth in our lifetime – Don't waste it! And me, take off the Rack of Torture soon . . . You have had Lytton with you and he easily made up for my absence. He did well enough . . . How I hate the coldness of life! It is not your fault Carrington Life is so arranged. Life has made you cold . . . You say in your letter you are "a wild Beast never to be tamed" . . . you are not a "wild" Beast but a frightened Beast and a timid Beast . . . If you had known many men – had had many lovers then you could boast of this "Wildness" . . . But my poor Virgin you have known *no* man yet . . . I hate your Virginity.'

Then, just as he seemed finally to have lost her, she turned to him. Guilty over misleading him, she found herself more than ever affected by his unhappiness. Also reading 'Venus and Adonis', 'To his Coy Mistress' and 'The Extasie' was having its effect. 'If I find many more poems by Donne urging me to forsake my virginity I may fall,' she conceded (September 1916), '. . . I think he is a man of such rare wisdom that I take his words very seriously. Far more so than Philip and Ottoline . . . But I ought not write this to you.' Then what ought she to do? That autumn she decided to surrender her virginity once more, this time to Gertler. 'What wonderful times we shall have later! When we are freer with one another,' he responded (25 September 1916), '. . . such interesting intimate times, close moments – moments of ecstasy! . . . Oh! Love is a good thing!'

But Carrington was still cautious. Sex – or 'sugar' as she called it in her letters to Gertler – 'does make one appreciate those poets more fully. But I only like sugar some times, not every week and every day . . . I shall . . . only allow you three lumps a month.'

Since Clive still worked on Ottoline's Garsington estate, and Vanessa was settling with Duncan and Bunny into Sussex, Maynard had arranged to take over the Bells' Gordon Square house (occupying it with Sheppard who had been employed as a translator by the War Office) and rent the larger premises at 3 Gower Street to Dorothy Brett. That September Brett invited Middleton Murry and Katherine Mansfield to occupy the lower rooms and, for nine pounds a year, invited Carrington to move in upstairs. 'What fun we will have in Gower Street,' she wrote to Lytton (September 1916). 'She [Katherine Mansfield] will play all the games I love best. Pretending to be other people and dressing up and parties!' These parties and pretences, and her deepening intrigues with Lytton and Mark, were a protection against the terrible war which she so seldom mentioned in her letters. But one night, the sky suddenly went crimson, the houses and trees were lit up and a sound of savage cheering, rising and falling, filled the streets. 'Carrington shot out of her room and we both clawed at the hall-door and dashed out,' remembered Beatrice Glenavy.

'. . . There it was, creeping and dripping down the sky, head first . . . a great flaming torch, and away above it the little light of the plane, signalling to the guns . . . it sounded as if all London was cheering. Carrington burst into terrible sobbing and rushed back into her room. I felt almost unconscious with excitement, and was on a plane of living where human suffering no longer existed. It looked as if the remains of the Zeppelin had come down on Hampstead Heath . . . I wanted to get a taxi and go to where it had fallen, and went to Carrington to get her to come with me, but she was crying so bitterly she could not speak, so I left her.'[29]

As soon as she had settled into Gower Street, Carrington began questioning friends, studying maps and pedalling off on her 'iron steed' to look for Lytton's ideal cottage. She sent him appraisals and diagrams and regular reports of her expeditions: '40 miles in one morning did I bicycle for your sake revered uncle?' she wrote (16 September 1916). 'Searching the highways and hedges, for your blasted house!'

The plan was to raise money to buy a house on something like a company basis – some of Lytton's Bloomsbury friends taking shares (that is, paying an annual sum of money) in return for which they might use the place for weekends or as an occasional retreat. 'Have you heard of the scheme for a country cottage?' Lytton asked Maynard (14 September 1916). 'Would you be willing to join? Barbara has already found something that sounds as if it might be suitable. Oliver [Strachey] and Faith [Henderson] are going to take shares – also perhaps Saxon . . . Oh, Carrington, too.'

Barbara Bagenal's discovery was an unfurnished house in Hemel Hempstead, at an annual rent of forty-eight pounds and with 'a loft for conscientious objectors'. When this fell through, the search was vigorously taken up again by Carrington. 'I have maps of every square inch of the country now,' she told Lytton (8 September 1916). 'And correspondence with every auctioneer in Newbury, Marlborough, and Reading!' But her notions of what would accord with Lytton's literary sensibilities were so elevated that no estate agent could rise to them. 'Our country cottage still floats high in the air,' Lytton commented to Ottoline (1 October 1916) '– a cottage in Spain.'

From Wells he had gradually and with great indecision drifted back to London, which 'I found horrible – stuffy and chilly at the same time, and packed full and flowing over, with inconceivably hideous monstrosities. They push one off the pavements in their crowds, they surge round every bus, they welter in the tubes – one dashes wildly for a taxi, but there are no taxis left. In the night it's *pitch* dark; one walks wedged in among the multitudes like a soldier in an army . . . No! London is decidedly *not* a place to be in just now.'

Nevertheless, it was in London that Lytton was to remain. At Belsize Park Gardens, by the last week of October, he was able to announce that 'cet épouvantable Docteur Arnold est fini – praise be to God!' Almost immediately he began reading and making notes for 'The End of General Gordon', the final essay in *Eminent Victorians*.

Whenever she could get him to sit for her, Carrington went on painting Lytton's portrait which 'will be really a good picture', she believed (6 November 1916). By the end of the year she had finished it, Lytton's elongated hands raised before his dreaming face, as if in prayer, holding a book above the reclining body. 'I wonder what you will think of it when you see it,' she wrote in her diary on New Year's Day, '. . . now tonight it looks wonderfully good and I am happy. But then I dread showing it. I should like to go on painting you every week . . . and never never showing what I paint. It's marvellous having you all to oneself . . . I would love to explore your mind behind your finely skinned forehead. You seem so wise and very coldly old. Yet in spite of this what a peace to be with you, and how happy I was today.'

When Lytton was not dining with Maynard at the Café Royal, going off with Sheppard 'and a party of young men', or, among the roaring and gloating, to a boxing match in Blackfriars with Boris Anrep ('I was quite close – almost touching their terrific naked bodies'), he would accompany Carrington to parties at Barbara's studio in Hampstead and at Augustus John's in Chelsea, and take her over to Hogarth House in Richmond where Leonard and Virginia were soon to start the Hogarth Press.[30] He would also come over to Gower Street for teas with her and Brett and Katherine Mansfield. 'I shall like living with Katherine I am sure,' Carrington had predicted in a letter to Lytton. But the trouble was that Katherine waylaid all the men – Mark, Lytton, Bertie and others – and enticed them into her first-floor rooms. 'To our chagrin, *no one* gets further than Katherine!' Brett told Ottoline. '. . . all disappear like magic . . . I have my little instrument [hearing aid] trained on the cracks in the floor!' Middleton Murry was flirting openly with both Ottoline and Brett (herself in love with Ottoline) while Katherine made off briefly and secretly with Bertie Russell. By February 1917 Katherine was to leave Gower Street because, according to Ottoline, 'she had been made

Strachey in 1904, painted in France (see p. 97) by his brother-in-law, Simon Bussy.
rtesy of the National Portrait Gallery, London)

RIGHT Carrington's portrait of Strachey finished at the end of 1916 (see p. 380): '. . . now tonight it looks wonderfully good, and I am happy. But then I dread showing it'. (Private Collection, courtesy of the Bridgeman Art Library, London)

OPPOSITE The Mill at Tidmarsh, Berkshire, where Strachey and Carrington lived from the end of 1917 until 1924. Carrington painted this picture of the mill in 1918 (see p. 431), adding the black swans from her imagination. (Private Collection, courtesy of the Courtauld Institute of Art, London)

Henry Lamb's portrait of Strachey, finished in 1914, but further revised and added to (see p. 250 between 1919 and 1921. (Courtesy of the Tate Gallery, London)

uncomfortable by Carrington who spied on her; watching when she went out or came in and who . . . made up all manner of fantastic tales, that Katherine used to disguise herself and go out at night, seeking exciting adventures, that she acted for cinemas and that she had mysterious visitors.'

Lytton came and went: listening, staring, curious, incredulous. That November he subsided at Asheham nursing a winter illness and over Christmas went to convalesce with Ottoline at Garsington. Clive Bell and Aldous Huxley were there as residents; Bertie was invited, as well as Brett and Carrington. There was much discussion of the war, long walks over the fields, secret messages passed from one to another, the celebrating of Evensong and some literary entertainments which included performances of Lytton reading his 'Dr Arnold' and a mock-Russian play, 'marvellously witty and good', Carrington thought, devised by Katherine. Carrington herself played Marcel Dash, the grandchild of Dr Keit, a part taken by Lytton. 'We performed a superb play invented by Katherine, improvising as we went along,' Aldous Huxley wrote to his brother Julian (29 December 1916). 'It was a huge success, with Murry as a Dostoevsky character and Lytton as an incredibly wicked old grandfather.'

Back in the fogs of London, Lytton interrupted his work on General Gordon with reviews for the *New Statesman* and by reading Rabelais (about whom he was to write in the *New Statesman* a year later). *Gargantua and Pantagruel* 'has surged over me altogether', he informed Ottoline (6 February 1917). 'I read very little else. I find him far the best antidote yet discovered against the revolting mesquineries de ces jours. I read him in the tube, and he is a veritable buckler of defence, warding off those miserable visages, with their miserable newspapers. What an adorable giant, to drop into the arms of! And then the interest of the book, from so many points of view, is so great. I am glad I never really read it before; it is intoxicating to get a fresh enthusiasm when one's over eighty.'

By the end of March, he had begun to feel again something like his actual age – now thirty-seven. The weather brightened and grew warmer, 'and now I feel that I really must set to and seriously attack the General', he told Ottoline, who had gallantly invited him again to Garsington, this time without Carrington (23 March 1917). 'I'm afraid it would be fatal to leave my stool until I've captured his first line of trenches.'

Meanwhile Carrington's relationship with Gertler had slowly been moving towards a crisis. He had imagined that he would be seeing far more of her since she moved to Gower Street, but either she was away on unexplained rambles in the country, or else the house was crowded with other men. 'What with one thing and another we hardly ever meet alone,' he complained (January 1917). When they were together 'I am always nervous and awkward in your presence and tongue-tied' (February 1917). One of their new problems was contraception ('I really did try that thing. Only it was too big, and wouldn't go inside no matter what way I used it!'). Carrington promised not to be childish; promised to be less selfish and to make him happier: but sexual relations between them did not get better. 'I envy often amiable people who can love more simply, and get on,' she told him. '. . . I wish to God I was not made as I am'. Her dislike of sexual intercourse with Mark gave her the idea, her biographer Gretchen Gerzina suggests, that she could 'sleep with him without being "unfaithful" to Lytton'. All the same, she felt miserable at making Mark so unhappy. But what could she do?

What she could do, Gertler urged, was to live with him. 'I shan't worry you for much "sugar" if only I can see you and talk,' he promised (December 1916). But he added: 'if any other man touches any part of your beautiful body, I shall kill myself – don't forget that! I could not bear such a thing ... Some moments I wish one of us dead!' Carrington, however, felt certain that 'I could never live with you sexually day after day,' though conceding: 'I see no reason why another summer it should not be a few months.' Their intermittent love-making was deeply frustrating for Gertler, and became worse whenever Carrington explained to him it was only 'because you want me sexually that you are miserable' or comforted him with the news that it was merely 'my corporeal body [that] has left you'. The quarrels between them this winter multiplied. He scorned her for trying to look like a boy, with her short hair, lack of make-up and fondness for wearing trousers – then, regretting his anger, showered her with apologies. 'As for trousers, forgive me for having grumbled – I don't really mind. *I* may even take up wearing a skirt!'

If only they could reach 'a much broader relationship like old friends', Carrington believed (25 March 1917) she would not be so frightened of hurting him or of his retaliation. 'I want you to meet my friends & share my interests,' she explained. Yet when Leonard and Virginia lent her Asheham, she went there not with Mark, but with Barbara and Saxon Sydney-Turner, and they passed the time like children, tobogganing on tea-trays across the Downs. The conclusion to which Gertler felt himself driven was that their relationship 'has one fault and that is we do not contrive to be in the country enough together'. He therefore invited her again to Gilbert Cannan's enchanted Mill House at Cholesbury in Hertfordshire and she haphazardly extended the invitation to Lytton, promising him a fire in his bedroom. Sensibly he declined.

Carrington had been horrified by the publication of *Mendel*, Gilbert

Cannan's roman à clef dedicated to 'D.C.' 'How angry I am over Gilbert's Book,' she had written to Mark (1 November 1916). 'Everywhere this confounded gossip, and servant-like curiosity. Its ugly and so damned vulgar.' D.H. Lawrence had disliked it ('it is a piece of journalism, absolutely without a spark of creative fire'), though Virginia had found it 'interesting' on account of the facts it provided about the younger generation. But Cannan, too, was now in despair, having fallen in love with a South African girl aged nineteen. Unable to believe that such a beautiful woman really loved him, unable to rid himself of this requited passion or contain it within his marriage, he had suffered a breakdown. 'The bursting of the cloud of insanity . . . has been growing and growing . . . the facts are appalling,' he confided to Gertler. '. . . My dear old Mark, we do seem to go through these things together . . . I wish I had your toughness.'

But Gertler did not feel at all tough. He felt vulnerable to whatever Carrington wrote or said or did. Their relationship was brought to a crisis by two deaths. In the first week of February 1917 Gertler's father died. It was 'the worst day I've had in my life'. Carrington had been hoping to hear something of her brother Teddy, missing in action since the previous autumn, but the passing of his birthday that month without news finally convinced her that he was now dead. 'I am losing hope of Teddy,' she admitted (26 February 1917). 'Its beginning to depress me terribly sometimes.' Gertler desperately needed to assuage his grief with sexual love; but Carrington needed the comfort of solitude. They met, and he lost control. 'You could have avoided all that dreadfulness by just letting me go away quietly,' she wrote to him afterwards. '. . . It is not that I do not love you, it is that I was sad and could not make love to you. When one is in sorrow one feels isolated curiously, and to be forced into another's animal passion suddenly makes it almost a nightmare.'

So she turned for solace over her brother not to Mark but to Lytton. 'You will not mind if I want to see you often,' she wrote to him (26 February 1917). 'For its wretched being alone and knowing how he went – without ever having been seen or loved. He had the independence of a child like Poppet,[31] all his joys contained inside himself – made by himself.'

Lytton's kindness to her, his compassion and gentleness, was her one source of relief. Her adoration of him deepened. She knew that there must always be limits to their relationship, but it was a satisfaction simply to be with him whenever that was possible; and when it was not, to receive and memorize his marvellous letters. She believed that she understood him, inexplicable as he was, better than anyone. In his reply to her from Alderney Manor, where he was staying with Augustus and Dorelia John,[32]

Lytton ruefully apologizes (8 March 1917) for his inability to do more for her.

'I fear I *am* at times a trifle – unsatisfactory. Is it age, sex, or cynicism? But perhaps it's really only appearance – of one sort or another. The fellow, as they say, (only they don't) is good at heart. I wish I could be of more avail – I often think that if the layer of flesh over my bones were a few inches thicker I might be. But that is another of the tiresome arrangements of the world . . . Ma chère, I'm sure I do sympathise with your feelings of loneliness. I know what it is so horribly well myself.'

If only Mark were more like Lytton – and in some ways Lytton more like Mark! Carrington could not reconcile her attachment to them both. She shrank from making a decision between them. They were so dissimilar she could not possibly consider them as rivals. Yet a decision of some sort would have to be made.

For Easter Carrington went down to stay at Lord's Wood, her friend Alix Sargant-Florence's home on Marlow Common – 'a very nice house', as she described it to Gertler, 'one of the best sort. With great comforts and a most beautiful bathroom you ever saw with coloured tiles.' The other guests were Lytton and James, Harry Norton and Maynard Keynes. 'I hope you will not think things have been done on too grand a scale,' Alix wrote to her mother (3 April 1917). 'But we want so much to make the party a success & every member is a glutton – Lytton (fussy), Maynard (voracious), James (systematic), Norton (hypochondriac), Carrington (healthy) & myself (greedy).' The sun shone, Carrington, happily dressed in breeches, roamed the great woods, painted the greedy intellectual Alix, read Plato 'and was very excited over it', and in the evening listened to James playing Bach and Beethoven at the pianola. Afterwards Lytton remembered (10 April 1917) 'quaffing Chianti twice a day, gorging Périgord Pie, dreaming by the fire and perpetually putting off the Grande Expédition'. Sometimes they read plays representing Bloomsbury's comic and tragic views of the world – Vanbrugh's *The Relapse* and Shakespeare's *Troilus and Cressida* – 'which was great fun', Carrington wrote. 'Only I was so agitated when it came to my part that I could hardly enjoy it as much as I should.'

Soon Carrington was to find 'a brilliant new game, completely shutting my eyes', she told Lytton (3 August 1917), 'and being a blind girl led by Alix'. It was natural for her to follow Alix whose love for James, which had begun at The Lacket eighteen months ago, seemed so similar to her own love for Lytton. This Easter party at Lord's Wood was the opening of

Alix's three-year campaign to win James – a campaign that had to overcome James's infatuation for Noel Olivier as well as to absorb Alix's own affairs with Bunny Garnett (inspiring him with 'a longing to commit murder and rape') and Harry Norton which Virginia mockingly analysed as 'Copulation every 10 days in order to free his suppressed instincts!' Never knowing when she was beaten, Alix knew very well what she wanted, and though the difficulties of her campaign revealed 'her sepulchral despair – poor woman', she pursued this quest of James, Virginia observed, with an 'air of level headed desperation'.[33]

These few days at Lord's Wood had a decisive effect on Carrington. On her last day there she wrote two letters, one to Mark telling him something of her feelings for Lytton and arranging to meet him on the following Monday afternoon; and the other to Lytton – who had just left Marlow – asking to see him the evening of the same day. On Sunday she travelled up by train to London, and the next morning woke from a disquieting dream of her brother Teddy drowning at sea. She took a bus to Penn Studio, where she found Gertler calm and ghostly. At first they talked nervously about pictures. Then he asked her what she intended to do, how she wanted to plan her life. She had been prepared for all sorts of scenes, and his control disarmed her. For she had decided to leave him. 'I became more and more wretched and wept,' she scrawled in her diary. 'It seemed like leaving the warm sun in the fields and going into a dark and cold wood surrounded by trees which were strangers. I suddenly looked back at the long life we had had between us of mixed emotions. But always warm because of his intense love and now I had to leave it all and go away.'

For the first time Gertler seems to have become aware that Carrington meant this meeting to signal the end between them; and he too broke down and sobbed. His tears were terrible and made her feel hateful to herself. 'For he wanted to die and I thought how much this love mattered to him,' she wrote, 'and yet in spite [of] its greatness I could not keep it, and must leave. His loneliness was awfull.'

Shortly afterwards they left the studio and had tea together in a café, hardly speaking at all. He asked her whether she intended to go and live with Lytton and she told him that she did not.

'But he may love you,' Gertler protested.

'No, he will not,' she answered flatly.

This seemed to make their separation easier for him to accept. But he still begged her to go on seeing him as a friend, a brother, though both of them knew that such an arrangement could not work. As the time came for them to part they grew embarrassed. 'How very much I cared for him suddenly came upon me,' she wrote. 'The unreality, the coldness of

Lytton.' They went by bus through the rain to the British Museum. It was a relief to be on the move and they laughed sometimes on the way. When they arrived, Carrington left him, 'frightfully sick with a bad pain in my side'.

She returned to her rooms, which she was now sharing with Alix, had a hot bath and dressed for the evening. Lytton was already downstairs having tea with Alix and her mother. Carrington joined them, but felt too sick to pay much attention, though she observed with a mixture of fascination and dread how, despite knowing what she must have gone through with Mark, Lytton 'sat there quite calmly, quibbling and playing lightly with his words'. Later, the two of them went out to dinner, and Carrington was glad to prolong the conversation about Lytton's friends and illnesses. But soon, the weight of what was being left unspoken began pressing upon her. The time they took over dinner was appalling. Should she speak up now in the restaurant or wait until Lytton took her home? He seemed unaware of her anxiety.

Then, when they got back to Gower Street and had settled down in front of the fire, he finally asked her what had happened, and she tried to explain.

'I thought I had better tell Mark, as it was so difficult going on,' she said.

'Tell him what?' Lytton inquired.

'That it couldn't go on. So I just wrote and said it.'

'What did you say in your letter?'

Carrington hesitated. 'I thought you knew.'

'What do you mean?'

'I said that I was in love with you. I hope you don't mind very much.'

'But aren't you being rather romantic?' Lytton asked. 'And are you certain?'

'There's nothing romantic about it,' she answered wryly.

'What did Mark say?'

'He was terribly upset.'

Lytton looked alarmed. 'Did he seem angry with me?'

'No. He didn't mention you.'

'But it's too incongruous,' he protested. 'I'm so old and diseased. I wish I was more able.'

'That doesn't matter.'

'What do you mean? What do you think we had better do about the physical?'

'Oh I don't mind about that.'

Lytton paused. 'That's rather bad,' he said.

As their discussion progressed, Lytton again brought up their physical incompatibility and the responsibility for what they were doing. 'They will think I am to blame,' he said. Carrington repeated that she knew what she was doing and that if there were fault, it was hers. 'I wish I was rich,' Lytton remarked, 'and then I could keep you as my mistress.' But this angered Carrington, and she told him that no amount of money would make any difference, to which he ruefully assented.

'Then he sat on the floor with me,' Carrington wrote in her diary, 'and clasped my hands in his and let me kiss his mouth, all enmeshed in the brittle beard and my inside was as heavy as lead, as I knew how miserable it was going to be.'[34]

Carrington hoped that he might stay the night with her, this night of all nights, but soon he got up and said he must leave. Alone, she was suddenly overpowered by 'the misery at parting and my hatred of myself for caring so much. And at his callousness – He was so wise and just.'

A little later she wandered downstairs to Alix, and began talking with her long into the night – of how to cope with her worship of Lytton, of how to arrange their lives together, of how to avoid the necessity for secrecy and deception.

Why had this happened to her? And although no answer presented itself, and 'there was no consolation', she felt relief at being able to discuss the problem with someone who comprehended so well. And as she talked on, later and later, it seemed as though in a little while a solution must be found, and then a new and wonderful life would begin. And it was clear to her, as it had been to another before her, that the end was nowhere yet in sight, and that the most tortuous and difficult part of it was only just beginning.

THIRTEEN

Tidmarsh

Suppose the kind gods said, 'Today
You're forty. True: But still rejoice!
Gifts we have got will smooth away
The ills of age. Come, take your choice!'

What should I answer? Well, you know
I'm modest – very. So no shower
Of endless gold I'd beg, nor show
Of proud-faced pomp, nor regal power.

No; ordinary things and good
I'd choose: friends, wise and kind and few;
A country house, a pretty wood
To walk in; books both old and new

To read; a life retired, apart,
Where leisure and repose might dwell
With industry; a little art;
Perhaps a little fame as well.

Lytton Strachey (1 March 1920)

I

DRAMA AND UNCERTAINTY

Carrington had spoken to Mark Gertler about Lytton as frankly as she could. But she had not been able to tell him everything. She had said goodbye, yet it had sounded to him like an *au revoir*. So after the studio and the café, they met again the following evening at the Eiffel Tower restaurant in Percy Street. Gertler turned up a few minutes late, and they murmured politely across the table until Carrington blurted out that the two of them had really better not see each other any more. He agreed and they fell silent. Not knowing what to say, she mentioned her talk with Lytton the previous night.

'How did that go off?' Gertler asked.

'All right.'

'Then what did you do?'

'Went to my rooms,' Carrington replied; and added: 'I told Lytton then.'

'And what did he say?'

'He was sorry.'

'Was that all he said?' Gertler laughed.

But Carrington felt indignant. 'Well, it wasn't his fault. What more could he say?'

'Fancy just saying that. Nothing more.'

'No.'

'Good God. And he doesn't care?'

'No. I knew he did not.'

This upset Gertler. 'I never want to see you again,' he said. 'So will you mind if I leave you directly after dinner?'

'No.'

The conversation up to this point had been subdued. But all at once Gertler raised his voice: 'To think after all these years, in 3 months you should love a man like Strachey twice your age and emaciated and old. As I always said life is a crooked business.'[1]

He did not blame her. He was not angry. But he could not bear to think of someone so beautiful, and so desired by himself, involved with a homosexual. This was why he could not see her again.

After a long silence, Gertler got up and left, and Carrington walked back to Gower Street alone. Before going to bed, she wrote him a letter (14 April 1917):

'Would you mind not telling anyone (except your friend Monty[2] or Kot[3] if you wish to) about it, anyway for the present. As it was too great a thing to let them know about, and jeer.'

She promised to return his books and asked his forgiveness 'for causing you so much sorrow', signing herself 'Your friend Carrington'. In reply she received some well-mannered messages from 'Ever your friend Mark Gertler'. He hoped her 'friendship with Lytton is a happy one' and urged her to treat him as 'a loving brother. I have taken my right place in relation to you.' After the shock of parting, 'I am thankful for what has happened', he assured her. 'I shall commence right away to build up my future life, brick by brick . . . My work will be the basis. From now on my life will be a more decent and spiritual thing than it's ever had a chance to be before.'

The effect of these letters on Carrington was unexpected. She had thought that her anguished decision in favour of Lytton would deliver her from the emotional chaos of the winter. But in the last two 'nightmare' weeks of April her confusion grew worse. Never had she felt so alone. Lytton was unfailingly kind but incapable of being demonstrative – especially as his affections were not much stimulated by sexual feelings. His spidery stillness, his riveting silences – only occasionally would he stir to unfold and reorganize his complicated angular limbs – still hypnotized her.

Although he did his best to help Carrington, Lytton still thought she was being alarmingly unrealistic and he made no attempt to play a part which he could not keep up. She had, he reasoned, better know the worst from the start. Such scrupulousness made her more aware of Gertler's long struggle over herself. Mark was striving to be 'absolutely self-contained', but had asked for 'the tiniest bit of friendship' until 'quite soon I shall be able to release you altogether'. Less certain suddenly that she wanted to be released, Carrington promised to 'try and make you happy all I can' (28 April 1917), adding that she had 'just been reading King Lear by Shakespeare. I think it his best work.' He sent her flowers. She came round with *King Lear*. 'I enjoyed our last meeting so much,' he wrote (15 May 1917). 'How nice of you to read King Lear to me.' She was sure now 'it is impossible for us to part always'. It had felt so good to be 'back again together at last with our foolishness and comic jokes'. Soon they were going for walks and spending evenings together – and she was filled 'with absolute horror' at the idea that she might be pregnant. For although she could not have sex with Mark every day, yet the occasional night, or weekend, or even week she thought she could manage after all. 'You see how contradictory it all is,' she explained early that May. 'But I love seeing you so much more now.'

So, by this circuitous route, Gertler achieved what he had sought through bringing Lytton and Carrington together. Within a month of their last farewells, she was his mistress. 'I will see you as much as I can,' she promised. Yet she was still tantalizingly elusive since her availability depended upon Lytton, about whose 'cynical frigidity and discipline' she sometimes complained, but to whose whims she responded with breathless servility. No wonder Gertler had attempted to get her pregnant. He tried not to censure Carrington, but his loathing of Lytton grew intense.

In May, when Mark was invited by Carrington and her friend Alix Sargant-Florence to Lord's Wood, he found on his arrival that Carrington was on the point of leaving for a hastily-convened party with Lytton,

Barbara Bagenal and Saxon Sydney-Turner. They were off to Chilling, Logan Pearsall Smith's house at Warsash on the Hampshire coast, which Oliver and Ray Strachey were then renting. In her letters to Mark, Carrington went to some trouble describing the marvellous little woods full of primroses and bluebells. Chilling, she assured him, was one of 'the most lovely houses and places' she had ever seen. 'It's Elizabethan, very old. in the fields with an orchard behind the house with trees in blossom. Dear friend I am so happy because it is all very beautiful . . . Did you enjoy staying with Alix!'

Almost every day she bathed naked in the sea with Oliver and Barbara, while Lytton and Saxon observed them from the beach. Sea-planes in their squadrons came swooping down low over the waves where they swam then went soaring into the blue sky. Lytton was still working at 'The End of General Gordon', and Carrington herself doing woodcuts for the Hogarth Press. The two of them would go for walks along the sea-shore, Lytton reciting *Romeo and Juliet* ('which I thought very beautiful'), *Henry IV*, and 'also some Greek History'.

Gertler fumed silently. 'You have been slightly brutal not to write to me,' Carrington chided him. But she was so happy that 'I am overlooking it and writing to you'. A solution to her problems, indefinable as yet, had never seemed nearer. 'If only like a magician I could frizzle up my parents into ether,' she wrote to Lytton after returning home to Hurstbourne Tarrant (26 May 1917), 'and waft them to some remote town, and then encase you in the old wall nut tree so you could never escape me . . .'

2

SUMMER MANOEUVRES

On his arrival back at Belsize Park Gardens, a tedious ordeal awaited Lytton. The Government was combing through all those who had until then been exempted from military service, and he was required to re-establish his case from the start. This time he hired counsel to represent him, restated in three measured paragraphs his conscientious objections, and arranged for Philip Morrell to appear as a character witness, though Maynard (who appeared as a witness for James Strachey) had recommended St Loe Strachey in place of the 'blundering' Philip. When the hearing took place his barrister did not allow Philip Morrell into the room – 'which I'm sure was a great mistake, as if he had appeared the Chairman would have recognised him, and seen that I was "well-connected", which, as it was, he didn't grasp'. The conscience part of the case was soon adjourned pending a medical re-examination by the army doctors, and a few days later Lytton appeared again at the White City, where he was shuttled about between doctors for some six hours – 'fortunately without any clothes on for most of the time'. Once again he was given what amounted to exemption from any kind of service. His medical grading was confirmed as C4, he was relegated to the reserve, and ordered to reappear every six months for further check-ups 'unless I put in a conscience claim', he told Carrington (9 June 1917). '. . . At present I incline to letting sleeping dogs lie.'

To recover from this 'fearful business', he hurried down to Garsington over Whitsun, 'leaving poor General Gordon alone and neglected on my writing table'. Asquith was there, now deprived by Lloyd George of his premiership, and looking 'a very diminished deflated figure'. But primarily Lytton was absorbed by two other guests, Augustine Birrell who had resigned as Chief Secretary for Ireland after the Easter Rebellion the previous year, and the twenty-two-year-old poet Robert Graves, who together seemed to represent the past and future. 'Old man Birrell – decidedly a Victorian product,' he wrote to Carrington (28 May 1917). 'Large and tall and oddly like Thackeray to look at – with spectacles and sharp big nose and a long upper lip that moves about and curls very expressively – white hair, of course, and also rather unexpectedly sensitive and even sometimes almost agitated fingers. Altogether, a most imposing façade! . . . Underneath – there really seems to be almost nothing. The ordinary respectabilities and virtues, no doubt, and a certain bookishness, gleaned from some rather narrow reading, and then – blank.'

Robert Graves was on sick-leave from the front. 'The fashion for façades has its drawbacks,' Lytton remarked. 'For instance there is the youth Graves, with one lung shot away, keeping himself going on strychnine, and with strange concealed thoughts which only very occasionally poke up through his schoolboy jocularities. Terribly tragic I thought. I found him (I need hardly say) attractive – tall and olive-brown complexioned, with a broken nose and broken teeth (the result of boxing) – dark hair and eyes.'

From this time on, whenever they were apart, Lytton would send Carrington long amusing letters telling her what he was doing, all he saw and heard, so that she could almost feel she had been with him. And she would write back spidery unpunctuated pages like improvised poetry, overlaid with drawings, dramatizing her adventures for his entertainment, and filling the spaces with declarations of her love. 'Do you know everytime I see you now I love you even more,' she wrote to him that summer. And again: 'More beloved than any creature please come next week again. I could kill you dead with my hugs to-day.' More than ever she felt her lack of formal education and literary knowledge. 'I wish I could write properly to you,' she told him (June 1917), 'but you know its almost too hard.' 'I consider your letters perfect – so pray don't improve them,' he replied – though he sometimes could not resist correcting her spelling. So she went on pouring out the chaotic feelings within her, enriching her mongrel style with Lytton's phrases, imitating his French *mots* and expletives. And always she begged him to send her back one more of his wonderful letters. He responded nobly. His crafted correspondence, with its air of lightness, its contrived ironies, its risqué passages and moments of comic melodrama, was like a classical ballet compared to Carrington's uncontrolled country dancing. But his writing gained in freedom, flexibility and range from being matched with such a partner. And her letters, for all their lack of co-ordination, created their own life, like a magic mirror that reflects across time, gesture, speech, movement, tone.

Carrington was anxious that those who knew of her attachment to Lytton should not gossip about it, especially 'all those fly catchers at Garsington'. What she dreaded was their pity. 'You must not think I am unhappy,' she wrote to Barbara Bagenal at the end of May. 'For I am often very happy only it is just that I cannot bear sometimes not seeing him even for a day ... If it is fine I am going for a jaunt to Cambridge with him, Barbara, I am so excited.'

At Cambridge, early that June, the two of them stayed with Harry Norton. Lytton piloted Carrington round the Fitzwilliam Museum, Rupert Brooke's Old Vicarage at Grantchester, and the colleges – 'I was rather excited over King's Chapel windows,' she told Noel (3 June 1917). 'But mostly over the architecture of Wren at Emmanuel, and also the Library Trinity.' She realized the significance of this introduction to Lytton's spiritual home which had formed his mind and given him happiness when growing up. But to Mark Gertler, who had felt an outsider when visiting Cambridge, she did not mention this trip. It was difficult keeping secrets in Bloomsbury. She told Mark of her bicycle trips round the country, but denied that she was looking for a cottage to share with Lytton. To Lytton himself she was to write (10 August 1917) that 'your only serious rival' was his brother James still awkwardly poised between Noel Olivier and Alix Sargant-Florence.

On his return to London, Lytton made another effort to assist General Gordon to his end. 'I find that if one works there's hardly any time for anything else,' he had told Ottoline (24 October 1916). But now there were frequent interruptions – theatres, operas and, most interesting of all, a private view of Augustus John's drawings at the Alpine Club. Unlike Carrington and Gertler, Lytton interested himself in the spectators. 'Such a strange well-dressed and respectable crowd,' he told John's old flame Ottoline. 'The great man appeared in the middle of it, dressed in a neat but not gaudy Khaki suit, with his beard considerably trimmed, and altogether a decidedly colonial air. On the whole, I must say I prefer him en bohème.'

What distracted him most from 'The End of General Gordon' was the worrying condition of his mother. For some time Lady Strachey had been experiencing pain in her defective left eye, and in July she was advised to undergo an operation to have it removed. While she was in hospital, and subsequently during her convalescence at Durbins, Belsize Park Gardens was shut up, and Lytton went to stay for some days with Carrington. That June, Dorothy Brett had given up the ménage at Gower Street explaining that Carrington's 'mode of life is too untidy, too much of a turmoil ... it disturbs me to have it splashing over me.' Maynard sent a bill to Brett calculating that (7 June 1917) 'since you took occupation of Gower Street, the house has cost me £142, against which I have had from you so far £53 3s 6d ... it's a beastly business having to do with houses.' Brett thoroughly agreed – then forwarded the bill to Carrington (14 July 1917) 'as the damage is to the furniture and I had my own!' It would teach her a lesson, 'but I don't know what they will do as Carrington has no money ...' What Carrington did was to borrow money from her brother Noel and a little from Gertler before settling into new lodgings at 60 Frith Street, in Soho. 'Lytton has been living with me this last week here since Wed.,' she wrote to Barbara Bagenal. 'He went on Sat. evening to Durbins. So I am still so happy that I thought I would write to you. Just to inform you that I've never been so happy in my *life* before ... It was fun persuading Mrs Reekes, my housekeeper, that Lytton was my uncle. But I think the general uproar that went on in the early morning in his room Rather upset her belief in me!'

It had been strange for Lytton waking up each morning with a 'virginal bodyguard' to kiss. She had to warn Mark that Lytton was temporarily in the building. 'I don't know if you'll like it,' she wondered (July 1917). '... Although he wants to see you again badly.' What she didn't like was Lytton's ability to leave her for days or even weeks without a qualm. For all she knew, he let out a sigh of relief at their parting. His frigidity, she wryly remarked to Mark, kept one pleasantly cool in the hot weather. 'Yes, I say it frankly,' she wrote, 'Lytton will be away for two months. So you will have no more reason to curse him or me. For you will have me every night you want to. What confessions we honest people make!' As a confession this was certainly indiscreet but, as it turned out, untrue. To save money she was obliged to retreat to Hurstbourne Tarrant, where she went on painting her friend Alix, planned a walking tour with her brother Noel, and wrote letters to Mark on botanical matters. 'If you ever want me, I shall always come to you, at a moment's notice,' Mark volunteered (June 1917). 'I know you are going through troublesome times now and I feel your troubles as I would my own.' But Carrington could not decide whether she wanted him to come or not. 'What a mess I've made of your life for you!' she exclaimed. Mark however would not accept this. 'It is not true,' he replied (15 June 1917); 'besides, my life is only just beginning . . . I should always find something or somebody to suffer about . . . We are all in the same rocky boat.' Also on board this rocky boat was Lytton to whom Carrington sent many loving letters this summer. 'I lap them down with my breakfast,' he told her (7 August 1917), 'and they do me more good than tonics, blood capsules, or iron jelloids.'

At Durbins, the atmosphere was subdued. Lady Strachey, 'attended by a pug-faced nurse', was still weak after her operation, and needed attention. She had always loved jigsaws and soon had a board made with stand-up rims and all the pieces turned over the right way so that she could put them together by touch. Lytton's principal companion was his sister Marjorie who was planning to compose a pamphlet on The Management of Spectacles and Pince-nez while making Love. 'We seem to get on very well,' Lytton told Mary Hutchinson (24 July 1917), 'in the kind of way in which brothers and sisters do, when they're not in love with each other.' Over the summer Roger Fry's house was a convalescent home for Lady Strachey. Lytton too found it a good base for the writing of General Gordon. 'For he is still around my neck, the old albatross!' he told Ottoline (14 August 1917). 'But he won't be much longer, I'm thankful to say.' By the third week of August his mother was much better, and Lytton prepared to leave Durbins to join Leonard and Virginia at Asheham. 'I find myself plunged in the gulf of Gordon, from which it is impossible to emerge for 2 or 3 days,' he wrote to Virginia. 'Then I hope the crisis will be over – though there'll still be some finishing paragraphs to be applied. Please expect me on Thursday.'

'The End of General Gordon' was completed later that month at Asheham, where he read it over to his friends. From there he moved on to see Vanessa, Duncan and Bunny Garnett who in 'confusion and horror' had left Wissett the previous autumn and were now established with Vanessa's two sons, Julian and Quentin, at Charleston, a farmhouse only four miles from Asheham. Virginia had been urging her sister to take this house beneath the South Downs and was soon herself taking pleasure in its ragamuffin atmosphere. 'It's most lovely, very solid and simple, with flat walls in that lovely mixture of brick and flint that they use about here and perfectly flat windows in the walls and wonderful tiled roofs,' Vanessa had written to Roger Fry when moving in her troupe of boys and men (16 October 1916). 'The pond is most beautiful, with a willow at one side and a stone or flint wall edging it all round the garden . . . there's a small orchard and walled garden . . . the rooms are very large and a great many.' 'It will be an odd life,' she wrote, '. . . but it seems to me it ought to be a good one for painting.' Charleston was to become Duncan and Vanessa's masterpiece, like a picture in which they lived. They covered almost every piece of furniture, every door, mantelpiece and curtain, every plate and cup with their designs; they hung their own pictures as well as works by Gris, Matisse, Picasso, Rouault, Sickert, Vlaminck. 'Nessa presides over the most astonishing ménage,' Virginia was to write (8 May 1919); 'Belgian hares, governesses, children, gardeners, hens, ducks, and painting all the time, till every inch of the house is a different colour.' From here Duncan and Bunny were able to continue with their 'work of national importance' on a farm near by. Even in wartime Charleston was a place for family parties, summer picnics, country walks, amateur plays, gramophone music and late night gossip. But it was also a place for work. There was a staff to cook meals, do housework, look after children, while Vanessa and Duncan covered empty surfaces with their flowers and nudes, Clive went ahead with his books and articles for the *New Statesman* and Maynard, for whom Charleston became a regular weekend refuge, was to write *The Economic Consequences of the Peace*.

This was Lytton's first visit to Charleston. 'Vanessa expects you to accompany me,' he had explained (31 July 1917) to Carrington, who answered that she looked forward to being 'wrapped in the folds of your octopi arms' (n.d. August 1917). But when she saw the house with its litter of easels and paintboxes, palettes and brushes, turpentine and tubes of paint, its decorations spreading everywhere like a vegetable growth, she felt an acute longing for the company of Mark. 'It was so good to be with artists who talked about painting,' she wrote to him. '. . . Do not leave me, Mark!'

Lytton was preoccupied with literary subjects, reading out the latest versions of 'Cardinal Manning' and 'Florence Nightingale' and deciding, after his trial reading at Asheham, that 'The End of General Gordon' needed reworking. 'That terrible General isn't yet done with,' he complained to Pippa (23 August 1917). During the reading Duncan had fallen asleep after a hard day's farming, and Vanessa thought his subversive informality was achieved by means of too many clichés. But

David Garnett was impressed, realizing, he later wrote, 'that Lytton's essays were designed to undermine the foundations on which the age that brought war about had been built'.[4]

Bunny Garnett was a genuine disciple of Lytton's, looking up to him as something of a moral and literary mentor. Their friendship during these war years partly depended on Bunny's good looks and talent for 'smoothing down my fretful quills with the softest hand – where the rest of the world seemed to be conspiring against me'. When Bunny was alone in Paris in the winter of 1915, Lytton had sent him a series of letters blending the message of his wartime journalism with something more personal. 'Mon cher,' he wrote, 'go to the end of your Rue de Beaune and look for the house at the corner, on the quai where Voltaire died, at the age of 84, having conquered both the rulers of this world, and of the next – and where (though the inscription doesn't say so, I think) he had lived fifty years before as a young poet. Consider that life and take courage.'

In his autobiography David Garnett recorded that Lytton 'often had an intuitive understanding of what I was feeling'. Lytton felt safe discussing with him some of his problems, which, for fear of ridicule, he was less willing to disclose to other Bloomsbury friends. Bunny had been one of the first to hear about Carrington. What could possibly be the outcome of this astonishing affair? Lytton wondered. But no one could answer that.

Their adventures continued that autumn with an expedition to the West Country, advancing one of the sub-plots as they took along James Strachey and Noel Olivier. By early September the four of them reached Beeny Farm,[5] three miles from Boscastle in North Cornwall ('a small and dirty farm-house, with an old lame hag and a couple of cats to look after us' was how Lytton described it). Among the fleas, next to the pig sty, and without benefit of hot water, Lytton worked on Gordon while Carrington wandered out en plein air. 'The sea is quite near,' she wrote to her brother Noel. 'But unfortunately un-get-at-able as theres a precipace of grey stone some 400 feet in height.'

In the evenings she liked listening to Lytton as he read from Motley's *Rise of the Dutch Republic* and Gibbon on the Emperor Claudius 'who was no doubt about it a bad fellow'. Sometimes, too, not wishing to sit indoors 'like a poached egg', she would go into the cornfields and paint. But this made her think again of Mark who was staying at Garsington. 'This place suits me admirably!' he wrote robustly to her (12 September 1917). Philip was talking of converting one of his beautiful barns into a studio for him, and he had been experimenting in water-colours with Dorothy Brett. 'She understands me and my work or what I want to do better than anyone – I do love her for this,' he wrote. 'You can't think how much she helps me, even to domestic details . . . she even came on her own account to scrub my back in the bath! . . . Brett has real talent too.' Carrington, no longer welcome at Garsington, felt miserable when she read this letter. 'I long to be back with you and Brett,' she answered. 'There's a confession! . . . sometimes I feel strangely isolated having lost my companions.'

Gradually this summer Mark's love had been eroded by her attachment to 'that half-dead man', as he described Lytton. She had tried to tell him that (July 1917) 'When anyone runs Lytton down you ought rather to say "he must be better than we think since Carrington loves him".' But Mark did not see this. He felt nauseated by their affair.

'I do believe in *you*, but nothing on earth will make me believe in Lytton as a fit object for your love,' he wrote.

'If you had com[e] and told me that you thought L.S. was a wonderful man and that you had an admiration for him, I should have tried to dissuade you because I do not think that he is, I think very much to the contrary in fact. But you came and told me that you *loved* him . . . You have by your love for that man poisoned my belief in love life and everything, you by that love turned everything I once believed in and thought beautiful into ridicule . . . for years I wanted – you only tortured me, then suddenly you gave your love to such a creature, and you yourself said that had he wanted your body you would without hesitation have given it to that emaciated withered being, I young and full of love, you refused it. Tell me Carrington what am I to think of life now, you say you are happy, yes you are *But I am not*. I long to fly to another Carrington where I shan't smell the stench that fills my nostrils constantly from the combination of your fresh young self with that half dead creature who is not even man enough to take your body – your beautiful body – But thank God he cannot, because if that happened, I should be sick all day.

I do not believe in [the] L.S. kind – His atmosphere is as thin as his body – he is merely learned and scholarly but fundamentally empty . . . He will deaden you in time and that is what hurts me so. You are absolutely at his feet. You follow him about like a puppy, you have lost all self respect, I shudder to think of it . . .' [6]

Mark had written this in July, but he had not sent it to Carrington. Two months later, after hearing 'attacks on the Bloomsburians' at Garsington, and the news that, in copycat fashion, Alix was desperately in love with James ('alas poor Alix! What a sickly thing love is!'), he wrote (12 September 1917): 'I am afraid that your passion for L.S. estranges me more and more from you – I can't stomach it at all. It makes it almost impossible to see you . . . I don't feel the same about you as I used to.' [7]

His change of feeling wounded Carrington. Nevertheless she was determined that 'we shall at least be friends'. She looked forward to painting with him, reading Chekhov and Euripides together and practising their French on each other. After the war was over, they must also spend some time in the West Country. 'I have learnt so much now. I am humbled like the man in the Psalms "even unto the dust" – and do not hate me for my cruelty, it was impossible I should know what you felt.'

But Mark seemed unalterably bitter. 'You have treated me abominably, Carrington – always until the last moment – and it is hard for me not to hate you,' he wrote back (4 October 1917). '. . . you will be just the same in the future – you can't help it . . . You have sown seeds of bitterness inside me . . . I have to spend all my time now undoing what you have done to me . . . there is something in you which I must always hate.'

Lytton knew nothing of this exchange of letters as he waged his more peaceful campaign with General Gordon. By the third week of September his rewriting seemed complete, though he feared that further revisions might be needed after he read the new two-volume *Life of Sir Charles Dilke* by Stephen Gwynn and Gertrude Tuckwell with its description of Gordon's assignment in the Sudan. Nevertheless 'I am glad to say that Gordon is at last finished,' he wrote to his sister Pippa (27 September 1917). 'In spite of every effort, he is about half as long again as Florence N. I think the four will fill a good-sized book – but perhaps a very short one ought to be added . . . I'm now reading [Mandell] Creighton's Life – have you read it? I thought he might do for number 5; but I find he's not sufficiently unlike Manning – though full of interest.'[8]

By now they were at the end of their endurance with the fleas and pigs at Beeny Farm. Wires were dispatched to outlying farms, and acceptance was signalled back from a Mrs Box, some thirty miles north of them at Home Farm, Welcombe, near Bude. They set off with some trepidation. 'I imagined of course a new bungalow farm, with a methodist female with spectacles and no food to eat!!' Carrington wrote to Barbara Bagenal (21 September 1917). 'After a 14 mile drive from Bude in a motor car we arrived here. It's simply perfect. A big grass paddock and walled garden and, a small farmhouse. We have a room each, two sitting-rooms, an unlimited supply of food and cream, and big double beds.'

The farm was perched on the tip of a steep hill rising between two deeply-cut green valleys, one of which formed the frontier between Devon and Cornwall, and along both of which streams ran to sea beaches. It was surrounded by animals – four black and white cats, a collie dog, a big pink pig and two smaller dark ones, all very well behaved and all of whom Carrington named after her friends. The country with its immense sea-cliffs and rocks, its inland woods and brooks was so much vaster and wilder than traditional English landscape that she felt she was in a foreign country. She would bathe in the sea or lie in one of the swift silver rivulets under the hot sun and let the icy water rush over her body. She was painting 'veille mère Box' in her kitchen, the solid form of the old woman crowned with a glorious bonnet and wearing an expression of inward determination, conveyed with tenderness and insight. She felt she could go on living here for the rest of her life and had 'almost a headache every morning because I get so tired and exhausted. Simply loving so hard!' she wrote to her friend Barbara Bagenal. 'Today is so hot and the flies buzz round our heads ... Lytton also finished his Essay on General Gordon and read it to us. I think it is very masterly.'

By the time Carrington arrived back at Hurstbourne Tarrant later in October, she was again sure that the solution to her problems was close. All her instincts told her so. She glowed with the happiness of Devon and Cornwall. It was the first anniversary of her brother Teddy's death, and her parents had seldom seemed more remote. Lytton could offer comfort. She was impatient to be back with him, gazing up at his calm features, those soft eyes, and hearing again his voice – his jokes, his reading, the wit and strange charm of his talk. Not that she was reconciled to the end of her intimacy with Mark. 'May I come and see your paintings when I come back?' she had persisted (October 1917). Surely it would be possible to re-establish some private balance between these complementary figures. But, having just left him, she missed Lytton most painfully. 'Oh its wretched having lost you,' she wrote (18 October 1917), 'and not to have you tonight to talk to. Dearest Lytton I can never thank you enough for these weeks. I did not realize how happy I had been until this evening. It's strangely beautiful here [Hurstbourne Tarrant] with the drooping beech trees and apples lying in the wet grass – But more melancholy and autumnal than a grave yard. If only you were here – and so many wishes. You have spoilt me for too long and now I feel as if suddenly I had walked into a greenhouse in the winter ... Dearest Lytton I love you so much.'

Her intensity stirred within Lytton faint tremors of his old fears, and he answered guardedly, almost formally. 'I'm very glad you enjoyed the summer and so did I – very much indeed,' he told her, 'but I fear I am too crabbèd. I wish, too, I could be more effectual in other ways; but I am old, debilitated, and floating. However, you know all this.'

3

THE MILL HOUSE

Carrington's determination to find a country cottage for Lytton and herself had never seriously wavered. Whenever it looked like doing so, Lytton would reprimand her. 'Madam! You fiddle while Rome is burning' (28 July 1917). During the summer and early autumn of 1917 she had written to David Garnett and other friends who already knew of her liaison with Lytton, asking them to keep their eyes open for somewhere comfortable and cheap. She herself bicycled everywhere, stopping pedestrians and other bicyclists in the streets to inquire if they knew of any empty farms or small houses. The vague plan which had been hatched a year before to rescue Lytton from Belsize Park Gardens was now complete in all its details, and ready to take wing. Oliver Strachey, Harry Norton, Saxon Sydney-Turner and Maynard Keynes had all agreed to participate in a scheme. Each of them, together with Lytton himself, was to put up twenty pounds a year in order to rent and maintain the place. This represented a subsidy to Lytton, who was to act nominally as caretaker and, with Carrington as housekeeper, live there permanently. It would become another of those Bloomsbury outposts, and along with Asheham, Charleston and Eleanor House, offer an alternative to the baroque rusticity of Garsington.

Barbara Bagenal volunteered to act as treasurer, collecting contributions by quarterly instalments and paying off the rent.[9] Other non-contributing friends might, of course, be invited down by the caretaker and housekeeper whenever the shareholders were not in residence. 'It appears on the whole a reasonable project,' Lytton explained to Clive Bell (6 November 1917). 'I shouldn't be able to face it alone; female companionship I think may make it tolerable – though certainly by no means romantic. I am under no illusions. But in the present miserable, chaotic, and suspended state of affairs, it seems to me the best that can be done. A little quiet work is really almost all that one can look forward to, just now.'

According to Noel Carrington, his parents had acquired the habit of frequently moving house from his father's practice of 'striking camp' in India. They were planning to move again in the autumn of 1917 when Carrington's mother handed her an estate agent's offer to view a Mill House in the tiny village of Tidmarsh, a mile south of Pangbourne in Berkshire.

She went over to see it the next day, Saturday 20 October. 'It's very romantic and lovely,' she reported to Lytton. '. . . very old with gables and some lattice windows . . . A charming Miller showed me over it . . . Electric light in every room. I'm wildly excited. Horray!' She enclosed a drawing for him.

The Mill House had been built on to the end of a large weather-boarded water-mill, the mill stream of which was banked to a high level and bounded one side of the garden. The mill-wheel still worked fitfully and the corn-chandler's warehouse above it was in operation. Inside, though rather damp and in need of some renovation, it was nicely decorated, and contained modern fireplaces and 'new oakbeams'. There were three 'Vast Big rooms', a kitchen, bathroom, six bedrooms ('2 Very big') and a box room. The grounds on two sides of the house extended over an acre and a half, and included a small orchard, a sunken Roman bath kept replenished by the gushing mill water, and a shady tennis or croquet lawn. It was near a church and a post office, took thirty-five minutes to reach by express train from Paddington, was being offered for three years' lease at a rent of fifty-two pounds per annum (equivalent to £1200 in 1994) and 'sounds too good to be alright!'

To Lytton also it sounded ideal. In such a place he might make a home for himself. 'It's this wretched separation of everybody that makes one uncomfortable,' he told Clive Bell (6 November 1917). 'But my hope is that if the house at Tidmarsh comes into being, it may be possible by the summer to have some pleasant reunions in the old style, whether the war's going on or not.' For writing 'un peu de recueillement' was essential. 'My notion is not to retire altogether,' he assured Clive (4 December 1917), '– but for 2 or 3 weeks at a time; and to spend happy intervals gadding about among such people as are left.' He hoped to remain industrious without becoming bored, to write something of value without bankrupting his personal life: in short, to enjoy the best of all worlds.

All the same, though this was what they wanted, both Lytton and Carrington had qualms about the Tidmarsh experiment. Already there was gossip. 'My plans for the future are quite devoid of mystery,' Lytton insisted to Clive. After describing the project in some detail, he ended up a little peevishly: 'This rather dreary explanation will I hope satisfy you that all is above board. Please don't believe in the hidden hand.' In the next few months he was more than once called upon to provide this dreary explanation against rumour and conjecture. There was some difficulty, too, in breaking the news to his mother. Lady Strachey did not voice her disapproval – that was not her way. But her distaste was to be sensed in what she failed to say. 'A curious scene at Belsize Park,' Leonard Woolf reported to Lytton a few weeks after the Mill House had been taken

(January 1918). 'V[irginia] and I at tea with her Ladyship. V. very innocently: "Well, Lady Strachey, and what do you think of Tidmarsh?" An awkward pause and some very indistinct remarks from her Ladyship. A pause. Then across the table to me: "What do *you* think of it all?" (She was referring to the general European situation, but I naturally thought she referred to Tidmarsh).'

Back at Hurstbourne Tarrant Carrington concocted a special story for her parents. Tidmarsh, she told them, was to be a new retreat for Slade girls where they could live cheaply and devote their time to painting; and this casual explanation appears for a time to have satisfied them, preoccupied as they were with their own plans for moving to Cheltenham. But with others, there was no easy way out. The Bloomsberries initially distrusted her. By going off to live with Lytton she must have known, too, that she would further antagonize some of her oldest friends – Dorothy Brett, for example, whose company she sadly missed. She was also certain to attract the rancour of Ottoline, who, to Lytton's perplexity, was showing renewed interest in Mark Gertler. 'What does it mean?' he asked Clive Bell (6 November 1917). 'I should have thought, a priori, that they would have found it impossible to have anything to do with each other ... though, I suppose, after all, their interweavings don't go much further than an after-lunch pianola romp.'

The most pressing of all Carrington's worries was Mark himself. She simply could not tell him

Lytton, who still rather admired Mark 'in a certain way', wanted to explain everything so that they could invite him down to Tidmarsh in the summer. But Carrington persuaded him that this was out of the question. She knew Mark better than he did. He had written ribald verses and made obscene drawings of Lytton. He could be dangerous too. Lytton was half-attracted, half-fearful. In any event Carrington must do what she thought best. 'It all rather alarms me,' he admitted (9 December 1917).

'. . . I find *him* very attractive – I really do like him – and would like to be friends with him; but the worst of it is that I can't feel any faith in him . . . It's a nuisance to have to be on one's guard, when one doesn't in the least want to be. – And it's so silly – his way of going on – because there's no point in it. However I don't suppose it can be helped.'

At first Carrington merely tended to mislead Mark. But so many stories of her and Lytton had been buzzing round lately that he was sceptical. 'No, I'm not going away with Lytton!' she exclaimed (November 1917). 'But my people are leaving Hampshire, and are going to live in a town,

Cheltenham, So I've got to go home for a little while, when they move to help them and take away my goods and furniture. Then I'll be back again in London all the winter I expect.'

Within this basic misconception, it was child's play to plant a lie. 'Oliver Strachey has taken an old water Mill House near Reading, so I am going to let him keep all my furniture for me. Until I have a place in London of my own. Its such a nice Mill House, and it will be good to have a retreat – like you and Brett have Garsington.'

And there the matter temporarily rested.

While Carrington was busy making the Mill House 'almost as good as Charleston', Lytton went back to Belsize Park Gardens where his mother and various sisters had reassembled. As the war went interminably on, his old friends seemed fewer and less accessible. In France, the British army had begun its Ypres offensive but had become stranded in the Flanders mud before a remorseless German bombardment under ceaseless rain. Over Britain, the German aircraft intensified their raids – Zeppelins killed twenty-seven people in London on one attack. The Government warned everyone to cut down on unnecessary motoring and announced that it would censor all pacifist publications. 'The amenities are getting so few and feeble, and the horrors steadily increase,' Lytton wrote to Clive (20 October 1917). 'Last night was spent waiting in vain for a bombardment – a most gloomy proceeding; and I suppose one that must be looked forward to now as the usual thing.' His longing for the new regime at Tidmarsh mounted daily, and to Mary Hutchinson – 'the only sympathetic person in London' – he confessed (31 October 1917): 'London fills me with disgust; and I am hoping to leave it for ever (minus a day).'

The world seemed to be entering another era – and the change was marked by a farewell party for Augustus John, the bohemian rebel of the Edwardian age, now a major in the Canadian army with an embarrassing likeness to George V. Lytton deplored this move from the roadside into the West End, for the first time seeing himself as a more radical force than the erstwhile opponent of commercialism. 'Poor John!' he lamented to Clive (4 December 1917). 'Did you by any chance go to that show of his at the Alpine Club? The impression produced by the reduplication of all that superficial and pointless facility was most painful. Naturally he has become the darling of the upper classes, and made £5000 out of his show. His appearance in Khaki is unfortunate – a dwindled creature, with clipped beard, pseudo-smart, and in fact altogether deplorable. All the same, late on Saturday night, there were moments when, in spite of everything . . . mais assez! –'

With forebodings of tedium he also visited an exhibition of Max

Beerbohm's caricatures at the Grosvenor Gallery in Mayfair, feeling that he had already seen enough caricatures to last him a lifetime, 'but I was quite carried away', he told Clive (4 December 1917). 'He [Max] has the most remarkable and seductive genius – and I should say about the smallest in the world.'

Otherwise he spent his days at Belsize Park Gardens going over, for the very last time, the entire manuscript of *Eminent Victorians*. Having discarded the idea of adding a short life of Mandell Creighton, he toyed briefly with the notion of writing on Watts – one of his original twelve candidates – but this also came to nothing. The preparation, research and composition of the book had extended over five years, and its completion now coincided with a landmark in his own biography, something for which he had been struggling ever since he left Cambridge – the end of family life in London. It was a fitting moment to conclude his work as a tetralogy. As he read the finished version of these essays, he realized that no additions were necessary. In their balance of mood and tone – variations on a single theme, comprising, in the opinion of Sigmund Freud, a treatise against religion – he saw that this series of four portraits corresponded to the four movements of an orchestral symphony, or perhaps more appropriately to the more intimate pattern of a string quartet:

'Cardinal Manning' – *Allegro vivace*
'Florence Nightingale' – *Andante*
'Dr Arnold' – *Scherzo*
'The End of General Gordon' – *Rondo*

By the time Lytton had finished his corrections, Oliver Strachey had signed the lease of the Mill House, and Carrington, helped by her friend Barbara and the local postmistress, was busy making it habitable. They painted walls, stained floors, hung pictures, created carpets and raided Hurstbourne Tarrant for furniture, plants, china and food. 'This is going to be a good life here,' Carrington promised Lytton (9 December 1917). 'The work of furnishing', Virginia observed in her diary (13 December 1917) 'falls of course upon Carrington; but Barbara is a good second.' Carrington was an admirer of Cobbett. 'Her very English sensibility, in love with the country and with all country things,' wrote Gerald Brenan, who visited Tidmarsh two years later, 'gave everything she touched a special and peculiar stamp.'[10] In Lytton's bedroom – later called 'the Adam and Eve Room' – she let herself go, painting on one wall the lifesize, naked figure of Adam, faced, on the opposite wall, by the naked Eve.

To help with the cooking and housework, and to do the laundry,

Carrington employed a village woman, Mrs Legge, whose son Donald worked in the garden. In the third week of December, Lytton rather nervously ventured down to begin what Carrington had promised would be (9 November 1917) 'a regular life at Tidmarsh, supported by glasses of milk, & vigorous walks'. It was extremely cold – 'pipes frozen and various supplementary horrors' – and many of the rooms were still in a state of wild disorder. 'Carrington is most energetic,' Lytton informed Ottoline (23 December 1917). '. . . I (as you may imagine) am less so.' While continuous pandemonium sounded from within, outside everything lay motionless in the stationary grip of winter. 'I really think the house will turn out quite a pretty one,' Lytton wrote to Ottoline. '. . . the sun has come out for the first time, and I feel what a blessing it is to be in the country.'

A letter which Lytton sent Virginia Woolf on 21 December, describing the rigours of settling in, arrived in so damp a condition that it was partly illegible.

'Here I am in considerable agony. Nature turned crusty, the "pipes" congealed, and it has been so cold that my nose (to say nothing of other parts) dripped in icicles . . . My female companion keeps herself warm by unpacking, painting, pruning the creepers, knocking in the nails, etc. . . . I try to console myself with Queen Victoria's letters . . . I still have the notion that I may be able to work in this seclusion, when all the nails have finally been knocked in. Nous verrons.

. . . Ah dearie, dearie me, I am nodding over the fire, and she's sewing an edge to the carpet with a diligence . . . Ah, la vie! it grows more remarkable every minute.'

Their first guests at Tidmarsh were Gerald and Fredegond Shove. Then, on Christmas Eve, Harry Norton arrived carrying with him, in a neat satchel, one large turkey and four bottles of claret. For Christmas itself James Strachey and Alix Sargant-Florence joined the party. 'I am gradually settling down (amid a good deal of loose paint and calico) to a regular rural existence,' Lytton told Clive Bell on the last day of December, 'and before long I hope to be really involved in work.' Later that day he returned to London, where he had arranged to have an interview with the publishers Chatto & Windus.

Left on her own, watching the cats playing on the lawn, listening to the mill-wheel creaking round and the water crashing intermittently into the tank from the pump below, Carrington now knew something of the way in which the next fourteen years of her life with Lytton would turn out. It was wonderful to be away from the 'pickle Jammy gloom' of London, but there would be many sacrifices. Seldom again would she have so much time for painting. Though Lytton admired her work, encouraging her to exhibit it (helping to select the pictures), arranging for her to have a studio in their houses and, after his own income was secure, offering her £100 a year to buy time for her painting, yet she felt diffident and sometimes used housework as an excuse to avoid the challenge of painting. She became an excellent gardener, improving the orchard of apple and cherry trees, adding to the vegetable beds, cultivating plants in her 'greenery-house' and filling the place with tulips and dahlias, aconites, sunflowers and anemones. Though she usually had a maid to help her, she did much of the cooking herself. She prepared large and delicious country meals for Lytton and his friends – home-made wines, game, and raspberry jelly and good helpings of green vegetables from the garden; and there were lavish breakfasts at Tidmarsh, Bunny Garnett remembered, with 'ham and eggs, kedgeree or kippers, coffee, a large bowl of fresh cream just skimmed from the pans of milk, hot rolls . . . marmalade, damson cheese . . .' ; and teas of farm butter, honey in the comb, rich plum cakes baked in the oven, skilful jams and warm loaves of currant bread, all neatly laid out on the table with a pink lustre tea-service. But behind the scenes, in the kitchen, it looked as if a bomb had exploded. It seemed a wonder that Lytton was not poisoned. Carrington's delicious rabbit-pie, for example, could be devastating in its after-effects, according to Diana Guinness who after one generous plateful 'had to have the Doctor at 3 A.M. – thought I was dying – I had to stay on some more days and that was how I became so fond of Carrington.'

As Lytton's *garde-malade*, she could be equally attentive and alarming – Barbara Bagenal once preventing her at the last second from serving him half a tumbler of undiluted iodine. But she had set out to make herself indispensable to him, and gradually she became indispensable. She was his housekeeper, his confidante, his nurse, his messenger, his loving friend. He would tell her when he wanted a cup of tea, and she would tell the maid – if he was alone, he might go without. She enveloped him with a devotion which struck others as excessive and possibly dangerous. But he thrived like a plant in a greenhouse.

By consent, both retained something of their independence. But it was precarious. 'My companion (whatever she may *say*) is of a decidedly watchful temperament,' Lytton told Mary Hutchinson (19 June 1918). 'I glide among shoals, rocks, quicksands, eddies, waterspouts.' His flights sometimes looked like a schoolboy's truancy, for Carrington would willingly have become his prisoner and sometimes hated his departures which, she nevertheless realized, were necessary for their unconventional union. When she was left alone in these first days of 1918, the Mill House seemed full of strange noises, either rats or ghosts, and both equally terrifying.[11] At night she would hurry up to bed early, lie there listening, and long for sleep. These mysterious night sounds seemed to echo the insecurity beneath her happiness. For in spite of everything, she never felt confident that her life with Lytton would last, and secretly hoped that one day he would ask her to marry him.

With all these fears and uncertainties, it was still a good life. Towards Lytton's young men Carrington felt no jealousy. They adored her; she enjoyed their playful company. These years at Tidmarsh were probably the happiest in their lives. Her happiness was Lytton's happiness, and all her energies were given to what they both wanted. She was certain, too, that though he might feel little sexual desire for her, yet she would be better for him than anyone else. Never again would he be so enfeebled by illness or so prostrated by secret misery and depleted vigour. She would see to it that he had measured doses of quinine, Bemax and Sanatogen and sensible clothes and plenty of cushions and Extract of Malt and rhubarb powder and eucalyptus oil and all the other supports and syrups the world had to offer.

4

'*TOUT EST POSSIBLE*'

While Carrington was busy preparing the Mill House, Lytton had been looking round for a publisher for *Eminent Victorians*. Several years earlier, Geoffrey Whitworth, the art editor of Chatto & Windus, had asked Roger Fry to write a book on Post-Impressionism. Fry had declined, but added that his friend Clive Bell was then engaged in writing just such a work, and that he would ask him to send it to them. In due course the book, entitled *Art*, was accepted and became a success. 'And how very strange to be published by Chatto and Windus!' Lytton had commented shortly before its appearance (9 November 1913). 'I thought they did nothing but bring out superannuated editions of Swinburne variegated with the Children's Theological Library and the Posthumous Essays of Lord de Tabley.'

Now, four years later, everyone was conspiring to move him towards these strange publishers – 'including Mr Robert Nichols,[12] who hurried up to me the other evening, and assured me that they were just the people for my book, with its delicate ironical flavour, etc., etc. as if he had read it all years ago'. Clive Bell had recently spoken of *Eminent Victorians* to

Whitworth and his associate, the novelist and critic Frank Swinnerton. So early in December, Lytton sent it to them.

He was not confident about its acceptance and cannot have been prepared for the publishers' reaction. Whitworth read it first, then passed it on to Swinnerton, who, finding the typescript in its cover of crimson paper on his office desk one morning shortly before Christmas, began casually to turn its pages.

'They were so enchanting that I continued, and when night fell I could not leave the book, but took it carefully home ... I had hardly taken the typescript up again after dinner when ... there was an air raid by Germans. The whirring of aeroplanes overhead, the rattle of machine-gun fire, and finally the frightful thunder of a gun in the field at the bottom of our garden, would all have served to distract a mind less happily engaged; but as it was, with curtain closely drawn to prevent the escape of light, I consorted that evening with Cardinal Manning, Thomas Arnold, Florence Nightingale, and General Gordon. The nineteenth century had come alive again.'[13]

Both Whitworth and Swinnerton were 'as excited before publication as the world was after it', especially since, outside Cambridge circles, the name of Lytton Strachey was little known. Frank Swinnerton recalled his primer on French literature, but knew nothing of its author. His enthusiastic acceptance of the book reached Lytton shortly before Christmas. Lytton replied (30 December 1917) asking for £50 (equivalent to £1150 in 1994) to be paid to him on the day of publication, as an advance against his royalties. 'I think the portraits would be an important feature of the book,' he wrote. '. . . The portraits I have in mind are to be found in books which are easily procurable; would you be able to obtain reproductions of these? I should add that I think there should be five portraits, and not four, as a portrait of Newman (there is a very suitable one in Wilfrid Ward's biography) seems to me indispensable.'[14]

Early in January, Lytton called at the offices of Chatto & Windus, leaving a vivid memory with Frank Swinnerton.

'His excessive thinness, almost emaciation, caused him to appear endless. He had a rather bulbous nose, the spectacles of a British Museum bookworm, a large and straggly dark brown beard (with a curious rufous tinge); no voice at all. He drooped if he stood upright, and sagged if he sat down. He seemed entirely without vitality ... Sad merriment was in his eye, and about him a perpetual air of sickness and debility.'[15]

Lytton was delighted by Swinnerton's and Whitworth's praise of his work. But between the acceptance of his typescript and the publication of his book, he was overrun with doubts. Perhaps the style was too richly adorned, the adjectives too thickly encrusted; perhaps the tone was over-emphatic; perhaps the characters would fail to 'convince'. He sent a copy of 'The End of General Gordon' to Philip Morrell, who liked it, and another to Virginia who replied that it was masterly. 'It's amazing how from all these complications, you contrive to reel off such a straight and dashing story,' she wrote, 'and how you weave in every scrap – my God, *what* scraps – of interest to be had, like (you must pardon one metaphor) a snake insinuating himself through innumerable golden rings . . . I don't see how the skill could be carried further.'[16]

Wherever he went this winter he would read aloud some pages from his book, finding this a good method for testing the flow and effective-ness of his conversational prose style. At Tidmarsh he read to Carrington, and at Hampstead to some of his family. Over Easter, leaving Carrington behind, he spent a few days at Asheham, where he again read to Leonard and Virginia and his fellow guests, James Strachey and Noel Olivier, who had recently qualified as a doctor. 'We had a short, & to me, very intimate talk; intimate in the sense that he [Lytton] will understand from the sight of the tail what the whole body of the thought is in one's mind,' Virginia noted in her diary (5 April 1918). 'These thoughts were for the most part about books; but books include a good deal of life.' Lytton seemed 'painfully anxious' about Leonard and Virginia's opinions of *Eminent Victorians*. 'I suspect that he is now in-clined to question whether Eminent Victorians, 4 in number, & requiring 4 years for their production, are quite enough to show for his age, & pretensions,' Virginia thought. She also suspected he might be comparing himself unfavourably with Leonard who (rather to Virginia's dismay) had involved himself in international relations and the Co-operative Movement. But was her reaction affected by another sort of comparison between Lytton and Leonard? Certainly Lytton had created an awkwardness between them by requesting that she review *Eminent Victorians*. She had agreed without thinking, then reflected that she did not much want to write 'under surveillance'. She mentioned her doubts to Lytton but he gently returned to the subject and she hesitated – then coaxed out of Bruce Richmond, editor of the *Times Literary Supplement*, a refusal on principle. 'He has to make it a rule that reviewers don't review their friends,' she explained to Lytton (23 April 1918). '. . . I rubbed it well into Richmond that it was a work of surpassing merit.' This was all done with tact and sensitivity, yet it slightly clouded their intimacy.

'My life passes almost entirely among proof sheets, which now flow in upon me daily,' Lytton told Ottoline (3 March 1918). 'It is rather exciting, but also rather harassing. All sorts of tiresome details, and minor crises – about covers, illustrations, contracts, and so on – keep turning up; but my hope is that in about six weeks or so "Eminent Victorians" will burst upon an astonished world.' He was also contributing political reviews and articles to the pacifist periodical *War and Peace*, which Leonard was temporarily editing, and trying out another play.

For much of this time, Lytton stayed in London, where he had recently joined the left-wing 1917 Club. Named after the February Revolution in Russia, the club had been conceived by Oliver Strachey and Leonard Woolf, and came into existence the previous December, taking the lease of No. 4 Gerrard Street in Soho, 'in those days the rather melancholy haunt of prostitutes daily from 2.30 onwards', Leonard Woolf recalls. Its membership, which later became largely theatrical, was then a mixture of the political, the literary and the artistic. 'It's quite a comfortable and attractive place,' Lytton assured Carrington, ' – very nice rooms, and tolerable furniture and tea and toast to be had.' The club also furnished him with a ringside view of much that was going on in contemporary politics, and an opportunity to study some of its more illustrious members, such as Ramsay MacDonald, its rather uneasy first president.

While in London this winter, Lytton attended Bertrand Russell's trial at Bow Street, feeling that the more friends who showed themselves in court, the better it would be for Russell. The trial arose out of an article Russell had written for the No Conscription Fellowship weekly, *The Tribunal*, advocating acceptance of a recent peace offer made by Germany. The laughter in court at some of the prosecution's misdirected sallies and the amusing quotes from Russell's article may well have stimulated the ferocity of the magistrate Sir John Dickinson, who sentenced Russell to six months' imprisonment in Brixton jail.[17] 'I have never encountered such a blast of vitriolic hatred,' Russell later commented on Dickinson. 'He would have had me hanged, drawn and quartered if he could.' Lytton echoed this view in a letter to Ottoline 3 March 1918).

'It was really infamous – much worse, I thought, than those other proceedings before the Lord Mayor – even more obviously unjust, gross and generally wicked and disgusting. The spectacle of a louse like Sir John Dickinson rating Bertie for immorality and sending him to prison! ... James and I came away with our teeth chattering with fury. It makes one abandon hope that such monstrosities should occur, openly, and be accepted by very nearly everybody as a matter of course.'

Later that March Lytton was summoned to yet another medical examination, this time conducted by the civil authorities. He had no clear notion of what to expect. The general outlook of the war was not good, and there was little reason to believe it would end in a mere seven months' time. 'How long will this madness last?' he asked Ottoline. It seemed incredible that the killing still went on. 'I should like to take chloroform until the declaration of Peace,' he told Mary Hutchinson. The Russian Communist Party had signed a humiliating peace treaty with Germany which, beginning its offensive with the second battle of the Somme, was shelling Paris. In Britain, the government had rationed meat and butter, was attempting to raise a new War Loan of £600 million, and introducing a Military Service Bill with the maximum conscription age of fifty. In his articles for *War and Peace*, Lytton once more attacked the 'theology of militarism' which was imposed by fanatics from all sides on moderate men and women, and which would soon melt away leaving everyone vacant and unbelieving. 'Extremists and fanatics and desperadoes may make a noise or disturbance,' he wrote (*War and Peace*, May 1918), they may even at times appear to control the course of events; but in reality they are always secondary figures – either symptoms or instruments; whatever happens, the great mass of ordinary, stolid, humdrum, respectable persons remains the dominating force in human affairs.'

His own health was now under the scrutiny of ordinary persons instead of the military authorities. At his medical board, he was declared to be permanently unfit for all forms of military service. 'It is a great relief,' he admitted to Ottoline (20 March 1918). '. . . The whole thing was infinitely better managed than before – far more civilized, and careful, and the doctors positively polite and even sympathetic. This comes of the military having nothing more to do with it.'

Whenever Carrington came to London – which was not often – she would try to see Mark and tell him how much better it was to live in the country than in the foggy old metropolis. They had somewhat patched up their differences of the previous autumn after Gertler asked to be forgiven for his outbursts. 'I don't blame you for anything really, and I feel quite friendly to you,' Mark had written (1 November 1917). '. . . I only hope that in the future I shan't worry you and interfere with your relations & affairs – but I'm sure I shan't now as I feel differently about it all.' She too implored him to forgive her for everything. So he forgave her, she forgave him and 'I long to be back and see you again,' she wrote from Tidmarsh at the end of 1917. '. . . I find being Mary, and looking after a house a confounded bore . . . I shall not bother any more about the old house and the furniture, but start painting.' Both of them felt uneasy about this new phase in their relationship. Carrington blamed Mark for the lies he seemed to draw out of her. 'I wish you weren't sometimes my enemy,' she told him, 'I could tell you so much more and frankly. But your moods terrify me into silence.' He too was terrified by these moods. 'I sometimes think my real life will not commence before my passion for Carrington ends,' he confessed (26 December 1917) to his friend Kóteliansky.

They began the new year with excellent intentions. Carrington was sure he would love the Mill House when he came there. She would invite him down when the others, Oliver Strachey and Harry Norton and Saxon Sydney-Turner, were away and he could see the orange sun shining in the stream and lighting up the trees. Up in London, Mark was seeing the cellist, Guilhermina Suggia, who soothed him by playing Bach. 'As she played I thought of you!' he wrote to Carrington (10 February 1918). '. . . I shall never forget you and shall never stop loving you!'

But that February he finally discovered that Carrington was living at Tidmarsh with Lytton. His first reaction was explosive. On the evening of 14 February, after a party given by Jack and Mary Hutchinson in Hammersmith, Lytton and Carrington were walking off down the blacked-out streets, when the dark figure of Gertler loomed from the shadows, overtook them, and launched an attack upon Lytton. Fortunately a number of other guests were near by and, running up, succeeded in separating them. 'Anything more cinematographic can hardly be imagined,' Lytton told Clive (18 February 1918), 'and on looking back it wears all the appearance of a bad dream. All the same it was at the time exceedingly painful, especially as a little more presence of mind on my part might have prevented the situation; but it all came about with a speed. Poor Mark! The provocation was certainly great, and I was very sorry for him. However, as he was obviously drunk, perhaps he was rather less conscious than one supposed. Characteristically, Maynard came to the rescue, and eventually led him off, and pacified him, with amazing aplomb . . . Carrington had fled under the protection of Sheppard, who kept on repeating, during the height of the crisis – "Who *is* it? Who *is* it?" in a most pained voice; and Harry [Norton] supported my trembling form from the field. It was really an intervention of Providence that they should all have come up at the psychological moment, as Heaven knows what mightn't have happened.'

The next evening Lytton was dining at the Eiffel Tower restaurant with David Garnett, when Mark came up and apologized.

Lytton giggled and replied: 'It was nothing at all. Please don't worry yourself about it.'

'I don't think', David Garnett later commented, 'that it was what Gertler wanted to be told.'

'I am so sorry about that scene,' Carrington apologized next day to Lytton. But it had been the sight of Mark that filled her with guilt. The haunting look of loneliness and despair in his face, deepened by the tubercular ill-health which was to keep him in and out of sanatoria for the rest of his life, clearly showed his suffering. 'Please do not worry about last night,' she wrote to him the following morning. 'I am only *very* sorry if I gave you the cause of your distress. It was quite unintentional.' But what was to be done? 'I am rather worried about you altogether,' she wrote to him again a few days later. He must, she recommended, make new friends in London. 'I felt it was so much my fault for leaving you for so long and making you unhappy.'

'It was a great blow to me, your moving to the country,' he replied (20 February 1918). This was not the end between them, but it was the beginning of the end. Carrington's love for Lytton did not prevent her loving Mark, but it made such love 'impossible for me', Mark explained (24 February 1918). For another two years the accusations, inquiries, concessions, the declarations and vindications, exasperation and regret locked them painfully and intermittently together before, like shipwrecked vessels, they drifted free. 'It is like a dying candle which is nearly finished,' Gertler told Kóteliansky (18 February 1918), 'but which shoots up every now and then, a brilliant flicker, more for the moment than it ever was when it was long and fresh, but still it is dying.'

Perhaps it was fortunate for Carrington that there was so much to occupy her at Tidmarsh. Life there was a procession of visitors – Oliver, who sat for his portrait; James, who had caught influenza and abandoned his career in medicine after three weeks as a medical student to become drama critic of the *Athenaeum*; Alix Sargant-Florence, puzzling over Rabelais with the aid of six dictionaries; Barbara Bagenal and her husband Nick, who would sometimes stay on to keep Carrington company while Lytton was away; Middleton Murry, very gloomy over his wife Katherine Mansfield's health, and very excited over his own prospects as editor of the *Athenaeum*; Saxon Sydney-Turner chuckling over Euripides; and Maynard who, Lytton told Clive (18 February 1918), looked 'very prosperous, but not very well I thought, and full of the L[loyd] G[eorge] crisis'.[18] He thought it possible that

'a vote of censure might be moved in the House by infuriated back-bench Tories, that the Govt. might then fall and be succeeded by a Law-Asquith combination including tout ce qu'il-y-a de plus respectable, but not pacifist, though destined to make peace. I doubt it – and I doubt still more, if it did come off, whether it would be any good. To be caught in the clutches of a second Coalition, and a respectable one this time, seems to me a dismal fate. But it's difficult to believe that the Goat [Lloyd George] won't clamber over this fence as he has so many others.'

When she was free of guests, Carrington would vanish into the attic to paint pictures that no one was allowed to see, or disappear outside to busy herself among the potatoes and the hens. 'We are trying to grow vegetables – and hens,' Lytton wrote to Dorelia John (10 May 1918). 'Neither seem to come up with sufficient rapidity – damn them – and in the meantime living costs about £100 a minute.' He spent the month before publication of *Eminent Victorians* at Tidmarsh composing an essay on the courageous and eccentric pre-Victorian traveller Lady Hester Stanhope for the *Athenaeum*, and a rather wicked pen portrait of Asquith, not for publication. He had also been reading for the first time Charles Greville's *Memoirs*, the full text of which he was later to edit, and the six volumes of the Goncourts' *Journals*, which Virginia had put him on to.

While waiting for his own book to appear, he browsed through several other new publications, among them a study of Byron ('what a splendid subject he would be for a really modern and artistic biography!') and Sidney Colvin's biography of Keats. In spite of the biographer's pomp and tepidity, the tragedy of Keats's short life came through overwhelmingly. 'It seems to me one of the most appalling stories known,' he wrote. 'One of the worst features of it is that one gathers that he had never once copulated. Is it possible, though?' He also read Desmond MacCarthy's articles from the *New Statesman*, *New Witness*, *Eye Witness* and *The Speaker*, collected under the uninviting title *Remnants*. 'I suppose you've seen Remnants – a book in the best of taste,' he wrote to Clive (10 May 1918). 'But it's difficult not to think that the milk has been standing a very long time, and that, though the cream is excellent, there's not much of it. However, nowadays, it would be absurd to complain of anything that is genuinely charming. His Asquith doings fill me with astonishment. I can still hardly believe that he likes those people or can think it worth while to flatter them.[19] Perhaps really he only finds them amusing to pass the time of day with – one can *just* imagine that – and that it may be rather fun to meet the Lord Chief Justice.'

Soon enough Lytton's own incursions into society would provoke a similar wonderment among his Bloomsbury friends. But for the time being he was content at Tidmarsh. Many years before he had written to Maynard (27 February 1906): 'When I have a home of my own, I should write up "Hope" over the door.' Now that at last he had a home of his own, his motto, he told a friend, was to be: '*Tout est possible.*' 'We have many projects,' he boasted to Clive (16 April 1918), ' – to build a fire-place, a book-case, a theatre, to learn Spanish, to attach the pump to the mill-wheel by a leather band, to buy 24 geese, to borrow a saddle from Farmer Davis and saddle the Blacksmith's pony with it and ride into Pangbourne, to write a drawing-room comedy, a classical tragedy in the style of Euripides, and the History of England during the War. But le temps s'en va, mon cher, and we are left idling in front of the fire.'

In the spring of 1918 a few ingredients to his happiness were still missing: a new love-affair; some fame to soothe away the mortifications of his early years; the necessary money to make this way of life permanent; and the end of war.

PART IV

'I have now passed the "mezzo del cammin di nostra vita" and am
rather surprised to find that existence continues to be highly interesting
in spite of that fact. I used to think in early youth that one's
development would come to an end in one's thirties – but I don't find
it so – on the contrary, things if anything seem to grow more interesting
instead of less. Also, they grow more satisfactory. One seems, as one
goes on, to acquire a more complete grasp of life – of what one wants
and what one can get – and of the materials of one's work, which give
a greater sense of security and power. I think I now see where my
path lies.'

Lytton Strachey to Lady Strachey (1 March 1916)

FOURTEEN

A Life Apart

'Brethren,

The President has asked me to propose the toast of "Eminent Victorians" . . .There was once an eminent Victorian called Mr W.G. Ward, who used to say "When I hear men called 'judicious' I suspect them: but when I hear them called 'judicious and venerable', I know they are scoundrels". Similarly when I hear people called "Victorians", I suspect them. But when I hear them called "Eminent Victorians" I write their lives. So an Eminent Victorian might be defined, on this principle, as the sort of person whose life would be likely to be written by Lytton Strachey. And perhaps that's as near as one can get.'

Lytton Strachey, Speech to the Apostles, proposing 'Eminent Victorians'

I

SUCCESS, MONEY, OTHER PEOPLE

Eminent Victorians was published on 9 May 1918. The timing was perfect. Everyone was weary of big guns and big phrases, and Strachey's ironic sifting of those Victorian pretensions that seemed to have led to this appalling war was specially appealing to younger readers. 'I remember very vividly my first sight of it,' wrote Hugh Kingsmill, then a prisoner-of-war in his twenties. '. . . the title *Eminent Victorians* caught my eye. "I must examine this old bore," I said, and made off with the book. That I assumed the title was unironic illuminates the state into which biography had fallen: and the immediate impression the brevity, coherence, and verisimilitude of the book made on me suggests the indebtedness to Lytton Strachey of everyone who has written biography within the last thirty years [1919–1949].'[1]

Strachey had developed his ideas on biography while working for the *Spectator*. At the beginning of 1909, reviewing Guglielmo Ferrero's *The Greatness and Decline of Rome*,[2] he wrote:

'When Livy said that he would have made Pompey win the battle of

Pharsalia, if the turn of the sentence had required it, he was not talking utter nonsense, but simply expressing an important truth in a highly paradoxical way, – that the first duty of a great historian is to be an artist. The function of art in history is something much more profound than mere decoration ... Uninterpreted truth is as useless as burned gold; and art is the great interpreter. It alone can unify a vast multitude of facts into a significant whole, clarifying, accentuating, suppressing, and lighting up the dark places with the torch of the imagination. More than that, it can throw over the historian's materials the glamour of a personal revelation, ... every history worthy of the name is, in its own way, as personal as poetry, and its value ultimately depends upon the force and the quality of the character behind it.'

In his preface to *Eminent Victorians*, he used another metaphor to describe his exploration below the surface of the past. The historian 'will row out over that great ocean of material', he explained, 'and lower down into it, here and there, a little bucket, which will bring up to the light of day some characteristic specimen, from those far depths, to be examined with a careful curiosity.'

'Guided by these considerations, I have written the ensuing studies. I have attempted, through the medium of biography, to present some Victorian visions to the modern eye. They are, in one sense, haphazard visions – that is to say, my choice of subjects has been determined by no desire to construct a system or to prove a theory, but by simple motives of convenience and art ... I have sought to examine and elucidate certain fragments of the truth which took my fancy and lay to my hand ... To quote the words of a Master – "Je n'impose rien; je ne propose rien; j'expose".'

This quotation from the French – which critics were to assume came from Voltaire – was no more authentic than the attribution Lytton had made to Livy in the *Spectator* nine years earlier. Like the translated Chinese poem, 'perhaps too modern to be included in Professor Giles's anthology', which he placed at the end of his *New Quarterly* review of *Chinese Poetry and English Verse*, they were Stracheyesque inventions. 'It occurred to me that I might make one of my well-known pseudo-quotations,' he had written to his brother James (23 July 1908) when composing his essay on 'Voltaire's Tragedies' for the *Independent Review*. Here he had observed that Voltaire was 'capable, for instance, of writing lines as bad as ... *Vous comprenez, seigneur, que je ne comprends pas*', though this line was actually written by his sister Marjorie.

These jokes, so agreeably subversive of academic discipline, were examples of his oblique historic methods. He did not break with traditional narrative and create new forms as the modernists, Eliot and Pound, Yeats and Conrad were doing. He used old forms, but parodied the values they represented by inversion and pastiche, and undermined them with modern psychological innuendo. He also introduced caricature into twentieth-century biography. Extending Strachey's metaphor, Desmond MacCarthy likened *Eminent Victorians* to an aquarium full of odd fish and a host of smaller fry. Robbed of their awful surroundings in the depths, they no longer appear the formidable creatures of sea-legend. With their crazy grimaces, their futile perambulating to and fro, their comic retinue of dabs and squids, they have become a circus spectacle. Only the good-natured, uncompetitive sole, content to lie modestly in the sand – like Lord Hartington whose miniature portrait in 'The End of General Gordon' belongs to the same family as P.G. Wodehouse's Lord Emsworth – is seen with any real affection.

The war had acted as a catalyst on *Eminent Victorians* which began without a thesis but acquired a theme. Strachey had started his 'Victorian Silhouettes' in the spirit of detached irony, but was moved by circumstances to a moral conviction that gave his book its artistic cohesion. For his 'fragments of truth' were less 'haphazard visions' of the previous century than his Preface suggested, the Victorian quartet being, as Noël Annan pointed out, 'the dupes of two false moral systems: ecclesiastical Christianity and the religion of success'.[3]

'This is the greatest fight ever made for the Christian religion,' the Bishop of London had announced in 1915. While pseudo-Christianity was deluging Europe in blood, Strachey planned his counter-attack. In 'Cardinal Manning', he sought to discredit nineteenth-century evangelicism by exposing the vanity of an ambitious prelate who had risen to be an intellectual force in Victorian England. Then, by removing Florence Nightingale from the pedestal where she posed as the legendary lady with the lamp, and replacing her with a twentieth-century neurotic who sacrificed others, he struck at popular Victorian mythology, in particular its conscience-saving humanitarianism. His dislike of Dr Arnold, the most influential teacher of the Victorians, was probably intensified by his own unhappy schooldays. In this essay his target was not only the public school system, where games were next to godliness and on whose playing fields future wars were reputedly to be won, but the whole movement of nineteenth-century liberalism based, not on principles of progress, but on variations of old and debased regimes. Finally, he took on the Church Militant and showed General Gordon becoming a willing instrument not of God but of the extreme imperialist faction of the British Government. For a war-shocked generation soon to return from the battle front, sickened by the chauvinism of clergymen assuring them that God had been in the trenches on their side, General Gordon's messianic religiosity was all too familiar. Evangelicism, humanitarianism, liberalism, education and imperialism, these aspects of Christian culture from the recent past were Strachey's targets.

*

'Pass a person through your mind, with all the documents, and see what comes out. That seems to be the method,' Walter Raleigh wrote to him. 'Also, choose them, in the first place, because you dislike them . . . No one can condemn except on the basis of a creed. Your creed comes easy to me. . . . I can't tell you how I like the book, – every word.'[4]

Lytton was astonished by the laudatory reviews. 'I'm getting rather nervous,' he admitted to Ottoline Morrell (3 June 1918), '– the reviewers are so extraordinarily gushing that I think something must be wrong.' Was it possible, he asked James, that they had confused him with the editor of the *Spectator*? Still the success rolled on, until it seemed as if he might also make some money from his book. 'I'm really rather disappointed that none of the Old Guard should have raised a protest,' he told Mary Hutchinson (30 May 1918). 'I did expect a *little* irritation. Is it possible that the poor dear creatures haven't a single kick left?'

He need not have worried. When the *Spectator* delivered its denunciation, he felt relieved; and he was encouraged, too, by a fulmination from Edmund Gosse in *The Times Literary Supplement*. 'As for Gosse,' he exclaimed, 'after having spent all his life saying disagreeable things about other people (his father included) – to turn round in self-righteous wrath, because someone criticizes Lord Cromer!'[5] Many of the charges brought against the book were marvellously trivial. Critics speculated as to whether Florence Nightingale's bedroom was really as 'shaded' as Strachey made out or whether it admitted the sun. They wondered if Dr Arnold's legs had been made 'shorter than they should have been' so as to reduce the headmaster's moral stature, and if Arthur Clough actually did have 'weak ankles'. They quarrelled as to whether Lord Cromer had kept up with the classics and if indeed General Gordon drank sherry or perhaps brandy-and-soda while reading the Bible.

But there was a genuine uneasiness over what he had done and what his influence might be. 'You can feel reading the book that he is pleased that Miss Nightingale grew fat and that her brain softened,' Duff Cooper wrote to Lady Diana Manners. But he rather guiltily added (7 and 8 July 1918): 'I have enjoyed it enormously.' Duff Cooper concluded that Strachey was less of an historian than a pamphleteer. But G.M. Trevelyan wrote to assure Lytton (12 August 1918) that 'You have got a real historical sense which few professional historians have and hardly any literary people who dabble in history. You have not only historical sense, as Carlyle and Belloc have – but *judgement* which they have not.' He did not 'think the book "cynical"' but felt that Lytton had 'found a method of writing about history which suits you admirably, and I hope you will pursue it'.

Part of this assurance reflected Trevelyan's politeness and part of it may have been a natural reaction to the book's beguiling readability – 'I read it at one long sitting in the train across North Italy with the most intense pleasure, approval and admiration.' But his apparent admiration faded once the influence of *Eminent Victorians* – 'cheap . . . nasty . . . absurd one-volume biographies' – made itself clear.

Their relations had been strained during the war by Lytton's pacifism. As his biographer David Cannadine makes clear, 'Trevelyan had in fact been appalled by the supercilious and dismissive tone of *Eminent Victorians*. He hated its zestful iconoclasm and self-conscious irreverence, thought its impressionistic approach the height of scholarly irresponsibility, and disliked the unsympathetic treatment of his subjects' private lives. Trevelyan believed in great men and women, and he was enraged that Lytton cut them down to size in such a sneering and dishonest manner ... Lytton had poisoned history, traduced the Victorians.'[6]

The serious objections to *Eminent Victorians* from historians were to be aimed at its suspect scholarship, its flippant tone, and the moral basis from which these deformities arose. And it was true that Strachey had given several hostages to fortune, usually signalling this risky business by letting his poised and witty style slide into passages of melodrama or sentimentality. He had run together passages written years apart so as to make Cardinal Newman appear a dove-like victim of his devouring eagle, Cardinal Manning. 'Your criticism of the "eagle and dove" passage went home,' Lytton admitted to Augustine Birrell (2 June 1918). 'It is certainly melodramatic, and I should like to alter it. I think perhaps my whole treatment of Newman is over-sentimentalized – to make a foil for the other Cardinal.' In two influential essays written more than ten years after Lytton's death,[7] the Cambridge historian F.A. Simpson suggested that in his theatrical reconstruction of Manning's audience with the Pope ('It is easy to imagine the persuasive innocence of his Italian voice . . .'), Lytton tampered with the evidence supplied by Manning's biographer E.S.

Purcell to contrive a sinister mystery. Nevertheless, though Lytton is certainly cavalier with his sources, it was actually Purcell himself who formulated the mystery surrounding Manning's visit to the Vatican. 'In fact Strachey is much more reliable than he seems', conceded Hugh Trevor-Roper who directed his own criticism at 'The End of General Gordon'. Strachey's account of Gordon 'retiring into his tent "for days at a time" for secret communion with the Bible and the bottle is the richest flourish in his brilliant picture of that strange, unpredictable, complicated character', he wrote. '. . . The real object had not been a brandy-bottle, but a prayer-book. Unfortunately "brandy-bottle" is funnier than "prayer-book"; Strachey could not resist the final touch of absurdity; and his brilliant portrait of a crackpot crusader is, by that one dangerous detail, overdone.'[8]

Strachey used no unpublished sources and provided no references. His chief source on Manning had been what Hugh Trevor-Roper called the 'devastating book' by Purcell that was 'packed with secret dynamite'. Here was the 'buried gold' he dug up, and it has been devalued only to the extent that subsequent scholarship has called Purcell's authenticity into question. Any inaccuracies in Purcell, as F.A. Simpson explained to the author, 'were only published after Strachey's death, so that it was not his fault not to know about them'. Later evidence on Gordon, however – such as a statement by Lord Carnock to his son Harold Nicolson, and a letter by Gambetta's secretary Joseph Reinach quoted by Roy Jenkins in his *Life of Sir Charles Dilke* (1958) – has confirmed the authenticity of Strachey's portrayal of Gordon as a secret drinker which he had taken from the suspect memoirs of Colonel Chaillé-Long, *My Life in Four Continents*.

But such criticisms by eminent historians were to inflict long-term damage on Strachey's reputation. The general reader was taught to think of *Eminent Victorians* as a 'debunking' biography and its author as, in the words of the American historian Douglas Southall Freeman, 'one of the most pernicious influences in modern biography'. Though now pejorative, the word debunker was an American colloquialism meaning someone who took the bunkum or humbug out of a subject – not such a bad thing after all. But Strachey was also blamed for what were regarded as the works of imitators: Harold Nicolson's *Tennyson*, Philip Guedalla's *Palmerston*, Hugh Kingsmill's *Matthew Arnold*, Richard Aldington's *Lawrence of Arabia*, as well as some of the biographies by André Maurois, Emil Ludwig and Van Wyck Brooks. 'Lytton Strachey's chief mission, of course, was to take down once and for all the pretensions of the Victorian Age to moral superiority,' wrote Edmund Wilson (21 September 1932). '. . . The harshness of *Eminent Victorians* without Strachey's wide learning and bitter feeling . . . had the effect of cheapening history, something Strachey never did – for, though he was venomous about the Victorians, he did not make them any the less formidable . . . But neither the Americans nor the English have ever, since *Eminent Victorians* appeared, been able to feel quite the same about the legends that had dominated their pasts. Something had been punctured for good.'[9]

*

'I shall soon have to make a triumphal progress through the British Isles,' Lytton announced to Ottoline; and he reassured Clive Bell (27 May 1918) that 'I remain calm even in the face of the praises of the Daily Telegraph and Mr Asquith.'

The immediate sales of *Eminent Victorians* were boosted by Asquith when, in the course of his Romanes Lecture delivered at Oxford that summer, he gave the book what Lytton called 'a most noble and high-flown puff'. He had been sent it by Ottoline. The ex-prime minister was still a widely influential figure, and no better publicity could have been looked for than his flattering commendation. 'This must be circulated,' Lytton wrote off to Carrington (June 1918), 'and it's to be hoped and indeed presumed that every member of the great Liberal Party will buy a copy.' He happened to be staying at Garsington on the Saturday when Asquith was delivering his speech, and drove over with Ottoline to hear it. 'It must be confessed that the lecture was a horribly dull one,' he afterwards told his mother (21 June 1918), '– but one can't be too severe after such a noble piece of advertisement. Apparently he was very enthusiastic about the book, talking about it to everyone. I didn't see him to speak to. The sight inside the Sheldonian was rather splendid – with red gowns – and Curzon (the Chancellor of the University) enthroned on a chair of state, in the highest pomp.'

It is possible that Asquith might not have spoken quite so warm-heartedly of 'Mr Strachey's subtle and suggestive art'[10] had he known that a fortnight earlier, on the publication of his *Occasional Addresses*, it had been applied privately and no less trenchantly to himself.

'The fundamental material of Mr Asquith I take to have been a middle-class, North-Country solidity, eminently respectable, almost non-conformist, moderate, cautious, humdrum, and with a not unintelligent eye on the main chance. Then came the influence of Balliol and Jowett, which infused the timid Oxford culture and the timid Oxford worldliness into the virginal undistinguished mass. After that the Bar, with its training in agility of case-putting and its habit of pomposity . . . the final influence brought with it some odd contradictions. The Margot set – rich, smart, showy, and self-indulgent – got hold of Mr Asquith. The middle class legal Don became a *viveur* who carried a lot of liquor and was lecherous with the ladies. The result was certainly curious. Who would guess from this book of his [*Occasional Addresses*] with its high minded rotundities and cultivated respectabilities, that the writer of it would take a lady's hand, as she sat behind him on the sofa, and make her feel his erected instrument under his trousers? (this I had very directly from Brett).

His public career suggests a parallel with Walpole. But one gathers that under all Sir Robert's low-minded opportunism there was a certain grandeur, and that his actual capacity was supreme. In Asquith's case the inveterate lack of ideals and imagination seems really unredeemed; when one has peeled off the brown-paper wrapping of phrases and compromises, one finds – just nothing at all. And as for his capacity, it was perhaps not much more than the skill of a parliamentary tactician. He could never deal with a serious difficulty.'[11]

Despite his book's success, Lytton heard nothing from the publishers. Chatto & Windus had brought it out at the price of ten-and-sixpence (equivalent to £11.50 in 1994), allowing Lytton 15 per cent of this on the first thousand copies sold, and 20 per cent thereafter. They had also undertaken to pay him the fifty pounds he had requested as an advance on royalties, on publication. But the days went by, and no money arrived. 'It's rather awkward,' he admitted to Clive on 27 May. 'Ought I to write to Geoffrey Whitworth? Perhaps if I'm patient it'll come all right – but perhaps not. I should be glad of your advice.' The following day a letter from Geoffrey Whitworth did turn up. It made no mention of the advance, but explained that *Eminent Victorians* was going so well that 'we are *being forced to think about* a reprint'. Meanwhile, Clive Bell advised Lytton to bring up the matter of his money without delay. He did so, and by return of post – exactly three weeks late – received a cheque with apologies.

After this false start, the relationship between Lytton and Chatto & Windus grew to be extraordinarily cordial. They are always seeking out ways and means to pay him extra money, always improving the clauses in his contracts, and subsequently breaking them for his increased benefit. They press him not to hurry with his next book; they offer to deal with the tax authorities on his behalf; they invite him to witness the printing of his books[12] and send him innumerable dust jackets and alternative bindings from which he is asked to select his favourite. Then out of the blue they write to congratulate him in general terms, and urge him to submit all negotiations to the Society of Authors. Lytton too is extremely courteous.

He makes pressing inquiries after the health of the partners, apologizes for legitimate corrections to proof copies; he recommends a friend to join the firm, and rescues his *Landmarks in French Literature* for them from Williams and Norgate which, in 1927, went bankrupt.

By February 1920 nine impressions of 1000 copies had been issued in Britain and Chatto & Windus brought out a second edition of over 5000 copies in the summer of 1921. It was published in the United States by Putnam who issued a further seventeen impressions during the 1920s after the first printing in September 1918 of a little over 1000 copies. In both countries it continued selling steadily throughout Lytton's life – approximately 35,000 hardback copies in England and more than 55,000 hardback copies in the United States – and was translated into French, Polish, Romanian, Spanish, Italian and Japanese.

Lytton was anxious to have a good French translation and consulted his sister Dorothy Bussy. That summer Dorothy was in England, spending much of her time with André Gide, then living at Merton House in Cambridge as the guest of Harry Norton.[13] Gide had come over with Marc Allegret, carrying a letter of introduction to the Strachey family from Auguste Bréal. During his stay, he had seen something of Lytton and rather more of Dorothy, who was helping to improve his English, and would later translate many of his books. Cambridge, in the summer holidays, half-emptied of undergraduates and half-filled with wounded soldiers, was not at its best, and Gide passed much of his time reading and bicycling about the countryside. Lytton's book had been recommended to him by Arnold Bennett. '*Eminent Victorians* lies on our sitting-room's table and is constantly "en lecture",' he wrote to Dorothy. '. . . I'm not at all sure this book may find in France many readers.'[14]

'I admire it and think it very good,' Ottoline wrote (29–30 May 1918) to Bertrand Russell in Brixton gaol, 'but it *hurts* me . . .' She had been offended by the book's satirical analysis of religion, and Russell, though filling his cell with laughter while reading *Eminent Victorians*, loyally agreed with her that it was objectionable to have these legendary figures of their youth served up for public merriment. He had felt Lytton to have been too quiet a pacifist, but now that his anti-war convictions declared themselves with the publication of this jeremiad, he resented its power to hurt Ottoline. For Bertie could still feel jealous of her old fondness for Lytton, as he had been piqued by G.E. Moore's closeness to Lytton with all its homosexual implications for the Apostles. 'I hate all the Bloomsbury crew, with their sneers at anything that has live feeling in it,' he told her (1 August 1918). '. . . I wish you had more congenial "friends".'

Eminent Victorians was to be one of the seminal Bloomsbury texts. 'Something had to have changed in people's attitude to themselves and to the world for such a book to have been conceived and written,' writes Keynes's biographer Robert Skidelsky.[15] It was the product of a new age, transposing G.E. Moore's philosophical refutation of Idealism into a criticism of Victorian ideals. It was to influence the style of *The Economic Consequences of the Peace* (1919) and *Essays in Biography* (1933), persuading Keynes to be 'more indiscreet than he was by nature', wrote David Garnett; 'to have the courage to print what he would have said in conversation'.[16] It helped to create the post-imperialist climate in which Leonard Woolf wrote *Empire and Commerce in Africa* (1920) and E.M. Forster *A Passage to India* (1924). 'It might be described as the first book of the "twenties",' wrote Cyril Connolly, who called it 'the work of a great anarch, a revolutionary text-book on bourgeois society written in the language through which the bourgeois ear could be lulled and beguiled'.[17]

Contrasting the two men's ambitions, Virginia suggested in her diary (17 June 1920) that Lytton was seeking cultural influence rather than Maynard's political power: 'he wants to deal little words that poison vast monsters of falsehood.' These little words creep all through *Eminent Victorians* and give it the peculiar tone of disparagement that so disturbed and excited readers. 'The tone was officer-class,' commented the poet and biographer Ian Hamilton; 'the sentiment was other rank.'[18] There was another feature too about this virtuoso style, with its ornate overstatements, its laconic recording of incongruities, its unpredictable transpositions, its ironic crescendoes and plummetings into bathos. The pitch was 'midway between the male and female ranges', the critic Barry Spurr observed. Like the novels of Ronald Firbank and E.F. Benson, Wilde's epigrams, the plays of Joe Orton, the drawings, designs and fashions of Beardsley, Beaton and Erté, the style is 'Mandarin in drag, Camp Mandarin one might say, in which Strachey impersonates its mannerisms and humorously exaggerates its gestures . . . [in] this pursuit of the artificial and the theatricalization of experience – identified by Susan Sontag as the essential components of the homosexual sensibility'.[19]

It was what Bertrand Russell termed this 'diseased and unnatural' element in Strachey's writing that unsettled readers. In stripping away so effectively the pious camouflage of his parents' world, was he not replacing one kind of falsity with another, substituting their piety with what a future Master of Balliol was to call a 'contemptible snigger'?[20] It was certainly true that, in his fashion, Strachey was as disreputable a literary figure as Boswell. His achievement in *Eminent Victorians* was to release twentieth-century biography from under the 'Damocles sword of Respectability' which Carlyle had protested in his review of Lockhart's *Life of Scott* 'hangs forever over the poor English life-writer (as it does over poor English life in general'. Some of Strachey's methods too were hardly respectable. 'Discretion', he remarked, 'is not the better part of biography.' He still believed, as he had written in the introduction to his dissertation on Warren Hastings, that 'in general, books are read solely for the pleasure that they give', and that 'the mixture of a lie doth ever add pleasure'. He had been referring here to his historical adversary Macaulay, but his own style, as Bertrand Russell noted, 'was not unlike Macaulay's'. Russell used this comparison to reach his conclusion that Lytton 'was indifferent to historical truth'.[21] But there is a characteristic difference from, as well as a debt to, Macaulay: a substitution of sexual for political ideology. The historian Peter Clarke has pictured Strachey 'with his eye pressed to the keyhole, recording for posterity what the butler saw'.[22] It is certainly an indiscreet posture, but one capable of discovering more truth than the pompous historical butler 'absorbed by his duty of rating the events he announces in the order of their conventional importance while keeping his private thoughts . . . to himself [and] too busy ushering in his facts, too replete with his ceremonious virtue [to] dwell on the disparity between their conventional and their human values'.[23]

Strachey's preface to *Eminent Victorians* was to be read as a manifesto for twentieth-century biographers. 'Human beings are too important to be treated as mere symptoms of the past,' he wrote. 'They have a value which is independent of any temporal processes – which is eternal and must be felt for its own sake.' Of all the qualities of a good historian, incisive moral accuracy was the most vital. Strachey was rebuked for his inaccuracy, his gratuitous mockery, for example of Dr Arnold, but 'how could any mockery be too much for such a man?' questioned the biographer John Stewart Collis. '. . . It is complained that he quoted things out of context and made them look bad. "It is very startling," said Dr Arnold, looking round the boys at Rugby, "to see so much sin combined with so little of sorrow." How do you make that remark look good? – and he did say it.'[24]

Though Strachey was a true heir of Boswell in the revitalizing of biography, his example was not closely followed. He was writing shortly before the growth of economic and social history, and his interest in character and human nature was often regarded as frivolous. A new academic industry was to revive the Victorian tradition of historical biography, its method of enormous and elaborate accretion now supported by a bedrock of references. Nevertheless Strachey's influence was to persist as 'a destroyer of illusions and a liberator of forms', concluded the biographer Richard Holmes. 'What he released was a generation of brilliant experimenters in biographical narrative, who at last began to ask *how* lives can be genuinely reconstructed . . .' [25]

With *Eminent Victorians*, he had let a genie, gleeful and irreverent, out of the bottle, and many potential subjects of biographies were alarmed. 'I've been reading *Eminent Victorians*,' wrote Rudyard Kipling. '. . . It seems to me downright wicked in its heart.'[26]

2

THE BEAU MONDE

For the first time in his life, Lytton was to be a person of independent means. During the 1920s his average income was between two and three thousand pounds per annum (equivalent to around £55,000 in 1994). The first use to which he put his money was the repayment of past loans from Harry Norton and others, and the making of improvements to Tidmarsh – among them the fulfilment of an early Abbotsholme ambition, the building of an earth closet in the garden. Success suited him. Wyndham Lewis has given a fanciful picture of him in his country cottage – a benevolent but rather inhuman old maid of a man, responding coquettishly to his few selected guests (of whom Wyndham Lewis was not one), and languidly dragging his daddy-long-legs from room to room. 'The big lips under his beard were dreamy and large and a little childlike, his big brown eyes were bovine but intelligent. He knew to what "tribe" he belonged, but probably did not practise the rites of the tribe. He liked watching.'

This public image is corrected by the testimony of Carrington. 'I am glad at any rate the public does not share my feelings about your appearance and character!' she wrote to him that July, while making a pilgrimage with her brother Noel to Rothiemurchus. 'Since you are bored with praise of your creations, I will tell you that I think you are the most eminent, graceful person. The most worthy, learned and withal charming character. And I shall always love you in your entirety . . . Visions steal up – of those hot days when you wore your Fakire clothes – in the orchard – The one afternoon when I saw you in the bath – When I lay on your bed on Thursday And smelt your hair, and broke the crackling beard in my fingers.'

Both Lytton and Carrington were glad to have escaped from 'the buffeting of London'. 'Mine is a "vita umbratilis", as Cardinal Manning said,' Lytton told Clive Bell (27 May 1918), '– a life in the shade or a shady life, – whichever you prefer.' Carrington filled the house with cats and the garden with flowers. She taught Lytton the art of picking vegetables for his meals, and how to weed while sitting in a chair. But whenever she left him there alone, he felt daunted by the magnitude of these tasks: peas were manageable, but 'the beans frighten me', he admitted, and the raspberries caught him in their nets. As for the hens, there seemed no possibility of catching one. 'I am in favour of making them tipsy,' he explained to her (7 July 1918), '– it seems to me, short of shooting them, the only plan.' Carrington would often have nightmares while away from Lytton, but he would write to comfort her. 'This is only to give you a kiss. No time for anything more' (12 June 1918).

That summer Carrington painted a large (28 in. by 40 in.) oil picture of what Virginia now called 'the Mill on the Pang'. It is a haunting image. The geometry of the house is lucid and the imaginative use of colour, dominated by glowing orange roofs and a blue sky mirrored in the mill stream, gives the composition a strange intensity. On the stream, which disappears into a tunnel under the house at the centre of the picture, are two black swans, one bent towards the other. The painting has the surreal quality of a dream which mysteriously conveys both happiness and danger.

'I've come to the conclusion we must never leave this earthly Paradise,' Carrington later wrote (29 April 1922). In the delicious heat of that first summer, Lytton would have been content, so he felt, to sit among the laburnums, lilacs, buttercups and apple-blossom, dressed in his Brahmin's robe (though with his mind not altogether Brahminical), serenely dreaming the hours away – if only so many people were not still being slaughtered over the horizon. Would the war *never* end? Yet there seemed little purpose to be served by brooding over it.

There was a procession of visitors. G.E. Moore came and Lytton's sisters Pippa and Marjorie, also his brother Oliver with a new girlfriend Inez, James too who 'weeds with two fingers' and Noel Olivier avidly reading Havelock Ellis on sexual inversion, Clive Bell and Mary Hutchinson, and that odd inseparable trio Saxon Sydney-Turner, Nick and Barbara Bagenal – 'all are incredibly aged. Nick and Barbara (the one without a kidney, and the other with a child) totter and potter like an old couple in an almshouse; and Saxon is wonderfully young for eighty-seven.'

A memory of them at the Mill House comes from another guest, Gerald Brenan, the following summer. The afternoon was heavily overcast, the trees steeped in vivid green, and the purplish clouds throwing the interior of the house into a gloomy shade.

'Carrington, with her restless blue eyes and her golden-brown hair cut in a straight page-boy bob, came to the door . . . and I was shown in the sitting-room. At the farther end of it there was an extraordinary figure reclining in a deep armchair. At first glance, before I had accustomed my eyes to the lack of light, I had the illusion – or rather, I should say, the image came into my mind – of a darkly bearded he-goat glaring at me from the bottom of a cave.† Then I saw that it was a man and took in gradually the long, relaxed figure, the Greco-ish face, the brown sensitive eyes hidden beneath thick glasses, the large, coarse nose and ears, the fine, thin, blue-veined hands. Most extraordinary was the voice, which was both very low and in certain syllables very high-pitched, and which faded out at the end of the sentence, sometimes even without finishing it. I never attuned my ears to taking in everything that he said.'[27]

But what struck Brenan was the attention Carrington lavished upon this fabulous creature. 'Never have I seen anyone who was so waited on hand and foot as he was by her,' he wrote, 'or whose every word and gesture was received with such reverence. In a young woman who in all other respects was fiercely jealous of her independence, this was extraordinary.'

With Lytton 'elegant in his dark suit, gravely remote and fantastic, with something of the polished dilettante air of a sixteenth-century cardinal', Brenan could not hit it off at all. And although Carrington, with her pre-Raphaelite clothes and her coaxing voice and mischievous smile, attracted him physically, he did not take to her because he had heard that she had made cruel fun of a close friend, John Hope-Johnstone, a myopic wanderer who before the war had tutored the children of Augustus John.

So, by the time he left, he had no premonition that he was to be caught up into the irregular mainstream of their two lives, and that for seven years Carrington would be the vital person in his own life.

*

After the success of *Eminent Victorians*, Lytton was soon taken up, much to his delight and slightly to his shame, by the aristocracy. 'The upper-classes rouse my curiosity, and for the present, I think I shall proceed with my enquiries,' he confided to Carrington (26 June 1918), who loved to hear his ironic descriptions of the beau monde. 'What I really need is the Gentleman's Complete Guide to Society' (7 July 1918).

From these glamorous sorties he would return to Carrington amid the ducks, geese, hens, rabbits, bees and kittens of Tidmarsh, and unfold his varnished tales of London society. He was like a dragonfly, Virginia

† in a letter to the author (14 September 1966), Gerald Brenan emphasized that this passage records 'the first impression of a young man, just demobilised from the army, in a bad light, and that it reflects more on my *naïveté* than on him. As soon as I had got over my first shock, I felt his elegance and distinction.'

thought, 'which visits dahlias, limes, holly-hock and then poises, quite unconcerned, in the lid of a broken tea-pot'. That summer he found himself a weekend guest of Lady Astor at Cliveden, of Lady Desborough at Taplow Court, of Lady Horner at Mells Manor in Somerset. He was invited to luncheon-parties and dinner-parties by the celebrated hostesses of the day – Lady Colefax and Lady Cunard, Princess Bibesco and Lady d'Abernon. Carrington was not included in these invitations. 'What a good thing it was I fell in love with you before you were famous . . . [or] I might have been refused,' she chided him (9 June 1918). But she had her own friends – Alix, Barbara and others – and on the whole this arrangement suited them.

Society fascinated Lytton. From a distance, it stood out as clear and well-defined – desirable or absurd according to the angle of vision. He read about it in the newspapers, and was mesmerized by the whirl of self-flattery. But move into its glittering vortex, and the illusion of its reality melted away. It was nothing – a glow in the mind. Yet even a glowing nothing could provide escape from oneself. Lytton hardly knew whether to be pleased or disgusted at this new state of affairs. 'I go next Saturday to the Duchess of Marlborough's,' he wrote to Ottoline (7 July 1918), '– is it the beginning of the end?

'Personally I don't think you or Tolstoy need be alarmed. In the first place, *they* won't like *me*; in the second place *I* won't like *them*. You know I am not altogether uncritical! Curiosity is what chiefly moves me. I want to see for myself. I met the D. of M. in Maud's [Lady Cunard's] ante-room at Drury Lane, and thought her (from a hasty inspection) more distinguished than the rest. Can you give me any tips about her? Lady Randolph [Churchill] was also there – an old war horse, sniffing the battle from afar.'

Another member of this Drury Lane party was Margot Asquith who 'had the cheek' to ask Lytton for a copy of his *Eminent Victorians*, and who invited him round to tea so that he might make the presentation. Yet he seems to have thought her a more valid personality than he had at first supposed – less exagérée and 'even faintly civilized'. But, like so many of these people, she was more like a creature in a play than a real human being – and someone to put in one of his letters to Carrington. 'Her mauvais ton is remarkable,' he told her (26 June 1918).

'There she sits in her box (cadged) and thinks she's the very tip-top, the grande dame par excellence, and all the rest of it – and every other moment behaving like a kitchen-maid – giggling, looking round, and nudging Elizabeth [Asquith – Princess Bibesco]. As for music, of course it's never occurred to her that such a thing exists. Yet, as one looks at her small weather-beaten (perhaps one should say life-beaten) countenance, one wonders – there does seem a suggestion of something going on underneath.'

People who only half a dozen years earlier had wondered how on earth Lady Ottoline Morrell could put up with such a queer fish in her drawing-room and more recently shuddered over his pacifism, now entreated him to visit them. In the second week of August he was invited down with Maynard to The Wharf, as house guests of the Asquiths. 'I'm not much looking forward to the outing,' he confessed to Clive (10 August 1918), 'there is a certain frigidity in those altitudes.' But curiosity drew him on, and once he had dived in, he floated enjoyably. He wanted them to like him; and he was prepared to like them a little in return. 'Maynard supported my tottering footsteps with great tact,' he reported to Ottoline (8 September 1918).

'Margot was extremely kind, and the Company (though not particularly brilliant) was entertaining. There were no great nobs. The Old Man was highly rubicund and domestic – also, I thought, a trifle sleepy. It was chiefly a family party – Violet,[28] Cys[29] and his wife, Anthony,[30] Elizabeth[31] – diversified by Lady Tree and one or two nonentities. Violet and I were very friendly. She certainly has changed enormously – so much more tolerant – at times almost humble, I thought, and even her appearance seems to have entirely altered, the angularity having disappeared, and something of the plenitude of the matron taken its place ... Am I a backslider? I don't think so, and she seemed to be almost intelligent. Even Elizabeth I got on better with (isn't it shocking?) and Margot's goodness of heart rather won me. But what I enjoyed best was the family side of the party – playing foolish letter-games after dinner with the more frivolous (including the Old Man) while the serious persons – Maynard, Margot, Elizabeth and Texeira de Mattos ... gave themselves over to Bridge. You see what I have sunk to! I even enjoyed going off to Church on Sunday evening with Lady Tree – can you imagine the spectacle. And Margot gave me a volume of her diary to read, which was really very interesting, as it had a detailed account of the Cabinet-making manoeuvres of 1906, and I sat up reading it till 2 o'clock in the morning.'

His final comments on Asquith himself show a softening in his attitude of only four months earlier. 'From what I could see, it appeared to me almost incredible that he should ever play a big part in politics again – the poor old fellow! The worst of it is he'll hang on, and block everything. Though to be sure, even if he did vanish, who could succeed him?'

After The Wharf, Lytton raced on to the next encampment on his social safari – a sixteenth-century castle perched on an abrupt rock off the Northumberland coast, the home of Edward Hudson, proprietor of *Country Life* – 'a pathetically dreary figure . . . a fish gliding underwater, and star-struck – looking up with his adoring eyes through his own dreadful element . . . A kind of bourgeois gentilhomme also.' At the end of an alarming journey, in a tumble-down dog-cart at sunset across three miles of desert sea-sand partly in flood and dotted with sunken posts to indicate the route, he arrived in the pitch dark at this fortified rock, nervous, dishevelled and weary, to find the rest of the house-party in evening dress tucking into a banquet of lobster and champagne. Lindisfarne, which had been converted into a 'dream castle' by Sir Edwin Lutyens, struck him as rather a poor affair, except for its actual situation 'which is magnificent', he told Mary Hutchinson (7 September 1918), 'and the great foundations and massive battlements, whence one has amazing prospects of sea, hills, other castles etc. – extraordinarily romantic – on every side. But the building itself is all timid Lutyens – very dark, with nowhere to sit, and nothing but stone under, over and round you, which produces a distressing effect – especially when hurrying downstairs late for dinner – to slip would be instant death. No, not a comfortable place, by any means.'

Predominant among the guests was Guilhermina Suggia, the celebrated cellist, who had befriended Mark Gertler and to whom Lytton at once took a fancy.[32] She seemed to possess the two qualities in women of which he stood in greatest awe – talent and energy. Women instrumentalists were at that time a rare species, and Suggia was rarer still in that she held the cello between her legs, like a male player, instead of in the side-saddle position women were expected to use. 'She is very attractive,' Lytton informed Mary Hutchinson, 'owing I think chiefly to (1) great simplicity – not a trace of the airs and graces of the "Diva" with a European reputation – no bother about playing or not playing – almost a boyishness at times; and (2) immense vitality – her high spirits enormous and almost unceasing – which of course is a great pleasure, particularly to a quiescent person like me.

'I suppose, besides this, that she's a flirt; but it is difficult to say, and there are so many grades of flirtation. Certainly she is full of temperament – of one kind or another; and there was one evening when she got tipsy – tiens!

Her music was of course marvellous – and I got such masses of it! I used to go with her, her mother (a pitiable old remainder biscuit) and the accompanist, to her bedroom; she would then lock the door (to prevent the ingress of Hudson, I fancy) and practise – for hours – playing Bach suites one after the other, and every kind of miracle, with explanations and comments and repetitions, until one tottered down at last to lunch (for this used to happen in the morning) in a state of ecstasy. Then in the evening after dinner she gave her full dress performances. It was really all an extraordinary joy.'

The other guests were less eminent. There was Lady Lewis who distressed Lytton by talking endlessly about his wonderful *Early Victorians*; and a couple of inconceivably rich Americans, crude and amiable (he played a banjo, while she pored silently all week over Lytton's book with results that were not communicated to him). There was also Suggia's mother – 'a subject in itself for a Balzac novel!' – unable to speak a word of any known language, perpetually neglected and perpetually smiling; and George Reeves, the attractive piano accompanist, who was forced by Hudson to go off on unlikely fishing excursions with Lytton in the early dawn. William Heinemann, the publisher, was also present, gushing forth his reminiscences of Whistler and Ibsen, and elaborately old-world improper stories which never failed to make Lytton shriek with laughter. 'I found him a fascinating figure,' he confided to Mary Hutchinson, '– one that one could contemplate for ever – so very very complete. A more absolute jew face couldn't be imagined – bald-headed, goggle-eyed, thick-lipped; a fat short figure, with small legs, and feet moving with the flat assured tread of the seasoned P. and O. traveller. A cigar, of course. And a voice hardly English – German r's; and all the time somehow, an element of the grotesque.'

After a week at this improbable castle, 'surrounded by cormorants and quicksands', Lytton made his escape and was joined by Carrington. Their adventures across Northumberland over the next ten days, 'with Carrington like a large woolly sheep trotting beside me', took them to the beautiful village of Elsdon, where they put up for a week at The Bird and Bush Inn, then south through Durham and York before eventually, on 14 September, arriving back at Tidmarsh. 'I think it very cheering to be with people who are thoroughly happy – for whatever reason,' Lytton wrote to Bunny Garnett (24 September 1918) in anticipation of Clive and Mary coming to stay. Such an observation was in complete contrast to those undergraduate and post-graduate days when the 'affectionateness' of the Bussys and 'couples in the road with their silly arms round their stupid waists' would irritate him by the unwitting emphasis they placed on his solitude.

One symptom from the past that lingered on was invalidism. His chief complaint that autumn was agonizing shingles, which reduced him to 'a mere wraith – a ruined spectre . . . a state of deliquescence'. Carrington somehow intensified her attentions until 'the worst appears to be over'. Lytton wrote to Mary Hutchinson. '. . . Me voici in bed, after breakfast, supported by pillows, and murmuring like Florence Nightingale "Too kind – too kind" to Carrington's ministrations.'

Carrington was jealous of anyone else looking after Lytton, fearing that they would do it more efficiently than she could. When he went to stay with Jack and Mary Hutchinson at their new home at Robertsbridge in Sussex that October, she bombarded him with packages of shortbread, bundles of flowers, and parcels of warmer and yet warmer clothes; and before he left Tidmarsh, she sent a characteristic letter to Mary full of convalescent scholarship.

'I am sure you will be able to provide Lytton with so many more comforts – Clive says you have four handmaids to wait upon him! – than he gets [in] this barbaric house, that I feel I cannot tell you of much. But I will go through his day 8.30 breakfast in bed 2 eggs, toast, and jam *without pips* in it. If that is possible! – 11 ock glass of hot milk with biscuits – Lunch his doctor recommends his having rice or macaroni as vegetable with meats. and milk puddings – Siesta in afternoon – tea at four ock – and so on till 10.30 when he has a bowl of bread and milk before going to bed – and a glass of milk with biscuits by his bedside in case he wakes up in the night – Lytton adds that you will then be required to sleep in the next room and wake at. one o'ck, two o'ck, five o'ck when he taps on the wall. and come in to bath his arm or sympathise with his groanings! – I will send him armed with his food books, and sugar. But really his wants are few, and as I said after this rude existence, and my appalling house management, and nursing, he is bound to be happy with you! . . . My constitution and appetite is that of an Ox, So nursing Lytton hasn't exactly impaired my health! . . . I am really so happy. Mary, that he is going to stay with you as I know you will care for him as noone else would . . . I cant write proper letters like you written. But I only want to thank you rather especially for everything.

   with love

     yr

       affec

         carrington'

Lytton was at Robertsbridge on 11 November – Armistice Day. When the news of peace came through, he found it difficult to believe. After the long years of war, he could hardly recall what peace was like. What did the papers write about when there was no war? Perhaps the weather made headlines. Carrington, who had gone up to London to see Barbara Bagenal, then in a nursing home having her baby (like 'a Japanese grub in the cot beside her'), expresses something of the same blank bewilderment in a letter to her brother Noel, written next day from the 1917 Club. When the guns were fired at eleven o'clock, she had thought it must be some joke, or an elaborate new bombing device thought up by the Germans.

'But it soon turned out to be Peace, with a big P. instantly everyone in the city dashed out of offices and boarded the buses. It was interesting seeing how the different stratas of people took it travelling from Hampstead seeing first the slum girls, and coster people dancing. Pathetic scenes of an elderly plumber nailing up a single small Flag over the door. Then the scenes became wilder as one reached Camden Town and more and more frantic as one [approached] Trafalgar Square office boys and girls, officers, Majors, waacs all leaped on taxis, and army vans driving round the place waving Flags. In the Strand the uproar was appalling. I was to meet Monty Shearman in [the] Adelphi for lunch and it was almost impossible I found to get there! He then took me off to the Café Royal to meet some other rejoicing friends of his . . . then lunch at the Eiffel Tower restaurant.'

Lytton himself came up to London to join in the euphoria. After a first stunned silence at the booming maroons, people had gone mad. The streets were solid with crowds, and everywhere there was noise. In their immeasurable relief, the population of London burst their throats to swell the general din. Motors hooted, handbells rang, police whistles shrilled – everyone felt the urge to do something ridiculous.

The evening was humid and rainy. Almost all Bloomsbury had assembled in Monty Shearman's flat in the Adelphi, where a large party was going on. 'Everyone was there,' Carrington wrote to Noel, 'The halt, the sick and the lame. Even old Lytton [who] was on his deathbed in Sussex rushed up, and joined in the merriment.' The rooms were packed with a familiar but constantly changing company – Clive Bell, Diaghilev and Massine, Roger Fry, Duncan Grant, the Hutchinsons, Maynard Keynes, Lydia Lopokova, Ottoline Morrell, Osbert and Sacheverell Sitwell and Mark Gertler. While Henry Mond strummed away on the piano, Bunny Garnett paired off with Carrington and danced and danced.

Lytton also was seen to dance, after his irregular fashion. 'I remember the tall, flagging figure of my friend Lytton Strachey,' Osbert Sitwell wrote, '... jigging about with an amiable debility. He was, I think, unused to dancing ... As I watched him, I remember comparing him in my mind to a benevolent but rather irritable pelican.'[33]

Lytton passed the next four winter months mostly at the Mill House. Life was sometimes cold and damp, but never solitary. For Christmas James and Alix came down, and so did Harry Norton. 'We eat large chickens,' Lytton wrote to Ottoline (27 December 1918), 'which pretend to be turkeys not very effectively, and drink grocer's wine. Such is the force of convention.'

Immediately afterwards Carrington went off for the funeral of her father, who had died at the age of eighty-two after ten paralysed years in a wheelchair. 'It was ghastly to see a little yellow ghost with a saint-like marble face lying in a narrow coffin,' she wrote to Mark Gertler, remembering how he had suffered over his father's death. 'Instead of that splendid old man in his wheelchair by the fire. And then that hard china-faced sister – and my mother with her sentimental attitude – was almost more hurting.' She stayed there a week, a week of nightmare, growing increasingly upset. She had never felt death so cruelly before, and it sickened her by its awful indignity and ruthlessness. Her father had been so simple and good-hearted until he lay now in a narrow wooden box beside his empty bed, a napkin over his face. When she lifted the napkin, 'oh Lytton, there was not his face, but a face very small, and pale yellow. So dim and icy cold. Then I knew how much I loved him ... oh Lytton why didn't I love him more when he could feel?' Her sister and her mother had never seemed so trivially female with their concern about their black coats and dresses, their indecent interest in his relics. 'They were simply like two pieces of furniture conversing.' She felt better once her father was hidden beneath the ground and she could think of his spirit floating back to India. 'I am glad he has escaped from it all,' she wrote (1 January 1919). She arrived back at Tidmarsh tired and empty-headed. Lytton was now the only family she recognized and his home would be her home. 'Dearest,' she wrote to him (1 and 22 January 1919), 'I am glad that there is you for me to love ... you've meant more to me these last few days than ever before ... you become more precious to me every day.'

For the first few months of the new year, the two of them stayed at the Mill House like a couple of hibernating animals. 'I find London impossible,' Lytton told Leonard and Virginia (29 January 1919). As for his friends in the smart set, he appeared to have abandoned them altogether – for the time being. 'I have decided definitely to give up the gay world, to become an anchoret,' he informed Clive (18 February 1919), 'to read nothing but the various lives of the Prince Consort, to gaze out of [the] window at the snow, and to put another log on the fire.'

At the same time he had started work on a new book.

3

QUEEN VICTORIA AND OTHER ESSAYS

While moving into the Mill House in December 1917, Lytton had begun to 'console' himself with Queen Victoria's letters. 'I am reading Victoria's diary, when a young maid,' he noted (11 December 1917), '– most absorbing, but not long enough.'

The first suggestion that he should make Victoria the subject of his next book had come from Walter Raleigh, shortly after the publication of *Eminent Victorians.* 'We want your method for some stately Victorians who have waited long for it,' he wrote on 13 May 1918. 'First the great Panjandrum – Victoria Herself. This is obvious. How can an adjective have meaning that is not dependent on the meaning of its substantive? . . . It's really wicked of you to leave those stout volumes alone, when you could put the gist of them within reach of us.'

Lytton's initial idea had been to write a second series of pen-portraits, treating the scientists who had been among his original list of twelve candidates. It was not until the end of 1918 that he seems finally to have decided on Queen Victoria. She was, he told Clive (28 December 1918), 'an interesting subject, but an obscure one . . . It's very difficult to penetrate the various veils of discretion. The Prince Consort is a remarkable figure; but Sir Theodore Martin's life of him in five stupendous volumes is not to be recommended to the general public. Have you heard of Emily Cranford? There's a book by her on the queen which is not without merit – Irish and full of gossip about the forties – very disordered, but in parts distinctly good.[34] I'm beginning to think that most of the good books are overlooked. For instance the Private Life of Henry Maitland [by Morley Roberts] is surely highly interesting – but who mentions it? I found it the other day, quite by chance, and found it absorbing.'

By the New Year, Lytton had completed enough reading and research to feel reasonably certain that, as he phrased it to Chatto & Windus (3 January 1919), the subject of his next biography would be 'The Life of

Her Late Majesty'. Writing the following day to his mother, he is more diffident. 'I am beginning a serious study of Queen Victoria; but it's difficult to say as yet whether anything will come of it.' Lady Strachey was taken aback by this news. 'I don't much fancy you taking up Queen Victoria to deal with,' she replied.

'She no doubt lays herself open to drastic treatment which is one reason I think it better left alone. She could not help being stupid, but she tried to do her duty, and considering the period she began in, her upbringing, her early associations, and her position, this was a difficult matter and highly to her credit. She has won a place in public affection and a reputation in our history which it would be highly unpopular, and I think not quite fair, to attempt to bring down.

What about Disraeli? He is near enough our own time to be topical, and too near to have been thoroughly dealt with as yet. His two reputations, the early one and the later which has developed into a legend, are quite contradictory, and until they have been welded together, are in my opinion equally false.'[35]

But Lytton had made up his mind. For six months he had been reading biographies of Albert the Good, of Victoria herself and all manner of works on Victorian politics and history. His letters to Pippa sometimes contain lists of books for her to send down to him at the Mill House when he was unable to get up to the London Library. Perhaps the most interesting of all the works that came his way was Sir Herbert Maxwell's two-volume edition of *The Creevey Papers*. 'How can anyone read novels when there are Creevey Papers to be had – in which there is every variety of human, political, and historical interest, sur le vif – I don't understand,' he wrote to Clive (18 February 1919).[36]

This preparatory reading took almost twice as long as the writing of his biography. Over the next two years he would stay at Belsize Park Gardens, or with his brother Oliver at 96 South Hill Park and occasionally at the Savile Club for weeks at a time, working at the London Library and the British Museum Reading Room, and then returning to Tidmarsh with a few pages of notes in an exercise book and some sheets of foolscap full of quotations. Huge parcels of books would arrive regularly at the Mill House from booksellers and libraries, and be explored day after day – six or eight or ten hours' reading a day. At the end of each volume, a dozen pencil entries on half a sheet of paper would represent the material he had extracted. 'His critical faculty was so highly developed by the time he came to write biography that he rarely noted down a superfluous fact, and still more rarely had to return to a book once read for some fact he had previously rejected,' recorded Ralph Partridge (8 October 1946). 'Still, the reading to be done was immense; and he never skipped through books, and never trusted an index to pick out references to his subject. An outline of the book he intended to write was in his head before ever he began his course of reading, but not a word went on paper until the reading was finished. Then very likely he would take a holiday abroad before settling down to write.'

While working on *Queen Victoria* he dared not squander vital energy on unrelated articles. At the same time, he could seldom resist dashing off poems and plays. There is a photograph of him and his sister Marjorie convulsed in laughter, with the caption 'Reading Lytton's tragedy'. During the summer of 1918 he had come up with 'Quasheemaboo' or 'The Noble Savage', a drama which he composed for Madame Vandervelde and Jack Hutchinson to act in at a charity gala. 'The plot of the play was suggested to me by you once,' he reminded his mother (5 June 1918), '– probably you've forgotten all about it – A wife who has become a successful actress without her husband knowing it. When she tells him he disbelieves her, whereupon she gets up a melodramatic scene, which completely takes him in – and then she rounds upon him. So if it's taken up, and performed on the Music Hall stage and brings in millions, you shall have half the profits!' Though never professionally performed, it is an amusing farce with some musical possibilities.

Shortly after the appearance of *Eminent Victorians*, he had been invited by J.C. Squire to write for the *New Statesman*. 'The idea of contributing to the New Statesman would be more pleasant to me if I could sympathise rather more with its war-policy,' he had replied. 'This, so far as I can make it out, seems to be a species of unconscious jingoism.

'Your ideals are no doubt admirable but what you are really promoting is the policy of the knock-out-blow – that is to say the wicked and impossible policy of the Northcliffe Press. That this is so is shown (to take one instance) in the tone of your remarks this week about Lord Lansdowne.[37] Whether you agree with him or not, you ought to be able to see that he is an honest man, and a man who is at any rate trying to use his reason. But evidently you see neither of these things, for you attack him in a style for which I can really only think of one epithet – blackguardly. It appears to me that the only possible explanation is that, whatever you may say, and whatever you may think, you are in fact a Northcliffian.'

Squire angrily repudiated these charges, but Lytton did not contribute to the *New Statesman* until, in 1931, under the new editorship of Kingsley Martin and as the amalgamated *New Statesman and Nation*, it became again an influential and argumentative journal of dissent.

By the year 1919, he had begun to associate himself with the *Athenaeum*, which had then reached a peculiar stage in its erratic history. 'It was about the end of 1828 that readers of periodical literature, and quidnuncs in those departments, began to report the appearance, in a Paper called the *Athenaeum*, of writings showing a superior brilliancy and height of aim,' wrote Carlyle in his *Life of Stirling*. But by the twentieth century, both brilliancy and height of aim had long since vanished, and as a monthly 'Journal of Reconstruction', the *Athenaeum* had barely survived the war. In 1919, however, it was given a drastic new lease of life when Arthur Rowntree purchased the paper and reconstituted it as a weekly 'Journal of English and Foreign Literature, Science, the Fine Arts, Music and the Drama'. By what the biographer F.A. Lea described as 'a stroke of inspiration', Rowntree offered the editorship to Middleton Murry, then an undischarged bankrupt. Brilliancy and height of aim were quickly restored, but during the two years that Murry reigned as editor, the paper lost almost ten thousand pounds.

Before visiting Tidmarsh, the letter Murry wrote Lytton (12 February 1919) rallying him to the *Athenaeum*'s happy band of contributors is a collector's item, showing a nice muddle of humility, touching bewilderment, great earnestness and the dependence upon other people to make a name for him.

'I have been made editor of the new Athenaeum – heaven knows what beneficent bee entered the bonnets of the owners – which is shortly to arise like the phoenix. I shall try to make it as good as I can. But to do that it is necessary that you should become a regular contributor . . .

But, my dear Lytton, it is your duty to the coming generation. I do think that a new Athenaeum is a great opportunity, and I know that unless you will join, we shall be unable to make the use of it which we ought to make. Therefore, though it will be a bother, and though the work will be no better paid than elsewhere, please be conscientious in your responsibilities and say you will.'

Murry's sincerity impressed Lytton, reducing his slight scepticism. In any event, there could be no doubt that Murry was preferable to Squire. 'I think he ought to make a good job of it, with his extraordinary competence qua journalist. I said I'll try and write a little for it – I should like to write a great deal, but I'm too slow, and then how does one put

put things? And perhaps on the whole books are more important than magazines.'

When Murry left Tidmarsh, he took with him 'Lady Hester Stanhope', and over the next six months Lytton sent him one piece of dramatic criticism, 'Shakespeare at Cambridge', and three more biographical essays. In 'Voltaire' and 'Walpole's Letters' he was treating familiar subjects. Both had been his constant reading since Cambridge days, so that he had come to know their long-vanished faces as well as those of living friends – 'one of those enigmatical friends about whom one is perpetually in doubt as to whether, in spite of everything, one *does* know them after all'. Otherwise he liked portraying eccentric and inexplicable lives which contrasted romantically with his own but answered some inner sense of abnormality. 'Lady Hester Stanhope' and 'Mr Creevey', both minor historical figures of triumphant unconventionality, ascended into this category. In all these essays Lytton shows less interest in public achievement than in the quirks of personality, which he gracefully sets off against the pastures of social and political high life.

'I find the Athenaeum a great addition to existence. Don't you?' he asked Ottoline a fortnight after the publication of 'Lady Hester Stanhope' (17 April 1919). 'It really, as they say, "supplies a long felt want".' But over the latter term of Murry's editorship, the paper began to lose its early momentum and Lytton's enthusiasm cooled. The proprietors also felt the paper to be in need of 'new blood' in the form of a new editor. Early in 1921, Murry resigned, and that February the *Athenaeum* merged with the *Nation*. Also financed by the Rowntree family, the *Nation* had been founded in 1907, and was skilfully edited by H.W. Massingham. The paper's political impact, however, was weak, and it had not prospered financially. Moreover, a new body of Liberals, known as the Grasmere Group and numbering among its members Sir William Beveridge, Philip Guedalla and Maynard Keynes, concerned over the absence of a good Liberal weekly, had started discussions with the Rowntree family, who were themselves growing restive under the mounting losses. It was agreed that fresh money would be found to reduce the burden upon the Rowntrees, if a radical alteration was made in the political outlook of the paper. Massingham then resigned as editor and Keynes was elected chairman of the new board. The first issue of what some critics have regarded as a special pulpit for the Bloomsbury Group came out on 5 May 1923 under the editorship of the economist Hubert Henderson, 'a small, testy, unheroic man, vaguely on the look out for offence', Virginia called him, who seemed as 'disappointed by Lytton' as by herself. But the literary section of the re-formed *Nation and Athenaeum* was kept free from the political part of the paper, and this freedom – reminiscent of that in the *New Quarterly* and *Independent Review* – suited Lytton well. During the next five years he contributed seventeen signed essays which were to comprise almost the whole of his sixth published volume, *Portraits in Miniature*.

4

MEMOIR OF AN INFANTRY OFFICER

On the afternoon of 10 August 1918 there arrived at the Mill House a powerfully built young man with light-blue eyes who was to enter intimately into their lives. This was Ralph Partridge,[38] a wartime friend of Noel Carrington. Leaving Oxford early in the war he had joined the army, been awarded a Military Cross and risen at the age of twenty-three to the rank of major, commanding a battalion. Noel Carrington had taken his sister and Ralph on a visit to Scotland that summer. His vitality, good looks and easy ways delighted her. 'The young man Partridge had just come back from Italy, the one I was telling you about the other evening,' she wrote to Lytton (4 July 1918). '. . . He adores the Italians and wants after the war to sail on a schooner to the Mediterranean Islands and Italy, and trade in wine without taking much money and to dress like a brigand. I am so elated and happy. It is so good to find someone who one can rush on and on with, quickly. He sang Italian songs to us on the platforms and was in such gay spirits – and used his hands gesticulating . . . I hope I shall see him again.'

But should Lytton see him? 'I wonder if you will like Partridge,' she wrote a little uncertainly (8 July 1918). 'Noel said he would probably like to come to Tidmarsh very much if we asked him.' Her brother, anxious to see her life arranged more conventionally, continued arguing the merits of 'the nice creature Partridge', and Lytton felt a flutter of interest. 'The existence of Partridge sounds exciting,' he wrote (6 July 1918). 'Will he come down here when you return, and sing Italian songs to us, and gesticulate, and let us dress him as a brigand? I hope so.'

It was agreed that Carrington should invite this young officer over to the Mill House. But the visit was not a success. Partridge's experience of the war had been very different from Lytton's and he advanced at once into a heated argument, claiming that all the carnage did not matter, that he himself had no objection to being killed fairly and squarely by the enemy, and that all pacifists were skulkers and ought to be shot. Lytton hardly joined in the discussion. But Carrington, angry that he should have been

445

exposed to such rudeness, fiercely and incoherently argued the cause of 'passifism', and finally, in despair, led Partridge off outdoors where his militaristic views might discharge themselves harmlessly into the open air.

Partridge himself seems to have remained unaware of his *faux pas*. 'I have been initiated into the Mill House,' he notified Noel Carrington the following week (17 August 1918), 'but as a great part of the μυστήρια [festivities] took place on the river, I viewed the proceedings very favourably. Old man Strachey with the billowy beard and alternating basso-falsetto voice did not play a great part.' In a letter to his friend Gerald Brenan, he described Carrington as 'a painting damsel and a great Bolshevik who would like to strike a blow for the Cause', while Lytton is dismissed as 'of a surety meet mirth for Olympus'. Partridge's name does not crop up in Lytton's correspondence this year except cursorily in one letter to Clive Bell as 'some Major Partridge or other', a friend of Carrington's. Carrington herself had been disappointed. Partridge didn't appear 'very interested in Books or poetry or painting,' she complained to her brother Noel (12 August 1918). '. . . He was surprised that Lytton had written that Book. as he said he didn't think he looked as if he could have . . . Then he didn't see very much in the book except that the style was "rather good" – Then he was prejudiced against Lytton slightly for his beard and appearance. and confessed it.'

Immediately the war was over, Ralph Partridge returned to Oxford, where he was supposed to be completing his law studies and from where he would bicycle over the twenty miles to Pangbourne for weekends. He had fallen in love with Carrington, and she felt pleased by his attentions. He was 'not very attractive to look at', she had warned Lytton, his face reminding her 'of a Norwegian dentist' (9 June 1919). 'I am sure you wouldn't like the Partridge,' she told Bunny Garnett (22 January 1919). Yet secretly she had taken to him strongly and so, to her surprise, had Lytton.

Partridge was tall, broad-shouldered, athletic and, as Carrington had initially written, 'immensely big'. He had the same male magnificence as Thoby Stephen and George Mallory, and 'seemed born to lead anything from a Polar expedition to an infantry assault', wrote his friend Gerald Brenan. '. . . He was very sure of himself and did not easily submit to authority that he regarded as stupid or incompetent.'[39] His Rabelaisian laugh, his incredible blue eyes, his reckless taste for adventure, as well as all his practical efficiencies, inspired Lytton with a kind of hero-worship. There was little question of any sexual relations between them, since Partridge was exclusively heterosexual. Indeed, his mind ran much on women, many of whom adored him; and he had many romantic conquests, especially among actresses and chorus-girls. Yet Lytton seemed to like him all the more for this.

Such were Ralph Partridge's resplendent qualities; and had this been all there was to him, then Lytton's passion would not have amounted to anything new. But this was not all. Despite his conventional opinions, Ralph was something of a rebel, and in his casual remarks delivered in a half-jocular, half-ironic voice, Lytton was able to observe the workings of a strong undeveloped mind. Though he was far more aggressive in argument than he realized, his outlook was unsentimental and realistic. He had a tenacious memory and a passion for acquiring facts that made him a rewarding pupil.

Lytton soon set about educating this young man, instilling in him some of his own tastes in literature and views on sexual ethics. The result was that, for all his individualism and disinclination to submit to authority, this robust man-of-the-world fell largely under Lytton's sway. From a bluff and breezy extrovert, he changed into a rather cultivated man of letters, who would work for the Hogarth Press, review for the *New Statesman* and finally become an author. So dramatic was the change that people who knew him only later in life could scarcely credit his earlier history. During the First World War he had been in his element in the front line; twenty years later, as a conscientious objector, he was attacking militarism with the same passion that he had previously used against Lytton and other pacifists. This conversion was partly due to Lytton who, as it were, helped to make a new man of him, only to find that his infatuation for the ebullient army major he first met had somewhat faded.

There was one other trait in Ralph Partridge's character which to Lytton's mind sanctified any philistine errors of taste and judgement, and this was his lack of ambition. Though naturally athletic, he was congenitally lazy. At Oxford he had taken up rowing, but when asked to row for the Varsity eight declined to do so on the grounds that it interfered with a holiday he was planning. Later, when invited to represent Great Britain in the Olympic Games, he again refused since the training was inconvenient. Lytton was charmed. What it must be to have the opportunity to turn one's back on such things! For some time Partridge embodied a new vision of his ideal self. 'Lord!' he exclaimed to Carrington (11 June 1919), 'Why am I not a rowing blue, with eyes to match, and 24? It's really dreadful not to be.'

On most evenings when the three of them were alone together at Tidmarsh, Lytton would read aloud – this being an important part in the curriculum of schooling his young friends. Carrington still found great difficulty over the longer words, but she had a feeling for poetry and came to absorb a good deal of it, particularly the Elizabethan song books. Meanwhile, Ralph was gradually shedding his boorishness and, with his natural intelligence, picking up a wider education. But his attention was fixed less on Lytton than on the rapt and enigmatic figure of Carrington. She was still something of a mystery to him, yet all the more desirable for that. He was accustomed to quick conquests over women, and to an equally precipitate loss of interest in them – either that, or else they did not respond to him and he did not like them. But Carrington was different. He found it impossible to understand her slavish attachment to Lytton.

Ralph tried everything he knew to make Carrington his own property. When the winter began to thaw and the warmer weather spread through the garden, he would appear in front of her stark naked and twist himself into contortionist positions so that she could make sensational drawings of his magnificent outlines. She felt grateful. It was thrilling for her in more confusing ways too. 'I've been drawing R.P. naked in the long grass in the orchard,' she told Lytton (May 1919). 'I confess I got rather a flux over his thighs, and legs so much so that I didn't do very good drawings.'

Through these early weeks of 1919, Ralph tried to persuade Carrington to go on holiday with him. But she did not wish to leave Lytton who, however, urged her to go. So, in the third week of March, more for his sake than Ralph's, she went with him for a month to Spain, accompanied by her brother Noel and Ralph's sister Dorothy, 'one of those perfectly nice characters, without any surprises'. Nearly all her brief separations from Lytton were enforced in this peculiar way. 'I was never in all these 16 years happy when I was without him,' she wrote at the end of her life. 'It was only I knew he disliked me to be dependent that I forced myself to make other attachments.'

Carrington's absence brought home to Lytton just how much he had come to depend upon her in the indecipherable business of running the house. Without her help, he appeared lost – comically and infuriatingly lost. 'This morning I visited the butcher's,' he wrote to James (7 April 1919), 'and stood for some hours among a group of hags and every sort of "joint" and horror. At last my turn came, and I asked if they had any mutton – of the butcher's wife. She said "Yes". I produced my coupon, on which she became rather mysterious, moved about, then brushed past me murmuring "wait a minute" in lurid tones. So I did. At last, on the departure of one of the hags, she said: "That was the food controller's wife." So I suppose we'd been committing some illegality, though what it can be I've no idea, as my principle is to understand nothing of such matters.'

To avoid the perplexities of 'shopping', Lytton took himself off for a week to the Cove Hotel at West Lulworth, with its memories of Rupert Brooke, where he could be sure of being looked after properly. He had expected to see James installed there, but finding no sign of his brother was obliged to 'sit solitaire, cheek by jowl with a quite silent (luckily) and half-witted military couple in a most higgledy-piggledy hotel,' he complained to Ottoline (27 March 1919).

'. . . There are splendid Downs going down into cliffs – all so pale and peaceful – into the sea, which yesterday was a Mediterranean blue. The sun was streaming down. I stretched myself full-length upon the grass and basked. It seems incredible; and indeed I thought at the time there was some trickery about it – and so there was. As I was basking, an old seagull swooped past, and positively laughed in my face – a regular mocking jeering laugh – as much as to say "you wait" – and lo and behold in the night the weather completely changed, and now we are back in the old story of hurricanes and deluges – ugh! And to be penned in with the Major and Mrs Major all day – oh! I shall struggle out and breast the elements, I think, what e'er betide.'

He caught up with James and Alix at Lyme Regis, spending Easter with them at a lodging-house. 'Behold me basking in the sun,' he wrote to Bunny Garnett (5 April 1919), 'on the Marine Parade, the sun sparkling below me, aged spinsters, discharged army youths etc. etc. floating round me.' Alix was now renting 41 Gordon Square in London into which she had invited James. There would be quarrels, reconciliations, moments when the strain became unbearable and Alix appeared 'on the point of killing herself', as Virginia reported to Vanessa. Yet Alix's strategy of attrition was beginning to work. 'She deserves to win,' Virginia concluded.

Lytton returned to Tidmarsh with relief. The last weeks, though not unpleasant, had seemed like a relapse into those aimless nomadic days before the war.

'I am so happy here, and the sun is so good and hot,' Carrington wrote (15 April 1919) from Madrid. '. . . I feel it is like some dream.' The four of them had walked up to thirty miles a day as they moved from Cordoba to Seville and on to Toledo and Madrid. 'I have seen sights one hardly dreamt of,' she told Gertler (30 April 1919). 'And people so beautiful that one quivered to look at them – and then those El Grecos at Madrid and Toledo – and yet one has to keep it all inside.' The primitive country with its startling colours, and also the Goya portraits, revived her desire to paint. Though Roger Fry and Clive Bell never mentioned her work, Virginia was about to make 'a large showpiece by Carrington' one of 'the chief decorations' at Monk's House in Sussex, and Lytton continued to encourage her. ('Don't you think the time has come to think seriously of beginning to show your pictures?' he was to ask that summer.) 'One day I really hope I shall be an artist,' she told him, '& then you'll see my affection.'

She seemed also to be growing fonder of Ralph. At the beginning of the year she had described him as 'self-satisfied and narrow-minded . . . [his] callousness, and lack of reverence for life, and death appalled me.' His bullying way of arguing still exasperated her (she appealed to Lytton for lessons in arguing), but he had an appealing vein of fantasy, she discovered, as she watched him pass them all off as a troupe of English acrobats. 'I must say R.P. was rather good at lying,' she wrote to Lytton (18 April 1919). But Dorothy Partridge was horrified and accused Carrington of ruining her brother.

As for Ralph, he had made up his mind that as soon as he came down from Oxford he must somehow persuade this strange girl to marry him.

5

HIGH LIFE, LOW LIFE AND LITERARY LIFE

The spring and summer months drew Lytton forth from his country hibernation. 'My smart life proceeds apace,' he informed Mary Hutchinson (15 May 1919). 'I find it mainly simply comic, and distinctly exhausting. No pasturage for the soul, I fear! Lady Cunard is rather a sport, with her frankly lower-class bounce; she makes the rest of 'em look like the withered leaves of Autumn, poor things. But she herself I fancy is really pathetic too. So lost – so utterly lost! – She takes to me, she says, for the sake of that nice dear Bernard Keynes, who's such an intimate friend of hers . . .

'after lunch, Lady C. suddenly said she must go and fetch Princess Bibesco (not Elizabeth – another) from the French embassy opposite.[40] She dashed off to do so. Reappeared very quickly, with the Princess, and – who do you think? – George Moore. He looked too preposterous – like a white rabbit suddenly produced by a conjuror out of a hat. He was furious, of course, and went away at once. Apparently, he had told Maud [Lady Cunard] over and over again "I do not want to come" – but it was useless – he was carried off – propelled into Mrs [Saxton] Noble's arms, and then, out of Maud's clutch for a moment, vanished.'

The whirl of party-going left Lytton feeling rather blasé – 'a blasé literary man I've become, I fear,' he told Carrington (16 May 1919). He was never truly at home in this milieu. The glitter of it all would amuse him for short stretches of time, but the descriptions of what he saw and heard are animated by dislike. In another letter to Carrington (14 May 1919), he describes a visit to Mrs Ava Astor, the wealthy widow of Colonel J.J. Astor, soon to marry Lord Ribblesdale.

'Yesterday I went (at my own suggestion) to tea with Mrs Astor. For the first time my courage began to ooze. The immense size of that Grosvenor Square house – double doors flying open, a vast hall with a butler and two female footmen permanently established in it, vistas beyond of towering pilasters and a marble staircase and galleries – it struck awe into the heart. Then a door quite close at hand was swiftly opened, and I was projected into a large square room, in a distant corner of which, on a sofa, was a lady whom in my agitation I hardly recognised – the colour of hair seemed to have quite changed – and as I advanced three small dogs rushed out at me snapping. I at last reached the sofa and we had a long but not amorous tête-à-tête. The poor dear woman is terrified of Bolshevism – thinks Mr Smillie[41] will lead the mob against her – and asks anxiously "Do you think they'll all go red?" I read her a lecture on the unequality of wealth, and left her trembling to get ready for the Opera.'

One can detect in such a passage the unreconciled stages of Lytton's social attitude – the awe, the surprised amiability, the radical reproof. When unknown and miserable long ago at Lancaster Gate, he had hated London society. But now that it had begun to take notice of him, he wanted to assure himself that he was equal to its attentions. For all their superior blood, their expensive clothes, he thought them rather an insensitive herd.

These fashionable circles, which only a year before were preoccupied with matters military and political, had now turned their attention back to the arts. Early that summer, Diaghilev's company, with Picasso, Massine, Stravinsky and Ansermet, arrived in London to give their spectacular performances of *La Boutique Fantasque*, *Le Tricorne* and *The Good-Humoured Ladies* (to which 'the Bird Partridge' took Carrington) and was immediately taken up by the society hostesses. Bloomsbury also shared in the festivities, and it was to introduce this confluence of artists, dancers and musicians into their circle that Clive and Maynard gave a supper-party for them at 46 Gordon Square.[42] Among the guests were Picasso, Derain, Lopokova and some forty young or youngish painters, writers and students. 'Maynard, Duncan Grant, our two maids and I waited on them,' Clive Bell later recalled. 'Picasso did not dress. We rigged up a couple of long tables: at the end of one we put Ansermet, at the end of the other Lytton Strachey, so that their beards might wag in unison.'[43]

Twice Lytton visited Garsington and found it 'terribly trying'. 'I was often on the point of screaming from sheer despair, and the beauty of the surroundings only intensified the agony,' he wrote to Virginia (27 May 1919). 'Ott I really think is in the last stages – infinitely antique, racked in every joint, hobbling through the buttercups in cheap shoes with nails that run into her feet, every stile a crisis, and of an imbecility . . . She is rongée, too, by malevolence; every tea party in London to which she hasn't been invited is wormwood, wormwood.'

Lytton's name also regularly appears in the visitors' book at The Wharf. A couple of times that summer the Asquiths invited him over for weekends. 'My heart sank and sank – and sank still further on reaching this house, which is really a worse house than Charleston to arrive at,' he confided to Carrington (June 1919). 'No sign of Margot – only a faded group of completely unknown people.

'I lost my head – opened a door, and found myself projected into a twilight chamber, with four bridge players in the middle of it. Complete silence. Margot was one of them. At last, after a long time, in which nobody even looked in my direction, she said, "Oh, how d'you do?" – I fled – fled to the other house, where my bedroom is – opened another door, and there, at the end of the room, alone and dim, was the Old Man. He was as usual most cordial, and conducted me with incredible speed all round the garden, and then back again to the other house. He's a queer nervous old fellow, really.'

Lytton came away murmuring 'never again, never again', but a month later he was back. 'It's perhaps slightly better than the last time,' he admitted to Carrington (17 July 1919). 'There's a middle-aged Scotch woman who plays chess with me while the others play bridge, and there are not quite so many absolute imbeciles. The "painters" are that creature Ranken[44] . . . and a little sporting fellow – an ostler – called Mullings[45] [*sic*], I gather, who, I also gather, paints race-horses for a living . . .'

He also encountered Lord Haldane,[46] who had been lord chancellor and secretary of state for war under Asquith and who was 'so incredibly urbane as to be almost a character in a French play – or as Mr Asquith suggested an Abbé', Lytton wrote to Ottoline (3 June 1919). 'In both of them I was struck by the fact of their talking of nothing but the past; what happened in August 1914 etc. seems to absorb them still. But really nowadays there are other things to think about.'

He liked to observe these great people, to give comic imitations while he talked about them with more than his old assurance. Watching him as he sported so gracefully, bringing down such rare fruits from the poison tree, Virginia acquitted him of any wish to impress her with this social flutter. 'He told us of a visit to Irene Vanbrugh, with his comedy,' she observed in her diary (16 May 1919); 'how the singing of her canary birds almost drowned his voice.' Though Ottoline had professed some alarm at what was happening to him, Virginia felt it would be absurd not to let him enjoy his butterfly's season. It was obvious, listening to his flittings from grand house to grand house 'as if he were an ordinary house fly', that 'his sting is in perfect order', she told Saxon Sydney-Turner (30 May 1919). Besides, as she had reassured Ottoline that same month (21 May 1919), 'the truth is of course, that no one humbugs Lytton for the wink of an eyelid'.

His mellowness was renewing Virginia's affection for him which, she liked to believe, 'has never been seriously in abeyance'. Yet the success of *Eminent Victorians* had troubled her. Leonard thought it a remarkable book and so apparently did the rest of the world, but 'I'm not interested in what he writes', she put in her diary (31 January 1919). When he had first sent it to her and Leonard, she had immediately questioned him (24 May 1918) as to 'how many copies you've sold, how many guineas, how many Countesses, how many adorations and whether at heart you're still the same.' She did not begrudge him the guineas, or envy the adoration. But the copies sold! 'Boils, blisters, rashes, green and blue vomits are all appointed by God himself to those whose books go into 4 editions within 6 months,' she had written to him the following autumn (12 October 1918) while he was ill at Tidmarsh. 'Shingles, I can assure you, is only a first instalment . . .' Lytton had 'laughed outright very loud five times' when he read this letter, Carrington reported. 'And the second time he read it, ten minutes later he laughed seven times.'

When they were together, Lytton and Virginia could always resolve these troubles into games, but he had been so sought after in the year following the publication of *Eminent Victorians* that there had been little time for Bloomsbury. 'It is so long since I have seen Lytton that I take my impressions of him too much from his writing,' Virginia noted in her diary on 17 April 1919. Looking at his writing she asked herself how it could be that he had 'dominated' a generation at Cambridge and was now the toast of literary society if, as she judged, he lacked originality? Was it simply jealousy that made her chary of praising his work? 'Do I compare the

6 editions of Eminent Victorians with the one of The Voyage Out?' Inevitably there was a tinge of jealousy. She could not help feeling a little rewarded when, telling Lytton of the good opinions of her second novel *Night and Day*, she thought she saw 'a little shade – instantly dispelled, but not before my rosy fruit was out of the sun'. She had treated his triumphs in much the same way, urging him to switch from his Victorians and 'write plays – stories – anything to break the mould' (25 May 1919). And he informed her that she was the 'inventor of a new prose style, & the creator of a new version of the sentence' and that he was sometimes 'disgusted by his own stereotyped ways: his two semi colons; his method of understatement; & his extreme definiteness'. So when he returned to his Bloomsbury friends, and they sat in the garden or by the fire at Monk's House and Tidmarsh, Virginia reflected that 'it doesn't much matter if his writing is not profound or original; one begins perhaps to suspect that it may be more original than one thinks'.

'It makes me melancholy to see so little of you and Virginia,' Lytton had written to Leonard at the end of 1918. Though his fame had changed him 'as love might', Virginia observed, making him 'immensely appreciative, even tender', and though he had been 'permanently shone upon' by the smart world, yet he was disaffected by what he saw as the professional unhappiness of great people – 'they are perpetually bored', he discovered. According to Clive, Virginia, Lytton, Roger, Vanessa and himself were 'the most hated people in London; superficial, haughty, giving ourselves airs . . .' But for all its superiorities and inferiorities, Bloomsbury remained real and interesting to Lytton in a way that aristocratic society never became, and he returned to it all with some relief. 'It's a mercy to be back here again, even though the Duchesses seem to have dropped me,' he wrote to Virginia from Hampstead (27 May 1919). 'I *was* rung up just now, though, and by – who do you think? – Vanessa, who's in Gordon Square apparently. I dine there tonight.'

Vanessa had given birth to her third child, a girl, the previous Christmas at Charleston. 'Its beauty is the most remarkable thing about it,' Bunny Garnett had written to Lytton (25 December 1918), adding prophetically: 'I think of marrying it; when she is twenty I shall be 46 – will it be scandalous?' Unlike Vanessa's two boys, Julian and Quentin, who 'scuttled about like mice, until distracted by stockings and presents',[47] the girl's father was not Clive, but Duncan (who was to end his sexual relations with Bunny shortly afterwards). It seemed best to keep this a secret – an open secret within Bloomsbury. Clive did not want to unsettle his parents and Vanessa was anxious to protect Duncan, then in his early thirties, whom she still looked on as an adolescent. It was 'the conventionality of this deception that is surprising,' their daughter wrote sixty-five years later. '. . . the only voice of criticism was that of Bunny Garnett, who told Vanessa that in depriving me of my true father she was making a rash decision . . . Owing to my likeness to Duncan, even my grandmother Ethel [Grant] must soon have had her suspicions. I was the only person successfully kept in the dark.'[48]

A more urgent problem seemed to be the choosing of names. What would be a really deep and inscrutable singular name? It wasn't easy. '"Aziola" would be a good name, for it indicates, according to Shelley, "nothing but a little downy Owl" – but probably the suitableness wouldn't last,' Lytton wrote to Vanessa (1 March 1919), '. . . Do you think Virginia would be out of the question? Perhaps it would cause confusions – I don't know. But I think there ought to be a Virginia in the next generation.[49] Also, no doubt, it would give great pleasure. Otherwise, what do you say to Elizabeth? – A truly magnificent name: and it has the additional advantage of having so many agreeable shortenings . . . Victoria (what about *that* for a name?).' The baby was registered as Helen Vanessa to which, on Virginia's recommendation, her mother added Angelica which 'has liquidity and music, a hint of green in it'.[50] So by that name she became known, first as Angelica Bell, then as Angelica Garnett.

*

Beyond Bloomsbury, Lytton would occasionally see other writers such as W.H. Davies, 'gnome and poet', and Aldous Huxley who 'looked like a piece of seaweed' but was 'incredibly cultured'. During the spring of 1919, Huxley and he visited Osbert Sitwell, then a patient in a military hospital in London. They made a lugubrious couple, Sitwell remembered, their 'silent elongated forms . . . drooping round the end of my bed like the allegorical statues of Melancholy and of a rather satyr-like Father Time that mourn sometimes over a departed nobleman on an eighteenth-century tombstone. Lytton's debility prevented him from saying much, but what he did say he uttered in high, personal accents that floated to considerable distances, and the queer reasonableness, the unusual logic of what he said carried conviction.'[51]

Another literary acquaintance was T.S. Eliot. They had not taken to each other when introduced a few years before but after a second meeting at Garsington on 12 May 1919, Lytton discovered that 'he's greatly improved – far more self-assured, decidedly intelligent, and, so far as I could see, nice.' Two days later they met again in London, and Lytton reported to Carrington (14 May 1919): 'Poet Eliot had dinner with me on Monday – rather ill and rather American: altogether not quite gay enough for my taste. But by no means to be sniffed at.' In a letter to Mary

Hutchinson (15 May 1919), he describes his friendship with Eliot as having reached a fluctuating stage. 'I do like him, though,' he added. 'He's changed a great deal since I last saw him – a long time ago. But the devitalisation I'm afraid may lead to disappointments.'[52]

These fears seemed well founded. That May Lytton read *Prufrock and Other Observations*, which The Egoist Ltd had brought out two years earlier, and sent Eliot a letter which, he hoped, might advance their friendship. In his reply (1 June 1919) Eliot touched on the processes of his writing.

'Whether one writes a piece of work well or not seems to me a matter of crystallisation – the good sentence, the good word, is only the final stage in the process. One can groan enough over the choice of a word, but there is something much more important to groan over first. It seems to me just the same in poetry – the words come easily enough, in comparison to the core of it – the *tone* – and nobody can help one in the least with that. Anything *I* have picked up about writing is due to having spent (as I once thought, wasted) a year absorbing the style of F.H. Bradley – the finest philosopher in English – "App[earance] and Reality" is the Education Sentimentale of abstract thought.'

Turning from his own writing to Lytton's letter, Eliot (who was then working for Lloyds Bank) comments:

'You are very – ingenuous – if you can conceive me conversing with rural deans in the cathedral close. I do not go to cathedral towns but to centres of industry. My thoughts are absorbed in questions more important than ever enter the heads of deans – as *why* it is cheaper to *buy* steel bars from America than from Middlesbrough, and the probable effect – the exchange difficulties with Poland – and the appreciation of the rupee. My evenings in Bridge. The effect is to make me regard London with disdain, and divide mankind into supermen, termites and wireworms. I am sojourning among the termites. At any rate that coheres. I feel sufficiently specialised, at present, to inspect or hear any ideas with impunity.'

For some time Lytton hesitated to communicate with Eliot again. 'I do intend to spur myself up though,' he assured Mary Hutchinson (17 July 1919), 'as I don't want to drop him. Only I fear it will take him a long time to become a letter writer.' Early in August, he reopened the correspondence, and Eliot answered saying how propitious it was that he had written before he, Eliot, disappeared into central France, where no letters could reach him. 'I have not been away but in London, in my office or among my books or (several times) in bed,' he went on (6 August 1919), 'and have frequently imagined you sitting on the lawn at Pangbourne or in a garden, conducting your clinic of Queen Victoria with perfect concentration ... You have frightened me because I always expect you to be right, and because I know I shall never be able to retaliate upon your finely woven fabrics. I have lately read an article of yours on Voltaire which made me envious.' Ten days later he sent Lytton a postcard from the Dordogne, where, he was careful to point out, he had been walking the whole time and so had no address at all. Wandering through the Corrèze he was happy and sunburnt, surrounded by 'melons, cèpes, truffles, eggs, good wine and good cheese and cheerful people. It's a complete relief from London', where one bled slowly to death.

In the months and years that followed, Lytton made more overtures to a closer relationship, and although these were apparently welcomed by Eliot, some hindrance to its further development persisted.[53] Eliot during these years was under the paralysing strain of his unhappy first marriage, and Lytton sometimes found his company 'grim'. He held a muted admiration for his work, though feeling some of it to be lugubrious and, quite frankly, religious. Eliot remained fascinated by Bloomsbury's 'nonconformity within a culture to which nevertheless they firmly belonged'[54] and which he wished to join. But he later insisted on skipping the generation of 'Wells, Shaw, Strachey and Hemingway' which had surrendered to the emancipated views of the time.[55]

Bloomsbury had by this time tentatively taken up Eliot – the Hogarth Press in 1919 publishing his *Poems*, and four years later *The Waste Land* – but his dry authoritarian manner made him something of an enigma to them. 'When we first got to know Tom, we liked him very much,' remembered Leonard Woolf, 'but we were both a little afraid of him.' In the summer of 1922, various members of Bloomsbury set up the Eliot Fellowship Fund, a scheme designed to release Eliot from his work at the bank. A circular was distributed to all potential subscribers asking them to contribute at least five or ten pounds a year for a minimum term of five years in return for first editions of all Eliot's future volumes. But shortly after the circulars had been drafted Eliot demurred, and a postscript had to be written explaining that 'circumstances have arisen which make it necessary that Mr Eliot should be allowed to use his own discretion as to continuing or relinquishing his present work at the bank'. Nevertheless, the committee decided to go ahead as best it could, since it remained beyond dispute, even by Eliot himself, that 'any addition to his income would not only remove from him considerable anxiety which the expense

457

of illness has brought upon him, but would make it possible for him to give more time to writing than he can now do'.

Lytton was prepared to help financially. But, hedged about by Eliot's own sombre caveats, the Fellowship Fund struck him as being rather ludicrous, and he sent Leonard and Virginia a parody of the Bloomsbury circular (December 1922).

THE LYTTON STRACHEY DONATION

It has been known for some time to Mr Lytton Strachey's friends that his income is in excess of his expenditure, and that he has a large balance at the bank. It is impossible, if his royalties continue to accumulate at the present rate, that he should be in a position to spend them entirely upon himself, without serious injury to his reputation among his more impecunious acquaintances. For this reason it is proposed that he should set aside the sum of £20,000 (twenty thousand pounds) to be known as the 'Lytton Strachey Donation', the interest upon which shall be devoted to the support of such persons as the Committee shall think fit to select.

All those in favour of this scheme are requested to communicate with Lady Ottoline Morrell, Garsington, Oxford, adding the sum which they themselves would wish to draw from the Donation annually. No sum less than £20 (twenty pounds) a year should be asked for, though demands for capital sums of £5000 (five thousand pounds) and upwards will be entertained.

POSTSCRIPT

Since the scheme in the accompanying circular was proposed it has come to the knowledge of the Committee that circumstances have arisen which make it impossible that Mr Lytton Strachey should be prevented from using his own discretion as to the disposal of his ill-gotten gains. It is however certain that many persons would benefit even from such small sums as 5/- (five shillings) or 2/6 (two-and-sixpence), supposing that Mr Strachey were willing to disburse them. Under these circumstances the Committee propose to continue the scheme in its present form, without, however, imposing upon Mr Strachey any conditions as to how his money should be spent.

It was through Eliot that the Hogarth Press was offered the uncompleted manuscript of James Joyce's *Ulysses*. Leonard and Virginia decided to try and publish it in about 1918, but since no English printer was willing to risk prosecution, they were eventually forced to abandon the enterprise. Leonard refers to the novel as 'a remarkable piece of dynamite', and Lytton supported its uncensored publication, but Virginia was on her guard. When Lytton signified that he was willing to support the Eliot Fellowship Fund, she replied (24 August 1922):

'One hundred pounds did you say? You shall have a receipt. Cheque payable to Richard Aldington or O. Morrell as you prefer. My own contribution, five and sixpence, is given on condition he puts publicly to their proper use the first 200 pages of Ulysses. Never did I read such tosh. As for the first 2 chapters we will let them pass, but the 3rd 4th 5th 6th – merely the scratching of pimples on the body of the bootboy at Claridges. Of course genius may blaze out on page 652 but I have my doubts. And this is what Eliot worships, and there's Lytton Strachey paying £100 p.a. to Eliot's upkeep.'[56]

Was this Virginia's jealousy again, or did she envy a literary power whose coarseness, Quentin Bell suggests, 'made her feel suddenly desperately lady-like'? A few months later she was again stirring up support for Eliot – this time over his appointment as literary editor of the *Nation and Athenaeum*. The chief strategist in putting over this plan was Maynard, who had met with great opposition from his fellow directors, none of whom had heard of Eliot. The only way he saw of disarming this opposition was to convince the directors that Eliot was well thought of by contemporary writers – like Lytton Strachey – who would contribute to their paper should Eliot be appointed. It was Virginia who, on 23 February 1923, wrote asking Lytton once more for his assistance. 'I have to approach you on a delicate matter – to wit, poor Tom,' she explained.

'. . . As you are aware the Eliot fund business has proved a fiasco; and this certainly seems to be the only possible solution of the problem. In fact, the poor man is becoming (in his highly American way, which is tedious and longwinded to a degree) desperate. I think he will be forced to leave the Bank anyhow. So if you would write me a line giving some sort of promise that you would write, or at least would be more inclined to write for him than another we should all be very grateful.'

Lytton pledged his support directly to Maynard, who described the negotiated arrangement, with Eliot as assistant literary editor as 'poise and counterpoise', adding in a private note a fortnight later (9 March 1923): 'Pretty complete victory. Ramsay Muir[57] and Guedalla have committed suicide and Mrs Royde Smith[58] has been assassinated.' From the point of view of Eliot's appointment, this victory was Pyrrhic, since Eliot 'spun out the situation into endless complexities' and the paper could not wait. Shortly afterwards, he was made editor of the newly founded *Criterion*, a paper which, standing for classicism in literature and religion, was alien to Lytton, Maynard, Virginia and Leonard who, filling the vacuum left by Eliot, found himself Lytton's part-time employer as literary editor of the *Nation and Athenaeum*.

6

THE QUESTION OF THINGS HAPPENING

Queen Victoria 'is a fine subject', Lytton wrote to Vanessa (1 March 1919), 'but she widens out alarmingly'. Using the British Museum Reading Room and the London Library, he sometimes stayed so long in town that it was rumoured he had taken special lodgings near the Albert Memorial to keep in the right mood for his work.[59] 'London continues to be very agreeable,' he admitted to Ottoline (30 May 1919), 'but I doubt whether I shall stay there much longer. A little work is really becoming necessary, and it's quite impossible to do a stroke in that charivari – I envy Harriet Martineau, whose autobiography I've been reading (rather an interesting book). She worked six hours a day writing political economy, and then every evening explored the beau monde. But in those days people were made of steel and india-rubber.'

'Lytton every time you come back I love you more,' Carrington wrote that summer (18 June 1919). She never thought him querulous or felt that he laid too many ties on her. Nor did the sense of living so much for his health, of having to assemble so many comforts round him, depress her. Visiting Tidmarsh later that year, Virginia noticed his books 'primly ranged & carefully tended as an old maids china', but as they talked together, 'so quick, so agile in our jumps and circumventions',[60] these surroundings receded and it was clear to her that Lytton 'has in the centre of him a great passion for the mind'. This too was what Carrington reverenced. 'All his adventures and experiences are mental, and only enjoyed by himself,' Carrington had noted in her diary (4 February 1919). 'Outwardly it's like the life of one of the hens. Meals dividing up the day, books read in the morning, siesta, walk to Pangbourne, more books. A French lesson with me, perhaps dinner. Reading aloud. Bed and hot water bottles, and every day the same apparently. But inside, what a variety, and what fantastic doings.'

Adventures and experiences of another sort arrived with Ralph

Partridge who would bicycle over after breakfast and pose for her. 'Drawing the bird Partridge in my studio was not without its bass accompaniament this afternoon,' she confided to Lytton (18 June 1919). As the mill-wheel creaked round and the water came cascading at intervals into the tank from the pump below, they made love together. 'I suppose it means a large bed in the cottage at Marsland if one is to put up with him for a fortnight,' speculated Carrington, who was planning a summer holiday with him and her brother Noel at Welcombe, next to the Box farm where she and Lytton had stayed with Alix and James two summers ago.

It was a good holiday. They put up at a remote cottage called West Mill which was wonderful for painting. 'The walls are white and one can sit with lovely still lives on the tables coloured jugs with flowers, bread, bottles of ink and teacups long after the meal is finished – and letters are written,' she told Mark Gertler (July 1919). 'Outside the window one looks up a long valley with high hills either side covered with trees . . . The other way the cottage faces roaring sea, only a few minutes walk with large crags, and cliffs.'

Mrs Box, aged seventy-two, was full of vigour, driving the cows to and from the marshes. 'She held up both her arms and waved them with a stick in one hand. And then ran towards me!' She sized up Ralph as a 'most lovely young man', and said that he and Carrington made 'a nice pair'. Most days they swam in the sea then lay on the rocks in the sun; and Carrington painted in high winds and wrote long letters to Lytton. She was anxious that her love-making with Ralph should not affect their relationship. 'The major remains exactly the same,' she assured Lytton (14 July 1919). '. . . His extreme kindness however makes him fairly easy to get on with.' If only he were silent, she added in Bloomsbury housestyle, or invisible during the day, life would be perfect since 'there's no denying that the Major with all his dullness is in the Shakespearean use of the word "A most excellent bed fellow"' (12 July 1919).

Knowing that Lytton's approval was essential to the future of their affair, and suspecting Carrington of being too defensive about him, Ralph sometimes worried that Lytton did not like him. But 'I like him more than anyone else – he seemed so modest,' Lytton reaffirmed (19 June 1919); '. . . I wish he had rather more forehead.' And of course there were other wishes and fancies and queries. 'I suppose he [Ralph] would be shocked if I suggested that you should give him a kiss from me?' Lytton asked Carrington (11 July 1919). 'The world is rather tiresome, I must say – everything at sixes and sevens – ladies in love with buggers, and buggers in love with womanisers, and the price of coal going up too. Where will it all end?'

*

Over the summer Lytton pressed on with *Queen Victoria*. 'Now I am fairly in it, or should I say Her, immersed, pegging away daily, and quite, so far enjoying myself,' he told Mary Hutchinson (17 July 1919). During the fine warm evenings he would sit out among the rambler roses in the mill-garden and, when not thinking of Ralph and Carrington in Cornwall, dream wistfully of Shaftesbury Avenue, Soho Square, the little passage into the Charing Cross Road, and the Tottenham Court Road, along to the tall trees of Gordon Square – and so on endlessly. Every shop window, every paving stone, he could see, especially when the light began to thicken, the street-lamps and illuminations to come on, though still weaker than the fading daylight, and all sorts of lovely creatures would flit from shadow to shadow across the roads. How he had hated London in the past: how inviting it seemed now in his quiet garden! 'I can hardly bear to think of it, I love it so much – to distraction.'

He soon finished the first two chapters of *Queen Victoria* – 'Antecedents' and 'Childhood'. 'I have been absorbed by Victoria for the last month,' he informed his mother (19 August 1919), 'and have now written the opening part – as far as her accession. So far the variety of curious characters and circumstances keeps me going – the difficulty will be much greater, I expect, after the death of Prince Consort.'

The Stracheys were beginning to organize their move later in the year to a new home, 51 Gordon Square, where Lytton's sister Marjorie started a small school which several Bloomsbury children attended. During the 1920s, Gordon Square was largely taken over by the Bloomsbury Group and their friends. Duncan Grant and Vanessa Bell made good use of No. 37 for a time; James and Alix Strachey lived on the top floor of No. 41, where Lytton, Ralph Partridge and Carrington also had occasional rooms;[61] into the flat below them Lydia Lopokova had moved during 1922, before her marriage to Maynard Keynes, when she transferred to No. 46; the ground-floor flat was occupied during one ballet season by Ernest Ansermet. No. 42 was in 1925 the home of Oliver Strachey and his daughter Julia. Near by, in Taviton Street, and subsequently Brunswick Square, lived Frances Marshall, Bunny Garnett's sister-in-law, later to move into 41 Gordon Square. No. 46, which had been taken by the Stephen family in 1904, was now the property of Maynard, though Clive and Vanessa and Duncan retained some accommodation there. Adrian Stephen and his wife Karin, both psychoanalysts, inhabited No. 50, as did, for a long time, Arthur Waley. And now Lady Strachey and her daughters were moving into No. 51. 'Very soon I foresee that the whole square will become a sort of college,' Lytton wrote to Virginia (28 September 1919). 'And the rencontres in the garden I shudder to think of.

'The business of packing, deciding what is to be sold, what sent to Tidmarsh, what given to the deserving poor etc. has been fearful, and is still proceeding, the brunt of it of course falling on the unfortunate Pippa. I am fit for very little more than wringing my hands. In the intervals I go to the British Museum, and try to dig up scandals about Queen Victoria. Altogether a distracting life, and the comble was reached in the small hours of Friday morning, when the policeman's wife who acts as caretaker gave birth to a baby just outside my bedroom door.'

With the help of Arthur Waley, then working in the Department of Prints and Drawings at the British Museum, and of H.A.L. Fisher, a trustee of the Museum, he had been given leave to look through the ninety-one small quarto volumes of Charles Greville's diaries, the printed version of which had omitted some observations upon Greville's private affairs, and 'reflections upon the character and conduct of Queen Victoria'. On 9 October 1919, he wrote to Fisher: 'I have made a certain number of extracts from parts of the Memoirs that have not been published – dealing chiefly with Victoria's attitude towards the Tories in the first years of her reign . . .

'I should be very glad to be able to refer to these in my book (I should not want to make long verbatim quotations) – and I think you will agree with me that there is really no reason at all why I shouldn't. Greville was very cross with the Queen for taking sides in politics – snubbing Wellington etc. – and it was natural that [Henry] Reeve should refrain from publishing these passages while H.M. was alive. But now the conditions are different – and the attitude of Queen Victoria in 1840 (which, incidentally, she changed a few years later) is merely a matter of historical interest and Court politics of 80 years ago.'

Once this had been accomplished, Lytton went back that autumn to Tidmarsh where he stayed 'penned down' for the next six months. In the intervals between working at the biography, he was arranging his library, which, having been brought down from Belsize Park Gardens, now covered the walls and floors of practically every room at Tidmarsh – while he sat in the midst of this confusion, happily cataloguing the titles in various coloured inks on a series of ruled cards. 'I see now the joys of Bureaucracy – the endless fascination of arrangement, dockets, specifications, lists . . . I completely understand the Webbs.' In this fashion the days succeeded one another interrupted by a succession of friends and 'shareholders', including some of Lytton's sisters, his brother Oliver with his girlfriend, a mute and sealed Saxon, the terrifying Ottoline, Clive and Mary who treated Carrington as a domestic, and E.M. Forster with his 'curious triangular face, and a mind, somehow, exactly fitting'.

Lytton regularly turned from his work to read new books.[62] Most exciting of all this winter were two books by his friends. The first was Virginia's new novel, *Night and Day*, which, he told Ottoline (15 November 1919), was a work not to read, but to re-read – 'there seemed so much in it that one could only just effleurer as one went along, and longed to return to. She [Virginia] was here last week, and appeared to be very well and cheerful, and of course more amusing than ever.' And to Pippa he wrote (13 November 1919): 'The visualization of faces does make it difficult to judge of. But I think Mrs Hilbery is a chef d'oeuvre.'[63]

The other highlight of these winter months was Maynard's *The Economic Consequences of the Peace*.* Maynard had written it during the months of August and September down at Charleston, and had read from it while Lytton was staying there. On his return to Tidmarsh a few weeks later, Lytton wrote to Maynard (4 October 1919): 'I seem to gather from the scant remarks in the newspapers, that your friend the President [Woodrow Wilson] has gone mad. Is it possible that it should be gradually borne in upon him what an appalling failure he was,† and that when at last he fully realized it his mind collapsed? Very dramatic, if so. But won't it make some of your remarks almost too cruel? – Especially if he should go and die.'

Although Maynard felt strongly that his sketch of Woodrow Wilson formed an essential part of his argument, and that, if the peace settlement was to be properly understood and the situation rectified, Wilson's character must be elucidated, he nevertheless did moderate some of his pages before publication in December. 'Your book arrived yesterday, and I swallowed it at a gulp,' Lytton wrote to him (16 December 1919).

'I think it is most successful. In the first place, extremely impressive; there is an air of authority about it which I think nobody could ignore. I was rather afraid at Charleston that it might appear too extreme, but I don't think this is at all the case. The slight softenings in the Clemenceau and Wilson bits seem to me distinct improvements, adding to the effect, rather

---

* This book made Keynes internationally famous. It was smothered, to use Maynard's own words to Lytton (23 December 1919), 'in a deluge of approval . . . letters from Cabinet Ministers by every post saying that they agree with every word of it, etc, etc. . . . Well, I suppose this is their best and safest line.' In fact this book 'incurred great odium in official circles', Roy Harrod wrote, and lost him influence with the Treasury for ten years. 'He attacks anything sound or established or generally accepted,' objected an American Treasury official, '. . . he is utterly irresponsible. He doesn't care how much harm he does.'

† At the Paris Peace Conference; Keynes attended as principal representative of the Treasury.

than otherwise. Then the mass of information is delightful. I had never, for instance, had any definite idea as to what the Provisions of the Peace Treaty really were – it was impossible to gather from the newspapers, and the import of the Treaty itself would have been clearly incomprehensible – so that your exposé, apart from the argument, was most welcome; and of course this is only one of a great number of extraordinarily interesting sets of facts. As to the argument it is certainly most crushing, most terrible. I don't see how anyone can stand up against it . . . One thing I doubted . . . whether, on your own showing, even your proposed terms were not far too harsh. Is it conceivable that the Germany which you describe should be able to or in fact would pay 50 million a year for 30 years?'

Work on his own book was now advancing steadily. Every morning, he would work for about three hours usually putting down some three hundred words in ink, with hardly a correction. He composed in his head, not sentences but entire paragraphs before committing them to paper. 'Queen Victoria, poor lady, totters on step by step,' he wrote on 9 December. 'As she's still in her youth, what will she be like in age at this rate? I can only hope that she may proceed in inverse fashion – growing speedier and speedier as she gets older, and finally fairly bundling into the grave.'

By the following spring he had completed the chapters on 'Lord Melbourne' and 'Marriage', and possibly the fifth chapter also, 'Lord Palmerston'. At any rate, he felt that before setting to work on the second half, he would fortify himself with a few weeks' holiday abroad.

7

SOUTH FROM PANGBOURNE

'I am curiously happy just now,' Lytton wrote to Maynard on 16 December. Not only was his writing going ahead well, but the conditions of his life appeared better than ever before. He was seeing a lot of Ralph. Sometimes he would brave the winter winds to go over and watch him row at Oxford; and often Ralph came across to Tidmarsh for the weekend when they would read Elizabethan plays and poetry together. 'Lytton gets on so much better with him now,' Carrington confided to her brother Noel, who was leaving to work for the Oxford University Press in India (12 December 1919). 'In fact they are great friends, and have long discussions on Einstein's theory whilst I darn the socks.'

Carrington too was fonder of Ralph. 'He has become so much more charming and has given up his slightly moral character which used to tire me,' she wrote (15 December 1919). 'So we never quarrel now, and have become a perfect pair of pigeons in our affections. I certainly will never love him but I am extemely fond of him . . .' At night he slept in her bed, and by day she put him to work in her studio ('I am doing a large oil painting of him every day') and in the garden where 'I import dung', he wrote to Noel, '. . . I sift cinders, clip hedges, burn, overturn and level to the ground all that comes in my way'.

Lytton had by now fallen deeply in love with Ralph. Several times a week he would write to him, and these letters reveal the teasing manner in which he spun it out. On 11 January 1920, he wrote:

'I wished you had been here at dinner yesterday to enjoy the jugged hare with some wonderful jelly concocted by Carrington out of the remains of the Burgundy – delicious! – When are you coming back? . . . I see that if I had any sense I should have had you nailed up by the ear in the Tidmarsh pillory, so that you couldn't have escaped until everyone was quite tired of you. I warn you this is what you must expect when you return – it won't hurt *very* much, and will be an interesting experience. Imagine me sitting up in bed, in my muffetees. The wind howls, the rain pours, and the horror of Sunday covers the earth.'

Three weeks later he is writing to him again (3 February 1920): 'If you don't appear either tomorrow or Thursday, I shan't see you for a hundred years, it seems to me. My beard will be snowy white, and your ears will have grown so intolerably perky for want of pulling that they'll have to be clipped by the executioner.

'. . . I am feeling very cheerful and well. My dearest creature, don't bother too much about my health. The exhaustion that shatters is the kind that's caused by miserable baffled desires – in a black period of my life I was nearly killed by it; but now, dear, I am buoyed up and carried along by so much happiness! On this subject two generalisations have occurred to me. Generalisation no. 1. – The secret of happiness is to want neither too much nor too little.

Generalisation no. 2. – No one can master this secret, under the age of 39.'

Sometimes Lytton felt tempted to ask too much from 'my sweet Ralph', and then, especially when Carrington was not with them, was overcome by anxiety on Ralph's behalf – 'don't suspect darknesses, please'. When

Carrington and Ralph spent a few days together in Oxford, leaving him at Tidmarsh, the solitude closed in round him and he wrote to Ralph (February 1920). 'My dear one, I am feeling rather dejected and lonely, and feel that I must press your hand before I go to my solitary couch. Carrington's too . . . It seems so good when we're all three together that I grudge every minute that keeps us apart.'

Carrington was delighted that her two men should have taken so well to each other. It was 'an immense improvement', she wrote (2 January 1920). 'As Lytton delights in teaching everyone literature. Its made R happier, & less diffident, and I can have him here as often as I like.' She felt able to play a still more intimate part in Lytton's emotional life. If she could attract friends whom he liked, then her place with him was secure. And Lytton did not resent Ralph's passion for Carrington – indeed their happiness seemed only to swell his own. For the time being all of them adhered to the first of Lytton's generalizations – not to ask for too much or too little – so that each one gained added enjoyment from the pleasure of the other two. There were no real moments of awkwardness between them – indeed they made fun of such possibilities. 'I send my fond love,' Lytton ended one of his letters to Ralph (February 1920), 'and all the kisses and etceteras that I didn't dare to send you by Carrington for fear of their being intercepted en route.'

The situation, however, could not stay so finely poised for ever. Ralph had been completely won over by Lytton's gentleness, his thoughtfulness, his alert and clever mind. He was charmed by him: but he was in love with Carrington. Towards the end of this winter, he started to put pressure on her to marry him. She strongly resisted, while Lytton, who wished everything to remain exactly as it was, looked on anxiously, wondering how things would turn out, but not attempting to influence them.

Thus the first shadow had been thrown across their relationship; but almost at once it dissolved when, that March, the three of them took off for six weeks' holiday in Spain. They were to stop at all the places that Carrington and Ralph had visited the previous year – Carrington insisted upon this; for only then could she share with Lytton her past experiences there. In addition to this itinerary, they planned to spend a few days with Ralph's friend, Gerald Brenan, who the previous autumn had sailed from England with a hundred pounds in his pocket to set up house at the primitive Berber village of Yegen, in Andalusia. This was to be the highlight of their journey.

Ralph, who acted as courier, had booked three berths on a boat that left Liverpool on 18 March. They stopped off for a day at Corunna, and finally disembarked at Lisbon. From here they continued their journey through the night by train across the Spanish border and to Seville, Lytton travelling first class, the other two, hot and smelly on wooden seats among the peasants with their 'terrified fowls', third class. 'At the best of times travelling in this country is hard,' Lytton wrote to Mary Hutchinson (11 April 1920), 'all the train journeys last for twelve hours at a minimum, and the slowness of one's advances is heart-breaking. We had a fearful night coming out of Portugal – the 1st class carriage blocked with sucking babies and drunken commercial travellers – poor Ralph reduced to sleeping on the portmanteau in the corridor, etc. etc. But still, one does progress, and the sights one sees are worth the horrors.'

These horrors multiplied as they pressed on into the empty yellow interior of Spain. By the time they reached Seville, Lytton was exhausted, but Ralph's strict schedule, omitting to take account of his companion's lack of soldierly stamina, did not allow for much civilian recruitment. Soon he was hurrying them on to Cordoba – 'a most wonderful town', Lytton informed Pippa (1 April 1920). Everything was more spectacular than he had expected. But Cordoba he loved best of all, describing it in a letter to Mary Hutchinson as

'oriental – a network of narrow narrow streets, and a very big and beautiful mosque, in the middle of which the astonishing Christians have stuck a huge rococo church – the effect is dizzying. One evening we went in after sunset, and found a mass in progress. A full orchestra was at work in the baroque building, a tenor was singing an aria by Mozart, and all round, dimly lighted by a lamp here and there, were the pillars and arches of the antique mosque, stretching away in every direction into far distant darkness. It was incredibly theatrical and romantic, and I felt like Uncle John, very very nearly a Roman Catholic.'

Ralph's time-table permitted them three full days in Cordoba. Then they were up and off again, and after more agonizing hours of Spanish travelling, came to Granada, which was 'astounding', Lytton declared, '– very high up, with immense snow mountains directly over it, and the Alhambra – huge dark red walls and towers – dominating the town. Before long, one observes picture-postcard elements in this, and the detail of the Alhambra is sheer Earl's Court, but the general grandeur of situation and outline remain.'

They arrived in Granada on 2 April with Lytton feeling 'very chirpy'. But his chirpiness did not last long. As the party had fought their way onwards and upwards over the bone-coloured rocks and hills and across the bare mountains, so their difficulties steadily mounted. Every day there was some fresh crisis or disaster – and the victim of every crisis and disaster was Lytton, who became more alarmed the further they left civilization behind. Already it seemed to him that he had been away from England several years. 'I am breaking S[trachey] of his milksops,' Ralph had confidently predicted to Noel Carrington; but at Granada Lytton suffered a relapse. The ruthless Spanish cuisine, with its emphasis on potato omelettes, dried cod, and unrefined olive oil, played havoc with his digestive system; he caught Spanish influenza; he nearly trod on a Spanish snake; he mislaid his pyjamas; he injured his knee and announced that he was liable to faint at any moment, though requiring no assistance to recover. 'I began the study of the Spanish language last Thursday,' he had written to Ralph on 11 January, '– but I haven't quite completed it yet – there's still time for you to put on the finishing touches ... Te envio un baccio.' Such eloquence was confined to paper. And to England. In Spain nothing would induce him to order even a glass of water and he relied on Ralph who, he admiringly wrote to his mother, 'can grapple with the Spanish language in a most talented way'. Whenever he lost sight of his two companions he was seized with dumb panic.

Their nerves frayed by these setbacks, Carrington and Ralph had now begun to quarrel. Outwardly these were lovers' quarrels, but the underlying bone of contention was Lytton.

At Granada their fortunes took a steep plunge. It was here that they had arranged to join Gerald Brenan, who planned to escort them across Los Alpujarras – a wild tract of country between the Sierra Nevada and the hills which lie to the north of the Mediterranean – up to his small mountain cottage. Delayed by chronic mismanagement of his own affairs Brenan failed to arrive, and so there was nothing for them to do but wait uncertainly in the Hôtel de Paris. They went to the mosque, to a bull-fight, and a concert. 'Monday we spent trying to find Brenan,' Carrington wrote to her brother Noel. '. . . Lytton refuses to go until he has R.P.'s good word for his safety. which R.P. can't give until he sees Brenan.'

Lytton himself uttered no complaints over Brenan's absence. The trek up vertical zigzagging tracks and across the most primitive region of Spain struck him as the pinnacle of folly. His spirit of adventure, so keen at the outset of their voyage, had been worn away by mishaps and he felt wary of courting more calamities. He saw Brenan as 'an amiable lunatic', he told Mary Hutchinson, '. . . who has come to live here in pursuit of some Dostoievsky will o' the wisp or other, and whom Partridge had engaged himself to come and visit with solemn vows'. Despite the hideous prospect of this ascent, he neither wanted to spoil it for the others nor to be left at Granada alone (or even with Carrington, in whose capabilities he had little confidence). So he determined to accompany them should Brenan turn up.

Ralph had meanwhile sent an urgent telegram to his friend reminding him of their arrival in Granada and adding that, unless he contacted them, they would be leaving in two days. This message brought Brenan, weak with influenza, scrambling down the mountains just in time to miss them – by half an hour – at their hotel, and barely in time to sprint up with them in the departing bus. The four of them then boarded another crowded motor-bus and for several frantic hours roared along the unmetalled roads in a haze of exhaust fumes and with a series of explosions until they reached Lanjaron, 'a small health resort in the hills'. Here they discussed the problem of transporting Lytton up to Yegen. He sat in a cane armchair drinking cognac, silent and bearded, and betraying no enthusiasm for the various ways and means that were being debated. Finally, it was decided to engage a carriage for the following morning to carry them all to a village called Orgiva, where they would procure mules to transport them along the last few miles of their trek. Brenan, however, had forgotten about the spring floods. All went well until they reached the Rio Grande, which was virtually impassable. On arriving at the ford, the mules went in almost up to their girths amid the racing water, and Lytton drew back in alarm. The party then wearily retreated to the hotel, deciding to make a fresh start by another route early the following morning.

Everyone's nerves were more than ever on edge, and the evening passed in general low spirits and an air of recrimination – Lytton gloomily resolute, Brenan much ruffled, Carrington and Ralph full of reciprocal accusations. 'The conveyance of the great writer to my mountain village began to assume more and more the appearance of a difficult military operation,' Brenan afterwards recorded. 'Carrington, caught between two fires, became clumsily appeasing and only Lytton said nothing. As for myself, I never doubted my powers to go anywhere or do anything of a physical sort that I wished to, but under my friends' bombardment I felt my unfitness for assuming responsibility for other people.'[64]

At nine o'clock next morning they tried again. The day was very hot, and thirty miles of precipitous country lay before them. No sooner had they dismounted from the carriage and descended into the river valley, than Lytton, who was suffering now from piles, discovered that he could not ride on mule-back. Every half-mile or so they would arrive at a river, he would perilously mount his animal, be agonizingly conveyed across, and then climb off again – all the while balancing an open sunshade high above his head. This procedure repeated itself with monotonous frequency throughout the day, so delaying progress that at last they agreed to break their journey and put up for the night at the small village of Cádiar. But one look at the best bed available at the *posada* and they changed their minds, dragging themselves off again along the same river which they continued, as in a nightmare, to cross and recross with their mules, on and on by narrow tracks, up and up, higher and higher, until the day began to fade and stars appeared in the sky.

The last part of their march, up a mountainside of some two thousand five hundred feet, took place in twilight. This dramatic climb, along a steep path bordered by precipices, was made by Lytton clinging side-saddle. On reaching the top, Carrington and Brenan hurried ahead over the last six miles to give warning of the great man's arrival and see to it that a meal was prepared. Ralph and Lytton reached the steep cobbled paths of Yegen half an hour later – at about ten o'clock that night – having travelled a good twelve hours with only one halt in the middle of the day. 'My God. I was never so glad to reach any place in my life as I was Gerald's cottage that night,' Carrington wrote to Noel. And Lytton, in a letter to Mary Hutchinson, exclaimed: 'oh it was a scene! – the sun scorching, the wind whistling, the rain drenching, at last the night coming on – Lady Hester wasn't in it: the emotional crises, too, of the strangest sort – until we arrived in pitch darkness and almost dead at our singular destination . . . Well, I hardly guessed that I should ever live to be led to such a spot by the beaux yeux of a Major!'

But once there, Lytton began to feel that the expedition had almost, if not quite, been worthwhile. The desert hills all round were covered with olives, oranges, figs and vines, chestnuts and bright green poplars. To the north stood the snow-topped Sierra Nevada, far away to the south they could see the blue glimmer of the sea over which the sun rose each morning, and everywhere lay vast stretches of hill and rock and chasm. 'Look at a map of Spain, and find Granada,' he instructed Mary Hutchinson (11 April 1920). 'Thence draw a line of 40 miles in a southwesterly direction, across the Sierra Nevada, and you will arrive – here. Yegen is a village among the mountains, high up with a view of the Mediterranean in the distance, and all round the most extraordinary Greco-esque formations of rocks and hills. Never have I seen a country on so vast a scale – wild, violent, spectacular – enormous mountains, desperate chasms – colours everywhere of deep orange and brilliant green – a wonderful place, but easier to get to with a finger on a map than in reality!'

Lytton passed most of his days at Yegen recovering from the journey and preparing himself for the trials of his return. Only once did he go out among the traffic of donkeys and mules with their loads of grapes and hay.

Otherwise he kept to the house which, with its low ceilings of plaster and beams, was luxurious by local standards – it even had a hole in a plank down into the chicken run to serve as a lavatory. 'I am treated with the utmost consideration, of course,' he wrote, 'and I am enjoying myself greatly, but I shan't be sorry when this section of our trip is over, and we return to comparative civilization.' Only during the last day, cheered presumably by the prospect of leaving and triumphing over the flies and fleas, did he become almost lively. Though Ralph seemed angry, Carrington and Brenan were in high spirits, bathing and going off for picnics. Despite the general strain of their visit and her unflagging concern for Lytton's health, it was for Carrington a peculiarly happy week. She had met Brenan a few times in England and already thought of him as a romantic adventurer. They immediately struck up a friendship, and looked as naturally 'charming and innocent and amiable' together as a pair of children. He was twenty-six that April – a year younger than Carrington – six feet tall, athletic, full of nervous energy yet strangely detached. Carrington enchanted him. She found him mysteriously attractive. 'He is such a charming person,' she wrote to Noel, 'very like Teddy in his good humour and charm. But oh so vague about distances, and any idea about time! We spent some of the best days there with him that I've ever spent in Spain.'

Soon they were off, 'beginning with a mule journey,' Lytton explained to his mother, 'then going in a delightful diligence by a horse and a mule, then in a motor-bus over another incredibly horrible road to Almeria, which is on the coast, and where civilization begins again.' From here they travelled on by train – Lytton lying on the floor of the compartment among the orange peel – to Toledo, where, in hot sunshine, Holy Week was being celebrated. Osbert Sitwell, recently risen from his sick-bed, was also visiting Toledo with his brother Sacheverell, and caught sight of Lytton and Carrington on the opposite side of a narrow street leading up to the Plaza from the Cathedral. Between them, like a slow-moving stream, passed the procession of worshippers, and it was not until half of it had filed by that the Sitwells saw 'the lean, elongated form of Lytton Strachey, hieratic, a pagod as plainly belonging as did the effigies to a creation of its own. Well muffled, as usual, against the wind, and accompanied by his faithful friend and companion Carrington ... who, with fair hair and plump, pale face, added a more practical, but still indubitably English-esthetic note to the scene, he was regarding the various giants and giantesses with a mute and somewhat phlegmatic air of appreciation.'

Lytton did not at first notice the Sitwells, partly concealed by the jostling throng of excited people moving between them, and Osbert was able to study him carefully.

'His head was crowned with a wide-brimmed brown hat . . . Humour and wit were very strongly marked in the quizzical expression of his face, and also, I think, a kind of genuine diffidence as well as a certain despair and, always, a new surprise at man's follies . . . the sense of a cultured, scholarly man that permeated his entire outward aspect, all these characteristics and qualities were, though highly individual, essentially English . . . as he stood there, thinly towering, impressive undoubtedly, but with an undeniable element of the grotesque both in his physique and in his presentation of himself, it was at him one looked, and not at anybody else.'[65]

While Osbert was forming these impressions, Lytton suddenly caught sight of him and Sacheverell, and signalled to them with a look of amused recognition. At that moment, the two lines of spectators on either side of the road broke behind the procession, the Sitwells were whirled away in one direction and Lytton and Carrington swept out of sight in the other.

The next day Lytton, Carrington and Ralph moved on to Madrid, 'which I think has little to recommend it besides the Prado', Lytton informed his mother, 'but that is a large exception'. They put up at the Hotel Terminus and nearly every day they would visit the Prado. 'Almost too much to see: Goya, El Greco, and Velasquez. One gets torn literally inside . . . These pictures make me want to give up everything and become an artist entirely,' Carrington wrote to Gerald (18 April 1920).

On 21 April, they left for Paris where they stayed at the Hôtel d'Orléans, in the rue Jacob. An hour after arriving there, they ran into Nick and Barbara Bagenal, and all five of them went off 'very cheerily' to Versailles, where Nick and Barbara were taking a course in French literature. 'Lytton was of course in his element. And gave us a superb History of the French Kings and their intrigues,' Carrington wrote to Noel. The tribulations of the past weeks were forgotten as he took them to lunch at Foyot's, to a concert of classical quartets, and to see the pictures at the Louvre.

On the Saturday afternoon, Ralph raced back to England to see his mother who was ill. That evening Lytton wrote to him: 'My Angel, It was so miserable parting from you that I hardly knew what to do. After being with you for so long and so very very happily, it was dreadful to know that you had gone. But dearest we shall soon meet again – very soon after you get this – if not before! Paris is delightful – such a warm evening, and everything even more attractive under the night sky than the day one; but we miss you terribly – the little café where we dined again tonight seemed to have lost half its charm without the courier to order dinner and enjoy the wine with and to speculate over the whores. My dear one, I have enjoyed it all immensely, and how can I ever thank you enough for what you have done for me during these five weeks? It is indeed good to think of how many wonderful memories we have now between us – from the porpoises in the Bay of Biscay to the Fra Angelico in the Louvre!'

The following Tuesday Lytton and Carrington caught the Dieppe train and were met that same evening at the station by Ralph. 'He is very unhappy which makes me despair also,' Carrington afterwards wrote to Gerald (5 May 1920). '. . . Yet I know, even if I did not think of myself, to marry him would not make it any better . . . I almost feel like flying with my paint boxes and leaving all these complications and simply changing my life and settling at Yegen.' 'You have seen Yegen,' Gerald replied, 'and will come back again. That's the main thing.'

As for Lytton, such were the miraculous healing powers of love that taking Ralph and Carrington out to dinner that evening, he raised his glass to the memory of 'the most glorious of holidays'.

8

THE END OF *QUEEN VICTORIA*

On their arrival back in England, the three of them went their separate ways – Ralph to row and complete his studies at Christ Church, Carrington into a London hospital for a minor operation on her nose, and Lytton to the Mill House, where he was soon 'plunged in Queen Victoria'.

The composition of his biography dominated the next eight months. But occasionally he would escape to London, staying in his sister Pernel's room on the second floor of 51 Gordon Square while she was at Newnham; or to Garsington where 'there was almost enough to eat' and Oxford where he watched Ralph rowing in the eights ('a horrid ceremony – crowds of dreadful women – mothers and sisters – veritable harpies – gloating over the young men's tortures'); or, as Maynard's guest, to Cambridge where the difference between war and peace seemed almost a difference between death and life. Once war had ceased, Cambridge had gone through a transformation. The sap began to flow again, and the exuberance of youth burst out. It was extraordinary to see college courts with caps and gowns in them, and the boats tearing after one another on academic streams.

'Life is more agreeable here than ever,' Maynard had assured him – though lamenting that 'my bed is depressingly disengaged all this month' – and he invited him over to King's where he would meet a new generation of Apostles and the recently ennobled Lord Chalmers, an ex-Treasury official who had chaired the Inland Revenue Board and was shortly to be appointed Master of Peterhouse. Lytton was soon writing an account of his visit to amuse the convalescent Carrington.

'Lord Chalmers is a pussycat of an old buffer with white hair and great urbanity – a plum on a wall, very far gone – squashy, decidedly. He makes long elaborate speeches, likes dragging in the eminent dead, and when he does so usually turns to me with a slight bow and says – "a friend of Mr Strachey's" – how Pozzo can take such obvious absurdity at all seriously quite beats me. We had a most pompous dinner yesterday in Hall, with the "Combination Room" afterwards – the wine-bibbing dons assembled round a long mahogany table, and drinking port, slowly, glass after glass (not very good port, I thought). Then I went to Trinity, and talked for some hours with [F.L.] Lucas, who appeared to me decidedly fascinating – though exactly why I'm blessed if I know. The young, otherwise, seem to be rather in retirement, though Maynard promises me a luncheon with [Scanes] Spicer and Sebastian [W.J.H.] Sprott (he tells me a real person) ... Cambridge is certainly a cosy, sympathetic spot after the grim grandeurs of Oxford – quite middle-class, which is always such a relief – at any rate for a day or two.'

In early June, after visits from James Strachey's two 'wives', Noel and Alix, Carrington had left the hospital and returned to the Mill House, racked by headaches, and feeling very sorry for herself. Lytton also hastened back to take care of her – 'so far I have induced her to keep in her bed,' he told Ralph. 'With rest and feeding-up (if these can only be administered!) I think she ought to be all right again before long.' In less than a fortnight she was, with her usual energy, looking after Lytton.

These were uneventful and industrious months. Ralph, in his last term at Oxford and heavily occupied with his rowing and his reading (he had switched from law to literature), was scarcely to be seen, and there was nothing for it but to work. 'It seems melancholy here without you,' Lytton confessed to him (9 June 1920). 'Truth to tell, I miss you very much.' His correspondence this summer shows him following a 'life of complete regularity and painful industry here – piling page upon page – well!' he wrote to Ralph (29 July 1920). 'I hope somebody some day may be amused by it, but I feel damned uncertain.' Queen Victoria was 'proving a tougher mouthful than even I had expected', he told Mary Hutchinson (14 August). 'I must masticate and masticate with a steady persistence – it's the only plan.' By the beginning of September, he had become 'perfectly paralysed by Victoria,' he admitted to his brother James. 'My brain spun round and round, and I thought I was going to sink into imbecility. So it became necessary to have a rest.'

He decided to refresh himself by a comparative tour of rural Bloomsbury. In exchange for various parcels of sugar, gingerbread and clean clothes, he sent Carrington an account of the eccentricities of Charleston, in particular 'a Bloomsbury Experiment with Time' (4 September 1920). 'Typically, Maynard has insisted on ... you'd never guess what; altering the time! So that the clocks are one hour in advance even of summer-time, with curious consequences.

'For one thing Jessie disapproves, won't have it, and has let the kitchen clock run down, so that the servants have *no* time. Then Clive is fitful on the subject, and insists upon always referring to the normal time; and altogether the confusion is extraordinary. How mad they all are! Maynard, though he sees what a rumpus it causes, persists. Vanessa is too feeble to put him down, and Clive is too tetchy to grin and bear it. The result is extremely Tchekhofesque. But luckily the atmosphere is entirely comic, instead of being fundamentally tragic as in Tchekhof. Everyone laughs and screams and passes on.'

From the topsy-turvydom of Charleston, Lytton moved on to Monk's House, the cottage to which Leonard and Virginia Woolf had recently moved, in the village of Rodmell, on the bank of the River Ouse. Here, though the diet seemed extraordinary – jam and potatoes and bottled plums – the atmosphere was more equable in spite of its peculiar dilapidation. 'This country seems to me the best in the world,' he wrote to Ralph (11 September 1920). 'I went for a perfect walk yesterday with Virginia. Oh, for a great farmhouse here, with many large panelled rooms and a walled garden, and barns, and horses for my two children, and a pianola, and multitudes of books, and a cellar of wine, and ... but my imagination runs away with me. Well! Some day it may occur!'

After a week at Monk's House, he travelled on to Jack and Mary Hutchinson's home in West Wittering. 'The house is minute,' he told Ralph (16 September 1920), 'with two children at the noisiest age ramping over it, and the tête-à-tête with Mary Hutch grows difficult as time goes on. The complete absence of sex-instinct is such a bore, unless there's a great deal of intellect to make up. When there's a slight flirtation – even an infinitesimally slight one, it makes such a difference!'

Such were the nuances of Bloomsbury in Sussex, and his investigations completed, Lytton came back to Tidmarsh. 'Here I sit,' he wrote to Mary

Hutchinson (4 October 1920), 'over the fire, trying to nerve myself for the coup de grâce on Victoria: but I hesitate ... she quells me with her fishy eye.' He had hoped to finish the book before Christmas, but it 'seems to me still rather doubtful whether I shall kill Victoria or Victoria me', he told Maynard. He was sending each chapter on to Ralph, who would type it out and correct the spelling. From one of his letters to Ralph (23 November 1920) it appears that he had altered his description of the Prince Consort's death, and this delayed him. 'I live the life of one submerged beneath horse hair sofas and collapsed crinolines,' he told Middleton Murry (22 September 1920). On 6 December, Geoffrey Whitworth of Chatto & Windus came down to Tidmarsh so that together they might plot and plan the book's publication. Lytton promised to deliver a complete typescript early in the new year, ready for the spring list. He gauged the length to be around ninety thousand words – ten thousand shorter than he originally intended.[66]

Arrangements for the American edition of *Queen Victoria* were more complicated and, in the long run, less satisfactory. Maynard, whose *The Economic Consequences of the Peace* had been recently issued by Harcourt Brace, had persuaded Lytton to write to Putnam's, who had published *Eminent Victorians*, politely notifying them that they would not be handling his next book. Then Maynard opened up negotiations with Harcourt Brace, and after some exchanges of letters and telegrams, reported back to Lytton that he had secured an outright offer for the American rights amounting to seven thousand dollars (equivalent to around £35,000 in 1994) which could be safely invested to bring in something between one hundred and fifty and two hundred pounds a year for life. 'I hardly know what to advise,' he added (30 November 1920). 'But for you there seems a good deal of virtue in certainty. You would still have the whole of the English rights intact to gamble with. What shall I cable back?'

Lytton was doubtful whether this sum was really enough, especially since it was to include serial rights for a number of extracts in the *New Republic*.[67] Already from Putnam's he had received, on a 20 per cent royalty basis, over seven hundred pounds (equivalent to £13,000 in 1994) from the immediate sales of *Eminent Victorians* – and there had been no question of a serial. But he was impressed by what Maynard said about the advantage of certainty on an outright sale of copyright, and asked him to try for ten thousand dollars for all rights, or up to five thousand dollars excluding serial rights. Harcourt Brace cabled back that it was willing to make the ten-thousand-dollar payment (equivalent to around £50,000 in 1994) providing they were given the Canadian rights also. Since Chatto & Windus amiably agreed to this, the contract was then signed. And so, to everyone's satisfaction, a deal was concluded that over the years disentitled Lytton and his literary executor to many thousands of pounds in royalties.

On 24 January, Lytton wrote to Geoffrey Whitworth telling him that the book was almost finished. There remained one more task, and that was rather peculiar. It consisted in fitting on the final paragraph, the famous death-bed scene of the Queen which was the very first paragraph he had written and towards which the rest of the book had been pointed.

At last he was a free man. On 25 January, he came up to 51 Gordon Square, where he was to spend most of the next three months, 'leading a life of idleness and proof-reading'. He had also been reading a couple of books by friends – Leonard Woolf's *Empire and Commerce in Africa* which he thought 'terrific'; and the *Oedipus Tyrannus* of Sophocles translated and expounded by Sheppard.[68] 'All is well,' he assured Carrington (24 February 1921), 'and the weather so marvellous that anything but idleness seems out of place.' He had been asked by the *Nation* to review Margot Asquith's autobiography, but disliked it too much. A more fascinating volume, which had been sent to him by a future biographer, Hesketh Pearson, was Frank Harris's notorious *Life of Oscar Wilde*. 'It has a fair amount of rather new information,' he had written to James (November 1920), 'though of course, it's not nearly detailed enough, and it isn't really *very* well done. However the story is a most remarkable one. The admirer is called Mr Hesketh Pearson, and is apparently some sort of agent for Frank Harris in England. He sent me the book in order, as he said, to find out what the greatest English biographer thought of the greatest American one – a slightly double-edged compliment, I fear. But *is* F.H. American? Or what?' Pearson's letter, like a parody of Lytton's dramatic prose style, declared that there was 'no dark and sinister motive' behind his gift – an assurance which somewhat alarmed Lytton. 'I'm rather afraid he [Pearson] may want me to write some wretched review or puff,' he complained to Carrington (3 November 1920), 'so I shall tell him that I can't do that, but otherwise will graciously accept the book.'

Released from his imprisonment at Tidmarsh, he now set his face towards a period of easy entertainment. He went to Cambridge to see again the young embryos and Apostles and read a paper to the Heretics. Occasionally, too, he would return to the Mill House for a weekend, bringing with him some of these new undergraduate friends – Sebastian Sprott who was reading moral sciences at Clare College while having an affair 'up to the middle, not head over ears', with Maynard; 'good prim priggish bright-eyed Peter' [F.L.] Lucas as Virginia called him, who, according to Maynard, was 'far and away the most brilliant of the younger classics up here' at King's; and, also at King's, a pretty student surgeon-oculist, James Doggart, a favourite of Sheppard's.

One new older acquaintance was Max Beerbohm who, the previous June, had sent him a letter executed after his most polished and whimsical manner – 'rather amusing and very elaborate,' Lytton commented, 'but how to answer it. Christ alone knows. Of course completely for publication.[69] All very nice, in its way, when done by somebody else, but a bore, a dreadful bore, when one has to sit down oneself in cold blood and compose.' Early this spring, Max came to London to arrange for an exhibition of his drawings, and asked Lytton whether he 'might professionally stare at him'. A few days later Lytton called round to see him at the Charing Cross Hotel. 'He rang me to ask me to go and see him, explaining that he drew a caricature of me, and wished to "verify his impressions",' Lytton afterwards explained to James (14 April 1921). 'I went yesterday, and found him, very plump and whitehaired, drawn up to receive me. "Let us come out on to the balcony, where we shall have a view of the doomed city." He begged me to turn my profile towards him, and for a minute or two made some notes on the back of an envelope. He was infinitely polite and elaborate, and quite remote, so far as I could see, from humanity in all its forms. His caricatures are to be exhibited in three weeks – "if England still exists".'

Though they were never close friends, Max looked on Lytton almost as a younger brother. In an age, it seemed to him, that was vulgarizing art, Lytton's good taste remained intact. Max felt that he was to Lytton what Oscar Wilde had been to him. 'You are wonderful,' he had written to him after the publication of *Eminent Victorians* (28 July 1918). He saw Lytton as a modified edition of himself, someone who had made small advances in the fastidious and refined craft of letters. 'He was no longer velveteen-jacketed,' Max noted with surprise when Lytton arrived at his hotel. 'He was dressed now in the worldier manner, which, I told him, seemed to me less characteristic, and he willingly agreed that he should remain velveteen-jacketed in my drawing.' What Max, with his static and mannered ways, did not see was that Lytton was moving with the times. Even if it was true that the Apostolic rather than the Victorian world was damaged by the war, still he reflected this change in *Queen Victoria*. For Max himself, the earthquake of the war had broken apart the formalized world of his youth. His pleasures – like Lytton's – were mainly those of travel and society. But in his monotonous retirement at Rapallo, he had rationed such activities. For Lytton, on the other hand, London and the Continent had ceased to exist as places of interest and adventure only in the war years themselves. Now that peace was restored and he had money of his own to spend, he looked forward to travelling and exploring society. The post-war world, which so horrified Max, filled Lytton with a renewal of optimism. The carnage, the philistinism, the reign of terror, stupidity and press dictatorship were over, and something better must surely take their place. The world was opening up again. He planned a few weeks after the publication of *Queen Victoria* to stay with the Berensons in Florence.

It was a year since his journey into Spain. This time he would be travelling without 'the children', Carrington and Ralph, and leaving behind an explosive situation. 'When *our* lives come to be written,' he observed, 'they'll be even more peculiar than the Victorians'.'

9

MOONS AND HONEYMOONS

'What I always feel', Carrington had written at the end of 1918, 'is that we are meant to persevere through this somewhat awkward time because later things will be better for us.' Two years later everything was more awkward and the need for perseverance still greater. It was important, she lectured Ralph (8 May 1920), 'to concentrate on the happiness we had, instead of all the time aiming for something we hadn't.' It seemed wrong, she observed to Lytton (3 September 1920), 'that with a surplus of affections for so many human beings that there can't be combined happiness for more than two people at a time.' Surely this was what Lytton had meant by his 'Generalisation no. 1'. She had mastered this secret though nowhere near the age of thirty-nine. But Ralph hadn't.

Having come down from Oxford and failed to get a job as assistant to the Fabian economist G.D.H. Cole, Ralph had been engaged by Leonard Woolf to act as his part-time secretary and compositor in the Hogarth Press. 'It is nice to think that you have such good work,' Gerald Brenan wrote to him (5 October, 7 November 1920). '. . . you shall have the offer of anything I have to publish.' But such a job, minutely remunerated,[70] seemed hardly suitable for the enormous fists of the burly ex-major – 'I don't see Partridge setting up the type,' Lytton commented. But Ralph himself appeared 'cheerful'. The job took him a step nearer marrying Carrington – indeed, he could see no obstacle to their immediate marriage except Carrington herself. For she still obstinately resisted his proposals, partly because she rejected the imprisoning regime of wedlock, and partly because she felt that Ralph, for all his affection for Lytton, did not really belong to her world. Few of her artistic friends and few of Lytton's at first liked him, though many came to do so later. Bloomsbury was sceptical too about his role in the Tidmarsh 'family', and recoiled from his intrusions into Gordon Square. Yet despite all this opposition, Ralph was amazingly persistent, and Carrington began to fear that her own stubbornness might soon alienate Lytton, endangering their life at Pangbourne. He had said nothing, of course. She would not expect him to do so. But she sensed his growing disapproval of their fractious relations. 'All this decision business has upset me,' she wrote (3 September 1920). 'I feel rather unhinged by it.' As Ralph's exasperation mounted so did Carrington's anxiety.

'Lytton dear, do you know what comfort you are to me,' she had written to him while he was staying at Charleston that autumn. 'I feel as long as you live on this earth I can never mind anything.' Knowing the cause of her distress, Lytton answered with all his customary tenderness. 'My dearest, I am sure that all is really well between us, which is the great thing. Some devil of embarrassment chokes me sometimes, and prevents me expressing what I feel. You have made me so happy during the last 3 years, and you have created Tidmarsh, as no one else could have – and I seem hardly to have said thank you. But you must believe that I value you and your love more than I can ever say.'

Yet even now Carrington was not altogether reassured. If Ralph, becoming fed up with her refusals to marry him, were to leave, then Lytton too might wish to go. If his sense of pity held him back, then he would certainly feel an involuntary resentment against her for driving away the man he loved. She therefore put forward a compromise. She would live with Ralph, on a more or less experimental basis, until Christmas. Since he was now working in London, this meant that the two of them must stay during the weekdays in James and Alix's apartment at 41 Gordon Square, going down together to Tidmarsh for weekends. James and Alix had left for Vienna to be analysed by Freud. 'Each day I spend an hour on the Prof's sofa,' James explained to Lytton (6 November 1920), '. . . it's sometimes extremely exciting and sometimes extremely unpleasant . . . The Prof himself is most affable and as an artistic performer dazzling . . . Almost every hour is made into an organic aesthetic whole. Sometimes the dramatic effect is absolutely shattering.'

Carrington 'almost believed' in what she called 'anylises', though observing that she had 'a complex' about spelling the word. But she had been impressed by James and Alix's decision, after a year together at 41 Gordon Square, to marry.[71] James had spoken of it as a necessary formality to avoid complications with passports and hotel rooms. Even so, Carrington wondered if the same thing might not happen to her and Ralph.

'It seems to me that your trying the G. Square experiment is probably right,' Lytton assured Carrington. To everyone's relief, the worst crisis had been postponed. 'On Fridays Carrington and the Major appear, departing again on Monday,' Lytton explained in a letter to James (November 1920). 'How long the arrangement will last I haven't an idea. I rather fear that she may find it doesn't suit her – that the ménage at Gordon Square is too purely domestic – but I don't know.' Whatever happened, he reassured Carrington, 'you must rely on my affection.'

There were some advantages, living in London. That autumn Carrington painted Lytton's mother, who bought the portrait for £25. 'I am painting her against a book case sitting full length in a chair, in a wonderful robe which goes into great El Greco folds,' she wrote to Lytton (21 November 1920). 'It is lined with orange. So the effect is a very sombre picture with a black dress, & mottled cloak, & then brilliant orange edges down the front of her dress. She looks like the Queen of China, or one of El Greco's Inquisitors.' 'The more I look at her Ladyship,' Lytton wrote back after the portrait was completed (21 February 1921), 'the more I admire it.'[72]

But on the whole London life struck Carrington as fraudulent. She hated being shut in by all the buildings when she could have been painting in the fields. 'I feel dreadfully depressed now, installed high up in this gloomy grey Square,' she confessed to Lytton soon after moving in (25 October 1920). '... *You* said the middle of the week would go so quickly, but the weekends, they go quicker far. And I saw so little of you ... [Ralph] is so good to me. He tries to make me happy. But I have to hide my pain, which makes it harder. For I do miss you so frightfully ...'

She was never adept at concealing her emotions, and Ralph, well aware of her loneliness, and himself growing dissatisfied at their arrangement, developed 'a mania for getting married'. He found himself with very little free time away from the Hogarth Press where he was 'putting his ox's shoulder to the wheel', Virginia noted, and he had very little money. 'I am in an extraordinary position myself just now – financially very bad ... It tinges my whole life with mournful anticipations,' he confided to Gerald (31 December 1920). '... If only people were not killed I should love soldiering; but the element of risk is perhaps the greatest pleasure of all, and that would be absent.'

Watching Ralph and Carrington together, Virginia observed (31 August 1920) that he 'is a superb body – shoulders like tough oak; health tingling beneath his skin. Merry shrewd eyes'; she 'is ardent, robust, scatterbrained, appreciative ... A little ashamed of P., I thought her. But what shoulders! what thickness of bone!' By the new year, she felt Lytton was growing 'wearied' by their continual bickering. 'Perhaps after all, said Lytton, one oughtn't to allow these attachments. Our parents may have been right.' She concluded that 'Carrington is losing Lytton and spurning poor Ralph.'

Everything seemed to improve after Lytton came to London and moved down the road into 51 Gordon Square. 'We get on very amicably now,' Carrington reported. But whenever Lytton went away the quarrelling started up again. Marriage, Ralph argued, would make no outward difference to *her* life – indeed, in some respects, such as travelling abroad with him, it would make things easier. But she dreaded the prospect of having children. What were the trivial difficulties of travelling abroad once a year compared to a brood of Partridges, with a mother and a father bird, for ever chirping at one? 'Oh dearie dearie I wish one never grew up,' she complained to her brother Noel (11 May 1921), 'or else One could live in a land where conventions, and parents n'est existe pas.'

By May, they appeared to have reached deadlock. The strain between them was very great. Infuriated by her evasions, Ralph threatened that if he did not marry her he would go to Bolivia and become a sheep farmer. Was he bluffing, or had the moment of decision arrived? Carrington could not tell. He sounded desperately serious. She did not know whether to laugh or cry. She did not know *what* to do.

It was at this point that Lytton chose to remove himself to Italy. He had not interfered in their drama, though its outcome would affect him profoundly, and now his letters to Carrington omitted any reference to her drastic predicament with Ralph. Instead he wrote of visiting the Sitwells at Montegufoni, 'a truly outstanding place'; and of Geoffrey Scott at the Villa Medici,[73] a superb eighteenth-century villa higher up in the hills. But chiefly his correspondence was taken up with descriptions of his host, Bernard Berenson, and his famous villa at Settignano, I Tatti. 'The house is just what I imagined – large – full of beautiful objects one can hardly look at, and comfort that somehow is really far less comfortable than Tidmarsh ... His Lordship looks like an imbecile butler, and I should think was one. Lady B. is a sad pseudo-beauty ... There is a distinct air of civil war about, which is slightly unpleasant.'

In another letter, a few days later, he writes: 'B.B. is a very interesting phenomenon ... a most curious complicated temperament – very sensitive, very clever – even, I believe, with a strain of niceness somewhere or other, but desperately wrong – perhaps suffering from some dreadful complexes – and without a spark of naturalness or ordinary human enjoyment.

'And this has spread itself over the house, which is really remarkably depressing . . . one is struck chill by the atmosphere of a crypt. Oooh! – And so much of it, too – such a large corpse – so many long dead corridors, so many dead primitives, so many dead pieces of furniture, and flowers, and servants, such multitudes of dead books; and then, outside, a dead garden, with a dead view of a dead Tuscan landscape . . .'

Back in England relations between Ralph and Carrington had reached a crisis. Shortly after Lytton left for Florence, Ralph suffered a breakdown and poured out his long accumulation of grievances to Leonard and Virginia. 'He was very shrewd & bitter about C[arrington],' Virginia wrote in her diary (15 May 1921). '. . . he said she was selfish, untruthful, & quite indifferent to his suffering. So people in love always turn & rend the loved, with considerable insight too.' Of course he was biased, but he was obviously speaking the truth too.

Leonard and Virginia had noticed how his work at the Hogarth Press had been affected by the strain. Despite his 'shoulders like tough oak', he dropped a whole box of type and then sent out for review Virginia's volume of short stories, *Monday or Tuesday*, without a date of publication. What sort of 'motherly advice' should Virginia give him? The previous summer she had thought 'it would be a good thing', as she confided to Vanessa (24 August 1920), 'to bring about a legitimate union'. Since then she had got to know him rather better. He was 'a bit of an ogre & tyrant', she imagined. 'I wdn't marry Ralph – A despot,' she had noted in her diary on 12 December. But should Carrington marry him?

Leonard had little doubt over what must be done. He saw Carrington as 'one of those mysterious, inordinately female characters made up of an infinite series of contradictory characteristics, one inside the other like Chinese boxes . . . It was impossible to know whether the Chinese boxes were full of intricate psychological mysteries or whether in fact they were all empty.' As for Ralph, he appeared a typical public schoolboy and English Don Juan, with a good deal of childlike vulnerability. 'Beneath the rather ebullient, hail-fellow-well-met, man of the world façade there was a curious stratum of emotionalism.' Easily moved to tears, he had now reached a condition of hysterical craziness over Carrington. It was obvious that drastic steps must be taken. Ralph 'must go to Carrington and put a pistol at her'.[74]

Though it was a less simple matter for Virginia (Ralph, she observed, 'wants more control than I should care to give – control I mean of the body & mind & time & thoughts of his loved'), she supported Leonard with a mingling of excitement and unease. 'I was in the thick of it,' she confessed to Vanessa (22 May 1921). ' . . . Poor Carrington.'

Carrington had now returned to the Mill House, having been commissioned to paint the signboards of some public houses in Reading.[75] It was here, after his session with the Woolfs, that Ralph caught up with her on Friday 13 May. They met in a workmen's café. The terrible deterioration in Ralph's appearance appalled Carrington. His mouth twitched; he looked ill. Seeing him in this wretched state, she felt fonder of him than ever she had done in his more aggressive moods. But she felt guilty too. As with Gertler, she was the culprit. It was her selfishness that had caused him such anguish.

In a flat voice, Ralph began by saying that he knew she was not in love with him, nevertheless he thought that her affections were strong enough to make him happy. He loved her and he could not go on any longer in uncertainty and pain. He would definitely leave the country if she would not marry him. He had already written to Lytton in Florence. He then repeated to her what Virginia had said: that Lytton was frightened of her becoming dependent on him, that he was going to spend more time alone in London. This revelation deeply affected Carrington. Always, in future, she would feel a terror of being physically on Lytton's nerves. Therefore she decided, partly for Lytton's peace of mind, but also for Ralph's happiness, that she would have to give in. That afternoon in the café she told Ralph that she would marry him, though still hoping even now that, having agreed in theory to become Ralph's wife, she might somehow defer putting the decision into practice.

Both of them were exhausted, Ralph elated, Carrington resigned, as they drove back that night to Tidmarsh. The next morning, Carrington sent off a long letter to Lytton.

'I have known all along that my life with you was limited. I could never hope for it to become permanent. After all Lytton, you are the only person who I have ever had an absorbing passion for. I shall never have another. I couldn't now. I had one of the most self abasing loves that a person can have. You could throw me into transports of happiness and dash me into deluges of tears and despair, all by a few words. But these aren't reproaches ... these years at Tidmarsh when we were quite alone will always be the happiest I ever spent. And I've such a store of good things which I've saved up, that I feel I could never be lonely again now. Still its too much of a strain to be quite alone here waiting to see you or craning my nose and eyes out of the top window of 41 G.S. to see if you are coming down the street, when I know we'll be better friends, if you aren't haunted by the idea that I am sitting depressed in some corner of the world waiting for your footstep ...

I saw the relief you felt at Ralph taking me away, so to speak, off your hands.

I think he'll make me happier, than I should be entirely by myself and it certainly prevents me becoming morbid about you. And as Ralph said last night you'll never leave us. Because in spite of our dullness, nobody else loves you nearly as much as we do.

So in the café in that vile city of Reading, I said I'd marry him . . . After all I don't believe it will make much difference and to see him so happy is a rather definite thing. I'd probably never marry anyone else and I doubt if a kinder creature exists on this earth . . .

I cried last night Lytton, whilst he slept by my side sleeping happily – I cried to think of a savage cynical fate which had made it impossible for my love ever to be used by you. You never knew, or never will know the very big and devastating love I had for you. How I adored every hair, every curl on your beard. How I devoured you whilst you read to me at night. How I loved the smell of your face in your sponge. Then the ivory skin on your hands, your voice, and your hat when I saw it coming along the top of the garden wall from my window. Say you will remember it, that it wasnt all lost and that you'll forgive me for this outburst, and always be my friend . . . Ralph is such a dear, I don't feel I'll ever regret marrying him. "Though I never will change my maiden name that I have kept so long," – so you mayn't ever call me anything but Carrington . . .

You gave me a much longer life than I ever deserved or hoped for and I love you for it terribly. I only cried last night at realizing I never could have my Moon, that sometimes I must pain you, and often bore you. You who I would have given the world to have made happier than any person could be, to give you all you wanted . . .

I see I've told you very little of what I feel. But I keep on crying, if I stop and think about you. Outside the sun is baking and they all chatter and laugh. It's cynical, this world in its opposites. Once you said to me, that Wednesday afternoon in the sitting room, you loved me as a friend. Could you tell it to me again?'

This letter, which was brought out to Italy by Lytton's sister Pippa, took six days to reach him. He wrote back immediately so that Carrington's agony of mind should not be prolonged. He told her that he thought this marriage would be best for them all; and in his effort to make her as happy as the circumstances allowed, came as near as his nature permitted to overcoming that 'devil of embarrassment' which choked the expression of his feelings. All the tenderness of their relationship is conveyed in these two letters.

'But I hope that in any case you never doubted my love for you. Do you know how difficult I find it to express my feelings either in letters or talk? It is sometimes terrible – and I don't understand why it should be so; and sometimes it seems to me that you underrate what I feel. You realise that I have varying moods, but my fundamental feelings you perhaps don't realise so well. Probably it is my fault. It is perhaps much easier to show one's peevishness than one's affection and admiration! Oh my dear, do you really want me to tell you that I "love you as a friend"! – But of course that is absurd, and you *do* know very well that I love you as something more than a friend, you angelic creature, whose goodness to me has made me happy for years, and whose presence in my life has been and always will be, one of the most important things in it. Your letter made me cry, I feel a poor old miserable creature, and I may have brought more unhappiness to you than anything else. I only pray that it is not so, and that my love for you, even though it is not what you desire, may yet make our relationship a blessing to you – as it has been to me.

Remember that I too have never had my moon! We are all helpless in these things – dreadfully helpless. I am lonely and I am all too truly growing old, and if there was a chance that your decision meant that I should somehow or other lose you, I don't think I could bear it. You and Ralph and our life at Tidmarsh are what I care for most in the world – almost (apart from my work and some few people) the *only* things I care for . . .

. . . you seemed in your letter to suggest that my love for you has diminished as time has gone on; that is not so. I am sure it has increased. It is true that the first excitement, which I always (and I suppose most people) have at the beginning of an affair, has gone off; but something much deeper has grown up instead.'

Carrington and Ralph were married on Saturday, 21 May, at the register office in St Pancras. Carrington described herself in the register book as an Artist (Painter) of Tidmarsh Mill House, Pangbourne; Ralph was a Private Secretary, living at 41 Gordon Square. The witnesses were Lytton's sister Marjorie and a young army and Oxford friend of Ralph's, Alan McIver. 'If people ever took advice I should feel a little responsible for making up Ralph's mind,' Virginia confided in her diary (23 May 1921). 'I mean I am not sure that this marriage is not more risky than most.'

But perhaps, Lytton hoped, it might turn out well. 'Everything is so happy now,' Carrington had written to him (20 May 1921). '. . . So you mustn't be worried about your children.' As a wedding gift, Leonard had presented Ralph with a month's holiday from the Hogarth Press, and Lytton sent them both train tickets to join him in Italy. They spent their wedding night in Paris, then travelled down to Siena and Perugia where 'we got rather drunk and had one of our brawls'. But by the time they reached Assisi these brawls had passed.

'We are taking very little,' Carrington had informed Lytton (20 May 1921), 'as if it's not too hot we shall walk.' They walked for three days over the Apennines to Rimini and on to Ravenna, and somewhere along the way Carrington lost her wedding ring. She had never liked it much – it was so narrow and plain – but the loss rather clouded their day.

On 6 June they joined Lytton and Pippa for an 'enchanting week' in Venice. 'I enjoyed Venice enormously,' Lytton later (29 June 1921) told Ottoline. '. . . and I can hardly bear the thought that it is still going on in all its fascination and that I am not in the middle of it.' Ralph and Carrington also seemed to be enjoying themselves. 'Rex is happy,' Carrington wrote to her brother Noel, 'and that is the main thing.' But in a letter to Gerald Brenan, who had come to symbolize all that she had given up for Ralph and Lytton, she wrote enticingly: 'I wish badly you could be with us. Then it would be perfect . . . We'll live at the good Mill and keep a little room in Gordon Square and always a bed for Geraldo . . . I couldn't have married anyone else, unless perhaps . . . But you shall never know that perhaps. G.B. Perhaps? or perhaps not!'

Over her honeymoon Carrington wrote four long letters to Gerald. Ralph nearly always went through her correspondence, she explained (8 June 1921), so if Gerald wished to write her a love letter 'put a red stamp on the outside upside down,' she advised, 'then the faithless wife can conceal it before he reads it.'

FIFTEEN

Eminent Edwardian

one of the most pathetic
sights however
is to see the ghost of queen
victoria going out every
evening with the ghost
of a sceptre in her hand
to find mr lytton strachey
and bean him it seems she beans
him and beans him and he
never knows it

Don Marquis, 'archy goes abroad'
from *archy's life of mehitabel*

'The agitations are of course terrific. Do you think there is no end
to love affaires and one can never say "c'est fini"?'

Carrington to Alix Strachey (11 May 1925)

I

THE GREAT PANJANDRUM

Reviewing a book called *Fifty Years of a Good Queen's Reign* in the *Pall Mall Gazette* in 1886, Bernard Shaw had called for a new class of royal biography. 'The truth is that queens, like other people, can be too good for the sympathies of their finite fellow-creatures,' he wrote. 'A few faults are indispensable to a really popular monarch . . . What we need now is a book entitled "Queen Victoria: by a Personal acquaintance who dislikes her" . . . The proper person for the work would be some politically indifferent devil's advocate who considers the Queen an over-rated woman and who would take a conscientious delight in disparaging her.'[1]

Such conscientiousness was widely expected from Lytton Strachey's *Queen Victoria* thirty-five years later. Among contemporary biographers he was the outstanding devil's advocate. Though he had not been a personal acquaintance of the Queen, he had acquired 'private information', referred to in his footnotes, from Lady Lytton (widow of his godfather, the first Earl) who had been one of her ladies-in-waiting. He had no political ideology and he was known for taking intense delight in revealing 'the hidden quality of things'.[2] What other writer of non-fiction could so disparage a public reputation by linking it incongruously to the subject's private life, especially the sexuality of that private life? He was anxious, he had promised his cousin Edith Plowden, not to make Victoria appear 'ridiculous' since she was a 'great queen'.[3] At the same time he was writing to his brother James (20 November 1920): 'It's quite clear that Queen Victoria was a martyr to analeroticism.' The biographical difficulty, he added, lay in steering 'the correct course between discretion and indiscretion' – that is providing a serious sexual subtext to the regal panoply of his narrative.

Strachey's originality as a biographer partly derived from his sexual temperament and psycho-sexual insights. In *Eminent Victorians* he had shown the inflated ambitions of Cardinal Manning and the destructive energies of Florence Nightingale flaring out from the suppressed fires of their sexuality. He also attributed Thomas Arnold's failure as an educational reformer to sexual fears beneath his attitudinizing moral righteousness. 'Was he to improve the character of his pupils by gradually spreading round them an atmosphere of cultivation and intelligence?' Strachey asked. 'By bringing them into close and friendly contact with civilized men, and even, perhaps, with civilized women? By introducing into the life of his school all that he could of the humane, enlightened, and progressive elements in the life of the community? On the whole, he thought not.' Finally he allows us to see the extreme imperialist section of the British Government easily misleading General Gordon, whose lack of self-knowledge arises from a lifelong retreat from his true sexuality, the nature of which Lytton hints at several times ('his soul revolted against dinner-parties and stiff shirts; and the presence of ladies – especially fashionable ladies – filled him with uneasiness'). He was to give a similar interpretation of the Prince Consort's character in *Queen Victoria*.

Queen Victoria is presented like a romantic novel beneath whose surface moves a current of subversive irony. 'You've discovered a new style which gives the essential and all-pervading absurdity of most human and all official life without losing anything of its pathos,' Roger Fry wrote to him (18 April 1921). 'You're so kind and so unsparing. It seems to me more nearly a true perspective than anyone's yet found.'

The characters arrange themselves into three categories. There are the unseen powers and immaterial beings who lurk in shadowy recesses and mysteriously control the event-plot; there are some highly-coloured portraits-in-miniature of nineteenth-century prime ministers who believe they control events; and then there are the heroine and hero round whom all these events cluster.

The Duchess of Kent, Baroness Lehzen, King Leopold I and Baron Stockmar are all used by Strachey as mechanical tricks of his trade to dramatize the battle for political power behind the scenes. As latent supremacy passes from one to the other, so the kaleidoscope of the biography shifts. While Victoria is growing up a fierce struggle develops between the child's mother and her governess – and it is the governess, Lehzen, who emerges triumphant. 'Discreet and victorious, she remained in possession of the field,' Strachey writes. 'More closely than ever did she cleave to the side of her mistress, her pupil, and her friend; and in the recesses of the palace her mysterious figure was at once invisible and omnipresent.' In international affairs Victoria's uncle, King Leopold of the Belgians, tries to gain ascendancy over the young Queen. It is, however, Leopold's 'confidential agent', Baron Stockmar, who at length carries all before him. If Victoria is the Baroness's pupil, Albert is the genie whom the Baron summons out of his bottle to enact his every wish. After Albert and Victoria's marriage a Punch-and-Judy show starts up, Stockmar and Lehzen violently activating the royal marionettes upon the stage until Punch-Albert-Stockmar is acclaimed the winner. Lehzen 'lost ground perceptibly', Strachey records. Then Stockmar gives the Prince the annihilating powers of his magic: 'He spoke, and Lehzen vanished for ever.'

Strachey's creation of Stockmar as an Invisible Man who holds prodigious sway over Albert was based on the mythical version which Stockmar himself conceived in a trance of retrospective optimism. With his trap-door exits and entrances, he is the good fairy of this pantomime, while the royal couple become two mandarin figures nodding or shaking their heads as their master pleases. The satisfaction of Stockmar's 'essential being lay in obscurity, in invisibility', we are told, '– in passing, unobserved, through a hidden entrance, into the very central chamber of power, and in sitting there, quietly, pulling the subtle strings that set the wheels of the whole world in motion'. The end of Stockmar is heralded by the death of Albert. Deprived of his medium, the Baron is suddenly redundant: a magician without a wand; a ventriloquist without a dummy. 'The Baron, by his fireside at Coburg, suddenly saw the tremendous fabric of his creation crash down into sheer and irremediable ruin. Albert was gone, and he had lived in vain.' No longer animated to new life by the master puppet-maker, Victoria can only go through her old tricks again. Her friendship with Disraeli is a distorted mummery of her earlier love for Melbourne; her dislike of Gladstone recalls her coldness to Peel. Sedately she enters her second childhood.

Victoria's early years, under the domination of her mother the Duchess of Kent, are likened to those of a novice in a convent. 'The child grew into the girl, the girl into the young woman; but still she slept in her mother's bedroom; still she had no place allowed her where she might sit or work by herself. An extraordinary watchfulness surrounded her every step.' Above all, the young Victoria was protected from the contaminating presence of men. Yet the female atmosphere that enclosed her, Strachey suggests, may have given rise to an unforeseen reaction: 'perhaps, after all, to the discerning eye, the purity would not be absolute. The careful searcher might detect, in the virgin soil, the first faint traces of an unexpected vein.' For all the care taken over her upbringing, 'there was something deep within her which responded immediately and vehemently to natures that offered a romantic contrast with her own.'

It is this hidden sexuality that Strachey explores when describing Victoria's relationships with her prime ministers. He makes the romantic contrast between the young Queen and Lord Melbourne particularly striking. We see Lord M. not only through the fascinated gaze of Victoria, but also with the admiring eyes of her biographer. The result is the most vivid impressionistic study in the book. Charles Greville described Melbourne as 'a man with a capacity for loving without having anything in the world to love'. This undirected capacity for loving suddenly focuses upon the Queen. Strachey picks out images that suggest the romantic sexuality of their attachment: 'the autumn rose, in those autumn months of 1839, came to a wondrous blooming. The petals expanded, beautifully, for the last time. For the last time in this unlooked-for, this incongruous, this almost incredible intercourse, the old epicure tasted the exquisiteness of romance.' Robert Peel possessed none of Melbourne's sex-appeal. He seemed embarrassed by women and his manner was unattractively pompous in their company. Since he made little impression on Victoria, he occupies little space in her biography.

After her marriage, Victoria (whose simple pleasures, Strachey tells us, were mostly physical) lost her 'bold and discontented' look, and her infatuation for Lord Melbourne gently faded. Obsessed by her husband, her response to any man was decided by his opinion alone. The jaunty and volatile Palmerston, to whom she might otherwise have been attracted, repelled her because he represented all that was most hostile to the Prince Consort in the spirit of England. But Strachey introduces the gipsyish figure of Tsar Nicolas I of Russia to remind us that Victoria was aroused by handsome men.

After Albert's death this power of appreciation again blossomed: whenever Victoria's sexual instinct came into play Albert's posthumous endorsement was taken for granted. He had preferred Gladstone to Disraeli, yet because Gladstone behaved towards her as if she were a public meeting rather than a woman, she could never warm to him as she did to Disraeli, who gave her back her feminine self-confidence. Strachey passes swiftly over Gladstone as he had done over Peel, but his portrait of Disraeli is almost as sympathetic as his Melbourne. 'After the long gloom of her bereavement, after the chill of Gladstonian discipline, she expanded to the rays of Disraeli's devotion like a flower in the sun.'

Strachey's Victoria is a woman who becomes dependent on men. Though shrewd, she has none of the political genius of Queen Elizabeth. Her politics belonged to the eighteenth century. She suspected political zeal and was more at ease in her later years with her Highland gillie John Brown and her Indian attendant Munshi Abdul Karim than with politicians. To overcome Albert's mute protest from the grave, she invented an obscure spiritual bridge – 'the gruff, kind, hairy Scotsman was, she felt, in some mysterious way, a legacy from the dead. She came to believe at last – or so it appeared – that the spirit of Albert was nearer when Brown was near.'

Victoria's deepest happiness came from her marriage to Albert, which forms the central panel in the biography. She was swept off her feet by a violent sexual upheaval described in highly charged romantic language: 'Albert arrived; and the whole structure of her existence crumbled into nothingness like a house of cards. He was beautiful – she gasped – she knew no more. Then, in a flash, a thousand mysteries were revealed to her.'

Although the Prince was a mirror of manly beauty in the eyes of the Queen, his constitution was not strong and 'owing either to his peculiar upbringing or to a more fundamental idiosyncrasy he had a marked distaste for the opposite sex'. Strachey told Hesketh Pearson that he had intended to suggest that Albert was homosexual. This must be taken as the key to several passages which bring out Albert's melancholy and isolation: 'A shy young foreigner, awkward in ladies' company, unexpansive and self-opinionated, it was improbable that, in any circumstances, he would have been a society success . . . Really, they thought, this youth was more like some kind of foreign tenor . . . From the support and the solace of true companionship he was utterly cut off.'

Strachey sees in Albert something of his own loneliness. His Prince Consort has the power of arousing an idolatry that does not answer his emotional needs. But he could not turn elsewhere for companionship. This was his 'curious position' to which Strachey returns in a later paragraph: 'The husband was not so happy as the wife. In spite of the great improvement in his situation, in spite of a growing family and the adoration of Victoria, Albert was still a stranger in a strange land, and the serenity of spiritual satisfaction was denied him ... Victoria idolized him; but it was understanding that he craved for, not idolatry ... He was lonely.' The fascination of this marriage for Strachey is clearly disclosed when he asks: 'was he the wife and she the husband?' and answers, 'It almost seemed so.' From resembling a foreign tenor Albert changes during the course of his marriage into an idealized butler. By adapting himself body and soul to the role of Prince Consort, he sacrifices what is original in his character and becomes the caricature of a worthy man. What pricked Strachey's curiosity was the underlying ascendancy of Victoria. Only when we see Victoria through the eyes of her declining husband are we made to feel a repugnance for her.

After the death of Albert, and during Victoria's old age, Strachey's attitude softens to the Queen. His last two chapters contain a full inventory of her shortcomings – her imperialism and religious obscurantism, her disapproval of the memoirs of Greville, her insistence on etiquette, her complacency, pride, egotism, insensitivity. It is a formidable list – yet Strachey seems more amused than censorious. Victoria's middle-class morals were really, we are led to believe, a development of her family affection. Her passion for John Brown contributes to that most loved of English qualities, eccentricity. Her collecting instinct, which is described in terms of an obsessional neurosis, has its roots in her fear of death, so that our hearts are touched. Even her indefensible insistence upon changing the form of the verdict in criminal cases involving insanity is partly excused as being due to her memory of Albert's feelings on the subject. This picture of the Queen's old age is framed with the abiding love of her people. In many ways she did not merit such devotion. She was out of step with her times and often insufferable to those near her. Yet the extraordinary loyalty persisted, so that each limitation of character Strachey points to only serves to increase our wonder at this spell. In the penultimate chapter he writes:

'The Queen was hailed at once as the mother of her people and as the embodied symbol of their imperial greatness, and she responded to the double sentiment with all the ardour of her spirit. England and the people of England, she knew it, she felt it, were, in some wonderful and yet quite simple manner, *hers* ... At last, after so long, happiness – fragmentary, perhaps, and charged with gravity, but true and unmistakable none the less – had returned to her.'

This tenderness can partly be attributed to Strachey having associated the Queen with his mother. It seemed that the 'cool and unsparing portrayer of the Victorian notables was no longer the aloof scrutineer', wrote the critic Ivor Brown. 'Following the Queen herself down the decades he found himself at last engaged in a sentimental journey.'[4] The relief in the country was prodigious. Strachey had come to curse, remarked G.M. Trevelyan, and stayed to bless. 'Much as I liked your last book,' he congratulated him (6 May 1921), 'I think it beats it a lot.'

Strachey's treatment of Victoria proved the truth of Bernard Shaw's assertion that 'a few faults are indispensable to a really popular monarch'. The biography inaugurated a new and legendary view of the Queen – a whimsical, teasing, half-admiring, half-mocking view that found in Victoria a quaintly impressive symbol of a quaintly impressive age. The book, which was translated into more than twenty languages, was an instant success. In Britain the first five thousand copies were sold out within twenty-four hours and another four impressions printed within the year; in the United States it was even more popular, going through seventeen impressions during the 1920s. Many critics came to regard it as a masterpiece of biography, a technical *tour de force*. 'To mould this vast material into a synthetic form,' wrote Harold Nicolson; 'to convey not merely unity of impression but a convincing sense of scientific reality; to maintain throughout an attitude of detachment; to preserve the exquisite poise and balance of sustained and gentle irony, and to secure these objects with no apparent effort . . . this, in all certainty, is an achievement which required the very highest gifts of intellect and imagination.'[5] Strachey had not only re-created the Queen, he had extended the architecture of biography. 'He it was who first saw the possibilities of this new medium,' wrote David Cecil. 'He it was who evolved the technical equipment for its expression. We may extend his building, but we must always construct on his foundations. He was the man who established the form.'[6]

Strachey had revolutionized the art of historical biography by showing that it could use one of the *genres* of fiction, but few biographers or historians followed this direction. 'The fate of this wonderful book has been extremely sad,' wrote the novelist and critic Nigel Dennis. 'It appeared when kings and queens were on the way out among historians, yielding sovereignty to economics and social studies. As Strachey's overwhelming interest was in the characters of Victoria and Albert, his book was regarded as frivolous – a stigma that it has kept to this very day.'[7] In the opinion of the historian E.H. Carr, Lytton's work was a contribution to literature rather than history. 'To Lytton Strachey, historical problems were always, and only, problems of individual behaviour and individual eccentricity,' explained Hugh Trevor-Roper. '. . . Historical problems, the problems of politics and society, he never sought to answer, or even to ask.'[8] Also the form of romantic novel into which Strachey had shaped his biography was already a debased form in fiction and did not commend itself to serious contemporary novelists. Wyndham Lewis poured scorn on his celebration of 'the quiet little great', at the head of which 'dazzling *élite* is usually some whimsical, half-apologetic, but very much sheltered and coddled projection of himself'. E.M. Forster found his 'skippy butterfly method' limiting, and Virginia Woolf agreed that it was 'flimsy'. She had been pleased to have the biography dedicated to her, but 'my jealousy is twinged' she admitted after seeing its great critical and commercial success. 'I expect', Forster hazarded, 'he *has* written an important work,' and this eventually became Virginia's conclusion too. Strachey had probably done for the old Queen 'what Boswell did for the old dictionary maker', she wrote at the end of the 1930s. 'In time to come Lytton Strachey's queen Victoria will be Queen Victoria, just as Boswell's Johnson is now Dr Johnson. The other versions will fade and disappear. It was a prodigious feat.'[9]

As for Lytton, he came to doubt whether he had put enough subversive energy into his subtext. When his brother James reported from Vienna that Sigmund Freud preferred *Eminent Victorians* to *Queen Victoria*, he replied (15 February 1922): 'I was delighted to hear of the Doctor's approval of *Eminent Victorians*, and I agree with his preference of it to Q.V.'

2

KISSING AND FISHING

'Private life continues to flow on very smoothly,' Lytton wrote to James. 'The curious ménage or ménages work, I think, quite well. Ralph is really a charming creature, and seems quite content, and Carrington appears to be happy.'

Lytton himself was more than ever the social lion, faithfully sending Carrington accounts of the other animals as he wandered through this grand menagerie. After dining with the Sitwells, he was taken off 'to an incredibly fearful function in Arnold Bennett's establishment', he wrote (28 June 1921). '*He* was not there, but *she* was – oh my eye, what a woman!

'It was apparently some sort of Poetry Society. There was an address (very

496

poor) on Rimbaud etc. by an imbecile Frog; then Edith Sitwell appeared, her nose longer than an ant-eater's, and read some of her absurd stuff; then Eliot – very sad and seedy – it made one weep; finally Mrs Arnold Bennett recited, with waving arms and chanting voice, Baudelaire and Verlaine till everyone was ready to vomit. As a study in half-witted horror the whole thing was most interesting. The rooms were peculiarly disgusting, and the company very miscellaneous ... Why, oh why, does Eliot have any truck with such coagulations? I fear it indicates that there's something seriously wrong with him.'

The demands of Lytton's social life may have made him less alert that summer to impending changes to their ménage-à-trois. Carrington's 'visionary days' at Yegen had stayed bright in her mind. In her daydreams she saw Gerald Brenan as a creature romantically cast adrift like herself. It was his innocence she loved. He did not even realize she was flirting with him when she wrote beguilingly to tell him that she could be '*very fond* of two or three people', that she thought of him 'with great emotion', and that when he came to visit her at Tidmarsh she would feed him with 'strawberry ices, & cream, & cheese straws' and he would be allowed to 'drink Lytton's port'.

Though Gerald was 'always being delighted' by Carrington's letters, they overwhelmed him with his own loneliness. 'You are', he wrote (8 May 1921), 'one of the few, almost the only, young lady (I have met few!) whom I might have fallen in love with.' But she had been his friend Ralph's girl, and now she was his wife. 'If anyone is to be congratulated upon engaging on such a perilous enterprise as matrimony, I think you're the man,' he wrote to Ralph (1 June 1921). '... I can't help adding that D.C. is scarcely less lucky.' But Gerald did not feel lucky. 'I am sorry for my own sake,' he told Carrington, 'because have love affairs I simply must, and whom shall I ever find as charming as you?'

That summer Gerald's great-aunt adopted him as her heir and sent over a little money so that he could visit England. He arrived in mid-June. 'I suppose we'll meet in July and clasp each other's honest palm,' he had written to Ralph. On 2 July he spent a night at Tidmarsh and five days later bicycled over from his parents' house to the White Horse at Uffington, for a picnic with Carrington. Ralph was unable to join them because of his work at the Hogarth Press, and Lytton, who distrusted picnics, stayed in London. Carrington and Gerald were therefore alone.

It was possible that day to taste the full flavour of an English summer. The sun burnt the grass, made the air tremble around them, sucked up the juices of the trees. Not a leaf stirred. The sky was a motionless dull purple as they ate their picnic on the crumbling slope of a hill, under a haystack near a little misty wood. 'We talked and suddenly she put her arms round me and kissed me. I let her, but afterwards felt angry because I was Ralph's friend and because she meant nothing to me . . .' A fortnight later Gerald came to stay at Tidmarsh for the weekend. He was determined that nothing more should spring from this episode. 'Then as I sat in an armchair I saw her move across the window with the evening light behind her, and I knew I was in love. It was like the first attack of flu to a Pacific Islander – I was completely, totally under from the first moment. I had fallen for her in the same way in which she had fallen for Lytton, and just as violently. And she was in love with me.'

Of these startling developments Ralph Partridge suspected nothing. He had welcomed his friend's arrival in England with the greatest amusement and delight. Gerald was 'the apotheosis of vagueness in man', he reported to Noel Carrington (17 July 1921). 'He eats, moves and sleeps, entirely unaware of the natural laws which govern these processes. He will talk anyone into a coma and withal is always interesting. Also he may very likely write a good book before he breaks his neck day-dreaming.'

Once the weekend was over, Gerald returned to London and Carrington followed him for a two-day 'orgy of kissing'. 'There is no need for me to tell you how fond I am of you,' he wrote to her (29 July 1921), 'for you can see that every time I look at you – nor of what kind my affection is, for that I only vaguely know myself. There are moments when you appear so entirely, so tormentingly beautiful that I begin to lose my head a little . . . [you are] a creature so beautiful that it would be a sort of madness not to fall in love with you.' At the beginning of August Carrington left for a holiday in the Lake District with Lytton and Ralph, and Gerald prepared to take his solitary journey back to Yegen. Then a telegram arrived from Carrington asking him to join them. Without hesitation he put off his journey to Spain and set off northwards to Watendlath Farm, near Keswick in Cumberland. By this time, the party also included Marjorie Strachey, who had turned up 'in pitch darkness and a howling tempest . . . having lost a reticule containing £6', James and Alix recently returned from Vienna, much in love, busy playing chess and translating Freud.[10] 'My family leaves me gasping,' murmured Lytton. The seven of them herded together into the small back parlour of Farmer Wilson's sheep farm. 'I am sitting, as you may guess, rather comatose, in a small cottage apartment,' Lytton wrote to Virginia (23 August 1921), 'green mountains out of the window, the stuffed head of a very old female sheep over the window.'

For Gerald these next twelve days sped by in a dream of surreptitious excitement. Everything that was beautiful and sad seemed crowded into this short period of his life. When the sun shone they would all clamber about the stony hills, until Lytton's feet were covered with blisters and 'I can only wear silk socks and slippers in which I totter occasionally into the air'. On rainy days the two Strachey brothers stayed crouched over the fire – Lytton reading Beckford's *Biographical Memoirs of Extraordinary Painters*, and James, 'on an enormous air-cushion balanced upon a horsehair sofa', ruminating on the psychology of day-dreams. But whatever the weather, Ralph would go determinedly out to fish – he had 'caught two sardines so far' – and he was accompanied by Carrington and Gerald, carrying fish-hooks and hard-boiled eggs wrapped in newspaper. While Ralph sat, rod in hand, beside the river, the other two would kiss and cuddle behind a bank close by or farther off in a barn on the dry crackling bracken. Gerald was soon riven by guilt about this deception. He had looked forward to an intense platonic attachment leading perhaps to some poems. But within a few hours of his arrival at Watendlath Farm, everything except love was driven from his head. He was like a man drowning in the sea. That he should love his best friend's wife became a torture – and yet he could not give up loving Carrington. There was only one right course. He would go and explain to Ralph exactly what was happening. Surely Ralph would understand. For in their desire not to be unfaithful to him they thought of themselves as being special friends and would have been shocked to have heard their liaison referred to as 'an affair'. Nevertheless Carrington, who knew Ralph better, would not agree to divulging anything. So the kissing and the fishing continued. Carrington luxuriated in this exquisite concealment, while Gerald lived in a romantic ecstasy, feeling an increased affection, almost a gratitude, towards his friend. Each night Ralph would take Carrington to bed; each morning Gerald would wander in and sit talking on the bed 'in a strange state of mind'. As for Ralph himself, he felt pleased that Carrington and Gerald were so amicable. He had fewer rows with his wife now that his friend had joined them. They were just like one another, he thought, vague, imaginative, hopelessly impractical – they even peeled apples in an identically clumsy way.

The others too paid them little attention. In one of his letters to Mary Hutchinson, Lytton complains that the sole adventures in the vicinity appeared to be meteorological (25 August 1921), 'and – so far as I can see – there is precious little love-making'. The only sign from the Outer World, he informed Pippa (30 August 1921), 'has been a vision of Mr Stephen McKenna trailing over the mountain-tops in company with a lady in magenta silk'. Altogether, it seemed, their holiday had turned out pretty uneventful.

Then, after Ralph almost caught Carrington and Brenan together, Gerald agreed to leave. 'You can't think how I minded sending you away,' Carrington apologized to him (30 August 1921). '. . . my heart was almost breaking and my eyes crying when you left.' 'It was getting more than I could stand,' Gerald agreed (5 September 1921). 'I was no longer satisfied at being with you, not even kissing you – I did the only possible thing in coming away.' But Ralph was angry that his friend had left and blamed Carrington for driving him away. She loved Ralph, but she had used Gerald for unconscious revenge against his bullying and her dependence on him for the happiness of Tidmarsh. Sometimes 'I pour coals of contempt on my head for not taking more risks,' she wrote to Gerald (30 August 1921), 'for not being more adventurous, for not spending more time with you.' Then her mood would change and she would (14 September 1921) 'Pray God the truth will never leak out.'

As for Gerald, he felt that they were soul-mates and that Carrington had married the wrong man. 'Oh, if I had never come back to England,' he lamented, 'if I never had, if I never had! I should then have been living an eventless life in Spain, calling myself happy . . . I have lain awake sometimes thinking that soon I shall see you no more for 8 months, and I feel absolutely sick at the thought. I do not want, as things are, to be with you any longer; but to be without you is horrible. It is like going out suddenly into complete darkness.'

3

VIEWS AND REVIEWS

'One wonders whether one has been quite wise in coming North,' Lytton had written to Virginia from Watendlath Farm (23 August 1921). Now early in September, he floated south again, staying with the Woolfs at Monk's House, the Hutchinsons at Eleanor House, and the Bells at Charleston, where 'I read for the first time the (almost) complete account of Oscar's trials,' he told Carrington (September 1921). '. . . It is very interesting and depressing. One of the surprising features is that he very nearly got off. If he had, what would have happened I wonder? I fancy the history of English culture might have been quite different, if a juryman's stupidity had chanced to take another turn.'

There were plenty of invitations this autumn: from Ottoline and Lady Astor, the Sitwells, Lady Colefax and Princess Bibesco. At Cambridge, as Maynard's guest, he met another batch of post-war undergraduates, and grew absorbed again by Apostolic affairs. Among those who became his friends and whom he began inviting back for weekends to Tidmarsh were George ('Dadie') Rylands,[11] a feline, fair-haired Etonian of great poise and elegance of dress, with a flair for stagecraft, then in his first year at King's and much under the influence of Sheppard; a brilliant and precocious logician Frank Ramsey, whose brother became Archbishop of Canterbury; and the three eldest Penrose brothers, Alec, 'a complete womanizer', as Lytton once called him, Lionel, the geneticist, and Roland, the art critic and biographer of Picasso. 'He [Alec] is a man of character (rare nowadays), and determined to be aesthetic,' Lytton informed James (28 November 1921), 'but I rather fear with no very great turn that way ... Lionel Penrose (younger brother) is at John's, and a complete flibbertigibbet, but attractive in a childish way, and somehow, in spite of an absence of brain, quite suitable in the Society.'[12]

Shortly after the publication of *Eminent Victorians*, Geoffrey Whitworth had suggested to Lytton that he bring out a volume of selected essays, as an interlude between his two biographies. 'Such a book would be sure of success,' Whitworth believed (4 April 1919), 'even though it might be slight in bulk.' But Lytton had already begun *Queen Victoria* and the scheme was dropped. After his biography had appeared, Lytton's mind did not immediately revert to this idea. He discussed various biographical projects with Virginia, in particular the 'History of the Reign of George IV', which she considered to be a magnificent subject for him. But there were difficulties. 'The worst of George IV', he said one afternoon over tea at Verreys, 'is that no one mentions the facts I want. History must be written all over again. It's all morality.' 'And battles,' Virginia added.

While he was thus undecided, Chatto & Windus wrote to remind him of Whitworth's original proposition for a volume of essays, this time making him a definite offer. Lytton at once accepted and opened up bargaining with his American publishers, Harcourt Brace. 'I don't think you heard the end of my negotiations with Mr Brace,' he reported to James (28 November 1921), '– they were perfectly hectic, and I spent days in which I alternated between the vast halls of the Hotel Cecil and the office of the Authors' Society, where poor Mr [Herbert] Thring[13] assisted me with his advice and exclamations.

'Mr Brace was a very pale, worn out American, with the inevitable tortoises, and we had a high old time, struggling and bargaining in the strangest style. I made a gallant effort to recapture the copyright of Victoria, but I found that he wanted more for it than I was willing to give, and it ended by my agreeing to let him have my next book (on very good terms) and the offer of two others, in exchange for £1500 down [equivalent to £27,000 in 1994]. It was an extraordinary, prolonged and feverish battle, at the end of which Mr Brace nearly dropped dead, as with shaking hand and ashy face he drew out his cheque-book. He had begun by offering £1200; but at the last moment I was able suddenly to raise my terms, and in a jiffy I had made £300. I can only hope that in some mysterious way I haven't been let in – but Mr Thring supported my every movement.'

Once these arrangements had been settled, Lytton returned to Tidmarsh where, over the next two months, he busied himself choosing from the many reviews and articles he had written since Cambridge days. Finally, he selected fourteen essays – including those on Beddoes, Blake, Sir Thomas Browne, Samuel Johnson, Rousseau, Shakespeare, Stendhal and Voltaire – all composed between 1904 and 1919, to make up this volume, passing each of them through a fine comb of textual emendation and making extensive alterations to the earlier ones such as 'Racine' in which he rewrote no fewer than twenty-three passages. Some of his corrections were trivial; others smoothed away awkward or redundant phrases which stood out when he read them aloud. 'Still others', records C.R. Sanders, who made a line-by-line comparison of the essays in the first and second versions,[14] and documented all discrepancies, 'are motivated by the desire to convert journalistic articles and reviews into literary essays.' Footnotes were dropped or drastically reduced, adjectives cut, some new illustrative material and the occasional amusing comment were added, and the number of parallel constructions increased.

The most interesting revisions were stylistic. They were of two kinds: those which tightened his prose, and those which added emphasis to the original narrative. Some long transitional passages were either trimmed or thrown out altogether. Opinions concerning living authors were sometimes toned down or occasionally qualified by the insertion of a 'perhaps'. A few long paragraphs were broken up to make for easier reading, but more often Lytton would fuse two paragraphs together so as to achieve an effect of greater weight. He also provided several quotations only alluded to in the earlier text.

He had thought of calling the collection *Views and Reviews*, but rejected this after discovering that W.E. Henley had already used it. 'Help! Help!' he implored Pippa (31 January 1922). 'The title question is pressing, and I am almost desperate. What do you think of "Books and Brains" – with "French and English" added underneath on the title page? A mixture of pure literature and biography should be indicated . . . Send a p.c. if you or

Lady S. have any suggestions.' Two days later he decided on *Books and Characters* – 'tame but harmless', as he told Pippa adding 'French & English' to the title page.

Books and Characters was dedicated 'To John Maynard Keynes' and came out on 18 May 1922 in Britain and a month later in the United States. The press notices were generally favourable, often praising the literary criticism at the expense of the biography. A reviewer in *The Times* congratulated Lytton on having 'cleared the honour of the nation. He has repaired past sacrileges by publishing the finest essay upon Racine which has ever been written in English … Mr Strachey's is perhaps the finest critical intelligence at work in English literature to-day.'[15] Middleton Murry, in the *Athenaeum*, described him as 'neither iconoclast nor hero-worshipper' but a 'man with a critical intelligence of the first order' who 'goes about redressing the injustices of time'.[16] To Aldous Huxley, he appeared 'a superlatively civilized Red Indian living apart from the vulgar world in an elegant park-like reservation', who rarely looked over the walls at the surrounding country. 'It seethes, he knows, with crowds of horribly colonial persons. Like the hosts of Midian, the innumerable "poor whites" prowl and prowl around, but the noble savage pays no attention to them.'[17]

Books and Characters led to a reissue of *Landmarks in French Literature* the following year, and consolidated his reputation as a post-Swinburnian literary critic in the manner of Walter Raleigh and Edmund Gosse rather than a biographical innovator. Many readers were grateful for this step. 'He had achieved some of his best, least popular work, in *Landmarks in French Literature* and *Books and Characters*,' Hugh Trevor-Roper was to write, '– early works which by their sympathy seem more mature than his later, more famous studies.'[18]

His growing eminence was marked by the award of a Benson Silver Medal and an invitation from the Royal Society of Literature to become a member of its Academic Committee.[19] This last offer he rejected and after sending back a polite letter of refusal disclaiming his 'election', he asked Edmund Gosse, himself on the Academic Committee, to act as his interpreter. 'It would be futile to argue the pros and cons of Academics and similar bodies in general,' he explained to Gosse (30 December 1922), 'and I realise that a good case may be made out for them; but so far as I am personally concerned I am convinced that I should really be out of place in one. This is as much a matter of instinct as of reason. Perhaps it is regrettable, but the fact remains that, as Saint-Simon said of himself: "Je ne suis pas un sujet académique" … if I am ever able to do any service to Literature, it will be as an entirely independent person and not as a member of a group.'

In the United States, *Books and Characters* went through five more impressions that year, and in Britain the first printing of five thousand copies was sold within a month, forcing Chatto & Windus to order another five thousand copies immediately and later embarrassing them to the extent of selling fifteen thousand more copies in their Phoenix Library. Between the spring of 1918 and the autumn of 1921, Lytton had earned almost eight thousand pounds (equivalent to around £140,000 in the early 1990s), but had escaped income tax.[20] 'The authorities here seem to have overlooked my existence,' he had confided to Maynard (11 November 1921), 'and if this happy state of things could continue, so much the better.' But he knew that it could not, and when Maynard came down to Tidmarsh with 'his attendant slave' Sebastian Sprott that Christmas, Lytton asked his advice. Maynard also gave him a 'detailed list of stocks of every kind, in which he insists that I shall put all I have. There is no choice but to submit, and face bankruptcy.'

Following the publication of *Queen Victoria*, Lytton had languished somewhat. 'I put it down to the Winter – the agony of thick underclothes, etc. etc.; but of course it may be sheer deliquescence of the brain,' he confessed to Virginia (6 February 1922). 'Anyhow, from whatever cause, I am sans eyes, sans teeth, sans prick, sans . . . but after that there can be no more sanses, – and on the whole I feel more like a fish gasping on a bank than anything else. It is terrible. I hope wildly that a change will come with the swallows . . .'

He had recently joined the Oriental Club, of which his father had been a prominent member,[21] and this new status, he felt, suited very well his winter senility. The place was like a luxurious mausoleum. 'Very ormolu,' Carrington noted in one of her letters to Noel. 'Full of old Indian Dug Outs.' And Lytton, in a letter to Virginia (6 February 1922), described it as 'a vast hideous building . . . filled with vast hideous Anglo-Indians, very old and very rich. One becomes 65, with an income of £5000 a year, directly one enters it. One is so stout one can hardly walk, and one's brain works with an extraordinary slowness. Just the place for me, you see, in my present condition. I almost pass unnoticed with my glazed eyes and white hair, as I sink into a leather chair heavily with a copy of the Field in hand. Excellent claret too – one of the best cellars in London, by Jove. You *must* come! I'll write again soon, if you can bear it.' But when he did write again, four days later, it was the same tale of lassitude. 'The horror of getting up is unparalleled, and I am filled with amazement every morning when I find that I have done it. To my mind there is clearly only one test of wealth, and that is – a fire in one's bedroom. Until one can have that at any and every moment, one is poor. Oh, for a housemaid at dawn!'

Towards the end of February, Ralph took Carrington to Vienna to see James and Alix, who was ill with pleurisy, while Lytton, who paid for the journey, moved up to Gordon Square. Without an anaesthetic, the doctors had to cut a section of Alix's ribs away to clean her lungs 'and she can use only one lung to breathe with now,' Carrington wrote to Lytton. 'But ever since the operation she has been getting a little better ... Poor James is very exhausted.' She cooked special meals on a small burner for James, but was not allowed to see Alix, whose temperature rose whenever Carrington's name was mentioned.

In London, life 'has been proceeding in its usual style of utter dullness punctuated by hectic frenzies', Lytton wrote to Carrington on his forty-second birthday. 'One of the latter occurred last night – a very absurd party at Lady Astor's to meet Mr Balfour – a huge rout – 800 extremely mixed guests – Duchesses, Rothensteins, Prime Ministers, Stracheys (male and female) – never did you see such a sight!

'As it was pouring cats and dogs the scene of jostling taxis and motors in St James's Square was terrific – it was practically full up. No one could get out it was so wet – for hours we sat ticking and cursing and occasionally edging an inch or two nearer the portals of bliss. To add to the confusion, various streams entered the Square by the side streets, and mingled with the cars. However the police and the good nature of the English lower classes saved the situation. If such a thing had happened in Paris it would have been simply Pandemonium. As it was, it was merely a great bore. The P.M. was leaving as we entered. Horror of horrors! The Rt. Hon. gentleman did *not recognise* Lytton Strachey! – though he bowed very politely – as did Mrs Lloyd George – an unparalleled frump. Mr Balfour was very complimentary behind large demi-ghostly spectacles.'

When Carrington returned from Vienna, Lytton joined her and Ralph back at Tidmarsh. All of them seemed precariously happy. 'I miss him so much when he leaves,' Carrington had written to Gerald (12 October 1921). 'I love his appearance so much & there is an emptiness in the rooms & garden when he has left.' But Ralph, who was not enjoying work at the Hogarth Press, sometimes talked of going to North Africa as a war correspondent. As for Lytton, his amorous adventures and those of his friends seemed to have become ominously suspended.

4

VALENTINE'S DAY

Over the past six months, since Gerald sailed away to Spain, Carrington had been writing to him every few days; and he had replied. Although Ralph insisted on reading their correspondence, he still suspected nothing – principally because there were postscripts to these letters, on separate sheets of paper, which he never saw. Now, at the beginning of April, they were all to meet again, Lytton and Carrington and Ralph and Gerald, at Larrau, as guests of Valentine and Bonamy Dobrée, in the Basses-Pyrénées. Carrington and Ralph had spent their wedding night with the Dobrées when they lived in Paris; and Gerald had stayed with them at Larrau on his way back from England the previous autumn, pouring out his feelings about Carrington to Valentine but failing to notice Valentine's passionate interest in himself. Early in 1922 the Dobrées had visited Spain, and it was then that Valentine laid her plans with Gerald for this spring reunion. She promised to 'distract' Ralph so that Gerald and Carrington could be together – and even stole into his bed so that she could expound her plans more intimately. But Gerald 'couldn't fall in love' with anyone but Carrington, and climbed out of bed to write to her about their new arrangements. Both of them were mad with excitement. 'I only want to be happy with you,' Carrington answered (12 March 1922), '& have as few regrets as possible. I have a feeling we might achieve this at Larrau.' She felt additionally excited by the involvement of Valentine. 'Everything she does moves me strangely.' In fact she could not understand Gerald preferring herself. Valentine 'is so much more talented beautiful, & charming than your Doric', she pointed out. Nevertheless she was secretly 'bringing out enough money for you to come back to England with', she told him. '. . . Lytton is so delightful. This time I insist on you knowing him better.'

To Ralph's joy the Dobrées' house overlooked a trout stream. It seemed to Carrington a perfect place to re-enact the kissing and fishing of Watendlath Farm. They arrived with Lytton on 5 April and Gerald, an amazing figure leaping down the bare mountains and through the woods, appeared out of the mists four days later. All around were deep valleys coated with the greenest grass, and everywhere grew tall bracken spreading itself into arches. Beech forests covered the headwaters of the streams, and above these, standing out against the sky, pointed the sharp peaks of red and yellow rock. 'We are pretty high up among the hills,' Lytton wrote to Pippa (7 April 1922), '– a charming house full of the local furniture – armoires and cupboards innumerable – in a small village, with steep heights on every side. Everything seems quite nice, though not exciting. There is hope of fishing, when the streams, which are at present Niagaras, subside . . . I am writing this in a basque bed, but now I shall have to get up and go downstairs and face the family. Le père de Madame (an Anglo-Indian planter, I gather) is rather distressing. He once went out to shoot Bustards in Nagpore, but never found any . . . However, Madame herself is very agreeable and sings Italian songs very nicely after dinner.'

'Valentine's diplomacy will count for much,' Carrington had written to Gerald. But the dark voluptuous Valentine was not a natural diplomat. It was strange that she had ever married her dry dull diminutive donnish husband[22] – 'a nimble second-rate man', Virginia called him – unless it was on account of his complaisance. She was rumoured to have been Derain's mistress and had been lovingly painted by Mark Gertler who stayed with her in Paris and was soon to come out to Larrau. She gave 'a touch of genius', Gertler said, to everything she did. Carrington, who had got to know her at the Slade, thought her as remarkable in her way as Alix.

A late snow had fallen on the lilac blossom, and while Ralph fished below, and Lytton sat silently listening to Bonamy Dobrée trying out passages from his book on Elizabethan tragedy, Gerald, upstairs in the attic, would pose for Carrington. Unfortunately Ralph appeared to have taken a violent dislike to Valentine, and was persistently rude to her, so that the atmosphere grew embarrassingly strained. But Carrington seemed more drawn to her than to Gerald who at a critical moment won back her sympathy by lapsing into impotence. Even more inexplicably, at least to Lytton, Valentine started flirting with Ralph. On the last day of their visit, to everyone's astonishment, Ralph and Valentine fell into each other's arms.

No sooner had this happened than, the very next morning, Lytton, Ralph and Carrington packed up and hurried away via Toulouse and Provence, back to England. They were pursued across the Continent by the passionate Valentine, and the distracted Gerald, who, absent-mindedly rejecting Valentine's advances a second time, was delayed by having to collect a sleeping bag and the camping kit which he had abandoned on his journey from Yegen in the deep snow of the Roncesvalles Pass. They were entering 'a vertigo of ever-intensifying complications'.

Gerald, his moods swinging wildly between elation, jealousy and despair, put up at Pangbourne during May, while Ralph proceeded openly to carry on his impetuous affair with Valentine in London, adopting a very disparaging attitude to Carrington. For some weeks it looked as if the whole Tidmarsh regime was about to disintegrate. Carrington, in despair, appealed to Lytton, who counselled patience, in the meantime sending Bonamy Dobrée some books on the Elizabethan dramatists. Up to this time, Gerald had kept his relations with Carrington confined to a more or less platonic level, out of a rather tarnished sense of loyalty to Ralph (whom he nevertheless knew to have been previously unfaithful). Now, when Ralph and Valentine went off for a few days together, he and Carrington began a sexual affair. Carrington was frightened that they might 'spoil the pleasure we get from being friends by having complications and too many secrets from Ralph'. Confusions, she warned Gerald, disrupt intimacies. It was as if she had a presentiment that everything would go wrong. 'I have lost something which seems to prevent me giving myself away completely ever again,' she wrote (early June 1922). All the same, she reassured him: 'in some ways I can give you everything and I do give you a great deal of love.'

Then the storm burst. While they were away together, Valentine revealed to Ralph that his wife and his best friend had fallen in love. She told, him of the love-making that had taken place at Watendlath Farm, and that, in the Pyrenees, Gerald, Carrington and herself had hatched an adulterous 'Larrau Plot' by which she should flirt with Ralph so as to leave Carrington and Gerald alone together. Valentine had not forgiven Gerald for his offhand rejections of her and, sensing her sexual superiority to Carrington, used all she had been told, and much she imagined, to establish her relationship with Ralph. But though he believed everything she told him, he would never feel much for her again. To Barbara Bagenal he confided that, regretfully, he would have to kill Gerald. He also rushed round to Mark Gertler to obtain particulars of Carrington's sexual involvement with him. But his first actions were still more dangerous. He drank half a bottle of whisky and drove furiously down to Tidmarsh in a car that Lytton had recently given him. It seemed that he considered it quite proper for him to have a love-affair with a married woman, though outrageous for Carrington to take a lover. But there was more to it than this – there was the humiliating deception – Valentine with her 'touch of genius' had told him that everyone knew of the affair except himself. He liked to think that he believed in openness at all times – and in comparison to Carrington he was remarkably open. She cherished her secrecy and would conceal small quite unobjectionable matters to safeguard her privacy. The key to Ralph's character lay in his belief that marriage and friendship meant trust and communication. His frenzy on hearing Valentine's revelations was caused less by questions of technical infidelity – though these became important – than by the dissimulation. The knowledge of this deceit damaged his marriage to an extent that no patchings up could really heal.

After a tremendous argument with Carrington in the Mill House, Ralph dispatched a telegram to Gerald demanding to see him in London. When they met at Hogarth House he announced that unless Gerald could promise him that he had had no sexual intercourse with Carrington, he would leave her and end the marriage. Gerald, who had been secretly briefed by Carrington at the 1917 Club, concentrating his mind on Watendlath and Larrau to the exclusion of what had happened over the last month at Tidmarsh, admitted to a romantic flirtation, but denied any 'interference'. Although his instincts were still to tell his friend the truth, he felt that he had no right, by doing so, to endanger Carrington's life with Lytton. Besides, since Ralph was asking about an earlier period he was telling him the literal truth. Ralph, now somewhat at a loss, replied with stern uncertainty that he would have to consider what he would do, but that if he decided to go on living with Carrington, then Gerald must return to Spain and give his word never to communicate with her again. Gerald promised. There was nothing else that he could do. The first person in Carrington's life was always Lytton, and Gerald himself could never hope to take Ralph's place. So, briefly and for the last time, Gerald returned to Tidmarsh to tell Carrington what had happened. Over lunch with her and Lytton his hands trembled so violently he could hardly hold his knife and fork. His life seemed in ruins. He returned to London and waited for Carrington to see him once more before he set sail for Spain on 14 June. But she did not come. Instead he was besieged by Valentine which added to his distress, but came as a relief to his parents as evidence that he was not homosexual. 'I am very sorry for him,' Lytton wrote to Ralph. 'He has injured himself very badly, and his life at the best of times was not a particularly pleasant one.' The day after he sailed, Lytton sent Gerald an encouraging letter.

'Things are still unsettled here and the first necessity is to clear the atmosphere. Letters between you might seem ambiguous to Ralph, and all ambiguities just now are to be avoided.

. . . I hope you will go on writing. From the little I've seen of your work, it seemed to me to differ *in kind* from everything else going about by writers of your generation. To my mind there is a streak of inspiration in it, which is very rare and very precious indeed.

. . . Things have turned out unhappily; but never forget that, whatever happens, and in spite of all estrangements, you are loved by those you love best.

Yours ever affectionately,
Lytton Strachey'

This letter shows the compassion of someone who had himself suffered in love-affairs. It also illustrates what Bloomsbury, at its best, meant by civilized behaviour in personal relations, and how difficult others sometimes found it to accept this behaviour. For Bloomsbury refused to accede any rights or claims to jealousy. 'Please forgive me the unhappiness I have caused to you as well as to others and do not think too badly of me,' Gerald wrote to Lytton the night before his departure. 'And thank you for the kindness you have always shown me. It has been a great pleasure to me to have known you and to have caught a glimpse at Tidmarsh of people who cultivate a free, happy and civilised life. Now that I have lost my part in it, I see all its attractions.'

He had lost his best friend and the love of his life. But though he felt guilty at having contributed to their unhappiness, the turmoil still seemed senseless and unnecessary. He could not change his love or friendship, and he could not altogether regret what he had done.[23] 'But that, among reasonable people,' he wrote to Lytton from Spain (14 July 1922), 'I who am fond of Ralph, can be – O wonderful irony! Too fond of C, and that without being the cause of their seeing less of each other or of their affections diminishing, and without my wishing for anything new for myself – that by these good and innocent means can be so great a source of unhappiness to all of us – is nothing less to me than madness, madness, horrible madness . . .'

5

DIPLOMATIC ASIDES

The task of reintroducing a spirit of affection into Tidmarsh during the next eighteen months was predominantly Lytton's. Finding some common ground on which to renew their relationship presented a difficult exercise in diplomacy. First of all he had to reconcile Ralph to Carrington. Neither of them would consent to see the other until he had negotiated a face-saving settlement. He started off by assuring Carrington that he sympathized absolutely with her feelings, and that, however things might turn out, he would never leave her. Nevertheless, he insisted that she must keep this confidence to herself, and for a while at least, look with extraordinary leniency upon Ralph's indiscretions. 'Lytton was superb and tried to smooth it out,' Carrington reported to Alix Strachey (19 June 1922). '. . . [He] says R's complex about my virtue is almost insane. It has made him dreadfully wretched and reduced him to a man of nerves . . . R now says he can't face living with me at moments because I am such a fraud etc. Lytton thinks it will be alright in time.' But he warned her not to have any more affaires if she wanted to go on living with Ralph. 'As they were not even affaires,' she explained to Alix, 'romances I suppose is the only word . . . and as I have had no others, it isn't much sacrifice to give up this imaginary life of [a] rouée. I am now feeling as you'll see rather grim – perhaps the end of this rather wretched business will be I'll paint and be some good as an artist.'

Ralph himself, having tentatively agreed to return to Tidmarsh on certain conditions, was staying in the basement of Hogarth House pending Lytton's negotiations on his behalf. 'I think I was able to make her realize your feelings and point of view,' Lytton wrote to him (June 1922). 'Of course, she was, and is, terribly upset. She said that you were essential to her – that Gerald was not at all – that this crisis had made her realize more than ever before the strength of her love for you. I explained your dread of a scene, reconciliations, etc., and said you wanted to sleep in the yellow room. She quite understood. I am sure that she loves you deeply. Be as gentle with her as you can when you come.

'We must try now to forget all those horrid details, and trust to the force of our fundamental affections to carry us through. At any rate, we know where we are now, which is a great thing.

. . . As for me, my dear, I can't say how happy your decision to try going on here has made me. I suppose I *could* face life without you, just as I could *face* life with one of my hands cut off, but it would have been a dreadful blow . . .

. . . my nerves are rather on the jump, and I am longing for your presence – the best restorative I know of! I sympathise with you so absolutely, so completely, my dear, dear love. Sometimes I feel as if I *was* inside you! Why can't I make you perfectly happy by waving some magic wand?

Keep this letter to yourself.'

The route having been paved for Ralph's return, Lytton did what he could to make life at Tidmarsh delightful. He would invite over for week-ends the most amusing of his new Cambridge friends whom Ralph liked and who adored Carrington, and older luminaries such as E.M. Forster who spread a calming influence. He had also bought a car and since neither Carrington nor he understood it and 'R.P. is a born driver', this increased their joint dependence on Ralph together with his sense of responsibility towards them – though Lytton assured him that 'of course you know the little car belongs to you'. Then, after Ralph complained about his job at the Hogarth Press – his poor income and prospects – Lytton stepped in and tried to reason his case with Virginia. 'There have been various conversations on the Hogarth question – with rather indeterminate results,' he reported to her (19 September 1922). 'I think the poor creature is really anxious to continue, but foresees difficulties. He is already brushing up his energies! On the whole I gather that he thinks less printing and more business might be a solution. Perhaps if some department in the business could be handed over in toto to him he would fling himself into it with more zest. But this is only a vague suggestion, and so please don't draw conclusions from it. I suppose he will write himself before long. The distance from London question is a very trying one.'

Lytton was 'extremely adroit' when speaking up for Ralph. It was clear that he was still tremulously in love with him, taking pleasure in his simplicity though acting in a fatherly way on behalf of both Ralph and Carrington. 'One cannot treat lovers like rational people,' he reminded Virginia, remembering his own tortures over Duncan and Henry. Of course it was probably true that Ralph's uncertainties at the Hogarth Press were exacerbating the difficulties of his marriage. 'It's all very distressing,' Virginia wrote to Vanessa (22 December 1922), 'as I feel slightly responsible for that marriage . . . And if it is true that we are all responsible for the sins of all, surely we ought to sink together?' Nor can it have been easy for a vigorous and educated young man to spend so much time in the Hogarth basement among the parcels and printing press. Yet Ralph threw away so many of Lytton's valid points, debasing his arguments when, for example, hinting that he would get Lytton's next bestseller for the Hogarth if he was promoted; or, if he got the sack, describing how he would set up a rival publishing house at Tidmarsh with Lytton's money. Such schoolboy craftiness put Virginia on edge. 'We wont be downed by the prestige & power & pomposity of all the Benson medallists in England,' she burst out (7 January 1923). '. . . Love is the devil.'

Love had a specially devilish effect on Ralph. 'We have a mad bull in the house – a normal Englishman in love,' Virginia had noted in her diary (23 June 1922), '& deceived.' At the best of times he was, as Carrington had observed, 'ill suited for any continuous labour'. Now he grew oddly undependable – lazy, industrious, grumpy, amiable, belligerent, disarming – all within a day. On the whole Virginia took Carrington's part. She was far subtler – and besides Virginia did not 'like to see women unhappy'. There could be no doubt that Carrington had lied, 'but then one must lie to children', and Ralph in the grip of his bullying passion was a child. His thoughtless remarks and insensitive actions made her blood boil whenever they inconvenienced Leonard, who would sometimes, she could see, turn white with rage. What she could not see, and Carrington did see, was that the Woolfs were 'perfect people to know as friends, but rather difficult as overseers, & business people'. In any case, publishing was a part time profession for them and only a part time hobby to Ralph. His grumblings and bellowings from the basement rose through the house and when he came upstairs, he was often bristling like a bear. 'I don't like the normal when it is 1000 horse power,' Virginia wrote (23 June 1922). 'His stupidity, blindness, callousness, struck me more powerfully than the magic virtues of passion . . . It was the stupidity of virility that impressed me – & how, having made those convenient railway lines of convention, the lusts speed along them, unquestioning.'

That December, after a weekend at Tidmarsh, Leonard agreed that Ralph should give three months' notice. 'The breach with the Woolfs, long anticipated, has at last been achieved – by whom I can't say,' Ralph wrote (22 December 1922). '. . . I didn't comprehend them and they didn't comprehend me, two years ago, or we should never have embarked on partnership.' There was some discussion about a Tidmarsh Press to bring out Lytton's extravaganzas, but instead Lytton was to employ him as his secretary to answer correspondence, deal with the Inland Revenue, publishers, editors, and assist with proof reading. 'I thank you for trying so valiantly at Tidmarsh to come to a happy ending,' Carrington wrote to Virginia (21 December 1922). 'But perhaps reviewing everything now it will all turn out for the best.' Virginia would have given 'a good deal to combine with Lytton in producing literature', but there had been no more practical chance of achieving this perhaps than of achieving a successful marriage with him – and to have his subtle ideas blared through Ralph's brass trumpet was exasperating. In some ways she was sorry to see him go because she liked the association with Tidmarsh. But the parting has been reasonably amiable and she was able to reassure Carrington (25 December 1922) that 'all friendships remain intact'.

This was only one of the problems Lytton had to solve. To outward appearances the triangular ménage at the Mill House went on very much as before. 'You have no idea what a perfect life we lead here,' Carrington wrote to her brother Noel (25 July 1922). '3 Hives of Bees, 30 ducks, 30 chickens, a Forest of delicious raspberries, and peas, and a Roman Bath to bathe in out of doors. Annie who is a gay little girl of sixteen, exquisitely lovely, who cooks and housekeeps for us all and then Lytton who is a paragon of a friend, who buys new books for our delight. The new car is a great joy. We go lovely rides in it . . .'

But under the surface, everything was still in crisis. For Carrington these summer months were miserable, and she was often in tears. Her deceits and subterfuges shamed her. She feared that she had lost Lytton's confidence and that it would be impossible to pick up the pieces of their shattered lives together. At the same time there seemed no alternative but to go on living at the Mill House where 'everything was completely awfull for me'. She missed Gerald's letters 'more than I ever thought, in my wildest moments, I should, and when one mustn't talk of it, it keeps on tormenting my head. But I won't talk of him because it only makes me remember him more.' Each day she wrote him an account of her feelings and everything that had happened since he left. 'I shall write a life of myself at intervals in the form of letters to you,' she recorded (14 June 1922). But she would not send it to him 'for, perhaps a whole year'. She was so worn out that she no longer knew what was in her mind or anyone else's mind. She still believed there existed enough between them all to make it worth going on, though perhaps it was only a matter of time before the final break-up. 'We've forty years probably to think it all over!' she wrote to Gerald. '. . . I feel a captive now. My spirit has gone . . . the play is over, the audience has left; the epilogue has been said.'

Lytton went on calming and reassuring her, but she felt that Ralph's love had changed to hatred. Sometimes he was completely silent, looking so ill and upset she could not bear to see him. At other times he was gripped with such a frenzy of rage that his face would grow distorted beyond recognition. Thoughts of Carrington and Gerald were a torture to him. He longed to drive them from his imagination, yet he could not really dislike Gerald, could not cut himself off from Carrington. 'As a friend I cannot love her,' he wrote, '. . . as a lover, not a husband, she is so tainted . . . yet she has been three quarters of my life to me for many years, and I can't operate on myself for the removal of such a vital portion without intolerable pain.'

He was openly continuing his affair with Valentine, bringing her down to Tidmarsh and sleeping with her there, while suggesting that Carrington go off to Vienna to be 'cured' of her lies and delusions by Dr Freud. 'I can tell you it was pretty intolerable,' Carrington admitted in a secret letter to Gerald later in the year (19 October 1922). Valentine seemed determined to 'push matters as far as she can', blowing upon the embers of Ralph's jealousy to bring the Tidmarsh regime crashing down. It was all the more tormenting for Carrington since she had herself felt a strong sexual attraction to Valentine: 'It follows from my lustful sapphism.' At first she could only believe that Valentine had acted 'unconsciously' and did not 'mean all this pain'. But now she saw her as a female Iago beside Ralph's impersonation of Othello. 'Its only when he gets with her, & she writes to him everyday, that Tidmarsh seems rather dull, & Lytton and me "cold fishes",' Carrington wrote in her journal for Gerald. Lytton had told her that Valentine was incapable of making Ralph happy, that had they loved each other they would already have gone away, and that Ralph was still sleeping with her chiefly from motives of revenge. It was impossible to welcome such a mischief-maker into their lives, he said, and the affair would soon die a natural death.

A little later that summer Bonamy Dobrée finally lost his patience and summoned his wife back to Larrau. She went, taking a new lover, Mark Gertler. Mark had always hated Ralph (he used to call him 'the Policeman') and may have felt there was some retributive justice in supplanting him. But to Lytton it seemed the best opportunity yet for Ralph and Carrington to get on terms again. This might more easily come about, he believed, if he himself were not there looking on. He therefore made plans to leave for a fortnight in Venice with Maynard's lover Sebastian Sprott. But before leaving, he invited 'bright little Barbara' Bagenal down to Tidmarsh to keep an eye on Carrington.

Lytton and Sebastian put up at the Casa Frollo in the Giudecca, a 'nice sort of broken-down place, which will just suit us', Lytton had told his sister Pippa (22 June 1922). The one drawback was a typically Venetian one – noise. 'An ice factory, if you please, is next door, and naturally chooses the hour of 3 a.m. for its most agitating operations – sounds of terrific collapses and crushes shake the earth, and I awake in terror of my life.' Otherwise everything was as beautiful as the previous year when Ralph and Carrington had joined him for their honeymoon. 'Venice is very lovely – but oh dear! *not* so lovely by half as it was last year,' he wrote to Carrington (July 1922). 'Such a difference does the mind make upon matters! Sebastian is really charming – most easy to get on with, most considerate, very gay, and interested in everything that occurs ... Of course he is young – also, somehow, not what you might call an "intimate" character – which has its advantages too. Nor is he passionate – but inclined if anything to be sentimental, though too clever to be so in a sickly style. His sentimentality is not directed towards me ...'

Lytton's own sentimentality was directed towards a 'sublime' gondolier named Francesco, whom he had already eyed on his earlier stay there. 'Francesco carries one to the Piazzetta in about 10 minutes, according to wind and obstacles,' he wrote to Ralph (24 June 1922).

'He is exactly the same as ever. It was luck being able to have him ... a few weeks after we went away last summer a new rule was made by which no one was allowed to hire a gondolier for more than a day at a time – except old clients – under which heading I mercifully come! Apparently Berenson last July tried to take Francesco as I did, with the result that a mob of enraged gondoliers collected booing and shouting, and he was nearly torn limb from limb. But *I* was at once recognised, and no mob assailed me . . . the rule was made by the degraded gondoliers, who found they were losing all their custom. It seems to me next year they'll do away with the blessed privileges of "old clients" as well – the pigs . . . Sebastian enjoys everything very much, and keeps up a constant chatter of a mild kind, which just suits me at the present moment. I can't say he looks ultra respectable, with a collarless shirt, very décolleté, and the number of glad eyes he receives is alarming. However so far his *behaviour* has been all that could be desired.'

The news from Tidmarsh during these weeks was bleak. Ralph had suggested that the only way of reviving their relationship was for Carrrington to have his child – his parents would certainly then give them some money. But this seemed to her impossible. At moments she even contemplated ending her life. Barbara was 'very understanding and I think her calmness and simple affection has a wonderful influence,' she wrote to Lytton. But she was sleeping badly and realized in his absence how much she relied on Lytton. 'Thank you, Lytton for all you have done for me, and for him, trying to make us both happy,' she wrote (21 June 1922). 'You alone prevented me many days from committing acts of madness and flying away somewhere.'

It did not sound as if they were drawing any closer and at moments Lytton felt discouraged – 'a feeling that everything is too difficult and fearful – a feeling of the futility of life'. But such moods passed, and his letters to Carrington are cheerful while those to Ralph reveal more of his anxieties. Was he returning from Venice too early? Would it ease matters if he stayed at Gordon Square for ten days before coming down to Tidmarsh? Had Ralph already forgotten him? The uncertainties of the last months had stimulated Lytton's affection. 'I hug you a hundred times and bite your ears. Don't you still realise what I feel for you? how profoundly I love you? . . . I wish I could talk to you now . . . I am always your own Lytton.'

As soon as he got back, he resumed patching and repairing their broken marriage, trying everything he knew to expel the uneasy atmosphere that still hung over the Mill House. During August he sublet Tidmarsh and took Ralph and Carrington on a five weeks' motor tour of Devon and Wales. But things went badly. After three weeks 'we have had exactly two fine days, and on one of them the motor broke down, so that we spent most of it in a garage.' They were constantly on the move from one dreadful and exorbitant hotel to another. 'I think my next work will be a fulmination on the Hotels of England.'

In the third week of August, they took rooms for ten days at Solva, near St David's. 'It is on the snout of Wales – a sea coast in the Cornwall style with rocks, coves, and islands, and would be perfect if there were any sun to see it in,' Lytton wrote to Pippa (18 August 1922). It was a relief to be settled at last in this empty spot – but not for Carrington and Ralph. Once there was no succession of calamities to distract them from their personal antagonisms, the tension mounted quickly; then exploded. All the time they had been travelling, Carrington could sense Ralph's thoughts fixed on Valentine, who was coming back to London. At Solva, angry scenes broke out. Carrington complained that since she had sacrificed Gerald, Ralph should give up Valentine whom she cursed for 'all this havoc!' Ralph retorted that he had no objection now to her and Gerald being friends – and at once sat down and wrote off a letter to Gerald to tell him so. 'If you're as wretched as I am, I'm heartily sorry for you.' According to Ralph, Carrington had subtly imposed this law of non-communication upon herself so as to put him in the wrong with Valentine. So they argued, and as the days passed and the arguments blazed on, the sun began to shine and the atmosphere between them gradually cleared.

On the first day of September they motored back to Tidmarsh. That same day Valentine returned with Mark Gertler to London, and Carrington, dreading another period of misery leading to an ultimate crisis, broke down. All that she most valued seemed to be slipping away from her. 'I love R very much,' she burst out in a letter to Gerald (19 October 1922). 'I suppose that when a person dies, or nearly leaves one for ever one becomes very aware of all one's feelings . . . I also love Lytton and I also love our life here, when I see other peoples lives I see how good this is . . . I care enough for it to put a good Deal of energy into opposing any enemy who threatens it.' The crisis she feared never materialized. By the end of October she and Ralph appeared to have reached some accommodation. So long as Carrington did not resume relations with Gerald, Ralph promised not to see Valentine. 'You say you mistrust Valentine,' he told her, 'and think she is wicked. I tell you that I mistrust Gerald, and think, not from wickedness but from thoughtlessness and vagueness he may imperil my happiness.'

No one was more responsible for this amnesty than Lytton. 'Lytton is still my Caesar, or whatever the expression is,' Carrington wrote that autumn. 'Through all the scenes, the wretchednesses, he has been amazing. If it hadn't been for his friendship I should have rushed away. He makes one see that one ought never to let other people's meannesses wreck one.'

Ralph, too, had stayed with Carrington during these terrible months because of a sense of loyalty to Lytton. Now his rage against Carrington evaporated and he seemed a different person to the tormented figure of the summer. 'My mind is perfectly restored to its balance,' he wrote (23 October 1922) to Gerald who also received confirmation from Carrington (1 January 1923) that 'Ralph has completely altered'. That winter he finally gave up Valentine and reaffirmed his intention to go on living at Tidmarsh. 'My relation with D.C. has reached the stage that can only continue by a mutual compromise,' he explained to Gerald (27 November 1922). 'It may look strong, but it has all these old patches which would open if any new crisis came.' Though he was not wholly easy in his mind, discounting the healing effects of time and believing they had passed through a minefield of misunderstandings ('Don't let's have any more mysteries'), yet their respective positions had by the end of the year 'been declared, re-declared, confirmed and receipted' so voluminously that he felt strongly re-attached to Carrington. But it was a different kind of attachment, less possessive, and one that would eventually invite further complications for them both.

As for Carrington herself nothing mattered compared to 'our Triangular Trinity of Happiness'. She no longer dreaded or feared Ralph, or felt that she had helped to ruin him. 'Oh Gerald you will never know what it was to be on the battlefield,' she wrote (14 November 1922). She wished she could see Gerald again soon. 'Is all this,' she asked him (1 January 1923), 'to have a Tchekov ending?'

6

AN IBSEN ENDING

'I am stiff – frozen stiff – a rigid icicle,' Lytton had written to Virginia from Pembrokeshire (22 August 1922). 'I hang at this address for another week, and slowly melt southwards and eastwards – a weeping relic of what was once your old friend.'

He had made out an elaborate schedule for his autumn visitings, joining Clive and Vanessa at Charleston and dividing the next week between them and the Woolfs at Monk's House. 'I pretend to read, and really do nothing but chat,' he wrote (27 September 1922). 'Clive and I go for vast walks over the downs, which have grown more beautiful than ever. Oh for a farmhouse at the foot of them, for my very own.' He looked forward to the winter which always seemed to bring with it a suspension of amorous entanglements. His spirit, so he confided to Mary Hutchinson (22 August 1922), had been almost broken by the events of the spring and summer. 'It would be indeed charming to see you again, and exchange confidences. But I hope you will lay in a good supply of wood, coal, mackintoshes, umbrellas and galoshes – rum punch for the evenings, too; followed, very likely, by glasses of porter in our bedrooms, warmed by red-hot pokers. I pray for Winter, when we shall be snug once more, and the sun will shine, and we will only *occasionally* shiver.'

Ottoline had been besieging him with invitations, so after leaving the Hutchinsons, Lytton went off for a 'pretty grim' weekend to Garsington, the other guests being the poet and critic W.J. Turner and his wife – 'a very small bird-like man with a desolating accent, a good deal to say for himself – but punctuated by strange hesitations – impediments – rather distressing; but really a nice little fellow, when one has got over the way in which he says "count"', he patronizingly wrote to Virginia (19 September 1922). 'Ott. was dreadfully dégringolée, her bladder has now gone the way of her wits – a melancholy dribble, and then, as she sits after dinner in the lamplight, her cheek-pouches drooping with peppermints, a cigarette between her false teeth, and vast spectacles on her painted nose, the effect produced is extremely agitating. I found I wanted to howl like an Irish wolf – but perhaps the result produced in you was different.'*

From Garsington he took himself off to the Manor House, Mells, for some days with Lady Horner. 'The house is a very charming one – the true country-house style, and the Horner famille seem a cut above the ordinary run of the upper classes. Lady H. has heard of Beaumont and Fletcher, and Katherine A[squith][24] dabbles in theology.' The following week, he left for a brief visit to Berlin with James, who was attending a congress on psychoanalysis, with Sigmund Freud in the chair – 'it seems a good opportunity of being shown round'. Later, the two brothers visited Potsdam and Sansouci, and saw the Voltaire *Zimmer* prepared by Frederick the Great, its walls decorated with monkeys, and with Voltaire's books still on the shelves.

In the new peaceful atmosphere, Lytton was more than content to pass

---

* On the same day Lytton wrote to Ottoline herself: 'It was a great pleasure to see you and to have some talks – I only wish there could have been more of them. Needless to say that I enjoyed my week-end very much. It was delightful to find Philip in such good trim, and I liked making the acquaintance of Turner. I hope your health is really taking a turn for the better at last. What a disgusting arrangement one's body does become when its machinery goes out of order.'

the winter at Tidmarsh. 'The winter is too terrible,' he wrote playfully to Maynard (28 November 1922). 'I can neither feel, think, nor write – I can only just breathe, read, and eat. I am impotent – my hair has turned perfectly white – my beard has fallen off...' But the winter, as he predicted, had brought a sweet cessation to their emotional dramas. Over Christmas, Maynard and his surprising mistress, the tiny Russian ballerina Lydia Lopokova, came down to stay, and Lytton wrote a short playlet for Carrington to produce for them in her toy theatre. So, quietly and harmlessly, the old year came to an end with Tidmarsh, like a vessel which had weathered a great tempest, gliding on its course.

*

The new year opened amiably with Lytton making few expeditions from the Mill House. One of these was to Cambridge, where he saw a performance of *Oedipus Rex* given by the Marlowe Society. Among the audience were many of his new undergraduate friends – F.L. Lucas, Stewart Perowne and Dadie Rylands, who had already made something of a name for himself in *The Duchess of Malfi*, acting the part of the Duchess. Cecil Beaton noted the scene in his diary. 'During the interval, the audience rushed to the club room to shout and smoke. Lytton Strachey peered at everyone through thick glasses, looking like an owl in daylight. He is immensely tall, and could be even twice his height if he were not bent as a sloppy asparagus. His huge hands fall to his sides, completely limp. His sugar-loaf beard is thick and dark, worn long in the fashion of an arty undergraduate.'[25]

He also made another visit to see Ottoline. 'Now I am off – est-il possible? – to Garsington,' he announced to James (February 1923). Ottoline's invitations were frequent and insistent, and despite his acid comments about her to others, Lytton remembered well enough her kindness to him in the past. She had now grown much less sympathetic to him, yet an afterglow of the old enchantment still glimmered round her house. Besides a core of the old Bloomsbury guard, there was usually an influx of clever pink-and-white undergraduates from Oxford with the guests. Among these younger men were Edward Sackville-West, David Cecil, L.P. Hartley, Lytton's cousin John Strachey and C.M. Bowra. One hot Sunday afternoon John Rothenstein records:

'I found myself with two companions, likewise Oxford undergraduates, in a house where none of us had been before, pausing at an open french window that gave upon a lawn, at the farther end of which a tea-party was in progress. We paused because the lawn was not so large that we could not discern among the tea-drinkers the figures of Lytton Strachey, Aldous

Huxley and Duncan Grant, as well as that, so awe-inspiring upon a first encounter, of our hostess Lady Ottoline Morrell. At that moment this modest patch of grass seemed to us an alarmingly large area to cross beneath the gaze of so many august eyes. So it is that I can still picture the group: Lytton Strachey inert in a low chair, red-bearded head dropped forward, long hands drooping, finger-tips touching the grass; Aldous Huxley talking, with his face turned up towards the sun; Duncan Grant, pale-faced, with a fine, untidy black hair, light eyes ready to be coaxed from their melancholy, and Lady Ottoline wearing a dress more suitable, one would have thought, for some splendid Victorian occasion, and an immense straw hat ... After listening to the discourse of Lytton Strachey and several others I vaguely apprehended that in this Oxfordshire village were assembled luminaries of a then to me almost unknown Cambridge world.'[26]

Early in March, Lytton went up to Gordon Square to be with his mother, who was now going completely blind. 'I hope it will not be long before I get sight of you,' she had scrawled with a shaky hand, in her last letter to him (February 1923). '... I am not able to see what I write, but I hope you will be able to read. Ever, dearest, Your Loving Mama.'

As the spring approached, Lytton again grew concerned over Ralph and Carrington. Ralph was already seeing a lot of 'new people, a younger generation than Bloomsbury ... rising talent, dancers and party-goers; the 1917 Club, new faces ...' Carrington suspected him of having 'at least four intrigues on foot with various lovely creatures in London' – certainly there was what Virginia called a 'Champagne love affair' with Marjorie Joad, the soi-disant wife of Professor C.E.M. Joad, whom Ralph was training to take his place at the Hogarth Press. The new regime at Tidmarsh was not yet resilient enough, Lytton judged, to withstand more shocks, and as soon as Ralph was at 'liberty from Woolfdom', he made plans for them all to travel abroad.

In the third week of March, the three of them set off for Algeria to join James and Alix at the Établissement Thermal, in the tiny inaccessible village of Hammam-Méskoutine a few miles south-west of Bône, where Alix was recovering from bronchitis. 'Apart from the unfortunate circumstances, it is a pleasure to be here,' Lytton wrote to Pippa (27 March 1923). '... The hotel is almost by itself in very beautiful country, with mountains all round, and masses of vegetation, and wild flowers such as I have never seen before. Oranges, lemons, palms, and bananas grow in the garden, and hoopoes hop from bough to bough.' As for the Arabs, they appeared highly romantic though infinitely unapproachable. The other residents at their hotel were English couples, invalids all, who had come there for the sake of the natural springs – 'extraordinary boiling hot affairs, which come bursting and bubbling out of the ground, giving off steam, and literally too hot to put your finger in'.

No sooner had Lytton set foot in Algeria than an extraordinary change came over the northern African continent. Its climate altered. While the Easter crowds in London sat out with their iced drinks in Regent's Park, the Algerian population shivered round their native fires. The weather was unprecedented, as it so often is, and far worse than anything ever recollected by the Oldest Inhabitant. While Carrington and Ralph went off for a week to inspect Constantine and Biskra, and James looked after Alix, Lytton did a little semi-recumbent work. On 12 April, he sent Maynard his essay on 'Sarah Bernhardt' for the first number of the newly reconstituted *Nation and Athenaeum*. 'She is *most* suitable,' replied Maynard (27 April 1923) who had also dispatched a review copy of Harold Nicolson's 'Stracheyesque' *Tennyson*. But at this Lytton demurred. 'I'm sorry to say I can't face Lord Tennyson,' he wrote back (16 April 1923). 'Harold N's book is so disgusting and stupid.' Virginia too tried to read Nicolson's *Tennyson* but, she informed Lytton's sister Pernel, had flung the book of this skilful imitator 'onto the floor in disgust'.

The five of them left Hammam-Méskoutine for Tunis on 15 April, travelled on to Palermo, in Sicily, and after a week went north to Naples. 'We have been having a very enjoyable though rather exhausting time,' Lytton wrote to Maynard from Parker's Hotel (5 May 1923). 'I am now recruiting in this slightly dreadful place. The sun shines, the sea glitters, the trams ting-tang along – and this evening at 6.30 St Januarius's blood will liquefy. But I fear that, like Cardinal Newman, I shan't "have time" to go and see the miracle.'

From Naples they progressed to Rome, and from Rome returned to Pangbourne – 'more or less alive', Lytton wrote to Maynard from Tidmarsh (28 May 1923), 'but furious at having been fool enough to exchange the heats of Rome for this fearful refrigerator'. The next week he was at Garsington again for what turned out to be the most disastrous weekend of all. To Carrington (who since her marriage had not been invited – Ottoline not wishing to see her any more, Mark had explained), Lytton did not reveal that Leonard and Virginia were also there. Instead he wrote of Ottoline's new medical attendant, an anti-Semitic quack 'quite in advance of England', who had renounced the pre-war practice of 'stuffing' for severe diets relieved by injections of bees'-stings and sour milk. 'It has been even worse than I anticipated,' he complained (3 June 1923). 'Appalling! A fatal error to have come. I see now only too clearly.

'The only other guest a miserable German doctor – a "psycho-analyst" of Freiburg – ready to discourse on every subject in broken English for hours.[27] The boredom has been indescribable. Most of the conversation is directed towards the dog, when the doctor is not holding forth. Imagine the ghastly meals. Then Philip at the pianola, then Philip reading out loud his articles in the Spectator, then Dr Marten on mysticism – "it can be explained in a few sentences" – followed by an address for 40 minutes by the clock. After which Ottoline joins in. Horrible! horrible! . . . Julian [Morrell] has become a kind of young lady – plays Bach and cuddles the dogs all day. Mr Ching came and played Bach. Pipsey is to play Bach after dinner. My brain totters. Soon I shall be playing Bach myself . . . If there had been a telephone in the house, I really believe I should have rung you up and fled. I am tempted to start walking as it is.

'"Psycho-analysis" is a ludicrous fraud. Not only Ottoline has been cured at Freiburg. The Sackville-West youth was there to be cured of homosexuality. After 4 months and an expenditure of £200, he found he could just bear the thought of going to bed with a woman. No more. Several other wretched undergraduates have been through the same "treatment". They walk about haggard on the lawn, wondering whether they could bear the thought of a woman's private parts, and gazing at their little lovers, who run round and round with cameras, snapshooting Lytton Strachey. Query, what did Ott go to be cured of? Whatever it may have been, she is pronounced by all the youths to be "better – much better". Probably after playing Bach this evening, I shall hurry to Freiburg myself. I shall certainly be badly in need of some "treatment". But I admit that I would rather receive it at the hands of P[hilip] Ritchie than of the German doctor. I must go downstairs. He will explain to me the meaning of asceticism "in [a] few sentences" – and then Ottoline will join in. The bell rings. Terror and horror!'

Philip Ritchie, the eldest son of Lord Ritchie of Dundee, soon to embark on a legal career with the novelist C.H.B. Kitchin[28] in the chambers of Lytton's old friend, C.P. Sanger, was then an Oxford undergraduate. Together with some of his friends, he had come over to tea that Sunday afternoon and 'was the one charming element', Lytton claimed. 'He told me shocking gossip about everyone, and in my gratitude I nearly flung my arms around his neck.'

As the warmer weather seeped in and rumours of summer circulated, Lytton's refrigerated spirit quickly thawed. Virginia observed that he seemed buoyant and had declared, with an embracing optimism, that they had twenty years of creative work still before them. 'Why not let oneself be content in the thought of Lytton – so true, gentle, infinitely nimble, & humane?' Virginia mused after their Garsington weekend. 'I seldom rest long in complete agreement with anyone. But here I think one's feelings should be unqualified.' He seemed absolutely happy and therefore, she thought, must be writing something that pleased him. In any event he had recovered from the long prostration that followed his writing of *Queen Victoria*. 'I have pledged myself to write once a month for that fiend Maynard,' he told Dadie Rylands (14 July 1923). Though he claimed to have been 'lured' into this 'perfectly mad occupation', it proved rewarding. Maynard, whom he had visited at King's early that June, arranged for him to be paid forty pounds for each contribution (equivalent to £1000 in the 1990s) – 'a splendid remuneration', Lytton acknowledged – and had also 'made a precarious arrangement with the *New Republic*' for each of these articles to appear in the United States, from where he would receive almost as much again.

Now that he was writing regularly once more, there was less time for social entertainments and he turned down a number of invitations with positive relief. Life at Tidmarsh was unclouded. During the whole of July, he emerged for only a single weekend house-party – with the Duchess of Marlborough at Blenheim, the potent architecture of which ravished him. 'Nobody was particularly interesting (except, perhaps, the Duchess)', he confided to Mary Hutchinson (11 July 1923), '– it was the house which was entrancing, and life-enhancing. I wish it were mine. It is enormous, but one would not feel it too big. The grounds are beautiful too, and there is a bridge over a lake which positively gives one an erection. Most of the guests played tennis all day and bridge all night, so that (apart from eating and drinking) they might as well have been at Putney.'

There was a procession of visitors to Tidmarsh – Pippa, Boris Anrep, J.H. Doggart, Frank Ramsey (twice), Sebastian Sprott, Dadie Rylands (who was soon to join the Hogarth Press), and the son of Lord Justice Tomlin, Stephen Tomlin, a brilliant and erratic sculptor, bisexual, good-looking and intermittently depressive.

So far there had been little sign of friction between Carrington and Ralph, but Lytton was not taking chances. His policy was still to keep them all on the move. At the beginning of August with Sebastian Sprott ('very interesting ... But perhaps too much of a bugger for your taste', Carrington informed Gerald), Lytton and Ralph and Carrington and Barbara Bagenal crammed into the car and careered off on an ambitious tour of France. From Boulogne they drove to Amiens, then hurtled on to Rouen and Chartres, whose cathedral Lytton rated 'superior to any other I have seen'. From here they motored south to Le Mans, then swept

Spray House.

ront sitting room at Ham Spray House. The painting above the mantelpiece is by Duncan

LEFT *Virginia Woolf with Lytton Strachey, at Garsington.*

RIGHT *Carrington with Stephen Tomlin, Fryern Court 1920s.*

Senhouse: 'May I have the little snapshot of you with pipe and handkerchief'.

Strachey instructing Carrington how to read Gibbon.

LEFT Poppet John and Carrington at Fryern Court, c. 1930.

RIGHT Ralph and Frances Partridge on a visit to Suffolk in the 1930s.

OPPOSITE Carrington in the garden at Ham Spray House.

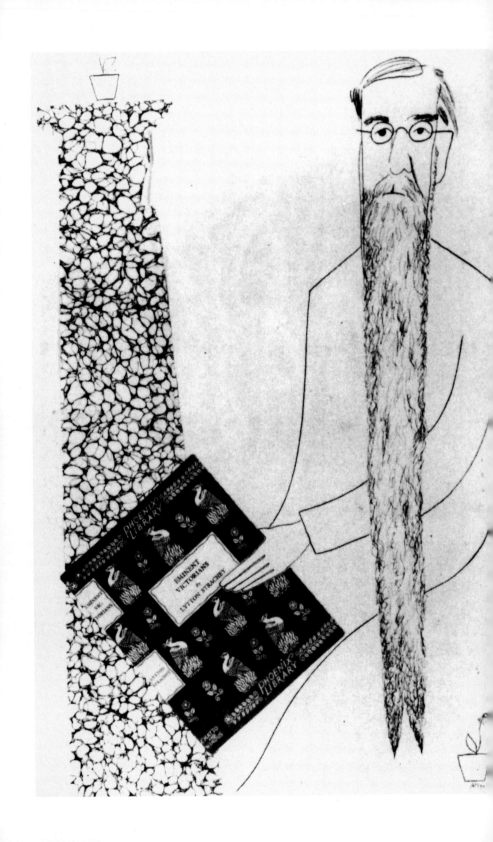

1916

Her Revenge. or the Fable of the Poet & the Banana Tree

But the Tree had her revenge, for the poet overate himself with Bannas. and the Doctor came too late The Moral of this tale is therefore, Poets do not be Buggers, & refuse to climb the Banana Tree!!

OVE *Facsimile of a letter (c. 1916) from Carrington to Lytton Strachey.*

T *Lytton Strachey, by Adolf Hoffmeister.*

ERLEAF *Lytton Strachey, c. 1930 at Ham Spray.*

eastwards via Orléans to Dijon, where Sebastian left them to join up with a young friend at Basle. Lytton's destination was the Cistercian Abbaye de Pontigny, on the Yonne, where he had been invited to attend the annual 'Entretiens d'été'. At these conferences, which used to last some ten days, writers and professors from a number of countries would assemble to discuss moral and literary problems. Lytton had been invited by André Gide, who was himself on Le Comité provisoire des Entretiens d'été, and who had written in his all but illegible hand to assure Lytton that they were anxiously awaiting 'votre présence à cette réunion "d'éminents" – penseurs des pays divers, qui doit avoir lieu cet été – du 16 au 27 août, à l'abbaye de Pontigny (celle-même où Thomas Becket trouvait asile) . . . J'aurais le plus grand plaisir à vous y voir et à vous présenter quelques amis qui ont un vif désir faire votre connaissance.'

The original plan had been for Ralph to continue touring the country with Carrington and Barbara while Lytton was stationed at this 'highbrow club'. But learning that his father was dying, Ralph dashed back to England, depositing the two women at an inn near Vermonton, and promising to motor out and collect them all at the end of the month.

Meanwhile Lytton was being introduced by Gide to his fellow *penseurs*,[29] in particular the strong French contingent which included Georges Raverat, Paul and Blaise Desjardins, Charles du Bos (who was later to write a long critical essay on Lytton), Jacques Rivière, Roger Martin du Gard, Jean Schlumberger and Max Lazard. They were all immediately startled by his resemblance to the Henry Lamb portrait which they had regarded as a caricature. 'On the first day,' recalled André Maurois, 'we were alarmed by his tall, lanky frame, his long beard, his immobility, his silence; but when he spoke, in his "bleating falsetto" it was in delightful, economical epigrams.'

Lytton too was startled by his experiences at Pontigny. The sanitary arrangements at the abbey were 'crushing and inadequate'; his breakfast featured not a single egg; and his bedroom turned out to be nothing more nor less than a monk's cell. He felt melancholy, too, at being separated from Ralph, and at his own 'constant and immense difficulty in effecting any kind of communication with the natives'. Like a schoolboy pitchforked into a new school, he was lonely and bewildered. Some of the older boys seemed particularly aloof. 'Gide is hopelessly unapproachable,' he told Carrington who was busy painting every day (26 August 1923). 'He gave a reading last night of one of his own works – in a most extraordinary style – like a clergyman intoning in a pulpit. It was enormously admired.' In a letter to Ralph (25 August 1923) he explains that he is overwhelmed by 'a sort of sentimental sunset Verlaine feeling'. He enjoys 'some secret love-affairs of course – confined, equally of course, to my own breast'. One of these secret passions was for the austere Blaise Desjardins – 'largish, pale, unhealthy, who sings very well – but apparently particularly dislikes me, hélas!' There were also some pseudo-adventures in which he was the object of other people's admiration.

'La belle Américaine, with the short black hair . . . she is an "artist" – has asked me to sit to her – has read my article on Racine, which she thinks wonderful – gazes at me with slightly melancholy eyes, etc. etc. . . . I shall only, I fear, turn out a disappointment. Her husband is an agreeable American-speaking Frenchman . . . I am beginning to wonder how we shall weather through another week. Translation hardly seems to be a subject adapted for 10 days of discussion! I only wish I were translated myself, like Bottom. Sometimes I feel as if I *had* been! And my Titania? – La Belle Américaine? Peut-être.'

Invariably the best part of each day was the morning, when he was allowed to sit in the excellent library and, without superintendence, read. But even then, owing to the lack of morning eggs, his exhaustion was considerable. At moments, either from early faintness or the soporific effect of the afternoon debates, the old abbey appeared like a dream. He listened to the discussions with an air of politely scornful indulgence. 'The "entretiens" which occur every day from 2.30 to 4.30 (what a time to choose) are rather appalling,' he complained to Ralph. 'Almost perpetually dull – and then the constant worry of one's being expected to speak and never doing so. Up to now I have allowed exactly three words to issue from my mouth – in public; so that I am growing very unpopular.'

Some of the subjects were in themselves pretty vacant – 'LES HUMANITÉS, sont-elles irremplaçables pour former une Élite?' or 'Y-a-t-il dans la Poésie d'un Peuple un trésor réservé impénétrable aux Étrangers?' During the long conference on 'THE MEANING OF HONOUR', lapping one of his grasshopper legs over the other, he nodded off. 'And what in your opinion, Monsieur Strachey, is the most important thing in the world?' suddenly inquired Paul Desjardins. There was a long and painful pause. Then from the slumbering beard there issued a tiny treble: 'Passion!' This was one of his three words, and as he uttered it the solemn circle of intellectuals, relieved for an instant, burst into laughter. Pressed during another discussion on the subject of 'LES CONFESSIONS' to contribute something, he stood up and announced: 'Les confessions ne sont pas dans mon genre,' then sat down. Another day, towards the end of an analysis of Gidean 'actes gratuits', his still small voice from the back of the hall was overheard inquiring plaintively: 'Est-ce qu'un acte gratuit est *toujours* désagréable?'

Many of the French *éminents penseurs* did not know what to make of this strange francophil in their midst. Possibly he was too English to be fired by abstract ideas. 'Looking at him there,' André Maurois wrote, 'we had the impression of an almost infinite disdain, of a wilful abstraction, of a refusal ... And yet sometimes, for one fleeting instant, a glance would flash behind his spectacles so vividly that we wondered if all this lassitude might not be the mask of a man really amused and keen, and more Britannic than any Briton.'

At the end of the month Ralph reappeared to rescue Lytton, collect Carrington and Barbara, and motor them all back to England. They drove in leisurely stages up to Paris and then back to England where Lytton made off for what was now his customary September trip to Charleston. The summer was almost over, and still no serious trouble had broken out between Carrington and Ralph. To his great satisfaction the plan of extensive travel that year seemed to have worked. There were no quarrels because 'there is nothing to quarrel about. After all we have been married four years now,' Carrington had miscalculated in a letter to Gerald (1 June 1923). 'And I am thirty years old ... I think Ralph may become a bookbinder ... For the moment I am bored by myself.' She wasn't worried by Ralph's 'intrigues, and love affairs, after his book binding shuts up' in the evening at the Polytechnic in London; and he didn't trouble himself over her new passion for an American bisexual beauty, Henrietta Bingham, who had 'the face of a Giotto Madonna', sang 'exquisite songs with a mandoline' and mixed 'such wonderful cocktails' that Carrington 'almost made love to her in public'. But what did exercise them both was the curious predicament of Gerald.

Among the mules and little beggar children of Yegen, Gerald had passed his time since leaving England eating bread and grapes, reading Proust, writing down and tearing up his poetry, and going for enormous walks along the mountains of the Sierra Nevada, immersed in the ocean air, dreaming of Carrington. 'I could not bear to be cut off from all information about you,' he had written to Ralph (11 and 31 October 1922). '... our annual meetings and my correspondence with D.C. have been a kind of nourishment that I cannot easily dispense with.'

In April 1923 Leonard and Virginia had come out to stay with him. This was their first holiday abroad since their honeymoon eleven years ago and it turned out 'the greatest success', Virginia told Roger Fry (16 April 1923), '... we discuss literature 12 hours every day'.

But they also discussed Tidmarsh, and after Leonard and Virginia left,

Gerald concocted a scheme for reintegrating himself there. Since his correspondence with Carrington resumed, he had failed to catch her interest with references to the rather unconvincing flirtations with which he tried to assuage his loneliness at Yegen. Now he wrote to Leonard conveying some extraordinary news which Virginia quickly passed on to Carrington. 'Gerald tells Leonard that he has just got engaged to an American girl at Granada,' she wrote (27 May 1923). 'Have you heard? Perhaps its a joke.'

It was a joke of the most serious intent and it did its work very effectively. 'We are told you are marrying,' Ralph responded (29 May 1923). '. . . I am strongly against it . . . Virginia would tell us all about it . . . Curse Virginia . . . Curse her again.' The fact that Ralph was 'plunged into profound gloom' by the news, Carrington added (28 May 1923), 'shows how deeply he cares'.

But she was startled by how much she herself cared. 'It does in a curious way make rather a difference,' she admitted. She had begun dreaming of him again. 'I can't give my reasons for caring for you,' she volunteered (31 May 1923). 'Although it's illogical and impossible I do still care.' On his mountainous walks through the Sierra Nevada, Gerald had imagined his relationship with her as being 'of the same nature as that of Dante and Beatrice, the troubadours and their ladies, or Shelley with Emilia Viviani and Jane Williams.' Now, feeling spiritually so close to him again, Carrington explained: 'I am in love with Shelley and so I pretend Shelley lives in you and you can never do any wrong for me.'

Yet he had done something wrong. It was almost as wrong, and as provoking, as his engagement joke. He had invited pretty Barbara Bagenal to come out and visit him. 'Why can everyone go to Spain and stay with you except your rejected and deserted QUEEN OF NOTHING?' Carrington demanded. '. . . I wish, so very much, I could come out with Barbara to Yegen.' Ralph felt the same. 'I nearly made up my mind to come out to you and Barbara,' he wrote (29 May 1923).

So why should they not both go? The real obstacle was Lytton. He would not go himself (the last journey had been 'DEATH' he assured Virginia) and he foresaw all manner of complications – added pain for Gerald and extra strain (after all his diplomacy) on Ralph and Carrington. Perhaps, he suggested, Ralph should go this year, and Carrington next year. 'I think it's best I write to Gerald quite frankly and tell him what I feel and the difficulties . . . you explained to me,' Carrington reluctantly agreed (27 August 1923). 'But there's no immediate hurry . . .' Ralph, however, was not to be persuaded by Lytton, for there was a still more powerful advocate recommending this expedition.

Frances Marshall was the sister-in-law of David Garnett and Lytton's 'niece-in-law' (her elder sister Judy having married Lytton's nephew Dick Rendel). She was twenty-three, sparkling and intelligent, and quite unlike the superficial pretty girls with whom Ralph had been carrying on brief affairs over the past year. She had read philosophy at Newnham and now worked at Francis Birrell and David Garnett's Bloomsbury bookshop in Taviton Street. It was here that she had first seen Ralph striding in with books from the Hogarth Press. 'Ralph's carrying on some intrigue in London at the moment,' Carrington notified Gerald (15 September 1923). But when she met this 'black haired beauty . . . a beautiful Princess that lives in Birrell & Garnett's bookshop', she liked her and was not upset by the relationship. Lytton positively welcomed it, since it made Ralph so charming. Unlike that 'seasoned adventuress' Valentine (whose name they had been delighted to discover was really Gladys), Frances loved Tidmarsh, taking to Carrington and being alarmingly impressed by Lytton.

Though subjected to a high-powered courtship by Ralph, Frances would not let his advances go too far – a precaution that earned his respect and deepened his fondness for her. As he began to fall in love, so his attitude to Gerald softened. It was Frances's influence that made him so set on taking Carrington out to Yegen. He was determined to remove any particles of bitterness that still lay between them all. He had told Frances everything and knew that their vertical love-making would have a better chance of becoming horizontal love-making if Gerald and Carrington resumed their own relationship. So, with Frances as his secret agent, he persuaded Lytton to relent. 'It's all settled dearest, we BOTH will come!!!!!!' Carrington immediately told Gerald.

Their three weeks in Spain at the end of 1923 and the beginning of 1924 were an entr'acte that, while settling nothing, created the atmosphere for the next scene of their drama. They went to parties, danced, swam, ate persimmons to the sound of guitars, read Eliot and Joyce, and had 'fascinating conversations ranging on every subject', Carrington wrote back to Lytton (23 December 1923), '. . . and then more hectic conversations'. It seemed to her, as she set off into the landscape with her painting materials, that these two men, Ralph and Gerald, could spend every day arguing even in perpetual sunlight. They were the most adamant characters – and yet they never really fell out. Gerald was intending, with his great-aunt's help, to return to England in the spring, and Ralph gave him his blessing to kiss Carrington as he kissed Frances. 'I do not dispute the attraction you have for each other, nor am I now made unhappy by it, because I am more reconciled to my own relation with her than I was,' he explained to his friend (21 January 1924). Besides, he believed that whatever happened, Carrington 'won't let Lytton go, or me, at any price'.

'Everything is so perfect,' Carrington had told Lytton (23 December 1923). '. . . Oh why, why, can't you be whisked here on a magic carpet . . . How happy you would be with us.'

Frances had arranged to meet them on their way back in Paris where Lytton joined them too. He came with marvellous news. For some months Ralph and Carrington had been speculating about the possibility of moving with Lytton from Tidmarsh. 'It is tame, without a doubt, hopelessly domestic, provincial, unimportant, smug and ridiculous,' Ralph had pointed out after getting back there from Italy the previous summer (29 May 1923). 'There is a cringing subservience all round – the flowers, the furniture, the tame birds and the wild birds, all very respectful and very well trained, but crushing, with the whole weight of England.'

Carrington found herself agreeing with him. 'I've grown bored with these damp meadows, & the Ibsen-esque drip of the rain, & the night mists from the Fjiord.' The rooms were too cramped for her painting and too damp for Lytton's health, she complained: but really she had absorbed too much pain at Tidmarsh to feel it was still an 'earthly Paradise'. 'I think its a mistake to become sentimental over any place,' she had excused herself to Gerald (31 May 1923), '& I can't quite get over my hatred for this garden & the dull green fields . . .'

But Lytton still felt very fond of the Mill House. Despite all the difficulties, he had been happy there. 'Old age I suppose, but for whatever reason the solid calmness of Tidmarsh exactly suits me,' he confided to Carrington (1 January 1924). Nevertheless he had agreed to join in their house-hunting the previous October, and Carrington quickly found what she wanted. 'I am in love with a house,' she announced. Ralph, too, was enraptured. 'Such a house', he exclaimed in his letter to Gerald (17 October 1923). 'A dream house under the downs near Hungerford, a refuge for old age. We gibber about it all day long.'

It was called Ham Spray House. 'That's a good title to begin with,' Carrington had written to Gerald (23 October 1923).

'It is within a mile of the village of Ham & the village of Inkpen and a stone's throw (if one threw well) from the most marvellous downs in the WHOLE WORLD – Tibet excluded – Inkpen Beacon. It is four miles from Hungerford. We saw a ram shackle lodge, a long avenue of limes but all wuthering in appearance, bleak, & the road a grass track. Barns in decay, then the back of a rather forbidding farm house. We walked to the front of it & saw to our amazement in the blazing sun a perfect English country house. But with a view onto downs before it that took our breaths away . . . Inside the house was properly built, simple & good proportions. It faced south so one would never shiver with the damp & cold as one does here. And there were eight bed rooms, & numerous queer lofts, & outhouses, also a small cottage separate from the house.'

The difficulty was price – a prohibitive £3000! 'What can we do? I feel in terrible despair!' Carrington asked Lytton (27 November 1923). 'I can hardly bare to let it fade, and yet it seems impossible . . .' By the time Ralph and Carrington went off to Spain, negotiations were still ploughing on. 'I believe I've bought Ham Spray for £2,300 [equivalent to around £55,000 in 1994] – but it still totters,' Lytton wrote to his brother James on 4 January. As soon as the agreement was settled, he sent a telegram to Spain and then met Ralph and Carrington in Paris with all the details. Ham Spray House had no drains or electric light and was in need of general repairs. But Carrington had already redecorated all the rooms in her imagination.

The builders started work there in the early spring. Carrington would go over nearly every day to plan her decorations and the layout of the garden. 'We are beginning to be busy over our new house,' Lytton told Ottoline on 24 April. '. . . It is altogether rather agitating, and complete financial ruin stares me in the face. I suppose I shall have to write another masterpiece.' Even with some help from a legacy which Ralph had received on his father's death, it was all turning out to be fearfully expensive, and Carrington admitted that they were 'on the rocks for d'argent'.

But she was in her element painting and decorating the walls, staining the floors and doors. As the rooms blossomed her spirits rose. 'All is beautiful!' she assured Lytton (16 July 1924). 'And we are growing happier.' Ralph was continuously driving her and their guests from Tidmarsh that spring – Leonard and Virginia, Sebastian, Dadie, Maynard, Frances Marshall and others – to the new house, and they would be put to work on any job that needed doing. Lytton's letters are full of the bustle of these months. 'We spent yesterday at our new house,' he wrote to Bunny Garnett (23 May 1924), 'with various persons, among them Tommy [Stephen Tomlin] and Henrietta [Bingham] – I liked her more than before. She white-washed amazingly and never said a word.'

When they left Tidmarsh on 15 July, Ham Spray was still not really habitable. Lytton stayed away as much as possible during these first weeks, fleeing with Pippa for a fortnight to Brittany. Tidmarsh would always have a special place in his memory. One night in July 1928, he almost wept as some music on the phonograph recalled their life there. 'Among others, there was a string quartet by Schubert, which brought back Tidmarsh to me with extraordinary vividness. I felt the loss of that régime very strongly, and in fact ... nearly burst into tears. I hope and pray that our new grandeur ... won't alter anything in any way.'

Carrington felt differently. Though she often blamed herself for the complications she had forced into Lytton's life, and had terrible nightmares about his leaving her, she was feverishly excited over Ham Spray. 'We must hope that the perfection of our lives will be so great in the sun and on the Downs that we will never regret it,' she rallied him (10 January 1924). 'I feel certain myself that we will master the situation. The real thing that matters is the indissolubility of our affections. The addition of hot sun, a verandah and the most beautiful country can only add to an already existing state of perfection. We love you *so* much.'

SIXTEEN

Ham Spray House

'I lead a dog's life between Queen Elizabeth's love affairs and my own.'

Lytton Strachey to Dorothy Bussy (11 June 1927)

'What is love? 'Tis not hereafter – no; but it also isn't heretofore. Is it even here? Ah, well! – But the odd thing is (among all the other oddities) that one occasionally manages to enjoy oneself.'

Lytton Strachey to George Rylands (12 August 1927)

I

PAPER-GAMES AND PUSSY-CATS

Ham Spray was a pleasantly modernized country house of the Jane Austen period. Its long veranda looked south past copper beeches, huge ash trees and a splendid ilex, across a lawn and fields to the Newbury Downs which, like an 'enormous green wave', stood poised half-a-mile away above the plains of brown and green farmlands. The house was larger than Tidmarsh ('where every bedroom communicates with every other') and its length and narrowness made it difficult to keep warm. Lytton introduced a number of improvements – tepid central heating, an 'electric light engine', a hot-water apparatus – and later converted the loft at the east end into a studio for Carrington. At last, by his own definition, he could count himself a wealthy man, having an open fireplace in his bedroom, its chimney-piece designed by Boris Anrep with, stretched across the lintel, a mosaic of a naked swimming hermaphrodite, with a resemblance to Carrington, peeping seductively over his shoulder into the room. Lytton was also supposed to have fitted up an appliance by which the wires of his bed were electrically heated, so that he was agreeably grilled all night – one of many apocryphal stories that began to circle round him.

Lytton's study too was upstairs. Its walls were lined to the ceiling with French and English authors alphabetically regimented and mostly belonging to the eighteenth century. A large writing-desk stood in the centre of the room and, hanging over the mantelpiece so that it dominated everything, was a picture of Voltaire by Huber, showing him seated at a table, his hand raised in benediction above a group of friends, and extending his blessing to people in the study. Lytton never used a typewriter and disliked dictation. Pacing up and down he constructed each paragraph in his mind before sitting down and putting it on to paper in a neat flowing hand. 'I write very slowly, and in faultless sentences,' he said when asked about his revisions.

The routine at Ham Spray was simple. After breakfast Lytton worked; after lunch he lay down; after tea he would usually go, stick in hand, for walks over the Downs; and in the evening, after dinner, he either played poker or piquet 'to say nothing of other games' in the downstairs front drawing-room, or listened to music – usually Mozart, Beethoven or Haydn – on the ramshackle phonograph. Sometimes he would read aloud in a surprisingly deep, emotional voice to Ralph and Carrington from favourite books or his own manuscripts, his left hand making curious prancing movements in the air, all three of them, with Tiber the cat, sitting round the fire.[1]

Under Carrington's hand, every room at Ham Spray was gradually transformed. She made patchwork counterpanes and quilts, Victorian-style designs from coloured tinfoil paper, she decorated doors and chimney-pieces, and made paintings on glass and china. Upon the tiles, the plates, the cups and saucers, appeared passion-flowers and sunflowers, legs of mutton, 'cellos, fishes, birds, ships, shells, archers, hunting scenes, abstract shapes, orchestras of cats and other marvels. Besides her own decorations, there were also some of Henry Lamb's drawings, paintings and panels by Duncan, and a mural by the surrealist John Banting showing a 'pregnant' Ralph bearing a twin. The walls of many of the rooms were hung with 'Fanny Fletcher's Papers' – hand-blocked wallpapers made with carved potatoes and in characteristic Bloomsbury shades, thick browns and terracottas, rusty reds, mauves, olives and cloudy yellows, eggshell blue or pale green.

Though she employed a young girl to do housework, Carrington still did much of the cooking. She also worked in the garden, educating her Latinate plants (Bacca loculis, Bummonia uncanta). She planted May trees and vines, a lily-of-the-valley bed, a tulip garden. At times she appeared entirely absorbed in her plant and animal kingdom. 'The loveliness of this country seems to make one permanently happy,' she wrote to her friend Barbara Bagenal. 'I am indifferent almost to everything except looking at the downs, and wandering in the garden. There are so many things to do, in the end I do nothing but lie on a sofa like a cat and look at Bulb catalogues, think of gardening, think of painting, contemplate writing letters, talk to Lytton, read the newspapers and gaze eternally out at the downs.'

Ham Spray had been registered in Ralph's name, as he was so much younger than Lytton. This may also have helped to deepen Carrington's feeling of security there. It seemed impossible to believe that, whatever 'vexations' might assail them all, her life with Lytton could now be uprooted. Things that happened beyond the circle of their home became of diminishing significance to her. By the end of the 1920s she had allowed her appearance to deteriorate, looking unkempt and haggard, using no lipstick or make-up. But she never lost the intensity of her emotions in these later years and her sexual instincts grew more obviously lesbian. 'I feel now regrets at being such a blasted fool in the past, to stifle so many lusts I had in my youth, for various females,' she confessed to Alix Strachey. Her 'drunken passion' for the beautiful Henrietta Bingham revived and intensified. This 'Kentucky princess' with her perfect oval face, dark symmetrical hair, and amazing eyelashes shading brilliant blue eyes, opened Carrington's mind to her own bisexual nature. 'I dream of her six times a week dreams that even my intelligence is appalled by, and I write letters, and tear them up, continually,' she told Alix (11 May 1925). Yet these passions did not seem to worry her, '– in fact,' she declared, 'I have seldom felt more self-possessed, and at peace with my lower self'. Perhaps this was the outcome of approaching middle age. 'One of the comforts of being over thirty, I find, is at last to know what one feels, and only do the things one wants to do!' she explained to Mark Gertler (7 October 1925). '. . . in reality I am very happy, I love the country, and house so passionately that I find nothing outside it seems to affect me very much. I do more painting than I used to, and now I have a fine studio here.'

Carrington and Lytton appeared a strangely endearing couple at Ham Spray, with only a glimpse of danger far off in the landscape. 'I have the memory of them both in their pleasant, large room at evening half-shadow,' Iris Tree wrote. 'Books, paintings, the sweep of the Downs through the windows, an ancient gibbet on high hill tops, the garden overlooked by a weeping ilex tree, roses outside and in. And Carrington, rose-cheeked, pouring tea, laughing upwards from under her thatch of hair, licking her lips with a delicate greediness for delicious things and topics. Lytton wrapped in a shawl, purring with delicate malice and enjoyment of thoughts succinctly worded, his hands stretched out transparent to the flames in the firelight.' In the village of Ham, he was looked up to with a peculiar mixture of awe, anger, affection and amusement as he sat out on the village green surrounded by village lads, dealing out forbidden cigarettes.

Their life at Ham Spray was grander than in the 'tomb of funguses' at Tidmarsh. There was good food and wine, greater comfort, endless talk. No longer did it appear to be quite the 'life retired, apart' which Lytton had eulogized on his fortieth birthday. He entertained more, and his guests were more varied. During the day he was as frail as ever, and he could still freeze a party with his dreadful silence. But as evening came, he seemed to wake up, enjoying the company of his many young companions and often playing the fool – putting his beard in his mouth, feigning extreme senility and acting up with fantastic high-spirits. 'He had a particular taste and gift for nonsense, and when playing some paper-game in the evening, would throw across at one an improvised quatrain about a friend or a pussy-cat,' remembered Raymond Mortimer. In summer there were badminton matches on a converted tennis court, bathing in the river, games of bowls on the lawn and complicated croquet; and indoors, unexpectedly fierce ping-pong contests. For the evening's entertainment, he would sometimes produce one-act playlets for his guests to perform, in which the ingenious plots hurried the bewildered actors into hermaphrodite confusion. Also popular were the amateur film shows, such as a Wellsian fantasy produced by Carrington and Stephen Tomlin and filmed by Bernard Penrose, which David Garnett remembered:

'The setting was Dr Turner's private lunatic asylum, where the inmates were experimented upon and reduced to the condition of animals, the subject being Saxon Sydney-Turner's sinister attempts to experiment upon the innocent heroine who was played by Rachel MacCarthy,[2] wearing a daisy chain. The scene of Saxon, as Dr Turner, peering round the bathroom door at her, had a macabre quality which I have never seen achieved in any other film. My sister-in-law Frances [Marshall] also achieved a success as a human quadruped lunatic wearing riding-boots on her arms.'[3]

A spell seemed to exude from the rich green country and linger over Ham Spray. 'I am tremendously happy whenever I think of my extreme good fortune,' Carrington wrote to Gerald Brenan (23 January 1925), 'I mean living in such a lovely place & with such amiable companions & then to have London as an extravagance whenever I feel in the mood for change . . .' But could the spell hold its magic against their misadventures and anxieties? To the novelist Rosamond Lehmann, Lytton confessed in an agonized voice that he would willingly surrender all his literary success for the gift of physical beauty. But now he could at least surround himself with good-looking friends and absorb pleasure from their beauty. He loved diffidently to finger their bare arms, pinch their cheeks, run his fingers through their hair, touch their ears. The critical severity of his mind melted away and he would endow them with glowing qualities though he knew their brains were really 'made of strawberries and cream'. 'Is there any reason why we should be bored *all* afternoon?' he asked his seventeen-year-old nephew Richard, then on holiday from Rugby and supposed to be working at some dull holiday task. 'Let's go to the theatre!' – and he took him off to the kind of show that would appeal most to a schoolboy, and which he very obviously enjoyed too. But he could not always hit it off with adolescents, who still found his appearance, and sometimes his manner too, formidable and perplexing. The first steps to any intimacy were still painfully difficult for him. Another nephew, the artist John Strachey, remembers him 'suddenly showing me an 18th century French print of a young woman having an enema, accompanying this gesture with a terrifying giggle. I daresay that he was trying to get on some sort of terms with me. Unfortunately the attempt was a failure and I became more scared than ever.'

He regarded conversation as the pleasantest occupation in life, 'and indeed', Lionel Penrose commented, 'with the Stracheys this ideal could be realised'. They talked of history, literature and the arts, and their literary and artistic friends. Lytton had a gift for making the past actual as he spoke and of discovering hidden excellences in others, a quality to which Virginia paid tribute when, after his death, she remarked to Clive: 'Don't you feel there are things one would like to say and never will say now?'

But he was not liked by everyone. His passion for ribald joking, schoolboy puns and charades was sometimes embarrassing; and he could be arrogantly intolerant to those whom he took against, sometimes on very inadequate grounds. Stephen Spender, who used to be taken to Ham Spray by Wogan Philipps and his wife Rosamond Lehmann, found him the most astonishing of the Bloomsbury Group. 'He combined strikingly their gaiety with their intermittent chilliness,' he recorded. 'Sometimes he would play childish games such as "Up Jenkins", which we played one Christmas. Often he would gossip brilliantly and maliciously. At times there was something insidious about his giggling manner; at times he would sit in his chair without saying a word.'[4] Harold Nicolson would speak of him as a bearded and bitchy old woman;[5] to Herbert Read he was 'rather a wistful, querulous figure'; Sylvia Townsend Warner remembered 'his breath was as cold as the Erlking's'; and George Santayana was 'not an admirer of Strachey. I knew him.'[6]

But none of these knew him very well. Some who disliked him had hardly met him. T.E. Lawrence, for example – whom Lytton himself considered a 'tawdry' character and writer – appears to have based his dislike largely on Lamb's portrait.[7] Most extreme of all is the inspired virulence of Wyndham Lewis. On 22 July 1926, he sent Lytton a mysterious letter. 'Dear Strachey,' he wrote from 33 Ossington Street, Bayswater. 'It is a very long time since I saw you. I should very much like to see you soon, to discuss two or three literary matters with you.' He suggested that they should meet 'incognito, or rather unobserved', in an unfrequented part of the town, for dinner, 'say at the Great Eastern Hotel Restaurant, called I believe the Great Eastern Restaurant; or for tea in some obscure tea-shop – say near the Law Courts or Covent Garden Market'; and that provisionally they should not divulge these arrangements. There is no record of Lytton having kept this rendezvous, nor of Wyndham Lewis going to Ham Spray; but almost thirty years later – having scrutinized Lytton with his caricaturist's eye (this probably being one of the literary matters he referred to in his letter) he published a novel, *Self-Condemned* (1954), in which the character of Cedric Furber, a rich, lonely bachelor in his forties, strict and fussy and old maidish, is founded on Lytton. The description he gives of this heavily bearded idiot-child living down at his country home is a brilliantly perverse view of disintegrating futility:

'Certainly Mr Furber's mask most successfully suggested a distinct, and possibly a new zoological species ... A long shapeless black beard ... stretched downwards from the base of his nose, and threw the onus of expression upon his eyes ...

While he was with this queer creature René always felt that he was engaged in field work as an amateur naturalist. It was like being a bird-watcher, and Mr Furber a great dreary owl ... Was he a soft, good-natured, "impish", old shit? No: he was not susceptible of a worldly classification after that manner. One cannot speak of an owl as a shit, for instance.'

But Lytton was no longer the great dreary creature of earlier days. He was 'by no means ugly', Frances Marshall discovered now that she was getting to know him. 'Tall, willowy, and with very long and beautiful hands, he displayed a peculiar elegance in the way he used to walk, or rather stalk, across the lawn under a white sunshade lined with green, and fold his long legs away into a deck chair. His velvety brown eyes were full of expression.'[8] On hot days in the summer, he would appear in an enormous sun-hat and advance from the veranda, stepping across the lawn with the slow elegance of a secretary bird. Then he subsided into a deck-chair, an ageless figure, his legs tightly pressed together, his knees on a level with his head, his diaphanous hands resting on baggy trousers; and he would begin to talk. There was a strange contrast between his quietness and the overstatement, when his immobility was suddenly shattered by lavish gesticulations. To his niece, the novelist Julia Strachey, he was 'the most vivid personality I have ever seen'.

Without shedding his mischievousness, he was regaining something of the romantic imperialism of his Cambridge and *Spectator* days. David Cecil recalled him speaking with mild affection of the British Raj. In a high voice and with grave face, he exclaimed to Frederick Laws: 'When I read Dr Renier's book *The English – Are they Human?* I felt just like the British lion. I waved my tail and I roared!'

On the surface his religious opinions also appeared to have eased. He considered that Christianity, which throughout history had been such a bitter enemy of humanitarianism, was now largely a spent force: no longer controversial or even interesting. Perhaps, for that reason, militant atheists were also out of date. 'One may say what one likes (more or less) on religion now,' he wrote to his nephew Richard (5 May 1926), 'but perhaps that is because no one's very much interested in it. There are other, more intimate subjects, which can't be mentioned – or only in the most recondite fashion.'

Some of these more intimate subjects were on his mind as he pursued his recondite researches in the British Museum. He would use Pernel's rooms at 51 Gordon Square as she continued her career as tutor, director, lecturer and then Principal at Newnham College in Cambridge. While the younger members of Bloomsbury – its second generation soon to be headed socially by Angelica Bell – gave late-night parties at the studio in Fitzroy Street,[9] the old Bloomsbury Group re-formed round 52 Tavistock Square, where Leonard and Virginia lived on the top two floors above the Hogarth Press. Lytton was seldom drawn into the rowdy Fitzroy Street parties, but he often turned up at the more sedate after-dinner gatherings in Tavistock Square. Roger Fry, Duncan Grant, Maynard Keynes and Lytton himself were the great aces of these evenings, and, more occasionally, Desmond MacCarthy and Morgan Forster. Sometimes they would assemble at Vanessa's house – congregations usually not exceeding seven or eight in number, including one or two from the younger generation.

Lytton's entertaining in London was often done at his clubs, the Oriental and later the Athenaeum. John Lehmann, who had been introduced to him by Dadie Rylands (both of them worked at different times for the Hogarth Press) has told how he would encourage Lytton to recount wicked stories of Leonard Woolf. 'I was in a glow of pleasure and amusement,' he wrote, 'as Lytton, in his high, thin but authoritative voice ordered an excellent wine and we settled down to a long discussion about the past of Bloomsbury and Lytton's Cambridge days, about poetry (which Lytton wrote copiously, though modestly and in secret), or modern French literature, in which he sadly found all the vices of German literature and very few of the great traditional French virtues. I also visited him at Ham Spray, and explored endlessly in his library while he worked, and afterwards would go for walks with him, during which we renewed our discussion – or rather I renewed my eager questioning and he his judicious and witty answers to the ever-unsatisfied disciple.'[10]

The atmosphere at Ham Spray, with its enveloping and pervasive calm, seemed specially sympathetic, and in these surroundings Lytton's personality, never completely liberated in his writings, conveyed itself most memorably to his friends. 'One remembered afterwards his doubts and hesitations, his refusals to dogmatize, his flights of fantasy, his high, whispering voice fading out in the middle of a sentence, and forgot the very definite and well-ordered mind that lay underneath,' Gerald Brenan wrote. '. . . One observed a number of discordant features – a feminine sensibility, a delight in the absurd, a taste for exaggeration and melodrama, a very mature judgement, and then some lack of human substance, some hereditary thinness in the blood that at times gave people who met him an odd feeling in the spine. He seemed almost indecently lacking in ordinariness.'[11]

The treble voice and great tawny beard, the impudent smile that would flit across his face to greet some barbed observation, the stillness, the soft and steady gravity of the eyes brooding behind tortoiseshell spectacles, were all parts of a physical personality that affected the house with its presence. This tall figure, recalled F.L. Lucas, 'who walked the fields of Ham Spray, had a foreign touch about his appearance, as of a Russian landowner; or like some pictured Jehovah, terrifying to strangers, who would yet relax at any moment into an amused Epicurean Zeus'.

2

ATTACHMENT

'We are established here pretty solidly now,' Lytton wrote to Ottoline on 8 November 1924, 'and it seems a very satisfactory place – surrounded by all that is most romantic.' For their first Christmas at the new house, Lytton composed a transvestite farce for the guests who, besides Carrington, Ralph and Frances, included the delightfully hectic Dadie Rylands from Cambridge and the burly mosaicist Boris Anrep who brought down an enormous Russian Easter cake bristling with almonds. 'So the months passed,' wrote Frances, 'with Lytton arranging books in his library, Carrington beautifying the house with charming tiles and painted papers, Ralph cutting down trees and binding books.'[12]

Yet even in this first year their 'curious ménage or ménages' were to be torn by new strains and aberrations. Outwardly Carrington and Ralph had regained their affection for each other, while Lytton 'grows more and more benign, and charming', Carrington told Alix (11 May 1925), 'which means I suppose one is on the brink of some unseen volcanoe'.

The danger came from what Lytton had called their romantic surroundings. Much expanded since the pioneer days of 'the Tidmarsh experiment', the nucleus of their lives had grown oddly unstable. Each of them looked outside this triple relationship now for sexual fulfilment, while not wishing to damage the Ham Spray union which they all prized. Yet their independent passions and adventures did affect it.

At the time they moved from Tidmarsh, their planetary system had Lytton at its centre, Ralph and Carrington revolving round him, and Gerald and Frances spinning in a wider orbit around the three of them. In the months that followed two other people began exerting their influence from a greater distance. The first of these was Lytton's new love, Philip Ritchie: 'clever and amusing', Frances called him, 'a devotee of chamber music and discussions on abstract matters'. But Carrington disliked him. It seemed to her as if he spoke of nothing but buggery, rape, tarts and catamites, relishing bawdiness as an escape from his prudish upbringing. Besides he 'isn't nearly so fond of Lytton as he pretends to be', she informed Alix. 'Perhaps he doesn't pretend, & Lytton imagines it himself.' Lytton saw that Philip's visits to Ham Spray were not popular with Carrington and Ralph. 'Please, however, both of you, try to like – or at any rate not dislike – my Philip,' he appealed to them (17 October 1924). 'I assure you he's a great rarity. It's true that he's not immediately attractive to look at, and that he probably has no taste in pictures; but he's intellectual (a good point); and he's sensual (also good); and he gives not the slightest value to anything but what is really valuable (very good indeed).'

A far greater disturbance, Lytton believed, was being set up by Carrington's dangerous new love, Henrietta Bingham. Operating from the London School of Economics in Holborn and her own secret house in

Knightsbridge, she went about breaking the hearts of many men and women. Her enigmatic smile, caressing syllables, glowing skin, held no appeal for Lytton who sensed her destructive powers; but they captivated Stephen Tomlin and Carrington, both of whom were soon to become her lovers. 'Really I had more ecstasy with her and no shame afterwards,' Carrington later confided to Gerald Brenan (21 July 1925).

This was the last thing Gerald wanted to hear. He had travelled from Spain at the beginning of April 1924 convinced that he had got over his love for Carrington. But 'I have never been able to control my sexual life properly,' he admitted to Ralph shortly before starting on his journey (4 February 1924), 'and this has been a constant motive of despair with me.' Carrington had met him at Victoria Station, taken him to the Belgravia Hotel and made love to him there that night. 'I simply cannot tell you how happy you made me yesterday,' she wrote to him (3 April 1924).

But in the weeks and months that followed she was to make him despairingly unhappy. He became mesmerized once more by her pink cheeks and seductive voice, that thick brown hair clipped like a yew hedge and those blue eyes with their disconcerting glance of innocence. By June he had moved into a flat in 18 Fitzroy Street lent to him by Roger Fry, and there he waited for Carrington to come to him. But she did not come – or hardly ever, it seemed to him.

Next to Lytton, Carrington had loved Gerald probably better than anyone because while he was in Spain he shared with Lytton the inaccessibility she found so attractive. 'You know my secret life is with you,' she told him (June 1924). 'I doubt if I shall ever meet anyone again who will exercise the special magic . . . I feel very intimate with you.' This magical place in Carrington's imaginative world began to fade after he turned up in England demanding to see her all the time. To preserve the mystique of his elusiveness she made herself hard to catch. Gerald would spend 'all day in bed', his biographer Jonathan Gathorne-Hardy records, 'often weeping, in an agony of misery and despair, or nervously, rapidly pace the room under acute tension, waiting, expecting, listening . . .' [13]

What was he to do? 'I should like my room to be available to you and Frances,' he volunteered to Ralph (25 June 1924). But he had not bargained on his room being used, while he was at the British Museum investigating the life of an austere sixteenth-century Spanish saint, by Carrington and Henrietta Bingham who, Carrington explained, 'killed my desires for les jeunes garçons pretty completely'. Would there have been fewer misfortunes, she wondered, had she been entirely Sapphic? It was ironic that Henrietta, who really meant so much less to her than Gerald, should have so fundamentally altered her sexual feelings.

'If I could make you unhappy I would,' Gerald retaliated. '. . . I simply see in you an object which (for what motive I don't understand) causes me most elaborate suffering.'

If she could have made him happy she would. But in spite of their enduring affection for each other there was something between them that went on producing unhappiness. Whenever she was going to see him, she would still feel a sensation, a quality of love, that was different from the love she felt for anyone else. Afterwards she hated the arguments that burst out between them. The trouble was that sexual intercourse had become Gerald's one proof that she still loved him. 'I know I can't make you happy in the way you want,' she explained (7 November 1924), 'and I can't bear to be the person who makes you unhappy.' She tormented herself with guilt until, her friend Julia Strachey observed, it 'surrounded her like a cloud of mosquitoes wherever she went'. The only comfort she could offer Gerald was the fact that (25 July 1924) 'Henrietta repays my affections almost as negatively as you find I do yours. In the end I expect you will find Saint Teresa your best and most faithful mistress.' But Gerald's biography of Saint Teresa was not going well. The more he worked, the more dismaying similarities he found between his religious subject, with her charm and complexity and self-doubt, and Carrington herself. There seemed no escape.

But that August he did escape to a cottage on Romney Marsh in Kent where he was to tutor Boris and Helen Anrep's two children over their summer holidays. 'You had much better conduct your life in the future without considering me,' Carrington had advised him (25 July 1924). Yet now, when he went away without considering her, she was greatly upset. It appeared that Frances knew more of Gerald's plans than she did. Besides, Stephen Tomlin had carried off Henrietta to Scotland that month so she could have come to visit Gerald as much as he liked. Or so she said. 'It means I see that I shall not see you for 2 months at least,' she chided him (4 August 1924). But because he was growing elusive again, she pursued him into Kent, staying four days at Romney Marsh early in September, fighting all day, the Anrep children remembered, and fucking all night.

The Anreps' marriage was on the point of breaking up. Boris had moved his exotic eighteen-year-old mistress into the family home, and Helen was preparing to move out and live with Roger Fry. Remembering Roger's previous liaison with Vanessa, Gerald wondered whether these new arrangements were not good examples for Carrington of cohabitations being happily ended and new relationships begun. During 1925, as Ralph grew closer to Frances, so he ceased having marital relations with Carrington. But this appeared to stimulate Carrington's affection for him. 'I am sorry I can't feel quite the same as Helen does towards Boris or as Vanessa does to Roger,' she apologized to Gerald (30 June 1925).

She was anxious that Gerald should not exercise his amazing talent for indiscretion and lay bare all their problems before Ralph. 'I won't want him and F[rances] to revel over our misfortunes,' she wrote (7 October 1924). In London, Gerald was seeing a lot of Frances these days. 'Is that an affair now?' Alix inquired. But James, who had spotted a back view of them getting off a train thirty yards away, made the instant diagnosis that they were not lovers. Whether at the circus in Olympia, or on the Giant Racer at Wembley, or together in the music halls, Gerald was talking to Frances about the philosophy of Hegel and the unresolved personality of Carrington. 'He was an amusing and altogether delightful companion,' Frances remembered, '. . . [but] I knew that some of his remarks about Carrington were made in the hope that they would eventually reach her ears, so that I felt rather like a loaded gun, which may do an equal amount of damage whether it goes off or not.'

Carrington was troubled by Frances's influence over Ralph. 'His relations are so easy, he never finds Frances lacking in any quality,' she confided to Gerald (6 August 1924). 'He can't understand our difficulties and if he does he simply thinks either you are mad, or that I deserve what I get because I behave so badly.' Yet Ralph had problems of his own. He felt a responsibility for Lytton and Carrington, yet he also felt them to be barriers between himself and Frances. 'I'm like a lost soul without you,' he had lamented to her (22 June 1924) when preparing to move into Ham Spray. Frances's visits to Ham Spray were not really enjoyable. Both Lytton and Carrington saw her as a potential danger to their way of life – for all her excellent qualities, she was not really their type of person: too unrealistically straightforward and remorselessly well balanced. They hoped that Ralph's passion for her would pass. Perhaps he feared it too. 'I feel uneasy,' he wrote to her in London (17 July 1924), 'because I'm engaged on something that you can't really share with me, it's such a waste of time and an irritation on the nerves. I *shall* be glad when I get back into the world again.' For Carrington the world was Lytton and Ham Spray; for Ralph it was London and Frances.

In the summer of 1924 Frances started seeing another man. He shared her gift for dancing, was unmarried and free to give her children. 'I mind a great deal about Hamish,'* Ralph told her. '. . . I am desperately in love with you.' He had often spoken to her about their own long-term future, but she was aware of 'the strong obstacle to our happiness together

---

* Philip Nicols, referred to as 'Hamish' in her memoirs.

represented by Lytton, Carrington and Ham Spray combined, whereas in the case of Hamish the way was clear and unobstructed'. So the tension heightened, every excitement set up in one part of the molecule between any two of its atoms agitating them all.

Lytton watched these shifting crises helplessly as one might watch violent changes in the weather. Recently his health had deteriorated – no one knew why. 'Apparently Lytton used to get ill like this,' Ralph reported to Frances. '. . . We now anticipate that he will go back to this earlier condition, if we do not make still gloomier prophecies. It takes two to look after him, and a doctor.' Despite himself, Ralph could not help being irritated by Lytton's infirmities, on top of Carrington's irresponsibilities and the wild vagaries of Gerald. He began to fret against the restrictions of his life at Ham Spray. But could he leave? Carrington's jealousy over Frances, though suppressed, was causing her to hold more tenaciously on to her husband. She never willingly gave up anyone – not Gerald, not even Gertler – and she dreaded that if Ralph went to live with Frances, Lytton might leave her.

From Friday night to Sunday they gathered to argue, debate and analyse their predicament; and from Monday back to Friday they carried on exchanging jokes, scandal and advice on page after page of writing-paper. As they paced the veranda at the weekends, sat in the garden, circled round the ping-pong table, their talk of psychoanalysis and masturbation, the vice of jealousy and the virtues of inquisitiveness, the nature of bisexuality and the general peculiarities of love-affairs would make fantastic jumps from private speculation to general propositions: then be arrested in mid-air by some *pièce de résistance* such as a recitation by Lytton from Stendhal's *Psychologie de l'Amour*, or a charade by Sheppard imitating Ottoline pretending to be as petite as Lydia Lopokova, or a new batch of Marjorie Strachey's obscene nursery rhymes. These, and Lytton's theatrical farces, gave temporary relief to their perplexities like incidental music in a Restoration comedy.

Nothing could have dramatized the mystery of love and the fickleness of sexual passion so bathetically as the entrance into Ham Spray of Lytton's old flame Henry Lamb. Of his dazzling pre-war beauty not a trace remained on the now battered face. 'He looks like an Army doctor who has seen "life" perhaps on the Tibet frontier,' Carrington notified Gerald (22 January 1925), 'or who has suffered from low fevers in Sierra Leone and also has a past murder, or crime, which makes him furtive and uneasy.' He was still in love with the extraordinary Dorelia John, but against her prevailing beauty he appeared a very faded piece of wallpaper. Yet Carrington welcomed him because he could talk astutely about painting and was an encouraging critic of her work.

Philip Ritchie, with his irregular features and endearingly gauche manner, was far more interesting to Lytton – like a superior version of his young self. On one of the weekends at Garsington, Lytton was introduced by Philip to his closest friend, another Oxford boy called Roger Senhouse, a romantic creature 'with a melting smile and dark grey eyes'. The two of them appeared inseparable and by the spring of 1925 they had become regular weekend visitors to Ham Spray. So new atoms were regularly added to the complex molecule and though the structure still held, the quivering commotion this-way-and-that intensified.

It became a necessity to escape occasionally from this pressure-cooking atmosphere. At Lady Horner's manor house in Somerset, Lytton tentatively experimented over a flirtation with the novelist Stephen McKenna and was flirted at more boldly by a French governess who directed at him a stream of admiring letters. In London he joined Bunny Garnett's new Cranium Club[14] where many of the younger 'Bloomsberries' would meet once a month and, according to Carrington, 'try and discuss Einstein but actually sing "Rendel my Son" at the piano'.

During those spring and early summer months of 1925 they began manoeuvring in search of a resolution to their problems. While Gerald prepared to take rooms near Ham Spray in the village of Shalbourne, Ralph carried Frances and Carrington off to France, and Lytton recovered his composure with Sebastian Sprott at Lyme Regis.

Separated from Carrington and Ralph, Lytton was better able to show those feelings that he found so difficult face to face – feelings which, even now, they might be tempted to overlook. 'Among other things I've felt a certain inability to express my feelings properly,' he admitted in a letter to Ralph (3 April 1925), '– I don't know why – and I've been afraid you may have thought, or dimly imagined, that they might have changed in some way – owing to Philip [Ritchie], perhaps, or other things. But it is not in the least so. All I feel for you is exactly the same, only strengthened by the passage of time; and it would be useless for me to try to say how much you and Carrington are to me. I can hardly imagine how I would exist without you both. Perhaps all this is unnecessary, and merely the result of the depression and fear of low vitality. But in any case you will understand.'

Love, that convenient monosyllable, was what Lytton was indicating – though he could not bring himself to write it down. But another word defines their situation better: *attachment*. They were attached to one another by many ties of understanding, affection, need. Lytton cherished Ham Spray, and wanted above all things to preserve their way of life there, now being threatened by the bombardment of so many external forces. In Gerald Brenan and Frances Marshall he saw two disruptive influences;

but he recognized their right to enter into the life there along with Philip Ritchie or Roger Senhouse. If the present unwieldy molecule, its atoms dedicated to eternal motion, could be held together by the gravitational pull of his own attachment, then their stability would hold.

But how long could these vibrations go on without pulling apart the perilous architecture of their lives? Besides spreading his own happiness to others, Lytton could do nothing but watch as the entire structure shook in perpetual ferment.

3

A MODERATE SUCCESS

These impending dramas were briefly halted in the summer of 1925 by the production of Lytton's 'tragic melodrama', *A Son of Heaven*, the 'Chinese concoction' which he had composed a dozen years before in the hope of making himself a quick and brilliant fortune. Now that money and fame had come from his biographies, the theatre managements, which had been so enthusiastically unhelpful in the lean years, were eager to consider the play afresh. The right time to stage it, they declared, had finally arrived: the right time for them, perhaps, but not for Lytton. He could no longer take this juvenile stage thriller seriously. His interest revived briefly on learning that the Lord Chamberlain (who may well have seen himself as Head Eunuch in the play) objected to certain passages, but when the Stage Society approached him with an offer to produce it, he turned them down. Harcourt Brace, however, set themselves up in the United States as agents for the play, and the impecunious Desmond MacCarthy confidently predicted that, adapted as a film, it would make Lytton a millionaire. Mrs Patrick Campbell, too, seems to have taken some interest in Lytton as a playwright, and on being assured by him that there was no star part for her in *A Son of Heaven*, begged him to write another play for her, providing him as she spoke with a description of her role in it. But he stared at her with such depth of silence and incredulity that the thought crossed her mind that he might have died of a sudden stroke. 'Well, will you, Mr Strachey?' she insisted after a long pause, whereupon he turned and piped in his tersest treble: '*No!*' But to a more modest request he felt obliged to accede. This was to allow two public charity performances at the Scala Theatre to raise funds for the London Society for Women's Service, of which his sister Pippa was the secretary.

A Son of Heaven, which takes place in the Winter Palace of the Chinese

547

imperial court at Peking during the Boxer Rising, is a 'lively historical cocktail of tragi-comedy, romance, melodrama, satire, insight and prejudice', in the words of the critic George Simson, who was to see its dramaturgy as a proving-ground for the New Biography. It has a variety of styles, borrowing something from the psychological methods of Racine as well as from the entertainments of Gilbert and Sullivan and the Edwardian music halls. His heroes do 'not die with a bang or a whimper', Simson observes, 'but of confusion'. In the middle of this confusion, the playwright serving as Herald, an observer and participant, lets us enter the drama whenever he can and, when he cannot, uses his voice to fill the narrative gaps, 'a character onstage and an interpreter and shaper of events'.[15]

The Scala production of *A Son of Heaven* was described by the Indian critic K.R. Srinivasa Iyengar as 'a moderate success'. Considering the quality of the acting and the violent altercations which, up to the opening night, rocketed between cast and director, even a moderate success seems remarkable. With its palace intrigues set against rich oriental magnificence, its cast which includes an Empress who speaks like a grander version of Elizabeth I (and who compares herself favourably to Queen Victoria), a sensitive Emperor, Princes, Ministers and Manchus all deep in subterfuge, a chorus of superstitious eunuchs and a masked executioner (played by Ralph Partridge), it can be produced either as a glorious historical extravaganza dominated by the Empress Dowager (who had been partly based on Lytton's aunt Lady Colvile); or alternatively, with a little dextrous cutting, as an intimate twentieth-century drama somewhat in the Granville Barker tradition in which the throne-room of the Winter Palace re-creates Whitehall, Westminster and the Buckingham Palace of Edwardian England, and where the theme focuses on the *fainéant* Emperor.

The leading part of the Empress Dowager, which Lytton had originally created for the comic actress Fanny Brough, was taken by Gertrude Kingston, a well-known performer of the old professional school,[16] who saw the work as neo-classical melodrama. The director was Lytton's Cambridge friend, Alec Penrose, who, being much influenced by the work of Edward Gordon Craig, felt that the play should be choreographed as a ballet. Inevitably these two principal figures took great exception to each other and, since neither was willing to concede anything, the result was an appalling clash of styles and a succession of ear-splitting rows. Gertrude Kingston thought the producer's theatrical notions amounted to so much new-fangled nonsense and disregarded his instructions. He was powerless to do anything with her since she was the mainspring of the whole affair.

During rehearsals a crisis would break out every few days threatening to capsize the production, and Lytton, in his now familiar role as mediator and diplomat, would hurry up to London to sort things out.

These rehearsals were made no easier by the rest of the cast – young amateur actors from Cambridge and the neighbourhood of Gordon Square, including three future academic professors. Professor Geoffrey Webb[17] played the part of Wang Fu, a provincial official, and also a European soldier; Sheppard was got up as a Manchu; Professor Dennis Robertson[18] was Li, Head Eunuch in the palace, whose retinue of lesser eunuchs included Lytton's artist-nephew John Strachey. Lytton's novelist niece Julia, as chief lady-in-waiting, was dressed in Chinese court costume, with red lips like two aces of hearts set tip to tip, and fluttered through her part very prettily. But Gerald Brenan, a palace guard, who had only to say 'Yes, your Majesty!' was so nervous on the first night that he said, 'No, your Majesty!'

Most of the actors had parts singularly ill-suited to their characters and were obliged to play love-scenes opposite people for whom they felt a special aversion. From the very first, there was much competition for certain roles, much bartering of parts, much carping and rivalry. At Ham Spray nothing but the play was talked of for several weeks. 'Do you want a super part?' Ralph asked Frances (25 May 1925). 'I am put down to be a Russian, a Boxer, an executioner and a Eunuch – fellow eunuchs are to be Adrian [Stephen] and Frankie [Birrell] and Mouldy [Webb]. Alec takes it all very seriously. Lytton tries hard not to show any interest but is unmistakably excited ... I anticipate a great deal of bother and very slight fun in the end.'

With only a few days to go, it looked as if the production might have to be called off. 'There's a Pirandello plot going on in Lytton's play,' Ralph explained (7 July 1925), '– the Empress together with the chief Eunuch are plotting against Bea Howe in real life as on the stage, and wish to turn her out together with Alec. Lytton was telephoned for and had to rush up yesterday afternoon to get at Dennis Robertson and the conspirators. There is a ferment at 51 Gordon Square – Pippa and Ray [Strachey] at their wits' end, how to appease Gertrude and yet maintain Alec. Lytton went up swearing to maintain the constitution, but also in great sympathy with the rebellion.' Once again a crisis was averted, the actors and director appeased; and the play was at last ready for production.

Perhaps the best features of the Scala version were the incidental music, composed by young William Walton,[19] the costumes and the sets – of the Throne Hall of Heavenly Purity in the Winter Palace, the palace garden and the courtyard in the palace precincts – designed by Duncan

Grant somewhat after the style of a D'Oyly Carte *Mikado*. The general atmosphere was of a pleasant teashop, James Agate commented, 'and one reflected that Sir Arthur Sullivan would have turned the whole thing into a delightful entertainment'.[20] The programme cover, 'A Son of Heaven' executed in Chinese characters, was done in mauve and red by Vanessa Bell.

The worst feature was the mutilation of Lytton's text. Enormous cuts had been made, including some of the chief speeches, in such a way that the original faults of the play were glaringly paraded. Reviewers noticed two plays within *A Son of Heaven*. The first, a rattling Elizabethan melodrama, reached its climax in the final act, amid a staccato profusion of tremendous moments. The second, somewhat in the style of Chekhov, was a gentler tragi-comedy. But the realism and the romanticism were never integrated as they are in Lytton's essays and biographies. He had used the biographical portrait by J.O.P. Bland[21] for his Empress Dowager, and she was the only figure to come fully to life. Beside her, the helpless young Emperor was a waxwork. 'He brought the Son of Heaven right to the front when he ought to have remained part of the background,' wrote Desmond MacCarthy. '. . . The Old Buddha should dominate the play completely. Even if the second theme had been able to rival in interest the other, it would have only pulled the play out of its proper centre of gravity, for the secret of good play-writing is the elaboration of a single theme, not the ingenious dove-tailing of two.'

The London critics gave the play quite favourable notices. St Loe Strachey, much reconciled to his cousin's work since *Queen Victoria*, described the occasion as highly distinguished, and in his *Spectator* review demanded that *A Son of Heaven* be transferred to the West End. But though Gertrude Kingston wanted to put it on in the United States, and Sybil Thorndike, who saw it at the Scala, was 'enormously impressed' and eager to follow up her triumph in *Saint Joan* by acting the 'very wonderful part of the "Old Buddha"',[22] nothing came of these plans during Lytton's lifetime.[23]

But twenty-four years later, in the spring of 1949, *A Son of Heaven* was revived for a run of three weeks at the New Lindsey Theatre, where it was produced by Vera Bowen, a Russian producer of plays and ballets and a close friend of Lydia Lopokova. This professional presentation was far superior to the Scala version, smoothly integrated and, James Strachey remembered, 'really very moving'.[24]

4

SOME MORE PLOT AND FRESH STIRRINGS

The opening performance of *A Son of Heaven* took place on the evening of Sunday, 12 July. But Lytton was not there. A few hours before the curtain went up, he fled the country, travelling through the night to Innsbruck, where he met Sebastian Sprott with whom he had planned a walking tour of the Dolomites. But on the third day, loaded down by an enormous pack strapped across his shoulders, he subsided between two precipitous cliff walls. They then returned a few yards down the road to a café, after which their expedition degenerated into a commonplace bus tour. By the time they had arrived at Cortona, they were both heartily sick of buses. 'It's a most wearing method of travelling,' Lytton complained in a letter to Carrington, '– there are crises at every turn – one never knows whether one will get a seat – then one's packed in with countless Germans got up like escaped convicts – and finally the machine breaks down on the top of a mountain 10,000 feet high and 18 miles from anywhere. This is what happened to us. There we sat, as night fell, among the convicts, the rain thundering down on the canvas roof – horror on horror! However, we got in safe at last . . . Sebastian is charming, and makes existence possible by his command of the German tongue.'

On Wednesday, 5 August, while Sebastian hurried on to Florence, Lytton set off by an early train for London and at the weekend returned to Ham Spray. 'He seems very much the same,' Ralph admitted (9 August 1925), 'rather worn by his journey from Munich, and very pleased to be back.' Carrington, who still minded these wanderings abroad, was enraptured at seeing him again. Now she could take enjoyment once more in the pleasant things around her – 'a very hot sun all day, the exquisite beauty of the downs, Lytton's very supporting affection'. He had, she pointedly reminded Ralph (20 September 1925) 'such finesse of tact that he responds very quickly to one's moods'.

While Ralph spent much of the time book-binding and dreaming of Frances, Carrington cooked, painted and ministered to Lytton who settled down to catalogue his library. He was doing little writing, and the only new books which gave him pleasure seemed to be those of his friends, especially Maynard's brilliant memoir of Alfred Marshall.[25] If the domestic scene appeared calmer to him, this was because, James had told Alix (7 March 1925), he 'is serenely unaware (or pretends to be) of any difficulty'. But it was also because so many loved ones had absconded. The first of these, in mid-May 1925, was Henrietta Bingham. 'I did not lose her through pride,' Carrington had confessed to Alix, '. . . but through excess of L[ove] . . . I suspect she found my affections so cheap that she doubted they could be worth very much.' In a sense this was true. Henrietta had been psychoanalysed by Ernest Jones who discovered, James confided to Alix (7 May 1925), that the reason why she 'threw over Carrington was that she (Carrington) wasn't a virgin'. The irony of the situation prompted some bitterness in Carrington. 'I keep on forgetting she is cruel, & indifferent,' she told Gerald, '& I can only remember her Beauty, & her charm.'

It was really Gerald who felt most bitter. Carrington had refused to spend nights at his lodgings in Fitzroy Street because it was so noisy and smelly there. At about the time Henrietta returned to the United States, Gerald had moved to Shalbourne so that he could see Carrington more often at Ham Spray. But theirs was always the weakest link in the Ham Spray molecule. 'I cried in bed because of the sadness and dreariness of our day together,' she wrote to him after one agitated meeting (1 June 1925). '. . . I could hardly bear the difficulties which seemed to surround us . . . Directly I am away from you, I hate myself for being so unfriendly . . . I shall never have a friend like you again.' It was the old problem: whenever he felt sexually aroused she felt nothing; whenever he was absent, she was filled with romantic longings. It was not their fault, she wrote. 'It was simply an irony of fate, that drew out suddenly from a past bundle of suppressions, these feelings of mine for H[enrietta]. Which are of course perfectly futile and senseless.'

These torments had made Gerald behave very oddly. He would seize upon Ralph, interrupt his book-binding, implore him to tutor him in ping-pong, make him practise three, four and five hours a day, then suddenly contract tennis elbow and give it all up. Still he had not set down a word of his biography of St Teresa. Instead he would take down twenty books at a time from the shelves, read half a page here and there, put them back and then, half an hour later, return, take down the very same books again and go through the same performance. He wandered in distraction from room to room and from book to book. After an hour indoors extolling the glory of the open English country, he would pass another hour walking in the fields describing the architectural virtues of Fitzroy Street and the advantages of a grimy environment for the literary temperament. According to his mood, he would treat everything with microscopic earnestness or the utmost triviality. He was the soul of indiscretion among visitors, and when there was no one else to abuse, would denounce the cat Tiber – its lack of character, its bad manners, its ugliness, its inexplicable habit of scratching him when he baited it. One way and another he unsettled everyone.

Lytton tried hard to be sympathetic but was heard to say that people in love should not live together, since they drove each other mad. Gerald certainly appeared mad. On Carrington's insistence, he went to consult Dr Ellie Rendel, the daughter of Lytton's eldest sister Elinor, and she in her deep pessimistic voice, prescribed veronal and, when that failed, advised him to 'eat mercury every three days and after meals strychnine and hydrochloric acid'.[26] The prospect of such 'violent foods' cheered him a little, but did not break his obsession.

At a party following the last performance of *A Son of Heaven*, Gerald had become very drunk, flirted with Ralph's old girlfriend Marjorie Joad, and then raged at Carrington for avoiding him. Ralph had already left the party, so at two o'clock in the morning, carrying a heavy rucksack, Carrington struggled towards King's Cross station, Gerald running after her begging to be allowed to carry her luggage. But she would not let him. Her face was very pale, he remembered, 'her eyes enlarged and fixed in an icy misery', and she kept on telling him to go home. But Gerald's tragedy was that he had no home.

Surely this had to be the end of their affair. 'I see *my* complexes only bring out your worst features,' she wrote to him from Ham Spray (19 July 1925). 'Gerald, I think I am unfitted as a human being to have a relation with anyone. Sometimes I think my obsessions and fancies border on insanity.' Gerald too looked desolate, 'an agitated figure, often on the verge of tears'. Everything had to end, yet neither of them could see how to give the other up. Their heads spun in unhappy confusion. 'Let us calm down a little,' Carrington pleaded. Both of them were fearful of the consequences of separation, but in the last week of July Gerald made a supreme effort. 'I have definitely broken with Carrington,' he announced to Ralph (27 July 1925). '. . . You will not mind if I avoid seeing you for some time.'

But Gerald's friendship with Ralph, which had been poisoned by his jealousy of Ralph's earlier married life with Carrington, now began to mend. The two men, bound together by all they had suffered, grew more fond of each other. Gerald's despair reminded Ralph of his own position some three and a half years ago. 'He [Gerald] is far more bitter about her than I am,' he wrote to Frances. 'The wounds are fresh in him, but scars in me.' Sometimes Gerald's convulsions of passion shocked Ralph. He would pour out all his long accumulation of rage against Carrington's maddening ways – her broken promises, her indifference when pursued, her ardour when pursuing. Yet how dreary she made other women seem! Her power to hurt was perhaps her greatest fascination. In a sudden panic, Gerald begged Ralph to restrain Carrington from taking new lovers. At the same time he affected to be contemptuous of more peaceful love-affairs and for that very reason, Ralph feared, might despise his with Frances.

By the time Lytton returned from Italy, there was no sign of Gerald, though a good deal of speculation about him. Philip Ritchie had also disappeared – to Monte Carlo – and never wrote to Lytton. 'I confess at the moment I am depressed,' he confided to Mary Hutchinson. 'Such a lull everywhere.' James and Alix came to stay, and E.M. Forster and J.R. Ackerley. Also Henry Lamb, still trailing after Dorelia. 'He positively crouched, and begged for the crumbs that fell from Lytton's beard,' Carrington noted. 'Rather ironical ... That he should now beg to be allowed to come over again, when 10 years ago *he* made Lytton cringe at a look.'

Another old friend to visit them this autumn was Bunny Garnett, bringing with him a copy of his new novel, *The Sailor's Return*. 'I think it is a beautiful work of art,' Lytton congratulated him (20 September 1925), '– most skilful in its conception and treatment. Your power of omission seems to me particularly remarkable. I only wish (personally) that the subject had been rather different – I am slightly rubbed the wrong way by simple domesticity, babies and rattles.'

To Virginia he had likened this novel to 'a perfectly restored Inn – Ye Olde ... everything tidied up and restored'. He had also been reading Virginia's *Mrs Dalloway* and criticized the discordance between its beautiful ornamentation and banal happenings. 'I like him the better for saying so,' Virginia wrote in her diary, '& don't much mind.' Then there was Aldous Huxley. '"These Barren Leaves" fluttered from my hands,' he told Ottoline, 'before I had read more than four of them.' *The Tales of Genji*, translated by Arthur Waley, was faintly pleasurable, 'very beautiful in bits – Country wine, made by a lady of quality – Cowslip brandy'.

On 20 September, Lytton started off on his familiar 'Autumn Manoeuvres', missing out Monk's House this time, and going straight to Charleston. 'Clive, whose clothes are really too shabby even for me – sprouting bits of cloth at the shoulder-blade, – buttons hanging on threads from the trousers – is an indefatigible walker,' he wrote to Carrington (24 September 1925), '– out we go for hours over the downs. In the evenings we sit up till half past one chatting.'

He had seen too little of Leonard and Virginia recently, largely because he had been so occupied with the amours of Ham Spray. Leonard had begun to cool towards him, finding Morgan Forster now a more congenial companion. Virginia conceded many of Leonard's criticisms. 'He is cautious,' she agreed. 'He is valetudinarian.' But the fact remained that

Lytton was still one of the half-dozen people of significance in her life, and when they got together, as they did at Charleston this autumn, and talked about everything under the sun: 'love, and beauty, and prose and poetry . . . about our friendship; and age and time and death and all the rest of it', then something intimate and incandescent rose between them. Virginia resented the insipid young men of the milk-and-water kind like 'poor feeble Philip [Ritchie] for instance, who is precisely like an Eton boy in an Eton jacket: give him an ice & a sovereign', because they kept Lytton away from her. When in love, she saw, he 'feels a little ridiculous, uneasy, & does not relish the company of old cynical friends like ourselves'.

But the gossip this September was all about another Bloomsbury love-affair. How to account for Maynard's sensational marriage to Lydia Lopokova?

On 25 August, they had married at a London register office and gone off for a couple of weeks' honeymoon to Russia, where Maynard could meet Lydia's parents. Bloomsbury was 'shocked'. How could Maynard, Lytton wondered, have attached himself to this 'half-witted canary' who bobbed and flitted about the furniture, chirruping away and failing to conceal her incomprehension of the English language? Whatever could have possessed poor Pozzo? He actually seemed to be in love with her – and she with him! It was really quite extraordinary.

Perhaps Duncan had some excuse for resenting the emergence of a second great love into Maynard's life. But it was the others who were really malicious. As Maynard's mistress, Lydia had added something childlike and bizarre to Bloomsbury – she was a more welcome visitor than Clive's over-chic mistress Mary Hutchinson. But '*don't* marry her', Vanessa had instructed Maynard (1 January 1922). If he did so Lydia would give up her dancing, Vanessa warned, become expensive, and soon bore him dreadfully. But what Vanessa and the other Charlestonians chiefly minded was Lydia's effect as Maynard's wife on Bloomsbury itself. Living a quarter-of-a-mile from Charleston at Tilton House on the edge of the South Downs, she would sweep in and stop Vanessa painting – and these interruptions were always so scatterbrained! Vanessa appears to have been made uneasy too by thinking of the emotional effect Lydia's marriage might have on Duncan, and of the encouragement it might give Clive who was wondering whether to divorce her and marry Mary.

But Clive also disapproved of Lydia. She was so profoundly unintellectual. To Maynard's fury, he could not help ticking her off when she dared to mention Proust about whose work he was Bloomsbury's expert. Lydia did her best, tried studying Shakespeare, pretended to be as serious as Alix Strachey, but it seemed hopeless. 'I think it's rather tragic for Maynard,' concluded Roger Fry.

All these objections were concentrated into the letters, diaries and conversation of Virginia. She thought the marriage a fatal mistake. To some extent she was expressing a general objection to marriage, arising partly perhaps from her own inadequacy as a wife and partly from her resentment of Clive's marriage to her sister. Once she had referred to Clive as a male parakeet and now she called Lydia a female parakeet. For the fact was that Maynard's new wife had no 'head piece', possessed 'the soul of a squirrel' and was encircled by grand conventional ballet friends who had already corrupted Maynard, making him 'very gross & stout . . . [like] a queer swollen eel'. Such vacuous companions would soon convert the Keyneses' homes at Tilton and Gordon Square 'the resort of dukes and prime ministers'. It was all right for Lytton to make raids on such great people and come away with amusing cameos of them. It was another matter for them to invade Bloomsbury.

Lytton shared some of these misgivings, though he was never impolite to Lydia (indeed he was 'very kindly and amiable', she remembered) and invited her and Maynard to Ham Spray. But they did not go because, feeling uneasy perhaps over Maynard's and Lytton's past, Lydia said she disapproved of Carrington's immoral ways. Lytton had never wholly forgiven Maynard for stealing Duncan away from him and could not resist seasoning the gossip as he passed it on. Maynard, he reported, had laid claim to a certain picture by Duncan; Vanessa argued that it was hers, and Duncan, called in to adjudicate, naturally supported her. Passions rose high. Maynard, they maintained, didn't *need* the picture. He had no aesthetic taste and he was far too rich. Besides, he had other pictures. So they planned to transfer it with their other belongings from 46 to 39 Gordon Square. But Maynard, foreseeing what might happen, had screwed the picture to his bathroom wall and so frustrated their plot. Vanessa was furious, but still determined not to be outwitted. Apparently mollified, she invited Maynard for a weekend to Charleston, and while he was on his way down, herself travelled up to London armed with her old latchkey to No. 46 and a screwdriver. She unscrewed the picture, carried it across to No. 39, and then returned quietly to Charleston that afternoon without a word. These were not actions that could easily be forgiven, and Maynard's association with Charleston weakened.

Lytton had a chance to judge the new ménage when, after leaving Charleston, he visited Tilton for a few days. 'The Keynes visit was rather lugubrious, somehow or other,' he told Carrington (29 September 1925). 'For one thing the house was so hideous. Then Lydia is a pathetic figure, to my mind – and so plain. Maynard is as engrossed as usual in his own concerns. He was very interesting on Russia and Wittgenstein; but there is a difficulty of some kind in one's intercourse with him – he seems rather far off . . . Would you believe it? Not one drop of alcohol appeared. The Charlestonians declare that il gran Pozzo is now immensely rich – probably £10,000 a year [equivalent to £230,000 in 1994]. I can believe it – and water, water everywhere! Such is the result of wealth.'

What Lytton and the others failed to recognize was the great physical and emotional effect of Lydia's devotion on someone who had always believed himself to be irreparably unattractive to women. It was true that he had for a time tried to get the best of both worlds by combining his romance with Lydia and his continuing liaison with Sebastian Sprott. But when Lydia finally objected, Maynard shed Sebastian as a sexual partner. There is no doubt that she loved him sexually – her letters are full of praise for his 'wet warm kisses' and 'subtle finger' – and when Virginia predicted that 'age and familiarity' would 'entirely crush' Maynard's love for her, she demonstrated Bloomsbury's lack of sympathetic insight into human relations where its insight was reputed to be specially sharp.

So there was little wonder that, as Virginia observed, Lytton wished to divert this Bloomsbury searchlight from Ham Spray. 'Perhaps,' she had speculated (19 April 1925), 'Philip Ritchie is waning.' But after Lytton caught up with Philip at Eleanor House that autumn and carried him back to Ham Spray, they appeared as affectionate as ever – except perhaps when Lytton was even more affectionate to Philip's friend Roger Senhouse. Roger charmed everyone except Virginia who suspected that, like Lydia, he was 'almost imbecile' (though, unlike Lydia, 'rather attractive perhaps'). She resented having to be nice to Lytton's series of new pink boys – it really didn't suit her. But Carrington much preferred Roger to Philip. 'I was melted by him this weekend,' she told Julia Strachey that summer. As for Carrington herself, now that Henrietta and Gerald had left, she was melting somewhat before Julia. 'I love having Julia here,' she later (27 December 1926) wrote from Ham Spray to Gerald. 'She is a gay sympathetic character. Her turn of humour is very fascinating.' But Julia's new lover happened to be Henrietta's old lover, the mercurial Stephen Tomlin who, greatly attracting Lytton and repelling Ralph, spiralled round the Ham Spray molecule causing shock waves everywhere.

Having bought Ralph a car, Lytton was to give Carrington something she had long dreamed of owning: a horse. After coming back from fifteen-mile rides, she would write to tell Gerald how much 'I wish I could have had you on a brown cob beside me. I have never seen the landscape so lovely.' It was exciting too, when walking along the top of the Downs, to spot this little white horse in its field and know that it was hers. She felt like a thirteen-year-old girl. 'Belle is very happy in her field,' she later reported to Lytton (19 September 1926), 'I pay her visits and she comes up, and lets me pat her.'

By these simple means Lytton hoped to fasten their régime together. But late in 1925 they began to pitch and flounder towards a new crisis. After one weekend Morgan Forster complained that he would never return to Ham Spray because Ralph had been so surly. Genuinely astonished, Ralph hastened to repair the damage.[27] But the incident signalled his own worries over Frances and 'Hamish'.

At the beginning of October Frances and Ralph went off for a month to Spain. This had been Ralph's idea and 'tactically it was a brilliant move', Frances later recognized. On their return, after weeks of lovemaking, their one desire was to spend their lives together.

But how could they extricate themselves from this clinging web of human relationships at Ham Spray? 'My mind is perpetually dodging back to my feelings for you,' Ralph wrote to Frances. 'I move about in a trance hardly knowing what to do.' Taking advantage of a weekend trip by Lytton to F.L. Lucas's home in Cambridge, Ralph treated Carrington to a long discourse about these problems and his thoughts on solving them. For many months now, he informed her, they had been battling together in a storm of arguments. The truth was, he had discovered, the two of them were incompatible. She always liked getting her own way, and that way had to be different from everyone else's; while he could not bear letting her have her way without aggressive protests, which was his attempt to get *his* own way. Neither of them yielded to the claims of the other, and the best relationship they could hope for would be that of brother and sister, never again husband and wife. He could not part from Frances whom he loved, he explained, and must take steps to put their liaison on a more permanent basis. Since Frances obviously could not come and live at Ham Spray, he must go up to London.

Carrington stood before him, awkward and miserable, like a schoolgirl being reprimanded by her headmaster. This was what she had been dreading. She begged him not to abandon his life at Ham Spray altogether. How could she keep Lytton once he thought Ralph no longer took any interest in her? Ralph denied that his intention was to abandon them. But his priority must be Frances, he added, who accepted his commitment to Ham Spray and was not asking him to divorce Carrington. What, then, should be done? The time had come to admit Lytton into the secret, for much depended on how he would react to the news.

After he returned from Cambridge, there was a long interview between the three of them. Ralph, who had been dreading this ordeal, mechanically repeated all he had said before. Carrington, now that Lytton was beside her, 'was calmer but so sad'; while Lytton himself listened carefully to everything, without a sign of emotion. Although he was no longer deeply in love with Ralph, he believed Ralph's practical support and strength of character were indispensable to the well-being of Ham Spray. 'But does Ralph *always* know what to do?' Morgan Forster had timidly asked. 'Yes,' Lytton replied. 'He has an instinct which tells him how other people are going to behave. He never does the wrong thing.' The present situation, however, was clearly beyond Ralph's control, and Lytton felt inhibited from saying everything he wished by the presence of Carrington. His best tactics, he reasoned, would be to go and see Frances, who might prove less intransigent than Ralph.

The meeting between Lytton and Frances Marshall took place the following evening at the Oriental Club. Lytton at once made his own views clear. If Ralph were to go and live permanently in London with her, he warned, then he could not guarantee staying indefinitely at Ham Spray with Carrington. There was a danger that the Ham Spray molecule might disintegrate entirely, leaving Carrington stranded. 'What would become of her?' he asked. Frances answered that, though she had no wish to drive a wedge between them all, it was surely not unreasonable for her to want to live with Ralph. Nevertheless she left the Oriental Club 'pierced by a poison dart', she recorded. 'So far I had not felt I was acting like a criminal.'

Lytton returned to Ham Spray. He could do no more. He wanted to bring home to Ralph and Frances the possible long-term results of any action they might take. Beyond that he would neither help nor hinder them. It was their own decision.

Despite Lytton's belief in his sound sense, it was Ralph's perpetual policing of these liaisons between Gerald, Carrington, Frances and himself that had exacerbated their problems. In an attempt to evade his management, Carrington appealed to Julia Strachey with whom she hoped Frances could share a flat and give Ralph visiting rights. 'I love you Julia for being so understanding and giving me a straw to cling to,' she wrote early in 1926. '. . . If only one's feelings weren't so involved there is a fascination in intrigue and plots that is unequalled.'

When this intrigue came to nothing, Carrington abandoned plots and wrote directly to Frances. 'We each know what we have all three been feeling these last months. Now it is more or less over. The Treaty has to be drawn up.

'I have to face that owing to a situation, which cannot be got over, I must

559

give up living with Ralph. I simply now write quite frankly, to beg you to try ... and see if it's not compatible with your happiness to still let me keep some of my friendship with Ralph. I can't get away from everything because of Lytton ... The bare truth from my point of view is that if Ralph leaves me completely, it really means an end to this life. I can't ask *him* to go on seeing me down here, because he really feels it depends on whether *you* can bear it. If you can't, nothing can be done. If you can, you must know it would mean everything to Lytton and me.'

Frances expressed herself as 'profoundly shocked' by this letter. Had she not told Lytton at the Oriental Club that she had no wish to drive a wedge between him and Carrington by carrying Ralph permanently away? For too long now the two women had only communicated indirectly through Ralph and the knot into which their shared happiness was tied hardened as it became more difficult for them to talk frankly to him. It was easy in black moments for each woman to see the other as a monster. But at last the knot began to unravel. Frances explained that though she had objected to Lytton's theory that the present situation could simply continue with her as a visitor to Ralph's life, 'I never never never feel that if R should live with me I should not want him to see you very often and go on being very fond of you ... it is to my interest that he should have to give up as little as possible of his happiness in order to live with me.'

After these two letters, and the rotating correspondence between everyone else that closely followed in the wake of them, their misunderstandings began to lift. Lytton took Carrington away to Falmouth for a few days' holiday, and when they returned the winter days of suspense seemed over. 'Today the hot sun, the innumerable birds singing, the flowers which suddenly have all come out made me so happy I couldn't work indoors,' Carrington wrote to Ralph (13 February 1926). 'I had to run about in the garden and put down sods on the empty flower bed, but in reality running round the garden out of high spirits. Lytton came out and pretended to be an old gentleman tottering on the esplanade.'

Ralph, who had feared that Frances might even now turn back to 'Hamish', was also much relieved. 'I thought you'd given me up because you didn't care any more,' he miserably confessed to her. Frances too was relieved, knowing that Carrington wanted to go on seeing Ralph after he had settled with her in London. The problem of how to accomplish this was suddenly solved that spring when James and Alix offered to lease them the handsome L-shaped first-floor flat at 41 Gordon Square. They would have Maynard and Lydia, Adrian and Karin Stephen, Clive Bell, Dadie Rylands and almost all the Strachey family as their close neighbours. 'I feel so happy that I haven't any misgivings,' Ralph told Frances. He now regarded himself as married to Frances, he explained to Gerald who had gone away to France. Lytton too 'seems very pleased that we are going to 41 and did not say a single crabbing word', Ralph added to Frances, 'except that if he had known they were so cheap he would have taken the rooms himself.'

Carrington called it 'a miracle'. In another year perhaps she would be 'as indifferent as Alix to people'. She had been half in love with the turmoil though the circumstances had been 'shattering' for her 'and also for me', Lytton volunteered to Sebastian Sprott (7 May 1926). 'Everyone has behaved with great magnanimity, & I don't see that blame attaches anywhere – but it's unfortunate.' As Frances went shopping for distemper and brushes, painting one wall pink and another green, moving in the Kelim rugs, pictures, furniture, double bed for this new experiment, and Ralph went up to help her, Ham Spray fell strangely quiet. 'C & I', Lytton wrote, 'live here in a vacuum.'

5

FIDDLING WITH ELIZABETH

'How long were the pauses between his books!' Desmond MacCarthy exclaimed. Lytton thought carefully about his literary future during these pauses. What should he do next? There was no lack of suggestions, or of his objections to them. As MacCarthy observed, he kept the chessboard of literary success in the corner of his study and would, so to speak, often stroll over to it, amused at his own hesitation, and wonder which piece he might move next – a queen, a bishop, or a knight? Or perhaps a little attack meanwhile with pawns against the public?

Since moving into Ham Spray, his output had been slight – though it had included his Leslie Stephen Lecture on Alexander Pope. He had long felt an affinity with what he had called Pope's 'crooked habit of mind', seeing it as a 'manifestation of that deformed and sickly state of being which had dwarfed and twisted his body, and made one "long disease" of his whole life'.[28] Writing as one *névrosé* about another, he implies that there is a relationship between a writer's physical condition and the literary style in which he works. Was it not possible that Pope achieved his elaborate 'correctness' with all its smooth transitions and brilliance of texture as a partial compensation for his ill-dressed bodily imperfections? Was there not a peculiar satisfaction for him in assembling the machinery of the heroic couplet as a device for torturing his aristocratic victims into shapes more humiliating than his own? In much that Lytton writes about Pope, a parallel with his own life and writing may be inferred.

The technical aspect of Pope's work was 'perhaps the most important side of all', Lytton wrote when reviewing George Paston's biography for the *Spectator* in 1909. It was to the technical evolution of verse forms that he addressed his Leslie Stephen Lecture fifteen years later: analysing the contribution made by the English classical couplet to the development of English poetry after the possibilities of Elizabethan blank verse were played out; uncovering the language of passion in this ordered symmetry; and concluding that these attributes constituted the 'high seriousness' and 'adequate poetic criticism of life' that Matthew Arnold ('Dr Arnold's son', Lytton called him) had denied Pope.

He was anxious about delivering this lecture before a large audience at Cambridge, wondering whether he should use a microphone. 'We have no loudspeaker,' the vice-chancellor A.C. Seward replied, 'and from what I have heard of the use of that instrument in London I feel rather shy of suggesting an installation of one here.' His anxieties redoubling, Lytton developed a sore throat, diagnosed by his brother James as an hysterical formation aimed at the lecture. But his aim had been too eager and on the afternoon of Saturday, 6 June 1925 he delivered his lecture with no sign of difficulty. Near the beginning, hearing Pope described as a fiendish monkey at an upstairs window ladling out spoonfuls of hot oil on to his victims, the audience started into delighted laughter. 'If it had been my privilege to be present,' Edmund Gosse sombrely recorded, 'I must have buried my face in my hands.'

Gosse included his 'Pope and Mr Lytton Strachey' in a volume of essays, *Leaves and Fruit*, dedicated 'to Lytton Strachey with Affectionate Admiration'.[29] This was the latest gesture in a relationship between these two biographers that was animated by little enough admiration and rather less affection. Gosse's disapproval of Lytton, partly concealed by an array of fine mannerisms, was rooted in the belief that, unlike Pope, he had been disloyal 'to the dignity of literature'. It was the incompatibility of generations that so awkwardly linked them. Gosse had crossed swords with Lytton over the 'errors of discretion' in *Eminent Victorians*, but welcomed *Queen Victoria* as 'a riper, a more finely balanced, a more responsible study than its predecessors' that established him as 'the earliest of the biographers to insist that a cat, and still more a careful student of the whimsicalities of life, may look steadily at a queen'. But as his biographer Ann Thwaite comments, Gosse himself had paved the way for this change in biography.

Lytton liked Gosse's *Father and Son* 'though not him', he had hurriedly added. He was so cautious, Lytton felt, perhaps insincere too. When someone asked him whether Gosse was homosexual, he had answered: 'No, but he's Hamo-sexual,' referring to his special friendship with the sculptor Hamo Thornycroft. Henry James described Gosse as having 'a genius for inaccuracy' and many of his inaccuracies, removed from under their covering of literary dignity, had been shown up by the criminologist critic Churton Collins. After reading Evan Charteris's *The Life and Letters of Sir Edmund Gosse*, Lytton wrote to Max Beerbohm (15 April 1931): 'I observe that at one point he [Gosse] characteristically gives Swinburne a widow. Luckily Churton Collins is dead.'[30]

They kept up a polite façade whenever they met, Gosse discharging his discourtesies into the press, Lytton reserving his incivilities for his friends. When Gosse inquired whether he regarded himself as an Edwardian, Lytton decorously replied: 'I am an Edmundian.' But, having once had his name fatally misspelt 'Edmund Goose', he became ever afterwards for Lytton 'Goose Gosse'.

Several of the alterations Lytton made to the essays appearing in *Books and Characters* were designed to show Gosse as less gooselike. He sent him a copy, and Gosse, then safely in his seventies, replied that Lytton was 'the best writer under fifty'.

Such compliments did not please Virginia as she looked on. Occasionally 'grocer Gosse', as she called him, came up in Bloomsbury conversation. She knew that Lytton thought her rather 'narrow-minded' about him, and she suspected Lytton of being rather too sentimental. 'It is said that you are getting up a subscription to give Edmund Gosse gold sleeve links on his 100th birthday,' she teased him (26 January 1926). But not long afterwards, in merely his eightieth year, Gosse died, and was succeeded as leading reviewer on the *Sunday Times* by Desmond MacCarthy.

*

During the 1920s Lytton resisted many openings and sacrifices. He turned down offers to write prefaces for Paul Valéry's *Le Serpent* and to C.K. Scott Moncrieff's translation of Proust's *A la recherche du temps perdu*, and though he did finally agree to provide an introduction to each volume of the *New Cambridge Shakespeare* (edited by Arthur Quiller-Couch and John Dover Wilson), this agreement collapsed after Cambridge University Press refused Chatto & Windus the rights to reprint his introductions. Eventually, the one commission he completed was an introduction to his friend Dadie Rylands's Hogarth Press anthology *Words and Poetry* (1928).[31]

There were other things also he positively did not do. He did not reduce the six-volume Monypenny and Buckle *Life of Disraeli* to a two-volume edition for a fee of one thousand pounds; and when his old university at Liverpool inquired whether he would like to succeed Oliver Elton in the Chair of Literature, he politely declined. He wanted to do more writing and for some months deliberated semi-seriously over a Life of Christ. 'Quite a good book has just arrived – Le Mystère de Jésus, by Couchoud,' he eventually told Ralph (3 April 1925), '– it finally relegates the poor fellow to the region of myth, and seems to me to be the last nail in the coffin of my book. What a nuisance! I think I shall have to take definitely to the drama'.

Again he studied the chessboard; and it was not a stage drama that he at last fixed upon. For in October 1925, a new idea came to him. He would compose a book of love-affairs; Queen Elizabeth and the Earl of Essex; Voltaire and Madame du Châtelet; Byron and his half-sister; Mr and Mrs Browning; and finally, if he had the nerve, Verlaine and Rimbaud. Such a scheme would yield admirably to the principles of biography formulated by Dr Johnson in his *Lives of the Poets*: to 'pass slightly over those performances and incidents which produce a vulgar greatness, to lead the thoughts into domestic privacies and to display the minute details of private life.' Lytton was eager to proceed with this project – in any case he needed, so Ralph told him, the extra money to pay his colossal super-tax. He started reading about Queen Elizabeth at once.

Two months later his plans had changed. The story of Elizabeth and Robert Devereux, Earl of Essex, so absorbed him that he decided to devote a volume to it. He would follow up his portrait of one Queen by this study of another. But it was going to be an altogether different sort of book, an experiment to transform biography from the solid craft of his *Victoria* into the more impalpable sphere of poetic drama – that elusive world moving between fact and fiction, fantasy and reality, that was the world of his own love-affairs.

Lytton began *Elizabeth and Essex* on the morning of 17 December 1925. 'He has written two pages of Queen Elizabeth,' Carrington informed Ralph the following day. 'He says he has forgotten how to write and finds it almost impossible!' For a month he worked at the book nearly every day. 'I have been having quite a tussle with the Virgin Queen,' he admitted to Ralph (6 January 1926), 'and am feeling at the moment perfectly exhausted.' Of all his books, *Elizabeth and Essex* was to be the most ambitious. Nothing he wrote gave him so much difficulty or wore him out so completely, and for over a year he had doubts as to whether he could bring it off. After six months' slow labour, he took himself off with his sister Pippa for a few days to Paris where 'the great, the exciting, the absorbing news was that – Cocteau had become a Roman Catholic,' he wrote to Ottoline (10 June 1926). 'Compared with that the collapse of the franc was nothing.'

He needed these recuperative holidays. At the end of another burst at *Elizabeth*, he travelled up to Hexham, in Northumberland, to spend a few days with the novelist Rosamond Lehmann and her two (present and future) husbands. 'Mr and Mrs R[unciman] share the establishment with a young man called Wogan Philipps – quite nice – and then there was Dadie – and that was the party,' he wrote to Carrington (19 June 1926).

'Leslie [Runciman][32] is to me extremely attractive – in character, even, as well as appearance. But I don't suppose many would agree with this. He is pompous, moody, flies into tempers, and is not mentally entertaining by any means. Perhaps you would be bored by the poor fellow. But oh! he's so strong, and his difficulties are so curious – and his eyelashes . . . there's a childishness about him that – I daresay all grown-up people are childish in some way or another – I find endearing. Rosamond is a much brighter character . . . though not as good-looking – gay, enthusiastic, and full of fun. She and Dadie get on like a house on fire. Wogan lies vaguely and sympathetically at their feet. And dear Leslie makes a pompous remark, to which no attention is paid, looks divine, scowls, until I long to fling my arms round his neck.'

He continued his journey north into Scotland where he was to be awarded an honorary doctorate in Law by the University of Edinburgh. 'I shan't exchange a sensible word with a single soul till I depart,' he complained to Carrington. '. . . Sir Alfred [Ewing][33] is a pawky little Scotch body, his wife a very plain, unfortunately, high-minded individual, without a spark of humour. Lord Allenby – a large, stupid man – is my fellow guest in the house.[34] It was certainly very wise of me to refuse the dinner, which is going on at the present moment, and where they all are, poor creatures, drinking bad champagne and listening to facetious speeches. This is a fine 1800 house, in a beautiful circle, – but oh! the taste of its internal decorations! How deplorable are the well-off!'

Two days later, the honorary doctorates were formally awarded.[35] 'The musical chairs went off very quietly this morning,' Lytton wrote later that day to Rosamond Lehmann, '– since then there has been a lunch and garden party, and in a few minutes a dinner party begins. What is left of me will return to-morrow – to face Lady Astor – and her son Bobbie[36] (who is not so bad). Nothing could be more complete than the contrast between this and Anick Cottage.'

By the end of the month he was back at Ham Spray. The love-story of Elizabeth and Essex was already involving him far more emotionally than his *Queen Victoria*. It kept prompting memories of his early love-affairs and mingling with the day-dreams of current infatuations – especially for the young Roger Senhouse. At times he appeared – like Virginia beginning her phantasmagorical *Orlando* – to enter a world of imagination, so that it became difficult to disentangle what was real from fantasy. For a few moments he might fancy himself possessed by something of Elizabeth's regal femininity – while before him stood the young and spirited Essex! Then all was vacancy and a sense of effort. In the aftermath of these strange moods, he felt bereft of identity, floating in a trance. 'A kind of dreaminess has descended upon me,' he wrote to Bunny Garnett (11 August 1926), 'only momentarily, I fancy – but there it is – I drift and drift; very pleasant, though shocking for my morale ... Circumstances have slightly changed, but hardly feelings, I think. As for me, so far as I can see I have always been identically what I was at the age of two. Rather monotonous for the rest of the world, perhaps!'

Now that Ralph came down only at weekends – almost always with Frances – and he was left during the week in the private world of *Elizabeth and Essex*, he needed the company of other friends if only to reaffirm his connection with the contemporary world. He eagerly accepted invitations, staying with Edward Sackville-West at Knole as the first of a new series of autumn visitations. 'Knole was interesting – beautiful on the whole externally, with the College-like courts and charming gardens and park,' he told Roger Senhouse (2 September 1926), 'but the inside was disappointing – too much hole-and-corner Elizabethanism; one longed for the spaciousness of the 18th Century; and the bad taste of countless generations of Sackvilles littered it all up. Eddie, it seemed to me, continued the tradition in his ladylike apartments ... We had quantities of music, both on piano and gramophone – interrupted from time to time, rather characteristically I thought, by – a cuckoo-clock! I found the self-centredness of my host a little chilling; and am very glad not to be the heir of Knole.'

Then Lytton veered off northwards again to visit Sebastian Sprott, who had recently left Cambridge to take up the post of lecturer in psychology at University College, Nottingham. 'I arrived here[37] on Friday with R[oger],' he notified Mary Hutchinson (11 October 1926). '... Nottingham is the oddest, grimmest place in the world, but with a certain hideous grandeur – Enormously large.' In a letter to Pippa the same day, he described the town as being 'grim and vast in a way I had hardly expected. The Explanation of England, probably.' There was little to do except sit on the edge of the gas-fire reading Elizabethan books, or wander through the streets where 'so far I've seen nothing either in the shops or out of them, to deserve more than passing attention'. Fellow lecturers of Sebastian's came to tea, but they seemed a melancholy crew, particularly Professor Weekley, Frieda Lawrence's ex-husband – 'a pompous old ape, "You keep a manservant, Sprott?" and so on'.

At last, after a couple of days with F.L. Lucas and his wife 'Topsy' in Cambridge, he came to rest at Ham Spray. The year seemed to be holding its breath before taking its final dive into winter, and he knew that he should be diving into *Elizabeth and Essex*. Yet a terrible lethargy swamped him. 'It seems to me that the world has stopped going round,' he confessed, 'but I am too lazy to bother about it.' He turned instead to Emil Ludwig's *Life of the Kaiser*, 'which is quite well done – interesting and fairly intelligent, though the translation might be better', to a new edition of *Les Fleurs du Mal* 'with a most interesting Preface by Valéry [who] ... persists in maintaining that Poe is a genius of the front rank' and to Arnold Bennett's *Lord Raingo* – 'distinctly neolithic; but, *qua* flint spearhead, quite well done'. It was now a year since he had started *Elizabeth and Essex*. 'Nobody can be more disgusted by my delay than myself,' he admitted to Chatto & Windus (13 December 1926). 'I am in hopes that I may be able to finish something on Queen Elizabeth before very long – certainly in less than a year – I hope much less. ... The Elizabeth book would be a very short one – dealing with her love-affair with Lord Essex at the end of her life. I should of course wish you to publish it if you liked the idea; but I feel rather doubtful about the whole thing.'

The explanation was that he had become 'run down'. The remedy was a fortnight in Rome with Roger Senhouse – 'a short jaunt with a divine creature!' he described it to Bunny Garnett (21 December 1926). 'I believe the breezes of the Channel and the sunlight of Rome will set me up completely,' he confidently predicted (16 December 1926). The two of them arrived on Christmas Eve under a blue sky and brilliant sun. They had booked a big double room in the Hotel Hassler, 'the best in Rome, high up over the steps that go down to the Piazza di Spagna ... so that everything is spread before us – St Peter's dome and a hundred churches ... We live in the height of luxury – private bathroom, etc., for £1 each day, including food. R. is a perfect companion – appreciates everything, and is continuously charming to me. He says he is enjoying himself very much, and I think he is – certainly I am.'

The holiday went so very well that he began to fear unforeseen snags.

Something, surely, *must* go wrong – a slight chill on the entrails at least. But no, the days sped past, full of miraculous sunshine and unbroken pleasure – it was really rather disturbing. 'Everything has equalled my wildest hopes,' he announced to Ralph (3 January 1927). '. . . We lounge in the Forum, pant grilling up to the Coliseum, sit toasting on the Pincio. – I hardly dare describe the generous heat . . . On Friday we took our lunch with us and motored out into the Campagna, and ate among ancient tombs on the Appian Way and the cypresses and pines with their spreading tops, drinking chianti in the blazing sun, while lizards crept out of the Roman masonry and flicked their green tails at us.' In the evenings they would return to the Hassler, 'where old Morganatic English females crouch and creep', to play piquet and read Dante. They also saw 'a delightful Roman opera', and one day Lytton was guest of honour at a luncheon given by Princess San Faustino, who explained how to assist the unemployed by cultivating the soya bean, a magic substance, the Princess assured him, from which factories and cars, synthetic chocolates and bath salts, could be miraculously manufactured. Working this idea up, as course followed course, to an exciting climax, she turned at the end of the meal and appealed: 'Mr Strachey, what do you think of my schemes?' 'I'm afraid I don't like beans,' he apologized.

After the delights of Rome, Ham Spray was a waste of snow. But quickly acclimatizing himself, Lytton was soon extolling the beauties of the enormous Downs in their perpetual shadow, and the opalescent fields and trees. The weather seemed to be surpassing itself, positively showing off, as if 'to demonstrate that, after all, there's not much to choose between England and Italy'. While Carrington spent her days out of doors, snowballing with Ralph or riding her 'flea-bitten mare' Belle, Lytton would sit in his study 'busy with Elizabeth'. He was determined to achieve something before the end of the summer. Determined. Yet he still seized opportunities to turn aside to something less exacting – a not very serious essay on Racine revealing him to be homosexual (which was burnt by a housemaid in London), a comic portrait-in-miniature of the seventeenth-century Master of Trinity Dr North for the *Nation and Athenaeum*, and even a long poem for Tiber about a mouse. 'I can only write nonsense to-day,' he confessed to Roger Senhouse on 7 February. 'I wish I could write Elizabeth as well. If only she could be reduced to nonsense – that would be perfect. The whole of Art lies there. To pulverize the material and remould it in the shape of one's own particular absurdity. What happiness to do that! I must try again.'

Dadie Rylands, 'to pamper my passion for Eton', had sent him M.R. James's reminiscences – 'a dim affair', he described it (26 January 1927).

'. . . Only remarkable as showing the extraordinary impress an institution can make on an adolescent mind. It's odd that the Provost of Eton should still be aged 16. A life without a jolt.' He also read Emil Ludwig's *Napoleon* – 'interesting though really second-rate'. But the books which chiefly occupied him were three modern novels by his friends. David Garnett's *Go She Must!* was 'beautifully written, and some of the descriptions exquisite – the whole thing, so far as I can see, wonderfully well done – only – it's almost impossible to read. At least so *I* find. There seems to be no interior tide flowing through it, to carry one along. But that may only be because of some personal disability on my part. I only know that I suffer agonies of boredom – and admiration – on every page.'

Rosamond Lehmann's first novel, *Dusty Answer*, was more readable. 'It seemed to me to have decided merit,' he wrote (11 May 1927), 'and for a first novel remarkable. The disadvantage to my mind is that it is too romantic and charged with sunset sentiment. A youthful fault, I suppose. Not sufficiently "life-enhancing". But very well and carefully done – without horrors in taste (a rare thing nowadays) and really at moments moving.'

Most original of all was Virginia's *To the Lighthouse*. 'But it really is a most extraordinary form of literature,' he wrote to Roger Senhouse (11 May 1927). 'It is the lack of copulation – either actual or implied – that worries me. A marvellous and exquisite arabesque seems to be the result. I suppose there is some symbolism about the lighthouse etc. – but I can't guess what it is. With anyone else, the suggestion would be fairly obvious, but it won't fit into the sexless pattern by any manner of means.'

There were platoons of visitors to Ham Spray that winter and early spring – Dadie Rylands 'reading Shakespeare with a violent cold in the nose'; the 'very whimsical and charming' Morgan Forster; James and Alix arguing 'on Dr Freud and the artist'; Raymond Mortimer and Francis Birrell 'whirling like loquacious windmills'; Julia Strachey 'like some strange bird but with habits unlike any other birds'; John Lehmann who 'with quite a slight adjustment of his features might have been a great beauty'; Lytton's sister Pippa, 'a most sympathetic character'; and then Saxon Sydney-Turner, 'a crane-like figure, for ever smoking – pipe in hand on one leg – or else perched on the arm of a chair, reading Plotinus in the original', who typically succeeded in avoiding the cab sent to meet him at the station, and walked the whole way from Hungerford, bag in hand – 'the sort of thing he thoroughly relishes!'

Once in a while came more spectacular invasions and misalliances. 'As I was returning from my walk in the afternoon,' Lytton recounted in one of his letters to Roger Senhouse (9 February 1927), 'an aeroplane was seen to be gyrating round the house.

'3 times it circled about us, getting lower and lower every time. Intense excitement! The farm hands, various females, Olive[38] and her mother, all the cats, and myself, rushed towards it, and Carrington was left solitary in her bed, like Antony "whistling in the air". Finally the machine came down in a field exactly opposite the lodge gates at the end of the avenue. There I found it – a group of rustics lined up at a respectful distance. I took it upon myself to approach – but in a moment perceived that the adventure would end in a fizzle. No divine Icarus met my view. Only a too red and stolid officer together with a too pale and stolid mechanic. They had lost their way. I told them where they were, asked them to tea which they luckily refused, and off they went. It *might* have been so marvellous! – What surprised me was the singular smallness and compactness of the contraption – not nearly as big as a motor bus.'

Early in February, Lytton had told Roger Senhouse that 'my own work goes fairly well, though slowly'. As the weather grew colder again, there was nothing for it but to rush up to London and drown his inertia in a sea of parties. He had lunch with Lady Curzon, dinner with Ethel Sands, tea next day with Lady Horner with whom he met 'old Haldane, as urbane as usual, talking of Newton and Einstein in such a style that it was impossible to make up one's mind whether he understood a word of what he was saying'. He also went to a lecture given by Roger Fry at the Queen's Hall. 'The hall was completely full – about 1800 people – and the lecture lasted from 8 to 10.30! – It was full of interest of course, the best thing being a quotation from Michael Angelo on Flemish art – really brilliant – I'd no idea he was a wit.'

He arrived back at Ham Spray with a renewed keenness for work. Steadily, though at a declining pace, he struggled on as if through a desert. Following the oasis of an Easter holiday, his rate of progress slowed still further, and for a time he actually considered abandoning *Elizabeth* altogether. But there was another oasis at Whitsun, and then a few days' frisking round London – a meeting with Emil Ludwig, a hectic evening as guest of honour at the 1917 Club, dinner with Dadie Rylands at Boulestin's, tea with Lady Lavery, and an amusing luncheon-party with Lady Aberconway where he came across Somerset Maugham, 'a hang-dog personage, I thought ... with a wife. Perhaps it was because I've eschewed such things for so long that I was amused – the odd mixture of restraint and laisser-aller struck me freshly...'

Once more the gaiety of London seemed to inject him with new energies. 'My state is I believe ameliorated,' he allowed (17 June 1927). 'I have written a fair amount, and hope to continue – a most unpleasant form of occupation in my opinion – but one simply has to!' It had become obvious that he could never complete the book by the end of the summer. After more than eighteen months of laborious exertion, he had written twenty-five thousand words – barely more than a third of what would be the final narrative. 'I am afraid I cannot give a very satisfactory report of Her Majesty,' he told Charles Prentice at Chatto & Windus (5 July 1927).

'It seems impossible that she should be finished off before October, and I hardly think it would be safe to think of publishing before Christmas – and perhaps really the Spring would be a more likely time.

So far as I can judge the affair is nearly half-done, and should come to about 50,000 words; but I am extremely vague about this. My experience has always been that things grow longer and take more time than one expects beforehand.

. . . Please do not expect too much! "Rather a dull production", I expect!'

He continued to 'crouch in my writing-room fiddling with Elizabeth'. Jack and Mary Hutchinson came down for a few days, and there was much talk about the old subjects – Freud and love, Sainte-Beuve and love, Cambridge and love. 'I cannot work,' he wrote in despair to Topsy Lucas (27 July 1927), 'perhaps tomorrow I shall be able to – but I've been idle for days and days. It's a wretched state of affairs . . .'

Sebastian Sprott arrived and busied himself 'like a squirrel' tipping into a series of concertina files the enormous correspondence Lytton had preserved.[39] 'He hopes to put all Lytton's letters & papers in order,' Carrington told Dorelia, '& I hope he may be induced to spring clean the house.' For weeks he persisted until 'order rises out of chaos', Lytton wrote to Dadie Rylands (12 August 1927). 'Correspondence after correspondence is sifted, arranged, and bound up. I feel when it's all finished the only thing left for me to do will be to sink into the grave – it's all so neat and final.' He could seldom resist leaving his desk where things were far from final, to glance through these sheaves of correspondence, gliding back on a river of nostalgia past Ottoline's 'gigantic mountain', and 'an exquisite, though too small collection' from Virginia, past the vanished visions of Sheppard and Woolf, through the cloud of years to older and still older memories of Maynard and Hobber at Cambridge, Papa and Mama at Lancaster Gate. 'Oh, such a plunge into the past! – and so many pasts! Hectic undergraduate days – absurdly melodramatic,' he wrote to Mary Hutchinson (27 July 1927).

571

'George Mallory later – rather sweet. A bundle from Rupert Brooke – nice, decidedly. Some vague Duncan letters – very amusing. The Bunny [Garnett] budget. And so on – until the present seemed to fade into some kind of mirage, and unreality reigned. I'm afraid my biography will present a slightly shocking spectacle! In the middle of it all, as I was dreaming over a snapshot of George I'd forgotten all about – so alluring! – the door opened, and who should come in but – Henry [Lamb]! Yes – that ghost. But accompanied, this time, by a far from spectral entity – his Pansy – a gay, sturdy, light-haired, dark-eyed young lady – positively attractive! (Her brother, so Henry says, is no less so – oh! oh!). He seems set up – perhaps that will end happily – perhaps she will be able to quell his evil spirit.'[40]

The past seemed to enfold him, absorbing and dissipating his precious store of energy, as the youthful cult of self-absorbing illness returned with a long line of minor maladies which held Carrington in alarmed suspense. In some respects, like nearly all the Stracheys, Lytton's constitution was resilient – he would sometimes walk his friends into the ground over ten or twelve miles – yet his curiously unstable temperament was beset by many agues and fevers. While he was working on *Elizabeth and Essex*, his emotional excitements scarcely diminished – indeed they may have multiplied. He complains in his letters of his nerves being 'edgy and disordered'. Possibly an explanation lay in the fact that some of his ailments, like Elizabeth's, were of an hysterical origin, and that his probing into her neurosis may have aggravated his own condition. Certainly this book emptied his own resources as no previous book had done.

Everything came to a standstill at the end of August. With immeasurable relief he turned to some old favourites – Montaigne's essays, the *Confessions* of Rousseau in a 'first edition [that] omits some vital passages owing to prudery', and Swift's poems – 'that man certainly had a dirty mind, in the literal meaning of the word. But no doubt if he liked one it would have been extremely exciting.' His investigations into sixteenth- and seventeenth-century England had whetted his appetite for 'the singular punishments they went in for in those days'. Much of his correspondence over this period contains exultant descriptions of these horrors[41] – of an eighteenth-century French Penal Code, for instance, which laid out the punishment for blasphemy.

'For the first time, offenders were fined: for the second, third and fourth times, more and heavier fines; for the fifth time the pillory; for the sixth time, the upper lip was cut off; for the seventh time, the lower lip cut off; "et si par obstination et mauvaise coutume invétérée, ils continuent" . . .

the tongue cut off. After that the imagination of the law gives out. There is also a section on "Délits commis dans les Bois" . . .'

He had collected a shelf of books on buggery, including a dissertation by a seventeenth-century Jesuit in Latin on how women could sodomize one another. On another shelf near by, there was Katherine Mansfield's *Journal* edited by Middleton Murry, which he described as 'quite shocking and incomprehensible. I see Murry lets out that it was written for publication – which no doubt explains a good deal. But why that foul-mouthed, virulent, brazen-faced broomstick of a creature should have got herself up as a pad of rose-scented cotton wool is beyond me.'

By early September, he was 'more cheerful, and with a faint prospect of being able to do a little work'. But it was not at *Elizabeth* that he planned to work – not just yet. Instead he was adding to his collection two further portraits-in-miniature, on Carlyle and Gibbon, and contributing a review of the second volume of Sidney Lee's *King Edward VII* to the *Daily Mail*.[42] His health and spirits were now 'positively bouncing upwards', he assured Virginia (16 September 1927). In the third week of September he went with Carrington to visit Augustus and Dorelia John in their 'curious establishment on the other side of Salisbury. You never knew anything quite so singular,' he told Dadie Rylands, '– so vague – so utterly lacking in amenities – so (every now and then) fascinating. There were two girls – two boys – some sort of governess – such silences and driftings! Dorelia herself is a most wonderful person. I am fondly attached to her – but she moves on an unfortunate plane.'

A few days later, on 20 September, he exchanged this old Bohemian encampment for one of Bloomsbury's rural outposts. 'Clive is nice, as he invariably is when not feeling the need to show off,' he wrote to Roger Senhouse (22 September 1927) from Charleston, '– Vanessa very superb – and Julian, whom I haven't seen since he was quite a boy – he's now on the brink of going to Cambridge. He's a very nice creature, was once most beautiful, but all now is ruined by a most unpleasant fatness. A Socialist – despises Art – so I'm told . . .'[43] After dinner we gossip and play the gramophone.' While he was there, the Woolfs came over from Rodmell, and Virginia, 'looking very young and beautiful', declared that they must all write their memoirs, on an enormous scale, and have them published in volume after volume in ten years' time.

Lytton had decided, on leaving Charleston, to invite Carrington for a week in Weymouth. 'I feel sure I shall like Weymouth,' he wrote. The town was entirely without pretensions, 'hardly altered, one feels, from the dim days of old George III'. He bought a heavy Kodak camera, and sauntered about snapping 'enormous photos' – of the wishing-well at Upwey, of 'an absurd statue of George III, with a sort of Piazza del Popolo effect behind it', and the lighthouse at the end of Portland Bill, 'a desolate region, extremely suitable for convicts'. Even the lodging-house where they were staying delighted him. 'Our landlord is the Mayor of Weymouth,' he boasted. '. . . Life in lodgings is really very fascinating, it seems to me. Everything is fixed – so unconnected with real existence – so comfortably hideous. I could go on here for weeks and weeks.'

Sitting beside him Carrington liked to peer over and see what Lytton was reading, perhaps then read it herself or pass on the news to others. 'Lytton reads. What does Lytton read?' she had teased Gerald. Sometimes as he sat in the firelight playing with his beard, some new novel would slip from his fingers. 'I don't know whether I'm hopelessly classical, or simply out of date, or an irredeemable purist, or what,' he explained to Topsy Lucas (30 October 1927). '. . . There are so many modern writers I can't see the point of, whom so many other people like very much, that it looks to me as if there were certain qualities I'm impervious to.' Nevertheless he was rather struck by William Gerhardie's *The Polyglots*[44] which was 'really very amusing, in the Dickens-Dostoyevsky-[Norman] Douglas style', also enjoyed a pamphlet against anthologies by Robert Graves and Laura Riding, and ('not quite so amusing') Evelyn Waugh's *Decline and Fall*.

As for his own writing, it was going remarkably well if somewhat in the wrong direction. After Carlyle and Gibbon, he planned two more portraits-in-miniature, on Macaulay and Hume. But *Elizabeth and Essex*, which he had not looked at since the middle of August, hung fire. 'I have been unwell all this summer,' Lytton explained to Charles Prentice (4 October 1927), 'and the result is that Elizabeth is not nearly so far advanced as I had hoped. It is most annoying; but I seem to have recovered now.'

But there was another reason for his procrastination. Over the past year, his life had been jolted by a series of shocks. As he was driven back from Weymouth to Ham Spray that autumn, however, his prospects appeared brighter than for many months. He was strangely happy.

He was in love again.

6

WAITING FOR ROGER

'A tranquillity has settled on Ham Spray recently,' Carrington wrote to Julia Strachey at the beginning of 1927. While Lytton sat 'writing away' indoors, she would plant innumerable bulbs 'all upside down' Lytton conjectured, play with her cats, canter across the country on Belle, toboggan down the hills together with Olive the maid, and set off fireworks in the garden ('the only good rocket C. managed to send off sideways,' Lytton observed). Now that Ralph and Frances had settled into Gordon Square, she felt closer again to Lytton. 'I've loved being with you alone lately,' she wrote to him (19 September 1926). '. . . I love you for being so kind to me always.' It seemed ridiculous after ten years to be telling him such things, 'but every time you go away it comes back to me, and I realize in spite of the beauties of the Ilex tree and the Downs, Ham Spray loses more than half its beauty . . .' Each time he went away, he would write to her, and then come back with 'the most amusing gossip. I laughed for nearly 2 hours over his stories.'

All was calm: though she provided some good gossip herself by going off to Dorset with Stephen Tomlin. She scarcely bothered to conceal this affair, even in her letters to Gerald Brenan, or her growing attraction to Julia Strachey with her elegant long legs, Eton crop, and high fashion. It was 'maddening', Carrington assured Gerald, to 'have (or rather don't "HAVE") a lily white lady with Chinese eyes & arms of purest milk sleeping night after night in my house, & there's nothing to be done but to admire her from a distance, & steal distracted kisses under cover of saying good night.'

That winter the tranquillity was fleetingly ruffled by Gerald's return from France, and the departure of Stephen Tomlin and Julia Strachey for a 'trial marriage' in Paris. 'Stephen Tomlin has carried off victoriously the lovely Princess Julia,' Carrington told Dorelia. '. . . I am glad as they [are] both my favourites.' Gerald was her favourite too, but she was less glad over his return. 'I complicate my own life, beyond endurance,' he had complained to Ralph. Wandering between Toulon and Paris, he abandoned his biography of St Teresa, toyed with a picaresque novel about a commercial traveller and actually finished a series of satirical astrological predictions which, Carrington informed him, entertained both Lytton and Desmond MacCarthy. Gerald now wished to restart his 'love-affair' with her, and though she was 'most reluctant to jump back onto the treadmill of their relationship', her biographer Gretchen Gerzina writes, she could not altogether refuse him.

Jealous quarrelling had hardly begun to warm up between them when the affair was interrupted by Carrington falling dramatically from her horse, being 'picked up for dead and carried by 10 stalwart men to a car and driven to the hospital amidst a gaping crowd of admirers'. That spring she slowly recovered at Ham Spray under the hands of a 'terribly sadistic' masseuse recommended by Lytton's niece Ellie Rendel, while Lytton himself sat playing with the new wireless set James had given them and looking 'very comical moving the "condensers" with his "ear phones" on his head', Carrington told Gerald (6 April 1927).

She had resolved to concentrate all her attention this year on her painting and to 'regard people as species of birds for my bird book which I am making'. Part of her work involved decorating in turbulent vermilion and flat apple green Gerald's spacious apartment on the top floor of 14 Great James Street; after which she moved to the ground floor of 41 Gordon Square, below Ralph and Frances, where Lytton had decided to rent a *pied-à-terre*. But was she cutting her own throat by 'making Lytton's room so elegant and lovely', she asked Gerald. 'Will he now fly to Gordon Square with R[oger Senhouse] every Monday and leave me désolée at Ham Spray?' He did not answer, and she could not tell.

*

For almost two years Lytton had wavered in his affections between Philip Ritchie and Roger Senhouse and, wavering, committed himself deeply to neither of them. Philip appeared to be his favourite: such sweet irregularity had suggested somehow a more available being than his strikingly beautiful friend. Besides, his way of looking at things 'fits very deliciously with my particular taste', Lytton told Mary Hutchinson (17 September 1924). But Philip had turned out something of a disappointment. 'I find him very interesting and increasingly attractive,' Lytton had told Sebastian Sprott (8 September 1924), 'and I suppose he likes me in some sort of way.' But he became anxious lest his friends should be driving Philip away. 'Do please do your best to like Philip,' he had urged Sebastian (1 October 1924). 'You struck me as decidedly sniffy about him. But I promise you he is very nice and also intelligent. He ... was rather afraid of you – so you mustn't be too crushing.' But whatever the reason, Philip remained elusive. And it was impossible to get properly involved with someone who so often disappeared abroad without explanation, never answered letters, and seldom put off other admirers.

Circumstances too had favoured a sentimental attachment with Roger. In August, the young man had come to stay at Ham Spray for what turned out to be four decisive days. After he left, Lytton wrote excitedly to Mary Hutchinson (11 August 1926). 'Ma chère, I have just had a most unexpected piece of good fortune – a free gift from Providence. The other day I gave a slight push to a door which I had longed to turn the handle of for about two years but hardly dared even to touch. To my amazement, it opened; and I found myself in an exquisite paradise. I am still in it, so to speak. Nothing more charming could be imagined. Perhaps you will guess the initial of the door – if so, you will see at once that this is an extremely confidential communication!'

People still believed Lytton to be a dry Bloomsbury cut-out. Yet even in middle age, he had 'more love in his little finger', as Virginia knew, than existed in the new generation of Bloomsbury critics who accused him of 'not loving mankind'. The fact was that nature had implanted in him an amorousness so irrepressible as to be often embarrassing to his friends. His susceptibility to Roger was plain for them to see – the handsome, elegant youth, with his open manner, his boyish spirit, his words and looks of admiration, fascinated Lytton. The descendant of a long line of Senhouses of Maryport in Cumberland, Roger had recently come down from Magdalen College, Oxford, to work for an import and export firm at Hays Wharf in the London Docks. He spoke with the melodious accents of Eton College which sounded so sweetly in Lytton's ears, arousing that exaggerated loyalty which non-Etonians sometimes feel for the old school. A manservant called Peel looked after him, rather as Bunter looked after Lord Peter Wimsey. Roger was a connoisseur of books – later to be the partner of Fredric Warburg in the firm of Secker and Warburg, and a friend of Genet, a translator of Colette. He was unambitious but his curiously gentle manner concealed much hectic adventurousness. He had a powerful physique, steel-blue eyes and firm jaw, all of which promised a decisiveness in action that was wildly misleading. Swept hither and thither by the breezes of his moods, the accidents of circumstance, the crosscurrents of learning and lasciviousness, he lived and moved in superb uncertainty.

Something about him – the lie of his dark-brown hair perhaps – reminded Lytton of George Underwood, the second of his 'desperate passions' at Leamington College. There was a resemblance between his feelings for Roger and for that freckled schoolboy of over thirty years ago. Recently he had noticed Underwood's name in an Army List and reflected that by now he must be a senior officer of fifty with a wife and family – a short, podgy, good-natured figure, bald yet with a few tufts of fading ginger hair, very popular in the mess. But when he glanced across at Roger, he felt again the feverish excitements and jealousies of youth. To be back in that simple past, a boy again at Leamington; to escape into the prolonged innocence of boyhood, its insignificance and dreams – that was love.

Or was it? Lytton was now approaching fifty, while Roger was in his early twenties – a dangerous concatenation of ages. Yet for the moment – it was the autumn of 1926 – all was well. There were long talks, long walks across the Berkshire Downs, and in the evening laughter and music, until

577

at last Ham Spray was empty, and they were left, the two of them, playing cards before the fire. In London, Lytton would often drop in on Roger at his flat, and every week – almost every day – they exchanged affectionate letters. There was a tender, playful quality to their friendship. Lytton composed love-poems for him, sonnets, acrostics and limericks. Sometimes he addressed his envelopes in verse:

> Deliver this to SENHOUSE (Roger)
> I prithee, postman debonair!
> He is the handsome upstairs lodger
> At number 14 BRUNSWICK SQUARE.[45]

'How to describe my happiness?' Lytton wrote to Mary Hutchinson from Nottingham where he had taken Roger to stay with Sebastian Sprott (11 October 1926). 'It is simply shocking – that's all that can be said. Sebastian is charming, but ignorant.' There was, in these first few months, a particular reason for trying to preserve the secrecy of their affair. Neither of them knew what would be Philip Ritchie's reactions once he found out. They dreaded hurting him. Besides, wasn't Lytton now working the very same trick that Maynard had pulled on him twenty years ago with Duncan? Not quite, perhaps, but something close to it.

The news could not be withheld from Philip indefinitely, and once the two of them had decided to go off to Rome together in the new year, there was no choice but to own up. Even so, they allowed him to know no more than was necessary. 'R[oger] has told P[hilip] about it – as vaguely as possible,' Lytton informed Mary Hutchinson (17 December 1926). 'P[hilip] was extremely charming and sympathetic, R[oger] says, and didn't bother with cross-examinations. Please, if he talks about it to you, don't know much more than the bare fact. The details are so harrowing – to him and everyone else. Don't even know anything about dates. He's coming here tomorrow. Rather agitating! Really rather a singular, not to say shocking, situation.'

Seldom had Lytton felt happier than in Rome. If only time could have stood still and drawn out those weeks through vague ages of summer. But relationships must either move or perish. After they had left the sun and blue skies of Italy, this sweet prologue to their friendship reached its end, and the first scene of the ensuing drama opened against the wintry climate of England.

As his memories of George Underwood suggest, the quality of Lytton's love-affairs did not greatly alter throughout his adult life. Spasmodically, he did feel some degree of sexual attraction towards women – Maria Nys,

Katherine Mansfield, Nina Hamnett and, of course, Carrington herself –
but women usually alarmed him. Since the way to heterosexual happiness
was blocked,[46] he returned for most love-affairs to the adolescent period
of his life. All his infatuations – with their common ingredient of hero-
worship – were embedded in a sense of unsureness – were, in effect, a
regression to the days of his youth. Yet they were not all the same. The
people he fell in love with were still the type of men he would himself have
liked to be, men who possessed attributes in which he felt himself to be
sadly deficient. But the attributes he admired were various, sometimes
contradictory, and fluctuating.

The evidence of his love-poems points to other changes. The poems
written at or soon after leaving Cambridge show his obsession and
revulsion over the physical act of love-making and reflect the mood of this
black period of his life. His later verse tends to divide lust from love,
treating lust with some degree of ribaldry and love as something chiefly
phantasmagorical, not subject to the decay of physical deterioration. Lust
is no longer a 'guttural voice' that rhymes with 'dust' to signify the grave of
noble aspirations: it is something less earnest and more thrilling. Very
characteristic of the lighter vein in which he presents erotic themes are
some lines of verse which he sent to Roger Senhouse in the summer of
1929.

> How odd the fate of pretty boys!
> Who, if they dare to taste the joys
> That so enchanted Classic minds,
> Get whipped upon their neat behinds;
> Yet should they fail to construe well
> The lines that of those raptures tell
> – It's very odd, you must confess –
> Their neat behinds get whipped no less.

This verse, of course, is written primarily to stir sexual amusement.
They are the lines of a happier, freer and more pleasure-loving man. He
needed sexual stimulation not so much to arouse desire between himself
and another man, but to pacify those pangs of prurient yearning which had
so often in the past made a dungeon of his love-life. Once this need had
been met, he was released from his physical longings into a floating region
of the spirit. It is this delirious universe of self-oblivion that his later love-
poems celebrate. In 'The Haschish', which he composed before the
outbreak of the war, he pictures himself liberated from what he again
describes as 'this wrong world', and transferred into a disembodied

condition, rapturously unencumbered by the bonds of logic and reason.[47] Despite many lines that seem to imply the occult and immortal nature of this dreaming, it consists principally of shedding egotism and vanity. The most touching lines of the poem are those in which Lytton expresses his wish for self-forgetfulness, for a deliverance out of the cocoon of his sick body and the hateful London life that walled him in.

> Let me eclipse my being in a swoon,
> And lingering through a long penumbral noon,
> Feel like a ghost a soft Elysian balm,
> A universe of amaranthine calm,
> Devoid of thought, forgetful of desire,
> And quiet as joined hearts which still suspire . . .
> – Looks that are felt, and lusts as light as air,
> And curious embraces like September flowers
> Vanishing down interminable hours,
> And love's last kiss, exquisitely withdrawn,
> And copulations dimmer than the dawn.
> Who now shall fret?

It is only when chloroformed in this way that lust and love can unite to the satisfaction of Lytton's fastidious nature. The guiltless vision he evokes becomes highly conventional, taking on the classical poetic diction of late Victorian sentiment, as he tries to convey a more palpable picture of homosexual bliss, and sees the

> forms of golden boys
> Embraced seraphically in far lands
> By languid lovers, linking marvellous hands
> With early Virgins crowned with quiet wreaths
> Of lily, frailer than the air that breathes
> The memory of Sappho all day long
> Through Lesbian shades of fragmentary song . . .

In 'Happiness', written while he was at work on *Eminent Victorians*, the sensation of love is again described as if it has been provoked by some drug – not an aphrodisiac, but an anodyne or opiate inducing drowsiness. Happiness, he implies, is most likely to come to those who have mastered impatience, and whose senses are no longer fretted with desire, either for lust or power. It is

oftenest known
To those in whom the waiting soul has grown
A little weary, and whose deep desires
(as in black coal sleep unextinguished fires)
All joy's rich possibilities ignore
And, not despairing, not expect no more.

He had reached the stage of expecting no more when Roger suddenly re-ignited these unextinguished fires. The new flame burnt brightly, erratically, almost without control, giving out a rather different light from earlier conflagrations. During his Cambridge days, Lytton had, in schoolboy fashion, associated sex with excrement and been obsessed by the idea of sodomy. Among his post-Cambridge writings, however, can be traced the development of more sophisticated deviations, and the suggestion that he could become erotically aroused by other parts of the body, especially the ears. There are a few references to ears in the Duncan Grant correspondence, and, a little later, a curious pleasure in contemplating 'the strange divine ears, so large and lascivious – oh!' of George Mallory. But it is not until his infatuation for Ralph Partridge that ears occur regularly in his letters. By the time he is writing to Roger Senhouse, they seem to have taken on a lickerish significance (he refers to them as 'lollipops'). He is always threatening to tweak or pinch Roger's ears for some misdemeanour, or slice off one or possibly both as punishment for some imagined crime; and he describes with horrified delight the mutilations to ears practised in the sixteenth and seventeenth centuries.

Such fetishes were part of the fantasy life to which, for the first time, he now seems to have abandoned himself. In his affair with Duncan Grant he had tried to force a reality out of his day-dreams by assuming, almost literally, the form and personality of the man he loved. With Henry Lamb, he had resorted to sexual infantilism only in moments of crisis or reconciliation, so that fantasy and actuality had run alongside in a makeshift partnership that eventually broke apart. With Ralph Partridge he had attempted to alter the object of his love so that they might become closer in everyday life – though after he had partly succeeded in this conversion, his initial amorousness dwindled into a more ordinary friendship. But in the company of Roger Senhouse, he stepped into a wish-fulfilment world where both of them could adopt fictitious identities and play out vicarious roles. It was a more imaginative method of escaping from himself and merging with his loved one – a method that arose out of Roger's surrealist nature. They would pretend they were David and

Absalom, Nero and his slave, a member of Pop (the Eton Society) and his fag, a parent and child – the invention was inexhaustible, the variety endless, and it was Lytton who took the lead. 'Why can't we return to our primeval forest, and swing from the boughs entranced in happiness?' he demanded (13 March 1927). 'We should live on three nuts a day, and sleep together, far up, in the middle of some marvellous palm. Never to touch the ground, Roger – how divine! Wouldn't that alone be worth all the intellect of humanity?' Then he would conjure up a domestic scene for them to enter. 'Won't you take me on as your servant instead of Peel?' he begged (December 1926). 'I have always longed for such a job. To have no will of one's own, no importance, no responsibility, hardly even a soul – how very satisfying it would be. If I shaved off my beard nobody would recognise me. "Disappearance of a well-known Author" – and it would be delightful.'

For Lytton, the feeling that he could be absorbed into a multitude of imaginary-historical scenes and forms and places added to his life an unexplored enchanted territory, into which he might be carried almost at will. The aesthetic tastes which he and Roger shared – especially for literature and music – became invested with strange sexual properties. Books and their bindings began to haunt Lytton's dreams. 'One's feelings towards certain books certainly approach the libidinous, as Dr Freud would say,' he observed. In Rome, during their fortnight of intense happiness together, they had read Dante, and afterwards Lytton discovered that simply by passing lingering hands over this book he could evoke a wave of sensuality. To trail his finger-tips over the delicious morocco bindings sent through him a shiver of excitement – 'for which I am sure Dante would have reserved a particularly ingenious circle of Hell – if only such a vice could have occurred to him'. Even reading together from a French first edition that had belonged to the 'Grand Dauphin' – the eldest son of Louis XIV – transported Lytton. No longer was he a middle-aged twentieth-century author, but the heir apparent to the French throne; and there beside him sat – not a handsome Etonian bibliophil – but the king himself! It was an experience too improbable for the most exaggerated novel – unless Virginia were to write it. 'I fear I am almost too happy when I am with you,' Lytton confessed to Roger (February 1930). '. . . Oh dear, the intricacy and intensity of existence reduces me to a shadow. Every moment is peculiar beyond words.'

Music too could work the same strange spell between them. When they listened to Mozart together, chamber music mostly, it almost seemed as if he and Roger were the instruments themselves – the violin, its very strings and bow, with its exquisite taut movement, rhythmically back and forwards, in and out. Music really was the food of love, though it was curious that they did not feel the same when playing Vaughan Williams. 'I expect that's only because I once knew his female relatives,' Lytton speculated.

Such experiences were beyond words, but when, at the end of the first chapter in *Elizabeth and Essex*, he describes the highest point of rapture in the Queen's love-affair with her courtier, it is with a musical metaphor that he awkwardly tries to evoke this.

'When two consciousnesses come to a certain nearness the impetus of their interactions, growing ever intenser and intenser, leads on to an unescapable climax. The crescendo must rise to its topmost note; and only then is the preordained solution of the theme made manifest.'

After their Roman holiday what could be more natural than to plan for the future? But when Lytton wrote off to Roger telling of his new rooms at 41 Gordon Square the reply was vague and vacillating. Lytton had expected to see his own sentiments mirrored back to him. What he actually saw was something blurred and diffuse. 'It's really rather a wonderful combination of things we seem to have discovered, or perhaps invented,' Lytton had written to him. But Roger was not quite so sure. He felt frightened of being shifted into a position where his own affection would fail. By consenting to go to Rome with Lytton – who had paid for everything – he found himself bound by something more than airy friendship or flirtation. All these further plans might bind him still tighter. So he began to prevaricate.

Lytton was bewildered and hurt. Appealing to Roger was like trying to make an impression on cotton wool. On an impulse, while in London, he telephoned him 'feeling like a detected murderer'. But to his surprise Roger sounded extremely friendly, and they arranged to go to *Così fan Tutte* together. The reconciliation was delicious, but even so Lytton remained puzzled. 'I feel a good deal happier, though rather alarmed,' he told Mary Hutchinson (25 March 1927), '– I don't quite know why – please support me!'

There were good reasons for this alarm, and much need, during the next weeks and months, for the support of his friends. Even as the two of them sat listening to Mozart that evening, a letter was on its way to Ham Spray setting out many of Roger's apprehensions. Where were these spirals of fantasy, these adventures of mind and imagination, leading them? he asked. Lytton would contrive roles and situations which were so gripping, so enjoyable, that Roger was completely swept up by them. They were so amusing too, and since they gave Lytton such evident pleasure, pleasurable to him also. But then reality, destroying all his aspirations, would send Lytton down a terrifying abyss. These sudden plunges appalled Roger. He did not himself experience this dreadful recoil, for he had not the same craving for make-believe, but he saw their effect on Lytton and was sucked into the complicated passage of emotions. Although not fully understanding what was going on, he still felt lost, upset, and in some way responsible for the anguish that would suddenly strike at Lytton. What should he do? Their physical needs and inclinations were so very different. It was all right when Carrington was there, and it was not so bad when Lytton came up to London, at which times Roger would, in some degree, take Carrington's place. But he was apprehensive about going down alone to Ham Spray. Literally, he feared that Lytton might go mad. He would urge Roger to more and more extravagant fantasies, would grow extraordinarily worked up; yet there was no release. Even in his most extreme states, he was still inhibited. Roger knew that Lytton's attitude towards him was not one of simple sexual desire but rather of limitless sympathy. He dreaded paining Lytton, who was at all times so vulnerable, who remembered everything he said and gave it unintended significance.

'Lytton, I cannot bear to wound you in any way at all,' he wrote, '– it has an instantaneous effect upon me – and yet I am continually finding myself upon the point of doing so by some inconsiderate word or action, and if I hurt you and see that I have, I feel a sense of shame that makes me nervous.

'I want always to feel entirely open, straightforward and undisguised in front of you, but I discover too often that I have cloaked my proper feelings, and that I am falling into a part that is not true to my nature . . . You are, Lytton, so overwhelmingly charming and considerate to me that I am quite at a loss to know how to reciprocate it, for were I to mention at any time dissatisfaction with what was taking place, I know the pains you would devote to amend it . . . I know you say that you get all that satisfies you from things as they have existed for the last months, but I who keep watch, as it were, can only realise that what I have loosely termed "things" might be so very much better.'

The effect of this letter upon Lytton was extraordinary. He could not conceal his agitation. 'I am in almost complete despair,' he lamented to Mary Hutchinson (1 May 1927). 'All is shattered!' He read only one meaning into Roger's hesitant words: that he did not love him. And he had been so certain of this love too! Just when happiness seemed within his grasp, when he had practically been able to see with Roger's eyes, set their two hearts beating in unison, the good moment had gone. And it had gone with such suddenness that 'I can hardly believe in any of it', he told Sebastian Sprott (2 June 1927). 'Why should such things be?' Had he really forced Roger out of his true nature, or had Roger's charm misled him? 'Yes, Roger's charm. But what pray is charm, I should like to know?' Lytton ruefully inquired of Mary Hutchinson. His character appeared to take colour from whatever it touched. From day to day, he was never the same person – now affectionate, now offhand as if faintly embarrassed to find himself the idol of an ageing invalid. Lytton did not know where he was.

The next four and a half months were overhung with uncertainty. He was driven by a harrowing restlessness. He could not bear to be left alone, but hurried from Carrington to Mary Hutchinson and Topsy Lucas, from Dadie Rylands to Stephen Tomlin, frantically drinking in their words of comfort and reassurance.

In these friends he was fortunate. All that friends can do in such circumstances, they did. 'I am surrounded by infinite kindness and devotion,' he wrote to Dadie Rylands (18 July 1927), 'but how can I not sometimes feel lonely?' At Ham Spray a new orientation of human affairs was spinning into place, with Lytton, in his disappointed passion for Roger, turning momentarily back to Ralph Partridge. Memories of their old intimacy – 'so intensely romantic and moving – rushed back upon me, and I felt strangely upset', he confided to Mary Hutchinson (9 August 1927). 'There he was, downstairs, the same person, really, I couldn't help feeling; but six years or seven had gone – and where were we now? – I longed to say something – but it was impossible to do more than murmur some vague word or two, and he returned to London.'

That summer, he tried to ease his heartache with a few light flirtations. 'Yes, love is tiresome,' he admitted to Topsy Lucas (27 July 1927), 'but life goes on, and things do happen – quite fresh and exciting – even though one is chucked by some R[oger] or other.' The most abiding consolation and companionship came from Dadie Rylands and Stephen Tomlin. The latter, being bisexual, for a brief spell occupied a virtuoso position in the Ham Spray régime. But Ralph – and this was later to be of tragic importance – strongly objected to 'Tommy' having an affair with Carrington, fearing he was someone more likely to destroy than to create happiness. At the end of July this tenuous affair lapsed when Tomlin finally married Julia Strachey.

'I am leading a decidedly queer life,' Lytton confided to Mary

Hutchinson (19 July 1927). 'Both T[ommy] and D[adie] are devoted to me – and I to them; they please me in every way – though, to be sure, the ways are different!. . . My relation with T[ommy] is exciting – there is strength there – and a mind – a remarkable character; – but there is a lull in the proceedings, for he is to be married on Thursday (I believe). There is also a lull with D[adie], who has gone to Cambridge – a delightful, gay affair that one. So you see altogether I have plenty to think about in my seclusion . . . Was there ever such a world? Such lives? Such peculiarities?'

Carrington had assured Julia in mid-July that she was glad 'you are going to marry Tommy who if you didn't marry I should seriously think of marrying myself, for he is such a charmer'. Looking at the two of them before the wedding, they appeared to her 'very devoted and happy so I hope it will (at any rate for some time) turn out successful', she wrote to Saxon Sydney-Turner (15 July 1927).

But nothing was any longer successful between her and Gerald. He was still jealously devoted, and visiting Ham Spray that summer – his first visit for two years – had felt humiliated before Ralph and Frances by Carrington's ostentatious failure to come to his bedroom. They had planned at the end of July to meet again at the Uffington White Horse where they had first kissed six years ago. But at the last moment Carrington veered off to stay with Alix and James in Munich. 'I feel at the moment it's no good you seeing me,' she wrote to him (13 August 1927). '. . . I was wrong in thinking last autumn that I was capable of sustaining a lover-relation.' It was the same conclusion she had reached two summers ago, but now it really was the end; or rather almost the end, for they both agreed that they had 'full liberty to break all rules and be as capricious as one likes', Carrington later wrote (11 February 1928). 'So there are no irrevocable endings, final letters, unforgivable insults, or closed doors.'

Lytton was still working at *Elizabeth and Essex*, but could find no escape from his troubles, for imbedded in the story he saw much that reflected his own tragic history. This may partly have been the cause of his painfully slow progress. He had been unhappily in love before, yet managed to carry on steadily with his writing because it afforded him relief from his emotional problems. *Elizabeth and Essex* magnified the pain.

The absence of Roger gradually became insupportable to Lytton. At the end of June, Philip Ritchie came down to stay with him to recover after an attack of tonsillitis, and a momentary calmness fell upon Ham Spray. But soon all was gloom and hesitation once more. Occasionally Lytton would see Roger, and sometimes they appeared as close as ever – disagreement vanished, the gloom lifted, hope returned. But Lytton could never tell how things would turn out from one meeting to the next. 'As for my young man, whom I went to on leaving you,' he wrote to Mary Hutchinson (15 July 1927), '– he was unexpectedly delightful – really most coming on – the villain!'

Was there some pattern to Roger's behaviour? Lytton thought there was. The farther apart from each other they were, the more affectionate Roger appeared. Lytton was going through what Carrington's lovers had gone through. 'I think of R[oger] still – no doubt too much – I wish I didn't,' he confided to Mary Hutchinson (27 July 1927). 'Things must take their course and it seems unlikely that I shall see him again before the autumn. There must no doubt be something tiresome about me, when seen very near at hand; but his reactions have I think been a trifle extreme.'

No sooner had Lytton regained some equanimity than Roger shattered it by turning up at Ham Spray. The day of his arrival marked an exact year since the visit on which Lytton first 'found myself in an exquisite paradise' – and Roger now 'kept the anniversary by sleeping, for the first time, by himself', Lytton revealed to Mary Hutchinson (9 August 1927).

'However, such coincidences are ridiculous ... He looked far from well – pale and puffy – no beauty that I could see – really almost someone different. So dreadfully fat! – All went well, he was most amiable. I behaved with the highest propriety, he seemed to enjoy himself, and positively on going away gave me an entirely unsolicited kiss. A queer creature, certainly. Decidedly charming ... We spent a happy hour comparing Rabelais in the original with Urquhart's translation. He picked wild flowers and branches from shrubs on our morning walk – more flowers in the garden – and went back with a huge armful – to my mind a sympathetic thing to do, and what no one else I know (except Carrington) would dream of doing. Aren't things strangely – exasperatingly – mixed? What does one want? What does anyone want? – Really? Ah! – so little – and so much –'

Everything, having repeated itself, seemed to have come to a stop. 'The Lytton-clock needs winding up,' he told Dadie (15 August 1927). 'The hands remain immovable in mid-career, and Ham Spray is the realm of Chastity.' Early in September, Roger left for a holiday in Germany, dispatching a stream of postcards and long letters to Lytton that 'positively sent his love!' But what, after all, was love? A feeling of vast relief spread over him after Roger left – at least he could enjoy some peace for the next few weeks. But all too soon he started to torture himself with thoughts of what Roger was doing. The letters and postcards were not at all clear. They could be read in so many ways. Then life was so dull without him. 'Do you think of me sometimes?' he asked. '. . . are you beginning to forget that I exist? As for me, I can hardly believe that I do – exist I mean.'

Things might have drifted on indefinitely but for a sad event that September. Following a relapse from his tonsillitis, Philip Ritchie suddenly died. 'I had imagined him well and possibly in Scotland,' Lytton wrote to Dadie (15 September 1927). '. . . It is crushing and miserable. Carrington too feels it terribly – she is infinitely sweet and good. Roger is not back yet . . . I feel very troubled about him. Fate has been unkind to him, certainly. I wish to be with him and comfort him, but it is an added irony that he may feel unable now to make use of my devotion.'[48]

The irony was that, even in this adversity, Roger could not abandon his capacity for surprising Lytton. Far from being unable to make use of Lytton's devotion, he relied upon it absolutely. The death of Philip wiped out all the previous months' estrangement and suspense. The two of them met as soon as Roger arrived back in London. He was in a wretched state, full of morbid self-reproach which Lytton helped to dispel by showing how disproportionate it was. 'It is such a great mercy, Dadie,' he afterwards wrote (21 September 1927), 'the cloud that was between us has gone away, and it was possible for me to do all I could to console him and show him my affection quite naturally; and he was perfectly charming and affectionate.'

While Lytton was away at Charleston and Weymouth, they corresponded every day. This shared sorrow promised to give new strength to their relationship. 'But you know, my dearest,' wrote Lytton before returning from Weymouth that October, 'it is impossible not to feel an undercurrent of sadness – more than before; about Philip; and about more general things – the dangers and difficulties of all human life – the miserable pain of separations and misunderstandings – the wicked power of mere accident over happiness and goodness – I know you feel all this and as for me, when I reflect upon these things, I can't help crying, and then Roger, I sink into our love which comes like the divine resolution of a discord, and all is well.'

7

TOGETHER

'All is well' sounded a cheerful refrain to many of Lytton's letters over the following months. 'It is delightful to find oneself down here again,' he wrote from Ham Spray to Topsy Lucas (29 January 1928). '. . . Roger continues to be perfectly charming, and I am curiously happy.' They had agreed that neither of them should write letters unless they wanted to. But Lytton was continually itching to send his love to this 'dearest creature' and slip secret kisses for the preposterous 'monkey's lollipops' into envelopes, or whisper how much he was longing to see his dear cherub or rogermuffin or baboon or monster again at Ham Spray. But he is careful never to blame Roger for not writing as much as he writes, never to bore him with too many invitations or history lessons. His requests are modest ('May I have the little snapshot of you with the pipe & handkerchief . . . if it's not destined for someone else?'); he teases him ('I must whisper it – sometimes – and you mustn't get angry – you are . . . come quite close to me . . . rather a goose!'); and he fills his letters with whatever he thinks will make Roger smile – stories from books, descriptions of people. Sometimes his apprehensions and resentments may be felt, but he cautiously hides them away so as to cause no trouble. 'All is well now between Roger and me,' he concluded in a letter to Dadie (15 October 1927). '. . . I have complete confidence in his affection. In all ways, too, I am much calmer. It is the greatest relief . . . thank you for all your sympathy, and kindness during that miserable time.'

At Ham Spray that autumn he was either still 'mewed up, struggling with Gibbon', or 'reading the whole of Hume's History as mum as a mouse'. By 2 November he had finished Gibbon and 'am pegging away at Macaulay', he told Roger, '– Hume, you see, left to the last – and hope to dispatch him (mac) before Friday'. Two weeks later he reported to Dadie: 'I have been working like ten cart-horses lately, and have now finished all four of those bloody historians. A great relief! – And now once more I find myself face to face with that moblèd queen.'

Having put himself to the plough he was determined not to be diverted, not even by an eruption of visitors from the expensive classes – including Osbert Sitwell, Christabel Aberconway, Siegfried Sassoon and Stephen Tennant, all of them preoccupied with 'dressing up'. Lytton described the scene in a letter to Roger (27 October 1927).

'The night before they had all dressed up as nuns, that morning they had all dressed up as shepherds and shepherdesses, in the evening they were all going to dress up as – God knows what – but they begged and implored me to return with them and share their raptures. When dressed up they are filmed – and the next week-end, I suppose, the film is exhibited. Can you imagine anything more "perfectly divine"? One would have expected them to come in a vast Daimler, but not at all – a small two seater (open) with a dickey behind was their vehicle – they came very late, having lost their way on the Downs, and I shudder to think of the horrors of their return journey. Strange creatures – with just a few feathers where brains should be. Though no doubt Siegfried is rather different.'

'I brace myself for Bess,' he wrote to Roger (15 November 1927). Earlier that month he had met his American publisher, Donald Brace, in London, and told him that it now seemed unlikely that he could finish the book before March. Brace in any case wanted the British publication delayed until the autumn. 'He said that this would make it much easier to prepare the way for the American sale,' Lytton explained to Charles Prentice (6 November 1927), 'which apparently is necessarily a long business – partly because of the size of the country – but also, I cannot help thinking, because of the slowness of the wits of its inhabitants.'

For the next three months he laboured with hardly an interruption at *Elizabeth* 'who marches forward with infinite slowness'. Frances Marshall who, with Ralph, still came down to Ham Spray most weekends, notes in her journal at this time that Lytton was always 'busy writing'. One entry in her journal catches very sympathetically the atmosphere of these winter months.

'Arrived at Hamspray with the black kitten. Roger Senhouse the only visitor. Lytton seems very much in love with him. Philip's death seems in some way to have brought them together. The effect on Lytton is to make him very gay and charming. Walked in the fields while Carrington galloped about on Belle. In the evening we let off some fireworks – an exquisite display of pink and green fountains under the pampas grass.'

This same day (12 November 1927) Lytton wrote to Dadie Rylands: 'He [Roger] gives me so much happiness that I hardly know what to do about it. I sometimes feel inclined to stand on my head, and do cart-wheels all down the Downs. Do you think that would be a good plan?'

Over Christmas, Tommy and Julia (she like 'a Veronese beauty', Carrington thought, or 'a large Swiss dowager' according to Lytton) came down, with Frances and Ralph, and they were joined by James. Carrington spent the days 'lighting fires, thinking of new ways of cooking turkey bones and mincing ham', she told Dorelia. It was idiotic to complain, of course, since she might easily have been so much worse off. But sometimes she resented being 'interrupted in my studio to turn off the water and put logs on the fires and order all these meals, and to hear these perpetual shrieks in the sitting room and nobody stirring a finger to do any work in the house'. It was maddening to feel that she might be painting better when it was so difficult to concentrate in these conditions. She never minded bringing Lytton 'things on a tray'. But after keeping an ear on the telephone, an eye out of the window, her mind on the clock for the crowd of weekend acquaintances, and for even regular visitors like Frances, 'a sort of overboiling seizes me sometimes', she told Alix.[49]

That year a Christmas tree was put up in the back room for the 'petit peuple' from the village who held a boisterous party round it – while, a little way off, Lytton moved like a shadow among his books. Overnight a heavy fall of snow filled the ditches and lanes with immense drifts and extraordinary shapes, like giant mushrooms, columns and sand-dunes. 'We had to fetch food on sledges,' Carrington wrote. A brilliant sun shone in the white fields and trees, and a transparent blue sky extended from horizon to horizon, without a cloud. The horses in the farmyard cantered about, jumping imaginary obstacles in their efforts to keep warm. Within Ham Spray too every psychological cloud seemed to have evaporated. 'Lytton, who had an assignation with Roger [in Brighton], was anxious to get away in spite of all difficulties,' wrote Frances (28 December 1927), 'and a procession set out to walk in to Hungerford.'

'Lytton in a fur coat and waders, R[alph] in top boots, a ruck-sack and a crimson hat trimmed with monkey fur, James with his head entirely enveloped in a scarf, we must have looked a bizarre collection. The scene was fantastically beautiful; after Inkpen the roads were full to the top with snow; the blue sky brought out curious pink lights in it and deep blue shadows, cottages were grotesquely hung with post-card icicles, and the snow was marbled all over with ripplemarks made by the wind. At Hungerford the world seemed suddenly ordinary again; people stepped into the train wearing bowler hats, and gaped to see a troupe of Bulgarian peasants, headed evidently by their Prime Minister in his fur coat.'

The new year of 1928 opened with undimmed radiance. 'Good Queen Bess' slowly trundled forward; Roger's charm, in its unaccountable fashion, continued unabated, and alongside it ran Lytton's own fragile happiness. On the weekend of 11 February, the two of them made a lightning trip to France, crossing the Channel in a terrific thunderstorm from Tilbury to Dunkirk, and hurrying on to Paris where, as the outcome of almost five years' intermittent correspondence, they were to meet Norman Douglas. Lytton, who had read nothing of Douglas's work before 1923, was introduced to it that year by Carrington – a passionate admirer of all his novels and travel books. Two years later he told Ottoline (16

February 1925) that 'I've become a great admirer of all his works; though I hardly dare say so, owing to the scoffs of the cultured.'

Urged on by Carrington, he had opened up the correspondence in October 1923, writing to say how much he had admired *Siren Land* (1911), *Old Calabria* (1915), *South Wind* (1917), *Alone*[50] (1921) and *Together*, which came out earlier that year.[51] This letter led to a long sequence of those reciprocal civilities to which authors are so poignantly inclined. 'I value your opinion more highly than that of any English writer,' Douglas answered (9 November 1923).

'Your books are so full; there is so much of so many things in them – so much experience, so much learning, so much art, so much humour, so much philosophy, and so much proof that there is so much, so very much, more underneath, that is unexpressed . . . in fact for me, your opinion is a thing apart from that of others, even as your writings belong to a category by themselves . . . do let me thank you for the real pleasure – joy, I should say – which I have derived from your books. A thing of art, unquestionably.'

By the end of this year they had already exchanged photographs – 'his [Douglas's] photograph seems to me much more prepossessing than I had expected,' Lytton admitted to Dorothy Bussy (25 November 1923). 'I had imagined something large, Scotch and coarse.' Douglas had also sent Lytton the revised edition of *Siren Land* and Lytton had responded with 'a charming letter of thanks and appreciation', lamenting only the absence of a map.[52] Not to be outmatched in the offering of literary garlands, Douglas dispatched 'a very nice letter' of his own. 'I wish you would write a biography of Heliogabalus, for example, drawn from new sources discovered yourself during a recent visit to Egypt,' he volunteered (3 December 1923). 'Come here, and we'll do it together. Or the private journal of the Emperor Claudius.'

The heady compliments and mild whimsy trickled on over the next year and, in February 1925, Douglas forwarded Lytton four copies of his privately printed brochure *D.H. Lawrence and Maurice Magnus. A plea for better manners*,[53] a theme nicely in harmony with their correspondence. 'I hope you will not dislike it,' he wrote (4 February 1925). 'It is the first thing I have written since October 1923, so you see you are not the only person afflicted with the complaint of non-productivity . . . I heard a rumour that William Beckford, Esquire, might soon be engaging your attention. That would be wonderful. You are the only person who could handle that proposition. A lovely subject!'

Throughout this time there had been several tentative arrangements for them to meet. 'Now come here if you can,' Douglas wrote from Italy on 25 September 1927. 'Florence is taboo for me also, at present. I am living at Prato and only go in for an afternoon now and then, thickly veiled and wearing blue glasses and a carroty beard. This will last, I daresay, till after Christmas. But there is no reason why you shouldn't come to the neighbourhood, anyhow.' When eventually they did meet some four months later, the suggestion had again come from Douglas. 'Now just think if you can't run (or fly) over to Paris for a week-end,' he invited Lytton (31 January 1928). 'I have to go there about the 10th, and have some 58 teeth pulled out, and 63 new ones put in, and I am sure you are the very person to hold my hand. Besides we can go to Pruniers in the intervals. Nancy Cunard is there; I hope you like her?[54] So do come along.'

After so much epistolary warmth, Lytton felt nervous of 'this truly frantic project', and was glad to have Roger with him. 'I am excited and terrified, as you may imagine,' he wrote to Dadie (9 February 1928). 'Good God! The crossing! The cold! The streets of Paris! And – most serious of all – Norman Douglas! Will he be charming, vulgar, too talkative, too vague, or what? – Perhaps a womanizer after all! Who knows? And what, oh what, shall I say? How *am* I to carry it off? A silent owl in an ivy bush. I shall beg Roger to wear a false beard, and shave mine off, so that we may change parts. And I'll let you know the upshot.' These preliminary fears were soon whipped to a frenzy by several last-minute calamities. 'There is great agitation as his [Lytton's] drawers and vests haven't come back from the wash and the wind roars so fiercely that he is terrified all the ships will sink,' Carrington told Dorelia (10 February 1928). 'But I expect it will be great fun boozing at Foyots.'

Douglas had written to ask whether Lytton could suggest someone who might help him collect 'the obscenest and most blasphemous Limericks (university or Stock Exchange?)'. He wished to make a full anthology 'for scholarly purposes of course', which would be privately printed 'with copious notes'. It was as adviser on limericks that Roger was going out with Lytton.[55]

After the rough passage, Lytton arrived feeling like 'a mere piece of wet brown paper'. Douglas, however, turned out to be most sympathetic, speaking with a pseudo-Scottish accent and behaving not at all in the florid manner that his letters had somehow suggested. He seemed to understand at once Lytton's aversion to 'those trailing café parties' and, so that Lytton should have an opportunity to recover, they arranged to meet at Foyot's for dinner. That evening, Douglas arrived, wearing a sombre black coat but there was no black coat on his conversation. 'N.D. was

rather older than I expected,' Lytton afterwards wrote to Mary
Hutchinson (22 February 1928), '– not flamboyant (as I had rather feared)
– in fact rather the opposite – very neat – something (as Roger said) of a
schoolmasterish effect in *appearance* – one of those odd benevolent
unexpectedly broad-minded schoolmasters one sometimes comes across.
Superb in restaurants, ordering food, and so on.

'A curious, very marked accent – partly Scotch, perhaps, partly – I don't
know what – distinctly fascinating. The talk was mainly on a certain
subject. Roger played up admirably, quite admirably, and made everything
go much more easily than would otherwise have been the case. He seemed
to be not particularly literary – which was slightly disturbing; and I think
just a trifle too old – I mean belonging to a generation almost too distant
for really intimate approach – a touch of Sickert – but perhaps I'm wrong
. . . A slight effect you know of having been not very well treated by life.
He's been very unlucky with publishers, and has made hardly anything out
of his books. One would like to surround him with every kind of comfort
and admiration and innumerable boys of 14½.'

The following day, Lytton and Roger went over to the Hôtel d'Isly in
the rue Jacob, where Douglas was staying with Victor and Nancy Cunard.
'Their relations were not very easy to disentangle,' Lytton reported.
'Christian names reigned – and they were all three living in the same hotel.
N.D. insisted on coming to the station to see me off – insisted on paying
for every meal – and eventually tried to tip the porter!'

The more Lytton thought of Douglas on his arrival back in England, the
more he felt that there was something sad about him. He was a kind man,
and he lived in want. He tried to interest Chatto & Windus in Douglas's
work, especially his novel on religion, *In the Beginning*, a limited edition of
which had been privately printed in Florence the previous year. 'Of course
I don't know in the least whether such a thing would be possible for you,'
he wrote to Charles Prentice (15 February 1928), '(nor did I say anything
to him about it), but the suggestion seemed worth making, and I hope you
won't mind my doing so. I feel he is exactly the sort of writer your firm
would like to be connected with, and that he on his side would benefit
greatly if this could happen. In my opinion he is a most distinguished
person, and it's a scandal that his last three books should produce no more
than £12 a year in royalties.' As a result of this letter, Chatto & Windus
became Douglas's publishers, bringing out *In the Beginning* later that
year, and subsequently a number of his other books, including his
autobiography, reprints of his earlier works, and *An Almanac* (1945),

a volume of Douglas's favourite passages from the whole corpus of his work.

From now on, until *Elizabeth and Essex* was finally off his hands, Lytton decided he must go nowhere. He refused all invitations – including one to a Birth Control Ball and another to a charity performance of a play dictated from the Other World by Oscar Wilde. 'I feel I must stick to this wretched grindstone, or all will be lost,' he explained to Mary Hutchinson (22 February 1928). 'Its serpentine prolongation is getting past a joke.' He had reached the thirteenth chapter, and all was proceeding well, though it 'really is horribly difficult'. On 6 March he wrote to Roger: 'The Bess crisis is pretty serious – a regular death-grapple![56] But I hope the worst will be over by the end of the week ... Bemax supports me.'

After two-and-a-half years of intermittent struggle, he was within sight of the long-prepared last paragraph. A fit of impatience seized hold of him. Every day he worked longer hours – but 'virtue never pays', he had told Ottoline, his stamina gave way and for a fortnight he was unable to write anything. Carrington nursed him and by Easter he felt well enough to go and stay with Dadie at his home in Tockington, near Bristol, arriving back at Ham Spray with four closely written sheets of paper – another chapter completed.

'At the moment I am almost dead with exhaustion from this fearful tussle with the Old Hag,' he told Roger (19 April 1928). On the last day of the month, the tussle came to an end. 'I am glad to be able to tell you that my book is finished,' he wrote to Charles Prentice, 'and the last bit is being typed now.'[57]

The next week he travelled up to London and delivered the typescript to Chatto & Windus. It was the first Thursday in May. When he left the office, late that afternoon, the plans for publication were agreed. The sun shone in the streets as he stepped out back to Bloomsbury. He was a free man again.

8

END OF AN ERA

'It was a terribly exhausting book to write,' Lytton later told Ottoline (29 November 1928), '– I don't know why – I was sadly depressed most of the time.' Over the next three-and-a-half years, he was to write only four new essays and his notes to *The Greville Memoirs*. It appeared as if some inner spring had lost its elasticity. 'I had not realised what a weight Elizabeth had been on me – especially for the last few months,' he confided to Roger (25 May 1928) '. . . My spirits are beginning to bounce about again as they ought.' During the last months of *Elizabeth and Essex*, he had told Topsy Lucas (30 October 1927) that he wished 'I never had even to pretend to do any work – I believe I should whirl round in a perpetual circle of pleasure'. For the rest of the year he could revolve to his heart's content in a smooth ellipse of travel and indolence. Laziness, he told Lumsden Barkway, was 'an accomplishment which I have thoroughly mastered! I could give you lessons in the art.'

During the last year he and Carrington had developed their rather separate though overlapping lives. She no longer enjoyed the perpetual stream of London conversations which seemed to have no end and no beginning. But visiting Augustus and Dorelia John at Fryern Court by herself was particularly 'to my taste'. There she would gallop round the country on wild horses with the Johns' two ravishing daughters, sit drinking and gossiping round the huge fire in the evenings with the enigmatic sons and fascinating Dorelia, and in the intervals do some painting in the shadow of that old monster Augustus. 'I am happy all day long,' she wrote to Lytton (10 April 1928). 'In fact if it wasn't for a bearded El Greco saint living in an Ilex bower, I think I could spend rest of my days here, painting pictures and riding.'

She was happy too with Julia and Tommy at their stone cottage at Swallowcliffe in Wiltshire. 'Really it's equal to Ham Spray in elegance and comfort, only cleaner and tidier.' These were happy intervals in a period of advancing worries. She was worried by thoughts of loneliness, ageing, death – wondering whether she should make a Will and then feeling too embarrassed to ask anyone to witness it. Some nights she had terrible dreams. Once she was crawling through a choking grey mist unable to make herself heard, knowing how angry Ralph and Frances would be at her stupidity. Another time she was wading through green scum towards a wizard who laughed and told her the water was 'reeking with syphilis, & I felt drowned'.

Watching her perched on the edge of a chair, smoking her cigarettes with elbows poised high, like 'half-unfurled wings', her face turned from the light, Julia Strachey thought of her as a modern witch, 'a lover of marvels, a searcher for the emotionally magnificent life', or a changeling 'glowing with sympathetic magnetism and droll ideas'.

'She wore the progression of youth into age (which is the usual lot of humanity and can be a quite respectable overcoat) like something hired, "off the peg", thrown on "all anyhow", and of a most farcically clownish fit . . .

From a distance she looked a young creature, innocent and a little awkward, dressed in very odd frocks such as one would see in some quaint old picture-book; but if one came closer and talked to her, one soon saw age scored round her eyes – and something, surely, a bit worse than that – a sort of illness, bodily or mental, which sat oddly on so unspoilt a little face, with its healthy pear-blossom complexion. She had darkly bruised, hollowed, almost battered sockets; and the strange eyes themselves, wide, clear and light as a Northern sky, were not particularly comforting, because of her look of blindness – a statue's blindness, screening her own feelings.'[58]

She had felt specially vulnerable while Lytton was obsessed with Roger and preoccupied with his work. She preferred him ill in bed where she could look after him, to being day after day in his study 'tête-à-tête with Her Majesty'. She told him of her moods of 'absolute despair' and he pretended to think they were due to a bad attack of influenza that winter. But as soon as he had handed in *Elizabeth and Essex*, he took her off for a month's tour of Provence. 'We have enjoyed Aix very much indeed,' he wrote back to Roger (17 May 1928), '– it's a truly delightful place – utterly dim – with house after house of extraordinary beauty.' They put up at the Hôtel Nègre-Coste, and each day, in architectural ecstasies over house fronts and doorways, they would wander through the fascinating streets, or explore the antique shops where 'egged on by C' he bought various items of furniture for Ham Spray, including a large chest-of-drawers ('Oh dear, oh dear! The gigantic packages!'). While Lytton sat in the cafés sipping vermouth-and-soda and reading *Kenilworth*, Carrington swam in the mineral baths or went through the town, filling her head with 'a hundred ideas for painting' as she watched 'curious black widows, old men with white moustaches, and portfolios, nuns herding petities peuples in white dresses to confirmation and the students of the University of Aix arguing with each other outside the cafés.' One morning they motored over to Cassis to have lunch with Duncan and Vanessa in their small house 'La Bergère'. 'They seemed very cheerful, but wouldn't show us any pictures,' Lytton wrote to Roger (17 May 1928). 'Rather a singular ménage.' But Vanessa believed that Carrington was having a lowering effect on Lytton and making his conversation listless.

There is no sign of listlessness in his letters. 'That horrid feeling of exhaustion has passed away,' he wrote to Dadie. 'C. has been a charming and infinitely accommodating travelling-companion. Luckily her propensity for wild-cat actions has calmed down, so it's all been plain sailing.'

On 18 May they left and were driven – 'by a perfect driver who steered his course with complete aplomb round all the precipices' – through Les Baux, to Arles, where they met Brian Howard,[59] apparently sent out there to write an article on the great gathering of gypsies at Saintes-Maries. Carrington wrote to Ralph (20 May 1928):

'Of course I should love to go to the great concourse of gypsies next Thursday at Santa Maria. Where they offer a sort of Fête to their patron saint, Saint Sara, but Lytton I can see *dreads* the gypsie world, so I don't feel I can ask to go = They say the gypsies allow nobody to their revly rites in the cathedral, and *tear* Foreigners limb from limb, if they are discovered at the ceremony. When Lytton asked Brian Howard if he would mind (being torn to pieces), he replied in a décrepid voice, – "well – I suppose it might have its fascination and attractions". He hopes to secret himself in the Cathedral and take some photographs by the help of an introduction from "Country Life" to the Archbishop. He seemed very dim and had never taken a photograph before.'

They hurried on to Nîmes, where amid much buzz and gaiety they settled into the Hôtel du Cheval Blanc, where 'there are no men servants – only females. Except one very old walrus waiter. Lytton was rather agitated when he found himself having his trunks carried by a female!' In spite of their tiredness, they rushed out at once to inspect the theatre and the arena. 'Very remarkable both,' Lytton noted in a letter to Roger, 'but the latter seemed oddly small after the Coliseum . . . the central space seemed too constricted to hold any crucified miscreants at all comfortably – hardly room for a lion to turn round in – and besides rows of neat green garden chairs were ranged about in preparation for some horrid concert business tomorrow.'[60]

Then they were off, via Pont du Gard, to Avignon. A sultry heat had settled over the country. After several days they battled up through this motionless weather to Paris where it was still more torrid. Lytton crept out from the Hôtel Foyot, half dead with giddiness, to get a little air under the trees in the Luxembourg Gardens. But it was no use. In an hour he limped back to his bed to be fed by relays of food from the restaurant.

He longed passionately now for soothing grey English skies, and mild inevitable English rain. 'On the soil of Old England, I shall be well again.' Yet the prospect of further travel made him shrink back in alarm, and eventually it was Ralph, driving a large new Sunbeam which Lytton had bought, who came out to rescue them.

It was a relief to be back amid the cool and quiet of Ham Spray. For a few days Lytton pondered over whether he might compose an idyll about Eton – 'a mixture of Tennyson and T.S. Eliot' – but decided against this once the proof sheets of *Elizabeth and Essex* arrived from Chatto & Windus. He went through these three times, besides having them checked separately by Goldie Dickinson and Roger Senhouse, and it was at this stage that he inserted the Essex poem at the end of Chapter VII. There was also the business of indexing, choice of illustrations and preparation of a limited edition for the United States – 'I spend my days signing my name at 4 guineas a signature for the Americans.'[61]

It was a relief to turn to other people's books. He had been reading T.S. Eliot on Shakespeare ('interesting remarks, but not quite enough') and F.L. Lucas's edition in four fine red volumes of *The Complete Works of J. Webster* which, though done with extraordinary erudition and industry, was 'in some ways a juvenile book'.

Among contemporary novels there were Aldous Huxley's *Point Counter Point* and D.H. Lawrence's *Lady Chatterley's Lover*. He had liked Huxley's collection of short stories, *Mortal Coils* (1922), but his novel 'seems to me worthy but not at all interesting. Is this my fault?' he asked Topsy Lucas (7 October 1928). By the time he had finished the book, he felt that the fault lay principally with the author. It was, he told Dadie Rylands, 'a bad book, in my opinion. The man can't write; his views are rotten; and the total result of his work is a feeling of devitalisation and gloom.'

About *Lady Chatterley's Lover* his feelings were more mixed. 'In many ways I liked it,' he told Roger (23 October 1928), '– the ordinary Lawrenceisms were less in evidence – and it was excellent to attack that subject frontally. But I complain of a sad lack of artistic intention – of creative powers thrown away – of an obsession with moralising. To say nothing of a barbaric, anti-civilization outlook, which I disapprove of.' He had been persuaded to read it by Norman Douglas, who wrote asking him for his opinion (30 July 1928) and, on learning it, replied (12 September 1928): 'As to Lawrence (D.H.) – you are perfectly right. He writes too quickly; a perfect diarrhoea, or rather cholera; besides he can't control his impulses. Lady Chatterley is better than I expected.'

Some of the money Lytton received on delivery of *Elizabeth and Essex* he handed to Carrington for the redecoration of Ham Spray. It was an imaginative way of quelling her anxieties about the future. 'Life is nothing but a whirl of carpenters, engineers and schemes for improvements,' she told Julia. One improvement was the transformation of her studio which became 'a lovely room, like the bows of a ship with 4 windows and painted a lovely pale blue', she wrote to Gerald (30 August 1928). 'But you will never come here and see it.' She was never so happy as when she was painting, and this new studio would 'completely change my character', she hoped, into 'a very hardened recluse' who painted pictures all day.

To avoid the hammering commotion Lytton carried off Roger for a short Scandinavian holiday. 'We have had all sorts of meals in all sorts of restaurants – have spent hours in second-hand bookshops, with no result – have walked through endless streets and gardens – and so far have seen no sights,' he wrote to Carrington from Copenhagen (8 August 1928). '. . . The inhabitants are pleasant, but oh! so lacking in temperament! Duty seems to guide their steps, and duty alone.'

At the end of the week, they moved on to Stockholm. The fearsome medicinal halls at Saltsjöbaden, to which Lytton paid a brief nostalgic visit, appeared unchanged from when he had been there eighteen years before, but Stockholm itself was more evidently a capital city. 'There is a great deal of water in every direction – broad limbs of the Baltic permeating between the streets – so that there really *is* some resemblance to Venice,' he wrote to Carrington (14 August 1928). 'The blueness of the water in this northern light is often attractive, and there are quantities of white steam ferry boats moving about, which adds to the gaiety of the scene.

'The best building to my mind is the royal palace, which stands on the central island of the town – a large severe square pale brown 18th century structure, dominating the scene. Then, slightly remote on a broad piece of water, is the new Town Hall – distinctly striking – very big – and of an effective bigness, built in dark red brick, with one very high tower at the junction of two wings – one (facing the water) longer than the other . . . The worst of it is, however, that in spite of a certain grandeur of conception, there is no real greatness of feeling about it. It is extremely clever and well thought out, but the detail is positively bad – in bad taste, and sometimes actually facetious – and there is no coherency of style – classical, gothic, oriental, byzantine, modern Viennese, etc. etc., so that one has no sense of security or repose. It is a pity, as the site is so good, and the hulk *is* impressive – which is certainly something; but the more I looked the more certain I became that it was infinitely far from real goodness.'

The days sped by and soon he was back at Ham Spray where a pitiless band of workmen, under Carrington's leadership, was making final alterations. Each hour their activities grew more ferocious in a crescendo of noise, confusion and expense. 'No peace, no repose on this earth I plainly see,' Lytton grumbled (30 August 1928). 'One rushes out of doors to escape from the eternal maelstrom only to find oneself set upon by ten million wasps, who, having demolished every particle of fruit in the garden, now begin to devour human beings.' While the pandemonium lasted, Lytton fled up to London where he continued to lead 'a shockingly lazy life'. There were lunches at the Ivy, dinners at Boulestin's, long conversations in the Oriental Club – strawberries – asparagus – cider cup, and copious parties. At Argyll House, one of his fellow guests was the eighty-year-old ex-prime minister A.J. Balfour. 'I like watching him,' Lytton told Roger, '– the perfection of his manners – the curious dimness – the wickedness one catches glimpses of underneath. But of course any communication of ideas is totally out of the question. One might as well talk to the man in the moon.'

In Bloomsbury, he went to the evening gatherings of the 'Woolves' and Bells. Observing him at intervals over the past year, Virginia had often seen him looking like 'an invalid after an attack of love'. This business with Roger, she believed, was the worst bout of love he had suffered since his affair with Duncan. There was something desperate about it. Of course she was only guessing since he never said anything. 'I often glide into intimacy with Lytton about books,' she had written (6 June 1927). 'He is enthusiastic, his mind bare, his attention extremely alive, about books; whereas, about love, its more cryptic.' But what of his latest book which, like hers, was a love story. 'I have every reason to suppose that his Elizabeth is a masterpiece,' she had written dubiously to Clive (31 January 1928). He had been paid a fortune – £6000[62] it was rumoured – for the American serialization in *Ladies' Home Journal*. Certainly it would 'enchant the fashionables'.

That autumn there were also literary afternoons given by Ottoline at her new house in Gower Street. This was the last phase in her career as patroness of the arts, and not even the presence of W.B. Yeats – 'with grey coat-tails and wide-ribboned pince-nez that recalled an old fashioned American politician' – could quite recall her original brilliance. On Lytton's first visit, the guests included Aldous Huxley and the Irish poet and chatterbox James Stephens, 'a little gnome-like Irishman,' he described him to Roger (9 November 1928), 'with a touch of the nautical, quite nice, but gassing away thirteen to the dozen with endless theories and generalizations. One of those essentially frivolous minds that mask themselves under a grand apparatus of earnestness and high-mindedness.'

Lytton's second visit to Gower Street went off rather better, except for a painful circumstance at the beginning. 'I made a pompous entry – late – everyone sitting round at the table – a general remuement, etc. and some slightly dazed looks,' he told Roger (8 January 1929). 'I didn't know why, but on at last taking my seat found that *all* my front buttons were undone, from top to bottom ... There was also cet éternel Stephens, Max [Beerbohm] himself was most quiet – like a great round pussy-cat. He was snowed under by the Irishman, though.'

Ottoline persisted with her invitations, but Lytton did not often go back to Gower Street. He felt some prickings of conscience over Ottoline. 'Dear Marquise, I value very very highly my friendship with you,' he had written to her before the war (1 July 1911). But since the war he had visited her because she wanted him to rather than because he did, and sometimes 'I cannot face it,' he told Mary Hutchinson (10 December 1919). He excused himself by saying he could not tear himself away from Ham Spray, though Ottoline had been told his diary was full of smart engagements. 'It is the happiness of success,' she generously concluded (15 July 1931), 'of what he did not get when he was younger. He must drink his champagne and I doubt if he will ever return to our modest cups of tea.'

One of his smartest engagements was an alarming house-party at Rushbrook Hall, near Bury St Edmunds, a large handsome red-brick Tudor building, with a moat, converted into a Queen Anne Renaissance style – the seat of Lord Islington.[63] He had been invited there out of the blue, and boldly accepted – only to regret his decision the minute he arrived. The sight of a small neatly prepared bridge-table, as he passed through an enormous sitting-room on the long march to his bedroom, confirmed his very worst fears. All the old sensations returned; his exasperation at the vapidity of the upper classes, made more acute by the difficulty of putting his finger on the actual spot of degradation – perhaps, after all, it was something wrong with the glands. How could he shine in such company? 'I had envisioned some sort of crowd, into which one could disappear,' he wrote to Topsy Lucas (7 October 1928), '– but there are only 2 other guests – Lord Hugh Cecil and Evan Charteris.[64]

'The conversation is ceaseless, impossible to join. Lord I. is a country gentleman of about 60. Lady I. an ex-beauty, a brilliant mimic (oh dear!) and a featherhead. Evan C. is a middle-aged man about town – mild, pungent, dull and amusing. Lord Hugh – you can imagine – a very unreal figure with all the regulation Cecil charm. During a long discussion last night on the pros and cons of capital punishment, his view was that there was only one objection to it – that (as at present arranged) it involved a voluntary executioner. Medievalism itself! –'

Once Carrington's redecorations were completed, the stream of visitors to Ham Spray started up again – Morgan Forster, Raymond Mortimer and Francis Birrell, Lytton's niece Janie Bussy, Gerald Heard,[65] who delighted everyone by his 'unexpected intensity', Arthur Waley, 'admirable, triumphant, talking away like anything and rather less remote than usual', Saxon Sydney-Turner, who strolled about 'looking very shrewd and nervous, amiable and ill, and reading Isocrates in the original', the ebullient Boris Anrep who 'bubbled along in a perpetual fountain of amusement' and told 'an absurd story of William Jowitt[66] in Paris ... that solemn handsome personage.

'He confessed that his one pleasure was whipping women, but he didn't know how to manage it – could G. tell him what to do, and where to go? G. handed him over to one of his numerous friends, who had every renseignement at his finger tips. W.J. could not quite make up his mind what he would like best. the friend described a certain lieu, where the naked ladies entered the room on all fours, pecking grain from the floor like chickens, while the customers lashed their behinds. W.J. was struck by this ... and yet ... did not after all feel *quite* sure that it was exactly what he wanted. And so it went on, until at last the four hours were up, and he went back to England. The poor fellow's debauches are always of this nature.'

The year, which had opened in a glow of happiness, ended sadly. Early in December, Lady Strachey, now in her eighty-ninth year, developed bronchitis. There was little hope of a recovery. She had been fading gradually throughout the year and, unable to see the world around her, focusing her mind increasingly upon the past. Incidents from her London life of over fifty years back lived vividly in her imagination – Browning's indignation at being called 'Robert' by a troop of unknown American women; Tennyson reciting his poetry in a surging monotonous voice; the night Salvini lost his shaven wig in the middle of Alfieri's *Samsone*; George du Maurier singing French songs with a meticulous accent in his tiny mosquito voice; the quiet and serious manner of George Eliot and Carlyle's Homeric shouts of laughter. And farther back, and more vivid yet, she could retrace that incredible voyage out to India – the water-spouts and flying fish, the albatross wheeling overhead, the tremendous storms and unearthly sea calms, and her mother playing the cottage piano on board the *Trafalgar*. Those days in India were more real and dear to her than ever – Lord Lytton, the viceroy, in his blue silk dressing-gown, and Lord Roberts mending her sewing-machine; and those amateur theatricals in Calcutta, and the time she chased the leopard with a croquet mallet.

Blindness had emphasized her remoteness from post-war England. Old age was 'like looking out on a garden once filled with life in all its variety and emotion,' she had written, '. . . and now all has vanished, nothing is left but a space, empty of all but graves, among which wander a few time-worn figures; while the faint echoes of once familiar sounds, reaching the ear, tell us of a new-crowded space outside our ken.'

This autumn she had become subject to alarming fits of fainting, and was too frail to walk more than a few steps without assistance. Leonard and Virginia, strolling along the pavement of Gordon Square one November day, glanced up at her window and saw her blind figure sitting on the balcony, with Pippa close behind. They waved up, and on being told of their gesture, she leant forward and opened her arms in a vast maternal gesture.

Death came fairly peacefully. 'It was very miserable,' Lytton wrote to Sebastian Sprott (22 December 1928), 'but fortunately she was not ill for long, and at last died quietly in a state of unconsciousness.' For two weeks she lay in bed looked after night and day by Pippa. Lytton visited her often, and tried to take some of the strain off his sister. They took it in turns to read to her. 'But they're the only bits I like!' she exclaimed when they left out the chapter headings. 'I have been rather numbed and exhausted with this wretched business,' Lytton admitted to Roger, 'and at the same time emotionally perturbed and chaotic.' Each day she grew a little weaker, a little more forlorn, though she had curious bursts of energy almost to the end. On the afternoon of Thursday 14 December, she died in her sleep. Although her death had been expected, Lytton still felt a shock. 'It is impossible to escape the grief, though one has discounted it so long,' he wrote to Topsy Lucas (21 December 1928). 'The prospects of old age are indeed miserable. Yet some manage to keep a hold on life till the last moment – and then vanish suddenly; but they are the lucky few.'

SEVENTEEN

Another World

'Human life in its last stages is certainly a miserable affair. And
yet we are horrified when Death comes to put an end to it.'

Lytton Strachey to Carrington (19 November 1931)

I

ELIZABETH, C'EST MOI!

'I hope by this time you've finished Orlando,' Lytton had written to Roger
Senhouse on 23 October 1928. In a long article for the American *Bookman*
(February 1929), Raymond Mortimer was telling United States readers
that *Elizabeth and Essex* and Virginia Woolf's *Orlando* were 'the two most
remarkable books of the autumn season.

'She has revolutionised fiction and he, biography . . . neither the novel nor
the biography will ever be the same again . . . The weapons they have
turned on the Victorians were forged in Victorian homes . . . the ethic
implicit in them . . . is a pagan ethic . . . In style they are a world apart but
in mind the authors have this mysterious quality in common . . . It has
some relation to a voice that is never too loud, a scepticism that remains
polite, a learning that is never paraded and a disregard, that never
becomes insulting, for the public taste. It is a quality of inherited culture.'

In seeking to define their kinship, Raymond Mortimer had reached
back through the generations as well as to the styles and techniques of *Mrs
Dalloway* and *Eminent Victorians*, *To the Lighthouse* and *Queen Victoria*. But
he was unable to analyse the mysterious atmosphere, to some extent
shared, of *Orlando* and *Elizabeth and Essex* 'not because it is non-existent,
but because it is indefinable'. It was indefinable partly because the source
of both books was a private emotional experience – Virginia's love-affair
with Vita Sackville-West and Lytton's with Roger Senhouse – transferred
to the page as self-projected dreaming. Instead of being confined by their
culture, both writers were now experimenting with ways of leaving the

polite world, mingling gender and time, and challenging public taste with deviant fantasy.

'Isn't it possible', Lytton asked Dorothy Bussy (3 January 1930), 'certain minds can build up these edifices out of their sensibilities and their dramatic power?' At Ham Spray there had been talk of Virginia's inadequate psychology, her lack of body language and inability to differentiate between people and places – all turned into something special, nevertheless, by her genius. At Monk's House it was observed that Lytton, for all his brilliant gifts and successes, had not become the 'great Voltairian historian or biographer'[1] his contemporaries at Cambridge expected. In her diary (25 November 1928), Virginia calls *Elizabeth and Essex* a 'lively superficial meretricious book', and confesses to being 'secretly pleased' that it was bad, though also to a feeling of depression at such mean pleasure. It was not until the following June that she discussed it with Lytton, and though she could see that he minded her criticism she liked him the better for this, seeing also that what she said mattered to him despite the clouds of praise from Dadie, Roger, Carrington and the rest. 'And I felt, among the discreditable feelings, how I had no longer anything to envy him for,' she noted (15 June 1929); '& how, dashing off Orlando I had done better than he had done; & how for the first time I think, he thought of me, as a writer, with some envy.'

Their talk was 'a relief' to her; and there would be more relief to come once she had subsumed her discreditable feelings, or 'disagreeables' as she called them, in a literary theory that made Lytton's comparative failure a matter of the confining nature of the genre in which he worked rather than his limited sensibilities or weak dramatic power. For this solved the problem of how such a remarkable intellect as his, with its suppleness and flickering wit, had not achieved something more original; and it proved the deconstructive thesis of her own biographical pastiche – that the 'riot and confusion of the passions and emotions' could not be fitted into an orthodox biographical form and that (as George Gissing had written) 'the only true biography is to be found in novels'.

In her essay called 'The Art of Biography', composed more than six years after Lytton's death, Virginia argued that 'biography is the most restricted of all the arts'. Where 'the novelist is free; the biographer is tied.' She used Lytton's *Queen Victoria* to show what biography could do, and *Elizabeth and Essex* to show what it could not do. 'In the *Victoria* he treated biography as a craft; he submitted to its limitations,' she reasoned. 'In the *Elizabeth and Essex* he treated biography as an art; he flouted its limitations.

'Could not biography produce something of the intensity of poetry, something of the excitement of drama, and yet keep also the peculiar virtue that belongs to fact – its suggestive reality, its own proper creativeness?

Queen Elizabeth seemed to lend herself perfectly to the experiment . . . to the making of a book that combined the advantages of both worlds, that gave the artist freedom to invent, but helped his invention with the support of facts – a book that was not only a biography but also a work of art.

Nevertheless, the combination proved unworkable; fact and fiction refused to mix. Elizabeth never became real in the sense that Queen Victoria had been real, yet she never became fictitious in the sense that Cleopatra or Falstaff is fictitious . . .'

By talking frankly to Lytton about *Elizabeth and Essex*, Virginia was doing no more than he had done over *Mrs Dalloway*. 'You should take something wilder & more fantastic,' he had said, 'a frame-work that admits anything, like Tristram Shandy.' This she had now done with a happy pantomime whose beginnings in the sixteenth century overlapped with the period of his own highly-coloured 'tragic history', presenting an ageing Queen Elizabeth very similar to his Queen and an eponymous hero who, with his 'strength, grace, romance, folly, poetry, youth' inevitably brings to mind the Earl of Essex.

'I want to revolutionize biography in a night,' Virginia had declared. Yet her love-tribute to Vita implies a recasting of life itself, as much as a change in our way of looking at it. Perhaps such an escapade – for it was an escape from factual imprisonment – could never be repeated, and its contribution to the future of biography – a contribution arising from suggestion rather than example – was after all quite close to that of *Elizabeth and Essex*. 'That failure,' she wrote, 'because it was the result of a daring experiment carried out with magnificent skill, leads the way to further discoveries . . . he has shown us the way in which others may advance.'[2]

*

'A quarter of an hour later – it was ten o'clock – the Earl was at the gate. He hurried forward, without a second's hesitation; he ran up the stairs, and so – oh! he knew the way well enough – into the presence chamber, and thence into the privy chamber; the Queen's bedroom lay beyond. He was muddy and disordered from his long journey, in rough clothes and riding boots; but he was utterly unaware of any of that, as he burst open the door in front of him. And there, quite close to him, was Elizabeth among her ladies, in a dressing-gown, unpainted, without her wig, her grey hair hanging in wisps about her face, and her eyes starting from her head.'

This closing passage from Chapter XII of *Elizabeth and Essex*, describing Essex's forbidden return from Ireland on 28 September 1599, reproduces the opening scene from the blank verse play, *Essex: A Tragedy*, he had written in 1909, the action of which covers Chapters XIII to XVI of the biography. Many of the book's dramatic happenings are framed by such theatrical entrances and exits. When, for example, in Chapter XI Essex is appointed Lord Deputy of Ireland, Strachey gets him and Robert Cecil off the pages as follows: 'With long elated strides and flashing glances he left the room in triumph; and so – with shuffling gait and looks of mild urbanity – did Robert Cecil.'

Strachey writes in places as if giving directions to a group of actors. In the scene where Elizabeth makes her speech to an assembly called by the Speaker of the House of Commons, he uses her exact words but also provides instructions as to how they should be delivered and heard:

'There was a pause; and then the high voice rang out'.
'She stopped, and told them to stand up, as she had more to say to them'.
'Pausing again for a moment, she continued in a deeper tone'.

He closes this scene at the end of Chapter XVI with a dramatic curtain.

'She straightened herself with a final effort; her eyes glared; there was a sound of trumpets; and, turning from them in her sweeping draperies – erect and terrible – she walked out.'

Whenever possible, Strachey treats his readers as direct onlookers – which is to say, as an audience. He endeavours to transform every source – letters, diaries, documentary accounts – into visual material. For example he brings in word for word a letter from Essex to Elizabeth, interrupting the text several times ('as he wrote, he grew warmer'; 'now he could hold himself in no longer'; 'the whole heat of his indignation was flaring out') so as to give readers the impression they are actually watching Essex write the letter.

Frequently he uses indirect speech to present the facts as seen by the characters themselves and to carry their tone of voice: 'The Attorney-Generalship fell vacant, and Essex immediately declared that Francis Bacon must have the post,' he writes in Chapter V. Then, slipping into Essex's own thoughts and attitude, he continues: 'He was young and had not yet risen far in his profession – but what of that? He deserved something even greater; the Queen might appoint whom she would, and if

Essex had any influence, the right man, for once, should be given preferment.'

In these soliloquies, Strachey conceals himself behind his characters who present their one-sided view of a situation or verdict on another character, passing from statements of facts to stream of consciousness without any verbal conjunction – though often using a dash: or sometimes a colon to mark the connection. These meditations (perhaps the best example occurs in Chapter XV where the Queen, thinking back on her relationship with Essex, deliberates over his pardon) have their origin in the monologues of the Elizabethan stage.

For it was as a five-act Elizabethan drama that he had constructed his biography. *Elizabeth and Essex* is his *Antony and Cleopatra*. 'There is only one thing which could have blinded a man in Antony's position so completely as we now know he actually was blinded,' he had written, 'and that thing is passion.'[3] Passion is the supreme motive in *Elizabeth and Essex*. Essex, whose sensual temperament and genius for friendship are brought out in a style that emphasizes his similarity to Antony, leaves and returns to his Queen as Antony leaves and returns to Cleopatra; and like Antony he dies a violent death. Elizabeth is no Cleopatra, but each in her fashion was 'a lass unparallel'd', the Queen of England's variations of mind and temper making a dramatic equivalent to the 'infinite variety' of the Queen of Egypt. In Sir Robert Cecil, the mastermind of the drama (who performs a function similar to Baron Stockmar's in *Queen Victoria*) there is a close approximation to the calculating Octavius. Shakespeare closes *Antony and Cleopatra* with the triumph of Octavius; Strachey, in the carefully weighed passage with which *Elizabeth and Essex* ends (a reversal of the famous retrospective last paragraph in *Queen Victoria*), employs another device from the Elizabethan stage, picturing Cecil brooding over the destiny of England and the future of his own house. With some qualifications, the comparison can be extended to Essex's loyal friends, Sir Christopher Blount, Henry Cuffe, Lord Southampton and Sir Charles Travers who may be likened to Shakespeare's Eros and Scarus. But Strachey simplifies his menagerie of characters. Francis Bacon, 'the serpent', is a blacker villain than Enobarbus; and Sir Walter Raleigh, 'the fox', is far more sinister than Lepidus.

Lytton dedicated *Elizabeth and Essex* to James and Alix Strachey who had by now established themselves as, in Freud's words, 'my excellent English translators'.[4] He did not read German and was not affected by the early American translations of Freud by A.A. Brill as he had been affected by Constance Garnett's translations of Dostoyevsky whose novels were the chief psychological influence on *Eminent Victorians*. As late as 1923 he is describing psychoanalysis as 'a ludicrous fraud'.[5] But during the mid-1920s, as psychoanalysis gradually permeated Bloomsbury and came of age in England, he began to change his mind. Adrian and Karin Stephen had decided to become analysts after the war; the Hogarth Press published the translations of Freud's works after 1924 (Sebastian Sprott was to translate Freud's *New Introductory Lectures*); and Lytton began reading and discussing his work with James and Alix.[6]

The book's Freudian thesis was partly a method of deepening the general pattern of Shakespearian predestination by adding a stream of unconscious inevitability to the mood of sixteenth-century superstitious fatalism. Strachey uses a number of dramatic incidents, such as the tempest which the expedition against Ferrol encounters, as omens to Essex's final tragedy, and reinforces this Elizabethan theatrical device with a subtext of unconscious processes. He had come to accept the general premise that infant sexuality and the adult operation of the sex instinct infiltrate human thought and action. In particular he used Freud's ideas concerning father–daughter relationships to account for the underlying attitude of Elizabeth to Essex's execution. There are several passages in the earlier chapters of the book that prepare us for the description of her sensations on sending Essex to his death. Strachey imagines, rising within her, the spirit of her father, Henry VIII, who had executed his wives, one of whom was Elizabeth's mother:

'He would find that she was indeed the daughter of a father who had known how to rule a kingdom and how to punish the perfidy of those he had loved the most. Yes, indeed, she felt her father's spirit within her; and an extraordinary passion moved the obscure profundities of her being, as she condemned her lover to her mother's death. In all that had happened there was a dark inevitability, a ghastly satisfaction; her father's destiny, by some intimate dispensation, was repeated in hers; it was supremely fitting that Robert Devereux should follow Anne Boleyn to the block. Her father! ... but in a still remoter depth there were still stranger stirrings. There was a difference as well as a likeness; after all, she was no man, but a woman; and was this, perhaps, not a repetition but a revenge? After all the long years of her life-time, and in this appalling consummation, was it her murdered mother who had finally emerged? The wheel had come full circle.'

When Strachey left the Mother Empress for the Virgin Queen his manner changed. 'We are aware for the first time disagreeably', wrote Edmund Wilson, 'of the high-voiced old Bloomsbury gossip gloating over the scandals of the past as he ferreted them out of his library. Strachey's curious catty malice, his enjoyment of the discomfiture of his characters is most unpleasantly in evidence in *Elizabeth and Essex*.[7] The writing is full of sexual allusion and innuendo – a critic in *The Criterion*, the Reverend Charles Smyth, described it as 'preoccupied with the sexual organs to a degree that seems almost pathological'.[8]

To dramatize the psychological disturbances of Elizabeth's childhood and show how these may have influenced her decision over the execution of Essex, Strachey conjectured an early traumatic experience. 'Manhood – the fascinating, detestable entity, which had first come upon her concealed in yellow magnificence in her father's lap – manhood was overthrown at last, and in the person of that traitor it should be rooted out. Literally, perhaps . . . she knew well enough the punishment for high treason.'

In *Elizabeth and Essex* there are as many references to the mutilation of ears related to fear of castration, as to castration itself. Strachey ends Chapter V, which covers the relationship between Essex and Francis Bacon, with the *divertissement* of Mr Booth 'who, poor man, had suddenly found himself condemned by the Court of Chancery to a heavy fine, to imprisonment, and to have his ears cut off'. Though this anecdote takes the reader away from the main theme of this chapter, it adds to the brutal and capricious picture Strachey creates of this age. It was as if, with a shiver of delight, he imagined himself living in sixteenth-century England, his ghost flitting between these gorgeous and alarming figures.

'Who can reconstruct those iron-nerved beings who passed with rapture from some divine madrigal sung to a lute by a bewitching boy in a tavern to the spectacle of mauled dogs tearing a bear to pieces? . . . the flaunting man of fashion, whose codpiece proclaimed an astonishing virility, was he not also, with his flowing hair and his jewelled ears, effeminate? . . . A change of fortune – a spy's word – and those same ears might be sliced off, to the laughter of the crowd, in the pillory; or, if ambition or religion made a darker embroilment, a more ghastly mutilation – amid a welter of moral platitudes fit only for the nursery and dying confessions in marvellous English – might diversify a traitor's end.'

Strachey's Elizabethanism is a personal evocation peopled by extravagant phantoms which act out the instincts that four hundred years later had receded into our subconscious – a never-never-again land with which we were connected by residual memories and in whose strange atmosphere we are invited triumphantly to lose ourselves.

*

In an early issue of *Scrutiny*, T.R. Barnes attributes Strachey's 'middle-brow' success to the fact that, with 'appropriately Freudian and free-thinking reasoning, [he] appealed to that desire for fantasy satisfaction through "character" or substitute lives, which is the basis of commercial fiction,' and concluded that, 'being incapable of creation in life or in literature, his writings were a substitute for both.'[9]

Rebecca West took a similar line when criticizing *Elizabeth and Essex* for breaking 'too flagrantly the rule that a work of art must never be an obvious compensation for the deficiencies of the author's existence. It was too plainly the revenge taken by the suppressed romantic elements in a character committed by a majority vote to a cool and classical way of living, and it had the turgid and disconcerting quality of adolescent dreams that have been dreamed too long.'[10]

This game goes on – since to use psychoanalysis is to invite its further use. The Canadian poet and critic John Ferns was to suggest that 'Strachey felt that his manhood had been denied and thwarted by a female presence that he could not get beyond . . . [he] was unable to struggle free of the oedipal web. If one sees *Elizabeth and Essex* in the Freudian terms that Strachey himself used in writing the book, one might ultimately identify Elizabeth with Strachey's mother and Strachey himself with Essex.'[11]

Alternatively, and at the time he was writing, he saw Essex, through the Queen's eyes, as the sort of person he desired to be – a pale and sorrowful scholar, shivering in the agonies of ague as he lay in the darkness of his bedroom, then flowering into this 'handsome, charming youth, with his open manner, his boyish spirits, his words and looks of adoration, and his tall figure, and his exquisite hands, and the auburn hair on his head, that bent so gently downwards.' Reading the book when it was first published, Maynard Keynes wrote to him (3 December 1928): 'You seem, on the whole, to imagine yourself as Elizabeth, but I see from the pictures that it is Essex whom you have got up as yourself.'[12]

Elizabeth and Essex has added to Lytton Strachey's influence as a liberator of biographical forms, and its intermittently thin texture may have been due less to psychological factors, which have enriched the book's subtext, than to physical deterioration. His correspondence over the period he was writing the book shows an enfeeblement of his health which seems detectable in many passages. There are some ironical flashes from the author of *Eminent Victorians* such as the portrait in Chapter X of King Philip, spider of the Escorial, 'spinning cobwebs out of dreams' who is troubled on his death-bed by a fearful thought: 'Had he been remiss in the burning of heretics? He had burnt many, no doubt; but he might have burnt more.' There are some charming metaphors from the author of *Queen Victoria*, such as the picture of Elizabeth's vacillating disposition, which he likens to a ship: 'Such was her nature – to float, when it was calm, on a sea of indecisions, and, when the wind rose, to tack hectically from side to side.' But the contrivance is held together by a connecting tissue of weak puns, shaky transitions, and the running-on of empty words.

'On the whole, it seemed certain that with a little good management the prosecution would be able to blacken the conduct and character of the prisoners in a way which would carry conviction – in every sense of the word.'

'The state of affairs in Ireland was not quite so bad as it might have been.'

'They [the Spanish ambassadors] had come into contact with those forces in the Queen's mind which proved, incidentally, fatal to themselves, and brought her, in the end, her enormous triumph.'

Between these deserted spaces he places his dramatic set-pieces, 'whipping the flanks of the language', as Virginia observed (25 November 1928), '& putting it to this foaming gallop, when the poor beast is all spavins & sores'.

The minor figures, often likened (as in all his books) to birds and beasts, and skilfully arranged in his Elizabethan tapestry, were now recognizable as stock characters from the Strachey repertoire. There is the brilliant enigma, an all-but-invisible Master Mind, here attached to a humpback and suspended in an endless state of purposeful inanimation. This assiduous quill-pusher is Robert Cecil, a man of superhuman intelligence bent double over his accumulation of papers as he directs the momentous affairs of the nation with fractional gesticulations of his feet and hands. Then there is the Bad Man of the tragedy, Francis Bacon of the 'viper-gaze'. Bacon is determined to prove a rascal. 'It is the *Lion and the Snake*,' commented Wyndham Lewis (27 November 1928) referring to his own *The Lion and the Fox* (1927) where he pictures Othello as the simple-hearted noble lion and Iago as the wily Machiavel. 'Essex as the embodiment of simple-minded chivalry and poor Bacon as the "Machiavel"! What a villain! One is almost inclined to believe after reading S[trachey]'s book, that he wrote Shakespeare's plays and did all the other things he is accused of.'[13]

Strachey's fox was the 'dangerous and magnificent' Walter Raleigh who, as an implacable enemy of Essex, is cast as 'ominous prophet of

Imperialism'. He needed this characterization so as to help identify Essex as 'the spirit of ancient feudalism' symbolizing a romantic, doomed way of life in the England of Elizabeth. She is 'the supreme phenomenon of Elizabethanism', served by rational new men such as Bacon and Cecil. All this is to give historical significance to the love story whose tragic hero had found no place in G.M. Trevelyan's recent *History of England* (1926).

Trevelyan had paid tribute to Strachey four years earlier for 'doing history a great service by connecting her again with literature and by interesting the public in her themes'. But, he added: 'I should be sorry if those who know most about history, those who give their whole lives to the study of history, relinquished the interpretation and exposition of history entirely to novelists and literary men who were not primarily historians.'[14] The further Strachey moved from the mainstream of history, the happier Trevelyan felt. *Eminent Victorians* had seriously disturbed him; *Queen Victoria*, he told Strachey (6 May 1921), 'beats it a lot'. With *Elizabeth and Essex* he relaxed completely. 'I have just finished Elizabeth,' he wrote (25 November 1928).

'We have not waited 7 years in vain, and your long hesitations over a subject have been rewarded by a success as great as crowned Elizabeth's long hesitations in her happier years. She is a much subtler and much greater subject than Victoria and one more completely suited to your genius. The idea of telling the tale of her and of her age not by full biography but by this particular episode was most happy.

It is much your greatest work. And its success bears out my theory as against your own – or what used to be your view. You used to tell me that your strength was satire and satire alone, so you must choose people you did not much like in order to satirize them. I thought the argument bad then, and now the time gives proof of it. Your best book has been written about people to whom you are spiritually akin – far more akin than to the Victorians. And it is not a piece of satire but a piece of life.'

This was not the general view. 'Lytton must look to his laurels,' Logan Pearsall Smith was writing to Mary Berenson. '. . . he has made no use of his real gift – his exquisite sense, like that of Voltaire or Gibbon, of human absurdity, of the unbelievable grotesqueness of men's actions and beliefs on this planet. It is a rare and shining gift and should not be laid under a bushel.'[15]

As Trevelyan must have known, professional historians would take little notice of what A.L. Rowse nevertheless called Strachey's 'brilliant and insufficiently appreciated book'. Here and there a surprising reference appears: Conyers Read in *The Tudors* points to 'some brilliant glimpses of her [Elizabeth] and her court' in *Elizabeth and Essex*; J.B. Black in *The Reign of Elizabeth 1558–1603* (part of *The Oxford History of England*) calls it a 'penetrating and suggestive study'. But it is not cited in a standard work such as J.E. Neale's *Queen Elizabeth* and was generally regarded as, in Logan Pearsall Smith's words, 'melodrama rather than history'. Or were historians too academically confined? G.B. Harrison, whose *Robert Devereux, Earl of Essex* (1937) was written as a riposte to *Elizabeth and Essex*, thought it a 'fine scenario but not history'.[16] The dovetailing of letters and conversations, Harrison wrote, were 'privileges denied to the pedestrian scholar'. Strachey was up to his old tricks. By leaving out passages without indication and transposing the rhythms of what he does quote (as if editing a dramatist's speech to assist an actress), he represented Elizabeth's last speech to Parliament, for example, as shorter and more striking than it actually was – though the sense was the same.

'I am deluged by E & E correspondence,' Lytton wrote to Dadie Rylands (29 November 1928). The most interesting letter of all came from Sigmund Freud, written in Vienna on Christmas Day. 'I am acquainted with all your earlier publications, and have read them with great enjoyment,' Freud wrote. 'But the enjoyment was essentially an aesthetic one.

'This time you have moved me deeply, for you yourself have reached greater depths. You are aware of what other historians so easily overlook – that it is impossible to understand the past with certainty, because we cannot divine men's motives and the essence of their minds and so cannot interpret their actions. Our psychological analysis does not suffice even with those who are near us in space and time, unless we can make them the object of years of the closest investigation, and even then it breaks down before the incompleteness of our knowledge and the clumsiness of our synthesis. So that with regard to the people of past times we are in the same position as with dreams to which we have been given no associations – and only a layman could expect us to interpret such dreams as those. As a historian, then, you show that you are steeped in the spirit of psycho-analysis. And, with reservations such as these, you have approached one of the most remarkable figures in your country's history, you have known how to trace back her character to the impressions of her childhood, you have touched upon her most hidden motives with equal boldness and discretion, and it is very possible that you have succeeded in making a correct reconstruction of what actually occurred.'

*

'It's being very successful,' Lytton wrote to Topsy Lucas a week after publication (30 November 1928), 'and I gather from Prentice that the only difficulty is to get enough paper and binding material for the multitudes of editions that will have to be printed. However a good many copies will have to be sold to keep pace with my growing extravagance. Aubusson carpets, for instance – I am plunging wildly in that direction – egged on, of course, by Carrington.'

In Britain, where *Elizabeth and Essex* was published on 23 November, over forty thousand copies had been printed and most of them sold within six months. In the United States, where it came out on 1 December, the book made publishing history. Two big presses and one small press were used, and with each revolution of these three presses one book was printed. Harcourt Brace prepared a first edition of thirty thousand copies and a week after publication twenty-five thousand more copies were sent out. By Christmas seventy thousand copies had been shipped and not once had the book been reported out of stock. This was a record for the production and distribution of a big non-fiction book. In the second week of January, William Harcourt wrote: 'For three weeks your book was being manufactured *night and day*,' and the situation had become 'unprecedented'. Ninety thousand copies were in print, and still the demand continued, until the eventual sales of *Elizabeth and Essex* reached one hundred and ten thousand hardback copies in Britain, and in the United States one hundred and fifty thousand hardback copies.[17]

'I have made incredibly huge sums out of E & E,' Lytton told his sister Dorothy Bussy (February 1929). But when Vanessa Bell asked him whether he liked such success, and the celebrity which it brought, the best answer he could manage was: 'It's vaguely agreeable.' It had come too late, he said to Virginia, 'to make us hop on our perches'. Nevertheless – and this was strange – his financial winnings did not fan his popularity among other writers, but would spur on a posthumous reaction against his books with more allegations of their meretricious middle-brow popularity.

2

TWO TO COME AND ONE TO GO

Lytton was in 'very good spirits', Carrington reported that winter. 'I think he was very set up by the success of Elizabeth.' The motor car was broken (Lytton had suggested converting it into a summer house), cook had vanished, the pipes were frozen solid, and it was so devastatingly cold they sometimes stayed in bed all day. But they had used Lytton's royalties to install some central heating at Ham Spray, and this 'sort of pads over the deficiencies of wayward lovers and cold hearted young men'.

Roger Senhouse came and went and came again, 'sweetness and vagueness incarnate'. Some of Lytton's friends had begun to wonder whether Roger had any character of his own, whether he wasn't all make-believe. But Lytton felt an extraordinary tenderness for him, really an absorption. 'I seemed to be living in some sort of golden trance,' he wrote to Sebastian Sprott. He thought of Roger constantly, riding the seas of doubt and expectation, sometimes in tears, then settling into a calmer sense of it being 'my metier to accept his peculiarities and peccadilloes'. Though fearful of being thought possessive or tiresome, he could not stop himself writing letters to his dearest creature, angel, monster, antelope, every two or three days. 'Look here, the magic carpet is waiting at the door, you've only to step on to it, and you'll be here in five seconds.' Sometimes it almost seemed as if Roger had indeed stepped on to this magic carpet, that the door of Lytton's study were opening and Roger was about to walk in filling the room with the beauty and comfort of his presence. Such moments came after specially happy hours together when, though still missing him, Lytton was left with the lingering sense that 'you are somehow with me – as if you could hear me, if I raised my voice – as if I could almost touch you if I could stretch out my hand a little further than usual'. He knew his imagination 'is naturally couleur de rose', and perhaps it was heightened by the new central heating among the shelves.

Lytton made many proposals to establish their relationship on a surer basis. He suggested that they make a catalogue of the Ham Spray library together ('how the hours and days would rush by! The perfect employment surely, for 2 people in the winter!'). He offered to buy Roger a Citroën car for £185 (the equivalent of £4500 in 1994) so that he could get down there more easily ('would you really not like it? A bulky cheque has this moment come from Chatto's – so now's the time'). He questioned whether in the future they might share rooms somewhere in London ('I would get any house you liked and fall in with all your wishes'). He also offered him a loan if he decided to leave his well-paid but unsatisfying import-export job and take up some more congenial business ('a bookshop perhaps'). Surely the risk would be better. 'I cannot believe that starvation would be the result! You might have to be comparatively poor, but there are worse things than poverty and one of them, it seems to me, is lack of freedom.'

But Roger avoided all Lytton's plans to re-arrange his life, and there was never any telling what he would do next. It was like being perpetually at a fancy-dress ball. 'I believe you would make an excellent trapezist,' Lytton decided (16 January 1929), 'or instructor in discobolos-throwing, or Russian Emperor, or whipped guardsman!' In good times these mercurial feats intoxicated Lytton with 'a sort of stupor, made up of happiness, remembrances, a pleasant exhaustion'.

He had never believed in past years that his expectations of love could really materialize, but during some days-and-nights with Roger he felt they were exceeded. This was what he had waited for and dreamed of. To be with Roger as the last experience of the day made Lytton so tremulously joyful that he did not know how to put his feelings into words. Yet it was impossible to let a day pass without a few words.

'Your perfectly divine elasticity lures me on and on – I fear I am almost too happy whenever I am with you . . . the intricacy and intensity of existence reduces me to a shadow. Every moment is peculiar beyond words . . . my love rushes out to you, and wraps you round and round, and keeps you very near me in spite of Time & Space . . .'

But time and space and other elements of reality gnawed away at their relationship. 'I am here', Lytton wrote (15 January 1929), 'to listen to everything you like to say to me.' But so often there were inexplicable silences and Lytton's confidence began to waver, his imagination to play tricks. Over the same period that he was proclaiming his love, he also communicated his sadness and perplexity:

'Please don't be too vague, and let me have an answer . . . It was impossible not to feel anxious . . . I've lost count of the letters I've sent you already of this kind . . . I've quite given up speculation about you! . . . Roger dear, you don't realise how little you say. You sometimes think you have told me things which in fact you have left to my instinct & imagination to pick up as best they can . . . I only hope it doesn't mean the prospect of our some day living together for some length of time is being obliterated.'

One special crisis cropped up in the autumn of 1929. 'Was I rather tiresome perhaps about crabs?' Lytton inquired on 2 September. Over the next week the story continued:

'Thank you so much, dearest creature, for the medicaments and the charming letter of instructions . . . If it hadn't been for your decision and competence – your determination to deal with the hideous truth – I shudder to think what my condition would have been . . . could you get me another bottle ... some moments of maddening irritation recur ... I suppose you wouldn't look in en route for the Schneider Cup and have a local inspection! ...

... a painful circumstance has arisen. The previous applications had a terribly violent effect on my unfortunate skin, which has been excoriated and inflamed over rather a long area ... I can't be absolutely sure that the original monsters have been eradicated. Its terribly difficult for me to see ... with the aid of that special mirror I could detect nothing ... I shall have to wait to be quite sure till I see you.'

'I beg you not to think I'm depressed,' Lytton assured him shortly afterwards (1 October 1929). As the winter started, he wrote apprehensively to Dadie (23 December 1929): 'The drear months are now beginning, and we shall have to give each other the support, love, lust etc that we can ... Where are the heats of next July?' Despite their setbacks – Roger's sudden departures and non-appearances, the cancellation of holidays and the sheer painfulness of Lytton's adoration – they survived the winter and next July Lytton was writing to Roger (30 July 1930): 'I hope things may improve – at any rate it's cheering to think how much worse they might be! With love on both sides all must be well really.'

*

Carrington was attempting to overcome her own difficulties with a campaign of painting. She painted portraits of the dashing fourteen-year-old Vivien John and the enigmatically married Julia Tomlin; she decorated Dadie's gothic rooms at King's College with apricot and grey-pink classical pastiches, and a little room for Dorelia at Fryern Court with identifying labels on the drawers ('Twine & String', 'Silk & Cotton', 'Rags & Bones'). She also set about designing an imitation bookcase over an unused door at Ham Spray with a series of ironic titles (*The Empty Room* by Virginia Woolf, *The Lad* by Leonard Woolf, and the ambitious *Deeds Not Words* volumes I & II by A. Carpenter). Every year she started with these resolutions to paint, then reached the summer with a sense that 'my life has been frittered away without producing anything worth looking at'. But she went on painting.

She was still ravaged by nightmares. In one she was 'having my neck cut off, & blood running down my chest'. In another 'terrible enemies pursued me into the kitchen & tried to put my eyes out with a small bent fork'. Though she loved Ham Spray and the smooth enfolding landscape, she felt marooned as if on a quiet green island whenever Lytton was elsewhere. It was strange how much of everything he took away with him.

The rooms looked different, and half the purpose of living seemed to evaporate. 'My life is conducted on a fugue basis,' she had told Gerald Brenan (30 August 1928). 'I go forwards a few bars and then retreat and pick up the old theme.'

Their new living experiment, with Ralph and Frances spending weekdays in Gordon Square, had not really suited her. She felt excluded when they were away, irritated when they came down. She could hear them talking and laughing in the bathroom together and their happiness emphasized her solitude. Ralph was sometimes exasperated by her moods. It seemed impossible to think up anything that pleased her. Was it not time she began acting her age? But a sense of ageing, a sense of death, time running out and love-affairs ending, was part of her nightmare.

Lytton had also been disappointed by the Gordon Square arrangement. He found it impossible to see Ralph except in the company of Frances. Every time Ralph came down to Hungerford he brought her; and at the end of their stay they would leave together. Lytton did not dislike Frances, but he could not easily get on with her, and nor could Carrington. The two women had never been real friends. Frances, it is true, felt an admiration for Carrington. But the most that Carrington felt for Frances was gratitude for having accepted so readily Ralph's links with Ham Spray – gratitude complicated by a lesbian attraction which leapt over her guarded feelings with sudden rushes of tenderness. They were therefore not simply rivals for Ralph's love, but two people who, because of circumstance, found the independent lines of their happiness knotted together in a way that they could not unravel.

The situation was particularly awkward for Carrington. She never complained to Lytton about this latest arrangement for fear it should change to something worse. But he could sense her discomposure. The atmosphere between the four of them at weekends had become heavy with a weight of unspoken feeling which all Ralph's parades of jocular friendliness could not dispel.

Towards the end of 1928, Lytton decided to try and remedy matters. 'My dearest,' he wrote to Ralph (6 November 1928), 'I am writing this without telling Carrington, and perhaps you may think it best not to show it to Frances, but of course you must do just as you like.

'I have felt for some time rather uneasy about F[rances] – but have been unable to bring myself to say anything. What worries me is her coming down here with you so much, and staying for so much of the time you are here, so that we see so little of you alone. It is not quite what I had expected would happen – and I think not exactly what you intended either.

I am afraid you may suppose that this indicates some hostility on my part towards F[rances]; but this is far from being the case. Can you believe this? I hope so. I hope you will trust that I am telling the truth, and believe in my affection for you, which is something I cannot describe or express. I feel it too deeply for that. I know that this must be painful to you, but it seems better that I should tell you what is in my mind than that I should continue indefinitely with a slight consciousness of a difficulty not cleared up between us. Perhaps it can't be cleared up – but at any rate I think it's better open than secret. I don't want to force you into anything unwillingly. If you feel that you can do nothing – then it can't be helped. If you feel that you cannot answer this either by writing or in talk, do not do so, I will say nothing more about it, and all will be well between us. But conceivably it might be possible for you to suggest to F[rances] that it would be better if she came down rather less often – and if that could be managed the situation would be very greatly eased. It is for you to judge what you can do. I trust your judgement. I only feel that you may perhaps have allowed things to drift from an unwillingness to take an unpleasant step. I don't know. And please do not do anything under a sense of "pressure" from me. I press for nothing. I only ask whether perhaps it may be possible, without too much pain, to make me happier.'

It was impossible for Ralph to ignore this appeal. 'If Lytton supposed Ralph wouldn't show me this letter he betrayed unusual lack of understanding of his character,' Frances tartly commented. 'Of course he did, and it was the only occasion I have ever seen him really furiously angry with Lytton.'[18] He knew how this rejection had hurt Frances, who partly attributed a mysterious illness early in 1929 to Lytton's letter. Though she did not feel quite as Ralph felt, she loved Ham Spray. But her ambiguous position there – neither guest nor host – had come to symbolize a state of limbo, and the suppression of her maternal instincts was a purgatory. All this pained Ralph who, the following week, argued it out with Lytton at 37 Gordon Square – after which 'things went on much as before', Frances noted, 'except that Ralph and I both stayed away from Ham Spray rather more'.

What made everything more difficult for Carrington was her final break with Gerald that month. They had tried to pick up the old theme again that summer and play it with more sweetness and resolution. But neither of them was any longer certain what they wanted. She thought it was 'nice' seeing him again, but did not want to lose 'the curious pleasures' of her privacy at Ham Spray. He loved her, but desperately wanted to be free from the 'agony and misery' she always brought him. For months they swayed between rows and reconciliations.

The end came over a trivial incident involving a bundle of old ties. Lytton had recently taken it into his head to go through his wardrobes and cupboards discarding clothes he no longer needed. But Carrington, who never liked getting rid of anything or anyone, felt it would be bad luck simply to throw out Lytton's old suits and socks. Then she had a brainwave – a solution to please everyone. She would offer these hallowed articles to Gerald who could not afford such things. He angrily refused the offer. But Carrington, who liked making parcels, wrapped up a couple of Lytton's old ties anyhow and sent them off to Gerald 'to tie our love'.

It was the last straw. To be handed Lytton's cast-off clothes symbolized for Gerald the second-hand place he had for so long occupied in Carrington's affections. Besides, they were such awful ties, one a frightful *shiny wood-silk* – 'quite *impossible to wear it*', he complained bitterly to Frances. He and Lytton had practically nothing in common with each other, yet Gerald had felt obliged to live in Lytton's shadow and now he was being invited to dress up in his old clothes. It was the end. He threatened to send Carrington some knickers from a prostitute he knew; he made plans to take 'honourable revenge' on her in his writings. What he actually did was to wrestle with an enormous parcel containing all the presents she had given him – books, paintings and ingenious pictures on glass using coloured inks and silver sweet papers – and leave it with the irritated Ralph in Gordon Square. So they parted. 'She could not bear anyone to reproach her because she was all too prone to feel guilty,' he later wrote, 'and that was how I lost her.'

But she continued to haunt him in such a way that the touchstone of all his future loves was to be their likeness to her. 'If I ruin my life,' he swore to Ralph (23 October 1929), 'I shall blame Carrington.' At times she seemed like a Vampire; at other times he sensed that she had 'awakened' something in him. For twenty years she would return to him in strange dreams from which he would wake up wondering at the mystery of their lives, then 'lie in the darkness, swept again by the sweetness and sadness of their remembered love'.[19]

*

From the late 1920s Carrington kept an intermittent commonplace-book-and-diary – thoughts, emotions, incidents, hurried on to the page in any order, mixed with drafts of letters, beginnings of stories, pasted-in poems, brief notes, outpourings – on the stiff, beige-coloured cover of which she inked in with her child's hand its misspelt title: *D.C. Partride, Her Book*.

This volume exhibits the vast disorganization of her life. She was drinking more and sometimes 'the spelling seems rather drunk'. Using Roger Senhouse's firm, Lytton and Ralph were now importing wine from France by the barrel and bottling it in the cellar: then while 'the cat is away the mice will make hay', Carrington teased Lytton (21 May 1929), illustrating her letter with a picture of mice triumphantly emptying the bottles. It was good training for her visits to Augustus John and his family, particularly a journey she took with them in the late summer of 1929 to France in preparation for which 'I got very drunk on hock, in spite of all my intentions to keep a clean palate for Burgundy' and eventually 'to my shame, I passed away insensible after drinking some glasses of vodka, and had to be removed home by Dodo . . .' She drank to banish violent pangs of terror, inexplicable depression. 'What absolute despair can seize one without warning or apparent cause,' she wrote in her diary. 'Lytton maintains it is the adrenalin glands not working.'

Lytton's nearness brought some order and security to her existence. But when he went party-going and weekending she would fall into the doldrums, and Ham Spray seemed 'a good setting by Synge', she told James, 'but a poor setting for a lonely middle aged old haggis'. 'I cannot try to say all you are to me,' Lytton succinctly reassured her while he was with Roger (August 1929). She increasingly needed his reassurance. 'I wish I had a lover,' she had written to Julia. Lytton of course was a very able substitute, 'curious as it may seem'. Sometimes she could not bear the thought of anyone coming near her – and of course he never touched her. But listening to him read in the evenings gave her a serene happiness. 'I get tremendous pleasure you know by living here,' she told Sebastian Sprott. 'It's so lovely, and Lytton is such an angel to me.' All the same, a lover would give her a measure of independence and after Gerald's departure enrich her life with secrets again. 'My life is rather too untouched by human hand at moments,' she admitted.

All her passions and affections seemed to be attempts to re-create some childish situation. She treated Lytton almost as if he were an adopted father, and saw the young men with whom she had affairs as semi-substitutes for her dead sailor brother, Teddy. Gerald had never been a convincing replacement. But after he left, she took up with someone who was better fitted to approach her ideal. This was Bernard Penrose, nicknamed Beacus, youngest of the four Penrose brothers. Beacus had trained as a cadet in the British India Steamship Company, and lived as Able Seaman and Second Mate before the mast, sailing the clipper route round Cape Horn in one of the last four-masted windjammers and voyaging to the Arctic on the 'rum and bible' mission ship *Harmony*. He had been psychoanalysed by John Rickman in Vienna to cure him of this fever of seafaring, but he was incurable. He was now twenty-six – ten years younger than Carrington – had a square muscular body and brick-red face.

Beacus was to be 'the last great passion'[20] of Carrington's life. He was unlike any of her previous lovers. He thought her 'a mysterious, brilliant woman', but he was not in love with her. Often he treated her casually, not seeming to care where she went or what she saw, and always 'quite incapable of understanding my odd cravings and feelings about him'. Nor was he ever at ease in Bloomsbury. 'I suppose you wonder sometimes why I am so fond of him,' Carrington later (June 1931) wrote to Rosamond Lehmann, who understood such things.

'It's really very little to do with him actually, but because he is so like my brother who was killed . . . I am awfully self-conscious of being a romantic, and rather stupid. My brother was very silent and removed. I hardly ever was allowed to be intimate with him and I always put it off, thinking one day I'd be able to show him how much I cared and then it was too late . . . it took me ages to ever believe he was dead.'

Being so young himself, Beacus brought back youth into Carrington's life. And there was something else. Though he was maladroit in Bloomsbury, he became a different person when sailing with her on his square-rigger to Plymouth or the Scillies. Was being at sea a feeling you could ever describe to others? When Beacus spoke to Carrington he found himself recalling some of his experiences. Carrington loved to hear these stories of schooners and barquentines, and halcyon days on fine sailing ships, and moments of strange lucidity on fo'c'sle watch. So he told her his sea-adventures: of the time when, in the grey-green morning light, the masts, yards and rigging were solid with ice up to the tops; of the gentle aroma of soil, livestock and woodsmoke off the rocky South Irish coast; and of the marvellous beauty of the Aurora Borealis, forerunner of dangerous gales, shining like brilliantly illuminated curtains over the North Pole. And after listening to him she made pictures of gallant vessels plunging through crested foam under icebergs and perpendicular white cliffs to tropical destinations.

There was a novelty and excitement about everything they did – drinking pink gins in sailors' pubs along the waterfront, making films with his motion picture camera, kissing in taxis and holding hands in the cinema, then speeding through the summer countryside in his navy-blue racing Bentley and, happiest of all, spending nights on his Brixham trawler, the *Sanspareil*, in Southampton harbour, with its black cat keeping watch over them on deck until they woke up together in its shiny mahogany cabin. 'It's an infinitely romantic ship,' she told Julia (December 1928),'with brown varnished cupboards and cut glass handles and a little fire place with a brass mantelpiece. I don't think I've ever enjoyed an evening more in my life, the rain beating down on the deck above, sitting in the cabin lit by lamplight, cooking eggs and sausages over the fire and drinking rum . . . He is so in love with his ship that he moons about in a trance opening cupboards and eulogising over its beauties, in his slow voice . . . The black puss is a great charmer and sat on the rails of the little balustrade that goes round the bunks peering with green eyes at the midnight feast.'

She called Beacus 'Seagull', though frequently he was her 'unworthy gull', incurious and unapproachable, as she had been with Ralph and Gerald and Mark (with whom she was again corresponding). With her 'gypsy's warning', she sensed that Beacus must be making love to other women, younger women, and 'I felt I was ugly'. Sometimes, too, when he seemed particularly monotonous, she would resent the time with him 'which might have been more happily spent with Julia and Tommy, or Dorelia and Augustus'. Then her mood abruptly switched and she would decide that for the time being his 'remoteness just suits me. For I feel I am not being "observed" all the time, that No reactions are expected. That whatever happens is alright. A moon shining in the window across the bed. In the morning seeing a tousled face lying beside me, and then embraces, and more Love. But the sky is light, it has to come to an end and reality must return.'

Lytton noticed that she was sometimes 'unhappy with her Figure-head', as he later phrased it in a letter to Mary Hutchinson (15 March 1931). He could see that she found Beacus boring, and he was hardly surprised. 'But he is a Figure-head,' Lytton conceded, '– and that is almost enough to make up for everything.' It was the unsteadiest of relationships, and whenever reality did return she knew it must be doomed because 'the whole thing is a chimera', she admitted to Lytton, 'a mirage of my own making'. Other people's loves were perpetually inexplicable. Lytton, who sometimes felt bemused over his own past affairs, had mocked Ottoline's unceasing demands for love-attention, and exclaimed incredulously over the spectacle of Maynard and Lydia as singing lovebirds – and had himself been mourned by the Visigoths in a duet of despair after he fell head over heels for what Vanessa called (22 February 1927) the 'incredibly boring . . . well meaning . . . empty headed' Roger Senhouse. But as extraordinary as any of these wonders was this mirage of Carrington's. How to understand this 'most deplorable case' of what was called love? 'He

[Beacus] is entirely made of wood,' Lytton protested to Sebastian Sprott (19 March 1926). His insignificance 'positively opens up vistas of human pointlessness hitherto undreamt of'.

But not to Carrington for whom Beacus opened up other vistas. Into HER BOOK she put all the desire, anxiety, excitement he released about which she could never speak to him.

'A short love affair. Then a month thinking about little else. A weekend to Cornwall. The pleasure of leaving London invisibly in the rain, like a ghost, curious how little interest anyone takes in trains, and then a sudden panic as usual. "I am too old, it is ridiculous. Probably it is all a mistake". At Exeter the car outside and then later on the Platform. And my misgivings returned. As I felt it would all be a delusion. One of my own day dreams which had no relation to anybody else's head. At Oakhampton. The disappointment because the bedroom wasn't exactly as I had imagined. I had "seen" a big tester bed, a large low room with Dark mahogany furniture, and burning fire . . . Instead a neat spare room in my Mother's style with no fireplace and everything white and polished. I felt Nothing can survive this. But curiously enough, it did . . . I lay in bed and read Tristram Shandy, while he drank in the bar. When I said it doesn't matter tonight he never questioned, or enquired. Not very much curiosity. Yet that is probably the main attraction. Perhaps the most beautiful moment with a shirt in dark close fitting trousers and a brass belt. Do men know the beauty of their appearance as exactly as females do?'

Her infatuation grew into an obsession and her obsession into a panic. Each day was important – it could not last many days. Yet somehow it lasted. Waiting for it to end was such misery that she sometimes longed to take the initiative, 'cut this nautical knot & retreat back to my former solitude'. Because they saw each other so irregularly, one night of lovemaking 'sets me up for days afterwards'. The potency of this 'animal affection' was 'partly the effect of having laid two years in the coffin untouched,' she confided to Julia (January 1930). '. . . It's difficult to go back to coffin life again and with my numerous complexes not very easy even if one wanted to, to get a transfer ticket to some one else.' Whenever she sensed him moving away from her, she would feel herself 'sinking back into that previous state of not being a female', she explained in HER BOOK. 'Hating undressing, hating getting into bed.' A curious numbness then moved over her, as if the present already seemed to lie in the past.

The affair was brought to a sudden crisis late in 1929 when Carrington discovered she was pregnant. 'If, when I am 38, I am not an artist,' she had written to Gerald (October 1920), '& think it is no good my persevering with my painting, I might have a child . . .' At her next birthday (29 March 1930) she would be entering her thirty-eighth year. But now that her youthful speculation presented itself as a reality, the impossibility of it became clear. She was an artist and wanted to persevere with her painting in the new Ham Spray studio. It was too late for a child. 'She was in utter despair,' Frances wrote. '. . . Ralph had long conversations with her and with Lytton, and came up to bed very much worried . . . it was unthinkable that she would go through with it.' It was probably this event more than anything else that led to Frances's breakdown that winter. She still longed for a baby of her own; and here was Carrington, raging and suicidal and going for violent rides along the Downs in order to bring about a miscarriage. For the first time she did what Lytton and Carrington had wanted her to do. 'I made myself as scarce as possible while these critical discussions went on,' she wrote, 'and Lytton was so nice to me in the taxi to Gordon Square that I felt my efforts to be accommodating had not been in vain.'[21]

Carrington liked children, but she was disgusted by childbearing. Only for a child of Lytton's, or so she believed, would she have been prepared to go through with it – and that was out of the question. As for Lytton himself, he had never previously objected to Carrington's and Ralph's lovers, except for that *femme fatale* Valentine (or was it Gladys?) Dobrée. For over a dozen years Carrington had been making sacrifices for his welfare. No one so naturally self-willed as she was could have so immolated herself without many unconscious longings for liberty. Her affair with Beacus was the most extreme expression of these longings, and though Lytton did not really like 'the wretched Beacus', as he called him in one of his letters to Roger, he knew that he had no right to object. 'You give me a standard of sensible behaviour which makes it much easier to be reasonable,' she wrote to thank him (4 and 5 November 1929). '. . . I love you so much, and I shall never forget your kindness lately to me . . . Really your understanding is magnificent. Nobody can be so reassuring, or so endearing.'

Lytton did not tell Roger of her pregnancy, and for a time Carrington did not tell Beacus. She had wanted to have secrets again in her life, and this was the biggest secret of all. So she held on to it. 'As he hugged me in the kitchen,' she wrote in HER BOOK, 'I thought "you little guess what you hug between us!"'

Ralph arranged for her pregnancy to be terminated in a London nursing home later that November, paying most of the expense himself. 'I really don't see why such foolishness should be rewarded,' Carrington wrote gratefully. Beacus, too, as he sailed away to the Mediterranean, acknowledged that Ralph had been 'damned nice'. He admired Carrington's way of life and sometimes wished she had kept the child and that he had married her.

It was the climax of their relationship: but it was not the end. 'I still rather adore my strange gull, & pub life among the sailors,' Carrington confessed to Lytton the following spring (17 April 1930). Observing Beacus and Roger at Ham Spray one weekend, she was suddenly struck by 'the similarity between Lytton['s] and my position. Both unable to do anything because we long for our bed companions who were equally indifferent . . . about coming to bed.'

But as Carrington practised her lamp-trimming and her nautical language with Beacus on the *Sanspareil*, and as Lytton bent over Roger to assist him with *The Times* crossword puzzle in a Brighton hotel, they both came to a similar conclusion. 'All decent people remain young for an incredible length of time and suffer accordingly,' Lytton had told Roger (16 January 1929). Carrington too accepted this suffering. 'In spite of my miseries I would not have had anything different,' she was to assure Lytton (31 December 1930). 'Would you?'

3

AMBITIONS

'It is really shocking, I am becoming a nature-lover and observer – fatal!' Lytton had written to Roger early that winter (12 November 1928). 'The intellect fades in proportion.' In the aftermath of *Elizabeth and Essex*, idleness had become his chief occupation. There were always plenty of improbable schemes in the air for a new *magnum opus* – Voltaire or Julius Caesar. The poet Robert Nichols urged him to tackle Louis XIII – 'one of the most extraordinary beings who have ever lived'. J.B. Pinker, the literary agent, coaxed him with the secret Life of Shakespeare. Peter Davies, the publisher, offered him a contract to write a short devastating book on Edward VII. As an antidote to *Elizabeth and Essex*, he considered writing a biography of more limited appeal, on General Booth, founder of the Salvation Army, or even on the heretical Master of Balliol Benjamin Jowett. He also contemplated the idea of a book on George Washington, from which he was apparently put off by the prospect of having to learn 'that almost incomprehensible and quite intolerable language – American'. Occasionally he thought of an admirable Victorian, such as Charles

Darwin, as a subject; or toyed with something shorter, like a history of the world.

There had been talk of a new Bloomsbury weekly magazine which Lytton proposed should be called the *W.C.1*. Desmond MacCarthy had approached him in March 1929 asking him to write for his new monthly periodical, *Life and Letters*, which was to be published by the *New Statesman* publishing company as a rival to J.C. Squire's *London Mercury*. Lytton replied giving as his choice of subject either *King Lear* or Bishop Creighton, and MacCarthy chose Creighton. To *Life and Letters* Lytton also contributed his essay on Froude (originally entitled 'One of the Victorians'), this being the last of his series 'Six English Historians', and 'Madame de Lieven', the last but one of his portraits in miniature. His final essay, 'The Président de Brosses', did not come out until April 1931 in the amalgamated *New Statesman and Nation* which, following the financial failure of *Life and Letters*, came under the editorship of Kingsley Martin, for whom Lytton promised to write regularly.

He had become the most unprolific of writers, but he was always reading. Every time he travelled up to London, he would scour The Times Book Club, finding there that spring I.A. Richards's *Practical Criticism*, which he thought 'fascinating', W.P. Ker's posthumous *Form and Style in Poetry* ('full of learning and sense') and Edwin Muir's 'excellent' *Structure of the Novel* which he preferred to Forster's *Aspects of the Novel*, 'but I imagine few will agree with me'. Soon he returned again to his old favourites, to Chesterfield, to Virgil, to Moore's *Principia Ethica* – 'such pleasant reading' – and Gibbon. 'My laziness is becoming more scandalous than ever,' he happily told Roger (13 September 1929). 'I do nothing but read Gibbon – first in the quarto – then in Bury's edition.'

The dearth of contemporary literature was 'serious'. But his admiration for Virginia's *A Room of One's Own* was unqualified. It was 'a masterpiece', he told Dorothy Bussy. Also a masterpiece was Richard Hughes's first novel, *A High Wind in Jamaica*, about which he wrote to many of his friends. 'My chief conversation will be, now and henceforward, on the subject of a High Wind,' he informed Roger (1 October 1929), 'insisting that everyone should read it who hasn't and that everyone should admire it who has.' Eighteen months later, Lytton met Hughes one afternoon at Ham Spray. 'Yesterday there was an incursion in the shape of Richard Hughes, who arrived with Faith Henderson, with whom he was staying,' he wrote to Roger (5 May 1931). 'Slightly sinister, we thought – but perhaps only timid under a mask.' To Richard Hughes it was Lytton who appeared sinister. 'My first impression was of the extraordinary beauty of the inside of the house,' he wrote, '– a beauty based on little original architectural distinction. Lytton, I think, spent most of his time deep in a chair – he was certainly ill at the time – but I was too frightened of him to look at him closely; my general impression, however, was that he looked as if he had been designed as the perfect objet d'art to go with the background of the house.' With characteristic shyness Lytton did not mention his admiration for *A High Wind in Jamaica*, and Hughes never suspected it. 'How cock-a-hoop I should have been at the time had I known it!'

The blue weather continued to fasten him at Ham Spray, where he was visited by Pippa. The two of them had been appointed joint executors and trustees of their mother's will, a long and complicated document, under which Lytton himself was left two thousand pounds (equivalent to £48,000 in 1994), minus any sum which he had received from her during her lifetime.[22] Later that year, Lytton arranged with Pippa to move back into 51 Gordon Square, taking over the ground floor which he converted into a self-contained flat. On 13 June he also made what was to prove his own last will, in which he bequeathed ten thousand pounds (equivalent to £240,000 in 1994) together with all his pictures and drawings to Carrington, and a further one thousand pounds (equivalent to £24,000 in 1994) to Ralph, the residue of the property – with the exception of the books given to Roger – being left to his brother James, whom he appointed his executor.

The weeks slipped by like a recurring dream. As the days lengthened and grew warmer, Lytton's idleness became more strenuous. It was impossible to enjoy leisure thoroughly unless there was plenty to do. He went up to London to watch Edith Evans act in Reginald Berkeley's *The Lady with the Lamp*, a play about Florence Nightingale which 'seemed to me entirely based on E.V. except for some foolish frills added by the good gentleman', and to lunch, unsuccessfully, with Lady Cunard who 'talked the whole time, so that Max [Beerbohm] was never once allowed to open his mouth. Idiocy! Idiocy!'

While Carrington went to France and Ralph dealt with Lytton's publishers and managed his finances, Lytton returned to King's – 'such sunshine – such crowds of young gents – such benignity', was invited to still more lunches, more enormous tea-parties and then went off for 'a perfect week-end with Roger' to Bath. They stayed at the Pulteney Hotel in Laura Place – 'a perfect spot – and quite a sympathetic établissement', he told Carrington (3 June 1929), 'with a lift boy no less sympathetic, who at last said to me (in a broad West Country accent) "Excuse me, zurr, bout are you the zelebrated author?" . . . We inspected all the favourite sights – including Prof. Saintsbury at No. 1. the Crescent – his white hair and skull-cap were visible as usual through the window.'[23]

They all did a lot of travelling that year. At the beginning of July, Lytton and Carrington set off with Ralph and Sebastian Sprott for a fortnight in Holland. It was a peculiar trip. On board ship the four of them crouched cheerlessly drinking gin and watching their Dutch and German fellow passengers who sat in long rows of deck-chairs, drifting off for heavy meals and otherwise staring stonily at the horizon as it tilted gently above the rail and then slipped below it.

They arrived at Rotterdam, examined the zoo, then hurried on to The Hague to look at the Van Goghs. The mood of all four of them was still sombre and, hoping for a rapid uplift in their spirits, they left for Leyden, which Nancy Cunard had told Lytton was 'wonderful'. Again they were disappointed, and made their way to Amsterdam, where they remained a week, 'looking at cheeses'.

'I have been rather maddened by the sporadic behaviour of the party,' Ralph burst out in one of his letters to Frances (4 July 1929). '. . . all are piano, piano, I don't know why. Perhaps we are all very old indeed, or perhaps we are growing a little Dutch.' Ralph himself was anything but piano, boiling over with small grievances. Each member of the party seemed resentful of what Ralph termed the 'selfish egotism of the others'. He himself was severely missing Frances, wondering why he had consented to come on this purposeless journey; Sebastian, usually a perfect *compagnon de voyage* was unfathomable, unforthcoming; Carrington behaved tiresomely, her thoughts reeling back across the sea to Beacus; while Lytton, anxious over Roger, contributed his most alarming silences. Beside each one moved the unseen presence of a loved-one whose company hovered more closely than any actual companion.

'Have you ever been to this hydroptic country?' Lytton asked Mary Hutchinson (4 July 1929) from Amsterdam.

'. . . It makes an odd mixture of impressions. The few days before I left England were curiously filled with experiences, and they are as much present with me as the beautiful seventeenth-century doors and windows – so solid, so rich – that line the waterways, and the Rembrandts and De Hooghes in the picture galleries, and the delicious dinners at a pound a head that one stumbles into quite accidentally, having intended simply to have a snack at an A.B.C. . . . but it is true that I am troubled about Roger – in an unexpected way. It is not easy to know one's own mind – not easy to balance instinct and reason – not easy to be sensible and in love. Do not mistake me, though – I am *not* unhappy – only speculative, a little dubitative, faintly uneasy, perhaps. I wake up at three o'clock in the morning and lie awake for an hour, trying drowsily to disentangle the puzzle of my mind and heart – and then sink to sleep again, having accomplished nothing and not in the least put out ... there is nothing but hazard, intensity, and interrogation.'

When Lytton returned from Holland he found that Roger had abruptly left with a friend for the South of France. Days passed in silence and speculation. A weekend on which they had planned to go away together came and went – and still there was no news. 'I am in rather a state about R., as you may imagine,' he confessed to Mary Hutchinson (25 July 1929). 'The possibilities are so various – the poor thing may be ill – or the wretch may be dreaming – or the little devil may have sailed for Greece in Mr B[urton]'s yacht. In any case there's nothing to be done, but twiddle one's thumbs, and seek such consolations as are available.'

A few days later a letter arrived from Cannes, written in Roger's most cramped style, which mentioned that he had been obliged to postpone his return home because of constipation! 'Surely, surely, something better might have been thought of as an excuse for another week in the South of France,' Lytton complained to Dadie Rylands (29 July 1929), '– but such are our friend's strange fancies. I ... have grown inert – cannot really bother any more ... I shall twiddle my thumbs like an aged Barbary Ape.'

All further speculation became futile. He determined to act sensibly even in love and shake off the heartache with some literary work on *The Greville Memoirs* which he had long been putting off. To his friends he seemed 'rather low and flat' that summer, but 'this does not mean that I am depressed or worried – quite the reverse,' he assured Dadie (2 August 1929). 'I feel extremely cheerful, and seem to have emerged on to some upper plateau from which I can contemplate all the eventualities with equanimity. It is something of a miracle, and a great relief.'

*

'Do you know how ambitious I am?' Lytton had asked Roger (16 January 1929). 'Don't breathe a word of this to anyone, but I long to do some good to the world – to make people happier – to help to dissipate this atrocious fog of superstition that hangs over us and compresses our breathing and poisons our lives. But it can't be done in a minute.'

'I believe that the great fault of the English nation is its hankering after compromise,' he had written to Ottoline Morrell (8 December 1910) '– and it's quite a new thing: it was not compromise that repealed the Corn Laws and cut off Charles the First's head.'

According to his brother James, he aimed to write one more biography then 'burn his boats' by declaring his homosexuality, and campaigning for sexual egalitarianism – even if it meant casting adrift from society and living abroad. He had supported financially many *avant-garde* and philanthropic causes, from birth-control to relief of war victims, and thought of himself as 'left-wing' but not a socialist. Yet he had never wanted to step into politics professionally. 'So glad I'm not a Prime Minister!' he wrote in one of his letters to Roger. 'So happy to be what I am.' What he wanted to do was to infiltrate his libertine and libertarian beliefs through literature, into the bloodstream of the people, and by such oblique methods that readers accepted it all quite naturally. The polemics of *Eminent Victorians* had been created by the war; in *Queen Victoria* he had carefully laid down a subversive sexual subtext; and then, more boldly in *Elizabeth and Essex*, written sexual deviation into the mainstream of English history.

The main threat to personal freedom, Lytton believed, was an incursive post-war tendency to interfere with the private life of the individual which had begun during the war itself. Through the 1920s this desire to regulate others persisted. In the United States, where the war fever had been most virulent and the losses of men smallest, and where the dragooning of vast masses of fellow citizens had come as a new experience, the cessation of conscription had left a want which was supplied by the enforcement of prohibition. In Italy, Germany and Russia autocracies were formed, the unconscious aim of which was to recover in another war the national prestige lost in the Great War. France alone left its citizens in peace, for France, unlike the United States or Britain, knew conscription before the war, and unlike Italy, Germany and Russia, emerged from the war with its prestige enhanced.

In Britain, state interference with the individual had for many the charm of novelty. The Defence of the Realm Act lingered on, vexing the ordinary man and encouraging energetic busybodies to plan more penetrating invasions into people's lives. It was this type of governmental officiousness that exasperated Lytton.

One example had been the Oscar Levy affair. Dr Levy, a distinguished philosopher, scholar and man of letters, had left England in 1914 and returned again in 1920 on business, staying on because of ill-health. After a few months he was threatened with deportation under the Aliens Restriction Act – a law that was due to expire at the end of 1921. In the early autumn of that year, Lytton had joined the Bloomsbury Committee which was making protests against his expulsion, and signed a petition to Lloyd George pointing out that Dr Levy had relinquished his German citizenship and had nowhere to go. 'The police expulsion of so eminent a man', this petition concluded, 'is surely a grave reflection on English civilization.'

All sorts of rumours were broadcast – that Levy had been connected with espionage during the war, that he was in counter-intelligence or the secret service. The Government confirmed or denied nothing, though granting a short delay of the deportation. Lytton was not optimistic. He disliked joining movements and committees and felt ill at ease among his allies. 'I have become involved in the great pro-Dr-Oscar-Levy movement,' he had reported to Ralph (5 October 1921).

'. . . I was summoned this afternoon to the headquarters of the movement at 34 Gordon Square, one of the principal props of which turned out to be Mr [David] Bomberg, painter . . . Another Jew welcomed me, and I rather gathered that I too was a Jew – which made me uneasy. At last I tore myself away, but I am in dread of being pursued for the rest of my life by this strange collection. As for poor Dr Oscar Levy I can't believe that with such supporters his chances are very good.'

So it turned out. On 25 October, Dr Levy left England for France, the French consultate having given him permission to enter the country and stay there without time limit. Once again French civilization had shown itself to be superior to English.

One of the chief dangers to the liberty of the individual in the 1920s was the rising popularity of autocratic controls. Autocracies, whether they were called Fascism, Bolshevism or Puritanism, claimed that they subordinated the prurient desires of the individual to the service of the community. To Lytton's mind, they in fact subordinated these individual desires to the passion for power of a few emotional misfits with enormous vigour and no internal resources. He objected to autocracy for much the same reason as he had objected to militarism. For all autocracies, however excellent the ideals with which they started, inevitably move towards war, partly because war is the simplest expression of power, and partly because the suppression of your own citizens cannot continue for long without a common enemy abroad.

In Britain, the most threatening form of autocracy was Puritanism. In the field of literature and the arts, this Puritanism took the form of censorship exercised by people who seemed to fear that society would at any moment sink into vicious iniquity. Throughout his career as a literary critic, Lytton waged an offensive against the expurgated text. In reviewing the first four volumes of Mrs Paget Toynbee's sixteen-volume edition of Horace Walpole's letters, he complained vehemently against certain omissions. 'The *jeune fille* is certainly not an adequate reason, and, even if she were, the *jeune fille* does not read Walpole. Whoever does read him must feel that these constant omissions are so many blots upon perfection, and distressing relics of an age of barbarous prudery.'[24]

Some fifteen years later, in 1919, Lytton reviewed Dr Paget Toynbee's two-volume *Supplement to the Letters of Horace Walpole*, and again protested at the numerous passages dropped on the score of propriety. 'Surely,' he exclaimed, 'in a work of such serious intention and such monumental proportions the publication of the *whole* of the original material was not only justifiable, but demanded by the nature of the case.'[25] Toynbee defended his policy in the correspondence columns of the *Athenaeum*. Great care, he assured his readers, had been taken over his responsibilities as editor. Improprieties would be too mild a word with which to describe the excised passages, which might be compared 'to the grossest of the avowals contained in the unexpurgated editions of Rousseau's Confessions'. The manuscripts had been deposited under sealed cover in the Bodleian 'where they will be available to any future editor of the letters at the discretion of the Delegates of the Clarendon Press'.

Lytton returned to the attack the following week. 'If a surgeon were charged with having made an unnecessary amputation,' he wrote, 'and were to answer that after all the limb was still in existence, carefully preserved, under a sealed cover, and that, if need arose, it might be sewn on again by another surgeon, at a future date, the patient's friends would hardly feel that the reply was reassuring.' After expressing wonder at the type of literary man who would reproduce Rousseau's *Confessions* only in a truncated version, he passed to the general problem of censorship:

'It is, moreover, extremely hard to see what good purpose is served by the deletion of passages which, in the opinion of individual editors, are indecent . . . Literature is inundated with improprieties and grossnesses of every kind; the mischief – if mischief it be – has been done already. It is too late to be prudish: Catullus, Rabelais, and a hundred others stare us in the face; the horse is gone, and no locking of the stable door will bring him back again.'[26]

When, in 1926, Paget Toynbee brought out a further supplementary volume of Walpole's letters, there were more expurgated pages. 'The editor', complained Lytton, 'is still unable to resist meddling with the text. The complete edition is incomplete, after all.

'Apparently, we should blush too much were we to read the whole of Walpole's letters; those privileges have been reserved for Dr Toynbee alone. It was impossible not to hope that, after so prolonged tête-à-tête with his author, he would relent at last; perhaps, in this latest volume at any rate – but no! the powers of editorship must be asserted to the bitter end; and the fatal row of asterisks and the fatal note, "passage omitted" occur, more than once, to exacerbate the reader. Surely it would have been kinder not to reveal the fact that any deletion had been made. Then one could have read on, innocent and undisturbed. As it is, when one's irritation has subsided, one's imagination, one's shocking imagination, begins to work. The question must be asked: do these explicit suppressions really serve the interests of the highest morality? Dr Toynbee reminds one of the man who . . .* But enough; for, after all, it is not the fly but the ointment that claims our attention.'[27]

Lytton was continually spotting this fly in the ointment. Not only Walpole's correspondence, but Blake's poems, Pepys's Diary and Boswell's letters had been mutilated by academic editors who claimed to be rehabilitating the author's text. 'When', Lytton demanded, 'will this silly and barbarous prudery come to an end?'

In one instance he saw an opportunity for defeating such prudery. *The Greville Memoirs* is not listed among the four bibliographies of *Eminent Victorians*, but on 6 November 1917, while at work on 'The End of General Gordon', Lytton had written to Clive Bell: 'I spend most of my time reading Greville's Memoirs (do you know them?) – very dry, and as they are dry – just the kind of book that pleases me. He was a slow-going medium member of the governing classes of those days – the days of Sir Robert Peel and Lord Melbourne – and he writes with a restraint and a distinction.'

When he had come to compare the complete manuscript in the British Museum with the Silver Library edition – which he included among the 'Works Referred to in the Notes' at the end of *Queen Victoria* – he had been disgusted to discover just how badly tampered with even the fullest published version had been. He drew attention to this state of affairs both by a preliminary note in *Queen Victoria* acknowledging his indebtedness to the Trustees of the British Museum for their permission to make use of unpublished passages, and in the text of the biography itself, where he recounts Victoria's indignation at seeing the contents of the abridged version. Two years later, in 1923, he published his biographical essay 'Charles Greville' in the *Nation and Athenaeum*, stating that Greville's diary was good enough 'to make him certainly famous and possibly immortal'. In this essay, which provided the background history of the diary, he did not

* Passage omitted [Lytton Strachey's footnote].

exaggerate its literary merits, comparing it unfavourably with Saint-Simon. Many of its pages, he explained, were rather metallic in style and its political information was not always reliable. Yet, he added, it was of extreme value, since the sheer quantity of Greville's first-hand knowledge was enormous.

'He was not exactly a gossip, nor a busybody; he was an extremely inquisitive person, in whom, somehow or other, it seemed natural for everybody to confide. Thus the broad current of London life flows through his ample pages, and, as one turns them over, one glides swiftly into the curiously distant world of eighty years ago. A large leisureliness descends upon one, and a sense that there is plenty of room, and an atmosphere of extraordinary moderation. Reason and instinct, fixity and change, aristocracy and democracy – all these are there, but unaccountably interwoven into a circumambient compromise – a wonderful arrangement of half-lights ... So Greville unrolls his long panorama; then pauses for a little, to expatiate in detail on some particular figure in it. His portraits, with their sobriety of tone and precision of outline, resemble very fine engravings, and will prove, perhaps, the most enduring portions of his book.'

In his conclusion Lytton suggested that 'perhaps the time has now come when a really complete edition of the whole work might be produced with advantage; for the years have smoothed down what was agitating and personal half a century ago into harmless history. When the book first appeared, it seemed – even with Reeve's tactful excisions – outrageous. The later Victorians were shocked ... To turn from their horrified comments to the Greville Memoirs themselves is almost disappointing. In those essentially sober pages the envenomed wretch of the Victorian imagination is nowhere to be found.'[28]

Unknown to him at this time, a copy of the diaries made by a clerk employed by the original editor, Henry Reeve, had found its way, after the death of Reeve's widow, to the United States. Shortly after the appearance of Lytton's essay in the *New Republic*, this unabridged manuscript fell under the notice of P.W. Wilson, formerly a writer on the *Daily News* and a Liberal member of Parliament, who, in 1927, brought out in two volumes a collection of extracts from it, containing some new material. This publication gave rise to an even more anomalous situation. The manuscript diary, which filled ninety-one small quarto books bound in red morocco, had originally been published in three instalments, totalling eight volumes altogether, in 1874, 1885 and 1887. P.W. Wilson's compilation, while apparently supplying Reeve's omissions, contained only a series of rearranged fragments from the diary, and provided no means of distinguishing the new material from the old. So there was still no satisfactory text.

In a letter to *The Times*, Lytton proposed that, in order to resolve 'this curious state of affairs',[29] a full and accurate edition of the diaries should at once be prepared. Next day, he received a wire from the publishers Allen & Unwin inviting him to edit a complete version of the memoirs. The task commended itself to him on several grounds. He was already familiar with the social and political world between 1814 and 1860, and working in such a world would come as a relief from *Elizabeth and Essex*. He might look forward to many civilized hours of methodical occupation.

But after a month of indecisive negotiations, the British Museum Trustees backed away. Greville's niece, Lady Strafford, then aged ninety-seven, would probably institute proceedings, they advised Lytton. In these circumstances they could not be a party to his scheme. 'What a world!' Lytton explained in exasperation to Carrington.

The following summer Lady Strafford died. Almost immediately Lytton applied again to the Trustees who, this time, put up no obstacles. Work began late in August. 'It is very agreeable here,' Lytton wrote to Carrington from London (11 September 1928). 'The weather is most soothing – and so is the work in the British Museum. We have been so far most industrious. I enjoy it very much and R[alph] is an excellent work-companion. The only question is whether I shall ever be able to give it up. It seems to me an ideal way of spending the hours – and we can hardly bear to tear ourselves away from the beloved MS at 1/4 to 5, which is closing time.'

Another version is given by Frances, who had recently left the Birrell and Garnett bookshop and was shortly to undergo 'a rest-cure'. In her diary entry for 15 September she wanly noted: 'R[alph] has now become to all intents a business man, going to the British Museum every day until 5, and as he lunches at present with Lytton I don't see him from morning till evening, which is the strangest sensation.' Frances could see that Ralph was thrilled to be doing the groundwork for this new edition under Lytton's supervision. 'I am quite envious,' she had noted (7 September 1928). Before the end of the month she herself was to change into a business woman, joining the others at work in the Manuscript Department. 'R[alph] and I are both now working on the Greville MSS in the British Museum,' she recorded (21 September 1928).

'We sit side by side on a shelf just wide enough to hold a table and two chairs, in the upper part of the Documents Room, looking down upon Magna Carta. The streams of schoolchildren and others who buzz around that memorable object might be distracting, except that our work is so utterly absorbing. On our table lies the previous, incorrect and much expurgated edition of the *Memoirs* made by Henry Reeve, and the first few volumes of the diary itself brought up from their locked safe by a museum official in the morning and taken back there at night ... I see now how important it was to get every formal question settled from the very start, and never let oneself forget the decisions made.'

Having decided these questions of misspellings, cross-references, abbreviations, and the methods by which to distinguish old notes from new, and to indicate hitherto unpublished passages, Lytton planned that Ralph and Frances should transcribe the missing and disputed pages of the memoirs, and every so often Ralph should come down to Ham Spray bringing with him the material they had prepared, which he would then annotate. 'I have been working with Ralph nearly every day at the British Museum,' he told Roger (19 September 1928). 'Now Frances takes my place in the afternoons, and before long she will altogether I think. It is very pleasant work. Various amusing details keep turning up, sometimes in a childishly easy cipher.'

Presently, as he had predicted, Lytton ceased going to the British Museum almost entirely, Frances taking over from him in the mornings also. This arrangement, which gave Frances much-needed work, also enabled Lytton and Carrington to see rather more of Ralph by himself, easing tension at Ham Spray. Already, by the end of January, the three of them had made considerable headway. Ralph 'brought an enormous quantity of Greville MSS', Lytton wrote to Roger (2 February 1929), 'and I see that the moment is rapidly approaching when I shall have to plunge into that ocean in good earnest'.

First there was the problem of publishers. 'I am beginning to fear that I may have some trouble with the publishers about printing *everything* – which is what I want to do,' Lytton confided to Roger (19 September 1928). There was little sensational appeal in such a book, and the sales could hardly be large. On the other hand, Lytton reasoned, all the public libraries and educational institutions would have to stock it, and his edition – if it did contain *everything* – would never be replaced. The firm which stood most to gain was Heinemann, having been responsible for bringing out the English edition of P.W. Wilson's two piecemeal volumes. Early this year, Ralph called at the Heinemann offices and persuaded them to agree, in principle, to bringing out the full text.[30] A few months later, Harcourt

Brace wrote to Lytton inquiring whether they might publish the American edition. 'It is very interesting to hear that your firm contemplates the publication of the new and complete Greville,' Lytton replied to Donald Brace (24 October 1929).

'. . . it would be a serious undertaking; I think it will take about ten large volumes; probably it would bring you more glory than profit! From my point of view, nothing would please me better than that you should undertake it. Our relations have been so pleasant that I would welcome any extension of them, and there is the minor point that a republication of the introduction would be facilitated . . . It is really the size of the affair that is the vital point – both from the point of view of the publisher and from that of the reader, who will not buy it unless he is a serious student; the plums of scandal and surprise – and there *are* some – are too few and far between to allure anyone else.'

From the summer of 1929 onwards he gave a regular part of his time to 'my Greville grubbings' and over the next two years his correspondence carries intermittent notes of 'continuing to grovel in Greville'. This year, too, saw the publication of *Leaves from the Greville Diary*, a potted version in one volume, with an agreeable introduction by Lytton's old friend, Philip Morrell. This book, by drawing attention to the need for an authoritative edition, acted as a spur to Lytton and his team. In 1930, he arranged with Gabriel Wells of New York for the American manuscripts to be transferred back to England and placed in the Bodleian Library at Oxford. By the time of his death, all the passages omitted from Reeve's edition, including those in cipher and those scratched out with a pen, had been transcribed from the original manuscripts. 'The latest and best edition by Reeve,' Roger Fulford wrote, 'that in the Silver Library published by Messrs Longmans in 1888, had been collated with the manuscripts and his frequent liberties with the text corrected. The notes are almost all Mr Strachey's – though here and there it has been found possible to add to them in the light of information published since his death.'

Lytton also attacked the censorship of contemporary authors, identifying himself with those campaigning against the prosecution of Radclyffe Hall's lesbian novel, *The Well of Loneliness*, though he does not seem to have thought very highly of the book's merits. When, on 23 March 1929, Gilbert Murray wrote a letter to the *Nation and Athenaeum* deploring the cult of obscenity in modern writing, which he claimed, had a peculiar power for destroying the imaginative values in its vicinity, Lytton replied, calling up in evidence to refute this statement two classical writers, Rabelais and Swift. 'Both in "Pantagruel" and in "Gulliver" it is obviously this very element [obscenity] which acts as a stimulus to the authors' most profound observations and most astonishing flights.'[31]

In the past he had petitioned against the suppression of D.H. Lawrence's novel *The Rainbow* and now found himself supporting Lawrence once again. Lytton's distaste for Lawrence seems to have been sharpened by Lawrence's inverted puritanism. On 14 June 1929, an exhibition of his pictures, organized by Philip and Dorothy Trotter, had opened at the Warren Gallery in Maddox Street, London. After some thirteen thousand people had been to the gallery, the police suddenly arrived and carried off thirteen of the pictures, storing them in a cellar of the Marlborough Street Police Court before having them burnt. 'I suppose you heard about the police raid on Lawrence's pictures at the Warren Gallery?' Lytton wrote to Roger (15 July 1929). 'I saw Dorothy and her spouse at Boulestin's one evening, and heard her account of it.

'The police appear to have been singularly idiotic, but D[orothy] herself, it seems to me, was almost equally so. They were on the point of seizing a drawing by Blake of Adam and Eve as obscene, and she was silly enough to tell them it was by him, and so make a cheap score; but if she had only let them do it, there couldn't have been a better exposé of their methods. Next day I had lunch with Mary [Hutchinson] and she showed me the book of reproductions from his pictures. They are wretched things – no drawing or composition so far as I could see – and in fact no point – not even that of indecency; there were some pricks visible, but not a single erection, which one naturally supposed would have caused the rumpus.'

Shortly afterwards he went round to the Warren Gallery with Geoffrey Scott. The exhibits were 'poor' and in his view the whole show had been a mistake. 'At least you think the pictures respectable?' queried Scott in the context of the impending trial. 'Much too respectable!' Lytton answered.

Immediately after the police seizure, Philip and Dorothy Trotter had started to get up a petition, but sensed, as Philip Trotter wrote, 'a winter wind from Bloomsbury in the dudgeon of Lytton Strachey and the silence of Roger Fry'. The Trotters were careful not to invite Lytton's judgement on the artistic merits of Lawrence's paintings in the petition.

'Since many pictures of admittedly great artistic value contain details which might be condemned as "harmful to the morals of those who are unstable or immature", we protest in principle against the destruction of pictures on that ground. The burning of a book does not necessarily destroy it, and condemned books have sometimes taken their places among the classics, but the burning of a picture is irreparable.'

This petition sought to change a law that permitted an anonymous informer, spurred on by the sensationalist section of the press, to put into action the machinery by which a painter's work was placed in peril of destruction. After a brief hesitation, Lytton added his signature to those of Leonard and Virginia, Vanessa and Duncan, Maynard, Vita Sackville-West, Roger Fry, Clive Bell and Augustus John, to help 'protect contemporary art from the grave menace implied in the terms of the summons issued in regard to Mr Lawrence's work'. However, this issue was never pressed, since at the trial St John Hutchinson, acting on Lawrence's instructions, offered to withdraw the pictures, assuring the court that they would not be shown again.

These were small but necessary battles against the moral evasion and mendacity that debased public opinion and had overshadowed Lytton's sexual life. After the war this 'atrocious fog' of peril and opprobrium was beginning to lift with the break-down of old class divisions. When Sebastian Sprott spoke to him about 'Len', 'Ernie', 'the Blackamoor' and other exotics of the Nottingham underworld, and then brought his working-class lover to Ham Spray ('large, decided, in mind and feature – not beautiful, though, and probably with false teeth. The Nottingham accent . . . has an odd barbarous effect. When he dealt [cards], he licked his thumb in a very winning manner'); or when Morgan Forster came with news 'of having achieved a complete success with a member of the lower classes, aged 24', showing plainly that 'never has he been so happy, and he is 53', Lytton sensed that sexual barriers were beginning to come down along with social barriers. The trial of Oscar Wilde was thirty years past and seemed to belong to a different age. The 'New Age', which Lytton had confidently predicted after Moore's *Principia Ethica*, now appeared to be advancing again with the influence of Freud and Marx – an economic and psychological reformation that aligned new understanding of our interior lives with new ideas of how to arrange the society in which we lived. In these readjustments to our thinking, Lytton saw a renewed opportunity for escaping the 'superstition that hangs over us and compresses our breathing and poisons our lives'. And if, by helping to release homosexuality from legal danger and social disgrace, he could change the future destinies of people like himself, then his secret ambition would be accomplished.

4

A SUMMER INTERLUDE

Ever since Carrington took up with Beacus, the 'sweet canary Don' Dadie Rylands had stepped forward as the principal confidant of Lytton's heart. Whenever the love and lust Lytton desired from Roger were being withheld, it was Dadie who chiefly provided the support he needed. 'I enjoy what he provides – an atmosphere of the schoolroom,' Lytton had explained to Sebastian Sprott (31 August 1925). 'If only one could beat him, it would be perfection.' Sympathetic to Lytton's varying bouts of ill-fortune, Dadie was none the less critical of his weaknesses. 'I suppose you realize that he's (unconsciously) jealous of both of us,' Lytton was to warn Roger (30 July 1930), '– that he wants (unconsciously) to supplant each of us with the other.' Yet he was so affectionate, and 'enhances life so immensely', that such unconscious motives might be discounted 'so long as one realizes their existence, & keeps a good look out (which I'm sorry to say I haven't always done)'. This was an oblique apology to Roger for various indiscretions. But mostly Lytton had been loyal enough. When Dadie irritably complained of the dismal pattern of his *affaire* with Roger, Lytton would defend himself with just the lightest hint of reproof (20 November 1929): 'People must gang their ain gate . . . And I also feel that it's specially my business to understand and make allowances for that peculiarly sweet creature. So you see . . .'

Dadie could not always be expected to see. During the spiritless months of winter, he was very close to Lytton. But by July, Lytton was again much happier, and their friendship receded a little. There were moments when Lytton felt slightly ashamed of having to confess that, for the time being, he had no further misdemeanours to unfold. Intermittently that summer, the vision of Roger spread across the whole horizon, obliterating other friends. 'To me our relations have always been among the greatest blessings of my life,' he wrote to him (30 June 1930), '– that I have never doubted. The truth is I'm gorged with good fortune, and really if I can't be extremely happy it's a scandal.'

There had been something strangely debilitating about Lytton's health over the winter. He was continually plagued by 'collywobbles' or 'a wuzzle buzzle of a cold'. Unable to wait patiently for the far-off heats of July, he had decided to break out of his hibernation at Ham Spray that spring and go to Rome. The idea immediately brought him to life. Roger, after prolonged indecision, came to the conclusion that he could go, and then that he could not. Finally Lytton invited Dadie to accompany him instead. They booked in at the Hotel Hassler and New York – where Lytton had previously taken Roger – Dadie carrying with him a portable edition of Shakespeare, and Lytton some novels of Trollope and most of Proust. But once they had done *The Times* crossword each day ('my theory now', Lytton had decided, 'is that life is not so much a pattern as a crossword puzzle') there was little opportunity for reading. When the sun shone, they would march off on long sightseeing expeditions. 'The beauty of everything is very great,' Lytton wrote to Carrington (13 April 1930), 'but it is a rigorous vigorous life one has to lead – so difficult ever to dream in Italy – and the Italians, one gathers, do nothing else! I don't understand it.'

Their social life in Rome proceeded as a caricature of the London scene – 'upper-class vagueness and unreality, American frenzy, intellectual sodomy etc. etc.', as Lytton described it in a letter to Ralph (19 April 1930). 'It is rather amusing, but it would be much nicer to lie under a tomb in the Campagna, or linger among the cypresses of Tivoli.' One afternoon the two of them went to have tea with a countess who politely inquired whether Dadie was Lytton's son; another day they encountered Lady d'Abernon who, 'poor soul, appeared out of space, and disappeared again after a slightly painful interchange of civilities'. They dined at the British Embassy with Maurice Baring; they met Beverley Nichols one evening and his American millionaire companion, Warren Curry, both of whom 'after wandering in despair over Europe and Africa, now openly quarrel standing in the street outside hotels'.[32] The climax to their social life was 'a particularly mad lunch party at Lord Berners,[33] where an Italian princess 'dressed in flowing widow's weeds, and giving vent to a flowing stream of very dimly veiled indecencies, kept the table in a twitter'.

Almost every day Lytton and Carrington wrote to each other; he telling her how homesick he felt and asking whether she would like to join them in Rome; she, half-tempted to do so, nevertheless reassuring him that he 'mustn't think I mind in the least you being in Rome. I mean I do. But at the same time I shall be very happy so you mustn't think of me.' He returned in the last week of April and spent May at Ham Spray. 'I feel I *must* stick to Greville for this month,' he wrote (11 May 1930). At weekends there were relays of relatives and friends – the Bussys, the Lambs, the MacCarthys, Sheppard and Norton, Alix and James, Julia and Stephen Tomlin who had made a remarkable bust of Lytton, 'a highly impressive, repulsive, and sinister object', Lytton had described it to Dadie while Tommy was at work on it (9 August 1929). 'Perhaps it is the pure truth.'[34] Clive Bell also turned up and 'chirps away with swinging legs which reveal a strange span of drawers below the knee, as ever'; and Boris Anrep who, pacing the rooms, described some enormous fishes he had seen off the coast of Brittany, round as footballs, and with a cruel triangular mouth which, if you wedged a brick into it, gave a crack! – and spat it out as powder.

Lytton divided this summer between Ham Spray and his flat in 51 Gordon Square. William Plomer, meeting him in London for the first time, left a description of what he looked like in this last phase of his life. The beard and spectacles, Plomer observed, made him appear older than his real age of fifty.

'Although he was lanky and Edward Lear was rotund, I imagine that Lear's beard and spectacles may also have seemed to create a certain distance between himself and others. About Strachey's eyelids, as he looked out through the windows of his spectacles over the quickset hedge of his beard, there was a suggestion of world-weariness . . . I did not think of him in terms of a sum of years but as an intelligence alert and busy behind the appendage of hair and the glass outworks. A glint came into his eyes, the brain was on the move as swiftly as a bat, with something of the radar-like sensitivity of a bat, and when he spoke it was sometimes in the voice of a bat.'

He was more than ever in demand at London social events, submitting to them with a characteristic mixture of enthusiasm, malice, curiosity and goodwill. 'I've been plunging in the oddest manner among the Upper Classes,' he reported to Dadie (8 July 1930). Among the very oddest of these functions was a tea-party given by the Duchess of Marlborough, the purpose of which was to assemble the most eminent writers in the land and record photographic groups corresponding to Conversation Pieces. If these proved sufficiently inspiring, it was planned to have paintings made of them. A miscellaneous crowd assembled in the gilded salons of Carlton House Terrace – among them Augustine Birrell who in his eightieth year 'seems extraordinarily vigorous, and in fact younger than anyone else'. While the duke, who absolutely forbade the use of a spiked tripod on his parquet floor, or of flashlight bulbs in case their smoke discoloured the ceiling, argued to a position of stalemate with an American photographer, the writers waited in their formal group. 'The exhaustion was terrific,' Lytton complained, 'the idiocy intense.'

Wherever he went, he wrote to Carrington. 'I had quite an interesting time last night,' he told her (28 May 1930) after a dinner-party with Bryan and Diana Guinness. '. . . On the way I fell in with the endless stream of motors going to the "Court", each filled with a sad bevy of débutantes – and an occasional redcoat.

'A considerable crowd lined the Mall, gaping at this very dull spectacle. I found again a large party – about 18 – with Eddie Marsh, but not Lady Cunard – again sat next to Diana [Cooper]. Once more Harold Acton figured – I feel myself falling under his sway little by little. At last, after a rather dreary dinner, we reached Rutland Gate, where, as I'd feared, Pa and Ma Redesdale[35] were in evidence. However, it was really a pleasant and a very young party – everyone looked very nice and behaved very well, it seemed to me – such good, gentle, natural manners – no stiffness – no blatancy – more like a large family party than anything else. The effect was rather like a choice flower-bed – each tulip standing separately, elegant and gay – but a ghostly notice glimmered – "Please do not pick".'

Lytton could still fall into curious dilemmas. One incident that summer took place in the National Gallery 'where I went yesterday to see the Duveen room – a decidedly twilight effect: but spacing out the Italian pictures produces on the whole a fair effect,' he wrote to Carrington (10 June 1930). 'There was a black-haired tart marching round in india-rubber boots, and longing to be picked up.

'We both lingered in the strangest manner in front of various masterpieces – wandering from room to room. Then on looking round I perceived a more attractive tart – fair-haired this time – bright yellow and thick hair – a pink face – and plenty of vitality. So I transferred my attentions, and began to move in his direction when on looking more closely I observed that it was the Prince of Wales – no doubt at all – a Custodian bowing and scraping, and Philip Sassoon also in attendance. I then became terrified that the latter would see me, and insist on performing an introduction, so I fled – perhaps foolishly – perhaps it might have been the beginning of a really entertaining affair. And by that time the poor black-haired tart had entirely disappeared. Perhaps he was the ex-king of Portugal.'

To recover from excitements such as these, he fled down to King's to stay with Dadie. But the pace of life in Cambridge, with its river-parties and dinner-parties, its theatres crammed with young men, grew almost as hectic as London. He hurried on for a few days to Taplow Court, a large mansion in the French château style, set high amid green lawns overlooking the Thames near the wicked weekend town of Maidenhead – the home of Lady Desborough, the most celebrated hostess of the age. The names of the guests staying with her over the previous weekend would appear on Monday mornings in *The Times*: a long list of statesmen, diplomats, proconsuls, fashionable beauties, terminated generally with one or two men of learning or letters. Lytton, however, does not appear to have been impressed by this clientele, which included 'a knot of dowagers and [J.M.] Barrie. Also Lord D[avid] Cecil, who struck me as being too much at home among the female antiques.

'Desmond was there too – a comfort; but I came away feeling pretty ashy. Lord Desborough[36] himself was really the best of the crew – a huge old rock of an athlete – almost completely gaga – I spent the whole of Sunday afternoon with him tête-à-tête. He showed me his unpublished books – "The History of the Thames" – "The History of the Oar" etc., etc. He confessed he had read the whole of Shakespeare. – "And, you know, there is some pretty stiff stuff in him"!'

A visit to Ireland a few weeks later gave Lytton the opportunity for more social misadventures. He had been invited by Bryan and Diana Guinness to Knockmaroon, a large comfortable house in Castleknock, on the farther side of Dublin from the enormous Phoenix Park. In preparation he purchased an aggressive suit of orange tweeds and, splendidly attired, travelled by a luxurious train over the sea to Kingstown, where, 'owing to the incompetence of the idle rich', there was no one to meet him. He was obliged to board an uncomfortable train to Dublin, and then a lawless taxi which 'wandered for hours in the purlieus of the various Maroons and Knocks – the rain all the time pouring cats and dogs'. At an advanced hour of the evening he raced in, with the speed of a fast bowler, to be met with looks of faint horror from the massed ranks of guests. 'Oh dear me!' he exclaimed in a letter to Roger (9 August 1930). 'My new tweeds were far too loud, and, when I burst in rather unexpectedly, quite horrified (I could clearly see) Lady de Vesci – but no matter, she left for England almost at once (whether in consequence of my tweeds or for some other reason) accompanied – this I regretted – by her son (or so I gathered) Lord Rosse, a foolish young man, but not unattractive.'

The company, which rapidly diminished the longer Lytton stayed (until, after ten days, there seemed to be no one else there) included Nancy Mitford, the 'amusing' sister of Diana Guinness whom he made shriek with laughter all the time, Henry Yorke[37] and his wife ('rather nice, I think') and the 'little Guinnesses', his hosts. 'He is so small . . . as to be almost invisible; but she is I suspect more interesting, but probably too young to provide any real sustenance.' Dominating this company, looked up to by all and evidently enjoying everything tremendously was Henry Lamb, who had arrived with his 'very agreeable' wife Pansy. The change that had taken place in him was extraordinary. 'Henry will obviously be my great support in this gathering,' Lytton wrote to Carrington (9 August 1930). '. . . [He] is a great success. They all adore him, and he is evidently quite happy. A strange unlooked-for transformation . . . How curious to be thrown together with Henry after all these years, and in Ireland, too, where such a fearful crisis was once enacted between us.'

In rapid succession Lytton was whisked off to a ball at the Viceregal Lodge, assisted along a mountain-climbing expedition, escorted round the Dublin National Library and taken to the Abbey Theatre, 'where Diana G. grew so restive over the brogue and the boredom that she swept out in the middle of the performance with the whole party at her heels'. Some aspects of this drawing-room life, in particular its mixture of decorum and impropriety, did surprise him. 'The state of civilization here is curious,' he reported to Roger, '– something new to me. An odd betwixt-and-between-ism. The indecency question, for instance – certain jokes are permissible, in fact frequent – but oh! there are limitations. And I must say I am always for the absolute. And the young men invariably leap to their feet when a young woman enters the room.'

The warm weather appeared to have given him fresh energy, 'and also – may I say it?' he asked Roger (4 September 1930) after his return from Ireland, 'the new warmth, chez toi has filled me with vigour and delight'. Roger was off to Scotland that September, Carrington planned to stay with the Johns and the Tomlins as well as spending some secret days at sea with Beacus, and so to prolong the summer warmth, Lytton set off to join Dadie, Rosamond Lehmann and her husband Wogan Philipps in France. 'Our movements have been peculiar and almost continuous,' he wrote to Roger (9 September 1930), '. . . a strange existence, this, so altogether cut off from the world – life on a raft, in fact, in mid-ocean, with 3 companions – a drifting, vague, and yet concentrated life.'

They arrived at Trébeurden, rode on to Brest ('le pot de chambre de la France'), continued to a minute seaside village, Les Mouettes, near the fishing town of Douarenez ('a place to while away the hours in, sipping cointreau, quite indefinitely'), and splashing through perpetual rain came to Quimper and on by road to Chartres where there was a fair 'with whirligigs and oiseaux and mechanical organs', and the sun finally shone. 'The cathedral there is a hundred times better than the rather pretentious object at Bourges,' Lytton wrote to Roger (15 September 1930).

'It was wonderful coming into it yesterday in the dark, only able at first to discern dim shapes of pillars and those astonishing blazes of stained glass. Gradually, as our pupils expanded, we saw more & more – all the glorious proportions at last, and the full sublimity. Oh, my dearest creature, I wished so much for you to be with me as I stood at that most impassioned point – the junction of the transept & the nave, where the pillars suddenly soar and rush upwards to an unbelievable height, and one is aware of the whole structure in its power and its splendour. The christian religion itself positively almost justified! And I made wishes for you, too . . .

I . . . have loved the movement and oddity . . .'

However sweet they were to him, he sometimes longed to be travelling with Roger. At other times he wished that Carrington had joined their raft. 'I think of you so often and love you more than I can say,' Carrington wrote to him (14 September 1930). And Lytton wrote to Roger (9 September 1930): 'I think of you a hundred times a day, and want you to be here to listen to a thousand comments on things that pass & things in general.'

Carrington met him at Southampton as he sailed in grandly on a four-funnelled liner, *The Olympic*, from Cherbourg. 'I only wish I could send you some of my own bouncing strength,' he wrote to Roger (23 September 1930). 'I never thought in days gone by that I should have any to spare for other people.'

He seemed to be enjoying an Indian summer and was 'in his most urbane mood', Vanessa noted. He went again to Charleston where the 'inevitable dolce far niente' still reigned, and somersaulted through more hoops of London entertainment, meeting a young Welsh short story writer, a young Italian novelist and a young English poet. 'Such a scene at the Ivy where Caradoc Evans, rather the worse for drink, apostrophized me in Anglo-Welsh for 3/4 of an hour,' he told Roger (23 September 1930).

'. . . "Truly to God" was one of his favourite phrases – "Truly to God, Mr Strachey, you can write English – English – you know what I mean – you *know* – yes, Mr Strachey, English, truly to God!" It was only ended by his mistress, a vast highly coloured woman in the Spanish style [Countess Barcynska], taking the whole party in her car to the house [51 Gordon Square] – where I cleverly escaped, without letting the others in. So you can see one does have a certain sort of adventure . . .'

His adventure with Alberto Moravia was a more sober affair, and took place in 'that palace of faded grimness', the Reform Club, to which they had both been invited by Morgan Forster. 'E.M.F. assured me that he [Moravia] really was good-looking,' he told Roger (15 November 1930).

'– however (knowing the peculiarity of his taste) I wasn't surprised to find a human weasel awaiting me under the yellow-ochre Ionic columns of the central hall. Otherwise he wasn't so bad, as foreigners go. He's apparently written a novel that is so shocking that even Beryl de Zoete refuses to translate it. "I deescra-eeb nékeed weemin" was his explanation. (Rather a disappointing one!)'[38]

It was at Ipsden House, some forty miles from Hungerford, near Wallingford, where he had been invited by 'Ros and Wog', that Lytton met Stephen Spender 'whom I liked very much', he afterwards told Roger (27 December 1930). With his red cheeks, blue eyes and a romantic expression Spender seemed 'a gay, vague, lively creature – youthful and full of talk. Has written a homosexual novel,[39] which he fears will not be published. Thinks of living in Germany with a German boy, but hasn't yet found a German boy to live with. Writes poems after lunch, and reads them aloud to Rosamond.' On Boxing Day, 'Ros and Wog' and Stephen Spender motored over for dinner to Ham Spray where the other guests were Clive and Vanessa, Ralph and Frances, and Carrington's brother Noel. 'It was a curious little party, but I enjoyed it,' Lytton wrote.

'Got some talk with S.S. who was very amusing and nice. Then we played Up Jenkins – rather a fearful game. Then the wireless was turned on, and dancing took place – Clive tottering round with Frances, Wogan gyrating like a top with Carrington – and for a moment with me! ... The latest scandal is that the Woolves (aided and abetted by Dadie, of all people) are trying to lure John Lehmann to join the Hogarth Press, and put all his capital as well as to devote his working hours to doing up parcels in the basement. And the large ape is seriously tempted.'

Lytton was still feeling unaccountably happy and light-headed. With an influx of energy he ended the year finishing the last essays for 'my little Spring book'. It was 'quite a pleasure to be working again', though he had difficulty thinking of a title. 'As at present envisaged, there will be a dozen small biographical essays, and ½ dozen historians ... Do you think "Little Lives"' would do?' he asked Roger (25 November 1930). By the beginning of 1931 he had settled on *Portraits in Miniature and Other Essays*. 'I think of writing a book moulded on Malinowsky,[40] called "The Sexual Life of the English",' he told Roger while correcting his proofs (20 March 1931); 'it would be a remarkable work, but no doubt would have to be published in New Guinea. In the meantime "Portraits in Miniature" is progressing in its tamer fashion.'

5

THINGS THAT PASS AND THINGS IN GENERAL

Chatto & Windus brought out *Portraits in Miniature* on 14 May 1931 in two simultaneous versions – a limited large-paper edition of two hundred and sixty copies (of which two hundred and fifty were for sale) costing two pounds; and a regular trade edition of twelve thousand seven hundred copies costing six shillings. Both in Britain and the United States (where Harcourt Brace published it on 16 July) the book sold well and was also well received. Edmund Wilson called it 'one of Strachey's real triumphs'[41] and Virginia Woolf noted in her diary (19 May 1931) 'Lytton's book: very good. That's his line. The compressed yet glossy account which requires logic, reason, learning, taste, wit order & infinite skill – this suits him far better, I think than the larger scale, needing boldness, originality, sweep.'

He had dedicated *Portraits in Miniature* to Max Beerbohm.[42] It was an appropriate dedication. Both of them were natural miniaturists or, as Virginia preferred to phrase it, had 'a small talent sedulously cultivated' – something she could respect but need not fear. In fact she felt surprised, she told Vanessa (23 May 1931), by how good the book actually was, 'indeed rather masterly in technique', she admitted, 'and the essays read much better together than separate'. This she attributed to Lytton having 'combed out his rhetoric somewhat in respect for us'. Though he did weed out various 'indefatigables' and 'deliciousnesses', he made far fewer emendations to the text of *Portraits in Miniature* than of *Books and Characters*. These essays read better together because a theme runs unobtrusively through them tracing, in France and England, town and country, the evolution of the modern world from the sixteenth to the nineteenth century. In *Eminent Victorians* he had pulled down the powerful from their high places; in *Portraits in Miniature* he raised up the victims of history – obscure pedants and pedagogues, sectarians and solipsists, crackpots, biographers and other square pegs and odd birds – pushed by circumstances into awful shapes, and treats them with ironic tenderness. Here are the butterfly careers of Lodowick Muggleton, an incomprehensible prophet with a tiny band of crazed disciples; poor forgotten John North, Master of Trinity, a caricature of seventeenth-century academic learning; Sir John Harington, led by his sensitive nose to become the inventor of the water-closet; and Strachey's predecessor, that assiduous muddler in love and literature John Aubrey, seeking after Apparitions and Impulses, and transmuting 'a few handfuls of orts and relics into golden life'.

These, and many others, had been swept from the narrative of history ruled over by the 'Six English Historians' at the end of the book, and lay like dried specimens from the past, pinned by Strachey's curiosity, illustrating the waywardness of the human spirit, the frustrated offshoots and cul-de-sacs of ambition. Because their reputations have lapsed, their faiths decayed, their arguments been buried in the dust, their troubled spirits do not vex the twentieth century. They are the subjects of historical burlesque, 'shorn beings, for whom the word is not tempered, powerless, out of place', breathing the pure air of comedy and pathos.

'A biography should either be as long as Boswell's or as short as Aubrey's,' Strachey wrote in his essay on John Aubrey. 'The method of enormous and elaborate accretion which produced the *Life of Johnson* is excellent, no doubt; but, failing that, let us have no half-measures; let us have the pure essentials – a vivid image, on a page or two, without explanation, transitions, commentaries, or padding.' But it was difficult to cover his historians without any explanations and transitions. His method was to exhibit one facet of each – the detachment of Hume, the balance of Gibbon, the philistinism of Macaulay, the morality of Carlyle, the provincial protestation of his disciple Froude, and the dryness of Mandell Creighton. Where his similarity to them is gratifying (Hume and Gibbon) he is sympathetic, and where it becomes uncomfortable (Carlyle and Macaulay) he grows more critical. Seventy-five years later we are better informed about Hume and Carlyle and know that Macaulay's emotional life was more complicated than he allows; but these vignettes still exemplify Strachey's view that history is a literary art.

No one arranged so anxiously for the demise of his characters. For Strachey the dying historian was an aesthetic necessity. The most remarkable death of all was that of Froude's tormentor, the red-bearded Professor Edward Augustus Freeman who was himself mercilessly attacked by another 'burrower into wormholes', Horace Round. The effect of Round's vitriolic articles on Freeman was alarming.

'His blood boiled, but he positively made no reply. For years the attacks continued, and for years the professor was dumb. Fulminating rejoinders rushed into his brain, only to be whisked away again – they were not quite fulminating enough. The most devastating article of all was written . . . Freeman was aghast at this last impertinence, but still he nursed his wrath. Like King Lear, he would do such things – what they were yet he knew not – but they should be the terrors of the earth. At last, silent and purple, he gathered his female attendants about him, and left England for an infuriated holiday. There was an ominous pause; and then the fell news reached Brighton. The professor had gone pop in Spain.'

Strachey wanted to ruffle the sensibilities of Freeman's counterparts among modern academic historians – and he appears to have succeeded. Shortly after his essay on Froude appeared in *Life and Letters*, he wrote gleefully to Roger Senhouse (17 December 1930):

'Virginia has just met Lord Esher who had told her that *he* had just met George Trevelyan, who was foaming at the mouth with rage. "Really! I should never have believed that a writer of L.S.'s standing would use an expression like that – went pop!" So some effect has been produced, which is something.'

In the summer of 1931, *The Week-End Observer* ran a competition for the best profile of Lytton Strachey done in his own manner. After reminding readers of his 'Six English Historians', it added: 'Let us suppose that to these a seventh is added – that of Mr Strachey himself.' Signing herself 'Mopsa', Carrington sent in an imaginary death scene which won first prize. 'If Mopsa be thought cruel,' wrote the organizer Dyneley Hussey, '– and I was in two minds whether on that score she might not have to be ruled out – the victim is, after all, only getting as good as he gives.' It is an apt mimicry of Lytton's style, with its planted *mots*, its insinuations, and its flippant moment of extinction, composed with the loving malice of someone who was moved at times by a furtive wish to escape. 'We might have had such a happy life without these Stracheys!' she had written to Alix.

'Crouching under the ilex tree in his chaise longue, remote, aloof, self-occupied, and mysteriously contented, lay the venerable biographer. Muffled in a sealskin coat (for although it was July he felt the cold) he knitted with elongated fingers a coatee for his favourite cat, Tiberius. He was in his 99th year. He did not know it was his last day on earth.

A constable called for a subscription for the local sports. "Trop tard, trop tard; mes jeux sont finis." He gazed at the distant downs; he did not mind – not mind in the very least the thought that this was probably his last summer; after all, summers were now infinitely cold and dismal. One might as well be a mole. He did not particularly care that he was no longer thought the greatest biographer, or that the Countess no longer – or did she? Had he been a woman he would not have shone as a writer, but as a dissipated mistress of infinite intrigues.

But – lying on the grass lay a loose button, a peculiarly revolting specimen; it was an intolerable, an unspeakable catastrophe. He stooped from his chaise longue to pick it up, murmuring to his cat "Mais quelle horreur!" for once stooped too far – and passed away for ever.'[43]

Death was much in Lytton's thoughts over these last few years. Apart from Philip Ritchie and Lady Strachey, many friends had recently died – several of them Apostles.

> How fast has brother followed brother,
> From Sunshine to the sunless land.

In the spring of 1922, he had gone to the cremation service of one of the eldest and most eminent brothers – Walter Raleigh. Lytton had not seen Raleigh for two or three years, but the occasion prompted many memories of the old days at Liverpool and Cambridge.

When Jane Harrison, the classical anthropologist who had courageously gone with him to Saltsjöbaden in those far-off days before the war, died in the spring of 1928, he mourned not just the demise of an old friend, but the deprivaton to the world of a fine talent. 'I've been feeling rather sad about Jane Harrison's death,' he told Roger (18 April 1928). 'She was such a charming rare person – very affectionate and appreciative, very grand, and very amusing. Her humour was unique ... I had not realised that she was quite as old as 77. What a wretched waste it seems that all that richness of experience and personality should be completely abolished! – Why, one wonders, shouldn't it have gone on and on? – Well! there will never be anyone at all like her again.'

The extinction of anyone whose faculties were still intact struck him as a ridiculous arrangement. There were so few people of genuine talent. Geoffrey Scott, for instance, who died in August 1929, he had never greatly liked. But he respected his intelligence and felt the loss to English scholarship – especially since his work on the *Private Papers of James Boswell from Malahide Castle* was incomplete. There was a danger now that the Boswell papers would be shipped from Europe to some pottling old translantic professor to tinker with over the years. 'One doesn't see who can grapple with them,' he wrote to Roger (18 August 1929). 'I only hope they won't be handed over to some wretched American.'

The most serious shock of these years was the sudden death of Frank Ramsey. He had been suffering from an undiagnosed disease of the liver, entered hospital for an operation, and never recovered. He was twenty-six years old, perhaps the most brilliant philosopher of his generation and with the main body of his work hardly begun. Like Moore at the turn of the century, he had revived the Society and started a vintage Apostolic era after the war. In Maynard's view he was a genius, a humorous and unassuming genius who claimed that the aim of philosophy was not to answer questions but to cure headaches. 'I am terribly distressed about Frank,' Lytton told Dadie Rylands (19 January 1930), who had also known him well.

'It is truly tragic. He was one of the few faultless people, with a heavenly simplicity and modesty, which gave a beauty to his genius such as I have never known in anyone else. He had all the charm of childhood, yet one never doubted for a moment when one was with him that one was in the presence of a very great mind. The last time I spoke to him was – do you remember? – when we met him coming out of the Provost's Lodge, and he told us, with those delightful fits of laughter, about the cat that came into his lecture room. I am miserable – miserable – to think that I shall never be able to make him laugh again, never hear him again at the Society, never again be able to say to myself, after reflecting on the degradation of humanity "Well, after all, there is Frank". The loss to your generation is agonizing to think of – and the world will never know what has happened – what a light has gone out. I always thought there was something of Newton about him – the ease and majesty of the thought – the gentleness of the temperament – and suppose Newton had died at – how old was he? – twenty-six? – I am afraid Richard [Braithwaite][44] will be particularly upset – will you please give him my love?'

The following month, another Apostle, Lytton's friend C.P. Sanger, collapsed and died after a short illness. Like Ramsey, like Moore, and a few others, he had combined great talent with natural modesty, 'unworldly without being saintly, unambitious without being inactive, warm-hearted without being sentimental', Goldie Dickinson called him. Lytton had never forgotten Sanger's kindness when he had gone up to Trinity. 'A nervous breakdown was the apparent cause,' he explained to Roger (11 February 1930).

'I fear it was the result of a long process of over-work, underfeeding, and general discomfort – a wretched business. He had an astonishing intellect; but accompanied by such modesty that the world in general hadn't any idea of his very great distinction. And he was so absolutely unworldly that the world's inattention was nothing to him. I knew him ever since Cambridge days, when he constantly came for week-ends for the Apostles' meetings – and then in London, when, at first, they lived in a little set of rooms at Charing Cross – and afterwards by a curious chance, Philip

[Ritchie] became an added link between us. How he loved Philip, and how often he used to talk to me about him, with mild expostulations over his illnesses! – And so all that is over now, and I shall never go to New Square again.'

The deaths of these friends prompted many bitter-sweet memories which had been given a new sharpness that spring when Sebastian Sprott came down to Ham Spray to arrange the last of Lytton's bundles of correspondence. As before, Lytton could not resist dipping into these old papers, though they stirred many complicated and uncomfortable sensations. Why, he wondered, should it sometimes depress him so much to go through these letters? It was like putting on a pair of distorting spectacles that presented – or did it redress? – an illusion of the past.

The past appeared more exciting now than the present. Ottoline had written him a letter that April which recalled many incidents long closed and half-forgotten. He seldom saw Ottoline these days – just occasionally in Gower Street, where she presided as a faded relic of a great hostess. In her prime, she had been a splendid figure, generous, comic and encouraging; but disaster seemed to spread over her relationships like a winter blight. She referred in her letter to the ashes and poisonous vapours lying over what might otherwise have been so good; yet the ashes and vapours, Lytton believed, had been of her own making. He felt some uneasiness over answering her letter. Clearly a certain amount of sentiment was called for, and some sincerity too – but how to mix them tactfully? After ten days' hesitation, he replied in what was to be the last long communication between them, partly truthful, agreeably clouded with metaphor, the conclusion to a long friendship now extinct. He wrote (8 April 1931):

'For me, getting to know you was a wonderful experience – ah! those days at Peppard – those evenings in Bedford Square! I cannot help surmising that if H[enry] L[amb] had been a *little* different – things would have been *very* different, but perhaps that is an impossible notion. Perhaps we are all so deeply what we are that the slightest shift is out of the question. I don't think I want to go back. It was thrilling, enchanting, devastating, all at once – one was in a special (a very special) train, tearing along at breakneck speed – where? – one could only dimly guess – one might be off the rails – or at Timbuctoo – or in Heaven – at any moment. Once is enough! . . . I have been astonishingly happy now for a long time – if only life were a good deal longer – and the sunshine less precarious!'

Something of Lytton's mood may be glimpsed from an entry made by

Carrington in HER BOOK, dated 20 March 1931. 'At tea Lytton said to me. "Remember all the bird Books and flower Books are yours", I said "Why?" "Well, after I am dead it would be important." Then I said, and "all my pictures, and objects are yours". and he said "Really?" almost as if he didn't believe me. I said "but if you died first –" but I felt suddenly serious, and gloomy, and Lytton noticing the change, like a wind sweeping across the lawn through the laurels, changed the conversation.'

But the interior dialogue persisted. He did not expect to die – most of his family were long-lived, and he was only fifty-one that March. But there were other reasons, besides the deaths of his friends, to account for these forebodings. Throughout 1931 he was almost perpetually ill. These illnesses did not in themselves appear to be serious, but they seldom left him and their cumulative effect was very enfeebling. He had been familiar with sickness all his life but now the sensations were unspecific. As if partly anaesthetized or suspended in a dream, he felt his physical consciousness of things separating from his emotional awareness. It was not so much pain he experienced as the blurred invading presence of some discomfort that he could not precisely locate, which made all movement unpleasant, and sitting or bending curiously difficult. At first his physician, Dr Starkey Smith, diagnosed internal piles and prescribed some suppositories. Later, changing his diagnosis, he arranged for Lytton to be attended by a professional masseuse and treated with an ultra-violet lamp. The wandering symptoms came and went, and returned in a more complicated form, accompanied by headaches, a slight temperature and a buzzing in the ears. 'I feel inclined to retire into a monastery,' he concluded after four months of these disorders (31 April 1931), 'but on second thoughts that couldn't be much good really – a nunnery, possibly . . .'

In his letters, Lytton makes light of this illness. He is always hopeful of a quick improvement. But occasionally he comes near to admitting the darker implications of his condition: 'I suppose I am gradually recovering,' he wrote to Roger (26 January 1931), 'but there are still moments when I feel as if I were at the bottom of a well with only the dimmest chance of getting out.'

He was frightened of appearing fussy and tiresome to his friends, especially to Roger whom he issued with bright bulletins of his progress which often had to be adjusted by disappointing statements of fact. 'As for my health,' he declared on 20 March 1931, 'it's now becoming the Grand Bore of Christendom, and I fear to refer to it. However, I'll just remark that I'm perhaps rather better – but not yet right. I feel quite well – and then seem to sink back into a buzzing ineptitude.'

He passed much of the year at Ham Spray. How English it all was and how well it suited him. 'There is a romantic beauty about everything here which ravishes my heart,' he had told Mary Hutchinson. He was reading Keats, 'who is perfect', and whose poetry heightened his sensitivity to the unemphatic green shapes all round, making him feel at one with them. 'Last night', he wrote to Roger on 29 June, 'just after sunset, an extraordinary light, as of some vast motor car appeared behind the trees on the top of the downs – a blaze between the trunks – we gazed – and then realised that it was the moon, that was just there – it moved rapidly upwards and sideways – a surprising and romantic spectacle, until at last it was balanced – a golden circle on the edge of the hill.'

Life went on in the quietest style, and 'the question of the next book to read is the only pebble that ruffles the surface of the pond,' he told Roger (17 April 1931). 'Yesterday there was an event though – 2 visitors by aeroplane – viz. Dorelia and Kaspar John. The latter took C. up for a turn – she adored it; but *I* refrained – the attraction, somehow or other, was not sufficient.' After her flight, Carrington tried to coax Lytton into going up, but he seemed not at all keen to 'have a go'. Caspar promised to deal gently with one of so gentle a nature and Dorelia asked Lytton how he would be able to discipline Carrington if he wilted where she had braved, and so the argument went on until they reached the safety of the house. The dreaded two-seater aeroplane was now out of sight in a field beyond the trees, and with renewed confidence Lytton rounded on his tormentors, and declared he was the wrong *shape* for flying and that his beard would certainly foul the controls. Then he coiled himself down into an armchair and there was no more to be said.

He still made small trips to London and to Cambridge where there was no diminution of social life, though 'it's the social life of a preparatory school to my mind'. With a new young friend, Alan Searle – 'my Bronzino Boy' as he called him – he visited Oswald Balfour[45] at the White House, in Thorpe-le-Soken, Essex, but was not sorry to leave after two nights. The Bronzino had behaved very tiresomely, to his mind, getting himself bitten in the stomach by their host's bulldog, and then collapsing into hysterics; an intolerable Dickensian charwoman called Mrs Scroggins had appeared and bearded Lytton with tales of village politics; and the rest of the house guests seemed a painful crew – Nature's second fiddles. Towards the first violin Oswald Balfour himself, an unmarried field officer with superior connections, Lytton felt not the least attraction 'except physically in a very odious way. The English upper class characteristic of going in for character as opposed to mind is annoying,' he observed to Roger (4 July 1931), 'even when it crops up in such queer (in every sense of the word) surroundings.'

It was a relief to return to Ham Spray. He was reading the ex-prime minister A.J. Balfour's *Chapters of Autobiography* which was 'very well done in its way – that is the way that tells you nothing of any real interest – curiously 18th century, in fact – so clear and limited. But the silly fellow was a Christian, and that I cannot forgive.' He also tried 'one of my imitators', Philip Guedalla's Life of Wellington, *The Duke*, but could not finish it. 'After going through the Peninsular War and Waterloo, I've given up,' he told Roger (7 October 1931), ' . . . Queen V[ictoria]'s letters are much better in every way – so full of incident and feeling, and so idiotically to the point.'

Among recent fiction, there was a new novel by Somerset Maugham – to whom he had been introduced by Alan Searle – the notorious *Cakes and Ale*. It 'is causing some excitement here', he explained to Dorothy Bussy (November 1930), 'as it contains a most envenomed portrait of Hugh Walpole, who is out of his mind with agitation and horror. It is a very amusing book, apart from that – based obviously on Hardy's history (more or less) – only marred, to my mind, by some curious lack of distinction.' Apart from that he had returned to the 'pretty strenuous business' of reading Proust, and so had Carrington who found the end of Baron Charlus 'almost too terrible', she told Lytton (12 May 1931). 'It has the appalling horror of Lear.' She had designed some bookplates for Lytton's library, but sticking them in with him at Ham Spray, and remembering him bidding for books at Sotheby's, it occurred to her that 'these books will one day be looked at by those gloomy-faced booksellers and buyers. And suddenly a premonition of a day when these labels will no longer [be] in the library came over me.[46] I linger to ask Lytton not to stick in any more.'

Carrington had begun the year with yet another new resolution to paint. 'I cater for every taste,' she had told Alix. As well as her glass and silver-paper pictures ('Victorian beauties, soldiers, tropical botanical flowers, birds and fruits are a few of my subjects'), she had been designing decorative tiles for bathrooms and fireplaces (under Beacus's influence 'mostly of shells, fishes and ships') and selling them through shops and by commission. (Beacus's brother Alex Penrose ordered a tiled fireplace which she did heraldically in a Dutch delft style showing a fountain pen crossed with a rose.) Few people guessed 'What Bloody Sweat went to produce these trifles light as air'. Most of her serious painting now depicted 'the botanicals' in her Ham Spray garden where she laboured every week with her cats ('I wish cats could be trained to weed gardens'). She also painted a rare cactus given to her by Dorelia, and the fairground at Marlborough where, one amazingly beautiful day, she went with Alix, shooting at bottles and swinging on the merry-go-round while Alix flew about 'on those little electric motor cars and charged everyone to pieces', she wrote to Frances (September 1931).

Her love affair with Beacus persisted though it had not prospered. When he criticized her 'awful' white stockings and asked her to wear black silk ones for him instead 'I realised our PATHS lay differently,' she confided to Julia (June 1931). Sometimes when Beacus arrived at Ham Spray she would stare at him and question whether this was really the person who had obsessed her while he was away. 'Can this be the nose, the mouth I craved for? ... This the body?' she demanded in HER BOOK. There were still evenings together lit by mysterious happiness, but perhaps at thirty-eight she 'should be settling down over tea-cups, bottling gooseberries', she reflected, instead of having 'Shelley cravings to sail and leave these quiet rural scenes for Greek Islands'.[47]

The end of the affair came that summer when, visiting Ham Spray again, Beacus fell ill with jaundice and had to be nursed by her for almost a month, while Lytton crept about in the next room and eventually made off for London. 'Rather ironical to realize one's mission in life is Florence Nightingale!' she wrote to Sebastian Sprott (July 1931). 'However I learnt everything there was to know about him and in some ways cured my illgotten passion.' When Beacus recovered and sailed away it was 'all off' between them, and Carrington sensed she had severed her last connections with youth. In some ways she was relieved. Happiness was largely a matter of the timing of relationships, she observed in HER BOOK. This one had come too late. She was feeling remorse lately at neglecting Lytton. She never tired of nursing him as she had with Beacus and now that her 'lusts had run dry' and her 'high jinks' were over, she planned to make it up to Lytton. Each year she had grown happier with him and, while she was recovering from her emotions over Beacus, she felt closer to him than ever. At the end of that summer she was looking forward to a more contented life among the rooms and gardens she had created for them both at Ham Spray. Everything was designed for the future.

Lytton's love-affair with Roger was also playing itself out. 'I think of you a great deal, my dearest angel – a great deal – and of everything about you,' he had written (20 March 1931). 'I long to be with you, to talk to you, to pull your lolls [ears], to be happy – Ah well! It is a blessing to be able to write to you and to get your letters.' Despite his illnesses, Lytton was always ready to pack his bags and dash off anywhere in the world with Roger. The pity was that there were so few chances. 'These ages of absence are very desolating – will you recognise me when you see me?' he wondered (21 April 1931). 'My retroussé nose and sky-blue eyes have probably by now quite faded from your memory, and I daresay if an imposter arrives on Monday, obviously disguised in a beard & spectacles, you'll be completely taken in.'

Seeing each other so seldom, their relationship became more bookish. 'So here I am in my solitude,' Lytton wrote from Ham Spray (12 May 1931), 'buried in books – chiefly about old atheists – such strange stories are told of them! The Elizabethans grow more and more peculiar ... Perhaps on the whole we live in better times, but it's difficult to calculate.' Some ingenious compromise between the sixteenth and twentieth centuries, he sometimes thought, would have suited him best. Indeed this was what, in their make-believe, he had tried to fashion between Roger and himself. From the strange stories that lay in his old books, he had made their secret code, translating the cruelties of human nature into gentle games. These fantasies multiplied while the actual relationship shrank so that they gradually became a substitute for that relationship rather than a stimulus to it.

He had known Roger for seven years, and his capacity for being surprised by this handsome invisible lover was nearly exhausted. Tenderness and great affection he still felt, but his early adulation had dispersed itself too often into the empty spaces created by Roger's elusiveness. There were still moments when his special charm made all things seem possible, but 'I've had the feeling that our relationship was coming to an end – or perhaps just fading away,' Lytton wrote to him (18 August 1931). '... What is it that you want? I'm afraid it may be some kind of impossible mixture of the occasional & the profound – or at least impossible for me who am neither a saint nor an acrobat.'

Ralph and Frances were still working at *The Greville Memoirs* in London and visiting Ham Spray less often, partly because Ralph's mother in Devon was ill with cancer, and partly because, having been 'turned out' of 41 Gordon Square because of expanding psychoanalysis, they had moved into a beautiful Queen Anne house, 16 Great James Street, which housed the Nonesuch Press. 'We are very contented here,' Ralph assured Gerald (25 February 1930).

Ralph and Frances had come up with a scheme to shut up the house this coming winter and, all four of them, sail for Malaga. Meanwhile they went off for a short holiday in the South of France. Carrington and Lytton remained 'crouching over the embers' at Ham Spray. He had felt some hesitation over their winter plan and she was full of forebodings. 'It is still lovely here,' Lytton wrote, 'and peace has descended – everyone has gone – C & I are left alone in this vague garden with its weeds and roses – ah! one draws a long breath, and looks out dreamily at the dreaming downs.'

6

FAREWELL TO FRANCE

That summer Lytton had begun 'a thing on Othello' intended as the first in a series of essays on Shakespeare's plays. It was 'fiendishly difficult to do', he had told Roger Senhouse, 'as it's all solid argument – and is perhaps rather mad'. The argument has an air of unreality as of someone turning away from actual life – from the illness and disenchantment that filled his own life. The *Othello* into which he draws himself is not an intense and tragic love poem within the play, nor does his 'solid argument' touch on the imaginative solution between a belief in virtue and knowledge of human nature. The Strachey *Othello* is a piece of impeccable stagecraft that is peopled by magnificent phantoms and driven by the aesthetic requirements of ancient Greek theatre. Iago, that great challenge for critics, becomes a contrivance designed for artistic balance in which the notorious 'motivelessness' blends with 'dramatic necessity'.

'I shall try to finish it,' Lytton wrote to Roger. But the essay was written with the last reserves of his strength, and they were exhausted before he was able to finish.[48]

A less arduous flight from reality was what Frances was to call his 'unusually adventurous step of going abroad alone'.[49] He wanted to cut adrift from people. He was tired of humanity, tired of common sense, tired of everything except dreaming. Solitude seemed to relieve his weariness – and solitude with plenty of comfort, good food and travel might renew his spirits. For the time being Carrington, having parted only recently from Beacus, was too full of her own guilt-ridden worries to be overloaded with his. Dadie Rylands could not safely be trusted as a brother-confessor with matters that concerned Roger. It was better to travel alone. For the first time since 1902, Lytton started keeping a diary. 'A Fortnight in France', as he labelled the exercise book into which, each night, he committed his reflections and the impressions of his journey, is the most unselfconscious of his autobiographical writings, and before the end of September, when he returned to England, it had helped to purge his temporary distaste for life.

He started out for Paris on 3 September, arriving later that day at the Hôtel Berkeley, in the Avenue Matignon. After many weeks of strangely febrile tension, he could pause and look round. More than once that summer, his visionary existence had felt more real than the physical world around him. He was drowsy with love-sickness, remembering vividly that brief interlude in Paris some twenty-five years ago with Duncan, up those forty-two soaring flights of stairs in the Hôtel de l'Univers et du Portugal, and other visits, the most recent of them with Roger to see Norman Douglas. He was alone this time, but not lonely.

'After the decidedly dreary and by no means cheap dinner at the restaurant here, I struggled out to a glass of coffee at the Rond Point,' he wrote that night in his bedroom. '. . . and then, not very conscious, strolled down the Champs Elysées towards the Place de la Concorde, in the darkness. Lights in the distance caught my eye, and then I remembered the new illuminations.

'I went on, begining to be excited, and soon came to the really magical scene; the enormous Place – the surrounding statues – the twin palaces on the North side – and in the middle the astonishing spectacle of the obelisk, a brilliant luminous white, with black hieroglyphics, clear as if drawn by ink, all over it. A move to the right revealed the Madeleine; and then, looking back, I saw the Arc de Triomphe, brightly lighted, with the avenue of lamps leading to it. A most exhilarating affair! It was warm, the innumerable motors buzzed, the strollers were many and – so it seemed – sympathetic.'

The following day he left Paris by train for Rheims, literally 'a godforsaken city'. Large areas, including the cathedral, had been wiped out by the war. 'Naturally with the cathedral bashed God goes,' he observed; 'but what's more serious is that nearly everything else has gone as well. I had imagined a few neat German bombs had blown up the sacred building and that that was all. Far from it – the whole town was wrecked. A patched-up remnant is all that remains – the patches dated 1920. Miserable!'

Next morning in the drizzling rain, Lytton set off with overcoat and umbrella to explore the town more thoroughly. 'The Cathedral, what with pre-war restorations, war destructions, and post-war restorations, presents a deplorable spectacle,' he wrote. 'I doubt whether even in its palmiest days it was anything very much – except, probably, for the glass. I tottered away from it to lose myself in dreary streets, jumping sky-high at one moment before the startled gaze of an elderly inhabitant – an attack of the Strachey twist.'

These attacks of 'the Strachey twist' no longer worried him as they did when he was young. He had learned to meet them with an ironic inquiry, as if he were watching someone else. Passing down the rue St-Honoré in Rheims one day, he inspected his own image mirrored back to him in a shop-window, like some woman *d'un certain âge* before her dressing-table. 'I saw for the first time,' he recorded, 'how completely gray my hair was over my temples. So that has come at last! I was beginning to think it never would. Do I feel like it? Perhaps I do a little – a very little. A certain sense of detachment declares itself amid the agitations that continue to strew my path.'

This, then, was the consolation of a middle age he had once dreaded. A numbness had spread over everything, protecting him from the heartache that only a short time ago could drop him into such despair. It was an agreeable change. Buoyed up by this curious composure, he felt that he could never again be much upset by romantic ordeals. Roger had again gone off with his friends to the Riviera but Lytton was recovering as Carrington was recovering from Beacus.

'I hardly feel as if I *could* now be shattered by him as I was ... I am really calm – that dreadful abysmal sensation in the pit of the stomach is absent. What a relief! Whether this means that I am out of love or not I can't pretend to say. I hope it means that my feelings are at least more rational. The inexpressible charm of his presence, the sweetness of his temper, his beautiful affectionateness – why should these things make it difficult for me to accept the facts that he must be allowed to have his own tastes, and that his tastes happen not to be what I would have wished?'

He felt perplexed by his own calmness. Could his chloroformed fading away be what they called 'the prime of life'? Was this maturity? On thoughts of age he drifted back to thoughts of death. What was his attitude to death? Perhaps it was like leaving a party. 'If one's in love with life,' he wrote, 'to leave it will be as terrible as the dreadful moment when one has to leave one's beloved one – an agony, long foreseen – almost impossibly fearful – and yet it inevitably comes. And really it is a kind of death whenever the beloved object goes; which is why sleeping together is such a peculiar solace – death is avoided – one loses consciousness deliciously alive.'

On Monday 7 September, he caught a train at Rheims station, stopped off at Châlons to inspect the cathedral, and then travelled to Nancy. It was 'a perfect town', like a miniature rococo Bath, laid out with enchanting squares, a triumphal arch or two and a delightful little park called the Pépinière – regular alleys of trees, amateurish lawns, neat flowerbeds, a fountain, some statues. Unfortunately the Grand-Hôtel in the Place Stanislas was moribund. The lift never moved; the hot water was cold; even the door-key dropped to pieces. But, though nothing worked, he resolved to stay a few days. He wanted to wander in that glorious rococo square, under those arches, along the alleys in the Pépinière – and sip vermouth on the cobblestones, dreaming of Voltaire.

So time agreeably slipped by. The only out-of-the-way episode took place over dinner on his first evening. It was one of those trivial incidents that Lytton relished and showed a reawakening interest in his fellow beings. 'The table next me was reserved for one,' he wrote that night in his diary. 'Presently the guest arrived – one of those thin-lipped intellectual epicures, who correspond exactly to some of our friends who interest themselves in art.

'Enjoyment the one thing that is *not* present. With my neighbour, the severity and pedantry of taste was carried to its most ascetic pitch. He ate his melon like a scrupulous rabbit, and then, in flawless French, entered into elaborate and distressed dissertations with the waiters. "Où est le maître d'hôtel?" etc. The French was in fact so flawless that I decided he must be an Englishman. The clothes seemed certainly English. No decoration in the button-hole. The only slightly suspicious object – and this really ought to have decided me – was a rather effeminate wrist watch. But I came to the conclusion that he must be some distinguished member of the Civil Service – one of those infinitely cultivated and embittered eunuchs who, one must suppose, govern the country, and perhaps afford the most satisfactory explanation of its present plight. But really the wrist watch ought to have shown me that I was wrong. However, at last I determined, coûte qu'il coûte, to satisfy my curiosity. After a great deal of complicated manoeuvring of orders and counter-orders, he ate a fig. I also had figs; but before eating mine, I turned to him and said, in the most off-hand and idiomatic English style possible – "Are these all right?" I calculated that if he'd been French he would have been quite at sea. As it was, there was a moment's hesitation, and he answered, with the precise politeness that one expected, "They're excellent." The question seemed solved, and I ate my fig, which, as a matter of fact was not very good. But then doubt suddenly assailed me – "May I ask you another question? Are you an Englishman who speaks French very well, or a Frenchman who speaks English very well?" A faint – a very faint smile – appeared (for the first and last time) and he answered "I'm Italian." This completely ruined me. The eventuality had never occurred to me; and I saw at once that he belonged to that dreariest of classes, the cosmopolitan, that he was doubtless merely a diplomat. At the same time – naturally, given his status – not the remotest sign of unbending: he coldly continued with his cigar. I had got into an impossible position – was being tacitly told that I was a tiresome intruder – and all I could do was to depart in silence as soon as I could and with whatever dim dignity I could muster.'

Three days later, Lytton went for the night to Strasbourg. 'I'd no idea how thoroughly teutonic this town was,' he noted, 'everyone speaks German in the streets – everybody is German – the place is simply German – and how the French managed to get up such a hullabaloo about it I can't understand.'

After walking around the streets for two hours, he was glad to get back to the Hôtel de la Maison Rouge and have a bath before dinner. Of course such comforts meant, in those days of inflation, paying twelve shillings a day for one's room, instead of eight shillings; but even so, it was well worth it. The inter-war depression made the survival of these luxuries seem very doubtful. 'All the more reason to snatch them while one can,' Lytton decided, '– to plunge into a hot bath immediately, before the revolution comes and all the water's permanently cold!'

The following day, he journeyed back to Nancy. The dingy outskirts with their smelly and decayed streets reminded him strongly of the slums in Liverpool. Another revolution would have to come. 'France, with all her gold, seems pretty poverty-stricken,' he observed. 'The beggars here are such as I've rarely seen – they look as if they'd all sat to their fellow townsman Callot – visions of utter horror and degradation. The soldiers are uncouth rustics with red noses and (about half of them) wear spectacles – which doesn't seem quite the thing.'

One morning in Nancy, as he was sitting outside a café sipping a glass of grenadine and seltzer, 'my mind pleasantly blank', a passing motor slowed down and a woman, slightly familiar in appearance, looked in his direction, then seemed to whisper his name to her male companion. 'The motor stopped, and I automatically got up, thinking it might be Diana Cooper, but – such is my vagueness for faces – not at all sure.' Only after she had introduced her remorselessly shaved and spherical companion as Dr Rudolph Kommer – her enigmatic 'dearest friend' – did Lytton's hesitation disappear. 'The truth was she was looking younger,' he observed, 'more cheerful, and less like the Madonna than usual'.[50] They got out, and insisted on my motoring with them to the Café Stanislas – more expensive. There we sat for some time.' After Duff Cooper's return to London in August to be made under-secretary of state for war, Diana Cooper explained to Lytton, she had stayed on in Venice with Laura Corrigan, enjoying the season there and meeting many younger people who, as she put it, frolicked her along with them. Now she was driving back to London '– with this ghastly-looking dago – an odd couple, but somehow or other not in the least compromising. But why?' Lytton questioned.

'Perhaps he was paying ... She was very agreeable; but I had, as I always do for some mysterious reason with her, the sensation of struggling vainly to show that I'm not a fool – mysterious, because really her own comments are very far from being out of the ordinary. K (or C) was polite. They admired Nancy; but it was too early for lunch and they had to hurry on to catch the boat to-morrow [12 September] at Calais. They went to their car, and then I observed that there was another member of the party – a kind of chauffeur, who sat in the dicky behind. He grinned a good deal – rather tendentiously I thought; perhaps he was K (or C)'s man – in every sense – and I daresay the brightest of the three.'

Two days later, Lytton returned to Paris where he went to an exhibition of Degas portraits at the Musée de l'Orangerie in the Tuileries. 'The pictures were fascinating,' he wrote that evening in his diary, '– so exquisite, witty, and serious – and there were admirable sculptured studies too, in bronze. Then a stroll down the Tuileries Gardens – how supremely enjoyable it all was! My old dread and dislike of Paris melted into nothing in the shining sun. A rainbow in the fountain – the long alley beyond – the magnificent Louvre closing in the distance – nothing but radiance and exhilaration.'

The truth was that Paris had become for him a city of *le temps retrouvé*. He went again to the Luxembourg Gardens. The trees were beginning to turn, and he remembered that time – almost exactly twenty years ago (but at the very end of September 1911) – when he had strolled along these same well-ordered avenues after his visit to Henry Lamb in Brittany, following a night journey through Nantes, and felt an extraordinary current of vitality and excitement push through him. As he walked on, he remembered another curious visit, not so long ago, with Carrington, in the intense heat, when, half-dead with exhaustion, he had crept out to try and get a little air under the trees, but, not succeeding, limped back again to this same Hôtel Foyot, where he remained in bed until Ralph came and rescued them.

Carrington and Ralph. For two weeks he had been cut off from them without news, and realized how he had come to miss England and all the extraordinary pleasures of Ham Spray. The absence of letters had produced a strange vacuum round him. Yet it had also given him the relaxation he needed, stimulating his appetite for the complexities of human relationships, the rigours of work, and all that made up ordinary life. Suddenly he longed to be back in England. Carrington, Ralph, Frances, Ham Spray – it would be delightful! And when winter came, perhaps they could after all make that expedition to Malaga, avoiding the discomfort of the winter which was past a joke now that he was nearly fifty-two.

8

THE FINAL SILENCE

The autumn was crowded with social engagements. Lytton dined with Somerset Maugham, and with Lady Cunard, Desmond MacCarthy and Noël Coward. He met William Gerhardie and Victor Cazalet at a party given by Syrie Maugham in the King's Road,[51] and Charlie Chaplin at one of Ottoline's Gower Street receptions. In the country he saw 'Ros and Wog' and a good deal of the 'little Guinnesses' at Biddesden, their country house near Andover. Carrington had been there, too, painting a *trompe l'oeil* window showing an eighteenth-century cook peeling an apple opposite a cat seated on a table which stares at a canary in a cage. It was to be a surprise for Diana Guinness when she returned from London after giving birth to her second son. For once Carrington was pleased with her work, which Lytton praised. He had bravely gone up to see Diana in the London nursing home. 'In those days one did not put a foot to the ground for 3 weeks after the birth,' she wrote. 'I told the nurse to take the baby to her room "because Mr Strachey can't abide babies". However, when Lytton and I were in the midst of our chatting she came in with the child in her arms and insisted on holding it practically under poor Lytton's nose. He said politely: "What a lot of hair!" To which she replied in a rather scornful way: 'Oh, that will all come off." Lytton gave a faint shriek: "Is it a wig?"'

He was greatly cheered by seeing Roger in London. The following month, the two of them ventured down for a weekend to Brighton, staying this time at the Bedford Hotel since 'it seemed to me rather unadventurous not to try something new'. Whether this would be enough to revive Roger's interest remained undecided.

'Don't come back too exhausted,' Carrington warned him; 'remember our literary weekend. You are responsible for the dazzling conversation.' At the beginning of November they were expecting Aldous and Maria Huxley at Ham Spray, and Carrington was threatening to 'put opium in the pies to mitigate Aldous's brilliance'. But the weather turned out beautiful and the visit went off well. 'They were evidently out to be agreeable,' Lytton reported (7 November 1931), '– especially Maria, who hasn't quite got over her early Ottoline bringing-up. Aldous is certainly a very nice person – but his conversation tends to be almost perpetually on high levels with a slightly exhausting effect.'

This exhaustion, which came over him very easily now, he put down to 'too much wit and too little humour perhaps'. Yet he was suffering from restlessness – 'one of the worst cares of life!' and with an overpowering urge to enjoy himself rushed up once more to London. Dining with Clive Bell one evening shortly after arriving in Gordon Square, he complained of feeling off colour, and left early, saying that they must meet again soon. At the weekend, accompanied by Pippa, he travelled down by train to Ham Spray. At Paddington he discovered by chance that Clive was journeying to Wiltshire in the same coach. 'He came to see me in my compartment,' Clive recorded, 'where I was alone, and we had some talk . . . At Reading he rejoined his party. At Hungerford I watched him walk along the platform on his way out. That was the last time I saw Lytton.'[52]

On his return to Ham Spray, he went to bed with what appeared to be a bad attack of gastric influenza. On 4 December, in one of his last letters, he wrote to Roger: 'I'm sorry to say I'm still sadly pulverised – have been for some days in bed – now creep about, but in an enfeebled semi-miserable condition. I cannot feel that I'm really on the mend yet. A sudden reversion to a state of affairs that I thought had gone about 15 years ago! . . . This is a gloomy recital, I fear! – In a way particularly annoying because there doesn't seem to be anything serious the matter. Only an eternal lack of equilibrium inside. Hélas! Luckily there are a lot of books to read.'

There was Somerset Maugham's *The Painted Veil* – 'class II, division I' – Burns's Letters to Mrs Agnes Maclehose – 'an amusing, curious book, published in the '40's' – and Leonard Woolf's first volume of *After the Deluge* – 'on Civilization, History, Humanity, Life etc. . . . I find it quite readable.' Virginia, too, had sent him a copy of her latest novel, *The Waves*, but he shrank from immersing himself. 'It's perfectly fearful,' he admitted to Topsy Lucas (4 November 1931). 'I shudder and shiver – and cannot take the plunge. *Any* book lying about I seize up as an excuse for putting it off – so at the moment I'm in the middle of Lucien Leuwen (Stendhal) – said by the French to be one of *the* masterpieces . . . well, well! – '

During the last week of November and the first two weeks of December, there were days when he seemed to start a recovery, but the general drift was downwards, and soon he was hardly able to read anything. Although his pulse stayed steady, his temperature fluctuated wildly, sometimes soaring to 104° and then tumbling down to 96° within a day. He was able to retain very little of what he ate, and could only be fed on what Carrington termed 'sparrow's food' – rusks, mashes and tumblers of brandy. He lost weight and strength rapidly. For almost two months the struggle went on. 'Lytton is so good,' Carrington wrote. 'He lies without moving day after day and never complains . . . He is marvellously brave and the doctors are all astonished by his courage and spirits.' He was dying with the aid of many physicians – at one time or another four specialists, two general practitioners and three nurses. Dr Elinor Rendel, Lytton's niece, who was not officially called in but fulfilled the part of a gloomy Greek chorus by commenting on the medical team's combined utterances, pronounced his case to be one of typhoid, due to the 'deep well water' at Ham Spray. But 'every suggestion she has made has been wrong', Ralph noticed.[53] Lytton's regular consultant from Hungerford, Dr Starkey Smith, appeared positively doubtful. Lytton was ill – no doubt at all of that; he was *seriously* yet not *dangerously* ill. Also he was never without 'a good fighting chance'. So there was little cause for alarm. Possibly, Starkey Smith conceded, Lytton's illness was a bad attack of colitis or alternatively one of four groups of paratyphoid. 'Nobody has ever seen a case like it,' Virginia commented, 'and nothing goes as they expect.'[54]

Meanwhile the only treatment that he could be given was a strict diet and constant nursing. The house filled up. Three professional nurses moved in and took it in turns to look after him. One was named Mooney, another McCabe, and the third, who was deaf, Phillips. Lytton made up nicknames for all of them: Clytemnestra; Old Mother Hubbard; Mousie. Pippa and James soon came down to join Carrington and Ralph who had gone to Ham Spray at once. 'Lytton asked me this morning how long I could stay and I said I would stay until he was better,' he wrote to Frances (10 December 1931). '. . . Carrington cries every time she goes to see him, as soon as she gets out . . . I talk to her hour after hour to prevent her rushing panics . . . I hate our being separated, but you shall come here if it goes on.'

The routine of a long illness set in. Frances came down and stayed in a room above the Post Office in Ham so that she could take some care of Ralph. 'Always a very emotional man, easily moved to tears, and deeply devoted to Lytton, he had been left with his powers of resistance reduced to practically nothing by the constant strain of trying to support Carrington in her even more agonising state of dread.'[55] Driving from Hungerford station and, during the following days, while walking through the fields together, Ralph would ceaselessly weep in front of her, before resuming his officer-like control at Ham Spray. Not a weeper herself, Frances could not help feeling some resentment over the devastating effects this Strachey illness was producing on him. Was there not a *folie de grandeur* in summoning all those eminent specialists to Ham Spray, as well as in the bulletins of Lytton's condition that were appearing each day in *The Times* and that were apparently rated so important? Why in any case were there so many Stracheys hanging round? Lytton had only wanted James and Pippa, and the others merely complicated Carrington's predicament. Frances could see that Lytton's suffering was 'really awful' and that it excited extremely strong emotion; nevertheless, it seemed to her there was 'a vein of hysteria in the agitation' that surrounded his bed. The reason, as Vanessa pointed out, was that for Bloomsbury Lytton was the first person they had all known since adolescence to be on the point of death.

'We are at your service at any moment day or night, Leonard and I,' Virginia wrote to Pernel Strachey (30 December 1931). On the whole visitors were not encouraged to come over since 'nothing more can be done in the way of human kindness', Carrington explained to Sebastian Sprott. But many found relief simply by driving to Hungerford. Saxon silently strolled in one day; Clive and Vanessa came over; Leonard and Virginia arrived: but Lytton was too ill to see them. Carrington and Ralph kept everyone informed by telephone and letter of each little improvement, every new emergency. 'I feel so relieved when each day is over,' Carrington confessed to Rosamond Lehmann.

The Bear Hotel at Hungerford had filled up with Lytton's sisters and brothers, 'all grey, all woollen, all red nosed, swollen eyed, quiet, exact',[56] battening down their family love as they pored over detective stories, played chess, finished crossword puzzles by the fire, and occasionally relieved their despair in bursts of cackling laughter or strident quarrelling as they waited for the doctors.

The burden of anxiety fell mainly on Ralph, Carrington, Pippa and James. Ralph attended to the electric light, the water supply, the fetching and carrying from Hungerford or Newbury. Carrington, who could only respond to the situation emotionally, was also, in a sense, a patient, and it was with her that Ralph felt he had to deal. Held by a terrifying dread, she would not stir beyond the garden, and avoided most callers. At nights, she hardly slept at all, or if she dozed off, woke every few minutes from nightmares and would listen to the owls hooting round the house or stand at the window gazing at the white frost. 'I feel nothing as bad can happen again,' she told Mary Hutchinson. By day she would sit at Lytton's bedside, sponging his face with scent and water and reading Jane Austen to him. Outside his room she pitched herself into the running of the house, the cooking, gardening, even painting. Weeds were pulled up, nettles flung on the bonfire. Enormous glass pictures emerged from her studio. For hours Ralph, who was none too controlled himself, continued talking to her, while the self-controlled Pippa took her place at Lytton's bedside.

It was Pippa whom Lytton probably liked to see most. As he sank deeper into his illness, his mind reverted, like Queen Victoria's, to scenes from his childhood, and these he was best able to communicate to his sister, who had nursed him through early illnesses. She had always adored Lytton, but never betrayed her grief. Her screeching laugh, too, seemed to cheer him. Once, when his temperature had reached 104°, Ralph entered the bedroom to find him weakly but coherently discussing with her the merits of McTaggart's philosophy. 'He remains reasonable, calm,' Virginia wrote to Ethel Smyth after hearing this story (4 January 1932), 'will even argue about truth and beauty and thus vindicates the race of scholars.'

James was also admirable in emergencies. Less alarmist than Ralph yet unexcelled by anyone except Carrington in his devotion to Lytton, he sat reading novels when there was nothing practical to be done. His pink unruffled presence, supported by Alix who was 'terrifyingly strong', reassured Carrington. 'James is such a truthful *exact* person,' she noted, 'that I believe everything he says and looks'.

On 9 December, the bacteriologist and physician-extraordinary to George V, Sir Maurice Cassidy – 'very grand specialist, bluff, 50, toothe-moustache', Carrington described him – took over the case. He was called in by Starkey Smith, who had been with him at medical school. After driving down from London, he examined Lytton with great thoroughness, concluded that he was suffering from ulcerative colitis – adding that his heart, lungs and pulse were all satisfactory – and carried off with him two samples of blood. His cheerful matter-of-fact manner inspired everyone with fresh confidence. The following night, his report came through via Starkey Smith: the samples had shown nothing. At various stages over the next week he examined six more blood cultures, but they too proved negative. Nevertheless, he felt convinced that Lytton was suffering from some sort of enteric fever. On 17 December, Ralph took him further samples to be analysed, but with the same result. By then Cassidy's optimism had begun to ebb. The state of affairs seemed more inexplicable and grave than at any other time. On the advice of Lionel Penrose, the family also consulted Leonard Dudgeon, professor of pathology at the University of London, who was a renowned diagnostician and 'the grandest pathologist in the world', Carrington told Sebastian Sprott. After a most elaborate examination, he confirmed the ulcerative colitis verdict. Throughout these weeks, this diagnosis was on the whole maintained, though at Christmas the possibility of paratyphoid was again admitted, and everyone in the house was instructed to be scrupulous over hygiene.

Meanwhile, Lytton continued to get steadily worse. The danger which Cassidy and the other doctors feared was the risk of perforation, which is constantly present in enteric fever. The worst of this condition was that it might go on for months. It had no curve and no crisis; the danger period might be almost as lengthy as the sickness itself. The critical stage gave little warning usually of its approach, Cassidy declared, and could occur at any time, day or night, regardless of temperature or pulse or any haemorrhages. An immediate emergency operation would then become essential. Plans for this operation had already been made. If Lytton were to collapse entirely and his temperature sink well below normal, Ralph was to telephone Starkey Smith, who had instructions to summon John Ryle, the surgeon at Guy's Hospital specializing in gastro-intestinal illnesses, to Ham Spray at once. The operation would then be performed in Lytton's bedroom. At some moment an injection of blood would be needed, not a transfusion, and Ralph was shown how to provide this. Since no anti-toxins were then known, nothing more could be done.

The house was submerged in ponderous gloom. Carrington and Ralph, Pippa and James were obliged to conduct an entirely defensive campaign. The continual strain reminded Ralph of the worst days of the war. 'I feel back in the trenches myself,' he told Frances (13 December 1931), 'there are the same orders for the day to carry out, telephone messages from headquarters, visits from the Colonel and Staff, N.C.O.'s to question and tell to carry on doing what they do infinitely better than ever you could, and at the back of one's mind the anxiety at night, the possibility of something unexpected and certain to be unpleasant being sprung upon one. I sleep as lightly as a feather. During the dark hours I breathe with only the top half of the lungs, and when I see daylight I take a deep breath and eat a hearty breakfast.'

It remained to be seen whether Lytton, with all his tenacity, could withstand the double strain of prolonged high fever and low diet. For a further week his constitution held out. 'All the doctors are amazed by his strength,' Virginia wrote, '. . . I always feel a toughness and sanity in Lytton, for all his look of weakness.'[57] He knew that a great deal depended upon his own efforts, and so long as there was hope of recovery he concentrated his will-power upon this objective. But each day his symptoms remained unaltered or grew worse, and his strength inevitably declined. He understood about the possibility of enteric fever from which his cousin, Sir Arthur Strachey, had died nursed by Pippa out in India, and the question of whether the struggle was worth continuing, of whether recovery was at all possible, must have occurred to him. 'If it's only keeping me alive a little longer don't,' he said. The crisis came, very alarmingly, on Christmas Eve. His condition sank swiftly and he appeared to be dying. Cassidy, Ryle and an anaesthetist were sent for from London, but everyone had by this time given up hope. Everyone except Carrington. 'I simply wouldn't believe that he could be defeated,' she said, 'and I still can't.'

Then, when it appeared almost impossible that he should do so, he rallied. The doctors now decided to administer injections of a new serum. Lytton was told that if he could maintain the fight a little longer, there was every hope of his fever subsiding. He did his best. Carrington had been shattered by his acceptance of death, moving around the house, numbed and desperate, scarcely recognizing people. But now she saw Lytton take up the fight once more. Miraculously, by the evening he had grown a little better, and over the next few dangerous days, though fearfully weak, he managed to hold his own.

It was an exquisite relief. Everyone was worn down after the weeks of misery, but inclined to be hopeful again. It appeared as if the Strachey constitution had triumphed and that forty-eight hours of improvement must mean something solid. At least Lytton was not sinking into unconsciousness again. 'Although the Stracheys and Stephen's may fight like cat and dog,' Virginia wrote reassuringly to Pernel Strachey, 'I cant help thinking we are of one flesh when it comes to a pinch.'

Feeling so close to him (after Leonard 'I don't suppose I care for anyone more than for Lytton,' she wrote. '... He's in all my past – my youth'), Virginia had sat in Monk's House with Leonard over Christmas Eve when they both believed Lytton to have already vanished from their lives, talking of the loss of friends, feeling a sense of age, speculating on their own deaths, suddenly bereft and crying together. But next day when Vanessa telephoned to tell them of the New Serum and the tea with milk and brandy Lytton was drinking, and then over the next week, as he slowly seemed to mend, their optimism rose irresistibly. 'Now again all one's sense of him flies out & expands & I begin to think of things to say to him,' Virginia wrote in her diary.

'... I am therefore freely imagining a future with my old serpent to talk to, to laugh at, to abuse. I shall read his book on Sh[akespeare]; I shall stay at Ham Spray; I shall tell him how L[eonard] & I sobbed on Christmas Eve ... we have lived through every grade of feeling – how strong, how deep – more than I guessed, though the cavern of horror is well known to me ... Lytton too, always reasonable, clear, giving his orders; & dying as he thought; & then as reasonably, finding some strength returning, deciding to live ... one has taken him back after those sepulchral days.'[58]

At the end of the year he was still maintaining this slight advantage, and having once escaped death so narrowly, his fight for life fired all his friends with hope. Describing the New Year celebrations at Ipsden, Rosamond Lehmann wrote to her brother John: 'That evening was the first for a week when the feeling of being in a bad dream lifted a bit – as we had just heard that a miracle had happened and Lytton pulled round after being given up by everybody. I now feel he will live, though the danger is still acute. The bottom would fall out of the world for us if Ham Spray were no more.'

'Lytton goes on, now better, now not so well,' Virginia noted in her diary on 13 January 1932, '... & now I say it is not the end.' Carrington too felt they had emerged from a dungeon. Although always in discomfort and sometimes in pain, Lytton lay, day after day, swallowing his 'vile black medicines' without a murmur. 'D'you know,' remarked Cassidy, 'I'd quite dote on that chap if I saw much of him.' Knowing the awful strain his illness was imposing upon the others, Lytton tried to lighten it by a wry cheerfulness and the kindly messages he sent everyone. He was too weak to speak much, but towards Carrington he was now careful to remain in good spirits, whenever possible greeting her with some joke. At night he had to be given sleeping draughts and these, he claimed, induced a whole series of amusing dreams. 'I've spent the whole night skipping,' he told her one morning, 'so curious. I didn't know I could skip. It was rather delightful.'

He thought about literature, not so much about people. He talked of Shelley's youth; and with deep satisfaction, he would recite lines of poetry:

Lorsque le grand Byron avait quitté Ravenne ...

It was the music of such lines, a river of sound, that soothed him. He also tried to compose poems of his own. 'But it's so difficult,' he sighed. 'Poetry is so very difficult.'

'Don't think about poetry,' Pippa advised him, 'it's too tiring. Think of nice simple solid things – think about teapots and chairs.'

'But I don't *know* anything about teapots and chairs.'

'Well,' replied Pippa, 'think of people playing croquet, moving quietly about on a summer lawn.'

Lytton seemed pleased. 'Ah yes, that's nice.' Then a pause. 'But I don't remember *any* reference to croquet in French literature.'

Once, in the early hours of the morning, when he was alone with one of the night-nurses, he began trying under his breath to compose a poem.

'Don't you weary yourself, Mr Strachey,' she commanded. *'I'll* write all the poetry that has to be written.'

There was a long silence. Then the nurse overheard two whispered words, incomprehensible to anyone not recognizing the slang of thirty years before: 'My hat!'

The poems of these last two months Lytton transcribed, very faintly in pencil, into a small exercise book.

> Let me not know the wherefore and the how.
>> No question let me ask, no answer find;
> I deeper taste the blessed here and now
>> Bereft of speculation, with eyes blind.
> What need to seek or see?
> It is enough to be.

> In absolute quiescence let me rest,
>> From all the world, from mine own self, apart;
> I closer hold the illimitable best,
>> Still as the final silence, with calm heart.
> What need to strive or move?
> It is enough to love.

Love was his religion, and he could only accept a god who would sanctify those loves, so singular, so plural, which had formed the most enduring passions of his life. Another of these poems, cast in the traditional form of a prayer, is really a hymn to sexual passion addressed to an officially unknown god:

> Lord, in Thy strength and sweetness,
>> Be ever by my side
> Close as the foot to fleetness
>> The bridegroom and the bride.

> Through sickness and through sadness
>> Still let me see Thy face;
> Bestow upon my gladness
>> Thy consummating grace;

> Fill with a golden clearness

My crowded hours of light;
And hallow with Thy nearness
My most abandoned night!

The satirical last line springs unexpectedly upon the Christian God of married love. Yet his disbelief is swept back by the emotional intensity in these poems, especially in the last one of all with its final *double entendre*:

Insensibly I turn, I glide
A little nearer to Thy side . . .
At last! Ah, Lord, the joy, the peace,
The triumph and the sweet release,
When, after all the wandering pain,
The separation, long and vain,
Into the field, the sea, the sun,
Thy culminating hands, I come!

The days passed: his condition remained the same. While he lay motionless in his bedroom, willing himself to live a little longer, a little longer, letters from his friends poured in, and these were read out to him by Pippa and Carrington. The last one which he was able to read for himself was from Virginia to Carrington. Ham Spray, she wrote (18 January 1932), was really 'the loveliest place in England . . . I want very much to come again.' To Vita Sackville-West she had written: 'I should mind it to the end of my days if he died.'

'There seems no end to this illness,' Ralph wrote to Gerald Brenan. By the second week of January, another celebrated specialist was called in on the recommendation of Ottoline. This was Sir Arthur Hurst, 'a weird little man', Carrington told the Guinnesses. 'I feel great confidence in his queer excited manner, and he looks extremely intelligent.' Hurst, who inclined to Cassidy and Dudgeon's original diagnosis though admitting the possibility of paratyphoid, recommended certain variations in Lytton's treatment, and said he had seen similar cases recover. But by now Lytton had shrunk to such a shadow of himself that to those who were visiting him for the first time since November and who saw the extraordinary fragility of his appearance, it seemed scarcely possible that he could ever get well again.

Three days later, his condition began to deteriorate once more. By this stage no one knew what to believe. Following the various symptoms, hour by hour, they lived on an endless switchback of hope and despair. One new anxiety had been added to the previous ones. Ralph discovered from one of Carrington's letters torn up in a waste-paper basket and written during the earlier crisis in Lytton's condition, that should he die, she meant to commit suicide. Ralph had no doubt that she was set on this course, and if allowed to, would kill herself. Who, that knew her, could doubt the violence of her desires or, in spite of all obstacles, her determination to carry them out? Ralph felt certain, however, that she would choose certain ways of suicide and reject others – those, for example, which were disfiguring. James openly accused her of planning suicide, and she denied it. But her denial meant nothing. They secretly searched her studio, that studio which 'is a mirror of my existence on earth. Untidy, disorganized and incomplete', and took away a medicine that was poisonous.

On the afternoon of Wednesday, 20 January, while Carrington was bathing his face, Lytton whispered: 'Carrington, why isn't she here? I want her. Darling Carrington. I love her. I always wanted to marry Carrington, and I never did.' It was not true; but he could not have said anything more deeply consoling. Afterwards she remembered 'it was happiness to know he secretly had loved me so much and told me before he died.'

Later he fell asleep for an hour, his mouth open, and she watched him, as she had done so often, with terror in her heart, thinking that if he died, she could not live. At a quarter to three, she observed a change in his face. 'I suddenly noticed his breathing was different although he did not wake up. And I thought of the Goya painting of a dead man with the high light on the cheek bones.' She ran out and called nurse McCabe who asked her to telephone Dr Starkey Smith and find out how much strychnine Lytton might be given. After telephoning, Carrington rushed back and held his arm while the nurse injected the prescribed dose. Presently his breathing deepened, and Carrington ran off to tell James and Pippa. When Lytton regained consciousness, Pippa told him that the doctor would soon be calling again. 'I shall be delighted to see him,' he said weakly. 'But I'm afraid I shan't be able to do much socially.'

That afternoon, for the first time, Carrington gave up hope. 'It became clear to me that he could not live,' she scrawled in HER BOOK. Dr Starkey Smith arrived and gave Lytton another injection. 'I saw from his face he had no hope,' Carrington noted. 'He slept without any discomfort or pain. A hatred for nurse Phillips came on me. I cannot remember now anything except watching Lytton's pale face, and his close shut eyes lying on the pillows and Pippa standing by his bed.'

At four o'clock, Ralph returned from a late picnic with Gerald Brenan, who was now living in a tiny thatched cottage at East Lulworth with the poet Gamel Woolsey. Carrington had invited Gerald over to tea, saying she particularly wished to see him. Hardly were the two men at the door when James came out. There had been a fresh crisis, he told them, and Lytton was sinking fast. Ralph hurried in, and Gerald drove to the post office to send off telegrams, since James did not want to use the telephone in the house for fear of being overheard by Carrington. Then he motored back, went in, and sat waiting in the drawing-room. Presently he heard Carrington's low and musical voice, more exquisitely modulated, more caressing than ever. He did not feel able to look at her, but she came up behind him and took his hand.

It had been decided, in the event of a crisis occurring, to send for another of Carrington's lovers, Stephen Tomlin. This was Ralph's idea; he wanted to mobilize anyone who might help to ensure her safety. They had got in touch with him and he was standing by. While Tommy was in the house, it was felt, Carrington would not attempt to take her own life. It was a cruel but clever expedient, for its success depended upon Tommy being so unbalanced and neurotic, so prone himself to suicide, shattered by his brother Garrow having been killed flying only the previous month, by the failure of his marriage to Julia Strachey and by all the supports in his life tottering, that Carrington's sense of responsibility would be aroused, and she would pull herself together to attend to him. Tommy's principal relations with other people contained a strong element of dependence. Lytton was not merely one of his closest friends; he relied, in some almost filial way, upon his existence. In the event of Lytton's death, Carrington would have to control herself and Tommy.

'Be nice to Gerald, he has been of great help,' Ralph told Frances. Stephen Tomlin having been sent for, Gerald drove off to Hungerford station in Ralph's car to meet him. 'He stepped out of the train looking more than usually undecided and pale and we set off in silence for Ham Spray,' Gerald recorded in his diary. 'But D.C., though apparently glad to see him, would not hear of him staying there and declared she could not understand why he had come.' So the two of them went back to the Bear Inn at Hungerford, where they sat up late, talking. 'When at last we went upstairs to bed, he asked if he might sleep in my room, since he could not face the idea of sleeping alone,' Gerald wrote. 'I consented and then, instead of lying down in the other bed, to my embarrassment he got into mine and like a child that is afraid of the dark and cannot bear to be separated from others, burst into tears. It was impossible not to be touched by his misery and I regretted that I was not a young woman so as to be able to console him more effectively.'

At Ham Spray that night special watches were arranged by Lytton's bedside. Pippa was to remain there till midnight; Carrington would replace her until three o'clock; Ralph would then relieve Carrington and carry on for the next three hours, until James took over for the last three. At three o'clock Carrington passed James on the landing on her way to Lytton's bedroom. Neither of them had slept. During the early part of her vigil, Carrington had asked nurse Mooney whether there was any chance of Lytton living. She seemed surprised at the idea. 'Oh no – I don't think so now,' she replied. Carrington leant over the bed and gave Lytton a kiss on his forehead: it was damp and cold. Ralph, also unable to sleep, came in with a cup of tea, and sat down by the fire. Carrington went over and kissed him too, said she was going to her bedroom and asked him not to wake her, since after weeks of her 'non-sleeping disease', she was exhausted. James, she noticed, had gone downstairs to the front room. She walked quickly along the passage and down the back stairs.

It was half-past three. The house was very quiet, and outside the moon shone in the yard through the elm trees and across the barns. She walked over to the garage. The door was stuck fast open, and she could hardly move it. Every jerk seemed to shriek through the night air. At last she scraped both doors closed. She got into the car, and accidentally touched the horn. 'My heart stood still, for I felt R[alph] must have heard as the landing window was open. I stood in the yard watching for a light to go on in the passages. After some time I crept back again, & made every preparation all ready that I could start up the car directly the milking engine started in the Farm yard.'

Then she waited, feeling very cold in her dressing-gown. Outside, there was not a sound. Her plan was to stay there until half-past four, at which time every morning the farmers started up the milking-machine, the noise of which would drown the car engine. Half-past four came by the car clock, and still nothing happened. Then she remembered it ran ten minutes fast. She went outside again and continued to wait. At half-past five she suddenly heard sounds from across the yard, and movements in the milking-shed. She ran back to the garage, shut the door, and a few moments after the milking-machine had started up, switched on the car engine.

'I was terrified by the noise . . . There seemed no smell. I got over in the back of the car & lay down, & listened to the thud of the engine below me & the noise of the milking machine puffing away outside. At last I smelt it was beginning to get rather thick. I turned on the light in the side of the car & looked at the clock only 10 mins had gone. However Ralph would probably not come exactly at 6 ock. The windows of the car looked foggy & a bit misty. I turned out the light again, & lay down. Gradually I felt rather sleepy, and then the buzzing noise grew fainter, & further off.

Rather like fainting I remember thinking . . . I thought of Lytton, & was glad to think I shouldn't know anymore. Then I remembered a sort of dream which faded away . . .'

Shortly before six o'clock there was another crisis in Lytton's condition. Thinking that he must be dying, they sent for Carrington, and not finding her in her bedroom, they searched the house. Going out to the garage, Ralph saw her lying behind the exhaust pipe of the car, the engine still running. She was unconscious. He carried her up to her room and immediately summoned Dr Starkey Smith. Had he found her ten minutes later, she would have been dead.

The doctor gave her an injection. There was a terrible buzzing in her ears, she woke up, saw Dr Starkey Smith still holding her arm with the syringe, and cried: 'No! No! Go away!' pushing his hand off until he seemed to vanish 'like the cheshire cat'. Then she looked up and saw her bedroom window. It was daylight. 'I felt *angry* at being back after being in a very happy dream. Sorry to be awake again . . . something wrong with my eyes. I couldn't see my hands or focus on anything.' Ralph was there. He held her in his arms, and kissed her, and asked: 'How could you do it?' It had never occurred to him that she would attempt anything with Lytton still alive. She would wish, he thought, at all costs to be there at the last moment, and that was why, when Lytton was on the point of death, he had gone to look for her.

She had promised him not to try anything. But she must have been aware that, the moment Lytton died, she would be closely guarded, and that Stephen Tomlin, waiting a few miles away with Gerald Brenan, would be brought into the house. By some obscure train of feeling, she had hoped, through the offer of her own life, to rescue Lytton's. 'It is ironical', she scribbled in HER BOOK, 'that Lytton by that early attack at 6 'ock saved my life, when I gave my life for his, he should give it back.'

But Lytton was not dead. Although everyone had tried to keep from him the gravity of his illness, he was not deceived. He accepted the idea of extinction with a quizzical humour, very typical of him. 'If this is dying,' he remarked quietly, 'then I don't think much of it.'

Early that morning, Stephen Tomlin was urgently called to the house. Other friends and relatives arrived, their cars crunching backwards and forwards on the gravel. The fine frosty weather that had gone on without a break since Christmas still lasted. It was intensely still – the sort of weather Lytton had always loved. A soft mist lay over the meadows and hung in the elm trees. The sunlight, sprinkling through their branches, spreading across the lawn, seemed to linger and delay, before touching the walls of the house, and streaming through the windows. The nurses popped in and out, arranging things. The others, strained, silent, seemed held in surreal immobility. It was impossible for them while they waited not to contrast this beauty with Lytton dying, or to wonder what result might follow for the three, bound together in precarious equilibrium, whom he left behind.

In London they were coming back from a Bloomsbury fancy-dress party, a tightness round their lips, a sense of something spent. 'One misses people more and more,' Duncan said. It was the stupidity of death that Virginia thought intolerable. Vanessa had asked what they would have liked if one of them were dying, and they all agreed that the party should go on. 'It is like having the globe of the future perpetually smashed – without Lytton,' Virginia wrote, '– & then, behold, it fills again.'

Carrington lay that morning in her four-poster bed. Ralph took Frances up to see her 'still very white, but with the hectic colour in her cheeks that comes from inhaling gas'. They kissed and Frances felt 'the thick softness of her hair against my cheek'. At midday she got up and went into Lytton's room. He was still sleeping, breathing deeply and fast. Pippa sat near his bed. 'I went up and sat in a chair, and watched him,' Carrington wrote. '"So this is death" I kept on saying to myself.' She was witnessing and recording what she had longed to escape. Two nurses moved about behind the screen. Ralph came, and sat on the floor.

'I felt completely calm,' she wrote. 'His face was very pale like ivory. Everything seemed to be transfixed. The pale face of nurse MacCabe standing by his bed in her white clothes, Pippa watching with those sweet brown eyes all tear stained and her face mottled. The noise of the electric light machine outside. I sat there thinking of all the other mornings in Lytton's room and there was "Pride and Prejudice", that I had been reading the afternoon before still on the table – It seemed as if time had lost all its properties, as if everything was marked by Lytton's [heart] beating . . . Suddenly I felt very sick and ran out to my bedroom and was violently sick into the chamber pot . . . I went back to Lytton's room, and sat on the chair. About 2 o'clock or 1.30 Lytton grew worse and his breathing became shorter. I stood holding Pippa round the waist. Lytton never opened his eyes. I could not cry . . . James came in and stood behind us with Ralph . . . Nurse Philipps suddenly came forwards and said: "I think you ladies had better go and sit down, you can do no good here." I was furious and hated her . . . A blackbird sung outside in the sun on the aspen. We stood there . . . Sometimes his breathing almost stopped. But then he breathed again fainter. Suddenly he breathed no more and nurse MacC. put her hand on his heart under the clothes and felt it. I looked at his face it was pale as ivory. I went forward and kissed his eyes, and his forehead. They were cold.'

EPILOGUE

'Talk of Carrington: how long shall we talk of Carrington?'
Virginia Woolf *Diary* 18 March 1932

A post-mortem, carried out at James's insistence on the afternoon Lytton died, revealed that a cancerous growth had formed in the stomach, completely blocking the intestine and actually making a perforation (through which food must have been passing) into the colon. All the doctors had been wrong.

Ralph explained to Carrington that Lytton could never have lived. 'It makes a difference,' she wrote in HER BOOK. His body was left for a day lying on the bed, the lines of fatigue and infirmity frozen deeply into his face. Carrington went in and out. 'The room looked so lonely. The fire had gone out, and everything had been removed,' she wrote. Ralph gave her some bay leaves and she made them into a wreath, trying it on her own head ('it was a little large') then putting it round Lytton's. 'He looked so beautiful. The olive green against the ivory skin. I kissed his eyes, and his ice cold lips.'

Next day they took her in the car to Savernake. She had always loved the forest but its familiar beauty now stirred her pain. 'She got out of the car and took a few steps, walking like a weak invalid,' Frances noticed. She could think only of Lytton, his pale face with its green leaves against the pillow. 'I knew while we were away men would come with the coffin and take Lytton away,' she wrote. 'That was what I could not bear.'

The body was removed for cremation at Golders Green,* and a bronze plate commemorating him was later placed in the Strachey Chapel, at the church of St Andrew, Chew Magna, in Somerset.

James and Pippa left for London, Frances took Ralph for two quiet days to stay with Rosamond and Wogan in Wales, while Stephen Tomlin

---

* Apart from functionaries, the only people present at the cremation were James Strachey and Saxon Sydney-Turner, who insisted on coming. 'There was, of course, no ceremonial of any kind,' James reassured the author. But Maynard Keynes thought James had carried unconvention too far. 'No service, no farewell,' he said to Virginia Woolf, '. . . with Lytton there was no mark to say This is over.' Virginia, too, felt unsatisfied. 'He has no funeral, I don't know where his ashes are buried,' she wrote in her diary (4 February 1932). 'There is no commemoration any more, except when we meet & talk; or in the usual ways, alone at night, walking along the streets . . . The solid statue that father left – that exists no longer.'

moved into Ham Spray to look after Carrington. 'They kept her going for the time,' Ralph wrote to Gerald on his return (30 January 1932), 'but she is still terribly low in spirits and in health.' For some days, she stayed in bed, but even with the strongest sleeping draughts she scarcely slept. The nights which never seemed to end, and the days which ended all too soon, prostrated her with headaches and nightmares. Each morning she felt as if Lytton had died again: and each day his loss was harder to bear. 'I am not facing things,' she admitted to Rosamond Lehmann, 'I can't for a bit . . . I find it difficult to go on with ordinary life, and I almost hate anybody else who can, although I know it's unreasonable to expect the world to stand still.'

'I hope when I die I shan't leave such cruel gaps in other people's lives,' Ralph wrote to Frances (15 February 1932). Like a warder he kept watch on Carrington, understanding her feelings better than anyone, sharing some of them. She appeared to be recovering, leaving her room, going into the garden. But he remained worried. 'She's doing too much clearing and tidying, particularly of the corner of the shrubbery by the ilex,' he wrote to Frances. She was hoping to bury Lytton's ashes there among the daffodils and snowdrops. But was she also planning to have her own ashes buried there? 'The truth is that it is practically impossible to discover D.C.'s intentions,' Ralph admitted.

'So the days passed in a state of acute anxiety,' Frances recorded. All Ralph could do was to arrange events and marshal friends so as to re-engage Carrington in the process of living. But he took it for granted that she would again try to kill herself. It was rare, 'outside Elizabethan plays, for a situation to be so clear cut', he told Frances. 'If I left a loaded revolver or an ounce of opium on the table and went for a long walk there is little doubt what I should find on my return.'

Of all the friends he invited to Ham Spray it was Stephen Tomlin who appeared most successful in halting her from making another attempt at suicide. 'He persuaded me that after a serious operation or fever, a man's mind would not be in a good state to decide on such an important step,' she wrote in HER BOOK. 'I agreed – So I will defer my decision for a month or two until the result of the operation is less acute.' He had not really altered her mind but 'you made this last week bearable which nobody else could have done,' she wrote to him towards the end of January. 'Those endless conversations were not quite pointless.'

With Stephen Tomlin, also, she liked reading some of the poetry she and Lytton had shared, especially from an Elizabethan anthology he had given her. One short poem in this volume, 'Misery' by Thomas Howell, she had heavily marked, turning down the page on which it was printed.

Corpse, clad with carefulness:
Heart, heaped with heaviness:
Purse, poor and penniless:
Back, bare in bitterness:
O get my grave in readiness,
Fain would I die to end this stress.

On the second day after Lytton's death, she had asked to see Gerald. 'I had been somewhat dreading this,' he wrote, 'for – besides the pain of seeing her in such distress – I guessed beforehand that our past estrangement, present uneasy terms and above all the fact that in the past it was Lytton who had really come between us, must at present make any real communication impossible . . .

'I sat in the chair by her bed: and she began to question me about my life, about our cottage, about Gamel [Woolsey]; her tone was not unkind nor even insincere, but so remote, indicating such a gulf between us, that it was clear that no natural form of conversation was possible. I asked her about her plans – she answered vaguely. It seemed to me that she was cut off not merely from myself but from everyone, and that for the time being neither sympathy nor pity were acceptable.'

Into the pages of HER BOOK she poured out her emotions, not to unburden herself, but to set them down so that she should never forget the very least of them. They read like a long unanswered letter. 'Oh darling Lytton you are dead, and I can tell you nothing.' She could not care about anything, could not think of anything except the living past.

'I was never in all these 16 years happy [when] I was without him . . . He was, and this is why he was everything to me, the only person to whom I never needed to lie, because he never expected me to be anything different to what I was, and he was never curious if I did not tell him things . . . No one will ever know the utter happiness of our life together. The absurd and fantastic jokes at meals, and on our walks, and over our friends and his marvellous descriptions of all the parties in London and his love affairs and then all his thoughts he shared with me.'

Pain was her only link with Lytton, and she could not bear the thought that she might get over her pain. To this affliction was added remorse imposed upon herself as a punishment for having (as she thought of it) neglected him over the last year or two for Beacus Penrose. Yet even had there been no Beacus, there must necessarily have been unmerited guilt, since guilt was threaded into her personality. Had she not felt a premonition that Lytton might die after writing her parody death-scene for *The Week-End Observer*? She blamed herself, less for particular acts, than for secret thoughts; for moments of depression or bitterness, and hours spent needlessly away from him.

On all these accounts, it appeared doubtful whether she could be persuaded to continue living. Ralph hoped that, if she could be got through a few months, she might unthinkingly attach herself to life. But he knew that the foundation was gone, and that for years to come there would be moments of depression when she might easily decide to end it. For the moment he thought it essential that she should not be left at Ham Spray by herself. When Gerald left, Julia Strachey came down, and the compassionate supervision of her life went on.

Up in her bedroom Carrington was scribbling innumerable letters in a quivering hand to Barbara Bagenal, Mark Gertler, Diana Guinness, Rosamond Lehmann, Roger Senhouse, Mary Hutchinson, Dorelia John and others and, until rebuked by James, sending them Lytton's possessions as keepsakes. In return they could give her only limited help. 'I write in an empty book. I cry in an empty room.'

There were many rumours around Bloomsbury. It was said that Lytton had left Carrington no money; that Ralph was abandoning Frances; that Frances was somehow to blame for the unresolved problems. People needed to be reminded that Lytton had left Carrington £10,000 together with his pictures and natural history books. But to Ralph's alarm she told him that she was making a will leaving this money to him and that she wished him and Frances to have a child.

Some people were urging Carrington to sell Ham Spray and make a fresh start. They did not understand that to her mind this would be like another death. To Ralph it looked as if these rooms would 'never recover from Lytton'. But Carrington already minded terribly the changes that were taking place. 'All your papers have been taken away,' she wrote in HER BOOK (16 February 1932). 'Your clothes have gone. Your room is bare. In a few months no traces will be left.'

Ham Spray actually belonged to Ralph, but he made it clear that what happened to the house depended on Carrington's needs. A little later, perhaps in the summer, Frances and he might move somewhere else. 'The answer will be in D.C.'s hands,' he told Gerald (8 March 1932). In the meantime 'I *must* stay here with her if I can,' he insisted in a letter to Frances (11 February 1932), 'and I *must* assert that you and I are not all-sufficient to each other or all is lost.' It was melancholy work. He knew that any pretence at consolation was really a fraud. Her relationship with Lytton had been unique and she could not bear the loneliness without him. As she had said, he was the only person to whom she had 'no need to lie'. With the rest, lying was common currency. 'The truth is negligible now,' Ralph explained to Frances: 'it is silly to kill her by inability to tell a lie.'

After the first ten days, Frances spent most of her time in London. 'I can't help being terribly anxious about you,' she wrote to Ralph. She was prepared to do whatever he felt was best, but privately thought that Carrington would have preferred her to be there. For it was obvious that Ralph's grief, on top of her own, was almost too much for Carrington to bear. 'No death', he had written to Charles Prentice after Lytton's cremation (11 February 1932), 'has ever hurt me more than his.' Too often, he now realized, he had let his irritation make him behave unsympathetically to Carrington. Now he was prepared to give up his entire time to her. He considered himself to be married to Frances in all but name, yet cared for Carrington 'in a way I've never cared for anybody', he confided to Rosamond Lehmann (March 1932), 'and know I could never care again. She was an obsession to me – once she got into anybody's blood she was ineradicable.'

'He has been so kind to me,' Carrington told Rosamond, 'but I feel we only make it harder for each other in some ways.' She longed to be alone, to get relief from her pain by shutting herself in Lytton's library reading his letters, or simply wandering round the garden. 'But everyone seems to be my enemy,' she complained to Sebastian Sprott, 'and insists on treating me like an imbecile invalid.' With Ralph guarding her, and his watchfulness acting as a continual reproach, she had to behave sensibly when all she wanted was to 'enmesh myself in his [Lytton's] relics . . . If I could sit here alone just holding his clothes in my arms on the sofa with that handkerchief over my face I feel I would get comfort, but I know these things are bad.'

It was for this reason that she had asked Frances to take Ralph away somewhere. There was nothing that Frances would have liked better. But she knew Ralph believed that this was another example of Carrington's slyness. 'She declares that she wants solitude but I find that unbelievable,' he wrote, '. . . everyone but me finds her so plausible.' Even Frances, he saw, agreed with what he said only because she loved him.

The people who did not jar on Carrington during these weeks were Dorelia, Tommy and Julia. After the departure of Gerald, and in Frances's absence, it was imperative that the Tomlins – or Stephen Tomlin alone – should remain in the house. Ralph was the person to arrange this, but he was coming to resent the superior power of persuasion that Carrington's former lover was exercising over her. His old exasperation broke out, and Carrington could not resist, even at this time of abject misery, playing on the bad feeling between the two of them. 'We never spoke to each other after dinner,' Ralph wrote to Frances from Ham Spray (22 February 1932). 'Quite like old times.' A little later Tommy returned with Julia to London.

Any crisis that might have followed their departure was postponed by an invitation from Dorelia John, asking Carrington to spend some days at Fryern Court, so allowing Ralph to join Frances for a few days' convalescence in London.

Of all the 'consolers and substitutes' for Lytton, Dorelia was one of the most helpful. Carrington still thought of her as 'the most beautiful perfect woman in the world'. But she went through her week at Fryern as if it was a dream. Beacus visited her there, but she showed no feeling for him.

'By not allowing myself to think of the reality of the situation I can bear life. But then it is not life. It is a contradiction. I pretend to myself this week at Fryern that I am on holiday. I avoid allowing my thoughts to even approach Lytton. If for a moment they break through my fences I at once feel so utterly miserable that it is only by thinking there will be only a few more weeks, I can bear the pain. That there's nobody any longer to serve and love completely and entirely makes everything pointless.'

It had been planned that Dorelia should come back to Ham Spray, taking the Tomlins' place there for a time. But Augustus John fell ill and she had to cancel this visit. However, she arranged with Carrington that they should all three go off on a holiday to France in the middle of March.

On her return from Fryern Court, Carrington seemed rather better. She was, it appeared, pulling herself together. 'Do tempt her up to London,' Frances urged Ralph. She came, spent all her time with James and Alix, Julia and Tommy, and showed further signs of improvement. Ralph also left her alone one day at Ham Spray. He still felt anxious about her, 'yet I am practically helpless', he told Gerald. In the garden at Ham Spray she made a bonfire, dropping on to it a miscellaneous collection of Lytton's belongings, his clothes, pyjamas, and finally his spectacles – without which no one ever saw him – and watching them vanish in the curling smoke. Her activity in tidying the house, arranging books and papers, reassured everyone except Ralph. Desmond MacCarthy came down to see her, and tried to interest her in the publication of Lytton's unpublished essays and letters; and this, though premature, was a good plan. She started to read through his writings, and to connect Lytton's memory with the future. There were masses of poems and unfinished plays, but James, who was the literary executor, thought they were not very good. There were also many boxes of letters. But Lytton wrote so provocatively about everyone. How could they be published? Probably a volume of essays was the best that could be managed, though James wanted Virginia to write something.

Five weeks had now passed since Lytton's death, and the period of immunity Carrington had promised Stephen Tomlin was almost at an end. Still nothing held her interest. For she had no desire to be in a world where she could never see Lytton, where *he did not exist*. How could she recover from this deprivation? She did not want to recover. She wanted to drown her anguish in unconsciousness. 'Really I have decided,' she wrote in HER BOOK. She could not live on memories, but must 'get through these days, and pray there won't be very many more'. Alix had argued that she must live up to those standards in which Lytton believed. But she had only tried to maintain these standards to please him.

'Every hour some habit we had together comes back and I miss you,' she wrote to him in HER BOOK, ' – at night I dream of you in the day you are with me. I read over and over again our favourite poems but there is no one to talk about their beauty now. No use now devising surprises to please you. You were more dear to me every year – What is the use of "adventures" now without you to tell them to? . . . there is no sense in a life without you.' Lytton had been 'more completely all my life than it is possible for any person to be'. Virginia had sometimes disliked Lytton for absorbing her so totally. But as Carrington makes clear, he had tried to guard against this danger. 'Our separations were for me enforced,' she wrote. 'I was never in all these 16 years happy [when] I was without him. It was only I knew he disliked me to be dependent that I forced myself to make other attachments.'

From her Elizabethan anthology she cut out two of the stanzas which Chidiock Tichborne[1] had written in the Tower of London before his execution, and pasted them into HER BOOK:

> My prime of youth is but a frost of cares;
>   My feast of joy is but a dish of pain;
> My crop of corn is but a field of tares;
>   And all my good is but vain hope of gain;
> My life is fled, and yet I saw no sun;
> And now I live, and now my life is done.
>
> The spring is past, and yet it has not sprung;

The fruit is dead, and yet the leaves be green;
My youth is gone, and yet I am but young;
I saw the world, and yet I was not seen;
My thread is cut, and yet it is not spun;
And now I live, and now my life is done.*

The last entry in HER BOOK was two lines from another Elizabethan poem, 'Upon the Death of Sir Albert Moreton's Wife', by Sir Henry Wotton:

He first deceased, she for a little tried
To live without him, liked it NOT, and died

On the last day of February, Carrington and Ralph, Frances and Bunny, went over to the Guinnesses at Biddesden. 'I love my visits to Biddesden, and those gallops, even if they do end by falling off,' she wrote to Bryan Guinness. While there her horse had bolted, tearing along the tarred road and, swerving round a corner, throwing her on to a bank next to a pile of logs. The irony of so narrowly missing accidental death while passionately longing for death stayed with her. Afterwards, during a picnic in the woods, she asked if she might borrow a gun from Biddesden to shoot the rabbits that were destroying her Ham Spray garden. 'We all heard the request,' Frances remembered, 'but it was rather vaguely given, and I think everyone hoped it would be as vaguely forgotten.' For six weeks, in an agony of mind, Ralph had been plotting and devising schemes to fasten her to life. A week later, Carrington demanded that she be left alone at Ham Spray. Ralph remonstrated with her, begged her to let him stay by her side. But she insisted. In any case, she reminded him, she would be off with the Johns in a few days.

Ralph still felt that Carrington had something up her sleeve. 'I have, however, reached the point where I must cease to interfere with her any more,' he explained to Gerald (8 March 1932). 'When she tells me to go away I must go, or my staying becomes unpleasant for both of us. But it leaves me like a lost soul, fluttering outside her life, afraid to venture in

* There is a third stanza in addition to the two which Carrington pasted in:
I sought my death and found it in my womb,
I look'd for life and saw it was a shade,
I trod the earth and knew it was my tomb.
And now I die, and now I was but made;
My glass is full, and now my glass is run
And now I live, and now my life is done.

and afraid to fly away further – and this must go on until her life takes on some shape and consistency of its own.' At some level, too, he must have longed for almost any conclusion to these weeks of torment.

So he left, and Carrington was again alone in Ham Spray. She had apparently not taken a gun from Biddesden after the picnic. 'It was very much more in character for her to come back in secret for it later,' Frances wrote.[2] Afterwards there would be disputes as to how she got a gun, but Frances maintained she went back to Biddesden for it.

On Thursday 10 March, Leonard and Virginia Woolf came down to see her. 'I've been mistaken about Virginia,' Ralph wrote to Gerald; 'somewhere she keeps a warm heart.' When Lytton died, both the Visigoths (as he had called them) remembered their brother Thoby's death – how helpful Lytton had been, how unhappy he often was in those days before he met Carrington – and they understood her unhappiness now. 'One cannot think of Lytton without thinking of you,' Vanessa wrote to her (25 January 1932), 'and with all one's sorrow there is mixed the feeling of gratitude to you for having given him so much happiness . . . It is owing to you that there is nothing to regret in the past and his friends would love you for that if for nothing else. Darling creature, come before very long and talk to us . . .'

Virginia too had blessed Carrington for what she had given Lytton. 'I hope you dont mind my writing to you sometimes – it is such a comfort because there is nobody to talk to about Lytton who knew him as you did,' she wrote (31 January 1932). '. . . One hates so the feeling that things begin again in London without him . . . I always put away things in my mind to say to Lytton. And what it must be like for you . . . I could never give him what you did . . . I'll write about him some day, but it must be for you only.'

These letters were among the few that were of use to Carrington. Virginia, too, was finding Lytton's absence harder, not easier, to bear and, unlike Leonard who felt that killing herself would be 'histrionic', found suicide 'quite reasonable' – though of course it was better to 'wait until the first shock is over & see'.[3] In the meantime she wrote encouraging Carrington to go on living for the sake of Lytton's closest friends (2 March 1932):

'Oh but Carrington we have to live and be ourselves – and I feel it is more for you to live than for any one; because he loved you so, and loved your oddities and the way you have of being yourself. I cant explain it; but it seems to me that as long as you are there, something we loved in Lytton, something of the best part of his life still goes on.'

The day was sparkling when the Woolfs arrived at Ham Spray, but the interior of the house felt cold. 'We talked with effort,' Virginia remembered. They asked Carrington if she would do woodcuts for their writing paper like those she had done for Ham Spray, and also designs for Julia's first novel *Cheerful Weather for the Wedding*. They tried to gossip, and Carrington 'laughed once or twice'. But she was still very pale, Virginia noticed. The two women went upstairs and stood looking out at the great shapes of the Downs in the sunlight. Carrington explained that she wanted to keep Lytton's rooms exactly as they had been, but that the Stracheys had criticized her for being morbid. She seemed frightened of doing wrong, 'like a child that had been scolded'.

She had written to Roger Senhouse assuring him that 'Lytton loved you so much always, and talked so often to me of all the happiness he had with you. You altered his life more than anyone.' But to Virginia she now spoke of her anger with Lytton's silly young men because they did not value him properly. Of course Roger would have to take the books, but 'Lytton loved his old friends best,' she reminded Virginia.

They went round the rest of the house, looking at the pictures by Duncan, Augustus John, Henry Lamb and others, at Lytton's four-poster bed, the Anrep mosaic chimney-breast. Then, in the sitting-room, Carrington suddenly burst into tears. 'There is nothing left for me to do.' It was true, Virginia thought, as she took Carrington in her arms. But she said that she too sometimes felt useless, sometimes hopeless, when she woke in the night and thought of Lytton. 'I held her hands,' Virginia remembered. 'Her wrists seemed very small. She seemed helpless, deserted, like some small animal left.'

But when the Woolfs rose to go she was very quiet and did not ask them to stay. They went down into the front of the house and Carrington kissed Virginia several times.

'Then you will come & see us next week – or not – just as you like?' Virginia asked.

'Yes, I will come, or not,'[3] Carrington replied.

Next morning she woke – as she always did now – very early, made herself a cup of tea and ate an apple. When the post came, she opened her letters and looked at *The Times*, which was later found crumpled up in her cupboard. Then she put on Lytton's yellow silk dressing-gown, which no one had known her to wear before, and took up the gun. It was nearly eight o'clock. At the window she saw, walking on the lawn below, two partridges – it would have been like her to find a joke in shooting not one of them, but herself.

She had thought out her preparations carefully. First she removed her favourite rug so that it should not be splattered by the blood, and laid down an inferior rug in its place in such a way that it might appear that she slipped on it. Next she turned and stood with her back to the window, facing a tall mirror in which she could see her position. Then she placed the butt of the gun on the floor and the barrel against her side. Finally she pulled the trigger.

Nothing happened.

She had forgotten to release the safety catch. Now she did so, but this must have put her aim out, for when she pulled the trigger a second time the shot, though taking away part of her side, missed her heart.

The gardener heard a noise, and coming under her window, caught what he thought was the sound of groans. He hurried to the foot of the stairs and she called out to him, saying that she had slipped on the mat and asking him to fetch the woman who lived in the lodge at the end of the drive, and to summon the doctor. When the woman came, she repeated to her the same story and told her to telephone Ralph. To Dr Starkey Smith, she again said the same thing, and, since she was in acute pain, he injected morphia. He seemed upset – he had known her for several years – so she sent him down to get the key of the cellar and help himself to a drink. She also apologized for giving so much trouble. Although he could not examine her properly for fear of increasing the flow of blood, he saw that she was probably too seriously injured to recover.

Ralph had been to a party the night before, slept late in his rooms at Great James Street, and was awakened by the telephone message. David Garnett, who was sleeping upstairs at the Nonesuch office, luckily had his car, and drove him and Frances down at breakneck speed. They arrived about 11 o'clock with a trained nurse and found Carrington lying on the rug in her bedroom where she had fallen, still conscious and, in spite of the morphia, in pain. She told them that she hated life, that she wished to die, but even this she had bungled. Then on seeing how awful Ralph looked, she changed her story, claiming that it had all been an accident, and promising him that she would for his sake try to live.

'Nothing,' Frances later wrote to Rosamond Lehmann, 'I do believe, would have shaken her determination.' Yet there were also signs – unfinished letters, a diary filled up ahead with appointments – which seemed to indicate that she was half ready to go on living. Perhaps suicide can only be premeditated up to a point, and Carrington did not definitely make up her mind until that morning. Perhaps, too, she really was beginning to get over the worst of Lytton's death, and was driven to kill herself by some fear of gradually weakening intentions. Ralph was coming down to join her that evening; and the following week she would have been in the South of France with Augustus and Dorelia. This day was her last opportunity. There was, too, a need to convince those who had tried so diligently to nurse her back to life that, next to Lytton, they meant nothing.

As the pain increased, the doctor again gave her morphia. Towards midday she became unconscious, and at a quarter past two, she died. 'I went into the room and saw her dead,' David Garnett wrote. 'There was a very proud expression on her face.'

Presently David Garnett left and Gerald Brenan arrived to find Ralph 'scarcely able to control his feelings or speak coherently'. He went into the garden and sat in her grove under the ilex tree and the Portugal laurels. It seemed 'impossible for her not to be there'.

She had left a letter for Ralph in which she said that she hoped he would marry Frances and have children. A long list of presents she wished given to her friends followed, and instructions that her ashes were to be scattered in the garden* – she hoped with Lytton's. Her work in the garden, which a month ago had so heartened everyone except Ralph, had, as he suspected, been the preparation for her grave. She also set aside one hundred pounds for Stephen Tomlin to design her tombstone, but Ralph suppressed this, perhaps because he saw the disadvantages, so near to the house, of such a monument. This letter was not produced at the inquest, held on Monday 14 March, which found her death to have been due to a 'gun shot wound in the left side caused through accidentally slipping when holding a loaded gun in her hand'. There was no post-mortem.

Ralph and Frances, Alix Strachey and Gerald Brenan stayed on at Ham Spray until the inquest was over. 'Before they took her away, I saw her,' Gerald recorded in his diary, ' – or rather the terrible changes wrought in her by death. The same hard frost, the same icy weather prevailed as when Lytton had died, seven weeks before. As I lay awake in his room – for they had put me to sleep in his bed – I could hear the rooks calling all through the night among the frozen trees. It was not possible, even by walking into the next room where her body lay, to understand it.'

---

* Carrington was cremated, but thirty years later no one could remember whether or not her ashes had been scattered in the Ham Spray garden.

Thirty Years On

When I was writing this biography in the 1960s almost all the Strachey papers were privately owned. Apart from working at Lord's Wood, James and Alix Strachey's home, and at the Strachey family home, 51 Gordon Square, where I met Philippa ('Pippa') Strachey, I went to the houses of Lytton's friends and their families: reading through the correspondence to David Garnett at Hilton Hall; to Ottoline Morrell with her daughter Julian Vinogradoff in Gower Street; to Barbara Bagenal at her home in Rye. Most of the people I was writing about were still alive. I saw Noel Carrington at Lambourne, Duncan Grant at Charleston, Bertrand Russell in Wales, E.M. Forster and Sir John Sheppard at Cambridge, Sebastian Sprott in Nottingham and, in London, Boris Anrep, Clive Bell, Bonamy (but not Valentine) Dobrée, Mary Hutchinson, Rosamond Lehmann, Osbert Sitwell, Arthur Waley, Leonard Woolf. Roger Senhouse and Dadie Rylands lent me Strachey's letters to them. Gerald Brenan and Frances Partridge – the latter at some emotional cost – copied out pages of diaries and correspondence for me.

There was one manuscript anomaly. In *Other People: Diaries September 1963–December 1966* (1993), Frances Partridge records that Noël Annan, then Provost of King's College, Cambridge, spoke to her in 1966 about the Lytton Strachey and Maynard Keynes correspondence which was at King's under an embargo – though she herself remembered hearing it read one icy weekend at Charleston, and only realized just in time that this was 'a deadly secret'. In her diary entry for 22 January 1966, she wrote: 'Holroyd dined with me two nights ago and went through the Ham Spray albums; I'm pretty sure he told me then that *he* also had read the above letters, but the Provost of King's had not. I did ask Annan if Holroyd saw them when he came to King's and he said, "Oh no. I've not seen them myself."'

This strange situation arose out of a compromise that had been reached between Geoffrey Keynes and James Strachey. Geoffrey Keynes wanted the correspondence destroyed and James Strachey wanted it published. Eventually they agreed to deposit the letters at King's College on the understanding that nothing should be read until 1986. I saw them together in the early 1960s and I thought I detected in each of them a determination to outlive the other so that his own solution might prevail. In case of accidents, however, and before the deposit of manuscripts was accomplished, James Strachey had in 1948 made a secret microfilm of it all (to which he added Duncan Grant's letters to Lytton).* It may be that the Charleston reading was from the originals before they were sent to King's. I worked from the microfilms, seating myself in my room before that huge black instrument I had hired. But I soon grew worried by the awkwardness of publishing extracts from a collection that was being so sternly guarded. Before my book appeared, I therefore went to see the legendary librarian at King's, A.N.L. Munby, and explained the position. To my surprise he took it as a great joke which added to the fun of a librarian's career.

In 1967, a few months before my biography was published, James Strachey died. In the Bloomsbury style he had made many derogatory comments about my work to others, but this may have assisted him in dealing generously with me. I can see now that I must have been a disappointment to him. But he was determined to make the best of a bad job. Over the five years I knew him I had moved from apprehension and incomprehension, through a sense of gratitude, into a feeling of guarded affection for him. In so far as he began to feel some exasperated goodwill towards me, this was I think shared by his widow Alix Strachey.

Alix now became Lytton Strachey's copyright holder, and it was she who enabled me to edit the autobiographical *Lytton Strachey by Himself* in 1971. One episode connected with that book will illustrate her tolerance and generosity. She lent two Carrington portraits of Lytton to my publishers who wanted to use one or other of them as a design for the jacket. These pictures were afterwards to be taken by the publishers to the Upper Grosvenor Galleries, some five or six hundred yards away, for the first exhibition of Carrington's work. But when the pictures had been photographed, the publishers placing them by the front door for a couple of minutes while a van was backed up, both of them were in those couple of minutes stolen and, despite a reward being offered, they were never recovered. I felt mortified. But Alix Strachey took this 'rather frightful

---

* After James Strachey's death and the publication of my biography, Geoffrey Keynes instructed solicitors to recover these copies. 'You will, I am sure, fully appreciate my reasons for wishing to be in effective control of my brother's letters,' he wrote to me (4 October 1970). But since the ownership of Maynard Keynes's letters to Lytton Strachey had passed to James Strachey after Lytton's death, and since I had not infringed the fair usage clause of the Copyright Act, Geoffrey Keynes had to be 'content (if discontented)' with assurances of proper control of the material by the Strachey Trust. 'I feel quite clear that it is morally reprehensible, if not legally wrong, to make a copy of copyright material without permission,' he told me (23 October 1970. '. . . Your book has done just as much harm to my brother's image as if you had infringed copyright.'

news' over 'those wretched stolen pictures' with philosophical mildness, never showing any sense of grievance or voicing any complaint to me – though there were some wild enough rumours elsewhere. 'I suppose this sort of thing is going on everywhere all the time,' she wrote (26 September 1970).

In 1972 Alix Strachey created the Strachey Trust, a registered charity the main purpose of which was legally defined as 'the searching out by all available means of manuscripts and the establishment by mechanical processes or otherwise and the maintenance for the benefit of the public of a register of manuscripts so discovered being a register indicating the nature of the manuscript and where it is kept'. To this Trust, Alix gave all Lytton's papers, and, on her death in 1973, she also willed to the Trust Lytton's literary copyrights together with her own and those of James Strachey.

Alix had two 'pet fears'. The first was of 'dying in the gutter' and the second was of 'being led away in chains for doing something wrong about the Income Tax'. The creation of a Charitable Trust, and the making of a publishing programme with her retaining all copyright income during her lifetime, went some way to warming her 'cold feet'.

Her posthumous intention was to increase the accessibility of manuscript collections to scholars. The founders and original trustees of the Trust were myself, G.E. Moore's biographer Paul Levy, and the historian and translator from the French Lucy Norton, sister of Harry Norton to whom *Eminent Victorians* is dedicated. We were charged to address ourselves to 'the difficulty often encountered by biographers historians and others in discovering the existence and whereabouts of relevant manuscripts'. The Strachey papers were later catalogued and purchased by the British Library (with money, I like to think, from the British Museum's Bernard Shaw bequest). The Trust then used this money, together with some of its royalty income, to conceive, promote, and help finance the *Location Register of Twentieth-Century English Literary Manuscripts and Letters* which the British Library published in two tremendous volumes in 1988. These are to be followed in 1995 by a register of eighteenth- and nineteenth-century manuscripts and letters, after which the Strachey Trust will assist in the formation of a copyright directory.

With the aid of the twentieth-century location register it can easily be seen where many of the papers on which I worked thirty years ago, and which were then privately owned, have now gone. I have also used the register to trace manuscript material that was not then available to me. Rather than attempt to attach reference notes retrospectively, I tried to keep to my original system of putting dates and recipients of letters in the text and supplementing these with a number of additional references at the foot of the page.* But it seems appropriate and also useful to add here a list of manuscript locations.

MANUSCRIPTS OF LYTTON STRACHEY'S SEPARATELY PUBLISHED WORKS AND FELLOWSHIP DISSERTATION

Eminent Victorians, with four exercise books of notes and drafts, is in the British Library (Add MSS 54219–54223). For a description see Jenny Stratford 'Eminent Victorians' *British Museum Quarterly*, Spring 1968 pp.93–6.

Queen Victoria is at the Humanities Research Center, University of Texas at Austin. In addition to corrected manuscripts, HRC holds some type-scripts (with a few emendations), revised page proofs and research notes.

Elizabeth and Essex is in the library at Duke University, North Carolina (there is a one-page fragment at the Humanities Research Center, University of Texas at Austin).

Portraits in Miniature. An incomplete revised manuscript (84 pages) is at the Humanities Research Center, University of Texas at Austin. There is also a manuscript fragment at HRC with the final lines of the book, and page proofs containing corrections and additions.

Warren Hastings, Cheyt Sing and the Begums of Oude is in the Robert H. Taylor Collection at Princeton University. There is also a typescript there and another typescript at Trinity College, Cambridge.

MANUSCRIPTS OF POEMS, PLAYS, ESSAYS AND REVIEWS

A photocopy of *A Son of Heaven* is at Duke University and there are plays and juvenilia by Strachey in the British Library's nineteenth-century Strachey Papers (Add. MSS 60631–60654, 61825). A large number of early poems is in the Robert H. Taylor Collection at Princeton University, and many poems to Roger Senhouse are in the Berg Collection at the New York Public Library. Occasional poems appear in other collections including those at King's College, Cambridge (Sheppard papers), Reading University, and Eton School Library (Edward Marsh Manuscript Album

* From where they were rounded up and herded into tight formation at the end of the book by my editor, on the grounds that 'they distract the reader from the narrative'. Out of kindness to me, however, she has left a sample number to enjoy the free-range existence I had wanted for them.

fols 125–6) and the Humanities Research Center at Austin, Texas. Some of these poems were sold in the Charleston Trust sale and are printed in the Sotheby catalogue (21 July 1980. Lots 279–84); others were sold at the Society of Authors sale and are printed in the Sotheby catalogue (30 June 1982. Lots 333–7, 618–20). For a list of Strachey's poems in manuscript (and those that appeared in print) and the manuscript locations of occasional essays and reviews see Michael Edmonds *Lytton Strachey: A Bibliography* (1981).

OTHER MANUSCRIPTS, IN BRITAIN

The British Library, London
The correspondence between Lytton Strachey and James Strachey (Add. MSS 60706–60712), Duncan Grant (Add. MSS 57932–57933), Carrington (Add. MSS 62888–62897) and the Society of Authors (Add. MS 63334). There are also Lytton Strachey's letters to his sister Philippa Strachey (Add. MSS 60720–60721), Clive Bell (Add. MS 71104), E.B.C. Jones/'Topsy' Lucas (Add. MS 53788), and single letters to E.H. Blakeney (Add. MS 63087), D.H. Lawrence (Add. MS 48966), Sidney Lee (Add. MS 56087) and Christabel McLaren (Add. MS 52556). Also in the British Library are some of Lytton Strachey's letters to newspapers (Add. MS 60721) and a large collection of letters written to him and James Strachey formerly in the collection of the Strachey Trust (Add. MSS 60655–60734).

The India Office Library and Records, London
Letters from Lytton Strachey to his grandmother (MSS. Eur. F. 127/69), his mother (MSS. Eur. F. 127/341) and his brother Ralph Strachey (MSS. Eur. F. 127/444). These letters belong to the papers of Sir Richard Strachey and his wife Jane Maria Strachey (née Grant) and her father Sir John Peter Grant (called 'The Strachey Collection') which James and Alix Strachey deposited at the India Office Records in 1964. Since then the India Office Library and Records have become part of the Oriental and India Office Collections at the British Library.

House of Lords Records Office, London
Correspondence between Lytton Strachey and J. St Loe Strachey (33/6/118–126).

Victoria and Albert Museum National Art Library, London
Letters to Boris Anrep (86.PP.12).

Royal Society of Literature, London
Two letters to the RSL 1922–3.

King's College Library, Cambridge
The correspondence between Lytton Strachey and John Maynard Keynes
(with two additional letters from Strachey to Keynes on deposit from the
Royal Economic Society, Cambridge), and letters from Strachey to E.M.
Forster, John Hayward, Gertrude Kingston, George Rylands, J.T. Shep-
pard, W.J.H. Sprott and B. Swithinbank. There are single letters to Julian
Bell, Goldsworthy Lowes Dickinson, Miss Finlay, Lydia Keynes, Rosa-
mond Lehmann and Thoby Stephen (copy). King's College also owns
Strachey's Introduction to George Rylands's *Words and Poetry* and one letter from Rupert Brooke to Strachey.

University of Cambridge Library
Letters to G.E. Moore (Add. 8330), a single letter to Edmund Gosse
(Add. 7032/7) and to Philip Gosse (Add. 7031/51) and a copy by Strachey
of a letter from Edmund Gosse (Add. 7031/46).

Trinity College, Cambridge
Letters to R.C. Trevelyan (RCT $17^{113\text{-}114}$) and letters relating to R.C.
Trevelyan's *the pterodamozels: an operatic fable* (RCT $19^{33\text{-}56}$). Also a card to
A.J. Robertson (Add. MS. a.238^8).

The Bodleian Library, Oxford.
Letters to H.A.L. Fisher (MSS Fisher and MS Fisher 66, fols 71–72) to
P.J. Toynbee (MSS Toynbee d25 & 27), to Sybil Colefax (MSS. Eng.
c.3170, fols. 26–39 and c.3175, fol. 40), and a single letter to H.H.
Asquith (MS. Asquith 35, fol 105).

Merton College, Oxford
Letters to Max Beerbohm (Max Beerbohm Collection 5A).

University of Sussex Library, Brighton
Correspondence between Lytton Strachey (copies) and Leonard Woolf
(SxMs18.MHL), three letters (copies) to Virginia Woolf (SxMs18MHL
(VW)) (also three letters from Virginia Woolf to Strachey) and a single letter to Goldsworthy Lowes Dickinson (SxMs11/11/4). The library also
holds a photocopied set of the original Charleston Papers archive which,
until its auction at Sotheby's in 1980, was housed by King's College,

Cambridge. This includes letters from Lytton Strachey to Clive and Vanessa Bell and a single letter to Thoby Stephen.

University of Reading Library, Reading
Letters to Chatto & Windus (MS 2444) and Nancy Astor (MS 1416/1/2).

Brotherton Library, University of Leeds
Letters to Edmund Gosse.

Hertfordshire County Record Office, Hertford
Letters to Lady Desborough (D/ERv/C2500/1).

National Library of Scotland, Edinburgh
Letter to George Blake (Acc.4989) and to John Purves (MS 15561).

Mitchell Library, Glasgow District Library, Glasgow
Letter to Henry MacLaren (MS 152/97).

National Library of Wales, Aberystwyth
Letters to Dorelia McNeil (NLW MS 22789D fols 97–101) and one letter to Augustus John (NLW MS 22785D fol 138).

OTHER MANUSCRIPTS, IN THE UNITED STATES

Humanities Research Center, University of Texas at Austin
Letters to J.R. Ackerley, James H. Doggart, Mary Hutchinson, Ottoline Morrell, Philip Moeller, Ralph Partridge, Lady Strachey, Sir Richard Strachey and the Strachey family, and Leonard Woolf. There are also single letters to Ralph Alker, St John Hutchinson, John Lehmann, Frances Marshall, Philip Morrell and PEN. There is a letter to Virginia Woolf tipped into a presentation copy of *Landmarks in French Literature*, and a letter jointly to Carrington and Ralph Partridge. Among the correspondence to Strachey (which includes letters from Sir Richard and Lady Strachey, Mary Hutchinson, Ralph Partridge and Leonard Woolf) there is a letter from Thomas Hardy praising *Queen Victoria* which Strachey mislaid and which was not located by Sebastian Sprott in the 1920s.

Berg Collection, New York Public Library
Letters to Barbara Bagenal, Rupert Brooke, John Maynard Keynes, John Middleton Murry, Roger Senhouse and Leonard Woolf. There are also

single letters to Nick Bagenal, John Lehmann, Katherine Mansfield, Edward Marsh, J.B. Pinker, Edward Sackville-West and Edith Sitwell.

Robert H. Taylor Collection, University of Princeton
Letters to Vanessa Bell, Dorothy Bussy, Leonard Woolf and Virginia Woolf. There is a single letter to Richard Jennings.

Houghton Library, Harvard University
Letters to Gamaliel Bradford, T.S. Eliot and William Rothenstein. There are single letters to Mr Everett and Henry Goddard Leach.

Duke University Library, North Carolina
Three letters to Crosby Gaige and single letters to Percy Spalding of Chatto & Windus and to James R. Wells.

Columbia University, New York
One letter to Paul Reynolds.

MANUSCRIPTS IN CANADA

McMaster University, Hamilton, Ontario
One letter and a telegram to Bertrand Russell.

PUBLISHED WORKS

After Lytton Strachey's death, his brother and literary executor James Strachey authorized the publication of *Characters and Commentaries* (1933), a selection of thirty-three essays written between 1905 and 1931 which had not previously been collected. This volume, which reprinted the prefaces to *A Simple Story* and *Words and Poetry* as well as the Leslie Stephen Lecture on Pope, included Lytton's unpublished 'English Letter Writers' and incomplete 'Othello'.

The Greville Memoirs, edited by Lytton Strachey and Roger Fulford, was published in 1938. The groundwork for the seven volumes had been done by Ralph and Frances Partridge who also prepared an index volume.

There have been two editions of Lytton Strachey's Collected Works. In 1934 Chatto & Windus brought out six volumes – *Eminent Victorians, Queen Victoria, Books and Characters, Elizabeth and Essex, Portraits in Miniature* and *Characters and Commentaries* – in a single black box (400 sets). A uniform edition of Strachey's Collected Works with scarlet binding and a dust jacket designed by Edward Bawden was issued by Chatto & Windus in 1948. The titles were: *Landmarks in French Literature, Eminent Victorians, Queen Victoria, Elizabeth and Essex, Literary Essays* and *Biographical Essays*. The last two volumes, which were also published in the United States by Harcourt Brace, rearranged the contents of *Books and Characters, Portraits in Miniature* and *Characters and Commentaries*, omitting six essays that appeared in the latter volume and collecting for the first time 'Charles Greville' which had been published in the *Nation and Athenaeum* (11 August 1923) and was reprinted in *Biographical Essays*.

Leonard Woolf and James Strachey edited and introduced *Virginia Woolf and Lytton Strachey* in 1956, a selection of correspondence written between 1906 and 1931 with some omissions and some names concealed by randomly chosen initials.

In 1964 James Strachey selected and introduced *Spectatorial Essays*, thirty-five contributions to the *Spectator*, including some theatre criticism originally signed 'Ignotus', composed by Lytton Strachey between 1904 and 1913, representing less than half the total number of his writings for his cousin, the editor St Loe Strachey.

Strachey's entertainment *Ermyntrude and Esmeralda*, with an introduction by Michael Holroyd and illustrations by Erté, was serialized by *Playboy* in 1969 and published in book form in Britain (Anthony Blond 1969) and the United States (Stein and Day 1970). A limited edition of 250 copies in a slipcase was also issued by Anthony Blond, and translations appeared in Italy (Sugar Editore 1970) and France (Flammarion 1971).

Lytton Strachey by Himself. A Self-Portrait (1971), edited with an introduction and commentaries by Michael Holroyd, was a selection of hitherto unpublished autobiographical essays (including 'Lancaster Gate' and 'Monday 26 June'), occasional diaries from childhood to 'A Fortnight in France' written in 1931, and miscellaneous pieces such as Strachey's statement as a conscientious objector.

A second collection of unpublished work, *The Really Interesting Question and Other Papers* edited with an introduction and commentaries by Paul Levy was published in 1972. This volume brought together some Apostolic papers, verse, fiction and correspondence from the war and showed Strachey primarily as a writer on political and social matters. To celebrate the centenary of Strachey's birth in 1980, Michael Holroyd and Paul Levy selected and introduced twenty-four essays under the title *The Shorter Strachey*. They were chosen mainly from previous collections but also published for the first time his paper 'Ought Father to Grow a Beard?' read to the Apostles in 1902, and an essay on Warren Hastings probably written in 1907 when Strachey was considering restructuring his Cambridge dissertation into a book. Also collected for the first time was his memoir of Asquith which had been published in *The Times* on 15 January 1972.

Works about Lytton Strachey include: G. Köntges *Die Sprache In Der Biographie Lytton Stracheys* (Herman Bauer 1938); Max Beerbohm *Lytton Strachey: The Rede Lecture* (Cambridge University Press 1943); Charles R. Sanders *Lytton Strachey: His Mind and Art* (Yale University Press 1957); M.S. Yu *Two Masters of Irony: Wilde and Lytton Strachey* (Hong Kong University Press, 1957); Martin Kallich *The Psychological Milieu of Lytton Strachey* (Yale University Press 1961); Gabriel Merle *Lytton Strachey (1880–1932) biographie et critique d'un critique et biographe* (Librairie Honore Champion, 2 volumes 1980); John Ferns *Lytton Strachey* (Twayne's English Authors Series 462, 1988); Barry Spurr *Diabolical Art: The Achievement of Lytton Strachey* (Edwin Mellen Press 1994).

Michael Edmonds has compiled and introduced *Lytton Strachey: A Bibliography* (Garland Reference Library of the Humanities volume 231, 1981).

ACKNOWLEDGEMENTS

The list of people who helped me with the preparation of this biography in the 1960s has become a necrology, and I have not reproduced it again. But I would like to renew my thanks to Frances Partridge who has once more looked through my account of Lytton Strachey's later life and generously given me additional information.

The present edition has been written with the assistance of a number of institutions which appear in my bibliographical appendix. I am also indebted to Sally Brown, Jane Hill, Cathy Henderson, Robert Skidelsky, Frances Spalding, David Sutton, Winifred Thomson, Ann Thwaite; to Angelene Rackett of the Bank of England for advice about money conversions; and to the Courtauld Institute, the Bridgeman Art Library, the National Portrait Gallery, the Tate Gallery, Angelica Garnett and Lady Pansy Lamb for permission to reproduce illustrations.

The book has benefited from the care and house-style severities of my editor Alison Samuel. I am grateful to her and to Sarah Johnson who has found the time from her own writings to follow the twists and turns of my amalgamated typing and handwriting, and transfer it all on to disc.

MICHAEL HOLROYD
Porlock Weir, February 1994

NOTES

DOUBLE PREFACE

1   Clive Bell *Old Friends* (1956) p.40.
2   'We think it can be said that you are the first Englishman to win a Saxton fellowship,' the secretary wrote (15 January 1964), 'although the late Sylvia Plath, who was the wife of the British poet Ted Hughes, probably had dual citizenship.'
3   *The Letters of Nancy Mitford* (ed. Charlotte Mosley 1993) p.469.
4   *The Kenneth Williams Diaries* (ed. Russell Davies 1993) p.341.
5   In *Who's Who* David Garnett named Clive Bell as Angelica's father (and this is repeated in *Who Was Who* volume VII 1981–1990). In *The Dictionary of National Biography* 1981–1985, the entry on David Garnett by Frances Partridge names Duncan Grant as Angelica's father.
6   Dido Davies *William Gerhardie. A Biography* (1990) p.ix.
7   'I cannot bear my very private feelings served up to the public,' Duncan Grant wrote to Desmond Shawe-Taylor (11 July 1967), '. . . but the author, a well-meaning young man, blackmailed me by saying that it was necessary to Lytton's story, so for art's sake I gave way.'
8   *South-West Review* volume 70, number 2 (Spring 1985) p.149.
9   *Letters of Leonard Woolf* (ed. Frederic Spotts 1990) pp.560, 573.
10 See Goronwy Rees *Brief Encounter* (1974) pp.81–3.
11 'Strachey: Short and Sharp' *Now!* (29 February 1980) p.77.
12 Paul Johnson *A History of the Modern World* (1983) pp.29, 169–71, 347. Alternatively it may be argued that, by ostracizing intellectuals who were homosexual, the British establishment created its enemies within. Many of them, however, worked for British Intelligence during the Second World War at Bletchley Park. After the war they were again ostracized, and the number of homosexual prosecutions per year between 1945 and 1955 rose from 800 to more than 2500. This was partly due to an invasion of puritanism from the United States which combined Senator Joseph McCarthy's purge against communists in the arts and the Eisenhower Executive Order which banned homosexuals from federal posts. One victim of this wave of homophobia in Britain was Alan Turing, chief code breaker at Bletchley Park, who committed suicide in 1953.

CHAPTER I: LANCASTER GATE

1   His first wife, Caroline Bowles, had died in 1855 within a year of their marriage.
2   James Strachey liked to recall that his father was actually as tall as his mother – about five feet eight inches. But he held himself badly and therefore seemed smaller. Photographs of them together make him appear distinctly the shorter figure.
3   Legendary and apocryphal bard of a popular and allegedly primitive Scottish epic poem, *Fingal*, which was actually written by James Macpherson (1736–96).
4   James Strachey, who disputed some details in Leonard Woolf's description, told

the author that the whole change in his father's life to semi-invalidism only took place after 1897, when he was eighty. 'In that year, which was when he was knighted, he made the journey by himself from our then country house near Manningtree in Essex, I fancy, to Osborne for the investiture. He also took Pippa to the Naval Review at Spithead that year. What happened was that he got an attack of dysentery after a visit to Belgium, and nearly died. Though he recovered and went on working, he was never so active again.'

5 *Sowing. An Autobiography of the Years 1880–1904* (1961) p.188.

6 Lady Strachey's *Nursery Lyrics*, originally published in 1893 with illustrations by G.P. Jacomb Hood, was reprinted with additions in 1922 as *Nursery Lyrics and other Verses for Children* and illustrated by Philip Hagreen. *Poets on Poets* appeared in 1894. In 1887, she had brought out her children's anthology, *Lay Texts for the Young, in Both English and French*. A copy of this book was presented to Lytton when he was about fourteen. There are no religious authors included in the volume, and, presumably because he was too well known, no Shakespeare. Several of the quotations appear to contradict one another, but the qualities held up to be emulated are truth, reason, balance, virtue and aspiration. She also wrote a play for children, *Little Boy Blue*.

7 The first (abridged) edition of *Memoirs of a Highland Lady*, edited by Lady Strachey, appeared in 1898 and was reprinted four times that year. In 1911 she published a shorter version, and it was from this text that the 1950 edition (prepared by Lytton's friend Angus Davidson) was based. Andrew Tod, editor of the comprehensive version taken from the manuscript in the National Library of Scotland, writes in his Introduction (1988) that: 'Not surprisingly, in the light of her time and station, Lady Strachey invariably pruned all references to sexual misdemeanors ... there was a steelier and racier side to her [Elizabeth Grant's] reminiscences, less in tune with the moral complacencies and certainties at the end of the century ... realistic and honestly matter-of-fact accounts, of servant immoralities at Rothiemurchus and the resulting regular pregnancies.'

8 *Nation and Athenaeum* XXXIV (5 January, 24 February, 1924), pp.514–15, 730–31; XXV (12 July, 30 August, 1924), pp.473–4, 664–5. See also XXXIV, p.514.

9 *Lytton Strachey by Himself* (1971) p.24.

10 James Meadows Rendel (1854–1937), Chairman of the Assam Bengal Railway and an expert on Poor Law administration, who married Lytton's eldest sister, Elinor.

11 Beatrice Chamberlain (1862–1918), the eldest daughter of Joseph Chamberlain and his first wife Harriet Kenrick, was a half-sister to Neville Chamberlain, later Prime Minister.

12 In May 1959 the Stracheys' old home became part of Douglas House, the large American Forces Club which occupied Nos. 66–71 Lancaster Gate. Though the shell of the building remains the same, the interior was fused with the houses on either side and became unrecognizable. It is now part of the Charles Dickens Hotel.

13 Lytton's unpublished autobiographical essay 'Lancaster Gate', written in 1922 for the Memoir Club, traces the influence of this house on himself. His magnification of the place (in contrast with which the proportions of every other house he lived in seemed tiny) was probably hysterical in origin. See *Lytton Strachey by Himself* pp.16–28.

14 The moving spirit behind this measure was Lytton's father. See *Memorandum on the Introduction of the Metric System in India* by Pitamber Plant, with a Foreword by Jawaharlal Nehru (Indian Government Publication, 1955). On the first page of this manual, the author remarks that Colonel R. Strachey's 'brilliant notes and memoranda (Appendices B1, B2, B5), in particular his Minute of Dissent (B2), are classic in their quality, imbued with scholarship, practical wisdom and above

all a noble earnestness which not only invokes admiration but inspires. No aspect of this complex subject has escaped his notice and none has received but the most patient and careful treatment. With ninety years separating his writings from now, it is remarkable that they are as much relevant and enlightening today, during our present consideration of the problem, as they were when the subject was in his care.' See also pp.8, 20, 53–104. The combined labours of Sir John and Sir Richard Strachey had a lasting influence over the policy and the constitution of the Indian Government, and the two brothers were celebrated in a Kipling poem. In the Preface to the third edition of *India: Its Administration and Progress*, Sir John Strachey recorded that 'for many years we took part, often in close association, in its government, and it would be an affectation of humility to profess that this part was not an important one. There is hardly a great office in that state, from that of Acting-Viceroy, Lieutenant-Governor, or Member of Council downwards, which one or other of us has not held, and hardly a department of the administration with which one or other of us has not been intimately connected.'

15 *The Autobiography of Bertrand Russell, Volume One 1872–1914* (1967) p.72.
16 The Doune was the home of the Grants, the most celebrated of whom was Mrs Smith of Baltiboys, author of *Memoirs of a Highland Lady* (1898). Her brother, Lady Strachey's father, Sir John Peter Grant, had modernized the house in the 1870s.
17 In his memoirs, *The Good Old Days* (1956), Lytton's cousin Patrick Grant wrote: 'During the summer months the house was packed, often with the whole Strachey family, my first cousins. Inspired perhaps by having read that famous book *The Fifth Form at St Dominic's*, Lytton Strachey and I decided we must produce and edit a magazine. Being almost unable to pronounce Dominican, I called it "The Domican". I have it still, and it represents, I think, Lytton's very first attemp[t]s at creative writing. Little did we guess that in the days to come he would become a famous author. His sister Pernel, afterwards I believe the Head of Newnham, was kind enough to write it out for us, and everyone, even including the butler, wrote stories or verses for it. Lytton's father, old Sir Richard, even painted a picture for us, but though it was a great success there was never a sequel to the first number.'
18 *The Diary of Beatrice Webb, Volume One 1873–1892, Glitter Around and Darkness Within* (ed. Norman and Jeanne MacKenzie 1982) p.277.
19 *Olivia* by 'Olivia' (1949), the title of which was suggested by the Christian name of Dorothy's sister who died in infancy. The picture of Lancaster Gate and of Sir Richard and Lady Strachey which is given by Dorothy in the opening pages of this novel should be read with some care. Though outwardly friendly, there was a degree of antagonism between mother and daughter which arose from the fact that Dorothy had turned down several eminent offers of marriage and then become the wife of the indigent French artist Simon Bussy. Comparing Lady Strachey with aunt E. (Aunt Lell) who 'was sensitive to art to the very finger-tips of her beautiful hands, and successfully created about herself an atmosphere of *ordre et beauté, luxe, calme et volupté*', she presents her mother as being without taste and responsible for that solid comfort within Lancaster Gate from which 'the sensual element was totally lacking'. Her view, too, of Lady Strachey being 'perhaps incapable of the mystical illumination' and of her home being purely intellectual, may partly have been brought about by the fact that, alone of the family, Dorothy had no ear for music. So, when all the rest of them trooped off to a Joachim Quartet concert at St James's Hall, she was left alone in the house. The trouble continued: Simon Bussy was also unmusical, and so was their daughter Janie. There was no piano in their home and no sound of music till fifty years later when the wireless arrived.
20 Richard John Strachey (1861–1935) became a colonel in the Rifle Brigade. In 1896 he married Grace, daughter of Field-Marshal Sir Henry Norman. They had no children.

21 Ralph Strachey (1868–1923) married Margaret Severs in 1901. Their first son was the novelist and writer of children's books, Richard Strachey. Their second son, John Strachey, was an artist who lived in Antibes. Their only daughter, Ursula, who married Cyril Wentzel, an actor and barrister, was herself on the stage, and later worked in the Foreign Office.

22 Oliver Strachey (1874–1960), musician, civil servant and joint-author with his second wife, Ray Strachey, of *Keigwin's Rebellion* (1916). He worked in the Foreign Office and the War Office during both World Wars and was employed as a code-breaker.

23 *Lytton Strachey by Himself* p.17.

CHAPTER II: 'FUNNY LITTLE CREATURE'

1 Mary Stocks, whose family was closely associated with the Stracheys, puts forward an interesting speculation about Lytton Strachey's parentage: that he was not a Strachey at all but a Lytton, the illegitimate son of his godfather. See *My Commonplace Book* by Mary Stocks (Peter Davies 1970). But Vincent Rendel describes this (*Times Literary Supplement* 11 December 1970) as 'malicious nonsense' which, he adds, 'has not even found its way into "Holroyd"'.

2 *Lytton Strachey by Himself* (1971) pp.59–60.

3 'The Cat' was first printed on 12 June 1902 in the Supplement of the *Cambridge Review*, p.xxiii and signed 'G.L.S.' Subsequently it was reprinted in *Euphrosyne* (1905), an anthology anonymously compiled by Clive Bell. It has also appeared in Mona Gooden's *The Poet's Cat* (1946), and in *A Dictionary of Cat Lovers* (1949), a symposium edited by Christabel Aberconway, containing scholarly notes on the 'Cat in Ancient Egypt'; and more recently in *The Chatto Book of Cats* (1993), compiled by Francis Wheen. In these later publications, the word 'pagan' in the opening line of the second stanza quoted above has been changed to 'northern'.

4 Dorothy Strachey had returned to England several weeks earlier.

5 *Lytton Strachey by Himself* pp.77–8.

6 Soon afterwards Lytton became highly indignant on learning that his uncle was resigning his commission and returning to civilian life. 'I am most disgusted with Uncle Charlie for leaving the army,' he told his mother.

7 There had been some question of sending Lytton to Eton, but Lady Strachey decided against this partly, it seems, because of her elder son Oliver's failure there, a love-letter from another boy having been discovered in his rooms. As an adult, Oliver was something of a womanizer – 'the most orthodox of all of us', as James Strachey described him.

8 Charles Kegan Paul (1828–1902) had been vicar of Sturminster until 1874, when he was converted to publishing. He translated books from the German and French, edited the letters of Mary Wollstonecraft and wrote a life of Godwin. In 1856 he had married Margaret Colvile, and was related, though marriage, to one of Lady Strachey's sisters.

9 Earlier that term he had acted another female role in a school production of *My Turn Next*. 'I had on a beautiful red silk dress with flounces,' he proudly told his mother.

10 'Sometime ago we have all been digging up potatoes in the field, we had to work pretty hard, because they all had to be got away before the frost came on' (Lytton to Lady Strachey, 29 October 1893).

11 In a letter to *The Times* (25 January 1932, p.17), four days after Lytton's death, Bishop Bidwell wrote: 'It is stated in his obituary notice that Lytton Strachey was educated "privately". As a matter of fact, he was a pupil of mine when I was chaplain and a form master at old Leamington College, which then ranked as one

LYTTON STRACHEY

of the minor public schools. I never saw or heard of him after he left till upwards of two years ago, when seeing my name and address in a communication to your columns, he wrote me a most delightful letter, of the sort that gladdens the heart of an old schoolmaster. He said that he had been wanting to express his gratitude (I am afraid little deserved) for years, but had lost track of me when I went abroad. He describes himself as my "somewhat wayward pupil". He certainly was, as I quickly perceived, different from the average boy, but my recollections of him as a boy are entirely pleasing, and I deeply regret his premature passing.' In his letter replying to Lytton (11 April 1929), Bidwell had written: 'I cannot tell you how pleased I was to get your letter. It is comforting to be remembered after all these years. Yes, *I* recall you perfectly as a boy, but mea maxima culpa I never identified the youth I knew with the celebrity of today.'

12 *Lytton Strachey by Himself* p.117.

CHAPTER III: LIVERPOOL

1 *Letters from Graham Robertson* (ed. Kerrison Preston 1953) p.505.
2 *Lytton Strachey by Himself* (1971) pp.89, 99–100.
3 *Ibid.* p.96.
4 Allan Wilson Grundy and Lancelot William Bird, two senior undergraduates who, in 1898, were both awarded BA degrees in the Faculty of Arts.
5 *Lytton Strachey by Himself* p.87.
6 Henry Sidgwick (1838–1900), the philosopher and free-thinker, who wrote textbooks on ethics and political economy, advocated higher education for women, and, in the words of John Maynard Keynes, 'learnt Arabic in order to read Genesis in the original, not trusting the authorized translators'. His wife, Eleanor Mildred Sidgwick (1845–1936), the Principal (1892–1910) of Newnham College, was a sister of Arthur Balfour, the Prime Minister.
7 Douglas William Freshfield, mountain climber and author, and his wife Augusta, sister of Mrs Cornish and eldest daughter of the Hon. W. Ritchie, later Advocate General of Calcutta, were friends of the Stracheys. Their house in London was in these years a hub of cultivated society.
8 Katherine Stephen, a cousin of Vanessa and Virginia Stephen, became Principal of Newnham, where Lytton's sister Pernel was studying. Athena Clough, her successor and Pernel's predecessor as Principal, was then a tutor there.

CHAPTER IV: FRATRIBUS

1 Duff was devoted to Lytton and on this account, James Strachey told the author, 'put up with my subsequent unsatisfactoriness'.
2 This name originated from his having been so announced by the butler at the door of the Lancaster Gate drawing-room.
3 Dons had only recently been permitted to marry and continue to hold their fellowships and many of the younger ones could not afford a wife. Undergraduates in Strachey's class, Noël Annan has written, 'were solemnly warned of the guileful way in which they might be entrapped by the tobacconist's daughter, and every college was a bachelor community. Such communities provide elaborate justifications for their ethos, and in this case the justification came from the classics.'
4 A.J. Robertson was a brother of D.H. Robertson, the economist and father of James Robertson, the conductor.
5 For two generations the Stracheys and the Stephens had been on cordial terms, and had a number of friends in common.

6 Sir G.O. Trevelyan (1838–1928), nephew and biographer of Lord Macaulay, was an eminent historian and parliamentarian. His works include *The Early History of Charles James Fox* (1880) and a history of the American Revolution in six volumes (1899–1914).

7 At that time Stephen Phillips's *Paolo and Francesca* had not been publicly performed. It opened under George Alexander at the St James's Theatre in February 1902.

8 This was what used to be called a 'Rest Cure' – invented in the 1880s by an American doctor called Silas Weir Mitchell.

9 Annie King was the daughter of Elizabeth Grant of Rothiemurchus (Mrs Smith of Baltiboys).

10 Virginia Woolf later recalled that she had been taken across to see the Stracheys by her father. 'Lady Strachey was in high glee. She had been routing about among the books, and had discovered a first edition, I think of Ben Jonson. "Look at that, Sir Leslie! Look at that!" she exclaimed, thrusting the book before him and pointing to an inscription on the title page, "Ex dono Auctoris". My father looked and admired, but a little grimly I thought and on the way home he said to me, "I didn't like to tell Lady Strachey, but the accent should be on the second syllable of auctoris, not the first."'

11 This statement is based upon an account given by Clive Bell in his memoirs, *Old Friends*. It is possible that he may have over-emphasized the significance of the Midnight because of his disappointment at not being elected to the Apostles. I have used the Midnight partly for aesthetic purposes, and partly because it was the first society to which Lytton belonged and, for a year or more, the chief one. After he had been introduced into the Apostles by R.G. Hawtrey in 1902, the Midnight ceased to exist. But even before this, its place had already been taken by the X Society – a play-reading club that met earlier on Saturday evenings. Leonard Woolf, Saxon Sydney-Turner, Thoby Stephen and Clive Bell belonged to it, together with a lot of miscellaneous characters such as Walter Lamb, D.S. Robertson (later Regius Professor of Greek), Hubback and Philby (the Arabian traveller and father of the 'Third Man' in the Burgess–Maclean affair). This group was still going strong after 1902 – 'I know because I went to a meeting much later,' James Strachey wrote, 'when I was up for a weekend from St Paul's and they read *Love for Love*, much to my excitement.'

12 Russell's reaction to the book was reported to Lytton by Ottoline Morrell a few days later. 'Thank you very much for passing on Bertie's message,' he replied (26 May 1918). 'I am delighted that he should have liked the book, and that he found it entertaining. If you're writing will you thank him from me, and say that I think it a great honour that my book should have made the author of *Principia Mathematica* laugh aloud in Brixton Gaol?'

13 C.P. Sanger, the barrister and conveyancer, author of *The Structure of Wuthering Heights* and an erudite edition of Jarman, *On Wills*.

14 In the first volume of his autobiography, *Father Figures* (1966), Kingsley Martin writes: 'McTaggart was an extraordinary figure in my day. He suffered from agoraphobia, and walked with a strange, crab-like gait, keeping his backside to the wall, as if afraid that someone would kick it – and maybe they did at school. He talked very quickly and was very hard to follow … He invited questions, but answered them so sharply and decisively that few were encouraged to ask another.'

15 Later Sir John Sheppard, the Provost of King's.

16 In a letter to his mother, Lytton wrote: 'I am going to get for my prize Merivale's *Roman Empire* (bound and stamped) and Swinburne's works – *au naturel*. This will be rather more than £10 – but I thought the magnificence of twenty-nine volumes was not to be resisted.' There was no collected edition of Swinburne's works in

those days. Besides these twenty-nine unbound separate volumes, Lytton finally bought a two-volume edition of Shelley.

17 *The Story of Nuncomar and the Impeachment of Sir Elijah Impey* (1885) by Sir James Fitzjames Stephen.

CHAPTER V: BEETLES AND WATER-SPIDERS

1 Lady Strachey had been told something of the Apostles by various friends and relations – Walter Raleigh, Sir Henry Maine, James Fitzjames Stephen and Arthur Strachey, all past members – and had grown fearfully keen that Lytton should be elected. Before he went up to Cambridge, she had passed on to him all she knew of the Society.

2 Gerald Balfour (1853–1945) was a Fellow of Trinity and member of Parliament for Central Leeds (1885–1906). Among the appointments he held were Chief Secretary for Ireland (1895–1900) and President of the Board of Trade (1900–1905). A popular man of great social charm.

3 Alfred Lyttelton (1857–1912), lawyer, statesman and popular socialite, was head of the Colonial Office (1903–5) but his chief eminence was as a cricketer. His play, remarked W.G. Grace, was 'the champagne of cricket'.

4 Benjamin Jowett (nicknamed 'the Jowler'), Master of Balliol from 1870 to 1893, said that he wanted to 'inoculate England' with his college alumni. He became one of the supreme influences in Victorian England. Arrogant and temperamental, with a shrill voice, squat figure and owl-like features, he was famous for his succinct rebuffs. He was Regius Professor of Greek at Oxford and responsible for a frigidly asexual translation of Plato.

5 Sir Ralph Hawtrey (1879–1975), economist at the Treasury (1904–45) and President of the Royal Economic Society (1946–8). Married Hortense Emilia D'Arányi – one of the musical sisters. 'I retain a vivid recollection of him [Lytton Strachey] and of his personality,' he wrote to the author (23 April 1963). At Cambridge he was chiefly known as a mathematician, and had great arguments with Moore, Russell and Harry Norton on metaphysics (logic and epistemology).

6 Oscar Browning (1837–1923), historian and historical biographer. Educated at Eton and King's College, Cambridge. In 1859 he had been made a Fellow of King's, and the following year took up a post as assistant master at Eton, then returned to King's in 1876 as lecturer in history. Hugely fat, he was a notorious socialite and 'character', a 'genius flawed by abysmal fatuity', as E.F. Benson called him. His last years were spent in Rome, where he was appointed President of the Academy of Arts. Among his many friends was Oscar Wilde. 'Do you know Oscar Browning?' Wilde asked Robert Ross (*circa* 13 October 1888). 'You will find him everything that is kind and pleasant.'

7 Sir Arthur Strachey (1855–1901), the second son of Lytton's uncle, Sir John Strachey. At Trinity Hall he had taken a degree in law, after which he went out to India and was made Chief Justice of the High Court at Allahabad. He died in Simla.

8 Lytton's paper was entitled 'Dignity, Romance and Vegetarianism'.

9 Alfred North Whitehead (1861–1947), mathematician and philosopher who, with Bertrand Russell, wrote *Principia Mathematica*.

10 Nathaniel Wedd, Fellow of King's College, where he was for many years Classical Lecturer and Assistant Tutor. Lionel Trilling, in his study of E.M. Forster, writes that 'the decisive influence on Forster was his classics tutor, Nathaniel Wedd, a cynical, aggressive, Mephistophelean character who affected red ties and blasphemy.'

11 Alfred Richard Ainsworth (1879–1959), who after leaving Cambridge took a job

as lecturer at Manchester University (1902–3) and then at Edinburgh University (1903–7), later becoming a Deputy Secretary at the Board of Education. He married G.E. Moore's sister and was, in part, the original of Ansell in E.M. Forster's *The Longest Journey*.

12 This almost certainly refers to the surprising presence at Westminster Abbey of a number of Edward VII's favourites, past and present – among them Sarah Bernhardt, Mrs George Keppel, Mrs Hartmann, Lady Kilmorey and Mrs Arthur Paget.

13 Sir Richard Strachey in fact turned out to be generous to the Bussys. He bought La Souco, a villa just below the Grande Corniche, overlooking the bay towards Monte Carlo, and gave it to them as a wedding-present.

14 *Cecilia Gonzaga*.

15 *Life and Labour of the People in London. 3rd Series. Religious Influences, volume 7*. Part of an eighteen-volume social survey – one of the first of its kind – compiled under the direction of Charles Booth, a friend of Beatrice Potter before her marriage to Sidney Webb.

16   Doctoribus Amicisque Cantabrigiensibus
           Discipulus Amicus Cantabrigiensis
                 Primitias
                 D. D. D.
                 Auctor.
To his teachers and friends of Cambridge, their Cambridge disciple and friend, the author, dedicates his first works.

17 'The scientific method has been introduced once and for all into Reasoning, and henceforward it will be almost impossible to go back. The Age of Reason has now begun.' Lytton Strachey to John Sheppard (undated).

18 Lytton and Sheppard had decided to take up dancing in order to equip themselves for a special dance that Lancaster Gate was giving before Dorothy Strachey's marriage.

19 Theodore Llewelyn Davies of the Treasury, a good-looking, austere, intellectual contemporary of Lytton's at Trinity, who drowned while bathing in the summer of 1905.

20 To anyone not brought up in Lancaster Gate, La Souco might have appeared quite fair-sized. It had originally been built by the Roquebrune carpenter for his own occupation, but was bought for the Bussys before it was finished, and was later extended – one main addition being a garage. Visiting it in August 1964, I was surprised to find that it had three spacious ground-floor rooms plus a dark and narrow kitchen, and three bedrooms, balconies and a bathroom upstairs. The villa lies just off the Grande Corniche below Roquebrune village, and looks directly across to Monte Carlo bay. It had a steep terraced garden, a number of olive trees and one towering cypress. Adjoining the house were a large studio and a walled patio with murals.

21 The Yen was Lytton's nickname for G.E. Moore.

22 James Strachey disagreed with the author that his brother was eccentric – an epithet which he felt to be derogatory. He took the view that Lytton was 'quite unshakeably rooted in commonplace sanity and reality', and that therefore a comparison with Oscar Wilde was unjust ('the only resemblance I can see is that they were both buggers'). His clothes too, James Strachey wrote, 'were always perfectly conventional except during the rather short Lamb–Augustus [John] period. My own very rarely used Savile Row tailor (an old gentleman now) told me a couple of years ago of his pride in having persuaded Lytton to go back to ordinary smart clothes (such as you see him wearing in the photograph with the globe). I think you get this from Bertie.'

23 At Cambridge, Leonard Woolf called him by a shorter version of his surname –

'the Strache'. For a short time at the beginning of the war, David Garnett used to call Lytton 'the Cowboy', because of the wide-brimmed hat he then liked to wear. But the name did not stick.

24 Of the above passage, based on Maynard Keynes's 'My Early Beliefs', and the previous passage taken from the first volume of Bertrand Russell's autobiography, James Strachey frankly disapproved. Sixty years later he wrote: 'It is quite untrue that metaphysical and logical arguments were out. When I was a brother, Maynard, Norton and Hawtrey (who came up very regularly) had constant hard-headed arguments about such things as sense-perception or truth or internal relations; and Whitehead, Sanger, Russell and Moore turned up often enough to affect the sort of conversation . . . you accept without reservation Maynard's forty years' later bleatings.'

25 No.6 Harvey Road, Cambridge, was Keynes's home.

26 'My disease is that I am so frank that nobody believes me and takes it for wickedness.' (Maynard Keynes to Lytton Strachey, April 1905.)

27 Professor Sir John Davidson Beazley, C.H. (1885–1970), the archaeologist and author of many works on ancient sculpture, painting and pottery, who was at this time an undergraduate at Christ Church.

28 *The Diary of Beatrice Webb, Volume Two, 1892–1905. All the Good Things of Life* (ed. Norman and Jeanne MacKenzie 1983) p.341.

29 Ruby J. Mayer.

30 Ralph Wedgwood became chief general manager of the London and North-Eastern Railway, 1923–41. He was knighted in 1924, and created a baronet in 1942. His daughter was C.V. Wedgwood, the historian.

31 Julia Strachey, Oliver's daughter, who married Stephen Tomlin, the sculptor, and subsequently Lawrence Gowing, the painter. She was the author of *Cheerful Weather for the Wedding* (1932) and *The Man on the Pier* (1951).

32 'English Letter Writers' was later published in *Characters and Commentaries* (1933) and reprinted in *Literary Essays* (1949). The manuscript is in the Humanities Research Center at Austin, Texas.

33 Edmund Anthony Beck, a Trinity Hall don.

34 R. Vere Laurence, then much under the influence of G.M. Trevelyan, in those days an austere teetotaller. Laurence himself was addicted to drinking and smoking, and before he died in 1934 had become an alcoholic.

35 Rosy Haigh, Lytton's bedmaker.

36 E.M. Forster, *Goldsworthy Lowes Dickinson* (1934) p.29.

CHAPER VI: POST-GRADUATE

1 Harry Stuart Goodhart-Rendel (he assumed by Royal Licence the additional name of Rendel) had a distinguished career both in musical and architectural fields. Among his many official appointments were Slade Professor of Fine Art at Oxford, Governor of Sadler's Wells, president of the Architectural Association and president of the Royal Institute of British Architects.

2 Charles Darwin, seven years younger than Lytton, a younger brother of Gwen Raverat, the author and artist, was a grandson of the great scientist Charles Darwin. He married Katherine Pember, while his younger sister Margaret became the wife of Maynard Keynes's younger brother Geoffrey. These Darwins were the children of Sir George Darwin, Plumian Professor of Astronomy at Cambridge, and a particular friend of Lytton's parents.

3 A.D. Knox, the second of the four Knox brothers, a brilliant classical scholar, afterwards Fellow of King's College, also famous for his fierce atheism, mysterious flights of spin bowling and wartime cryptography. In later years, Lytton became very friendly with him.

4 Sir Geoffrey Keynes (1887–1982), later to become a surgeon and Blake scholar, whose *Job* he converted into a ballet, choreographed by Lytton's cousin Ninette de Valois, and with music by Vaughan Williams. His bibliographies include volumes on John Donne, Sir Thomas Browne, Rupert Brooke and Siegfried Sassoon.

5 Lytton and Rupert Brooke had in fact met in the summer of 1898, when the Stracheys rented the country house called Ardeley Bury, near Stevenage and Rupert came to stay with James. They were both then aged between ten and eleven, and James remembered Lytton reading *Paradise Lost* to him in the garden. They met again in Brighton during the Easter holidays of 1900, but neither of them appeared to have remembered it.

6 The politically influential figure at Cambridge was Ben Keeling, who converted Hugh Dalton from a Conservative tariff reformer into a Fabian socialist. It was only after the First World War that communism became a topic of discusssion within the Society.

7 '"Comus" at Cambridge' *Spectator* 101 (18 July 1908).

8 The term was invented by Desmond MacCarthy's wife, Molly.

9 'In fact,' James Strachey objected, 'in our stockinged feet, we were both, at our best, exactly 6 ft 1 in. tall.'

10 Daniel Macmillan (1866–1964), elder brother of Harold Macmillan, later prime minister. A scholar of Balliol College, he subsequently became chairman and managing director of Macmillan and Co. Ltd, the publishers. Maynard Keynes listed him as a sexual partner at Eton.

11 Ray Costelloe was the daughter of Logan Pearsall Smith's sister, Mary Costelloe, who later married Bernard Berenson. Ray's sister Karin married Adrian Stephen, and her aunt Alys was the wife of Bertrand Russell. A leader in the Woman's Movement, Ray was the author of *Millicent Garrett Fawcett* (1931) and *The Cause* (1928). She and Oliver Strachey had two children, Barbara, who joined the administrative staff of the BBC, and Christopher, who, after a spell as a Harrow schoolmaster, became an expert in machine intelligence and in the early 1950s succeeded Alan Turing as the central innovative figure in British computing until his death in 1975.

12 Geoffrey Winthrop Young, poet and mountaineer. On leaving Eton, he had taken up a post as one of H.M. Inspectors of Secondary Schools (1905–13). Later he became renowned for scaling Alpine peaks after having lost a leg in the battle of Monte San Gabriele in the Great War.

13 Lytton celebrated the occasion with some verses entitled:
'*In Memoriam J.M.K. Ob.Sept.1906.*'
Here lie the remains of one
Who always did what should be done.
Who never misbehaved at table
And loved as much as he was able.
Who couldn't fail to make a joke,
And, though he stammered, always spoke;
Both penetrating and polite,
A liberal and a sodomite,
An atheist and a statistician,
A man of sense, without ambition.
A man of business, without bustle,
A follower of Moore and Russell,
One who, in fact, in every way,
Combined the features of the day.
By curses blest, by blessings cursed,
He didn't merely get a first.

A first he got; on that he'd reckoned;
But then he also got a second.
He got a first with moderate pride;
He got a second, and he died.

14 Alfred Plowden, a first cousin of Lady Strachey's, was a tremendously celebrated figure in the popular press during the early years of the century. Like Mr Justice Darling, he was famous for the jokes he made in court, and readers of the halfpenny papers could find them quoted almost every day. His daughter Pamela, a great beauty and the first love of Winston Churchill, married the second Earl of Lytton who was for a time acting-viceroy of India.

15 Published in May 1906. On 7 April, Lytton wrote to Duncan Grant: 'With some difficulty and agitation I finished my review of Blake. It is for the Independent, and will I hope appear in the May number. It annoys me to think of the poor result of so much effort. After it was finished I felt worn to the bone – a "poor, pale, pitiable form", as he says himself. But I'm now more or less cheerful again. My dear, he's certainly equal to the greatest of poets – though I somehow failed to say this properly in my damned review. His poems are the essence and sublimation of poetry.

Poor, pale, pitiable form
That I follow in a storm;
Iron tears and groans of lead
Bind around my aching head.

Isn't it a triumph? And almost too much?'

16 *The Really Interesting Question and Other Papers* (ed. Paul Levy 1972) p.127.

17 Quentin Bell tells me that Lytton was probably inexact in giving this description. Clive Bell never did and never could drive a car.

18 *The Brides' Tragedy* (1822) and *Death's Jest-Book* (1850), both by Thomas Lovell Beddoes.

CHAPTER VII: INTENTIONS

1 Mrs Fawcett was leader of the constitutional movement in favour of women's suffrage – a movement going back to John Stuart Mill. It was only fairly recently that Mrs Pankhurst and her supporters had started up a society which employed non-constitutional methods to gain the same objective. The Stracheys were old friends and colleagues of Mrs Fawcett, but they deplored the behaviour of Mrs Pankhurst's Women's Social and Political Union.

2 E.M. Sidgwick (1845–1936), the widow of Henry Sidgwick, who became president of the Society for Psychical Research, a body concerned with making scientific investigations of such phenomena as telepathy and séances. Though not a spiritualist, she eventually became convinced of the probability of survival after death.

3 Blanche Warre-Cornish, daughter of William Ritchie, was the author of two long novels and a rather tame monograph of R.H. Benson – Frederick Rolfe's 'Bobugo Bonson' – the Catholic writer and apologist.

4 This was published in *The Shorter Strachey* (1980) pp.225–32.

5 Sir Arthur Wing Pinero (1855–1934), prolific writer of farces and dramas influenced by Ibsen.

6 H.O. Meredith, known as 'Hom' among his Cambridge friends, a Fellow of King's who later became Professor of Political Economy at Queen's University, Belfast.

7 A collection of poetry translations from the Chinese made by Professor H.A. Giles of Cambridge, and originally published in 1898. Lytton was to write an

appreciation of this book in the summer of 1908, printed that autumn in the *New Quarterly* and the *Living Age*.

8 Lytton's essay on Madame du Deffand was not in fact composed until 1912.

9 Vanessa Bell's Friday Club, founded in the autumn of 1905, held most of its early meetings in her house at 46 Gordon Square. Inspired by the cultural milieu of some Parisian cafés, it became a centre where artists could talk shop, listen to lectures and discuss contemporary work. Between 1910 and 1914 it developed into one of Britain's liveliest exhibition groups.

10 Alice Knewstub, who had married William Rothenstein in 1899. According to her son, John Rothenstein, she was 'an inflammable compound of Toryism and anarchy'.

11 *Men and Memories. Recollections of William Rothenstein, Volume 2 1900–1922* (1932) p.179.

12 Among the plays he went to in these months was Herbert Beerbohm Tree's production of Wilde's *A Woman of No Importance*. 'It was rather amusing', he told Duncan Grant (2 June 1907), 'as it was a complete mass of epigrams, with occasional whiffs of grotesque melodrama and drivelling sentiment. The queerest mixture! Mr Tree is a wicked Lord, staying in a country house, who has made up his mind to bugger one of the other guests – a handsome young man of twenty. The handsome young man is delighted; when his mother enters, sees his Lordship and recognizes him as having copulated with her twenty years before, the result of which was – the handsome young man. She appeals to Lord Tree not to bugger his own son. He replies that that's an additional reason for doing it (oh! he's a *very* wicked Lord!). She then appeals to the handsome young man, who says, "Dear me! What an abominable thing to do – to go and copulate without marrying! Oh no, I shall certainly pay no attention to anyone capable of doing *that*, and –" when suddenly enter (from the garden) a young American millionairess, shrieking for help, and in considerable disorder. The wicked Lord Tree, not contented with buggering his own son, has attempted to rape the millionairess, with whom (very properly) the handsome young man is in love. Enter his Lordship. Handsome Y.M.: "You devil! You have insulted the purest creature on God's earth! I shall kill you!" But of course he doesn't, but contents himself with marrying the millionairess, while his mother takes up a pair of gloves and slashes the Lord across the face. It seems an odd plot, doesn't it? But it required all my penetration to find out that this *was* the plot, as you may imagine. Epigrams engulf it like the sea. Most of them were thoroughly rotten, and nearly all were said quite cynically to the gallery. Poor old Tree sits down with his back to the audience to talk to a brilliant lady, and swings round in his seat every time he delivers an epigram. The audience was of course charmed.'

13 Granville Proby (1883–1947), later Clerk to the House of Lords and Lord Lieutenant of Huntingdonshire.

14 Geoffrey Scott (1884–1929), the Boswell scholar, and author of *The Architecture of Humanism* and *The Portrait of Zélide*.

15 The Rt Reverend Monsignor Ronald Arbuthnot Knox (1888–1957), whose biography has been decorously written by Evelyn Waugh (1959). Author of many books on Roman Catholicism, and of *Studies in the Literature of Sherlock Holmes*, a work that gave impetus to Holmeseology. Translator of the Vulgate. When Lytton met him he was up at Balliol College and reputed to be the wittiest president of the Oxford Union within living memory. After he was converted to Roman Catholicism in the First World War, the *Manchester Guardian* wrote that Rome had 'landed the biggest fish since Newman'.

16 James Elroy Flecker (1884–1915), poet and dramatist, who left Trinity College, Oxford, in 1906 with only a Third in Mods and Greats, and returned the following year in an abortive attempt to live through writing. He became an

accomplished linguist, a great traveller and keen bibliophile. His poem *The Golden Journey to Samarkand* was much admired by Eddie Marsh, but D.H. Lawrence declared that it 'only took place on paper – no matter who went to Asia Minor'. His chief drama, *Hassan* (published posthumously in 1922), was produced with a ballet by Fokine and music by Delius. Reconverted to Christianity, he received communion on his death-bed at Davos in the first week of 1915.

17 Degen was the nineteen-year-old baker with whom Beddoes lived in close companionship for six months at Frankfurt.

18 Frances Spalding *Vanessa Bell* (1983) pp.63–5.

19 'The Rousseau Affair' was based on a two-volume publication *Jean Jacques Rousseau: A New Criticism* by Frederika Macdonald (1906). The principal revelations of this work related to the *Mémoires et Correspondances de Madame d'Épinay* (1818), the concluding quarter of which contains an account of Rousseau's quarrel with his friends, written from the anti-Rousseau point of view. This hostile narrative, as Mrs Macdonald showed, was in effect composed by Diderot and the Baron de Grimm. Lord Morley had published an earlier biography of Rousseau, taking the accuracy of the *Mémoires* for granted. Lytton's essay (incorrectly dated as 1907 in *Books and Characters*) did not in fact appear in the *New Quarterly* until 1910. 'What is going to happen to that appalling paper?' he wrote to Desmond MacCarthy (7 June 1910). 'I was furious to see my old Rousseau hash served up in it, and I shall never speak to you again if you don't pay me for it. I am dead for want of money, so I insist on being saved by £5.'

20 'Modern Poetry', *Spectator* 100 (18 April 1908) pp.622–3.

21 'Mr Yeats's Poetry', *Spectator* 101 (17 October 1908), pp.588–9.

22 'The Mollusc', *Spectator* 99 (30 November 1907) pp.867–8.

23 'Mr Granville Barker', *Spectator* 100 (28 March 1908) pp.499–500. Collected in *Spectatorial Essays* (1964) pp.194–7.

24 'Mr Beerbohm Tree', *Spectator* 100 (1 February 1908) pp.185–6. Collected in *Spectatorial Essays* (1964) pp.203–7.

25 'Mr Barrie's New Play' (*What Every Woman Knows*), *Spectator* 101 (26 September 1908) pp.444–5.

26 'Three New Plays', *Spectator* 100 (6 June 1908) pp.899–900.

27 *Spectatorial Essays* (1964) p.9.

28 Amabel Strachey (1894–1984), who in 1915 married B.C. Williams-Ellis, the architect and man of letters, was the eldest daughter of St Loe and Henrietta Amy Strachey. She was the author of many books for children, including *Darwin's Moon* (1966), a biography of Alfred Russel Wallace, and a memoir entitled *All Stracheys are Cousins* (1983).

29 Gerald Frank Shove (1887–1947), the economist, who became a lecturer in economics at Cambridge and a Fellow of King's, was at this time a keen left-wing socialist and syndicalist.

30 After a short tenancy at Belgrave Road, they moved to 21 Fitzroy Square. Then, in 1911, they shared a house at 38 Brunswick Square with Adrian and Virginia Stephen, Gerald Shove and Leonard Woolf. Later still they moved to 46 Gordon Square which they shared with Clive and Vanessa Bell.

31 This refers to *The Embarkation for Cythera*, painted by Antoine Watteau in 1712 (and now in the Louvre), which shows an imagined voyage to an island of love and blessedness.

32 'Loch an Eilein' is a Gaelic place-name meaning 'the loch of the island'. A famous beauty spot, it is incredibly romantic and much reproduced on picture postcards. The island-fortress in the middle of its placid waters was, as legend has it, the lair of the notorious Wolf of Radenoch, who in fact died several years before it was put up. The fortifications, now in ruins, were erected in the fifteenth and sixteenth centuries.

33 This portrait, which was exhibited at the Duncan Grant Tate Gallery retrospective exhibition of 1959, and again, in 1964, at Wildenstein's 'Duncan Grant and his World', now belongs to the Provost and Fellows of King's College, Cambridge.

34 'An Anthology' *New Quarterly* 1 (October 1908), pp.603–10. Reprinted in *Characters and Commentaries* (1933) and *Literary Essays* (1949).

35 Robert John Grote Mayor (1869–1947), Old Etonian, Fellow of King's College, Cambridge, and later principal secretary at the Board of Education. He was the brother of F.M. Mayor, author of *The Rector's Daughter*. Mrs Humphry Ward (1851–1920), popular novelist and author of *Robert Elsmere*. A niece of Matthew Arnold and a strong reactionary, her novels, especially the earlier ones, examined problems of faith and ethics with unsmiling sentimentality that was taken at the time for high intellect.

CHAPTER VIII: THE WRONG TURNING

1 The President of the Board of Trade at this time was Winston Churchill. Edmund Gosse had worked as a translator in the Board of Trade with Austin Dobson, the poet. Sidney Colvin, who had been Slade Professor of Fine Art at Cambridge and Director of the Fitzwilliam Museum, was now Keeper in the Department of Prints and Drawings at the British Museum.

2 In 1909, the House of Lords rejected the Liberal reforms implemented by the budget. Asquith dissolved Parliament and, in January 1910, won the election. Soon afterwards he introduced proposals for altering the powers of the House of Lords, but at that moment Edward VII died, and in the new reign a constitutional conference was held between the parties. This broke down in the autumn and Asquith dissolved Parliament a second time and held a second election in December 1910. Having won this too, he introduced the Parliament Bill, at the same time threatening to abolish the Lords' veto by advising the Monarch to create, if necessary, some five hundred new peers sympathetic to his measures. Rather than be flooded out in this manner, the Upper House gave way. Lytton bought *The Times* booklet reporting the debate in the House of Lords on the second reading of the Finance Bill of 1909, and marked a number of the more extreme passages to assist him with the dialogue of his novel. This was perhaps the start of Lytton's serious political interest. He became strongly anti upper class. Parts of the four chapters from *Lord Pettigrew* were published in *Lytton Strachey. The Really Interesting Question and Other Papers*, ed. Paul Levy (1972).

3 In the Savile Candidates Book No. 3, it is recorded that Lytton was proposed by J.E. McTaggart on 13 February 1908 and elected on 31 March. His referees were H.L. Stephen, W.H.C. Shaw (who had married Frances, younger sister of St Loe Strachey), H.G. Dakyns, Hilton Young, John Pollock, A. Chichele Plowden (Lytton's cousin), J.B. Atkins (a friend of St Loe Strachey's and assistant editor of the *Spectator*), and (the Rev.) H.F. Stewart, a Trinity don, friendly with Lytton and with Pernel who was then a Newnham don in the same modern languages department.

4 Mallory was constantly abashed by having to endure these 'disconcerting reminders' of his good looks, David Robertson, his biographer, tells us. He seems, at least before others, to have been embarrassed by Lytton's irreverence and coyness, but was somewhat in awe of his intellect, and amused by his wit, even when exercised at the expense of those 'simply absurd' objects, mountains. 'He [Lytton] is very, very queer,' Mallory wrote defensively to his fiancée, Ruth Turner (23 May 1914), ' – not to me, of course, because I know him as a friend, but to the world. He must be very irritating to many people. My profound respect

for his intellect, and for a sort of passion with which he holds the doctrine of freedom, besides much love for him as a man of intense feelings and fine imagination, make me put up with much in him that I could hardly tolerate in any other.'

5 Frank Sidgwick, the publisher, best remembered perhaps for his collaboration with Eddie Marsh on Marsh's *Memoir* of Rupert Brooke, and selections from Brooke's poetry. He was also responsible for bringing out Brooke's first book, *Poems*, which Sidgwick and Jackson published on 4 December 1911.

6 In his biography of Rupert Brooke, Christopher Hassall noted that this actually referred to Samuel Widnall, 'author and printer of several topographical books, and pioneer in photography; he was never ordained but affected the appearance of a clergyman, and in 1853 erected a Folly at the bottom of his garden, the ruinated fragment of what might be a medieval nunnery.'

7 Francis Birrell (1889–1935), journalist and drama critic, who after the war started a bookshop with David Garnett.

8 Francis Birrell's father, Augustine Birrell, the politician and man of letters, was Chief Secretary for Ireland in Asquith's Cabinet. He resigned after the Easter Week Rebellion in Dublin in 1916.

CHAPTER IX: THE CHANGING PAST

1 *Ottoline. The Early Memoirs of Lady Ottoline Morrell* (ed. Robert Gathorne-Hardy 1963) p.179.

2 The portrait was bought by the National Portrait Gallery in 1991 for a little over £100,000.

3 Francis Dodd (1874–1949), the etcher and painter of landscapes, who, in 1895, had gone to live in Manchester, and nine years later moved to London where he eventually became a Royal Academician and a trustee of the Tate Gallery (1928–35).

4 In later life Euphemia took up with the painter James Dickson Innes (1887–1914). John Rothenstein, in his *Modern English Painters, Volume 2: Innes to Moore* (revised edition 1962, pp.29–30) writes: 'They met in a Paris café [at 25 Boulevard du Montparnasse in May 1910] and ... made their way, largely on foot, to his favourite resorts on the foothills of the Pyrenees, and back to London, he contributing to their support by making drawings in cafés and she by dancing. Their attachment lasted until his death.' When he was dying in a nursing-home at Swanley in Kent, Horace Cole and Augustus John took Euphemia to see him. 'The meeting of these two was painful,' John records in *Chiaroscuro* (1952 edn, p.206). 'We left them alone together: it was the last time I saw him. Under the cairn on the summit of Arenig, Dick Innes had buried a silver casket containing certain correspondence. I think he always associated Euphemia with this mountain and would have liked at the last to lie beside the cairn.'

5 Ottoline's ancestor, Hans William Bentinck, first Earl of Portland (1649–1709), had entered William of Orange's household at the age of fifteen, becoming the Prince's loyal companion of a lifetime, his favourite, and his confidential agent. At William and Mary's coronation he was deluged with honours and rewards, but remained rather an unpopular figure in international politics. He married three times, his numerous children settling partly in Holland, partly in England.

6 Philip Morrell had lost his seat in the General Election of January 1910 but was returned as Liberal MP for Burnley in December 1910.

7 After studying law at St Petersburg and travelling widely through Europe, Boris von Anrep (1883–1969) had gone to Paris where he studied Byzantine art. In 1910–11, when Lytton first encountered him, he had moved to the Edinburgh

College of Art. In 1916 he joined the Imperial Guard and appeared, a terrific figure in full Russian Guard uniform, claiming that a battle at the Front wasn't nearly so alarming as one of Ottoline's parties. After the war he was to live for a time in Hampstead, but returned to Paris in 1926 and devoted himself to the revival of mosaic as an independent art. His chief public commissions in Britain include the mosaic pavement at the Tate Gallery, the floor, vestibule landing and pavement at the National Gallery (which depicts, among others, Virginia Woolf, Mary Hutchinson, Clive Bell, Osbert and Edith Sitwell, T.S. Eliot and Bertrand Russell), and mosaics for Westminster Cathedral, the Bank of England and the Royal Military College chapel, Sandhurst. In 1918 he married Helen Maitland (1885–1965), a close friend of the Johns and ex-girlfriend of Henry Lamb, who later left him to live with Roger Fry, whose wife, having become incurably ill in 1910, was to die in 1936.

8 *Ottoline. The Early Memoirs of Lady Ottoline Morrell* p.215.

9 The recommendation of Dostoyevsky may have come originally from Boris Anrep or indirectly from Augustus John. In August 1909, John dined with James Strachey, and in the course of their conversation made a long speech in favour of the Russian novelist, about whose work only a few intellectuals knew at this time. R.L. Stevenson had been greatly impressed by *Crime and Punishment* in the 1880s, but a wide interest in Dostoyevsky followed the publication of Maurice Baring's *Landmarks in Russian Literature* in 1910, and the translation of his novels by Constance Garnett between 1912 and 1920.

10 'A red-brown-gold beard', he described it in a letter to George Mallory, 'of the most divine proportions.'

11 *Ottoline. The Early Memoirs of Lady Ottoline Morrell* pp.213–14.

12 Leonard Woolf *Beginning Again. An autobiography of the years 1911 to 1918* (1964) pp.41–2.

13 *Song of Love. The Letters of Rupert Brooke and Noel Olivier* (ed. Pippa Harris 1991) p.212.

14 Paul Delaney *The Neo-Pagans. Friendship and Love in the Rupert Brooke Circle* (1987) p.154.

15 *The Times* obituary 26 April 1915. Paul Delaney suggests it was probably drafted by Eddie Marsh.

16 Published in *Lytton Strachey. The Really Interesting Question* (ed. Paul Levy 1972) pp.62–8.

17 James Strachey pointed out that Lytton never in his life wore gold-rimmed spectacles and never a velveteen coat – unless this is meant to include corduroy, which he did go in for during his Augustus John period.

18 Max Beerbohm *Lytton Strachey. The Rede Lecture 1943* pp.5–6.

19 The best-known portrait (oil, 90 x 70 in), for many years in the collection of Stanley Spencer's patrons, the Behrends, was bought in 1953 by the Tate Gallery under the terms of the Chantrey Bequest and has been on loan to the National Portrait Gallery. A painting of the background of this portrait, 'Hampstead Heath from the Vale of Health', was owned by Richard Carline. An earlier version, painted in 1912 (oil, 20 x 15½ in), was bought in 1923 by Siegfried Sassoon who wrote to Sydney Cockerell (24 November 1923): 'The other day I committed an extravagance and bought Henry Lamb's first small oil picture of Lytton Strachey (the study for the big one). It is delightful, and, I think, of historic value (I gave £60). Some day I will transfer it to the Fitzwilliam (L.S. being a Cambridge man it should be there). You can take this as a promise.' In fact Siegfried Sassoon gave this portrait to Lady Ottoline Morrell; it was exhibited at the Leicester Galleries in 1956 ('Pictures from Garsington', No. 32 in the Catalogue) and bought by Lord Cottesloe, who exhibited it in Leningrad at a British Council exhibition of British Painting. This was later sold to a private collector in the United States.

The Fitzwilliam Museum has a portrait painted in 1913 (20½ x 16 in) in which the head and shoulders exactly correspond to the Tate Gallery portrait. This was formerly owned by C.K. Ogden, and by J.E. Vulliamy, who presented it to the Fitzwilliam in 1945. The Ashmolean Museum, Oxford, has a 'Study for Portrait of Lytton Strachey' purchased by Lord Cottesloe in 1961; and the Victoria and Albert Museum acquired in 1962 a pencil drawing of Strachey seated in a chair. A red chalk drawing was sold at Christie's on 4 July 1953. Mrs Gilbert Russell owned another early portrait similar to that in the Fitzwilliam Museum and Mrs Julian Vinogradoff, daughter of Lady Ottoline Morrell, a painting of the head and shoulders (exhibited at the Café Royal Centenary Exhibition, 1965, and at the Arts Council Gallery, 1966, 'Vision and Design', commemorating the life, work and influence of Roger Fry).

20 See Keith Clements *Henry Lamb. The Artist and his Friends* (1985) chapter ten.
21 Stephen Spender *World Within World* (1951) p.76.
22 Osbert Sitwell *Noble Essences* (1950) p.7.

CHAPER X: TOWN VERSUS THE COUNTRY

1 'Dostoievsky' *Spectator* 109 (28 September 1912) pp.451–2. Reprinted in *Spectatorial Essays* (1964) pp.174–9.
2 *The Letters of Leonard Woolf* (ed. Frederic Spotts 1990) p.176.
3 Ada Beddington (1862–1933), author of six epigrammatic novels, who had married Ernest Leverson, the son of a diamond merchant. She became one of the closest and most loyal friends of Oscar Wilde, who always called her 'the Sphinx'.
4 Sir Charles Holroyd (1861–1917), Director of the National Gallery and first Keeper of the Tate Gallery, had four years previously lent his support in favour of Epstein's Strand statues.
5 A slightly different and shorter version of this statement appears in Jacob Epstein's *An Autobiography* (revised edition, 1963) pp.53–4.
6 James Strachey remembered that Willie Glass was little more than a gillie, though, like all Highlanders, exceedingly cultured. He was also mad, and said to be, like so many others, a descendant of an illegitimate son of Laird William, Lytton's great-uncle, a notorious loose liver. 'Glass' in fact is another version of 'Grant'.
7 *The Selected Letters of Bertrand Russell volume I. The Private Years, 1884–1914* (ed. Nicholas Griffin 1992) p.429.
8 *Ottoline. The Early Memoirs of Lady Ottoline Morrell* (ed. Robert Gathorne-Hardy 1963) pp.231–2.
9 *Ottoline. The Early Memoirs of Lady Ottoline Morrell* (ed. Robert Gathorne-Hardy 1963) p.233.
10 Ethel Sands, painter and 'rich ugly elder spinster' (Mark Gertler), had migrated to Paris to live with her companion Nan Hudson, and only returned on the death of her mother. For a time she lived at Newington, a square grey stone house inaccurately attributed to Inigo Jones, with exquisitely decorated rooms, a forecourt, formal garden and great stone gates. By the time Lytton got to know her she was living at 15 The Vale, Chelsea. The dining-room here was to have mural decorations by Duncan Grant and paintings by Sickert, and in the hallway there were mosaics by Boris Anrep, one of which was to show Lytton looking out from a cottage window towards Carrington, depicted from another mosaic window, looking up at him.
11 'A smoothing-over of the late crisis has taken place by means of long and amicable letters,' Lytton wrote to Virginia (1 December 1912), 'so if the dear fellow should go and see you, I hope you will be discreet and refrain from pouring salt on the

wounds by injudicious repetitions of long-cancelled abuse. I'm looking forward to see him again, but I have the greatest fears that he's cut his hair short, which would be a severe blow.'

12 Boris Anrep had chosen the Russian contingent of the Second Post-Impressionist exhibition, Clive Bell the English, and Roger Fry the French.

13 Lytton could not bring himself to tell Leonard Woolf what he thought of *The Village in the Jungle* for nearly six months, when he was safely out of the country. From Paris, on 23 April 1913, he criticized the novel in a manner that catches the racism prevalent among the Edwardians. 'I think I'm in a particularly difficult position for judging of it, because my tastes are not at all in the direction of the blacks etc. I'm sure most people have more of a fellow feeling for them. As for me, the more black they are the more I dislike them, and yours seems to be remarkably so. I did hope for one bright scene at least with some fetid white wife of a Governor, but no doubt that would have been quite out of key. Perhaps really for everybody the blacks are not a very interesting subject – but it's difficult to be certain . . . Oh Lord! how horrible it all is! – Fortunately there are other things in the world . . . Whites! Whites! Whites!'

14 Paul Delaney *The Neo-Pagans. Friendship and Love in the Rupert Brooke Circle* (1987) p.154.

15 Godfrey Harold Hardy (1877–1947), Fellow of the Royal Society and later Sadleirian Professor of Pure Mathematics at Cambridge. Lytton had first met him when an undergraduate at Trinity. 'I played bowls on the Fellows' Bowling Green which is behind the chapel and most charming,' he wrote to his mother (2 May 1901). 'Only fellows and their friends are allowed there – ours was Hardy, who got the Smith's Prize last year – he is *the* mathematical genius and looks a babe of three.' In 1940 he published a short book, *A Mathematician's Apology*, that is generally voted a masterpiece stylistically as well as in content.

16 Evidently Alice B. Toklas. Describing Lytton as 'a thin sallow man with a silky beard and faint high voice', Gertrude Stein wrote of this meeting in her *Autobiography of Alice B. Toklas*: '. . . we had been invited to meet George Moore at the house of Miss Ethel Sands. Gertrude Stein and George Moore who looked like a very prosperous Mellon's Food baby, had not been interested in each other. Lytton Strachey and I talked together about Picasso and the russian ballet.'

17 *Ermyntrude and Esmeralda* was published in 1969 by Anthony Blond with illustrations by Erté. An Italian translation came out in 1970, and a French translation in 1971. It also appeared in *Playboy* (1969).

18 Sir James Mackay, first Earl of Inchcape (1852–1932), the ship-owner; director and chairman of numerous shipping companies.

19 The second Earl of Lytton, then in his mid-30s, was distantly connected to the Grants through his marriage to Pamela Chichele-Plowden, daughter of the outspoken magistrate Alfred Plowden. He had just published a biography of his father, Edward Bulwer-Lytton.

20 MacCarthy in fact never completed this novel on school life. But a short story, *The Mark on the Shutter or A Small Boy's Conscience* – 'for me, the best short story ever written about a school' (Lord David Cecil) – may have been a distillation of his original idea. It is included in *Humanities* (1953).

21 The Omega Workshops had officially opened in July 1913 at 33 Fitzroy Square, these premises serving as showroom, design studios and actual workshops. The driving force behind the scheme was Roger Fry, who was helped by his two directors, Vanessa Bell and Duncan Grant. Among the young artists they employed part-time at thirty shillings a week to design and produce textiles, dress fashions, furniture and pottery were Wyndham Lewis, Edward Wadsworth, William Roberts and Henri Gaudier-Brzeska. Several of their fabrics were hand-painted with dyes. In some cases local carpenters were employed to do basic

joinery in white wood which the artists would then decorate; in others, designs were placed in the hands of large firms – furnishing fabrics sometimes printed in France, carpets sometimes woven by Royal Wilton, stained glass produced in Fulham. Amateur and experimental in execution, their products – which could be bought or made to order – aimed at giving employment to contemporary artists and educating the public taste to radically new aesthetic ideas. In June 1919, Fry closed the workshops and the company was forced into voluntary liquidation.

22 Will Arnold-Forster (1885–1951), a mild water-colourist, second cousin of Aldous Huxley, married Ka Cox in 1919.

23 Nijinsky was the choreographer of *Le Sacré du Printemps*. He did not dance in it.

24 A fine description of this food, and of the inn itself, is given by Leonard Woolf in *Beginning Again. An Autobiography of the Years 1911 to 1918* (1964) pp.153–4.

25 Arthur Ewart Popham (1889–1970), usually called Hugh Popham, had been at King's College and was later to become Keeper of Prints and Drawings at the British Museum. He was painfully shy, had first proposed unsuccessfully to Brynhild in 1910 ('I think it almost impossibly much to ask you to marry me'), and only married her in October 1912 when allegedly in reaction from an affair with Gerald Shove's mother. Their marriage struck great jealousy into Rupert who attempted to sabotage it by proposing an affair with Bryn. It also greatly upset Margery Olivier who, identifying with her sisters, imagined herself in love with both Rupert and Hugh Popham (as well as with James Strachey and Harry Norton) having what Leonard Woolf called 'a disease of advanced virginity in which one imagines proposals at every tea party'. After years of increasing mental instability, Margery was committed in 1922 to an asylum by her sister Noel, then a doctor, who certified her as having 'Dementia Praecox Paranoides'. She had been treated by Dr Henry Head (who also saw Virginia Woolf) and by Dr Caesar Sherrard with whose nephew, Raymond Sherrard, she fell in love. He later became the second husband of Bryn after her divorce from Hugh Popham. Bryn and Hugh's second child, Anne, married Vanessa and Clive Bell's second child, Quentin Bell.

26 *Song of Love. The Letters of Rupert Brooke and Noel Olivier 1909–1915* (ed. Pippa Harris 1991) p.250.

CHAPTER XI: THE LACKET

1 Leonard James Maxse, editor and proprietor of the *National Review*, was drawn into the Marconi affair through some articles written in his paper by W.R. Lawson which suggested that certain ministers in the Government were guilty of corruption. Maxse's statement before the Select Committee of the House of Commons was largely responsible for flushing out those ministers concerned and making them face public opinion. In due course he became a target of the Liberal press.

2 Lady (Sybil) Colefax, a fashionable hostess and camp-follower of the arts, who managed an ambitious social career with military self-discipline, was the wife of Sir Arthur Colefax, a pillar of the law, who haunted her entertainments like a smiling spectre.

3 The Second Grafton Group exhibition was being held at the Alpine Club Gallery, where Duncan Grant, Vanessa Bell and others were showing pictures.

4 Nina Hamnett (1890–1956) became a great cicerone to the art world of Paris and London and a leader of the *vie de bohème* which she described in her two volumes of autobiography, *Laughing Torso* (1935) and *Is She a Lady?* (1955). Among her friends were Modigliani, Gaudier-Brzeska, who did a sculpture of her body (now in the Victoria and Albert Museum), and Roger Fry, who employed her – together

with her husband Roald Kristian – in the Omega Workshops, and who painted her portrait. Among her enemies was Aleister Crowley, the Great Beast No. 666, against whom she successfully defended herself in 'one of the most extraordinary trials of the first half of the 20th century' (John Symonds).

5 'Aunt Fanny Stanley', though not really an aunt, was a proverbial figure of the faithful elderly female relative, on the Grant side of the family.

6 Kenneth Bell (1884–1951), Fellow of All Souls and of Balliol, who five years before his death was ordained a priest in the Church of England.

7 Professor A.F.B. Williams (1867–1950), historian and barrister. He was the biographer of Cecil Rhodes and William Pitt and author of *The Whig Supremacy 1714–60*, volume XI of *The Oxford History of England*.

8 The first editor of the *New Statesman* was Clifford Sharp, a notorious alcoholic, the other permanent members of the staff at this stage being Desmond MacCarthy (drama critic), J.C. Squire (literary editor) and Emil Davies (City correspondent). The paper, a brain-child of the Webbs, had been founded in 1913. Shaw, a part-proprietor, was expected to be the star contributor, but he insisted on writing anonymously and so sabotaged the Webbs' hopes of using his name to attract a thousand new readers.

9 Sir Matthew Nathan (1862–1939), civil servant and soldier, at this time Chairman of the Board of Inland Revenue. He was later appointed Governor of Queensland. In his pristine days, he had been one of Dorothy Strachey's unhappy suitors.

10 *The Letters of Walter Raleigh 1879–1922* (ed. Lady Raleigh 1926) volume II p.403.

11 'Coelum non animum', the Strachey family's motto, comes from Horace – '*Coelum non animum mutant qui trans mare currunt*' – which Lytton translated for this line of his poem. This motto was subject to some variation. In the eighteenth century, when it was the fashion to get dinner services made in China, the Stracheys at Sutton Court sent orders to the East for a set to be made with the motto on each plate. The whole dinner service arrived eventually, inscribed COBLUM NON ANIMUM. Pieces of Coblum china survived for many years at Sutton Court.

12 A rather different account of a second showing of this play, performed before an English audience, is given by David Garnett in *The Flowers of the Forest* (1955) pp.22–3.

13 Miranda Seymour *Ottoline Morrell. Life on the Grand Scale* (1992) p.206.

14 David Garnett *The Flowers of the Forest* (1955) p.31.

15 Ibid. p.17.

16 Unpublished essay by David Garnett quoted in Frances Spalding's *Vanessa Bell* (1983) p.136.

17 Robert Skidelsky *John Maynard Keynes. Hopes Betrayed 1883–1920* (1983) p.300.

18 'Send me your life of Manning at once or I shall go mad,' E.M. Forster wrote to him (17 May 1915). 'I will disinfect it.' A fortnight later he wrote again. 'I will return the Cardinal when I have read him again – a habit you censured some 12 years back. Meanwhile I wish you would send me Mademoiselle Nightingale and some short witty stories. I am certain you have some – they will be quite safe.'

19 Mary Barnes, daughter of Winifred Strachey (who married Sir Hugh Barnes), the fourth child of John Strachey (1823–1907). Her grandfather, Sir John Strachey, was a younger brother of Lytton's father. Her husband, St John Hutchinson, became Master of the Bench Middle Temple, Recorder of Hastings and a Trustee of the Tate Gallery. Lytton attributed the 'extraordinary sympathy' between Mary and himself to their common ancestry. 'There seems to be a subtle – an exciting – congruity between our natures: a unique affair,' he wrote to her (11 August 1926). And she wrote to him (21 February 1928): 'Sometimes I think you will have been the only constant human being in my life – my only certainty.'

20 Frances Spalding *Vanessa Bell* (1983) p.141.

21 Lytton Strachey to Carrington, 23 March 1917.

22 He had recently read the original draft of Forster's unpublished homosexual novel *Maurice*. 'I enjoyed it very much indeed – I think really more than the others,' he wrote to Forster (12 March 1915). 'The absence of the suburb-culture question was a relief ... I thought it seemed to go off at the end to some extent. The beginning – especially up to the successful combination of Maurice and Clive – I liked very much ... The Maurice-Alec affair didn't strike me as so successful. For one thing, the Class question is rather a red herring, I think. One suddenly learns that Maurice is exaggeratedly upper-classish – one wouldn't at all have expected it in the face of things – and then when the change comes, it seems to need more explanation ... because the ground isn't enough prepared: and Alec's feelings don't quite seize. As you describe it, I should be inclined to diagnose Maurice's state as simply lust and sentiment – a very wobbly affair; I should have prophecied a rupture after 6 months – chiefly as a result of lack of common interests owing to class differences – I believe even such a simple-minded fellow as Maurice would have felt this – and your Sherwood Forest ending appears to me slightly mythical ... The writing gets staccato (for the first time) at the end of Ch.xliv – just at the crisis ...

... A minor point is that I find it *very* difficult to believe that Maurice would have remained chaste during those 2 years with Clive. He was a strong healthy youth, and you say that, unless Clive had restrained him "he would have surfeited passion" (Ch.xv). But how the dickens could Clive restrain him? How could he have failed to have erections? Et après ça –? Well! I suppose it's just conceivable, but I must say I think you seem to take it rather too much as a matter of course ...

There remains the general conception – about which I don't feel at all certain. I don't understand why the copulation question should be given so much importance. It's difficult to distinguish clearly your own views from Maurice's sometimes, but so far as I can see, you go much too far in your disapproval of it ... Then, à propos of Maurice tossing himself off (you call it a "malpractice") (Ch.xxxii), you say – "He knew what the price would be – a creeping apathy towards all things". How did Maurice know that? And how do you? Surely the truth is that as often as not the effects are simply nil ...

It almost seems that you mean to indicate that Maurice's copulating with Alec is somehow *justified* by his falling in love with him. This alarms me considerably. I find the fatal sentence (Ch.xliii – British Museum) – "he loved Alec, loved him not as a second Dickie Barry, but deeply, tenderly, for his own sake, etc". More distressing still, there is never a hint afterwards that Maurice's self-reproaches during that period were exaggerated. I think he had still a great deal to learn, and that the très-très-noble Alec could never teach it him. What was wanted was a brief honeymoon with that charming young Frenchman who would have shown Mr. Eel that it was possible to take the divagations of a prick too seriously.

... you really do make a difference between affairs between men and men and those between men and women. The chastity between Maurice and Clive for the 2 years during which they were in effect married you consider (a) as a very good thing and (b) as nothing *very* remarkable. You then make Clive marry (without any change in his high-falutin' views) and promptly, quite as a matter of course, have his wife. (So that when he said to Maurice "I love you as if you were a woman," he was telling a lie.) I really think the whole conception of male copulation in the book rather diseased – in fact morbid and unnatural.'

CHAPTER XII: WAR AND PEACE

1 *Ottoline. The Early Memoirs of Lady Ottoline Morrell* (ed. Robert Gathorne-Hardy 1963) p.272.

2 'I really did not like Lytton Strachey,' Dorothy Brett told the author (9 March 1966). 'First of all he was so unpleasant to look at, to put it mildly, and he was secretively obscene. I did not know him intimately, I used to meet him at weekend-parties at Garsington, at parties in London. He was of delicate health, but as far as I could make out not delicate minded . . . I can remember an amusing incident at Garsington, when Lytton complained that Ottoline was stingy with the food. So the next morning, as a sort of ironical swatt at him, Ottoline had a breakfast sent up, consisting of eggs, sausages, bacon, mounds of toast, etc. To her chagrin he ate it all! From that day he was stuffed with food . . . The Bloomsburies scared me to death. I was much closer to Lawrence, Murry, Katherine, Gertler, who were not Bloomsburies. Virginia Woolf was the only one at all nice to me. I was a great nuisance with my deafness. I missed so much which irritated everybody . . . There was something to me creepy about Lytton. I have no objection to homosexuals, no prejudices whatsoever, maybe it was just his looks, I don't know.'

3 On 3 October 1919, Lytton wrote Katherine Mansfield a fan letter. 'Dear Katherine, The Government tells one only to write letters that are necessary – so be it! This is the letter of a loyal subject, because I can *think* of nothing more necessary than to tell you how much I admire your Athenaeum reviews, and how grateful I am to you for such charming weekly titillations . . . I should be very glad to hear any news of you – but I don't want to give trouble – only let me have a word or two some day.'

4 H.W. Massingham (1860–1924), editor of the *Nation*.

5 Later Sir Archibald Henry Bodkin (1862–1957) who between 1920 and 1930 was Director of Public Prosecutions.

6 This appeal was heard before the City Quarter Sessions, at the Guildhall, on 29 June 1916. Russell declined to pay the fine, but there was never any question of imprisonment since he owned valuable books that could be seized and sold. These books were saved by the action of Russell's friends, who subscribed the necessary hundred pounds and bid that sum for the first volume put up for sale at the auction.

7 *Selected Letters of Vanessa Bell* (ed. Regina Marler 1993) p.192.

8 Charles P. Sanger, the Apostle.

9 Nina Hamnett *Laughing Torso* (1932) pp.95–6.

10 Also living at Garsington was Sir Julian Huxley's future wife, Juliette Baillot, to whom Lytton was giving instruction in English verse.

11 Gretchen Gerzina *Carrington. A Life of Dora Carrington 1893–1932* (1989) p.8.

12 *Carrington. Letters & Extracts from her Diaries* (ed. David Garnett 1970) p.504.

13 Carrington often spoke of her brother 'Teddy' as a sailor and gave some of her friends the impression that he had been drowned at sea. He had left Cambridge when war was declared and with a group of rowing friends he volunteered for a minesweeper, joining the Navy as an A.B. After about eighteen months the Admiralty disbanded his unit. He then put in for a commission in the Wiltshire Regiment where his eldest brother Sam had served as a regular officer some years before the war, and where Noel had been serving since 1914. After a short training course he was sent out to France in 1916 and posted missing early in the battle of the Somme. There are other references in Dora's letters to Sam, wounded in August 1914, and to Noel, wounded in June 1915. But the loss of Teddy was a particular blow and did much to convert her to pacifism. Her relations with him were never really close, but he was the first young man she knew to be killed in the war and she felt passionately his loss. The last time he came on leave he was in sailor dress, and she made several drawings of him.

Noel was the author of *Design in Everyday Life and Popular Art in Britain*. He joined the Oxford University Press, became an editor of *Country Life* and also an editor of the Penguin series Puffin Picture Books. After the Second World War, he left publishing and farmed in Berkshire.

14 There are at the Slade two life paintings by Carrington, one for which she was awarded the Melvill Nettleship Prize for figure composition (1912) and another which won second place in figure painting (1911). In her last year she was given a prize for a painting from the cast.

15 'My name. Yes indeed its a closely guarded secret,' she wrote to Gerald Brenan (26 December 1920). 'For like all names it betrays my destiny. I can't help feeling I am doomed if once my name is known.' She experimented with various substitutes, signing some of her letters 'Doric' (or its inversion 'Cirod') and 'Kunak'. Lytton was to call her 'Mopsa' after one of the shepherdesses in *The Winter's Tale*.

16 Mark Gertler *Selected Letters* (ed. Noel Carrington 1965) p.235.

17 *The Diary of Virginia Woolf, Volume I 1915–1919* (ed. Anne Olivier Bell 1977) p.89.

18 *The Diary of Virginia Woolf, Volume II 1920–1924* (ed. Anne Olivier Bell 1978) p.88.

19 Viscount Snowden (1864–1937), then member of Parliament for Blackburn and champion of the conscientious objector. Later he became Chancellor of the Exchequer (1924; 1929–31). He had been one of the chief founders of the Labour Party, and second in the Party to Ramsay MacDonald.

20 *The Shorter Strachey* (ed. Michael Holroyd and Paul Levy 1980) p.40.

21 The German spy question recurrently caused Lytton some embarrassment, especially in the country. 'It is distinctly unfortunate being so noticeable a figure,' he complained to Vanessa Bell (6 August 1917). 'Ought I to shave my beard for the period of the war? But would even that lull the suspicions of the yokels?'

22 Like 'Lancaster Gate', this autobiographical essay was subsequently read to the Memoir Club and eventually published in *Lytton Strachey by Himself* (1971).

23 *Selected Letters of Vanessa Bell* (ed. Regina Marler 1993) p.199.

24 Later Viscount Tredegar (1899–1949). He was at this time an undergraduate at Christ Church, Oxford.

25 Violet Paget (1856–1935), the lesbian bluestocking who wrote books on aesthetics, politics and Italian art under the pseudonym of 'Vernon Lee'. In later life she grew rather deaf and was obliged to employ an ear trumpet which she raised when talking herself. She was famous also for appearing in the first line of a poem by Browning: 'Who said "Vernon Lee"?'

26 *The Shorter Strachey* p.40.

27 *Carrington. Letters & Extracts from her Diaries* (ed. David Garnett 1970) p.37.

28 'How and why Carrington became so devoted to him [Lytton] I don't know,' Dorothy Brett told the author. 'Why she submerged her talent and whole life in him, a mystery . . . most of her friendships I think were partially discarded when she devoted herself to Lytton . . . She pandered to his sex obscenities, I saw her, so I got an idea of it. I ought not to be prejudiced. I think Gertler and I could not help being prejudiced. It was so difficult to understand how she could be attracted.'

29 Beatrice Glenavy *Today We Will Only Gossip* (1964) pp.104–5.

30 The first publication of the Hogarth Press, Leonard and Virginia Woolf's *Two Stories* (1917) has four woodcuts by Carrington, for which she was paid fifteen shillings.

31 Poppet John, the daughter of Augustus John.

32 In her memoirs, *Two Flamboyant Fathers* (1966), Nicolette Devas records that she used to meet Lytton and Carrington with the Johns 'at Fordingbridge and neighbouring gymkhanas . . . If you saw Strachey in a wilting pose on frail legs, Dora Carrington was his shadow, a pace behind, at heel, devoted, worshipping . . . We called her the "North Wind" for the way she poked her face into the wind; her long black [sic] hair, cut with a square fringe, swished out at the back in a dark

pennant, while her black skirt, too, always seemed to be under the influence of the wind, blown against her gaunt figure.'
33 *The Diary of Virginia Woolf, Volume I 1915–1919* (ed. Anne Olivier Bell) pp.92, 60.
34 *Carrington. Letters & Extracts from her Diaries* (ed. David Garnett 1970) pp.63–5.

CHAPTER XIII: TIDMARSH

1 *Carrington. Letters & Extracts from her Diaries* (ed. David Garnett 1970) p.66.
2 Montague Shearman, barrister and connoisseur of pictures. He was one of Gertler's most loyal friends and patrons, often lending him his rooms in the Adelphi. An exhibition of Shearman's collection was held at the Redfern Gallery in 1940.
3 Samuel Solomonovitch Kóteliansky (1880–1955) had come to England in 1911 on a scholarship from Kiev to do research in economics for three months, and stayed for life at 5, Acacia Road, St John's Wood. Swarthy, with a pale sensitive face and fierce black glance, he was, as his friend D.H. Lawrence once said, 'a bit Jehovah-ish'. He made a career for himself as a translator of Bunin, Chekhov, Gorky, Kuprin and others, sometimes in collaboration with his friends Lawrence, Katherine Mansfield, Middleton Murry and Leonard Woolf, who used to render his strange English into their own prose style to be published by the Hogarth Press.
4 David Garnett *The Flowers of the Forest* (1955) p.153.
5 This cottage had been recommended to James Strachey by a Quaker lady in the Society of Friends office where he was doing Work of National Importance distributing milk to German wives.
6 See John Woodeson *Mark Gertler* (1972) pp.245–6.
7 *Mark Gertler. Selected Letters* (ed. Noel Carrington 1965) pp.151–2.
8 Lytton was to write an essay on Creighton (1843–1901), Bishop of London, in 1929. It was first collected in *Portraits in Miniature* (1931).
9 Once the scheme had been put into operation, Maynard Keynes every three months or so used to take Barbara Bagenal to the Café Royal and over lunch or dinner there go through the formality of checking her book-keeping.
10 Gerald Brenan *Personal Record 1920–1972* (1974) p.24.
11 The corn storehouse next door was a regular breeding ground for rats. 'One morning I was awakened by yells from Lytton's room,' James Strachey remembered, 'and went in and found something moving inside the bottom of his bed – a rat, which I caught in a chamber pot.'
12 Robert Nichols (1893–1944), the poet and dramatist, who was at this time working in the Ministry of Labour, having seen service on the Belgian-French front. His recently published book of poems *Ardours and Endurances* had been widely read and he was regarded by many as a new Rupert Brooke.
13 Frank Swinnerton *Autobiography* (1936) p.126.
14 In the first edition of *Eminent Victorians* there were actually six illustrations, the last one being a photograph of Gladstone.
15 Frank Swinnerton *The Georgian Literary Scene* (1951 edn) p.269.
16 But in her diary for 7 January 1918, Virginia wrote: 'I told him he wrote too much after the pattern of Macaulay. "I see you don't really like Gordon," he said. He was quite unmoved, contented, almost sleek.'
17 Sir John Dickinson (1848–1933), who had taken his law degree at Trinity College, Cambridge, was from 1913 to 1920 Chief Metropolitan Police Magistrate, Bow Street.
18 Lloyd George was convinced that the victorious allied armies in the east could defeat Germany, but was opposed by the Chief of the Imperial Staff, Sir William

Robertson, as well as by King George V, by Asquith, and by some members of the War Cabinet. He successfully took them on in the House of Commons and on 18 February Robertson read of his own resignation in the morning newspapers. 'The course of politics at the beginning of the week was deeply shocking,' Asquith wrote to his mother (22 February 1918). 'Bonar [Law] could have become prime minister if he had liked, but he funked it, and as no one else seemed inclined to take the job, the goat [Lloyd George] struggled through.'

19 Desmond had fallen in love with Lady Cynthia Asquith, the wife of H.H. Asquith's second son, the poet Herbert ('Beb') Asquith.

CHAPTER XIV: A LIFE APART

1 Hugh Kingsmill *The Progress of a Biographer* (1949) p.7.
2 'A New History of Rome', *Spectator* 102 (2 January 1909), pp.20–21. Collected in *Spectatorial Essays* (pp.13–17).
3 Introduction to the Collins Classic edition of *Eminent Victorians* (1959).
4 *The Letters of Sir Walter Raleigh 1879–1922* (ed. Lady Raleigh 1926) volume II pp.479–80.
5 In his Preface, Lytton had paraphrased part of an article on biography (*Anglo-Saxon Reviews*, VIII (1901) pp.195–208) in which Gosse wrote: 'We in England bury the dead under the monstrous catafalque of two volumes (crown octavo) and go forth refreshed ... These two great solemn volumes ... follow the coffin as punctually as any of the other mutes in perfunctory attendance.'
6 David Cannadine *G.M. Trevelyan. A Life in History* (1992) pp.43–4.
7 *Cambridge Review* volume LXV (4 December 1943) pp.120–22 and *Spectator* (7 January 1944) pp.7–8.
8 'Lytton Strachey as Historian' *Historical Essays* (1957) pp.279–84.
9 Edmund Wilson 'Lytton Strachey' *New Republic* 72 (21 September 1932) pp.146–8. Collected in *The Shores of Light: A Literary Chronicle of the Twenties and Thirties* (1952) pp.551–6.
10 During his Romanes Lectures, entitled 'Some Aspects of the Victorian Age', Asquith said: 'In a recently published volume – the most trenchant and brilliant series of biographical studies which I have read for a long time – Mr Lytton Strachey, under the modest title *Eminent Victorians*, has put on his canvas four figures (as unlike one another as any four people could be) ... They are in less danger than ever of being forgotten, now that they have been re-created for the English readers of the future (not in a spirit of blind hero-worship) by Mr Strachey's subtle and suggestive art.'
11 *The Shorter Strachey* (ed. Michael Holroyd and Paul Levy 1980) p.41.
12 Lytton was invited to see the printing machines in action, and the performance was arranged in such a way that, at its conclusion, a first copy of his book would be magnificently produced and presented to him. As he stepped into the room, however, where everything was busily taking place, the machinery broke down. Nothing could start it up again, publishers and printers fell back in confusion; but Lytton seemed relieved.
13 Gide had begun his stay at Grape House in Grantchester, but transferred to Merton House in order to be nearer Dorothy Bussy, then living at 27 Grange Road, Cambridge.
14 On 29 September 1918, Gide wrote to Lytton: 'Un contretemps absurde fait que je n'ai reçu que trop tard votre aimable invitation, alors que déjà tout était décidé pour mon départ. Le plaisir que je me promettais, de vous revoir et Miss Carrington, était si vif que peu s'en fallut pour que je me remisse mon voyage ... Du moins croyez la sincérité de mes regrets. Et pour me consoler, je vous lis.'

15 Robert Skidelsky *John Maynard Keynes. The Economist as Saviour 1920–1937* (1992) p.406.

16 David Garnett *Great Friends* (1979) p.140.

17 Cyril Connolly *The Modern Movement* (1965) p.41 and *Enemies of Promise* (revised edn 1961) p.59.

18 Ian Hamilton *Keepers of the Flame. Literary Estates and the Rise of Biography* (1992) p.238.

19 Barry Spurr 'Camp Mandarin: The Prose Style of Lytton Strachey' *English Literature in Transition 1880–1920* volume 33, number 1 (1990) pp.31–45.

20 Anthony Kenny 'Evolution of a Primate' *Oxford Magazine*, Sixth Week, Hilary Term (1986) p.15.

21 Bertrand Russell 'Portraits from Memory. J.M. Keynes & Lytton Strachey'. Broadcast on BBC Home Service 10 July 1952.

22 Peter Clarke 'Strachey, Prospero, and the Seventh Heaven' *London Review of Books* (22 May–4 June 1980) pp.22–3.

23 William Gerhardie *God's Fifth Column* (1980) p.18. See also *New Directions in Biography* (ed. Anthony M. Friedson 1981) p.24.

24 John Stewart Collis *An Artist of Life. The Life and Work of Havelock Ellis* (1959) pp.92–3.

25 Richard Holmes 'People who knead people' *Times Saturday Review* (11 May 1991) pp.16–18.

26 Charles Carrington *Rudyard Kipling. His Life and Work* (1955) pp.479–80.

27 Gerald Brenan *South from Granada* (1987 edn) pp.28–9.

28 Violet Asquith, the daughter of H.H. Asquith by his first wife Helen (*née* Melland); later Lady Violet Bonham-Carter, and later still Baroness Asquith. At Garsington she had attacked all conscientious objectors as unpatriotic cowards who ought to be deported – in which case, Lytton was provoked to reply, her militaristic views (and perhaps the Government's) were identical to those of the enemy Prussians. After this quarrel she had refused to speak to him.

29 Cyril Asquith, the youngest of Margot's stepchildren.

30 Anthony Asquith, usually known as 'Puffin' within the family; later a film producer.

31 Elizabeth Asquith, Margot's daughter, who married Prince Antoine Bibesco.

32 Suggia (1888–1950) afterwards confessed to being terrified by Lytton.

33 Osbert Sitwell *Laughter in the Next Room* (1975 edn) p.22.

34 Nevertheless this book is not listed in the bibliography or 'List of References in the Notes' at the end of Lytton's *Queen Victoria*.

35 In 1920 Lytton did write an article on Disraeli for *Woman's Leader*. A review of Monypenny and Buckle's six-volume biography, *Dizzy*, as it was called, consists of little more than an elegant admission of perplexity. 'The absurd Jew-boy, who set out to conquer the world, reached his destination,' ran the opening sentence. And he had little to add to this statement, since, as he told Hesketh Pearson shortly after the publication of *Queen Victoria*, Disraeli's mummy-like inscrutability baffled him. 'I can't make him out,' he admitted; 'his character is so utterly contradictory.'

36 Lytton's essay on Thomas Creevey appeared in *New Republic* (7 June 1919), *Athenaeum* (13 June 1919) and *Living Age* (19 July 1919) and was collected in *Biographical Essays* and *The Shorter Strachey*.

37 In a letter to the *Daily Telegraph* on 29 November 1917 (a letter previously turned down by *The Times*), the veteran Lord Lansdowne had sought to counteract the internal propaganda of both Britain and Germany, which, he felt, was helping to prolong the war unnecessarily. 'What are we fighting for?' he asked. The answer was to defeat the Germans, not out of mere vindictiveness, but honourably and in such a way as to prevent another war in the future. He defined Britain's war aims

with the aid of five guiding points. There was to be no annihilating knock-out blow; no imposition of an unwelcome form of government on the German people; no permanent economic sanctions after the war was over. Britain would work for international agreement on the 'freedom of the seas' question and help to set up a compulsory international pact to ensure peace. This letter provoked a hurricane of abuse from the Government and in the Press. Northcliffe, for example, endeavoured to discredit Lansdowne as a statesman, an Irish landlord, and an individual. But a minority of people applauded Lansdowne's courage and honesty.

38 Partridge's actual Christian name was Reginald – Rex for short – but Lytton invented the name Ralph for him, and soon everyone was calling him Ralph.

39 Gerald Brenan *A Life of One's Own* (1962) p.187.

40 Opposite Kent House. The Princess Bibesco Lytton referred to was probably Princess Martha Bibesco, the friend of Proust and author of *Proust's Oriane* and *The Sphinx of Bagatelle.*

41 Robert Smillie, president of the Miners' Federation of Great Britain (1912–21) who, in 1923, became Labour member of Parliament for Morpeth. A dour, granite-faced lowlander, he was said, by the few who knew him well, to be kindly and intelligent, and was much admired by Oliver Strachey.

42 Diaghilev had been fêted by London society (Lady Ripon, for example, and, of course, Ottoline) before the First World War. It is, however, a curious fact that Bloomsbury had not paid attention to him until his reappearance after the war. This was because it was only during the war that Diaghilev became involved with Picasso and Derain. His earlier painters, such as Bakst, were not liked by Bloomsbury. A feature of the return of Diaghilev was his new prima ballerina Lopokova.

43 Clive Bell *Old Friends* (1956) p.172.

44 William Bruce Ellis Ranken (1881–1941), old Etonian, ex-Slade student, and for many years vice-president of the Royal Institution of Painters in Water Colours. He was particularly known for his portraits of British Royalty – including Queen Elizabeth (wife of George VI) now the Queen Mother, and Queen Mary – and also for his interiors of Windsor Castle and Buckingham Palace. In 1936 he was one of four painters given facilities to paint the Coronation ceremony of King George VI in Westminster Abbey.

45 Sir Alfred Munnings (1878–1959), member of the Newlyn Group and President of the Royal Academy (1944–9), famous for his equestrian portraits.

46 The Rt Hon. Richard Burton Haldane, FRS, OM (1856–1928) was to regain the post of Lord Chancellor in 1924 under the first brief Labour Government, having split off from the Liberals.

47 Frances Spalding *Vanessa Bell* (1983) p.177.

48 Angelica Garnett *Deceived with Kindness. A Bloomsbury Childhood* (1984) pp.37–8.

49 Quentin and Olivier Bell named their eldest daughter Virginia.

50 Virginia Woolf to Vanessa Bell 23 March 1919. *The Question of Things Happening. The Letters of Virginia Woolf, Volume II 1912–1922* (ed. Nigel Nicolson 1976) p.339.

51 Osbert Sitwell *Laughter in the Next Room* (1975 edn) pp.38–9.

52 A few days after their dinner together in London, Eliot wrote to Lytton (19 May 1919): 'Dear Strachey, I find that I am being sent on a tour of the provinces, by my bank, as soon as I can get off, and that I shall probably be gone some weeks. So unfortunately there is no possibility of my asking you to dine with me in the near future, as I should have liked you to have done. I only fear that when I am settled here [18 Crawford Mansions, W.1] again you will be buried away in the country. Perhaps you will keep me in touch with your movements, and perhaps you will even let me have your opinions and Reviews of anything of mine you see in print.'

53 When Lytton wrote inviting him to spend a weekend with him at Tidmarsh, Eliot replied (14 July 1920) that he was delighted to hear from him and would love to

have come, 'but unfortunately I have some people motoring down for Saturday afternoon. Perhaps this is providential, as I ought to work Sunday on a book which is heavy on my conscience. How do you ever write a book? It seems to me a colossal task. *Perhaps* you will ask me again sometime?'

54 Peter Ackroyd *T.S. Eliot* (1984) p.74.

55 Nevertheless, in a letter inviting Lytton to a small party at 38 Burleigh Mansions, Eliot wrote (10 December 1923): 'And once again – although I admire and enjoy your portraits in the Nation, it is to my interest to say that they are not *long* enough to do you justice. So – although you once refused – 2 years ago – please remember that I should like to lead off a number of the *Criterion* with you, up to 5000 or 8000 words ... I have thought that you ought to do MACAULAY – but anything from you would ensure the success of a number, besides the pleasure it would give me. Could you?' Lytton did write an essay on Macaulay in 1927. It was published in the *Nation and Athenaeum* (21 January 1928), and it was 2,500 words long.

56 Lytton subscribed his hundred pounds some four months before writing his parody. In later years Eliot became a close friend of Dorothy Bussy and her daughter Janie.

57 Ramsay Muir (1872–1941), historian and Liberal member of Parliament for Rochdale (1923–4). Chairman and president of the National Liberal Federation. Author of *History of the British Commonwealth* (2 volumes, 1920 and 1922).

58 Naomi Gwladys Royde-Smith, prolific 'women's' novelist from Wales, and eldest daughter of the curiously named Michael Holroyd Smith. As literary editor of the *Weekly Westminster* – a paper that, in the pre-1914 days, enjoyed a great vogue – she had published much of Rupert Brooke's early verse. During the First World War she and Rose Macaulay conducted a joint salon for writers and artists, founded on that of Julie de Lespinasse, about whom she wrote a biography. In 1926 she married the actor Ernest Milton.

59 On 1 March 1919, Lytton wrote to Vanessa Bell: 'By-the-bye, what is your view of the Albert Memorial as a work of art? It's not easy to consider it impartially – one's earliest memories are so intertwined with it – surely we must have met on those steps in long clothes? – but surely there's a coherence and conception about it not altogether negligible? – Compared, for instance, to the memorial to Victoria opposite Buckingham Palace, it certainly stands out. At any rate, it's not a thing one can easily forget.' Quentin Bell comments on this letter that the Albert Memorial was 'the stock joke and aunt sally of the 1920s. Then a later generation Betjeman-wise in its day discovered or re-discovered it. Now the clever jokes at the A.M. are thought particularly "20ish" and are I fancy laid at Lytton's door. It's fascinating to find Lytton in 1919 coming so close in his judgements to the views of the post-Strachey epoch.'

60 *The Diary of Virginia Woolf, Volume I 1915–1919* (ed. Anne Olivier Bell 1977) p.312.

61 Alix Sargant-Florence and James Strachey had taken the whole of 41 Gordon Square in January 1919, and let off various bits of it at various times. 'We began by living on the top two floors, before we were married,' James told the author. 'Then we took on the second floor and then for some time when we were rich, the first floor as well. There was even a very short period when we had the whole house, during which we gave a celebrated party with two hundred guests. Then by degrees we receded again till in our final period we had only the top three floors ... Lydia [Lopokova] was on the ground floor and shook the whole house when she practised her entrechats.' In 1956, James and Alix Strachey gave up 41 Gordon Square and went to live at Lord's Wood, Alix's mother's house near Marlow.

62 He mentions Gide's 'decidedly remarkable' *La Porte Etroite*, Daisy Ashford's 'perfectly charming' *The Young Visiters*, Ethel Smyth's reminiscences, *Impressions*

that Remained ('extremely entertaining, not to say interesting. Curiously old-fashioned, too'), *The Education of Henry Adams* ('certainly very remarkable, though a trifle long'), Stephen Graham's *A Private in the Guards* enjoyable 'chiefly as a self-revelation, but also for accounts of things in the war', and Festing Jones's biography of Samuel Butler ('vol 2, after Miss Savage dies, decidedly falls off in interest, I think. *Her* letters are really excellent').

63 'Ah, how delightful to be praised by you!' Virginia wrote to Lytton (28 October 1919). 'I tell myself that of course you're always too generous about me, and one ought to discount it, but I can't bring myself to. I enjoy every word. I don't suppose there's anything in the way of praise that means more to me than yours.'

64 Gerald Brenan *South from Granada* (1987 edn) p.34.

65 Osbert Sitwell *Noble Essences* (1950) pp.11–13.

66 Since Lytton's estimate of one hundred thousand words held good until the early autumn of 1920, it seems likely that he had meant to deal with Victoria's old age at greater length, deciding on a more cursory treatment only while he was actually at work on the ninth chapter.

67 On 27 January 1921, Lytton wrote to his brother James in Vienna: 'My state has been appalling – given over to Victoria for weeks and weeks without cessation – a fearful struggle, its horrors being increased by the "relaxing" conditions at Tidmarsh – however it's now done – typed – and actually handed over to Chatto's. The relief is enormous; but the worst of it is that various crises are still pending. The American question is acute and complicated. Maynard has been acting as an intermediary with Harcourt, his American publisher, who, after some havering, offered 10,000 dollars for all the American rights complete. At that time this was worth nearly £3000 – and I thought it would do, and accepted. But since then the wretched dollar has sunk [and the pound had strengthened], so that it's now worth only about £2660. But still the contract has not been fixed. There are also various difficulties about serialisations – in England and America and their dates. The Times (also via Pozzo) is being negotiated with, but nothing has been settled yet. In the meantime, Chatto has payed me £750, as advance royalties, payable on receipt of the MS. The arrangement is that I get 20% on the first 5000 copies, and 25% after that – viz. on the selling price of the book, which will probably be 15/-. So that the advance royalties covers the first 5000 copies. If I get £700 for the serial rights – which is conceivable – I may net something between £4 and £5,000 – which doesn't seem so bad – though I still shiver in my shoes over the American question which continues to hang in the wind. I suppose I shall have to invest it – which seems rather dull – and I daresay the best thing would be to buzz it all straight off. I wish to goodness you had been here to assist me in these terrific transactions. And as for the proof correcting, I shudder to think of it. C & W. say they'll have it out on April 7th. As for the work itself, I hope it's readable, and that it steers the correct course between discretion and indiscretion. I feel rather doubtful as to whether the presentment of her Majesty forms a consistent whole: the tone seems to shift so wildly – from tragedy to farce, from sentiment to cynicism: but let's hope it all forms up. It's almost impossible for me at the present moment to get an impartial view of it. The strain of such a long continuity has been extreme. I don't feel as if I should ever be able to face such a bulky affair again.'

68 'I've just finished your African book, in the greatest excitement,' Lytton had written to Leonard (14 June 1920). 'It seems to me a most important work – done with superb power and perfect clarity, and marvellous, devastating detachment... I go about now with a positively darkened view of humanity. From some points of view Africa is worse than the war.'

'I am reading the Oedipus Tyrannus in a new edition that Sheppard has brought out, with a translation (which is what I read – with an occasional puzzled glance at the other side of the page) and an elaborate and rather interesting commentary,' Lytton wrote to Ralph Partridge. 'In the entire list of the world's masterpieces, my fancy is to place it second, though I wish I could understand the Greek better than I do – and when I think of all the hours and years I spent learning the paradigms of the irregular verbs, and construing Thucydides!'

69 In which case it had better be published here. 'Dear Lytton Strachey, Some time in 1913, at this address, my wife and I acquired a young fox-terrier. We debated as to what to call him, and, as Henry James had just been having his 70th birthday, and as his books had given me more pleasure than those of any living man, I, rather priggishly perhaps, insisted that the dog should be known as James. But this was a name which Italian peasants, who are the only neighbours we have, of course would not be able to pronounce at all. So we were phonetic and called the name of the dog *Yah-mès*. And this did very well. By this name he was known far and wide – but not for long; for alas, he died of distemper. Now that we are to re-establish here, we haven't another dog; dogs aren't so necessary to one as they seem to be in England, and they have an odd and tactless way of making one feel that one *is* in England – perhaps because they don't gesticulate and don't speak one word of Italian and seem to expect to find rabbits among the olive-groves and to have bones of Welsh mutton thrown to them from the luncheon table. But the other day we were given a small kitten – charming in itself and somehow not distinctive of local colour. The old question arose: what shall we call it? Again I laid myself open to the charge of priggishness, perhaps. And again you will perhaps think I have taken a liberty. But – well, there it is: no book by a living man has given me so much pleasure – so much lasting pleasure in dipping and re-reading since I wrote to you – as your "Eminent Victorians". And the name of that kitten is, and the name of that cat will be: *Stré-chi* (or rather Stré-cci). I do hope you don't mind. I am sure you would be amused if you heard the passing-by peasants enticing it by your hardly recognisable name. We will re-christen it if you like.'

This letter was written from Villino Chiaro on 7 July 1920. Lytton, in his reply, expressed his sense of honour at this appellation, and two years later, in June 1922, Max took up the sequel to this story in another letter. 'The kitten of whom I told you last year is now a confirmed cat. He is much larger than he seemed likely to become, and is vigorous and vagrant, but not, I am sorry to say, either affectionate or intelligent. It is not known that he ever caught a mouse; he dislikes rain, but has no knowledge of how to avoid it if it falls; and if one caresses him he is very likely to scratch one. He is, however, very proud of his name, and sends his respectful regards to his Illustrious Eponymisto Inglese.'

In the course of this same letter, Max refers to Lytton's essay 'Voltaire and Frederick the Great' as an 'abiding masterpiece', and adds: 'So is "Madame du Deffand".'

70 Ralph Partridge's salary was £100 a year plus 50 per cent of the net profits. His earnings in 1920 were £56. 6s. 1d., and during 1921 he earned £125 (equivalent to £2200 in the early 1990s).

71 Noel Olivier had turned down several proposals of marriage including one from Adrian Stephen and, following Rupert Brooke's death, told the still-adoring James Strachey that she would never marry for love. She became a doctor, then in 1921 married a fellow medical practitioner Arthur Richards, a year after James married Alix Sargant-Florence who had been at Bedales with Noel. Between 1924 and 1940 Noel had one son and four daughters (to the last of whom, Tazza, James was godfather). In the spring of 1932, at the age of thirty-nine, Noel wrote to James saying that she now realized that she had really loved him all along. She was thankful that she had come to realize this before it was too late. Their roles were now reversed: she passionate and beseeching, he cautious and rather

guilty. Their intermittent affaire lasted until 1940. After James's death in 1967, the index and bibliographical volume of his *Standard Edition of the Complete Psychological Works of Sigmund Freud* was compiled by Noel's eldest daughter Angela Richards Harris.

72 The portrait is now in the permanent collection of the National Gallery of Scotland.

73 Immediately before the war Geoffrey Scott had been looking after the decorations and furniture of various new rooms at I Tatti, where he fell in love with Nicky Mariano, later Berenson's librarian and companion. Mary Berenson had planned that the two of them should marry, live together near by and act as her husband's helpers and advisers, but during the war Geoffrey Scott had married Lady Sybil Cutting (who later became the wife of Percy Lubbock). During his stay at I Tatti, Lytton saw something of Nicky Mariano, who remembered that Berenson urged him to take up Pius IX as his next subject, a suggestion by which he seemed to be tempted.

74 Leonard Woolf *Downhill all the Way* (1967) pp.69–72.

75 'What good news of the greyhound!' Lytton wrote to her (6 July 1921). 'It will be splendid if you become Sign Painter in Ordinary to the Counties of Berks, Wilts and Hants! I am longing to see it in position.' She painted several other signboards in the neighbourhood, including that of John Fothergill's inn, the Spread Eagle at Thame.

CHAPTER XV: EMINENT EDWARDIAN

1 'The Year of Jubilee' *Pall Mall Gazette* (16 November 1886). Collected in *Bernard Shaw's Book Reviews* (ed. Brian Tyson 1991) pp. 213–18.

2 A.B. W[alkley] 'Flamboyancy: Sidelights from Mr Strachey' *The Times* (18 May 1921) p.6.

3 *The Times* (28 January 1932) p.6. Letter from Edith Plowden.

4 Introduction to Collins Classics edition of *Queen Victoria* (1958).

5 *The Development of English Biography* (1927) pp.148–50.

6 In his article on biography for *The New Universal Encyclopedia*, Peter Quennell cites Lord David Cecil and Harold Nicolson as being two of Lytton's 'few genuinely gifted pupils'. David Cecil, who was to contribute the entry on Lytton to *The Dictionary of National Biography*, was at his most admiring when compiling and introducing *An Anthology of Modern Biography* (1936), but in his biography of Max Beerbohm (1964) wrote that Max had overrated Lytton, feeling perhaps that he had done so too.

7 *Sunday Telegraph* (2 March) 1980.

8 *Historical Essays* (1957) p.281. See also E.H. Carr *What is History?* (1964 edn) p.48.

9 'The Art of Biography' *Atlantic Monthly* (April 1939). Collected in *The Death of the Moth* (1942) and *Collected Essays* volume 4 (1967).

10 James Strachey was to become the translator and general editor of the Standard Edition of the *Complete Psychological Works of Sigmund Freud* (24 volumes Hogarth Press), in the preparation of which he was assisted by Alix and by Anna Freud (Freud's youngest daughter). On 9 March 1921, he wrote to Lady Strachey that he and Alix were translating 'a series of Freud's "clinical" papers. There are to be five of them, each giving a detailed history of a specially interesting case and an account of the treatment. They were written at intervals during the last twenty years – the first in 1899 and the last quite recently – so that they give a very good idea of the development of his views. Altogether the book will probably be about 500 pages long. It is a great compliment to have been given it to do. And he

736

thought of the plan on purpose to be of help to us in two different ways. First of all, it'll give us a specially intimate knowledge of his methods, as we are able to talk over with him any difficulties that occur to us in the course of the translation; and we now go on Sunday afternoons specially to discuss whatever problems we want to. In the second place, our appearance as official translators of his work into English will give us a great advertisement in psychological circles in England.' The translation of *Group Psychology and the Analysis of the Ego* was published in 1922. After its completion, James told Lytton (22 January 1922), 'we've been passed as fit to practise by the Prof.'

11 George Rylands (b. 1902) later became a Fellow, Dean, Bursar and Lecturer at King's College, a Governor of the Old Vic, and Chairman of the Directors and Trustees of the Arts Theatre, Cambridge. His best-known book is the Shakespeare anthology, *The Ages of Man* (1939). Lytton claimed to be 'luckily (*almost* entirely) immune from his [yellow] hair'.

12 Lionel Penrose, FRS (1898–1972), Galton Professor of Eugenics, University College, London, and author of *The Influence of Heredity on Disease* (1934) and *The Biology of Mental Defect* (1949, 3rd edn 1963), was, as Lytton soon became aware, one of the cleverest of his Cambridge friends.

13 G.H. Thring was a solicitor who, from 1892 to 1930, worked as secretary to the Society of Authors and was famous for his ferocity to publishers. 'We have had him cheap, and he has been devoted to the Society, incorruptible and hardworking,' Bernard Shaw wrote to H.G. Wells on Thring's retirement (21 February 1930), '. . . his method of taking up cases included fixing his teeth in the calves of both parties.'

14 See 'Lytton Strachey's Revisions in *Books and Characters*', *Modern Language Notes* (April 1945) pp.226–34; and 'Lytton Strachey Improves His Style', *College English*, VII (January 1946) pp.215–19.

15 *The Times* (18 May 1922) p.16.

16 *Athenaeum* (3 June 1922) pp.346–7.

17 Aldous Huxley *On the Margin* (1923) p.142.

18 Hugh Trevor-Roper *Historical Essays* (1957) p.284.

19 Under the endowment of A.C. Benson (1 May 1916) medals were to be awarded in respect of meritorious works in poetry, fiction, history, biography and belles-lettres. A selection committee was appointed each year by the Fellows of the Royal Society of Literature, which alone had the right to recommend recipients.

20 The accounts from Chatto & Windus show Lytton to have received by the end of March 1922 £4,867.2s.0d. on the sales of his books in the British Empire, £1,105.11s.0d. on sales in the USA (which does not include the outright sum of £1,500 from Harcourt Brace), and £99 in respect of French and Swedish rights. To this should be added a small amount from the continuing sales of *Landmarks in French Literature*, something from his contributions to the *Athenaeum*, etc., and possibly also an income from private investments.

21 There is in the Oriental Club a portrait of Sir Richard Strachey painted in about 1888 by Lowes Dickinson, the father of Goldie Dickinson.

22 'Dobrée . . . has mildly literary and pedantic tastes. He is dull but harmless – I fear is writing a series of sixteenth-century lives in the style of Eminent Victorians. She is rather more interesting – perhaps a Saph – much attached to Carrington – but oh, not what might be called clever. She paints – à la Modigliani, etc. The place is pretty high up in the Pyrenees – a largish village with steep hills in every direction – snow to be seen in the distance . . . I think I should be able to last out another 10 days or so . . .' Lytton to James Strachey (9 April 1922).

23 Gerald sent Carrington several long letters during the next few months via either Lytton or John Hope-Johnstone. On 11 June 1922 he wrote: 'I have one request. When you are able to talk to Ralph about me, tell him what you know to be true,

that my only treachery was to conceal from him my affection for you. That this affection did not begin suddenly but insensibly, that though I could not bear to end it by telling him, I tried to lead it into safe channels. That I hoped in the end, with time, seeing that my feelings are different from his and that I live so far off, to reveal it to him and that he would tolerate it ... My friendship with Ralph is at an end; that I accept, but what I cannot endure is that he should think it never existed. I was devoted to him as I have been, I think, to no other man; I do not believe I would willingly have injured him.'

In another letter, posted two days later, he added: 'Whatever I think of, my thoughts return to *you* and make me feel how much and how sweet a happiness I am deprived of ... You do not know how much I love you, how much I shall always love you. There is nothing about you which does not charm me or that could ever grate upon me; your face, your body, your character, your habits are perfect – not because they conform to any exterior standard of perfection but because they make up a unity of their own which is good and beautiful. Am I allowed to tell you that? I may fall in love, I may have other friendships and liaisons, but I shall not forget you, because my feelings for you neither exclude other affections nor can be excluded by them. What I feel for you I shall feel for no one else, and to you I shall always be different to what I am to other people. One part of me belongs unalienably to you, and when I am with you or when I am thinking of you everything else in me is obliterated.'

Some months later, when friendly relations between himself and Ralph had been resumed, Gerald wrote to Carrington from Yegen (15 September 1922): 'I have acted badly and foolishly, and you foolishly – but from now onwards let us be the only people to act sensibly, and with a view to the greatest possible happiness, for all concerned, in the future. Love. Gerald.'

24 Lady Horner's daughter, married to Raymond Asquith.
25 Cecil Beaton *The Wandering Years. Diaries 1922–1939* (1961) p.26.
26 John Rothenstein *Summer Lease* (1965) pp.91–2.
27 Dr Marten was one of the strangest characters Ottoline attracted to Garsington. 'Other friends of mine consulted him,' Robert Gathorne-Hardy records, 'and in later years we half suspected that he made experiments on English patients who had been so lately enemies of his country. With his practice he combined some superficial psychoanalysis. I asked Ottoline if he found anything peculiar about her. "I find", she droned with humorous solemnity, "that my brothers play an undue part in my life."'
28 In his novel *Crime at Christmas* (1935), which is dedicated to Kenneth Ritchie, C.H.B. Kitchin wrote: 'It is my fate, in Bloomsbury, to be thought a Philistine, while in other circles I am regarded as a dilettante with too keen an aesthetic sense to be a responsible person.' This sentence, Mr Kitchin confirmed in a letter (5 July 1965), 'has certainly an autobiographical overtone and largely sums up my social situation during the twenties. I was introduced to Bloomsbury by Philip Ritchie, who was a close friend of mine, and met most of the leading lights in that circle, but being in those days a tiresome mixture of shyness and conceit, I never felt sufficiently at home in it to form intimate contacts with its members. Strange to say, Virginia Woolf, the most formidable of them all, developed, I think, a slightly protective attitude towards me and it was thanks to her good offices that the Hogarth Press published my first two novels, *Streamers Waving* and *Mr Balcony*. I doubt if any other publishers would have considered them at that time.' Kitchin's reputation as a writer was made with his third book, *Death of My Aunt*, but Lytton preferred his first two novels and his fourth, *The Sensitive One*.
29 Among the German contingent was Heinrich Mann, brother of Thomas, and then almost as celebrated as a novelist.

CHAPTER XVI: HAM SPRAY HOUSE

1 Besides Tiber (or Tiberius) there were various families of cats at Tidmarsh and Ham Spray, including Agrippa, Nero, Ptolemy and, christened by Carrington, Biddie, Stump, and Rabbit Cat. Tiber, the chief cat, was named after Matthew Arnold's lines: 'So Tiberius might have sat, Had Tiberius been a cat.'

2 Rachel MacCarthy was the daughter of Desmond MacCarthy. She later married Lord David Cecil.

3 David Garnett *Flowers of the Forest* (1955) p.46.

4 Stephen Spender *World Within World* (1951) pp.143–4.

5 Harold Nicolson's wife, Vita Sackville-West, also disliked Lytton. On 3 August 1938, she wrote to her husband from Sissinghurst: 'The drooping Lytton must have done its [Bloomsbury's] cause a great deal of harm. I hated Lytton.'

6 'Personally I can't bear Santayana, I confess,' Lytton complained to Katherine Mansfield (3 October 1919), '– but that must be considered as a mere personal idiosyncrasy.'

7 In a letter to Robert Graves dated 1 October 1927, T.E. Lawrence compared Lytton Strachey unfavourably with Bernard Shaw. 'It's hardly fair to bracket him [Shaw] with Lytton Strachey,' Lawrence wrote. 'The only portrait which I've seen of him, lately, (deliberate portrait) was that one of William Archer prefixed to three of Archer's plays: and it was direct and wholesome. Strachey is never direct: and not, I think, in himself wholesome. But I don't know him, and my memory of his features tangles itself with my memory of Henry Lamb's marvellous portrait of an outraged wet mackerel of a man, dropped like an old cloak into a basket-chair. If the portrait meant anything it meant that Lytton Strachey was no good.' See *T.E. Lawrence: Letters to His Biographers. Robert Graves and Liddell Hart.*

8 Frances Partridge *Memories* (1981) pp.77–8.

9 No. 8, Fitzroy Street, a studio once occupied by Whistler and by Sickert, into which Duncan Grant had moved after the war. Not all the parties here, at Taviton Street, or at 46 Gordon Square were confined to Bloomsbury and Cambridge. David Garnett remembers seeing Picasso talking to Douglas Fairbanks senior at one gathering; and at another, everyone formed an enormous circle, while, at the centre, two particular guests were left to introduce themselves – Lytton and the film actress Mary Pickford.

10 John Lehmann *The Whispering Gallery* (1955) p.187. Lytton was proposed by Max Beerbohm, and seconded by Goldsworthy Lowes Dickinson, for the Athenaeum in 1930. He was elected the following year under Rule II which allows the committee to invite a distinguished person to become a member without need of election.

11 Gerald Brenan *South from Granada* (1987 edn) pp.35–6.

12 Frances Partridge *Memories* (1981) p.101.

13 Jonathan Gathorne-Hardy *The Interior Castle. A Life of Gerald Brenan* (1992) p.203.

14 The Cranium Club was named after Thomas Love Peacock's Mr Cranium in *Headlong Hall*, who personifies the cult of phrenology.

15 George Simson 'Eminent Chinese: Lytton Strachey as Dramatic Herald from the Court of Pekin' *Etudes Anglaises*, no. 4 (October–December 1980) pp.440–52.

16 It was for Gertrude Kingston that Bernard Shaw had written his one-act piece of buffoonery *Great Catherine* (1913), a music-hall divertissement, set at the court of the Empress Catherine, that displays his generosity rather than his genius. As well as being an actress and founder of the Little Theatre in London, Gertrude Kingston devoted herself to giving conferences on Political Speaking, getting up illustrated books for children and painting in lacquer.

17 Geoffrey Webb (1898–1970), who had been at Magdalene College, Cambridge and was a friend of Roger Fry, became Slade Professor of Fine Art at Cambridge

(1938–49) and a member of the Royal Fine Arts Commission (1948–62). Among his books are a biography of Sir Christopher Wren (1937) and *Architecture in Britain: The Middle Ages* (1956).

18 Sir Dennis Robertson (1890–1963), then a Fellow of Trinity College, Cambridge, afterwards Sir Ernest Cassel Professor of Economics in the University of London, adviser to the Treasury (1939–44) and president of the Royal Economic Society (1948–50). As a past president of the Cambridge Amateur Dramatic Club, he was the one good performer in *A Son of Heaven*.

19 Composed two years after *Façade*, when Walton was still influenced by Bernard van Dieren, Schoenberg and Stravinsky, the music has unfortunately 'long ago disappeared', Walton told the author. The tympanist in the scratch orchestra was Constant Lambert.

20 Other critics have taken exception to this description of James Agate's, believing that the designs were more in the style of a Diaghilev–Picasso ballet.

21 J.O.P. Bland (1863–1945), who had worked in China since 1883 and been a representative of the British and Chinese Corporation Ltd, was correspondent successively in Shanghai and Peking (1897–1910) for *The Times*. Among his works was *China under the Empress Dowager* which he wrote in 1910 with Sir Edmund Backhouse, and a biography of Li Hung-Chang (1917) which Lytton reviewed in *War and Peace* and which was of use to him in 'The End of General Gordon'. During the early 1920s, Lytton wrote to Bland asking whether, in his opinion, he ought to allow *A Son of Heaven* to be produced, and Bland, replying as though the Shavian revolution in the theatre had never taken place, advised against it, 'for the reason that you have a big reputation, and this play would, I fear, give the heathen cause to blaspheme. You have followed the historical course of events so precisely, and reproduced the chief actors in the Boxer Crisis in such a manner, as to necessitate, I think, accuracy in depicting them; and this is lacking. A Chinese Empress who talks of kissing (oh, là-là!) and of masked balls at court would never do! – and no Chinese woman would say the things Ta-hé says. The play, in fact, while interesting and picturesque, is to me unconvincing, because it lacks the correct oriental atmosphere, and the characters talk like Europeans.'

22 'I wonder if you would allow me to read your play?' Sybil Thorndike inquired. 'There are not many such parts this year for women – men get all the tremendous parts – (except in the Greek plays) I want to play a Queen Elizabeth one of these times. I've read 8 different plays and have been offered them – Bernard Shaw says she's too successful for him to tackle with interest – I hope that somebody might do her.'

23 Lytton's attitude to *A Son of Heaven* seems to have changed somewhat after the Scala production. In a letter to Frances Marshall (9 August 1925), Ralph Partridge wrote: 'Lytton said he was struck by the highbrowness of all his dear friends, as shown about his play, the way they scorned anything that didn't aim at "the heights" of art (though all writing for *Vogue* themselves); he wants to write another play now, but thinks they'll be severe on him if he's not as lofty as Shakespeare, as serious as Ibsen.' When Gertrude Kingston tried to get the play performed in the United States, he wrote to her (14 July 1926): 'I really don't mind what cuts or alterations are made, if you approved of them. I have always thought that what was needed was a hero – a young, clean-limbed Englishman (or whatever they're called) in the English Embassy, who would rescue Ta-Hé at the critical moment, etc., etc. – but I don't see how that's to be added now.'

24 James Strachey to George Simson (20 August 1962). In 1950 and 1951, *A Son of Heaven* was successfully transmitted on radio by the BBC several times on various home and overseas programmes in a version arranged by Harold Bowen (1896–1959), an Arabic scholar and husband of Vera Bowen (1889–1971).

25 On 21 October Lytton wrote to Maynard: 'It was very kind of you to send me your Life of Marshall, which I have read with the greatest interest and admiration. It seems to me to be one of your best works, and I only regret that it should be buried in an addendum to the Economics Journal. I wish there were more such things – just the right length and esprit – written in English. What a world it opens up! What strange people were the married monks of the nineteenth century! By-the-bye you don't say – perhaps in the circumstances you couldn't – whether he used French letters. Or was he (or she) naturally sterile? That they should have no offspring seems to have been an essential part of their system of existence. I am alarmed, horrified, impressed – almost over-awed – by such a life. Mon dieu! how wildly different are one's own experiences! The emotions and embraces in which I found myself involved as I read your Memoir – what, oh what, would the subject of it have said of them? After all, he took what was really an easy road to Heaven. And did he get there?' In his answer Keynes said that he didn't think that Marshall 'used letters', but that he became sterile soon after marriage.

26 Jonathan Gathorne-Hardy *The Interior Castle. A Life of Gerald Brenan* (1992) p.203.

27 Forster had rather fallen for Ralph. 'I had a long walk with Morgan [Forster] to the Gibbet and on to the top of Walbury Camp,' Ralph wrote to Frances (undated); 'there was a terrific wind and the country looked bleak but sympathetic. I could hardly manage to talk to Morgan, though I tried *earnestly* – that's the word. I like him for liking me, but I'm completely in the dark as to his real character. His language is so linked up with his mother and his aunts that it's like a dialect which I can't talk. I agreed that I'd behaved badly to him on his previous visits, and said that that made me inclined to have a grudge against him. We talked about friendship but not with conviction or much interest. He likes it without intimacy. I with, otherwise it seems to me almost too mild . . . he likes so much and I so little that it's hard to agree.'

28 'Alexander Pope' *Spectator* 103 (20 November 1909) pp. 847–8. See also *Spectatorial Essays* (1964) pp.147–52. The Leslie Stephen Lecture, *Pope*, was published by Cambridge University Press in June 1925, and by Harcourt Brace in the United States in September 1926. It was subsequently included in *Characters and Commentaries* (1933) and *The Shorter Strachey* (1980).

29 'I am overwhelmed by your proposal to dedicate your new book of Essays to me – overwhelmed, honoured, and touched,' Lytton wrote to Gosse (16 May 1927). '. . . I shall come with great pleasure to lunch at the Marlborough Club on Friday – but you must be prepared for my being, on the one hand, quite above myself, and on the other, suffused with blushes!'

30 On page 476 of Evan Charteris's biography, Gosse is quoted as writing: 'the fact is that piracies of Swinburne's copyright – which Messrs Heinemann bought from the poet's widow at great cost – have been frequent.' In the opinion of Ann Thwaite, Gosse was referring to Clara Watts Dunton, author of *The Home Life of Swinburne* (1922).

31 This introduction was reprinted in *Characters and Commentaries* (1933) and collected in *Literary Essays*.

32 Walter Leslie Runciman (1900–89), afterwards Viscount Runciman of Doxford, who became director-general of BOAC (1940–43), had his marriage to Rosamond Lehmann dissolved the following year (1927). In 1928, Wogan Philipps (afterwards Baron Milford), a communist, farmer and painter, became Rosamond's second husband.

33 Sir Alfred Ewing (1855–1935), a scientist noted for his researches into magnetism, was Principal and Vice-Chancellor of the University of Edinburgh (1916–29).

34 Viscount Allenby (1861–1936) – formerly Field-Marshal Sir Edward Allenby and

nicknamed 'the Bull' – was later made Rector of the University of Edinburgh. On this occasion he was being awarded an honorary doctorate in Law. 'Lord Allenby was in the train with me,' Lytton wrote to Rosamond Lehmann (20 July 1926), 'and is in the house with me now – a large, stupid man, whom one would like to stick pins into – but it would be useless – he would never feel them.'

35 In this laureation address, Professor James Mackintosh referred to Lytton as 'an eminent Georgian who first made his mark in contemporary literature by his witty and subtle biographies of Eminent Victorians. The book was the outstanding literary triumph of the last year of the war; its acid analysis of character and its brilliant irony delighted a generation grown somewhat weary of the ideals and idols of its forerunner. Three years later his *Queen Victoria* made a still more favourable impression by its sympathetic and illuminating portraits of the revered Queen and the Prince Consort and its penetrating and suggestive criticism of the spirit of the time. Although he disclaims the role of historian, Mr Strachey has blazed a trail through the thicket of this crowded epoch for which every future explorer passing that way will have reason to thank him. He is eminently worthy of our Order of Merit in the department of letters, if only for restoring to the delectable but almost forgotten art of biography its proper style, proportion and attitude.'

36 Robert Gould Shaw (1898–1970), Nancy Astor's favourite son by her first marriage, was later imprisoned for a homosexual offence, though his conviction was not reported by the newspapers in deference to his stepfather, Waldorf Astor, proprietor of the *Observer*. The Astors owned a sporting property on the island of Jura where Nancy languished and Waldorf fished during the summer.

37 29A Clumber Street, Nottingham.

38 Olive Martin, who helped Carrington with the cooking and housework and remained at Ham Spray until her marriage in the 1930s.

39 'It occurred to me that you might come here and act as my secretary during August,' Lytton wrote to Sebastian Sprott (17 June 1927). 'I have long (genuinely) been in need of someone to arrange my letters & papers, which are in a horrid muddle . . . I don't know whether you could bear to stay here for so long etc. etc. A salary of 3 guineas a week would be attached to the situation – but would that be enough of a dédommagement? Consider of it – and forgive me if I seem to you too crude.'

40 'Dadie has been here, and now Henry Lamb and his Pansy are with us for 2 nights,' Lytton wrote to Roger Senhouse (4 September 1927). 'Rather lugubrious, though I like her – she is a sister of Longford's – perhaps you knew him at Oxford? – very pretty, strong and gay – but so young that it's difficult to discover what's inside her, and I hardly think that H.L., who seems to be surrounded with an aura of pale purple depression, will do much to open her out.'

41 'I must tell you a curious tale of the 17th century that I've just come upon . . .' Lytton wrote to Dadie Rylands (8 September 1927). 'It was discovered by Archbishop Laud that the Headmaster of Westminster had written a letter to a Bishop in which he referred to "that little meddling hocus-pocus". The letter was found among the Bishop's papers, and Laud (rightly) flew to the conclusion that it referred to himself. He had the Headmaster arrested and taken before the Star Chamber, where he was condemned to be fined £5000, and . . . to have his ears nailed to the pillory at Westminster in the presence of his scholars! – Can you imagine a more marvellous half-holiday for the whole school? Only conceive of it! – But, most unfortunately, the Headmaster made off, and the sentence was never carried out, and the dear boys were disappointed. If one had lived in those gay days how careful one would have had to be! – even more so than now I fancy.'

42 'A Frock-Coat Portrait of a Great King', *Daily Mail* (11 October 1927) p.10. For this review Lytton was paid fifty pounds. It has not been reprinted in any of his collected volumes.

43 At Cambridge, Julian Bell became an Apostle, also turning his talents to poetry and left-wing politics. Deeply attached to his mother, he was reacting against the liberal humanitarianism and the pacifism of Bloomsbury, and tried to escape the clash between his sense of loyalty and his unsqueamish instincts by taking, in 1935, the job of Professor of English at the Chinese National University of Wuhan. Two years later, he returned home, where Vanessa Bell was trying to secure for him the post of company director, at a hundred pounds a year, of a family business importing feathers from China. He himself was eager to fight in the Spanish Civil War, and so a compromise was reached whereby he drove an ambulance with the Loyalist Forces in Spain. He was killed on 18 July 1937 at Villanueva de la Canada, in the battle of Brunete.

44 'He [Gerhardie] is a new discovery of Mary [Hutchinson]'s,' Lytton told Sebastian Sprott (1 November 1927). 'Distinctly amusing and talented, but unluckily a 100 per cent womaniser as well as 75 per cent Russian (something wrong with the arithmetic there).'

45 Lytton addressed letters to a number of his friends in verse. For example:
       Kind *Cambridge* postman, please do not
           Forget through loitering, love, or talk
       To leave this letter with the SPROTT,
           Who lives at *7 Brunswick Walk.*

46 In a letter to Sheppard (7 April 1903), Lytton had hinted at an incest taboo: 'I think of when I was a child, when I rushed headlong to my mother and clasped her and kissed her with all my strength, and wonder whether I shall ever again love anyone as much as that, with as wild an ecstasy as that, and with as many tears.'

47 James Strachey urged that there was never any question of Lytton actually being a hashish eater. In those days, in England, hashish was not so much a drug (*Cannabis Indica*) as a purely literary substance from the *Arabian Nights* (though later celebrated in France in more realistic fashion by Baudelaire). Lytton was 'far too respectable ever to *dream* of going in for that sort of thing', and would have disapproved of the journalistic existence the drug now enjoys. 'The Haschish' and 'Happiness' appeared in the *New Statesman and Nation* (26 June 1937) pp.1045–6.

48 Ritchie had developed a cold before his operation, but the surgeon decided to go ahead. Two days afterwards a severe haemorrhage occurred. He then underwent a second operation to stem the bleeding. A London specialist was called in; but the poison had already got into his lungs and some seven weeks later, on 13 September, he died of septic pneumonia.

49 'I am always divided as to whether it is a great bore or rather pleasant,' Carrington wrote to Dorelia about the Ham Spray visitors. 'I think it's probably a mixture of both.'

50 'I have a special love of *Alone*. How did you manage to fill it with that romantic beauty? The variety of moods in it is indeed extraordinary; and yet the totality of the impression is completely preserved,' Lytton wrote to Norman Douglas. 'I am delighted to hear you like *Alone*!' Douglas replied. 'So do I. What you discover in it to please you is no doubt the result of that ridiculous war, driving me into myself. I really felt *alone*, surrounded by a legion of imbeciles hacking each other in pieces. An exhilarating sensation; and one that has not quite faded away. May it never do so.'

51 'We are reading a new novel by Norman Douglas in the evenings,' Carrington wrote to Dorelia John (10 February 1928). 'Tell me, have you got it? It's rather Greek, and very lecherous.'

52 A revised edition of *Siren Land*, Norman Douglas's first serious book, was published by Martin Secker that winter. 'As for Siren Land,' Douglas wrote to Lytton (9 November 1923), 'seven of its twenty chapters were cut out by the

publisher as being "too remote from human interests". *Without consulting me*, he also pulped the entire edition save what had already been sold, which is an infamous proceeding, as one would gladly have bought a copy or two to give to friends. It cannot be helped; one is in the hands of these brigands. Secker has now brought out a new one; the copies reached me last night and I am sending you *one* right away. You will find it stodgy in places, and precious, and unintelligible here and there; but it testifies to an appalling industry.'

53 This pamphlet was written in 1924 as a reply to D.H. Lawrence's Introduction to *Memoirs of the Foreign Legion* by Maurice Magnus. Lytton forwarded one of his copies to Ottoline. 'I think it may amuse you,' he wrote (11 February 1925), 'even if you haven't read the book à propos to which it is written; for years I've thought that some such protest was wanted; and N.D., it seems to me, has done it effectively, in his own particular style. But I doubt whether "friend Lawrence" will see the errors of his ways.' In the *New Statesman* (20 February 1926) Lawrence, 'weary of being slandered', defended himself against Douglas's charges.

54 After the First World War, Nancy Cunard had gone to live permanently in France, set up her own Hours Press at Réanville and published (1928–31) some twenty volumes of contemporary authors. She later wrote her memories of Norman Douglas and some reminiscences of George Moore.

55 Roger Senhouse was of no use to Douglas over the limerick book. On 30 July 1928, Douglas wrote to Lytton from the Abruzzi mountains, where he had fled with 'two youngsters', asking whether 'our young friend' could be induced to send him some limericks. 'I should be ever so glad, as the book is under weigh (? way) and I want as much variety as possible.' On 12 September 1928, he again wrote: 'I have *finished* the limerick book. It will shortly be printed and bound, and a copy shall go to you. So you needn't bother the poor Roger (appropriate name).' A little later that year one hundred and fifty copies of *Some Limericks* were privately printed in Florence for subscribers only. They were all signed, bound in amber-coloured canvas, and sold at five and even ten guineas each – after which all sorts of other private editions have been brought out. Douglas planned two sequels – *More Limericks* and *Last Limericks* – but because the police court in Florence, stirred up, it was commonly believed, by the British Home Office, threatened to take criminal proceedings, he judged it wiser to publish no further limericks. As to *Some Limericks*, Nancy Cunard commented: 'They have to be seen to be believed, rollicking, scatological and dire, as they are, in their schoolboy mirth, stockbroker or Army-wit, and all of them frightfully funny. But not so funny as the learned note that accompanies each (and its variants), where the author (or collator) examines them closely, often in a pseudo-scientific manner … The Index is a gem in itself' (*Grand Man* pp. 286–7).

56 Lytton uses this same phrase in a letter (3 March 1928) to Lumsden Barkway, who had written to him on his forty-eighth birthday. 'I am in the death-grapple with a vile book on Queen Elizabeth, and dare not relax my grip. It was delightful and astonishing of you to remember my birthday. Yes – I am 48 – it seems absurd, and I should suggest that there must be a mistake of twenty years in my birth certificate, if it were not that *you* would arise as a witness against me! … The odd thing is that my hair refuses to give any evidence – so far as I can see – it remains preposterously brown. But I always felt I was a kind of Samson – *all* my strength is in my hair! …'

57 The typing was done by Ethel Christian's of Southampton Street, to whom Lytton would send batches of his manuscript at intervals.

58 *Julia. A Portrait of Julia Strachey by Herself and Frances Partridge* (1983) pp.119–20.

59 Wit, poet, and friend of the famous, Brian Howard dazzled Eton, Oxford and London during the 1920s and 1930s by his exotic manner of living. In the opinion

of Evelyn Waugh, who pilloried him as Anthony Blanche in *Brideshead Revisited* and Ambrose Silk in *Put Out More Flags*, he was like Byron 'mad, bad and dangerous to know'. He committed suicide in 1958.

60 Carrington, in a letter to Ralph (21 May 1928), gives a fuller description of their adventures: 'Lytton's impatience to see everything the moment he arrives, is always extraordinary! Inside the arena we found a curious Bull fight going on. A young bull entered the arena to the sound of Buggells; and about a dozen young men – not drest up – just in shirts, and cotton trousers started darting from side to side, in front of the Bull. At last one braver than the rest, (very attractive with light red shoes . . .) rushed up to the Bull and seized a red cockade off its head between its horns, and got away with it. Then they all tried to touch the Bull's horns. It was a curious game. I found it difficult to believe there was any danger. The Bull seemed so bewildered, and slow, like a very poorly cross old widow, having to play "Touch" with a gang of little scaramouches.'

They then went off for a large tea in the Boulevard Hugo where Carrington ate 'so many cakes I felt almost ill'. Afterwards they walked to the gardens which were 'crowded with all the nobility of nîmes in their grandest clothes', and Lytton climbed the Hill of Pines to look at the monument at its summit -'all monuments look their best about 5 o'clock, I've noticed' – and finally, before retiring to their hotel, they sat by one of the lakes, listening to the evening music from the Pavilion, and sipping vermouth – 'It was a Bosky scene.'

61 A signed limited edition of *Elizabeth and Essex* was issued in Britain and the United States on 24 November 1928 costing four pounds or twenty dollars. It consisted of 1060 copies of which 20 were printed on green paper and issued without numbers. The publisher in Britain was Chatto & Windus, and in the United States Crosby Gaige.

62 The fee of $30,000 (equivalent to rather more than £6000) was a record price for serialization of a book in 1928. In the early 1990s it is approximately equivalent to £145,000. The version of *Elizabeth and Essex* printed by the *Ladies' Home Journal* 'is extraordinarily mutilated', Lytton complained to Charles Prentice (21 September 1928), '. . . rather like an execution for High Treason'.

63 Sir John Poynder Dickson-Poynder (1866–1936), politician and administrator, who had been governor of New Zealand (1910–12) and was created first Baron Islington (1910). Among his later appointments had been Under-Secretary of State for the Colonies (1914–15), Parliamentary Under-Secretary for India (1915–18) and Chairman of the National Savings Committee (1920–26). In 1926 he had officially retired.

64 Lord Hugh Cecil (1869–1956), Conservative politician famous for his ecclesiastical oratory, was later appointed Provost of Eton.

Sir Evan Charteris (1864–1940), barrister and biographer, later became Chairman of the Trustees of the National Portrait Gallery (1928–40), Chairman of the Tate Gallery (1934–40) and a Trustee of the National Gallery (1932–9). Among his books are a biography of John Sargent (1927) and *The Life and Letters of Sir Edmund Gosse* (1931).

65 Gerald Heard (1889–1971) was at this time the author of *Narcissus: An Anatomy of Clothes*, a book which attempted to work out historically the connection between architecture and costume. Later, as H.F. Heard, he gained fame as the writer of mystery stories, and, as Gerald Heard, the author of studies in theological and scientific subjects. In 1937 he was to leave England for America where he became a close friend of Christopher Isherwood and Aldous Huxley, who portrayed him as the mystic William Propter in *After Many a Summer*. Bishop Barkway, in a letter to the author (20 May 1963), writes of 'a side of his [Lytton's] nature which he kept tightly concealed from others, but it is characteristic of the many conversations he had of the deepest of all mysteries. Once in the "Backs" he

confided to me how much he was attracted to the oriental point of view. It was then a fore-shadowing of the interest in the Indian religions such as is manifested by Gerald Heard and others like him in this time.' But Gerald Heard has recorded that 'L.S. never said anything to my knowledge re Oriental Religions. He did once suggest he would write a Life of Christ but in a Queen Victoria key, and one did suggest it wouldn't be a successful composition.'

66 William Jowitt (1885–1957), lawyer, left-wing politician and lord chancellor, who was knighted (1929), created a baron (1945), a viscount (1947) and an earl (1951).

CHAPTER XVII: ANOTHER WORLD

1 Leonard Woolf *Downhill all the Way* (1967) p.251.
2 Virginia Woolf 'The Art of Biography' (1939). See also *Collected Essays* volume 4 (1967) pp.221–8.
3 'A New History of Rome' *Spectator* (2 January 1909) pp.20–21. *Spectatorial Essays* pp.13–17.
4 Sigmund Freud *Collected Papers* volume 3 (1925) p.21.
5 Vide supra p.523.
6 Alix wrote to Lytton on 1 December 1925, a week after he began writing *Elizabeth and Essex*: 'James says that what I said about vaginismus wasn't quite correct. It appears that it isn't only a hysterical pain in the vagina, so that it hurts very much to have a penis put in it or sometimes even touch it; but also an actual constriction of the sphincter of the vagina (also hysterical & independent of any physical defect or disease) which makes it physically impossible for anything to get in. This constriction, I gather, is often painful & of a convulsive nature. It is not under the control of the will, & no amount of determination will affect it. It comes on, of course, precisely when the penis approaches the vagina.'

In Chapter II of *Elizabeth and Essex*, Lytton wrote: 'in Elizabeth's case, there was a special cause for a neurotic condition: her sexual organization was seriously warped . . . The crude story of physical malformation may well have had its origin in a subtler, and yet no less vital, fact. In such matters the mind is as potent as the body. A deeply seated repugnance to the crucial act of intercourse may produce, when the possibility approaches, a condition of hysterical convulsion, accompanied, in certain cases, by intense pain.'

7 Edmund Wilson 'Lytton Strachey' *New Republic* (21 September 1932) p.47. *The Shores of Light* p.553.
8 *Criterion* VII (July 1929) pp.647–60.
9 *Scrutiny*, volume II, no. 3 (December 1933).
10 'Lytton Strachey: Father of Modern Biography', *New York Herald Tribune* (7 February 1932).
11 John Ferns *Lytton Strachey* (Twayne's English Authors Series 1988) p.101.
12 Lytton rejected the portrait of Essex at Trinity College, Cambridge, as being too cerebral. 'It is certainly very fine,' he wrote to Charles Prentice (3 August 1928), 'but I had not remembered how extremely intellectual the face was.' He chose instead a more idealized likeness from Woburn Abbey.
13 *The Letters of Wyndham Lewis* (edited by W.K. Rose 1963) p.185.
14 'History and Literature' *History*, IX (1924) pp.81–91.
15 Lytton continued to prefer *Eminent Victorians* to his other books. On 20 May 1929 he wrote to Sebastian Sprott: 'I'm glad you like Em.V. It always strikes me as bright – but many prefer the more "sympathetic" style of my later works – wrongly, to my mind.'
16 G.B. Harrison to the author (6 January 1967). In this letter Harrison refers to his review of *Elizabeth and Essex* in the *Spectator* ('Elizabeth and Her Court' 24

November 1928). The *Spectator*'s literary editor, Celia Simpson (who later became the second wife of John Strachey, the politician and writer), finding the review less eulogistic than she expected, rewrote the first and last paragraphs herself. 'I only discovered the changes when they sent me a proof . . . I was only a beginner at that time, and since this was my first invitation to review for the *Spectator*, I was too timid to make a proper protest.'

17 Strachey's bibliographer, Michael Edmonds, has calculated that *Elizabeth and Essex* 'was printed 42 times in other languages', including an edition into the Spanish language for an advance of fifteen pounds – 'a deplorable result of the Spanish Armada', Lytton observed. There were dramatic adaptations too. In Germany, Ferdinand Bruckner made a stage version which was adapted for the English theatre by Ashley Dukes. In the United States there was a film of the book and in Britain a radio dramatization by Louis MacNeice. Benjamin Britten also took advantage of the dramatic element in the book for his opera *Gloriana*. 'He had a special liking for *Elizabeth and Essex*,' wrote William Plomer, 'and a strong interest in the character and fate of Essex . . . Like Britten, I was impressed on re-reading the book, by its dramatic qualities, its vividness, and Strachey's sense of character and situation.'

18 Frances Partridge *Memories* (1981) p.119.

19 Jonathan Gathorne-Hardy *The Interior Castle. A Life of Gerald Brenan* (1992) p.232.

20 *Carrington: Letters & Extracts from her Diaries* (ed. David Garnett 1970) p.386.

21 Frances Partridge *Memories* (1981) p.168.

22 Lady Strachey's estate had been valued at £36,810 11s. 8d. Twenty years earlier Sir Richard Strachey had left only £6,470 16s. 8d. – possibly because he had made over some of his capital to his wife. Lady Strachey had also, in the meantime, inherited the estate of her sister Elinor (Lady Colvile).

23 George Saintsbury (1845–1933), historian and literary essayist, friend of Mandell Creighton and noted especially for his writings on French literature. On retiring from his post of Regius Professor of Rhetoric and English Literature at the University of Edinburgh, he had gone, in 1916, to live at 1 Royal Crescent, Bath, where his *Notes on a Cellar Book* was written – leading to the foundation of the Saintsbury Club.

24 'Horace Walpole' *Independent Review* 2 (May 1904) pp.641–6. Reprinted in *Characters and Commentaries* and *Biographical Essays*.

25 'Walpole's Letters' *Athenaeum* (15 August 1919) pp.744–5. Also, 'Some New Letters of Horace Walpole' *Living Age* 302 (27 September 1919) pp.788–91. Reprinted in *Characters and Commentaries* and *Biographical Essays*.

26 'Suppressed Passages in Walpole's Letters' *Athenaeum* (5 September 1919) p.853.

27 'The Eighteenth Century' *Nation and Athenaeum* 39 (29 May 1926) pp.205–6. Also *New Republic* 47 (16 June 1926). Reprinted in *Characters and Commentaries* and *Biographical Essays*.

28 'Charles Greville' *Nation and Athenaeum* 33 (11 August 1923) pp.593–4, also *New Republic* 35 (15 August 1923) pp. 325–7. Reprinted in *Biographical Essays*.

29 'Greville Memoirs. Access to Original Manuscript. Mr Lytton Strachey's Plea'. *The Times* (12 November 1927) p.8.

30 P.W. Wilson's version of the diaries had been so ill received that Heinemann felt obliged to offer to undertake a complete edition of the text. When Lytton died, the negotiations fell through. What happened then was described to the author by Roger Fulford. 'Some time after my first book was published – which was in 1933 – I was approached by Mr James Strachey to know if I would complete the book and, if need be, find another publisher. Mr Thomas Balston, who had been responsible for the publication of my first book and was at that time the active mind in Duckworth's, agreed that his firm would publish it, and it may well have

been that he suggested my name to Mr James Strachey. Plans with Duckworth advanced and, owing to the cost of production, we contemplated doing it in the old-fashioned way with subscribers' copies. When Mr Balston left Duckworth (I think in 1934) that firm declined to complete the project. Mr Balston most generously put me in touch with Mr Daniel Macmillan and Macmillans agreed to publish it, and carried out their undertaking. The cost of the finished book and the numbers printed were nothing to do with me. It is obvious that the commercial hazards at that time were very great and, if Macmillan's book was expensive, at least it was published.

'Part of the explanation for the high price which this book fetches in the second hand market is that it was beautifully produced by the Cambridge University Press. Mr and Mrs Ralph Partridge behaved with great generosity; they had done a great deal of work on the text and on the footnotes, this was neither acknowledged financially nor on the title page of the finished book.'

Thomas Balston wrote: 'I am still very proud of my small part in its production, and of having immediately realised how very great its importance would be to the many historians who would be working on that period in the next fifty years or so ... I am also glad that I thought it so important that I sent it to the C[ambridge] U[niversity] P[ress], then with Walter Lewis as their typographer the best printers in England, and of course, very expensive.'

The Greville Memoirs was published in September 1938 in eight volumes (the last an index volume). Six hundred and thirty sets were printed and each set cost £15 or $60. 'When so much labour and learning have been expended upon this edition,' wrote Raymond Mortimer, 'it is deplorable that the ordinary reader should still be obliged to use the old mutilated text.' He criticized Macmillans for having condescended 'to this method of publication, against which Lytton Strachey himself would certainly have been the first to protest'. In 1963 Roger Fulford brought out an abridged volume in the Macmillan Historical Memoirs series.

31 'Obscenity in Literature', *Nation and Athenaeum* 44 (30 March 1929) p.908.

32 This description was a typical piece of Stracheyesque extravaganza, Beverley Nichols assured the author. 'It is true that I knew a young American called Warren Curry who came over to England to study for a short while and stay with me. But we certainly never wandered "in despair over Europe and Africa". We never went near Africa, and our only excursion abroad was a brief trip to Rome where, far from quarrelling, we had a very enjoyable week-end.'

33 Sir Gerald Tyrwhitt-Wilson, fifth Baronet and fourteenth Baron Berners (1883–1950), musician, artist and author, whose ballet music 'Luna Park' was this year being performed in C.B. Cochran's revue. He had been honorary attaché in Rome (1911–19) and after the war often stayed at 3 Foro Romano, his house overlooking the Forum.

34 Lytton had commissioned Stephen Tomlin to make this portrait and paid him an advance commission of £30 in December 1928. When it was completed early in 1930 he gave a party at 51 Gordon Square so that his friends could inspect it. 'It seemed to me very successful,' he wrote to Bunny Garnett (3 November 1929). In April 1930 Brinsley Ford bought the cast which is now in the Tate Gallery, and was the second of an edition of three. Another cast was inherited by Pippa Strachey after Lytton's death, and a third was acquired by David Garnett. In the late 1970s Anthony D'Offay made a further edition of eight copies.

35 The parents of the celebrated Mitford sisters, Diana, Jessica, Pamela, Unity and Nancy who, in her novel *The Pursuit of Love*, caricatured her father as Uncle Matthew, a man who 'knew no middle course, he either loved or hated, and generally, it must be said, he·hated'.

36 Lord Desborough, the father of Julian Grenfell the poet, was one of the most

esteemed all-round sportsmen of his generation. He swam the Niagara pool, slaughtered a hundred stags in a single season, played cricket for Harrow, ran the three-mile for Cambridge, ascended the Matterhorn three times by alternative routes and fenced in the Olympic Games.

37 Henry Green (1905–73), the novelist, who had already published both *Blindness* and *Living*. He remembered Lytton as being extremely well dressed, 'as bright as a button' and 'a real charmer'. In particular he was struck by the fact that Lytton always listened attentively to what everyone said, would encourage them to speak on, and then, when they had finished, utter a few words that might completely deflate them. His technique was superb. Yet people did not appear to feel aggrieved; for there always seemed more absurd than malevolent humour in what he said.

38 *Gli Indifferenti* had recently come out in Italy but was not translated and published in England until 1935, when it appeared under the title *The Time of Indifference*. Alberto Moravia's regular English-language translator was Lytton's friend Angus Davidson.

39 Stephen Spender's autobiographical novel, *The Temple*, which contained caricature portraits of W.H. Auden, Christopher Isherwood and the photographer Herbert List, was not published because, Spender's publisher Geoffrey Faber explained, 'besides being libellous, [it] was pornographic according to the law at that time.' In 1962 Spender sold the manuscript to the University of Texas and in 1988 published a partly rewritten version of the novel.

40 Bronislaw Malinowsky (1884–1942), the Anglo-Polish anthropologist whose *The Sexual Life of Savages in North-Western Melanesia* had recently been published.

41 Edmund Wilson *The Shores of Light* (1952) p.553.

42 'I feel immensely proud that you should wish to dedicate a book to me,' Max Beerbohm wrote (21 March 1931). 'Much older though I am than you, my admiration for your prose, since I first knew it, has had the fresh wild hot quality that belongs rather to a very young man's feelings for the work of a great congenial veteran.'

43 Carrington cut out her winning entry and pasted it into HER BOOK on 18 July 1931. Lytton sent her a congratulatory telegram and she replied: 'Darling Lytton, My most venerable Biographer, knitter of coatees, most dissipated of masters, do you know your wire gave me more pleasure than anything in the world? ... Terrible to think I nearly lost my two guineas through cruelty! Ralph is really more delighted than I am, I believe!'

44 In 1931, Professor Richard Braithwaite (1900–86), later Knightsbridge Professor of Moral Philosophy at Cambridge, edited a volume of Frank Ramsey's posthumous papers entitled *The Foundation of Mathematics* – 'mostly quite incomprehensible', Lytton claimed (7 October 1931), 'and even those recommended (by Braithwaite in his introduction) to the "general reader" seem to me alarmingly obscure. I'm glad to see that G.E. Moore (in a preface) confesses that (owing no doubt to his stupidity) he can make neither head nor tail of them. One *can* see an extraordinary eminence, though, showing through the fog.'

45 Lieutenant-Colonel Oswald Balfour, who had been military secretary to the governor-general of Canada (1920–23) and was to become chairman and director of several steel companies.

46 The books in Lytton's library dated before 1841 were left to Roger Senhouse and sold at Sotheby's on 18–20 October 1971 as part of Senhouse's library after his death. The modern books were left to James Strachey, and a number of these were sold at Sotheby's on 14 December 1965. Carrington's bookplates have the name 'Lytton Strachey' against a lattice background and occur in three sizes. They replaced a more elaborate bookplate dated 1899 with the name 'G.L. Strachey'.

47 *D.C.Partride*. HER BOOK undated (British Library).
48 The unfinished 'Othello' was first published posthumously in *Characters and Commentaries* and reprinted in *Literary Essays*.
49 Frances Partridge *Memories* (1981) p.192.
50 Lady Diana Cooper had played the role of the Madonna in Max Reinhardt's famous New York production of *The Miracle* in 1924.
51 Syrie Maugham, daughter cf Dr Thomas Barnardo the celebrated physician and philanthropist, was one of the most fashionable interior decorators of her day. In 1927 she had been divorced from Somerset Maugham, who was her second husband, her first being Sir Henry Wellcome, a noted American scientist. William Gerhardie, who remembered this party, wrote to the author that 'I asked Cazalet, since he knew everybody, to introduce me to the most glamorous débutante present. He confessed that as she was rumoured to be engaged to a royal duke, and was highly sought after, he must seek an appropriate moment; meanwhile fobbing me off with Lytton Strachey. When Strachey was in the heat of relating his experiences of driving in a taxi into the courtyard of Buckingham Palace, and the anti-climax of being fobbed off with the king's secretary Lord Stamfordham, Cazalet came back to say that the débutante was now available, and Strachey was left mournfully alone. I never saw him again . . . As for poor Cazalet, he crashed to death in an aeroplane accident (suspected of political sabotage) in his capacity of dispenser of affectionate reassurance to the Polish wartime leader, General Sikorski, sitting beside him.'
52 Clive Bell *Old Friends* (1956) p.41.
53 *Best of Friends. The Brenan–Partridge Letters* (ed. Xan Fielding 1986) p.107.
54 *The Sickle Side of the Moon. The Letters of Virginia Woolf, Volume V 1932–1935* (ed. Nigel Nicolson 1979) p.5.
55 Frances Partridge *Memories* (1981) p.196.
56 *The Diary of Virginia Woolf, Volume IV 1931–35* (ed. Anne Olivier Bell) 1 January 1932 p.62.
57 *A Reflection of the Other Person. The Letters of Virginia Woolf, Volume IV 1929–1931* (ed. Nigel Nicolson) p.421.
58 Diary entries 25, 27, 29 December 1931, 1, 13 January 1932. *The Diary of Virginia Woolf, Volume IV 1931–35* pp.55–7, 62–3.

EPILOGUE

1 Chidiock Tichborne (1558?–86) had joined the Babington conspirators and was one of six to whom the deed of killing Queen Elizabeth was allotted. He was seized in St John's Wood on 14 August and lodged in the Tower. At his trial on 13 and 14 September he pleaded guilty. Six days later he suffered the full penalty of the law, being disembowelled before life was extinct. But his final speech moved many to compassion, as did the pathetic letters he wrote to his wife Agnes on 19 September.
2 Frances Partridge *Memories* (1981) p.209.
3 *The Diary of Virginia Woolf, Volume IV 1931–35* 30 January 1932 p.66. See also 17 March 1932 p.83.
4 *The Diary of Virginia Woolf, Volume IV 1931–35* 12 March 1932 pp.81–3.

INDEX

Abbey Theatre, Dublin (1930): 'brogue and boredom' 648
Abbotsholme, Derbyshire: The New School 29-35
Aberconway, Lady (Christabel) 570, 589
Abingdon, Oxfordshire (1916) 365
Ackerley, J. R. 554
Acton, Sir Harold 646
Agate, James 550
Ainsworth, A. R. 73, 83, 84, 103, 147, 160, 163
Aix-en-Provence (1928) 597
Albany Review see Independent Review
Albert, Prince Consort 34, 440, 477, 490, 491, 492-4
Aldington, Richard 459
Lawrence of Arabia (1955) 424
Algeria (1923) 521-2
Allegret, Marc 427
Allen & Unwin (publishers) 638
Allenby, Lord 565
Allenswood, Southfields 15, 16
Alpine Club Gallery, London 251, 299, 394, 404
Amsterdam (1929) 631
Annan, Lord (Noël) 101, 421, 695
Anrep, Boris: and Henry Lamb 226, 230, 237; Lytton develops a crush on 272; and the hostility of Bloomsbury 272; at a boxing match with Lytton 380; visits Tidmarsh 524; designs a Ham Spray chimney-piece 533; brings a Russian Easter cake 541; his marriage breaks up 543; 'bubbles along . . .' 603; describes fishes the size of footballs 644-5; the author visits 695
Anrep, Helen 543, 544
Ansermet, Ernest 451, 452, 462
Apostles, the (Cambridge Conversazione Society; The Society): activities and aims 76, 77-8, 82, 83, 85; and Henry Sidgwick 77, 99; Lytton's election 76-7, 78-9; Lytton's papers 79-82; Lytton elected secretary 85; and Moore's impact 86-7, 89-92, 103; Lytton and Keynes in the ascendant 103, 104, 105, 128; Hobhouse's election 106, 108-9; James Strachey and Harry Norton join 124; in decline 127; their revaluation of Sidgwick 139-40; and Rupert Brooke 124, 235; Lytton explains his newly developed beliefs to 249-50; and Wittgenstein's election 272-5; Lytton toasts 'Eminent Victorians' 419; post-war 474-5, 500-1, 654-5; author criticized for giving an 'inaccurate impression' of xiv; mentioned 111, 122, 123, 137, 147, 167, 176, 179
Archer, William 173
Ardeley Bury, nr Stevenage 51
Aristophanes: *The Frogs* 36
Aristotelian Society 278-9
Arles, France (1928) 598
Arnold, Matthew 140, 297, 562

Arnold, Dr Thomas *see under* Strachey, Lytton: *Eminent Victorians*
Arnold-Forster, Katharine (*née* Cox) ('Ka'): describes James Strachey 236; her squashy appearance and powers of attraction 240; her relationships with Rupert Brooke and Henry Lamb 240-4; assists after Virginia's suicide attempt 298; marriage 290; mentioned 267
Arnold-Forster, William 290
Arts Theatre, Cambridge 290
Asche, Oscar 265
Asheham, nr Rodmell, Sussex 289, 290, 291, 293, 338, 351
Asquith, Anthony 434
Asquith, Lady (Cynthia): Lawrence to 335, 336
Asquith, Cyril ('Cys') 434
Asquith, Elizabeth *see* Bibesco, Princess
Asquith, Herbert Henry (Lord Oxford and Asquith): Lytton meets at Bedford Square 302-4; brings Britain into the War 310; not a realist 321; announced as 'another gentleman' 330; and conscription 339, 340-1; Lytton studies at Garsington 364-5; his attitude to Keynes 365; like 'a seraph in a heavenly ecstasy' 373-4; Lytton's views on 373-4, 414, 415, 425-6; 'a very diminished deflated figure' 392; boosts the sales of *Eminent Victorians* 425; his Romanes Lecture 425; plays foolish letter-games 434; Lytton's attitude softens towards 434-5; 'a queer nervous old fellow' 452
Occasional Addresses (1918) 425, 426
Asquith, Katherine 519
Asquith, Lady (Margot) 433, 434, 452; her autobiography 478
Asquith, Lady (Violet) 434
Astor, Ava (later Lady Ribblesdale) 451
Astor, 'Bobbie' *see* Shaw, Robert Gould
Astor, Colonel J. J. 451
Astor, Lady (Nancy) 433, 500, 505, 565
Athenaeum 414, 415, 443, 444, 503, 539, 635
Aubrey, John 651, 652
Auden, W. H. xii; his revisions xxii

Bacon, Sir Francis 608, 609, 611, 613, 614
Badley, Dr J. H. 29, 235
Bagenal, Barbara (*née* Hiles): at Garsington 331; at Asheham with Carrington 351-2; spells out H-O-M-O-S-E-X-U-A-L to Carrington 353; with Lytton, Carrington and Nick Bagenal in North Wales 371-2, 373, 374; finds a country house for Lytton 379; her parties 380; at Asheham with Carrington and Sydney-Turner 382; bathes naked at Warsash 391; as treasurer for the Mill House rent 401; helps make the Mill House habitable 405; prevents Carrington from giving Lytton neat iodine 407; visits Mill House 414; 'incredibly aged' 431; her baby like 'a Japanese grub' 438; in Paris 473;

751

Lansdowne, Lord 442
La Souco *see* Roquebrune
Laurence, R. Vere 111, 116
Lavery, Sir John 259
Lavington, Wiltshire (1908) 178
Law, Andrew Bonar 341, 414
Lawrence, D. H.: on Bertrand Russell 69; antagonistic towards the Apostles 92; on Ottoline Morrell 222; on Brooke's war sonnets 245; dislikes *Landmarks in French Literature* 247; 'in the dusty rear' 288; and Brooke's death 328; Ottoline invites to Bedford Square 327-8; elects her as his new patron 328-9; on Garsington 325, 328, 330, 336; at Ottoline's 42nd birthday party 327; disgusted by her Bloomsbury friends 76, 333, 334-5; Russell loves him 'more and more' 335; tears up Russell's lectures 335; *The Rainbow* suppressed 335-6; his portrayal of Ottoline in *Women in Love* and the end of their friendship xviii, 333; encounters Lytton 333, 334; Gertler discusses his troubles 356; caricatures Carrington in *Women in Love* 356-7; advises Gertler 358-9; dislikes Cannan's *Mendel* 383; his pictures seized 641-2; mentioned i, xxii, xxiii, 315
Lady Chatterley's Love (1928, 1932) 599
The Prussian Officer (1914) 327
The Rainbow (1915) 335-6, 641
Sons and Lovers (1913) 327
The White Peacock (1911) 327
Women in Love (1921) 222, 333, 337, 356, 377
Lawrence, Frieda 327, 328, 329, 334, 377, 567
Lawrence, T. E. 538
Laws, Frederick: Lytton to 539
Lazard, Max 525
Lea, F. A. 443
Lear, Edward 645
Leathes, (Sir) Stanley 57, 73-4, 178
The Cambridge Modern History (vol. 5 1908) 178
Leavis, F. R. xxiv, 92, 140
Lee, Sidney 156
King Edward VII (2 vols 1925, 1927) 573
Shakespeare and the Modern Stage (1906) 156
Lee, Vernon (Violet Paget) 370
Legge, Donald (gardener at Tidmarsh) 406
Legge, Mrs (housekeeper at Tidmarsh) 406
Lehmann, John 246, 539-40, 569, 650; Rosamond to 675
The Whispering Gallery (1955) 246
Lehmann, Rosamond: 'full of fun' 565; in France with Lytton 648, 649; introduces Lytton to Stephen Spender 650; takes Spender to Ham Spray House 537; feels Lytton will live 675; Frances and Ralph stay with in Wales 683; the author visits 695; mentioned 668
Dusty Answer (1927) 569
Carrington to 624, 671, 684, 686, 687
Frances Partridge to 693
Ralph Partridge to 687
Lytton to 536-7, 565-6
Lehzen, Baroness 491
Leighton, Frederic: impotent 140
Lenin, V. I. xxiv
Leopold I, King of the Belgians 491
Lespinasse, Madame Julie de 160; Lytton's essay on 147, 150

Leverson, Ada 258
Levy, Dr Oscar 633-4
Levy, Paul 91, 697
Lewis, Lady 436
Lewis, Wyndham: feels ostracized by the Bloomsbury Group 226; is revolted by Lytton 232; Lytton finds his pictures execrable 271, and his article 'affreux' 277; in Dieppe 292; caricatures Lytton 362-3, 538; describes Lytton in his country cottage 430; pours scorn on Lytton 496; invites Lytton to a secret rendezvous 538; on *Elizabeth and Essex* 613
The Apes of God (1930) 362-3
The Lion and the Fox (1927) 613
Self-Condemned (1954) 538
Lietz, Dr Hermann 29
Life and Letters 629, 653
Lincoln College, Oxford 54
Lindisfarne (1918) 435
Liverpool 45-6; University College (later Liverpool University) 43-9, 52-3, 564
Livy (Titus Livius) 419-20
Lizard, The, Cornwall (1903) 88-9
Llandudno, Wales (1916) 373, 374
Lloyd George, David: not a realist 321; 'verging towards the madhouse cell' 338; Lytton wants him publicly castrated 340; his ignominy and treachery 341; like a prehistoric monster 342; and Keynes 343; as prime minister 392, 414-15; does not recognize Lytton 505; and the Oscar Levy affair 633
Lloyd George, Mrs ('an unparalleled frump') 505
Location Register of Twentieth-Century English Literary Manuscripts and Letters (1988) 697
Loches, France (1898) 49-51
Lockeridge, nr Marlborough *see* Lacket, The
Lockhart, J. G.: *Life of Scott* (1837-8) 138, 429
London: before the war 299, 302; in the First World War 335, 338, 378-80
London Mercury 629
London Society for Women's Service 547
Longmans (publishers) 640
Lopokova, Lydia: on Armistice Day 438; at Clive and Maynard's supper-party 451; her flats in Gordon Square 462; stays at Tidmarsh with Maynard 520; her marriage to Maynard 555-7; mentioned xxii, 545, 550, 560
Lord's Wood, Marlow Common xiii-xvi, xviii, xx, 384, 385
Louis XIII, King of France 628
Lowe, Mr (a racehorse trainer) 268, 270
Lowe, Mrs 268, 269-70, 277
Lucas, F. L. 475, 478, 520, 540, 558, 567
The Complete Works of J. Webster (1927) 599
Lucas, 'Topsy' 567, 585
Lytton to 571, 574, 585, 588-9, 596, 599, 602, 604, 616, 669
Ludwig, Emil 424, 570
Life of the Kaiser (tr. 1926) 567
Napoleon (tr. 1926) 569
Luke, Peter xv
Lulworth, Dorset: (1910) 214; (1911) 239, 240-1; (1919) 449
Lutyens, Sir Edwin 435
Lyme Regis, Dorset (1919) 449
Lyttelton, Alfred 78
Lytton, Edward Robert Bulwer, 1st Earl of ('Owen Meredith') 4, 154

Lytton's character witness 391-2; his barn
conversion for Gertler 397; likes 'The End of
General Gordon' 410; causes Lytton
'indescribable boredom' 523; mentioned 519*n*
Leaves from the Greville Diary (1929) 640
Mortimer, Raymond xii, 536, 569, 603, 605
Motley, John: *The Rise of the Dutch Republic* (1855)
397
Mozart, W. A. 312, 582
Così fan' tutte 583
The Magic Flute 287
Muggeridge, Malcolm i, xv
Muggleton, Lodowick 651
Muir, Edwin: *Structure of the Novel* (1928) 629
Muir, Ramsay 459
Munby, A. N. L. 696
Munnings, Sir Alfred ('Mullings') 452
Munthe, Axel 220
Murray, Gilbert 215, 234, 640
Murry, John Middleton: and D. H. Lawrence 328,
334; in Gower Street with Katherine
Mansfield 378; flirts with Ottoline and Brett
380; 'as a Dostoyevsky character' 381; gloomy
over Katherine's health 414; editor of the
Athenaeum 414, 443-4; on Lytton 503; as
editor of Katherine Mansfield's *Journal* 573
Lytton to 477
Musk, Lord 197

Nancy, France (1931) 664-6
Naples, Lytton visits: 1913 283-4; 1923 522
Napoleon: 'the *lowness* of him' 257-8, 569
Nash, Paul: on Carrington 355
Nathalie, ex-Queen of Serbia 65
Nathan, Sir Matthew 303
Nation 310, 478
Nation and Athenaeum 444-5, 460, 522, 568, 636,
640
National Council against Conscription (NCC) 339,
343
NCC *see* National Council against Conscription
NCF *see* No Conscription Fellowship
Neale, Sir John: *Queen Elizabeth* (1934) 615
Neeve, Mr and Mrs 210-11
Nelson, Geoffrey 314
Nevinson, C. R. W. 355
New Lindsey Theatre: production of *A Son of
Heaven* 550
Newman, John Henry, Cardinal 409, 423, 522
New Quarterly 68, 155, 156, 165, 168, 172, 185,
420
New Republic 477, 524, 637
New Statesman xx, 68, 296-7, 301, 305, 335, 336,
381, 396, 415, 442-3, 447, 629
New Statesman and Nation (formerly *New Statesman*)
443, 629
New Witness 415
Nichols, Beverley 644
Nichols, Robert 408, 628
Nicolas I, Tsar of Russia 492
Nicols, Sir Philip ('Hamish') 544, 545, 558, 560
Nicolson, Harold viii-ix, xiv, 424, 495; on Lytton
537
Tennyson (1923) 424, 522
Nicolson, Nigel xiv-xv
Nietzsche, Friedrich 305
Nightingale, Florence *see under* Strachey, Lytton:
Eminent Victorians

Nijinsky, Vaslav: 'that lovely serpent' 226, 278;
'certainly not a eunuch' 291; still enthralls
Ottoline 302
Nikisch, Arthur 287
Nîmes, France (1928) 598
1917 Club 411, 438, 509, 521, 570
Noble, Mrs Saxton 450
No Conscription Fellowship (NCF) 339, 344, 345,
411
North, Dr John, Master of Trinity 568, 651
Northcliffe, Lord 309
Northcliffe Press 442
North Molton, Devon (1907) 160, 161, 162-3
Norton, Harry: as a Cambridge freshman 123; joins
The Apostles 124; in love with James Strachey
148; helps at Suffrage demonstration 156;
Lytton sees as middle-aged 158; with Keynes
in Paris 160, 161; at the North Molton
reading-party 163; 'The horror of Sunday!'
with his family 170; still in love with James
Strachey 212, 239, and Vanessa Bell 239; his
loans to Lytton 267, 277, 295; lunches with
Lytton 278; evolves a new theory of cubic
roots at Wissett Lodge 368; almost shares a
bedroom with Carrington 372; a
hypochondriac at Marlow 384; and copulation
every ten days 385; has Lytton and Carrington
to stay 393; participates in Mill House scheme
401; brings turkey and claret 406; supports
Lytton's 'trembling form' 413; Gide stays with
427; Lytton repays 430; *Eminent Victorians*
dedicated to 697; mentioned 147, 148, 174,
210, 272, 439, 644
Norton, Lucy 697
Nottingham (1926) 566-7
Nys, Maria *see* Huxley, Maria

Olive (a maid) *see* Martin, Olive
Olivier, Bryn *see* Popham, Bryn
Olivier, Daphne 235, 292, 315, 316
Olivier, Marjorie 235, 292
Olivier, Noel: and Rupert Brooke xxii, 235,
239-41, 244; and James Strachey 245;
camping in Norfolk 292; 'agreeably bouncing
and cheerful' at Rothiemurchus 293; revives
Rupert's enmity for Lytton 293; her 'deadly
slight affection' for James 293; at The Lacket
315; her last letter to Rupert 315; her affair
with James continues 385, 393, 397; qualifies
as a doctor 410; avidly reads about sexual
inversion 431; visits Carrington in hospital 475
Olivier, Sir Sydney 235
Olympic, The 649
Omega Workshops, the 290, 352
Oriental Club 504, 539, 559, 601
Orton, Joe 428
Osborne, John xv
Oxford University 78; *see* Balliol; Lincoln
Oxford University Press 179

Paderewski, Ignace 287
Painter, George: *Marcel Proust* (1959, 1966, 1989)
xxii
Paley, George Arthur 155
Pall Mall Gazette 489
Pallavicino, Countess 142
Palmerston, Lord 492

'Voltaire's Tragedies' 420-1
'Walpole's Letters' 444
'Who would love only roses among flowers?' 376
Strachey, Marjorie (sister): with Lytton at Hyde
   Park Kindergarten 14-15; at Allenswood 15;
   collaborates on literary enterprises with Lytton
   18; in the south of France 67; has outrageous
   opinions 178; argues with Lady Strachey 178;
   looks after Lytton and her niece at
   Roquebrune 229; her lewd readings of nursery
   rhymes 239; invents a party game 271; as a
   Post-Impressionist sphinx 288; with nothing on
   but a miniature of the Prince Consort 289; in
   a minuet with Lytton 312; gets on well with
   Lytton 395; writes one of Lytton's pseudo-
   quotations 421; witnesses Carrington's
   wedding 487; turns up in Cumberland 498;
   writes obscene nursery rhymes 545; mentioned
   348, 431, 442, 462
Strachey, Oliver (brother): at Eton 19; at Balliol 51;
   tours the world 107; at Brahms's funeral 107;
   joins the East India Railway 107; Lytton and
   Moore at his new household 107-8; returns to
   India 126; nurses Lytton at Corfe 229; marries
   again 233; badgers Lytton 247; a Harlequin in
   Bloomsbury 288; rents Durbins 350; plays
   Bach 370; bathes at Chilling 391; his help in
   the leasing of Mill House 401, 405; and the
   1917 Club 411; sits for his portrait 414;
   mentioned 47, 129, 231, 232, 251, 348, 379,
   413, 431, 441, 462, 463
Strachey, Pernel (Joan) (sister): at Allenswood 15;
   Lytton visits 53; meets Simon Bussy 87; at
   Lancaster Gate 178; finds the Saltsjöbaden
   clinic 'very singular' 214, 215; as Principal at
   Newnham College 539; mentioned 298, 323,
   348, 474
Lytton to 61, 62
Virginia Woolf to 522, 671, 674
Strachey, Philippa ('Pippa') (sister): Lytton hopes
   she will marry Moore 86; types Lytton's
   thesis 98; nurses him in Paris 145, 146;
   'unconscious' 147; organizes the 'Mud March'
   156, 157; nurses her father 177; with Lytton
   to Boulogne and the St Loe Stracheys' 177-8;
   endures a fortnight at Lytton's Swedish clinic
   215; types Landmarks for Lytton 235; lends
   Lytton five pounds 237; visits The Lacket 298,
   323; looks after Lytton at Durbins 370; sends
   books down to Lytton 441; and the move to
   Gordon Square 463; brings Carrington's letter
   to Lytton in Italy 486; Lytton flees to Brittany
   with 531; secretary of the London Society for
   Women's Service 547; and the Scala version
   of A Son of Heaven 547, 549; to Paris with
   Lytton 564-5; 'a most sympathetic character'
   569; nurses her mother 604; as joint executor
   of her mother's will 630; with Lytton till his
   death 669-78 passim, 682; her screeching
   laugh 672; advises him not to think of poetry
   675; the author meets 695; mentioned 431,
   524, 683
Lytton to 37, 38, 95, 96, 147-8, 215, 297, 348,
   350, 396, 399, 464, 468, 499, 502-3, 506,
   515, 517, 521, 566-7
Strachey, Ralph (brother) 19
Strachey, Ray (née Costelloe) (Mrs Oliver Strachey)
   129, 229, 233, 350, 370, 391, 549

Strachey, Sir Richard (father): birth and career 3;
   meets and marries Jane Maria Grant 3-4; his
   relationship with Lytton 4-5, 19, 177; reads all
   day long 5, 13; made Grand Commander of
   the Star of India 6; Dorothy describes 17;
   writes to Lytton about being bullied 35-6;
   Bussy paints 87; refused a pension 155; a
   dangerous pedestrian 5-6; his death 177;
   Lytton describes his world 20; mentioned 9,
   37, 52, 62, 269, 504
Strachey, Richard (nephew) 537, 539
Strachey, Richard John (brother) 18-19
Strachey, Ruby (sister-in-law) (Mrs Oliver
   Strachey) 107, 126
Strachey, William (uncle) 11-12
Strachey Trust, the 696-7
Strafford, Lady 638
Strasbourg (1931) 666
Strauss, Richard 286
   Der Rosenkavalier 278
Stravinsky, Igor 451
   Le Rossignol 245
   Le Sacre du Printemps 291
Strindberg, Johann August 279
Strong, Professor Herbert 45
Suez Canal (1893) 26-7
Suffrage movement 156-7, 215
Suggia, Guilhermina 413, 435-6
Sunday Times 563
Suthery, Mr (classics master) 38
Sweden: Saltsjöbaden clinic 206-10, 214-15, 600;
   Stockholm (1928) 600
Swift, Jonathan: 'a dirty mind' 572; stimulated by
   obscenity 641
Swinburne, Algernon Charles 49, 55, 61, 83, 208,
   408, 563
Swinnerton, Frank 409-10
Swithinbank, Bernard W.: Lytton cultivates his
   friendship 112; punts with Lytton up to
   Twickenham 113; Duncan Grant eclipses 115;
   founds the Pleiads 127; too shy 127;
   summoned to help in the 'Mud March' 156-7;
   his passion for Dilly Knox 158; lunches on
   strawberries and cream 167; intends to
   become inspector of Fijian brothels 167-8; 'the
   most beautiful person' Lytton has ever seen
   189-90; the end of their friendship 190, 201;
   returns from Burma, 'all youth gone' 299-300;
   mentioned 148, 191
Keynes to 139, 140
Lytton to 60, 112-13, 122, 127, 134, 163, 170,
   171, 179, 184-5
Sydney-Turner, Saxon: still-born into the Midnight
   Society 58, 59, 61; in the Civil Service 73, 93;
   introduces Lytton to Beddoes 164; 'probably
   no one less entertaining in the world' 176; the
   perfect Jamesian figure 195; Lytton sees more
   of 212; Henry Lamb has a soft spot for 226;
   as a eunuch 288; rather eerie in Norfolk 292;
   like a simmering kettle 352; at Asheham 382;
   at Warsash 391; participates in Tidmarsh lease
   401; chuckles over Euripides at Tidmarsh 414;
   'incredibly aged' 431; in an amateur film show
   536; 'crane-like ... for ever smoking' 569;
   'looking very shrewd ...' 603; Lytton too ill to
   see 671; mentioned 70, 148, 160, 251, 379,
   413, 464